EARLY PENNSYLVANIA LAND RECORDS

Minutes
of the
Board of Property
of the
Province of Pennsylvania

by
William Henry Egle

HERITAGE BOOKS
2008

HERITAGE BOOKS
AN IMPRINT OF HERITAGE BOOKS, INC.

Books, CDs, and more—Worldwide

For our listing of thousands of titles see our website
at
www.HeritageBooks.com

A Facsimile Reprint
Published 2008 by
HERITAGE BOOKS, INC.
Publishing Division
100 Railroad Ave. #104
Westminster, Maryland 21157

Originally published
Harrisburg, Pennsylvania
1893

— Publisher's Notice —

In reprints such as this, it is often not possible to remove blemishes from the original. We feel the contents of this book warrant its reissue despite these blemishes and hope you will agree and read it with pleasure.

International Standard Book Numbers
Paperbound: 978-0-7884-2279-9
Clothbound: 978-0-7884-4890-4

MINUTES

OF THE

BOARD OF PROPERTY

OF THE

PROVINCE OF PENNSYLVANIA.

EDITED BY
WILLIAM HENRY EGLE, M. D

HARRISBURG:

1893.

[The Minutes of the Board of Property, herewith given, comprise only a portion of what, in many respects, are valuable documents. Several of the early volumes are illegible, while others cannot be found and hence the record begins with Minute Book C.]

MINUTE BOOK "C."

MINUTE BOOK OF PROPERTY COMMENCING ABOUT THE YEAR 1685, BOOK C. IN THE SECRETARIES OFFICE.

William Penn, Proprietary and Governor of the province of Pennsylvania and Counties annexed, &c.

WILLIAM PENN:

To my trusty and loving friends William Markham, Thomas Ellis and John Goodson, or any Two of them I heartily salute you.

For as much as there will be Occation to Dispose of Lands, both to Purchasers and Renters, as they are commonly Distinguished, and that the former Commissioners for that Service have served in that Charge a Sufficient Time, and Reposing Special Trust and Confidence in your care, prudence and Integrity, I Do hereby Impower you, or any two of you (my Secretary being one) in my Name and for my behoof, to grant warrants and Survey Land, and Pass Patents for the Lands so surveyed, so as it be according to Custome and the regulation formerly settled and observ'd, hereby revoaking all other Commissions of this Nature heretofore Granted, Requiring all Persons to yield you the regard and respect that belong to the trust I repose in you, and so I recommend you to God's grace and protection and bid you heartily farewell.

Given at Worminghurst Place in old England ye 21st of the 11th Month, 1686.

A Proclamation concerning the Caves of Philadelphia, By William Penn, Proprietary and Govern'r, &c.

WILLIAM PENN, P. G'r:

Whereas I did at first, in regard of the infancy of things and specially out of tenderness to the poorer sort, permitt divers Caves to be made in the Bank of Philadelphia, fronting Delaware River, for a present accommodation, and perceiving that they are commonly disposed of from one to another as a kind of Property, and taking farther notice of the great Detriment that is like to insue to the Street by the continuation of them, as well as the Disorders that their great Secresy hath given occasion to loose People to commit in them, I do hereby desire and strictly order and warne all the Inhabitants of the said Caves to depart the same within two Months after the Publication hereof, And require my trusty and loving friends and Commissioners, William Markham, Thomas Ellis and John Goodson, or any two of them, to see that the same be accordingly effected. And that no Damage may redound to the Publick by my former Indulgence; the said Commis'rs are thereby ordered to cause a Survey to be taken of the State of the Said Caves that such who have lived in them may be obliged to secure the Bank and Street from any Damage that may happen from them. It being but a reasonable thing that those who have had the benefit thereof should Indemnifie the Publick, of which all Persons concern'd are to take notice and yield their due obedience as they will answer the contrary at their Perrill.

Given at Worminghurst Place in old England ye 24th of ye 11th Month, 1686.

A Proclamation concerning cutting of Timber and clearing of Lotts in Philadelphia and Suburbs, By Wiliam Penn, Proprietary and Governor, &c.

WILLIAM PENN, *P. G'r:*

Since Justice in all things ought to be observed, It ought not for that reason in the least thing to be neglected, and for that end I took great care whilst I was in the Province among the rest to prevent peoples cutting Wood. and especially Timber off from other men's Lotts; and foreseeing the Scarcity that would quickly follow, I did appoint a Woodman, who was instructed to grant such trees as belonged not to any private Person, and in such number as the case deserved, and for his paines to receive 6d pr. Tree. Now inasmuch as I am credibly informed that some of the People of Philadelphia have been very Irregular and Injurious herein, I do hereby desire and strictly Order my loving friends and Commissioners, William Markham, Thomas Ellis and John Goodson, diligently to inspect this matter and to cause such as shall from time to time, be found offenders, to be effectually and Impartially presented according to Law in that case provided. And because one of the evil consequences of destroying the Timber so irregularly, has been the growth of Underwood, which does not only hinder the Towne Stock of the benefit they might else have and render the Town more a Wilderness, but if not cleared and prevented may become a common Nusance by being a covert for Vermin, and too often for loose and evil Persons. I have thought fit to require my said Commissioners, and they are hereby ordered to present this to the Inhabitants of the Town whose accommodation has been for the most part the cause of this Inconveniency; And they also are hereby required to take some effectual course to clear the ground of such Under-Woods with all convenient speed.

Given at Worminghurst Place in old England ye 26th of ye 11th Month, 1689.

A Proclamation concerning Seating of Land, By William Penn, Proprietary and Governor, &c.

WILLIAM PENN, P. G'r:

Since there was no other thing I had in my Eye in the Settlement of this Province next to the advancement of Virtue, than the comfortable Situation of the Inhabitants therein and for that end, with the advice and consent of the most eminent of the first Purchasers, ordained that every Township consisting of five thousand Acres should have tenn familys at the least, to the end that the Province might not be like a Wilderness as some others yet do by vast vacant tracts of Land, but be regularly improved for the benefit of Society in help, trade, education, Government, also Roads, travill, Entertainment, &c., and finding that this single constitution is that which eminently prefers the Province in the esteem and choice of Persons of great Judgment, Ability and Quality to embarque with us and second our beginnings. I do hereby desire and strictly order my trusty and loving friends and Commissioners, William Markham, Thomas Ellis and John Goodson, or any two of them, that they inspect what Tracts of Land taken up lye vacant and unseated and are most likely to give cause of exception and Discouragement to those y't are able and ready to seate the same and that they dispose of, if not seated by the present pretenders within Six Months after the Publication hereof, provided always that the usual time allowed for Plantations be already expired and that this extends not to those persons that have forfeited their Lands in the Annexed Countys to whom I a year and an halfs time after my arrival to settle at the old Rent and have nevertheless neglected to do the same, And the said Commissioners are hereby further desired and required to take the greatest care that Justice and Impartiality be observed towards all in the disposal of Land, as well in reference to quality as quantity, that what is Right in the Sight of God and good men may always be preferred, for it is the best and lastingest Bottom to act and build upon.

Given at Worminghurst Place in old England the 24th of the 11th Month, 1686.

The 7th of ye Third Month was published ye Governor's Proclamation (viz:) that about ye Caves and y't about the cutting of Timber and Clearing of Lotts in Philadelphia, &c.

A a meeting of ye Commissioners ye 13: 3mo., 1687. Present William Markham, Thomas Ellis and John Goodson.

The Governor's Instructions was read which was directed to William Markham, Thomas Ellis and John Goodson, which follows Verbatim:

W. PENN, P. G'r.:

Trusty and well beloved friends I heartily salute you; I have thought fit, having made you my Proprietary Deputies or Commissioners, to let you know my mind about the Execution of that Trust I have reposed in you which you shall receive in these following Paragraphs and doubt not your strict, faithful and diligent execution of my Will and Pleasure in ye same from time to time.

1st. That no warrants of resurvey be granted by you for Land within five Miles of the River Delaware, or any Navigable River.

2dly. That all over plus Lands upon Resurveys granted by the former Commissioners not already granted finally or not patented be reserved to my use and Disposal.

3dly. That you take especial Care that where the Timber of mine or my Childrens' Lots is not cut down it be carefully preserved. And for as much as I am informed y't ye great Oake on ye left hand of ye Center in my Son's Lott or no Lott and so mine is felled, That I so often and solemnly warned People not to fell. I Desire and require you to inform yourselves who did it and Indict him for the same to ye utmost rigour; and hearing, that a Windmill is setting up in the Town of Philadelphia which is my Royalty to the Prejudice of Water Mills before they have half paid their Charges, which is unjust and Detrimental to ye said owners of the Water Mills, and that the Owners thereof may be considered, I do hereby order you to prevent the said Wind mill at least till further Order.

4thly. And whereas I formerly granted a warrant for forty

Thousand Acres for the Welch People to lie contiguous on the West side of ye Schoolkill, And that I am informed incursions have been made upon those Lands contrary to Equity, As also that Charles Ashcome refuses to make regular returns To Thomas Holme, Surveyor General, or pay him his old dues, which was one-third from the first of his serving under him. These are to will and require you to look into the same, and to do Justice both to the Welch and to ye Surveyor General. Charles Ashcome promiseing me to pay ye said one-third Part of ye Money for survey to the said Thomas Holme, and in Case the said Charles Ashcome shall be disorderly or refractory you are hereby impower'd to displace him, otherwise to continue him in his Imploy.

5thly. No Lands to be laid out next or Adjoyning to y't Inhabited and that in every Township one Share be reserved for the Proprietary with all ye Indian Fields that are in the said Township.

6thly. That wherever you have any Knowledge of Mines of any Sort or but a probable report of the same you do not offer to grant the same to any Person whatever without my express warrant for the same, and therefore that you put a stop to ye Irregular grant that was made to Charles Pickering and John Gray, alias Jathan (now discovered to be a Benedictine Monk of St. James's Convent, as they call it, commanded over by ye King), and their Adherants. And that in my Name you warn them all to desist as an Irregular Survey, for which Thomas deserves from a Surveyor General to loose his Office if I am rightly informed. And also that you send me of the best you can get of ye said Mines by ye first opportuntiy.

7thly. That you make a Schedule of my rents and Call my Steward, James Harrison, before you and Inform him of my Right by giving him a Copy of the said Schedule, and that you take Cognizance of his Receipts and Disbursements as my former Commissioners for my little Revenue were Impowered to do. And for the same y't you Receive as a fee ten Bushels of English Wheat Each of you yearly, remembering that the last day of ye year Eighty-five my New Rents were due and I desire and order you to see that they are paid by inferior Servants that James Harrison, my loving Steward, Employs in that Service, that so my family may be maintained, my Improvements go on and what is owing Discharaged; the last day of this Month there will be two years due, which I expect to a farthing, for that is like to be my supply at last. And because my new Rents are to be paid in Money or Silver, not in Produce, I do hereby order you to tell my Steward and under Stewards so, to whom you are on behalf of the whole of my Income Inspectors or over Seers. For the Proclamation concerning the Caves I would have it forthwith Published, for y't of the Land being seated use your Discretion so that ye Time may not exceed three Months after its arrival, I mean for its Publication; the other Proclamation relating to Timber and underwood ought to keep Company with that of the Caves of which pray take effectual care.

Lastly be careful that the Surveyors Intrench not upon any of my manners nor my Childrens' or Kindred's and y't in all things you be meek yet Just, Ready to hear yet set your Times and keep them exactly and I beseech ye God of Wisdom to direct and protect you, and leaving you to his grace, I bid you heartily farewell.

Given at Worminghurst Place in old England ye 1st day of ye 12th Month, called February, 1686.

Ordered y't ye Secretary Draw up an Instrument for ye Commissioners to sign to put in Execution the Governor's order about ye Welch tract.

Capt. Thomas Holme, Surveyor General, gave the Commissioners a Certificate under his hand, That he gave no order for ye Laying out any Land within ye Welch Tract.

The Proclamation for Seating of Land sent ye Commissioners by ye Governor, bearing Date 24th 12 Month, 1686, was Read, in order for ye Commissioners to give their opinion for the Publication thereof; after debate it was concluded that seeing ye Proprietary hath left it to the Discretion of ye Commissioners, so that ye Publication exceed not three Months after its arrival. It was ordered y't ye Publication be suspended till further Order.

Information being given to ye Commissioners, That one Jo. Allen, hath Seated a Tract of Land untaken up Lying on ye River Delaware, Contrary to order, or without its being Surveyed to him. Ordered, that the Secretary send to ye said Jo. Allen to appear before ye Commissioners the next sixth day come se'nett to show Lawful Reasons for his so doing or Prossess will go out against him in ye Proprietary's Name.

John Day complains against David Powell for his Surveying or laying out to another a Tract of Land that was first laid out for him, ye said John Day. The business appearing somewhat Intricate, John Day is desired to state his Case in Writing against ye next Time the Commissioners Sit, at which Time David Powell promises to answer the same.

David Powell, Hugh Roberts, Griff. Owen, Edward Jones, Wm. Edwards, Price Jones and Rowland Ellis appearing before the Commissioners in ye behalf of ye Welch friends, the Minute of Council was Read to them w'ch ordered that ye Surveyor General should make the returns to ye Secretaries' Office of ye Land Surveyed by Charles Ashcome in the Welch Tract for Thomas Barker and Company, being four Thousand Acres. And they being asked by the Commissioners whether the Welch friends were consenting thereunto and willing that ye 4000 Acres should be confirmed unto Thomas Barker and Company, they denyed that any of them had given Such consent and did unanimously desire in ye behalf of themselves and of the rest of the friends Concerned in that Tract that it might not have Confirmation. Information being given to ye Commissioners that one, ——— ————, that lives upon a tract of Land between the North End of Philad'a and the Proprietary's Mill, ye w'h tract is held by him for one hundred Acres and y't he, ye said ——— ————, is disposeing or hath disposed of several small Parcels of ye said Land before ye over plus (of w'ch ye Commissioners are informed there is a considerable quant'ty) is taken out thereof. It is therefore ordered that a warrant be forthwith made for ye Surveyor General to resurvey ye said tract of Land in order to accommodate ye Governor's Mill with the Over-plus.

The Commissioners doth order and appoint a weekly Sitting to be ye Sixth Day of every Week, commencing ye next Sixth Day come se'nett, w'ch will be ye 24th Instant, to which Day they now adjoin till 9 in ye fore Noon.

———

At a meeting of ye Commissioners ye 24th 4th Mo., 1687. In ye Council Room at Philadelphia. Present: William Markham, Thomas Ellis, John Goodson.

John Allen appeared according to ye order of ye Commissioners at their last sitting, and not giving Sufficient Reasons for his Peremptory Seating ye Land, it was ordered y't he, ye said Allen, depart ye said Lands he has thus seated opposite to all Law, Rule or Method, in some Reasonable Time, w'ch we allow to provide himself in, or he shall be prosecuted at ye Proprietary's Sute.

Ordered y't Edward Morgan have a Warrant for 100 Acres of Land in ye County of Chester upon Rent.

Ordered y't Tho. Fitzwater have a Warrant for 300 Acres of Land in ye County of Chester upon Rent.

The Petition of Edward Turner was read requesting a Lott near David Brintnell's, ye Surveyor informing ye Commissioners y't it was ye Governor's Land. Answered they could not dispose of it without particular order from the Governor.

Ordered y't warrants be made for Derrick Vandenburgh, 400; John Hanson, 200; Cornelius Hanson, 200, and Hermans Vangilder, 200 Acres of Land upon Rent in ye County of New Castle.

The 25th 4th Mo., 1687. The Secretary writ this following Letter to Tho. Peirson, formerly Deputy Surveyor of New Castle County:

THO. PEIRSON: The Commissioners understanding y't you Surveyed unto John Boulton, John Webster and John Rily Each 300 acres of Land in ye County of New Castle, They expect you forthwith acquaint them by what Power you did the same or they will suppose you had none, and therefore order a Process to go out against you in ye Proprietary's Name for your so doing.

W. MARKHAM, Secretary.

At a meeting of the Commissioners, In ye Council Room at Philad'a ye 22d of ye 5th Month, 1687. Present: William Markham, Thomas Ellis, John Goodson.

The Petition of Caleb Pusy, Keeper of Chester Mill, was read setting forth that Thomas Cobourn, of the County of Chester, was about to set up upon the same Creek a Mill above his, w'ch would be to his great Damage, therefore begs Relief.

It was ordered y't ye Case should be heard ye next Sixth Day, w'ch will be ye 29th Ins't, before ye Commissioners, and notice thereof to be given to Tho. Cobourn that he might then appear, w'ch was done in Manner following:

FRIEND THO. COBOURN: Caleb Pusy, Keeper of Chester Mill, having Exhibited a Complaint against Thee for thy being about to set up a Water Mill on ye same Creek, ye w'ch being a Royalty belonging to the Proprietary, and as his Commissioners Thereof, cognisable before us have thought fit (before we give our Judgment Therein and that thou shouldest not complain of Severity) To let thee know we have appointed ye next sixth Day, w'ch will be ye 29th Instant, for hearing the Master In Difference between you about the Premises by 9 in ye forenoon at ye Governor's House in Philadelphia, and so we bid you farewell. Dated at Philadelphia ye 22d of ye 5th Mo., 1687.

WILLIAM MARKHAM,
JO'N GOODSON.

The Time being expired w'ch was granted in a Proclamation Published ye 7 of ye 3d Month last Past, for the Inhabitants of ye Caves in Philadelphia to provide themselves other nabitations and having received fresh Instructions from ye Proprietary and Governor about ye same ye Commiss'rs did, in order to execute both ye former and ye latter Instructions, Publish this followng Declaration :

By ye Proprietary Deputies:

WHEREAS, a Proclamation was Publish'd by order of ye Proprietary and Governor ye 7th of ye 3d Month last past, strictly ordering and warning all ye Inhabitants of ye Caves in Philadelphia to depart ye same within two Months after ye Publication thereof;

These are therefore to give notice to all ye aforesaid Inhabitants y't on ye next second day by nine in ye forenoon the Commiss'rs will meet in ye Council Room at Philadelphia to put in Execution ye said Proclamation where any Inhabitant of ye said Caves may there show reason why their Caves might not forthwith be Destroyed. Dated at Philadelphia ye 22d 5th Mo., 1687.

WILLIAM MARKHAM,
THOMAS ELLIS.

WILLIAM PENN, *P. G'r.:*

I heartily salute you on contrary winds giving further time both of Information and Consideration in Reference to the things I have already writ to you about. I have thought fit to let you know that for as much as some of ye Buildings in ye Bank, as Benj'n Chambers, &c., have been more costly than ordinary, tho' Irregular and his particularly without leave, and y't some may interprett Such Buildings in the Bank unconcern'd in ye word Caves in ye Proclamation, Know y't even in such Cases you permit none to stand with out at least one hundred pound security for good behaviour in them and preservation of ye Bank, and Rent at half ye Value (real) yearly of ye same, to be yearly paid to me or my order so long as I shall permit them to reside there and y't this Indulgence extend to none ye Building of whose Caves is not worth Thirty Pounds and that are not of. Sober Conversation. In ye next Place, Since my last by ye same Conveyance 1 am informed of high Discontents in several, especially New Comers, That those Purchasers that are already there, have taken up their proportions next to y't w'ch is planted, and have not, nor are not yet able to seat the same but keep it for market and y't at a much higher price than I set, to the great discouragement of such as are come there, w'ch must End with prejudice to ye Publick. I do therefore, hereby most Earnestly desire and Strictly charge you, y't you allow not one day's Time after ye Publication of ye Proclamation for seating Land, and y't you publish it ye next Day after ye Receipt thereof, with this Limitation in practice, y't you reserve to present pretenders half of their Proportions till further order; and though I doubt not but you may meet with contradictions from some of the greater Purchasers, Govern not yourselves by that for 'tis just, 'tis wise 'tis equal; and having had so many Years instead of one to perform the Regulation in, if they forthwith comply not with it prosecute your Instructions to the full. The whole world of Sober Men will Justifie our proceedings therein. And in Case any should stand upon their Terms and go to Law, you are my Court for Land and I need not submit to ordinary Courts, whether I am Proprietor of my own Land or not; however if you think it safe to ye Regulation and my Just Interest to Refer it to a Jury you may, for Surely Such Engrossings must needs go for a Grievance and that cannot be popular. But when I consider 'tis no law but a Custom and Original Settlement Proprietarily made by me at first, I don't see the need of Submitting it to such a Tryal; if you should, I say you are my Commissioners of Property and that they have is theirs by my Regulation, Even Purchasers, for by English Deeds no place is fixed to them. This Manage with Zeal and Wisdom, persuade ye parties, if y't succeeds not, Command ye Surveyor, and fix the familys that Present, For the province shall not wait the Leisure of their Ability to seat it, Nor shall it be a wilderness for any man's humour or covetousness; they shall not stand between me and ye Province, and both, And the People that would settle it; and because that I would y't my Relations should comply with the Publick regulation so far set forth as they can, being infants, propose if they have ten Thousand Acres in a Place a Thousand to ten poor familys to settle the same, if but five Thousand then five Hundred to five familys to settle the said five Thousand Acres. For being Children, and I on the Publick account here, and having exhausted myself much there, and not supplyed by the Publick and Proprietary to boot, I think I may be excused, both as to me and mine. If any seat their Land let Care be taken that they have not the best places, and that for Nearness of the Land and goodness they pay some acknowledgement after three Years, that is more than Ordinary; I leave that to you especially ye Secretary to effect. If you can get them for less land 'twere better, I mean of Inheritance, tho' you add on a Lease of 7 or 11 years a hundred Acres apiece, w'ch might be 150 Acres for each family. What holes had I made if I had taken up for my relations and self near the Town or next to the old Planters, or according to Agreement, the tenth Part for myself. You may do as much for my relations by my Wife ye Penningtons I mean. I do also hereby order you to take up in the most convenient Place, y't is to say the Canoable branch on the west Side of ye Skoolkill, about Thirty Miles from ye Town, Ten Thousand Acres for my Daughter, Gulielma Maria Penn, ye Younger, get a Patent past for the same; 'tis that which goes towards the Susquehanna, by which they rode when R. Fretwell went to view that River, and seat it after the same manner, 50 acres Inheritance and 100 on Lease for 11 years for each family, or rather than not encourage ye poor give them half for an acknowledgement and half upon Lease of ye 150 acres, but so as their settlements be regular, and after ye exacted Methods of Townships and tryed to do service to their respective Mannors, when held according to patent. For my Brother Lowther's Children Advance backwards and add 2,000 acres more, w'ch makes 4 Mannors at 3,000 acres to a Mannor for his 4 Children, Margarett, William, John and Anthony, and on each 4 Familys as before. I do further strictly order you to inspect all former grants and surveys that no Irregularities may pass without your Scrutiny and Censure, for I am informed that in some Places Lands have been squandered away to nobody knows who for fees, and y't Warrants go to Markett, which is a most disorderly and condemnable thing. Whatever is Irregular vacate; for I shall be very strict. So recommending you to the protection of ye Almighty God I bid you heartily farewell.

Given at Worminghurst Place in old England ye 8th of ye 12th Mo., 1686. For my trusty and loving Friends and Companions, William Markham, Thomas Ellis and John Goodson, In Philad'a.

At a meeting of the Commissioners in the Council Room at Philad'a ye 25th of ye 5 Mo., 1687. Present : William Markham, Thomas Ellis, John Goodson. According to Notice given ye last sitting of ye Commissioners there appeared of ye Inhabitants of ye Caves on the Bank :

John Otter.	Thos. Prichard.
Benj'n Chambers.	Edward Morgan.
Hen. Furnis.	Alse Guest.
Anth. Weston.	Morris Morgan.
Nath. Allen.	Hen'y Hughes.
Hugh Marsh.	Tho. Roberts.

Samuel Hersent appeared in the behalf of John Swift and Jere Elfrith.

John Otter, Benj. Chambers, Nathaniel Allen and Alse Guest, their Caves were esteemed to be worth the Building, thirty pounds, and the Commissioners treated with them ac cordingly; the rest desired they might have more time allowed them that they might provide habitations for themselves. It was granted till ye 19th of ye 7th Month next provided, they sign to a Writing (should be drawn) ye next sitting of ye Commissioners, w'ch will be ye 29th Instant.

John Otter and the rest were appointed to come the same time and sign a writing which shall be prepared about their ———.

Upon the Petition of Walter King it was ordered that (seeing he had a Warrant from the Proprietary for 700 Acres of Land to be laid out at the place he now lives, and tho' on the neglect of Thomas Fairman in not finishing his Survey before he had placed several others so near him that when he had finished the same he found left but 500 Acres for the said Walter King, the which was returned unto the Surveyor General's Office by Thomas Fairman; And also the said Walter King making it appear unto the Commissioners that he had due to him one hundred acres of Land more than he had yet surveyed to him, and desiring it might be compleated within the said Tract returned by Thomas Fairman for 500 Acres, if upon a resurvey it should appear so much therein to be) a warrant to be granted to resurvey ye said tract to accommodate him accordingly.

Ordered y't Richard Mason have a warrant for 500 Acres of Land in ye County of New Castle upon Rent in Lue of a warrant he had formerly for the same quantity in Chester County; he being a man able to seat the same.

This day was signed the Instrument that was ordered to be drawn the 13th of ye 3d month last about the Welch Tract which follows Verbatim:

We, the Proprietary Deputies, having taken into consideration the request to us made by several persons, both in the behalf of themselves and others, concerned in a Tract of Land about forty Thousand acres w'ch was laid out by vertue of a warrant from the proprietary and Governor bearing Date ye 13th day of the first month, 1684, for the Purchasers of North and South Wales and adjacent Counties of Herefordshire, Shropshire and Cheshire. Wherein they set forth y't after the Legal Execution of the said Warrant several Incroachments have been made within the bounds of the said tract of Land by others that had not Right therein, and also then having produced to us a ceritficate from under the Surveyor General's Hand, y't he hath not by any order, directly or indirectly caused the said Warrant to be violated or Infringed. And what Land so ever hath been surveyed and laid out by Charles Ashcome or any other of his Deputy Surveyors within the said

Tract of Land was not done by order from him, Against which Incroachments the Persons concerned in the said tract have craved Justice from us that their Rights might be Maintained according to the true Intent and meaning of the aforesaid Warrant granted them by the proprietary and Governor. We having therefore well weighed the Matter, truly considered the case and rightly understanding the Governor's Intentions in granting the said Warrant, Do by vertue of the Authority granted us, Publish and declare that what Land so ever hath been surveyed and laid out within the Tract of Land aforesaid (as it is bounded, Beginning at the Skoolkill thence running West South West on the City Liberties two thousand two hundred fifty-six Perches to Darby Creek, thence following up the several courses thereof to New Town nine hundred Eighty-eight Perches to a Corner post by Crumb Creek, Thence down the several Courses thereof four hundred and Sixty Perches, thence West and by South by a line of Trees two thousand and Eighty Perches, thence North North West by a line of Trees nineteen hundred and twenty Perches, thence East and by North by a line of Trees Three thousand and forty Perches, thence East and by South one thousand one hundred and twenty Perches, thence South South East two hundred fifty-six Perches, Thence East North East Six hundred and forty Perches, Thence South South East one thousand two hundred and four Perches, thence East North East Six Hundred Sixty eight Perches to the Skoolkill, thence down the several courses thereof to the Place of beginning) (otherwise than to the Purchasers Concerned therein as aforesaid, viz: ye Purchasers of North and South Wales and adjacent Counties as Herefordshire, Shropshire and Cheshire), to be Illegal, Irregular and not according to Proprietary Method (except such Land as was Survey'd before the said Tract was laid out), and therefore do forewarn all persons Concerned who pretends to Land which hath been Surveyed or laid out within the said Tract and not qualified purchasers as aforesaid or whose Land was not Surveyed or laid out to them before the Tract aforesaid was laid out, to forbear seating or any wise occupying the Land so Illegally & Irregularly laid out. All which Illegal and Irregular proceedings we do in the Proprietor's name, reserving to himself his future Orders, thereby Condemn, Disanull and Make voyd. And all People concerned therein is to take notice hereof, as they will answer the Contrary at their Peril.

Dated at Philadelphia ye 25th day of ye 5th Month, 1687.

WILLIAM MARKHAM,
THO. ELLIS,
JO'N GOODSON.

The Commissioners upon Reading ye Proprietaries Instructions bearing Date 8th of ye 12th Mo., 1686, w'ch ye Proprietary expected should have come with the Proclamation brought by Ed. Blackfann, fell into Consideration about the Proclamation for the Seating of Land. For having by a former Instruction Received with the Proclamation three Months Time allowed their Discretion and not to exceed it to publish the same in, and that in the Proclamation Six months Time after Publication thereof was allowed for Seating ye Land, and having before given out amongst the Purchasers that there was such a Proclamation, with the whole Tenor thereof, and that there was such great Expectations of its Coming forth in Manner and Form as it was, And would create great Animosities if altered. They therefore concluded that a Proclamation should be drawn answerable to that of the proprietaries without allowing any of that Time which was allowed by the proprietary for their Discretion to publish it in, but only to allow in it so much Time as if the Proprietor's Proclamation had been published the Day of the Receipt thereof.

A Proclamation by the Proprietary Deputies.

Since the Proprietary had no other thing in his Eye in the Settlement of this Province next to the advancement of Vertue, than the comfortable Situation of the Inhabitants therein, and for that End with the Advice and Consent of the most eminent of ye first Purchasers, Ordained that every Township consisting of five Thousand acres should have ten familys at the least to the end the Province might not lie like a wilderness as some others yet do by vast vacant Tracts of Land, but be regularly improved for ye benefit of Society in help, trade, Education, Government, also Roads, travel, Entertainment, etc., and finding that this single Constitution is that which eminently prefers the province in the esteem and Choice of Persons of great Judgement, Ability and quality, to embarque with us and second our beginnings. We thereby publish and give Notice y't ye Commissioners will inspect what Tracts of Land Taken up, lye vacant and unseated, and if any of the said Tracts, lying vacant and unseated, shall not be seated according to the Regulation aforesaid, within Three Months after the Date thereof, provided the usual Time allowed for seating the same be already expired. The said Tract will be disposed of to Those that are able and ready to seat the same. Dated at Philadelphia ye 26th Day of ye 5th Mo., in the 3d year of the Reign of King James ye second, and 7th of ye Proprietary's Government, Anno Dom., 1687.

WILLIAM MARKHAM,
JOHN GOODSON.

MINUTE BOOK "C." 17

Two of these were set up in Philadelphia, one given the under sheriff of Chester County and one sent to James Harrison for Bucks.

At A Meeting of the Commissioners in The Council Room the 29th of ye 5th Mo., 1687, at Philadelphia.
Present, William Markham, John Goodson.
Several of the Inhabitants of the Caves which were not to stand upon Rent Appeared, but all Refused to sign to the obligation the Tenor whereof was: 1st. to depart out of the Caves at or before the 19th day of 7ber next. 2dly. To keep good orders in the meantime. 3dly. To repair the Damage tnat hath been done the said bank by building them.

John Otter, Nath. Allen and Alce Guest, Signed their obligation as Renters, but Benj. Chambers Came not. The Tenor of their obligation was: 1st. to pay the half Value of Yearly rent as it shall be valued by 4 indifferent men to be mutually chosen, it to Commence the 19th 7ber next. 2dly. Keep good order. 3dly. upon order to depart out and leave the same. 4thly. to repair the Bank. Upon the refusal of the foregoing signing the obligation the Messenger was sent to the Attorney General to acquaint him that the Commissioners desired to speak with him about Six in the afternoon at the Secretary's office.

Thomas Cobourn not appearing according to Notice given him the 22d Instant, These following orders were made:

PROVINCE PENSILVANIA.

To THOMAS COBOURN, of Chester County:

Whereas we, the proprietary Deputies, (upon Complaint made to us by Caleb Pusy, that thou wert about to set up a Mill in Chester Creek to the great Damage of the Mills there, under the Charge of the said Caleb Pusy, which hath been of vast Charge to the Owners thereof, and but of Little profits (yet) toward the defraying any Part thereof) did, on the 22d Instant, obligingly send to thee to give thee Notice thereof and to desire thou wouldest ye 29th following, answer the said Complaint before us in the Council Room at Philadelphia. But instead thereof, thou sent a Letter of the 26th Instant by which we perceive thou dost not only contemn the Proprietary's authority and Endeavour to subvert his Dominion over all the water and Soile within this, his Province of Pensilvania, as he is chief Proprietary thereof, but likewise intendest to persist on the Building the Mill aforesaid to the Damage of the other Mill and Contempt of the Proprietaryship.

2—VOL. XIX.

We therefore, in the Proprietary's name, will and require thee to desist from building the said Mill (without positive order from the proprietary for the same), or any way hinder the true Course of the Water of the said Creek, or any part thereof, by drawing it out of its own proper Channel, or stop or any other way molest the same upon thy Peril. Given under our hand and proprietary's Seal this 30th of the 5th Mo., in the third Year of the Reign of King James the second, and seventh of the Proprietary's Government, 1687.

WILLIAM MARKHAM,
JOHN GOODSON.

The original was given in the secretary's office to the under sheriff of Chester County the 30th Instant to be delivered to Thomas Cobourn.

PROVINCE PENSILVANIA.

By the proprietary Deputies.

We do by the authority of the proprietary, will and require thee, Thomas Cobourn, of the County of Chester, in the Province aforesaid, to forbear setting up any Mill on the Creek called Chester Creek, without order from the Proprietary for the same. And we do further, by the authority aforesaid, will and require thee not any way to stop, hinder or molest, or any way Divert the course of the water of the said Creek in or from its own proper Channel, as thou wouldest answer it at thy Peril. Given at Philadelphia the 30th of the 5th Mo., 1687.

WILLIAM MARKHAM,
JOHN GOODSON.

This was given the under sheriff at the same time the former was, with order to read the same to Thomas Cobourn and then nail it up at the Mill he is building.

Post Meridian.

Present, William Markham, Jno. Goodson.

David Lloyd, ye attorney General, according to Request, in the forenoon met the Commissiones, they consulted about a Method to prosecute those who would not go quietly out of their Caves, it was the attorney's opinion to prosecute them for a Nusance.

It was ordered y't ye Messenger should go to Every respective Cave and warn ye Inhabitants to depart the same within one Week, and those that did not should be prosecuted accordingly.

At a Meeting of the Commissioners in the Secretary's office at Philadelphia the 5th of the 6th Mo., 1687.
Present, Wm. Markham, Tho. Ellis, John Goodson.
The Petition of Benj. Chambers was read.
The Commissioners answer, was that they had formerly considered his Case but they were obliged to follow the Proprietary's Instructions. That they had formerly offered him an Instrument to Sign as others had done, whose Caves were admitted to stand during the Proprietary's Pleasure, but he evaded it. They do now again offer him the same and will also give him under their hands, that if there be such a writing under the Proprietary's hand as he alledges (by w'ch he granted part of the Bank to ye Purchasers), that he shall have the benefit thereof so far forth as it Concerns him, but if he did not forthwith comply he should be returned to the Attorney General to be prosecuted.

At a Meeting of the Commissioners in the Council Room at Philadelphia ye 12th of ye Sixth Month, 1687. Present, Wm. Markham, John Goodson.
The Proprietary's letter in the behalf of Thomas Hudson was Read for an Hundred acres of Savana, and ordered accordingly.
Upon the second reading of Benj. Chambers's Petition, in the behalf of the Society, for fifty acres of Land at Frankford, out of Walter King's purchase, and the certificate under the hand of the Surveyor General, a warrant for ye same was Granted.

At a Meeting of the Commissioners in ye Council Room at Philada. ye 19th of the 6th Mo., 1687.
Present, all the Commissioners.
The Petition of Joseph Asheton was read, setting forth tnat Tho. Fairrman had resurveyed his Land without order, Either from the Commisisoners or from the Surveyor General.
Upon w'ch the Commissioners did declare that those practices are very pernicious, both to ye Proprietary and people, and shall be severely looked after and course taken to bring offenders in y't and ye like nature to condigne Punishment.

Post Meridian at John Goodson's house.
Present, all ye Commiss'rs.
The Commiss's advising with the Attorney General about proceeding against the Persons y't yet remain Contemptuously in Caves, it was concluded y't Since the quarter sessions is to

be ye 7th Day of ye next Month they would forbear till then, and then present them to the grand Jury y't shall be found still to continue ye Contempt.

At a Meeting of the Commissioners in ye Council Room in Philadelphia ye 8th 7th Mo., 1687.
Present, all the Commiss'rs.

The Persons yet remaining in Caves having had notice given them, Appeared; they all Ingaged to depart forthwith Except Henry Furnis, who, by arguments the Commiss's Could use, Could not prevail with him, whereupon a Note was drawn and sent to the Attorney General Signed by all ye Commiss'rs to present the said Henry Furnis to the Grand Jury.

The Commiss'rs Signed The Commission following:
By the Proprietary Deputies of ye Province of Pensilvania and Counties annexed.

Whereas the Proprietary hath reposed in us the Care of his profits and Revenue arising within this Province and Counties annexed, and considering that that arising by Cattle, Horses, Swine, etc., unmarked, would be of no small advantage if Carefully and diligently looked after, which hitherto has been either neglected or abused, not only to the Loss of the Proprietary, but greatly Injurious to several whose Cattle hath been taken up, Worked and other ways abused. To prevent all which we have thought fit, to constitute and do hereby constitute, authorise and appoint Wm. Croasdell, chief Ranger of the County of Bucks, Impowering him to act therein according to Law, and to observe such Instructions as he shall from Time to Time Receive from the Proprietary, his Deputy or Deputies, or others appointed by him to manage his Proprietaryship. The said William Croasdell, before he Enter upon this service, is to give one hundred Pounds security in ye Secretary's office for his faithful performance of his Duty therein, and we do hereby revoak all former grants of this Nature. This Commission to be in force till further order. Dated at Philad'a ye seventh day of the 7th Mo. in ye 3d Year of ye Reign of King James the second and seventh of the Proprietarys' Government, Annoq'e Dom. 1687.

Wm. Markham,
Tho. Ellis,
Jno. Goodson.

General Instructions to be observed by Rangers, a Copy whereof Each Ranger within this Province and Territory is to have and observe.

To A. B. Ranger of ye County C. D.

1st. Thou art to Apply thy self to ye Clerk of ye County of w'ch thou art Ranger and desire of him a Coppy

Law 86.   out of the Records of what Marks of Cattle have been registered and likewise to inform thyself of ye Clerk from Court to Court what Marks have been Entered therein from Time to Time.

2. Thou art to account all strays whose Marks are not recorded and to secure them accordingly.

3. Thou art not to take up any Sort of Cattle whose Mark is recorded without having a Note under the Hand of the owner thereof to Justifie thy so doing with ye Mark Expressed therein of what he desires thee to take up for him.

4. That all Cattle whatsoever not marked at a Year old
Law 178.   are Deemed Strays and as so thou art to secure them.

5. Thou art not to Mark any unmarked Cattle unless with the Proprietary's Brand Mark but upon Extraordinary occasion.

6. Thou art not to Range nor hunt for any Cattle in any other County but what thou art Ranger of, unless it be in pursuit of what has been first found within your Precinque.

7. If thou shalt have Knowledge of any Person that hath marked or hereafter shall Mark horse, mare, Kine, Swine, etc., after the Age appointed by Law, or that any way shall damnifie the proprietary in any Thing Cognisable in your office, Thou art forthwith to acquaint the Secretary therewith, That Course may be taken with the offenders.

8. Thou art to keep an exact accompt of what Cattle thou takest up, as well marked as unmarked, and how thou hast disposed of them. A Copy of w'ch accompt thou art once in half a Year to transmit to the Secretary, and once in a Year to make up your Accompts with him and oftner if Required.

By the Proprietary Deputies.

Whereas, Thomas Hooton produced to us an order of Council bearing Date the 18th of ye sixth Mo., 1687, Impowering him to prove the will, and administer upon the Estate of Christoph'r Taylor, We do in the Proprietary's behalf, not only respectfully concur with the said order, but request the same of the said Thomas Hooten.   Dated at Philad'a ye 11th Day of ye 8th Mo., 1687.

WILLIAM MARKHAM,
THOMAS ELLIS,
JON. GOODSON.

MINUTE BOOK "D.

MINUTE BOOK OF PROPRIETY COMMENCING THE SEVENTH DAY OF THE TWELFTH MONTH, 1689-90, THIS IS BOOK D IN THE SECRETARIES OFFICE.

At a Meeting of the Commiss'rs the 7th of the 12th Month, 1689-90.

Present, all of them, viz: Wm. Markham, Rt. Turner, Jno. Goodson, Sam'el Carpenter. The Proprietary s Commission Directed to them was read and is as Followeth, Verbatim, (viz:)

To My Trusty and Loveing Friends:

Wm. Markham, Rt. Turner, Jno. Goodson and Sam'el Carpenter, Greeting:

Reposing Special Confidence in your care and integrity, I do hereby Nominate and Appoint you my Commiss'rs of Propriety for the province of Pennsylvania and Territorys, to act according to former Commiss'ons. Letters and Instructions and such as from time to time you shall receive. Also To be in the Nature of a court of Exchequer for the better collection of my Arrears of rent and for Auditing my Receiver's Accounts, to sitt as often as you see cause on either Occasion and to do all that which to Either Capacity does in Law, Equity or just prerogative belong, three whereof shall be a Quorum, Requiring all persons to give you the respect due to this great trust. Given at Hammersmith this 16th, 2 month, 1689.

WM. PENN.

Resolved Unanimously that they would serve the Proprietor in the Powers of the Aforesaid Commission, so far as in them lies, and they may be Justifyed by law, and in Order thereunto did agree, that the seventh day of Each week should be the Certain days of their sitting, to Commence the 15th Instant, and that publick Notice thereof be giv'n.

Order a Letter to be sent to Jacob Hall to Acquaint him that if he Can show reason why patt. should not pass to D. Rockford for 3000 Acres of land he caviated as Trusty for one Hud-

---

It was sent by D. Rockford, 7, 12 mo., '89-90.

At a meeting of the Commiss'rs ye 15th of ye 12 Month, 1689-90. Present, all the Commissioners.

The petition of Charles Pickerin was read, setting forth that he having purchased the right of Wm. Rakestraw, and that John Wheeler's house on the front of Dellaware Stood upon the Lott that properly belong'd to the said purchase, and seeing the Proprietary had sold the said Lott, he requested the bank before the same, which being formerly grant'd to another, it was ordered he should have a proportion of bank amongst the Schoolkill friends, Viz: 30 foot.

John Sinnock Verbally requesting that the Commiss'rs would order the bank before his front Lott on Dellaware side in Philadelphia, might be surveyed and laid out unto him upon the same terms as is to other purchasers; Ordered a Warr't to be made for the same quantity, 102 foot.

Thomas Bracy Verbally requests that the bank before the front Lott on Dellaware, in Philad'a, that was laid out for his purchase. The Commiss'rs understanding the said Bracy had made Exchange with the proprietor, his Lott, for land in Chest'r County; Ordered that the bank before the said lott be laid out and not disposed of to any until the Proprietaries pleasure be further known. Quantity, 102 foot.

Rob't Turner Requests that he having purchased of Rob't Taylor and Rich'd Crosby their Lotts on the front of Dellaware, in Philadelphia, that he may have the bank before said Lotts layd out to him on such terms and Obligations as other purchasers; Ordered a Warr't for the same quantity, 40 foot.

At the Requests of these persons following, viz: Chris. Pennock, Tho's Duckett, Wm. Southby, Melisent Hodgkins, Wm. Baldwin and Mary Sibthorp, whose Lotts fell, or are now Inhabitants at the Schoolkill, that the commissioners would grant to each of them a proportion of the bank of Philad'a on Dellaware side; it was Ordered that these should be laid out to Each of them on such terms As Others hath been, the Quantities following Between Sasafras Street and Vine Street, Viz:

	Foot.		Foot.
Chri's Pennock,	33	Thomas Duckett,	30
Melisent Hodgkins,	30	Wm. Southeby,	30
Wm. Baldwin,	33	Mary Sibthorp,	33

and in regard John Day's front Lott, is between the Aforesaid streets, and the said Day not being in the province, it was ordered that 33 foot of the bank before the said Lott should be Surveyed, laid out and resurveyed for the said John Day, or till further Orders from the proprietaries or his Commiss'rs as the proprietary or his Commiss'rs Shall seem Meet.

At the request of Sam'l Cart, in the behalf of his father' Joshua Cart, that the Commiss'rs would grant to his s'd father the Bank before the front Lott on Dellaware side of Philad'a, the w'ch Lott he purchased of Rob't Grenaway; Ordered a Warr't be made for the same.

At the Request of Rich'd Turner for a lott In Mulberry Street to make an orchard on, was granted on the Common Rent as a Renter.

The request of Henry Haslings and Rich'd Buffinton, prefer'd by John Brislow, requesting a tytle to their Land they bought, quantity 400 Ac's, in the County of Chester; Wm. Markham Declares he sold them the said land when he was Deputy governor, and was paid for it by boards Delivered for the Proprietarys. The Surveyor General's Deputy informs he can find no such land Entered in the Surveyor Gen'll Office, tho' the land hath been seated about seven years; Ordered a Warr't for the Survey in order for a patent.

Dennis Rockford requests that they would grant him Tenn foot of Bank to be added to 20 foot Granted him the first Instant in consideration that ye said 20 foot was laid out where there was a great breach made; it was ordered that a warr't be made for the tenne Foot Addition.

Henry Laykin, by Petition setting forth, that having some time lived in Philad'a upon a Lott Laid out to Charles Lee Purchaser, and there being a Vacant Lott Joyning thereto Requests to take up the said Lott upon Rent, the Surveyor General's Deputy informs that both those Lotts were laid out at first to the said Lee as Purchaser but afterwards the Proprietor Ordered that each Lott should be Divided in halves as being two large and that ever since the said Lott hath been Vacant; ye Commiss'rs granted the same and ordered a Warr't.

Thomas Pert by his petition Setting forth that he bought the front Lotts of Rowland Ellis and of Thos. Ellis in Philad'a on Dellaware side being 42 foot and made great Improvements thereon Requests the Grant of the Bank before the said Lott, which the Commissr's Granted on such terms as others.

Humphrey Murray requesting an Addition of ten foot to his lott of 99 in Mulberry Street for the Makeing a ditch and quick sett hedge, he having made great Improvements upon the same and that a return of the whole might be made to the Secretary's Office; the same was Granted ye ten foot to lye on ye west side of his Lott and to be 20 English.

Michael Harland and Alphonses Kirk Verbally requesting the Commissr's to grant each of them 200 Acres of land in the County of New Castle upon old rent in regard it was many miles from any River and a tract of land formerly laid out for one David Sharply, who never Seated nor ever heard of since in the province; the Commiss'rs being desirous of promoteing the Settlement of the Country w'ch for some time hath declined, Granted the same provided it be not within seven miles of any Navigable water.

Nathaniel Cartmill and Timothy Atkinson Verbally requesting that each of them might take up 200 Acres of land in the Mannor of Rockland; the Commiss'rs granted the same at a penny p'r acre Rent, being Unwilling such good Husbandmen should leave the Government.

Rich'd Moore an Inhabitant and husbandman of West Jersey being desirous to purchase 200 Acres of land in the Township of Concord in the County of Chester the which Land was formerly Laid out Upon Rent unto Rob't Adams now deseased and to the Land Unsituated nor any tytle made to the said Adams for the same nor hath any Relation or Adm'or appeared in the said Adams' behalf; The Commiss'rs Order'd that a return of the bounds of the said land should be made to ye Secretary's Office in order to make a title and sale of the said Land unto the said Rich'd Moore, he paying for the same sixteen pounds Current of this province half in silver.

John Sowghust Requesting that he might take up the Bank before the front Lott in Philad'a on Dellaware side that was Laid out in Right of his father's purchase; the same was granted him.

Several persons who have served out their time in this province Requesting us that we would grant them some Convenient place that they may Seat together upon one Entire tract; it was resolved and Ordered that a Resurvey be made of Maj'r and Jasper Farmer's land lying on the Schuylkill in the County of Philad'a, And a Convenient tract of the overpluss be sett apart for the same, And likewise to proportion or lay out unto the said Maj'r and Jasper Farmer, their Heirs, Assigns, &c., the five thousand Acres purchased by the said Maj'r and Jasper Farmer in such manner as they shall agree Upon.

———

At a Meeting of the Commissioners the 22d of 12th mo., 1689-90. Present, Wm. Markham, Rob't Turner, John Goodson.

At the request of Wm. Powell, Alex'r Beardsley and Phill. England that the Commissioners would grant each of them a proportion of the Bank on Dellaware side of Philad'a, the Surveyor General's Deputy informing the Commiss'rs that there were untaken up between 30 and 40 foot lying between Thomas Peart's and Dennis Rockford's bank lotts; Ordered that the same be Divided Equally Between them.

Griff. Jones as Agent and in the behalf of Thomas Barker and Samuel Jobson that the Commiss'rs would grant them to take up the Bank before their lotts on Dellaware side of Philad'a, which was Granted.

Daniel Hall requesting his head land as Serving out his time to Henry Waddy the said Waddy being before the Commiss'rs Justifyed the Same and Requested that 50 Acres more upon Common Rent might be added to it; it was granted.

Joseph Paul having purchased the right of Edward Blenman (viz:) one thousand acres, Requests Warr'ts to take up the lotts Liberty land and four Hundred Ninety-two the said purchase in Bucks, which was granted.

Francis Gray by his wife and Recommendatory note from Lloyd, Requested ten trees for his Building on the Bank; the Commiss'rs debateing about it did agree that it were better to grant Warr'ts for the felling of timber whereby they may be Limited, then fall as the people doe such great quantitys and no way to prevent it, the request was granted.

Ordered that if there be any Convenient part of the bank to be Disposed of that John Fuller have the Refusall.

Letter from Wm. Byles in answer to what the Secretary had writt to Jacob Hall by Order of the Commiss'rs ye 7th of 12th Month, '89-90, was brought to the Commiss'rs and Read; Ordered it be Communicated to Den. Rockford when he Applyes himself again to them.

Several persons some who have built others who are about to build on the Bank and understanding that the Proprietor's Concession for building there was but 4 foot above the bank have requested the Commiss'rs for leave to build as high as their Conveniency will permitt. Sam'll Carpenter being absent the Result was that when they met all together they would give their Answer.

Ordered that Edmond Benett have a Warr't for the takeing up his Liberty land according to his purchase of 1,000 acres.

Wm. Salway Requesting that the Commiss'rs would grant him part of a Cripple or Swamp before his own Land at or near Tawakawny for the Setting up a Fulling Mill; the Surveyor General's Deputy being present he produced the Draught of that part of the Cripple Requested, which was 34 acres.

The Commissioners to Incourage the Manufactory Intended Ordered that he have a Warr't for the same.

Benjamin Chambers by request made to the Commiss'rs for takeing up the bank on Dellaware side of Philad'a, Setting forth that he hath purhased of James Kennerly 30 foot, of Wm. Waid 25 foot, and belonging to his own purchase 20 foot, in all 75 foot, which was granted him.

At a Meeting of the Commiss'rs ye 1st day of ye 1st Month, 1689-90.

Present, Wm Markham, Sam'l Carpenter, John Goodson.

Wm. Markham purchaser of 5,000 ac's Requests a Warr't to take up 500 of the same in the County of Philad'a, which was granted.

Thomas Fitzwater Requesting that he might purchase the 150 acres of land he took upon Rent in the Mannor of Springetts Berry with an addition to it of fifty acres; Resolve that the said Thomas Fitzwater paying to Israel Hobbs twenty pounds (to whom the Proprietary is in debt) they will make him a purchase title to the 200 acres.

Richard Townsend having purchased of John and Thomas Parsons the windmill upon the Bank before the front Lott of Joseph Growdon and being Desirous to remove the said mill request that we would grant him one hundred foot of bank before the proprietor's son's Lott that lies at the South side of the said Growdon's to sett the Mill upon, which was granted.

Dennis Rockford's Patent for 200 acres of land in Philad'a County in right of Herriot, Date the 24th 12th mo., 1689-90, was signed by William Markham, John Goodson and Samuel Carpenter.

William Rakestraw Complaining that he had Extreamly suffered for want of the front lott that belonged to his Purchase the Commiss'rs offered him Sixty foot of the bank next on the north side of James West's; the said Rakestraw Desired till the next Sitting in Court to Consider of it, which was granted.

Wm. Carter having Requested the Commiss'rs for a Square of Philad'a Containing 16 Lotts one whereof he hath by Patent granted unto   bearing date the   Day of the month 16   the which square is bounded as followeth: on the south with Mulberry Street on the west With the 12th Street from Dellaware on the north with   Street and on the east with 11th Street from Dellaware. The Commiss'rs have granted him the fifteen lotts within the said Square that are not taken up according to his Request for a Horse pasture for the term of twenty-one years, Obliging himself to Clear it fit for and sow grass and at the end of twenty-one years to leave the same in such posture of fencing as he hath Generally Used whilst in his possession, Yielding and paying to the Proprietary, his Heirs, &c, Ten Shillings in good Merchantable wheat as it shall be sold for Silver in Phild'a the first year Excepted, which is to be free.

The request that was read at the last Sitting which was signed by Several that had taken up lotts on the Bank, Requesting permission to build higher than the Proprietary's Regulation did allow, the Commiss'rs Replyed that they desired all those persons that have any lott on the Bank would meet the Commiss'rs the next sixth day come Se'nett in the forenoon to discourse further about it.

Wm. Nicholas Requesting to take up 100 acres of land in the County of Kent it was granted him where not already taken up.

Henry Furnis Requesting the use of a piece of the Proprietary's land at the north end of Philadelphia upon the side of the Creek to land his Timber on, it was granted until further Order from the Proprietary.

By the Commiss'rs Order the Secretary writt to the Justices of Chester County setting forth that one Richard Moore had purchased of the Commiss'rs a tract of Two Hundred acres of Land in the Township of Concord the which land was formerly taken up by one Rob't Addams upon Rent butt he said Addams being dead and none appearing to settle the said Land nor secure the Proprietary of his Rent nor was there any yet paid nor Improv'ts made nor any Patent ever granted for the same. The Commiss'rs disposed of the Said Land tho' to the Loss of all the past rent due to the proprietary and therefore hoped the said Justices would not exact any Tax that the said land was burdened with for any time before the date of the said Moore's tytle.

At a Meeting of the Commiss'rs the 8th day of the 1st Month, 1689-90.

Present, William Markham, Rob't Turner, Jno. Goodson, Sam'l Carpenter.

Wm. Rakestraw haveing Considered of what was offered him the last Meeting Requested that he might have the 60 foot of bank (which was the quantity then offered him) made up 100 next to James West's and Liberty to make Ropes on the Proprietary's Land during the Proprietary's pleasure, which was granted and if the Proprietary shall sett out lotts there that he shall have one on the same terms others shall have which is left to the Proprietary, all which the said Rakestraw doth willingly accept as a full satisfaction for his Disappointments and Loss in want of his front Lott belonging to his Purchased land with the bank thereunto belonging and doth accordingly acknowledge himself fully satisfyed there with.

Christopher Pennock brought the Surveyor General's Return of a 1,000 ac's of land surveyed by Virtue of two Warr'ts from the Propietary dated in the year 1683 being Part of Fran. and George Rogers' purchase sold unto Geor. Collet desireing a Patent for the same, which was granted.

MINUTE BOOK "D." 29

The Petition of Several people in and about the Center was Read, Refer'd to next seventh day, Wm. Markham being Absent [gone to the Election at New Castle.]
James West Requesting 40 foot of the Bank where the penny pott house stands as an addition to sixty foot formerly Layd out to him for a Conveniency to build ships and Vessels upon, he haveing bought the penny pott House of the Widdow; his request was granted he complying with his promise (viz): to make a Convenient Slipp with timber and fill it up with Earth and Pitch it with stone against the street which is to be left 100 foot wide.

At a Meeting of the Commiss'rs the 15th of ye 1st Mo., 1689-90. Present, Wm. Markham, Rob't Turner, John Goodson, Sam'l Carpenter.

The Petition of The Inhabitants in and about the Center which was Read the last Sitting and Refered to this, was again Read and whereas they mention in their petition that by report the Proprietary had sent Orders for the Granting to the Inhabitants at the Center each five acres of land; the Commiss'rs did Assure them that they never received any such order. However did assure them that they were very willing and Ready to Accommodate them so far as safely they may doe, but in regard the Surveyor was Not in Town, Refered it till the next seventh day meeting.

The Pattent that was Ordered to be drawn for Chris. Pennock at the last sitting was this day signed by all the Commiss'rs and bears date the 13th Instant.

Henry Lakin who had a Warr't bearing date the fifteenth of the 12th Month Last as p'r minute of that day may appear, since which the surveyor at the last sitting informed the Commiss'rs that there was 198 foot front in that land which was supposed to be but two lotts, which Exceeded the bounds Limmited in the Warr't. The Commiss'rs considering the great Improvements thereon have granted the whole unto the Heirs, Executors or assigns of Charles Lee Deceased, paying unto the Proprietary, his Heirs &c.. for one whole Lot thereof one shilling English and for the rest tenn shillings English Yearly Rent forever.

Patrick Robinson, Attorney, and in the behalf of James Kingsburrie Requests that they would grant unto the said Kingsburrie a 25 foot lott in Dellaware front street first belonging to John Rowland Purchaser then to Henry Gibbs and by the said Henry Gibbs sold to James Kingsburrie which lyes between

Ben. Chambers and Joseph Phipps, see more at large by the request, The which was granted him.

Ordered that a Warr't be made for Derrick Vandenburgh for 500 acres of land in the County of New Castle upon New Rent.

Ordered that Rich'd and Henry Wright have each of them a warr't to lay out to each of them a lott in the town of New Castle.

Ordered that Zach. Vandercooling have a Warr't for a lott in New Castle.

Ordered that a Warr't be made for Ben. Chambers for the bank he requested the 22d 12th mo. Last.

At a Meeting of the Commiss'rs the 21st of the 1st mo., 1689-90. Present, Wm. Markham, Rob't Turner, Jno. Goodson, Sam'l Carpenter.

Appeared the persons Concern'd in the bank of Philad'a on Dellaware side for themselves and the Absent.

The Commiss'rs proposed that the thirty foot Street intended should be thirty foot in the Clear and Clear of all porches, Celler Stayres, payles, &c, to be a Common publick Street forever to which the Bankers assented Unanimously. That a pair of accessable Stairs be made between Street and Street in the Center or as near as may be beginning at the east side of the 60 foot Street and to go throw and Down to the 30 foot Street and from thence to the extent of 250 foot in River Dellaware or at least to low water mark and further if they build further out and that the said Centrall Stairs be built and kept in Repair by the said Bankers Dwelling between the said two streets and that there be at least left ten foot of ground between Each two streets for the said publick Centrall stairs.

That the old patents for the Bank be brought in and a rough Draught be made of a new one for their perusal.

That none ought to build or lay the foundation of any house to be built on the Bank without the Direction of the surveyor Gen'll or one of the Commiss'rs, that none may Build Irregularly through Mistake.

At a Meeting of Commiss'rs ye 22d 1st Month, 1689-90. Present, Wm. Markham, R't Turner, Jno. Goodson, Sam'l Carpenter.

Ordered That Walter Fossett have a Warr't to Resurvey the tract he lives on in order to have a patt.

MINUTE BOOK "D."   31

Ordered that Will'm Dungan have a Warr't to resurvey the 100 acres formerly lay'd out unto Jonathan Wescard, vid. No. 24: WM. TE JG.

The petition of Several of the Inhabitants of the Rocksland was Read requesting to Each 100 acres of land they hold 10 acres of Marsh, which was granted.

Signed a Warr't for Wm. Markham purchaser for 513 acres of land upon part of the overpluss Land formerly laid out to Major and Jasper Farmer, the which warr't is in the Lieu of a Warr't signed for the said Wm. Markham for 500 acres bearing date the 1st of the First month the which was Cancelled, vid y't days Minute.

Ordered that Humphrey Edwards have a lease of 21 years for thirty acres of that Overpluss he lives on at a Bushell of wheat; the land lys on the Creek Opposite to the Proprietary's Mill.

At the request of Wm. Crews it was ordered that the 62 foot lott he took up and built his pott House upon be made up 100 at the Rent Eight Shillings English.

Ordered that Joseph Paul have his Lott laid out on the front where it fell.

Wm. Weight having a Warr't in Right of Rob't Jefferson for 100 acres of land in the County of Bucks Requests that he may have a Warr't to lay it out in the County of Philad'a, which was granted, he bringing in his former Warr't No. 4 in 1687.

The Surveyor Gen'ls Deputy Reports that there is of the Bank to the Northward of the north end of Philad'a on Dellaware side between the Bridge and Vine street Includeing the street 1,070 foot.

Rich'd Turner Requesting to take for 21 years 3 Lotts between the 7th and 8th streets Lying Contiguous to a Lott he formerly took up upon Rent, to plant an Orchard, it was granted, for which he is to pay 3s English p'r Annum, and at the Expiration of the 21 to leave it well Fenced and planted.

Ordered that Rich'd Wall and Timothy Clemment have laid out to Each of them 30 of the Bank next to R'd Townsend at the south end of the town.

Ordered that John Ogle have a Warr't for 200 acres of land on the southwest side of Brandywine Creek in New Castle County.

Ordered Wm. Salway have 50 foot of the Bank on the Proprietor's land at the North end of Philad a.

At a Meeting of the Commiss'rs the 28th of the 1st mo., 1690. Present, Wm. Markham, John Goodson, Sam'l Carpenter.

Ordered that an Instrument be drawn for the bankers to sign and to Insert that the 30 foot Street be such in the Clear and that if any will have Stairs and Door-cases, &c., that they leave six foot at least for the same.

That it be discoursed at the next sitting about leaving 100 foot on the north side of the 30 foot street at the Dock, next the River for a Common Landing forever and how John Tyzack may be Accommodated Elsewhere.

At a Meeting of the Commiss'rs ye 5th 2d month, 1690. Present, Rob't Turner, Jno. Goodson, Sam'l Carpenter, Wm. Markham.

Ordered that Thomas Fitzwater have a warr't for 50 acres of Land to be laid out on the N. W. side of his and Thomas Duckett's land in the Mannor of Springfield.

Benj. Chambers Requesting that he might have 100 foot in breadth Joyning to the N. E. part of James Hunt's Lott on the bank of the Proprietor's Land at the North End of Philad'a, It was granted him he being obliged to Leave 40 foot for a Street through it from one Street to the other. Vid No. 33.

Jacob Telnor requested he might have a Warr't for 2 lotts proportionable to his purchase of 5,000 acres, which is Refered to Next sitting.

John and Zacha. Whitpaine Requests the Commiss'rs would grant Each of them 30 foot of the Bank the great house they Live in.

Wm. Stockdale Requests to take up 200 acres of land in the Mannor of Rocksland which was granted him at 1d p'r acre

Andrew Doz the Proprietor's Serv't at his Vineyard haveing Several times Requested us to put an end to his Business, we agreed that in Consideration of his service and Disbursement upon the Vineyard and in full satisfaction of all Dues and demands for the same from the Propri'r, that he shall have a Pattent for two Hundred acres of land Including the improvements and Vineyard in it for him and his Heirs forever at old rent, But upon Condition that He keep up and Improve the Vineyard so long as he shall live, and Furnish the Proprietary with vines as he shall have Occasion for his own use and whereas the said And'w Doz has charged the Proprietary with twenty dozen Bottles of Clarrett with the Bottles which he values at twenty-four pounds we agree that he shall be paid for the same he making it appear to be just and Right.

MINUTE BOOK "D."

At a Meeting of the Commiss'rs ye 10th 2d Month, 1690. Present, Wm. Markham, Rob't Turner, Jno. Goodson, Sam'l Carpenter.

Sold unto Thomas Duckett one hundred acres of Land in the Mannor of Spingfield the which Land was formerly taken up upon Rent by a Warr't bearing date ye 10 of 12 Month, 1687-8. The price tenn pounds to be paid unto Israel Hobs on the Proprietary's account.

———

At a Meeting of the Commiss'rs the 12th 2d mo., 1690. Present, Wm. Markham, Robt' Turner, John Goodson, Sam'l Carpenter.

A Pattent was signed for Katherine Farmer now Katherine Billopp dated the 10 Instant for 1,250 arces of Land being her former Husband's, Jasper Farmer's part in the tract of 5,000 acres purchased by Maj'r Farmer, Patrick Robinson Ingageing to pay the quit rent due since the date of the first pattent granted by the Proprietary for the whole 5,000 acres.

Eliz. Tibby Complaining that Joseph Walker has Surreptitiously Obtained a Pattent for part of her lott (as vacant land) and is about to build on the same Ordered that he be acquainted not to proceed until that matter be cleared.

Jacob Telnor's business that was before the Commiss'rs the 5th Instant was reassumed, he produced the proprietary's Letter in his behalf, a lott was granted him Joining upon Vine Street of an Hundred foot in Breadth fronting the first or front Street and in length as far as an Intended Street Midway between the front and second street, and further ordered that he have 20 ac's of liberty land more adjoining to the 60 acres formerly granted him, Upon his Ingagement that if the Proprietary approve not thereof that he will submitt himself and Obide by the Proprietary's Judgment therein.

Francis Cook Haveing Credit by acc't on the Proprietor, desires to purchase a small Lott in the High street if any there, which is Defered to the Next meeting and in the meantime to Inquire of the Surveyor what Land is unlaid out there.

Benj. Chambers Requests 3 squares Near Randall Spikeman's for a pasture which is granted him on the same Conditions Wm. Carter had his, he likewise desires he may make use of some trees to make the Bridge at the north end of the front Street w'ch was granted him.

Ordered that Edm'd Bennett have a Warr't to lay out for him a piece of swamp adjoining to his Land in Bucks County.

At a meeting of the Commiss'rs ye 19th of the 2d Month, 1690. Present, Rob't Turner, Will'm Markham, Jo'n Goodson, Sam'l Carpenter.

It's Ordered (and agreed unto by Benjamin Chambers) that there shall be 40 foot left between James Hunt's Lott and Benj. Chambers' lott at the North end of the bank of Dellaware for a passage out of the Street below the bank, into the street above the bank, the said Benj. Chambers proposes to make a Cartway for publick use up the bank as well as underneath, the Commiss'rs allowing as an addition ten foot more to his Ninety formerly granted him, which was granted.

Signed a Pattent for John Goodson for two hundred acres of land, Dated this day, Lying within the bounds of the liberty land sold by the Commiss'rs unto the said Jo'n Goodson for twenty pounds, the which sum he was ordered to pay unto the Carpenters that wrought at Pennsberry for part of work done there.

Thomas Hardin, Jo'n Denzy and Charles Wair desires each of them a bank lott at the south end of the Town granted unto each 30 foot adjoyning to R'd Walls and Timothy Clemments.

Thomas Miller requests a bank lott granted to him 28 foot adjoining the Bank Lotts aforegoing.

Timothy Clement and R'd Wall, vide 22d 1st Month for the grants of their Warr'ts.

———

At a meeting of the Commiss'rs ye 17th day 3d Month, 1690. Present, Rob't Turner, John Goodson, Sam'll Carpenter.

Thomas Fairman Requests that the Commiss'rs would grant Liberty to take up some of the Overpluss Land that may Remain as overpluss upon the Division of More land amongst the Children of Docter Moore Deceased, he haveing a Certificate under the Hand of John Holme (who married the widdow of the said Moore) as Consenting thereunto. The Commiss'rs in Consideration that the said Fairman has right to take up about sixteen hundred acres of land Did agree thereunto, provided he take the whole overpluss, the bad with the good.

———

At a Meeting of the Commiss'rs the 7th of the 4th Month, 1690. Present, Wm. Markham, Rob't Turner, John Goodson, Sam'l Carpenter.

Ordered that a Warr't be made for the 50 acres of land Thos. Fitzwater purchased of the Commiss'rs as an addition to 50 he formerly had Laid out for him, vid ye 1st of ye 1st Month, 1689–90.

Ordered a Warrt' to be made to lay out for John Countis in Chesnut Street upon rent.

Thos. Fitzwater requesting to purchase 50 acres of land more in the Mannor of Springfield at 5'l the 50, it was granted and a Warr't for the Laying out the same.

Ordered that James Pillar, Thomas Hardin and John Denzy have each of them a Lott in Strawberry alley.

Ordered that a Corner lott of Strawberry alley in the High Street for Sylas Crispin.

Ordered a Warr't for the laying out half the vacant Lott next to the lott laid out unto the Plymouth Friends in the High Street, unto Wm. Markham in lieu of his front lott on the Schoolkill which was Disposed off by us to William Bowling.

James Sandelands and Lasse Cock in the behalf of themselves and Sweeds, Requests that they may have a Pattent for the Church Land at Upland, for the Resurvey of which the Proprietary gave his warr't and was Resurveyed accordingly. Ordered that the Surveyor General make Return of the resurvey in order for a Pattent.

James Fox and Fran. Rawle Requests they may have a Pattent for the 5,000 acres they Purchased now called the Plymouth Town, and that the Six Hundred Acres which was formerly Intended for a Town be Returned as part of the said 5,000 acres. Ordered that a Warr't be made for the Returning the 5,000 acres of land in manner aforesaid.

Ordered that Fran. Cook have the other half of the Vacant lott next to the Plymouth Friends Lott in the High Street, the other Half being granted unto Wm. Markham, vid min. 12th, 2d Mo., 1690.

The Petition of Rich'd Townsend was Read setting fourth that he had a piece of Land granted him by the Proprietary the which he cannot gitt Returned out of the Surveyor Gen'lls Office by Reas. Thos. Brasie hath Cavett it and Clames it to be his own, it was ordered that the said Thomas Brasie he being then in town be sent for to answer to the said Petition which was done, and tho' Spoak to he came not.

Elizab. Storter requests that she may have the whole Lott of 99 foot as it was first Surveyed to her in the fourth street from Dellaware and a Pattent for the same, and that Jno. Rush who had a grant from the Proprietary for half of it may be accommodated some other place, w'ch was granted.

Ordered that 5 foot on the south side of Letitia Penn's Bank lott be allowed towards the Common Stairs.

Ordered that Andrew Doz have a Warr't as formerly granted to Resurvey 200 acres of the Proprietary's Vineyard Plantation, and that if there Be 50 acres vacant Land adjoining to it as is

Supposed that it be laid out unto Jacob Dewberry at the yearly rent of two pence per acre.

Ordered a Warr't for John James for a lott in Strawberry alley in Lieu of his Lott on the bank on the Proprietary's Land at the North end of Philadelphia.

At a Meeting of the Commiss'rs the 14th 4th Month, 1690. Present, Wm. Markham, Rob't Turner, John Goodson.

Ordered that George Harmer have half the Lott untaken up in High Street at the end of Strawberry alley, the whole Lott being 41 foot fronting High Street, and backwards 80 foot, and that James Pillar have the Other part.

John Holston Requests that he may purchase of the Proprietary 50 acres of land adjoyning to two Hundred he formerly Bought and was laid out in Chester County; Granted, the price Fifty Shillings and that the 50 and 200 acr's be Returned as one tract.

George Keith producing his Deeds from the Proprietary for 500 acres of land requests a Warr't for the same to be laid out on the Overpluss Land of the 5000 acres that was laid out to Maj'r and Jasper Farmer; a Warr't was Ordered for the same.

Upon the Complaint of James Hunt that Jonas Neelson did hinder his mowing of hay upon a Meadow lying near his Plantation to w'ch meadow the said Neelson had no Tytle, there fore the said Hunt Requests a proportion of the said Meadow upon the old Rent.   Ordered that he have a Warr't for $\frac{1}{8}$ part of the Meadows between Kingsesson Creek and Lands Creek, Reserving to Andrew Patterson what he reserved in his writing to Lassie Cocks.

Ordered that James Atkinson have what Bills, Bonds or any other obligation or Debts due to the Proprietary towards the discharge of the Proprietary's Debtor part of Acc't to the said James Atkinson.

Ordered that Anthony Taylor have a Warr't for a Lott in Strawberry alley.

Rob't Turner having made appear to the Commiss'rs that he hath the right of John Gee and Companie's Purchase of 5,000 Acres of land and that a Warr't was granted unto the said John Gee and Company by the Proprietary, bearing date ye 16th 3 mo., 1684, for the Laying out one thousand Acres thereof in the County of Bucks, the said Rob't Turner desires that the said 1,000 Acres may be changed for the like quantity in Philad'a County, and in the name of Rob't Turner as Purchaser thereof. Ordered a Warrant be made for the same, he paying the Quitrent due in Arears.   The remaining part of

MINUTE BOOK "D."

this Paragraph is Copied upon the Tenth and 9 lines in Page 16 ———.

John Goodson, in the behalf and as Attorney for Thomas Coxe, purchaser of a thousand acres of land, Requests that 914 Acres thereof may be had out of the overpluss of Maj. and Jasper Farmer's Land, in Lieu of the like Quantity formerly Laid out in another place. Granted, he Paying the Quitrent due in Arears for the land formerly Surveyed.

Ordered that notice be again sent to Tho's Brasie giveing him two Meeting days to give in his answer as p. minute of ye last Siting; notice was accord'y Sent in writing, Signed by the Seretary.

At a Meeting of the Commiss'rs ye 26th of the 2d Month, 1690. Present, Wm. Markham, Rob't Turner, John Goodson, Sam'el Carpenter.

The writings about the Regulation of the bank of this day's date was Signed by the Commiss'rs, and Several of the persons concerned in the Lotts on the bank Signed the Counter Part.

A Receipt was this day Signed by the Commiss'rs to Jo'n Goodson for twenty pounds which was for two hundred Acres of land he bought of the Commiss'rs, the which sum he had paid by the Commiss'rs Order unto Israel Hobbs and Oliver Dunkley for work done by them at Pennsberry.

Wm. Bowling Setting fourth that he had Layd out the greatest part of his Estate on his Lott at the Schoolkill so that he cannot, as others have done, Remove from the same, Therefore Requests that he may have a piece of Land Layd out to his Lott to lnlarge it. Wm. Markham being Willing to part with his Lott on the Schoolkill for part of a Lott in the High Street, it was Ordered that the said Markham's lott on the Schoolkill be laid out to him, he yearly paying to the Proprietor.

At the Request of Tho's Fairman, Ordered a Warr't to lay out an hundred acres of land he purchased of Walter King.

Upon the Request of Wm. Pyles, granted a warr't to lay out to him fifty acres of Marsh Contiguous to his Eight Hundred Acres of upland in Sussex County.

At a Meeting of the Commiss'rs ye 3rd of ye 3rd Month, 1690. Present, Rob't Turner, John Goodson, Sam'el Carpenter.

Wm. Rakestraw desired to have some land near to his house to accommodate him; Granted a Square behind his lott, between the eight Street from Schoolkill and broad Street, and

Between Sassafras and Vine Street, upon the Usual terms, (viz:) tenn Shillings p'r Square.

Arthur Cook Desires a Warr't one thousand acres of Land in part of his purchase which was granted.

Thomas Fairman Requesting a Pattent for his Brother Robert's Seven hundred acres of land he bought of Thomas Holme, and laid out about five years since by warr't from the Then. Commiss'rs. Ordered that Return thereof be made to the Secretary's Office and Patented.

[This Sheet was put into the Book by reason the paper that had the rough minutes of these 2 days, Viz't, 26th 2d mo. and 3rd of 3rd Mo., 1690, was in the hands of Sam'el Carpenter and not returned to the secretary till he had entered some minutes of after days. Wm. Markham, Secretary.]

The Address of Archibald Mitchell, John Kinsey, Abell Noble, Joseph Ransted, Abrah. Hardiman and George Emlin was Read, Requesting an Abatement of their Quitrents For their Lotts in Chestnut Street, they being Rated above any other tho' Much Less; it was granted, and that each should pay 5 shillings, English, whereas they paid before 7s 6d.

James Pillar who had granted to him the 7th Instant, a Lott in Strawberry Alley, Requests he may have the other half of that Lott that was this day granted unto George Harmar in Lieu of that he took up in Strawberry alley.

At a Meeting of the Commiss'rs the 21st 4th Mo., 1690. Present, Wm. Markam, Rob't Turner, John Goodson.

The Petition of Thomas Cross and Caleb Pusie was read Complaining against Thomas Coburn's Mill on Chester Creek, it stoping the Course of the water and Overflowing their land, Answered that for what damage they have Received the law ought to right them.

David Lloyd Requests that the Commiss'rs would not grant a Pattent for the Sweeds' Gleeb Land at Chester before there be a hearing of the Difference in that Case between him and the Sweeds. Ordered that Notice be given unto James Sandeland that the Commiss'rs have appointed this day fortnight to hear it, and the like notice to be given to Tho's Erasie to be hear the same time.

Ordered that Wm. Gieach and Adam Butcher have each of them a Lott in the third Street near Wm. East's.

Ordered that James Mortamore and Sam'el Nicholls have each of them a Lott in the third Street.

It was Agreed that the lott Layd out to Francis Cook in the High Street should be at the yearly Rent of two English Shillings, besides paying twenty pounds Current Silver money of Pennsylvania between this and the next fall of the Lease.

Ordered that a Warr't be Drawn for the Laying out of New Street and Dock Street, at the North part of Philad'a, According to the Old minutes,

---

At a Meeting of ye Commiss'rs the 28th 4th Mo., 1690. Present, Robert Turner, John Goodson, Sam'el Carpenter.

George Harland Verbally requested to have his hundred Acres where he now lives Upon Brandy Wine Creek in New Castle County, Chang'd from New to old Rent in Consideration of the great Distance the said Land is from Any Navigable part of a River; it was granted him.

Thomas Giles Requests to take up 200 Acres in New Castle County which was formerly Layd out to Tho's Hughson, haveing left this Goverment Several years, have neither improved it nor hath patt. for it, nor paid Quitrent, the which was granted and upon old Rent, it Lying 7 miles at least from any Navigable water.

Also he desires a warr't to take up 500 Acres of land near the Aforesaid land on old Rent he haveing many Children, which was granted on the Aforegoing Consideration.

Ordered that Thomas Hill have a Lott in the third Street between High Street and Wm. Harde's.

Ordered that Thomas Master have a Lott in the 3rd Street to plant an Orchard, and in Convenient time to be built on, which was agreed to.

Gave to James Atkinson a bill on John Russell for Nine Pounds that is due for Lands purchased of the Proprietary.

Wee haveing Discoursed Sam'el Jennings (According to the Proprietary's Instructions in a Letter to Rob't Turner) about the Receiver's place, he was willing to accept of the same, provided he may have Sufficient power to act and be made Capable to performe the same from the Secretary's and Surveyor Gen'll's Office, Wm. Markham Secretary not being present to be Advised with about it.

At a Meeting of the Comss'rs the 1st 5th Mo., 1690.
Present, Wm. Markham, Rob't Turner, John Goodson, Sam'el Carpenter.

Griffith Jones haveing a bill of Exchance of £50 Sterling money of England bearing date the 11th March, 1689-90, Drawn by Capt'n John Blackwell upon the Proprietary at London, payable unto the said Griffith Jones, Requests that Rather than send it home the Commis'rs would take it up and satisfie him, here Rob't Turner proposed to Discharge the said bill upon good Security, Either to be paid his money again or have land to his Satisfaction for the same. The Commiss'rs did resolve that the said Rob't Turner shall be forthwith paid to his Satisfaction accordingly.

At a Meeting of the Commiss'rs ye 5th of ye 5th mo., 1690. Present, Wm. Markham, Rob't Turner, John Goodson, Sam'el Carpenter.

The Petition of Hans Petterson was Read Complaining that the Surveyor Gen'll had Surveyed part of a Marsh from him unto Wm. Leister and Adam Sharply. Ordered that the Surveyor attend the Commiss rs to Answer the Complaint.

Rob't Ashton Requests a piece of Marsh, quantity about Thirty acres, lying between his plantation and the River, which piece of Marsh is now made an Island by a New Creek breaking out of George's Creek and bye that the mouth thereof in New Castle County; the Commiss'rs granted the same, provided that if Edw'd Blake, whose plantation is in the same Creek, be Desirous of having part thereof that he may be Accommodated, the Rent, penny English p'r Acre.

Joseph Phipps Requests that Benjamin Chambers might have the bank before his, the said Phipps' front lott on Dellaware, he having acknowledged that the said Benjamin Chambers hath made him Satisfaction for his Right therein.

Henry Lakin Requesting that the quitrent of his Lotts which was agreed upon ye 15th of ye 1st mo. '89-90 may be leased. It was agreed that one lott should be as a purchased Lott, the other two at eight shilling, English, p'r An.

Ordered that Nicholas Pierce have a Warr't for the Lott that was laid out for John James upon the Bank at the north end of the Town.

At a Meeting of the Commiss'rs the 12th 5th Mo., 1690. Present, Wm Markham, Rob't Turner, John Goodson, Sam'el Carpenter.

The Deputy Suveyor of New Castle County According to a Summons at Last Sitting appeared. Hans Peterson made it Sufficiently appear that He and his Predecessors had Enjoyed the 30 Acres of Marsh twenty years, and produced the Coppy of a Warr't Signed by Ed. Cartwell, bearing date the 8th of June, '70, for the Laying it out, and that that Marsh is no part of Vedreeda Hook marsh, but Cherry Island Marsh. The Deputy Surveyor of New Castle County did acknowledge that as he was Surveying the said Marsh he was Informed that that piece he was Surveying was Hans Peterson's, upon which he forbore untill Will'm Leister for whome he was Surveying prest him to it bear him Harmless therein, upon which the Deputy Surveyor proceeded to Execute his Warr't tho' the Warr't did direct the laying out a proportion of Marsh Called Vedreed Hook marsh, and made return of the Survey into the Secretary's office by which the said Wm. Leister Obtained a Pattent; upon Debate of the Matter it was ordered that Wm. Leister appear before the Commiss'rs this day month that the matter may be more Clear.

The Petition of Rich'd Tucker was read Complaining that he wants tenn acres of his Hundred he had a Pattent for from the proprietary Refered to this day month, and Rob't Longshore is desired to acquaint Dot'r Ernestcho to be hear then his land lying Contiguous to it.

Thomas Brasie not appearing tho' Notice often given him to answer the quere he entered in the Surveyor Gen'el's office and Rich'd Townsend. The Complainant Requesting he might be no longer Delayed but have a pattent for his 50 Acres of land in Chester Township. Ordered that the Cavett should be void and the said Townsend have a Pattent.

Ordered that Wm. Philipps have a Lott in New Castle at ususal Rent, he building on it and fenceing it in within six months after the Date of Survey.

Ordered that John Maccoom have a Lott in Philad'a upon Rent near the Burial ground.

At a Meeting of the Commiss'rs the 2d of ye 6th mo., 1690. Present Wm. Markham, R't Turner, John Goodson.

Oliver Dunkly Complaines that Fran. Cook hath not yet paid him any part of the Bill Drawn upon him for tenn pounds, but still delays the same. Ordered that the said Cook be writt unto to acquaint him that the Intent of the Commiss'rs Disposing of that lott in the High Street was to pay Oliver Dunkly, and that if he Cannot Comply they Intend to dispose of it other-ways.

At a Meeting of the Commiss'rs ye 9th of 6th Mo., 1690. Present, Wm. Markham, Rob't Turner, John Goodson, Sam'el Carpenter.

It is Requested by the Commiss'rs that Rob't Turner and

42   MINUTE BOOK "D."

John Goodson on Second day next, take a view of what timber hath been Cut upon the Proprietary's and his Children's land within and Near Philad'a, and what Timber Shall be found Cut down and Lying upon the Place that they would dispose of it as they shall see Convenient for the Proprietor's best Advantage.

The Petition of John Blunston was read requesting that no Pattents be granted by the Commiss'rs to the Damage of Wm. Sherlow.

The Petition of Henricus Williams was Read requesting a Small piece of land near the town Marsh not taken up, at New Castle. Granted, provided it exceed not two Lotts and pay rent proportionable to Lotts.

The Request of Edw'd Blake and Rob't Dyer was Read requesting a Warr't to Resurvey a piece of land Called the out Lett, in New Castle County, about three miles from the town, for which there is an old Pattent, quantity an 100 Acres, more or Less. Ordered that a resurvey be made of the said piece of Land according to the bound Mentioned in the said Pattent.

Henry Bowman setting forth that he haveing warrt's for 700 Acres of Land, the which was Layd upon a tract of land on the north side of Ceedar Creek in the County of Kent, the which Tract the Proprietor had taken into his Mannor. Therefore requests that the said Warr'ts may be laid on a piece of land adjoining to the land the said Bowman bought of Tho's Skidmore and Tho's Williams which was 400 Acres upon Ceedar Creek so that the said 400 Acres and 700 be joyned, vid. Wm. Clark's Certifycate Concerning the same, this day Read, whereupon it was granted.

James Claypool Requesting to take up a Lott in New Castle, granted upon Usual Rent.

Ordered that Hans Justason and Israel Helms, Jun'r, have between them 300 Acres of land in the Proprietor's Mannor of Rocksland in the County of New Castle, upon rent on the N. W. side of the King's Road.

According to an order of ye 12th of 5th Mo., Last, Wm. Leister appeared and answered the Complaint of Hans Peterson, But Hans not produceing any tytle but that of mowing it about twenty years and made no proof that it is a distinct Marsh from Vedreeda Hook Marsh, The Commiss'rs did Declare the said Lerster's Pattent to be good.

At a meeting of the Commiss'rs the 16 of the 6th Month, 1690. Present, Wm. Markham, Rob't Turner, John Goodson, Sam'el Carpenter.

Patrick Robinson as Attorney to Rich'd Collett, Presented

a bill Drawne by the Proprietary upon Cap't John Blackwell, Receiver Gen'll of the province of Pennsylvania, (payable to the said Collett or his order) for thirty, forty or Fifty pounds as the said Collett or his Order Shall demand. The Commiss'rs promises the payment out of the first Effects of the Proprietor's.

Upon a Debate between Otto Ernestcho and Rich'd Tucker before the Commiss'rs the Latter made appear that he had purchased of the Proprietor one hundred acres of Land, which was Ordered to be Laid out on the overpluss land of Calcoon Hook, but finds he hath not his Quantity, but that the said Otto, whose land Joyns to the said Tucker's Land, has more than his Due, It is therefore ordered that a Resurvey of their lands be made in Order each may have his Due.

The Petition of Humph. Murry and James Fox for themselves and in the behalf of others Concerned in a flock of Sheep in Philad'a was read, Requesting a Convenient piece of land somewhere about the town for the Keeping them. Ordered that about Sixty Acres be laid out in Squares between the Broad Street and so far towards Dellaware as Conveniently may be, so that it be between Dock Street and Walnut Street.

Samuel Carpenter having made use of the Butt ends of 9 trees that had been fallen in the Proprietary's Land is willing to Allow twenty Shillings for the same, and Rich'd Hilliard who did fall them is to have the tops of 5 of them.

At a Meeting of the Commiss'rs the 23rd of 6th Month, 1690. Present, Wm. Markham, Rob't Turner, John Goodson, Sam'el Carpenter.

John Hart Requests that he may take up for Wm. Bringly and Ann Ollife purchasers of 1,000 Acres their Lotts, and his Own he having purchased 1,000 Acr's. The Deputy Surveyor Gen'll acquaints the Commiss'rs that Bringly and Ollife are Distinct purchasers, each 500 Acres, and that their Lott as well as Jno. Hart's, fell on the Schoolkill.

Ordered a Warr't be made for the laying out George Symcock's Liberty land he being purchaser of 500 Acres.

Upon Request of Thomas Duckett, granted to him a piece of land, quantity about sixteen Acres lying between his Land Widdow Fincher's, joyning upon the River Schoolkill and upon John Gardner's and Joseph Brown's Lotts, a Lease for twenty-one years at tenn Shillings English, per Annum.

At a Meeting of the Commiss'rs the 30th of 6th Mo., 1690.
Present, Rob't Turner, John Goodson, Samuel Carpenter.

Jno. Hart requests two Squares in Philad'a for a pasture which is granted, upon the Usual rent, that is at the same terms as Wm. Carter's is.

A meeting of the Commiss'rs the 13th 7ber, 1690.
Present, Wm. Markham, Robt. Turner, John Goodson, Sam'l Carpenter.

Ordered that Christ'r Sibthorp have a Warr't for twenty foot of bank adjoyning unto ye John Fuller's bank lott, and thirty-one foot to John Fuller adjoyning to him.

Ordered that Jonas Smith have his bank Lott layd out.

At a Meeting of the Commiss'rs the 20th of 7th ber, 1690.
Present, Wm. Markham, Rob't Turner, John Goodson, Sam'l Carpenter.

Ordered that a note be writt to Sam'l Jennings the Proprietary's Recei'r Gen'll to pay unto Dan'el England four pounds and ten pence Due to him for Shingles used at Pennsberry.

The Petition of Mary Jeff's was read, Directed to the Proprietary and prefered to him in England, Humbly Requesting him for an Order to his Com'rs Here to allow of her Surrendring up of 1,500 Acres of land her deceased Husband Had taken up upon Rent in the County of Bucks in Expectation of several out of Ireland to Seat it. The Proprietary by his Endorsm't on ye Petition Ordered the Commiss'rs to Comply there with which was Accordingly done.

Sold to Sam'l Rowland a piece of land at the west side of the Dock at the South end of Philad'a bounded Eastward with the Dock street, westward with the 2d Street, in Breadth 16 foot, it being the back part of that Lott which was granted unto Griff. Jones, for the Setting the blew Anchor house upon, the price Six pounds to be paid to Andrew Doz, and yearly Rent one English Shilling.

It was agreed and ordered by the Commiss'rs that what land Shall be taken up in New Castle County and it be 7 Miles from any Navigable water, it Shall go at old Rent.

Ordered that Annica Lawson have 17 Acres of Vedreeda Hook marsh.

Ordered that John Gardner have 12 Acres of Land layd out on the South Side of the Cause-way at the ferry on the west side of the Schoolkill.

At a Meeting of the Commiss'rs the 27th of 7th Month, 1690. Present, R't Turner, John Goodson, Sam'l Carpenter.

Rob't Turner and John Goodson Reports that they had lately viewed part of the proprietor's Lands near and Adjoyning to the Town of Philad'a and found great Spoil and waste made of the timber; there-for,

Ordered that power be given to Benj. Chambers and Even Oliver to Seize any timber cut in the wood or Shall be Cut without Order, and to Endeavour to find out the Persons Offending.

Henry Baker having an hundred Acres of Purchased Lands to take up, Desires he may have it at the great Swamp about a Mile from his own house in Bucks County. Refered to the next meeting, that if any of his Neighbours wants accommodation therefrom they may have the like priviledge.

Benj. Chambers Desiring two squares more may be Layd out for him adjoyning to his three squares formerly granted. Ordered Accordingly at the same Rent the other three is and like terms.

Rob't Turner Request in behalf of John Gee and Company to have a Lott by the Dock side at north end of the town next to the bridge, which was ordered Accordingly.

Ordered that Tho's Fairman have a Lott next to Jo'n Gee and Company.

Rob't Longshore in Behalf of Tho's Holme in right of Sam'l Clarridg whose Lott fell at Schoolkill Desires a Lott opposite to John Gee's Lott afore mentioned.

Thomas Fairman Having Right to take up purchased land, Requests a piece of Cripple opposite to his Meadow at Shaxamaxent and is Willing to allow four Acres of purchased land for one of Cripple, which is granted.

At a Meeting of the Commiss'rs the 4 day of Oct'r, 1690. Present, Wm. Markham, Ro'bt Turner, John Goodson, Sam'l Carpenter.

Cornelius Empson, Requesting in Writing a part of Brandywine Creek for his Mills, The Commiss'rs Desired that Cornelius himself may be first Discoursed by them.

Ordered that Henry Baker have a Warr't for one hundred Acres of land he purchased, Laid out in the Proprietor's Mannor, above the Falls of Dellaware, includeing the great Swamp, provided that if Joseph Milner will have a third part of the said Swamp the said Henry Baker shall accommodate him therewith at Reasonable Terms.

A Lett'r was Read Directed to the Commiss'rs from the Proprietary in the behalf of John Day, bearing date the 8th 10th Mo., 1689, ordering 500 Acres of Land should be laid out for the said Day, Resolved a Warr't should be made according to the tennor of the said Letter.

At a meeting of the Commiss'rs the 10th of 8thber, 1690.
Present, Wm. Markham, John Goodson, Samuel Carpenter.

The Secretary is desired by the first Oppertunity that he see the Surve'r of New Castle County, divide the Land that belongs to John Grub in Rocksland Mannor from that the Proprietary bought of Isaac and David ——

Wm. Salway having had granted to him a piece of Swamp near his house on Dellaware by Frankford Creek on ye 22d 12th Mo., Last, the Pattent was Signed this day for the same it being 36 acres at 2d per acre per annum.

Ordered that Daniel England have layd out for him a vacant piece of land at the N. E. End of the Town of New Castle, it Running along the small Creek side.

Peter Trago alledges that Charles Ashcome formerly surveyed unto Joseph Edg. 50 Acres of land in the County of Chester for which he, the said Ashcome, never had Warr't and that the said Edg had now Deserted it, he, the said Trago Requests that he might take up the said land which was granted.

At a Meeting of the Commiss'rs ye 18th of 8th Mo., 1690. Present, Wm. Markham, Rob't Turner, John Goodson.

Andrew Robinson in the behalf of himself and others, that they may take up 5,000 Acres of land and that the Commiss'rs would Dispence with the Regulation of its lying Contiguous to other lands already laid out, promising that they will seat the same according to regulation and procure Sufficient old purchasers tittles to lay on the whole tract, the which was granted.

The Petition of Several of the Inhabitants of the Town and County of Philad'a Requesting Liberty to build a Publick Wharfe against the end of Walnut Street. Ordered that a rough Draught of a Pattent for the same be made to be Considered off.

Caleb Pusie Complains Against Tho's Coborn for Stoping the water of the Mill at Upland Creek. The Comiss'rs considering what orders have been made about the same, and notice given to Coborn to Decline building on the said Creek or hinder the Current of the water of the said Creek, and that the said Coborn hath take no notice thereoff. Therefore ordered that notice be given to the Attorney Gen'rll that he prosecute the s'd Coborn according to Law.

Severall Inhabitants near Schoolkill Complaining of Severall illconvenientcy that may Accrue to them if Tho's Duckett should take up the land which was granted him ye 23d of 6th mo., Last, whereupon it was Ordered that the Surveyor Gen'll forbear laying it out until further Ordered.

———

At a meeting of the Commiss'rs the 25. of the 8thber, 1690. Present, Wm. Markham, Rob't Turner, John Goodson.

John Marshall having purchased of Henry Gibbons 50 Acres of land which Gibbons had by Warr't from the Proprietor at 1d p'r acre Rent, Requests that he may Purchase the said 50 Acres, which was granted, he paying 2. 10. 0 Silver in 4 Months time or three pounds for the said 50 Acres with the overpluss, vid. 3 mo., 1689, No. 174.

Sam'l Sellars Requesting to purchase his land he lives on at Darby in the County of Chester, which is now at a penny p'r Acre it being 100 Acres, which is granted him at £5 Current Money of this Province, of which he payed Present in Silver two pounds one Shilling and Six pence, which was Delivered to John Goodson to be paid to Andrew Doz on acc't of the Proprietor, and one pounds five Shillings by bill upon Edw'd Dowly, Silver, the rest to be paid in wheat in two months time, both to be paid to Edw'd Hunlock Merch't at Burlinton on acc't of the Proprietor.

Whereas Peter Trago obtained a Warr't the 10 Instant for a piece of land in the County of Chester, which was formerly laid out by Charles Ashcom unto one Jos. Edg, pretending the said Edg to have relinquished it, but the said Edg Appearing and Setting forth that he had built a house and was burnt out, which Several of his neighbours did testifye, it was ordered that the said Edg have the land Confirmed to him as one that has Served his time in the Country (viz:) unto Tho's Mincher.

Benjamin Chambers brought a Return of the Survey of 5 squares to have it Confirmed to him for the term agreed as with Wm. Carter, and to pay for each square tenn Shillings p'r Annum to Commence the first day of the first month 169½.

By the Commiss'rs for granting Lotts and lands they takeing into Consideration the great Quantity of Land lying wast and unsetled within a tract of about 40,000 Acres, Commonly known by the name of the Welch tract, the want of Seating and Improveing of which has been of great Dammage to the Proprietary and of Exceeding Loss and hindrance to the well seating and Strengthening the Province, Several Honest, able and Substantiall persons having either Leaft it for want of such convenient Seats that are unsetlett in that Tract, or hindred from Seating, Such as have been formerly layd out unto them in it. In order to an accommodation both to the service of the Proprietor, the good of the Inhabitants of the said tract, and the common Benefit and well fare of the Province, Resolved that notice be given unto David Powell, or some othe: purchaser concerned in the said tract, that they show cause why the land not laid out or not seated and Improved, (within the said tract) according to regulation, may not be disposed off as other lands within this Province, for the Hearing of which the Commiss'rs Intends God willing to Sitt in Philad'a the 19th of the next Month.

At a Meeting of the Commiss'rs ye 1st of 9ber, 1690. Present, Wm. Markham, Rob't Turner, John Goodson.

Ordered that two Warr'ts be made Each for 50 Acres of Land in the County of Philad'a unto Thos. Fairman in Right of Wm. Stanly, the which land, Viz: 100 Acres was formerly laid out by Warr't in Right of Walter King.

Ordered a Warr't to be made for the Laying out unto John Fuller, 31 foot of Bank next to Christopher Sibthorp.

Francis Smith haveing produced to us a Conveyance of 1,250 acres of land from Charles Lloyd and Margaret Davis, unto Joseph Harris and from the said Harris to the said Smith, Ordered a Warr't for the Laying out the said land in the Welch tract.

At a Meeting of the Commiss'rs the 8th of 9ber, 1690. Present, Wm. Markham, Rob't Turner, John Goodson.

A Petition by Several of the Inhabitants of Philad'a being presented last Sitting for Liberty to build a free wharfe before Walnut Street for the Publick Service, It was ordered that a Rough Draught of Pattent should be prepared, which was Accordingly done, Read and perused by the Commiss'rs and amended. Therefore it was Ordered to be Engrossed with its amendments and past into a Patent.

Ordered a Warr't be made to lay out the Liberty Land of Henry Slighton, Edw'd Blake and he purchased together, 500 Acres of land, but Blake had formerly taken up his proportion of liberty Land.

MINUTE BOOK "D."

At a Meeting of the Commiss'rs the 15th of 9ber, 1690. Present, Wm. Markham, John Goodsoh, Sam'l Carpenter.

Tho's Fitzwater having at Several Times purchased of the Commiss's 310 Acres of land in the Mannor of Springfield in two tracts, (viz:) one of a 150, ye other of 160 Acres for which he was to pay after the Rate of Ten pounds p'r 100 which amounts to £31 for part of pay he this day gave up to the Commiss'rs a bill Drawn on them by Israel Hobbs, Dat ye 1st 1st mo., 1689-90, and Accepted by Sam'l Carpenter the same Day (being one of the Commiss'rs) the which bill was Accepted as part of payment, it being for twenty pounds.

The Request of Cornelius Empson (setting forth the great Charge he hath been at in setting up a Mill for Corn, Sawing and fulling on Brandy Wine Creek in the County of New Castle) was Read, and therein Complains Against Hans Peterson that he was about Setting up a Mill on the same Creek opposite to the said Cornelius's Mill, with Intention to make use of the said Cornelius's Dam, and thereby Draw the water of the said Creek from his Mill, Therefore Requests that if Hans Peterson will build a Mill that he might be ordered to build it Either above or below the said Dam; that the water of the Creek may be Servisable to both of them, Resolved that an Order be sent to the Said Hans that he forbear building any mill on the said Creek or Diverting any of the water of the said Creek out of its proper Course or Channell.

There being about 100 Acres of land in the Mannor of Springfield Lying between the Land of Tho's Fitzwater and Tho's Duckett's Land, the said Tho's Duckett Requests that he might purchase the same which was granted him at 10 p. 100 Acres.

Ordered that George Willard have a Wrr't to take up 200 a, of Land in the County of Bucks he being purchaser of 1,250 Acres.

By the Proprietary's Commiss'rs: Where as we are given to understand that Hans Peterson is about to build a Mill on Brandywine Creek not only to the Dammage of a Mill already there Built, But an Incroachment upon the Proprietary's Prerogative or Privelege the whole right and property of the water of the said Creek being in him. Wee Doe therefore, in the Proprietary's name, will and Require thee, Hans Peterson, not to Erect, build or Sett up any mill on the said Creek nor by any means whatsoever Draw the water of the said Creek out of its true and Natural Channell it now runs in or Inlarge the same without leave first obtained from the Proprietary, his Agents or Commis'rs as thou Wilt answer the Contrary at thy Perrill. Given at Philad'a the 15th 9ber, 1690.

At a Meeting of the Commiss'rs the 19th 9ber, 1690. Present, Wm. Markham, R't Turner, John Goodson, Sam'll Carpenter.

4—Vol. XIX.

Griff. Owen, with several other Purchasers who have an Interest in the Welch Tract was this Day with the Commiss'rs, according to notice sent to David Powell bearing Date the 25th of ye Last Month. They requested a longer time to Give their answer to the Commiss'rs Proposall, which was granted untill the 13th of ye Next Month.

The Commiss'rs takeing into Consideration the Request of Jos. Wilcox for a Conveniency to Sett up a Rope yard, did Resolve that he ought to be encouraged thereunto, and Ordered that he have a Lott next to Jacob Telnor's to the northwards of the Slipp at the north end of the town of Phila'a (Viz:) in the Front street 50 foot front, to run Backward Westwardly unto a new Street now Called Cable Lane, with the same breadth of 50 foot to be granted to him and his Heirs, &c., for Ever at the yearly Rent of 2s 6d.

And for a Rope yard or walk, to begin on the West side of the said Cable lane, over against the said Lott and with the same breadth of 50 foot, as if Continued with the Lines of the said lott, Straight unto the third Street, Skiping or passing over the streets already laid out, which is not to be Surveyed unto him; granted him and his Heirs for Ever for a Rope yard at the yearly rent of 5s English p'r an.

At a Meeting of the Commiss'rs the 22nd of 9ber, 1690. Pres't, Wm. Markham, Rob't Turner, John Goodson.

The Petition of Wm. Clark was Read Setting forth that one Thos. Fenwick hath taken up a tract of land on the South Side of the Indian River in Sussex County, by a grant from Mary Land, the which tract is in the Mannor Laid out by the Proprietary's Order, and requesting that he may have a grant from the Commiss'rs to take it up and he will forthwith seat it to prevent the other. The tract being Six hundred acres, whereupon it was granted upon old Rent.

Granted unto Wm. Clark a Lott in the Proprietary's Land at the north end of Philad'a in Vine Street between Cable lane and Second Street.

Wm. Bethell requests the Commiss'rs would grant him to Cutt Six Cord of wood; granted provided he cut no timber trees that are fitt for Building.

Franc. Rawles Requests he may Cut for his Bakeing such trees as he shall find already Cut Down in the Woods.

Ordered that the Surveyor Gen'll Resurvey that tract of land

MINUTE BOOK "D." 51

Called Shaxamaxsen and make Return thereof to the Secretary's Office.

Ordered that And'w Griscom and James Pillar have their bill of Three pounds paid out of the first money Received, it being for Viewing and appraising the work done by Isr'll Hobbs and Oliver Dunkly at Pennsberry.

Ordered that Joshua Barkstead have a Lott of 50 foot broad near the Runn, at the North end of the Proprietor's Land at the North end of the Town, next to Rob't Turner's.

Ordered that a Warr't be Directed to Joshua Barkstead to take an exact Survey of Sussex and Kent County, with all the lands laid out there in Order to make a Draught of the Whole Countys.

At a Meeting of the Commiss'rs the 29th 9ber, 1690. Present, Wm. Markham, Rob't Turner, John Goodson, Sam'l Carpenter.

Wm. Markham Requests to take up two Hundred acres of Land on old rent in the County of Kent, which was granted him.

Thos. Willard Requests 4 timber trees for the finishing his house in Chestnut Street; was granted.

Ordered that John Chandler have 4 trees (for his trade of Wheelright) of those that are already fallen.

Ezech. Meedham Requesting Warr'ts to take up two hundred acres of Land in the County of Kent upon old Rent; it was ganted to be laid Out in two tracts, viz: 100 in Each.

Upon the reading of the Petition of Thos. Jones of Sussex County, Setting forth that one Wm. Burton, of Virginia, Obtained from S'r Edmond Andros a Patt. for one thousand acres of Land in the County aforesaid at a place Called the Long neck, after which, in the year 1677, Obtained from the said Andros a grant for Six hundred acres adjoyning upon the said Burton's Land, and was Confirmed to him by the Proprietor, Wm. Penn, Esqr., by Pattent about Eight years since, and further that the Surveyor hath Resurveyed the said tract of Land of 1,000 acres without any Warr't or Order, as the Petitioner Supposes, and thereby within the bounds of the Resurvey hath included almost all the Six Hundred acres of the Petitioner's aforesaid and that the whole as the Resurvey has been made amounts to above two thousand acres.

The Commiss'rs takeing into Consideration the great abuse Committed by the Surveyor of Sussex and Kent Countys (if the alligation of the petitio'r be true), Ordered that the Surveyor Doe forthwith Send to the Commiss'rs a true and Exact Draught of the Land he Resurveyed for Wm. Burton, Called the Long neck, with the true Quantity of the same in order to

Doe Speedy Justice as Well to the said Burton as the petitioner, of which thou art not to faile at thy Perrill. Given at Philad'a the 29th 9th Mo., 1690.

The foregoing Order was sent by the Petitioner and Directed to Wm. Clark, Surveyor, &c.

At a Meeting of the Commiss'rs ye 6th 10thber, 1690. Present, Wm. Markham, R't Turner, John Goodson, Sam'l Carpenter.

Sam'el Sellars paid £1 13s 6d in full of his purchase of Land made the 25th 8thber last, ye which sum of £1 13s 6d was paid Unto Wm. Markham on acco't of Edw'd Hunlock.

John Marshall paid towards the land he purchased the 25th 8ber Last the sum of twenty shillings, the which sum of twenty shillings was paid unto Wm. Markham on acc't of Edw'd Hunlock; there remains due from the said Marshall two pounds.

Daniel Jones Requests a lott adjoyning to him in Walnut Street, which was granted him & in Consideration of its incommodiousness at 3d English p'r an.

Jonathan Duckett Requesting a Warr't for some timber to build his house on the bank at Philad'a, Was granted Six trees.

Jo'n Brook Requests to have the Swamp adjoining to the west side of the 7 street opposite to James Poulter's, which was granted him (Reserving the Street) With a Lott of dry land adjoining, the whole amounting to about 8 lotts; in Consideration of the great Charge he must be at in makeing it fit to plant, have put the rent at Six English Shillings per annum.

At a Meeting of the Commiss'rs the 13th of 10ber, 1690. Present, Wm. Markham, R't Turner, John Goodson, Sam'l Carpenter.

Thos. Fairman haveing purchased of Wm. Stanly 4,000 of 5,000 acres, which was old purchase, and having as he acknowledges sold unto Jo'n Swift 200 acres of his 4,000 Requests that the said John Swift may have a Warr't to take up the said 200 acres in lieu of a Warr't formerly granted unto Thos. Fairman bearing date ye 31 of ye 3rd mo., 1689, which warr't is said to be lost; this was granted.

Sam'l Rowland, who purchased a piece of ground in Philad'a of the Commissr's ye 20th 7ber Last, for which he was to pay unto And. Doz Six pounds, brought to the Commiss'rs a Receipt under the said Andrew Doz's hand for five pounds, promising to pay unto ye said Doz the Remainder in a very sort time, whereupon he had his Pattent signed.

Nich. Scull, by the hands of Rob't Longshore, presented a bill Drawn by him, the said Skull, upon Zach. Whitpaine bearing date the 9th 10 mo., Instant, and accepted by the said Whitpaine to pay in Six weeks time after the Date five pounds to the Commiss'rs, or Order it being in part of payment for 100 acres of land the Commiss'rs Sold him in the Mannor of Spingfield, the full price sold for being tenn pounds; the which bill was Endorsed payable to Edw'd Hunlock.

John, Thos. and Edward Jones, Joynt Purchasers of 5,000 acres of Land Requests a Warr't for their Liberty Land.

Andrew Griscom in the Behalf of John Murray Requests two trees to help finish the said Murry's house.

Sam'l Carpenter in the behalf of himself and others Concerned in Partnership with a Stock of Sheep Requests that the Commiss'rs will grant them as many black oaks as will fence in tenn acres of land for a Sheep pasture, w'ch was granted in any sort of wood Except white Oak.

John Marshall paid five Shillings and Six pence, which was given to Wm. Markham for Edw'd Hunlock, Vid Last Day Sitting.

William Carter Requests a Tree to make Laths on, which was Granted.

Girff. Owen, with several others, Inhabitants of the Welch tract, Came and gave in a Paper to the Commiss'rs, which follows verbatim. Vid 25th 8ber and 19 9ber Last:

Wee, the Inhabitants of the Welch tract in the Province of Pennsylvania, in America, being Descended of the Antient Britains, who always in the land of our Nativity under the Crown of England have Enjoyed that liberty and priviledge as to have our bounds and Limits by ourselves within, the which all cause Quarrels, Crimes and Tittles were tryed and wholly Determined by officers, Magistrates, Juries of our own Language which were our Equals, Having our faces towards these Countrys, Made the Motion to our Gov'r that we might Enjoy the same here, which thing was soon granted by him before he or we ever came to these parts, and when he came over he gave forth his Warr't to lay out 40,000 acres of land to the intent we might live together here and enjoy our Liberty and Devotion in our own Language as afore in our Country, and so the 40,000 acres was Surveyed out and by his own Warr't, Confirmed by several orders from the Commiss'rs of ye Propriety, and Settled upon already with near four score Settlements, and as we have good grounds to believe if the way had been Clear from troubles there might had been so many Setlers upon it by this time as in Reason it could Contain, and besides as it is well known there was Several Scores of our men Serv'ts who was very desirous to have out their head land according to promise, but could have none with any convenientcy that was worth to settle upon, whereby many are like to Desert the province and to go to other Countrys, also some of our Friends that have Concerned themselves with the first that came to this country have lived a while here and Returned again for their families, Friends and Relations, that had Disposed themselves to come over with all speed if Providence had permitted, and as far as we are given to understand are Still waiting for the oppertunity to their great Dammage, and now to Deprive these of their lands and Libertys which they Depend upon when Coming here (and that in their absence) Wee Look upon it to be a Verry Unkind Dealing, like to Ruining many Families as also a Subtill undermining to Shutt that Door against our Nation which the Lord had opened for them to come to these Countrys, for we can declare with an open face to God and man that we Desired to be by ourselves for no other End or purpose but that we might live together as a Civill Society, to endeavour to deside all Controversies and debates amongst ourselves in a Gospell order, and not to entangle ourselves with Laws in an unknown Tongue, as also to preserve our Language, that we might ever keep Correspondence with our friends in the land of our Nativity. Therefore our request is that you be tender not only of Violating the Governor's promises to us but also of being Instrumentall of depriveing us of the thing which were the chief Motives and Inducements to bring us here, and that you would be pleased as far as in you lies to preserve us in our properties by removeing all such incroachments as are made upon the Lines and Boundarys of our said tract, and by Pattent or otherwise in Due form of Law to Establish and Confirm the same unto us, so that we may not by any further pretences be interupted in the peaceable Enjoyment thereoff, according to the Governor's true intent, and then we shall with all readiness become responsable for the Quitrent accruing to the Proprietor, the Commencements whereoff we shall referr and submitt to his Consideration, and if these our reasonable Desires be not answered but our antagonists Gratifyed by our being exposed to those uncertainties that may attend, wee shall choose rather than Contest to suffer and appeal our Cause to God and to our friends in England.

At a Meeting of the Commiss'rs ye 20 of 10ber, 1690. Present, Wm. Markham, Rob't Turner and Jno. Goodson.

The Commiss'rs ordered that the paper that was given in the Last Sitting by the Inhabitants of the Welch Tract should be read over again, which was accordingly Done, and having Considered of the same and found not to answer the propositions made by the Commiss'rs to them, Ordered that the Commiss'rs propositions be Drawn up in writing to be Delivered to them, which follows Verbatim:

By the Proprietary Com'rs.

To the Inhabitants of the Welch tract:

The Proposition that was made to you by us was, That there being 40,000 acres of land actually Surveyed and laid out and known by the name of the Welch tract, and there being Regular Returns thereof made in form and Manner as other purchasers Lands are by which we know (and by no other means can) how to charge each Tract of Land with its Quitrent, and therefore in course and according to the Method which has hitherto been used, we have Charged the said Tract of 40,000 acres as other tracts of the like purchase are, But least it should Surprise you, or give Suspition of an unneighbourly or unfriendly act, we gave you time notice for a conferrance with us about it and afterwards a Considerable time to make your answer, which you gave in writing the 13th Instant, The which we have very Deliberately Considered, and find the Maj'r part of the writing not Cognisable by us, Or within our province, which is only to Confirm and grant Lands, &c., and settle the affairs of the Proprietor's Revenue, nor Indeed does any part of it answer our proposition, but Verry Obliquely and with much ambiquity, which shows more of Skill and Cunning then a Direct and Sincere answer.

Whatever the Proprietor hath promised, we Question not but he will perform, and in whatever he has given us power we are Ready to doe, and when you please to Demand willing to Confirm to you the said tract by Pattent as we doe unto other purchasers according to the warr't and Survey, the which if you Refuse, and others accept, You Cannot think it hard if we grant your Refusal to them who have Equal right with you by purchase to take up land. To this we desire you will be speedy and plain in your Answer as we are with you in our proposition, for we are Resolved what in us lyes God willing to Remove all Rubbs and hindrances in the way to a quiet and easy Settlement off the Proprietor's Revenue within his Province. Dated at Philadelphia the 20th 10th Mo., 1690.

The Request of Patt. Robinson for a Warr't for the overplus of the tayle of his Dellaware front street Lott, between the east side of the 30 foot Street and the tayle of his said Lott upon the east side of the Dock upon 6d English rent according to the regulation of the Dock, was granted, the said Pat. Robinson having produced to us Thos. Budd's Rec't for £3 8s 0d, being 16d per foot for each 51 foot.

Upon the Request of Randall Spakeman to grant him a lott in the Proprietor's Land on the north end of Philad'a. The Commiss'rs granted to him 50 foot adjoyning to Joshua Barkstead's Lott.

Liberty was given to Jos. Brown to Cut 100 Cords of wood for burning of bricks, but no white oaks.

John Goodson Complaining that there was a minute Standing against him in the Collum of the Warr't book at No. 228, Dated the 2d of 11 mo., '89-90, Concerning the Bank Lott, before Alex. Parker's front street Lott, which was prejudicial to his Quiett possessions of the said bank Lott or at Leastwise Cause some Dispute, the Commiss'rs therefore Doe by this Minute make void and Null the Minute in the Collum aforesaid, affirming that the said bank lott was granted to no other nor to no other end then is expressed in the Pattent for the said Bank Lott bearing date the 15th of the 7th Month, 1690.

The Commiss'rs Granted unto Jo'n Loftus 50 of Bank next to Randall Spakeman on the Proprietor's Land at the north end of Philad'a.

The Commiss'rs having about 7 mo's Since Verbally promised unto Edw'd Shippen of Boston on Condition that if he would live in and be an Inhabitant of this Province, to sell unto him a tract of land, quantity about 205 acres, adjoyning upon the south Bounds of the Town of Philad'a, at the price of 100 pounds Current Coin of this Province, and that he should have a year's time to Consider of it, This Day Arthur Cook produced to the Commiss'rs a letter from the said Shippen to himself Desiring him to take up the said tract for him and to Clear and fence part of it, for that he was resolved to live in this Province and Shortly Intended hither, and at his arrival would pay the Money, whereupon it was Ordered a warr't Should be Directed to the Surveyor Gen'll to lay out the said tract.

At a Meeting of the Commiss'rs 27th 10ber, 1690.

Present, Wm. Markham, R't Turner, John Goodson, Sam'l Carpenter.

John White of Bucks County this Day bought of the Commiss'rs 37 acres of land which was the over pluss of Sam'l Cliff's, the price £9 Silver to be paid on the 7th Day of the Next 12th Month; a warr't Ordered for the laying out the said Land.

MINUTE BOOK "D." 57

At a Meeting of the Commiss'rs ye 3rd 11 Mo., 1690-1.
Present, Wm. Markham, R't Turner, Jo'n Goodson, Sam'l Carpenter.

At the request of Dennis Rockford that we would end the Difference between him and Wm. Byles, Attorney to Thos. Hudson, concerning 3,000 acres of Land in the County of Bucks, Ordered that notice be sent to Wm. Byles to appear before the Commiss'rs the 17th Instant to show reason why the said Land Should not be Confirmed to Dennis Rockford.

Ordered that Dan'el Cook have two trees towards building his House in Chestnut Street.

Ordered that Benj. Chambers have 30 trees for the fenceing in the 5 Squares he Leases of the Proprietor, White oaks Excepted.

Jo'n Bristow, one of the Executors of Thos. Brasie, Requests the Renuing of a Warr't formerly granted the said Thos. Brasie for a piece of Land in Chester County, which Warr't is said to be Lost, which was Dat. the 17th 12 mo., 1685, No. 125, which was granted.

———

At a Meting of the Commiss'rs the 10th 11 Mo., 1690-1. Present, Wm. Markham, R't Turner, Jo'n Goodson, Sam'l Carpenter.

Granted to John Carter 10 Trees to build on his Lott in the High Street.

John Bowls Requesting the purchase of a Small Cripple adjoyning to his Land on the west side of the Schoolkill, which was granted, he paying after the rate of £10 p'r 100 acres.

Ordered a warr't to lay out to Robert Thomas and Randall Vernon their lotts and liberty land.

The Inhabitants of Shaxmaxsen appeared to give their answer whether they would purhase the overpluss Land of their, the which they did in the Negative.

Humphrey Edwards, who married the widdow of Jurian Hartsfield, who sold a tract of land unto one Smith, and some other, the which Tract the Commiss'rs Caused to be Resurveyed and found to have 245 acres overpluss, three hundred and fifty being the quantity granted by Pattent from S'r Edmond Andros the said Humphrey Edwards Requests he may Rent of the Proprietor 30 acres of the said Overpluss Land, which was improved by his predecessor, which was granted him for 21 years at a Bushell of Wheat per annum.

The Inhabitants of Monohocken requesting the Cripple lying between their Meadows and the River Dellaware may be Laid out unto them, it was granted and Ordered that a Warr't be

Made for the Laying out unto each of them so much Cripple as Shall be found to lye before each man's Meddow and land or as Near as possible, not altering what has been laid out unto Wm. Salway; the Rent as their land is. Ordered that Erick Cock and Wm. Salway have a Warr't for the Cripple between their land and Frankford Creek.

At a Meeting of the Commiss'rs ye 12th of 11th Mo, 1690-1. Present, Wm. Markham, R't Turner, Jo'n Goodson, Sam'l Carpenter.

Ordered that a Warr't be made for the Subdividing of the Land of Shaxamaxen amongst the Inhabitants according to their Proportions, allowing for the King's Road, as has generally been alowed by the Proprietor.

Rob't Turner being willing to take up the Overpluss land of Shaxamaxen in part of payment of the bill he took up Drawn on the Proprietor by Capt. John Blackwell, allowing for it at the Rate of twenty p'r Cent and at a bushell of wheat Rent p'r 100 Acres p'r Annum; Ordered a Warr't for the same with the proportion of Meddow and Cripple to the said Overplus and all the Cripple and Swamp from John Bowyer's Line Northward to the end of Shaxamaxen: Land to be laid out to best Conveniency for the said Rob't Turner, the price of the Cripple to be 5 P. p'r hundred Acres and Rent one Bushell of wheat p'r 100, to be laid out as an appurtenance to the Tract he lives on; Ordered a Warr'tt to lay out unto Robert Turner a Vacant piece of Land Joyning to poor Island.

Nich. Nellson requests that in Regard that its intended a Mill should be built upon the Mill Creek Near the north end of Philad'a and having a piece of Meddow in the said Creek that thereby will be Drowned, that he may have in Lieu thereof the Cripple below the Bridg on the North east side of the said Creek.

William Salway haveing granted him a piece of Cripple as p'r Warr't bearing date the 22d 12 mo., 1689-90 for a fulling Mill, and having finished his Said Mill, and finding not water sufficient to sett it to work requests a small piece more of the said Cripple wherein a Small run is, in Order to Carry the water off the said Runn to the Mill, which was granted the former way.

At a Meeting of the Commiss'rs 17th 11th mo., 1690-1.
All of them Present.

William Rawles having purchased 200 Acres of land in Bucks County of Job Howell which the said Howell took up upon

Rent by Warr't from the Proprietor, the said Wm. Rawles requests (that) he being a very poor man, and the rent of the Land so great that it discourages him from Seating the same, and that he had already paid unto Job Howell 6 P., The Commiss'rs will grant him to purchase the same and give him some time for payment. Resolved that he pay for the said two hundred Acres Tenn pounds at two payments, Five pounds in one year's time, and five pounds the Next year, and that Job Howell pay the Quitrent Due for the said Land unto this Day he never having improved it.

Thomas Curtis having formerly obtained a grant for twenty foot of the bank on the Proprietor's land at the north end of Philad'a, requests that in Lieu thereof he may have a Lott in the third Street trom Dellaware next to Wm. Geetch, he not being able to build an wharf on the Bank as required. It was granted him, Thirty-Three foot in Breadth.

Granted Henry Badcock Six timber trees towards the inlarging his house.

Madlen Morris having a lott to the westward of the Broad street at the Center, and there being about thirty foot Square ground which remained of Lotts when laid out, he requests to take up the same as an addition to his lott aforesaid at the proportionable Rent, which was granted him.

Alexand'r Line requests the Meddow and Cripple fronting his Land in Shaxamaxen, Land in Lieu of so much fast land belong to his plantation.

———

At a Meeting of the Commiss'rs ye 24th 11th mo., 1690-1. Present, Wm. Markham, R't Turner, Jo'n Goodson, Sam'll Carpenter.

Daniel Howell having built upon the Bank of the River Dellaware Northward of Philad'a before Daniel Pegg's Land Under pretence that the said Pegg had leased unto him the said land,—It was debated by the Commiss'rs, and resolved that it was not within the bound of the said Pattent of Dan'll Pegg's, but ought to be at the Proprietor's Disposal, and therefore Ordered that Notice be given to the said Howell that he forbear to build any further upon the Bank or wharf any further into the River than what he has already done upon his Perill, or at least to the Incommodation of that place which has been Intended for a dock.

Dan'll Pegg was offered the refusal of the overpluss land of that tract at the North end of Philad'a, etc., valued at 100 P., excluding what was formerly taken out of the South part of the Tract, alowed him a week's time to Consider of it and give his Answer.

Ordered Joseph Brown have Liberty to Cut 100 Cord of wood more, According to a former grant, etc.

Robert Longshore Requests that he may take up of Cripple before his house on the Schoolkill, which is about 50 or 60 Acres, at a Bushell of wheat p'r 100, which was granted, provided he incommode not his Neighbours and do forthwith Ditch and Improve the same.

William Boulding Requests the land that fronts his Lott on the Schoolkill between the River and his house at One English Shilling Rent, which was granted.

Granted Evan Oliver the Brick shades at Salford's Brickkills, they being ready to Drop down.

Elizabeth Shorter and Rich'd Townsend haveing a right to 8 acres of Liberty Land, Viz: Each four Acres, and through Ignorance took up ye whole in their plantation Tract, requests that no advantage may be taken thereof but they may have it at a reasonable rate to purchase, which was granted, paying tenn shillings for the same.

At a meeting of the Commiss'rs ye 31st 11th Mo., 1690-1.
Commisioners Present:
Cap't Wm. Markham, Rob't Turner, John Goodson, Sam'l Carpenter.

Granted John Delavall and others (the overseers for the Building of ye Wharf against Walnut Street), twenty trees towards ye same.

Peter Yoakham, Mounce Jonesson, John Joneson, Neels Joneson and Wm. Clayton, each having a proportion of land in a Tract seated on the Schoolkill Called Aronamink, Requests that a part of a Cripple lying near or bounding upon the said tract may be laid out unto them. It was granted in Manner following, Viz: That they make such improvements as Rob't Longshore was obliged to Doe at his takeing up part of the same Cripple at the last sitting, and also that they leave a Sufficient passage through the said Cripple to and from other Lands that Lys without that Cripple, to the nearest fast Land.

Jno. Goodson Reporting that he hath paid unto Andrew Doz the Tenn Shillings on Acco't of Rich'd Townsend and Elizabeth Shorter, According to the Minute at last sitting, Ordered he have a Warr't for the eight acres of liberty land therein expressed.

Joseph Wilcox requests that he may have Six trees, and one sufficient for makeing Clapboards to build on his Lott on the

MINUTE BOOK "D." 61

Proprietor's Land, which he took up for a Rope yard. which is granted, the six trees not to be above one foot through.

Agreed with Dan'll Pegg and Tho's Smith's Widdow, for the overpluss of land as p'r the last sitting, that they pay fifty pounds in Silver at or before the first Day of the third Month, And twelve pounds in Current Money forthwith to Content and the remainder of the £100, being thirty-eight pounds, to be paid at or before the first Day of the 8th Month next, and Humphrey Edwards to enjoy 30 Acres of the Land he Lives on as tennant to them as was agreed by the Commiss'rs. The said Edwards not makeing waste of timber or firewood, and Accommodation for a Mill by the new Casway reserved of about Six Acres, And also the Commiss'rs doth allow that what conveniency upon their view the front of the land upon the River, may be granted them.

This Day made up Andrew Doz's Acco't and there was Due to him to Ballance, 13P. 15s 18d. A Bill was drawn upon Dan'll Peggs and Widdow Smith For the payment thereof on acco't of their Purchase of the overpluss Land.

At a Meeting of the Commiss'rs the 14th of 12th Mo., 1690-1. Present, Cap't Wm. Markham, R't Turner, John Goodson.

Cap't Markham Reports that he had received of John White, of Nesheminah Creek, nine pounds, it being for thirty-Seven Acres of land, being part of the overpluss land of Sam'l Clift's in Bucks, having given the said White a receipt for the same, and had paid it to Edw'd Hunlock, of Burlington, on the proprietor's Acc't.

Granted Henry Furnis a Lott upon the Proprietor's land on ye North end of Philad'a Joyning to the second Street and fronting upon the Creek.

Upon the Request of Wm. Rakestraw, granted him a half square on the same terms as Wm. Carter and Benja. Chambers had theirs, according to proportion, being bounded to the Northward with Mulberry Street, Eastward With Broad Street, Southward with back lotts, and Westward with the Eighth Street, to be added to that; granted the 3rd 3rd mo., 1690.

Randall Sparkeman requests that he may have Liberty to Cut wood upon the proprietor's Land for the next summer's work for burning of bricks. The Commiss'rs in Consideration of the great rent he paid for the tenn acres, Viz: 5,000 of Bricks p'r Annum, And this being the Last year he was to stay on it, granted him to Cut 60 Cord, but not to Cut any Timber Trees or White Oke.

Benja. Chambers being before the Commiss'rs they Acquainted him that he might Remember the Hundred foot of bank granted him the 5th of 2d Mon., was upon the terms of Makeing a Cart Way or Street through it from the front Street to the thirty foot Street under the Bank, and they Expected he would fourthwith goe about it, but finding Nothing yet done towards it, did resolve y't he have Six Months time to perform it or else to be Disposed of as the proprietor or his Commiss'rs Shall think fit.

Ordered that Wm. Southbe have A lott adjoyning to the Common Landing at the end of the Second Street fronting the River on the Proprietor's Land.

At the request of Ellis Jones that the Commiss'rs would grant unto him a Lease of 21 years for eight acres of Land near the Proprietor's Mill at the yearly Rent of 12d p'r Acre.

The Purchase of the new burying ground is Twelve pounds Rent one Ear of Indian Corn p'r Annum.

At a Meeting of the Commiss'rs the 8th of 12th Mo., 1690-1. Present, Cap't Wm. Markham, R't Turner, Jo'n Goodson, Sam'll Carpenter.

Wm. Jenkins having Produced to the Commiss'rs his Deeds from the Proprietary for 1,000 Acres of Land Requests a Warr't to lay it out in the Welch Tract.

Upon information that John Grub Makes daily Havock and Spoyle of the Timber upon his Land in the Bout under pretence of its being undivided,—Resolved that his part be Laid out to him with all Convenient Speed and that in the mean time notice be sent to him to Desist on his Perill.

This Day accounted with James Atkinson and there remains due to him twenty-one pound fourteen Shillings and four pence.

Ordered that John Chandler have a Lott of fifty foot wide near the Second Street fronting the Runn at the North end of the Proprietor's Land.

John Marshall who purchased a piece of land brought to Compleat the pay for it a Coverlid, for Which the Commiss'rs Acquitted him, Viz: the 13th [Nov.] and 6th of Dec'r last.

Whereas there appears 20 Acres of Land to be overpluss in a tract held by Otto Ernest Cock and Richard Tucker for 200 Acres in the township of Darby which is Sold to Richard Tucker, he paying thirty Shillings for the Same and to be laid out adjoyning to the said Tucker Land, and Otto is to have his 100 Acres laid out as Conveniency Shall Permitt.

Joshua Tillery Requests to Rent 50 Acres of land which the Proprietor Purchased lying about a Mile above the falls of the Schoolkill, it was granted him for 100 Years at 3d p. Annum p. acre.

At a Meeting of the Commiss'rs the 7th of 1st Month, 1691.
Present, Cap't Wm. Markham, R't Turner, Jo'n Goodson, Sam'll Carpenter.

The Secretary reports that the Bill drawn upon Zacha. Whitpain by Nich. Scull for Five pounds in part of paym't of Twenty pound due to the proprietor from the said Scull for two hundred acres of land Purchased of the Commiss'rs is accepted and Credit given to ye Proprietor for it by Edward Hunlock.

Nicholas Scull having had formerly a Verbal Grant to purchase 100 Acres of the Overpluss of Maj'r and Jasper Farmer's Land, the which overplus land lyes about the Sandy Runn, he requests a Warr't for the same, he paying Purchase Tenn pounds.

David Lloyd was sent for about the Sute at Chester, etc.
The Secretary is Desired to be at Chester Court.

At a Meeting of the Commiss'rs the 21st of 1st Mo., 1691.
Present, Cap't Wm. Markham, R't Turner, John Goodson.

The Secretary reporting the transactions at Chester Court according to the Minute at last sitting. Ordered that a Memorial be put in writing to be delivered to Da'd Lloyd, which followeth, Verbatim:

By the Proprietary Commiss'rs,
To David Lloyd, Attorney Gen'll:

Upon the 7th Instant we acquainted you that there was a house, lott and Land in the Township of Chester, Als: Upland, which in the year 1681 was taken in possesison as an Escheat by the then Deputy Governor William Markham, (now Secretary) for the use of the Proprietor, the which house, Lott and land became an Escheat by the Death of one Marmaduke Randal, who Deceased Without will or heir or at least none at that time Appeared, The Proprietor after his Arivall in his Province, being in Possession of the said Escheat made an Exchange with one Tho's Bracy, Purchaser of 5,000 Acres of land for his Lotts and liberty Land in Philadelphia Town and County, and gave him possession thereof, and that Robert Eure, by a pretended Will of the said Marmaduke Randall to

Elisabeth Bangs, now wife to the Said Rob't Eure, laid Claim and had Commenced Suit in the Court of Chester for the said House, Lott and Land of the which house, Lott and land the Proprietor was obliged to make good tittle unto Tho's Bracy, his Heirs, &c., or return unto him his Heirs, &c., the Lotts and liberty land aforesaid, And therefore we Desired thou wouldst appear to defend that Cause according to thy Office in Chester Court the tenth Instant, to which thou gavest no Satisfactory Answer, whereby we might hope thou intendest to perform it, Only said it was necessary Some of us should be there to see how it went, and that thou wert to be there Accordingly we Desired the Secretary to be there who went and at his Return reported that he was all the First day of the Court there, but saw not the Attorney Gen'll, but During his stay there Rob't Eure had by some Stratagem gott Possession of the house, this we thought fitt and Necessary to acquaint thee with and to Desire thou will't either take such care in that matter that the Proprietor may come to no Damage thereby, or lett us have thy refusall that we may take our measures Accordingly. Dated at Philad'a the 21st of the 1st Month, 1691.

Here Ends Book D in the Secretaries Office Compared by m.

Jo'n Hughes.

MINUTE BOOK "E."

BOOK OF MINUTES OF THE PROPRIETARIES COMMENCING FROM THE 7TH OF THE 12TH MONTH, 1689-90, AND ENDING THE 21ST OF THE 1ST MON., 1691. RECEIVED OF SECRETARY PETERS AND RECORDED THE 21ST DAY OF JULY, 1759, BY ME, JO'N HUGHES.

N. B.—This is book E in the Land Office.

At a Meeting of the Commissioners the 24th of the 1st Month, 1691.

Present, William Markham, Robert Turner and John Goodson.

The Commissioners having Sent for David Lloyd to Deliver him the Memorial that was Ordered the 21st Instant but he was not in Town.

At a Meeting of the Commissioners the 28th of ye 1st month, 1691. Present, Cap't William Markham, Robert Turner and John Goodson.

The Surveyor General's Deputy having brought in a Draught of the Proprietor's Land at the North end of Philadelphia, the Commissioners Took it in Consideration and Did Resolve that all those that have taken up Lotts on the Bank before the said Delaware River side, and do not, within three Months after this Day, build and support the Bank and Wharf out to make out the Thirty foot Street according to the Regulation of the Bank of the Town, The Lotts shall revert to the Proprietor.

Upon the reading the Petition of Mary Bradshaw, Widdow of James Bradshaw, Deceased, &c., It was ordered that Henry Hollingsworth should have ordered accordingly during pleasure.

John Roads requesting to purchase Fifty Acres of Land in the Proprietor's Mannor, of Springfield, it was granted, he paying Five Pounds for the same.

Otto Ernest Cock requesting to take up the Swamp or Cripple between his six Acres of Land he bought of John Ladd and the Mill Creek between Philadelphia and Shakamakson, which

5—VOL. XIX.

was granted him at the prise of two Shillings, Curr't Money, p. Annum.

Thomas Roberts took the Key belonging to the House of Thomas Callowhill from the Commissioners of Propriety, promising to pay to the said Callowhill, his Heirs or Assigns, Tenn Shillings p. Annum, and the Key was delivered the last setting to the Commissioners by Henry Moore.

Thomas Fairman haveing purchased fifty Acres of Land of Walter King, and the Deputy Surveyor General informs that will compleat the takeing up of the said Walter King's Land purchased, A warrant was ordered for its being taken up in Philadelphia County.

At the request of some persons for Trees to repair the Bridge in Chestnutt Street, it was granted they should have three Trees, but such as are already fallen and not claimed by any Warrant from the Commissioners.

The Petition of Mary Bradshaw was read, ordered that the proffitts of the Surveyor's place of New Castle County be continued to her, as it was to her Husband, untill further Orders.

At a meeting of the Commissioners ye 11th of the second Month, 1691.

Present, Robert Turner, John Goodson, Samuel Carpenter.

Ordered that a Patent be Made for John Calvert in his Own Name for 700 Acres of Land in Chester County, being Granted by the Proprietor the 13th of the 1st Month, 1683, Unto Thomas Calvert 300 Acres, John Calvert 300 Acres, and unto Margaret Calvert 100 Acres, being now Made Appear to us that the whole 700 Acres is properly ye s'd John Calvert's.

Ordered Richard Tucker's Patent be made According to Return, being One Hundred and Twenty acres.

At a Meeting of the Commissioners ye 25th April, 1691.

Present, Cap't William Markham, Robert Turner and John Goodson.

Richard Deane, Thomas Parsons and John Parsons, Request Each a Lott on the East Side of the Third Street, Between Walnut Street and Spruice Street, Each 30 Foot at 5s a ps. Sterling Rent; Cadwallader Lewis the Like.

Jeremiah Elfrith and Peter Sherborn, at their Request, is Granted them Each a Lott joyning together on the Bank on the South Side of the Dock, 44½ foot Front, They wharfing out and Leaving a Space between their wharf for Security of

Boats and Vessels; and that Charles Ware have 30 Foot next them.

Andrew Griscome and James Piller's bill that was brought in the 22nd of the 9thber, Last, was this Day indorsed to Samuel Jennings to Allow it to Andrew Griscome Upon Account of Quitrent; the Bill is Three Pounds.

By the Minute of the 28th of the 12th Month, Last, Richard Tucker was Indebted unto the proprietor 30s for Land Bought, &c., the which being certified to us Under the hand of s'd R'd Dean, that it was paid by Thomas Smith to Samuel Carpenter's Order, and Credit Given the Proprietor by Samuel Carpenter; for it a Receit was Given for it.

The Bank before Sasafras Street being very much Decayed, it is therefore Ordered that forthwith publick Notice be Given to the Magistrates and Inhabitants of Philadelphia that they Support and Maintain the Same, and where it has Broaken into the Front Street it be Repaired, Otherwise the Commiss'rs will grant it unto Such as will perform the Same.

At a Meeting of the Commis'rs ye 2nd of the 3rd Month, 1691. Present, William Markham, Robert Turner and John Goodson.

Silas Crispin Requesting, in the behalf of his Brothers and Sisters, James, Joseph and Benjamin Crispin, and Jeane, Ellinor, Elizabeth and Amy Crispin, a warrant to take up the 3,000 Acres Granted unto them by the proprietor By a Deed bearing Date the 8th Day of August, 1687, wherein the Proprietor Apointed William Markham, Thomas Ellis and John Goodson, his Attorneys, Jointly and Severally, to Deliver Seizin thereof, Accordingly the same was granted and Ordered a warrant should pass for the Same forthwith.

Abraham Hooper requests to take up a Lott in the third Street next to Thomas Parsons, &c., that at the Last Sitting Took up Lotts which was Granted Upon the Same Terms and Quantity; The Like is Granted to John Fallows and James Coat, each a Lott.

This being the Day appointed for the Welch friends to give their answer to the Commiss'r's propositions of the 20th of December, Last, there appeared in behalf of the Welch, Griffith Owen, Hugh Roberts, Robert Owen, John Bevan, with many Others. The Welch Friends' answer is, that they are willing to pay hence forward Quitrent for the whole 40,000 Acres, but not since the Date of Survey, the which Answer not being Satisfactory or Direct to the proposition,

Resolved that the Lands already laid out in the Said Tract unto other Purchasers be Confirmed unto them.

Granted that James Fox Take up a Lott, Taken up Upon the Runn at the North End of Philadelphia on the proprietor's Land.

Caleb Pusy having purchased the 50 Acres of land that was laid out unto Richard Townsend, in the township of Chester, in which tract there is found to be about 20 Acres over pluss, the said Caleb Pusy desireing to Purchase the same, which was Granted, the purchase to be Fifty Shillings.

William Southeby requesting that he may have liberty to gett Stone from of the Proprietor's Land on the Schoolkill, it was granted him for one year's time.

At a Meeting of the Commissioners ye 9th day of ye 3rd mon., 1691.

John Tank desires his land in the township of Shakamaxunk may be returned into the Secretary's Office in Order to a patent; Ordered that the same be accordingly done.

William Watson requesting a Lott in Philadelphia; Granted him one adjoining to Timothy Clement.

In Order to Answer the proprietor's late desire, that Acco'ts should be sent him of his Rents and Revenues, It's agreed that we bring in Our Acco'ts of what we have received and paid and that notice be given to all others that have received any Rents or Revenues of the proprietor's, that they would bring in their Acco'ts to the Commissioners or the Receiver Gen'l, without fail the 21st Instant and that those that live more remote may have notice to bring in their Acco'ts with all speed, persons to give notice to, that has been Concerned, that comes at present to our Minds, are James Atkinson, Phineas Pemberton, Wm. Yardly, James Sanderland, Caleb Pusy, George Foreman, the Execut'rix of James Bradshaw, George Martin, John Hill, William Berry, James Nevell.

Copy of what was written to them, Viz:

These are to desire and require thee to bring in or send to us a true acco't of whatsoever thou hast received and paid for the Proprietor by the 21st Instant, of which pray fail not.

At a meeting of the Commiss'rs the 30th of ye 3rd month, 1691, present, Capt'n William Markham, Rob't Turner, John Goodson.

Arthur Cook appeared in the behalf of Edward Shippen as his Attorney and requested a patent for his land laid out by Virtue of a Warr't bearing date the 20th day of the 9th Month, 1690, the said land being granted conditionally that the said

Edward Shippen shall Seat and Settle himself in this province as an Inhabitant thereoff, the said Arthur Cook doth offer to Engage to the Proprietor in a bond of two Hundred pounds that the said Edward Shippen shall settle within this province, as an Inhabitant thereof, within one year and a half after the date hereof, Death or Sickness Excepted, or the land with its improvements to be returned to the proprietor, &c., and likewise that the sum of one hundred pounds which is the purchase of the said land to be paid to the propriet'r, &c., or his Commissioners, or their order within 4 months.

Ordered that a Warrant be made for 1,000 Acres of Land for Arthur Cook in Chester County in part of his purchase.

Ordered thirty foot on the Bank to Pat. Robinson, being an Addition to Timothy Clement's by reason of the Largeness of the Bank in that place, and likewise to Jeremiah Elfrith, twenty-nine and a half, and next adjoining to Watson 30 foot, and then Adjoining to enter Sherborn, allways Observing the former Regulation that in that place is ordered.

Ordered Thomas Fareman to have the Twenty foot Lott on the Bank which was given up by Thomas Curtis.

At a meeting of the Commiss'rs the 20th of ye 4th Month, 1691, present, Capt'n Will'm Markham, Rob't Turner, Jno. Goodson, Sam'l Carpenter.

Some of the Inhabitants of the tract of Land called Shackamaxon, requesting Patents for their respective divisions of the said tract, but it being Objected by Thomas Fairman that of the 1,000 Acres, they had title to no more than 600 Acres. It was Ordered that they should bring to the Commiss'rs at their next siting their receipts for their Quitrents from the first time, that it might appear how long they have paid their quitrents for 1,800 acres.

Timothy Clement having formerly a grant for 30 foot of Bank at the South end of Philad'a, which was accordingly laid out with the usual Length of 250 foot, which length would not reach the river Deleware, and therefore the regulation of the Bank as in other parts of Philad'a could not be performed, which aforesaid lott after Improvements Made thereon by the said Clements was sold by him to Patt. Robinson, who hath requested to grant the said lott to him in his own name, together witn a convenient number of feet at the east end thereof that the same may be recommodated with the River Delaware as in other parts of the Bank, which was granted to be laid out as followeth, that is: at 150 foot Distance Eastward of the front parallell thereto Runn a street of thirty foot Broad, then next lay out forty-five foot for Building thereon, then next thereto a Street of thirty foot Broad, then extend into the River 175 foot.

Valentine Bird, Ord'r 30 foot opposite to Dan'l Jones' at 5s p'r annum Rent.

Ordered a Patent for 31 foot of Bank for John Fuller. Ordered a Warrant to Joshua Tillery for 40 foot of Bank to Corner of Sassafras Street which was formerly granted to Robert Turner and by him sold to the said Tillery.

Ordered that Robert Turner and Samuel Carpenter bring in their acco'ts next fifth day, on which day the Commiss'rs, with the receiver Generall, intend to meet together to Settle with them.

Ordered that the People at Darby have notice to be here next seventh day to meet the Welch Friends, in order to Settle the Welch Tract. Ordered that Jeremiah Elfrith and Peter Sherborn have each of them 29½ feet.

At a meeting of the Commiss'rs 27th of ye 4th Month, 1691. Present, Capt. Wm. Markham, Rob't Turner, Jno. Goodson, Sam'll Carpenter.

John Martin requests to have 90 foot of ground fronting the fourth Street and adjoining to the Back of the lott he lives on in Walnut Street, w'ch was granted him for 5 years, he paying 3 English Shillings p'r Annum.

The Inhabitants of Shackamaksen appeared and brought their Receipts to make appear what Quantity of land they have paid quitrent for and for what time; Michael Neelson and Gunner Rambo brought their receipts, whereby it did appear that Michael Neelson had paid quit Rent for 450 acres before the Proprietor had any Title to this province, and Gunner Rambo for — acres, whereupon it was Ordered Michael Neelson and Gunner Rambo should have their Patents for their said Lands.

At a meeting of the Commiss'rs the 27th 4th Mo., 1691. Present all.

Griffith Owen, with several of the Welch Friends, appeared for themselves and other Inhabitants and those concerned in the Tract of Land of about 40,000 acres called the Welch tract, and did offer to pay quit Rent from hence forward for the whole 40,000 acres, and thereupon Challenged a Patent for the whole to themselves; the Commiss'rs Ordered the Minute of the 2nd 3d mo. last about the same business to be read, which was accordingly done, and that it was now too late for them to alter that result, having past their words Already to Confirm those Tracts to the purchasers that have been laid out within the said 40,000 acres who are ready and willing to pay their quit Rent from the time of survey, whereupon it was Ordered a Warrant for takeing of the Caveats entered in Surveyor General's Office of the Lands within the said Tract following, Viz: of Sneeds, Thomas Bracy, John Hort, the Society and Francis Fisher, that returns of them may be made into the Secretary's Office.

Alce German requests to take up a Lott upon Rent in some Convenient place, which was granted to be between 20 and 30 foot front, if any such place can be found.

At a meeting of the Commiss'rs ye 18th of ye 5th Month, 1691. Present all.

Whereas at the first Laying out of Philadelphia, the Front lots on the North side of Mulberry Street, by reason of the River from that place upwards, inclineing more Easterly then in other places, were ordered to Extend Eastwardly thirty foot more than other Lotts to the South of it, and from the North Eastwardmost Corner of the said Mulberry Street to the North Eastwardmost corner of the High Street a straight line to Run, whereupon the Lotts between the said Mulberry Street and High Street are of greater Length then those who are to the southward of the High, which Lengths is not mentioned in their Respective platts, But the Owners of the said Lotts having requested a Confirmation of the said Extraordinary length as an addition to what was granted them by Patent; the same was granted.

At a Meeting of the Commiss'rs the 12th ye 7th mo., 1691. Present, Robert Turner, Samuel Carpenter, John Goodson.

Samuel Jennings, Receiver General.

John Barclay gives an acco't of money Disbursed by him for the use of the Proprietor for Surveying Charges, and also shewed Us a draught of the land lying on Seaboard Side, in east Jersey, where One thousand two hundred acres of Land is agreed to be laid Out to each proprietor, and upon Inquiry made we have Unanimously agreed to have the Proprietor's 1,200 acres to be laid out adjoining to the Pertition line betwixt the Jerseys, which, when done with 500 acres more already laid out, the Charges in the whole amounting to £4 15s which the Receiver Generall promises to pay unto the said John Barclay when he shall have Effects in his hands, or if he have Occasion of anything of his ship goods it shall be paid presently, and for as much as it is further agreed by the Proprietors of East Jersey that each proprietor shall have 10,000 acres more, But John Barclay reports to us that it's not to be done without Warrant from their Governor, and at preasent there being none it Cannot be done now, but it may be will advise of it. Memorandum to Inquire for the Governor's Deeds for Two Prorprietys in West Jersey.

At a meeting of the Commiss'rs ye 19th ye 7th mo., 1691. Present, Capt'n Wm. Markham, Rob't Turner, John Goodson.

A Patent was signed for the piece of Ground that by the Front street's not running strait was more then Robert Turner's patent for the Lott afore Mentioned, and that one English silver six pence shall be the rent thereof, &c.

Isaac Warner Requesting to be made Ranger for the County of Philadelphia; he was refered to Sam'l Jennings, the Receiver Gen'll, to be Commissionated by him.

Ordered that the Inhabitants of Shackamaxson have notice to attend the Commiss'rs the next setting day, to make appear their Titles to their Land.

Arthur Cook's Bond for the payment of £100 to the proprietors upon acc't of Edward Shippen for Land Bought joining to the line of the Town of Philadelphia.

John Martin having had a grant for 3 Lotts, as p. Minute, Requests the addition of one Lott more upon the same terms, which was granted.

On the fifth of the 7th Month last the Indians being paid what was due to them for land that was bought in New Castle County and Chester County, they did desire that Brandywine Creek may be Opened that the fish may have their passage Up, which they say was according to their Contract with the proprietor. Ordered that a Lett'r be sent to the County Court at New Castle to take Course therein according to Law.

John Otter requesting a piece of ground not taken up near Thos. Hards, which was granted.

Ordered that publick notice be given that all those that have any Bank Lott or Lotts between the ship and the Bridge at the North End of Philad'a do make Improvements thereon by wharfing and Building according to regulation within six months after the date hereof or they will be disposed of to others.

Received the 5th of the 7th month, 1691, of and from Robert Turner, John Goodson and Sam'l Carpenter, Commiss'rs appointed by Wm. Penn, Absolute Proprietary and Governor of the province of Pennsylvania, &c., &c., Samuel Jennings, his Receiv'r General, the full Value of thirty Kersy Coats, Eight Kittles, Tenn shirts, three hundred pound of tobacco and an anchor of Molasses, which is in full payment and Satisfaction of all the land lying between Upland Creek and Duck Creek and as far back into the wood as in any manner of ways belongs and appertains unto us or any or either of us according to a Certain Deed signed by us unto Wm. Penn, aforesaid, and his Heirs and assigns therein mentioned, as Witness our hands the the Day aforesaid.

Witness Present,	Seconing	X his Mark.
LACE COCK,	Toughis,	X his Mark.
RICHARD ROADS,	Appehon,	X his Mark.
ROB'T LONGSHORE,	Sickhoys,	X his Mark.
PETER YOAKAM,	Neughhayon,	X his Mark.
	Nepoughhas,	X his Mark.

At a meeting of the Commissioners ye 26th 7th mon., 1691. Present, Capt'n Wm. Markham, Rob't Turner, Jno. Goodson, Sam'l Carpenter.

A Patent Signed to Thos. Janney for 550 acres in Bucks County.

A Patent signed to Pat. Robinson, as deriveing right from Timothy Clement for a thirty foot Bank lott at 3s 0d Sterling, and for a Front Lott at 18d English, both Contained in one patent Dated 25th of ye 7th Mo., 1691.

A Bank Patent signed to Rob't Turner, Executor to John Fuller, for the use of his Legatees for 31 foot, Dated the 24th of the 7th Month, 1691. Rent 3 shillings English.

Upon the Complaint of the Inhabitants of Shakamaxing at the request Thomas Fairman produced to them, Lawrence and Martha Cock's Deed of Sale and Conveyance to Elizabeth Kinsey, Now Wife to Thomas Fairman, full his Right, Title, Claim and property to a Certain Plantation farm or parsell of Land Containing 300 acres, lying and being on the west side of Delaware River at Shaxamaxing, the whole Dividend and Quantity of land being of late Resurveyed for the Inhabitants of Shaxamaxing in Generall, Contains 1,800 acres, by which Resurvey the Share and Interest of Lawrence Cock, as being one of the said Inhabitants of Shax'ing, amounts to 300 acres with L. Cock's share and Interest to the Marshes or Meadows Belonging to the said Land and all the Houses. The Deed is Dated the 30th March, 1678. Acknowledged in Upland Court ye 12th 9th Mo., 1678.

A Patent Signed to Andrew Robeson in Right John Longhurst for 12 acres of Liberty Land, Dated the 25th of the 7th Month, 1691.

A Patent Signed to William Clark on the Proprietor's Land, 100 Foot Front. Dated 25th 7th Month, 1691. Rent 5s English.

Granted to Thomas Dennis and Valantine Bird the Hollow that Lyes between their Two Lotts in Walnut Street, and be Divided Equally between them.

At a Meeting of the Commiss'rs ye 3d of October, 1691.
Present, Capt. William Markham, Robert Turner and John Goodson.

A Patent Signed to Robert Webb for 40 acres of Liberty Land in Right of Elizabeth, his wife, Late Barber. Dated

A Patent Signed to Jeremiah Elfrith for a Lott at the South End of Philadelphia. Rent 18d English. Dated the 24th 7th mon., 1691.

A patent signed to Peter Sherborn for a Lott in the South End of Philadelphia. Rent 18d English. Dated the 27th 7th month, 1691.

A Patent signed to Jeremiah Elfrith for a bank Lott at the South end of Philadelphia. Dated the 1st of Oct'r, 1691. Rent 4s 6d.

A patent signed to Peter Sherborn for a bank lott at the south end of Philad'a. Dated 20th Octob'r, 1691. Rent 4s 6d.

Granted to Robert Webb a Warr't for the High Street Lott proportionable to John Barber's Purchase of 2,500 acres, he having married the said Barber's Widdow.

John Dunn being desirous to sett up the trade of Tanning in the Town of New Castle, Requests for the conveniency thereof two Lotts in the said town backwards toward the Marsh at the upper end of the said Town, which was Granted.

At a meeting of the Commiss'rs ye 10th day of Oct'r, 1691. Present, Capt'n Wm. Markham, Rob't Turner, Jno. Goodson, Sam'll Carpenter.

George Heathcoat setting forth the Inconveniency of Land near Wellcome Creek, it lying in a very Long and narrow Slip, whereby he is put to great charge in fenceing and Difficulty in Comeing to it, and no conveniency for sheep and Cattle, and therefore he requests that wee would Grant him to purchase a piece of Land adjoining to it to make it more commodeous for such a charge as he intends to lay out upon it, to be considered of at next setting or as soon as the Surveyor general has Brought a Draft of Pennsbury.

Upon the debate to preserve the wood and timber upon the proprietor's Son's and relations' Land, it was ordered that none presume to Cut or Carry away any timber or firewood from off the said Lands upon pain of such penaltys as the Law Directs, and what timber or wood is already cut and upon the Land, be forthwith seized (as also what shall be hereafter cut without sufficient Orders) by the woodmen, the one-half to be Seizures.

At a meeting of the Commiss'rs the 17 day of Oct'r, 1691. Present, Capt. Wm. Markham, Rob't Turner, John Goodson and Sam'l Carpenter.

John Martin Requests that we would grant him to take up four Lotts as Near as Conveniency will permit to his now dwelling house in Chestnut Street, to fence in and improve upon the same During the Proprietor's pleasure, paying for the same four shillings p'r annum during the time he shall hold the same, which was granted accordingly.

The Commiss'rs debated how to preserve the Wood, both upon the proprietor's and his son's Land about the town, and also the wood within the lines of the Town; it was resolved and ordered that the People Should have Liberty to Cut up what trees were already falling within the lines of the Town and Cut Brush and Carry of w't Cordwood is already Cut, But not to fall any tree exceeding that Commonly Termed Brush; it is further Ordered that none upon their peril presume to Cut any Trees upon the proprietor's or his son's Land nor remove or Carry away any that is already Cut there, and what Cord wood is already cut upon the aforesaid Land be seized by the woodmen, the one-half thereof to the seizer, the other to the person that Cut it.

James Hunt Requests a piece of Cripple at Kingsess, Lying between his land and the Creek, which was Granted, he paying one Bushell of Wheat Quit Rent p'r annum.

A patent was signed to Nichoas Pierce Dated the 13th Instant, for his lott on the Bank of the proprietor's land at the North end of the town, in which he is obligded to be his share in making and maintaining a common pair of stairs between New Street and Bridge street.

At a Meeting of the Commiss'rs the 24th Oct'r, 1691.

John Green by his wife Seteth forth That he having purchased a house and lott in Walnut Street, of one Thomas

Leasly, laid out for him as purchaser quantity 74 foot, the patent thereof being signed by the proprietor. Rent 5s. 8d. English, Requests that the Rent may be no more than the other Purchasers; upon Supposition that it was a mistake It was granted, and ordered it to be 1s 6d p'r annum; the 6d was allowed him to be bought of for 6s to be paid Shoes by Daniel Jones.

John Ellott requesting that we would grant him to take up the swamp and Cripple Lying between his land Called Long Hook and Darby Creek and Mill Creek, and likewise twelve acres more of Cripple lying ajoining to Carcoonhooke Island Bridge and before his Plantation, which we have granted, he forthwith Improving the same and paying yearly one Bushell of Wheat proportionable to 100 acres.

Thomas Millard having a Grant formerly of a Lott on the bank on the Hill at the south end of the Town of Philad'a, Viz: thirty foot, a Warr't was Sygned for the same with caution to preserve the Street made by the Last regulation.

Upon the petition of Sarah Smith, Widow, of Sussex County, Setting fourth that Luke Watson having formerly laid out for him 2,000 acres of Marsh by warrant from the proprietor by which and the Deputy Surveyor's Errors or mistakes She hath been much Damnified, as also by her Neighbour, Luke Watson, takeing hay from her after her Charge of Cuting it, to her Extream Loss of Cattle, therefore requests a Warr't to resurvey the said marsh and that she might have the Overplus.

At a Meeting of the Commiss'rs.

Present, Capt. Wm. Markham, Rob't Turner, Jno. Goodson, Sam'l Carpenter.

Thos. Fairman complaining that in the Division of the land of Shaxamaxin, Rob't Turner's line runs through his plowed Land or Cleared field, which took part of it from him; the Commiss'rs acquainting the said Rob't Turner with it, the said Turner consented and desired that his line might be altered so that the whole Cleared field might be left without his Bounds.

John Buckly and Oliver Cope requests a piece of Land lying contiguous to theirs in the County of New Castle, of which they produced a Draught of the Survey'r, which was granted them.

Granted a Warr't to Captain Markham for his Liberty land.

On the 6th 10th Month, 1690, there was granted unto Daniel Jones a lott in Walnut Street; he requests that there may be added to the said Lott 24 foot more in breadth and the whole to be Rented according to the accomodation of the Ground, it Lying so in a Vally not fit for Building on; the whole was granted at 4s 6d p'r annum English.

At a Meeting of the Commiss'rs the 7th 9ber, 1691.
Present, Capt. Wm. Markham, Rob't Turner, John Goodson.

A Warrant was made to bring before the Commiss'rs, or any One of them, the Body of R'd Roberts for Cutting wood off the Proprietor's Land.

The Commiss'rs finding Ben. Chambers Very Careless or Wilfully negligent in securing the wood and timber upon the Proprietor's Land according to the trust Reposed in him, It is therefore thought requisite and ordred that Even Oliver have the Care of the wood and timber on all the lands Belonging to the proprietor, His Children or Relations.

Griffith Jones requests to grant him the marsh about his plantation on the side of the little Creek, as it is between the points of fast land Running into the said Marsh; it was granted to run with a straight line from Point to point.

Joseph Wood and John Ellot appearing before the Commiss'rs, Joseph Wood Complaining that the Plantation he now lives on at Darby had no conveniency for Hay but what was surveyed unto John Ellot by Virtue of a Warr't dated the 24th last, the said Ellot Being present, did agree and Consent that the said Woods should have all the marsh or Cripple granted him that Day provided he May have confirmed unto him that part of it from his White oke bounded tree upon Darby Creek down to the Great Rock.

Richard Roberts was brought before us according to the foregoing Warr't; he Confest he and his man had Cut Down Two or Three trees, promising not to do the like again, Whereupon the Commiss'rs Ordered that he be not prosecuted for this offence unless he be again accused, and therefore Discharged him, he paying Charges.

The Commiss'rs Considering how far up the Creek above the Proprietor's Land at the North end of ye Town shall be Deemed Bank, Resolved it Should be up to the third street, and the Regulation of all the Bank before the proprietor's Land aforesaid be under the same Regulation in all respects and Rents as ye Town Banks is.

Robert Longshore laying before us his disappointment in his purchasing a right of 5,000 acres in England of a purchaser there, in the libertys of Philad'a thereunto belonging, and he humbly requesting Us that we would grant him to take 80 ac's of Liberty Land on the East side of the Skullkill and that the same be Confirmed to Joshua Carpenter by patent, for which he will either pay unto us for the same or otherwise Purchase so much Liberty Land on the East side of Skullkill to answer the aforesaid Number of acres.

Resolved that he may have a warrant for the laying out of the same, and that the same be confirmed by us accordingly, and that the said Longshore do give his Bond of one hundred pounds to the proprietor, his Heirs and assigns, Conditionally that he shall purchase and procure Eighty acres in ye Libertys of Philad'a on the east side of Skuilkill, and when the same is so purchased and procured by him the same to deliver up to the proprietor, his heirs and assigns, or to his Commiss'rs on or before the 10th of November, 1694.

Granted to Robert Turner a lott in the **Proprietor's** land at the North of Philad'a, to be 102 foot front to the street than runs along the Bank to the Runn, and to Extend along the Delaware front Street within 20 foot of the New Cut there, made by the Occasion of the New Bridge.

At a meeting of the Commiss'rs ye 21st ye 9th Month, 1691. Present, Capt. Wm. Markham, Robt. Turner, Jno. Goodson, Sam'l Carpenter.

Granted unto Griffith Jones the lott of ground lying between Wm. Clark's Lott and Joseph Wilcox's Rope walk, bounded between Cable Lane and Second street.

Ordered a warrant to be made for the laying out of 200 acres of land purchased by Charles Pickering of John Southworth, including the Liberty land, according to the Deeds from Southworth to the said Pickering, and 40 acres of Liberty land in Right of Edward Carter, according to Deeds From Carter to Philip Tholmain.

At a meeting of ye Commiss'rs the 28 of 9mo., 1691. Present, Capt. Wm. Markham, Robert Turner, John Goodson, Sam'l Carpenter.

John Delavall and Albertus Brant reports to the Commiss'rs from the Dutch Minister of Flat Brush, Upon Long Island, that the said Minister had a desire to settle himself in this province and that there would be with him about 200 families, and should want About 40,000 acres of Land and that if they Could not be accommodated in the province they intended to the lower Countys, and if not accommodated there they intended to Maryland. John Delavall said the Minister told him that the persons engaged with him were sober, Industrous people. The Commiss'rs Answered they were willing and ready to incourage Such people and would discourse the Surveyor General's Deputy about a convenient Tract for their settlement and in two days they should have a more particular acc't from them. Ordered that the Surveyor Gen'ls Deputy Meet the Commiss'rs the 30 Instant at two in the afternoon.

Hester Bowyer, the widow of John Bowyer, presented a bill for work done by her Husband to the Proprietor s barge and boat, the sum £5 7s. 6d, which was allowed. Orders for payment was Endorsed to Sam'l Jennings, Receiver General.

Randal Spakeman requests a lott fronting Sassafras Street and about the Seventh Street Back from Delaware, w'ch was granted.

At a meeting of the Commiss'rs the 30th of ye 9th Month, 1691. Present, W. M., R. T., J. G.

The Commiss'rs Letter to John Delavall and Albertus Brant, Viz:

Friend {JOHN DELAVALL:
{ALBERTUS BRANT:

What you proposed to us the 28th instant concerning a Dutch Minister with about 200 families intentions of settling in this province Wee have Considered of, and being verry desirous to make the best provisions for such sober, Industrous persons, have unanimously resolved to give all the incouragement possible our Commission will permit, and in order to know the most convenient Tract for their settlement we have Discoursed the surveyor Generall's Deputy, and find several, which we believe and do not doubt but may accommodate them; if any of them will be pleased to view the places we shall provide persons to wait on them. Wee hope to hear further from you with all Convenient Speed Concerning this that we may order things accordingly.

We Remain y'r. Loving fr'ds.

Philad'a, 30th 9th month, 1691.

Resolved that all the land intended for a dock lying between the new Cut and the Lotts Laid out on the South side of the Creek, which is on the north side of the Proprietor's Land and the north end of Philad'a, if not made use of for such a service as a Dock as was intended it shall Ly in common for a Road, Street, or otherwise, as occasion shall serve, and not to be disposed or appropriated to any particular person to the prejudice of the publick.

At a meeting of the Commiss'rs the 22 of 10ber, 1691. Present, Capt. Wm. Markham, Rob't Turner, John Goodson.

The Commiss'rs appointed this day, at the Request of John Philley, to hear what he had to say; he Delivered a paper which was read.

Answered, the receiver Gen'll not being preseant and the paper chargeing him, &c., and it properly belonging to the receiver Gen'll, would not do anything in it till they speak with him.

At a meeting of the Commiss'rs the 26th of 10ber, 1691. W. M., J. G., S. C.

Albertus Brant informs that he and John Delavall had received an answer from the Dutch Minister upon Long Island and that he desired to know the lowest price, how far from Philad'a and how far from a Navigable Creek; to which the Commiss'rs sent them a Letter in Answer, Viz:

The 28th of the last month John Delavall and Albertus Brant acquainted us that thou and several of thy Country Men were Desirous of Settling in this province and that they required about 40,000 acres of land; we were as Desirous and willing to accommodate you, had a meeting on purpose, examined the surveys of all the lands, found some convenient tracts and gave them such answer as hoped would be to your Good likeing and content, and ever since have had great care to preserve those tracts for you. This day Albertus Brant was with us again, acquainted us that he and John Delavall had an answer from you of what they writ concerning it, In which you desired to know what quantity you could have together, what the price, how far from Philadelphia and how far from any Navigable River; wee suppose the answer before mentioned, which we gave to John Delavall and Albertus Brant they sent you, by which you may perceive that we expected some persons Impowered from you to view the land and treat about it; we think still that way the best and most expeditious and with no doubt be most satisfactory to you since some tracts are more commodious for situation than others, some for goodness of Land, and some Nearer than others to Philad'a, for which will arise, different prices. As to the quantity you may have near if not all in one tract and that upon the Skullkill; when you please to send any person or persons to view the tracts and treat with us about them they shall be kindly received and treated withal, and we shall appoint some to wait on them, if they please to view the Country.

We are your answered friends,
WM. MARKHAM,
JOHN GOODSON,
SAM'L CARPENTER

Philad', Dec'r 26th, 1691.

At a meeting of the commiss'rs the 9th of Jan'y 1691-2.
Present, Wm. Markham, Rob't Turner, John Goodson.

Samuel Atkins, as Atturney for Basilion Foster and John Haslegrove, purchaser, Requests Warr't for the takeing up the remainder of their purchase in the county of Philad'a and also their liberty land.

Evan Oliver informs that Rich'd Jennett, Miles Goforth and Zachariah Goforth hath cut down several trees from of the proprietor's land near the town of Philadelphia. Ordered that a Warr't be made by the Commiss'rs that they may be brought before them to answer the tresspass. Warr't was made and signed by Wm. Markham, Robert Turner, John Goodson.

The aforementioned Warr't was Executed by Joseph Ambler and the three persons brought before the Secretary, who Clared the two Goforths upon their father's passing his word for their not hereafter Cuting wood on the proprietor's land, &c., But Rich'd Jennett being very insolent in his behaviour before the secretary upon his examination was committed untill he shall find Security for his good behaviour or till he be Delivered by due Course of Law.

At a Meeting of ye Commiss'rs the 16 of ye 11th Mo., 1691-2.
Present, Capt'n Wm. Markham, Rob't Turner, John Goodson.

A Petition was preferred to the Commiss'rs by Will'm Salway, Griffith Jones, Jeremiah Elfrith, &c. Ordered that the Secretary draw up an Instrum't Whereby to assert the proprietor's rights, &c. Appointed to meet the 19th Instant About the same.

At a meeting of the Commiss'rs the 19th instant.

This following publick Instrum't of protest was drawn up, Viz:

By the Proprietary Commiss'rs.

Whereas complaints was made to us by Wm. Salloway, Griffith Jones and Jeremiah Elfrith that Thomas Lloyd, Humphrey Murrey and John Delavall with others did last Summer Several times come on their Bank Lotts and Interrupted their workmen by Commanding them to desist, pretending they built in the streets, and thereby the said Jeremah Elfrith was retarded in his Building the whole last summer to his great damage, as also that Wm. Salloway obtained a patent for a Bank lott and having Sold the same to him by Deed, yet when the said Will'm Salloway came to acknowledge the same in Court to Jeremiah Elfrith, David Lloyd, Clark of the said Court, Defaced the said Deed and Patent to us produced By Indorsing on the Back of the Deed those words, Viz: Caveated Because the Lot within granted is supposed to be the Cartable landing place of this town, and so hath Been accordingly ordered by the Governor and Council, therefore this Deed ought not to pass till further inquiry be made therein, which Enormities being taken into consideration, and we finding them So much to Infringe on the Rights of the Proprietor, which Obliges us to assert and Maintain his Authority by this Publick Instrum't and thereby maintain the power he had granted to us by his Commiss'rs for Disposing of all Lotts and Lands within this province and without any other Control but his Own, and therefore wee do hereby, in his name, assert the patents granted by us to the above named persons to be good and sufficient to them and do protest against the above named persons for all damages that has, shall or may Arise by their said Indorsement, Either to the proprietor, ourselves or those to whom we have granted any patents by Virtue of the said Commiss'n Dated at Philad'a the Day of Jan'y, 1691-2.

WM. MARKHAM,
ROB'T TURNER,
JOHN GOODSON.

At a meeting of ye Commiss'rs the 23 of January, 1691-2. Present, Capt'n Wm. Markham, Rob't Turner, Jno. Goodson.

James Fox and Tho's Millard requests timber trees for their Building on the bank; after Consideration of the great Destruction of the timber from off the proprietor's Land, the Commiss'rs resolved to Use their utmost Endeavour to preserve the same and to grant no permitts for Cutting any.

At a meeting of the Commiss'rs the 30th of Jan'y, 1691-2. Present, Cap't Wm. Markham, Rob't Turner, John Goodson.

John Murry requests two trees from off the proprietor's Land for making a Crane on his Wharf, the Commiss'rs refer'd him to Samuel Jennings, the receiver General.

William Hard requests a piece of ground adjoining to his

fronting the third Street 30 foot in breadth as an addition to his Lott, the whole to be 6s 6d English.

Ordered a letter to be writ to the Inhabitants of Shaxamaxen which follows Verbatim:

FRIENDS: We having been requested by several for a Road through your land from Philad'a to Wm. Salloway's Mills, the Glass house and meddow, we are not willing to conclude on it before you agree how it should be laid out for your greatest conveniency. We are
        Your Loving Friends,
          WM. MARKHAM,
          ROB'T TURNER,
          JNO. GOODSON.
To the inhabitants of Shakamaxen.

At a meeting of the Commiss'rs the 6th of Feb'y, 1691-2.

Present, Cap't Wm. Markham, Rob't Turner, John Goodson.

Henry Hollingsworth, Surveyor of New Castle County, being present, informs that John Grub makes great Havock of the timber on the proprietor's land in his mannor of Rocksland, the surveyor having had formerly a Warr't to Divide the said Land leaving to the said Grub his part, Viz: 200 Acres; Ordered that the Surveyor execute the said Warr't and make return thereof.

Henry Hollingsworth requesting to take up a lott in the Town of New Castle, was granted.

William Byles having purchased of the proprietor, for Francis Richardson, Two Hundred acres of land in Right's Town, and the said Richardson had paid Ten pounds for the same unto John Right by Ord'r of Ja's Harrison which 200 Ac's was to be laid to a Tract of 1,000 Ac's purchased by the s'd Richardson; ordered to Return the 1,000 and 200 in one tract.

George Millard, Merch't, Informs the Commiss'rs that there was laid out unto John Hough 125 Acres of Land which he purchased of the proprietor, which was Never Seated or Improved nor paid any Rent, and a note being produced under the hand of Peter Lester, who is the present owner thereof, that he is wiling to give it, the said Millard requests that he might take up the said Land as part of his purchase and he would pay the Rent due from the first laying it out, which was granted him.

Will'm Salway requests a Warr't to the surveyor Gen'll to return into the Secretaries Office of 300 Ac's of Land laid out for Will'm Lovell as part of 1,250 acres purchased by Rich'd Collings, of Bath, 300 acres being laid out in the Welch tract Without warrant.

At a Meeting of the Commiss'rs ye 13th of Feb'y, 1691-2. Present, Cap't Wm. Markham, Rob't Turner, John Goodson.

Whereas it appears to us that there was had and received for the proprietor's Use, by James Harrison, four Hogsheads of Rum Containing 345 Gallons at 22d p'r Gallon, is £31 12s 6d being the goods of Andrew Drury of Barbados, and that the said rum is not paid for nor charged in the said James Harrison's Acc't this day made up before us, we do therefore order and allow that the said thirty-one pounds, twelve shillings, six pence be paid out of the Effects of William Penn, proprietor, when called for by the said Andrew Drury, his executors, Admr's or Assigns. Given under our hands,

WILLIAM MARKHAM,
ROB'T TURNER,
JOHN GOODSON.

This day Phineas Pemberton presented the Acc'ts of James Harrison, deceased, relating to the proprietor's affairs whilst in the said Harrison's hands, to Wm. Markham, Rob't Turner, John Goodson, the proprietor's Commiss'rs, and Samuel Jennings, the receiver Gen'll, and we find upon Adjusting the same to remain due to the said Harrison's Acco't to Balla's, One Hundred and Six pounds, Three shillings, which we hereby Order and allow to be paid out of the effects of William Penn, Proprietor, to Phineas Pemberton, Adm'r to the said James Harrison. Signed by Wm. Markham, Ro't Turner, Jno. Goodson.

Ordered that there be laid out unto Sam'l Jennings forty foot of the bank before Letitia Penn's Front Lott on the South side.

John Bristow, as Adm'r to Tho's Bracy, requests that their being laid out in Chester 290 Acres of land unto the said Bracy in his lifetime, by Verbal Order of the Proprietor, desires a Warr't to return the same into the Secretary's Office that a patent be made thereon accordingly.

Will'm Dixon Requests to take up 300 Acres of land in the County of New Castle, Upon old Rent, granted Provided it be taken up 7 miles from any Navigable Runn of water.

James Paxon having taken up 200 Acres upon Rent, and William Paxon 100 Ac's Upon Rent, they desire to purchase the same, which was granted, they paying the quit Rent that is in Arears.

James Paxon requests a Warr't to resurvey his 200 Ac's and to have the Overpluss, granted, and to have the same returned as Overpluss. Wm. Paxon requests a Warr't for the return of his 100 Acres of land as Purchase, granted.

Will'm Radny acquainting the Commiss'rs of his intention of settling a plantation in the County of Sussex, and in ord'r thereunto was about purchasing of land and therefore requests a grant for 100 Acres of Marsh, to be laid out to the settlement he shall make, which was granted provided he Settle as intended within one year after the Date hereof.

Will'm Dire's petition was read requesting some pieces of Fast land that runs out of his land into the Marsh like tongues or Necks of land, which by reason of straght lines Was left out of the survey of his land, which was granted; And also 200 Acres of Marsh between prime hook bay and broad Kill, which was likewise granted in one Warr't.

A Letter was sent to Wm. Clarke in Order to Answer Sarah Smith, widow, her petition as fo. Verbatim :

William Clark : We have had several petitions from the widow Smith, of your County, Complaining grievously of the verry hard and Unneighbourly Usage from Luke Watson fencing out her cattle from the Marsh before her Land, under pretence the whole was granted to him by the Proprietor, therefore we desire thou wilt forthwith send us a Draught of the said marsh and a Copy of the Order you laid it out by, that we may make that Proprietary Regulation which in Justice we ought to doe; this is all at present from

Your real Friends,
W. M., R. T., J. G.

Philadelphia the 12th 12 Month, 1691-2.

There being a piece of land in the town of New Castle, And in the same Street that John Cann lives in, desires Us to grant him as an addition to the Lott he now lives on, And the whole tract be at two bushells of wheat p. Annum, the whole being less ground than any of the same Rent in the town, the Commiss'rs in Consideration of his good servise and faithfulness to the proprietor, granted it.

William Cloud, of Chester County, purchaser of 500 Acres of land, and the same being laid out to him on Naman's Creek, of which he hath given to his son Jeremiah 100 Acres, Therefore desires a patent for that 100 Acres that he might confirm the same to his son, himself being unwilling yet to take a patent for the whole 500 Acres before resurvey be made thereof, there being supposed to be more then what it was laid out for, which was granted.

John Gregg, by his request to the Commiss'rs seting fourth that he and his Brother having seated 400 Acres of Land on Brandy Wine Creek, in the County of New Castle, Upon New Rent, which they aledge is about 7 miles from any Navigable water and therefore requests the land may be at old Rent; the Commiss'rs in Consideration of its Distance from Navigable Water did grant the same.

Thomas Sawyer requests that he may have the 300 ac's of Land that was laid out unto Wm. Stockdale, the said Stockdale not intending to seat the same and that it may be upon old Rent, it lying at least 7 miles from any Navigable Water, did grant the same.

Toby Leach producing to the Commiss'rs the Proprietor's Rec't Dated the 21st 5th Month, 1683, for the money paid for his Land, Viz: 300 acres, which was Returned to the Secretaries Office in Philad'a, Thelman's time of being Secretary, as a Rentor and in quantity 350 acres; he likewise produced another Receipt from the Proprietor to his Brother-in-Law, John Ashmead, bearing the same date with the former, for 300 acres of Land purchased, but the said Ashmead had laid out in his tract but 250 acres, the whole being Six hundred acres, The said Ashmead being Dead, the said Toby, his admin'r and Trustee, doth allow and Request that the Division of the whole 600 acres made may Stand, Viz: 350 acres to Toby Leach and 250 to the Heirs of John Ashmead, was accordingly done and a patent made to Toby Leach, new purchaser for 350 acres.

At a meeting of the Commiss'rs at Philadelphia, 28th May, 1692.

Present, Rob't Turner, John Goodson, Sam'l Carpenter.

John Warrall requesting to purchase 200 ac's which was formerly taken up by Richard Barnard, in the County of Chester, at one penny per acre; Capt. Markham being absent it is defer'd.

George Emblin having bought of Thomas Harding his Lott formerly granted and laid out to him in Strawberry alley, 32 foot front and Eighty-two foot long, requests that the same may be Confirmed directly to him, which was accordingly gr't'd.

Tammany and several other Indians requests that we may pay them nine guns, Ten-Eight Duffill Machcoats, ten Blankets, which they pretend the Governor promised them in Consideration of the Gift of Land which Tammany gave the Governor, which said promise being not apparent pay is defered untill Capt. Markham Comes up from New Castle, and they again to give their attendance to us the 7 of June Insuing, and in the Meantime to give them two gallons of Rum and two Dozen of Rowles.

At a meeting of the Commiss'rs ye 11th of ye 4 Mo., 1692. Present, W. M., R. T., J. G.

Capt. Wm. Markham being present did agree to John Warrell's request about the purchase of 200 acres, But as to the Indians he knows nothing is due to them.

The Proprietor having formerly sent a warr't to the Commiss'rs directing that 100 ac's of Sewana, above the falls of Delaware, be laid out unto Thomas Hudson, and accordingly the Commiss'rs granted a Warr't to the Surveyor Gen'll for the laying out the same, which not being Executed, Ordered that a warrant be directed to the Surveyor Gen'll to execute and return the same into the Secretarie's office or Show reason to the Contrary.

Ordered a Warr't for the laying out Rich'd Davis' Lotts in Philadelphia at the request of David Powel and Likewise for his liberty land.

William Biles as Atturney for Tho's Hudson requests a Confirmation of the 5,000 acres of Land laid out in the County of Bucks part of which hath been a long time in dispute between the said Hudson and Dennis Rotchford, The said Biles pleads that the surveyor Gen'll granted two Warr'ts to his Under Surveyor for the County of Bucks, the one for 5,000 ac's to Hudson the other for 3,000 ac's to Rotchford, Rotchford getts the Surveyor of Philadelphia County to goe into Bucks County and lay out the said 3,000 acres, after which the attorney to the said Hudson By Virtue of his Warr't directed to the surveyor of Bucks County had by the right surveyor of the said County the said 5,000 ac's laid out, in which he took in 2,000 acres of the 3,000 of the land laid out by the Surveyor of Philadelphia County, not knowing a strange survey had been in his limits to execute a Warr't which was directed to himself.

Ordered that a patent be made for the society's Lotts in Phild., including the Bank lots, the whole at the Rent of three pounds English p'r annum, the Improvements on the Bank to be theirs for Ever, both of Phila'da and Schoolkill.

George Hethcott having often petitioned the Commiss'rs for a piece of land belonging to Chipassing adjoining to his plantation, which is supposed to be about 250 acres, being bounded with Wellcome Creek, the Main River of Delaware, and a line of the said land he hath setled in the County of Bucks. The Commiss'rs took into consideration the ill-conveniency of the s'd Hethcott's Tract for a plantation without an additon to it, with the improvements he hath made and is likely to make, as also to incourage him to promote the trade of this Country, have granted him the same upon purchase at thirty pounds Silver money or proportionable thereunto, be it more or less, and to pay the Usual Rent of a purchaser.

The said Geo. Hethcoat did upon the Confirmation of the aforesaid Land acquitt all his Interest and title to any other land in Chipassing excepting two Hundred acres Granted him by the Proprietor in England and 304 acres Granted him by ye Commiss'rs as by a writing under his hand and Seal at Philad'a the 15th of June, 1692, on the file may more fully appear.

At a meeting of the Commiss'rs the 18th of 4th Month, 1692. Present, Capt. Wm. Markham, Robert Turner, John Goodson.

Jane More, Widdow, requests to take upon a Rent three squares in the Town of Philadelphia for 21 Years at the Usual Rent of thirty years; It was granted provided She brings Security to pay the Rent for that time and to leave it in good condition, &c.

Ordered a Warr't for James Claypole to be Survey'r of New Castle town and County.

Phineas Pemberton, as Execut. to James Harrison, requests a Warr't to return into the Secretarie's Office 80 acres of Liberty Land that was laid out to James Harrison in Right of his purchase of 5,000 acres.

Philip England's petition was read seting forth that there was another Ferry set up nigh his, which was Contrary to the Propri. Commands in his license; the said petition was refered to the Governor Lloyd with his Indors't, Viz: Philad'a ye 18th of the fourth month, 1692, the within petition is refered to Governor Lloyd with our request that by his authority he will maintain the Rights of the proprietor in the Case set forth in the said petition; was signed By

WM. MARKHAM,
ROB'T TURNER,
JOHN GOODSON.

At a meeting of the Commiss'rs ye 30 of ye 4th mo., 1692. Present, Capt. Wm. Markham, Rob't Turner, Jno. Goodson.

Robert Turner desiring that he may have 26 foot front in the High Street joining to his lott there on Delaware side, He offering to give up his whole Lott on the Schoolkill side, Being one hundred thirty-two foot front and in right of John Gee & Company, Purchasers of 5,000 acres, whose right to land and Lotts he the said Turner have bought, which we have granted.

At a Meeting of the Commiss'rs the 6th of July, 1692. Present, Capt. Wm. Markham, Ro't Turner, John Goodson.

Richard Cantrell requesting a Warr't for a Lot of 30 foot upon Rent in the third Street near the burying place, was granted.

Israel Taylor requests a Warr't to Survey or lay out 300 acres of land, part of his father's purchase, which was granted in the County of Bucks; the Warr't was indorsed to be laid on the land laid out for John Gilbert, by Virtue of a Warr't from the proprietor dated the 9th day of the 9 month, 1683, he having not sealed it.

Edward Farmer, purchaser of 100 acres of land of the proprietor's Mannor of Springfield, adjoining to his own land, for which he is to pay Ten pounds; Ordered a Warr't for the laying out the same, not Exceeding 40 perches to the South East end of his land.

Captain Wm. Markham requests that he might have a Warr't to lay out his liberty land on Delaware side, though it fell on the East side of Schoolkill; the Surveyor acquainting there was land enough to satisfy the purchasers; it was granted.

The proprietor being indebted to James Moore, the said Moore requests he may purchase 100 acres of land in the Welch tract at the price of five pounds, he engaging to pay what it amounts to above the Debt in Money; it was granted.

Ordered a Warr't to be made for John Goodson, which was done as followeth:

Whereas by Virtue of a Warr't from the proprietary bearing date the 14th of the 12th Month, 1683, there was granted to be Surveyed unto John Goodson a Tract of land within the Libertys of Philad'a, on Dellaware side, answerable to the purchases of several persons therein mentioned, the whole proportion amounting to Seventy-Six acres in the said Libertys, to answer his Obligation to the proprietor; and whereas the said John Goodson Could not Purchase of every of the several persons aforesaid their respective Lotts in the said Libertys to answer the said Obligation, But hath to that end purchased the liberty land proportionable belonging to the purchasers, follow Several, whereof falling by Lott on the Schoolkill Side and therefore their Liberty Land there also.

But in Consideration of the Proprietor's Warr't afore Mention'd which Ordered Severall purchasers therein falling on Schoolkill Side, to be Notwithstanding laid out unto the said John Goodson on Delaware Side, Notwithstanding any order or Instruction thou hast to the Contrary (Viz:) unto John Goodson in right of John Sibly, whose wife is relict to John Martin, Purchaser of 500 acres, 8 acres in right of; Wm. Busby, whose wife is relict to Thomas Cery, Purchaser of 500 ac's, 8 acres in Right; to Rob't Adams, purchaser of 500 ac's, 8 ac's in Right of; Edw'd Martindall, purchaser of 1,000 acres, 16 acres in right of; Rich'd Worrell, purchaser of 500 acres, 8 acres in right of; Nicholas Walne, purchaser of 1,000 ac's, 16 acres in right of; Rich'd Buntes, purchaser of 250 ac's, 4 acres; and in right of his Own purchase of 500 ac's, 8 ac's; in right of all which aforesaid Numbers Amounting to Seventy-six acres which said Number, with 4 acres more, was according to the Proprietor's Warr't and Order formerly laid out in the Libertys in one tract.

These are therefore in the Proprietor's Name to will and Require thee forthwith to make or Cause to be made a return of the aforesaid Tract into the secretarie's Office in Order to have the same Confirmed by patent unto the said John Goodson.

To Capt. Thos. Holme, Survey'r Gen'll.

At a meeting of the Commiss'rs the 27th of 7 mo., 1692. Present, Capt. Wm. Markham, Rob't Turner, John Goodson.

The Commiss'rs met this day chiefly to settle the proprietor's particular Tracts of land laid out both for himself and Relations in Order to pass Patents for the same, but the deputy Survey'r Gener'll reporting that all was not executed nor returns drawn of those warrants that were Executed and that for others he had not warrants for the Laying them out. Ordered that a Warrant be Directed to the Surveyor Generall that there be forthwith Returns made into the Secretary's office of all the tracts as aforesaid already laid out by the proprietor's Warr't or Verbal Order, and that he forthwith execute all such Warr'ts he has by him Unexecuted, and that also to lay out all such Tracts of land as Sam'l Jennings the proprietor's Receiver Gen'll and Steward has Orders from the proprietor to have done; and whereas the receiver Gen'll aleges that his Orders are to have 100,000 acres of land in one tract for each of the Proprietor's Children, it is the opinion of the Commiss'rs that it is a mistake and that it was intended but 10,000 acres, of which the Surveyor Generall is to have notice that he may act accordingly.

John Buckly, Surveyor Gen'll of East Jersey, reports that Andrew Hamilton, Esqr., Gov'r of the said place, lately came from England, brought with him an order from the proprietors that every person having any right to land may have it laid out unto him, and that our proprietor having a right to land thereof which there is yet untaken up 9,500 acres, advises that it were convenient now to have it taken up least the best land and Conveniency be taken up by others.

Ordered that this report be recommended to the receiver Gen'l, Sam'll Jennings, with advise that what lotts or lands hath been laid out to the proprietor in that province, Patents may be got for them, and to be Mindfull that if any other lotts or lands are in right belonging to our Proprietor, besides the 9,500 acres aforesaid and not yet taken up be taken up and patented also.

Robert Longshore producing a Deed from John Sharples of his lotts in the Town of Philad'a and Liberty land, according to the purchase of 1,000 acres purchased by his father, deseased, of whom he rights himself Son and Heir, the which Deed bears date the 16th of May, 1692. Ordered that a warr't be made for the said Longshore to take them up.

At a Meeting of the Commiss'rs the 1st day of Oct'r, 1692. Present, Capt. Wm. Markham, Rob't Turner, Jno. Goodson, Sam'l Carpenter.

Israel Taylor presenting a bill of 5£ due to him for Survey work done at Pennsberry in the time of James Harrison, which bill was formerly before the Commiss'rs and payment Ordered but not being done, it was directed to Samuel Jennings to pay it, discounting Tenn shillings formerly Received of it.

Arthur Cook in the behalf of the widdow Dungan and Children, who holds about 600 acres of land amongst them at a penny Rent p'r acre, Requests that we would sell the same that it may be at equal Rent with the Purchasers, the people being verry poor and land very Barren, and they ready to leave the province, not being able to pay the Rent, and the said Arthur Cook in kindness to them and to keep them in the province, Intends to lend them the money, the which was Granted at five pounds p'r C't, and to pay all the rent in arrears.

Arthur Cook Seting forth in his petition that he had purchased in Sussex County Six hundred acres of land to which there was no marsh belonging, requests one hundred acres of marsh, for which a Warr't was Ordered to be laid out in the most convenient place, not hindering a convenient passage to the rest of the marsh.

William Clark having purchased a Tract of land in Angoloneck, in the County of Sussex, lying at the bottom of the Neck, fronting of which is a great quantity of marsh in which is some Islands or spots of dry land, and one fitt for a pasture which the said Will'm Clark requests to take up upon old Rent, with as much of the Marshes with the said Island may amount to 100 acres; granted, provided it be so laid out that it shall no way hinder or Incommode any setled there about, or shall settle there about, from makeing use of or takeing up any part of the remaining Marsh.

A Warr't Granted to Andrew Bankson to Survey several parcells of Land in the Township of Passiunk he had bought of several persons in Order to gett a patent for the whole.

Robert Turner having Purchased tenn acres of Marsh or

meadow of Thos. Fairman, the first dated the 16th day of the Fourth Month, 1691, the other the 12th of the twelfth month, 1691-2, thereunto relateing, and Rob't Turner now requesting that the same may be confirmed by Patent, with the marsh lying before the same between that and the River, which was granted accordingly.

Baptist Newcomb requests 100 acres of Marsh lying before his land in the County of Sussex; it was granted on the conditions as was made with Mr. Clark this day.

Phineas Pemberton seting forth his great want of fodder for his Cattle on the Plantation he now lives on in the County of Bucks, by George Hethcoat's purchasing that land he Used to mow his hay on, Requests that he may purchase another piece of land lying near or adjoining to the said Heathcoat's land between Wellcome Creek and Bridge Creek, Computed to be Two Hundred acres, which was granted at Tenn pounds per hundred acres.

The ground undisposed on, lying on the South side of the proprietor's Front Lott in Philadelphia may be granted unto Governor Lloyd, provided the persons to whom the same fell unto by lott do not claim the same.

———

At a Meeting of the Commiss'rs the 12th of 9ber, 1692.

Present, Capt. Wm. Markham, Rob't Turner, John Goodson.

James Moore having purchased 100 acres of land for 5£ did this day satisfy the Commiss'rs for the said 5£ in manner following, Viz't: 2£ 19s 8d being due to him for work done to the Proprietor's Mill and 2£ 1s 6d paid in cash unto Capt. Wm. Markham in part of the Ballance of Oliver Dunkly's account.

———

Examined, Compared and Corrected p.

                JO'N HUGHES.

July 21st, 1759.

These are to Certify that the foregoing Sheets contained in this Book, No. 10, in the whole amounting to One hundred and forty-nine Pages are true Copies of the Originals found in the Office of the Secretary's and that the same were carefully compared with the said Originals by me during my apointment as Recorder of Warrants and Surveys under the act of assembly passed in the 33 Year of his late Majesty's Reign entitled "An Act for recording Warrants and Surveys and for rendering the real Estates and properties within this Province more secure."

                p. JO'N HUGHES.

Signed in the presence of

          THOS. LEECH,
          JOHN MORTON,
          SAMUEL RHOADS,
          JAMES WRIGHT,
          HENRY WYNKOOP.

MINUTE BOOK "F."

A BOOK OF RECORDS, VIZ: DEEDS AND OTHER WRITINGS. THIS IS BOOK F IN THE SECRETARIES OFFICE.

Commission of Patrick Robinson.

Benjamin Fletcher, Captain Generall and Governor in Chief of the Province of New York, Province of Pennsylvania, County of New Castle and the Territories and tracts of Land depending thereon in America, Under Majesties William and Mary, by the grace of God, of England, Scotland, France and Ireland, King and Queen, Defenders of the Faith, &c.
To Patrick Robinson, Esqr., Greeting:
By Virtue of the Power and Authority Granted me by their Majesties Letters Patents Under the great Seal of England, bearing Date the twenty-first day of October, In the fourth year of the reign of our Sovereign Lord and Lady, William and Mary, by the grace of God, of England, Scotland, France and Ireland, King and Queen, Defenders of the faith, &c., I doe hereby erect and Establish the Office of Secretary of the Province of Pennsylvania and County of New Castle, And Reposing especiall trust and Confidence in the loyalty, learning and Integrity of you, the said Patrick Robinson, doe authorize, Constitute and appoint you, the said Patrick Robinson, to be secretary of the Province of Pennsylvania and County of New Castle, and as such to use, Exercise and Enjoy the said Office of Secretary in as full and ample Manner as any former Secretary hath held and enjoyed the same in the said Province or in the Province of New York or any of their Majesties Plantations in America. To have and to hold the said office of Secretary of the said Province and County and to use, Exercise and Enjoy the same by yourself or your Sufficient Deputy, to be approved of by the Lieutenant Governor of the said Province and County for the time being, and to have, take and Receive all Salleries, fees, perquisites, profitts, advantages, Previledges and appurtenances to the said office of Secretary belonging, or that may hereafter belong, during your good behaviour or untill

my pleasure shall be further known. In testimony whereof I have hereunto put my hand and Seal at Philadelphia the first day of May in the fifth year of their Majesties reign, Anno Domi 1693.

BEN. FLETCHER.

By his Excellency's Command,
    DAVID JAMISON,

Francis Gibbon's Letter of Attorney to Samuel Carpenter.

BARBADOS.

To all People to whom this present writing shall come:

I, Francis Gibbon, of the said Island, Merch't, Send Greeting; Know ye that I, the said Francis Gibbon, for Divers good Causes and Considerations, me thereunto moving, have made, assigned, Constituted, authorized and appointed and by these presents doe make, assign, Constitute, authorize and appoint and in my stead and place putt and Depute my trusty friend, Sam'll Carpenter, of the Province of Pennsylvania, Merch't, to be my true and lawfull attorney for me in my Name and to my use by all lawfull ways and means, to enter into and upon all and Singular Tract and Tracts of land, plantations, messages, tennements and Hereditaments, with their and every of their appurtenances to me in any wise appertaining or belonging, in the said Province of Pennsylvania or Territories thereof, and possession thereof, and of every part and parcell thereof for me in my name, to take and keep and being so possessed of the said tract and tracts of land, plantations, messages, Tennements and Hereditaments with the appurtenances, the same and every part and parcell thereof for me in my name and to my use, to bargain, Sell, allien, grant and Convey to such person or persons and for such Estate of Inheritance, fee simple, Life or years and for such sum and sums of money or other Consideration as to my said attorney shall be thought fit and Requisite, to and for my best benefit and advantage and the deed or deeds of Sale, grants and other writings or Conveyances of and for the same tract and tracts of land, plantations, messages, Tennements and Hereditaments with their and every of their appurtenances and every part and parcell thereof (so to be made) for me and in my name to Seal, Deliver and Execute according to law and the Consideration Money or other effects to be agreed upon, for the purchase of the premises aforesaid for me and in my name, and to my use, to accept, Receive and take, the same to consign or

MINUTE BOOK "F." 95

other wise Dispose of according to my order, and upon the receipt thereof any acquittances or Discharges for me and in my name, to make, Seal, give and deliver, and upon such sale as aforesaid to give and Deliver, Livery of Seizin and possession of the premises in due form of law, moreover one attorney or more with like full power and authority under him, my said attorney, to sett and substitute, and at his pleasure the same to revoke, Hereby giving and granting unto my said attorney all my full and whole power, strength and authority in and about the premises for me and in my name to doe, execute and perform all and every other Lawful act and acts, thing and things, Devise and Devises in the law whatsoever Needful and necessary to be done in and about the premises as fully, amply and effectually in every respect to all intents and purposes as I, the said Constituent, myself might or could do being Personally present, Ratifying, allowing and confirming all and whatsoever my said attorney or his Substitute or Substitutes shall lawfully do in or about ye premises by Virtue of these presents. In witness whereof I, the said Francis Gibbon, have here unto sett my hand and Seal the two and twentieth day of September, Annoque Domini, One thousand Six hundred ninety-two.

FRANCIS GIBBON. [Seal.]

Sealed and Delivered in the presence of Sam'll Harrison, John Pinyard, Luke Gale.

Philad'a the 9th 12mo., 1692, Samuel Harrison appeared before me and did Acknowledge his hand to the Above written Instrument, and attested that he saw the same Sealed and Delivered, Rob't Eure, Justice; the 18th day of May, 1693, before me, one of their Ma'ties Councill at Philad'a, personally appeared Jno. Pinyard and made oath upon the Holy evangalist that he saw the within Letter of Attorney Sealed and Delivered by the within Francis Gibbon as his act and Deed, and he with Sam'l Harrison and Luke Gale signed thereunto as witnesses, Taken before John Cann.

Know all men by these presents that I, Sam'll Carpenter, of Philad'a, Merch't, by virtue of the within Mentioned power and Authority to me, derived from Francis Gibbon, of Barbados, Merch't, do in my place and stead authorize, Substitute and appoint my Loving Friends, Cap't John Brincklo and Sam'll Burbary, both of Kent County, or either of them, Attorny or Attornies under me to acknowledge, make over and Confirm, in open Court according to law, unto Wm. Rodney of the said County of Kent, a Certain parcell or tract of land

Situate lying and being on the west side of Dover River in Kent County aforesaid, Containing Six hundred and Ninety-five Acres, Called and known by the name of Gibbon's point, for the only proper use and behoof of him, the said Wm. Rodney, his Heirs, Executors, Administrators or Assigns, from the said Francis Gibbon, his heirs, Executors and Administrators forever. As witness my hand and Seal at Philad'a this Eighteenth day of May, Anno Domi., 1693.

       SAM'L CARPENTER. [Seal.]

 Sealed and Delivered in ye presence of Jos. Pidgeon, Ro. Frensh Gallias.

 This Day Sam'll Carpenter in his own proper person appeared before me, one of their Majesties Councill at Philad'a, and Acknowledged the above mentioned Substitution to be his act and Deed, as witness my hand this Nineteenth day of May, 1693.

        GEORGE FORMAN.

Benjamin Griffith's Letter of Attorney to John Barclay.

Know all men by these presents that we, Benjamin Griffith, of Wood bridge, in the County of Middlesex in the province of East new Jersey, and Margaret Robinson of Elizabeth Town, in the County of Essex, in the said province, Executor and Executrix of the last Will and Testament of Wm. Robinson, late of Elizabeth Town Aforesaid, Deceased, have Nominated, ordained, Constituted and appointed and Authorized, and by these presents do Nominate, ordain, Constitute, appoint and Authorize our trusty and well beloved friend and Acquaintance, John Barclay, to be our true and lawful Attorney for us, and in our names as Executor and Executrix as above said, to ask, require, demand and Receive of and from all and all manner of persons, all such sums of money, debt, Dues, demands, goods, Chattles, Cloathing or any other thing or things of what kind soever they be, which are due, owing, belonging or appertaining or were due, owing, belonging or appertaining to the above said Wm. Robinson, and upon their or either of their refusall, them or any or either of them to proceed against in a Judiciall way, by process, arrest, Judgment, Condemnation, execution and Imprisonment, and upon agreement or Composition to release and Discharge and acquittances, or acquittances in our Names, to give, Seal and Deliver, and to act and perform all other lawfull acts and things for the recovering and obtaining of any of the above said premisses as we or any of us might or would lawfully doe if we were personally present, Ratifying, Confirming and holding firm and Stable all and whatsoever our said Attorney shall lawfully doe in and about the premisses. In witness whereof we have here unto Sett our hands and Seals this Thirtyeth Day of the third Month, one thousand Six hundred Ninety and three.

      BENJAMIN GRIFFITHS. [Seal.]
      MARGARET ROBINSON. [Seal.]

The day above said came before us the above Named Benjamin Griffith and Margaret Robinson and acknowledged this to be their act and Deed before us, Isaac Whitehead, Benjamin Price, Justices.

Recorded 5th of June, 1693.

John Sellwood's Letter of Attorney to Samuel Harrison.

Know all men by these presents that I, John Sellwood, of Ratcliff in the Parish of Stepney in the County of Middlesex, Citizen and weaver of London, for Divers good Causes me hereunto Moveing, have made, Constituted and appointed, and by these presents doe make, Constitute and appoint Sam'l Harrison, Master of the ship Called the Pennsylvania Merchant, now outward bound from the port at London, Intending, if God permitt, for Philad'a, or some other parts in America, to be my lawfull Attorney for me and to my use, to as't, demand, recover and receive of Henry Badcock, now Inhabiting in Philad'a or some other parts of America, all sum and Sums of money, goods, Debts, adventures or other Effects what soever that is due to me, the said Jno. Sellwood, from him, the said Henry Badcock, and upon non Payment of such sum or sums of money, I Doe give him my full power and Lawfull authority to this, my said Attorney, to sue, Arrest, Implead or Imprison him, the said Henry Badcock, his Ex'ers or Assigns, and again at his pleasure to revoke, Compound, agree or Determine all matters, reckonings, Accompts, debts, dues or demands whatsoe'r, Ratifying and Confirming all things that my said Attorney shall Lawfully do for me and in my name as amply and fully as I myself could do were I personally present. In witness whereof, I have hereunto sett my hand and Seal this four and twentieth day of the Month Called October, 1690.

      JOHN SELLWOOD, [Seal].

Sealed and Delivered in the presence of Jno. Sayer, Joshua Killingsworth.

Be it Remembered that the above named Jno. Sayer and Joshua Killingsworth did Attest that they saw the above named Letter of Attorney Signed, Sealed and Delivered by Jno. Sellwood, whereunto these Deponents have signed as Wittnesses; attested before me the 26th 3 m., 1691.

ARTHUR COOKE.

Recorded 8th June, 1693.

William End's Letter of Attorney to Philip Richards.

Know all men by these presents that we, Wm. End and Daniel Savery, both of Mayallow in the County of Cork and Kingdom of Ireland, Merchants, have Assigned, ordained and made, and in our stead and place by these presents, put and Constituted Our trusty and well beloved friend, Philip Richards, of New York, in America, Merch't, our true and lawfull Attorney for us in our Stead and name and to our use and behoof, to ask, recover and Receive of Miles Forster, formerly of Boston in New England, and now of East Jersey in America, the sum of Five hundred pounds, Sterling, due to us for the non payment of a bill of Exchange in London of Two Hundred and fifty pounds, which he drew on Luke Forster, payable the fourteenth day of May, 1680, for Value received of us as by one obligation, with Condition there under Written, bearing Date the fourteenth day of February, 1680, more plainly appeareth, Giving and by these presents granting unto our said Attorney our full power and lawfull Authority in the premises to doe, say, perform, Conclude and finish for us and in our names as aforesaid, all and every such act and acts, thing and things, divice and Devises, in the law whatsoever for the recovery of all of the debts aforesaid, as fully, largely and amply in every respect as we ourselves might or could doe if we were personally present, giving and granting unto our said Attorney full power and Authority to appoint any other under him to prosecute all manner of lawfull means for the recovery of the said Debt, and upon the receipt thereof accquittances or other Discharges, for us and in our names, to make, seal and deliver, Ratifying, allowing and holding firm and Stable all and whatsoever our said Attorney shall lawfully doe or cause to be done in or about the execution of the premisses by virtue of these presents. In Witness whereof we have hereunto sett our hands and Seals this first day of May Anno Domini, 1688.

WM. END. [Seal.]
DAN'L SAVERY. [Seal.]

Signed, Sealed and Delivered to the use of the Attorney above named in presence of us, John Barnes, Wm. Byrn, Jonathan Perril, Nota. Pub.

Recorded 9th of June, 1693.

Philip Richard's Release to Miles Forster.

Know all men by these presents that I, Philip Richard, late of New York, in America, but now of the town and County of Philad'a, in the province of Pennsylvania, also in America, Merchant, Attorney for Wm. End and Dan'l Savery, both of Mayallow in the County of Kork and kingdom of Ireland, Merch'ts, by Virtue of a Certain letter of Attorney granted by them under their hands and Seals to me, bearing date the first Day of May, 1688, Impowering him, the said Philip Richards, for them in their steads and Name, and to their use and behoof, to ask, recover and Receive of Miles Forster, formerly of Boston, in New England, thereafter of East Jersey, in America, and now of New York Aforesaid, the sum of five hundred pounds, Sterling, Due to them for the Non payment of a bill of Exchange in London of Two hundred and fifty pounds which he drew on Luke Forster, payable the fourteenth Day of May, 1680, for value Received of them As by an Obligation with Condition thereto under written, bearing date the fourteenth Day of January, 1680, In which Letter of Attorney they, the said Wm. End and Daniel Savery, did give and grant unto the said Philip Richards their full power and lawfull Authority in the premisses to do, say, perform, Conclude and finish for them and in their names as aforesaid for recovery of the debt as fully in all respects as them themselves might or could do if they were personally present, and upon receipts thereof, Acquittances and Discharges for them, and in their names to make, seal and deliver, Ratifying what their said Attorney should lawfully doe or cause to be done in and about the Execution of the Premisses by virtue of the Letter of Attorney, as the same of the date aforesaid, Recorded in the Secretary's Office of the said province of Pennsylvania, Book No. 1, A., Page 3d, the ninth day of June, 1693, for and in Consideration of the sum of three hundred and two pounds, tenn shillings, Lawfull silver money of the said Province of Pennsylvania, in hand, paid or Secured to be paid by the said Miles Forster to the said Philip Richards, Attorney, and for the only proper use and behoof of the said Wm. End and Dan'l Savery, and their Heirs, Executor, Administrators and Assigns. The receipt there of the said Philip Richards doth hereby Acknowledge; and thereof and of every part thereof doth acquit, exonerate and Discharge him, the said Miles Forster, his Heirs, Executors And administrators, forever by these presents hath for them the said Wm. End and Dan'll Savery, their heirs, Executors, Administrators and Assigns, remised, released, exonerated, quit Claimed and for ever Discharged, and by these presents doth for them the said Wm. End and Daniel Savery, their Heirs, Executors, Administrators and Assigns, release, remise, exonerate, quitt claim and forever Discharge him, the said Miles Forster, his Heirs, Executors and administrators, forever by these presents of the said Sum of Three Hundred and two pounds, tenn shillings, Money aforesaid, and that in full and Compleat payment and Satisfaction of the said Sum of two hundred and fifty pounds, Sterling, Mentioned in the said bill of Exchange and of the said Sum of Five hundred pounds, Sterling, Mentioned in the obligation Conditioned for the payment of the said two Hundred and fifty pounds, Sterling, Mentioned in the said Bill of exchange, and of the said sum of two Hundred and fourty pounds Mentioned and Contained in four other Obligations granted by the said Miles Forster to James Claypoole or his Attorney in England, for the uses of the said Wm. End and Daniel Savery, to be paid at fives goales, Viz: Sixty pounds thereof ye Eleventh of July, 1685, Sixty pounds the same day 1686, Sixty pounds the same day 1687, and Sixty pounds the same day 1688, which four Obligations were granted by the said Miles Forster to the said James Claypoole or his Attorney in England, for the use Aforesaid for the said sum of two hundred and fourty pounds, which with ten pound paid by the said Miles Forster to the said James Claypoole, made up the very self same sum and no other sum Contained in the said bills of Exchange and Condition of the said first Obligation, And also in full and Compleat payment and Satisfaction of all the by gone Interests of the said Obligations and protests of the said bills of exchange, As also of all Actions and Causes of actions, Suits, Bills, bonds, Writings Obligatory, debts, dues, duties, Acco'ts, Sums of money, Judgments, Executions, extents, Quarrels, Controversies, tresspasses, damages, Interests, protests, Claims and Demands whatsoever both in Law and Equity or otherwise howsoever, which they, the said Wm. End and Daniel Savery or their said Attornies ever had now have, or which they or their Heirs, Executors, Administrators or Assigns or any of them, in time to come, can or may have Claim, Challenge or Demand to for or against the said Miles Forster, his Heirs, Executors, Administrators or Assigns for or by reason or Means of any Matter, Cause or thing Whatsoever, or of what Kind soever the same be, Nothing Excepted or reserved from the beginning of the world to the day of the date of these presents, Obligeing me, the said Philip Richards, and my heirs to Warrant this present Discharge to the said Miles Forster, his Heirs, Executors, Administrators and Assigns against myself and against the Said Wm. End and Daniel Savery, and their Heirs, Executors, Administrators and Assigns, as also against all other persons whatsoever Claiming or to claim by, from or under them or either of them, their or either of their Heirs, executors, administrators and assigns forever. In Witness whereof I have hereunto put my hand and Seal this tenth day of June Annoque Domini, 1693.

PHILIP RICHARDS. [Seal.]

Sealed and Delivered in Presence of us John Holme, Pat. Robinson. Philad'a 10th June, 1693, personally appeared before me the above Named Philip Richards who did Acknowledge the within and above Written receit to be his Act and Deed.

PAT. ROBINSON,
Secretary.

Recorded 10th June, 1693.

Miles Forster's Obligation to Philip Richards.

Know all men by these presents that I, Miles Forster, of ye City of New York, in America, Merch't, doe owe, Stand Justly Indebted and firmly bound unto Philip Richards, of the Town and County of Philad'a, in the Province of Pennsylvania, in America, Merchant, attorney for Wm. End and Daniel Savery, of Mayallow, in the County of Cork in the Kingdom of Ireland, Merchants, In the penall Sum of Three hundred and two pounds, tenn shillings, lawfull Current money of New York, to be paid to the said Philip Richards, Attorney Aforesaid, but to and for the only proper use and behoof of the said Wm. End and Dan'l Savery, their Heirs, Executors, Attorney order Admin'ors and Assigns, In and to the which payment will and truly to be made I bind and Oblidge me, my heirs, Executors and Administrators firmly by these presents. In witness whereof I have hereunto put my hand and Seal this Twelvth day of June, Anno Domini, 1693. The Condition of this Obligation is such that if the Above bounden Miles Forster, or his Certain Attorney, Heirs, Executors, Admin'ors or Assigns doe and shall well and truly pay or Cause to be paid to the said Phillip Richards, Attorney for the said Wm. End and Daniel Savery, and for their and their Heirs, executors and admin'ors, their only proper Use and behoof the full and Just sum of one hundred fifty-one pounds, five shillings Aforesaid, att and upon the   Day of   , in the year 1693, And that without fraud, Covin or further Delay that then and in that Case the above said Obligation shall be void, otherwise it shall remain in full force and Virtue.

MILES FORSTER, [Seal.]

Sealed and Delivered in Presence of us, John Holme, Patt. Robinson. Philad'a 12th June, 1693, Personally appeared before me the within Named Miles Forster who did Acknowledge ye Obligation within written to be his act and Deed.

PAT. ROBINSON,
Secretary.

Recorded 12th of June, 1693.

Know all men by these presents that I, Miles Forster, of the City of New York, Merchant, do owe, stand Justly Indebted and firmly bound unto Phillip Richards, of the town and County of Philad'a, in the Province of Pennnsylvania, in America, Merchant, Attorney for Wm. End and Dan'l Savery, of Mayallow, in ye County of Cork in the Kingdom of Ireland, Merch'ts, in the penall sum of three Hundred and two pounds and ten shillings, Lawfull Current money of New York, to be paid to the said Phillip Rich'ds, Attorney Aforesaid, but to and for the only proper use and behoof of the said Wm. End and Daniel Savery, their heirs, Executors, Attorney order, admin'ors and Assigns. In and to the which payment well and truly to be made, I bind and oblige Me my heirs, executors and Admin'ors firmly by these presents. In witness whereof I have hereunto put my hand and Seal this twelvth Day of June, Annoq Domini, 1693.

The Condition of this Obligation is such that if the above bounden Miles Forster or his Certain Attorney, heirs, Executors, Admin'ors or Assigns, doe and shall well and truly pay or Cause to be paid to the said Philip Richards, Attorney for the said Wm. End and Daniel Savery, and for them and their Heirs, Executors and Admin'ors, their only proper Use and behoof the full and Just sum of one hundred fifty one pounds, five Shillings, Money Aforesaid, at and upon the   day of   , in the year 1694, And that without fraud, Covin or further Delay, That then and in that Case the Above said Obligation shall be void, otherwise it shall remain in full force and Virtue.

MILES FORSTER. [Seal.]

Sealed and Delivered in ye Presence of us, Jno. Holme, Pat. Robinson. Philad'a 12 June, 1693, Personally appeared before Me, the within named Miles Forster, who did Acknowledge the within obligation to be his act and Deed.

PAT. ROBINSON,
Secretary.

Recorded 12th June, 1693

Edward Claypole's Letter of Attorney to Patrick Robinson.

To all Christian people to whom these presents shall Come:

Know ye that I, Edward Claypoole, of the Island of Barbados, Esqr., have ordained and made and doe by these presents in my stead and place put and Constitute my Trusty Friend, Mr. Patrick Robinson, Inhabitant in the Country of Pennsylvania, to be my true and lawfull Attorney for me, and in my name and to my use to ask, Sue for, Levy, recover and receive from all manner of persons, debtors or accounttants, in the said Country of Pennsylvania, all such sum and Sums of money as now are or hereafter Shall become due to me upon the sale of any lands or otherwise whatsoever hereby giving, and granting to the said Patrick Robinson my full and whole power, authority and right in and Concerning the premisses, as also full power and Authority in my name, and for my use to bargain, Sell, alien and enfeoff any land, houses, Tenements, howsoever belonging unto me in the said Country of Pennslyvania, with their Appurtenances, and to dispose of any other goods for my use and to my best advantage that are or shall be recovered, and by this same power to give releases, Acquittances and other lawfull Discharges in and about the same and for the more effectuall Execution of the premisses or any part thereof for me, and in my name to doe, perform and execute all other act and acts, deed and Deeds, things in the law needfull and Necessary, as fully and amply as if I myself were personally Present and did the same, hereby ratifying and Confirming all and whatsoever my Said Attorney shall doe or cause to be done in and about the premisses. Sealed with my seal this fifth day of November, in the fourth year of the reign of our Sovereign Lord and Lady, Wm. and Mary, by the grace of God, of England, Scotland, France and Ireland, King and Queen, Defenders of the faith, &c., Anno Domini, 1692.

EDWARD CLAYPOOLE. [Seal.]

Sealed and Signed in presence of us, Geo. Walker, John Phillips.

Personally appeared this 5th January, 1692, before me, Cap't Wm. Markham, one of their Majesties of the Peace, for the town and County of Philad'a, the within named Geo. Walker, who did Solemnly attest that he saw the within named Edward Claypoole Sign, Seal and Deliver the Letter of attorney, within named, and that he saw the within Named John Philips sign Witness thereto.

WM. MARKHAM.

Recorded 12 June, 1693.

Richard Royston's Release io Charles Goss.

Know all men by these presents that I, Richard Royston, of Talbut County, in the Province of Maryland, Planter, for and in Consideration of Full and plenary Satisfaction had and Received as well for and in Consideration of a Certain quantity of Tobacco, Recovered of me at the Sute of Philip Lynes, of St. Marces, in the province aforesaid, on the account of Charles Goss, now of Philad'a, in the province of Pennsylvania, as for all and all manner of bonds, bills, suits, Actions, Cause and Causes of actions, Book debts, dues and Demands whatsoever, doe hereby exonerate, Release, Discharge and forever Quit Claim unto the said Charles Goss, of Philadelphia, in the province aforesaid, Mariner, as well of and from the said Philip Lynes as for and from all and all manner, Bonds, Bills, Suits, Trespasses, Accounts, Slanders, Actions, Cause and Causes of Actions, Records, Judgements, appeals, had moved or Depending, or that might have been had or moved, as well as of, for and from all Claims For Charges, Processes had or Depending in law or Equity, and for all and every Manner of thing or things, devise or devises in word or Deed, or on any accompt whatsoever that I, the said Richard Royston, have had, may, might or Could have against the said Charles Goss, his Heirs, Executors, Adm'nors or assigns from the beginning of the world to the day of the date of these Presents. In Witness whereof, I, the said Rich'd Royston, have to these Presents my hand and Seal Interchangeably Sett att Philad'a, in the Province of Pennsylvania, in America, this eighth day of October, In the year of our Lord, 1692.

RICHARD ROYSTON. [Seal.]

Signed, Sealed and Delivered in presence of us, Zechariah Whitpain, Jno. White, Joseph Willcox.

Pennsylvania, 15 June, 1693. Personally appeared before me the within named Jno. White and Jos. Wilcox who did solemnly attest and Declare as in the presence of God that they saw the within named Rich'd Royston sign, seal and Deliver the within mentioned Receipt of the said Charles Goss as his act and Deed.

PAT. ROBINSON,
Secretary.

Recorded 15th June, 1693.

Daniel Stone's Letter of Attorney to Charles Goss.

Know all men by these presents that I, Daniel Stone, of the Province of Pennsylvania, Ship Wright, for Divers good Causes and Considerations me hereunto moving, have made, Ordained and appointed and by these presents doe make, Ordain and appoint my friend, Charles Goss, of the said place, Merch't, my true and lawfull attorney for me and in my name to ask, demand, Levy, recover and receive all such sum or sums of money, goods, wares or Merchandizes whatsoever in America belongeth to me the said Daniel Stone and also to Summons, arrest, Sue, Implead, Imprison and Condemn, or to use any other means as is requisite either in Law or Equity, or the recovery of any such sum or sums of money due or hereafter may be due belonging or in any wise appertainnig unto me in America aforesaid, and upon Receipt thereof acquittances or other Sufficient Discharges for me and in my name to make, seal and Deliver, and I do hereby authorise my said attorney to make one or more attorney or attorneys under him and such authority as he shall give unto them or him the same, at his Will and pleasure to revoke further, I doe ratify, allow and Confirm all and whatsoever my said attorney shall lawfully doe or cause to be done in and about the premises. In witness whereof I have hereunto sett my hand and Seal the twenty-third day of May, Annoq. Domini, 1693.

DANIEL STONE. [Seal.]

Sealed and Delivered in presence of Jos. Willcox, Jasper Yeats, John Claypoole.

Pennsylvania, 15th June, 1693, personally appeared before me the above Named Joseph Willcox and John Claypoole; the first did Solemnly attest as in the presence of God and the other did swear upon the Holy Evangall'st of Almighty God that they saw the above named Daniel Stone Sign, Seal and Deliver the Letter of attorney within mentioned.

PAT. ROBINSON,
Secretary.

Recorded 15th June, 1693.

William Wright's Letter of Attorney to Charles Pickering.

Philadelphia.

Know all men by these presents, that I, Wm. Wright, of the aforesaid City, Inhabitant, for divers valuable Considerations me hereunto moveing, have nominated, ordained and appointed, As by these presents I doe Nominate, ordain and appoint my trusty and well beloved friend, Charles Pickering, of the aforesaid City, Inhabitant, to be my true and lawfull attorney for me and in my name, to ask, demand, Sue for, levy, recover and receive all such sum or sums of Money as is now due unto me from any person or persons inhabiting, residing or being in the province of New West Jersey or Elsewhere, to say within that Province Particularly, Wm. Dare, of Cohanzey, and if he or they or any of them shall refuse or delay to make Satisfaction when Demanded I doe by Virtue of the premises give and grant unto my said attorney full power and authority to Sue, Implead, Imprison and Condemn, and upon Composition and out of Prison again to deliver acquittances or other Discharges in my name, to give and in Case of Sickness or any other Occations one or more attorneys under him to substitute and at pleasure again to revoke and generally to doe, Execute, Accomplish and perform all other lawfull acts and things as to my said attorney shall be thought meet and Convenient in the premises, all which I will and doe ratify and Confirm and allow of as Valled and Effectual a manner as if realy done by myself were I personally present. In Testimony whereof I have hereunto sett my hand and Seal this twentieth day of June, 1691.

WM. WRIGHT. [Seal.]

Sealed and Delivered in presence of us, John Herves, George Leamb, Charles Ware.

Recorded 25 June, 1693.

MINUTE BOOK "F."

General Release of Charles Pickering to William Dare.

Know all men by these presents that I, Charles Pickering, of the Town and County of Philad'a, in the province of Pennsylvania, Gent., as well for myself as that I am attorney of Wm. Wright of Boston, in New England, doe hereby fully, freely and absolutely Exonerate, acquit and Discharge Wm. Dare, of Cohanzey, in the Province of West Jersey, Mariner, of and from all debts, dues and Demands Whatsoever that may have been formerly depending between the said Wm. Wright and the said Wm. Dare whether by bill, Bond, book accompt, or any other reckoning Whatsoever, as also of and from all actions or Cause of actions, Judgments, Executions, Bonds or arbitrations, awards and Controversies, whatsoever, by virtue of said power of attorney, dated the 20th of June, 1691, and that I from the begining of the world unto this present date, as Witness my hand and Seal at Philad'a this twenty-sixth day of the fourth month, June, 1693.

        CHARLES PICKERING. [Seal.]

Sealed, Signed and Delivered in presence of Philip Richards, Sam'l Hoult.

Recorded 26th June, 1693.

2d Exch. 6£ Sterling.   Maryland, May 14th, 1692.

At ten days sight of this my second Bill of Exch., my first and third not paid, pay or Cause to be paid to his Excellency, Lionell Copley, Esqr., Capt. General and Governor in Chief of their Majesties province of Maryland, or his order, the sum of Six pounds Sterling, being for the Moytie of two Shill. p'r hhd. Impost on Tobacco, Exported in the Ship Mary of Maryland.
        WM. BLACK.

To Mr. Patrick Ellis, merchant, near the Monument in London.

Exch. for 3£ 11s Sterling.   Maryland *ss:* August ye 24th, 1692.

At ten days sight of this my second bill of Excha. my first and third not being paid, pay or Cause to be paid unto his Excellency, Lionell Copley, Esqr., or his order the sum of three pounds Eleven Shillings Sterling; make good payment and place it to the account of the Tho. and Mary p. me.
        THOS. ELY.

To Mr. John Taylor, Merchant in London.

Exchange for 2£.   Maryland.

At ten days sight of this my second of Exchange, my first and third not being paid, pay or cause to be paid unto his Excellency, Lionell Copley, Esqr., or his order, the sum of two pounds Sterling, It being for fees for the Ship Marg'tt of London. Make good payment and place it to the said Ship. From your Serv't,

                                                ADR. ROACH.
To Mr. Benjamin Braine, Merchant of London, July 8th, 1692.

                        Maryland, September 5th, 1692.

At twenty days sight of this my second Bill of Exchange, my first and third not being paid, pay or Cause to be paid unto his Excellency, Lionell Claypoole, or order, the sum of twenty-Seven pounds, It being for the impost of one Shili. p'r hhd. Maryland for the ship Sam'l and Henry; make good payment and place it to the account of your Ser'vant.
                                                JOHN MEAD.
To Mr. John Facter, Merchant in London.

11£ 2s Sterling   Maryland, May 14th, 1692.

At ten days sight of this my second, my first and third Bills of Exchange not paid, pay or Cause to be paid unto his Excellency, Lionell Copley, Esqr., Gov'r of their Majesties province of Maryland, or order, the sum of Eleven pound two shillings Sterling, the Moitie of two shills. p'r hhd. Impost on Tobacco Exported in the Ship Reserve.
                                                WM. ROBERTS.
To Mr. James Lymery and Compa. in Bristoll.

Exch. for 14£.   Maryland, 9th June, 1692.

Upon ten days sight of this my second of Exchange, first and third not being paid, pay or Cause to be paid unto his Excellency, Lionell Copley, Esqr., Gov'r of their Majesties province of Maryland, or his order, fourteen pounds Sterling, the Moity of the two shillings p'r hhd. Imposition on Tobacco Exported in the Ship George, whereof Is Mr. S'r your son and Servt.
                                                JOHN CRANE,
To Mr. George Lapthorne, Merchant in Plimo.

For 8£ Sterling.   Maryland, 2d July, 1692.

At thirteen days sight of this my second bill of Exchange, my first and third not being paid, pay or cause to be paid unto his Excellency, Lionell Copley, Esqr., Capt. Gen'll and Gov'r in

Chief of the province of Maryland, or order, the sum of Eight pounds, being for the Moity of the two Shillings p. hhd. Imposition on Tobacco on board the Resolution of Plimo, as p'r advise of.

JOHN LUKE.

To Mr. John Addis and Compa., Merchants in Plimo.

All the said seven Bills are Indorsed thus: pay to Richard Haines and Compa., or order, it is mine, for Value received in Philadelphia of Charles Sanders and Compa.

L. COPLEY.

Recorded 27 June, 1693.

Prudence Wager and Mary Parker's Letter of Attorney.

To all People to whome these presents shall come:

Wee, Prudence Wager, of London, Spinster, and Mary Parker, of Poole in Dorsettshire, Spinster, Executrixes of the last Will and Testament of Alexander Parker, late of George Yard, in Lombard Street, London, Haberdasher, deceased, send Greeting: whereas by Indenture of Lease bearing date the one and twentieth day of October, and a Release bearing date the two and twentieth day of October, Anno Domi. one thousand Six hundred Eighty- one, made from Wm. Penn, of Worminghurst in the County of Sussex, Esq'r, unto the said Alexander Parker, He, the said Wm. Penn, for the Consideration therein mentioned did grant and Convey unto the said Alexander Parker and his Heirs One thousand acres of land in the Province of Pennsylvania in America, as by the said receited Indenture, relation being thereto had may more fully and at large appear, and whereas the said Alexander Parker by his last will and Testament under his hand and seal bearing date the Sixth day of the Mon. Called March, Anno Domi. 1688, and duly executed in the presence of three Credible Witnesses, did hereby give and devise and bequeath unto the said Prudence Wager and Mary Parker the aforesaid premises in these words, or words to this Effect Item: I give and bequeath unto my Executrixes all my real estate, lands and tenaments in the Kingdom of England and in the province of Pennsylvania to them and their heirs and assigns forever, by them to be sold for the best price they can gett and the moneys thereof ariseing to be added to my personall estate, and I hereby authorise them or either of them to sell the same for the use aforesaid and of his said will Constituted and appointed us, the said Prudence Wager and Mary Parker, executrixes, as by the same relation thereunto being had may appear, now these presents Witness, That we, the said Prudence Wager and Mary Parker, pursuant to the power given us by the afore-recited will, and also for divers good Causes and Considerations us hereunto moving, Have made, ordained, authorised, Constituted and appointed, and by these presents doe make, ordain, authorise, Constitute and appoint Jno. Goodson, of Philad'a, in the province of Pennsylvania, Chirurgeon, and Sam'l Carpenter, of the same place, Merchant, our true and lawfull agents, deputies and Attorneys for us in our names, and for our use to ask, demand, Sue for, recover and receive of and from all and every person and persons all such rents, Issues, profits and demands whatsoever now due or hereafter to become due unto us for and in respect of the said one thousand acres of land in the said province and also to use all lawfull ways and means for the recovery thereof, and to give such acquittances, releases or discharges as shall be thought needfull for or in respect of the same, and we do hereby further authorise and appoint our said attorneys Joyntly and severally to grant, bargain, Sell and Convey the said one thousand acres of land or any part thereof to any person or persons for any estate or estates and at such rates and prices as they can get for the same, they using their endeavour to gett the utmost value thereof, and we hereby authorise and appoint our said attorneys or either of them for us and in our names to make, Seal, deliver and duly Execute such Conveyances and assurances of the said premises or any part thereof as shall be reasonably devised, advised or required, and for such money or other valuable Considerations as they or either of them shall receive for the same to give releases and Discharges. In Witness whereof we, the said Prudence Wager and Mary Parker, have hereunto sett our hands and Seals this four and Twentieth day of May, Anno Domi. one thousand Six hundred and Ninety.

        PRUDENCE WAGER [Seal.]
        MARY PARKER. [Seal.]

 Sealed and Delivered by the above Named Prudence Wager in the presence of us, Harb't Springett, Jno. Price. Sealed and Delivered by the above named Mary Parker in the Presence of Thomas Kekwick, Sam'll Rallis. This was Executed in my Presence by Prudence Wager the Sixteenth of the fourth Month, 1690.

       Witness, WM. PENN, $P'r$ $G'r$.

Recorded 28 June, 1693.

Hugh Hall's Letter of Attorney.

Barbados:

Know all men by these presents that I, Hugh Hall, of the Island of Barbados, Merch't, have made, ordained, Constituted and by these presents doe make, ordain, Constitute and appoint my son, Hugh Hall, to be my true and Lawfull attorney In my name to ask, Demand and Receive from Daniel Fraes, of Kent County, in the province of Maryland, and John Jones, of the city of Philad'a, in the province of Pennsylvania, in America, all such sum or Sums of money Whatsoever as now is due, owing and belonging unto me from said persons by Vertue of their bond Jointly and Severally bound, and upon non payment or Delivery thereof, the above said persons or either of them, their Heirs, Executors or administrators, In my name to Sue, arrest, Implead and prosecute for the same, and upon such sute to proceed to Judgment and Execution, and thereupon the above said persons or either of them, their Executor or Admin'ors in prison to hold and keep untill Satisafction be made, with all Costs and Damages Sustained by reason of detaining the same, and upon payment or Delivery, the said person or persons or either of them out of prison to discharge and acquittances for the same or any part thereof, In my name to make seal and Deliver, and also to doe, perform and execute all and every other lawfull and reasonable acts and things whatsoever, both for obtaining and Discharging the same as shall be Needfull to be done. Giving and by these presents granting unto my attorney my full and absolute power in the premises, Ratifying and holding firm and Stable all and whatsoever my said attorney shall lawfully doe or cause to be done in and about the premises by Virtue of these presents. In Witness whereof I have hereunto sett my hand and Seal the twenty Day of May, Annoq. Domini, 1693. (Quinto Annoq. Regni Regis Gulielmi and Reginae Mariae Super Angliam Scotiam and Hiberniam Franciam Fidei Defensoris.)

HUGH HALL. [Seal.]

Signed, Sealed and Delivered in the presence of Nicho. Seaborne, James Foreman. Philadelphia, 15 July, 1692. Personally appeared before me the within Named Nicholas Seaborne who did Solemnly depose and Swear upon the Holy Evangells of Almighty God that he did see the within named Hugh Hall sign, Seal and deliver the Letter of attorney within mentioned and that this deponent did sign witness thereto, and also saw the within Named James Forman Subscribe his Name as Witness thereto.

PATRICK ROBINSON,
Secretary.

Recorded 17 July, 1693.

Power of Attorney from Executors of Baraby Brown.

Barbados:

Know all men by these presents, that we, Jo'n Parkinson, of the Island of Barbados, Gen't, and Frances Brown, Widdow, whole and sole Executrix of the last will and Testament of my late husband, Baraby Brown, of the said Island, Gen't, Deceased, have assigned, ordained and made, Constituted and appointed and in our steads and places by these presents doe assign, ordain and make, Constitute and appoint our trusty and well approved of Friend, Jasper Yeates, of the City of Philad'a, in the Province of Pennsylvania, Merch't, to be our true and lawfull attorney for us and each of us, in our names and to our uses to ask, Sue for, leavy, require, recover and receive all such sum and Sums of money, goods, Wares, Merchandize, effects or other thing or things of what nature or quallity soever which shall be due, owing, belonging or appertaining unto us or either of us for or by reason of any bargain, Sale, Contract or agreement had, made or done either by the said Baraby Brown, Deceas'd, or any other person or persons, whomsoever, from all manner of person or persons whatsoever, giving and by these Presents Granting unto our said attorney full power and authority for us, and in our names to Sue, arrest, Implead, Condemn and Imprison all such debtors refusing to pay the same, our names to make use of and our persons to Represent in all Courts of law or Equity, and before all Judges, Justices or other persons therein Concerned, and upon due payment and Satisfaction made out of prison to release and discharge, and upon receipt of any sum or sums of money, Merchandize as aforesaid, acquittances or other lawfull Discharges for us, and in our names to make, Seal and Deliver, and one attorney or more under him to make or Substitute and at his pleasure to revoke and make void as the nature of the business shall require and to our said attorney it shall seem necessary and Convenient, and Generally to doe, execute, prosecute and Determine all and every other act and acts, thing and things, Devise and Devises in the Law whatsoever to all Intents, Constructions and purposes as amply, fully and effectually as if we ourselves were from time to time actually Present, Ratifying, allowing and Confirming as good and firm all and whatsoever our said attorney shall lawfully doe or Cause to be done by Virtue of these Presents. In Witness whereof we have hereunto Sett our hands and Seals the Eleventh day of March, Anno Domi., 1692.

                        JOHN PARKINSON, [Seal.]
                        FRANCES BROWN. [Seal.]

Signed, Sealed and Delivered in the presence of. the word Widdow being first interlined, Abra. Carpenter, Solomon Bowin. Philad'a, May 7th, 1693, the above witnesses appeared before me and did acknowledge that they see the above said John Parkinson and Frances Brown Seal and Deliver the Letter of Attorney in Barbados.

ROBERT TURNER,
Justice.

Recorded 18th July, 1693.

Dr. John Haughton's Letter of Attorney.

Know all men by these presents that I, John Haughton, of the Province of West Jersey, Chirurgeon, for Divers good Causes and Considerations me hereunto moveing, Have made, ordained and appointed and by these presents do make, ordain and appoint my friend, Jno. Claypoole, of Philad'a, in the province of Pennsylvania, my true and lawfull attorney for me, and in my name and to my use, profitt and advantage, to ask, demand, levy, recover and receive, and to Sett, lett and Sell all my Land in the province of West Jersey with the appurtenances thereunto belonging, and thereupon to seal, deliver and acknowledge all deeds, Leases and Conveyances whatsoever for the same Lands and premises, Giveing and by these preents granting unto my said attorney my full power and authority to ask, demand, levy, recover and receive and dispose all such sum or sums of money, goods, wares and Merchandizes whatsoever belonging to me in America, and also to summons, arrest, sue, Implead, Imprison and condemn all and every such person and Persons as shall deny or do not satisfy all such debts and duties that are or shall be due and payable unto me in America, and upon receipt thereof accquittances or other Sufficient discharges for me and in my name to make, Seal and Deliver, and I doe hereby authorise my said Attorney to make one or more Attorney and Attorneys under him and such authority as he shall give unto him or them, the same at his will and pleasure to revoke, further I doe allow and confirm all and whatsoever my said attorney shall lawfully doe or cause to be done in and about the premisses. In witness whereof I have hereto sett my hand and seal The twelvth day of November, 1689, being the first year of their Majesties Reign and Ninth of the Proprietor's Government.

JOHN HAUGHTON. [Seal.]

Sealed and delivered in the presence of John King, Francis Cooke.

Recorded 18th July, 1693.

Letter of Attorney from Thomas Byfeld and others.

Know all men by these presents, that wee, Thos. Byfeld, James Braine, Richard Haynes, John Lamb and Benjamin Braine, all of London, Mercht's, and Joint traders Together in Company to America, for divers Considerations us thereto moveing have made, ordained and in our and every one of our steads and places put and Constituted and by these presents doe make, ordain and in our and every of our steads and places put and Constitute our trusty friends, Charles Sanders and Joseph Pidgeon, of Pennsylvania, in America, Merchants, to be our true and lawfull attorneys, factors and assigns Jointly and Severally, and the Survivor of them for us and in our names and to our use to ask, demand, Levy, recover and receive by Composition, Law or otherwise, of all and every person and persons whatsoever in the parts of America, whom it doth, shall or may Concern all such sum and sums of Money, debts, goods, Merchandizes, Commodities, effects, duties and demands of what nature or quality soever, as are or shall be owing, payable, belonging or to be delivered by or from the same person or persons, every or any of them to or for us or any of us our or any of our use or behoof concerning or anywise relating to our trading together as aforesaid, and also to pay all and every person and persons whatsoever in the parts of America whom it doth, shall or may concern all such sum and sums of money and demands as are truly owing and due to them or any of them on account or by reason or means of our said Joint trading, as our said attorney or the Survivor of them shall think fitting or have orders from us to pay, and also for us and in our or any of our names to answer and Defend all and Every action and actions which shall be brought or Commenced against us or any of us in any parts or places of America for or by reason or occasion of our Joint trading thither as aforesaid, and all other matters, affairs and things whatsoever Concerning the same in America to doe and perform as fully as we could do in person, and especially to call to account and account with Jno. and Zechariah Whitpain our late factors or attorneys for the parts aforesaid, and either of them, for touching and Concerning their or either of their proceedings and translations in and about all or any of the trusts, matters and things whatsoever Committed or referred to them or either of them, by us or any of us in or about our said Trading in Company as aforesaid, and for their or either of their breach of Covenant or Contract touching the same, and upon Ballance or end made of the same to give and deliver to them, the said Jno. and Zechariah Whitpain, full and ample Discharges of or for all bonds and Obligations by them entered into touching the premises, Giving and by these presents granting unto our said Attorneys Charles Sanders and Joseph Pidgeon, Jointly and Severally, and the Survivor of them, all our full power and lawfull Authority Concerning the premisses, all and every person and persons whatsoever whom it doth, shall or may Concern and every or any of them, their, either or any of their Executors, Admin'ors and goods, or any of them (if Need be) to sue, arrest, attach, seize, Sequester, imprison and Condemn and out of Prison to deliver, and to appear before all Justices and Ministers of the law and to compound, Compromitt, conclude, agree, recover and receive, and of the recoveries or receipts, or upon any end Composition or agreement to be made Acquittances or any other discharges in our or any of our names to make, Seal, and as our deed and deeds deliver, And one Attorney or more under them, the said Charles Sanders and Joseph Pidgeon and the Survivor of them to make, Substitute and Revoke and generally to doe, execute, prosecute and Determine all and every other act, thing and things whatsoever which in and about the premisses shall be needfull and Necessary or Convenient as fully and effectually as we might or could doe personally, holding and allowing for firm and Stable, all and whatsoever the said Charles Sanders and Joseph Pidgeon Jointly or severally, or the survivor of them or their substitutes, shall doe or cause to be done in the premisses, by virtue of these presents. In Witness whereof we have hereunto Sett our hands and Seals, dated the seventh day of November, Anno Domi. 1691, And in the third year of the reign of King William and Queen Mary of England, &c'a.

THOS. BYFELD,	[Seal.]
JAMES BRAINE,	[Seal.]
RICH'D HAYNES,	[Seal.]
JNO. LAMB,	[Seal.]
BENJ. BRAINE.	[Seal.]

Sealed and Delivered in the presence of Robert Ungle, Wm. Cumberland, Junior.

Recorded 18th July, 1693.

Conveyance of Joseph Pawle to John Jennett.

These Indentures made this Twenty-fourth day of the ninth Mon., November, being the fourth year of the reign of Wm. and Mary, King and Queen of England, &c., Annoq. Domi., 1692, Between Joseph Pawle, of the Town and County of Philadelphia, in the province of Pennsylvania, in America, Yeoman, of the one part, and John Jennett of the same place, Taylor, of the other part, Witnesseth that for and in Consideration of the sum of twenty pounds, lawfull Money of the said province, in hand paid by the said John Jennett to the said Joseph Pawle, the receit whereof the said Joseph Pawle doth hereby acknowledge and thereof doth accquitt and discharge the said John Jennett, his Heirs, Executors and admin'ors for ever by these presents, He, the said Jos. Pawle, hath given, granted, bargained, sold, enfeeoffed and Confirmed, and by these presents doth absolutely give, grant, alien, bargain, Sell, enfeeoff and Confirm to the said John Jennett a Certain lott of land in the said Town, Containing in breadth twenty foot and in length three hundred Ninety-Six foot, bounded Northward with vacant lotts, Eastward with Dellaware front Street, Southward with Daniel Smiths's lott, and to the westward with the Second Street, With all its rights, Members, Improvements and appurtenances whatsoever held, used and enjoyed therewith or reputed as any part of the same, And the reversions, remainders, rents and profitts thereof, and all the estate, right, title, Interest, use, possession, property, claim and demand whatsoever of the said Joseph Pawle of, in and to the said premisses, and all deeds, grants, warrants, Surveys, returns, Letters, Patents and other evidences and writings Concerning the same, All which are situate, lying and being, as is above said, and are now in the Possession of the said Joseph Pawle by virtue of a pattent of confirmation of the same granted to him, his heirs and Assigns therein mentioned, from the Commissioners of Wm. Penn, Proprietor and Governor of the said province, dated the twenty-eighth day of June, 1692, to have and to hold the said lott and premisses to him the said John Jennett, his Heirs and Assigns for ever, att and under the yearly rent from henceforth to become due to the Chief Lord of the Soil of the said lott and premisses, and the said Joseph Pawle doth Covenant, promise and grant for him and his Heirs that they, the said lott of land and premisses to him, the said John Jennett, his Heirs and Assigns against him, the said Joseph Pawle, his Heirs and Assigns, As also against all others Claiming by, from or under him, them or any of them, or by his, their or any of their, or their Heirs, their means, privity, Consent or procurement shall and will warrant and for ever defend by these presents, and that the said Joseph Pawle hath not done nor Suffered any act whatsoever whereby the said granted premisses is, are, Shall or may be by any means lawfull Impeached, Charged or Incumbered in any manner of way; and this Indenture further witnesseth that the said Joseph Pawle hath Constituted and hereby doth

Constitute John Persons to be his Attorney, to appear at the next County Court of Philad'a, and there in presence of the said Court to declare, acknowledge and deliver these presents to the said John Jennett or his Attorney according to law. In Witness whereof the parties first above Written to these presents have to these present Indentures their hands and Seals interchangebly put the day and date, first above Written.

JOSEPH PAWLE. [Seal.]

Sealed and delivered in presence of us, Pat. Robinson, Wm. Robinson. Received this twenty-fourth day of November, 1692, from the within John Jennett, the within sum of Twenty pounds, consideration Money within Exprest by me, Joseph Pawle. Witness Pat. Robinson, Wm. Robinson. Acknowledged in open Court held at Philad'a on the sixth day of the Tenth Mon, 1692. Witness John White, Dep't Clarke and County Seal. [Seal.]

Recorded 20th July, 1693.

Conveyance of David Brintnall to John Jones.

Know all men that David Brintnall, of Philad'a, Taylor, for the Consideration of five pounds, current money of Pensylvania, to him paid by John Baldwin who sold the lott hereby granted to John Jones, the receit whereof he, the said David Brintnall, doth hereby acknowledge, hath given, granted, enfeeoffed and by these presents Confirmed unto the said John Jones all that piece of ground in Philad'a Containing in Breadth twenty foot and in length two hundred fifty-five foot, Bounded Northward with Chestnutt Street, Eastward with Joseph Walker's ground, Southward with back lotts, and to the westward with the other part of the said David Brintnall's lott, granted him, the said David, by Pattent from the Commiss'rs of property, dated the sixth day of the fifth Month. 1688, to have and to hold the said piece of ground hereby granted, with all its appurtenances, unto the said John Jones and his Heirs, to the use of him, his Heirs and Assigns for ever, yielding and paying therefore yearly unto the said David Brintnall, his Heirs or Assigns the rent or sum of five Shillings in Old England Money, on the first day of the first Mon., Yearly for Ever, and the said John Jones for himself, his heirs, Executors and Assigns doth Covenant, promise and agree forthwith to make one whole side of the fence between the hereby granted premisses and the said David Brintnall's lott, and to Maintain the one-half thereof at his, the Said Jones' proper Charge, and at the Charge of his heirs and Assigns forever together with the whole End between the granted premisses and Henry Lakin's lott, and one-half of the Side fence between Joseph Walker's, and the said premisses which he, the said John Jones and his Heirs and Assigns are to Maintain forever, and the said David Brintnall and his Heirs the said piece of ground hereby granted with the appurtenances, unto the said John Jones and his Heirs and Assigns under the rent and Covenants herein mentioned and reserved against him, the said David Brintnall and his Heirs, against all Others lawfully Claiming or to Claim by, from or under him, them or any of them shall and will warrant and forever Defend by these presents. In Witness whereof he hath hereto Sett his hand and Seal the twenty-fourth day of the fourth Month, Anno Domi., 1693.

       DAVID BRINTNALL. [Seal.]

Sealed and delivered in the Presence of Francis Littell, Rice Peters, Da'd Lloyd. Acknowledged in open Court, Certifyed under the Clark's hand this 6th July, 1693. Patrick Robinson, Cl. Com.

Recorded 20th July, 1693.

Conveyance of William Dillwin to Mary Ryner.

This Indenture made the eighteenth day of the first month called March, Annoq Domi, 1693, and in the fifth year of the reign of William and Mary, King and Queen over England, &c., and thirteenth of the said Proprietor's Government, Between Wm. Dillwin, of the City of Philad'a in the province of Pennsylvania, Sadler, of the one part, and Mary Riner, of the place aforesaid, widdow, of the other part, Witnesseth that the said Will'm Dillwin, for and in Conisderation of the sum of thirty pounds, Current Silver money, to him in hand paid by the said Mary Ryner, the receit whereof he doth hereby acknowledge, hath given, granted, enfeeoffed and by these presents Confirmed unto the said Mary Ryner all his said bank lott in Philad'a with a house there upon, a building, Containing in Breadth twenty-five foot and in length, into the River, Two hundred and fifty foot, bounded Northwards with Thos. Willard's lott, Eastward with the river Dellaware, at the said Extent of two Hundred and fifty foot, Southward With Wm. Carter's lott, and to the westward with the front Street, so called, all which said lott and premisses being part of the lott granted by Pattent under the Commiss'rs hands unto Rob't Longshore, and by the said Rob't Longshore conveyed unto him, the Said Wm. Dillwin, as may more at large appear, by a Deed bearing date the first day of the fifth month, 1691, together with all the Buildings and improvements thereupon, and the reversions and remainders, Rents, Issues and Profitt thereof to have and to hold unto her, the said Mary Ryner, her heirs and Assigns for ever; provided always, that if the said Wm. Dillwin, his Heirs, Executors or Admin'ors, or some or one of them shall and will well and truly, pay or Cause to be paid unto her, the said Mary Ryner, her Heirs, Executors or Assigns, or to any of them, lawfull Interest for the above said sum of thirty pounds, or so much as he, the said Wm. Dillwin, shall have in his hands during the term of time or times after expressed at every half year's end, Begining from the day of the date hereof, with the sum or sums of Money herein after Mentioned, at the days and times hereafter limitted and appointed, that is to say, the sum of fifteen pounds, in lawfull silver money, at or upon the Eighteenth day of the first month, which shall be in the year of our Lord, 1696, and the sum of fifteen pounds of like lawfull money at or upon the Eighteenth day of the first month, which Shall be in the year of our Lord, 1697, with lawfull Interest as aforesaid, without fraud or Covin, that then these presents to be void and of none effect, And it is mutually Covenanted, Concluded and agreed upon by and between the said parties, to these presents, In Manner following, that is to say, that if default of payment of the said sum or sums of Money before Mentioned, with lawfull Interest as before Exprest, or any of them, or any part or parcell of them, shall be made in part or in all at any of the days and times before limitted for payment thereof, That then it shall and may be lawfull to and for the said Mary Ryner and her Heirs To enter on the above Mortgaged Premisses with all their appurtenances, and the same to have, hold and enjoy as her or their proper Estate, But untill such default be made as aforesaid That it shall and may be lawfull to and for the said Wm. Dillwin and his Heirs to have and enjoy the said Mortgaged Premisses with the appurtenances without the lett, sute or Interruption of the said Mary Ryner, her Heirs or Assigns anything herein before Contained to the Contrary thereof, in any wise notwithstandig and hath made his Attorney to deliver these presents in open Court according to law unto Mary Ryner or to her Certain Attorney. In Witness whereof the said parties to these presents have Interchangeably Sett the hands and Seals the day and year first above wrtiten.

WM. DILLWIN.   [Seal.]

Sealed and delivered in the presence of William Walker, Francis Cooke. Acknowledged in open Court, Certifyed under the Clark's hand this 6th July, 1693.

PAT. ROBINSON, *Cl. Com.*

Recorded 21st July, 1693

MINUTE BOOK "F."

Patent to Joseph Pawle.

Willam Penn, Absolute Proprietor of the province of Pennsylvania and Countys anexed by his Commission, dated the sixteenth day of the tenth month, 1689, Unto Wm. Markham, Rob't Turner, John Goodson and Sam'll Carpenter, or any three of them, Sendeth Greeting: Whereas there is a lott of land in Philad'a Containing in breadth twenty foot, and in length three hundred Ninety-Six foot, bounded Northward with vacant lotts, Eastward with Delaware front Street, Southward with Daniel Smith's lott, and to the Westward with the second Street, Granted by virtue of a Warr't from ourselves, dated the   day of the   Month, 1692, and laid out by the surveyor Generall's Order, the same day and year, unto Joseph Pawle in right of Edward Blardman, Purchaser of one thousand Acres of land, And the said Joseph Pawle requesting us to Confirm the Same to him by Pattent. Know ye that by Virtue of the Commission aforesaid Wee have given, granted and Confirmed, and by these presents for the said Wm. Penn, his Heirs and Successors, We doe give, grant and Con-firm to the said Joseph Pawle, his Heirs and Assigns for Ever the said lott of land To have —— ——, hold and enjoy the said lott of land to the only use and behoofe of the said Joseph Pawle, his heirs and Assigns forever, to be holden of the proprietor and his heirs as of the mannor of Springettsberry in the County aforsesaid, in free and Common Soccage by fealty only in lieu of all Services, he fenceing in and building on the same according to regulation, Yielding and paying therefor to the Proprietor and his Heirs att and upon the first day of the first month, in every year, at the town of Philad'a, one English Silver Shilling, or the Value thereof in Coin Current, for the said lott to such person or persons as shall be from time appointed for that purpose. In witness whereof we have Caused these, our Letters, to be paid Patents at Philad'a this twenty-eighth day of June, being the fourth year of the reign of Wm. and Mary, King and Queen of England, &c., and twelvth year of the proprietor's Government over the said province in America, Annoq Domi. 1692.

Wm. Markham, Robert Turner, John Goodson and Seal of the Province.

Recorded 21st July, 1693.

Robert Webb and Wife's Letter of Attorney.

To all people to whome these presents shall come, I, Robert Webb, of London, Gen't, and Elizabeth Webb, my wife, send

Greeting. Whereas I, the said Rob't Webb, and Elizabeth Webb my wife, being interested and intituled in and unto five and twenty hundred acres of land Situate in the province of Pennsylvania, in America, part of which is cast into a City lott or laid out in the front street of the town of Philad'a next the river Dellaware, and one other lott thereof is Sett out in the high street of the said Town, another part of the said five and twenty hundred Acres doth Consist of Liberty lands belonging to the town lotts or lands sett out of the said town, the remainder of which said five and twenty hundred Acres or the greatest part thereof being Still undivided or not sett out, which said lands were purchased by John Barber, late Husband of Elizabeth Webb, my said wife, of the Governor of the said province, and by him, the said John Barber, in and by his last Will and Testament given and bequeathed unto the said Elizabeth, my Wife, or otherwise she by legall right after his death became intituled thereto, the writings of which said Lands are now remaining in Pennsylvania aforesaid, in the hands of Zechariah Whitpain, or of Sarah his wife, And whereas I, the said Robert Webb, and Elizabeth Webb, my wife, being interested and intituled in Severall goods and moneys to the Value of one hundred pounds or thereabouts, And of and in three servants, two of them Men the other a maid Servant, and in Severall other small debts, all which were lately of and belonging to the said John Barber, Deceased, and are since by my marriage with my said wife, become due unto me and her, now these presents witness that I, the said Ro't Webb, and Elizabeth Webb my wife, for divers good Causes and Considerations us hereunto moveing doe make, ordain, authorize, Constitute and appoint Patrick Robinson of the City or town of Philadelphia aforesaid, our true and lawfull agent and Attorney for us, and in our names and for our use to ask, demand and receive of John Longhurst, of Philadelphia aforesaid, Carpenter, son and Heir of Jno. Longhurst, of the same place, deceased, and Executor of his last will and Testament, or admin'or of his goods and Chattles, and also of and from the Executors or Admin'ors of Philip Leyman, late of Philad'a aforesaid, deceased, and of and from Zechariah Whitpain aforesaid, and Sarah his Wife, and of and from all and every other person or persons whatsoever Indebted to us or either of us all such sum and sums of money, Debts, dues, duties, Servants, to or the profitt or advantage thereof, writing, Claim and demands whatsoever which are now due, owing or belonging to us or either of us, as my said wife is Executrix, Admistratrix or Legatie to or of the said Jno. Barber, or as are due, owing or belonging to us or either of us upon any other account whatsoever by or from the said persons above particularly Named, or any other person or persons in the said province or elsewhere, and upon non-payment or not receiving of the same or any part thereof to use all lawfull and Equitable means whatsoever for recovery and obtaining thereof in any Court of Law or equity as our or either of our Substitute or Attorney, and upon receit or recovery of the said premisses, or any part thereof, to give discharges in our or either of our names, and we do hereby further Authorise and appoint our said Attorney to Survey, take up, lay out, lett, sett our said lands in Pennsylvania, or otherwise transact or negociate in relation thereto or in Relation to any of our Debts, dues and demands, according to his discretion or as he shall think fitt, and we do hereby ratify and Confirm all and whatsoever our said Attorney Shall doe in or Concerning the said premisses, or any part thereof, and doe hereby, for his ease, give him power and Authority to Constitute one or more Attorneys under him. In witness whereof I, the said Robert Webb, and Elizabeth my wife, have hereunto sett our hands and seals this one and thirtyeth day of December, Annoq. Domi. one thousand six hundred Eighty-Nine.

       Robert Webb, [Seal.]
       Elizabeth Webb. [Seal.]

 Sealed and Delivered in the presence of Richard Morris, John Day. Sealed and Delivered in my presence, Wm. Penn.

 Know all men by these presents that I, the within Named Robert Webb, have further made the within Pat. Robinson my Attorney to sell all or any of my lotts and lands in the within province according to my Instructions, and to Sign, Seal and in Court to deliver Conveyances for the same to the purchasers thereof as amply as I could do myself if I were present, Ratifying what he therein does, witness my hand and seal at Philadelphia this fifth of October, 1691.

       Robert Webb. [Seal.]

 Sealed and Delivered in Presence of us, Thomas Fitzwater, Tho's Harris.

 Recorded 21st July, 1693.

Conveyance of Robert Webb to William Salsbury.

 These Indentures made this twenty-fourth day of Aprill, being the fifth year of the reign of Wm. and Mary, King and Queen of England, Scotland, France and Ireland, Defenders of the faith, &c., Annoque Domi., 1693, Between Robert Webb, of the County of Talbot in the province of Maryland, Merch't, of the one part, and William Salsbury, of the town and County of Philad'a in the province of Pennsylvania, in America, Carpenter, of the other part, Witnesseth that for and in Consideration of the sum of twelve pounds, lawfull Silver money of the said province in hand paid or secured to be paid by the said Wm. Salsbury to the said Rob't Webb, the receit whereof the said Rob't Webb doth hereby ackno'ledge, and thereof doth accquitt, exonerate and discharge the said Wm. Salsbury, his Heirs, Executors and Admin'ors for ever by these presents, Hee, the said Rob't Webb, hath given, granted, Aliened, bargained, sold, enfeeoffed and Confirmed, and by these presents doth absolutely give, grand, alien, bargain, sell, enfeeoff and Confirm to the said William Salsbury, his Heirs and Assigns A Certain lott of land on and before the bank of Dellaware in the town of Philad'a, Containing in breadth forty foot and in length two Hundred and fifty foot, Bounded northward with vacant lotts, Eastward with the river Dellaware att the said Extent of Two hundred and fifty foot, Southward with the Jerman lott, and to the westward with the new thirty foot Street, with all the rights, Members, Improvements, appurtenances and priveledges whatsoever of the said bank lott held, used and enjoyed therewith or reputed as any part of the same, in as large, ample and beneficiall Manner as he, the said Rob't Webb, ever held, now holds or in any time comeing may or shall hold the same himself, and the reversions, remainders, rents and profitts thereof and all the estate, right, title, Interest, use, possession, property, Claim and demand whasoever of the said Rob't Webb of, in and to the said bank lott and premisses, and all warr'ts, Surveys, Returns and Patents Concerning ye same, All which are Scituate in the said town of Philadelphia, and are now in possession of the said Robert Webb by virtue of a Pattent of Confirmation of the same granted to him, his Heirs and Assigns therein named, from the Commiss'rs of Wm. Penn, absolute proprietor of the said Province, dated the Sixth of October, 1691, To have and to hold the said bank Lott and premisses to him the said Wm. Salsbury, his Heirs and Assigns, and to the only use and behoof of him the said Wm. Salsbury, his Heirs and Assigns for ever att and under the yearly rent of four English Silver Shillings or value thereof in Coin Current, yearly, and each year to become due to the Chief lord of the Soil of the said Lott and premisses, and under all and Singular the other rents, Covenants, provisions, Conditions, reservations and restrictions on the part of the said Rob't Webb, his heirs and Assigns, preformable to the said Wm. Penn, his heirs and Successors, mentioned in the said patent, And the said Rob't Webb for him and his heirs, do Covenant to and with the said Wm. Salsbury and his Heirs and Assigns that the said bank Lott and Premisses to him the said Wm. Salsbury and his Heirs and Assigns against the said Robert Webb and his heirs, as also against all others Claiming by, from or under him, them or any of them, or by his, their or any of their or their Heirs, their means, privity, Consent or procurement shall and will Warrant and forever defend by these presents; And that the said Rob't Webb hath not done nor suffered any act whatsoever whereby the said granted premisses is, are, shall or may be by any means lawfully Impeached, Charged or incumbered in any manner of way, and this Indenture further Witness that he, the said Rob't Webb, hath Constitut'd and hereby doth Contitute James Peller to be his attorney to appear at the next County Court of Philadelphia, and there, in presence of the said Court, to Declare, acknowledge and Deliver these presents to the said Wm. Salsbury or his Certain Attorney, according to law. In Witness whereof the parties first above written to these presents have to these present Indentures their hands and Seals Interchangeably put the day and date first above written.

Rob't Webb. [Seal.]

Sealed and Delivered in presence of us, Pat. Robinson, Wm. Robinson.

Received from the within named Wm. Salsbury the within sum of Twelve pounds Consideration Money within exprest, by me, this twenty-fourth day of Aprill, Annoq. Domi., 1693.

Robert Webb.

Witness Patrick Robinson, Wm. Robinson. Acknowledged in open Court, Certifyed under the Clark's hand this 6th of July, Anno Domi., 1693.

Pat. Robinson, Cl. Com.

Recorded 22nd July, 1693.

Conveyance to James Peller.

This Indenture made this thirteenth day of June, being the Fifth year of the reign of our Sovereign Lord and Lady, Wm. and Mary, by the grace of God, of England, Scotland, France and Ireland, King and Queen, defenders of the faith, &c., Annoq. Domi., 1693, between Pat. Robinson, of the town and

County of Philad'a, in the province of Pennsylvania, in America, attorney for Edward Claypoole, of the Island of Barbados, Esqr., of the one part, and Jas. Peller, of the said town and County, Carpenter, of the other part, Whereas the said Edward Claypoole, by his letter of attorney, under his hand and Seal, did give and grant unto the said Pat. Robinson, full power and authority in his, the said Edward Claypoole s Name and for his use to bargain, Sell, Alien and enfeeoff any lands, houses, Tenaments howsoever belonging unto him in Pennsylvania, with their appurtenances, to his, the said Edward Claypoole, his best advantage and for the more effectual execution of the premisses or any part thereof, for him, the said Edward Claypoole, and in his name to doe, perform and Execute all and other act and acts, deed and deeds and things in the law needfull and necessary as fully and amply as if he, the said Edward Claypoole, himself were personally present, and did the same himself, thereby ratifying and confirming all and whatsoever his said attorney should doe, or Cause to be done in and about the premises, as the same letter of attorney under the hand and Seal of the said Edward Claypoole, bearing date the fifth day of Novem'r, Anno Domi., 1692. Proved by the Witnesses thereunto to have been the act and Deed of the said Edward Claypoole before Capt. Wm. Markham, Esqr., one of their Majesties Justices of the peace for the said County, the fifth day of January, Anno Domi., 1692. Recorded in the Secretary's office at Philad'a, Book A, 1, page 6, the Twelvth day of June, 1693, more at large proports; Now these present Indentures, witness that he, the said Pat. Robinson, attorney aforesaid (for and in Consideration of the sum of forty pounds lawfull Silver Money of the said Province, in hand paid, or secured to be paid by the said James Peller, to the said Pat. Robinson, attorney, and for the sole and only proper use and behoof of the said Captain Edward Claypoole, the receit whereof the said Patrick Robinson, attorney aforesaid, doth hereby acknowledge and thereof doth acquitt, exonerate and discharge him, the said James Peller, his Heirs, Executors and admin'ors forever by these presents), hath given, granted, aliened, bargained, Sold, Enfeeoffed and Confirmed, and by these presents doth absolutely give, grant, alien, bargain, Sell, enfeeoff and Confirm to the said James Peller, his Heirs and assigns forever a Certain part and proportion of that Southermost lower part of a Certain Dellaware front Street lott of land in Philadelphia, Containing in breadth in the whole fifty-five foot, and in length with the other lotts three hundred Ninety-six foot, and which Certain part and proportion of the said lower part of the said front lott of land in Philadelphia doth begin at the extent of two hundred foot distance from the west side of Dellaware front Street, and from thence downwards in length one hundred and Ninety-six foot westward to the East side of the second Street from Dellaware, and at the said Extent of two hundred foot distance from the west side of Dellaware front street in breadth fifty-five foot, and upon the east side of the said Second Street the whole breadth, that it will bear by reason of the swamp on the south side thereof, leaving on the north side thereof forty-seven foot as the breadth of the remainder of the said whole lott, being one hundred and two foot, and which Certain lower part and proportion of the said lott is bounded Southward with Richard Whitpain, deceased, his lott, and with the said swamp Westward, with the second Street Northward, with The remaining forty-seven foot of James Claypoole, deceased, his whole lott, and Eastward with the remaining part of the said Edward Claypoole's lott, with all the rights, Members, Improvements, appurtenances and priviledges whatsoever of the said lower part and proportion of the said lott held, used and enjoyed therewith or reputed as any part of the same, In as large, ample and beneficial Manner as he, the said Capt. Edward Claypoole, by his attorney aforesaid, or his predecessors and authors from whom he delivered his right ever held, now holds or in any time Coming may or shall hold the same themselves, and the reversions, remainders, rents and profitts thereof, and all the estate, right, title, Interest, use, possession, property, Claim and demand whatsoever of him, the said Capt. Edward Claypoole, of, in and to the same, and all deeds, grants, Charters, warrants' Surveys, returns, letters, patents, Judgments, executions, apprisements, Verdicts of Juries, returns of executions and deeds of sale proceeding thereupon, and other evidences and writings Concerning the said lower Certain part and proportion of the said lott in conjunction with the remaining parts thereof, all which are Scituate, lying and being as is above written, and is now in the tenure, possession and Occupation of him, the said Capt. Edward Claypoole, by force and Virtue of a certain deed of sale and Conveyance of the said lower part of the said lott, with the upper part thereof granted by Benjamin Chambers, Sheriff of the County of Philadelphia, to the said Patrick Robinson, attorney, and for the proper use and behoof of the said Capt. Edward Claypoole, his Heirs and assigns forever, dated the Second of June, 1691, acknowledged in the County Court of Philadelphia, the said day and year, under the Clark's hand and Seal of the County. Recorded in the Rolls office at Philadelphia the Sixteenth day of the said Month and year, book E, 2 Vol. 5: Page 155, by David Loyd, ibid: To have and to hold the said Certain part and proportion of the lott and premises to him, the said James Peller, his Heirs and assigns forever, as fully and absolutely in all respects as he, the said Captain Edward Claypoole, or his Predecessors and authors, from whom he derived his right ever held, now holds or in any time Coming may or shall hold the same themselves by force and Virtue of the said deed of Sale and Conveyance thereof granted by the said Sheriff to the said Capt. Edward Claypoole, and by force and Virtue of the grounds and Warrants whereof the same preceded in all points att and under the yearly rents, from henceforth to become due to the Chief Lord of the Soil of the said Certain part and proportion of the said lott of land and premises, and the said Pat. Robinson, attorney for the said Capt. Edward Claypoole, doe Covenant for them and their Heirs that they, the lowermost part and proportion of the said lott of land and premises to him, the said James Peller and his heirs and assigns against him, the said Capt. Edward Claypoole, and his Heirs and assigns, as also against all others Claiming by, from or under them, or any of them, or by his, their or any of their or their Heirs, their Means, Privity, Consent or Procurement shall and will warr't and forever defend by these presents, and the said Pat. Robinson, attorney, aforesaid, nor the said Capt. Edward Claypoole have not done nor suffered any act whatsoever, whereby the said granted premisses is, are, can, shall or may be by any means Lawfully Impeached, Charged or incumbered in any manner of way. In Witness whereof the parties first above written to these presents have to these present Indentures their hands and Seals Interchangeably putt, the day and date first above written.

           PATRICK ROBINSON. [Seal.]

Sealed and delivered in presence of us, Jos. Willcox, Thomas Jenner.

Received from the within Mentioned James Peller, the within written sum of fourty pounds Consideration Money, within Exprest by me this thirteenth day of June, Anno Domi. 1693

            PATRICK ROBINSON.

Witness, Joseph Willcox, Thos. Jenner; acknowledegd in open Court, Certifyed under the Clark's hand this Sixth July, 1693.

           PAT. ROBINSON, *Cl. Com.*

Recorded 24th July, 1693.

The Proprietary's Patent to Arthur Cooke.

William Penn, absolute proprietor of the Province of Pennsylvania and Counties annexed, by his Commission, dated the

Sixteenth day of the tenth month, 1689, Unto William Markham, Robert Turner, John Goodson and Samuel Carpenter, or any three of them, Sendeth Greeting.

Whereas Arthur Cooke, of the town and County of Philad'a, hath requested us to grant him a piece of land upon and before the bank of Delaware river, in the said town, Joyning upon the east side of Dellaware front street, and to run out into the river in order to erect a wharf or key, and to build houses thereupon for the better Improvement of the place, as well as for his own particular profitt. Know ye that (for the Further encouragement of the said Arthur Cooke) by virtue of the Commission aforesaid, we have given, granted and Confirmed, and by these presents for the said Wm. Penn, his Heirs and Successors, wee doe give, grant and Confirm Unto the said Arthur Cooke, his Heirs and assigns, a Certain lott of land on and before the said bank of Dellaware, in the said town of Philad'a, Containing in breadth thirty foot, and in length two Hundred and fifty foot, bounded Northward with vacant lotts, Eastward with the river Dellaware, at the said Extent of two hundred and fifty foot, Southward with Jno. Wheeler's lott, and to the westward with Dellaware front Street. Granted by Virtue of a Warrant from ourselves, dated the twenty-eighth of the tenth Month, 1689, and laid out by the Surveyor General's Order the day unto Arthur Cooke, To have, hold and Enjoy the said lott to the only use and behoof of the said Arthur Cooke, his Heirs and assigns forever, Yielding and paying therefore yearly, and each year during the space of Fifty-one years from the Said twenty-eighth day of the tenth Mon., 1689 and fully to be Compleated and Ended Unto the said Wm. Penn, his Heirs and Successors, upon the first day of the first month, March, in Every year, Three English Silver Shillings or value thereof in Coin Current at the Said Town of Philad'a to such persons as shall be from time to time appointed for that purpose, and att the expiration of the said term of fifty-one years the yearly value of the said lott of land, with its building and all its Improvements shall be reasonably valued and apprised by two men mutually to be Chosen, one-third part of which valuation and apprisement the said Arthur Cooke, his Heirs and assigns shall for ever thereafter pay to the said Wm. Penn his Heirs and Successors, also at and upon the first day of the said first month in every year, at the said town of Philad'a, to such persons as shall be from time to time appointed for that purpose, To be holden of the said Wm. Penn, his Heirs and Successors, Proprietors aforesaid, as of our Mannor of Springettsbury, in the County aforesaid, in free and Common Soccage, by feilty only in lieu of all Services, and we doe also give and grant that the keys or wharfs to be built upon the said land Shall be lawfull keys or wharfs forever for landing and Shipping all goods and Merchantdizes, giveing and granting unto the said Arthur Cooke, his Heirs and assigns full authority and power to Contract and agree with and to receive reasonable satisfaction from all persons making use of the same by shipping or landing of goods and Merchandizes, and by ships, boats or vessels Coming to, lying by and making use of the same, Provided always, that the said Arthur Cooke agree, his Heirs and assigns doe and shall regularly leave thirty foot of ground in the Clear for a Cartway under and along the said whole bank, and in Convenient time shall make the same to be a Common and Publick Cartway for all persons by day and by night for ever hereafter, and if the said Arthur Cooke be desirous to have Celler Stairs or Steps up or down into his house, that then he shall leave room to make the Same upon his own ground, without any encroachment upon the said Cartway, and if the said Arthur Cooke Shall unadvisedly build to the utmost extent of his bounds, then he shall expect no other Conveniency, neither for Celler Stairs nor steps then what he can make within his own house, and if the said Arthur Cooke shall not wharff out nor make the said thirty foot Cartway, that then the person that shall happen to be next unto and to join upon such shall and may make the said Cartway for the generall Service, and the said Arthur Cooke so neglecting, shall pay the whole Charge thereof to the person that makes the same, and that the said Arthur Cooke is and Shall be willing (so far as Concerns his said bank lott), the said thirty foot Cartway shall run upon one Stretch or Course from one publick Street to another as near as may be, and also provided that in the Center (or as neer the same as may be between Spruce Street and Walnut Street, the said Arthur Cooke shall Leave his proportionable part (answerable to his said whole lott) of ten foot of ground whereupon to make the same, one publick pair of Stone Stairs down from the east side of Dellaware front Street, Clear of all building), over the same and of an open passage into the said thirty foot Cartway, also of tenn foot broad and of the like Space of ten foot of ground for a passage (and Clear of all building over the same) out of the East side of the said thirty foot Cartway, and so downwards Eastwardly into the river Dellaware, at the said Extent of two hundred and fifty foot from the said East side of Dellaware Sixty foot front Street, with one pair of Stairs down into the said river, and which last pair of Stairs shall run out at least to low water mark, and that the said ground two pair of Stairs and passages be left purchased, built and kept in Repair from time to

9—VOL. XIX.

time for Ever hereafter at the proportionable Charge of the Said Arthur Cooke, his Heirs and assigns, between the said Spruce Street and Walnut Street, provided also that it Shall hereafter be in the Choice of the said Arthur Cooke, his Heirs and assigns, to make and leave or not to make and leave any Stairs, passage or ground for Stairs, or passage in his said bank lott unless he, the said Arthur Cooke, hath Covenanted with the persons from whome they have derived their right to allow them free access to the river and to the wharfs, and if it should happen that part or all of the said buildings and Improvements should be destroyed by Inundation, fire or other act of Providence after the said valuation and apprisement, then and in such case the said Commiss'rs doe grant for the said Wm. Penn and his heirs that they, the said Arthur Cooke, his Heirs and assigns, shall be Considered by abatement of rent proportionable to the loss sustained, and the said commissioners, with consent of the said Arthur Cooke, will have the said Wharff forever hereafter, for distinction's sake, be Called Wharff. In witness whereof the said Commiss'rs have Caused these, third letters, to be made Patents the Philad'a this Twenty-fifth day of June, being the third year of the reign of Wm. and Mary, King and Queen of England, &ca., in the tenth the Government of the said Wm. Penn over the said province in America, Annoq Domi. 1691. William Markham, Robert Turner, John Goodson and seal of ye Province.

Recorded 1st Angsut, 1693.

Conveyance of Arthur Cooke to George Thompson.

These Indentures made this twenty-eighth day of the ninth month, November, being the year of the reign of our Sovereign Lord and Lady, Wm. and Mary, King and Queen of England, Scotland. France and Ireland, Defenders of the faith, &c a., Anno Domi. one thousand Six hundred Ninety-two, Between Arthur Cooke, of the town and County of Philad'a, in the Province of Pennsylvania, in the parts of America, Merch't, of the one part, and George Thompson and Andrees Derickson, of the same place, also Merch'ts, of the other part, Witnesseth that for and in Consideration of the sum of three hundred pounds, lawfull Silver Money of the said province, in hand paid to the said Arthur Cooke, by the said George Thompson and Andrees Derickson the receit whereof the said Arthur Cooke doth hereby acknowledge, and thereof and of every part thereof doth acquitt, exonerate and discharge them, the said George Thompson and Andrees Derickson, their Heirs, Executors and admin'ors for ever by these presents. He, the said Arthur Cooke, hath given, granted, aliened, bargained, sold, enfeeoffed and Confirmed, and by these presents doth freely, fully and absolutely give, grant, alien, bargain, sell, enfeeoff and Confirm to the said George Thompson and Andrees Derickson equally between them and their respective Heirs and assigns, all that his, the said Arthur Cooke, his Certain Lott of land on and before the bank of the river Dellaware, in the said town of Philad'a, Containing in breadth thirty foot and in length Two Hundred and fifty foot, Bounded northward with vacant lotts, Eastward with the said river Dellaware at the said extent of two hundred and fifty foot, Southward with John Wheeler's, now George Heathcot's Lott, and to the westward with Dellaware front Street, together with all the rights, members, houses, buildings, wharff, passages, Improvements, appurtenances, and privileges whatsoever of the said bank lott held, used and Enjoyed therewith or Reputed as any part of the same, In as large, ample, extensive and Beneficial Manner as he, the said Arthur Cooke, ever held, now hold or in any time Coming may or shall hold the same himself, and the reversions, remainders, rents and profitts thereof, and all the estate, right, title, Interest, use, possession, property, Claim and demand whatsoever of him, the said Arthur Cooke, of, in and to the said bank lott and premises and all warrants, Surveys, returns and letters Patents Concerning the same, all which are Scituate, lying and being in the said town of Philada, in the said Province, and are now in the possession of the said Arthur Cooke by Virtue of a Warrant from the Commiss'rs of Wm. Penn, absolute Proprietor of the said Province and Countys annexed, bearing date the twenty-eighth day of the tenth Month, December, 1689, and laid out by the Surveyor Generall's order the same day unto the said Arthur Cooke, and by Virtue of a Patent of Confirmation following thereupon of the same granted by the said Commiss'rs to the said Arthur Cooke, his Heirs and assigns therein mentioned, bearing date the Twenty-fifth day of June, 1691, To have and to hold the said bank lott and premises to them, the said George Thompson and Andrees Derickson, Equally between them, their respective heirs, Executors, admin'ors and assigns for ever, and to the only proper use and behoof of them, the said George Thompson and Andrees Derickson, Equally between them, their respective Heirs, executors and admin'ors and assigns forever, secluding and hereby expressly excluding Survivorship and all benefitt and advantage thereof absolutely for ever, att and under the yearly Rent of three English Silver Shillings or value thereof in Coin Current yearly, and Each year to become due to the Chief Lord of the Soil of the said bank lott and premises, and under all and Singular the other rents, Covenants, provisors, Conditions, reservations and restrictions on the part of the said Arthur Cooke, his heirs and assigns, performable to the said Wm. Penn, his Heirs and Successors, Mentioned in the said Pattent, and the said Arthur Cooke, for him and his Heirs, doth Covenant, promise and grant to and with the said George Thompson and Andrees Derickson and their respective Heirs and assigns, that they the said bank lott and premisses to the said George Thompson and Andrees Derickson, and their respective heirs and assigns against him, the said Arthur Cooke and his Heirs, as also against all others Claiming by, from or under him, them or any of them, or by his, their or any of their or their heirs, their Means, privity, Consent or procurement Shall and will warrant and for ever defend by these presents, and that the said Arthur Cooke hath not done nor suffred any act whatsoever whereby the said granted premises or any part thereof Is, are, can, shall or may be by any Means lawfully Impeached, Charged or Incumbred in any manner of way, and these Indentures further witness that the said Arthur Cooke hath made and Constituted, and by the Tennor hereof doth make and Constitute John White to be his attorney, to appear at the County Court of Philadelphia, and there in the presence of the said Court to declare, acknowledge and Deliver these presents to the said George Thompson and Andrees Derickson, or their Certain attorney, according to Law. In Witness whereof ye parties first above written to these presents have to these present Indentures their hands and Seals Interchangeably putt the day and date first above written.

ARTHUR COOKE. [Seal.]

Sealed and delivered in Presence of us, Charles Goss, Albertus Jacob, Patrick Robinson, John Cox.

Received from the within Mentioned George Thompson and Andrees Derickson the within Sum of Three hundred pounds Consideration Money, within Exprest by me, Arthur Cooke. Witness John Cox, Charles Goss, Albertus Jacob, Patrick Robinson; acknowledged in open Court held at Philad'a on the Sixth day of the Tenth month, 1692, as Witness John White, Dep't Clark and County Seal.

Recorded 2d August, 1693.

Conveyance of George Thompson to And's Derickson.

These Indentures made this first day of July, in the fifth year of the Reign of our Sovereign Lord and Lady, Wm. and

Mary, by the grace of God, of England, Scotland, France and Ireland, King and Queen, defenders of the Faith, &c'a, Annoq Domini, 1693, Between George Thompson, of the Town and County of Philad'a, in the Province of Pennsylvania in the parts of America, Merch't, of the one part, and Andrees Derickson, of the same place, also Merch't, of the other part, Witnesseth that for and in Consideration of the sum of One hundred and thirty pounds, lawfull Silver money of the said Province, in hand paid by the said Andrees Derickson to the said George Thompson, the receit whereof the said Andrees Derickson doth hereby acknowledge and thereof doth discharge the said George Thompson, his Heirs, Executors and admin'ors for ever by these presents he, the said George Thompson, hath given, granted, aliened, Bargained, Sold, enfeeoffed and Confirmed, and by these presents doth absolutely give, grant, alien, bargain, Sell, enfeeoff and Confirm to the said Andrees Derickson all that his, the said George Thompson, his Just and equall Moiety and half part of a Certain lott of land on and before the bank of the river Dellaware, in the said town of Philad'a, Containing in breadth thirty foot, and in length Two hundred and fifty foot, bounded Northward with vacant lotts, Eastward with the river Dellaware att the said Extent of two Hundred and fifty foot, Southward with John Wheeler's, then George Heathcot's now ——— Carpenter's lott, and to the westward with Dellaware front Street, with the Just and Equall Moiety and half part of all the rights, Members, houses, buildings, wharffs, passages, Improvements, appurtenances and priviledges whatsoever of the said bank lott held, used and enjoyed therewith or reputed as any part of the same in as large, ample, Extensive and beneficial Manner as he, the said George Thompson, ever held, now holds or in any time Comeing may or shall hold the same himself, and the reversions, remainders, rents and profitts thereof, and all the estate, right, title, interest, use, possession, property, Claim and Demand whatsoever of him, the said George Thompson, of, in and to the said Moiety of the said lott and premises, and all warrants, Surveys, returns, letters, pattents and Deeds Concerning the same, all which are Scituate, lying and being as is above said, and which moiety is now in the possession of the said George Thompson by Virtue of a Pattent of Confirmation of the said whole lott, granted by the Commiss'rs of Wm. Penn to Arthur Cooke, his Heirs and assigns, bearing date the twenty-fifth day of June, 1691, and by virtue of a Deed of Sale and Conveyance of the said whole lott, Granted by the said Arthur Cooke to the said George Thompson and Andrees Derickson, equally between them, their Heirs and assigns therein mentioned, bearing date the Twenty-eighth day of November, 1692. Acknowledged in the County Court of the said County the Sixth day of December, 1692, under the Clark's hand and Seal of the County, To have and to hold the said just and equall Moiety and half part of the said lott and premises to him, the said Andrees Derickson, his Heirs and assigns, and to the only proper use and behoof of him, the said Andrees Derickson, his Heirs and assigns for ever, att and under the proportionable part of the yearly, to become due to the Chief Lord of the Soil of the said Just and Equall Moiety and half part of the said lott, and under all and Singular the other rents, Covenants, provisors, Conditions, reservations and restrictions, on the part of the said George Thompson, his Heirs and Assigns, performable to the said Wm. Penn, his Heirs and Successors Mentioned in the said Patent, proportionably to the said Moiety of the said lott, And the said George Thompson, for him and his Heirs, doth Covenant, promise and grant to and with the said Andrees Derickson and his Heirs and Assigns, that they, the said Moiety and half part of the said Lott and premisses to him, the said Andrees Derickson, and his Heirs and Assigns, against himself and his Heirs, as also against all others Claiming by, from or under him, them or any of them, or by his, their or any of their or their Heirs, their Means, privity, Consent or procurement, shall and will warrant and for ever defend by these presents, and that the said George Thompson hath not done nor Suffered any act whatsoever whereby the said Moiety or half part of the said lott and premisses is, are, can, shall or may be by any Means lawfully Impeached, Charged or Incumbred in any manner of way. In Witness whereof the parties first above written to these presents have to these present Indentures their hands and Seals Interchangeably putt the day and date first above written.

GEORGE THOMPSON. [Seal.]

Sealed and delivered in presence of us, Edmund Du Castle, John Duplouvis.

Received this first day of July, 1693, from the within Andrees Derickson, the above sum of one Hundred and thirty pounds Consideration Money within exprest by me, Geo. Thompson. Witness, Edmund Du Castle, John Duplouvis; Acknowledged in open Court. Certifyed under the Clark's hand this Sixth July, Annoq Domini 1693.

PATRICK ROBINSON, Cl. Com.

Recorded 2d August, 1692.

Receipt of Griffith Jones to Lawrence Cock.

Received from Lawrence Cock the full and Just sum of forty-two pounds, being in full for Seven years' rent of a Certain

MINUTE BOOK "F." 135

lott in Walut Street, from the first day of **January, 1691-2**, To the first day of January, 1698-9, Conform to a deed thereof granted by me to the said Lawrence Cock, Containing Six pounds p'r Annum, payable by him to me for the said lott forever, bearing date the Twenty-eighth of November, 1691. I Say received by me, Griff. Jones, this twentieth day of July, 1693.

GRIFFITH JONES. [Seal.]

Sealed and Delivered in presence of us, Pat. Robinson, William Robinson, Twentieth July, 1693; Acknowledged by said Griffith Jones to be his act and Deed Before me, Pat. Robinson, Secretary.

Recorded 2d August, 1693.

Bill of Exchange, Nicho. Milburne to Jasper Yeates.

Maryland the 9th June, 1693.

S'r: P. £ 20 Sterling at Thirty day's Sight, pay or Cause to be paid, this, my first p'r Exchange, my second and third not paid Unto Mr. Jasper Yates or order twenty pounds, Sterling, the value of himself make Current payment and place it to account of your friend and Servant.

NICHO. MILBURNE.

To Mr. James Braine, Merchant, in London. Indors'd, thus, pay the Contents to Edward Laschals, Jasper Yeates.

Recorded 2d August, 1693.

Conveyance of Daniel and Elizabeth Cooke to Geo. and Mary Parris.

These Indentures made this Seventh day of July, being the fifth year of the reign of our Sovereign Lord and Lady, William and Mary, by the Grace of God, of England, Scotland, France and Ireland, King and Queen, Defenders of the faith, &ca., Anno Domini, 1693, Between Daniell Cooke, of the town and County of Philad'a in the province of Pennsylvania in the parts of America, Carpenter, and Elizabeth his wife, of the one part, and George Parris of the same place, Marriner, and Mary his wife, of the other part, Witnesseth that for and in

Consideration of the sum of one hundred and Seventy pounds lawfull Money of the said Province, in hand paid or Secured to be paid by the said George Parris to the said Daniel Cooke, the receit whereof the said Daniell Cooke doth hereby Acknowledge, and thereof doth acquitt and Discharge him, the said George Parris, his Heirs, Executors and Admin'ors for Ever by these Presents, they, the said Daniel Cooke and Elizabeth his Wife, have given, granted, aliened, bargained, Sold, enfeeoffed and Confirmed, and by these presents doth absolutely give, grant, alien, bargain, Sell, enfeeoff and Confirm to the said George Parris, and Mary his Wife, and to their heirs, Lawfully procreate or to be procreate between them, their part of Certain lott of land in the City of Philad'a, which part Contains in breadth, forty foot, and in length, one hundred Seventy-eight foot, bounded Northward with the back of the High Street, Eastward with Henry Jones' and John Weal's lott, Southward with Chestnutt Street, and to the westward with the remaining part of John Redman's Lott, with all the rights, Members, houses, buildings, yards, orchards, Improvements and appurtenaces whatsoever of the said lott held, used and enjoyed therewith or reputed as any part of the same, and the reversions, remainders, rents and profitts thereof and all the estate, right, title, Interest, use, possession, property, Claim and Demand whatsoever of them, the said Daniell and Elizabeth Cooke, of, in and to the said premises, And all deeds, grants, Charters, letters, patents, escripts and other evidences and writings Concerning the said premisses only or only any part thereof or in Conjunction with other lands, all which are Scituate, lying and being as is aforesaid and are now in the possession of the said Daniell Cooke by Virtue of a deed of Sale and Conveyance of the said whole lott of land above Mentioned, from Charles Pickering to right of Wm. Rakestraw, purchasers, to John Redman, his Heirs and Assigns therein Exprest, dated the fifteenth day of May, 1686; acknowledged in open Court the Second day of June thereafter; Recorded in the rolls office at Philadelphia, Vol. 5, book E, folio 343, the Eighteenth day of the said Month and year, and by Virtue of a deed of Sale and Conveyance of the said part of the said lott, Granted by the said John Redman to the said Daniel Cooke, his Heirs and Assigns therein mentioned, bearing date the Seventh day of July, 1686; acknowledged in open Court the same day under the Clark's hand and Seal of the County; Recorded in the office of rolls and publick registrie at Philad'a, Vol. 5, book E, folio 374, the Eleventh day of the said Month and year, To have and to hold the said part of the said Lott of land, houses and premisses to them, the said Geor. and

Mary Parris, and to their heirs, lawfully procreate or to be procreate between them and to their Heirs and Assigns, and to the only use and behoof of the said George and Mary Parris and to their Heirs, lawfuly procreate or to be procreate between them and to their Heirs and assigns for ever, at and under the yearly rents, from henceforth to become due to the Chief Lord of the Soil of the said part of the said lott and premisses, and the said Daniel and Elizabeth Cooke doe Covenant, prom'se and grant for them and their Heirs that they, the said part of the said lott and premisses unto them, the said George and Mary Parris, and to their Heirs lawfully procreate or to be procreate between them and their Heirs and Assigns against them, the said Daniel and Elizabeth Cooke, and their Heirs, as also against them, the said Charles Pickering and Wm. Rakestraw, and their Heirs and Assigns rexive, as also against all others Claiming or to Claim by, from or under them or any of them, or their or any of their heirs, their means, privity, Consent or procurement shall and will warrant and for ever Defend by these presents, And the said Daniel and Elizabeth Cooke hath not done nor suffered any act, matter or thing whatsoever whereby the said Granted Premises or any part thereof is, are, can, shall or may be by any means lawfully Impeached, Charged or Incumbered in any manner of way. In Witness whereof the parties first above written to these presents have to these present Indentures their hands and Seals Interchangeably putt the day and Date first above written.

DANIEL COOKE. [Seal.]

The mark of ELIZABETH E COOKE, [Seal.]

Sealed and Delivered in presence of us, Jos. Pidgeon Pat. Robinson.

Received this Seventh day of July, 1693, from the within George and Mary Parris the within mentioned sum of One hundred and Seventy pounds, Consideration Money within Exprest by us.

DANIEL COOKE.

The Mark of Eliz. E Cooke, witness, Jos. Pidgeon, Pat. Robinson. Acknowledged in open Court, Certifyed under the Clark's hand this 4th day of August, 1693, by me.

PATT. ROBINSON, Cl. Com.

Recorded the August, 1693.

Pasiunk Patent.

Richard Nicolls, Esqr., Principall Commissioner from his Ma'tye, in New England, Governor Generall, Under his highness James Duke of York and Albany, &c., of all his Territories in America, and Commander in Chief of all the forces employed by his Ma'ty to reduce the Dutch Nation and all their usurped lands and Plantations under his Ma'ties Obedience, To all to whom these presents shall Come, Sendeth Greeting: Whereas there is a Certain piece or parcell of land Commonly Called or known by the Name of Pasiunk, Scituate, lying and being at Dellaware by the side of the Sculkill, Containing, by Estimation, one thousand Acres, be it more or less Bounded on the South with the main River, on the west with the Sculkill, on the North with the Plantation belonging to Peter Rambo, and upon the East by a Parcell of land Called Malboes Land; Now Know yee that by Virtue of the Commiss'n and authority unto me given, I have thought fitt to give and grant, and by these presents doe give, ratify, Confirm and grant unto Rob't Ashman, John Ashman, Thomas Jacob, Caleb Carman, Dunkin Williams, Francis Walker, Thomas Llewellyn, Frederick Anderson, Joshua Jacob and Thomas Jacob, their Heirs and Assigns, the aforecited piece or parcell of land and premisses with all singular their appurtenance, To have and to hold the said piece or parcell of land and premisses, unto the said Rob't Ashman and his Associates before Mentioned, their Heirs and Assigns, unto the proper use and behoof of the said Rob't Ashman and his Associates, their heirs and Assigns for Ever, Yielding and paying therefore, Yearly and every year, unto his Ma'ties use, tenn Bushells of wheat as a Quitrent when it shall be demanded by person or persons in Authority as his Ma'ties Shall please to Establish and Empower in Dellaware river, and the parts and plantations adjacent. Given under my hand and Seal at fort James, in New York, on the Island of Manhatans, the first day of Jan'y in the Nineteenth Year of his Ma'ties Reign, Annoq Domini 1667.

Richard Nicoll's Memorandum, before the signing and Sealing of this Pattent It is resolved that the first planters, namely, Mr. Rob't Ashman and his then Associates, shall have and Enjoy a large proportion the Allottment then others according to their Stocks and ability to Improve the said land, and in Case the above Mentioned Pattentees cannot agree in the Division of such lands Capt. Jno. Carre, Ensigne Edmund Withins and Mr. Wm. Tom shall putt a perriod to any Question hereafter by causing the lotts to be laid out and registered what every man's proportion amounts unto.

RICHARD NICOLLS.

Recorded by order of the Governor the day and Year above Written.

MATHIAS NICOLLS, *Secretary.*

This Patent is entred in the records of upland Patents, Folio 2, p'r Eph. Herman, 1678, Clr.

Recorded 5th August, 1693.

MINUTE BOOK "F."

Conveyance of James Peller to John Densy.

This Indenture made the fifth day of July, Annoq Dom. 1693, Between James Piller, of the County of Philadelphia, Carpenter, of the one part, and John Densy, of the Said place, Carpenter, of the other part, Witnesseth that for and in Consideration of the sum of Seven pounds, ten shillings, lawfull money of Pennsylvania, in hand paid by the said John Densy, the receit whereof he, the said James Peller, doth hereby Acknowledge, hath given, granted, aliened, bargained, Sold, enfeeoffed and Confirmed and by these presents doth absolutely give, grant, alien, bargain, Sell, enfeeoff and Confirm to the said John Densy, his Heirs and Assigns a Certain lott of land in Philadelphia, Containing in breadth twenty foot and a half, and in length Eighty foot, Bounded Northward with the high Street, Eastward with Silas Crispin's lott, Southward with John James' lott, and to the westward with George Harmar's lott, granted by Virtue of a Warr't from the Commiss'rs, &c., as may more fully appear by Patent under their hands and proprietor's Seal, dated the fifth day of October, 1692, with all the Improvements and appurtenances whatsoever thereunto belonging or held, used or enjoyed therewith, and all the estate, right, title, Interest, use, possession, property, Claim and Demand whatsoever of the said James Peller or his Heirs of, in and to the said lott and Premises, To have, hold and enjoy the said lott and premises to him, the said John Densy, his Heirs and Assigns, to the only use and behoof of him, the said John Densy, his Heirs and Assigns for ever, at and under the yearly rents thereof due and payable to the proprietor and his Heirs, and all deeds, Patents and other Evidences and writings Concerning the said Premisses, And the said James Peller doth Covenant, promise and grant for himself and his Heirs that they, the said lott and premises, to the said John Densy and his Heirs against the said James Peller and his Heirs, as also against all others Claiming by, from or under him or them, or by his, their or any of their Means, privity, consent or procurement shall and will Warrant and for ever Defend by these presents, and that the said James Peller hath not done nor suffered any act whatsoever whereby the said granted Premisses or any part thereof is, are, Can, Shall or may be, by any means, lawfully Impeached, Charged or Incumbred in any manner of ways. In Witness whereof the parties first above written to these present Indentures, their hands and Seals have Interchangeably putt the day and date first above Mentioned.

JAMES PELLER. [Seal.]

Sealed and Delivered in the presence of William Salsbury, Henry Flower, Wm. T Trotter, his Mark, Acknowledged in open Court, Certifyed under the Clark's hand this Sixth of July, 1693.

PAT. ROBINSON, *Cl. Com.*

Recorded 6th August, 1693.

Charles Butler's Pardon.

William Markham, Esqr., Lieu't Governor of the province of Pennsylvania, County of New Castle, and the territories and tracts of land Depending thereon, in America: To all to whome these shall Come sendeth Greeting: Whereas at a provinciall Court held for the County of Philadelphia, in the said province, upon the 24th day of September, 1691, Charles Butler was Indicted for Uttering and paying away Several pieces of false money of false mixt Mettall to the likeness of Spanish Coin, Called pieces of eight, which he some times before made or Coyned in the County aforesaid, intending, Craftily, falsly and traiterously to defraud the King and his people, without any authority or License from the King and Queen to him given Contrary to the laws in such Cases made and provided, whereupon the Petty Jury upon the 26th day of September, 1691, did find the said Charles Butler guilty of dispersing bad money, Upon which the said Charles Butler had Sentence pronounced against him, Viz't: that he should forfeit his goods and Chattells for Ever and the profitts of his land during his Life, and that be imprisoned during his life; And whereas the said Charles Butler by his Petition to me and the Councill did sett forth ye Severity of the said Sentence for being only found Guilty of dispersing bad money, and the records of the said Court having been examined in Councill, it was unanimously resolved that the said Sentence was severe, whereupon the Councill requested his Excellency, Benjamin Fletcher, &ca., or in his Absence, the Lieu't Governor, upon the said Charles Butler's application, to grant him a pardon, and whereas the said Charles Butler hath, by his Petition to me, begged Mercy and Compassion to be extended to him in his deploreable Condition by reason of the said Sentance, and that I would restore him by Pardon. Know ye therefore, that in the absence of his Excellency, Benj'n Fletcher, the Chief Governor, I have Pardoned, acquitted, for-given, discharged, released and through remitted, and by these presents doe pardon, acquitt, forgive, discharge, release and thoroughly remitt, to the said Charles Butler, the Crime and offence of dispersing bad money whereof he was Convict, As also the Judgments, Sentence, punishment and execution thereof Aforesaid, he, the said Charles Butler, giving into the Secretaries Office goods and Sufficient Security for his good behavior. In Witness whereof I have hereto putt my hand and Seal this Nineteenth day of August, being the fifth year of the reign of our Sovereign Lord and Lady, Wm. and Mary, by the grace of God, of England, Scotland, France and Ireland, King and Queen, Defenders of the faith, &ca., Annoq Domini, 1693.

WILLIAM MARKHAM.
By the Lieu't Governor's Command.
PAT. ROBINSON, *Secretary.*
Recorded 19th August, 1693.

Assignment of Samuel Miles to Thomas Hobbs.

The Originall Patent whereof the assignment follows, is Recorded at Philadelphia the fourth day of fifth month, 1691, Patent book, Page 287, Examined David Lloyd, Deputy, ibid. Know all men that the within named Samuel Miles, for the Consideration of fifteen pounds, Current Money of Pennsylvania, to him paid by Tho's Hobbs, of Philad', Yeoman, hath given, granted, assigned, and by these presents transfered and Sett over unto the said Tho's Hobbs the pattent within written, together with the lott of land within Mentioned and all his, the said Sam'll Miles' right, title and Interest of, in and to the same, To have and to hold unto the said Tho's Hobbs and his Heirs to the use of him, the said Tho's Hobbs, his Heirs and Assigns forever, and the said Sam'l Miles and his Heirs, the said lott of land with the appurtenances unto the said Tho's Hobbs and his Heirs, against him and his Heirs, and against all other persons whatsoever lawfully Claiming or to Claim by, from or under him, them or any of them shall and will warr't and for Ever Defend by these presents, and hath made Daniel Jones, his Attorney to deliver these presents in open Court According to law. In Witness whereof he hath hereto sett his hand and Seal the Twentieth day of the fifth Month, Annoq Domini, 1691.

SAMUEL MILES. [Seal.]

Sealed and Delivered in presence of John Southworth, Sam'l Bulkley, Edward Farmer; Acknowledged in open Court, Certifyed under the Clark's hand this fourth August, 1693.

PAT. ROBINSON, Cl. Com.

Recorded 26th August, 1693.

Patent for Isaac Warner's Lott.

William Penn, Absolute proprietor of the province of Pennsylvania and Counties Annexed, by his Commission, dated the sixteenth day of the tenth month, 1689, Unto Wm. Markham, Robert Turner, Jno. Goodson and Samuel Carpenter, or any three of them, sendeth Greeting: Whereas there is a Certain lott of land in the town of Philadelphia, Containing in breadth thirty-two foot, and in length Eighty-two foot, Bounded Northward with vacant lotts, Eastward with Strawberry alley, Southward with Anthony Tayler's lott, and to the westward with Thomas Harlow's lott, Granted by Virtue of a Warrant from ourselves, dated the twenty-Sixth of the Second Month, 1690, and laid out by the Surveyor General's order the twenty-fifth of the second Month, 1691, Unto Isaac Warner, and the said Isaac Warner Requesting us to Confirm the same to him by Patent; Know yee that by Virtue of the Commission aforesaid Wee have given, granted and Confirmed, and by these presents for the said Wm. Penn, his Heirs and Successors, We doe give, grant and Confirm to the said Isaac Warner, his Heirs and Assigns for Ever the said lott, To have, hold and enjoy the said lott to the only use and behoof of the said Isaac Warner, his Heirs and Assigns for Ever, To be holden of the proprietor and his Heirs as of the Mannor of Springettsberry in the County aforesaid, in free and Common Soccage by fealty only in lieu of all services, he fenceing in and building upon the same according to regulation, Yielding and paying, therefore, to the proprietor and his Heirs, att and upon the first day of the first month in ever year, at the town of Philad'a, Three English Silver shillings or Value thereof in Coin, Current, for the said lott, to such persons as shall be from time to time appointed for that purpose. In Witness whereof we have Caused these, our letters, to be made Patents at Philad'a this twenty-fourth of February, fifth Year of the reign of Wm. and Mary, King and Queen of England, &ca., and Twelvth year of the proprietor's Government over the said Province, in America, Annoq Domini, 1692-3. Wm. Markham, Robert Turner, John Goodson and Seal of the Province.

Assignment Thereof.—Isaac Warner to John White.

Indorsed thus: Know all men that the within Isaac Warner, for the Consideration of two pounds, fifteen Shillings, to him in hand paid, and Secured by John White of the City of Philadelphia, Wooll Comber, the receit whereof he doth hereby acknowledge, Hee, the said Isaac Warner, hath bargained, Sold, Assigned, and by these presents transferred the within Patent and lott of land therein Mentioned unto him, the said John White, his Heirs and Assigns for ever, and the said Isaac Warner and his Heirs, the said lott of land and premisses unto him, the said John White and his Heirs, against him and his Heirs, and against all other persons Claiming, Shall and will warrant and forever defend by these presents. In Witness whereof he hath hereto sett his hand and Seal the second day of March, Annoq Domini, 1693.

ISAAC WARNER. [Seal.]

Sealed and delivered in the presence of George Harmer, Fran. Cooke; Acknowledged in open Court, Certifyed under the Clark's hand this fourth day of August 1693, by me.

PAT. ROBINSON, *Cl. Com.*

Recorded 29th August, 1693.

Conveyance of John White to Nathaniel Thornton.

Know all men that John White, of Philadelphia, in the Province of Pennsylvania, Wooll Comber, for the Consideration of Five pounds, Current Money to him in hand paid, and Secured by Nathaniell Thornton, of the same place, Husbandman, the receit whereof he doth hereby acknowledge, hath given, granted, enfeeoffed and by these presents Confirmed unto him, the said Nathaniell Thornton, all that lott of land in Philad'a Containing in breadth Thirty-two foot, and in length Eighty-two foot, Bounded northward with vacant lotts, eastward with Strawberry alley, Southward with Anthony Tayler's lott, and to the Westward with Tho's Harlowe's lott, granted by patent under the hands of the proprietor's Commiss'rs, dated the 24th day of February, Annoq Domi 169$\frac{2}{3}$, Unto Isaac Warner, and by the said Isaac Warner, assigned over unto said John White together with all his right and interest in and to the aforesaid lott of land and premisses, To have and to hold the said lott of land and premisses with all the appurtenances unto him, the said Nathaniell Thornton and his Heirs, to the only use and behoof of him, the said Nathaniell Thornton, his Heirs and assigns for Ever, under the Yearly Quittrent accruing to the proprietor and his Heirs for the same, and the said John White and his Heirs have hereby granted the said lott of land and premisses, with all the appurtenances unto him, the said Nathaniell Thornton and his Heirs, against him, the said John White and his Heirs, and against the said Isaac Warner and his Heirs, and against all other persons whatsoever lawfully claiming or to Claim by, from or under him, them or any of them, shall and will warrant and for ever defend by these presents. In witness whereof he hath hereunto sett his hand and Seal the first day of the sixth month Called August Annoq Domi. 1693, being the fifth year of the reign of Wm. and Mary, King and Queen over England, &ca.

JOHN WHITE. [Seal.]

Sealed and Delivered in the presence of Robert Wallis, William Alloway; Acknowledged in open Court, Certifyed under the Clark's hand this fifth August, 1693.

PATRICK ROBINSON, *Cl. Com.*

Recorded 29th August, 1693.

Conveyance of Philip Richards to Daniel Cooke.

This Indentures made this first day of August, being the fifth year of the reign of our Sovereign Lord and Lady, Wm. and Mary, by the grace of God, of England, Scotland, France and Ireland, King and Queen, defenders of the faith, &ca, Annoq Domini, 1693, Between Philip Richards, of the Town and County of Philadelphia, in the province of Pennsylvania, in America, Merchant, of the one part, and Daniel Cooke, of the said place, Carpenter, of the other part, Witnesseth that for and in Consideration of the sum of Seventy-five pounds lawfull silver money of the said province, in hand paid by the said Daniel Cooke to the said Philip Richards the receit whereof the said Philip Richards doth hereby acknowledge and thereof doth discharge the said Daniell Cooke, his Heirs, Executors and admin'ors for ever, Hee, the said Philip Richards, hath granted, aliened, bargained, sold, enfeeoffed and Confirmed, and by these presents doth absolutely grant, alien, bargain, sell, enfeeoff and Confirm to the said Daniel Cooke, his Heirs and assigns, a Certain lott of land on and before the bank of Dellaware, in the said Town of Philad'a, Containing in breadth Twenty-seven foot, and in length two Hundred and fifty foot, Bounded to the Westward with Dellaware front Street, northward with Nathaniell Allen's lott, Southward with Alexander

Parker's Lott, and to the Eastward with Dellaware River att the extent of two hundred and fifty foot, With all the rights, Members, Improvements, appurtenances and priviledges whatsoever of the said bank lott held, used and enjoyed therewith, or Reputed as any part of the same in as large and beneficiall Manner as the said Philip Richards held, holds or in any time Coming may or shall hold the same himself, and the reversions, remainders, rents and profitts thereof and all the estate, right, title, Interest, use, possession, property, claim and Demand Whatsoever of the said Philip Richards of, in and to the said Lott and premises, and all warrants, Surveys, returns and Patents Concerning the same all which are Scituate in the town of Philad'a, in the said province, and are now in the possession of the said Philip Richards by Virtue of a Pattent of Confirmation of the same, granted to him, his Heirs and assigns therein named, from the Commiss'rs of Wm. Penn, absolute Proprietor of the said province, dated the twenty-fourth day of the tenth month, December, 1692, to have and to hold the said bank lott and premisses to him, the said Daniel Cooke, his Heirs and assigns, and to the only use and behoof of the said Daniel Cooke, his Heirs and assigns for ever, at and under the yearly rent of two English silver shillings and nine pence, or Value thereof in Coin Current Yearly, and each year to be come due to the Chief Lord of the Soil of the said Lott and premisses, and under all and singular the other Rents, Covenants, provisors, Conditions, reservations and restrictions on the part of the said Philip Richards, his Heirs and assigns, performable to the said Wm. Penn, his Heirs and Successors Mentioned in the said Pattent, and the said Philip Richards, for him and his Heirs, doe Covenant to and with the said Daniel Cooke and his Heirs and assigns, that they, the said bank Lott and premisses to him, the said Daniell Cooke and his Heirs and assigns, against the said Philip Richards and his Heirs, as also against all others Claiming by, from or under them or any of them, or by his, their or any of their or their Heirs their means, privity, Consent or procurement shall and will warrant and forever Defend by these presents, and that the said Philip Richards hath not done nor suffered any act whatsoever whereby the said granted premises is, are, can, shall or may be by any means lawfully Impeached, Charged or Incumbered in any manner of way, In Witness whereof the parties first above Written to these presents have to these present Indentures their hands and Seals Interchangeably putt the day and date first above written.

          PHILL. RICHARDS. [Seal.]

Sealed and Delivered in presence of us, Thomas Morris, Wm. Robinson.

Received this first day of August, 1693, for the within Daniel Cooke the within Mentioned sum of Seventy-five pounds Consideration Money, within exprest by me, Phill. Richards. Witness, William Robinson, Tho's Morris; acknowledged in open Court, Certifyed under the Clark's hand and Seal of the County By me.

PATRICK ROBINSON, *Cl. Com.*

Recorded 29th August, 1693.

Conveyance of Griffith Jones to Robert Wallis.

This Indenture made the twelvth day of the fourth, Called June, being the fifth year of the reign of Wm. and Mary, King and Queen over England, &c., Anno D'ni 1693, Between Griffith Jones, of Philad'a, in the Province of Pennsylvania, Merch't, of the one part, and Rob't Wallis, of the same place Plasterer, of the other part, Witnesseth that for and in Consideration of the yearly rent, after Mentioned, to be forever paid by the said Rob't Wallis, his Heirs and assigns, to the said Griffith Jones, his Heirs and Assigns, Hee, the said Griffith Jones hath granted, bargained, Sold, enfeeoffed and by these presents Confirmed unto him, the said Rob't Wallis, a certain part of his Dellaware front lott adjoyning to said Wallis's ground, Containing in breadth twenty foot and in length One hundred and ten foot, Bounded Westward and Northward with the remainder of the said Griffith Jones' lott, Eastward with the said Rob't Wallis' lott, Southward with Wm. Walker's lott, with the reversions and remainders, rents, Issues and profits thereof, to have and to hold the said lott of land as aforesaid, and premmisses, with all the appurtenances unto him, the said Rob't Wallis, his Heirs and assigns for Ever, Yielding and paying therefore yearly forever after the date hereof to the said Griffith Jones, his Heirs and assigns, the sum of fifty Shillings, either in Current silver money of this province or in good, sound Merchantable winter wheat, Delivered in Philad'a at Silver money price, beginning the first yearly payment thereof upon the twelfth day of the fourth month, Called June, 1694, and so forth thereafter Yearly forever, and if the said yearly rent shall be behind unpaid by the space of tenn days next after the twelfth day of June yearly as aforesaid, that then it shall be Lawfull for the said Griffith Jones, his Heirs and assigns, into the aforesaid lott of land or any part thereof to enter and to distrain for the said yearly rent of fifty Shillings with the arrearages thereof, and the distresses there found to Carry away, detain or sell at reasonable rates, untill full Satisfaction be made, and the over-plus return without sute at law, and if no Sufficient distress can be had or taken in and upon the premisses, or if any rescous or pound breach shall be made, or any replevins sued or obtained by reason of any distresses to be taken by these presents, that then it shall be lawfull for the said Griffith Jones and his aforesaid into the said lott of land and premisses, with all the appurtenances wholly to re-enter and the rents and profits to receive and keep, and to use the said lott and premisses untill the said yearly Rent, and the arrearages thereof (if any) and all Costs and Damages sustained be fully from time to time paid, and the said Griffith Jones and his Heirs the hereby granted Lott of Land and Premisses, with all the appurtenances unto him, the said Rob't Wallis and his Heirs and assigns, against him, the said Griffith Jones and nis Heirs, and against all other persons whatsoever Claiming or to Claim by, from or under him, them or any of them shall and will Warrant and for ever defend by these Presents. In witness whereof the parties aforesaid to these Presents have to these present Indentures their Hands and Seals Interchangeably Sett the day and year first above written.

GRIFFITH JONES. [Seal.]

Sealed and Delivered in the presence of Wm. Davis, Francis Cooke; acknowledegd in open Court. Certifyed under the Clark's hand this fourth August, 1693, by me.

PAT. ROBINSON, *Cl. Com.*

Recorded 30th August, 1693.

Conveyance of Thomas Masters to George Heathcote.

Know all men that Thomas Masters, of Philadelphia, Carpenter, for the Consideration of Sixty Pounds Current money of this province, to him paid by George Heathcote, of Philad'a, aforesaid, Merchant, the receit whereof he doth hereby acknowledge, hath given, granted, enfeeoffed and by these presents Confirmed unto the said George Heathcote all that piece of ground Scituate on or before the Bank of Dellaware, in Philad'a, Containing in Breadth thirty foot and in length two Hundred and fifty foot, Bounded Southward with Philip Howell's Lott, westward with Dellaware front Street, Northward with John Smart's lott, and Eastward with Dellaware River at the said Extent of two hundred and fifty foot, Together with another piece of Ground Containing in breadth Six foot, and in length from the Cartway under the bank to the extent of the other adjacent lott hereby granted, Southward with the said hereby granted lott, Westward with the said Cartway, Northward with John Smart's and Eastward with the said river at the said Extent, excepting out of the first Mentioned piece of ground two foot for an alley or passage between it and the said John Smart's lott, and excepting out of the Last mentioned six foot as much as the said George Heathcote shall see fitt, so as there be a Convenient alley left from the Cartway to the river along the said lott; To have and to hold the said two pieces of ground and premisses with the appurtenances, with all Deeds, Patents and Writings Concerning the same (except before excepted) unto the said George Heathcote and his Heirs, to the use of him, the said George Heathcote, his Heirs and assigns for ever, Under the like rents, Covenants, Reservations, Restrictions and Provisors as the said Thomas Masters or former owners thereof, and their Heirs might or ought to have held and enjoyed the same, and the said Thomas Masters and his Heirs, the Hereby granted premisses with the appurtenances (except before excepted) unto the said George Heathcote and His Heirs, against him and his Heirs, and against all other persons lawfully Claiming or to Claim by, from or under him, them or any of them shall and will warrant and forever defend by these presents. In Witness whereof he hath hereunto sett his hand and Seal the twenty-fourth day of the fourth Month, Anno Domini one thousand Six hundred Ninety and three.

THO. MASTERS. [Seal.]

Sealed and Delivered in the presence of us, after the words [against him and his Heirs] were Interlined in the four and twentieth line, John Delavall, Rich'd Dean, Da'd Lloyd.

Philad'a, the 24th of the fourth Month, 1693. Received then of the within Named George Heathcote Sixty pounds, being in full for the Consideration money within mentioned. I say received by me, Tho. Masters. Witnesses, John Delavall, Rich'd Dean, Da'd Lloyd. Acknowledged in open Court; Certifyed under the Clark's Hand this fourth of August, 1693, by me.

PATRICK ROBINSON, *Cl. Com.*

Recorded 30th August, 1693.

Conveyance of Annanias Turner to William Crews.

This Indenture made the twenty-eighth day of the ninth Mon., November, Anno Domini 1691, between Annanias Turner, of St. Joneses, in the County of Kent and Territories of Pennsylvania, of the one part, and Wm. Crews, of the town and County of Philad'a, of the other part, Witnesseth that the said Annanias Turner, for a reasonable Consideration, in hand paid, hath given, granted, bargained, sold and by these presents doth absolutely give, grant, sell, alien, Enfeeoff and Confirm unto him, the said Wm. Crews, of Philad'a, Pot-maker, his Heirs, Executors, admin'ors and assigns forever one lott of land Scituate and lying in Chesnutt Street, in the said Town of Philadelphia, Containing in breadth Thirty-one foot and a half and in length One hundred Seventy foot, more or less, bounded Southward with Chestnut Street, Eastward with Wm. Ellingsworthe lott, Northward with Pat. Robinson's lott and Westward with the said Wm. Crews' lott, being granted to the said Annanias Turner by a warr't from the proprietor's Commissr's, and accordingly laid out by the Surveyor Generall's order; to have and to hold the said lott of land, Together with the reversions and remainders, Issues and profitts unto the said Wm. Crews and his Heirs and assigns to the use of him, the said Wm. Crews, his Heirs and Assigns forever, and the said Annanias Turner and his Heirs, the hereby beforegranted premisses, with the appurtenances unto the said Wm. Crews and his Heirs, against him and his Heirs and assigns, and against all other persons whatsoever lawfully Claiming or to Claim by, from or under him or them or any of them, shall and will warrant and forever Defend by these presents, and hath made David Powell, his attorney, to Deliver these presents in open Court, In Witness whereof he hath hereunto sett his hand and seal the Day and Year above written. Sealed and Delivered in the Presence of us.

Memorandum: that before Sealing and Delivery hereof it was agreed that the said Annanias Turner should Clear and pay of all the Quit Rent, taxes and other Incumbrances of the said lott of land and make it a Clear estate to the said Wm. Crews, and further that the said Wm. Crews should be at all Charges of takeing out a Pattent from the Proprietor's Commiss'rs for the said lott of land and for the surveying of the same.

ANNANIAS **T** TURNER, his Mark. [Seal.]

Witnesses, George Keith, Wm. Bradford. Acknowledged in open Court; Certifyed under the Clark's hand this fourth day of August, 1693, By me.

PATRICK ROBINSON, *Cl. Com.*

Recorded 1st of September, 1693.

Patent to Wm. Markham for 80 Acres of Land.

William Penn, absolute Proprietor of the province of Pennsylvania and Counties annexed, by his Commission dated the Sixteenth day of the tenth Month, 1689, Unto William Markham, Robert Turner, John Goodson and Samuel Carpenter, or any three of them, sendeth Greeting; whereas there is a Certain piece of land within the liberties of Philad'a, begining at a Corner post of John Tyzack's land, Standing by the Schuylkill, Thence East North East by the same one hundred and four perches to a Corner Hickory, Thence North North West by the said Tyzack's land fifty and a half perches, Thence East North East by a line of Trees One hundred fifty-one Perches, Thence South South East by a line of Trees Seventy and a half Perches, Thence West South West by a line of Trees Two Hundred Sixty-three perches to a Corner tree by the aforementioned Schuylkill, thence up the several courses thereof to the place of beginning, Containing and laid out for Eighty acres of land, Granted by Virtue of a Warrant from ourselves, bearing date the day of February, 169$\frac{2}{3}$, and laid out by the Surveyor Generall's order the twenty-third day of the said Month and year, Unto Capt. Wm. Markham, Purchaser of Five thousand acres of land in the said Province, in part of his said purchase, and the said Capt. Wm. Markham Requesting us to Confirm the same to him by Patent; Know ye that by Virtue of the Commission aforesaid we have given, granted and Confirmed and by these presents for the said Wm. Markham, his Heirs and Successors, Wee doe give, grant and Confirm to the said Capt. Wm. Markham, his Heirs and assigns for ever the said Eighty acres of land, to have, hold and Enjoy the said land to the only use and behoof of the said Capt. Wm. Markham, his Heirs and assigns for ever, to be holden of the Proprietor and his Heirs as of the Mannor of Springettsberry, in the County aforesaid, in free and common Soccage, by fealty only in lieu of all Services, he Seating and Improveing the same according to regulation, Yielding and paying therefore to the proprietor and his Heirs at and upon the first day of the first month in every year, at the town of Philad'a, after the rate of one English Silver Shilling or Value thereof in Coin Current for Each hundred acres of land to such persons as Shall be from time to time appointed for that purpose. In Witness Whereof we have Caused these, our Letters, to be made Patents at Philad'a this twenty-fourth day of February, being the fourth year of the reign of Wm. and Mary, King and Queen of England, &c., and twelfth year of the Proprietor's Government over the said Province in America, Annoq Domi. 169$\frac{2}{3}$. Samuel Carpenter, Robert Turner, John Goodson and Seal of the Province.

Recorded 12th of September, 1693.

Conveyance of William Markham to John. Tyzack.

These Indentures made this first day of March, being the fifth year of the reign of our Sovereign Lord and Lady, Wm. and Mary, King and Queen of England, Scotland, France and Ireland, Defenders of the faith, &c., Annoq Domi. 169⅔, Between Capt. Wm. Markham, of the town and County of Philad'a, in the province of Pennsylvania, in America, Gen't, of the one part, and Pat. Robinson, of the same place, attorney for John Tyzack, of the City of London, in the Kingdom of England, Broad Glass-maker, of the other part, Witnesseth that for and in Consideration of the sum of forty pounds, lawfull Current Silver money of the said Province, in hand paid by the said Pat. Robinson as attorney and for and in name and behalf of the said John Tyzack To the said Capt. Wm. Markham, the receit whereof the said Capt. Wm. Markham doth hereby acknowledge and thereof doth acquitt and discharge the said Patrick Robinson and John Tyzack, their Heirs, Executors and admin'ors for ever by these presents, he the said Capt. Wm. Markham, hath given, granted, aliened, bargained, Sold, enfeeoffed and Confirmed and by these presents doth absolutely give, grant, alien, bargain, Sell, enfeeoff and Confirm to the said John Tyzack a Certain Piece of land within the Liberties of Philad'a, Beginning at a Corner post of the said Jno. Tyzack's Land Standing by the Schuylkill, Thence East North East by the same one hundred and four perches to a Corner hickory, Thence North North West by the said Tyzack's land fifty and a half perches, Thence East North East by a line of trees one hundred fifty-one perches, Thence South South East by a line of trees Seventy and a half perches, Thence West South West by a line of trees Two hundred Sixty-three perches to a Corner tree by the aforementioned Schuylkill, Thence up the several Courses thereof to the place of beginning, Containing and laid out for Eighty acres of land, With all its rights, members, ways, waters, water courses, Quarries, Mines, Mineralls, woods, trees, Improvements and appurtenances whatsoever of the said land held, used and enjoyed therewith, or reputed as any part of the same, and the reversions, remainders and Profitts thereof, and all the estate, right, title, interest, use, possession, property, Claim and demand whatsoever of the said Capt. Wm. Markham of, in and to the said land and premises, and all deeds, grants, warrants, Surveys, returns, Letters, Pattents and other evidences and writings Concerning the same, all which are Scituate, lying and being in the said town of Philad'a, and are now in the possession of the said Capt. Wm. Markham by Virtue of a Pattent of Confirmation of the same granted to him, his Heirs and assigns therein Mentioned from the Commissioners of Wm. Penn. Proprietor and Governor of the said province, dated the twenty-fourth day of February, 169⅔, to have and to hold the said Eighty acres of land and Premisses to him, the said John Tyzack, his Heirs and assigns for ever, at and under the yearly rent from henceforth to become due to the Chief Lord of the Soil of the said land and Premisses, and the said Capt. Wm. Markham doth Covenant, promise and grant for him and his Heirs that they, the said Eighty acres of Land and premisses to him, the said John Tyzack, his Heirs and assigns against him, the said Captain William Markham and his Heirs, as also against all others Claiming by, from or under him, them or any of them or by his, their or their Heirs the Means, privity, Consent or procurement shall and will warrant and forever defend by these presents, and that the said Capt. Wm. Markham hath not done nor Suffered any act whatsoever whereby the said granted premisses or any part thereof is, are, can, shall or may be by any means lawfully Impeached, Charged or Incumbered in any manner of way, and the said Capt. Wm. Markham hath Constituted Charles Weir to be his attorney to appear at the County Court of Philad'a and there in presence of the said Court to declare, acknowledge and Deliver these presents to the said John Tyzack or his Certain attorney, according to law. In Witness whereof the parties first above written to these presents have to these present Indentures their hands and Seals Interchangeably putt the day and date first above written.

         WM. MARKHAM. [Seal.].

Sealed and Delivered in presence of us, Benjamin Chambers, James Jacob. Received from Pat. Robinson, attorney, within mentioned, the within written sum of forty pounds Consideration money, within expresst by me, this first day of March, Annoq Domi. 169⅔, Wm. Markham. Witness, Benj. Chambers, James Jacob. Acknowledged in open Court held at Philad'a on the 7th of the 1st Mon., Anno Domi. 1693. Witness, John White, Dep't Clark, and County Seal.

Recorded 12 September, 1693.

Conveyance of Christopher Sibthorp to George Mannd.

Know all men that I, Christopher Sibthorp, of the town and County of Philad'a, in the Province of Pennsylvania, Braisor, for and in Consideration of the Natural affection I bare unto

George Mannd by reason of the dear love I had for his Mother, my late wife, deceased, for whose sake I freely give and grant unto the said George Mannd, Citizen of London, his Heirs and assigns, all that my tract of land, Scituate and being in a Certain township above Warmester, in the County of Bucks, within the said Province, Beginning at a post being the bounds of the Land of Sam'l Carpenter, and also of Alexander Parker's, thence by the said Parker's land North East three hundred and twenty perches to a post for another Corner, and thence Northwest by Vacant Land One hundred and Sixty-four perches to a post for another Corner, and thence Southwest by the land of Christopher Davice Three hundred and twenty perches to a post for another Corner, and thence Southeast by land laid out for Mary Blinstone One hundred Sixty-four perches to the first Mentioned Corner Post, Containing four hundred Ninety-two acres of Land, granted by deed of lease and release dated the tenth and eleventh days of October, 1681, from Wm. Penn, Chief Proprietor of the said Province, unto Thos. Scott, of London, and from the said Scott unto me, the said Christopher Sibthorp, my Heirs and assigns, by Virtue of Certain Deeds of Lease and Release bearing date in London the thirteenth and fourteenth days of March, 1684, and being by the Surveyor Generall's order legally Located as is above Described, the 16th day of the 9th month, 1686, together with all ways, Waters, woods, water Courses, Commons, profitts, Commodities and appurtenances whatsoever to the same premisses belonging and appertaining; To have and to hold all and Singular the premisses with the appurtenances to the said George Mannd, his Heirs, Executors, admin'ors and assigns to the only proper use, behoof and best advantage of him, the said George Mannd, his Heirs and assigns for Ever, Yielding and paying yearly and every Year to the proprietor and Chief Lord of the Soil thereof the quitt rents due and Coming due for the same, and the said Christopher Sibthorp for himself, his Heirs, Executors and admin'ors doth hereby Covenant to and with the said George Mannd, his attorney, Heirs, Ex'ors and admin'ors that he, the said Christ'r or his above written, have not done nor suffered to be done any matter or thing whereby the said granted premisses is, are, shall or may be burthen'd or Incumbred in any estate, title or Claim Whatsoever other then the annuell quittrents, before Exprest, and that at the ensealing and Delivery he hath full power and lawfull authority, as well in good affection to give, as also for other Considerations to sell and alien the premisses or any part thereof, and he and they doe further Covenant to and with the said George Mannd and his above written that they shall and will at any time from henceforth Warrant and Defend the said title against all persons Claiming or to Claim by, from or under him, the said Christ'r Sibthorp, his Heirs, Ex'ors and admin'ors, or any other person in right of them, and that at any time within Seven years after the date hereof hee and they shall and will at the request, Cost and Charges of the said George Mannd or his assigns make due and execute all such other and further assurances of the premises as in the Law shall and may be reasonably devised or required, so as the parties so requested be not Compelled unreasonably for the doing the same and so as no other warranty be Contained then what is herein Exprest, and it is further Covenanted and agreed by both the said parties to name, Constitute, authorize and appoint John Goodson, of Philad'a, to be a lawfull Attorney to receive these presents in open Court for the use within Mentioned. In Witness whereof I, the said Christopher Sibthorp, have putt and Interchangeably Sett my hand and Seal the twenty-eighth day of the first Month, being the fourth Year of the Reign of Wm. and Mary, King and Queen of England, &c., 1692.

CHRISTOPHER SIBTHORP. [Seal.]

Sealed and Delivered in the Presence of Tho. Hollyman, Isaac Dellbeech, Thomas Fairman. Acknowledged in open Court at Philad'a the Twenty-Second day of September, 1693, and Certifyed Under the Clark's hand.

PAT. ROBINSON, *Cl. Com.*

Recorded 23rd of September, 1693.

Conveyance of Attorneys of Thomas Holme to John King.

This Indentures made this fifth day of July, in the third Year of the reign of Wm. and Mary, King and Queen of England, &c., Annoq Domi. 1691, Between Silas Crispin, of the County of Philad'a, Gent'n; Pat. Robinson, of the City of Philad'a, Gent.; James Atkinson, of New Town in West Jersey, Gent., and Rob't Longshore, of the aforesaid City, Gent., of the one part, and John King, of the Said County, Mariner, of the other part; Whereas Thomas Holme, lately of Philad'a, in ye province of Pennsylvania, in America, and now of ye City of London in the Kingdom of England, Gent., by his letter of Attorney under his hand and Seal, dated the 13th day of October, 1690, did Constitute the said Silas Crispin, Patrick Robinson, James Atkinson and Rob't Longshore, or any two of them (whereof ye Said Patrick Robinsson to be always one of them) his Attorneys for him, the said Thomas Holme, in his name and Stead to sell all his City Lotts, Liberty land and all or any of his other lands in the Counties of Philad'a, Bucks and Chester in the said province or Territories thereof, in America, and to make, seal, deliver and acknowledge in open Court all such Deeds to any Persons and with such warrantie to bind him, the said Thomas Holme, his Heirs, Executors and Assigns as the said letter of Attorney duly proved by George Heathcote and Samuell Harrison, two of the Witnesses thereto before Francis Rawle, one of the Justices of the piece for the said County, upon the twenty-fifth day of May, 1690. Recorded in the rolls office at Philadelphia the Sixth day of the fourth Mon., 1691, in book D, folio 275, more amplie proports. Now these present Indentures witnesseth that for and in Consideration of the sum of thirty-nine pounds, Lawfull Silver money of the said province, in hand paid, or Secured to be paid by the said John King to the said Attorneys, in name, behalf and for the only proper use and behoofe of the Said Thomas Holme, the receit whereof the said Attorneys doe hereby Acknowledge and thereof doe acquitt, Exonerate and discharge the said John King, his Heirs, Executors and Admin'ors for ever by these presents, they, the said Silas Crispin, Pat. Robinson, James Atkinson and Robert Longshore, Attorneys Aforesaid, have granted, aliened, bargained, Sold, enfeeoffed and Confirmed, and by these presents doe Absolutely grant, alien, bargain, sell, enfeeoff and Confirm To the said Jno. King, his Heirs and Assigns, a Certain part and proportion of the said Thomas Holme's, his Dellaware front Street Lott in the City of Philadelphia Bounded Southward with Chestnutt Street, and which part and proportion of the said Thomas Holme's Lott doth Contain in breadth twenty foot and in Length Eighty-Nine foot, bounded Northward with Vacant lotts, Eastward with Dellaware front Street, Southward with Chestnutt Street and to the westward with the remainder off the said whole lott Att the said extent of Eighty-Nine foot, With all the rights, Members, Improvements, Appurtenances and preveleges whatsoever of the said part of the said lott held, Used and enjoyed therewith or reputed as any part of the same, and the reversions, remainders, Rents and profitts thereof and all the estate, right, title, Interest, use, possession, property, Claim and demand whatsoever of the said Tho's Holme of, in and to the said Premisses, and all deeds, grants, Charters, pattents and other evidences and writings Concerning the same, all which are Scituate as is above said and are now in the possession of the said Thomas Holme by Virtue of a Patent of

Confirmation of the said whole lott, granted to him, his Heirs and Assigns from the Commiss'rs of Wm. Penn, dated the twenty-eighth of May, 1691, proceeding upon an Assignment from Richard Croslie of his deeds of Lease and release for One thousand Acres of land and for all the lotts and appurtenances thereto belonging (purchased by him from the said Wm. Penn, to the said Thos. Holme, his Heirs and Assigns, dated the first of October, 1688, Recorded in the Rolls Office att Philad'a the second of July, 1690, fol. 229, 230, 231, 232, and produced to the Commiss'rs to have and to hold the said part of the said lott and premisses to the said John King, his Heirs and Assigns for ever, att and under the proportionable part of one English Silver Shilling due for the said whole lott, from hence forth to become due to the Chief Lord of the Soil of the sayd Lott and Premises, Yielding and paying therefore Yearly and Each year to the said Thos. Holme, his Heirs and Assigns forever, one English Silver three pence or Value thereof in Coin Current, Att and upon the first day of July, yearly for ever, and the said Attorneys in name and behalf of the said Thomas Holme and his Heirs doe Covenant that they, the said part of the said lott and premisses to him the said John King and his Heirs and Assigns against themselves and the said Thomas Holme and their Heirs as also against all others Claiming by, from or under him, them or any of them, or by his, their or any of their Heirs, their Means, privity, Consent or procurement shall and will warrant and for ever defend by these presents, and that the said Attorneys nor the said Thos. Holme have not done nor Suffred any act whatsoever whereby the said granted premisses or any part thereof is, are, can, shall or may be by any Means lawfully Impeached, Charged or Incumbred in any Manner of way. In Witness whereof the said parties first above written to these presents have to these present Indentures their hands and Seals Interchangeably putt the day and date first above written.

                              SILAS CRISPIN,   [Seal.]
                              PAT ROBINSON,   [Seal.]
                              ROB'T LONGSHORE,   [Seal.]
                              JAS. ATKINSON,   [Seal.]

Sealed and Delivered in presence of us, Henry Flower, Wm. Robinson. Received from the within mentioned Jno. King the within mentioned sum of Thirty-nine pounds, Consideration Money within mentioned by us, Silas Crispin, Rob't Longshore, James Atkinson. I, the within named John King, doe appoint Henry Flower my Attorney to receive from Silas Crispin, Pat. Robinson, Rob't Longshore, James Atkinson the deed within mentioned in open Court this fifth day of July, Annoq

Domi. 1691, John King. Witness Wm. Robinson; Acknowledged in open Court and Certifyed under the Clark's hand this twenty-second day of September, 1693.

PAT. ROBINSON, *Cl. Com.*

Conveyance of Attorneys of Thomas Holme to Arch'd Mickle.

This Indentures made this fifth day of the fifth Mon., July, being the third year of the reign of Wm. and Mary, King and Queen of England, &c., Anno Domi. 1691, Between Silas Crispin, Pat. Robinson, Rob't Longshore, all of the County of Philad'a, in the province of Pennsylvania, in America, Gent., and James Atkinson, of New Town, in West Jersey, Gent., of the one part, and Archibald Mickle, of the said County, Cooper, of the other part; Whereas Thos. Holme, Late of Philad'a and now of the City of London, in the Kingdom of England, Gent., by his Letter of Attorney under his hand and Seal did Constitute ye s'd Silas Crispin, Pat. Robinson, James Atkinson and Rob't Longshore, or any two of them (whereof the said Pat. Robinson be always one of them) his Attorneys for him, the said Thomas Holme, in his name and Stead to sell his City lotts, Liberty land and all or any of his other lands in the Counties of Philad'a, Bucks and Chester, in the said province or Territories thereof, in America, and to make, seal, deliver and acknowledge, in open Court, all such deeds to any Persons, and with such warrantie to bind him, the said Thos Holme, his Heirs, Executors and Assigns, as the said letter of Attorney, dated the 13th day of October, 1690, duly proved by two of the witnesses thereof, before a Justice of the Peace for the said County, upon the twenty-fifth day of May, 1690, Recorded in the rolls Office att Philad'a, the Sixth day of the fourth Mon. 1691, in Book D, folio 275, more amply proports. Now these present Indentures Witnesseth that for and in Consideration of the sum of tenn pounds tenn shillings, lawfull Silver money of the said province in hand paid, or Secured to be paid by the said Archibald Mickel to the s'd Attorneys. In the Name, behalf and for the only proper Use of the said Thomas Holme, the receit whereof the said Attorneys doe hereby acknowledge, and thereof doe Accquitt and discharge the said Archibald Mickel, his Heirs, Executors and Admin'ors for ever, They, the said Silas Crispin, Pat. Robinson, James Atkinson and Rob't Longshore, Attorneys Aforesaid, have granted, aliened, bargained, Sold, enfeeoffed and Confirmed, and by these presents doe Abolutely grant, alien, bargain, sell, enfeeoff and Confirm to the said Archibald Mickle, his Heir and Assigns a Certain part and proportion of the said Thomas Holme's his Dellaware front street Lott in the City of Philadelphia, Bounded Southward with Chesnutt Street, and which part and proportion of the Said lott doth Contain in breadth forty-four foot and a half Upon Chesnutt Street and in Depth, backward, Twenty foot, Bounded Northward with Vacant lotts, Eastward with Wm. Bevon's Lott, Southward with Chesnutt Street, and to the Westward with the remainder of the said whole lott att the said Extent of forty-four foot and a half, With all the rights, members, Improvements, appurtenances and priveledges Whatsoever of the said part of the said lott held, Used and enjoyed therewith and reputed as any part of the same, and the reversions, remainders, rents and profitts and all the estate, right, title, Interest, use, possession, property, Claim and demand whatsoever of the said Thomas Holme of, in and to the said premisses and all deeds, grants, Charters, Patents and other evidences Concerning the same, all which is Scituate, Lying and being as is abovesaid, and is now in the possession of the said Thomas Holme by Virtue of a Patent of Confirmation of the said whole lott granted to him, his Heirs and Assigns therein Me'tioned from the Commiss'rs of Wm. Penn, dated the twenty-Eighth day of May, 1691, proceeding upon an Assignment from Rich'd Croslie of his deeds of Lease and Release for One thousand acres of land, and for all the lotts and appurtenances thereunto belonging (purchased by him from the said Wm. Penn to the said Thomas Holme, his Heirs and Assigns, dated the first day of October, 1688, Recorded in the rolls Office at Philad'a the second day of July 1690, fol. 229, 230, 231, 232, and produced to the said Commiss'rs To have and to hold the said part of the said lott and Premisses to him, the said Archibald Mickle, his Heirs and Assigns for ever at and under the proporcionable part of one English Silver Shilling, due for the said whole lott from henceforth to become due to the Chief lord of the Soil of the said lott and premisses, Yielding and paying therefore yearly and each year to the said Thos. Holme, his Heirs and Assigns for ever, One English Silver three pence or value thereof in Coin, Current, att and upon the fifth day of July, yearly for ever, and the said Attorneys in name and behalf of the said Thomas Holme and his Heirs doe Covenant that they, the said part of the said lott and premisses to him, the said Archibald Mickle, and his Heirs and Assigns against themselves and the said Thomas Holme and their Heirs, as also against all others Claiming by, from or under him, them or any of them, or by his, their or any of their or their Heirs, their Means, privity, Consent or procurement, Shall and will Warrant and forever defend by these presents, and that the said attorney nor the said Thos. Holme have not done nor Suffered any Act whatsoever whereby the said granted premisses or any part thereof Is, are, Can, shall or may be, by any Means, Lawfully Impeached, Charged or Incumbred in any Manner of way. In Witness whereof the parties first above written to these presents have to these present Indentures their hands and Seals Interchangealy putt the day and date first above written.

SILAS CRISPIN, [Seal.]
PAT. ROBINSON, [Seal.]
JAS. ATKINSON, [Seal.]
ROBT. LONGSHORE. [Seal.]

Sealed and Delivered in presence of us, Wm. Robinson, Wm. Bevon: Received from the within Mentioned Archibald Mickle the within sum of ten pounds, ten shillings, Consideration Money within Mentioned by us, Silas Crispin, Robert Longshore, James Atkinson, Pat. Robinson; Acknowledged in the County Court held at Philad a the first day of the Seventh month, 1691; Certifyed under my hand and County Seal.

DA. LLOYD, *Cl. Com. pl'ce.* [S.]

Assignment Thereof.—Arch'd Mickle to Daniel Standish.

Know all men that the within named Arch'd Mickle, for the Consideration of twenty pounds, Silver money, to him, in hand paid, by Daniel Standish, of Philad'a, Bricklayer, hath given, granted, Sold, assigned, and by these presents sett over unto the said Daniel Standish all the lott of Land within mentioned Together with the Deed within written, To have and to hold unto him, the said Daniel Standish, his Heirs and Assigns forever, as fully and amply as the said Archibald Mickle and his Heirs may, might or ought to have hold and enjoy the same, and hath made Abraham Hardiman his Attorney to deliver these presents in open Court, according to Law, unto Daniel Standish or his Certain Attorney. In Witness whereof he hath hereunto Sett his Hand and Seall the twenty-first day of the seventh Mon., Anno Domi. 1693.

ARCHIBALD MICKLE. [Seal.]

Sealed and Delivered in presence of John Kaighm, Francis Cooke. Acknowledged in open Court, Certified Under the Clark's Hand, This twenty-Second of September, 1693.

PAT. ROBINSON, *Cl. Com.*

Recorded 25th September, 1693.

Conveyance of Edward Smout to Francis and Mary Cooke.

There is Recorded in the rolls Office at Philad'a the Twenty-fourth day of the fourth Mon., Called June, 1690, in Book E, fol. 139 and 140, by Thos. Lloyd, a Deed of Sale to Francis and Mary Cooke of a piece of lott in the Second Street of Philad'a, Containing in Breadth, fronting the second Street, Thirty-two foot, and in Length One hundred thirty-two foot, bounded on the Southward with Jno. Heaton's Lott, on the Northward with Wm. Markham's Lott, on the Eastward with the Second Street from Dellaware, and on the Westward with a Vacant Lott, and to their Heirs and assigns forever from Edward Smout, Sawer, dated the fifth day of March, 1689-90; acknowledged in open Court the fourth day of the said month and year, Indorsed thus:

Assigned by Francis and Mary Cooke to Daniel Standish.

Know all men that the within Mentioned Francis Cooke, with Consent of Mary, his wife, for the Consideration of Eighteen pounds to them, in hand paid, the receit whereof they do hereby acknowledge, hath granted, bargained, Sold, assigned and by these presents Transfirred the within Deed and Lott of Land Therein Mentioned unto Daniel Standish, of the City of Philad'a, Bricklayer, To have and to hold the within mentioned Lott of land and premisses with all their appurtenances Unto him, the said Daniel Standish and his Heirs, to the use and behoofe of him, ye said Daniel Standish, his Heirs and assigns for ever, under the yearly rent therein exprest, and hath made Abraham Hardiman their attorney to deliver these presents in open Court according to law Unto Dan'll Standish or his Certain Attorney. In Witness whereof they have hereunto sett their Hands and Seals the 13th day of the Tenth Mon., December, Anno Domi. 1692, Being the fourth year of the Reign of Wm. and Mary, King and Queen over England, &ca., and Twelth of the proprietor's Government.

       FRANCIS COOKE. [Seal.]
       MARY COOKE. [Seal.]

Sealed and Delivered in the presence of us, Alex'r Beardsly, George Gray, Archibald Mickell; acknowledged in Open Court, Certifyed Under the Clark's hand this twenty-second off September, 1693.

       PAT. ROBINSON, *Cl. Com.*

Recorded 25 of September, 1693.

MINUTE BOOK "F." 161

Conveyance of Mathias Hulsted to William Carter.

This Indenture made the first day of the Tenth Month, December, in the year, according to the English account, 1689, and in the first year of the Reign of King Wm. and Queen Mary over England, &ca., Between Wm. Carter, of Philadelpia, Blockmaker, of the one part, and Mathias Houlsted, of Passiyunk, In the County above said, of the other part, Witnesseth that ye said Mathias Houlsted hath bargained and agreed and sold unto Wm. Carter all that parcell of Meadow being and lying between the Creek Called Malboes Creek, all along by the Land of Wm. Carter and Wm. Snouden, begining at a Corner post on the North East side of the land of Wm. Carter, and so along by the Land of Wm. Snouden South West, and by the Swamp to the Southermost marked tree of the s'd Wm. Carter's Land, which lieth on the South West side of the s'd Wm. Snouden's Land, which is in Length One hundred and Thirty poles, and the East side bounded by the Cripple next ye the Creek abovesaid for the Consideration of twenty-four shillings, Lawfull money of Pennsylvania, to him in Hand already paid, the receit hereof hee doth hereby acknowledge Himself Fully Satisfyed and Contented and paid, and I doe accquitt, Exonerate and Discharge him, the said Wm. Carter, his Heirs and assigns for ever for the same, and I doe by these presents give, grant unto the said Wm. Carter, his Heirs, Ex'ors and assigns all my Right, Title and Interest to the same, to have and to hold the said piece of meadow to him and his Heirs, &c'a. for ever, and furthermore The said Mathias Houlsted doth hereby Covenant for myself, my Heirs and assigns to and with the said Wm. Carter, his Heirs and assigns that the said Wm. Carter, his Heirs and assigns shall or lawfully may for ever hereafter peaceably and quietly have, hold, use, occupy and enjoy the same and every part and parcell thereof, as Witness my hand and Seal the day and year first above Written.

MATHIAS HOULSTED. [Seal.]

Signed, Sealed and Delivered in presence of us, Lasse Cocke, Sam'l Atkins. Acknowledged in open Court, Certifyed Under the Clark's hand this twenty-second of September, 1693.

PAT. ROBINSON, *Cl. Com.*

Recorded 26th of Sept'r, 1693.

Conveyance of Mary Hillyard to Charles Sobers.

To all Xtian people to whome these presents shall come, Mary Hillyard, Widdow, relict and Executrix of the last Will and Testament of Richard Hilliard, late of the Town and County

11—VOL. XIX.

of Philad'a, in the Province of Pennsylvania, in America, Carpenter, Sendeth Greeting; whereas the said Richard Hilliard, my said late Husband, in his life time by his Last Will and Testament duly Signed, Sealed, published and Declared in the Presence of three or more Credible Witnesses, bearing date the twenty-third day of the seventh Month, Annoq Domi. 1692, did Constitute and appoint me sole Exec'rix of his said Will, and did hereby give, bequeath and Devise unto me all his Estate, both Reall and personall, paying to Each of his said Children five Shillings a piece at their Rexive ages of one and twenty years, if the same should be Lawfully demanded for and to the Intent fully and absolutely to Cutt of all pretentions of Right or Claim by them or any of them to the real and personall Estate so Bequeathed and devised to me by the Will aforesaid, as in and by the said Will remaining on Record in the register Gen'lls Office for the said province, refference being thereunto had more fully and at large appeareth. Now know ye that I, the said Mary Hilliard, for and in Consideration of the sum of One hundred and Ten pounds, Current silver Money of this province, to me in hand paid at and before the Sealing and Delivery hereof, the receit whereof I doe hereby acknowledge to have had from Charles Sober, of the said town of Philad'a, Chirurgeon, and accquitt, Exonerate and Discharge him, the said Charles Sober, of and from the s'd sum and every part and parcell thereof; absolutely by these presents have granted, bargained, Sold, aliened, enfeeoffed and Confirmed, and by these presents doe fully and absolutely grant, bargain, Sell, alien, Enfeeoff and Confirm unto him, the said Charles Sober, his Heirs and assigns forever, One Certain Lott of Land in the City of Philad'a, Containing in breadth forty-Nine foot and a half, and in Length two Hundred fifty-five foot, Bounded Eastward with the Front street from Dellaware, Southward with back Lotts, Westward with Thomas Jones' Lott, and to the Northward with Chesnutt Street, granted and Confirmed to my said late husband by Patent under the hands and Seal of the Commiss'rs of property, bearing date the twenty-ninth day of ye 11th Month, Anno Domini 1690, Together with all the houses, Ediffices and buildings thereon Standing, and all other the premisses with ye appurtenances to the said Lott belonging, or in any wise appertaining to me, given and devised by the Last will and Testament of my said late husband; To have and to hold the said Lott, houses and premisses with the appurtenances above mentioned to him, the said Charles Sober, his Heirs and assigns for ever, Freely and Clearly accquitted, Exonerated and Discharged of and from all former Bargains, debts, dues, Mortgages or any other Incumbrances whatsoever, and the said Mary Hilliard doth hereby Covenant and agree for herself, her Heirs, Ex'ors and admin'ors to and with the said Charles Sober, his Heirs, Ex'ors and admin'ors by these presents that the said Mary Hilliard hath good right, full power and absolute authority to sell and dispose of the said Lott and premisses to the s'd Charles Sobers, and that shee will Warrant and forever defend ye same unto him against all person and persons whatsoever Claiming any right, title or Interest in and to the same. In Witness whereof I, the said Mary Hilliard, have hereunto sett my hand and Seal this twenty-second day of Sept'r, Anno D'ni. 1693.

MARY HILLIARD. [Seal.]

Sealed and Delivered in the presence of Charles Pickering, Tho. Brock, Theo. Roberts. Acknowledged in open Court, Certified under the Clark's hand this twenty-second day of September, 1693.

PAT. ROBINSON, *Cl. Com.*

Bond for Performance, folio 43.
Recorded 27 of September, 1693.

Conveyance of Michael Nelson to John Goodson.

This Indenture made this first day of September, 1693 by and Between Michael Nelson, of Shakamaxunk, Husbandman, of the one part, and John Goodson, of the Town of Philad'a, in the Province aforesaid, of the other part, Witnesseth that for and in Consideration of the sum of twenty-one pounds, good and Lawfull Moneys of this Province, and truly paid unto him, the said Michael Nelson, by him, the said John Goodson, the receit whereof the said Michael Nelson doe hereby acknowledge and himself therewith fully satisfyed, Contented and paid for the same, he, the said Michael Nelson, hath given, granted, bargained, sold, aliened, enfeeoffed and Confirmed unto Him, the said Jno. Goodson, his Heirs and assigns forever, Seventy acres of Land Scituate, lying and being in the Township of Shakamakunk aforesaid, and is bounded to the North North West with John Goodson's Land, to the West south west with Cohocksink Creek, to the East North East with Thomas Fairman's Land, and to the South South East with the remaining part of the said Michael Nelson's land, with all the rights, Members, Improvements, appurtenances and Priveledges whatsoever of the said Seventy acres of Ground held, used and enjoyed therewith or reputed as any part of the same, and the reversions, remainders, rents and Profitts thereof, and all the estate, right, Title, Interest, use, possession, property, Claim and demand whatsoever of him, the said Michael Nelson, of, in or to the same or any part and parcell thereof, all which aforesaid Seventy acres of land are Scituate, Lying and being as afore is said and is now in the tenour, possession and Occupation of him, the said Michael Nelson, by Virtue of a Patent of Confirmation granted unto him, the said Michael Nelson, his Heirs and assigns therein Mentioned by Wm. Markham, R't Turner, Jno. Goodson and Samuel Carpenter, Commiss'rs Impowered by Wm. Penn, Esqr., absolute proprietor of the province aforesaid, &ca., ye 4th day of the first Mon., 1691, for Four hundred sixty and two and a half acres of Land, as the same more at large expresses of which the said 462½ acres of Land, the hereby granted Seventy acres of Land is part and parcell, To have and to hold the said Seventy acres of Land and all and Singular the appurtenances thereunto belonging unto the Sole only and proper use and behoofe of him, the said John Goodson, his Heirs and assigns for ever, att and under the Yearly Quitrent owing and payable and from henceforth to become due unto the Chief Lord of the soil of the said Land and Premises, and the said Michael Nelson doe Covenant, promise and grant for himself and his Heir that they, the said Seventy acres of Land and Premisses to him, the said John Goodson, his Heirs and assigns against him, the said Michael Nelson and his Heirs, as also against all others Claiming or to Claim by, from or under him, them or any of them, or by his, their or any of their Means, privity, Consent or procurement shall and will Warrant and forever defend by these presents, and that the said Michael Nelson have not done nor suffred to be done any act or thing whatsoever whereby the hereby granted Seventy acres of Land and Premisses or any part or parcell thereof is, are, can, shall or may be by any means lawfully Impeached, Charged or Incumbred in any Manner of way, and he, the said Michael Nelson, hath Constituted and doe hereby Constitute, appoint and Impower John Claypoole to be his lawfull attorney to appear at the County Court at Philad'a and there in presence of the said Court to acknowledge and Deliver this present Indenture unto him, the said John Goodson, or his Certain attorney, according to law in that Case made and provided. In Witness whereof both parties to these present Indentures have Interchangeably Sett their hands and Seals the day, month and year first above Written.

      MICHAEL **M** NELSON, his Mark and Seal.

 Sealed and Delivered in the presence of us, R. Longshore, Tho. Millard. Received of and from the within mentioned John Goodson the full and Just sum of twenty-One pounds,

MINUTE BOOK "F." 165

Consideration of the within Mentioned Seventy acres. 1 say received this first day of September, 1693, p. me, Michael M Nelson, his mark. Witnesses present, R't Longshore, Tho. Millard. Acknowledged in open Court, Certifyed under the Clark's hand this 22d of Sept'r, 1693.

PAT. ROBINSON, *Cl. Com.*

Recorded 28th September, 1693.

Conveyance of Philip Richards to Adam Burch.

These Indentures made this fourteenth day of August, being the fifth year of the reign of our Sovereign Lord and Lady, Wm. and Mary, by the Grace of God, of England, Scotland, France and Ireland, King and Queen, Defenders of the faith, &ca., Annoq D'ni. 1693, Between Philip Richards, of the town and County of Philad'a, in the province of Pennsylvania, in the parts of America, Merch., of the one part, and Adam Burch, of ye Same place, Cordwayner, of the other part, Witnesseth that for and in Consideration of the sum of four Hundred pounds, lawfull Silver Money of the said Province, in hand paid by the said Adam Burch to the said Philip Richards, The receit whereof the said Philip Richards doth hereby acknowledge, and thereof and of every part thereof doth acquitt, exonerate and discharge the said Adam Burch, his Heirs, Ex'ors and admin'ors forever by these presents. Hee, the said Philip Richards, hath given, granted, aliened, Bargained, Sold, enfeeoffed and Confirmed and by these presents doth absolutely give, grant, alien, bargain, Sell, enfeeoff and Confirm to the said Adam Burch, his Heirs and assigns all that his, the said Philip Richards, his Just and equall Easterly Moiety and half part of his Dellaware front Street lott of Land, in ye City of Philad'a, Scituate, lying and being between High Street on the North, and Chesnut Street on the south, The which Just and Equal Moiety and half part thereof doth Contain in Breadth thirty-one foot and in Length One hundred Ninety eight foot, Bounded to the Northward with Philip James' Lott, now ——— ——— Lott, to the Eastward with Dellaware front Street, to ye Southward with Alex'r Parker's, now John Goodson's Lott, and to the westward with the remaining westerly halfe part of the said Phil. Richards Lott, at the Said Extent of One hundred Ninety-eight foot, with all the rights, Members, Brick houses, Logg houses, Sheds, his half part of the pumpe and Implements thereof, house of Office, yards, orchards, fences, inclosures, Improvements and appurtenances whatsoever of the said Just and Equall Moiety and Half part of the said Lott held, used and enjoyed therewith or reputed as any part of the same, and the reversions, remainders, rents and profitts thereof, and all the Estate, Right, Title, Interest, use, possession, property, Claim and Demand of the said Philip Richards of, in and to the above said granted premisses, and all deeds, evidences, Warrants, Patents and other Writings Concerning the said Easterly Moiety or half part of the said Lott in Conjunction with the remaining part thereof, and which s'd Easterly Moiety or half part of the said Lott, with the remaining part thereof, is now in the possession of the said Philip Richards by Virtue of a Patent of Confirmation of the same granted to Dennis Rotchford in Right of Thomas Herriott, purchaser of five thousand acres of Land by the Commiss'rs of Wm. Penn, dated the twentieth day of the Second Mon., 1685, Recorded in the Patent office att Philad'a, Vol. A, fol. 82, the Tenth day of the fifth Mon., 1685, and by Virtue of a Deed of Sale and Conveyance thereof granted by the said Dennis Rotchford, with Consent of Mary, his Wife, to John Test, his Heirs and assigns, bearing date the Seventh day of December, 1685, acknowledged in open Court the third day of the Twelvth month, 1685, and recorded in the Office of Rolls and publick Registrie at Philad'a, Vol. 5, Book E, fol. 182, and by Virtue of a Deed of Sale and Conveyance thereof granted by the said John Test to the said Philip Richards, his Heirs and assigns, bearing date the third day of February, 1685. Acknowledged in open Court the said day and recorded in the Office of Rolls and publick Registrie att Philad'a, Vol. 5, Book E, folio 185, the thirteenth day of the twelth Month, 1685, To have and to hold the said Just and Equal Easterly Moiety and half part of ye said Lott of Land, houses and premisses to him, the said Adam Burch, his Heirs and assigns, and to the only proper use of him, the said Adam Burch, his Heirs and assigns for ever, att and under the proportionable half part of the yearly Quitt rents from henceforth to become due to the Chief Lord of the soil of the said Lott and premisses, and the said Philip Richards doth Covenant, promise and grant for himself, his Heirs, that they, the said Just and Equall Easterly Moiety and half part of the said Lott of Land, Houses and premisses to him, the said Adam Burch, his Heirs and assigns, against him, the said Philip Richards and his Heirs, as also against him, the said Jno. Test and his Heirs, as also against him, the said Dennis Rotchford and his Heirs, as also against all others Claiming by, from or under them or any of them or by their or any of their or their

Heirs, their Means, privity, Consent or procurement shall and will warr't and forever Defend by these presents, and that the said Philip Richards hath not done Nor suffred any act whatsoever whereby the said granted Premisses is, are, can, shall or may be by any means lawfully Impeached, Charged or Incumbred in any manner of way. In Witness whereof the parties first above Written to these presents have to these present Indentures their hands and Seals Interchangeably putt the day and date first above Written.

PHILIP RICHARDS. [Seal.]

Sealed and Delivered in presence of us, John Cox, Pat. Robinson. Received this 14th day of August from the within Adam Burch the within Mentioned Sum of Four hundred pounds, Consideration money, within exprest by me, Anno D'ni. 1693. Philip Richards. Witnesses, John Cox, Patrick Robinson. Acknowledged in open Court, Certifyed under the Clark's hand this 22d, 7 b'r, 1693.

PAT. ROBINSON, *Cl. Com.*

Recorded 2d of October, 1693.

Conveyance of John Test to Hance Peterson.

This Indenture made the Seventh day of Novem'r, 1687, in the third year of the reign of James the second, of England, &c'a., King, Between John Test, of the County of Philad'a, in province of Pennsylvania, Cordwayner, of the one, and Hance Peterson, of the County of New Castle, in Territories of said province, yeoman, of the other part, Witnesseth that for and in Consideration of the sum of Seventy-five pounds, lawfull money of said province, in hand paid or Secured to be paid by the said Hance Peterson to the said John Test, the receit whereof the said John Test doth hereby acknowledge and thereof doth acquitt, Exonerate and discharge the said Hance Peterson, his Heirs, Executors and admin'ors for Ever by these presents. Hee, the said John Test, hath given, granted, aliened, bargained, Sold, enfeeoffed and Confirmed, and by these presents doth absolutely give, grant, alien, bargain, Sell, enfeeoff and Confirm to the said Hance Peterson, his Heirs and assigns a Certain Lott of Land in Philad'a, Containing in Breadth fifty foot, and in Length One Hundred Seventy and eight foot, Bounded to the Northward with James Claypoole's Lott, to the Eastward with John Boult's Lott, and to the Southward with Chestnut Street, and to the

Westward with the third Street front, with all its Rights, Members, Houses, ffences, Gardens, orchards, Improvements and appurtenances, and the reversions, remainders, rents and profitts thereof, and all the Estate, Right, Title, Interest, use, possession, property, Claim and demand whatsoever of the said John Test of, in and to the said premises, and all deeds, grants, Charters, Letters, Patents, escripts and other evidences and Writings Concerning the said premises only or only any part thereof, all which are Scituate, lying and being as is aforesaid and are now in the possession of the said John Test by Virtue of a Warr't from James Claypoole and Rob't Turner Nominated, and appointed under the great Seal Commiss'rs by Wm. Penn, Proprietor and Governor of said Province, to grant and to Sign Warr'ts and Patent for Lands, dated the thirtieth day of the 11th mon., 1684, and laid out by the Surveyor Gen'lls order the 16th day of Said month and year to ye s'd John Test, Renter, and By virtue of a Patent of Confirmation thereof granted to him, the said John Test, his Heirs and assigns therein named, dated the 17th day of the 11th Month, 1684, To have and to hold the said Lott of Land, Houses and premises to him, the said Hance Peterson, his Heirs and assigns for ever, to the only use and behoofe of him, the said Hance Peterson his Heirs for ever, att and under the yearly rents to become due to the Chief Lord of the Soil of the said Land and premisses, and the said John Test doth Covenant, promise and Grant for himself and his Heirs that they, the said Lott of Land and premisses to him, the said Hance Peterson and his Heirs against him, the said John Test and his Heirs, and all others Claiming by, from or Under him or them or any others by their Means, privity, Consent or procurement shall and will Warrant and forever defend by these presents, and that the said John Test hath not done, acted nor Suffred any act, Matter or Whatsoever whereby the said Granted premises or any part thereof is, are, can, shall or may be by any Means Lawfully Impeached, Charged or Incumbred in any manner of way, and that he, the said John Test and his above written shall and will, within seven Years next Ensuing, at the Charge of said Hance Peterson, make or cause to be made all other Conveyances Needfull for the further Conveying of the said Land and premisses to the said Hance Peterson and his above written as by them or their Councill shall be Lawfully advised so as the persons thus requested be not Compellable to Travill from the place of their abode above Twelve miles for the doing thereof, and so as the same Contain no other Warrantie than is above Mentioned. In Witness whereof the parties first above written to these presents have to these present Indentures their Hands

and Seals Interchangeably putt the day and date first above written.
JOHN TEST. [Seal.]
Sealed and Delivered in Presence of us, Henry Flower, Pat. Robinson, 7th 9th ber, 1687. Received from the within Hance Peterson the within sum of Sevety-five pounds, Consideration Money, within Mentioned, John Test. Witnesses, Henry Flower, Patrick Robinson. 1, Hance Peterson, doe appoint Jno. Claypoole my attorney to receive from John Test a deed of a Lott of Land in Philad'a sold to me, dated the 7th of 9ber, 1687; witness my hand this 5th 7th ber, 1693, Hance Peterson. Acknowledged in Open Court, Certified under the Clark's hand this 22d, 7th ber, 1693.
PATRICK ROBINSON, *Cl. Com.*
Recorded 3rd October, 1693.

Conveyance of John Duplouvys to John Fleckne.

These Indentures made this first day of May, being the Fifth year of the reign of Wm. and Mary of England, &c., King and Queen, Anno Domini 1693, Between Jno. Duplouvys, of the Town and County of Philad'a, in America, Baker, of the one part, and John Fleckne, of the same place, Carpenter, of the other part, Witnesseth that for and in Consideration of the yearly Rent after Mentioned to be for ever paid by the said John Fleckne his Heirs and assigns to the said Jno. Duplouvys, his Heirs and Assigns, the said John Duplouvys hath Given, Granted, Aliened, Bargained, Sold, Enfeeoffed and Confirmed and by these presents doth Absolutely give, grant, alien, bargain, sell, enfeeoff and Confirm to the said John Fleckne, his Westerly Certain part and proportion of his, the said John Duplouvys, his whole Dellaware Front street Lott (being between Wm. Shardloe's and Nathaniell Sykes' Dellaware Front Street Lotts), and which westerly part and proportion of the said Whole Lott doth Contain in breadth twenty foot fronting the second Street, and in Length Eastward Sixty foot, Bounded Eastward att the said Extent of Sixty foot with the rest of the said John Duploavys' Lott, and Northward with Nathaniell Sykes' Lott with all the rights, Members, Yards, Orchards, ffences, Improvements, appurtenances and priveleges whatsoever of the said Westerly part and proportion of ye said Lott held, used and enjoyed therewith or reputed as any part of the same, and the Reversions, Remainders, Rents and profitts thereof, And all the estate, right, title, Interest, use, possession, property, Claim and Demand whatsoever of the said John Duplouvys of, in and to the said Westerly part and proportion of the said Lott and premises, And all deeds, grants, Charters, Surveys, returns, Letters, Patents and other evidences and Writings Concerning the same Westerly part of the said Lott in Conjunction with the remainder thereof, All which are Situate, lieing and being as Is above said, and are now in the possession of the said Jno. Duplouvys by Virtue of his Deeds of purchase of the same, to have and to hold the said Westerly part and proportion of the said Lott to him, the said John Fleckne, his Heirs and Assigns, and to the only use and behoofe of him, the said John Fleckne, his Heirs and Assigns for Ever, att and Under the proportionable part of the Yearly Quitt-Rents from hence forth to become due to the Chief Lord of the soil of the said whole Lott of Land and premises, Yielding and paying therefore, yearly for ever hereafter to the said John Duplouvys, his Heirs and Assigns, for the said Westerly part and proportion of the said Lott and Houses thereon, to be built, the sum of two pounds in good Lawfull Current Silver Money of the said province for the time being, The first year's actuall payment whereof shall be made to the said Jno. Duplouvys, his Heirs and Assigns by the said Jno. Fleckne, his Heirs or Assigns upon the first day of May, 1694, and so forth thereafter, Yearly for ever, and if the said yearly rent of two pounds shall be behind unpaid by the space of tenn days, next and Immediately after the said first day of May, yearly, that then and in that Case it shall be Lawfull for the said John Duplouvys and his Above written either into the said Westerly part and proportion of the s'd Lott and into the Houses thereon to be Built to enter and there to distrain for the said Yearly rent of two pounds and the Goods, Chattles and Distresses there found to Carry away, detain or Sell at reasonable rates for payment and Satisfaction to him, the said John Duplouvys and his Above Written, of the said yearly rent so to be behind unpaid and of the arrearages thereof if any shall be without Suit at law and the Overpluss to return to the said Jno. Fleckne or his above written, and if no sufficient Distress Can be had or taken in and upon the premises or if any rescous or pound breach shall be made, or any replevins Sued or obtained by Virtue of these presents, that then it Shall be lawfull for the said Jno. Duplouvys and his above written, into the said Westerly part and proportion of the said Lott of Land, to enter and the rents thereof to receive and keep and to use the same Lott, Houses and premises Untill the said Yearly Rent of two pounds with the arrearages thereof shall be unto the said John Duplouvys, his Heirs or Assigns fully, from time to time, paid by the said John Fleckne, his Heirs or Assigns, and the said John Duplouvys Doth Covenant for him and his Heirs that they, the said Westerly part and proportion of the said Lott and premisses, to him, the said John Fleckne and his Heirs and Assigns, against him, the said John Duplouvys and his Heirs, and against Jacob Telnor and his Heirs, as also against all others Claiming by, from or under them or any of them, or by his, their or any of their or their Heirs, their Means, privity, Consent or procurement, shall and will Warrant and for ever Defend by these presents, and that the said John Duplouvys hath not done nor Suffred any act whatsoever whereby the said granted premisses is, are, can, shall or may be by any means lawfully Impeached, Charged or Incumbred in any manner of way. In Witness Whereof the parties first above Written to these presents have to these present Indentures their hands and Seals Interchangealy putt the day and date first above written.

JOHN DUPLOUVYS. [Seal.]

Sealed and Delivered in presence of us, John Cox, Pat. Robinson. Acknowledged in open Court, Certifyed under the Clark's hand ye 22d of Sept'r, 1693.

PAT. ROBINSON, *Cl. Com*

Recorded 5th Oct'r, 1693.

Conveyance of William Salway to Griffith Jones.

These Indentures made this Tenth day of August, being the fifth year of the reign of Wm. and Mary over England, &ca., King and Queen, Anno Dni. 1693, Between Wm. Salway, of the Town and County of Philad'a, in the province of Pennsylvania, in America, Clothier, of the one part, and Griffith Jones, Merchant, of the Town and County aforesaid, of the other part, Witnesseth that for and in Consideration of the sum of twenty-three pounds lawfull Money of the said province, in hand, paid by the said Griffith Jones to the said Wm. Salway, The receit whereof the said Wm. Salway doth hereby Acknowledge and thereof doth discharge him, the said Griffith Jones, his Heirs, Ex'ors and Admin'ors for ever by these p'nts, He, the said Wm. Salway hath given, granted, aliened, bargained, Sold, enfeeoffed and Confirmed, and by these presents doth Abso-

lutely give, grant, alien, bargain, sell, enfeeoff and Confirm to
the said Griffith Jones, his Heirs and Assigns, a Certain piece
of Land in the Liberties of the City of Philad'a, begining at a
Corner post of Jno. Reynold's Land, then North North West
by the same One hundred and thirteen perches, thence East
North East by Griffith Jones' and Tho's Reynold's Land,
forty-five perches, thence South South East by a line of trees,
One hundred and thirteen perches, thence West South West
by a line of trees, forty-five perches, to the place of begining,
Containing and laid out for thirty-two Acres of Land, as also
an other piece of Land in the s'd Liberties Begining at a Cor
ner post of Nathaniell Allen's Land, Thence South South East
by the same One hundred and thirteen perches, Thence East
North East by a line of trees, Eleven perches and a half,
Thence North North West by a line of trees, One hundred and
thirteen perches, Thence West south West by the said Griffith
Jones' Land, Eleven and a half perches, to the place of Begining, Containing and laid out for Eight Acres of Land, with all
the rights, Members, Improvements and appurtenances whatsoever of the said Thirty-two and eight acres of land rexivle,
held, Used and Enjoyed therewith or Reputed as any part of
the same, and the reversions, remainders, rents and profitts
thereof and all thee state, Right, title, interest, use, possession, property, Claim and Demand whatsoever of the said Wm.
Salway of, in and to the said premisses, and all Deeds, grants,
Charters, Letters, Patents, Escripts and other Evidences and
Writings Concerning the Same, All which are Scituate, lying
and being as is above said, and the said thirty Acres of Land
are Now in the possession of the said Wm. Salway by Virtue of
a Patent of Confirmation of the Same granted to Nathaniell
Allen, his Heirs and Assigns therein exprest, dated the first
day of June, 1689, and the said eight acres of Land are now in
the possession of the said Wm. Salway by Virtue of a patent
of Confirmation of the same granted to Edward Lane, his
Heirs and Assigns, therein Mentioned, in the behalfe of Wm.
Lane, purchaser, and by Virtue of a Deed of Sale and Conveyance of the said Eight Acres of Land Granted by the said Edward Lane to the said Nathaniell Allen, his Heirs and Assigns
therein Mentioned, dated the twenty-Ninth day of Aprill, 1689;
Acknowledged in open Court the fourth day of June, 1689, and
by Virtue of a Deed of Sale and Conveyance of the said Thirty-
two Acres of Land and of the said Eight Acres of Land granted
by the said Nathaniell Allen to Rich'd Hillyard, his Heirs and
Assigns therein Mentioned, dated the fifth day of June, 1689;
Acknowledged in open Court, and by Virtue of a Deed of Sale
and Conveyance of the said forty Acres of Land, rexivle,

granted by the said Rich'd Hilliard to the said Wm. Salway, his Heirs and Assigns therein Mentioned, bearing date the 20th day of Sept'r, 1692; Acknowledged in open Court the fifth day of Oct'r, 1692, To have and to hold the said 40 Acres of Land rexivle with their appurtenances To him, the said Griffith Jones, his Heirs and Assigns, and to the only use and behoofe of him, the said Griffith Jones, his Heirs and Assigns for Ever, Att and under the Yearly Rents, to become Due to the Chief Lord of the Soil of the said 40 Acres of land and premisses, and the said Wm. Salway doth Covenant for him and his Heirs that they, the said thirty-two and Eight Acres of Land and premisses to him, the said Griffith Jones, his Heirs and Assigns against himself, as also against them, the said Edw'd and Wm. Lane, Nathaniell Allen and Rich'd Hilliard and their Heirs, as also aga. all others Claiming by, from or under him, them or any of them, or by his, their or any of their or their Heirs, their Means, privity, Consent or procurement, Shall and will Warrant and for Ever defend by these presents and that the said Wm. Salway hath not done nor Suffred any Act whatsoever whereby the said 40 Acres of Land and premisses is, are, can, shall or may be, by any Means, lawfully Impeached, Charged or Incumbred in any manner of way, and the said Wm. Salway hath Constituted and hereby does Constitute Charles Pickering to be his Attorney to appear at the Next County Court of Philad'a and there, in presence of ye said Court, to declare, Acknowledge and Deliver these presents to the said Griffith Jones or his Certain attorney, according to Law. In Witness whereof the parties first above written to these presents have to these present Indentures their hands and seals Interchangeably putt the day and date first above Written.

WM. SALWAY. [Seal.]

Sealed and Delivered in presence of us, Ro. French, Andrew Robeson, Sam'll Robeson. Received from the within Mentioned Griffith Jones the within written sum of twenty-three pounds, Consideration Money within Exprest by me this 10th day of August, Anno Dni. 1693

WM. SALWAY, [Seal.]

Being present Andrew Robeson, Sam'll Robeson, Acknowledged in open Court, Certifyed Under the Clark's hand this twenty-second of Sept'r, 1693.

PAT. ROBINSON, *Cl. Com.*

Recorded 6th October, 1693.

MINUTE BOOK "F."

Conveyance of Griffith Jones to James Stanfield.

These Indentures made this first day of July, Annoq Dni. 1693, Between Griffith Jones and James Stanfeild, both of the Town and County of Phild'a, in the province of Pennsylvania, in the parts of America, Merchants, of the one and the other parts, Witnesseth that for and in Consideration of the yearly Rent, after Mentioned, to be for ever paid by the said James Stanfeild, his Heirs and Assigns to the said Griffith Jones, his Heirs and Assigns, Hee, the said Griffith Jones, hath given, granted, aliened, bargained, Sold, enfeeoffed and Confirmed, and by these presents, doth Absolutely give, grant, alien, bargain, Sell, enfeeoff and Confirm To the said James Stanfeild a Certain part and proportion of his, the said Griffith Jones, his Dellaware bank lott, between High Street and Mulberry Street, and which part and proportion of the said Lott doth Contain in breadth twenty-two foot, and in Length two Hundred and fifty foot into the River Dellaware, Bounded Northward with William Salway's Lott, Southward with John Buzbie's Lott, Westward with Dellaware front street, and Eastward with the said River Dellaware att the said Extent of Two hundred and fifty foot, With all the rights, Members, Wharffs, Improvements, Appurtenances and previledges whatso'ver of the said twenty-two foot Lott held, used and enjoyed therewith or reputed as any part of the same In as large and beneficiall Manner as he, the said Griffith Jones, ever held, now holds or in any time Coming may or shall hold the Same himself, and the Reversions, Remainders, rents and profits thereof, and all the Estate, right, title, Interest, use, possession, property, Claim and Demand whatsoever of ye Said Griffith Jones of, in and to the said twenty-two foot Lott and premises, and all Deeds, grants, Surveys, returns and Patents Concerning the same in Conjunction with the remainder of the said whole bank Lott, all which are situate, lying and being as is above said, and are now in the Possession of the said Griffith Jones by Virtue of a Patent of Confirmation of the same granted to him, his Heirs and Assigns therein Mentioned, from the Commiss'rs of Wm. Penn, proprietor of the said Province, dated the third day of Aprill, 1689, To have and to hold the said twenty-two foot Lott and premises to him, the said James Stanfeild, his Heirs and Assigns, and to the only use and behoofe of him, the said James Stanfeild, his Heirs and Assigns for ever, att and under the proportionable part of the yearly Quitt-rent from henceforth to become due to the Chief Lord of the soil of the said whole Lott of Land and premisses and under all and Singular, the other Rents, Covenants, provisoes and Conditions on the part of the s'd Griffith Jones, performable to the s'd Wm. Penn, his Heirs and Successors, Contained in the s'd Patent, proportionable to the said twenty-two foot Lott, Yielding and paying therefore, yearly, for ever hereafter, to the said Griffith Jones, his Heirs and Assigns for the said twenty-two foot lott, Houses and wharffs thereon built or to be built, the sum of Three pounds, Six Shillings in Lawfull Silver Money of the said Province for the time being, yearly, for ever, Begining the first year's payment thereof att and upon the first day of July, 1694, and so forth thereafter Yearly for ever; and if the said Yearly Rent of Three p'unds, six shillings shall be behind unpaid by the space of Tenn days next and I'mediately after the said first day of July, yearly, that then and in that Case it shall and may be lawfull for the said Griffith Jones and his above written either into the said twenty-two foot Lott and into the Houses thereof to be built, to enter and there to distrain for the said Yearly Rent of Three pounds six Shillings, and the Goods, Chattles, distresses there found to Carry away, detain or sell at reasonable rates for payment and Satisfaction to him, the said Griffith Jones and his above written, of the said yearly Rent so to be behind unpaid and of the arrearages thereof, if any shall be without Suit at Law, and the overpluss to return to the said James Stanfeild or his above Written, and if no Sufficient Distress can be had or taken in and upon the premisses, or if any rescous or pound breach shall be made, or any replevins Sued or obtained of, for or by reason of any distresses to be taken by Virtue of these presents, That then it shall be lawfull for the said Griffith Jones and his above written, into the said Lott of land, houses and premisses to enter, and the Rents thereof to receive and keep and to Use the same whole Lott, houses and premisses untill the said Yearly Rent of Three pounds, Six shillings, with the arrearages thereof, shall be fully from time to time, paid by the said James Stanfeild to the said Griffith Jones, his Heirs and Assigns, and the said Griffith Jones doth Covenant for him and his Heirs that they the said twenty-two foot Lott and premisses, to him, the said James Stanfeild and his Heirs and Assigns, against him, the said Griffith Jones and his Heirs as also against all others Claiming by, from or under them or any of them or by his, their or any of their or their Heirs, their Means, privity, Consent or procurement shall and will warrant and for ever defend by these presents and that the said Griffith Jones hath not done nor Suffered any act whatsoever whereby the said Granted Premisses is, are, can, shall or may be by any means lawfully Impeached, Charged or Incumbred in any Manner of way, and the said James Stanfeild doth Constitute for him and his Heirs and Assigns, that att or before the expiration of one Year and a Day after the date hereof, they will build and Improve upon the said Lott. In Witness whereof the parties first above written to these presents have to these Present Indentures their Hands and Seals Interchangeably putt the day and date first above Written.

GRIFFITH JONES. [Seal.]

Sealed and Delivered in Presence of us, Joseph Wilcox, Pat. Robinson. Acknowledged in Open Court, Certifyed Under the Clark's hand this 22d 7ber, 1693.

PATRICK ROBINSON, Cl. Com.

Recorded 8th 8ber, 1693.

Obligation.—Mary Hilliard to Charles Sober.

Know all men by these Presents, that I, Mary Hilliard, widdow and Executrix of the Last will and Testament of Rich'd Hilliard, deceased, do Acknowledge myself to owe and stand firmly bound Unto Charles Sober, of Philad'a, Chirurgeon, in the penall sum of Two Hundred and twenty pounds, Current Silver Money of ye Province of Pennsyvania, to be paid unto him the said Charles Sober or his Certain Attorney, Heirs Ex'ors or Admin'ors to which said Payment well and truly to be made, I bind mee, my Heirs, Ex'ors and Admin'ors firmly by these presents, Sealed with my seal and dated this twenty second day of September, Anno D'ni 1693.

The Condition of this Obligation is Such, that if the Above Bounden Mary Hilliard, her Heirs, Ex'ors and Admin'ors shall and will from time to time and att all times hereafter, will and Sufficiently Maintain, make good, Justify, Warrant and for ever defend him, the said Charles Sober, his Heirs and Assigns in his and their peaceable and quiet possession, right, title and Interest of, in and to the Messuage, Lott and premisses to him, the said Charles Sober bargained and sold by the above Bounden Mary Hilliard, as in and by a Certain Bill of Sale thereof, bearing even date with these presents and Recorded in the Secretary's Office in Philad'a, the twenty-seventh day of September, relation being thereunto had more fully and at large appeareth, Then this Obligation to be Void or else to remain in full force, Effect and Virtue.

MARY HILLIARD. [Seal.]

Sealed and Delivered in the Presence of Us, Charles Pickering. Philip James, Theo'r. Roberts, George Parris.
Philad'a 20th 8th ber, 1692.

Personally appeared before me, Pat. Robinson, Secretary of the Province of Pennsylvania, &ca., the within George Parris, who did depose on the Holy Evangells of Almighty God, and the within Charles Pickering who did Attest that they rexivle saw the within Mary Hilliard Sign, Seal and Deliver the within Obligation as her Act and Deed, and that they Signed Witnesses thereto.

PAT. ROBINSON, *Secretary.*

Recorded 20th October, 1698.

Bill of Sale of ⅛ part of the Brigantine Friends Adventure.— George Heathcote to Rich'd Haines and Company.

To all Xtian People to whom this present Writing shall Come, George Heathcote, of Philad'a, in the province of Pennsylvania, in America, Merch't, Sendeth Greeting: Know ye that I, the said George Heathcote, for and in Consideration of the sum of One hundred and seven Pounds, Current Silver Money of the said province, to me in hand Paid, att and before the ensealing and delivery hereof, The receit whereof I doe hereby Acknowledge, Have bargained, Sold, assigned, and Sett over, and by these Presents doe fully and Absolutely bargain, sell, assign and sett over unto Rich'd Haines, James and Benjamin Braine, Thos. Byfeild and John Lamb, of London, Merch'ts, all that my Eighth part of the Briganteene, Commonly called or Knowne by the name of the friends Adventure, now riding att anchor in the port of Philad'a, in Dellaware River, whereof John King was lately Master, To have and to hold ye said Eighth part of the said Briganteene together with all the Riggin, Furniture, Takle and apparrell belonging thereunto as fully and amply to all Intents and Purposes as I could or might lay Claim or Interest there unto att her discharge att Philad'a, of her Late Voyage from England to them, the said Richard Haines, James and Benjamin Braine, Thos. Byfeild and John Lamb, their Heirs and Assigns for Ever, and I, the said George Heathcote, doe hereby for mee, my Heirs, Ex'ors and Admin'ors Covenant, promise, grant and agree to and with the said Rich'd Haines, James and Benj'in Braine, Thos. Byfeild and John Lamb, their Heirs, Ex'ors and Admin'ors by these Presents, that I will warrant and defend the said one-Eighth part of the Hull of the said Brigantine and all other the Premisses and appurtenances to the said Eighth part belonging to the said Rich'd Haines, James and Benj'a. Braine,

Thos. Byfeild and John Lamb, their Heirs, Ex'ors, admin'ors and assigns for one year and a day against the Claims and Demands of all persons whatsoever (danger of the Seas, fire, Enemy, Pirates, Restraints and Embargoe of Princes only excepted). In Witness Whereof I have hereunto sett my hand and Seal this twenty-fifth day of October, being the fifth year of the reign of King Wm. and Queen Mary over England, &ca., Annoq Domini, 1693.

GEORGE HEATHCOTE. [Seal.]

Sealed and Delivered in the presence of us, John King, Ro. French, Jas. Yeates. October ye 25th, 1693, Received then of the within Named Rich'd Haines, James and Benja'n. Braine, Thos. Byfeild and John Lamb, by the hands of Joseph Pidgeon, the sum of One hundred and seven Pounds, being the Consideration Money within Mentioned; I say received by me, Geo. Heathcote. Witnesses present, John King, Ro. French, Jasper Yeats.

Pennsylvania, 31st 8ber, 1693, Personally appeared before me the within and above Named John King and Ro. French, who did depose on the holy Evangells of Almighty God that they saw the within and above named George Heathcote Sign, Seal and Deliver the within Bill of Sale and above written receipt to Joseph Pidgeon, Attorney for the barganees within Mentioned.

PAT. ROBINSON, *Secretary*.

Recorded 31st of 8ber, 1693.

Letter of Administra'on to Miles Forster on James Bainer's Estate.

Benjamin Fletcher, Captain Generall and Governor in Chief of the Province of New York, Province of Pennsylvania, County of New Castle, and the Territories and Tracts of Land depending thereon, in America, To Miles Forster, the friend and Creditor of James Bainer, late of Carolina, but Coming to Philad'a, there Deceased, Greeting: Whereas the said James Bainer so as aforesaid, Deceased, hath lately dyed Intestate, haveing, while he Lived and att the time of his Death, goods, rights and Creditts within the said province by means whereof the full Disposition of all and Singular the goods, rights and Creditts of ye S'd Deceased, and the granting of the Administration of them as also the hearing of account or reckoning of the said Administration and the small discharge and dismission from the same unto me alone wholly, and not unto another Inferior Judge, are Manifestly known to belong, I desiring that the goods, rights and Credditts of the said deceased be well and faithfully Administred and Converted and Disposed of Unto pious uses, doe grant unto you, in whose fidelity in this behalf I verry much Confide, full power by the tenure of these presents, to Administer the goods, rights and Creditts of the said Deceased, and faithfully to dispose of them, also to ask, Collect, levy and Require the Creditts whatsoever of the said deceased, which unto the said Deceased while he lived and at the time of his Death did belong, and to pay the Debts in which the said deceased Stood Obliged so far forth as the goods, Chattles and Creditts of the said deceased can thereunto extend according to their rate Chiefly of well and truly administering the same and of making a full and perfect Inventory of all and Singular the goods and Chattles and Creditts of the said deceased, and exhibiting the same unto the registry of the Prerogative Court att or before the Eighteenth day of February next ensuing, also of rendering a full and true account or rekoning at or before the Eighteenth day of August, which shall be in the year of our Lord 1694, being sworn upon the holy Evangelists, and I doe by these presents ordain, depute and Constitute you administrator of the goods, Chattles and Creditts of the said Deceased. In testimony whereof I have Caused the seal of the Prerogative Court to be here unto affixed at New York the 18th day of August, in the year of our Lord 1693.

DAVID JAMISON. [Seal.]

Recorded 21st day of November, 1693.

Indenture of James Letort to John King.

This Indenture, made the Eight and twentyeth day of May, Anno Domini 1692, Between James Letort, son of James Letort, of Pennsylvania, of the one part, and John King, of Philad'a, in the province of Pennsylvania, in America, of the other part, Witnesseth that the said James Letort, Junior, doth hereby, by the Consent of his Mother, bind himself an apprentice to the said John King, to serve him, the said John King or his Assigns, either on board or on Shore, from the day of the date hereof, for during and unto the full and term of five years from hence, Next ensuing and fully to be Compleated and ended and the s'd John King doth hereby Covenant for him and his Assigns to find and provide for the said James Letort, Jun'r, Sufficient diet and to Treate and use him in all things According as is Customary and Usuall for Servants and apprentices bound out to Sea; Lastly, the said James Letort, Jun'r, doth hereby promise to Serve the said John King or his Assigns faithfully and Diligently during the said term, and that he shall not nor will not proloyne, Imbezle, Convey away or other wise defraud the said John King of any Money, Goods, Wares or Merchandizes belonging to him or in his Care or Custody for any other person or persons whatsoever. In Witness whereof the parties first above Named have to these present Indentures their hands and Seals Interchangeably putt the day and Year first above Written.

       ANNE LETORT. [Seal.]
     Sign, JAMES VW LETORT. [Seal.]

Sealed and Delivered in the presence of John Holme, Justice, Sam'll Atkins, Nathaniell Puckle, NM, H. G. Personally appeared before me, Pat. Robinson, Secretary of the Province of Pennsylvania, &c., the within Named John Holme and S'd Sam'll Atkins, who did Swear upon the Holy Evangells of almighty God that they Saw the within Named James Letort and Anne Letort Sign, Seal and Deliver the within Indentures to John King, within Named, as their act and Deed this 22d 9ber, 1693.

       PAT. ROBINSON, *Secretary.*

Recorded 22d November, 1693.

Conveyance of Rich'd and Eliza. Bassnett to Philip Richards.

These Indentures, Tripartite, made this twenty-first day of November, being the fifth year of the Reign of our Sovereign Lord and Lady, Wm. and Mary, by the Grace of God, of England, Scotland, France and Ireland, King and Queen, Defenders of the faith, An'o D'ni 1693, Between Elizabeth, late Framton, now Bassnett, relict and ex'rix of the estate of Wm. Framton, of Phila'da, Merchant, Deceased, and Rich'd Bassnett, of Burlington, in the province of West New Jersey, Inholder, now her Husband, of the first part, with Consent of Alice. Late Throckmorton, now Skelton, as relict and ex'rix of the Estate of John

Throckmorton, of Middle Town, in East Jersey, Yeoman, Deceased, and of Robert Skelton, now of Middle Town, aforesaid, Yeoman, Now Husband to the said Alice, adm'ors on the Estate of Joseph Throgmorton, Mariner, also deceased, of the Second part, and Philip Richards, of the town and County of Philadelphia, Merch't, of the Third part, Whereas shee, the said Elizabeth Frampton, by her Deed or Mortgage under her hand and seal duly acknowledged and Recorded for the Consideration of Three Hundred and tenn pounds, Lawfull Silver Money of Pennsylvania, therein mentioned, to be paid the first of August, 1689, did Mortgage to the said Joseph Throgmorton, his Heirs, Ex'ors, admin'ors and assigns a Certain Lott of Land in Dellaware Front street, in Philada, aforesaid, as also a bank Lott opposite thereto, ten acres of Land at the North End of the said Town and Five Hundred acres of Land in the Township of Cheltenham, in the County aforesaid, into which Mortgaged premisses he, the said Ro't Skelton (by reason that the said Mortgage was forfeited for non payment of the said sum of Three Hundred and tenn pounds, principall and Interest Included, upon the first of August, 1689), did peaceably re-enter upon the Sixteenth day of November Instant, and Whereas by a fair and Stated accompt Made up between the said Rich'd and Elizabeth Bassnett's, and Rob't and Alice Skelton, upon the day of the date hereof, They, the said Richard and Elizabeth Bassnett's stand Justly Indebted to the said Rob't and Alice Skelton's in the sum of Three Hundred and three pounds, Nineteen Shillings and three pence, Money afores'd, and Whereas the said Mortgaged premisses, by decay of the House, Wharffs, fences and want of Tenants, will not raise the Said Sum nor is not worth the same, and therefore the said Rob't and Alice Skelton's are willing to take the sum of two Hundred forty-seven pounds in good ready Silver Money of the Said Province, in full of the said Mortgage, and the said Richard Bassnett is willing, with the Consent aforesaid, to sell the said Mortgaged premisses for the said sum of Two Hundred and forty-seven pounds to the said Philip Richards, because it will yield no more. Now these present Indentures Witness that for and in Consideration of the said sum of Two hundred and forty seven pounds, lawfull Silver money of the s'd province, in hand paid by the said Philip Richards to the said Richard and Elizabeth Bassnett's, the receit whereof the said Richard and Elizabeth Bassnett's doth hereby acknowledge and thereof doe acequitt and Discharge the said Phillip Richards, His Heirs, Ex'ors and admin'ors thereof for Ever by these presents. They, the said Rich'd and Elizabeth Bassnett's, with the express assent and Consent of the said Rob't and Alice Skelton's, Witnessed by their Subscribing these presents, and as parties Hereto have given, granted, aliened, bargained, sold, enfeeoffed and Confirmed, and by these presents doe absolutely give, grant, alien, bargain, sell, enfeeoff and Confirm to the said Philip Richards the said Lott of Land in Dellaware front Street, in Philad'a, lying between Wallnutt Street and Spruce Street, Containing in breadth forty-two foot, and in Length, on the North side, two hundred fifty-five foot, and on the South side Two Hundred and one foot, Bounded Northward with Sabian Cole's Lott, Eastward with Dellaware front street, Southward with Sam'll Jobson's Lott, westward with the swamp or Marsh, with all the Houses, gardens, fences and Improvements thereon, being, as also the said bank Lott, in breadth forty-two foot, and in Length into the River Delaware 250 foot, directly oppositt to the said first Lott, With all the Keys and wharffs thereon being, with all the priviledges thereto belonging, as also the said Ten acres of Land at the North End of Philad'a, begining at Corner post Standing foot distance from the river Dellaware, and thence running North Sixty-one Degrees Westerly by the land of Daniel Pegg and Compa. to a Corner marked post, from thence running South Seven degrees westerly by the said Pegg and Compa's Land forty Eight perches to a Corner marked post standing Near to Cooachquenauque Creek, Thence Running North Twenty degr's Easterly through the swamp fifty-two perches to a Corner Marked post, Standing in the swamp and fifty foot distance from the river Dellaware, Thence running North Twenty degr's Easterly fourteen perches to the place of begining, as also the said five hundred acres of Land in the Township of Cheltenham, in the said County of Philad'a, begining at a Corner Marked Stake, being the Corner Stake of John Russell's Land, from Thence North East by the said Russell's line of Marked trees Four Hundred and eighty perches to a Corner post, from Thence North West by a line of trees One hundred Sixty-Seven perches to a Corner tree, from thence south West by a line of Marked trees four Hundred and eight perches to a Corner Marked post, from thence by a line of Marked trees South East One Hundred Sixty-Seven perches to the first Mentioned Marked post, With all their Rights, Members, ways, water-Courses, trees, houses, buildings, yards, orchards, wharffs, Keys, Improvements and appurtenances whatsoever of the said Lott, bank Lott and five hundred and ten acres of Land held, Used and enjoyed therewith or reputed as any part of the same, and the reversions, remainders, rents and profitts thereof, and all the estate, right, title, Interest, Use, possession, property, Claim and demand

Whatsoever of the said Rich'd and Elizabeth Bassnett's and Rob't and Alice Skeliton's, ex'rix and admin'ors aforesaid, of, in and to the said Lands, Lotts and premisses, and all Deeds, grants, warrants, surveys, returns, Letters, Patents and other Evidences and Writings Concerning the same, all which are Situate, lying and being as is above said and are now in the possession of the said Rich'd and Eliza. Bassnett's, and of the said Robert and Alice Skelton's, ex'rix and adm'rs aforesaid, by Virtue of their rexive rights and titles thereto, to have and to hold the said Lott of Land, bank Lott, Houses, Lands and premisses to him, the said Phillip Richards, his Heirs and assigns, and to the only use and behoofe of him, the said Philip Richards, his Heirs and assigns for Ever, att and Under the rexive yearly Rents from hence forth to become due to the Chief Lord of the Soil of the said rexive lott and lands above Mentioned, and the said Rich'd and Elizabeth Basnet, with Consent aforesaid, doe Covenant, promise and grant for them and their Heirs that they the said Lotts, Lands, Houses and premisses against themselves and their Heirs, as also against all Other persons Claiming or to Claim by, from or under them or any of them or by their or any of their or their Heirs, their Means, privity, Consent or procurement shall and will warrant and for Ever Defend by these presents, and that the said Rich'd Nor Elizabeth Basnet's, nor the said Rob't nor Alice Skelton's have Not done nor suffred any act whatsoever whereby the said granted premisses or any part thereof, is, are, can, shall or may be by any Means lawfully Impeached, Charged or Incumbred in any manner of way, and that the said Ric'd and Elizabeth Basnet's, with Consent of Rob't and Alice Skelton's, shall and will at all times Hereafter during the space of Seven Years next Ensuing the date Hereof att the request and Charges of the said Philip Richards, his Heirs and assigns, make, doe and execute such further and other reasonable act, matter or thing as by the said Phillip Richards, his Heirs and assigns, Shall be lawfully required for the better and more Clear Confirming and Conveying the said premisses with the appurtenances to the said Philip Richards, his Heirs and assigns for ever, according to the true Intent and meaning hereof, so as the persons to whom such request shall be made be not Compelled nor Compellable to travell above twelve miles from the place of their abode for the doing hereof, and so as such further assurance Contain no further nor other Warrantie then is herein before exprest and they, the said Rich'd and Elizabeth Bassnett's, with Consent of Rob't and Alice Skelton's, have made and Constituted John Claypoole their attorney to appear at the County Court of Philad'a and there in presence of the said Court to declare, acknowedge and deliver these presents to the said Phillip Richards or his Certain attorney, according to law. In Witness whereof the parties first above written to these presents have to these present Indentures their Hands and Seals Interchangeably putt the day and date first above written.

                          RICHARD BASSNETT. [Seal.]
                          ELIZABETH BASSNETT. [Seal.]

Robert Skelton Consents.   [Seal.]
Alice Skelton, A her Mark; Consents.   [Seal.]

Received this twenty-first day of November, 1693, from the within Phillip Richards the within written sum of Two Hundred forty-seven pounds, Consideration Money, within exprest by us, Richard Basnet, Eliza. Basnet. Witnesses, John Stout, Wm. Salway, John Test. Sealed and Delivered by Richard Basnet and Robert Skelton in presence of us, John Stout, Wm. Salway, John Test. Sealed and delivered by Elizabeth Basnet in Presence of us, James Marshall, Cha. Reade, John Stout. Sealed and delivered by Alice Skelton in Presence of us, John Stout, Moses Lipet Acknowledegd in open Court held at Philad'a the 6th day of Xber, 1693, as witness my Hand.

                                        JOHN CLAYPOOLE, *Clerk*.

Recorded 10th Xber, 1693.
Examined and Corrected p. Jo'n Hughes.

MINUTE BOOK "G."

MINUTES OF PROPERTY COMMENCING YE 19TH 9TH BER., 1701. THIS IS BOOK G IN THE SECRETARIES OFFICE.

William Penn, true and Absolute Proprietary and Governor in chief of the Province of Pensilvania and Territories there unto belonging. To my Well beloved Friends, Edward Shippen, Griffith Owen, Thomas Story and James Logan, sendeth greeting. For as much as the present Circumstances and Public Emergencies of the government of this Province and Territories and other Exigencies have laid me under an inevitable necessity to return for some time to England and being Desirous to secure all Persons in their Just Claims, and that all Matters of Property should be translated and carried on as well in my Absence as when present. Know ye, therefore, that reposing Special Trust and confidence in your fidelity, Justice, Prudence and Ability, I have constituted and appointed and do by these presents Constitute and appoint you, the said Edward Shippen, Griffith Owen, Thomas Story and James Logan my Property Deputies or Comis'rs of Property for the said Province of Pensilvania and Territories, Given hereby and Granting unto you, the said Edward Shippen, Griffith Owen, Thomas Story and James Logan, or to any three of you, full Power and Authority for me and in my name to grant by Warrants under your Hands or the Hands of any three of you, and the Great Seal of the Province all such Tracts or parcels of Rough, unseparated Lands, Town Lots, Tenements and hereditaments whatsoever within the said province and Territories (according to the Regulation hitherto made and practised and by me instituted in and about the same) as not yet Surveyed, Taken up or appropriated to any particular uses to such person or persons as by any former grant or purchase have right to any of the Lands, Lots, Tenements and Hereditam'ts aforesaid, and to every such other person and persons as shall be willing to purchase for competent sums of money or otherwise on valuable Considerations to take up any of the said Lands, Lots and premises under such Quitrents, Services, Acknowledgements and Reservations to me, my heirs and Successors, as to you, the said Edward Shippen, Griffith Owen, Thomas Story and James Logan, or any three of you, shall seem Just and Reasonable. And I do hereby Authorize and Impower you, or any three of you, by your Warrants or Orders to cause to be Surveyed, Resurveyed and Admeasured, according to a late Act of Assembly of this Government, made and passed for the confirmation of Property, all and Every the Tracts, parcels and Lots of Land within the said Province and Territories that have been already allowed or taken up, as well by the Outlines and Boundaries by which they were at first laid out as by the Lines of Subdivisions or any other way whatsoever as you shall see cause, and further to regulate and order all things whatsoever relating to the Survey, resurvey, Admeasurement, Division, Bounding or Location of Lands, whether in Lesser or greater Tracts or whole Counties, within the said Province or Territories, and all such overplus Lands in Measure which are or shall be found in any Particular Tract or Tracts above the Number Acres such Tract or Tracts were at first laid out for (allowance first being made for Roads, &c., according to such Law or Laws by me passed and made as are or shall be in force for that purpose) me and in my Name to Alien, Sell, Bargain and dispose as such Law or Laws doe or shall Direct for such Competent Sums, money or other valuable Considerations, as to you or any three of you shall seem Just and Reasonable. Also for me and in my Name to Nominate and appoint from time to time in every case and in all things whatsoever to act about cutting of or disposing of such overplus Lands according to any Law of this Government in that case made and provided doth direct, Also for me and in my Name to Bargain, Sell, Alien, Enfeeoff or Demise all such Concealed or vacant Lands as shall be found Interjacent between any Surveyed Tracts and all Meadow, Marshes, Cripples, Woods, not particularly appropriated upon such Terms, Quitrents, Services and reservations to me, my heirs and Successors, as you shall see most reasonable and Convenient, also to make satisfaction out of my other Lands and Estate (my appropriated Land Excepted) in the said Province and Territories as the Law in that case directs, for all such Deficiencies in measure as upon a Due Resurvey shall be found in any Tract or Tracts or parcels of Land to the respective persons thereby grieved, and for all such Lands, Lotts, Tenements and Meadows, Marshes and hereditaments as are already taken up within this Province and Territories and duely seated by Vertue of Grants or Warr'ts obtained from Governors or lawful Commiss'rs under the Crown of England before the King's grant of this Province to me (except the same was had by fraud or Deceit), and all Lots and Lands duely taken up by Vertue of Warrants obtained pursuant to Purchases made and had from me or in pursuance of any Commission or Power Granted to me by any other Person Except as before Excepted and all other Lands, Lots and Tenements whatsoever which the Owners or Possessors thereof have any Just, Lawful or equitable Claim to but are not yet Confirmed, and all such Lands, Lots, Tenements and other Hereditaments as in pursuance hereof shall be taken up or granted, whether rough, Unseparated Lands, Overplus Lands or concealed or otherwise Vacant Lands not hitherto particularly appropriated, I doe by these Presents Give and grant to you, the said Edward Shippen, Griffith Owen, Thomas Story and James Logan, or any three of you, my full, whole and absolute power, Right and Authority for me and in my Name, by Patents or Instruments under your Hands or the Hands of any three of you, and my great Seal of this Province To Give, Grant, Release and confirm to such person or persons to whom they are or shall be laid out or granted, or by whom they are respectively held as aforesaid, or to their Heirs or Assigns, and to their respective Heirs and Assigns forever all such Tracts and Parcels of Land, Lotts, Meadow, Marshes and other hereditaments, with all and singular their Appurtenances, To have and to hold the said Lands, Lotts, Meadows, Marshes and other hereditaments with their Appurtenances to such person or persons as aforesaid, their Heirs and Assigns forever, To the proper use and Behoof of the said Persons, their Heirs and Assigns forever, to be holden of me, my heirs and Successors, Proprietarys of the s'd province and Territories in free and Common Soccage, as of some of our Mannors, or Reputed Mannors, in the respective Counties within the said Province and Territories wherein they shall severally happen to Lye, under such Quitrents, Acknowledgements and reservations to me, my heirs and Successors aforesaid; And I do further hereby Give and Grant to you, the said Edward Shippen, Griffith Owen, Thomas Story and James Logan, or any three of you, for me and in my Name full Power and Authority to Lett, sett, Lease and farm out all such Parts and Parcels of my Mannor Lands, or Reputed Mannors, or any of my Lands in the said Province and Territories appropriated to my use as now or hereafter from Time to Time you shall receive instructions for from me under my Hand to such Person and Persons as shall be Willing to take up and hold the same under such Rents and Services and Reservations to me, my heirs and Successors, and for such Term or Terms of years as you shall see most convenient for the publick Benefit and Utility, And for my interest, And further if cause shall be seen to alien, Sell, Enfeeoff and Confirm any such parts or parcels of my mannor or other Lands as afores'd for an Inheritance to the respective Granted, their heirs and Assigns forever, by such Instruments under your Hands, or the Hands of any three of you, and my great Seal as aforesaid, which Grants, Patents, Leases and Instruments of Confirmation to be by you, the said Edward Shippen, Griffith Owen, Thomas Story and James Logan, or any three of you made as aforesaid. I do hereby fully and absolutely Ratify, Confirm and make valid to all Intents and purposes according to the respective Tenours of the same to be firm and unquestionable Titles to the respective granted, their Heirs and Assigns, and shall be good and effectual in Law against me, my heirs and Successors forever, Notwithstanding any Objection that may arise against the form of such instrum'ts or any other Objections against the Manner of Granting and confirming any such Lands or Lotts whatsoever, provided always that you shall not grant any such Instruments as aforesaid contrary to any Instructions that you shall or may from time to time receive from me, which Instructions shall be publick and upon Record in the office of Property, to be by you held in Philadelphia or in the Rolls Office of this Government, and I do further, by these presents fully and absolutely Authorize and Empower you, the said Edward Shippen, Griffith Owen, Thos. Story and James Logan, or any three of you, to Doe and execute or cause to be done and executed all and every such Act or Acts, thing or things whatsoever in and about the granting, Conveying, Setting, securing and Confirming all and singular the Lands, Lotts, Tenements, Meadows, Marshes and other hereditaments aforesaid, and every part and parcel thereof to such persons as have or shall have right to the same, and in determining all Manner of Differences and Disputes Concerning the Bounds, Survey, Settlement of any such Lands or Lotts, as aforesaid, that of Right do belong to me, to Determine, and all other things whatsoever to Doe and execute that by any Law or Laws of this Government relating to my Property I or my heirs ought or could do as fully and amply to all Intents and purposes as I or my heirs by my or their Act or Acts can or may do in any wise whatsoever. And for the more effectual Management of all my affairs of Property in the said province and Territories I do further hereby Give and Grant to you, the said Edward Shippen, Griffith Owen, Thomas Story and James Logan, full Power and Authority by your Commissions under your Hands or the Hands of any three of you to Constitute all Officers Immediately Depending on my Property as Surveyors, Rangers and all others whatsoever Independent from the Government in whom the trust of Executing any Matter or thing between me as the Proprietary and the people is reposed, with full Power, also together with my Receiver General if you shall see cause to call all, every or any Person or Persons to account within the said Province between me and whom any accounts of great Moment Doe Depend, also from time to time to make up accounts with my said Receiver General as you shall see occasion or as you shall receive orders from me, hereby avowing, Justifying and Maintaining whatsoever you shall Doe in pursuance or in Due Execution of this Commission, which is to continue in force till my further Pleasure shall be known. Given under my Hand and great Seal of this province at Philadelphia the 28th day of 8ber, in the 13th year of the reign of King William the 3d over England, &c., and the 21st of my Government, Annoq Dom. 1701.

An Additional Commission to the Foregoing.

William Penn, True and absolute Proprietary and Governor in Chief of the Province of Pensilvania and Territories thereunto belonging, To my Trusty and Well-beloved Friends, Edward Shippen, Griffith Owen, Thomas Story and James Logan, Sends greeting.

Whereas by my Commission, under my Great Seal, bearing Date the Twenty-eighth day of October last past, I was pleased to constitute and Appoint you my Commissioners of Property for the said Province and Territories, with full Power and Authority for me and in my Name to Grant and dispose of Lands, Lots, Tenements and Hereditaments to such Persons in the said Province and Territories as have right to take up or would purchase or Rent the same. Which Commission nevertheless not being In all Respects so full and Compleat as intended, I have therefore thought fitt for the more fully Investing You with All the requisite Powers Granted to me and my Heirs by the Royal Charter or Letters patent of King Charles the Second, bearing Date the fourth day of March, in the thirty-third year of his Reign, that more immediately relate to my Propriety of the said Province and the Lands and Soil thereof, to Give and Grant to you, and accordingly doe presents, give and Grant to you, the said Edward Shippen, Griffith Owen, Thomas Story and James Logan, or any three of you, my full and Absolute Power and Authority for me and in my Name by Vertue of a Special Clause in the said Letters patent for this End provided, to Erect into Mannors all and every Such Tract and Tracts of Land in the said Province as You shall think fitt and reasonable, And the same to endow with all the requisite Powers, Jurisdictions, Privileges, franchises and Immunities whatsoever that to a Mannor properly belong, according to the Law and Customs of England as far as they shall appear consistent with and agreeable to the Laws and Constitution of the said Province and Territories, To have, hold and enjoy the said Mannors with all the Powers, Jurisdictions, ffranchises and appurtenances whatsoever thereunto belonging to the respective Grantees, their Heirs and Assigns forever. I do also hereby give and grant to you, the said Edward Shippen, Griffith Owen, Thomas Story and James Logan, or any three of you, full Power and Authority for me and in my Name to give, grant, Bargain, Sell, Alien, Enfeof, Demise and confirm to such Person or Persons as have right to or are willing to purchase or rent any Part of the same, and to his and their heirs and Assigns forever All and all manner of Meadows, Marshes, Swamps, Cripples. Savannas, Pocosons, Sunken Lands, Islands, Creeks, Rivulets, Inletts, Wayes, Waters, Watercourses, Mines, Minerals, Woods, Underwoods, Copies, Timber and Trees, Hawkings, Huntings, fishings, fowlings and all other Commodities, Profits, Advantages and appurtenances whatsoever to the Land and Soil of the Said Province of Pensilvania and Territories or any Part thereof belonging or in any wise appertaining, not being yet disposed of nor otherwise appropriated, in such form and after such Manner as by your said Commission You are directed, Reserving always to me and my heirs three clear fifth of all royal Mines and such Rents and Services as have been ususal or you shall think fitt and reasonable. Which grants to be by you made I do hereby Ratify, Confirm and make good to all Intents and purposes as any other Grant, Instrument or Act whatsoever which by my said Commissions, You are Impowered to doe or execute, And shall further Ratify and confirm the same from Time to Time as occasion shall require. And I doe further hereby Authorize and Impower You, the said Edward Shippen, Griffith Owen, Thomas Story and James Logan, or any three of you, by your Commissions under your hands and the Seal of the Province to Constitute and appoint all necessary officers for collecting or receiving any Duty or Impost granted to me by Law, and former Commission to revoke as you shall see cause, also to constitute and ordain Steward, Bailiffs and other Officers, and all other Acts, Matters and Things whatsoever to doe and execute that you shall see necessary for the Preserving of my Property and securing my Revenue within the said Province and Territories during my Absence out of the same, or till my further Order. In Witness whereof I have hereunto Sett my hand on board the Ship Dolmahoy, in Delaware Bay, the first Day of the ninth Month, One thousand Seven hundred and One, and caused my great Seal to be also affixed.

WILLIAM PENN.

Under the Great Seal Appendant.

Instructions To my Commissioners of Property to be observed by them in granting of Lots and Lands in my Province of Pensilvania and Counties Annexed.

[Lesser Seal of the Province.]

Whereas I, William Penn, Proprietary and Governor of the Province of Pensilvania and Counties Annexed, have by my Commission under my great Seal, bearing Date the twenty-eighth day of October last, Constituted and appointed You, my trusty Friends, Edward Shippen, Griffith Owen, Thomas Story and James Logan, my Commissioners of Property for the Granting and confirming of Lands and Lotts in the said Province and Territories thereunto belonging to the Purchasers, Renters and Inhabitants thereof; Know therefore That I have thought fitt for your better Directions, Guidance, in the Execution of the said Commission to Injoyn the following Instructions for your Observation.

First. You shall Grant unto all Persons who have right to take up any Lands in the said Province by Purchase all their whole rights, and in such parcels and Quantities as they can most conveniently settle, and according to the Method of Townships appointed.

Liberty Land and Lotts You shall grant to first Purchasers according to their respective Rights.

Overplus Lands You shall Grant to the Possessors according as the Law directs, unless the Possessor shall agree to part with his right to compensate the Deficiency of his Neighbour.

Concealed Lands You shall Dispose of for the Value thereof in such Manner as will most accomodate the People, reserving such Tracts as you shall think fit to be applied to any particular uses for the benefit of my Family.

After the same Manner dispose of Marshes, Meadows and Cripples according to the Necessity and want of the Persons desirous to take them up, reserving sufficient for the accommodation of future Settlers.

And for the better accommodation of such as are willing to seat themselves on small parcels of Land, and near other Inhabitants, I am willing and doe allow That you dispose of out of my Mannor of Springetsbury, near Philadelphia, fifteen hundred or two thousand Acres of that part chiefly most remote from the Town, or as you shall think most convenient, reserving for my Demesne at least one thousand Acres adjoining to fair-Mount and the City, at least one Moiety of what you so dispose of to be upon lease for a Number of Years, and some Smaller Part if you see cause in fee.

For the same reasons and after the same Manner, You may retrench my Mannor of Pennsbury to five thousand Acres but not under.

Also out of my Mannor of Gilberts, you may dispose of Three thousand Acres. Out of my Mannor of Rocklands five thousand acres and no more. Out of my Mannor of Highlands Three thousand acres and no more. Out of my Mannor of Spring-Town four thousand acres and no more. All which Lands to be disposed of out of my Mannors as aforesaid you shall subject to such Services as are customary in Mannors in England, or as you shall otherwise see cause.

The Reversions of the Bank Lotts of Philadelphia from the front street Two hundred and fifty foot into the River, I do allow you to sell off for twenty Shilling p'r foot reserving always the Ground Rent.

The Yearly Rents of a penny p'r Acre You may reduce to one Bushel of Wheat for Six pounds p'r hundred, or to an English Shilling after the Rate of a twenty Years' purchase.

After the same rate you may sell of the old rents in the lower Counties reserving one English Shilling per hundred acres.

All which said Instructions being by you observed, I doe and shall from time to time ratify, Avow, Justify, Warrant and Maintain all your proceedings in pursuance of the said Commission according to the full and true Intent and meaning thereof. In witness whereof I have hereunto Set my hand and caused the lesser Seal of my Province to be affixed on board the Ship Dolmahoy in the River or Bay of Delaware, the first day of the ninth Month in the Year one thousand seven hundred and one. WILLIAM PENN.

The Acts and Proceedings of the Commissioners of Property in pursuance of the aforegoing Commissions and Instructions, Commencing 19*th* 9*ber,* 1701.

At a Session of the Commissioners at Philad'a the 19th of the the 9th Month, 1701, Post Merid. Present, Edward Shippen, Griffith Owen, Thomas Story and James Logan.

William Clark Produces a Petition Signed by himself, Directed to the Proprietary, requesting of him a Warrant for a small Piece of vacant Land of the same breadth with his Lott in Chesnut Street on which his New house stands, in breadth about forty or fifty foot, lying between the said Chestnut Street and Walnut Street at the head of the Dock at an easy yearly Rent forever, on which Petition the Propr'y in his own hand has wrote the following Words, viz:

I allow this at the rent of five Shillings.

WM. PENN.

Ordered that a Warrant be forthwith drawn and Signed for the same. Said William Clark produces also a Certificate of Survey signed by Thomas Pemberton, Deputie Surveyor, bearing Date (or the Land out) the 9th of the first Month, 1693-4, for five hundred Acres of Land lying on Indian River Pukahoe branch and the head of Cypress branch, laid out by said Pemberton in pursuance and by Vertue of a warrant from Thomas Holme, Surveyor General (no date mentioned or recited), which Certificate having been presented to the Proprietary he was pleased in his own hand to subscribe the following Words, viz: (twenty-three d. 8ber, 1701, Lett Wm. Clark have his patent for this Land, Wm. Penn). Subscribed also with these Words by the Secretary by the Prop'rs Order, viz: (allowed on old rent, J. Logan.)

Ordered that Patent be forthwith drawn to the said William Clark upon the said Certificate, and according to the Bounds therein expressed, he giving Bonds to suffer the same to be resurveyed at the Proprietaries or Commissioners Pleasure. Wm. Clark further produces a Certificate under the Hand of Thomas Pemberton, Deputy Surveyor of Sussex County, for the Survey of one hundred Acres of Marsh Scituate on the West Side of Delaware Bay and on the South Side of broad Creek in the said County, beginning at the Mouth of a Gutt proceeding out of Baptist Newcomb's Creek (so called), laid out to the said William Clark the 3d Day of March, 1694, by Vertue of a Warrant (as there recited) from Thomas Holme, Surveyor General, bearing Date the 9th of the 8th Month, 1693, which said certificate is subscribed by the Proprietary in his own hand in these following Words, viz: (Lett William Clark have this Included in his other Patent or in a distinct one for this Marsh Land, William Penn); and is also subscribed by the Secretary by the said Proprietor's Order in these Words: (allowed on old Rent, James Logan.) Which Patent he requests.

Ordered that a Patent be accordingly drawn for this forthwith, according to the Bounds in the said Certificate expressed, He giving Bond for this, also to suffer a Resurvey when the Proprietary or Commissioner shall think fitt.

William Ffutcher, by a Letter to his friend William Clark, dated Lewes, 4th September, 1701, and in pursuance of the said Letter the said William Clark for the said Ffutcher, sets forth that the said Ffutcher is by Vertue of a Patent from Governor Andros, bearing Date the 25th March, 1676, possessed of or claims a Tract of Land upon Rehoboth Bay, in the County of Sussex, reputed to contain or laid out for 900 Acres, for which he requests a Warrant of Resurvey, to be granted in his own name as also the overplus for his own use for which he will pay the Proprietor's Quittrents.

Ordered that a Warrant of Resurvey on the said 900 Acres be drawn and that the confirmation thereof and Grant of the overplus be further Considered when the said William Ffutcher's Right or Title to the same is produced when the quantity of the Overplus is known.

Memorandum, that 200 Acres of the aforesaid Tract belongs to the Heirs of Francis Richardson to which Capt. John Hill is obliged by Bond to make a Title.

The proprietary, By Indenture, bearing date the 16th of July, 1691, having granted to John Hough, of Macclesfield, in the County of Chester, Chapman, Three hundred and Seventy-five Acres of Land in consideration of twelve pounds, ten shillings, said to be to him in hand paid, to be laid out (as in the said Indenture is mentioned towards the River Susquehanna,) which Land Rich'd Hough, brother of the said John, doth affirm and declare that his said brother John, as well by a Deed under his hand and Seal as by several Letters, all which he hath to produce but not at hand, gave to him, the said Richard, for his own Children's Use, Which said Indenture the said Richard having produced to the Propr'y before his Departure particularly remarking these Words: (towards Susquehanna), the said Proprietary, in the presence of the Secretary (as the said Secretary declares), allowed that a Warrant should be granted for the said Land in any Part of the Province according to the common form. The said Richard thereupon requests a warrant as aforesaid.

Ordered, that a Warrant be accordingly Drawn for the said Land to Rich'd Hough, and that before it be confirmed, the said Richard produce his brother's Deed and what else may tend to strengthen his Title.

Samuel Clift, being by Vertue of a Grant from New York (as is and has been on all hands concluded and admitted), possessed of a Parcel of Land on Bristol over against Burlington, as the Proprietor's approval by Deed Poll, dated 23d 9th Month, 1682, Conveyed to Richard Dungworth fifty Acres of Land, part of the aforesaid, Scituate on the Mill Creek below the said

Dungworth's Dwelling house, which fifty Acres the said Dungworth, by one other Deed, dated the 13th of the 8th Month, 1693, Conveyed to Edmond Bennet, his heirs and Assigns forever, who deceasing, his Relict Elizabeth Bennet by Deed Poll, dated the fifth of the fifth Month, 1696, sold and Conveyed the said 50 Acres to Thomas Yardley which Deed Recites that the Proprietary and Governor, by his Warrant (no Date mentioned), again Granted the Same to the said Bennet as part of his Land Due to him by purchase (it being before On Old Rent), And that the said Edmond, by his Last Will, Dated the 5th 7ber, 1692, Devised it to the said Elizabeth, his wife and her heirs, who, by virtue of the Said Will, Sold it as afores'd to Thomas Yardley, who Requests a Warrant of Resurvey on the Same.

He also produces a Warrant from the Commiss'ers, bearing Date the 16th of the 2d Month, 1690, To Captain Thomas Holme for Six Acres of Marsh adjoining to the fast Land of Edmond Bennet, to be granted to the said Bennet, being the afore recited fifty Acres, in right of which Warrant the said Yardley having purchased the above, requests a Warrant also for the said six Acres or that it may be included in the other and he will pay its Value. Ordered that a warrant of Resurvey on the afore mentioned fifty acres be granted with an order in the same Warrant to Survey the six Acres of Marsh which he may purchase at its present Value to be judged by persons acquainted therewith, provided that no other person be injured thereby. Agreed Since, at 20 Shillings p'r Acre.

At a Session of the Commissioners at Philadelphia, the 24th of November, 1701, A. Merid. Present, Edward Shippen, Griffith Owen, Thomas Story, Jas. Logan.

A warrant for a Piece of a Lott in Chestnut Street, ordered to William Clark the 19th Instant, was signed, and another to said William for 112 Acres in Sussex, Ordered to-Day. A Warrant of resurvey on 900 Acres in the County of Sussex to Wm. Futcher, ordered the 19th instant, was signed.

A Warrant to Richard Hough for 375 Acres, ordered the 19th Instant, was Signed. A Warrant of Resurvey to Thomas Yardley, ordered the 19th Instant, was Signed.

A return from Edward Penington, Surveyor General, dated 4th 7 mo., 1701, in pursuance of the Proprietor's Warrant, dated 8th 11th Month, 1700, for the Survey of one hundred Acres in the City Liberties, in right of Richard Thomas's purchase, to Hugh Roberts, was presented in order to having a Patent granted. Ordered that a Patent be forthwith drawn thereupon.

William Clark Producing a Patent or Grant from S'r Edmond Andros, dated 29th 7ber, 1677, for one hundred and twelve acres of Land on Whoore hill and Pagan Creek, Sussex, to Cornelius Verhoofe, also a Deed from the sheriff (J. Vines), of the County to the said Wm. Clark for the said Tract of Land taken in Execution to satisfy a Debt due from the Estate of the said Cornelius to William Clark, Also a Release from Peter Groundick, dated the 20th 2d Month, 1686, who was executor on the Estate of the said Cornelius, which Land as actually Surveyed and laid out not agreeing with the Bounds mentioned in the said Grant, he requests a Warrant of Resurvey on the same. Ordered that a Warrant of Resurvey On the whole Tract granted by the said. Patent be forthwith drawn with an order therein to run the subdivision lines of that Part thereof sold to Jonathan Baily.

A Patent to William Clark for five hundred Acres of Land in Sussex, Ordered the 19th Instant, Was Signed.

A Patent to William Clark for one hundred acres of Marsh, Ordered the 19th Instant, was Signed.

Post Meridiem ejudusdem Diei.

A Return under Edward Pennington's hand, dated 7th 9th Mo., 1701, in pursuance of a Warrant from the Proprietary, dated the 16th 3d Month, 1701, for one hundred Acres sold John Lee in Concord, in the County of Chester being Vacant Land, at 30£ p'r hundred, but upon a due Survey is found to contain 136 Acres and 152 perches, and is so returned, on which the said John Lee requests a Patent and offers to pay after the rate of 30£ p'r hundred for the overplus.

Ordered that a Patent be accordingly granted, he paying as aforesaid, And whereas he insists on five Acres to be allowed. Ordered that the Consideration thereof be deferred.

Martin Zeal, Shoemaker, husband to Elizabeth, the Dutch Washerwoman, that has generally wrought which the Governor having long solicited the Proprietary for some Land to settle on, the Proprietary gave the said Martin a Paper wrote all in his own hand and by him signed in the following words: (I am willing to let Elizabeth's Husband have fifty Acres in my Mannor on the other Side of the Run near to the shoemaker, Lying upon the s'd Creek and Running back to William Biles's Line at 3d Sterling p'r Acre, to begin to be paid the third Year and so Forever after, holding the s'd Mannor and under the Regulation of the Court thereof when Erected. Wm. Penn.) Ordered that a warrant be Accordingly Drawn for the same and a patent Upon the Return.

William Dyre by his friend William Clark requests a Confirmation of 289 Acres of Marsh between the Broad-Kill and Prime hook, laid out by Thomas Pemberton, July 21st, 1693, and certifyed by William Clark 16th 7th Month, 1693, by Vertue of two Warrants from the Commissioners of Property, the one for 200 Acres dated 13th 12th Month, 1691-2, and another for 89 Acres 2d of June, 1693, which Marsh the said Dyre having sold to James Stanfield and his Executor, Francis Chadd, to William and Thomas Ffisher, and the said Dyre having given bond of one hundred pounds to make a Title, which Bond was also assigned to said Fisher's, they, the said Fishers, are now about suing the Bond, and Dyre like to be ruined thereby.

Which being considered and weighed and the Board being informed that the Proprietary was much adverse to the confirming of the said Marsh when requested by Dyre, and it being doubted whether the Commissioners had sufficient Power to confirm the said Marsh as requested, Ordered that the Matter be deferred till the Proprietary's pleasure can be known.

Will'm Dyre by said William Clark produces a copy of a Certificate of the Survey of a Tract of Land called Walker's Choice, situate on the South Side of prime-Hook, laid out June, 1681, by Cornelius Verhoofe, Surveyor, in pursuance and by Vertue of a Warrant from Whoorkill Court (as it said, no Date mentioned), for one thousand acres to Nathaniel Walker, on which Certificate is also subscribed the following Words:

"At a Court held at Deal, by the King's Authority, the above Survey is certified to be in part sealed, signed Luke Watson, and is also certified to be a true Copy from Cornelius Verhoofe's papers signed, Norton Claypoole, Clerk."

Also the Copy of a Deed poll under the Hand and Seal of John Winder, dated the 12th March, 1686, certified under Norton Claypoole's Hand, Clerk of the County of Sussex, to be a true Copy conveying from the said John to Nathaniel Walker all that Tract of Land in the said County Called Winder's Neck, containing eleven hundred Acres of Land, granted to the said John by the Name of Robert Winder by patent from N. York, dated 25th March, 1676.

Also a Copy of the said Nathaniel Walker's last Will, dated 7th April, 1683, in the second part of Codicil annexed to which the said Nathaniel devised and bequeathed all the said Land to s'd William Dyre in the following Words, vizt:

"Know all Men that I, the aforesaid Captain Nathaniel Walker, do give, will and bequeath unto my loving Brother in Law, Captain William Dyre, all my Lands and Tenements now in the Government of Pensilvania, lying and being at the

Whoore-Kill, a place formerly so called, since New Deal, and now called Lewis, either by purchase, Grant, Warrant, which Copy is attested under the Hand of Daniel Neech, Clerk, Com., North'ton, Virg'ia, where said Walker lived and seems to be a probate according to the form of that Colony.

Also, A Copy of the last Will and Testament of the above named Capt. William Dyre, dated 20th Ffeb'ry, 1687-8, attested under the Hand of Neh. Ffield, clerk of the County, and the County Seal, in which the said Land is devised in the following Words: ("Item, I will and bequeath unto my eldest Son, William Dyre, now at Boston, in New England, all my plantation or Land, situate and lying and being in the Broad Kill in Sussex County aforesaid, now called Rumble's place, containing two thousand Acres, be it more or less.") By which Grants, Deeds and Devises the said William Dyre having been poss'ed of the whole two thousand one hundred Acres aforesaid he requests a Resurvey upon the whole together with fifty Acres granted him formerly by the Commissioners.

Ordered that a Warrant of Resurvey be granted according to the first Survey and Outlines thereof together with the 50 Acres as requested.

William Rodney having petitioned the proprietary That whereas he had obtained Warrant from the Court of Kent for 500 Acres also bought of John Inians a Warrant from the same Court for the like Quantity and the said Warrants not being executed he requests a New Warrant to take up the said Land. On which petition the proprietary in his own Hand indorsed the following Words: ("I grant this to William Rodney but not for a presedent those Orders not executed being precarious. W. Penn.") But by this Endorsment it appears the proprietary designed only five hundred Acres which he promised in the hearing of Edward Shippen as he Attests and thereupon requests a Warrant to take up the same on old Rent.

Ordered that a Warrant be drawn to the said William Rodney for 500 Acres of Land in Kent County to be seated within two Years after the Date of survey.

———

At a Sessions of the Commissioners at Philadelphia the 26th 9ber 1701, A. Merid.

Present, Edward Shippen, Griffith Owen, Thomas Story, James Logan.

Robert Burton, in a Petition to the Proprietary, given in at Sussex, having set forth that he purchased of Andreas Dirrickson a Tract of Land in the Bottom of Angola Neck in Sussex, granted by the Proprietary's Patent to William Kanning for four hundred Acres (and Rent has been accordingly paid for it), but upon a Resurvey 'tis found there is not much above one-half of the said quantity of land within the Lines of the Patent, great Part of it falling upon the Water. He requested a Resurvey and Compensation for the Deficiency of his Land out of what other Land is to be found adjacent, which Samuel Preston, appearing for the said Robert says, the Proprietary was then pleased to promise and thereupon the said Samuel requests a Resurvey with an Order to include his Plantation left out in the Patent and what other vacant Land may be found to make up the said Quantity of four hundred Acres.

Ordered that a Warrant of Resurvey be granted on the said Land according to its true first Bound of Survey, and in Case there be any Vacancies to be found and the other prove deficient the said Deficiencies be made up out of the same, he having paid rent.

Wm. Fisher Producing a Copy of a Return of Survey out of the Surveyor's Office for a lot of twenty-five ffeet on Delaware ffront, laid out to William Powell, Purchaser of 1,250 Acres, in Pursuance (as is said) of the Proprietary's Warrant, dated 29th 1st Mo., 1684, Survey Dated 16th 10th Mo., 1692, the Return is by the Deputy only not subscribed; this Lot William Powell sold to Thomas Wollaston by Deed dated 1st 2d Mo., 1697, who conveyed it to the said William Ffisher by Deed dated 22d 7 Mo., 1697, who built a Brick House upon it about four Years agoe and requests a Confirmation.

Upon search 'tis found that William Powell's Lot fell on Skuylkill Side and is No. 16 in the ffront there by the Prints, the Proprietary's original Warrant is not to be found but a Copy of it in one of the Books in the Surveyor's Office (wrote as E. Pennington informs in Thomas Jenner's Hand, in which Warrant are the following Words): ("At the Request of William Powell, Purchaser of 1,250 Acres, that I would grant him to take up his Lots in the City both in the ffront on Delaware and in the High Street these are to.") The lot on which the said Warrant is executed seem to be Part of No. 38 in the Print, viz't: that Part of the said Lot on which Henry Maddock is placed and the said Maddock has taken up his Lot in another Place, so that there seems none wronged by it. All which being duly considered specially the Governor's special Warrant and that the man paid the full Value for it and has built and improved it, and if disappointed would be ruined, having a ffamily of Children, 'tis therefore ordered that a Patent be granted, provided it shall not be made a presedent.

Thomas Parsons, first Purchaser, producing Deeds of Lease and Release dated 23d and 24 of May, 1682, from the Proprietary to himself and his Brother Richard Parsons for one thousand Acres of Land, one Moiety of which he has taken up and has a Warrant for the Remainder, the Liberty Land to be deducted. He requests a Warrant to take up the same.

In the List of the first Purchasers, Thomas and Richard Parsons have but 500 Acres in the whole, and the above mentioned Deeds are all rased as often as the Words (one thousand) occurs and also the Sum or Consideration Money, both in the Deed and Receipt, But the said Thomas producing several good Arguments that the said Rasures were made before and not after signing, and the Proprietary himself (who was well acquainted with the Purchase and had the Deeds in his keeping at Worminghurst 'till his last coming away) having under his Hand and with his Knowledge signed Warrants for the Woodland, 'Tis upon the whole thought reasonable that it should be Ordered that a Warrant be granted to the said Thomas for twenty Acres of Liberty Land, his Lott falling on Skuylkill Side.

Richard Parsons, by Deed under his Hand and Seal, dated 29th June, 1685, released and transferred all his Right in the said purchase, therein called a thousand Acres.

David Lloyd and Isaac Norris, Executors of the last Will of Thomas Lloyd, having by Petition remonstrated to the Proprietary several Hardships they lye under in respect to the said Thomas's Estate and among other Things, particularly requesting that there might be granted to them one thousand Acres of Land in the Province in lieu of the like Quantity which belong to the Testator upon Indian River in Sussex, lately entered upon by the Mary Landers.

In answer to which the Proprietary in his own Hand on the other Side wrote the following Words: ("I allow that the thousand Acres may be granted elsewhere in lieu of that upon Indian River, and thereupon the said Executors request a Warrant to take up the same in the County of Philadelphia or Chester.

Ordered that a Warrant be accordingly drawn and a Patent thereupon when required.

John Ffurnese, of Philadelphia, Barber, producing a Certificate under the Hands of Samuel Carpenter, dated 8ber, 13th, 1701, and Joseph Ffisher That Robert Turner, late of Philadelphia, deceased, transported Servants by Indenture, Henry Ffurnis, John Ffurnis, Mary Ffurnis, Sarah Ffurnis, Rachel Ffurnis, Joseph Ffurnis and Daniel Ffurnis from the Port of Dublin to this Province of Pennsylvania, in the Ship called the Lyon of Liverpool, John Crumpton, Mas'r, and were landed at Philadelphia aforesaid 8th 8 Mo., 1683, for which said

Servants and in their Right purchased of them by the said John Ffurnes, he requests to take up their head Land, being in all three hundred and fifty Acres at a Halfpenny, Sterling, per Acre.

Ordered that a Warrant be drawn for the said John Ffurnese to take up thesaid Quantity of Land in the Township, of 6,000 Acres, ordered to be laid by a warr't from the Proprietary for Servants that came in the years 1682-83.

Signed a Warrant for 500 Acres of Land to William Rodney, ordered the 24th, P. M.

Signed a Warrant of Resurvey to William Dyre on 2,150 Acres of Land, ordered the 24th inst., P. M.

Post Meridiem ejusdem Diei.

Signed a Warrant for a thousand Acres to David Lloyd and Isaac Norris, Executors of Thomas Lloyd, ordered this Morning.

Signed a Warrant to Robert Burton for the Resurvey of 400 Acres in Sussex, ordered this Morning.

Signed a Warrant of Survey to Martin Zeal for 50 Acres in Pennsbury Mannor, ordered 24th inst., P. M.

At a Sessions of the Commissioners at Philadelphia the 1st day of 10ber, 1701, A. M.

Present, Edward Shippen, Thomas Story, Griffith Owen, James Logan.

John Walker, present Husband of Sarah, formerly wife of Thomas Langston, produces a Return of Survey, signed Thomas Holme, for a ffront Lot of 45 ffoot, bounded North with Robert Taylor, Southward (then) with a vacant Lot laid out to Richard Davis, first purchaser, 14th 8th Mo., 1692, in pursuance of two Warrants, one from the Proprietary dated 29th 1st Mo., 1684, for 25 foot and the other from the Commissioners dated 11th 4th Mo., 1692, for what Lots were yet unlaid out to Richard Davis in Right of his Purchase of 5,000 Acres.

Also a Deed from Jerem. Powel, dated 7th 7th Mo, 1697, conveying the said 45 ffoot to Thomas Langston, which Deed recites that the Attornies of the said Richard Davies had by a Deed duly executed bearing Date 16th 6 Mo., 1692, conveyed the Premises to him, the said . . . . . Thomas Langston sold it to William Southby and obliged himself to make a Title, in order to which the said John Walker requests a Patent of Confirmation.

The Deeds for the whole 5,000 Acres were to Davis, but Rowland and Ellis and   Owen, with some others, were joint Purchasers, and had Deeds of Partition signed by Davis from the other great Deeds for the whole 5,000. These under Purchasers, at least several of them, have had their Lots, so that this ought to be inquired into, but the Surveyor General himself having signed this,

Ordered that a Patent be granted.

John Barnes having produced into the Secretary's office 15th 1st Mo., 1700-1, a Return of Survey under R. Longshore's Hand dated 12th 11th Mo., 1688, for 242 Acres laid out 1st 12 Mo., 1685, in Pursuance of a Warrant from the Proprietary dated 29th 3d Mo., 1684, granted to himself in part of his Purchase of 500 Acres, and desiring a Confirmation, had a Warrant of Resurvey, dated 3d 2d Mo., 1701, upon the said 242 Acres, which being executed it was found to contain 281 Acres, that is 39 Acres above Measure out of which allowance being made for Roads, Everard Bolton to whom John Barnes has bargained the same at £14, P. C't desires to purchase the said Overplus.

Ordered that a Patent be drawn to John Barnes for the whole Land, Everard Bolton paying three Pounds for the odd Acres.

Signed a Warrant to Thomas Parsons for 20 Acres Lib. Land, ordered 26th ulto.

Post meridiem.

William Garret, of Chester County, having several times made application to the Proprietary (as the Secretary Remembers) for a Confirmation of a Tract of Land laid out to him in Right of John Love, purchase within the Bounds of the Welch Tract, and being at last referr'd by the Proprietary to his present Commissioners, they thought it necessary to have that whole affair between the Welch and the English of Chester first considered, and being discoursed, 'tis Ordered that some of the principal Men of the Welch be spoke to and desired to appoint Deputies with full power to manage that Affair before this Board, and that in order thereunto they first prepare an exact acco't of what Number of Acres the Welch, for whom that Tract was designed, have a Right to by their original Purchase and how much thereof is laid out and to whom, also who is yet deficient and that the Account of the Lands laid out be by Estimation unless there be a suspicion of Deficiency, in which Cases that a Resurvey be made.

John Dinzy, of Philadelphia, producing a Warrant under Wm. Markham and S. Carpt's Hand for a Lot in Strawberry Alley, dated the 4th 4th Mo., 1690, to be at the same Rent with others granted there.

The Lot he affirms was accordingly at that Time laid out

and fenced in. John Dinzy, by Deed dated 7th 10ber, 1697, sold his Right in the said Lot for £9 to Thomas Pritchard, whose Son Mathew, his Heir or Executor, by Deed dated 10th 2d Month, 1700, sold it with a House built thereon about 2 Years agoe to Christopher Blackburne, who request a Confirmation of it to himself.

Ordered that seeing there is no regular Return for Certificate of the Survey to be produced a Warrant be granted for the Survey or Resurvey of the said Lot, of the same Breadth and Length with the Rest and a Patent upon the Return at the yearly Rent of three shillings Sterling p. Annum, the usual Rent there.

The Commissioners of Property having by their Warrant dated 15th 12th Month, 1689-90, granted to John Day, first Purchaser of 1,250 Acres, 33 ffoot of the Bank of Philadelphia, over against or a little below his Lot of 25 ffoot in the Front Street, on which a Survey was made the same Day of the Date of the Warrant and returned the 15th 11th Mo., 1690, into the Secretary's Office, as by Copy of the said Return under the Surveyor General's Hand appears, The Executors of the said Day, viz't: John Parsons and his Relict, Han'ah Day, by Deed Dated 5th 7ber, 1698, conveyed the said Lott to Joshua Tittery, who requests a Patent thereupon.

Ordered that a Patent be accordingly granted according to the said Return at the usual Quit Rent and Terms.

Thomas Harley, Esqr., of London, having purchased of the Proprietary 5,000 Acres of land in this Province, as P. deeds of Lease and Release bearing Date 3d and 4th of July, 1682, which said 5,000 Acres the said T. Harley, by Deed Poll dated 15th Aug't, 1699, conveyed to Thomas Ffairman, The said Thomas Ffairman, by Deed dated 1st Day of 10ber, 1701 (viz. this Inst.), sold 2,500 Acres; one Moiety of the said Quantity to John Morris, who requests Warrants to take up the same in one Tract, designing to settle it all forthwith with some of his ffriends expected from Wales.

To which objection being made that the Proprietary would never grant above 500 Acres to any one person and no faster than it could be improved.

But the said Morris making it appear that his only Design was to have a sufficient Tract together for the accomodation of such whose only Inducement would be to have the Society of Neighbourhood.

Ordered therefore that in consideration of the Premises he shall have five several Warrants for 500 Acres, each to be settled within two Years after the Date of Survey, otherwise the Survey to be void, which is to be expressed in each Warrant.

Richard Cantrill, Brickmaker, requesting to take up for the carrying on of his Trade three Acres of Land within the Bounds of the City between the 6th and 7th, or 5th and 6th Streets from Delaware, on the Southernmost End and upon the furthest Street of the City or thereabouts, where the best Clay is, for 21 Years, at a certain Rent p. Year.

Ordered upon Agreement with the said Richard that he shall have the Quantity desired at the Yearly Rent of 40s P. Annum for the whole for the said Term of 21 Years Upon these Conditions:

That the said Richard shall build a Brick House of a Story and a Half high, thirty foot long and eighteen ffoot wide, the first story to be a brick and a half thick and the next one Brick, that he shall fence in the whole Ground and so leave it, with an Orchard of at least eighty good Apple Trees standing, and level all the pitts he diggs his brick, without any Water standing in the same, and the House, Orchard and Fences to be left in good Repair, to be delivered up at the Expiration of the said Term, and that accordingly a Warrant be forthwith granted for laying out the same.

To Thomas Parsons for 20 Acres Lib. Land.

At a Sessions of the Commissioners at Philadelphia the 3d Day of the 10th Month, A. M.

Present, Edward Shippen. Griffith Owen, Thomas Story, James Logan.

The Proprietary by Lease and Release dated 2d and 3d March, 1682 (it must be 1681-2), granted three thousand Acres of Land in the Province to Lewis David.

Lewis David, by Indenture dated 11th, idim, granted 1,000 Acres thereof to Henry Lewis.

Henry, Son and Heir of the said Henry Lewis, by Deed Poll dated 11th Mo., 1693-4, conveyed his Right to 20 Acres of Liberty Land app't to the said 1,000 Acres to Jonathan Ducket Who, by Deed Dated 5th 10ber, 1694, sold his Right to the said 20 Acres to John Ball.

John Rowland, first Purchaser of 1,350 Acres of Land by Deed dated 12 1st Mo., 1689, granted his Right to 25 Acres of Lib'ty Land appurtenant to his said Purchase to Jonathan Ducket aforesaid, and the said Ducket by the same Deed with the afores'd twenty Acres sold his Right to the said twenty five Acres of Liberty Land to the said John Ball, who Requests a Warrant to take up the said two Parcels in one.

The Right under Lewis David's Purchase appears clear, But by a Warrant in the Surveyor's Office it appears that

John Rowland had sold his Liberty Land to Charles Brigham, who took out the said Warrant for the same, dated 19th 5 Mo., 1684, so that no Warrant can be granted for that 'till John Ball give further Satisfaction concerning it to this Board. 'Tis therefore Ordered that the said John have a Warrant granted for the first 20 Acres, but that the other be deferred for the reasons Aforesaid.

The Proprietary by Lease and Release dated 18th and 19th 6 Mo., 1681, granted to John Day 1,250 Acres of Land in this Province; in Part of which the Surveyor General by Warrant dated 7th 8th Mo., 1682, ordered 500 Acres to be laid out to the said John Day, together with other Land to John Mason. But the Land in that Place where the said Warrant was to be executed falling short, there fell only 210 Acres to the said Day's Share.

John Day, by his last Will and Testament, dated   , devised the said 210 Acres to Han'ah, his Wife, making the said Han'ah and John Parsons his joint Executors, who by Deed dated 4th 5 Mo., 1696, sold the same to David Haverd, deceased, giving Bond to make the said David a Title thereto.

David Haverd dying intestate, left his Son John Heir to the said Land, to whom Mary, his Mother, Relict of the said David, together with the said Hannah, Relict of John Day, and now Wife to James Atkinson, requested it may be confirmed by Patent.

Ordered that a Patent be accordingly granted for the same in Case they produce a regular Return of Survey or Resurvey thereon, which they are to do.

The Proprietary by Lease and Release dated 13th and 14th April, 1683 (by a Print Signature), granted to Sypke Aukes, of Ffriesland, 300 Acres of Land under 1 Sh'l. Sterling p. 100 Acres p. Annum.

By a Deed dated 14 April, 1683, the said Sypke Aukes purchased off the said Quit Rent from 3s Sterling to 3d and ⅔ of a penny Sterling per Annum for the whole.

Sypke Aukes by Deed dated 5th 10th Mo., 1687, sold all his Right in the said 300 Acres to Renier Jansen, his Heirs and Assigns forever.

Renier Jansen by Deed dated 16th 6th Month, 1700, granted the said Land to Paul Woolf, his Heirs, who requests a Warrant to take up the same.

Ordered that a Warrant be forthwith granted to the said Paul Woolf according to the common fform, to be seated in 18 Mo's after Survey and a Patent on the Return.

John Carver having purchased of the Proprietary by Deeds of Lease and Release 500 Acres of Land (formerly produced) had the same laid out in the Year 1682, or thereabouts, upon Potquessing Creek, in the County of Philadelphia, which not being duly confirmed to him, he obtained of the Prop'ry a Warrant of Resurvey dated 15th 6 Mo., 1700, by Vertue of which the said Tract was resurveyed by Order of the Surveyor Gen'l 15th 5th Mo., 1701, and returned into the Secretary's Office 11th 6 Mo., 1701, for 590 a's being found to contain so much.

William Hibbs having purchased of Thomas Ffairman a Tract of Land contiguous to the above; there has been for some Time past a Contest between him and the said John Carver and his Brother William Carver about a Corner Post which Hibbs complains has been taken away and thereby the Bounds altered, upon which the said W. Hibbs put a Caveat into the Secretary's Office against the Confirmation of Carver's Land by Patent, and thereupon the said Patent was stopt and after some Debates this Day assigned for a Hearing of both Parties by a Summons signed by the Secretary accord'g to which they appeared.

William Hibbs being demanded the Reason of his Caveat and his Objections gave them to this Board, which being considered it was resolved that seeing the Proprietary's Warrant of Resurvey ordered Carver's Land to be Resurveyed according to the old Bounds and first Lines of Survey, which the Surveyor General being present affirmed he had executed to the utmost of his Power, being present himself at the Survey; it was to be presumed the Lines as returned were the true ones, unles it could be made appear to the contrary, which William Hibbs was not sufficiently able to do.

Yet for a further Trial of the Case it was proposed to the said Hibbs to take out a Warrant of Resurvey on his Land also, and the Neighbourhood being met at the Execution thereof the Surveyor General, who by the said Warrants would be obliged to return the true Lines between them, both would be able fully to determine the Difference by his Return being regularly made and by Authority.

But the said Hibbs declining to join with this Proposal, the only Expedient to satisfy him that could be thought of, and J. Carver hav'g proceeded regularly in order to a Determination, It is Ordered that J. Carver's Patent be no longer delayed but be granted forthwith according to the Return of Resurvey, and that he pay 10s per Acre for the Overplus, according to Agreement with the Proprietary, which was then reputed 60 Acres, and for 8 Acres more sold Rich. Waln.

John Carver having by Deed dated 30th 2d Mo., 1700, sold to N. Waln 8 Acres of Liberty Land appurtenant to his above said purchase, Requests a warr't to take up the same.

Ordered that a Warrant be accordingly granted, it being uncertain whether Carver's Land was laid out for 492 or 500 ac's, that it be reputed 492 A's, and that J. Carver pay for those 8 Acres as Overplus.

———

At a Sessions of the Commissioners at Philadelphia the 8th Day of the 10th month, 1701.

Present, Edward Shippen, Griffith Owen, Thomas Story, James Logan.

Peter Taylor, with his Brother William Taylor, purchased of the Proprietary by Lease and Release dated 3d 1 Mo., 1681, 1,250 Acres of Land between them, viz: each 625 Acres, of which there was layed out by the Surveyor Gen'ls Order before the Proprietary's arrival 350 acres to Peter, and the same Quantity to William, also 10 Acres of Liberty Land to each, so that there is 265 Acres remain'g due to Peter of his Share, who Requests a Warrant to take up the same.

Ordered that a Warrant be accordingly granted to be seated within two Years after Survey, vid off: Prop'y 27th 12 Mo., 1700.

Thomas Metcalf produces a Return of Survey under the Hand of Henry Hollingsworth, dated 19th 1 Mo., 1689-90, for 200 Acres of Land laid out by him by Vertue of a Warrant from James Bradshaw (as there recited,) bearing Date the 15th 1st Month, 1689-90, to John Dunn, Renter, 19th 1st Mo., 1689.

John Dunn, by Assignm't on the Back of the said Return, dated 12th 8ber, 1691, made over the said Tract to Anthony and William Sharp.

Anthony Sharpe deceasing without Issue, by his last Will, as is affirmed, bequeathed his Share of the said Land to William, his Brother, the Survivor William Sharp, by Deed dated 24th March, 1696, sold and conveyed the said whole 200 Acres to Thomas Metcalf, who requests a Patent on the said Return.

Ordered that a Patent be forthwith granted, he giving Bond in £100 to suffer a Resurvey at any Time within seven Years, at two Bushels p. 100.

(Rent paid to E. Gibbs 25th Mar., 1696, two bush'ls; to ditto 8th 4th Mo., 1698, by Alph. Hick, 4½ Bushels due; to the 1st Month next, 37 bush's and ½.)

Gabriel Beans, of the County of Bucks, produces Deeds of Lease and Release and a Receipt for the Consideration Money, dated 24th and 25th May, 1683 (the Proprietary's Name printed), for 450 Acres of Land sold to William Caras, who coming over into this Province from Liverpool in the Ship Britania, Anno

1699, deceased and left the Care of his only Son, Thomas Caras, to the said Gabriel, who in his Behalf requests a Warrant to take up the said Land for said Thomas, who is now Apprenticed in Town.

Ordered that a Warrant be accordingly granted for the said 450 Acres to Thomas Caras, to be seated in two Years after Survey.

John Guest, of Philadelphia, Esqr., claiming 200 Acres of Land in the County of Newc. by a Purchase made by his Mother-in-Law, Sarah Welch, of Jonas Askain, as by Deed dated 4th Dec'r, 1689, contiguous to which (as he informs) he has lately purchased 200 Acres more and being desirous to make up the whole 500 Acres Requests a Warrant to take up 100 Acres joining on the last mentioned Parcel upon old Rent, under such other reasonable Terms as the Commissioners shall think fit.

Ordered that a Warrant be accordingly granted to the said John Guest to take up 100 Acres at 1 Bushel of Wheat p. Ann. he paying such a ffine over and above as Land is generally sold for in the Neighbourhood.

The Proprietary by Deeds of Lease and Release dated the 19th and 20th Jan'ry, 1681, Sold to John Chambers 500 Acres of Land, who coming over into this Province had a warrant from the Commissioners dated 28th 4 Mo., 1686, for 490 Acres, which was executed.

John Chambers dying, his sole Daughter Elizabeth, by a Deed Dated 30th 8th Mo., 1686, sold all her Right in the same to Benj. Chambers, after which a Return of the said Warrant was made by Tho. Holme, dated 21st 2d Mo., '88.

Benjamin Chambers and the said Elizabeth (now Clemson) by Deed Poll dated 29th 4th Mo., 1699, conveyed all the said 490 Acres to Jonath. Hayes.

The Proprietary by Lease and Release dated 24 and 25 Jan'ry, 1681, recorded in the Rolls Office, Book A, Vol. 1, fol. 220, sold to Benj. Chambers 1,000 Acres, in part of which there was laid out on the 14th 2d Mo., 1688, by Vertue of a Warrant from the Commissoners bearing date 7th 2d Mo., 1688, to said Benjamin 610 Acres adjoining to the former, making the whole 1,100 Acres.

B. Chambers, by Deed dated 29th 4 Mo., 1699, sold the said 610 Acres to Jonathan Hayes, who stands possessed of the whole 1,100 Acres afores'd.

This Land being laid out in Plymouth Township or adjoining, or adjoyning to it on Skuylkill over against the Barbadoes Island on the Land reputed Wm. Penn Junior's Manor, the Proprietary scrupled to confirm the same to the Claimers, but

MINUTE BOOK "G." 209

Jona. Hayes soliciting the same before the Govern'rs Embarquem't, obtained a Paper all in his own Hand in the following Words:

26th 8ber, 1701.

"Let Benjamin Chambers and Jonathan Hayes be satisfied with 1,100 Acres in lieu of that surveyed on Skuylkill out of my Son's Manor, and if the Quantity cannot be had to their Satisfaction, that the s'd 1,100 Acres continue as surveyed, tho' I much desire it might be otherwise."

WM. PENN.

To the Commissioners.

Jonathan Hayes, who is invested with the whole Right of the said 1,100 Acres, requests a Confirmation of the said Land, remonstrating that he despairs of finding any in the Province besides that will be satisfactory to him in lieu thereof.

'Tis proposed to the said Jonathan notwithstanding that seeing the Prop'ry shewed his desire by that Paper of having other Land found for him in lieu of that already surveyed, the Commissoners would be deficient of their Duty if they should not endeavour it, and therefore Tho. Ffairman is ordered to shew him some which he acquiesces to go and view, and is to report his Mind at another Sessions.

The Proprietary by Lease and Release dated 22d 1 Mo., 1691, sold to Jos. Powel 250 Acres, to whom there was laid out in Part thereof 125 Acres in Providence, in the County of Chester, by a Warrant from the Surveyor Gen'l, dated the 9th 7th Month, 1682.

Esther Powel, sole Ex'rix, and Hannah and Mary Powel, Heirs of the said Joseph Powel, by Deed dated 4th 2d Mo., 1700, conveyed the said 125 Acres to Joseph Sharpless. Vid. Court of Inq'ry Com. Chester, Provide T. Joseph Sharpless (joins on Jno. Sharpless.)

The Proprietary, by Patent under his Hand and Prov. Seal, dated 28th 5 Mo., 1684, Confirmed to John Sharpless, purchaser, 300 Acres in Middletown, County of Chester.

Jane Sharpless, Widow, Adm'r'x, and John Sharpless, Heir of the said John Sharpless, deceased, by Deed dated 9th 4 Mo., 1696, conveyed the said 300 Acres to Joseph Sharpless. Vid. Rep't Com'rs Inq'ry, Chest'r, Middletown, Jos. Sharpless (it joins on Blake's Land.)

Joseph Sharpless requests a Resurvey on both the said Tracts in order to a Patent.

Ordered that a Warrant of Resurvey be accordingly granted and a Patent on the Return.

John Richardson, of Christina Hundred, Com. N. C., informing that there is a small Parcel of vacant Land between the

14—VOL. XIX.

Head Lines of Ffernhook and the Land of John Hussey and the Widow Haige, near Christina Creek, on the South Side adjoining on his Son John's Land, Requests a Warrant to take up the same to pay it's present Value.

Ordered that a Warrant be granted to John Richardson, jun'r, to take up 100 Acres of Land in the said Place at a Bush'l of Wheat P. ann., and to pay the Value over and above for a ffine.

William Paxon purchased of Henry Comley 100 Acres of Land in Middle Township, in Bucks, as by Articles and Bond, dated 1st 12 mo., 1695-6, who bought it of Tho. Marl, as by Deed dated 6th 1 mo., 1683, to whom it was laid out upon Rent by the Propr'y's Warrant jointly, with 300 Acres more to several other Persons, dated 24th 11 Mo., 1682, But the said Tho. Marl bo't off the Rent of the Prop'ry for £5, as by a Mem'dum under Philip Lehnmain's Hand Appears, dated 20 12 Mo., 1683, produced to the Secret'ry as by a former Minute of his Office appears.

The said Will m also purchased of John Duncan and Wm. Bryan 170 Acres as by Articles and Bond dat. 31 3 Mo., 1697, from Duncan, and 2 16 Mo., 1697, from Bryan, the whole of which was first laid out to the said Bryan by a Warr't from the Prop'ry (which cannot be produced) on Rent, his Name however is in the Map and 'tis credibly affirmed by his Neighbours. On these two Tracts the said Wm. Paxon took out a Warrant of Resurvey from the Proprietary dated 1st 12 Mo., 1700, which being executed 17th 2d Mo., 1701, there was found in both the said Tracts 330 Acres and 93 Perches by the Survey'r's Return dated 23d 5 Mo., 1701, for which he requests a Patent and to buy off the Rent.

Ordered that a Patent be granted for the whole said 330 Acres, he paying for the Overplus and 20 Year's purchased for the Rents.

The two Tracts ought to contain but 270 Acres, on which there being allowed according to Law, 10 P. C't, that is 27 Acres there is of Overplus, 33 Acres for which he has to pay 10£. and for the Rents 11£., P. C't, i. e. 18£. 14 s. at the signing of the Patent.

Signed Thomas Metcalf's Patent for 200 Acres in the County of N. Castle, ordered this Morning, on which he has given Bond to admit a Resurvey in seven Years at 2 Bush'ls of Wheat P. C. from the Date of Survey.

Signed 5 Warrants for 500 Acres each to John Morris, ord'd 1st Inst't, to be seated within two Years.

Joseph Wilcox, Heir to his ffather, Barnabas Wilcox's Estate, in this Province, informs this Board that his said ffather and himself coming into this Province about the same Time the Prop'ry first did in order to view the Encouragem'ts of it, his ffather proposed to purchase of the Prop'ry 800 Acres of Land, but the Prop'ry advised him to buy a whole thousand, promising him for an Inducem't the priviledge of a first Purchaser, that is 20 ffoot for a Lott in the ffront Street and proportionable in the High Street, to which Barnabas agreed, and thereupon went over with his Son Joseph to Bristol to bring over his ffamily, having first seen his Lots surveyed to him in the said Streets and in convenient Places, but upon his Return the next Year found the Lotts Surveyed to him before his Departure laid out to and in the Possession of others who had begun to improve them, Upon which making Application to the Proprietary for Redress, then making beginnings of a Settlement at Skuylkill, the Proprietary advised him to rest satisfied 'till his Return from England (being then shortly bound thither), which he designed should be speedy, promising Lotts to better Advantage on the said River where he intended the chief Settlement of the City should be. But the Proprietary not returning (as intended) for 15 Years, they had all that Time rece'd no manner of satisfaction. Sometime after the Proprietary's Return, Joseph making Application to him for Redress by a Letter deliv'd by Tho. Story in which he had recited so many Particulars as brought the whole Matter to the Prop'ry's Rememb'nce he obtained a Warrant and Patent for 50 ffoot on the 2d Street, adjoining on the Lot where he now lives on the Southermost Side thereof. But the Proprietary having promised upon his first Applications that he would rather, over than under, doe in compensation for his ffather's Disappointm'ts, and Joseph thinking the said Lott to be in no wise an Equivalent to the two other first laid out to them, he renewed his Suit to the Proprietary by a Second Letter acknowledg'd his ffavour in the said Grant and further requesting that he would yet still consider his promises, Exhibiting that he would not insist on them to the Utmost nor above one-half, but that if the Prop'ry would grant him fifty foot to be added to the fifty ffoot he now holds at the North End of Delaw. ffront Street used by him for a Rope Walk to extent to the 2d Street, at the common Rent of a ffront Lot in the City and remitt him his part in the last Tax which amounted to something above £4; he would be satisfied therewith and cease all further Demands.

To this the Prop'ry demurr'd, being unwilling to part with any Lots in the said Place being Land laid out for Lots for the Use of his own ffamily, and Joseph by a 3d Letter making further Application he was referred to the Commissioners and his Requests given in Charge to the Secret'ry the Morning before he left Philadelphia, Upon all which he applies here that his said Requests may be granted.

Resolved that seeing the Proprietary could not think w't he demanded proper to be granted forthwith if at all, 'tis fit this Board should consider of it more fully than Time will now permit, and endeavour by saving the said ffront to the Proprietary, to find some other Way of compensation if it may be effected, and 'tis referred to further Consideration.

At a Sessions of the Commissioners at Philadelphia, 10th 10ber, 1701.

Present, Edward Shippen, Griffith Owen, Thomas Story, James Logan.

Philip England having been settled (at the first founding of this City) by the Prop'ry at the End of the High Street on the River Skuylkill, in order to keep a fferry over the said River, for an Encouragem't to which the Proprietary had granted him some Acres Land on   , but not being sufficiently settled, Wm. Markham (because the other Commissioners refused to act therein), by Indenture of Lease bearing Date 30th Aug't, 1693, demised to the said Phillip the said fferry for 10 Years, together with eleven Acres of Land adjoining thereto, bounded to the North Eastward (as in the Lease) with a small Run, and vacant Land to the North Westward, with the River Shuylkill, to the South Westward with Wm. Bolding's Lott, and to the South Eastward with Skuylkill ffront Street, as also twelve Acres of Land on the West Side of Skuylkill formerly laid out to the said Philip England as Land to the said fferry belonging and the Priviledge of an Ordinary for all which the said Philip was to pay the yearly Rent of £7.

But soon after other fferries being set up over the said River, and Philip being thereby deprived of the Benefit of his said Lease, the Comm'rs, upon Application made to them by him at a Meeting held at Philadelph'a, 29th 7 Mo., 1694, Present, Robert Turner, Tho. Holme, Jno. Goodson, Samuel Carpenter and Ffrancis Rawles, remitted the aforesaid Rent both for the Time past and to come, except he could have the proposed Benefit of the fferry or 'till the Prop'ry's Pleasure should be further known, as appears by a Minute of the said Commissioners, sign'd by John Wilkinson, Clerk.

Upon the Proprietary's last Arrival, Philip frequently applying to have that Business settled, after great Importunities, at last obtained an Answer from the Prop'ry to a Request of his in the following Words in the Govern'rs own Hand: ("I allow thee the Land thou hadst in Lease at Skuylkill for 31 thirtyone Years at such Rent as the Commissioners of Property shall allow. Wm. Penn.")

Upon which 'tis ordered that a Lease be granted for the said Quantity of Land and Time to the said Philip, his Ex'ors, Adm'ors and Assigns, at the yearly Rent of 20s, without other Priviledge, and all former Grants to be void.

The Proprietary by Lease and Release, dated 21 and 22 April, 1682, sold to Sarah Woolman 250 Acres.

The said Sarah, by her Letter under Hand and Seal, dated 24th Ffeb'ry, 1686, constituted Will'm Carter, of Philadelphia, her Attorney to sell and dispose of the said Land for her Use.

The said William produces a Draught under T. Ffairman's Hand of 246 Acres situate on a Branch of Neshamineh, adjoining on Samuel Carpenter's Land, in which he informs the Warr't is not by which it was laid out, but that it was executed 26 6 Mo., 1684.

Requests a Patent or Resurvey on the said Land.

Ordered that a further Inquiry be made whether there ever was a Warr't granted for S. Woolman's Land, and that the Draught be further considered.

William Beaks purchased of the Prop'ry, in England, 1,000 Acres of Land in this Province by Deeds of Lease and Release (dated as in Jenner's Deed hereafter mentioned is recited), 26th and 27th July, 1681, In right of which Purchase the said William obtained from the Prop'ry a Warr't dated 22d 5 Mo., 1684, for laying out his Lots in the City, and Proportion of Land within the Liberties.

In the printed Draught of the City, Wm. Beaks' Lott fall on Skuylkill side, But there is produced a Return of the said Warrant under T. Holme's Hand dated 5th 10th Month, 1692, for 20 ffoot in the ffront of Delaw., bounded Northward with Th. Callowhill, and Southw'd, ('tis said) which vacant Lots being above Griffith Jones' about 200 ffeet above the High Street, survey'd unto Wm. Beaks, 28 9th Mo., 1691.

William Beaks (as is recited in Jenner's following Deed), by a Deed dated 16th Aug't, 1697, and acknowledged in Court at Philadelphia 10th Sept'r, 1697, conveyed his Liberty Land and Lotts to Thomas Jenner.

The said Jenner by Indenture, dated 1st 10br, 1697, (wrote and witnessed by Pat. Robinson), for the Consideration of forty Pounds, sold the said ffront Lot to James Stanfield, his Heirs for ever.

James Stanfield, by his last Will and Testament, duly proved, bearing Date 1st 7br, 1699, appointed his Brother, Ffrancis Chads, of Chester, Com., in this Province, Ex'or thereof, with a special Power to sell, dispose of and alien in ffee or otherwise, all his Lands, Lotts, and convey the same as he shall think fitt for the Payment of his Legacies and Bequests.

Ffrancis Chads, for the said purpose, having sold the said Lot to   , requests a Patent on the aforementioned Return in order to make a Title for the Performance of, which William Beaks' Lotts falling on Schuylkill Side, in the Print occasions a Demur, and Th. Jenner being concerned, encreases it.

But T. Holme's Return, signed by him in 1692, seems to clear Jenner; 'Tis located on a Vacancy found between Griff. Jones and Tho. Callowhill, whose Lotts in the Print join, so that none seems wrong'd by it.

Referred, however, to further Consideration, and Wm. Beaks' Deed to Jenner, ordered to be produced.

Signed a Warr't for 3 acres to R'd Cantrill, order'd the first Inst't.

Signed a Warr't to John Richardson, jun'r, for about 100 Acres vacant Land near Christina, ordered the 8th inst't.

Signed a Patent to Hugh Roberts for 100 Acres of Lib'ty Land upon the Indian Creek and the Mill Creek near Adam Rhode's Land, laid out by Vertue of the Prop'ry's Warr't, dated 8th 11th Mo., 1701, surveyed 26 4 Mo., 1701, to Hugh Roberts in Right of Richard Thomas, first Purchaser of 5,000 Acres, returned 4th 7th Mo., 1701, Ordered by the Comm'rs 24th 9br, 1701.

Signed a Patent to John Lee for 136 Acres and 152 Perches the 3 inst't. Ordered 24th 9th last, the Overplus not fully agreed.

Signed John Barnes' Patent the 3d inst't, for 281 Acres and 52 Perches in the County of Philadelphia, laid out to s'd Barnes 1st 12 Mo., 1685, in pursuance of a Warr't from the Prop'ry, dated 29th 3 Mo., '84, for 242 Ac es in Part of his original Purchase of 500 Acres, resurveyed 12th 3 Mo., 1701, in Pursuance of the Prop'ry's Warrant, dated 3d 2 Mo., 1701, and found to contain as aforesaid, Now sold to Everard Bolton, who agrees to pay £3 for the Overplus (being 15 Acres).

Signed a Patent to John Carver for 590 Acres, ordered the 3d Inst't.

Signed a Patent to Joshua Titterry for a Bank Lot, Ordered the 1st inst't.

Signed a Patent to Wm. Ffisher, ordered 26th Ult., for a Lott.

Signed a Warr't to Paul Wolf for 300 Acres, ordered the 3d Inst.

MINUTE BOOK "G." 215

At a Sessions of the Commissioners at Philadelphia, 15th 10b'r, 1701.

Present, Edward Shippen, Griffith Owen, Thomas Story, James Logan.

The Prop'ry having, by Deeds of Lease and Release dated 25th and 26th 7br., 1681, sold to Henry Waddy 750 Acres of Land, Job. Goodson for his ffather, John Goodson, who, with Jos. Paul, administ'rs on said Waddy's Estate, in this Province, produces a Warrant from the Proprietary dated 12th 8br., 1683, for a Lot in the Streets proportionable to that Purchase, and another dated 14th 5 Mo, 1684, for 12 Acres of Lib'ty Land Appurten't to the said Purchase and a Return

Also a Return dated 1st 3 Mo., 1691, for 188 Acres laid out by Vertue of a Warrant from the Proprietary dat. 14th 5 Mo., 1684, surveyed 20th 8 Mo., 1685, in the County of Bucks, adjoining to Christopher Davis and Sam'l Carpenter.

Requests a resurvey on the sa'd 188 Acres, also a Warr't of another Lot in the 2d Street.

Ordered that a Warrant be granted for the Resurvey. His Lot is No. 64, the last in the Second Street in the Draught.

Ordered a Warrant for the Same.

The Proprietary, by Deeds of Lease and Release, dat. 19th and 20th of Mar., 1682, (by his Agent in England) sold to Wm. Bennet 1,000 Acres of Land (the Gov'rs Name is printed in the Lease, Release and Receipt), In right of which Ezra Crosdale produces a Return of Survey of 400 Acr's, laid out by Israel Taylor in Newtown, Bucks, adjoining on Christo. Taylor and Rob't Burges on which he requests a Resurvey.

Ordered a Warrant forthwith.

Ezra's Right is to be produced with the Return of Resurvey.

There is lately laid out to Ann and Sarah Bennet 400 Acres more in Right of this Purchase.

The Proprietary, by Lease and Release, dated 26th and 27th 7 br., 1681, sold to Daniel Smith, of Marlborow, 500 Acres and by like Deeds, dated 17th and 18th Mar. 1681, sold to said Smith 2,000 Acres more, and by like Deeds dated 11th and 12th 8br., '81, sold to Thomas Hatt 500 Acres, which 500 Acres the said D. Smith, by Deed dated 17th April, 1686, purchased of said Hatt. See Dan'l Smith's Purchases at large, Pa., 48, and in right of the said Daniel's own Purchase of 2,000 Acr's he obtained a Patent for one thousand of the Comm'rs dated 8th 10 Mo., 1690, situate in the County of Chester, Also (in right of such Lands as he had to take up) a Warr't for one thousand Acres dated 24th 9 Mo., 1686, in Part of which there was surveyed to him 24th 7 mo., 1688, 360 Acres on Brandywine joining on Richard Collet, as by a Return produced dated 9th 2 Mo., 1690, And on Crum Creek in Chest'r, Com., 670 Acres as by.

On which two last Tracts of 360 and 670 Acres, being not yet confirm'd by Patent, Randal Spakeman, present Husband of the said Daniel's Relict and Adm'or on his Estate, requests a resurvey.

Ordered that a Warrant of resurvey be accordingly granted.

The Proprietary having, by Deeds of Lease and Release, dated 24th and 25th of Jan'ry, 1681, sold to Amy Child 500 Acres of Land in this Prov., Charles Read, present Husband of the said Amy, requests a Lot in the City appurtenant and proportionable to the said purchase.

In the printed City Draught her Lott is No. 146 on Delaw., in Mulberry Street, between the 5th and 6th Streets on the North Side, which, upon Inquiry made by him, is disposed of to others.

Ordered that a Warr't be granted for a Lott in some other convenient Place. He demands and expects it in the 2d Street which cannot be had, there being none such undisposed of.

Nathaniel Newlin, of Chester, Com., producing a Return of Survey, signed, Thos. Pierson for 600 Acres of Land surveyed 16th 8br., 1695, in the Manor of Rocklands, (as it now falls) in the County of Chester near Concord Line, by vertue of a Warrant (as is recited), dated 8th 9th Month, '94, from T. Holme, Also a Paper from the Propr'ry, wrote with his own Hand in these Words:

"James Logan,   5th 8br., 1701,   I recommend Nathaniel Newland to thy Regards on my Account about the Land he has in the Manor of Rockland whether he buy or continue to rent it.

"WM. PENN."

Requests a Confirmation of the said Land and in order thereunto a Resurvey

The Rent hitherto paid has been but one Bushel of Wheat p. 100 Acres, But at less than a penny p. Acre or 2 Bush'ls p. 100 it cannot be reckoned, which, if he would buy off, it must be purchased at the common Rate of other Rent Lands when converted into Purchase, viz: £11 p. 100

Ordered that a Warrant of Resurvey be granted, but that it be not confirmed 'till the former Commissioner's Minutes are reviewed or their Warrants be produced.

Joseph Todd, of Warminster, in the County of Bucks, having last Year purchased of the Proprietary 200 Acres of Land in the Township aforesaid, formerly laid out to James Poulter on Penny Acre Rent, but since quitted as under his Hand is made appear for £30 to be paid this present Year, which Land for the greater Certainty he procured David Powel to resurvey, who, in the Acco't of it under his Hand, gives it for 224 Acres.

The s'd Joseph requests a Confirmation of the said Land and is ready to pay the Money.

There is no Trace of a regular Survey appears to ground a Patent on nor any Warrant produced or mentioned to have ever been granted, 'tis therefore thought fitt to propose this and other like Cases to the Surveyor General to consider of some Means to save the Charges of Survey to the People when both the Proprietary or his Comm'rs are well satisfied about the Measure and only want some fform to ground a Patent on, But in the mean Time, 'Tis Ordered that the said Joseph stay no longer for his Patent, and but that it be drawn according to D. Powel's Draught and that he pay 50s for the Overplus over and above the said £30 of which there is allowed 9 Acres for Roads.

The Proprietary, by Deeds of Lease and Release, dated 12 and 13th April, 1682, sold 1,000 Acres of Land to Humphry Killinbeck.

The said Humphry, by Deeds of Lease and Release, dated 12th 7br., 1700, gave all the said 1,000 Acres to his Kinsman, Thomas Wickersham, 500 Acres thereof, and the City Lott to the said Thomas himself, and the other 500 to his four children, 200 to his eldest Son Humphry, and to Thomas, John and Ann, one hundred each, to be conveyed to them when at Age.

In Part of this, the said Thomas hath taken up 500 Acres, the Liberty Land deducted for the whole by a Warrant from the Propr'ry dated 21st 1st Mo., last, located near or towards Brandywine which he appropriates to himself, and requests a Warrant to take up the remaining 500 Acres for his Children.

Ordered that a Warrant be accordingly granted.

Signed a Warrant of Resurvey to Ezra Crosdale, Ordered this Day.

Signed a Warrant of Resurvey to Joseph Sharpless, Ordered 8th Inst't.

Signed a Warr't to Peter Taylor for 265 Acres, Ordered 8th Inst't, dated 10th.

Signed a Warr't of Resurvey to Nathan'l Newlin, Ordered this Day.

Signed a Warr't of Resurvey to Randal Spakeman, Ordered this Day.

Signed a Warr't to Judge Guest for 100 Acres or there'b'ts in N. C., order'd 8th Inst't.

George Pierce coming into this Province about the same Time, the Propr'ry last did grant him a Warrant for 400 Acres of Land unseperated, for which he made no Agreement with the Proprietary but was to give the same Rate with others, which Warrant being executed the   , He produces a Return thereof from the Surveyor General, dated   , on which he requests a Patent and to know the Terms.

Agreed with him at £11 p. 100, and thereupon ordered that a Patent be granted forthwith, he paying £44 as aforesaid.

At a Sessions of the Commissioners at Philadelphia, 17th of the 10th Mo'th, 1701.

Present, Edward Shippen, Griffith Owen, Thomas Story, James Logan.

The Proprietary at his last Departure from Newcastle, having, at the Request of Sam'l Carpenter and others, concerned in the Bank of Philadelphia, offered to sell the Reversions of the Third accruing to him for 20s p. ffoot.

Alice Guest produces a Patent for 24 ffoot of the said Bank dated 3d 3 Mo., 1692, on which she has built, Offers £24 for the Reversion and requests a new Patent.

Ordered that a Patent be granted accordingly.

George Lea having arrived in this Province about twelve Months ago with his Relations, Richard Webb, from Gloucester, in England, requests to take up 200 Acres of Land in the Manor of Rocklands in that Part thereof that falls in the County of Chester, on the South East Side of Nathaniel Newlin's Tract, mentioned the 15th Inst't p. 27, for which he is willing to pay £25 p. 100 Acres upon Agreement, within one Year after the Date of his Warrant, and Nathaniel Newlin offers to be his Security.

Ordered that a Warrant be granted to the said George forthwith for the said Number of 200 Acres as requested, and that it be confirmed to him by Patent upon the Return, the said Nathaniel being Security for the Payment of £50 as afores'd, Mem'd that 100 Acres of this is affirmed to be poor Land.

Nathaniel Newlin also requests to take up 200 Acres on the South West End of his Tract in the Mannor of Rocklands mentioned the 15th Inst't, p. 27, for which he agrees to pay £50 at the Delivery of his Patent.

Ordered that a Warrant be granted according to his Request and a Patent upon the Return, both the said Tracts to pay a shill. sterl., p. 100.

Daniel Ffalkner, the present Agent for the German Purchasers, having obtained a Grant from the Proprietary of 200 Acres of Land in the Liberties of Philadelphia, in Part of 300 Acres appurtenant by their Agreement with the Propr'ry to their Purchase of 15,000 Acres, of which 200 Acres they had obtained, 120 which they sold to John Ball since the Proprietary s Arrival, did further obtain a Warrant for the remaining 80 Acres which the said Daniel, together with Joannes Kelpius and Joannes Jawert, had sold to Robert Nailor, and therefore requested that the Warrant which bore Date the 13th 11 Mo., 1700, should be granted to the said Robert, and be located near Indian Creek adjoining on Geo. Collet in the said Liberties, But this Location being mentioned in the Warrant by an Imposition the Place having been before granted to Hugh Roberts who had a Right to 100 Acres in right of   Purchaser of 5,000 Acres, At the Request of the said Hugh the Proprietary issued an Order under his Hand and Seal, bearing Date the 1st 12 Month, 1700-1, countermanding and vacating the said location, but confirming the Grant of the said 80 Acres in all other Respects, Upon which Robert Nailor recanted his said Bargain, the said Alteration not suiting with his Exigencies; The said Daniel therefore, because the said Warr't was to Rob't Nailor, requests another Warr't from the Comm'rs for the said 80 Acres, to be granted to himself in Right of his Constituents, the said German Purchasers.

Ordered that a Warrant be accordingly granted.

The Propr'ry having, by Deeds of Lease and Release, dated 21 and 22d of the 1 Mo., 1681, sold to Peter Worral 500 Acres of Land, of which the said Peter has taken up only 300, in the County of Chester, he requests a Warrant for the remaining 200, and that it may be granted to Jno. Willis, who this Day has purchased his Right to the same.

Ordered that a Warr't be accordingly granted.

There having been a Difference long depending between Walter Ffaucit and Edw'd Pritchet, both of the County of Chester, about a Tract of Land formerly belonging to Neal Matson in the said County, in Ridly Township, of which the said Walter claims one-half but Edward the whole, and upon a hearing of the Parties the Propr'ry having granted a Warr't of Resurvey, ordering the Tract in Controversy to be divided in equal Shares between them, leaving to each such Parts as they had improved which Warr't has been executed by Isaac Taylor, Surveyor of that County.

Edw'd Pritchet upon the same, enters a Caveat ag'st the granting of a Patent to Walter upon the said Resurvey for reasons he hath to alledge, and requests a Day may be assigned to hear the same before the Comm'rs.

Ordered that this Day 3 Weeks, being the 7th of the 11 Mo., be assigned for the said Purpose and that the Secretary under his Hand give Walter Notice hereof.

Signed a Warr't of Resurvey to Chris. Blackburn on a Lot, Ordered 1st Inst't.

Signed a Warr't to Geo. Lea for 200 Acres, Ordered this Day.

Signed a Warr't to Nath'l Newlin for 200 Acres, Ordered this Day.

Signed a Warr't to Nicho. Waln for 8 Acres Lib. Land, Ordered 3d Inst't, signed.

Signed a Warr't for 500 Acres to T. Wickersham's Children, Ordered 15th Inst.

Signed a Warr't for 80 Acres of Lib. Land to the Germans, Ordered this Day.

Charles Whitacre, of the County of Chester, having obtained a promise from the Propr'ry to have the Refusal of 1,500 Acres of Land in the said County, said to be formerly laid out to Griffith Jones but by him quitted and now in the Proprietary's disposal, desires the Commissioners to sett a Price on the same.

And Upon Consultation had, the Prices sett £25 p. 100, upon which the said Charles refuses the said Land at that Price, but still craves that if they cannot dispose of the said Land at that Rate he might have the Refusal thereof when the Price is lowered, for which he has the Commissioners Promise.

At a Sessions of the Commissioners at Philadelphia the 22d of 10br., 1701.

Present, Griffith Owen, Thomas Story, James Logan.

The Proprietary having sold to John Sharpless, original Purchaser in England, 1,000 Acres of Land, there was laid out to him in Right of the said Purchase 24th 8 Mo., 1682, 330 Acres of Land by a Warrant from William Markham, dated 7th 6 Mo., 1682, and confirmed to the said Jno. by Patent from the Propr'ry, dated 28th 5 Mo., 1684, situate in the Township of Providence and County of Chester, which said 330 Acres, the said John deceasing, Jane Sharpless, his Relict and Adm'rx, and John Sharpless, his Heir, by a Deed dated 9th 4 Mo., 1696, conveyed to James Sharpless who requests a new Patent for it under the Great Seal, and offers to give Bond to admitt a Resurvey any Time within seven Years, which is granted and a Patent ordered.

Thomas Cooper having on presumption settled on a Tract of Land within the bounds of the Manor of Rocklands about two Years ago, requests a Grant of 200 Acres in the said Place for which he agrees to pay £25 p. 100, and two Years Arrears, one-half of the Money to be paid the 25th of the first Month next, and the Remainder the 29th of Sept'r next following, and afterwards one Shill. Sterl., Quit Rent p. 100, to give good Security when he takes out his Patent.

Ordered that a Warr't be granted according to the aforesaid Agreement and a Patent on the Return.

John Chaffan having seated on a Tract adjoining to the preceeding about two Years ago, requests a Warrant for 250 Acres on the same Terms with Thomas Cooper.

Ordered that a Warr't be accordingly granted vid: the foregoing.

James Chevers having seated about 3 Years on a Tract in the Manor of Rocklands, joining on Nathan'l Newlin's Land and Concord Line, requests a Grant of two hundred Acres in the said Place on the same Terms with Thomas Cooper and John Chaffan, only that he shall pay three Years Rent at a Penny p. Acre, which is granted.

Which is granted and ordered that a Warr't be drawn and signed.

Henry Gunston being seated on 50 Acres of Land in Burmingham in the County of Chester adjoining on the Line of the Manor of Rocklands, and finding the same too strait and small for a Plantation, Requests a Grant of one hundred Acres in the Manor adjoining to that he possesses, which is granted upon Agreement that he shall pay £30 for the same the 25th of the first Mo. next, and Tho. Cawdry, his Neighbour, offers to be his Security.

Ordered thereupon that a Warr't be granted and a Pat. on the Return.

Hugh Roberts, of Meirion, produces a Warr't of Survey under the Hands of Wm. Markham and John Goodson dated 1st 4 Mo., 1688, for two hundred Acres of Land to be taken up in the Welch Tract, purchased by the said Hugh of the said Commissioners of which he sold one hundred to Katherine Thomas, Relict of John Thomas, which being never executed he requests another Warr't from this Board for 100 to himself, and another for the other 100 to Thomas Jones, eldest Son of the said Katherine.

Inquiry being made into the Payment of the Consideration Money, Benjamin Chambers appearing, affirms that the Pennsylvanian Society Trade being in Hugh Robert's Debt and the Proprietary in the Society's Debt, the said Benjamin by the Comm'rs order, gave the Propr'ry Credit in the Society's Acco'ts (whose Agent he was) for £10, the sum agreed on for the 200 Acres.

Upon which 'tis ordered that Warr'ts be granted according to Request.

Nicholas Lockyer, of the County of New Castle, producing a Return of Survey under Henry Hollingsworth's Hand, formerly deputy Surveyor of the said County, for 86 Acres of

Land near New Castle Town, survey'd 7th 12th Mo., 1689, in pursuance of a Warr't from the Proprietary, dated 20th 12 Mo., 1682 (as is recited), said to be for 100 Acres, granted to Cornelius Johnson, but the said 86 Acres laid out to Elizab. Priestner, his Relict and Widow, also of John Priestner for which the said Nicholas, her present and 3d Husband, requests a Patent.

It being objected the Land was his Wife's and not his, James Claypoole being present certified that the said Elizabeth, after her intermarriage with her present Husband, did in their Court (of which he is Clerk) resign and give up all her Claim, Title and Interest in and to that and all her other Lands to her said Husband in Cons'rtion that he should give her the Priviledge to dispose of £100 at her Death to her Relations. The Rent also being discussed of, 'tis affirmed that the said Land has been taken up these 30 Years past, that his Wife's Mother (being also Adam Peterson's) was killed in a House standing on it by the Indians, and that their Writings being burnt they applied to the Proprietary at his ffirst arrival for a Title in order to which the said Warrant was granted, but that it lay dormant in W. Welch's Hands, which occasioned the Survey to be delayed. All which being considered,

A Patent is ordered on old Rent.

The Proprietary having, at his Departure from Newcastle promised Dorcas, present Wife to Geo. Hogg, 200 acres of Land, where she could find it vacant in the said County, for the Use of her Son Henry, Land by her former Husband; Land in Consideration of some Services done for the Publick and Losses sustained thereupon by her said fformer Husband, in the Presence of Edward Shippen, Griff. Owen and R'd Halliwell, whom he desired to be Witnesses for her upon her application to the Comm'rs.

And she, by her Letter, accordingly applying, and R'd Halliwell under his Hand, and E. Shippen and Griff. Owen, present, testifying as aforesaid.

Ordered that a Warr't be granted to the said Henry, Land for 200 acres in the said County where not already granted nor appropriated.

Richard Halliwell and Joseph Wood, in behalf of themselves and the rest of the Inhabitants of Newcastle concerned, presented to the Propr'ry a Petition at his last Departure from that Place in the following Words:

To the honourable William Penn, Esqr., absolute Proprietary and Governor of the Province of Pennsylvania and Territories:

May it please your Honor, That whereas the Members of assembly for the Lower Counties did request your Honour in behalf of the Inhabitants of this Town that you would be pleased to grant the Bank to such Persons as have Lotts fronting the River at the yearly Quittrent of one Bushell of Wheat for each sixty ffoot in Breadth and six hundred foot in Length from the New ffront Street, they improving the same with good Wharfs in seven Years after the Date of the first Grant, or else the same to revert to your Honor to be granted to such Persons as will comply with the same in the Time prefixt (which your Hon'r was pleased to promise should be done.)

We therefore, in behalf of our selves and the rest of the Town concern'd do further request that the same may be confirmed by some Order or writing under your Hand to your Commissioners that Warr'ts may be granted and the same to be laid out and Patented to such Persons as shall desire the same, and we shall as in Duty bound ever Pray, etc.

RICHARD HALLIWELL,
JOSEPH WOOD.

Undersign'd by the Gov'r thus:
Granted as here requested 31st 8 br., 1701.

WM. PENN.

In pursuance of which Petition and grant thereupon Joseph Wood, being possessed of a Lot in the said ffront of Newcastle, requests a Warr't for the Bank fronting his said Lott on the Terms mentioned in the Petition aforegoing.

Which is granted and ordered that a Warrant be drawn accordingly.

In pursuance of an order of this Board, issued the 1st Instant, for taking some Measures to regulate the Welch Tract, some of the Chiefs of that Nation in this Province having met and concerted the Methods to be taken in order to the Regulations aforesaid, It was agreed,

That in as much as the Welch Purchasers of the Propr'ry were, by large Quantities of acres in one Pair of Deeds, granted to one or two Persons only, under which several other Purchasers had a Share; the Gen'l Deeds of one Purchase should be first brought in with an acco't of all other Persons who had a Share in such Purchase, also an account in whose Possession the Respective Lands of every under Purchase now are, and that because all the Lands hitherto laid out (or most of them) in the said Tract were by Vertue of one Gen'l Warrant; particular Warr'ts of Resurvey should be granted to every Man upon what he now possesses, and that an exact account of all their Titles should be taken in distinct Minutes from these presents, to be kept fair in a Book or Papers for that Purpose, and accordingly the Propr'ry's Deeds to John Thomas and Edward Jones for 5,000 acres were brought in with all such necessary acc'ts as aforesaid, and the following Warr'ts of resurvey this Day signed, made up partly of the said Purchase and partly of others, but brought under this Head.

To Hugh Roberts for 549¾ acres in Goshen; 482 thereof of Jno. ap. Jno's.

To Robert Roberts and Owen Roberts 200 acres, each in Meirion.

To Edward Reese 205¼ acres in Meirion.

To Eward Jones' Survey on 200 acres in Goshen and a Resurvey on 151¼ in Meirion and 153 in Goshen.

To Edward Jones, jun'r, 306¼ acres, half in Meirion, ½ in Goshen.

Robert David 274¼ acres in Meirion and 234½ in Goshen.

Richard Walter 100 acres in Meirion.

Richard Rees als. Jones 137½ in Meirion and 75 in Goshen.

To Cadwallader Morgan 202 acres and ½ in Meirion.

To John Roberts, Malter, 306 acres and ½; ¾ thereof in Goshen, ¼ in Meirion.

To Hugh Jones 768 and ¼ acres in Meirion.

To Griffith John 194 acres.

To Rob't William 76¼ acres in Goshen.

To Ellis David 151 acres and ½.

To Thomas Jones, Robert Jones and Cadwallader Jones 1,225 acres; ½ thereof in Meirion and ½ in Goshen; left them by their ffather, John Thomas, the original Purchaser.

To John Roberts, Cordwainer, of Goshen, 78¼ acres in Goshen

Signed a Warr't for 20 acres of Lib. Land to John Ball, ordered 3d Inst.

Signed a Warr't for 200 acres to Thomas Cooper, ordered to-Day.

Signed a Warr't for 250 acres in Rocklands to John Chaffan, ordered to-Day.

Signed a Warr't for 200 acres in Rocklands to James Chevers, ordered this Day.

Signed a Warr't for 100 acres in Rocklands to Henry Gunston, ordered this Day.

Signed a Warr't for 200 acres in Newc. Coun. to Henry Land, ordered this Day.

Signed a Warr't of Resurvey to Jos. Wood, ordered this Day.

Signed a Warr't to Joseph Wood for his Bank Lot in Newc., ordered this Day.

Signed a Patent to Nicholas Lockyer for 86 acres, Ordered this Day.

At a Sessions of the Commissioners at Philadelphia the 24th of 10br., 1701.

Present, Edward Shippen, Griffith Owen, Thomas Story, James Logan, Sec'ry.

The Proprietary, by Deeds of Lease and Release, bearing Date the 15th and 16th of March, 1681, sold to Thomas and Samuel Bulkly 500 acres of Land, and Thomas Bulkly, by Deed dated 14th 3 Mo., 1684, released his whole Right in the said Purchase to his Brother, the said Samuel, in right of which Purchase there is laid out to him in the Map a Tract of about the said Quantity between the Branches of Skuylkill, above the Manor of Bilton, not far from Perquiominck, on which he requests a resurvey, vizt: 490 acres, and a Warrant to take up the other 10 acres in the Liberties, together with 5 acres more of Lib. Land sold him by Griffith Owen, being appurtenant to.

Ordered that a Warrant of Resurvey be accordingly granted on the said 490 acres and a Warrant to take up the said Lib'ty Land.

Joseph Hall, by Deeds of Lease and Release, dated 4 and 5th Apr., 1682, purchased 500 acres of Land of the Proprietary, and by like Deeds dated 3d and 4th of Aug't, 1683, conveyed to William Hobson and William Hall 250 acres, Part of the aforesaid for the Use of his Sister, Hannah Overton, and by an Instrument dated 7th Aug't, 1683, appointed Samuel Overton and Henry Maddock his attorneys for the other Moiety.

Hannah applying to the Prop'ry had his Promise under the Secretary's Hand dated 15th 8br, last, for her 250 acres, which she now requests of the Commissioners.

Ordered that a Warrant be granted for the said 250 acres.

The Propr'y, by Deeds of Lease and Release, dated 2d and 3d of Ffebr'y, 1681, sold to William Tanner 500 acres of Land, and by like Deeds of the same Date to John Tanner the same Quantity.

The said William and John, by one Deed dated 21 June, 1683, sold all their 1,000 acres to Benj. Clark, who by Deed dated 12 June, 1683, conveyed 500 acres, a Moiety thereof to Joseph Phips, whose Share has been reckoned the Purchase of John Tanner, and the other Moiety remain'g to B. Clark the Purchase of William Tanner.

In right of said John's Purchase there has been laid out to the said Joseph Phips in one Tract 300 acres in the County of Philad'a, near Nich. Skull's Land, on which he requests a Resurvey and a Warrant for 8 acres of Lib. Land to himself and the like Quantity to Benj. Clark.

Ordered that Warr'ts be granted accordingly.

Benjamin Chambers having several Times requested the Propr'ry before his Departure that in consideration of the Barrenness of the Tract of Land laid out in the County of Chester for 2000 acres to the Kentish Purchasers, He would be pleased to grant him at a moderate Rate to take upon the North Side of the said Tract for himself and Henry Green, two of the said Purchasers, 150 acres or thereab'ts of vacant Land, and at the Eastern End of the said Tract 200 acres for Peter Blan and James Hunt, the other two of the said Purchasers, out of the Land formerly laid out to Anthony Weston and Burgess, and by them deserted.

The Propr'ry granted the said Benjamin his Request, but not having leisure referred him to agree for the Price with and to take out Warrants from the Commissioners.

In Pursuance of which Grant (certified by the Secretary) 'tis agreed that the said Benjamin, upon the Survey of the said Land, shall pay after the Rate of twelve Pounds per 100, and thereupon 'tis Ordered that two Warrants be granted.

Signed a Warrant to Joseph Phips, ordered to-Day.

At a Sessions of the Commissioners at Philadelphia the 29th of 10br., 1701.

Present, Edward Shippen, Griffith Owen, Thomas Story, James Logan.

The Request of Joseph Wilcox, made and stated the 8th Inst., being fully considered and upon several Conferences had with the said Joseph largely debated, 'tis at length agreed between the Commissioners in behalf of the Proprietary and the said Joseph That he shall have in Satisfaction of his ffather's Disappointments in and about the Lotts promised his ffather upon his Purchase of one thousand acres, and in full of all his Demands thereupon twenty-five ffoot on the North side of his present Lott at the North End of the Town, on the Proprietary's Land extending from the ffront to the Second Street on Dellaware, and the same Quantity of twenty-five ffoot from the 2d to the 3d Street, and fifty foot from the End of his present Rope Walk on the East Side of the 3d Street, extending to the 4th Street, the whole with what he is already possessed of to be held at the yearly Rent of seven shillings and six Pence, Sterling, also that his Share of the two thousand Pounds Tax for the Govern'r, amounting to about £4, 3s, 4d, and that he shall further have Liberty to make Use of the Proprietary's Land beyond the granted Premises to the Length of two or 300 ffoot for the carrying on of his Trade, so long as the same shall not be otherwise disposed of or appropriated, in such Cases where the Ropewalk hereby granted, being in Length about 942 foot, shall prove too short, which Grant the said Joseph accepts in full Satisfaction as aforesaid, and in lieu of all claims or Demands of the Propr'ry (on the said account) whatsoever.

Whereupon 'tis ordered that a Warrant be granted according to this Minute and a Confirmation on the Return of Survey.

A Difference about a ffront Street Lott appurtenant to John Sharpless, his Purchase of 1,000 acres in which William Lawrence and Will'm Bowlin, both of Philadelphia, are concerned, being stated before the Secretary in his Office the 22d of the 12th Mo., last, as follows:

John Sharpless, original Purchaser of 1,000 acres, sold his Right to his City Lotts and Lib'ty Land to Wm. Morgan, but did not convey them. William Morgan obtained a Warrant from the Propr'y dated 29th 12 Mo., 1683, to take up his said Lots in pursuance of which T. Holme, Surveyor Gen'l, made his Return, produced under his Hand, dated 11th 12 Month, 1684, certifying that by Vertue of the said Warrant he had caused to be surveyed to the said Morgan a Lot in the ffront Street of twenty ffoot in Breadth, bounded Southw'd with Anth. Tomkins' Lott and Northward with a Vacancy, also a High Street Lott proportionable, both surveyed 8th Sept'r, 1684.

Robert Longshore purchased of the said Morgan his Right to the said Lotts and Lib. Land. but there being no Deed passed between Sharpless and Morgan for the same, Sharpless, by a Deed dated 6th May, 1692, conveyed his whole Right to both Lotts and Liberty Land appurtenant to his said Purchase to Robert Longshore, making no mention of the Location of the Lotts or the aforementioned Survey.

Robert Longshore being thus invested with Sharpless' Right, not regarding the Survey or Return aforesaid, upon application made to the Comm'rs of Property then in Power, obtained a Warrant dated 29th 7 Mo., 1692, to take up the said Lotts, which he being concerned in, the Surveyor's Office executed on a Lott in the ffront lying much more Southerly and therefore more Valuable, between the Lotts of Richard Davies to the Northward and Rowland Ellis to the Southward, being about 144 ffoot above Mulberry Street (and on another likewise more valuable in the High street), and by a Deed dated 8th 8 Mo., 1692, sold the last mentioned ffront Lott to William Lawrence, who since sold it to Timothy Stevenson, who several Years ago has built upon it.

After R. Longshore's Decease, Tho. Jenner marrying his Widow and by that means having an opportunity to Search the Surveyor's Office, found the first mentioned Return under T. Holmes' Hand, also Sharpless' Deed to Longshore, by Vertue of which (tho' without any Legal Power, having only married the Widow) he sold the first surveyed Lot in the front to William Bowlin and gave Bond to make him a Title.

Upon which both Lawrence and Bowlin sue for a Confirmaion of what they possess, viz: Bowlin for the true Lott without any Right (Longshore having before sold all his) and Lawrence with a full Right but on a wrong Lott that he Claims, properly belonging to Sir John Sweetaple's Purchase.

All which being duly considered, but especially that Lawrence, who has the Right, has by his assigns improved and built on his Lot.

'Tis ordered that the Lot of 20 ffoot in the ffront, now possessed by Timothy Stevenson, by him purchased of William Lawrence, shall be confirmed to one or other of them, that is to say to Stevenson if Lawrence has conveyed it and if not to Lawrence himself.

And that the Lott claimed by Wm. Bowlin shall be granted to S'r John Sweetaple or his assigns.

And that William Lawrence shall pay six Pounds in considera'ion of the more advantageous Situation of the said Lot than the fformer, which of Right belonged to Sharpless' Purchase.

Richard Hough producing a Return of Survey, sign'd Edward Penington, dated   last past, made in pursuance of a Warrant of Resurvey granted by the Proprietary dated on 250 acres formerly laid out in Right of the said Richard's first Purchase of 500 acres and 50 acres adjoining Part of a larger Tract laid out in the Right of Luke Brinsly's first Purchase, the whole being reputed 300 acres, situate in Makfield Township, in the County of Bucks, but found upon a Resurvey to contain 416 acres, of which there being 30 acres allowed by the Law there remains 86 acres to be purchased, for which he agrees to pay after the Rate of £20 p. 100, viz: £16 12s for the whole, there is also due from the said Richard for 9 acres of Meadow found in a Tract reputed 25 acres, Sold for 10s p. acre, £4, and for 44 acres of Vacant Land granted him by the Proprietary adjoyning to Richard's Land in the Manor of High Lands, at the Rate of £20 p. 100 acres, £8, which two last Parcels were confirmed to him by Patent from the Propr'ry, dated the   of 8br., last.

For the whole of which he is to give Bond to the Proprietary, being in all £ 28 12s, payable in six Months, and thereupon he requests a Confirmation of the first mentioned 416 acres, which is granted. For the Particulars of his Title See the Secretary's former Minutes of Property for the said County and Township.

The Proprietary, by Deeds of Lease and Release, dat. 21 and

22d 8br., 1681, sold to Nathaniel Pask 250 acres, who by like Deeds dated 5th and 6 July, 1699, conveyed the same to Thomas Bye.

The Propr'ry also by Deeds of Lease and Release, dat. 10th and 11th of 8br., 1681, sold to Edward Crew 250 acres, who by like Deeds dated 5 and 6 July, 1699, conveyed the same to Thomas Bye, both which Purchases have been taken up by the said Bye since his arrival in this Province.

The Propr'ry also by Deeds of Lease and Release dated 10th and 11th 8br., 1681, sold to Edward Simkins 250 acres, who by a Letter of attorney dated 7th Ffebr'y, 1700, impowered the said Thomas and Margaret, his Wife, to take up and dispose of the same.

Upon which he Requests a Warrant to take up the said last 250 acres, also Warrants for the Lotts appurtenant to the said Purchases, viz: for Pask's and Crew's to himself, and for Simkins to his self.

Ordered that first a Warr't be granted for the 250 acres and afterwards for the Lotts as there shall be occasion; Liberty Land to be deducted.

Philip Howel produces a Warrant under the Propr'ry's Hand and Seal, dated 6th of the 4th Mo., 1684, for a Lot to Cuthbert Hayhurst, proportionable to his Purchase of 500 acres, also a Deed from Wm. Hayhurst, Son and Heir of the said Cuthbert, dated 6th 1 Mo., 1699, conveying all his Right to the Lotts and Liberty Land appurtenant to his ffather's said Purchase to the said Philip.

Cuthbert Hayhurst is a first Purchaser of the said Quantity in the original List, Deeds dated 17th 18 Ffebr'y, '87; the Lott by the City Draught is No. 40, on Skuylkill; the Warr't mentions neither Side.

The said Philip also produces a Warrant from the Propr'ry dated 19th 4 Mo., 1684, for a Lott to Thomas Langhorn, Purchaser of 500 acres, and a Deed from Jeremy Langhorn, Son and Heir of the said Thomas, dated 1, 1 Mo., 1698, conveying (for £5) the Right of all the Lib'ty Land and Lotts appurtenant to the said Purchase to the said Philip, which Deed recites the Proprietary's Deeds of Lease and Release to be dated 7th and 8th of 9br., 1681 The Lott falls on Skuylk., No. 91.

The said Philip also produces a Warr't from the Propr'ry dated 2d 6 Mo., 16 3, to lay out a Lot to Ann Smith, on Delaware or Skuylkill side, where it might be most convenient, proportionable to her Purchase of 500 acres.

Also a Deed from Ffrancis Smith, of Brandywine, her Husband, dated 30th May, 1698, conveying to the said Philip a Lot in the 2d Street on the South side of Wm. Crosdale's, which

Lot notwithstanding was never surveyed (that can be heard of to the said Ffrancis, but was pitched upon by him by Vertue of the said Warrant. There is also a Warranty in the Deed for the said Lott.

For all which said Lotts the said Philip applying himself frequently to the Propr'ry, He was pleased to allow and accordingly left Directions in Writing that Ffr. Smith's Sale should be good.

Ordered therefore that a Warr't be granted to the said Philip for ye s'd Lot. But because the other two fall on Skuylkill Side they cannot be removed nor granted on Delaw., as requested.

Ordered further that 10 acres of Liberty Land be granted to the said Philip in Right of Jerem. Langhorn's Sale.

At a Sessions of the Commissioners at Philadelphia the 31st 10 br., 1701.

Present, Edward Shippen, Griffith Owen, Thomas Story, James Logan.

John Ogle, Son of Thomas Ogle, of the County of Newcastle, dece'd, having been long resident in this County before the Proprietary's arrival, and as he alledges suffered much with his ffather and ffamily by the Lord Baltimore's Invasion in the said County, and being yet without any Land of his own, notwithstanding he has twelve Children to maintain, requests a Grant of 500 acres near Whiteclay Creek, where he lately presumed to settle on the same Terms as the New Welch Purchasers in the said County have their Land; he craves being very near their Line.

Ordered that in consideration of the Premises the said John have a Warrant for 500 acres, for which he agrees to pay £62 10s within three Years after the Date of the Warrant, the first year to be clear of Interest, but for the second and third to pay after the Rate of 8 p. Cent., afterwards to be one Shilling Sterling p. 100.

Joseph Moore, of the same County and Place, being upon much the same Circumstances with John Ogle, and having purchased a blind claim from a late Inhabitant there, for about 200 acres, in the Lines of which he supposes there may be 300, requests a Warrant for the said 300 and 100 more upon Abrah. Brewster's Line near White Clay Creek, on the same Terms with J. Ogle.

Ordered that in Consideration of the said Joseph's Sufferings and the Propr'ry's known Respect to him he have a Warrant for 400 acres as requested and upon the same Terms of Payment with John Ogle, as desired.

John Portman, lately settled on a Tract between the Land granted to John Ogle and the New Welch Purchasers Line, Requests that he may have 200 acres granted there on the same Terms with the foregoing.

Ordered at the humble Suit and Request of Jno. Ogle and Joseph Moore that the said John Portman have a Warrant for 200 acres in the said Place, upon the same Terms with the said Ogle and Moore, and that in their Warrants and all others for Land for which a Consideration is to be paid there be one Clause inserted mention'g the agreement and another Clause making void, both the Warrant and the Survey in Case the agreement be not fulfilled and that upon granting a Patent for any such Land before the Money be paid the Land be mortgaged to the Propriet'ry for Security and the Mortgagors or Patentees be obliged to improve.

George White, Purchaser (by the original List) of 2,500 acres, took up in his Life Time, as is recited in the following Deed, 1,500 acres, and had at the Time of his Decease 1,000 acres remaining to be then taken up, which 1,000 acres by his last Will and Testament, dated 9th of 7br, 1687, he bequeathed to his Sons, Will'm, Ffrancis, Joseph and Benja. White, in equal Shares among them, viz: to each 250 acres.

Joseph White, the 3d son, by a Deed dated the 8th of this Inst., drawn by Phineas Pemberton, and reciting the Premises, conveyed his Right to the 250 acres left him by the said Will to Samuel Baker, who requests a Warr't to take up the same.

Ordered that a Warr't be accordingly granted.

John Bittle producing the Copy of a Warrant from the Commiss'rs dated 7th of the 4 Mo, 1690, for a Lot to be laid out on Rent on Chesnutt Street to John Countiss, who on the Back of the said Warrant or authentick Copy assigned all his Right therein to John Bittle, the assignment dated 13, 3 Mo., 1692, having first built on it before the Sale. Requests a new Warrant to resurvey it, granted at 5 Sterl. p. ann.

It lies on the North Side of Chesnutt Street, between 4th and 5th.

Signed James Sharpless' Patent; he gives Bond to admit a Resurvey, Ordered 22d Inst.

Joseph Moor, of Newcastle Coun, having petitioned the Propr'ry before his Departure that among other Things he would order him the Payment of £35 12 6 Sterl'g, recovered by the said Joseph by Judgment of Kent County Court, dated 1st 2 Mo., 1685, against William Berry, administrator on the Estate of Edm'd Warner, which said Sum the Propr'ry assumed to pay, he being principally the adm'or and Berry acting only under him, of which Money he has laid out 'till this present

Time, and the Propriet'ry delivering the said Joseph's Petition to the Secretary with Orders to answer him, the said Joseph requests the Secretary, as the Propriet'ry's Receiver, to pay the Money, upon which he demurring, craves the Commissioners advice in the Case.

And all things being duely weighed 'tis advised seeing the said Joseph pleads so great a Necessity that he dare not return home, William Grant having an Execution out against him for a Debt, and that the said Grant having given the Proprietary a Bond last Summer for the Payment of 77 Bushels of Wheat for his Quit Rent, which Bond, with six Pounds would answer Joseph's present Exigencies, that therefore the Secretary assign Joseph the said Bond and pay him the said Sum of six Pounds, and take his Bond for fifty Pounds, ten shillings, for the Repayment of £25 10 in Case the Proprietary shall not allow of it and that the Secretary inform him by first Opportunity.

Signed a Patent to James Sharpless for 330 Acres, ordered 10th Inst., Gives Bond.

Signed a Warrant to John Ogle for 500 Acres, ordered to Day.

Signed a Warrant to Joseph Moore for 400 Acres, ordered to Day.

Signed a Warrant to Jno. Portman for 200 Acres, ordered to Day.

Signed a Warr't to Sam'l Baker for 250 Acres, ordered to Day.

At the Request of Joseph Wilcox, for his Brother in Law, John Roads, that we would grant him to cut fifty Dead Trees, blasted two or three Years ago by the Locusts, off the Manor of Springfield, on which he joyns, for fencing of his Plantation, which Trees, if not cutt, will rot on the Ground and rather be of Damage than Benefit.

Ordered that the said John Roads have Liberty to cutt 50 Trees as aforesaid.

Signed two Warrants to Benj. Chambers for 150 and 200 Ac's, ordered 24th ulto.

At a Sessions of the Commissioners at Philadelphia the 5th Day of the 11th Month, 1701.

Present, Edward Shippen, Griffith Owen, Thomas Story, James Logan.

Joshua Story, of the County of Newcastle, requests to take up two hundred Acres of Land next adjoining to that lately taken up and seated by John Grantham for which he agrees to pay twenty Pounds p. 100 and a Bushell of Wheat Rent p. Ann., the Money to be paid at 3 Payments each, six Months Distance, the last within 18 Mos.

But Dorcas Hogg solicits that the Warr't granted the 22d ulto. to her Son Henry, may be located there, that being the Place designed by him at the Time of her Request it being the nearest vacant to his Brother Ffrancis.

Ordered therefore that the first two hundred next adjoyning to Grantham be laid out to Henry Land, and the next after to Joshua Story, to extend in Length from Mary Land Road to that leading to Elk River, and of a Breadth sufficient for the Quantity upon the Terms aforesaid.

John Calvert requests a Grant of two hundred Acres in the County of Newcastle next to Major Donaldson's and Jasper Yeats', at the same Rate and Terms with the aforegoing or more if there be more to be had.

Ordered that because the said Land is affirmed to be poor and the Timber much wasted a Warrant be granted for the same as requested, that is, for the whole Vacancy there, in Case it exceed not 250 Acres, but if it exceed that Number that he shall then have only the 200.

Peter Anderson, seated about 7 Miles below Newcastle on Mary Land Road, requests a Grant of fifty Acres joining to his Plantation on the other Side of the Road for which he agrees to pay ten Pounds and half a Bushel of Wheat yearly, the greatest Part of the Money to be paid in Hand, Ordered that a Warr't be granted as requested.

There being a small Parcel of Marsh on Red Lyon Creek and Delaware in the County of Newcastle equally claimed by Peter Anderson and Peter and Joshua Hansens, for their better accomoda'ion Anderson requests a Resurvey of the same.

Which is granted and ordered a Warrant.

Lands Purchased by Daniel Smith.

Acres.

Dan'll Smith purchased of the Propr'y by Deeds dated
14th and 15th 7br., 1681, ... 500
And by Deeds dated 17th and 18th of March, 1681, . . . 2,000
Of Henry Bernard by Deeds dated Mar., 1686, 500 acres,
who purchased of the Prop'ry by Deeds dated 7br.,
1681, 250 acres, ... 250
Of Thomas Sager and Susannah Bayly by Deeds dated
May, '86, 500 acres, who purchased the same of the Prop'ry by Deeds dated Aug'st, '81, ... 500
Of Joan Keal by Deed dated 4th May, '86, 500 acres, who
purchased of Edw'd Jeffries, who purchased of the Prop'ry by Deeds dated 19th and 20th 8br., '81, ... 500

Of Thomas Hatt by Deed dated 17th Apr., '86, 500 acres, who purchased the same of the Prop'ry by Deeds dated 11th and 12th 8br., '81, ... 500
Of Wm. Isaac 500 acres by Deeds dated Mar., '85-6, who by Deeds dated 15th and 16th Mar., '81, purchased the same of the Prop'ry, ... 500
Of Jno. Rety 250 acres by Deed dated July, '86, who purchased of the Prop'ry by Deeds dated 8th and 9th 7br., '81, 500 acres, but by the List 250, ... 250
Of Walter Edw'ds 250, who purchased the same of Enoch Flower, being part of his 2,000 acres purchase, ... 250
Of Jno. Bill 125, who purchased of Wm. Bayly, purchaser of 500, ... 125

 Purchased in all, ... 5,375

Of which 5,375 acres there has been taken up as follows, as far as by Warr'ts and Returns in the Surveyor's office appears:
By Warr't dated 24th 9 mo. '86, Surv'd 24th 7 mo., '88, in Chest'r Coun., ... 360
By Warr't Dat. 18, 8, '88, Surv'd 22, 2 mo., '89, Chest'r, . 1,000
By Warr't Dat. 24, 9, '86, Surv'd 24, 5, '88, Lib. Land, . 32
By Warr't dat. 24, 12, '84, Surv'd 4, 1 mo., '84, in Chest'r, to Hen. Bernard, ... 500
In right of Tho. Sager, &c., ... None.
By Warr't dat. 8, 12, '87-8, Surv'd 24, 5 mo., '88, Lib. Land to D. Smith, ... 8
By ditto, Surv'd 2, 12, '89, to Ditto, ... 492
There is also laid out adjoyning to Hatt's 178, the Whole being 670, ... 178

 Laid out Certain, ... 2,570
In right of E. Jeffries there was granted a Warr't dated 19th 10 mo., '84, for Lotts and Lib. Land to Wm. Farmer, the Lott returned Surveyed 26th 10 mo., '84, Lib. Land only 4 acres, and that uncertain, also for 250 acres, a Moiety of the s'd purchase, which if taken up is, . . . 254

 In all, ... 2,824

By the aforegoing Warr'ts and Returns there Seems to have been taken up 2,824 acres (of which 2,570 are Certain), and there remains of all Danl's Purchases 2,551 acres to be taken up, of which there is 32 acres Liberty Land, and the remaining 2,519 acres rough or Wood Land, for all which Randal Spakeman, adm'r on the Said Danl's Estate, requests for the Use of the Estate of Dan'l Smith aforesaid to have Warr'ts for the Location.

Ordered that Warr'ts be granted for about 2,000 acres or more as fast as it can be seated or Sold, but that the whole be not Yet quite granted 'till some greater Certainty of what has been taken up appears and that a Warr't for the Liberty Land be granted forthwith.

The Prop'ry, by deeds of Lease and Release, dated 26th and 27th 7br., '81, sold to Richard Collins 1,250 acres, who by Deed dated 29th 3 mo., 1683, convey'd the whole to Richard Wood, who by Deed dated 26th June, 1683, Sold one Moiety thereof to Will'm Lovell, who by an Instrum't dated 20th May, 1701, Constituted Joseph Kirl his attorney to act for him in and about the said Land.

In right of this said Purchase there was laid out to Lovel by Warr't Dated in the 8th or 9th Mo'th, 1683, 500 acres within the Welch Tract before it was Inclosed, adjoyning on Laetitia Mann'r, on which the said Joseph requests a Resurvey.

500 more lies in Southampt. in Bucks.

Ordered that a Resurvey be accordingly granted, provided it has Ever been duly laid out and is Claimed by no other person.

Christopher Taylor having purchased of the Prop'ry in England 5,000 acres of Land by Deeds of Lease and Release dated 27th and 28th of 8br., 1681, of which there was Laid out to the said Christopher by a Warr't from the Prop'ry dated   , 500 acres on the River Dellaware, in Bristol Township, between Wm. Haig's and Fra. Richardson's Lands, which being Resurveyed by Phin. Pemberton's Ord'r, is certified by him to Contain 562 acres upon a Strict Survey, of which 50 acres being allowed by the Law there is 12 acres Overplus.

Christo. Taylor, by Deeds not to be found, convey'd the s'd Land to Tho. Lloyd and Israel and Joseph Taylor, the only Surviveing Sons of the Said Christopher by a Writing under their hands upon the Draught of Resurvey acknowledge their Father's Sale and requests it may be Confirmed to the Ex'ors of T. Lloyd, but there being no Deeds to be found from Christopher to Thomas Lloyd 'tis Judged more proper to Confirm it to Israel, the Heir, that he may Convey it afterw'ds to David Lloyd and Isaac Norris, the Ex'ors of Thomas' last Will, or to their assigns, as they themselves shall think fitt.

Ordered therefore that a Patent be granted to Israel Taylor for the said Land, the Ex'ors answering for the 12 acres of Overpluss which is valued at   p'r acre.

David Lloyd, for himself and Isaac Norris, Ex'ors of T. Lloyd's Will, produces a Deed from Ann Salter dated 1st 4th, 1685, for a Tract of 60 acres and another Tract of one hundred acres, both in Bristol Township, Coun. Bucks, Sold by her to Tho. Lloyd being part of Sam'l Clift's old Rent Land. The 60 acres she purchased by Deed, dated the 7br., '84, of Walter Pomfry, who by deed dated 23rd 8br., 1682, purchased the same of Sam'l Clift's.

The other Tract of 100 acres she purchased by Deed dated 17th 3 mo., 1684, of Morgan Drewitt, who in the last said Deed is recited to have purchased the same of Sam'l Clift, being part of his 274 acres, resurveyed to him by a Gen'l Warr't from the Prop'ry dated 14th 4 mo., 1683. By the said Warr't there was Resurveyed to all the Old Settlers there who took up land before the Propr's arrivall att a bushell of wheat p'r 100 Rent, as follows:

To Edm'd Bennett,	321 *Acres*.
To John Otter,	200
To Edm'd Bennett in another Tract,	50
To Will'm Stanford,	164
To Sam'l Clift,	274

The Original Draught of Resurvey is in David Lloyd's hands. By a Resurvey made on the above mentioned 160 acres by Israel Taylor, by Order of Phin. Pemberton, it was found to Contain 190 acres, of which 16 being allowed by Law, there is 14 acres Overpluss, Valued at   p'r.

The said David and Isaac requests a Confirmation of the said 190 acres to them for the use of the Testator's will, which is granted, they Satisfying for the Overpluss.

Griffith Jones having purchased of the Prop'ry in England 5,000 acres of land by Deeds of Lease and Release dated 11th and 12th 8br., 1681, there was Laid out to him in Bristol Township, in the County of Bucks, by Vertue of a Warr't from the Prop'ry dated the 6th 12 mo., 1682, five Hundred acres confirmed to him by Patent dated 27th 4 mo., 1684, Survey'd 5th 1 mo., 1683, which said 500 acres the said Griff., by Deeds dated 3rd 8mo., 1685, to Thomas Lloyd, and being resurveyed by Israel Taylor, by Ph. Pemberton's Ord'r, is found to Contain 572 acres, of which 50 being allowed by Law there is 22 acres of Overpluss, Valued at   p'r acre.

David Lloyd and Isaac Norris, Ex'ors of T. Lloyd's Will, request a further Confirmation of the said Land if it shall be thought fitt. But the said Tract being Sufficiently Confirmed already and Nothing remaining but the Overpluss, 'tis

Ordered that care be taken to cut off the Overpluss or oblige the Claimers to pay for it, and if they please they may then have a Confirmation of the whole.

Thomas Murrey, attorney for Wm. Sharelow, by Vertue of an Instrum't dated 20th Jan'ry, requests a Warr't for the front and High street Lotts appurten't to S'r John Sweetaple's purchase of one thous'd acres, whose right the said Sharelow purchased, but the Deeds are not produced.

The Lott requested is that Claimed by Wm. Bolding (alias Bowlin), p. 40 in these Minutes, W. Lawrence being possessed of S'r Jno. Sweetaple's true Lott, upon which an Exchange is there Ordered q. V.

Ordered that a Warr't be accordingly granted to S'r John Sweetaple or his assigns, to be Confirm'd when the Deeds are produced.

Patrick Kelly being Seated on the Manor of Rocklands 3 years on presumption, near John Garret, in New Cast'e Coun., requests a grant of one hundred acres, for which he agrees to pay twenty-five pounds at two payments within 18 Months.

Ordered a Warr't as requested, he paying 3 years arrears at a penny p'r acre.

John Kenedy settled on the Mannor of Rocklands, without Newc. Line, upon a Tract joyning on Rob't Brown and George Garret, requests a grant of one hundred acres on the same Terms with P. Kelly, Viz: £25, to be paid after the same manner. Ordered a Warr't as requested, he paying arrears as above s'd.

Signed a Warr't to Joshua Story for 200 acres, Ord'd to-day.

Signed a Warrant to Jno. Calvert for 200 acres, Ordered to-day.

Signed a Warrant to Peter Anderson for 50 acres, Ordered to-day.

Signed a War't of Resurvey to Peter Anderson, Ordered this day.

Signed a Warr't to Patrick Kelly for 100 acres in Rocklands, Ord'd this day.

Signed a War't to John Kenedy for 100 acres in Rocklands, Ord'd this day.

———

At a Sessions of the Commissioners at Philad'a the 7th of ye 11th Mo'th, 1701.

Present. Edward Shippen, Griffith Owen, Thomas Story, James Logan, Sec'ry.

The Prop'ry haveing, by Deeds of Lease and Release, dated 29th and 30th of Aprill, 1683, Sold to Will'm Puryour one thousand acres of Land in this Province, the said Wm. by Deeds of Lease and Release dated 1st and 2d of 8br., 1684, Conveyed the same to Rob't Fairman, who by his Letter dated 8br., 3rd, 1684, Constituted his Brother Thomas Fairman his attorney to Enter upon and Dispose of the same.

Thos. Fairman by Vertue of the said Deeds and Power by a Warr't from the Comm'rs (Ja. Clayp. and Robert Turner) dated 24th 12 mo,, 1684, took up out of the Overpluss of Southampton Township (but in ye County of Philad'a) 500 acres, being now John Jones' Plantation, and out of the same by a Warr't dated 2d 12 mo., 1685, he also took up 300 ac's, the War't Mentioning so much, but T. F. says there is only 250 acres laid out by Vertue of that War't, which said 250 acres he by Deed dated 24th 5 mo., 1686, Convey'd to Ann Salter, who by Deed dated 28th 5 mo., 1686, Convey'd the same to To's Lloyd, whose Ex'ors David Lloyd and Isaac Norris, requests a Confirmation of the s'd Land for the Uses of the Testator's Will.

This Warr't for 300 acres Mentions that quantity to be the remand'r of Wm. Puryour's Purchase, and there is another Warr't produced from the same Comm'rs bearing the same date with the Last, Viz: 2d 12 mo., 1685-6, for 200 acres to T. F. in the right of the same purchase, which the said Thomas Fairman informs was laid out in Abington Township, Sold after Location to Walter King and Arthur Powel, now in the Posssession of Peter Taylor.

Ordered upon the said Ex'ors Request that a

John Ball haveing in pa. 15 made application for 25 acres of Liberty land in Right of John Rowland, but for some objections then rising the grant being deferred till further satisfaction could be produced. The said John applying again informs that he has been with John Rowland himself, who has given under his hand that he Never Sold any to Brigham, but that he made a bargain with one, —————, who quitted it again to him, the said Rowland, who was truly invested with the right when he sold the same to Jon. Duckett, and that upon the Utmost Inquiry that can be made there appears no foot steps that ever the said Liberty Land was taken up, He therefore requests a Warr't to take up the said 25 acres. Upon which 'tis Ordered that if John Rowland's whole purchase be not yett taken up, but that there be 25 acres Remaining, a warr't be granted as requested.

John Pierce Seated about 6 years ago upon the Mann'r of Rocklands, on presumption, near the Land of Will'm Tally, requests a grant of one hundred and fifty acres, for which he agrees to pay twenty-five pounds p'r 100 acres, and the arrears of Rent at a penny p'r acre for the time he has been on it, Viz: the said 6 years, afterwards to hold it at an English shilling p'r 100. One Moiety of the said Money to be paid the first of ye 3rd Month Next and the Remainder ye 29th of 7br, following.

Ordered that a Warr't be granted as Requested.

William Simpson being desirous to settle on a Tract in the

S'd Manor adjoining to the preceding, requests a grant of one hundred acres, for which he agrees to pay thirty pounds at the same times that John Pierce agrees to pay his, viz: one Moiety the first of the 3rd Month, the Remainder at the 29th of 7br., following, at 1s sterling p'r 100.

Ordered that a Warrant be accordingly granted. Mem'dum that the price of Land already taken up and Setled by presumption is agreed to be £25 p'r 100 and the arrears of Rent, But land now bought, £30 p'r 100.

Edward Pritchet, having in page 31 entred a Caveat against Walter Faucet's Obtaining a Patent upon the Resurvey made by Isaac Taylor, Surveyor of Chester Coun., in Pursuance of the Prop'rs warr't, and this day being appointed for hearing the reasons the said Edw'd hath to alledge, Both parties appeared, Pritchet with Jno. Moore, Councill for him, and Faucet with several of his Neighbours for Evidence.

The Case appeared thus:

Neals Matson, an old Settler, took up 100 acres of Land Confirm'd to him by a grant from Gov'r Lovelace, dated   , 1670, Bounded by the River Delaware, Crum Creek, Claus Andries' Land and a line Running North into the Woods, At a bushell of wheat p'r 100, which was after Confirmed to him by a Patent from Gov'r Penn in 1684. Not long after Matson's Settling there Henry Jacobson Seated himself at Matson's Instance and Desire upon part of the said Tract, each of them improving such parts of it as between themselves they thought fitt, choosing to seat thus Near for their greater Security from the Indians. So that upon the same tract then reputed only a hundred acres, each had his Plantation with distinct feilds and Improvements, Separate from Each other by fences and Known Boundaries and partitions, yet much Lock'd within Each other.

By articles of agreement, in the Nature of a Deed, dated in Feb'ry, 1683, Matson sold to Edward Pritchet his Plantation on Dellaware and Crum Creek in Consideration of £120, but without any other Certain bounds or quantity Specifyed, and by a Deed afterwards drawn, but without date, Certifyed by Rob't Eyres, once Clerk of Chester Court, under his Hand to have been acknowledged in Court (but without the County seal or date as is required by law), Matson further Confirmed his s'd plantation to Pritchet under more Certain Bounds than in the former Deed, yet not sufficient, and without Mentioning the Number of acres, together with which Deed she also Delivered to Pritchet his Patent.

Hen. Jacobson, about the year 1689, being about to sell his Plantation part of the said Tract, but haveing no Manner of

Title to shew from Matson, procured from him a Copy of Gov'r Lovelace's grant for the whole, and Under the said Copy a Deed of Sale or assignment from the said Matson under his Hand and seal dated 19th 4 mo., 1689, for one Moiety of the said 100 acres by Vertue of which the said Jacobson convey'd to Renier Peterson by Deed dated   , who sold the same to Walter Faucet.

Upon which the Difference is:

That Pritchet by the Gov'rs Grant to Matson, and Maston's sale of all his Plantation to him, claims the whole Tract, To which Faucit pleads that 'tis true Matson sold all the Plantation that was then his, but that Jacobson's plantation was not included in that sale, that being sold by Matson to Jacobson several years before and by him seated and Improved, Notwithstanding there had no Deed past for the same (which in those early days was not much practised) till Jacobson had Occasion for one, to make Peterson a Title.

Before the opening of the case before this Board, Pritchet, who entered the Caveat and for whom this Hearing was assigned, pleaded by his Council that this Difference lay Neither before the Prop'ry nor his Commiss'rs but was to be determined by the law, and therefore craved that all further proceedings of ye Board in this affair should be stopt, Upon which J. M. Departed.

But Pritchet having in his Caveat desired a day for the Hearing of his Reasons that he had to aledge was required to produce them, and thereupon he gave in that part of the Matter relating to himself, as stated above, and as it had often been exhibited to the prop'ry and to the Secretary in his Office.

W. Faucet produced several Evidences to strengthen his allegations as follows: first, an affidavit of Hen. Jacobson, now very ancient, taken before Corn. Empson, Justice of New C. Coun., dated 25th 4 mo., 1701, declaring that the said Dep't about 27 years ago bought of Neals Matson half of his Tract of Land, Bounded upon Delaw. and Crum Creek, that the said Land was divided between them, and that he (the Dep't) had possessed it 14 years before he sold it to Renier, and 7 years before Edw'd Pritchet came into that Country. But here Jacobson is Evidence in his own Case.

Isaac Taylor, the Surveyor, declares that 16 years agoe Edw'd Pritchet, then his Neighbour, often told him going by his plantation that such a feild (pointing to it) was H. Jacobson's, and such an one was his, and that he had often Shewn him their Divisions, by which Information and knowledge only he had now made this Resurvey of the improved parts, and that he never understood Pritchet made any pretence to these fields reputed Jacobson's till very lately.

Rob't Barber declares that while this Land was in Peterson's possession Pritchet would have employed him and expressly desired him to buy it of Peterson for him, and a Writing is also produced from Thos. Howell declaring that Pritchet advised him, the said Thomas, to buy it of Peterson and so be his Neighbour.

Several others also affirm that Pritchet never till very lately pretended to the whole but confessed that W. Faucet had right to 50 acres, which Isa. Taylor also declares he heard both Pritchet and his Wife this Last Summer acknowledge.

Sam'l Levis, designed an Evidence for Pritchet, says that several years ago (viz: about 1684) he heard a discourse at Ja. Sandilands That Matson had acted a very ill thing for he had Convey'd all his Plantation to one man when he had sold half of it long before to another.

Several of the Neighbours present also affirm that Pritchet (which he himself acknowledges) has offered W. Ffaucet £50 for his right, but this Pritchet says was to buy peace, or to satisfy for the Improvements w'ch he owns he had no right to in equity.

All which alligations on both sides being duly weighed it appears that Walter Ffaucet has a right to one Moiety of the Tract first reputed an hundred acres, but there being so much Intricasy in the Division made by this last Resurvey the Confirmation is deferr'd till further Consideration, some thinking it Necessary to be done by a Writt de Partitione facienda.

Signed a war't to Jos. Wilcox for his Rope Walk, &c., ordered 20 Ult.

Signed a war't to Rand. Spakeman for 32 acres of Liberty Land, Dan'l Smith 8 acres thereof in right of Smith's own purchase of 500 acres, 8 acres in right of Sager and Baily, 8 acres in right of Wm. Isaac, 4 acres in right of Hen. Bernard and 4 acres in right of Jno. Rety, all on Delaware side, Ordered 5th Instant.

Signed a War't to Thos. Bye and Marg't, his Wife, for 250 acres to Edw'd Simkins, Ordered 29th Ultim.

Signed a War't to John Bittle, Res. on a Lott, ord'd 31st Ult.

———

At a Sessions of the Commissioners at Philad'a the 12th of the 11 Month, 1701.

Present, Edward Shippen, Griffith Owen, Thomas Story, James Logan, Secr'y.

Evan Powell having bought of Rich'd Taylor 300 acres of land in the County of Philad'a, who bought it of Thos. Fairman, being part of the Overpluss of the Manor of Moreland, laid out as is said in Right of Stanly's purchase, to which 'tis feared the said T. F. can make no title, and if so, will prove the Prop'rs Land still, the said Evan therefore requests that if it be found Taylor and Fairman can make him no title to it, The Commiss'rs would grant him the previledge of purchasing it before any other, in Consideration of the Improvem'ts he has made thereon, which is granted. But T. F. offers to Clear the Title.

Nathaniel Allen having, by Deeds of Lease and Release dated 26th and 27th of July, 1681, Purchased of the Propr'y 2,000 acres of Land, of which there has been laid out to him 600 acres on Neshaminah and 750 in Warminst'r Township, both in Bucks, and 32 acres in the City Liberties, Nehemiah Allen, his son and Heir, requests warrants for the remaining 618 acres.

Ordered that Warr'ts be granted to take up the said 618 acres in two Tracts.

John Kinsey Produces an acc't Signed by Phin. Pemberton, taken out of James Harrison's Books, by which it appears he had bought and paid for 200 acres of Land of the Prop'ry, also a Copy of a Warrt out of the Surv'rs Office Signed by Ja. Claypoole and Robt. Turner, dated 4th 6 mo., 1684, for 200 acres bo't of Ja. Harrison and 100 more on rent to be laid out in the County of Philad'a, also a draught Under the Dav. Powell's hand of the said quantities, which the said David, Being present, affirms is located in the Welch Tract and thereupon the said John Kinsey requests a Resurvey in order to a Patent and to purchase of the rent of the 100 acres.

The arrears of rent on the 100 acres is £10 (viz: 16 years at 12s 6d p'r year) and the Purchase is £11 in all £21, which he agrees to pay.

Ordered thereupon a War't as requested and Patent, &ca.

John Walker's request made first Ult., entred pa. 10, for a Confirmation of a front Lott of 45 foot, being further inquired into and considered it is found that R'd Davis had no right nor pretence to either Lott or Liberty Land upon the acco't of his purchase of 5,000 ac'rs, he having made that purchase only in Trust and forthwith convey'd it all away to his employers, who have all taken up their Lotts in the several parts of the City according to their respective shares, as has fully appeared by that Purchase being Called over and Stated in the Minutes of the Welch Tract q. v., and Davies had a right only to 25 foot front appurten't to his own Purchase of 1,250 acres, part of the said 45 foot, which is allowed, but the other 20 foot is a Wrong grant and not to be Confirmed.

Ordered therefore that the Confirmation be deferr'd, and Jno. Walker is advised to buy some first purchaser's Right to a Lott app't to 1,000 acres and to locate it there, seeing he cannot well part with it being Inventoried for parcel of The. Langston's Estate, whose widdow he Married. When this Lott is Confirmed, whether only 25 foot or the whole 45 foot, Joshua Tittery producing a Deed from Thomas Langston, dated 2d 7br., 1698, for the back part of the whole 45 foot fronting the 2d Street and in depth   foot, is to have a Patent for the same.

And the rest to be Confirmed to Jno. Walker and his Wife Sarah, Relict of Thos. Lagnston, for the use of the s'd Sarah and her Daughter, Sarah Langston.

Francis Chadds' request, pa. 24 being further considered, especially upon his pleading an absolute Ruine to the Estate if they should be disappointed of that Lott for which they honestly paid without any Design of fraud, and had given bond to make a Title in a very considerable sum, also that it was Located by the Surveyor Gen'll, who had made a due return thereof in pursuance of a Warrant from the Prop'ry himself.

It is ordered that a Patent be granted, which was this day signed but dated the 29th Ult.

Francis Chadds having purchased of Daniel Smith 500 acres of Land upon Brandy Wine Creek, in Chester Coun., laid out in right of Hen. Bernard, first purchaser by the List, of 250 acres, and so it has been in ye Deeds, but now by a rasure is made 500 acres, which cannot be allowed.

And Dan'l having a Right to more land, He requests, together with Randal Spakeman, adm'ror Smith's Estate, that the whole 500 acres may be Confirmed to him, and that what is wanting in right of Hen. Bernard may be allowed out of some other purchase that Dan'l has a right to, and in Order thereunto Requests a Resurvey, which is granted and Patent.

Andrew Heath desires that when the land in Bucks, sold to him by the Gov'r for John Snowden and Peter Worral, in right of Will'm Venable, is to be Confirmed by Patent to him, the s d Andrew and Elizabeth, his Wife, and to John Hutchinson and Joyce, his Wife, and Frances Venables, the said Elizabeth being Relict and Joyce and Frances Daughters of the said William, which is approved of.

The Prop'ry having, by Deeds of Lease and Release dated 11th and 12th of Aug't, 1682, sold to Benja. Furly, of Roterdam, five thousand acres of Land in this Province, Dan'l and Justus Falkner produce a Letter of attorney to themselves from the said Benjamin, dated 23 of April, 1700, N.S., Impowering them, the said attorneys, to enter upon, Lease out or sell the said Land. Also a paper wrote in the Prop'rs own hand directed to the Secretary in these Words:

JAMES:

Prepare a War't for 4,000 acres for Benjamin Furly, out of which 3 War'ts for 500 acres Each for Falkner and Brother and Dorothy and Brother and Sister, which recommend to the Commiss'rs of Propriety if not done before I goe; 25th 8br., 170¹.

WILL'M PENN.

Which directions to the Secretary are in pursuance of Certain Powers and Orders exprest in the aforesaid power of attorney.

Upon this they request a War't of Resurvey on what Land there is already laid out to the said Benjamin in right of the said purchase and in the same war't to take up the remainder.

Ordered that a War't be granted as Requested.

There being a Vacant piece of Land in the Township of Bethel, in the County of Chester between Wm. Fleming's Land and ye line of the Manor of Rocklands, reputed to contain 150 acres, Wm. Garret requests a grant of one hundred acres thereof for which he has agreed to pay £30 on the 29th of 7br., next, which is granted in Case he think fitt to stand to the Bargain; has been setled 2 years.

William Fleming requests a grant for the remaining 50 acres upon the same terms, Viz: £15 to be paid at Michaelmas Next, which is granted as the above.

Signed Israel Taylor's Patent for 562 acres, Ord'd 5th Instant.

At a Sessions of the Commissioners at Philad'a the 14th of the 11 mo., 1701.

Present, Edward Shippen, Griffith Owen, Thomas Story, James Logan, Secretary.

John Chandler being sent over about 15 or 16 years agoe an Indented Serv't to the Prop'ry for 4 years, which he faithfully served at Pennsberry, under a Coven't In the Indentures formerly produced to the Secretary, that he should have 100 acres of Land at the expiration of his time, which he has not yet had but was promised by the Prop'ry before his departure that it should be granted to him, Requests a War't for taking up the same at ½ penny Sterling p'r acre Rent.

Ordered that a War't be accordingly Granted.

George Smedley, of the Township of Providence being seated on a Tract of land in the County of Chester, reputed and laid out for 250 acres, purchased of the Prop'ry when first here and paid for since his last arrival, had the same resurveyed by Hen. Hollingsworth, under whose hand he produces an acc't of the resurvey, making it to contain 295 acres, upon which said Survey he requests a Patent and agrees to pay for the Overplus, Seven pound ten shillings.

MINUTE BOOK "G." 245

Ordered that a Patent be accordingly granted, he paying the said £7 10s upon the delivery of the said Patent.

Cornelius Empson for himself and several others to the Number of 20 families chiefly of the County of Chester, proposes to make a Settlement on a tract of land about half way between Delaware and Susquehannah, or near the latter, being about 24 Miles distant from New Castle, on Otteraroe River, in Case they may have a grant of twenty thousand acres in the said place at a bushell of wheat p'r 100 rent, or five pounds purchase, to be after at a Shill. Sterling p'r ann., which being duly Considered and the advantages that might arise thereby by rendering ye adjacent Lands more Valuable and incouraging the Settlement of Susquehannah River, 'tis proposed that they shall have 15 or 20,000 acres at £8 p'r 100 or at 2 bushells of wheat rent p'r ann., the first year for their incouragement to be free of Rent, or one year Creditt to pay the purchase money. He agrees to the price of purchase or to a Bushell and ½ p'r ann., But is referred to their further Consideration.

Jno. Guest, Esqr., having in pursuance of a War't Ordered 8th Ult., caused a Survey to be made on the Tract of Vacant Land then granted and reputed only 100 Acres, finds the same to Contain 176 Acres, and being Desirous to purchase the Whole Vacancy Requests to know the price. Agreed because the Tract is so small and for an Incouragem't to his Improvem'ts that he shall have it at £8 p'r 100 and a Bushell of Wheat Rent, Upon which a Patent is Ordered when he shall apply, with a Due Return of Survey on the same.

There being a Tract of Vacant Land lying between the lands of Geo. Smedly, David Ogden, Thomas Minshal and Ridly Creek, in the Township of Providence and County of Chester, left out and untaken up hitherto because of its Excessive barrenness, Hen. Hollingsworth being Settled in a Mill adjoining with only Six Acres of Land belonging to it, Requests a grant of the said Land for the Conveniency of Firing, &c., and agrees to pay for ye same ten pounds p'r 100, which is Granted as Requested.

Jno. Wood, of Duck Creek, in the County of Newcastle, haveing before his Land and between it and the s'd Creek and Delaw. Bay a parcel of broken Salt Marsh which he would purchase of the Proprietary and proposed to the Secr'y, J. L., when down there last summer with the Prop'rs Commision to give in Exchange for the same 200 Acres of fast Land lying in the same Neck and upon some Expectations given him that his Request might be granted, procured the said Marsh to be survey'd and found it to Contain between 2 and 300 Acres, Requests now a War't to Authorize the said Survey and a Confirmation of the Proposalls Aforesaid, Alledging that the Prop ry, when he went ashore there at his last Sailing out of the Bay, promised that he should have it, Which being duly Considered 'tis thought fitt the grant should be deferr'd till a better Assurance of the Prop'rs mind therein Can be had.

Abraham Brewster, having upon Encouragem't from J. L., when in Newc. Coun. last summer, procured a survey to be made by Geo. Dakayne, Surveyor of the s'd County, on a tract of Vacant land found to Contain 247 Acres, Requests to know on w't terms he may have ye same.

Offered at £12 p'r 100 and a Bushell of Wheat Rent, with which, if he agree, a War't is ordered.

Humphrey Best and Joseph Wheeldon applying themselves last sum'er to the Secretary, J. L., in the County of Newcastle, when sent thither w'th the Propr's Commission for some Land on the west side of the King's Road Near the head of Duck Creek in the s'd County, on which they desired forthwith to settle and improve, and Best to sett up his Trade which is a Smith, And upon Encouragem't given them they accordingly Settled and procured the Surveyor of the County to run them out 400 Acres between them, To Authourize which Survey they Request a War't and that they may hold it at a penny sterling p'r Acre from the time of Survey.

Ordered that a War't be granted as requested.

Peter Oldson, being lately seated on a Tract of Land about 8 Miles from New Castle on Maryland Road, by some Encouragem't given him last Summer, Requests a grant of 100 Acres, for which (by his Ord'r to George Dakeyne, who Solicits for him) he agrees to pay Sixteen pounds at or before the 29th of 7br. Next, at two several payments, the first to be by the first of the 3 mo. and one Bushell of wheat yearly Rent ever after. Ordered that a War't be granted for 100 Acres in case the said Peter shall stand to the said agreem't.

Obadiah Holt being seated upon the same foot as Peter Oldson, on a Tract Next Adjoyning beyond him, Requests a grant for 150 or 200 Acres on the same terms as Peter Oldson is to have his.

Ordered that a War't be granted to the said Obadiah for the said quantity of Acres at £16 p'r 100, One Moiety thereof to be paid the first of ye 3d Mo'th Next, and the other the 29th of 7br. at a Bushell of Wheat Rent.

Andrew Anderson Requests a Resurvey on a Tract of Land on Apoquiniminck Creek where he is Seated, reputed 200 Acres.

Ordered that a Warr't of Resurvey be granted.

George Hogg, of the town of New Castle, requests a Warr't

for the Bank before his Lott in pursuance of the Gov'rs grant entred pa. 35.

Ordered that a Warr't be accordingly granted.

George Dakeyne, Surveyor of the County of New Castle, having Petitioned the Prop'ry, before his departure, for Six hundred Acres on Red lyon Run in the said County, which Petition the Prop'ry was pleased to underwrite in his own hand, Granted at two bushells of wheat or a Country penny p'r Acre. In pursuance of the said Grant the said George Requests a Warrant to take up the same.

Ordered that a Warrant be accordingly granted, But that the Rent be ten shillings Country Money, p'r 100, to which he agrees.

Ordered that Geo. Dakayne. in Consideration of the Prop'rs gracious Grant aforegoing and as an Acknowledgem't of his Gratitude for the same, shall Resurvey all the Lands from the Mouth of Christina Creek to Christina Bridge, and along the River Delaw. to Newcastle Town, being Chiefly those that follow Jno. Lewden's, Robt. Hutchinson's, The Swisses, John Hussey's and Compa., Ingilbert Lotts, Jno. Richardson's, Jun'r, Widdow Polson, De la Grange's, with several others adjoyning; John Hunt's, Peter Catt's and Several Vacant Plantations into which he is to Enquire and as far as possible know their Titles, Jacob Clauson's, Paul Polson's, Widow Smith's, Erick Erickson's, Widdow le Fevre's, all Pard hook Lands; Nicholas Lockyer's and all others within the said Bounds for which 'tis Ordered that a Warrant be forthwith Issued to the said George for the same.

At a Session of the Commissioners at Philad'a the 19th of ye 11th Mo'th, 1701.

Present, Edward Shippen, Griffith Owen, Thomas Story, James Logan, Sec'ry.

It haveing pleased God to remove our Surveyor Gen'll, Edw'd Penington, by Death on the 10th of this Instant, The Commiss'rs to whose care the said Office is Committed by the Prop'rs Commission, think fitt to take the disposall thereof into their Consideration, And having duely weighed the Prop'rs affairs of Property in this Province and Territories, as they now stand in Relation to that Act of Assembly passed at Newcastle and Confirmed at Philad'a, commonly called the Law of Property, and especially in respect to Resurveys, Ordered by the said Act; and having also Considered the Uneasiness and Complaints of the People upon Acc't of the Fees and Charges of that Office which has very much retarded the

Progress of Resurveys being made by the People, and Several of the Deputy Surveyors having Remonstrated to the Commiss'rs That the said Office is of no great Service to the People, Seeing it may be managed without any such Officer, and with no less Safety to both them and the Prop'ry, It is thought fitt to order, that unless the Prop'ry himself shall see cause to appoint a Surveyor Gen'll from England, or till his pleasure be further known herein, There shall be no such Officer appointed.

That in the Mean time the said Office with all the Books, records, War'ts and Papers belonging thereunto shall be taken into the Comm'rs hands, and remain Under their Care, and that the Secr'y shall Chiefly Superintend the same with the Assistance of an able, fitt hand, well skilled in Surveying.

That Jacob Taylor, now concerned in a school at Abington, be invited to take the management of the said office under the Secr'y or other Commiss'rs upon him.

That all warrants shall be directed to the several Surveyors of the respective Counties to be returned into the Surveyor's Office at Philad'a.

That for the greater Security both of Prop'ry and People the Original War'ts Shall not be scattered or sent into the Country, but kept in the Office as before, and be there also entred in the Books, and that Copies of the Originals, attested by the Secretary, shall be sent into the Countrey to the Surveyors.

That to make the said Warrants the more Authentick, in every Original Warr't Under the Province Seal and Commiss'rs hands, it shall be express'd That the said Original shall remain in the Surveyor's office at Philad'a, and that a Copy thereof, attested as aforesaid, shall be sent to the Surveyor to whom it is directed and that the returns made by the Several Surveyors into the Surveyor's office at Philad'a Shall be delivered when examined, therein to the Secretaries Office as before, in order to a Confirmation.

That all the fees in the Surveyor's office, complained against by the Assemby, shall be thrown off, and only the examination of the Draught and Return into the Secretaries office paid for.

That all riding Charges shall be thrown off.

That the price of Surveying Lands shall stand, But that Resurveys be reduced from 7s and 6d for the 2d hundred to 6s, 8d, but that for the support of the Office and payment of T. F's Salary and other Incident Charge each Surveyor shall pay to the Office 20d out of every Second and third Hundred, &c., and double the same out of the first and proportionably for Surveying of Lotts.

That what the said allowances made by the Surveyors shall

exceed the Necessary Charges of the Office, such overplus shall be allowed and converted to the payment of Chain Carriers and such others, in Resurveys made at the Prop'rs Charge.

That new Commissions and Instructions shall be granted to all the Surveyors.

That Each Surveyor give bond to the Prop'ry, with Securities, in the Sum of (at least) two hundred pounds for the due Discharge of their Office.

That all Chain Carriers be attested as before.

Thomas Fairman, by Deed dated 25th of February, 1698-9, sold to Isaac Jacobs 1,100 Acres of Land located in the Deed above the New Welch Tract, being part of Wm. Stanly's purchase of 5,000 Acres, and was bought by the s'd Thomas of Peter Bainton, who Married Rebecca, the said Stanly's widdow, Survey'd in a Tract of 2,500 Acres by Virtue of a Warr't from the Commiss'rs, dated 30th 7mo., 1684. Isaac Jacobs by the Name of Isaac Van Bebber, by Assignm't, endorsed on the said Deed dated 6th Mar., 1699-00, Sold the said tract of 1,100 Acres to Alexand'r Edwards, who is possessed of 900 thereof and sold the remaining 200 to Job Bates. The said Alexand'r requests a Resurvey on the Tract he holds, Viz:' 900 Acres.

Ordered that a War't of Resurvey be granted on the whole 1,100, and that the Division Line be run between Bates' and Edwards'.

John Guest, Esqr., having Purchased of Francis Cook, Ex'or of the last Will and Testament of Jas. Claypoole, dec'd, two parcells of Land in the County of Newcastle near White Clay Creek, one of 150 Acres bought by the said James of John Ogle, and the other of 180 Acres taken up by J. Claypoole by the Prop'rs War't upon Rent, Requests a Resurvey on them both in one and to know the price of what Overplus shall be found there.

Ordered that a War't be accordingly granted and the price is agreed ten pounds p'r 100 and a Bushell of Wheat Rent.

Jasper Yeats, Robert French and Francis Baldwin, Proprietors of the Mill on Naaman's Creek, Requests a grant of 100 Acres of Land on the south Side of the said Creek next the River to run in a Narrow Slip as far up as the King's Road or beyond it, that being Owners of the land on both sides of the Creek their Dam and Water may be the More Secure, for which they are Willing to pay the Utmost Value.

Ordered that the Place be first Viewed and Further Considered, and that in the Mean time it be granted to no other without their Knowledge.

Daniel and Justus Falkner, Attorneys for the Frankfort Company, produceing a Patent from the Prop'ry dated 28th 5

Mo., 1684, for a front, Second and third Street Lott on Society Hill, each of 102 foot in breadth in which the Rent as it now stands is 16s, Sterl., p'r Ann., but is made so by a rasure or alteration and appears to have been Eleven shillings, of which having Complained to the Prop'ry before his Departure he promis'd them Redress, and thereupon they Crave a new Patent upon ye Old Rent, viz: Eleven Shillings Sterling.

Which being duly Considered and Examined and there being no shew nor Colour of Reason why the said Rent should have been altered or made so high, and that Eleven Shills. is the utmost that can be Demanded according to the Proportion of other rents in ye Town.

'Tis Ordered that a New Patent be granted at 11s p'r Ann. as requested.

James Harland Requests a grant of one Moiety of a Tract reputed 3 or 400 Acres in Christina Hundred, on which he is setled but was never Survey'd, lying between the New Welch Tract, John Ogle's land and Judge Guest's, for which he agrees to pay twelve pounds, ten shillings p'r 100 and a bushell of wheat Rent Ever after, the money to be paid at three payments in 18 months.

Ordered that a War't be granted as Requested.

The Prop'ry having, at his Departure, Granted to Joseph Growdon that his Lands between Potquessin and Neshamineh should be erected in to a Manor, and as an order for the same left in his Directions to the Secr'y the following Words in his own Land: [That Joseph Growdon have a Manor as mean Lord for his 10,000 Acres, if he has his Father's Ord'rs, but else for 5,000 only], the s'd Joseph Requests that for the greater Conveniency of the s'd Manor it may be inclosed by the Natural bounds, Neshamineh, Delaware and Potquessin, and the Eastern line of Southampton Township, including all the lands Contained within the s'd bounds, as well those belonging to other persons as those laid out to or purchas'd by himself, All the Quitrents of which he would either buy of the Prop'ry or lay them on such Lands as he holds himself and so become Answerable for the whole, and in Order thereunto he requests a Resurvey on the said Lands being those that follow, Viz: The Land laid out to himself and Father for 5,000 Acres or thereabouts, his Tract at Bensalem on the River Laid out for 900 Acres (as he says) in right of the same Purchase with 250 adjoyning bought of John Test, A Tract purchased of Tho. Fairman for 600 Acres, A Tract he purchased of John Bowen for 250 Acres, upon old Rent, A Tract of 952 acres, late of Jno. Tatham, on old rent, A Tract of Sam'l Allen's, A Tract of 80 Acres sold by Tho. Fairman to Michael Fredrickson, A

Tract of 250 Acres, late of Nathan'l Harding, A Tract of Dunck Will'm's of about 250 A's, A Tract of 600 Acres laid out to Nathan'll Allen, A Tract of 400 A's, late of Walter Forrest, A Tract of 100 Acres of Jno. Gilbert's, Containing in all by his Estimation, about 12 or 13,000 Acres, the greatest part of which he has some kind of Claim to.

Which Request being taken into Consideration 'tis doubted whether the same will not overstrain the Prop'r's Directions and is therefore deferr'd to be further thought of or referred to the Prop'ry that his mind may be better known therein, In the meantime 'tis thought fitt that a Resurvey be granted on all the s'd Lands as Requested.

At a Session of the Commiss'rs at Philad'a the 21st of the 11th Month, 1701.

Present, Edward Shippen, Griffith Owen, Thomas Story, James Logan, Sec'ry.

There being a Tract of Vacant Land lying between the thousand Acres of Jno. Guest, Esqr., the Land of Jonas Arskin and white Clay Creek, on part of which Jno. King, upon Encouragm't given him the Last Summer, is seated, The said Jno. Guest requests a grant of the same for the better Accommodation of his s'd Tract of 1,000 Acres, and making his Land Contigious to the Creek, at such Rate as may be thought the Value thereof. Ordered that John King have the Refusal for an Accom'odation for a Settlement first, and that Judge Guest have the Refusall of the Remainder.

James Cooper, Hannah Cooper, Robert Scotchorn, Henry Giles, Francis Crompton, Dan'l Hybert, John Marshall, Robert Smith, Jno. Kirk, John Roads, Thomas Collier and John Ball, having all come in Serv'ts in the years 1682 and '83, as by Certificates from Jno. Blunston, &c., Does appear, Request their head Land, according to the Prop'rs Engagem't. Ordered to the first Six one War't, and to the last Six another for 300 Acres each, to be laid out in the Township allotted for Servants.

Ellis Jones producing a Return of 5 foot Surveyed to him the 17th of the 12th Mo'th, 1693-4, by the Surveyor Gen'll, by Vertue of a Warr't from the former Commiss'rs bearing date 20th 11 mo., '93-4, Sci:uate between Thomas Tunniclifs to the North and Rich'd Davies to the South, in the Front street of Philad'a, being in Length 426 foot, purchased by the said Ellis of the said Commiss'rs for five pounds, for ye paym't of which he produces a Receipt Under Rob't Turner's hand, dated 29th

4th Mo., 1694, by Order of the Commiss'rs and for the Prop'r's Use, Requests a Patent for the same. Granted as Requested.

William Bolding producing a Deed from Jerem. Powel and Th. Jenner dated 20th 8br., 1698, for a High Street lott, in breadth 33 foot, and in length 306 foot, bounded Eastward with Will'm Clow's Lott, South with back lotts, West with (then) vacant Lotts, North with the High Street laid out to Richard Davies, 30th 8br., 1692, by Vertue of the Gov'r's War't dated 29th 1 Mo., 1684, in Right of his purchase of 1,250 Acres, sold by Thos. Lloyd, William Powell, Hugh Roberts, John Humphry and David, Attorneys to said Richard to Jeremiah Powel, whose brother David Aforesaid Sold the Liberty Land and High Street Lott appurtenant to the said purchase of 1,250 Acres to Thomas Jenner, who jointly with Jeremiah Powel (there being no Conveyance from him before) by the first Mentioned Deed, Sold it to W. B. aforesaid; Requests a Confirmation, which is granted as Requested.

The Proprietary by Deeds dated   , Sold to John Barber 2,500 Acres now mostly belonging to his Widdow, Eliz. Webb, in right of which there was laid out 5th 3 Mo., 1683, by warr't Dated 28th 2 mo , 1683, a Lott in Dellaware front of 51 foot in breadth to the s'd Elizabeth, his Widdow, to whom the s'd John, by his last Will dated 20th 7 mo., 1682, bequeathed his whole Estate, some Legacies excepted. Constituting her sole Exec'x of his Will, of which Lott she being thus possessed exchanged it with her Father, John Longhurst, for another on the other Side of Sassafras Street, being the front Corner, by means of which Exchange the s'd Jno. Longhurst became possest thereof, who dying Insolvent, Zech. Whitpaine w'th several others obtained an Execution upon Judgm't by Court ag'st Jno. Longhurst, Heir to the s'd Jno., his Father, for the said Lott, and the said Zechariah Whitpaine for himself, Patrick Robinson, Attorney for Robt. Webb, of Maryland, Benja'n Chambers, Ex'or of Wm. Wade's last will, and Robt. Ewer, Attorney for Mercy Philips, to whom the said Lott was Conveyed by Jno. White, high Sheriff of Philad'a, by Deed dated 1st Mar., 1692-3, did by their Deed dated 8th Mar., 1692-3, convey the same to James Jacobs, of Philad'a, Cordwainer, who Requests a Patent for the same, which is granted.

Will'm Bolding produces a Deed dated 20th 8br., 1698, from Thos. Wollaston and Thomas Jenner for a Lott of 33 foot in breadth, and in Length 306 foot in high street, bounded Northw'ds with the s'd street, Eastw'd with Rich'd Davies, now in the possession of said Bolding, Westw'd with (then) Vacant Lotts, and laid out to Willi'm Powel, first purchaser of 1,250

MINUTE BOOK "G."

Acres, 16th 10 Mo., 1692, by Vertue of the Gov'r's Warr't, in the Office, dated 29th 1 Mo., 1684, who by Deed dated 1st 2 Mo., 1697, conve'd the same to Thomas Wollaston, who sold (as it seems) to Thomas Jenner, but not convey'd, who jointly with Wollaston, by the first recited Deed, conveyed the same to Wm. Bolding, who thereupon requests a Patent.

W. Powel's Lott fell on Skuylkill, but his front is confirmed wrongfully by us on Dellaware to Wm. Fisher, pa. 8, Haerendum ergo.

Edward Wilburn, of Concord, Blacksmith, Requests a grant of 94 acres of Vacant Land in the County of Chester, bounded by James Chevers, Widdow Budd and John Chaffan, within the Manor of Rocklands, but without Newcastle Line, for which he agrees to pay twenty-fiye pounds within Six Months.

Ordered a Warr't as Requested and a Patent on the Return.

Thos. Shaw, of Duck Creek, in the County of Newcastle, having procured a Warr't of Resurvey on a Tract of 100 acres purchased of Caleb Offly, which proved by exact Measure to Contain 107 acres, Requests a Patent on the same, which was granted.

Samuel Carpenter having produced in the Secri'es office, before the Prop'rs Departure, a Patent under the hands of Wm. Markham, Rob't Turner and Jno. Goodson, dated 19th 2 Mo., 1694, for 200 a's, Granted by War't from the Prop'ry 14th 4 Mo., 1683, and laid out by Ord'r of the Surveyor Gen'll (as is said in one Draught) 5th 5 Mo., 1690 [vid old setlers of Buckingham in D. L., and Is. Norris, pa. 50], to John Otter on Old Rent, Near Bristol, which 200 a's, by assignm't on the back of the Patent dated 20th 2 Mo., 1694, and by a Separate Deed Poll of ye same date, were convey'd by Said Otter to Sam'l Carpenter, also a Copy of a Return of Survey dated 6th 5 Mo., 1691, in pursuance of the Gov'r's Warr't dated 25th 5 Mo., 1684, for 25 acres in the County of Bucks, being part of the Overplus of Sam'l Clift's Land, laid out to Francis and Michael Rossel the same day of the date of the war't, also a Deed dated 1st 6 Mo., 1698, from Thos. Brock for 8 a's, being parcel of 30 acres Left by Sam'l Clift by Will dated 23rd 9 Mo., 1682, to his Son Joseph English, who sold 3 acres thereof to Francis Rossel, and the other 27 a's to s'd Brock, the first p'r Deed dated 10th 9 Mo., 1683, the other by deed Dated 6th 2 Mo., 1692, about the bounds of which 3 acres there being a Difference between said Brock and Rossel, in his Life time, and Rossel, by his last will dated 5th 8 Mo., 1694, having left all that his said Land with others to Sam'll Carpenter, said Brock convey'd 5 acres from himself with the said three acres included, in all 8 acres, to the end that all Differences thereupon for the future might be ended, also a Deed Poll dated 9th 1 Mo., 1696-7, from John Town for a Small Lott 63 foot Long, joyning on the Creek bought by the said Sam'l Carpenter, because of a Claim made by said Town to the ground on which one Corner of the Mill stands, the said Lott was purchased with other land by said Town of John Smith, by Deed Poll dated 8th 1 Mo., 1696-7, and by him of John White by Deed Dated   , to Whom it was granted by Patent; Said S. C. Requests a Resurvey on all the said Tracts in Order to a Patent; He produced also a Deed Poll dated 16th 4 Mo., 1696, trom Peter White and his Wife, Daughter of Joseph English, for about 3 acres and ½ appurtenant to the Mill Land but not Contigious to the above, who [i. e., S'd English] marrying the Daughter of Sam'll Cliff, became Heir to one Moiety of his Lands Left in this Province upon the Death of Said Cliff's son in England, declared Heir upon his Father's decease, for Cliff's Land, Vid ut antea, pa. 50, Requests a Confirmation of this also.

Ordered a Warr't of Resurvey on all the Tracts and Lotts aforegoing, the first 4 to be Confirmed in one and the Last as shall appear further.

Signed a Patent to Thos. Shaw, ordered this Day.

Signed a War't of Resurvey to Jos. Growdon, Ordered 19th Inst.

Signed a War't of Resurvey to Sam'll Carpenter, Ordered this day.

At a Session of the Commiss'rs at Philad'a the 26th of the 11th Month, 1701.

Present, Edward Shippen, Griffith Owen, Thomas Story, James Logan, Sec'ry.

The Prop'ry, by Deeds of Lease and Release dated 21st and 22d of Mar., 1681, convey'd to John Alsop 1,000 acres, who sold or made over the same to Tho. Tunnicliff by Deed dated 19th July, '84, in right and part of which by Vertue of a War't dated 26th 5 Mo., 1686, there was Surveyed to s'd Tunnicliff 29th of the same month 16 a's of Liberty Land, who by Ind're dated 19th 6 mo., 1687, convey'd the said 16 acres to Rob't Longshore, who by Deed Dated 3rd 10 Mo., 1687, sold the same to Chr'r Sibthorp.

Edw'd Blake, first purchaser of 250 acres, by deed dated 5th 6 mo., 1691, sold 4 acres, his proportion of Liberty Land (together with 4 following), to said Chr. Sibthorp.

Joseph Powel, Original Purchaser of 250 acres, by his attorney, Tho. Cross, Sold 4 acres, his proportion of Lib. Land, to the above said Ed. Blake, who by the above recited deed sold the same with the aforegoing 4 acres as aforesaid. Tho. Scott, purchaser of 500 acres, did also (as 'tis said) some way Transfer his right to 8 acres of Lib'ty Land, the Proportion of the said purchase, to Christo. Sibthorp; s'd Sibthorp purchased Scott's whole Right.

Tho. Cobb, first purchaser of 250 acres, transferring his Right in the same to Christ'r Davison, Sen'r, and his son of the same name, they, the said Christ'rs by Deed dated 16th 9 mo., 1685, convey'd their Right to the Lib'ty Land belonging to the said purchase to s'd Geo. Walker.

Wm. Neal, also purchaser of 250 acres, Convey'd the same to s'd Geo. Walker by a Deed now in the hands of Wm. Garret, to whom he sold all but the Lib. Land, which Lib. Land the said George took up.

Sam'll Bennett, first Purchaser of 250 acres, by deed dated 10th 1 mo., 1691, convey'd his proportionable part, viz: 4 acres, to Christ'r Sibthorp.

Christo. Sibthorp, in right of Blake, Powel, Scott and Bennet, took up 20 acres, which with the first Mentioned sixteen, he by Deed dated 6th, 12 Mo., 1698-9, convey'd to George Walker.

George Walker, by deed dated 1st 1 Mo., 1698-9 convey'd the afors'd 36 acres of Alsop, Blake, Powel, Scott and Bennet convey'd to him by Sibthorp, and the other 8 acres purchased of Davison and Scott to Nicholas Waln (in all 44 acres), who Request a Resurvey on the same, as also on 172 acres by him purchased of Joshua Carpenter and lying Contiguous with the Former in one Tract.

Ordered that a War't of Resurvey be accordingly granted.

Wm. Bolding producing a Return of Survey signed by Robert Longshore for 33 foot of the Bank of Philad'a, bounded Northward with Mellisent Hodgkin's, Southwards with William Southbe's, laid out by Vertue of a War't dated 15th 12 mo., 1689-90, and Survey'd the same day, Requests a Confirmation of the same by Patent, which is Granted.

The Prop'ry having, by Deeds of Lease and Release dated 21st and 22d of April, 1682, convey'd to Thos. Crossdale, of New Hay, in York sh., yeoman, 1,000 acres of Land, 500 of which was laid out to him in the County of Bucks, his Sons, Wm. and John Crossdale, by Deed dated 23rd 6 mo., 1698, convey'd the Proportion of Liberty Land belonging to the said Purchase to Nicholas Waln, Who verbally had bargained for it many years before, and now Requests a Warr't. The said Land in Bucks was several years agoe Resurvey'd by the Commiss'rs Order and found to contain 670 acres, for the Overplus of which they agreed with and paid the said Commiss'rs.

Ordered therefore that a War't be granted to the said Nicholas Waln for the said 8 acres on this Condition; that in Case it shall not be made appear that the said 8 acres was deducted out of the said 670 or allow'd, said Nicholas Shall pay the Value of the same; 250 more thereof was sold to Tho. Slackhouse, now in the Tenure of Robert Heaton.

Susannah Brandt, Widdow of Albertus Brant, deceased, and Daughter of Jacob Telner, purchaser of 5,000 acres, producing a Return of Survey dated 8th 3 Mo., 1693, for 80 a's of Lib. Land survey'd the first of ye — mo., 1692, in right of her Father's s'd purchase, Requests a Confirmation and in Order thereunto a Resurvey.

Jacob Telner being none of the first 100 purchasers, had no right to Lib'ty Land according to the Concessions, but for Encouragem't of the Linnen Manufacture, which he brought over, had a promise from the Prop'ry of the same privileges with the first purchasers.

And the said Susannah, immediately after her husband's Interm't, applying to the Prop'ry the night before his last Departure from Philad'a, he was pleased to order the Sec'ry that it should be Confirmed.

Ordered therefore that a Resurvey be forthwith granted, &c., and Patent.

Hugh Roberts being Seated on some of the Prop'rs Land within the Liberties on the West side of Skuylkill, obtained a Survey on 200 a's by the Prop'rs Warr't, but did not agree about the price till his departure, which he then Fixed should be £150.

Of this the said Hugh has paid £60 in hand, but not being yet able to procure the rest, desires he may be allowed Some Further time and have a Patent, he giving Bond for the said Remaining Sum.

Ordered that the said Hugh give Bond for the said £90 to be paid the 29th of 7br. Next, and that a Patent be thereupon Granted.

Edward Shippen having obtained a grant from the former Commiss'rs of one whole Square of ground within the City at the Yearly rent of £5 p'r annum for a pasture and resigned the same, requests a grant of that part of the Square made by the 3d and 4th Streets and Walnut and Spruce Streets, lying Vacant behind his Orchard, for the same use, there being no likelihood of its being improved or built on because of the great descent made by the Gutt or Dock, rendering the said Street impassable that way, for which he agrees to pay fifteen shillings of Country Money Yearly Rent for 51 years and then to Surrender it well fenced and improved with English Grass for pasture. Ordered that a War't and Pat't be accordingly granted.

By G. O., T. S. and J. L.

Signed a Patent to Timothy Stevenson for a Lott, Ordered 10 br. 29th.

At a Session of the Commiss'rs at Philad'a the 28th of the 11th Month, 1701.

Present, Edward Shippen, Griffith Owen, Thomas Story, James Logan, Sec'ry.

The Prop'ry, by Deeds of Lease and Release dated 26th and 27th July, 1681, convey'd to Tho. Coborne 500 a's of Land in Right of which there was laid out to the said Thomas in the County of Chester 492 acres. Joseph and Wm. Coborne, only sons of the said Thomas, and Ex'ors of his last Will by Deed dated 1st 6 Mo., 1700, Sold to Wm. Cuarton 10 acres, the Proportion of Liberty Land belonging to the said purchase, who requests a War't to take up the same. Ordered that 8 acres, the remainder untaken up, be granted and laid on the West Side of Skuylkill, as their Lott fell.

A Plantation of about 300 acres between Dragon and Red lyon Run, in the County of Newcastle, being left Vacant above fifteen years and run to ruine by the Death of Lewis David, the last Owner thereof, who deceasing intestate, and, as 'tis said, without Heirs, the said land is escheated to the Proprietary.

Joseph Hansen, of the said County, requests a grant of the same and agrees to pay £16 for every hundred acres the 25th of the first Month following.

Ordered that a War't be granted to the said Hansen as requested.

The Prop'ry, by Patent dated 5th 6 Mo., 1684, granted a bank Lott in breadth 42 foot and in Length 250 foot to Wm. Frampton, who dying insolvent, Rob't Skelton and Alice, his Wife, Relict and adm'x of John Throckmorton, Sole Ex'or of Joseph Throckmorton, recovered the said Lott with others by Execution for a Debt due by the said Will'm to the said Joseph, as by a Record of Philad'a Court dated   at large appears. Robert and Alice, his Wife, being so seized of the said bank Lott (together with the front lott in right of which the Bank was granted) by Deed dated 24th July, 1696, convey'd the same to Philip Richards, who by deed dated 3rd Jan'y, 1697, sold the said Lotts to Charles Read, who by Deed dated 3d 7br., 1700, convey'd them to Jonathan Dickinson, who in pursuance of the following petition and grant Requests to purchase off the Reversion of one-third part of the Bank coming to the Proprietary after the Expiration of 41 Years:

To William Penn, Prop'ry and Governor of the Province of

Pennsylvania and Territories, the Humble Petition of Sam'll Carpenter, Joshua Carpenter, Thomas Masters and Jonathan Dickinson, in behalf of themselves and others, Possessors or Owners of the Several Bank Lotts in Philadelphia, Sheweth:

That whereas thy Petitioners and others did take up and improve Several Lotts on the Waste bank of the said Town upon the Condition of certain Quitrents to be paid to thee and thy Heirs for ever, as also after about fifty-four years from the year 1684, the time of the first grant, to pay thee and thy Heirs one-third part of the Yearly Value of the Improvem'ts thereon for ever, with said Quitrents at first reserv'd.

And whereas thou hast been pleased to grant to the front lott Men of Newcastle the Privilege of Bank or Water Lotts before their respective Lands on reasonable rates, and not doubting of thy equall kindness and encouragement to the Inhabitants of Philad'a, who by their Industry and Charge have improved thy Interest therein, and for as much as the Conditions by which we hold the said Bank Lotts in Philad'a are not only discouraging of Improvem'ts but also in Case of Death and Necessity of the Undertakers to sell the same, what has been Laid out thereon will not yield near the Value because of the said Incumbrance. We therefore, thy Petitioners, Humbly Request that according to thy former proposal thou wilt be pleased to sell us thy Reversion or Remainder therein, Quittrents only excepted, we also request time for paym't of ye same, Viz: One-half within a year from such grant, the other half within one year after. If thou please to grant this, our Request, we shall Kindly accept thereof and desire thou wilt give Instructions to thy Commissioners of Property.

SAM'LL CARPENTER,
THOMAS MASTERS,
JONATH'N DICKINSON.

Newcastle 30th 8 Mo., 1701.

Which Petition is Indorsed as follows:

I grant this Petition and doe hereby Order and appoint my Commiss'rs of Property to sell off my Reversion in the Bank Lott in Philad'a, my Quittrents only excepted, unto the said Petitioners and others willing to purchase off the same and to Confirm the same taking for each foot twenty Shillings that is to say one-half to be allowed by those who hold the Water side part below the Street or Cartway under the Bank and the other to be allowed by those who hold that part between the said Cartway and Front street, performing within the Compass of one year after the date of this.

WM. PENN.

Upon which 'tis Ordered that the said Jonathan for £42 may buy off ye Reversion as requested and that a Patent be prepared for the same.

Elizab. Tibby, Widdow of John Tibby, first purchaser of 250 acres produces a Return of Survey dated 10th 5 mo. 1684, in pursuance of a Warr't dated 8th 2 mo., 1683, from the Prop'ry for a Lott in Walnut Street, on the North side Survey'd 13th 2 mo., 1683, to the said Jno. in right of the said purchase for which She requests a Patent. Thomas Tibby, Carp'r, Son to said Jno., as Heir has right to this Lott, but appearing before the Commiss'rs is willing that it be granted to his Mother during Life and to him, his Heirs and assigns after. Ordered as Requested.

The Prop'ry, by Deeds of Lease and Release, dated 11th 7br., 1681, sold to John Swift 500 acres, 492 whereof is laid out in the County of Bucks. The Prop'ry also by Deeds of Lease and Release dated 5th and 6th of 7br., 1681, sold to Wm. Bingly 500 acres of Land, which is also laid out in the same County, and the said Will'm, by Indenture dated 8th of August, 1699, convey'd the same with all appurtenances to said John Swift, which Deed was also signed by the Prop'ry Jointly with the said Bingly, because the first Deed was vitiated.

In right of which Purchase the said John Swift Requests a War't for 16 acres of Liberty Land, which is granted.

John Richardson, of Newcastle, having by Deed dated purchased of James Read a Lott in Newcastle.

Thomas Pierson, of Newcastle Coun., producing Returns and War'ts for 2 tracts of Land in the said County, now in his Possession, the one laid out for 200 acres on Christina, where he Now lives, the other for 400 on Peck Creek, running into White Clay Creek, requests a Resurvey in order to a Patent.

Ordered that a War't be granted and that before the said Tracts be confirmed the Title be fully Stated.

Signed a Patent to Jno. Richardson, Ordered this day, dated 26 Inst.

Signed a General War't of Resurvey on Christina Lands, ord'd 14 Inst.

Signed a War't to Jno. Pierce for 150 acres. N. C. Ord'd 7th Instant.

Signed a War't to Wm. Simpson for 100 acres, Ord'd 7 Inst.

Signed a War't to Abra. Brewster for 147 acres, Newc., Ordered 14 Inst.

Signed a War't to Hump. Best and Jos. Wheeldon for 400 acres Newc., Ord'd 14 Inst.

Signed a War't to Peter Oldson for 100 acres, Newc., Ord'd 14 Inst.

Signed a War't to Obadiah Holt for 150 acres, Ord'd 14 Instant.

Signed a War't of Resurvey to Andw. Anderson, Newc., Ord'd 14 Inst.

Signed a War't to George Hogg for his Bank in Newc., Ord'd 14.

Signed a War't to George Dakayne for 600 a's, Newc., Ord'd 14.

Signed a War't to John Guest, Esqr., Resurvey on 330 a's, Ord'd 19.

Signed a War't to James Harland for Vacant Land, Newc., Ord'd 19.

Signed a War't to Paul Garretson for part of the same, Ord'd 19 Inst.

Signed a War't to Joseph Hansen for 300 acres, Newc., Ordered this day.

Signed a War't of Resurvey to Tho. Pierson, Ordered this day.

At a Session of the Commiss'rs at Philad'a the 2d of the 12th Month, 1701.

Present, Edward Shippen, Griffith Owen, Thomas Story, James Logan, Sec'ry.

Thomas Crosdale, Purchaser of 500 acres, by Deeds of Lease and Release from the Proprietor, dated 21 and 22 Apr., 1682, obtained a War't of Survey on the City Lott appurten't to the said Purchase, dated 25th 11 mo., 1683, in Pursuance of which there was Survey'd to his Widdow, Ann Crosdale, 14th 5 mo., 1692, a Lott in the second Street on Delaware, bounded North-w'ds with Robert Lodge's and Southw'ds with then Vacant Lotts [now with Philip Howel's]. Sold by Wm. Crosdale, Heir, and John, his younger brother, by Deed dated 1st 10 mo., 1697, to David Powel, who has since Sold the Same to Rob't Adams for about £25, and in order to make him a Title requests a Patent.

This falling on part of the open Space between Hugh Derborow's and the Keithian meeting house, where Thomas Jones and John Swift have each a Promise of a Lott from the Prop'ry as well as Phil. Howel a Positive Grant, and to Supply the s'd Jones, Swift and Adams, there being only one Lott with this remaining, 'tis

Ordered that the said Lotts, consisting of Something above 100 foot, be divided into three Equal parts, and that each of them have one-third part for their Share, viz: about 34 foot or more, if there to be found, and that the Dificiency be Supply'd out of a Vacancy said to be at the back of the said Lotts in the 3d street, which if to be found, is also to be equally divided among them.

The Prop'ry, by Deeds of Lease and Release, dated 11th and 12th April, '82, sold to Tho. Barret and John Heycock 875 acres, of which 250 was Heycock's share, and the remaining 625 Acres T. Barret's, which 250 Acres the said Heycock took up in the Falls Township, in Bucks, about the year 1683, as also 50 A's on Rent Adjoyning.

The said John Heycock deceasing, Elizabeth, Relict of Wm. Venables, brother-in-law to Barret, and widdow of Lawrence Bannor, now wife of Andrew Heath, administered on his Estate, and by Vertue thereof by a Deed dated 4th 10 mo., 1694, Sold the said 200 Acres to Gilbert Wheeler, who by Deed dated 11th, 10 Mo., 1694, Convey'd the same to James Paxon, who obtained of the Prop'ry a War't of Resurvey on the said Land dated 24th 1 mo., 1700-1.

In pursuance of which War't the said Land being Resurvey'd the 15th of the 2d Month following, by Order of the Surveyor Gen'll, as by a Return under his hand dated 25th 5 Mo., 1701, appears, is found to contain 404 Acres, of which 30 being allowed by the Law, there remains 74 to be paid for. The said Ja. Paxon applying to the Prop'ry about the s'd overplus, the price was by him left to Ph. Pemberton, who sett £20 p'r 100, as by a Certificate under his hand appears, at which rate the said Overplus being about ¾ of a hundred amounts to £15 and the Purchase of the Rent of 50 Acres to £5 10s, the whole to £20 10s, for which he is to give Bond Payable , and a Patent is thereupon Granted.

The Prop'ry, by Deeds of Lease and Release, dated 4th and 5th July, 1681, convey'd to Rich'd ap Thomas 5,000 Acres of which there has been none laid out Saving 600 acres on part of 1,300 Acres laid out to Wood and Sharlow, and therefore not approved of by the Comm'rs, and 100 Acres of Lib. Land taken up by Hugh Roberts, his Son and Heir, Rich'd ap Thomas, therefore requests War'ts to take up the said Land in the Welch Tract.

The said Richard having been a Verry great Sufferer by his Father's embarquing for this Province and deceasing before or upon his Arrival, by which means he has been reduced to great hardships, 'tis Ordered that a War't be forthwith granted to take up 2,000 A's of Vacant land where to be found in the said Tract, and that War'ts be also Issued for the remainder as fast as he can be accommodated.

Hugh Davies coming over into this Province in the Ship Canterbury, had the Prop'rs promise of the same privilege

that other Servt's had at the first Setling this Province, viz:
50 Acres at ½d, Sterl'g, p'r Acre, for the taking up of which he
requests a War't as also to purchase 50 more to be added to it.

Ordered that a War't be accordingly granted for the head
Land, and that when he pitches on the place a price be sett
acccordingly for the other 50.

Signed a War't to Edw'd Shippen for part of the Square,
ord'd 26 Ult.

Signed . . . .

At a Session of the Commiss'rs at Philadelphia the 4th of
the 12th Mo'th, 1701.

Present, Edward Shippen, Griffith Owen, Thomas Story.

George Harland producing a Draught of one hundred Acres
of Land near Brandywine Cr. and a Warr't under the hands
of Wm. Markham, S. Carp'r and Jno. Goodson, dated 28th 4
mo., 1690, granting the s'd Land to be on old Rent, Viz: 1
bushell of Wheat p'r 100, provided it were 7 Miles distant from
Newcastle, requests a Resurvey in Order to a Confirmation.
Granted on Condition that he pay arrears of Rent from 1684.

George Harland having been Long helpfull to the Indians in
fencing and Improving a Settlem't made by them for some
years in a Neck or Bend of Bandywine Cr., within the Manor,
and being a great Sufferer by their vicinage as is certified by
Several of his Neighbours, requests a grant of 200 Acres of that
land over against his Plantation where the said Indians were
Setled, but have now left it, for which he agrees to pay £25 p'r
Hundred Acres.

Ordered that a War't be accordingly granted and Patent on
ye Return.

Michael and Thomas Harland, upon E. Penington's Arrival
in this Province, being desirous to take up and Settle on some
Vacant Land beyond the Inhabitants near Brandywine, had
encouragm't from the s'd Edw'd and Expectation given them
that on the Propr's arrival they might have the same privilege for the s'd Land as if vacant, upon which they entred
upon a Quantity of about 500 A's.

The Proprietary, after his arrival, having granted to Christo.
Pennock a War't for 500 Acres in right of the Rogers' Pur-
chase, dated   , the said Christopher Sold the same by a
Deed dated   , to Geo. Harland, who requests that the 500
A's taken up by his brother and Son aforesaid, may be re-
turned in pursuance of the s'd War't for which he pleads a
Grant from the Prop'ry before his Departure.

Ordered that the same be Granted, he paying £20 down in

Money as a Consideration, or that he hold the said Land at one bushell of wheat yearly Rent for every hundred Acres for ever.

George Harland produces a War't under the hands of Wm. Markham, Sam'll Carpent'r and John Goodson dated 28th 4 mo., 1690, for 500 Acres to be then Laid out on Old Rent, but is agreed to be paid from the Year 1684, on which he requests a Resurvey in Order to a confirmation, which is granted.

Thomas Hollingsworth produces a War't from the Commiss'rs signed by Wm. Markham, Sam'll Carp'r and Jno. Goodson dated 23rd 2 Mo., 1692, granting 400 Acres of Land on Brandywine at a Bushell of wheat p'r 100 (which (as is there recited) was granted at a Penny an Acre before to Valentine Hollingsworth), provided it were 7 Miles distant from Navigable Water. But 'tis affirmed That the first grant of this Land on new rent was to James Scott and Sam'l Hollingsworth who quitted it and that Valentine Never possessed it by Vertue of any other War't or grant than the first Mentioned of the 2d Mo'th, '92, he therefore Requests a Confirmation, and in Order to it, a Resurvey, which is granted on Condition that he pay Arrears of Rent from 1684 at a Bushell p'r 100.

Ordered a Warr't of Resurvey on G. Harland's 100 and 500 and . . . . this 400, and that it be directed to Hen. Hollingsworth and Patents on the Returns.

Toby Leech, Rich'd Wall, Jno. Ashmead and Everard Bolton purchas'd in this Province 1,000 Acres together by the Prop'ry of which the said Toby's share was 300 Acres for which he has now nothing to Shew but the Copy of a Return out of the office for the said Quantity, in which return he is termed renter, by some Mistake, for he had a Pat't for the said 300 Acres at the Common Rent of purchased Lands and produced it to the Proprietary and the Secretary about 18 Mo'ths ago when he paid his Quitrent for the same, he also produces several Witnesses who have seen a Receipt under the Propr's hand for the Purchase Money and therefore requests a new Patent (his old one and all his writings being burnt the last year with his House) and in order to it a Resurvey.

Ordered That a War't be accordingly granted, and upon the Return a Patent, he paying for the Overplus if any be found.

John Ashmead, Son and Heir of John Ashmead above mentioned, Purchaser with Toby Leach of 250 Acres, producing a Return of Survey from the office dated 10th 5 mo., '84, for the said 250 Acres Survey'd 30th 9 mo., 1682, by Vertue of the Propr's War't dated 10th 9 mo., '82, but has nothing More to Shew for it, his Papers having been likewise burnt, Requests a Resurvey in order to a Patent.

Ordered that a War't be granted and a Patent on the Return, he paying for the overplus, &c.

Thomas Minshal having procured of the Prop'ry a War't of Resurvey on 2 tracts of land in his Possession dated 17th 7br., 1701, the one of 315 Acres in Middletown, the other of 300 Acres in Providence, had the same executed by which the first is found to contain 380 A's and the other 373, in all 753 Acres, of which there being 60 Acres allowed by the Law, there remains 78 Acres to be paid for, which (being Very rough Land) he agrees to pay £23 and thereupon Requests a Patent which is granted. For the Title see Court of Inquiry for Chester from whence to be inserted here when the Patent is Signed.

John King having Seated himself on a Tract of Vacant Land by Encouragem't of the Sec'ry, about Midsummer Last, in the County of New Castle, joyning on John Gardiner and Muddy run, Requests a War't to take up 200 Acres for which he agrees to pay £22 10s, one-third thereof at 6 months, one-third at 12 months and the remainder at 18 Months, and a bushell of Wheat yearly Rent p'r 100 for ever.

Ordered that a War't be accordingly granted and a Patent on the Return.

Upon the Request of John Brewster, of New Castle, for ye Bank before his front Lott, Ordered that a War't be granted for so much as he has a good Title to in the said front.

Peter Dicks, of Burmingham, in the County of Chester, Requests a grant of 300 Acres of Vacant Land lying over ag'st him on the Southside of Brandywine for which he agrees to pay £50 and one shilling, Sterling, yearly Rent, £20 of the said purchase Money to be paid in hand and the residue in Six Months, Ordered that a War't be accordingly granted.

Signed a Commission to Isaac Taylor to be Surveyor of the County of Chester with Instructions, &c., Hee gives bond in £200 for the due performance of his Office.

Signed a War't of Resurvey to Fra. Chads on 500 Acres, Ord'd 12th Ult.

Signed a War't to Edw'd Wilburn for 94 Acres, Ordered 21st Ult.

Signed a War't to Geo. Harland for 500 Acres Seated by Michael and Thomas Harland, Ord'd this day, signed 16 Instant, and a War't to Peter Dicks for 300 Acres.

Signed a Warr't of Resurvey on three tracts, one to George Harland for 100 Acres, one to Ditto for 500 Acres, and one to Tho. Hollingsworth for 400 Acres, all ordered this day.

Signed a War't to John King for 200 Acres in Newc., Ord'd to-day.

At a Session of the Commissioners at Philad'a the 9th of the 12 Month, 1701.

Present, Edward Shippen, Griffith Owen, Thomas Story, James Logan, Sec'ry.

Philip Howell having purchased of Jer. Langhorne a Right to 10 Acres of Liberty Land (as in pa. 43 q. v.) requests a Warr't to take up the same.

Ordered because Tho. Langhorn, or his Widdow for him, took up his whole 500 Acres on Brandywine, that the said Jeremiah take but 490 Acres there, he having Requested a Resurvey on the said Land which is not yet performed, with which if he agree, then the said Philip to have the said Liberty Land. The said J. Langhorn's Land has never been returned, He Likewise requests a War't for 10 acres by him purchased belonging to Cuthbert Herst's purchase, but because the said purchase is all taken up and returned the said Philip is thereby wholly excluded.

The Family of the Swansons, to whom a Convenient quantity of Marsh, Meadow and Cripple, for the accommodation of their Plantations at Wickakoe, was granted by the Prop'ry by his War't dated   , having procured all the Marsh, Meadow and Cripple adjoyning on their Plantations and lying between them, Holland'rs Creek and the River, to be resurvey'd, find the same to Contain 180 A's, which they Crave, should be granted to them, but this being denied because so much exceeding the quantity allowed by the Prop'ry they refuse to accept of any, resolving to hold the whole without any grant.

A Lott in Newcastle adjoyning or Near to Wm. Howston's, formerly in the Possession of Wm. Philips, who died intestate many years agoe, seems escheated. Watts administered on his Estate and by that Claimed it but had no Title, John Parsons Solicites for a Title on Watt's behalf.

Another Lott Laid out to Maudlin Baunse in Beaver Street in the said Town, in breadth 62 foot, Survey'd 6th 4 mo., 1691, by H. Hollingsworth, by Vertue of a Warr't from the Comm'rs, seems also Escheated, the said Maudlin deceasing without Heirs, the said Watts Settled this w'th the former but without any right. To be enquired after.

Jacob Willis having formerly proved in the Sec'ries office that he came a Serv't into the Country at the first Setling of it to Wm. Clod, requests a War't for 50 Acres of Head Land as his right. Which is granted in Case it appear in the said Office.

Will'm Roberts Requests the Refusal of 500 Acres of Vacant Land Lying at the south end of Gwined Township or North Wales near Will'm and Rob't Jones, of which Expectation is given him, if free and not disposed of. Inquire of T. F., Granted to D. Lloyd and Is. Norris, 1703.

Margaret, Widdow of Peter Yocom, producing a certified Copy of a War't from the Prop'ry dated 4th 6 mo., 1684, out of the Surveyor's Office for 500 Acres of Land granted at a Half penny p'r Acre, In exchange for Land he quitted to Thos. Holme, at Pennipeck, which said War't was Laid on part of Laetitia Penn's Man'r, but never duly returned nor the bounds ascertained, David Powell having Survey'd it, 400 perches Long and 200 broad on Skuylkill, but Tho. Fairman 560 p'rches Long and 134 broad, Requests that the bounds may be ascertained and her due confirmed to her according to the Prop'ry's promise, before his Departure, in the Sec'ries hearing, to whom he gave it in charge. Ordered that Tho. Fairman resurvey the said Land and that a Patent be granted on the Return.

At a Session of the Commissioners at Philad'a the 11th of the 12th Mo'th, 1701.

Present, Edward Shippen, Griffith Owen, Thomas Story, James Logan.

The Prop'ry, by Deeds of Lease and Release, dated 2d and 3d of March, 1681, sold to Wm. Bostock 500 Acres In right of which John Simcock, Attorney to the said William, procured a Tract to be laid out in Edgmont, in the County of Chester, joyning on Francis and Philip Yarnal.

Capt'n Samuel Finney and Edw'd Sproston, Attorneys to Jno. Bostock, Brother and Heir to the said Wm. deceased, Request a Resurvey on the said Tract in Order to a Confirmation.

Ordered that a War't of Resurvey be granted forthwith and a Patent on the Return, they paying for the overplus if any.

Albert Henricks Possessed of 500 Acres on Dellaware in the County of Chester, below the town, for which he affirms he had a Patent from Gov'r Lovelace which being delv'd to the Prop'ry at his first arrival, it was never given him again.

Requests a Resurvey in Order to a New Patent for a Title to Capt'n Finney's Son, to whom he has sold great part of it.

Ordered that a War't of Resurvey be forthwith granted and a Patent on the Return, paying for the Overplus, &c.

John Millington and Mary, his Wife of Salop, by Deeds dated 14th and 15th of August, 1682, purchased of the Prop'ry 500 Acres which D. Lloyd, in whose keeping the Deeds are, affirms, T. Lloyd purchased of Millington, tho' he can find no Deed for it, and therefore desires it may be laid out in the

Welch Tract designed for those of Shropsh. as well as the
Welch in Millington's Name if we think fitt.

Henry Wright, of Salop, by Deeds dated 11th and 12th July,
1682, purchased of the Prop'ry 500 Acres.

Henry Lichfield, of Salop, by Deeds dated 24 and 25th July,
1682, purchased of the Proprietary 500 Acres.

Wm. Thrattle, of Salop, by Deeds dated 24 and 25 of July,
'82. purchased of the Proprietary 250 Acres.

Copies of all these Deeds as Well as Millington's are in D.
Lloyd's hands engrossed in parchment, being sent over to be
enrolled by T. Lloyd.

Beaks, for himself and some others, of the County of Chester, his Neighbours request a grant of that large tract of Vacant Land in the said County, formerly designed for Gr. Jones and laid out for 1,500 Acres for which they agree to pay £25 p'r 100, one Moiety the 29th of the 3d Month, and the other Moiety the 29th of the seventh Month following, and to leave out so much upon the Creek as shall be Sufficient for a Settlem't for the Indians, lately removed thither, which quantity Shall be adjudged as also the place allotted by Caleb Pusey and Natha'l Newlin to whom the care of Settling the said Indians was committed by the Prop'ry. Granted on the Terms aforesaid, the whole to be Survey'd first.

The Proprietary having by Deeds of Lease and Release, dat'd 8th and 9th 7br., 1681, Sold to William Cloud 500 Acres of Land, the said William upon his Arrival in '82 Settled on a Tract joyning on the south side of Naaman's Creek, which falling afterwards in the County of Newc. and Manor of Rocklands, he has been obliged to pay a bushell of wheat p'r 100 Quitrent, and he has no Security of the said Land because not within the bounds of the Province, Requests therefore that his Rent may be settled according to his purchase and the Land be secured to him, or that if he must pay the said Rent that 500 Acres be laid out to him elsewhere in pursuance of his said purchase. Ordered that a War't of Resurvey be granted on the said Land and a Patent on the Return paying for the Overplus if any, and that the said William, on the back of the abovementioned Release, sign a Release to the Prop'ry for the within granted 500 Acres upon which the Rent to be fixed at one shilling, Sterling, p'r 100.

Signed a War't to John Furnese for 350 Acres, head Land, Ord'd 26th 9br. last.

Signed a War't to Thomas Bye for 2 City Lotts, Ord'd 29th of 10br. last.

Signed a War't of Resurvey to Jos. Kirl on 500 Acres of R'd Wood, Ordered 5th 11 mo. Ult.

Signed a War't for 25 Acres Lib. Land to Jno. Ball, Ord'd 7th Ult.

Signed a War't to Nehem. Allen for 300 A's, Ordered 12th Ult.

Signed a War't of Resurvey to Jno. Kinsey on 300 A's, Ord'd 12th Ult.

Signed a War't of Resurvey to Wm. Cloud on 500 A's, Ord'd to-day.

Signed a War't to Abrah. Beaks, &c., for the tract of 500 A's, Ord'd to-day.

In pursuance of an Order of ye 22d of 10br. Last, pa. 36, made for the Regulation and Settlem't of the Welch Tract, the following Warr'ts of Resurvey were this day Signed:

To Lewis David a Resurvey on 190 Acres, in Duffrin Mawr, in Right of his Own Purchase.

To Griffith Owen 156½ in right of John Thomas, &c, and 145 in right of John ap John and Rich'd Davies.

To David Hugh 220 acres in Haverf'd in right of L. David.

To David Rees 260 Acres in Haverf'd in right of L. David.

To Nathan Thomas 81 Acres in Haverf'd and 100 Acres in the upper end of the tract, both in right of Lewis David.

At a Session of the Commissioners at Philad'a the 16th of the 12th, 1701.

Present, Edward Shippen, Griffith Owen, Thomas Story, James Logan, Sec'ry.

The Prop'ry having, by Deeds of Lease and Release, dated 10th and 11th June, 1683, sold to Isaac Jacobs 1,000 Acres the said Isaac by Deed dated   , Sold to Thomas Fairman 800 Acres, who by a Deed dated 4th of Aug't, 1699, in England sold to Captain Samuel Finney the said 800 Acres laid out in Philad'a County adjoining on Joseph Fisher's, Rob't Wilkins', Thomas Sydon's and the Susquehanna Road, on which said 800 Acres the said Samuel Finney requests a Resurvey in order to a Patent, first Warrant dated 14th 9br., '85. Ordered that a Warrant of Resurvey be forthwith granted and a Patent on the return, he paying for the Overplus, &c., Rent 1 Shilling p'r 1,000.

Benjamin Chambers, purchaser of 1,000 Acres in right thereof by Vertue of a Warrant from the Commiss'rs dated 28th 4 mo., 1686, took up his front Lott of 20 foot in breadth, bounded North with Sam'll Fox, and South with Rich'd Sutton's, formerly Jos. Phips, which Lott, by Deed dated 3d 4 mo., 1695, he convey'd to Richard Sutton who has now sold it to John Gilbert, but not convey'd it, and Requests a Patent for the same. A Deed from Sutton to Gilbert is to be forthwith made and dated the 17th Instant, upon which 'tis Ordered that a Patent be granted to John Gilbert.

The Prop'ry having, by 3 Several Warr'ts now in the Surveyor's Office, granted to Joseph Phips in the year 1683 and '84, a Lott in the front Street being the same on which the above mentioned Lott of B. Chambers bounds on the Northward, and by the last of the said Warrants expressly granted 25 foot, the said Joseph by Vertue thereof entred upon and was Possessed of the said Lott, 25 foot in Breadth, for Several years, and by a Deed dated 6th 2mo., 1693, Convey'd the same to Richard Sutton who is now posesssed thereof, and Requests a Patent of Confirmation in order to which a Warrant of Resurvey. Ordered that a Warrant be accordingly Granted and a Patent on the Return.

Andreas Rudman, in behalf of himself and the rest of his Countrey men, the Swedes, to whom the Prop'ry granted 10,000 A's of Land at a bushell of wheat Rent p'r 100, upon Skuylkill near Manatawny, Requests that the said Tract may be laid out higher up on the River Skuylkill and not Extend so far backwards as was at first proposed, the Country some few Miles off the River being in that Place so exceeding rocky and Mountainous that it is no ways habitable.

Ordered that the said Request be Considered and in order thereunto that the Surveyors be diligently inquired off concerning the same.

The Prop'ry having, by a War't under his hand, &c., dated 2d of the 7th Month, 1701, granted to James Thomas, of Meirion, to take up 300 A's of Land purchased of Wm. Jenkins, Old purchaser of 1,000 Acres, which Should have been in the Welch Tract but was not so mentioned in the said Warrant, he therefore requests a New Warr't for the s'd 300 Acres, ordering it to be laid out in the said Welch Tract, which is Granted.

Lewis Thomas, an Old Settler on Skuylkill in Philad'a. for the better accommodation of his Settlem't there, by Which (as 'tis said he had been a great Sufferer, obtained of the Former Comm'rs a Grant of 9 Acres of land adjoyning on the City Line on the North side (for which they affirm there is both a War't and Return in the Office) at 15 Shillings p'r acre, Purchase Money, and Sixpence p'r Rent p'r Ann. Ever after, which 9 Acres, together with his house and Settlem't to which it joyns, the said Lewis has sold to Wm. Carter, who requests a Confirmation, and in Order thereunto a Resurvey. Objected that it may discommode a Settlem't designed by the Prop'ry on Fairmount by cutting off Such a Slip between that place and the Town, upon Which Wm. Carter Offers to give bond to the Prop'ry to resign it to him or his Son if either shall, within the space of   Years next ensuing, make a Settlem't at Fairmount, and desire it of him, his Heirs, &c., the Prop'ry paying him what it shall Cost him with lawfull Interest.

Rob't Longshore, by Deed dated   , convey'd to Tho. Marl a Lott in the High Street of 26 foot in breadth, on the North Side, joyning on Wm. Lawrence, said in the Deed to be in right of R'd Davies's purchase, but by endorsem't dated 26th 4 mo., '97, on the said Deed by Tho's Jenner and Margaret, his Wife, Relict and Adm'x of said Longshore, is again Conveyed to said Marl in right of Jno. Sharpless of whom the said Rob't Longshore purchased a High Street and Front Lotts (Vide W. Laws, pa. 40,) by Deed dated 16th 3 mo., 1692. This Lott was Surv'd   by Warrant dated   . T. Marl Now possessed of the said Lott requests a Patent on the same. This Lott is also the 2d Survey of Sharpless's High Street Lott mentioned pa. 40, but the first being Vacant and this built on, 'tis Granted.

Dennis Konders, of German Town, Dyer, having in a Petition to the Prop'r'y dated 15th of 8br., 1701, exhibited that he having purchased 500 Acres [I suppose of Lenert Arets] of Land in this Province, had yet taken up but 225 A's thereof and had 275 Acres untaken up remaining, which 275 A's for the better Accommodation of 3 of his Sons now of age besides 4 Children more, born in this Country, he requests that the Prop'ry would grant him either out of the Overplus adjoyning on the German Town or out of his Manor of Springfield, to which the Governor answered in his own hand: [I am Contented to allow this Petition but not out of the Manor, being my Children's, who are of age.

Wm. Penn.

Upon which 'tis Ordered that when said Konders can find a fitt place that the Prop'ry has it in his Power to dispose of, a Warrant be granted according to the said Petition and Answer.

Francis Chads producing a Warr't under the hands of W. Markham, Rob't Turner and Jno. Goodson, dated 7th Jan'y, 1692, for 100 Acres in the Manor of Rocklands, upon Old Rent, if 4 miles distant from the River, which was forthwith executed about 6 or 7 Miles from Delaware and built upon, Requests a Confirmation and in Order to it a Resurvey.

Ordered that a Warrant be granted and a Patent on the Return, he paying for the Overplus if any.

The Proprietary, by his Warrant dated 5th 3 mo., 1684, Granted to Henry Baker, of Makefield, in the County of Bucks, to take up 300 a's of land in said Township, being Land bought of the Prop'ry here and paid for, which warrant was executed 25th 12 mo., 1685.

The Proprietary, by Lease and Release, dated 23d and 24th Aprill, 1683, Granted to Richard Hough 500 acres, of which, by Deed poll dat. 1, 4 mo., '88, he sold 250 to Hen. Marjoram, and he, by Deed dated 8th 4 mo., '96, convey'd the same to Hen. Baker.

On these 2 Tracts lying Contigious the Prop'ry Granted his War't of Resurvey dat. 11th 11 mo., 1700, which being executed and Returned by E. Penington, they are bound to Contain 859½ acres, of which 550 being their Right and 55 allowed by law, there remains 254½ a's to be Purchased, for which Sam'l Baker, Heir to the said Henry, now deceased, agrees to pay after the rate of £20 p'r Ct, and is £51 2s 6d.

The former Commiss'rs, Viz: Rob't Turner, W. Mark. and J. Goodson, by Pat't dat. 15th Mar., 1692, Granted to Tho. Hudson, of Cheshire, 100 acres of Savannah or Swampy Meadow, in the Manor of Highlands, in pursuance of the Prop'rs Letter to them for that purpose. Of the said Land Wm. Biles, attorney to the said Tho. Hudson, by Deed p. dat. 7th 12 mo., '98, conv'd 25 acres to said Hen. Baker.

The Proprietary, by his Warr't dated 11th 11 mo., 1700, Granted a Resurvey on the said 25 acres, which being Returned, 'tis found to Contain 32¾ a's and is 7¾ acres Overplus, for which said Samuel agreeing to pay 10 shill's p'r acre; it amounts to £3 17s 6d, and craves a Patent upon Each.

Ordered that Patents be granted accordingly, he giving Bond for £55.

The Proprietary having, by Deeds of Lease and Release, dated   , Sold 500 acres to Maurice Llewellin, 490 acres, of which has been taken up, the Liberty Land reserved, for which the said Maurice Requests a Warrant. Ordered that a Warrant be granted.

Signed a War't to Phil. Howel for Francis Smith's Lott, Ord'd 29th of 10br. last.

Signed a Warrant of Resurvey and Survey on 5,000 acres to Ben. Furly, Ordered 12th Ult.

Signed a Warrant to Hen. Hollingsworth for the Barrens, Ordered 14th Ult.

Signed a Warrant to Geo. Harland for 200 a's on Brandyw., Ord'd 4th Inst.

Signed a Warrant of Resurvey on Bostock's Land in Edgem't, Ord'd 11th Instant.

Signed a War't of Resurvey to Albert Henricks, Ordered 11th Instant.

Signed a War't to Rich'd Sutton for Jos. Phips' Lott, Ordered this day.

Signed a War't of Resurvey on 100 acres to Fr. Chads, Ord'd this day.

Signed a War't of Survey to Maur. Llewellin for 10 a's L. Land, Ord'd to-day.

In Pursuance of the Order made 22d of 10br. last, pa. 36, there were Signed the Following Warrants of Resurvey on Land in the Welch Tract:

To Edw'd Griffith on 300 acres in Meirion in right of J. Tho. and Edw'd Jones.

To Jno. and Evan Jones on 153½ a's in Goshen in right of J. Tho. and E Jones.

To Abel Thomas on 76½ a's in right of John Tho. and Edw'd Jones.

To Henry Thomas on 400 a's in Haverf'd and 180 in right of Lewis David.

To Jno. Lewis, Sen'r, on 350 a's in Haverf'd in right of Lewis David.

To John Lewis, Jun'r, on 100 a's in Haverf'd in right of Lewis David.

To Rich'd Hayes on 260 acres in Haverf'd in right of L. David.

To Jno. David Thomas on 210 a's in Duffein Mawr in right of L. David.

To Maurice Llewellen on 420 a's in Haverf'd in right of himself and L. David.

To Will'm Thomas on 153¼ a's in Radnor in right of Rich'd Davis.

To Jno. Roberts, malter, on 150 a's in Meirion in right of R'd Davis & Co., on old Rent.

To Bertha Rowles on 250 a's in Duffein Mawr in right of Tho. Ellis.

To Henry Saunders on 250 a's in the Welch Tract in right o" John Toyer.

At a Session of the Commissioners at Philad'a the Eighteenth of the 12th Mo'th, 1701.

Present, Edward Shippen, Griffith Owen, Thomas Story, James Logan, Sec'ry.

Jno. Chaffan having bought of the Commiss'rs (22 of 10br., pa. 33) 250 a's in the Manor of Rocklands at £25 p'r 100, one-half to be paid the 25th of the first Month next, and the other half the 29th of 7br. following, by a Deed under his hand and Seal dated 14th Instant, sold 50 a's, part thereof to John Beckingham on the West side of his Tract on the same terms he purchas'd himself; Tho. Cooper also having purchased 200 a's at the same time, adjoyning to Chaffin, by a Deed of the same date, sold to s'd Beckingham 50 a's on the East Side of his Tract on the same terms as he bought it.

In Pursuance of which Purchases J. Beckingham requests a Warrant to cutt off the said 100 a's, and undertake to pay for the same at the same rate that his Vendors were obliged, for which he offers Jos. Gilpin his Security. Ordered that a Warrant be accordingly granted and a Patent on the Return, and that a Bond for the Money be taken.

The Proprietary, by Deeds dated 8th and 9th, 1681, sold to Rob't Stevens 250 a's, who took it up in Bromingham, in Chester Coun., and after, by Deed dated 5th 1 mo., 1687, Sold to Nathaniell Lukins, who, by Indorsement on the said Deed dated 30th 7br., 1692, Sold all his Interest in Stevens' Purchase to John Willis, Son of Henry Willis, who is now Seated on the s'd Land, and having resigned the Lott appurt't to the said purchase to his Father, he, viz: Henry Willis requests a Warr't for the said Lott and that it may be laid out on a Vacant Spott inclosed within his Fence in Mulberry Street where he Lives.

Ordered that a Warr't be accordingly Granted; Rent 1 shilling.

Prudence West, Widdow of James West, having purchased the Lott at the North End of the City, granted to Albertus Brandt, informs that there is an Overplus within the fence of the said Lott of between 30 and 40 foot, desires to Purchase it if she may and agrees to pay 7s 6d p'r foot or £14 for the whole if 40 foot, upon which a Survey is Ordered and a Patent thereon.

John Streipers, of Crefeld, in Germany, by Deeds dated 9th and 10th Mar., 1682, Purchased of the Proprietary 5,000 acres at one shilling Sterling Rent p'r thousand, of which there has been Laid out 50 acres in the City Liberties, as 'tis said, and only 275 in Germantown, all the Rest being yet untaken up, and also sold to Leonard Arets 275 more, the whole 600 acres. The said Streipers, by an Instrum't dated 13th of May, 1698, Constituted Renier Tisen and Henry Sellen, of Germantown, in this Province, to be his attorneys, or the Survivor in Case of Death or either in Case of the Other's Ceasing to act, in which case, in the said Instrument, he gives a Special power upon the Death or refusal of the one to the other to associate to himself some honest Man to act with him in Conjunction, and said Tisen refusing, Henry Sellen associated to himself in Germantown Court Lenert Arets, who accepting, requests a Warrant for 4,675 acres of Streipers' Purchase remaining. Ordered that a Warrant be granted to be laid out on the Skuylkill near the Tract laid out To the Frankfort Company.

Lenert Arets, by Deeds of L. and Rel., Dated the 10th and

18—VOL. XIX.

11th days of June, 1683, purchased of the Proprietary 1,000 acres at the rent of one shilling for every hundred acres, i. e., 10 Shillings for the whole, The Prop'ry, by Indenture dated the said 11th of June, in consideration of £3 12s Released 9th part of the said Rent to the said Lenert Arets, his Heirs and assigns for ever, and by Deeds dated   , Sold to Dennis Konders, of Germantown, one Moiety of the said 1,000; there has been taken up in Germantown (as they affirm) 501 a's, of which Konders has 225½ and Arets 275½ acres, whereof 50 a's he gave to Renier Tisen, and of the 499 acres Remaining, there belongs to Konders 274½ acres and to Arets 224½, who requests a Warr't to take up the same; Konders Grant, vid. pa. 90.

Ordered that a Warrant be accordingly Granted.

John Guest, of Philad'a, Esqr., having been Several times treating about some Barrens and Vacant Land in the County of Newcastle 'tis at length agreed that he have a grant of all the land Lying between his large Tract of 1,000 a's and White Clay Creek joyning on Jno. King, John Gardiner, &c., and all the Vacant Land between the said Tract and Whiteclay Creek joyning on Neal Cook and Ja. Claypoole, for which he is to pay Nine pounds p'r hundred and a Bushell of Wheat yearly Rent for all that is not Realy Barrens, and for all the real Barrens that are not arable One bushell of Wheat Yearly Rent only, and no more, upon which agreem't 'tis Ordered that a Warrant be granted.

Griffith Jones, Purchaser of 5,000 acres, by Deeds dated   , 1681, had 2,920, part thereof laid out in one Tract on Land Survey'd and granted before to others, viz: on 1,000 granted to G. Claypoole, 1,000 Granted to Benja'n Furly, and 1,000 granted before to himself by another Patent, by which undue Survey being now disappointed of his Land where expected, he requests a War't to take up the said 2,920 acres on other Vacant Land with the allowance in Measure made by Law in Resurveys in case of Overplus, as there certainly Was Sufficient in the said Land of which he is disappointed.

Ordered that a Warrant be granted as Requested.

Rebecca Shippen, Relict of Francis Richardson producing by her friend a Patent from the former Commissioners dated 23rd March, 1692-3, for 1,200 acres in Wright's Town, in the County of Bucks, joyning on Jos. Ambler and John Martin, Survey'd 1st 10br., 1687, of which 1,144 a's lie in One Tract and the Remaining 56 acres in the Townstead,

Requests a Resurvey in Order to a New Patent, with allowance of Overplus. Ordered that a Warr't be forthwith granted and a Patent on the Return.

Daniel and Justus Falkner's, attorneys to Benja. Furly,

claim the Common proportion of Lib'ty Land in Right of his Purchase of 5,000 acres, Mentioned pa. 59, But that being none of the First hundred purchasers it cannot be now granted, Yet they insisting on it as his certain Right, 'tis Ordered that they have Liberty to pitch upon Some Convenient Tract of a Sufficient Number of acres within the Liberties, which shall be reserved, and in Case the said Benjamin, in 18 Months, make good his Claim from the Proprietary, it may be granted; Ordered also in their Request a New Warrant for the said Benjamin's Lott already Survey'd to him.

Thomas Hoodt, by Deed dated 13th 1 mo., 1693, Convey'd to George Thomas 100 a's of Land in Newtown, in Chester, part of 250 acres purchased by the said T. Hoodt of John Blunston, purchaser of 1,500 acres. John Blunston, Constituted attorney by Letter dated 4th 9br., 1692, for Joseph Potter, purchaser of 250 acres, by Deed dated 12th 1 mo., 1693, convey'd to the said Geo. Thomas 100 acres joyning on ye foregoing.

George Thomas going to Sea, by a Letter left behind him as his Will, devised the said 200 acres to Elizab. Brotheron, now Wife of Morgan James, which devise was afterwards Confirmed by a Decree of the Provincial Judges at Chester, dated 19th 2 mo., 1699, in Consideration that the said Morgan Should pay to Thomas Thomas, brother to the said George, £30, which because the said T. T. soon after fled in Gov. Webb's Vessel, was never paid by him, they are Ready to answer it when he demands it; 'tis said he (T. T.) is dead. Requests a Resurvey; Granted and a Patent.

The Proprietary, by Lease and Release, dated 21st and 22d 1 mo, 1681, sold to Allen Robinet 250 a's, in right of which there was laid out to him in Providence, Chester Coun., 245 a's by Ch. Ashcorn, in pursuance of a Gen'll Warrant from Th. Holme, dated 9th 7br., '82. The said Allen, by his Last will, dated 4th 4 mo., 1694, bequeathed the said Land to his Son, Samuel Robinet, and his Daughter Sarah, Wife of Rich'd Bond, who have Sold thereof to Randal Maline 50 acres and to Rich'd Woodworth 100 acres, Now Jos. Baker's, in order to Make a Title, to whom Sam'll Robinet procured of the Prop'ry a Warrant of Resurvey, dated 6th 1 mo., 1700-1, upon the Execution whereof by Hen. Hollingsworth ye said Tract is found to Contain 329 acres, of which 25 being allowed by the Law, there is 54 or 59 a's to be paid for, for which he agrees to give £18, to be paid the 10th of the 4th Month next and Tho. Powell to be bound for him. Requests a Patent thereupon, which is Ord'd forthw'th.

Signed a Patent to Edw'd Shippen for part of a Square, Ord'd 26 Ult.

Signed a Patent to Jno. Bittle for a Lott in Chestn. Str. ; r't 3s 6d, Ord'd 10br., 31.

Signed a War't of Resurvey to Alex. Edwd'son 1,100 a's, Ord'd 19th Ult.

Signed a War't to James Cooper, &c., Darby, Serv'ts, for 300 a's headl., Ord'd 21st Ult.

Signed a War't to Jno. Marshall, &c., Darby, Serv'ts, for 300 a's, Ord'd 21st Ult.

Signed a War't to Susannah Brandt on 80 a's Lib. Land, Or'd 26 Ult.

Signed a War't of Resurvey to Capt. Finney on 800 a's, Ord'd 16th Instant.

Signed a War't to James Thomas for 300 a's in the Wel. Tract, Ord'd 16th Inst.

Signed a War't to John Beckingham for 100 a's, Ord'd this Day.

Signed a War't to Griffith Jones for 2,920 a's, Ord'd this day.

Signed a Warrant to Rebecca Shippen, Resur. on 1,200 a's, Ord'd to-day.

Signed a War't of Resurvey to Morgan James on 200 a's, Ord'd to-day.

In Pursuance of the order made 22d of 10br. last, there were Signed the following Warrants of Resurvey on Land in the Welch Tract, viz:

To Ellis Ellis on 230 a's in Haverf'd and to Brigid Ellis 100 a's in right of Tho. Ellis.

To Daniel Humphrey on 200 a's in Haverf'd in Right of T. Ellis, L. David and J. Toyer.

To Rachel Ellis on 111 a's in Haverf'd and 250 in Duffrin Mawr, Tho. Ellis.

To John William on 209½ a's in Meirion in right of Tho. Ellis.

To Rob't Lloyd on 259½ a's in Meirion in right of T. Ellis and R. Davis.

To Thos. Lloyd, of Meirion, on 150 a's in right of T. Ellis and R'd Davis.

To John Evan, of Meirion, on 200 a's in right of T. Ellis and R'd Davis.

To Richard Moore on 245 a's in Radnor in right of R'd Davies's 5,000.

To John Evans on 2,200 acres in Radnor in right of R'd Davies's 5,000.

To John Morgan on 450 acres in Radnor in right of R'd Davies's 5,000.

To Henry Price on 300 acres in Radnor in right of R'd Davies's 5,000.

To Margaret German on 100 a's in Radnor in the same right.

To David Evan on 308 a's in 2 Tracts in Radnor in the same right.

To Richard Davies [or Prees] on 76½ a's in Goshen in the same right.

To Samuel Miles on 275½ acres in Radnor, part R. Davies, p't Purchas'd here.

To Rich'd Miles on 170½ acres in Radnor in the same right.

To David Meredith on 200 acres in Radnor in the same right.

To Steven Evans on 250 acres in Radnor in the same right.

To Thomas Howel 100 acres in Haverf'd in right of R'd Davies' 1,250.

To James Thomas, of Meirion, on 100 acres in the same right.

To Evan Harry on 164 acres, part in the same right and p't purchas'd here.

At a Session of the Commissioners at Philadelphia the 23d of the 12th Mo'th, 1701.

Present, Edward Shippen, Griffith Owen, Thomas Story, James Logan, Sec'ry.

George Biles, of the Falls, producing a Deed dated 10th 4 mo, 1696, for 300 a's of Land in New Bristol Township, in Bucks, bounded Westward with John Rowland, Northward with William Dungan, Eastward with Rand'l Blackshaw, Southward with Cha. Brigham, Laid out to   , Sold by Wm. Biles and his Wife Jane, Relict of Tho. Adkinson, to the said George, in Consideration of Certain Sums of Money Secured for the said Adkinson's Children by Bucks Court.

Also a Release from Isaac Adkinson, eldest Son of the said Thomas, now of age, dated 11th 4 mo, 1700, of all his Right, Claim, &c., in and to the said Land, upon which the said George Requests a Resurvey in order to make Solomon Warder, to whom he has sold it, a sufficient title.

Ordered that a Warrant be forthwith granted and a Patent on the Return, paying for the Overplus, the alienation from the Proprietary being further inspected.

Nicholas Waln, having been long treating with the Proprietary and with the Present Commiss'ts for 80 acres of Liberty land belonging to Rich'd Penn's Purchase of 5,000 acres, for which he Offers £80, but will not advance because Poor, in an ill Place and far from the Town. 'Tis agreed that he shall have it at the said Price upon Griff. Jones, (being Present) declaring that were it his he would take the same Money for it. Ordered therefore that a Warrant be forthwith granted and a Patent on the Return; to pay Ready Money.

Samuel Carpenter and John Parsons, to whom the arbitration of a Request made to the Prop'ry for Satisfaction for 200 acres of Land Surrendered by Wm. Clayton, of Chechest'r, deceased, to the Swansons, lying near the Town on Skuylkill, was left both by the Proprietary and Wm. Clayton, Son and Heir to the said William, Deceased, having awarded that the Prop'ry shall pay the said William Fifty pounds in Money and give him to the Value of £50 more in Land at Sasquehannah, and given the said award under their hands, 'tis thereupon Ordered that a Note be Drawn on Samuel Carpenter for the paym't of the said fifty pounds to Wm. Clayton, and that the Land at Sasquehannah, viz: 1,000 a's be granted him with the rest there.

Thomas Fairman and Job Goodson, in behalf of his Father, having had a Long Contest about 200 a's of Land laid out in the Overplus of Whitpains Township (so called), as J. Goodson affirms, first to him but (as T. Fairman affirms) never to any other but himself, who is now possessed of it by his assigns, And has given Bond to make the said a Title, and the case being fully Stated and all arguments and allegations on both sides heard and considered, 'Tis the Opinion of this Board that T. Fairman should hold the s'd Land and Job Goodson have 200 acres some Miles above it in the New Bristol Township, where T. F. affirms he actually Survey'd it to his Father J. Goodson, and that each of the Parties should choose one or two Good Men to Judge the Difference of Value between these 2 Tracts, which Difference T. F. should pay to the s'd J. Goodson as a Satisfaction for his disappointm't, With which if the said parties doe not Comply, they are Sett over to the Law.

The Commiss'rs, by Patent dated 26th 9 mo., 1695, Granted 500 acres to Rob't Longshore, Purchaser in Bristol Township, in the County of Philad'a, joyning on Germantown, Irenia Land, and Will'm Wilkins, of which by Deed dated 1st 4 mo., 1686, he sold to Samuel Bennet 200 acres, who by Deed dated 2, 4, 1695, sold 150 thereof to David Potts, who sold to Wm. Harman 50 acres now in the Possession of Peter Clever.

The said David Potts Requests a Warr't of Resurvey on the said 150 acres according to the True bounds of the Tract and to Cutt off 50 a's to said Harman or Clever. Ordered that a Warr't be accordingly granted for the said 50 acres to be cutt off as by agreement made between them and a Patent on the Return if required, they paying for the Overplus, if any.

John Swift having purchased of William Bingly 500 a's of Land (as in pa. 76, q. v.) of which 492 acres are laid out in Warminster, in the County of Bucks, Requests a Resurvey on the same in Order to a Patent. Ordered that a Warrant be forthwith Granted and a Patent on the Return, he paying for the Overplus, if any.

The Proprietary having granted under his hand 300 a's in the

Welch Tract to David Powel, formerly belonging to Daniel Harry, Renter, but quitted by him, also 100 acres of Vacant Land interjacent between two tracts of the said David's, with orders that he should have them upon Moderate terms and under their Real Value to be paid for, he requests a Warrant to Survey the said Lands.

Ordered that a Warrant be accordingly Granted.

The Prop'ry, by Deeds of Lease and Release, dated 14th and 15th 7br., 1681, Granted to John ap John and Thomas Wynne, their Heirs, &c., 5,000 a's, who by Several Mean Conveyances granted.

The Prop'ry, by Deeds of Lease and Release, dated 16th and 17th 7br., 1681, Granted to John Thomas and Edward Jones, who by Several mean Conveyances Granted the greater part thereof to other Mean purchasers, and the said Mean Purchasers together with the said Edward Jones and Thomas Jones, Son and Heir of the said John Thomas, by a Deed dated 27th 10br., 1693, Granted the Proportion of Lib'ty Land belonging to the said Purchase, viz: 100 a's to the said Wm. Edwards, who is now possessed of the same.

The Prop'ry, by Lease and Release, dated   , Granted to William Jenkins 1,000 acres, and by Like Deeds dated 19th and 20th Jan'y, Granted to Thomas Simmonds 500 a's, whose Son, John Simmonds, after his Father's Decease, Granted the said 500 a's To Thomas Merchant, who by an Instrum't dated 15th 2 mo., 1694, constituted the said Will'm Jenkins his attorney.

Wm. Jenkins, by Vertue of his Said Purchase of 1,000 acres, of which 20 a's is Liberty Land, and by Vertue of the said Letter of attorney, in behalf of Thomas Merchant, and in right of the said 500 a's (to which 10 acres Lib. Land belongs) convey'd 30 acres, the Proportion of both the said Purchasers, to said William Edwards, Survey'd the

The Prop'ry, by like Deeds dated 11th and 12th of 8br., 1681, Granted to Joshua Hastings 1,000 acres of Land, who by Deeds dated 24th 6 mo., 1700, sold to the said Wm. Edwards 20 a's of Lib. Land, the Proportion of the s'd purchase, Granted by a Warrant from the Prop'ry to the said William, dated 10th 11 mo., 1700-1, and laid out 2d of the 1 mo., following, at which time the afore recited 190 acres being resurvey'd were found to contain   acres, for which he requests a Patent.

Ordered that a Patent be accordingly Granted.

Signed a Patent to D. Haverd for 229 acres, Ord'd 3d of 10br., pa. 15.

Signed a Warrant to Henry Willis for a Lott Ordered 18th Inst., pa. 93.

Signed a Warrant to Nicholas Waln on 44 a's purchased of Geo. Walker, with which also a Resurvey on 172 acres of Lib. Land purchased of Joshua Carpenter, Ordered 26th Ult., page 72.

Signed a Warrant to John Chandler for 100 a's of headland, Ord'd 14th Ult.

Signed a Warrant of Resurvey to George Biles, Ordered to-day.

Signed a Warrant to Len't Arets for John Strepers on 4,675 a's, Ord'd 18th.

William Warner Settled on a Tract of Land on Skuylkill before the Grant of this Province, reputed 300 a's, Craves a Resurvey and that if it prove deficient that it may be made out of the adjoining, according to the Prop'rs promise. Ordered that a Warrant be granted as requested.

Signed the said Warrant to William Warner.

At a Session held at Philadelphia 25th 13 mo., 1701.

Signed a Patent to Ellis Jones for part of a Lott, Ordered 21st Ult.

Signed a Warrant to John Swift for 16 a's of Lib. Land, Ord'd 28th Ult.

Signed a Warrant to Nicholas Waln for 80 acres of Lib. Land Ordered to-day and 16 a's Ordered; page 17 and 71.

Signed a Warrant of Resurvey to John Swift on 492 a's, Ordered to-day.

Signed a Warrant to David Powel for 400 a's, Ordered to-day.

Pursuant to an agreement made the 14th of ye 11 mo. last, pa. 60, with Cornelius Empson, the said Cornelius Requests a War't for 15,000 a's upon the terms proposed by the Comm'rs, Viz: £8 p'r 100, to be paid within one Year and an English Shilling quitrent Ever after, or two bushells of Wheat p'r 100 at some Navigable Landing on Dellaware, the first year to be Clear of Quittrent, and accordingly a Warrant was Signed for the said 15,000 A's, dated 7th 1 mo., 1701-2, to the Persons following:

To Cornelius Empson 1,000 A's, To John Richardson 1,000 A's, To James Brown 1,000 A's, to Henry Reynolds 1,000 A's, to Wm. Brown 1,000 A's, To John Bales 1,000 A's, to Edward Beeson 1,000 A's, to James Cooper, of Darby, 1,000 A's, to Randal Jenny 1,000 A's, to Andrew Job 1,000 Acres, to John Churchman 1,000 A's, to Ebenezer Empson 1,000 A's, to John Guest, of Philadelphia, Esqr., 1,000 A's, to Joel Baily 500 A's, to Robert Dutton 500 A's, to Samuel Littler 500 A's, to Meser

Brown 500 A's, And the Proprietary for his Own Proper Use three thousand Acres if the Land will hold out, all in One Tract, with Sufficient Allowance for Roads, according to the Method of Townships, beginning at the Northern Barrens between the main branch of Northeast River and Otteraroe Creek, and bounding it to the Southwards with and East and West Line parrallel as near as may be to the Line of the Province, and Northward next the Barrens with a Line Also parrallel to the South Bounds and in the said Tract to run Eighteen Several Divisions of 1,000 A's, Each, to be taken by Lotts, and the Surveyor to Draw the Proprietary's three.

The Warrant directed to Hen. Hollingsworth.

Signed a Commission for Surveyor of Bucks to Jno. Cutler, dat. 10th Mar. Signed a War't to the said Jno. Cutler to execute the War'ts directed to P. Pemberton dated 10th 1st Month.

Signed a Warrant to Tho. Caras for 450 a's, Ord'd 8th of 10br. last, pa. 18.

At a Session of the Commissioners at Philadelphia the 23rd of the 1st Mo'th, 1701-2.

Present, Edward Shippen, Griffith Owen, Thomas Story, James Logan, Sec'ry.

Samuel Carpenter having Originally Purchased of the Prop'ry 5,000 acres of Land in this Province by Lease and Release, bearing date ye   , 1681, by Vertue of a Warrant from the Prop'ry dated 4th 6 mo., 1684, took up 4,420 a's, his full Complement (having taken up 580 a's before) adjoining to the following Tract of Joseph Fisher's and the Line of Bucks County, on which he Requests a Resurvey and a Confirmation.

Ordered that a Warrant be accordingly granted and a Patent on the Return, he paying for the Overplus in Measure, if any be found, twenty Pounds p'r C't.

The Prop'ry, by Deeds of Lease and Release, dated 22d and 23rd of March, 1681, Granted to Joseph Fisher 5,000 acres at the yearly Quittrent of one Shilling Sterling p'r 100 acres, and by Indenture bearing date 22d 6 mo., 1682, in Consideration of £18 Sterling reduced the s'd Quittrent to one Shilling p'r 1,000, at and under which Rent he now holds the same, in right of which purchase he took up 80 a's of Lib. Land and 500 acres in the County of Philadelphia, on which he now lives, and by a Warrant from the Prop'ry dated 14th 12 mo., 1683, 4,420 acres adjoyning on the abovementioned Land of Samuel Carpenter on which last Tract he requests a Resurvey and a Confirmation, agreeing to pay £20 for the Overplus, if any be found, above the allowance made by Law, also to Reduce the Rent of the said Overplus to the proportion of one Shilling p'r 1,000. Ordered that a Warrant of Resurvey be accordingly granted and a Patent on the Return on the terms aforesaid.

Rob't French, of Newcastle, having by Vertue of a Warr't from the Commiss'rs dated   of March, 1687-8, taken up 300 a's of Land in the County of Newcastle, about 11 miles from the Town, of which he produces a Draught under Ja. Claypoole's hand, Requests a Confirmation of the said Land at a bushell of wheat p'r ann. in Consideration that he now holds about 6,800 a's within this Governm't upon the same Rent, of all which he Never Yett took up any from the Prop'ry besides the said Tract. Ordered that a Patent be granted as Requested.

The Proprietary having been Long desirous to Purchase of Thomas Stacy deceased, and his Son John, his Heir, 300 acres of Land Scituate in West Jersey, on Dellaware River, over against Pennsbury, and at his departure having Ordered that the said John should confer with the Commiss'rs about the said Purchase, who accordingly appearing Some time agoe. informs that He would have Land in the Manor of Springettsberry in Exchange for the said Land, Value for Value, Upon which the Commiss'rs according to the Prop'rs directions chose Sam'll Jenning's in behalf of the Prop'ry, and the said John chose Peter Tretwell, doth of Burlington, in his behalf, to award the Terms and Difference of Value.

And the said John affirming that £300 has been offered to him for the said 300 a's, and the Commiss'rs Valuing the said Land in the Manor being the upper end Near Germantown at 30s p'r acre the said Sam'll and Peter Judging only by the Prices sett by each, Return that the Prop'ry should give 200 a's of the said Manor Land for the 300 a's desired. But the Commiss'rs demurring upon this through a Jealousy that the said John's Land is much Overvalued, Notwithstanding all pretences of Mines or Minerals to be found in the same, which chiefly Induce the Proprietary to make the said purchase, request the s'd John to give them Six Months time to write to the Prop'ry to know his mind therein, to which the said John agrees and promises that in that time he will not grant it to any other.

Robert Assheton producing a Deed from the Prop'ry dated the 30th of May, 1687, by which he granted to William Assheton, father to the said Rob't, for the use of his children 3,000 acres of Land in this Province, of which 3,000 acres the said Robert's share is 750 acres, and producing also a Deposition Sworn by the said Robert before Judge Guest and by him certifyed that the Prop'ry before his departure promised to the said Robert in lieu and in full Satisfaction of the said 750 acres 500 acres near Edward Farmer's, in the County of Philad'a, adjoining on the land lately granted by the Prop'ry to Robert and Sussannah Reading;

He thereupon Requests a Warrant for taking up the said 500 acres, But the Evidence not appearing Sufficient, and yet the said Robert Pleading his Exigencies to be great, 'tis Ordered that a Warrant shall be granted to the said Robert for the said 500 acres, if there be so much Vacant there, and that he shall give bond in £300 to produce Sufficient Evidence from the Prop'ry in 18 Months or at the Expiration of the said time to pay 150 pounds in Consideration of the said Land.

Martha Durant, Widow of John Durant, deceased, producing a Certificate Under the Prop'ry's hand that some time about . . . . , ... He, the said Prop'ry, Granted the said John and Martha 600 a's of Land in this Province, which he was Willing should be now taken up, Requests a Warrant for taking up the said Land, being now in a great Strait and having an opportunity of entring upon a Way for a Livelyhood provided she could obtain the said Land.

Ordered that whereas the Prop'ry is pleased to acknowledge that he Granted 600 a's to the said John and Martha, which being by Deed is irrevocable, and that upon the said John's decease, Martha Surviving, hath a right to the whole and that the said Martha is at present so Necessitous, a Warrant be forthwith granted to the said Martha for the said Six hundred acres and Confirmed by patent on the Return.

Josiah Ellis, of London, purchased of the Prop'ry by Lease and Release dated 1684, 1,000 acres of Land, to which there belongs a Lott of 20 foot in Breadth in the Front Street of Philad'a, on Dellaware Side, which Lott is part of No. 3 in the said Front Street, but is taken up and granted to others, in lieu whereof his Son, Josiah Ellis, of Philad'a, Taylor, requests a Warrant to take up a Lott in the said Street of the same Dimentions where it may be found Vacant, which is Granted.

Signed a Warrant to Judge Guest for the Barrens, &c., in N. C., Ord'd.

———

At a Session of the Commissioners at Philadelphia the 25th of the 1st Month, 1702.

Present, Edward Shippen, Griffith Owen, Thomas Story, James Logan, Sec'ry.

The Proprietary, by Deeds of Lease and Release dated 8 and 9 of 7br., 1681, Granted 250 a's to Rob't Stevens, who by a Warrant f'm the Commiss'rs dated 2d 10 mo., 1684, took up the same in Bromingham, in the County of Chester, and by a Deed dated the 5th 1 mo., 1687-8, Convey'd the said Land to Nath'll Lukins, who by Deed dated 13th 7 mo., 1692, convey'd the same to John Willis, who is Now Seated thereon and Requests a Resurvey in Order to a Confirmation. Ord'd that a Warrant be accordingly granted and a Patent on the Return, he paying for the Overplus. Also that the said Warrant be granted on 25 a's adjoyning, by him purchased by Deed dated 8th 1 mo., 1697, of John Bennet, who (as 'tis said) purchased 500 acres of John Jones, but is to be further cleared, when the Patent is Granted.

The said John Willis also requests a Grant for 100 acres adjoyning to the Corner of Mathias Prosser's Land near Brandy Wine, in the Manor of Rocklands, extending tow'ds the Indian Fields, or 200 a's of Land last Granted to George Harland for which he agrees to pay twenty-Five Pounds, one Moiety the 24th of the 4th Mo'th and the other the 29th of the 7th Mo'th ensuing. Ordered that a Warrant be accordingly granted and a Patent on the Return.

George Palmer, by Lease and Release, dated 26th and 27th 2 mo., 1682, purchased of the Prop'ry 5,000 acres of Land, of Which by his last Will bearing date 4th 4 mo., 1682, he devised to his Wife Elizab. 1,000 acres, to his Daughter Elizab. 800 a's, and to his Sons George, John, Thomas and William 800 a's to each. William by a Warrant from the Prop'ry dated , took up his 800 acres in Whitpain's Township, in the County of Philad'a, which by a Warrant from the Prop'ry dated 27th 1 mo., 1701, he procured to be resurv'd and 'tis found thereupon by a Return under E. Penington's hand to Contain 832 a's, for which he requests a Patent.

Ordered that a Patent be forthwith Granted.

Elizabeth, daughter of the said George Palmer, now wife of Ralph Jackson, having also obtained a Warrant of Resurvey of the same date on 300 acres Scituate in the said Township and is parcel of the abovementioned 800 acres granted her by her said Father the said Land is found to Contain 311 acres as appears by a Return Under E. Penington's hand, on which she requests a Patent. Granted to Ralph and Elizabeth Jackson.

Agreed with John Redman, Bricklayer, for £14 to underpin the Walls of the New Mill at the Town's end and that he shall repair all breaches and make good all Deficiencies and find all Labourers, the Prop'ry only to find lime and Stone. Agreed also for £20 for a Pair of Mill stones.

Memorandum: That with the Tract of 12 acres of Philip

England on the West side of Skuylkill there is enclosed within the same bounds 8 acres granted by Warrant from the Prop'ry dated 27th 10 mo., 1683, Surveyed 15th 7 mo., '84, and Confirmed by Patent 19th 6 mo., 1687, to the said Philip, who has since sold it Jno. Longworthy.

Signed a Generall Warrant of Resurvey on the Townships of Chichester, Bethel, Concord and Bromingham, in the County of Chester, with directions to make Returns of the whole Townships with all the district Courses and Corners of each division Line by which the several Tracts were at first laid out or otherwise, to Isaac Taylor.

Signed a Warrant of Resurvey to John Willis on 275 a's, Ordered to-day.

Signed a Warrant to John Willis for 100 a's in Rocklands, Ordered to-day.

At a Session of the Commissioners at Philadelphia the 30th of the First Mo'th, 1702.

Present, Edward Shippen, Griffith Owen, Thomas Story, James Logan, Sec'ry.

Ordered that Randal Spakeman have five Warrants for taking up Daniel Smith's land in the several Counties, 500 acres in Each Warrant, the Last

Ordered that the Deficiencies of Henry Marjoram's Land in the County of Bucks be Supplied out of the Overplus of the 625 acres sold to the Heirs of William Venables by putting a Warrant granted by the Prop'ry for that purpose forthwith in execution, but that all Improvem'ts, and Especially those made by Peter Worrall, be left to the said Land and that the Overplus shall be accounted all above the Number of 625 acres aforesaid.

The Prop'ry, by Lease and Release, dated 10th and 11th 8br. 1681, Granted to Caleb Pusey 250 a's of Land, of which 100 being laid out where he now lives; the remaining 150 were by a Warrant from the Prop'ry dated 14th 12 mo., 1683, laid out in Middletown, in Chester County, and by another Warrant of the same date 50 more added for which (he saies) he paid the former Commiss'rs.

John Hicks, of London, Cheesemonger, by Lease and Release, dated 10th and 11th 8br., 1681, purchased of the Prop'ry 250 a's which by a Warrant dated 7th 5 mo., 1683, were taken up in the said Township of Middletown, and the said Hicks by an Instrum't dated 3d August, 1689, Constituted Randal Vernon, Thomas Vernon and Walter Faucet, his attornies, to dispose of the Said Land, who by a Deed dated 10th 1 mo., 1691, convey'd the Said 250 acres to Caleb Pusey. Of this 250 acres Purchase, Caleb Pusey, by a Warrant dated 30th 5 mo., 1687, took up the same day 4 a's of Lib. Land so that the said tract should Contain but 246 a's [See whether John Goodson his Lib. Land in right of this].

John Pusey, of London, Dyer, by Lease and Release, dated 10th and 11th of 8br., 1681, purchased of the Prop'ry 250 acres, which by a War't dated 7th 5 mo., 1683, were Survey'd adjacent to the above in the said Township, and by an Instrum't dated 8th of August, 1682, appointed Caleb Pusey his attorney to enter and take up the said Land, who by Vertue thereof took it up as afores'd.

Frances Pusey, Widdow of the said John, by a Letter of attorney dated 2d of Feb'y, 1692, Impowered Randal Vernon, Thomas Vernon and Walter Faucet to convey the said Land with all appurtenances of the said Purchase, by Vertue of which the said three attorneys by Deed dated 1st 10 mo., 1694, convey'd the said 250 acres to Caleb Pusey.

William Boswel, of Southwark, Poulterer, by Lease and Release, dated 10th and 11th of October, 1681, Purchased of the Prop'ry 500 acres of Land, and by Deeds dated 19th and 20th of 10br., 1681, sold one Moiety thereof to Robert Hart, of London, Plaisterer, to whom it was Surveyed at the same time with the aforegoing by Ch. Ashcorn. Robert Hart, by an Indenture dated 27 of June, 1685, conveyd the s'd Moiety to Jacob Chandler of London, Basket maker, who by Deed dated 8th 1 mo., 1697, sold the same to Caleb Pusey, all which several parcels lying contigious in the Township of Middletown aforesaid, and now by Vertue of the said Purchases in the said Caleb's Possession He requests a Resurvey on the same, being 950 acres in the Whole, and a Patent on the Return. Ordered that a Patent be granted on the return as requested, he paying for the Overplus, if any be found, and first a Warrant of Resurvey.

Signed a Warrant of Resurvey to David Potts on 150 acres, Ordered 23rd 12th Mo'th.

The Proprietary having before his Departure granted to John Herick Sproegel 100 acres of Land in the Manor of Springfield at 20s p'r ann., which by the Prop'rs Order was laid out by Thomas Fairman, requests a Confirmation. Ordered that a Patent be granted on the said 100 acres at 20s p'r ann., and ten Pounds to be paid to the Prop'ry, his Heirs, &c., at the expiration of every fifty years after the date of the grant.

James Thomas, of Philad'a, Merch't, having built on a piece of Vacant Land by Mistake in the County of Sussex, requests a grant of 100 a's where his House now stands and where his Tenant, Tho. Townsend, is Seated, on the same Rent with the rest of his Lands there. Ordered that a Warr't be granted for

100 acres as Requested at 1 Bushell of Wheat p'r ann.; to Pay Seven years arrears for the time past.

Thomas Fairman produces an imperfect Deed dated 26th 5 mo., 1684 (but saies he has a Better), for 200 a's of Land Scituate beyond Shackamaxon (being the same on which Fr. Rawle is Seated), of which 200 he Sold to Rob't Turner 180 acres, and reserved the remaining 20 to himself. Rob't Turner, by Deed dated 12th 9 mo., 1689, convey'd to the said Thomas Fairman 21 acres lying on the North side of John Brock's Land and the King's road, bounded by the said Land and Road and Tumanaramaning's Creek [i. e. the Wolf's Walk], granted to the said Rob't Turner by way of Exchange by Peter Nelson. Rob't Turner also by Deed dated 16th 4 mo., 1695, convey'd back again 5 acres of the 180 mentioned above, purchased of Thomas Fairman, to the said Thomas, who is now Possessed of 3 aforementioned parcells, being in the whole 46 a's, on which he craves a Resurvey for his brother Robert Fairman's Wife, and that in Pursuance of a Grant from the Prop'ry left under his hand, all the Vacant Land adjoyning may be added to it, for which he is to allow Land in Exchange out of that at Shackamaxon for the accommodation of the Prop'rs Mill at the Town end.

Ordered that a Resurvey be Granted as Requested.

At a Session of the Commissioners at Philadelphia the 6th of the 2d Month, 1702.

Present, Griffith Owen, Thomas Story, James Logan.

Joseph Kirl having obtained a Warrant of Resurvey dated 11th of ye 12th Month, 1701, on 500 acres of Land in the Welch Tract, which being executed, the said Tract is found to Contain 597 acres, of which 50 being allowed by Law there Remains 47 acres to be paid for, for which he agrees to pay together with 18 Years Quittrents £20, i.e., twenty pounds the Rents. Ordered a Patent thereupon forthwith.

Joseph Kirl also Requests a Warrant for the Lib'ty Land appurtenant to Richard Collins' Purchase, Mentioned pa. 49, for which the said Joseph and Richard Wood took out a Warrant, but whether Survey'd or not he knows Not. Ordered that a Warrant be granted as Requested for 25 a's to the said Joseph and James Wood, Heir to the said Richard.

Joseph Kirl produces a Patent from the Prop'ry dated 12th 4 mo., '84, for 30 foot in the Front of Philadelphia, granted to Enoch Flower in Right of his first Purchase, being in Length on the North side from the Front Street to the East side of the Swamp 148 foot, and from the West Side of the said Swamp to the Second street 64 foot, and on the South side from the

Second street to the West side of the s'd Swamp 75 foot, and from the East Side thereof to the Front Street 135 foot; Rent 2s Sterling p'r ann. Enoch Flower, by his last Will, Dated 21st of the 6th Mo'th, 1684, appointed Seth Flower and the said Seth's son, Henry Flower, his Ex'ors. But Seth Flower being Resident in England renounced and left the whole to his Son, Henry Flower, who by a Deed dated 5th of February, 1700-1, convey'd to the said Jos. Kirl the Eastermost part of the said Lott together with the Swamp granted in pursuance of the General Grant to John Budd, on which he craves a Warrant to take up the said Swamp according to a late agreem't made with the Owners of the Lotts Joyning on the said Swamp and a Patent on the Return.

Joseph Kirl for William Lovel and Richard Wood having taken up 500 a's in the Welch Tract and 500 acres in South'ton, in Bucks, and now taken out a Warrant for 25 acres of Liberty Land in right and part of 1,250 acres Purchased by Rich'd Collins (vid pa. 49) requests a Warrant to take up the 225 acres remaining which is granted.

The Prop'ry, by Deeds of Lease and Release, dated Granted to William Sharlow 2,500 acres, in part of which by a Warrant dated 2d 5th Mo'th, 1683, there was Surveyed to him 30th 7 mo., 1684, 500 acres within the bounds of the Welch Tract. William Sharlow, by the name of W. S., of London, Merch't, by an Instrum't 30th 7br., 1691, appointed John Blunston his attorney to dispose of the said Land, who by a Deed dated 5th 10 mo., 1692, convey'd 150 a's, part of the said 500, to Thomas Potts, who by a Deed dated 2d 2 mo., 1695, convey'd the s'd 150 acres to David Hugh, who sold it to Robert Jones, of Meirion, Labourer, who again sold it to Robert Jones, of Meirion, Yeoman, and the said David Hugh not having Convey'd it before and the said Robert Jones, Labourer, by a Joynt Deed dated 20th 4 mo., 1699, convey'd the said 150 a's with all appurtenances to the said Robert Jones, Yeoman, who being Now in Possession thereof craves a Resurvey in Order to a Patent.

Ordered that a Warrant be forthwith Granted and a Patent on the Return, he paying for the Overplus if any.

The Prop'ry, by Pat't dated 16th 5 mo., 1684, Granted to Robert Marsh 500 a's of land in South'ton Township, in the County of Bucks, out of which the said Robert (as 'tis said) in his life time Sold 200 acres to William Waite, who Sold to Joseph Holding and is now claimed by John Nailor.

The said Robert, by his last will, dated 25th of July, 1688, devised his Land in South'ton among Others to his Wife Sarah and his Son Hugh, who by a Deed dated 14th 2 mo.,1693, convey'd the said Land, viz: the 300 acres remaining to John Eastburn, who desires a Resurvey on the said 300 acres in Order to ascertain the bounds between him and John Nailor.

Ordered that a Resurvey be granted and a Patent on the Return.

The Prop'ry, by Deeds of Lease and Release, dated 12th and 13th of December, 1698, joyntly with Vincent Vincent and Theod. Vincent, Esqrs., Sons of S'r Matthias Vincent, convey'd to Joseph Pike 10,000 acres of Land, being the same Tract that the Prop'ry by a Deed Poll dated 20th of Aprill, 1686, Sold to the Said S'r Matthias Vincent, which was Laid out Soon after the first Purchase, in the upper part of the County of Chester, in a Tract of 30,000 acres and the said Joseph Pike by his attorney, Thomas Story, obtained of the Proprietary a Warrant of Resurvey dated 29th 6th Mo'th, 1700, which was executed 18th 8 mo., 1700, and the days following, and Duly returned; and upon the said Return the Proprietary granted a Patent dated 17th 8th, 1701, in which three-fifths of all Royal Mines being Reserved to the Prop'ry, the said Tho. Story in behalf of himself and Samuel Carpenter and Isaac Norris, the other two attorneys, Constituted by an Instrument dated 20th 7th Mo'th, 1700, objects against the same, alledging that the Prop'ry by the words [all Mines, Mineral] and [Royalties], had Convey'd away all Royal Mines and therefore could reserve no more than what the King had Reserved to himself in the Royal Charter to the Proprietary, and therefore craves that the Commiss'rs would Order the said Patent (not being Yett Sealed) to pass under the great Seal with an alteration of the said Reservation from three-fifths of Royal Mines to one-fifth only. Ordered that the Proprietary should be Consulted thereupon, the Secretary affirming that the said Reservation was made by the Proprietary's Special Order.

The Prop'ry, by Lease and Release, dated 24th and 25th of August, 1682, Granted to Sam'll Rolle, of Balyfyn, in the County of Cork, in Ireland, Gen't, 5,000 acres of Land. Samuel Rolle, by Lease and Release, dated 17th and 18th of August, 1698, convey'd all the said 5,000 acres to Joseph Pike, his Heirs, &c a. In right of which there has been taken up by a Warrant dated 25th 5 mo. 1700, 500 acres in Philadelphia Coun., and by a Warrant dated 10th 7br., 1700, 500 More were taken up in the County of Chester and Confirmed by Patent 7th 8, 1701. The first mentioned five hundred a's were confirmed by Patent dated 19th 2 mo. 1701, and by a Patent dated 23d of August, 1701, was again Confirmed (as 'tis said by a Mistake) having the same bounds, Corners and Courses, so that there seems to be taken up only 1,000 acres, Notwithstanding the said three

19—Vol. XIX.

Patents. The above mentioned attorneys request Warrants for taking up the Lotts appurtenant to the said Purchase, and the remainder of the Land untaken up. Ordered that a War't be granted for his Lotts and Warrants for his Land in several Tracts of 500 acres each, one tract to be in one Township and no more.

Joseph Wood, of Newcastle, Sheriff, having obtained a Warrant from the Prop'ry Dated 31st of 8br., 1701, for taking up 200 a's of Land in the County of New Castle in lieu and in Consideration of the like quantity untaken up belonging to his Father's Purchase of 2,500 acres, for which 200 a's the Prop'ry when formerly here granted a Warrant designed to be executed upon the Swedes Mill Creek near Darby, but was prevented indirectly (as 'tis said) by Robert Longshore. The said last Warrant, viz: of ye 31st of 8br. last the said Joseph procured to be executed on a Tract of Vacant Land adjoyning on the backs of Hernhook Plantations and the King's Road, affirmed by James Claypoole to have been left Vacant there for the accommodation of the Inhabitants of Swanwick and in no wise belonging to the Commons, and therefore Craves a Confirmation. The said Joseph also requests a grant of a small Tract of Vacant Land interjacent between one Corner of the said Land and the King's Road, formerly Claimed (but without any Title) by William Marslender, for which he agrees to give after the Rate of £30 p'r 100. Ordered that the Surveyor make Return of the said Survey and that a Patent be granted thereupon, and that if the said Joseph can procure a Release or Quittclaim of all right to the said 41 acres from those who have pretended to it, a War't be also granted for the same and be returned and Confirmed together with the other.

Signed a Patent to William Palmer for 832 acres, Ordered 25th Ult.

Signed a Patent to Ralph and Eliz. Jackson for 311 acres, Ordered 25th Ult.

Signed a Warrant to Rand. Spakeman for 500 acres to D. Smith, in Chester Coun, Ord'd, p. 49.

Signed a War't to R. Spakeman for 500 a's to D. Smith, in the Prov., Ordered, pa. 49.

Signed a War't to R. Spakeman for 500 a's to D. Smith, to be seated in 18 mo'ths, Ord'd, pa 49.

At a Session of the Commissioners at Philadelphia the 13th and 14th of the 2d Mo'th, 1702.

Present, Edward Shippen, Griffith Owen, Thomas Story, Jas. Logan, Sec'ry.

The Prop'ry, by Deeds of Lease and Release, dated the 10th and 11th of August, 1682, Granted to Henry Wright, of Shrewsbury, Tobacconist, and Elizabeth, his Wife, 500 a's, in right of which by Vertue of a General Warrant from the Prop'ry for laying out the Welch Tract there was Survey'd to the said Hen. Wright by David Powel 490 acres within the said Tract the first of the 4th Month, 1685. Hen. Wright deceasing and Elizabeth Surviving, by a Deed Ind'r dated 27th of June, Convey'd the whole said 500 acres to her Grandson, Henry Wright, who by a Deed dated 7th March, 1701-2, convey'd the same to Philip Yarnal, who Requests a Resurvey in order to a Patent, also Lotts and Liberty Land appurtenant. Ordered that a Warrant of Resurvey be forthwith Granted and to make it 500 acres and a Patent on the Return, &c.

The grant not being within the first 100 purchasers there belongs no Lotts nor Liberty Land to it.

The Prop'ry, by his Patent dated 1st 1 mo., 1684, Granted to Gilbert Wheeler 180 a's upon old Rent, in Bucks, adjoyning on Wm. Biles', together with a small Island called Wheeler's Island, which being upon a New Regulation of the old granted Lands thereabouts Survey'd by D. Powel, there was a Mistake Committed either in the Return or Patent by which the lines are made to interfere and altogether preposterous, tho' the lines in the fields Seem regular enough as has been tried by Wm. Emlyn, according to which he requests a Resurvey in Order to a New Pat't.

Ordered that a Resurvey be accordingly granted and a Pat't on the Return.

The Prop'ry, by Lease and Release, dated 20th and 21st of March, 1681, Granted to William Yardly, of Rushton Spencer, in the County of Stafford, Yeoman, 500 a's of Land, which by a Warrant from Gov'r Markham, &c., dated 6th 8 mo., 1682, was on the 13th of the said Month laid out to the said William in Makfield Township, in the County of Bucks, and by a Patent from Wm. Markham and John Goodson dated 23d 11 mo., 1687, confirmed to the said Will'm for 500 acres.

Enoch Yardly, Son and Heir of the said Wm., Requests a Warrant of resurvey on the whole, being now all in his possession, as follows:

William Yardly, by his last Will and Testament, dated   , devised one Moiety of the said 500 a's, with all Improvements, to his son Enoch, and the other Moiety to his Sons Thomas and William, of whom the said Enoch Purchased the same by a Release under their hands dated   , and accordingly requests a Patent.

The Prop'ry, by Lease and Release, dated 21st and 22d of

Aprill, 1682, Granted to Nicholas Waln 1,000 acres, in part of which there was Survey'd to the said Nicholas by a Warrant from the Prop'ry 21st 1 mo., 1683, 250 acres on Neshamineh Creek, confirm'd by Patent from the Commiss'rs (together with another tract of 250 acres), dated 9th 11 mo., 1684. Of the said 25 acres Nicholas Waln Convey'd to Wm. Herst 50 a's and the remaining 200 by a Deed Poll dated 10th 1 mo., 1695, to John Stackhouse, who obtained from the Prop'ry a Warrant of Resurvey dated 22d 1 mo., 1700-1, which being executed it is found to Contain 312 acres. Of the said 307 acres 20 being allowed by Law there Remains 87 acres to be paid for at 7s 6d p'r acre, which he agrees to give and Requests a Patent on the same, which is granted.

There being, as 'tis said, a Deficiency in a Tract adjoyning granted for 250 a's to John Scarborow, 60 thereof now possessed by Tho. Beans, 80 thereof by H. Huddlestone, and 110 (Should be, but proves (they say) only 87 a's, viz: 23 Short) by Adam Harker, who if he takes a Warrant to Resurvey on the whole is to be paid for what is found Short after the same rate that J. Stackhouse pays the Proprietary.

Samuel Nichols Producing a return of Survey of a lott In the 3d Street, 30 ft. in breadth and 198 ft. Long, laid Out To him 1st 8br, '92, In pursuance of a Warrant from the Comm'rs of the same date, On Rent 3 Shill's Sterling, from said Survey.

The Prop'ry, by Lease and Release, dated 21st and 22d 2 mo., 1682, Granted to Henry Baily 1,500 a's, who by a Deed dated   , (as is affirmed by Nicholas Waln, who says he had the said Deed in his Possession but was lost in P. Pemberton's hands) granted 250 a's to Alexander Giles, who took up the same (which is laid out in the Map) upon Neshamineh Creek, in Bucks, and being seized thereof Died Intestate, leaving Issue 3 Daughters Elizab., Mary and Dorothy, Coparceners of the said Land. Elizab. being deceased, the whole right is Now in the other two, who have sold the whole to Robert Heaton, the Deed to be drawn bearing date   , the said Rob't Requests a Resurvey in Order to a Patent. The Deed from Baily not appearing the Title seems dubious, but it being so positively affirmed that a Deed has really been seen and Robert Running the Risque, a Resurvey is granted and a Patent on the Return, he paying for the Overplus.

Thomas Norbury, of Newtown, in the County of Chester, produces the Copy of a Warrant from the Office Signed by E. Pen., from the Proprietary dated 21st 9br., 1683, for 125 acres granted to the said Thomas, Purchaser (as is there s'd), but he having Never paid for it, Cal. Pusey making application to the Prop'ry before his Departure in behalf of the said Thomas as an object of his Charity, the Pro'ry was pleased to grant the whole for £10, as by a Certificate under Caleb's hand appears. The Land is Ordered in the Warrant to be laid out between Crum Creek and Darby Creek as now Scituated. He also produces a Like Copy of a warrant from the Proprietary dated 21st 9br., 1683, for 50 Acres to be laid out in the Place aforesaid to Stephen Hough, late Purchaser, who deceasing, the said Thomas Married his Widdow Francis, and in right of the said Marriage holds the said Land. The whole 175 Acres is granted for the said Sum of £10 by the Gov'r to Thomas Norbury who requests a Resurvey on the whole and a Patent on the Return.

Granted as Requested.

Peter Yocom having obtained of the Proprietary (as in pa. 84,) 500 A's of Land which were laid out on p't of Laetitia Penn's Manor by a Deed poll duly executed, bearing date 23d August, 1697, convey'd 250 Acres thereof to John Hew who requests a Warrant of Resurvey in Order to a Patent.

Ordered a Resurvey on the said Land, also upon the other 250 A's, Regulating and ascertaining the whole bounds and a Patent upon the Return, paying for the Overplus, &c a.

The Prop'ry, by Lease and Release, dated 26th and 27th 7br., 1681, Granted to Wm. Baily 500 Acres of Land (with the addition of W. B. of Gottacre, in the County of Wilts, Yeoman), who by his last Will dated 2d 8br., 1691, devised all his Lands in Pennsylvania to his Nephew Jacob Button, of Calne, in Coun. Wilts, Taylor, Jacob Button, by Indentures of Lease and Release, dated 3th and 4th of 8br., 1701, Convey'd the said 500 A's of Land, with all its appurtenances, to Jeremiah Collet, Junr., of the County of Chester, in Pennsylvania, Merch't, who Requests a Warrant to take up the same. Of this 500 Acres Wm. Baily Sold to John Bill 125 Acres who sold to Daniel Smith, as in Page 48, So that there remains only 375 Acres to be taken up, for which he requests a Warr't.

Granted and a Patent on the return.

Signed a Patent to Tho. Janvier, of Newc., for 4 Several Lotts joyned into two at 2 bushells p'r Ann., Ordered this Day and recited New Castle Minutes.

Signed a Patent to Philip Howel for 20 Acres of Liberty Land in right of Hen. Pawlin's first Purchase of 1,000 Acres laid out by a War't dated 26th 2 mo., 1701.

George Maris, Junr., of Springfield, having lately purchased the Remaind'r of 500 Acres laid out to George Simcock, Purchaser of the said quantity, Requests a Warrant of Resurvey on the same. Of the said 500 Acres Samuel Lewis holds 190 Acres,

Edm'd Cartlidge 100, John Meres 25, Fra. Yarnal 25, Jacob Simcock 50, and Peter Britton 88½, in the whole 478½ A's, Over and above which Andrew Griscomb, in the year 1691, obtained a Warrant for 8 Acres of Lib. Land, the proportion of the said Purchase, which if Survey'd, there remains only 13½ Acres of the said Purchase, but there appears about 60 acres in the Field. Ordered that a Warrant of Resurvey be granted at the request of G. Maris on the said Residue, but that by the same Warrant the Whole be Resurvey'd.

James Wallace, of Bristol, Merchant, having Purchased of the Prop'ry by Lease and Release, dated , 168 , 1,000 Acres of Land in this Province, Thomas Withers, of Chichester, appointed Attorney by Letter under the hand and Seal of the said James, bearing date , obtained a War't from the Prop'ry for 500 A's, which has been executed in the County of Chester, and now requests according to the Propr's Promise a Warrant for the remainder to be laid out in the next Township, w'ch is granted.

The Prop'ry, by Deeds of Lease and Release, dated 21st and 22nd March, 1681, Granted to Henry Maddock, of Hoomhall, Coun. Chester, Yeoman, and James Kennerly, of the same place Yeoman, 1,500 A's of Land in right of which by Vertue of a Warrant dated 29th 7 mo., 1682, there was laid out to them 800 or 850 Acres of Land in Springfield in the County of Chester; James Kennerly deceasing, w'thout Issue, Hen. Maddock Inherited, who by a Deed of Gift dated 28th and 29th 8th Mo'th, 1701, Granted all his right to Lands in Pennsylvania to his son and Heir Mordecai Maddock, who requests a Resurvey on the said Tract. Granted.

The Prop'ry having, by his Warr't dated 22d 9 br., 1683, Granted to Roger Hughs, Purchaser of 250 Acres, David Meredith of 100 A's, John Lloyd of 100 Acres, R'd Cook of 100 A's, each of them a Lott in the City proportionable to their Several Purchases, which were in pursuance of the said Warrant laid out in Chestnut Street; David Meredith, in behalf of himself and the others, Requests a Resurvey in Order to a Patent. Ordered a Warr't and Patent

Signed a Warrant to Jerem. Collet for 375 Acres, Ord'd Yesterday.

Signed a Warrant to George Maris for a Resurvey in Springfield, Ordered Yesterday.

Signed a Warrant to Tho. Withers for 500 A's in right of Ja. Wallace, Ord'd Yesterday.

Signed a Warrant of Resurvey to Mordecai Maddock Ordered Yesterday.

MINUTE BOOK "G." 295

At a Session of the Commissioners at Philadelphia the 20th of 2d Mo'th, 1702.

Present, Edward Shippen, Griffith Owen, Thomas Story, James Logan.

Bartholomew Coppock, Junr., having by Vertue of a Warrant from the Prop'ry Bearing date 17th 7th Mo'th, 1701, procured his Land in Springfield laid out for 400 Acres by Vertue of a Warr't from T. Holme dated 11th 7 mo., '82, in right of a Purchase made by the said B. Coppock of 500 A's, and Barth. Coppock, of the said place, Senr., of 250 A's, by Deeds of Lease and Release dated 21st and 22d of March, 1681-2, which said 400 As' being Resurvey'd by Isaac Taylor is found to Contain 520 Acres, of which 40 being allowed by Law, there remains 80 to be paid for. B. Coppock, Junr., holding only one Moiety of this, desires a Pat't for the same and agrees to give ten Shillings p'r Acre for his 40 Acres of Overplus to be paid.

Ordered a Patent forthwith.

Nathaniel Allen, by Deeds dated 26th and 27th July, '81, Mentioned pa. 57, Purchased of the Prop'ry 2,000 Acres, of which 600 A's being laid out on Neshamineh and 750 in Warminster.

Nath. Allen, by an Obligation dated 1st 5 mo., 1685, obliged himself, his Heirs, &c., in the sum of £50 to Wm. Noble, of Bristol, in England, with Condition that he, the said Nath'll, should Surrender to the s'd Will'm 300 A's of that Tract laid out in Warminster Aforesaid.

The said Nath. Allen, by his last Will dated 21st of August, 1692, devised the Whole said 750 Acres to his Son Nehemiah Allen, and to his Grandsons, Nath'l and Nehemiah, Sons of the said Nehemiah, and of his said Will he made his said Son Nehem., Tho. Bradford and Tho. Paschal Ex'ors. But Nehem. Allen well knowing the said 300 Acres, parcel of the said 750, were sold by his Father Nathan'll as afores'd, he, with T. Bradford, by Indenture, dated 30th 7 br., 1700, granted and Convey'd the said 300 Acres to Abel Noble, son of the said William.

By another Ind're of the same date the said Nehemiah Allen and Tho. Bradford, for the Consideration therein Mentioned, granted and Convey'd to the said Abel Noble the remaining 450 A's, upon which the said Abel requests a Resurvey on the said Whole Tract and a Patent on the Return, which is granted.

Thomas Fairman, of that Tract of 2,500 Acres, Purchased of Stanly s Relict, &c., Mentioned in page 65, over and above the said 1,100 Acres there disposed of, Sold to **Thomas Roberts** 200

Acres Situate above Job Bates', and by a Bond dated 9th 6 mo., 1701, obliged himself in the sum of £100 to procure him a Title, In Order to which and to make Titles to others to whom he stands under the same Obligations, the said Tho. Fairman Requests a Resurvey on the Remainder of the said Tract of 2,500 Acres, besides what is already Resurvey'd to Al. Edwards, &c., page 65, Viz: 1,300 Acres.

Ordered that a Resurvey be accordingly Granted.

Gunner Rambo, for himself and some other Swedes here Mentioned, Produces the following Paper Signed by the Proprietary:

Philadelphia the 28th of the 8th Month, 1701. Gunner Rambo, his Son John, and Peter Cock, making application to me for a Confirmation of the Land they Live upon, which was layed out to them within my Daughter's Manor on Skuylkill, in right of my Grant to Lasse Crock and his Children, and whereas it is presumed there is an Overplus therein, I hereby Order that the same be strictly Resurveyed at their charge, and that they pay my Commiss'rs thirty pounds p'r 100 Acres, they paying my Daughter a half penny p'r Acre for what is within their Bounds, and on these terms lett it be Confirmed.

WM. PENN.

Which land was, by a Warrant from the Prop'ry, formerly granted for 1,000 Acres to the said Lasse Cock, who granted 500 thereof to Gunner Rambo and left 250 to his Son John Cock, and 250 to another son Peter Cock.

All which being Resurvey'd by D. Powel and Tho. Fairman by an   from the Prop'ry, Gunner Rambo's Tract is found to Contain 603 Acres, of which 53 Acres being to be paid for is £16; Peter Cock's is found to Contain $404\frac{3}{4}$ Acres, of which . . . . All which Sums they Severally agree to give Bond to pay as Soon as they can possibly raise it and thereupon Request Patents. Ordered that when the Returns of Survey are perfected Patents be granted as Requested.

Mouns Cock, by Vertue of a Warrant from the Prop'ry, dated 2d of the 6th Mo'th, 1684, for 300 Acres, And by T. Holme's Order, took up the said quantity in the said Manor adjoyning to the preceding, for which the said Mouns being Much indisposed at the time of the Prop'r's Departure could not make application together with the aforesaid Gunner and his Cousins, and therefore now intreats that the said Inability may not turn to his Disadvantage, But that he may have the same favour Shewn him with the others. And the Case being the same, 'tis Ordered that a Resurvey be granted on the said Tract and a Patent on the Return, he paying for the Overplus after the same rate with the aforegoing.

Robert Edwards, Carter, having long sollicited the Gov'r for a Settlement in the Manor of Gilberts (which he granted, but the terms and Place never fully Concluded), again Requests a Grant of 300 Acres in the s'd Manor, for which he agrees to pay twenty pounds p'r hundred by a Bill to Engl'd at 50 p'r C't exch., and if that be not paid engages to pay Interest for a year or two till he be able to pay it here. Upon which 'tis Ordered that a Warrant be granted to the said Robert Edwards for the said quantity of 300 Acres in the said Manor, fronting Skuylkill, to begin on the line run there for a Town and by that to extend Northeast to Perqueomink, and from thence, by another line parrallel to the same, Including the said quantity, And a Patent upon ye Return, he giving Security for the payment.

The Prop'ry, by Original Deeds of Lease and Release, dated , 168 , Granted to Major Jasper Farmer and his Son, Jasper Farmer, 5,000 A's, in part of which there was Survey'd 14th 12 mo., 1689, by Vertue of a Warrant from the Commiss'rs dated 7th of the said Month and Year, 1,250 Acres unto Katherine (then Billop), Relict and Ex'rix of the said Jasper's, Junr., last Will, being part of 5,000 formerly laid out (as 'tis said in the Patent (to said Jasper Farmer and Company, and Confirmed by Patent from all the Commiss'rs dated 10th of April, 1690. And the said Katherine deceasing, Thomas Farmer, her Heir Requests a Resurvey on the s'd Land upon a Suspicion that the Boundaries mentioned in the said Patent are broke in upon. The said Land is Situate near the white Marsh on Skuylkill and is now in the possession of David Harry. Ordered that a Resurvey be granted and an Order for the Deficiency to be made up.

The Prop'ry, by his Warrant, dated 19th 10br., 1683, granted to Cha. Ashcom, Purchaser, 400 Acres of Land in the County of Chester, in pursuance of which Tho. Holme (to whom the said Warrant was directed) Impowered the said Charles (by a Warrant under his Hand dated 20th of the said Month) to lay out to himself the said quantity in the s'd County on the North side of Crum Creek, where not already Survey'd, which was executed in part 15th 5 mo., following, viz: on 330 Acres by the lines of John Simcock, Henry Thauten, &c., in Ridly Township.

Tho. Holme (by his Attorneys), for a Debt due from the said Cha. to the said Tho., obtained a Decree at the Provincial Court at Chester the 18th of the 2d Month, 1692, for one Moiety of £201, 11s, and in pursuance thereof an Execution, which was levied by Caleb Pusey, Sheriff of the said County, Upon 280 Acres, part of the Premises, and the said C. Pusey, as

Sheriff of the said County, by Indenture dated 20th 2 mo., 1693, granted and Convey'd the said 280 Acres to the said Thos. Holme for payment of the said Debt.

Tho. Holme, by Indr. Deed, dated 25th of March, 1694, in Consideration of £114, granted to John Cock the said 280 Acres, who by his Deed dated 26th 9 mo., 1700, Sold to Jacob Simcock the whole said Tract, eighty Acres parcel thereof excepted, which were before sold by the said John Cock to R'd Crosby. Jacob Simcock Requests a Resurvey on the said Land in Order to a Patent, which is granted.

James Hunt Claiming 75 Acres, one Moiety of 150 Acres, granted by Patent from Gov'r Lovelace, dated 10th 1mo., 1670, in Kingsessing, Also 100 Acres more Purchased of Lawrence Cock, who, as 'tis said, purchased of Andr. Peterson; Also 91 A's purchased of the Widdow Dolby, Peter and Wm. Dolby and John Massey by Deed dated 29th 12 mo., 1687, granted to Peter Dalbo in 3 parcels, one of 50, one of 20, and one of 10 Acres, by Patent from Fr. Lovelace dated 18th Feb'y '72, Requests a Resurvey on the said 266 Acres together with a Tract of about 45 Acres of Meadow or Marsh adjoyning, for which be obtained a Warrant from the Commiss'rs dated 14th 4th, 1690, for $\frac{1}{3}$ of the Meadow between Kingsesson Creek and Land Creek. Ordered that a Warrant of Resurvey be granted to the said James Hunt for the said 266 Acres, and that the said Marsh be also resurvey'd without making any Manner of Title to any more than the said 266 Acres.

George Smedly, having in Page 60, agreed to pay £7 10s for 20 Acres of Overplus Land, in which he Complains he was much Mistaken in the agreem't, affirming the land to be wholly Barren, and also produces a Certificate under the hands of Joseph Baker and others of the Neighbours, that his Land in General is not worth above £10 p'r 100, craves that he may be redressed and that the said agreement be cancelled, for he will never Stand to it. All which being Considered, and several proofs of the said Barrenness produced. Ordered that the s'd George shall pay only after the rate of £15 p'r 100, Viz: £3 for the said 20 Acres, which he now pays.

Henry Maddock, Purchaser, with Ja. Kennerly, of 1,500 A's, by Articles dated in England 7th 9 br., 1694, Sold to John Worral 387 A's, which John Simcock, Attorney for the said Henry, by Deed dated 11th 12 mo., '95, Confirmed to the said John Worrall, his Heirs, &c. The said Land was, by Vertue of a Warrant from the Commiss'rs, dated 12th 7 mo., 1684, laid out to Ja. Kennerly at the head of Chester Creek in Edgem't for the said quantity of 387 Acres, which being resurvey'd by Hen. Hol:ngsworth, at the instance of the said John Worral, is found to Contain 478 Acres, of which 38 being allowed by Law there remains 53 Acres to be paid for, for which, being barren or rough at that end where it should be cutt off, he agrees to pay £18, and requests a Patent upon the same. Ordered that a Patent be accordingly granted, the said John giving Bond to admitt of a Resurvey according to the Proprietaries Proposal.

The Proprietary, by Lease and Release, dated 23d and 24th 7 br ,1681, Granted to John Harries, of Goatacre, Wilts, Clothier, 1,500 Acres, of which ('tis said he sold 500 acres to Thomas Ducket and) by Deed dated 1st 8br., 1701, John Harries, son and Heir of the afors'd John Harris, and Edw'd Harris having Some Claim to part of the s'd Land, convey'd the remaining 1,000 A's to Philip Roman. In right of the said purchase there was laid out to the said John Harris and Edward Harris a certain Tract in Bromingham in the County of Chester for 750 Acres, as 'tis Said and is expressed in the Map, which being resurvey'd by Isaac Taylor in pursuance of a Gen'll Warrant for Resurveying, the s'd Township is found to Contain 900 Acres.

Philip Roman, by his Son-in-Law, Isaac Taylor, requests a Warr't to take up the Remainder, being 170 Acres, and a Pat't on the s'd 900 A's.

Ordered That a Warr't and Patent be granted as Requested.

Joshua Hastings, by Lease and Release, dated   , purchased of the Prop'ry 1,000 Acres, of which there has been laid out in Middletown, Coun. Chester, 472 Acres in one Tract, and in Nether Providence 340 Acres, which being resurvey'd by Vertue of a Warr't from the Prop'ry dated 17th 7 Mo., 1701, by Is. Taylor, is found to Contain 390 Acres and is Now sold to Robert Vernon and John Sharpless, the said Joshua having a right to more Land by Vertue of his said purchase, requests a Patent on the said 390 Acres and a Warrant for the remainder. Besides the aforegoing two Tracts, he has taken up 20 Acres of Liberty Land, which, together with the aforegoing, makes 882 Acres, and the Overplus of this Tract being   Acres, makes the whole   Acres, and the remainder to be taken up is

Ordered that a Patent and Warrant be forthwith Granted.

John Bowater, understanding that David Powel, in his late surveys in the Welch Tract, has run Several Lines over a Tract granted by the Commiss'rs Patent dated 8th 7br., 1692, to Mary Fincher, and by a Bargain and Sale from the said Mary, is Now in his Possession, Caveats against the said Land being granted to any Other person till he shall be heard. The said Land is Claimed by Griff. Owen, Hugh Roberts, &c., as 'tis said.

John Baldwin, of Aston Township, having proved a Right

to 50 A's of headland to himself and 50 for his Wife in the Secretaries Office, requests a Warrant to take up the same which is granted.

John Baldwin Came Serv't to Joshua Hastings, and his Wife Kath. Carter, to Isaac Blunston, they request it in Chester County.

Tho Sharp, of Kent County, having purchased of Wm. Johnston and Rich'd Whiteheart 300 Acres of Land Situate on the south side of Duck Creek, by Deed dated 9th 11 mo., 1691, taken up, as W. Clark affirms, by a Warrant from Kent Court, Request a Resurvey upon the same in Ord'r to a Patent, which is Granted.

The Tract laid out to Joseph Fisher for 4,420 Acres, Mentioned pa. 102, being in Pursuance of the Warr't there granted, Resurvey'd by David Powel and Duly returned, is found to Contain 5,062 Acres, of which 440 being allowed by Law there remains 202 to be paid for, which, at the price there agreed for, amounts to £40, and the reducing the Rent thereof to one Shill'g, Sterl'g, p'r thousand is £2 14s which the said Joseph is to pay, and a Patent is Ordered.

At a Session of the Commissioners at Philadelphia the 27 of the 2d Month.

Present, Edward Shippen, Griffith Owen, Thomas Story, J. Grey, Clerk.

The Prop'ry, by Deeds of Lease and Release, dated 26th and 27th Apr., 168 , Granted to John Blunston 1,500 A's in right of which there was laid out on the East side of Darby Creek 500 Acres, and on the west side of the same Creek 250 A's, and on Mill Creek 250 Acres More, in the City Liberties 30 Acres, in the upper end of Darby 180 Acres, and above Edgem't 290 Acres, all in the County of Chester, of all which he has Alienated 647 Acres to several persons, and holds the remainder, vid Court of Inq. for Chester. Requests a Resurvey on the said two parcels of 180 A's and 290 Acres, and a Patent on the Return, which is granted, he paying for the Overplus, &c.

John Gibbons, Jun'r, and Jeremiah Collet, both of the County of Chester, having long Sollicited for a Tract of Vacant Land in or upon the Edge of the Manor of Rocklands, which J. Collet first began to Clear and Improve and first petitioned the Prop'ry for, upon his arrival, but J. Gibbons (as he affirms) first petitioned the former Commiss'rs for it, and Claims a preference from thence, as well as from the Conveniency of it for his Plantation to which it is Contiguous, and that he being a Planter needs it, when J. Collet, a Merch't, has (as he alleges, much less occasion for it) and therefore Requests a grant thereof upon such terms as Shall be thought reasonable. Ordered that in Case the said J. Gibbons procure and produce to this Board a Release and Quittclaim from the s'd Collet of all his pretences to the said Land, it shall be granted as Requested.

The said John Gibbons further Requests that he may purchase 500 a's at the back of the Inhabitants on the Northside of Brandy Wine Creek. Ordered That the said Request be Considered.

Nicholas Hicks, born and bred a Gentleman in England, but through Misfortune come to Poverty, made application to the Prop'ry before his Departure for Relief, which he was willing to grant by taking him into his Service, but upon his Departure is now willing to seat himself on Some Small Tract of Land, and therefore requests a grant of one hundrd acres in Springfield Manor, which, in consideration of the premises, 'tis Ordered That one hundred acres, in a Convenient place joyning or near to Sprogel's tract, be granted to the said Nicholas Hicks under the Yearly Rent of 40s p'r annum.

The Prop'ry, by Lease and Release, dated 10th and 11th 8br., 1681, Granted to R'd Corsely, of Bristol, 1,000 acres, who by Indorsem't on the Release assign'd the same to Tho. Holme (assignm't dated 1st 8br., 1688). Tho. Holme, by his last Will, dated 10th 12 mo., '94, appointed Silas Crispin Sole Ex'or of the same, and left two Daughters, viz.: Esther, Wife of the said Silas, and Elinor, wife of Joseph Smallwood, the said Joseph Smallwood and his Wife Elinor, by an Instrum't dated 20th August, 1701, Released and Quittclaimed to the said Silas all their Right, Estate, Title, Interest and Demand whatsoever that they, the said Joseph and Elinor, then or ever had to any bequest or Legacy in the s'd Will Mentioned, or to any part or parcel of the Real or personal Estate of the said Thomas Holme, by any way or means whatsoever, by Vertue of which last Will and Release aforesaid, the said Silas became Seized of the right of the said one thousand acres. In right of the said Purchase and by Vertue of a Warrant for the Commiss'rs dated 19th 10 mo., 1684, there was Survey'd to Rich'd Corsely 500 acres in up'er Dublin Township, in the County of Philad'a, which said 500 acres the said Silas having Sold to Edward Cartlidge, and he to Thos. Siddon, Requested of the Prop'ry a Patent, which was granted, bearing date 21st Oct'r, 1701, but there being some Errors of ill Consequence in the Recital, Requests another according to ye above, w'ch is also granted.

The Prop'ry, by Lease and Release, dated , 1681, Granted to Joseph Growdon 5,000 acres, and by like Deeds dated   , to Lawrence Growdon 5,000 acres, who (as 'tis s'd) granted his Whole right to his only Son, the said Joseph.

Joseph Growdon Verbally granted to David Lloyd (as he affirms) one thous'd acres, part of the said purchases in right of his Marriage with his Daughter, who Requests a Warrant to take up the same. Granted.

James Price, having by Deeds dated 19th and 20th June, 1682, purchased of Rich'd Davies 300 acres [as in the Welch Minutes under R. D.], which have been Since Granted to David Price as in said Minutes. In right of the said purchase there was laid out to the said David Price a Lott in the City, as 'tis said, among the rest of the Country Men, in Chestnut street, w'ch, by a Deed dated 7th July, 1693 (not locating the Lott), he granted to William Thomas, of Radnor, who sold it (as 'tis said) to Tho. Lloyd, in whose behalf D. Lloyd requests a Confirmation of the same, and that it may be Survey'd together with D. Mered.'s, page 119, which is Granted.

There was no Deed passed from W. Thomas, he losing his Life by an accident soon after the sale; 'tis therefore Ordered that a Release or Deed be produced from the Widdow before a patent is granted.

Nicholas Skull desireing to buy 200 acres of Land adjoyning on his Own and running from his South West Corner along Tho. Fitzwater's line to Daniel Howel'r N. E. Corner, for which he agrees to pay forty pounds p'r hundred, one Moiety the 29th of 7br. next, and the other Moiety the first Month Next, and Interest for Six Months for one half. Ordered that a Warrant and Patent be granted.

Signed a Patent to Jonathan Dickenson for 40 foot of Bank. Ordered 28th 11th Mo'th, Ult.

Signed a Patent to Tho. Minshal for 735 acres, Ord'd pa. 82, 12 mo., 4th Ult.

At a Session of the Comissioners at Philadelphia the 4th of the 3rd Month.

Present, Edward Shippen, Griffith Owen, Thomas Story, James Logan.

The Prop'ry, by Lease and Release, dated 21st and 22 10br., 1681, Granted 500 acres to John Hughs, in wright whereof and by Vertue of a Warrant from Capt'n Markham, &c., dated 17th 6 mo., 1682, there was laid out to the said John Hughs 495 acres in Oxford Township, which was confirmed by Pat't from the Prop'ry, dated 18th 5 mo., 1684, to said Hughs, his Heirs and assigns for ever. The said Hughes, by Lease and Release, dated 2d and 3d 2d Month, 1688, granted the whole said 500 acres to Robert Ewer, his Heirs and assigns, &c., who by Deed dated 6th 10br., 1694, granted one Moiety of the afores'd 495 acres and one Moiety of the Liberty Land appurten't to the said purchase and by another Deed dated the same day, viz. : 6th 10 mo., '94, Granted the other Moiety of the said 495 acres and Liberty Land to Edm'd Orpwood, for which Lib. Land the said W. Buzby and E. Orpwood request a Warrant. There is in the Office a Warr't for the said Liberty Land granted to Jno. Goodson, but he by a Note under his hand declares he can not find that ever he bought it. Ordered that a further Inquiry be made whether Jno. Goodson ever had the said Liberty Land, and if not that then a Warr't be granted.

Joseph Fisher, Joseph Ashton, George Northrap and Edm'd McVeigh, with others of Dublin Township remonstrated that the Sasquehannah Road laid out through the said Township, designed to be laid out equally in the Middle of the said Township, is notwithstanding run too much to the Northw'd, by which Means the Settlem'ts on that side, viz: North of the Road are too Short and on the South too long and therefore requests that the same may be remedied. Ordered therefore that Seeing there has been in Most parts of the said Road only one line thereof run and that it should Contain in breadth 4 perches, that therefore the s'd Road be run the whole length through the s'd Township the s'd breadth, according to the first design, and that the said breadth be laid out on the South side of the said Line, and then if Occasion be that tne said breadth be added to the Deficient Lands.

Joseph Fisher informing that a Tract laid out to him in the said Township for 500 acres is Deficient in breadth, as he Supposes, as Well as in length, desires his deficiency may be made up out of the Overplus which was found in Ja. Atkinson's 200 a s, which Geo. Northrap holds. Granted, Geo. Northrap agreeing to it provided he shall be at no Charge.

Robert Lucas, by an Order from S'r Edm'd Andros, in the year 1679, took up a parcel of Land now in the Falls Township, in Bucks co'nty, 177 acres, which the Gov'r, by his Warr't dated 9th 3 mo., 1684, again granted and by Patent dated 31st 5 mo., 1684, Confirmed it to the said Robert, who devised the same to Edw'd Lucas, his Son and Heir (as 'tis said), Requests a Resurvey according to the old Lines. Granted.

William Warner having obtained a Resurvey and Survey of the Deficiency of 300 acres of Land in Blockley Township produces a Return of it and Requests a Patent, which is Granted.

Job Goodson, for his Father John Goodson and Thomas Fairman, not being yet able to agree upon the Terms proposed and Concluded page 98, and having another hearing doe at length fully conclude and agree that the said Job, in behalf of his Father, shall release all his right to the said 200 acres upon a Grant made from the said Commiss'rs of the like Quantity, to be laid out in some convenient place by the said Tho. Fairman, both which Tracts are to be Valued by indifferent persons and the Difference of Value to be paid by the said Tho. Fairman to the said John Goodson.

Edward Farmer Produces a Certificate under Wm. Markham's hand, dated 11th Jan'ry, 1700-1, declareing that on the 6th of July, 1692, there was granted by the Prop'rs Commiss'rs, Viz: Wm. Markham, Robert Turner and John Goodson, unto Edw'd Farmer, the purchase of one hundred acres of Land in the Manor of Springfield, not exceeding 40 perches, adjoynnig the Southeast part of his Land, he paying for it ten pounds, which 100 acres the said Edw'd affirms was, by a Warr't from the s'd Commiss'rs, laid out to him as aforesaid by Rob't Longshore, but that before he could obtain a Patent the Prop'ry had sent Orders from England that the said Manor Should not be disposed of, and according to the said Order, Sam'll Jennings having received part of the pay, refused the remainder, for which reason the said Tract does yet Remain unconfirmed and the account not Settled. Whereupon the said Edw'd Requests a Resurvey and Confirmation, alledging that the Prop'ry promised to be kind to him in it and that nothing but his Sudden departure prevented the same being confirmed by the Proprietary himself. Ordered that the Prop'ry's pleasure be known before any proceedings be Made herein, there seeming no room for a grant w'thout his particular Ord'r.

The Prop'ry, by Lease and Release, dated 10th and 11th 8br., 1681, Granted to Jonathan Stanmore, of London, Shoemaker, 250 a's. who deceasing, left it (as 'tis said) to his Wife Rachell. Rachel Stanmore, Relict of the said Jonathan, by an Instrument dated 12th 6 mo., 1699, Constituted Jas. Logan her attorney, who with a Particular Negligence and forgetfullness has hitherto Omitted to Discharge the Duty of a Faithfull Trustee and now at length humbly Craves his brother Comm'rs to grant him a Warr't for 245 acres of Land and 5 acres Liberty Land and a City Lott for this said poor Constituent. Ordered upon the said humble request that Warrants be accordingly granted.

The Prop'ry, by Lease and Release, dated   , Granted to Richard Snead, of Bristol, Linnen Draper, 1,500 acres of Land, in right of which there was laid out in the Welch Tract 1,276 acres by Vertue of a Warrant dated 13th 1 mo., 1684, and by a Warrant dated 13th 12 mo., 1691, 200 acres on Skuylkill, on Which Richard Parker, by Tho. Story, Requests a Resurvey. Granted the said 1,276 acres falling under the Welch Claims, is proposed to be quitted in case there can be any equivalent granted; and first they Claim the Overplus in the said 200 a's, which is also Granted.

The Prop'ry having Sold to Isaac Jacob 1,000 acres of Land, which he sold to Tho. Fairman, and T. Fairman to Capt. Finney, as in page 87, the said T. F. produces a Deed under the Prop'rs hand and Seal dated 11th June, 1685, in which the Prop'y sold off the Quittrent of 9s p'r ann. (and reduced the whole to 1s Sterl'g To Isaac Jacob.)

The Prop'ry, by Lease and Release, dated 26th and 27th of 7br., 1681, granted to John Jones, Mercer, and Michael Jones, Grocer, both of Bristol, 1,000 acres, Who by Deeds bearing date 28th and 29th August, 1684, granted 500 acres, part of the said Purchase, to Wm. Watson, late of Farne's field, in the County of Notingham, yeoman, his Heirs and assigns for ever.

By Vertue of a Warr't from the Comm'rs in the year 1684, there was laid out to the said Wm. Watson 500 acres (besides 10 acres of Liberty Land) in the New Bristol Township, on which (to be reputed 490 acres) he Requests a Resurvey and Patent. Granted.

The Prop'ry, by Patent dated 27th 4 mo., '84, Granted and Confirmed to Tho. Barker, purchaser of 1,000 acres, a Lott in Dellaware front, between Walnut and Spruce Streets, in breadth 20 foot. The Comm'rs, by Patent dated 28th Apr., 1691, Granted to the said Th. Barker, 20 foot of Bank fronting the afores'd lott. T. Barker, by his Letter of attorney, dated 4th 10br., 1694, authorised Geo. Heathcot to sell and Convey all or any part of the said Lotts, &c., who in pursuance thereof by a Deed dated 20th 3 mo, 1701, granted the said Lots unto Nehem. Allen, his Heirs and assigns, who by Deed Poll dated 27th 6mo. last, granted the said two Lotts to Hugh Cordry, of Philad'a, Blockmaker, his Heirs, &c., who requests a Warrant to Resurvey the said Lotts and ascertain the Bounds Situate in the Patent between James Claypoole's Lott and John Moore's. Granted.

John Rowland and Thomas, his brother, first purchasers, by a Deed jointly between them, dated 1st 4 mo., 1687, Granted to Gilbert Wheeler a Tract of Land in the County of Bucks, laid out for 300 acres, being part of a Tract granted by 2 Warrants, one from the Prop'ry bearing date 13th 9 mo., 1692, the other from the Comm'rs dated 7th 6 mo, 1685, laid out in the 7th Mo'th, 1685, and Confirmed by Patent dated 30th 7 mo., '85, for   Acres. The said Gilbert being Seated thereon, requests a Resurvey upon the same. Granted.

The Prop'ry, by Lease and Release, dated 17th and 18th Mar., 1698, Granted to Thos. Musgrove and John Brook 1,500 Acres (T. M. of Halifax and J. Brook, of Holnfrith, in Coun. York), Of which the Heirs of John Brook, since the Prop'rs arrival, took up his Share, viz: 750 Acres. Thomas Musgrove deceasing, Jonathan Cockshaw, who stands bound to see the Moiety of the said Land confirmed to T. Musgrove's Children, requests a Warrant for laying out the s'd Land to Thomas, Abraham and Elizabeth, Children of the said Thomas, and the said Jonathan's Nephews. Granted in two Warrants.

At a Session of the Commiss:onrs at Phildelphia the 11th and 12th 3d Mo'th, 1702.

Present, Edward Shippen, Thomas Story, James Logan, Secretary.

The Prop'ry, by Lease and Release, dated 21st and 22d 8 br., 1681, to Will'm Neale, of the Par. of St. Olave, in Southwark, Wool Stapler, 250 Acres of Land; said Wm. Neale, by Indenture dated 25th 10 br., 1683, convey'd the said 250 A's to Geo. Walker, of the Par. of St. Saviour, in Southwark, Fellmonger, said Geo. Walker, by Indorsem't on the last Mentioned Deed dated 20th 10br., 1701, Granted and Assigned all his right and Title to all the said 250 Acres (4 Acres laid out in the Liberties of Philadelphia only excepted) to William Garret, of Darby, in the County of Chester. The Comm'rs, by a Warr't dated 9th 4 mo., 1685, granted to George Walker to take up the said 250 Acres directed to Tho. Holme and at the Bottom to I. Taylor, on the back of which Warr't 'tis Indorsed by said Isr. Taylor that he actually Survey'd 200 Acres of the said land in the County of Bucks soon after the date of the Warr't between Atkinson's and Benj. East. The said William Garret requests a Resurvey on the s'd 200 A's. Ordered that a War't of Resurvey and Patent on ye Return be granted.

The Prop'ry, by Lease and Release, dated   , Granted too Sarah Fuller 1,000 Acres, of which she sold to John Barns, now of Philad'a,   Acres, laid out in Abington Township, Deed dated   , of the said   Acres together with 246 laid there, also of his own purchase, the s'd John Barns sold to John Roberts near 100 Acres to Wm. Roulledge 150, for the Use of the School 120, to Edw'd Eaton 50, and by Deed dated 17th 4 mo., 1698, to William Jenkins 437 Acres, on Which he craves a Resurvey.

Ordered that a Warr't be accordingly granted and a Patent on the Return, Overplus to be paid for. The Proprietarie's deed to John Barns dated

The Prop'ry, by Lease and Release, dated   , granted to Charles Lloyd and Marg't Davies 5,000 Acres, of which each had an equall Share; Charles Lloyd by an Assignment dated   , granted to Tho. Lloyd all his Right and Title to his share in the said Purchase. Of the other Moiety, there came also in the possession of the said Tho. Lloyd 1,250 Acres, as in the Welch Minutes at large q. v., and the Descent of T. L's Estate.

Isaac Norris and David Lloyd, Ex'ors of the said Thomas's last Will, by Deed dated 4th 10 mo., 1694, Granted and Sold to David Prees 118 Acres, s'd in the Deed to be in the Welch Tract, but under no other Bounds than the Demensions of the Lines, but lies in Meirion adjoyning on the Liberty Land, on w'ch the said David Requests a Resurvey. Granted and a Patent on the Return.

John Buckly, Seated on the Manor of Rocklands on Delaware, Requests the grant of 50 Acres of Vacant Land adjoyning on the Prop'rs tract, formerly William Stockdale's; but this not being thought fitt to be granted, 'tis Ordered that no other person have the preference, Also that a Power be granted to the said J. B. to oversee the Timber of the said Mannor.

Signed a Patent to Albert Henricks for 750 Acres. Ordered 11th 12 mo, for the 20 Acres of Overplus in which he has given a bill on John Finney for £20.

Signed a Pat't to Tho. Peirson for 1 Tract of 206 A's and another of 402 A's. Or'd.

Signed a Patent to Silas Crispin for 500 A's. Ordered 27th 2 mo. Last.

Signed a Warr't of Resurvey on 2 Lotts to Hugh Cordry. Ordered 5th Instant.

Signed a War't to Wm. Caurton for 8 Acres Lib. Land. Ordered 28th 11 mo.

Signed a Warrant of Resurvey to Wm. Caurton on 200 A's in Meirion. Ordered in the Welch Minutes.

Signed a War't to Nicholas Hicks.

At a Session of the Commissioners at Philadelphia 18th and 19th of ye 3d Mo'th, 1702.

Present, Edward Shippen, Thomas Story, James Logan.

The Prop'ry, by Lease and Release, dated 19th and 20th Mar, 1682, Granted to Wm. Bennet, of Parrish Harmonsworth, in Middlesex, husbandman, 1,000 A's of Land in part of Which there has been laid out to Sarah Bennet, since Sold to E. Pennington 400 A's, and to Ezra Crosdale 400 A's, upon which there remains 200 Acres to be taken up, purchased by s'd Ezra.

who requests a Warr't to take up the same, the Deed is not yet Drawn being deferred till the Land be Located. Ordered that a Warrant be accordingly granted and a Patent on the Return to said Ezra, he producing a Deed from the Heirs.

Robert Lucas Producing a Receipt under James Harrison's hand dated 24th 11 mo., 1684, in which the said James Declares he had accounted with Robert Lucas for 244 Acres of Land and Received £1 13s 10d, the Balllance in full for the same on the Gov'rs Acc't; Also a Warrant from the Prop'ry dated 27th 12 mo., 1682, for 200 Acres to Said Rob't Lucas, Surv'd 244 Acres in Falls, T. P. joyning on P. Webster. Robert Lucas, before his Decease, devised (as 'tis s'd) the said 244 Acres to his Wife Elizab., Who has since, by a Deed dated   , granted the same to Edward Lucas, who requests a Resurvey in Order to a Patent.

Ordered that a Resurvey be accordingly granted, and a Patent on the Return to the Person in whom the right shall appear invested, they paying for the Overplus if any, &c.

Ordered that the eight foot of Overplus in dispute on the south side of T. Callowhill's Lott, or the North side of Mary Knight's Lott, rendring the Situation of the two interjacent Lotts between said Callowhill's and Knight's uncertain, be joyned to Tho' Callowhill in part of Compensation ordered by the Prop'ry to be made by his former Comm'rs to said T. C. for his Disappointm't of his Bank Lott, and that a War't be forthw'th granted thereupon.

Ezra Crosdale producing a Return of Resurvey Signed by Ph. Pemberton, dated 13th 11 mo., 1701, in pursuance of a Warr't from the Comm'rs dated 15th 10 mo., last, of 440 Acres in Newtown, Requests a Confirmation; but first, there being a vacancy or parcel of Concealed Land at the head of the Township between that and Wright's Town through the Surveyors not running the head Lines, he requests a grant of the same, agreeing to give £20 p'r 100 and a Warr't thereupon. Ordered that a Warrant be granted for the said Vacancy adjoyning on the head of the said Ezra's Land, and upon the return a Patent to the said Ezra for both the Old and New Survey.

Robert Heaton having Accounted with the Gov'r the day before his last Departure from Philad'a for 100 Acres of Land taken up by him on Neshamineh Creek, but Never paid for till that day, there was found due for the same £15 7s 6d, in part of which he paid by discount £3 3s 4d, and in Money £10, and there remains due £2 4s 2d, which he agrees to pay, and Requests a Resurvey on the same. Ordered that a Warrant be accordingly granted and a Patent on the Return, he paying for the Overplus if any, &c.

Thomas and Cadwallader Jones having procured a Survey on a Second Street Lott of 34 foot and a third Street Lott of 20 foot (in lieu of one whole Second Street Lott of 51 foot of which they have been disappointed) in pursuance of a Warrant from this Board dated 6th 2 mo. Ult., produces Returns for the said two Lotts on which he requests a Patent, which is granted.

S'r Edm'd Andros, Gov'r of N. York, 1679, granted to John Wood a Certain Tract of Land near Dellaware Falls, which, after the Propr's arrival, being Resurvey'd by his Warr't dated 9th 3 mo., 1684, was found to Contain 478 A's, and for that quantity confirmed together with an Island in the River adjoyning called Wood's Island (whether included in the s'd Number of Acres is uncertain) by the Propr's Patent dated 31st 5 mo., 1684, to the said John Wood, whose only son and Heir, Joseph Wood, being now possessed thereof, requests a Resurvey on the Same. Ordered that a Warr't be accordingly granted and a Patent on the return, he paying for ye Overplus if any, &c.

Jos. Growdon, by a Deed poll, under his hand and Seal dated 17th 8 mo., 1699, Convey'd to Thomas Stackhouse, his Heirs, &c., 90 Acres of Land adjoyning on Jer. Langhorn's Land, being part of two tracts, the one granted to the said Joseph by Deed Poll from Edw'd Evans, dated 6th 1 mo., 1696, and the other granted by Griffith Owen, John Humphrey, Rowl'd Ellis and David Lloyd, Attorneys for R'd Davies, unto the said Joseph by Deed dated 6th 1 mo., 1698-9, Jeremiah Langhorn, Son and Heir, and Sarah Biles, Daughter (with her husband Wm. Biles, Jun'r) of Thomas Langhorn, by a Deed Poll dated 18th 8 mo., 1699, granted to the said Thomas Stackhouse, his Heirs, &c., one hundred Acres of Land, being part of 860 Acres sold to the said Tho. Langhorn by Francis Dove, Wm. Wiggans and Edw'd Sumwayes (purchasers each of 500 Acres) by Indenture of Lease and Release, dated 5th and 6th 7br., 1687. Ja. Claypoole and Rob't Turner, Comm'rs, by Patent dated 11th 12 mo., 1684, Confirmed to Ralph Ward, purchaser, 123 A's Situate in the County of Bucks, on Neshamineh Creek adjoyning on the Land of Philip Alford, laid out 21st 6 mo., 1682, by a Warrant from Wm. Markham dated 7th 6 mo., id.

The Comm'rs, by Patent dated 1st 10 mo., 1684, Confirmed to Philip Alford, Purchaser, 123 Acres Adjoyning on the aforegoing, laid out the 14th 6 mo., 1682, by Vertue of a Warrant from W. M , &c., dated 7th of the same Month, The s'd two parcels of Land containing in the whole, by Estimation, 246 A's, are the Original purchase of the said Ph. Alford of 250 A's of the

Prop'ry in Engl'd, as per Deeds of Lease and Release dated , of which 250, the s'd Alford by Deed dated , Convey'd one Moiety to said Ward.

Ph. Alford, by Indenture dated 6th 7 mo., 1687, Convey'd to Thomas Jenner, of Philad'a, Carp'r, all his Right, Title, &c., in and to his said 123 Acres. Ralph Ward and Thomas Jenner being possessed of the said 2 Tracts by a Joynt Deed, Ind'd, bearing date 17th 3 mo., 1694, Granted the whole said 246 A's to said Tho. Stackhouse, who after by a Deed Poll dated , convey'd ¼ p't of the whole next the Creek to Ezra Crosdale.

The Prop'ry (as is affirmed by the persons who paid the Money appearing) Sold in this Province to John Town 157 Acres, for which Nich. Waln declares he paid £5 in behalf of John Town in part and Ezra Crosdale ye remaind r as p'r a Receipt, and there upon granted a Warrant to the said J. Town for the same, bearing date 21st 12 mo., 1683, which warrant was executed and Returned, as in the office appears, joyning on the above Tract of Phil. Alford, which the said J. Town appearing confesses he has sold to the above mention'd T. Stackhouse and Ezra Crosdale, but no Deed pass'd, said Town being unable to make a Title, makes a Deed dated 10th 4 mo., 1702.

All the Several aforesaid Tracts in T. Stackhouse's possession containing 453 Acres he Requests a Resurvey on the same in Order to a Patent. Granted as Requested, he paying for the Overplus, &c.

The Prop'ry, by Lease and Release, dated 24th and 25th Jan'y, 1681, Granted to Amy Child 500 Acres Mentioned page 27.

Edward Stanton Intermarrying with the said Amy obtained from the Comm'rs. J. Cl. and R't T. a Warrant dated 18th 9 mo., 1686, for taking up the same w'ch was executed above the Manor of Highlands in Solebury Township.

Charles Read, Second Husband of the said Amy, in a Joint Deed with her, Dated 10th 10 mo., 1698, Sold and Convey'd the said 500 Acres of Land then called, but 492 Acres to John Scarborough, his Heirs, &c.

Since the first Survey of the said Land which was 10th Apr., 1698, the lines have been altered by the surveyors so much that the Bounds are altogether uncertain as is reported, the said John therefore Requests a Resurvey. Ordered that a Warrant be accordingly granted.

John Scarborough, by Lease and Release, dated 3d and 4th July, 1682, purchased of the Prop'ry 250 Acres in right of which he Obtained a Warr't from the Prop'ry dated 6th 2 mo., 1683, for a City Lott but was never executed. John Scarborough by an Instrum't dated 15th 8br., 1696, appointed his only Son,

John Scarborough, his Attorney, to Sell, Dispose off, enter into, &c., all his Lands and Lotts, &c., in Pennsylvania.

The said John Scarborough, Junr., Requests a renew'd Warrant to take up the said Lott. Granted for a Vacant Lott in the 5th Street and no other where.

Isaac Scheffer having purchased of Joseph Hansen the Tract of Land or old plantation between Dragon and Redlyon Runs in ye County of Newc., because the said Joseph could not Comply with his bargain desires to become answerable to the Commiss'rs for that Agreem't, but requests further time, w'ch is given for one Moiety to the 15th 9br. next, and for the other Moiety to 25th 1 mo. Next, with interest from the 25th 1st Month last past.

And the said Isaac, informing that there is a Vacant piece of Cripple or Marsh adjoyning between Peter Hansen and Mathias Vanderhyden, Requests a grant of the same upon the same Terms with the fast Land, viz: at £16 p'r 100 to be paid at the times above expressed, Which is granted, provided no person's just Claim be injured thereby.

The Prop'ry, by Lease and Release, dated   , Granted to John Harper, of   , 500 Acres of Land, in right of which there was survey'd (by a Warr't not to be found) 16th 6 mo., '82, 495 Acres in Oxford Township, the remaining 5 Acres Left for Liberty Land, the said John Requests a Warr't to take up the same. Granted. It falls on ye West of Skuylkill.

The Prop'ry, by Lease and Release, dated 26th and 27th of July, 1681, Granted to Henry Chomley or Comby, of the City of Bristol, Weaver, 500 Acres of Land in part of which there was Survey'd by Vertue of a Warr't dated 17th 11 mo., 1683, 200 Acres to the said Henry, but after taking out the Warr't and before Location, the said Hen., by an Instrum't under his hand and Seal dated 6th 1 mo., 1683, granted the said 200 Acres (which were then located) to Thomas Marl, of Philad'a, Carp'r, in the County of Philad'a, to the Northwest of Springfield Mannor. Tho. Marl sold it to Nich. Skull and he to Edward Burk, now Seated on it, and all the three, said H. Comby, T. Marl and Nich. Skull, joyning in one Deed, convey'd the said 200 Acres to the said Edw'd by Deed dated 8th 10br., '99, who requests a Resurvey in Order to a Patent.

Ordered that a Warrant be accordingly granted and a Patent on the Return. But desires it may be deferred till he make good his Title to 100 Acres more adjoyning.

The Prop'ry having Ordered £12 to be paid John Routlidge for his time at Pennsbury, the said John remonstrates that he served at the said place 8 months and that none Offered him less than £30 p'r Ann., w'ch he could easily have had, and therefore craves that he may be Considered. Upon which the Comm'rs, advising, are of Opinion that he ought to be allowed considerably More and at least after the rate of £24 p'r Ann., viz: £16 for his Said time.

Mem'dum. That Rich'd Burgess' Land in the County of Bucks is one Tract of 276 Acres above the Falls, One Lott in Newtown about 300 Acres, and one Lott and house in Buckingham or New Bristol, certifyed under P. Pemberton's hand. John Moor is his Attorney.

Signed a Patent to William Warner for 300 Acres. Ord'd.

Signed a Patent to George Smedly for 295 A's. Ordered 14th 11 mo. last.

Signed a Patent to Hen. Margerom.

Signed a Warr't to Ja's Hunt for ye Resurvey of 266 Acres. Ord'd 20th Ult.

Signed a War't to Rob't Heaton for the Res. of 100 Acres. Ordered to-day.

Signed a War't to Dennis Konders for 275 Acres. Ordered 16th 12 mo. last.

Signed a Warr't of Resurvey on 118 A's to David Prees. Ordered 11th Instant.

Signed a Warr't of Resurvey to Robert Lucas. Ordered Yesterday.

Signed a Warrant to Ezra Crosdale for 200 Acres. Ordered to-day.

Signed a Warrant to Ezra Crosdale for a Tract of Vacant Land. Ord'd to-day.

Signed a War't of Resurvey to Jos. Wood, of Bucks. Ordered to-day.

Signed a Warr't of Resurvey to Wm. Garret

Signed a War't to Isaac Scheffer for Marsh in Newc. County. Ord'd to-day.

Signed a War't of Resurvey to Tho. Stackhouse. Ordered to-day.

Signed a War't of Resurvey to John Scarborow. Ordered to-day.

Present, Iidem qui Antea.

Nehemiah Field, of the County of Sussex, having, when the Prop'ry was in the said County, entred his Title to 300 Acres of Land or Broadkill, requests a Resurvey on the same, and that P. Pemberton may execute the War't, the late Constituted Surveyor of that County living at 70 Miles distance.

Ordered that a Warrant be accordingly granted and a Patent on the Return, he making good his Title before that time.

Signed a Patent to Caleb Pusey for 980 Acres. Ordered 30th 1 mo. Last.

Signed a Patent to Christopher Blackburn for a Lott. Ord'd 1st 10 mo. last.
Signed a Warrant to Nehem. Field. Ordered to-day.

At a Session of the Commissioners at Philadelphia 1st and 2d 4th Month, 1702.

Present, Edward Shippen, Thomas Story, James Logan, Secretary.

The Prop'ry, by Lease and Release, dated 14th and 15th June, 1682, Granted to Joseph Jones, of South'ton, Black Smith, 500 Acres which has been laid out in the edge of Philad'a and Bucks County, now in the Possession of Peter Chamberlin, who, by Deed dated 4th 5 mo., 1687, purchased the same of the said Joseph, with all Rights and Previledges to the said Purchase belonging.

Peter Chamberlin, in right of the said purchase requests a Lott and Liberty Land, which he says has been deducted out of the Main Tract.

The Propr'y, in 1684, granted a Warr't for a Lott in right of the said Purchase, Yet he was not within the List nor the time of the first 100 purchasers.

Joseph Sharpless (Entred pa. 20) having by our Warr't procured 2 Tracts of Land in the County of Chester, one in Provid. Township of 125 acres, and the other in Middletown of 300 acres, the first of which is found to Contain 131 acres, with no Overplus, the other 420 acres, in which 30 acres being allowed by Law, there remains 90 acres Overplus, which he not agreeing to Purchase, 'tis Ordered that the Surveyor Cutt off the same.

Moredcai Maddock having procured a Resurvey, pa.   , on a Tract of Land in Springfield, laid out for 800 a's, the same is found to Contain 1,160, out of which there being allow'd 80 acres by Law, there remains 280 a's Overplus, for which not agreeing he desires it may be referr'd to 4 men to sett a price or cutt it off as the Law directs, but upon a further consultation 'tis agreed that he shall pay £100 for the whole, and a Patent is Ord'd thereupon.

John Swift producing a Return out of the Surveyor's Office of the Propr's warrant, dated   8th Month Last, and of another of the same date, for 2 Lots in the Second street, with an appendix on the Third Street, on Dellaware, Requests a Patent for the same, which is granted.

Joseph Phips, Junr., of the County of Chester, Seated on a Tract laid out for 200 acres, as is said, to George Goodyear, in upper Providence, purchased by the said George of the Prop'ry in this Province at his first arrival, for the payment of which the said Joseph produces a Certificate that the Prop'ry at Chester, when last there, acknowledged the receipt of the Money of the said George, requests a Resurvey upon the same in Order to a Patent, and that the warrant may be directed to Hen. Hollingsworth, who has already tried the quantity of the said Tract and finds about 80 a's Overplus. Ordered therefore that a Warrant be granted as requested, with a particular Order to cutt off the Overplus.

Nathaniel Newlin having procured of the Prop'ry a Warr't dated   , for laying out 375 acres of unseperated Land in right of an old Purchase, by Vertue of which Warrant, through Mistake, the Late Surveyor General issued his Warr't for 500 acres, in pursuance of which there was the said quantity Survey'd to him in Marlborow Township, Coun. Chester. He therefore requests that a price be sett on the 125 acres of Overplus, which is agreed £13 10s, and thereupon Ordered that a Return be made for 500 a's and a Patent thereupon.

The Prop'ry, in this Province (as is affirmed by Nich. Waln) sold to Thos. Constable and Walter Bridgeman 700 acres of Land which were Laid out by David Powel on Neshamineh, near Newtown, about the Year 1683, joyning on the Land then of Wm. Crosdale, now John Cowgill, but the said Land not being paid for for some Years after, and paid then by several Sums, upon which there is now a Difference between Nicholas Waln, who represents the said Claimants, and the Comm'rs concerning the Interest of the Money, for which there is about £14 demanded. The said Nicholas Waln Requests a Resurvey on the said Land in Order to a Confirmation, but cannot comply with the paym't of the s'd Sum; the whole therefore is deferr'd.

John ap Hugh having for some years past (about 4, 'tis said) been Settled on the Manor of Springfield, in which 'tis affirmed, by some Evidence, he had encouragem't to proceed in his Improvem'ts from the Prop'ry, requests to know on what terms he shall hold it and a Confirmation. Agreed and Ordered that one hundred acres be granted to the said John in the place where he is now Settled in Consideration of forty pounds, to be paid by him with Interest to the time of Paym't, and a Warrant thereon.

The Settlers on the Tract called Gwynned or North Wales, in the County of Philadelphia, purchased by them of Robert Turner for   acres, having agreed with the Proprietary before his Departure for the Overplus thereof at £20 p'r 100, at one Shill'g Sterl'g rent p'r 1,000, in part of which they have paid £60, Requests a War't to Resurvey the s'd Tract, w'ch is granted and Pat'ts Ord'd on the Returns.

Signed a Patent to James Paxon for

Signed a Patent to Nathan'll Newlin for 600 acres in Rocklands. Ord'd.

Signed a Patent to Nathan'll Newlin for 200 a's in Rocklands. Ord'd.

At a Session of the Commissioners at Philadelphia 8th and 9th of the 4th Month, 1702.

Present, Edward Shippen, Thomas Story, James Logan, Secretary.

George Hogg producing a Return from the Surveyor's Office of the Survey of a Bank Lott in Newcastle, 66 foot in breadth, fronting his Lott, in pursuance of a Warr't from the Comm'rs dated 22d 1 mo. last, Requests a Confirmation of the same upon the terms the Prop'ry granted the same on. Ordered that a Patent be accordingly granted.

George Hogg producing a Return from the Surveyor's Office of the Survey of 200 acres to his Wife's Son, Henry Land, by Vertue of a War't from the Comm'rs dated 23d of 10br. last, requests a Patent on the same, which is granted.

Governor E. Andros, by a Patent dated 25th Mar., 1676, Granted to John Moll a Tract of Land adjoyning on the Town of Newcastle, laid out for 100 acres, running by Otter Street, Maryland Road and the Marsh, of which Tract the said John Moll, by an Indorsem't on the said Patent, declares that he had Sold Gerrit Jansen als. Smith a Small Tract or parcel of about 4 or 5 acres, and to James Read a Tract lying between the King's Highway to Swarten Nutten Island, Otter Street and Maryland Road, and on the N. W. with the Main Woods, and to John Dun a Tract out of the said Patent, bounded on the Southeast with the Tract Sold to Ger. Jansen, now Wm. Howston's, Southwest with the King's High Way, N. W. with the Cripple, N. E. with the Marsh, by Deed dated 18th June, 1695. George Hogg, in behalf of John Dun's Orphans, requests a Resurvey on the said Tract in Order to a Confirmation.

Jacob Simcock producing a Return from the Surveyor's Office of the Resurvey of a Tract reputed 200 acres in Ridly, but found to Contain 254 a's, desires to agree for the 34 acres of Overplus. Agreed for the same to pay Sixteen pounds forthwith, and a Patent is Ordered thereupon.

Thomas Janvier having obtained a Warr't for the Bank before his Front in Newcastle, dated 1st 2 mo. last, produces a Return of Survey on the same, being 30 foot in Breadth, and requests a Pat't thereupon, which is granted.

Edw'd Jones, Wm. Jenkins and Philip Howel, on their attestations, declare that Humphrey Edwards, now of Gwynned, came into this Province about the Year 1683 a Servant to John ap Edwards, and Served his time to him faithfully and according to Indenture; The s'd Humphry Edw'ds thereupon craves a Warr't for 50 acres of Head Land, which is Granted.

Edw'd Jones and David Powel declare that Philip Howel, of Philad'a, Taylor, came into this province a Serv't to David Davis, Son of Richard Davies, and having Served about a Year, bought off the remainder of his time, and thereupon Craves a Warr't for his Head Land. Ordered that a Warrant be accordingly granted.

Joseph Jervais having, in the 12th Month, 1700, made application to the Prop'ry for the grant of a Tract of about 150 acres in Middletown, left Vacant because of its Barrenness, which the Prop'ry then granted at the Value and in the 7th Month, 1701, issued a Warrant for the Survey thereof dated 27th 7br., leaving the price to Caleb Pusey and Nath'll Newlin, who, by a Certificate under their hands fixed the said price at £12 p'r 100, and the Return being produced from the Surveyor's Office the said Tract is found to Contain the said Number of 150 acres exact, on which the said Joseph Requests a Patent, he securing the pay of £18. Ordered that a Patent be accordingly Granted.

Richard Tucker being recommended by the Prop'ry to the Secretary, desires a grant of two Lotts adjoyning on himself on the Southside of Walnut Street, between the 5th and 6th Streets from Dellaware, on Rent. Granted two Lotts as Requested at five Shill'gs Sterl'g rent each p'r ann.; upon Which a Warr't is Ordered and a Patent on the Return with a Clause saving to all persons their just right and Claims.

Signed a Patent to Hen. Land for 200 acres in Newc. Coun. Ordered 8th Inst.

Signed a Patent to David Powel for a Lott in Second street. Ordered.

Signed a Patent to John Swift for a Lott in the 2d street and another in the 3d. Ord'd.

Signed a Patent to Barth. Coppock for 338 acres. Ordered.

Signed a Patent to Phil. Howel for a Lott in the 2d Street. Ordered.

Signed a Patent to Jos. Jervais for 150 acres in Chest'r Coun. Ordered to-day.

Signed a Patent to Mordecai Maddock for 1,160 acres. Ordered to-day.

Signed a Warrant of Resurvey on   acres to John Du:. Ordered.

Signed a Warrant of Resurvey on   acres to Wm. Watson. Ordered.

Signed a Warrant of Resurvey to Wm. Jenkins on   acres.
Ordered.
Signed a Warrant to Jos. Phips of Resurvey on   acres.
Ordered.

———

At a Session of the Commissioners at Philad'a 15th and 16th 4th Month, 1702.
Present, Edward Shippen, Griffith Owen, Thomas Story, James Logan, Secretary.

The Prop'ry, by Lease and Release, dated 9th and 10th 3d Mo'th, 1682, granted 1,000 a's to Edw'd Blendman. The said Edw'd Blendman, by Deed dated   , granted 250 acres thereof to Nath'l Bryan, his Heirs, &c., and by Deed dated   , granted 250 acres thereof to Tho. Dickerson his Heirs. &c., and afterwards by Indorsem't on the Release, dated 23d Jan'y, 1688, granted the said whole 1,000 acres to Joseph Paul, Mentioning therein the other two grants afores'd, and after the said Nathan'll Bryan, by Deed dated   , granted his said 250 acres to the said Jos. Paul, his Heirs, &c. The Commiss'rs, by Warrant dated 22d 9 mo., 1686, granted 250 acres of the said Land to said Jos. Paul, in the County of Bucks, and by another warr't dated 22d 12 mo., 1689-90, granted 492 acres, and by another Warr't at the same time 8 acres Lib. Land to the said Jos. Paul, which s'd Warr't of 492 acres remaining unexecuted he requests a New one for the same.

Ordered accordingly, if the other be not Surveyed.

Peter Bezalion having built a house in the fall of the year 1700, on a Tract of Land over against Mahanatawny, requests a grant of a few hundred acres at a bushel of wheat p'r 100, which cannot be granted. Ordered however that the said Peter shall enjoy the said Settlem't quietly without Molestation till the s'd Land is to be Settled by such who would make a Plantation, and if he shall be Willing to doe the same shall have the refusall of a Convenient quantity there.

The Prop'ry, by Lease and Release, dated 17th and 18th June, 1684, Granted 5,000 a's to John Gray als. Tatham, of London, Gent., his Heirs and assigns, who Making his late Will and Testament in Writing by the Name of John Tatham, left all his Estate, real and Personal, to his Wife Elizab., makeing her sole Ex'rix, and died Seized of the Premises. The said Elizab. also made her last will and Testament in Writing and Constituted Pat. Robinson and Thos. Revel her Joynt Trustees and Sup'visors, with full power and authority to Sell and dispose of her estate for raising of Money for the paym't of the Legacies of her said last Will, but the said Pat. Robinson refused to take upon him the s'd Trust and is since dead, having first given up his s'd whole Trust to the said Thomas Revel, who by the name of Th. Revel, the Surviving Trustee, Feeoffee and Supervisor, appointed and Impowered by the last will and Testament of the s'd Elizab., Widdow, deceased, to sell and dispose of her Estate, real and personal, to the use and behoof of her said last Will as therein Mentioned, Granted to John Budd, of Philad'ia, Brewer, his Heirs, &c., 2,500 acres by Ind're, dated 20th 2 mo, 1702, part of the afores'd 5,000 a's. In right of which the said John Budd requests two Warr'ts, each to take up 500 acres, which is Granted.

Mem'aum, That T. Revel hath also sold to Wm. and Tho. Stevenson 2,500 acres more, located on the forks of Neshamineh, In right of the afores'd purchase, being part, as is affirmed, of 3,000 acres taken up in said place in the same right, out of which Jno. Tatnam, in his life time, granted 500 a's to

so that there remained but 2,000 acres to T. Revel to dispose of.

Upon a further Search and by a Draught in the Office the other 500 Seems laid out to T. Philips in right of Jefferson.

The Prop'ry, by L'rs Pat't under the great seal, dated , 1700-01, Confirmed to Marg't Cook, Widdow of Arthur Cook, in right of   's Original Purchase, 528 a's, in the County of Bucks.

M. Cook, by Ind. dated 7th 9br, 1701, together w'th her son, Jno. Cook, Granted ye s'd Tract to Thos. Hilborne, now of the s'd County, Yeoman.

The Prop'ry. by Ind'r of L. and Rel. dat.   '81, Sold to Hen. Pawlin 1,000 acres, who again granted the same to Rich'd Burgess, who convey'd 300 acres, part thereof, to Edm'd Cowgill and Israel Morris, by Deed dat.   , Convey'd 130 acres, part of the aforesaid, to s'd Tho. Hilborne, adjoyning on the aforegoing.

The late Comm'rs, by Patent dat. 23rd 1 mo., '87-88, Confirmed to John Otter in right of (it seems) his own Purchase 250 acres, who by Deed poll, dat. 4th 4mo., '94, Granted the same to Henry Baker, of the County of Bucks, Yeoman. H. Baker making his last Will and Testament devised the said Land to his son, Nathan Baker, but afterw'ds Sold the same to the said Tho. Hilborne, without altering his Will, and died. After the said Henry's decease Sam'll, his eldest Son and Heir, at the request of the said Nathan, a Minor of about 17 Years of age, Confirmed the said Land to the s'd Tho. Hilborne, who being now possessed of all the said 3 Tracts, requests a Resurvey upon the two last Tracts and Confirmation on the Return, which is granted, he paying for the Overplus if any be.

The Prop'ry. by Deeds of L. and Rel., dat.   , Granted to Edw'd Blenman, Original purchaser, 1,000 acres of Land, who by Deed dat. 10th 7br., 1685, Convey'd 246 a's part thereof, to Joseph Paul, now of this Prov., who by Deed dat. 1, 6 mo., '97 Sold the same to George Willard. The Comm'rs, by Pat. dat. 13, 7br., '86, Granted to Tho. Rowland 100 acres in right of his Original purchase. T. Rowland, by Deed dat. 10, 1 mo., '88, sold the same to Phil. Conway, who by Deed dat. 19th 2 mo., '90, convey'd the said 100 acres to Mark Bettridge, who by Deed dat. 24th 11 mo., '95, convey'd the same to the said Geo. Willard, who Requests a Resurvy and Confirmation of both the said Tracts in one.

Granted, he paying for the Overplus if any be found.

The Comm'rs, by Pat't dat. 26th June, 1689, Granted Unto Rob't Ewer, of Philad'ia, Merch't, a Certain bank Lott of 51 foot in breadth, fronting the front Lott of Wm. Shardlow, at 5 Shillings Rent p'r ann. and $\frac{1}{3}$ of the Value to revert after 50 Years. Robert Ewer, by Deed dat. 6th 9br. 1696, in Consideration of 500 acres of Land, Granted one Moiety of the said Lott, with all the Improvements thereon, to Nathan Stanbury, his Heirs, &c., who Requests to purchase off the said Reversion upon the Usual terms of 20 Shillings p'r foo and a Confirmation of the Whole.

Ordered that a Patent be prepared and granted according.

The Prop'ry, by Lease and Rel., dat. 1st and 2d 6 mo., 1681, Granted to Anthony Elton 500 acres of Land, to be laid out in this Province. Ant. Elton sold but not Convey'd 100 acres, part of the same, to Rob't Wheeler, of Burlington, 'and Anth. Elton, Son and Heir of the aforesaid Anthony, Confirming the said Sale, convey'd the s'd Land to the s'd Rob't, being Located near the forks of Neshamineh, in the County of Bucks. Rob't Wheeler having sold but not Convey'd the s'd Land to Joseph Large, the s'd Joseph requests a Resurvey and Confirmation of ye same, w'ch is Granted.

Signed a Patent to Nathan Stanbury for the Reversion of his Bank. Ord'd Yesterday.

Thomas Fairman having purchased of Stanley, Vid. his acco't, in right of which there was laid out to him in the overplus of Whitpain's Township 200 acres, by a Warr't from the Comm'rs dated   , now in the possession of Wm. Davies, Requests a Resurvey in Order to a Pat. Ordered as Requested.

Tho. Fairman having purchased a Tract of 2,500 acres of Stanley, Sold off the same to Several persons, and is now in the possession 900 a's of Alex'r Edwards, 400 Job Bate, Peter Boome 150, Richard Adams 150, Frank Hoven 100 a's, Gerard Peterson 200 a's, Thos. Roberts 400 a's and the remaining 400 a's in Thomas Fairman's Hands. They request a Warr't of Resurvey on the whole and to Subdivide to each particular their Quantity. Ordered a Resurvey.

Ordered that the Value of the Land lying between Allen Foster and Geo. Northrap Should be referred to.

Upon application of Andreas Redman, in behalf of himself and Others, 'tis Ord'd that they shall begin at a Marked Hickery about 300 p's above their former line.

Rob't Ashton 314 acres to be Patented.

Jeremiah Osborn and his Wife Eliz., formerly being proved to have Come Serv'ts into this province to Gr. Jones at his first Coming in, request their head Land. Granted.

The Prop'ry, by Lease and Release, dated 17th and 18th March, 1698, granted to Christop'r and John Atkinson 1,500 acres, who coming over in to this province in the Britannia, from Liverpool, both dyed, and Jno's Wife also, the said John leaving Isue, Wm., Mary and John. The Prop'ry, by Warr't dated 12th 7 mo.,1700, Granted to Mary and Alice Hind, Sisters to the said John's Wife and admin'or on his Estate, to take up 500 a's, which were laid out in the County of Bucks and returned by Edw'd P., 24th 4 mo., 1701; the said Mary and Alice request a Patent for the s'd Land to the Children, which is granted

Phil. Howel's Servants Lands granted to all that are proved.

Judge Guest, in pursuance of our Warr't, dated 23rd 1 mo. last, produces a return of 1,250 acre, of which 500 are given in as arable, for which he is to pay £45, and the rest at a Bushell p'r Hund'd, as the other 500, is Granted a Patent.

Randal Spakeman, pa. 27, having purchased a Resurvey on a Tract of 360 a's on Brandyw., and being Survey'd is found to Contain 415 a's, which s'd Tract John H. Sheriff, of the C. of Chester, for a debt recovered by Execution by Sev'rl persons to the Value of £104, Convey'd the same to Rich'd Webb for £121, who requests a Patent. Granted.

Thomas Fairman, by Deed dated 25th 12th '98-9, Conveyed to Matthew Vanbebber 200 a's, adjoining to the Land formerly of Robert Turner, and to the Tract of 1,100 a's Sold by the Said Tho. Fairman to Alex. Edwards, part of 2,500 a's, a Moiety of Standly's Purchase. M. Van B., by Deed—in the Bowels of the former, Dated the 6 Mar., '99-00, Conveyed the Same to Alex. Edwards.

Sarah Welch having purchased of Jonas Asskain 200 a's, pa. 18, sold the same to her Son, John Guest, by Deed dated the 30th 4mo., 1702, which was also resurvey'd, Vid. alias, being Resurvey'd 'tis found to contain 223 a's. Is. Norris and Da. Lloyd, by Deed dated 13 June, 1702, Sold the 250, Mentioned page 52, to John Swift, who request a Patent upon the same, the Measure being, as 'tis affirmed, very exact. Ordered as Requested.

Tho. Crosdale, of, Vid. pa. 72, took up for themselves 500 a's, which prov'd 670, and 250 was Sold to Tho. Stackhouse, now in the Possession of Rob't Heaton. Wm. Crosdale requests the remaining 250, as they call it, but it must be inquired what the other 670 was granted for. It was p'd for or must be.

250 acres granted.

Tho. Fairman having resurvey'd the 46 acres at half way house, the same is found to contain 58 a's, for which 12 a's he is to give   ,   a's to be added to the Governor's Mill.

Chris. Taylor purchased 5,000 acres, and by a Deed dated 10th 7 mo., 1685, Sold to Tho. Potter, of Shrewsberry, in East Jersey, 500 a's in Bucks, which the s'd Tho. Potter Convey'd to Tho. Lloyd as p'r a Mem'dum under T. Ll. and Tho. Potter's hand, dated 24th 5 mo., '85, appears. Isr'l Taylor and Jos. Taylor, Sons and Heirs of the said Chr. Taylor, by a Deed dated 2d June, 1702, Convey'd the said 500 a's to Is. N. and Dav. Lloyd, Ex'ors of the said Thomas, who request a Patent to the Uses of the Testator's Estate; the said Land was Survey'd by a Warrant dat'd the 12th 8br., '83, to Tho. Potter, and being tried by the said Isr. Taylor is found to Contain 555 acres.

John Palmer, of Wessahickon, having 112 acres of land, 80 thereof to Wm. Markham, and 32 to John Tyzack, desires to be rectifyed.

Gov'r to George Jackman 26th 7br, '81, 500 acres. G. J. of South'ton, Yeoman.

Geo. Jackman to Ja. Strealer, of Alsford, Grocer, now of Pennsyl'a, the same 500. 14, 15 May, '85, requests Lott and Liberty Land. Granted.

Tho. Stackhouse having his Tract of 453 acres Resurvey'd, 'tis found to Contain 505 acres, the Overplus he agrees to pay £6 for.

William Fisher requesting 100 acres Vacant Land in Slaughter's Neck, in Sussex, 'tis granted for £10 and a Bushell of Wheat Rent; to be laid out not to discommode any Others.

The Comm'rs of Property, by Patent dated 10, 1 mo., '88–89, granted to Pat. Robinson a Bank Lott fronting the Lott of Wiliam Haig, which he, the said Patr., Purchased, in breadth 51 foot, bounded Northw'd first with Jno. Wheeler's, but then Jer. Elfriths', Southw'ds, then Vacant ; P. R., by Indenture dated 16th 10 br., 1689, granted the said Bank Lott to Richard Russell, of Philad'a, Ship Wright, who by Deed Ind'd dated 8th 10br., '91, granted the said Lott of 51 foot, with the house and Wharff, to Jos. Kirl, of Philadelphia, Mariner, who requests to purchase off the Reversion for 51 pounds.

Paul Wolf producing a Return of 300 a's, Survey'd 29th 3 mo., in pursuance of our Warrant, requests a Patent. Granted.

At a Session of the Commissioners at Philadelphia 10th 5 mo., 1702.

Present, Edward Shippen, Griffith Owen, James Logan, Sec'ry.

John Burradale produces a Return of 500 a's Resurvey'd by Vertue of the Gov'rs Warrant, dated 25th 1 mo., 1701, on Brandywine, for which he craves a Patent. Granted.

Edward Griffith, Serv't to Hugh Roberts; Kath. Griffith, formerly wife, to H. Roberts; Jno. Hugh to Rees, Jno., Wm., Hugh, Sam'll to Tho. Ellis, Mary Hughes to Jno. ap Edw'd, Jno. Rob'ts and Wm. Roberts to Rob't David, Wm. David to John Bevan, Eliz. Owen to Widdow Thomas, Tho. David and Ann David to Widow Thomas, James Pugh to Steven Bevan, Thos. Rees to Evan Thomas, Susannah Griffith to Jno. Richards, Alex'der Edw'ds to Griffith Owen, all Coming into this Province in 1683 or soon after, by a Deed dated 8, 6 mo., Instant, sold all their rights to John Roberts, who requests Warrants, the said Rights being 750 acres, in 3 Warrants.

Tho. Norbury being deceased, before his Death he left all his Estate, some few Legacies excepted, in the power of Daniel Williams and Evan Lewis, both of Newtown, Chester, his Ex'ors, to sell for his Children's Use, the Pat't to be to said Executors.

The Prop'ry, by L. and Rel., , Granted to John Nixon 500 a's, and by a Warr't dated 6, 8br, '83, to take up 374 a's in right thereof, which was laid out in two parcels, viz: one of 74 a's, between Ridly and Crum Creek, the other of 300 a's on the west side of Darby Creek, formerly Confirmed by Patent, dated 26, 5 mo., '84; Survey'd 20th 8 mo, '83.

Jos. Nixon, by a Deed dated 12, 2 mo., '87, granted to B. Coppeck, Junr., the s'd Tract of 300 a's, who requests a Warr't to Resurvey the same, being Situate in Marple Township; Joyns on Geo. Maris.

William Dyer having, as in page , proved a right to 2,100 a's upon Returns of a Survey made in pursuance of Warr't for Wm and Tho. Fisher; there is in one Tract 1,100 a's, being part of the Tract of 2,100, besides which 1,100 there is also sold to Tho. Groves 418 a's, but on that Tract on Which the Patent is there Can be found but 175 a's in Tho. Fisher's possession and 150 a's in Corn. Weelbauck's, in all 325 a's, So that to make up the deficiency of this he requests the Overplus of the other, the Tracts being Contiguous.

At a Session of the Commissioners at Philadelphia the 17th 6th Month, 1702.

Present, Edward Shippen, Griffith Owen, James Logan, Secretary.

Peter Taylor, of Ches., having by a Warrant from the Prop'ry, dated   , procured a Resurvey on a Tract of his laid out for 350 acres, the same is found to Contain 421 a's, with 36 a's Overplus and the said Peter having also procured a Warrant from us, dated 10th 10br. last, for laying out the Remainder of his Purchase, Viz: 265 a's, which is not yet Executed requests that the said 36 a's of Overplus may be deducted out of the said 265 a's, and an Order thereupon Issued to J. Tayler, Surveyor for the same. Granted.

William Howston to have his 65 a's, in right of Jno. Moll, 55 a's; The other 10 and 45 acres adjoyning to be Confirmed in the same Pat't. Consid'n £15.

At a Session of the Commissioners at Philadelphia 8th 7br., 1702.

Present, Edward Shippen, Griffith Owen, Thomas Story, James Logan, Sec'ry.

Chr. Sibthorp purchased of Tho. Scott 500 acres, with all the app's. He was first purchaser, in the right of which by Vertue of a Warr't in the Office dated 26th 3 mo., '85, there was Survey'd to the said Chr. a Lott in the 2d Street, between Sassafras and Vine Street, on the West side; soon after the date of the Warrant fenced it and Dug a Cellar, but no return being made, requests a New Warr't for a Patent, which is granted.

John Morris having in pa. Obtained Warr'ts for 2,500 a's, there is return made of 1,000 acres, Survey'd in the County of Philadelphia, on which he requests a Patent. Granted.

Joseph Hedges, of N. C. Coun., requests 100 acres, at the head of the Tract formerly taken up by Geo. Hogg on new Rent, and now entred upon by some Dutch Men, Situate upon Redclay Creek, for which he agrees to pay £20 upon the Confirmation. Rent 1 Shilling p'r 100; 1st 11 mo.

At a Session of the Comm'rs at Philadelphia 14th 7 mo., 1702.

Present, Edward Shippen, Thomas Story, James Logan, Secretary.

John Hill, of Sussex, having in pursuance of a Warrant from the Prop'ry, dated 25th 8br. last, procured a Survey on 255 acres in Walker's Neck produces a Return thereof and Requests a Patent; he claims by right of a Warrant for 500 a's granted in '83, then entered in the said place. Ordered a Patent. Old Rent to be paid from the first entry, '86.

The Comm'rs granted by Warrant 21st 4 mo., '90, to Wm. Gieach and Ad. Butcher, each of them a Lott in the 3d Street, which were Survey'd the same day to Wm. Gieach a Lott of 33 feet in breadth, in length 198 feet, between Walnut Street and Spruce Street, bounded Eastw'd 3d Street, N. with Ad. Butcher's, West with back Lotts and Southward with Vacant ground, for which the said Wm. requests a Patent. Granted. Rent 3 Shillings Sterling p'r annum.

Da. Lloyd requests his Warr't of 1,000 a's to be laid out in C. County.

John Buckly, of Rocklands, having 100 acres granted in Rocklands by the Gov'r in '82, and 30 a's more by the Comm'rs in '91, at new rent, desires a Resurvey on the same and a Patent; agrees to pay after the rate of £7 10s p'r C't, to reduce the 30 a's to Old Rent. Granted the Warr't and a Patent in Case the Warr'ts and Returns be produced, also Land to make up the s'd Tract upon a Resurvey, 210 acres to be laid out joyning to the N. West end of it provided it hinder no other, nor in any particular conveniency to discommode the Manor, for which he is to pay £20 before Lady day next and old Rent.

Wm. Brakin, Lab'r, of N. C. Coun., requesting a grant of 100 A's Near Jno. Evan's near Redclay Creek, for which he agrees to pay £12 10s p'r C't and a Bushell of Wheat Rent p'r Ann., to pay 25th 10 br., 1703, with Interest from 25th 10 br., 1702.

Andrew Cock requests Joshua Story's bargain, pa. 47, which he has forfeited and further willingly resigned. Ord'd a New War't pursuant to that granted to Story.

Ordered that a Commision be granted to John Buckly to take Charge of the Gov'rs Timber in Rocklands and to Seize all cut upon any Land whatsoever that is not appropriated, &c., forthwith.

The Prop'ry, by L. and Rel., dated 24th and 25th 8br., 1681, granted to Fran. Plumsted, of the Minories, Lond., Iron Monger, 2,500 Acres of Land as by Copy of the Deeds certified by Jere. Jenkins, Notary publick, appears upon H. Springet's oath before the Mayor of London, F Plumsted, by his Instrum't of Procuration dated 13th 9br., 1700, constituted Mord. Moore, of Maryl'd, Merch't, his Attorney, to take up the s'd Land and doe all things Necessary about the same, and to Appoint Attorneys, Agents, &c. Mor. M. Requests Warr'ts to take up the same, the Lotts and Lib. Land are already taken up. Ordered that he shall have 3 Warrants for 500 Acres each, one in the first Township of each County.

Memorandum, Philip Howel's War't for 700 Acres, bot. of Rich'd Thomas.

Agreed with John Kinsey for the Overplus that will appear in his Land for £22 5s p'r C't, the price he gives to buy all the Quittrent off his penny Rent Land to be on Interest.

The Comm'rs, by Patent dated 30th 6 mo., 1690, granted to Philip James a Bank Lott, in breadth 40 foot, and in Length 250 feet, bounded N. with Alice Guest, and South with Nath. Allen.

Philip James, by Ind're, dated 30th 6, 1690, granted to Mathew Bonney, of Philadelphia, Baker, a certain part and proportion of the said Lot, Containing 1 breadth 16 foot, bounded Nw'ds with an alley of Six foot breadth dividing it from Al. Guest's, and South with the remaind'r of the s'd Lott.

Matw. Bonney, by Indorsem't on the said Indenture, dated 5th 3 mo., 1691, granted the said 16 foot to Anthony Morris, his Heirs, &c., who by Deed Ind. dated 25th 5 mo., '92, Convey'd the s'd 16 foot to John Colley, of Philad'ia, Hatter, and Susannah his Wife, their Heirs, &c., which said Jno. and Sus., by Indr., dated 16th 3 mo., 1701, granted to Mary, the Wife of Wm. Say, of Philad'ia, Baker, the Water Lott and hold the Bank. John and Sus. requests to purchase off the Reversion of their Bank and the s'd Mary Say off her Share, The Trusts not to be Mentioned.

John Harper, purchaser of 500 Acres by Deed dated , Vid. Oxf'd T., took up 495 thereof and requests a Warr't for the 5 A's Lib. Land remaining. Gra'd.

Wm. Say having in the year 1687 taken up 100 Acres on Rent above Highlands, in Bucks, in a Tract of 200 A's undivided between him and Rob't Wheeler, requests to buy it off and that he may be Considered for the remoteness. Granted at £17 10s, to be paid on the Patent delivering the draught from Jacob Taylor.

Whereas the Prop'ry granted a Warrant to the Surveyor Gen'll, deceased, to resurvey the Tract now Wm. Guest's, where he lives, formerly Abr. Mann's, which was begun but never performed, he therefore requests a Warrant renewed pursuant to the former directed to G. Dak.

The Prop'ry, by Deeds, dated 24th and 25th 8br., 1681, Granted to John Burge, of Haverf'd, Pembr., Clothier, 750 Acres, of Which there was designed to be laid out 300 in Haverf'd but fell short 60 Acres, now in the Possession of Richard Hay, and 250 More in said Township in the Possession of Humphrey Ellis, but the Quantities being uncertain 'tis Ordered that a Warr't be granted upon a full trial of what is already taken up to Survey the remainder.

The Prop'ry Sold Edward Pricherd 2,500 Acres by Deeds dated 14 and 15 April, '82, in right of which there was laid out to him in the Welch Tract on the West side of Skuylkill in one Tract 1,250 Acres, and in another in Radnor Township 1,250 Acres, Confirmed by Patent dated 18th 3 mo., '85.

At a Sessions of the Commissioners at Philadelphia 29th 7 mo., 1702.

Present, Edw'd Shippen, Tho. Story, Griff. Owen, James Logan.

Alex'dr Edwards having, page 65, procured a Warrant of Res. dated 18th 12 mo. last, on 1,500 Acres, of which he holds 900, the said 900 was resurvey'd by D. P. as by a Return from the Office, and found 996 of which 90 is Allowed by Law, and for the 6 Acres he agrees to pay 30 Shillings, desires a Patent; must pay his Tax.

Samuel Bradshaw, by Ind., purchased 500 Acres dated 11th 2 mo., '82, and by Warrant dated 24, 6 mo., '82, took up 250 Acres in right thereof and by a Deed dated 13th 4 mo., '92, sold to John Bowne, of Long Island, in the Province of N. York, 240 Acres which was laid out as by the Map in West T. Ch., but there being laid out to Tho. Whitby the said quantity in Willis. in right of his purchase of 500 Acres, which purchase he Sold to John Roads, who likeing Bowne's Land better than his Own and Knowing said Bowne had little to Shew for the Survey took possession of the said Tract in West Town and Sold it to Aaron James who now possesses part of it, leaving that in Newtown to John Bowne, being the Tract in the Map Ascribed to Tho. Whitby.

After the said John B's decease, having left John Rodman, of N. Y., Merch't, and John Blunston, of Darby, Yeoman, Trustees of his Estate, who were approved also by the Court of Queens County, in Long Island, who upon a Division and thereupon an Instrument of Settlem't and a Deed of Sale from Sam'll Bowne, Heir to said John, it was granted the above Tract to John Bowne, Younger Son of the said John Bowne in whose behalf the said John Rodman and John Blunston requests a War't of Resurvey on the s'd Tract in Ord'r to a Patent. Granted.

Wm. Vennables, upon his first Arrival, procured a Warrant from Tho. Holme in '82, for 300 Acres of Land to be laid out in Bucks near the Falls, but upon the Division of Lands there there happened to be left 600 and odd Acres all w'ch he possessed, but upon no Agreem't; soon after deceasing, his Widow Marryed a Second Husband and then a third, Viz: And'r.

Heath, who with her lived on the Plantation and brought up Venables' Children, being 2 Daughters, tne said Heath designing to remove, Sold to John Snowdon, of Bucks, 416⅔ Acres by a Deed Ind., dated Mar. 9, '97, Signed by the s'd Andr. Heath and his Wife Eliz., Signed Also by John Hutchinson and his Wife Joyce, one Daughter and Frances Venables, being of full age the other Daughter, the Remaind'r they Sold to P. Worral. No Title being ever Made to Venables, and Several Differences arising, the Prop'ry, before his departure, for the Confirming of the said land to said J. Snowdon and P. Worral granted to Venables' Children the said Tract for 625 A's as reputed at £5 p'r C't with Interest to 8br., 1701, which Money was then paid, and being resurveyed by the Governor's Warrant, dated 3d 1 mo., 1700-1, J. Sn's share is found to Contain , for which he desires a Patent, and is granted.

George Dakeyne producing a Return for 600 A's, granted pa. requests a Pat't. Granted.

At a Session of the Commissioners at Philadelphia the 5th of 8th ber., 1702.

Present, Griffith Owen, Thomas Story, James Logan, Secretary.

Geo. Wood, purchaser of 1,000 A's, procured of the Prop'ry a Warrant dated 2, 5 mo., '83, for 20 Acres L. L. John Blunston, purchaser of 1,500 A's, procured another of the same date for 30 A's. Tho's Whitby, purchaser of 500 Acres, by Deeds dated 12 and 13 Apr., '82, had a Warr't dated 6, 5 mo., 1702, for 10 A's, and Sam'll Bradshaw, purchaser of 500 A's, took up 10 A's together with the rest which were all Survey'd together, but the Warr't appears not. Jno. Bl., Geo. Wo., Sam'll Bradshaw and Ad. Roads, by Vertue of a power from Tho. Whitby, convey'd all the said 70 A's, being all located near Darby Continguous by a Deed Under all their hands and Seals dated 22d 4 mo., 1691, to Lewis Walker, of Haverf'd, who by Deed dat. 9th Mar., '93-4, convey'd the same to Lewis David of said place, who, by Deed dated the same day, convey'd the whole to John Ball, of Darby, who requests a resur. and Pat't. Gra'td.

The Prop'ry, by L. and Rel., 22, 2mo., '82, granted to Henry Bayly, of Grindleton, Coun. York, Yeom., 1,500 Acres of Land, whose eldest son, Hen. Baily, [say not Heir] by Ind. of L. and Rel., dated the 15, 10br., 1696, granted to Tho. Musgrove, of Warly, Coun. York, Clothier, 1,250 A's, the greatest part of it said to be taken up with Lib. Land and City Lotts, of which there was taken up by Vertue of a War't procured by his Attorney, N. Waln, dated 7, 2 mo., '85, soon after by Isr. Taylor, 600 Acres Near the forks of Neshamineh as in the Map, and 245 A's on Neshamineh by the S. Gen'r's War't, dated 6, 8 mo., '82, for this last was laid out 400 A's, and 'tis agreed that so it shall pass, 250 A's remaining of the said 1,250 untaken up, and 250 More, Also of 750 mentioned page   , at the request of Jon'a Cocksaw 'tis Ordered that a Warr't may be granted to the Widow for the Uses of Tho. Musg.'s Will, to be laid out in Philadelphia County, Also a Resurvey on the 400 A's the 600 being sold to —— Huddleston, of Dartmouth, of N. England.

The Prop'ry, by his Warrant, dated 17, 4 mo., '84, granted to James Moore, of Philad'a, Blacksmith, a Lott at the Center of 50 foot in Breadth, which was taken up and built on; the said Ja's Moore, by Deed dated 7, 10 mo., '93, granted the said Lott and House to Richard Worthin, who by Deed to be drawn and dated, Granted the same to Eliz. Price, who desires a Patent. Granted, The Deed being produced.

Tho. Withers having procured a Warr't from the Prop'ry dated 28th 10br., 1700, in behalf and for James Wallace, of Bristol, for 500 A's, part of his 1,000, and the same proves 515, Ordered that the s'd 15 Shall be in part of the remaining 500. Gr'd.

Jno. Bevan, purchaser of 2,000 A's by Deeds dated   , procured a Warrant for 25 A's of Lib. Ld. Wm. Howel, purchaser under Lewis David of 500 A's and Evan Thomas of 250, took up 15 A's. Wm. Genkins, purchaser under John Poyer of 250, and John Griffith in the same right of 250, took up 10 Acres. Tho. Ellis, purchaser of 1,000 Acres himself, and of 625 Acres from Several purchasers Under Richard Davies (as in the Wel. Min.), took up by War't 3, 11 mo., '87-8, 32½ Acres, and Lewis David, who kept to himself of his purchase of 3,000, took up 10 Acres, All which Dan'll Humphreys was Ordered to take up, and accordingly took up two Tracts of 50 A's each, in which there is Overplus of 7½ Acres, the said two Tracts were Confirmed by the Comm'rs, W. M., R. T., J. G., by a thing called a Patent, dated 5, 3 mo., '94, to the s'd Dan'll Humph. At the other's request this 7½ A's to be inquired after. John Bevan having taken up but 25 Acres has 3 More due to him for 150 which he sold to Jno. Rich'ds and rebought, and having Sold to Ralph Lewis 250 Acres, who never took up his 5 Acres, 'tis requested that for these 8 Acres the other 7½ A's be allowed.

The Prop'ry, by L. and Rel., dated 21st and 22d Mar., 1681, granted 250 Acres to Shadrack Walley, of Bicley, in the County Pa   , of Chester, Inn holder, &c., Laid out to the said Shad'h in New Town in the Cou. of Bucks.

The Comm'rs, by Lett'rs Patent, Confirmed 250 A's adjoyning to the last mentioned, to Benjamin Roberts to hold, &c., as by the said Lett'rs Patent under the Lesser Seal dated 5 Apr., 1688, appears by War't dated 18th 10br., 1683. Granted. Laid out 25th same Month and Year by Vertu whereof the s'd Ben. Roberts became Seized for the said 250 Acres and Dyed so Seized without Issue and Intestate, after whose decease the said 250 A's did of right descend to Mary Crow, of London, only Sister and Heir to the said Benj. Roberts, and whereas Humphrey Morrey, of Philad'ia, Merchant, and John Goodson, of the same place, Chirurgeon, as Attorneys for the said Mary Crow (by Vertue of her Letter of Attorney dated 7th 7br., 1693, impowering them to sell the said 150 Acres), granted the said 250 Acres to the said Shadr'ck Walley.

Joseph Wood's Patent, 200 A's in lieu of the same quantity, ye Remainder untaken up of 2,500 A's, purchased by Wm. Wood, by Deeds dated   , the Overplus in the first Tract being 65 A's together with the small Tract of 9 Acres which is now purchased at £30 p. C't, being New Land, The other Tracts of 50 A's was purchased of Wm. Marslander, of the Cou. of N. C., Yeom., by Deed Ind., dated   , who had the same, by Gift of Mary Block, Widdow, as p'r Deed poll, was at first derived from the Dutch.

The Prop'ry, by L. and Rel., dated   , granted 5,000 A's to Chris. Taylor, &c., Who by Deed of Sale dated 7, 11 mo., '83, Convey'd a Certain parcel thereof to his Son, Isr. Taylor, &c., Who by Deed poll dated 13, 1 mo., '89, granted a Certain p't thereof, lying in New Town in the Coun. Bucks, then reputed to Contain 200, to Jno. Coat, &c., who, by an Instrum't in writing, dated some time in August, '99, Assigned the said reputed 200 A's to his Son Sam'll, &c. W. M., R. T. and J. G., by a Certain Patent dat. 18 February, '92, granted 250 Acres lying in the s'd County to the s'd Israel, &c., who sold the same by Deed dated 14 Apr., '93, to James Yeats, &c., who by Deed dated 16th 9br. '96, granted 23 Acres thereof to the said Sam'll Coat, &c., Who by Deed dat. 10th 1 mo., 1702, granted the said 2 parcels of 200 A's and 23 of Land to Shad'k Walley, of New Town afores'd, Yeoman, &c., who requests a Resurvey on the said Tracts, containing together in all, by the above Min's, 723 Acres and a Patent.

William Snead, of Philadelphia, Victualler, Cla'ms 200 Acres by him bought of the Governor about 18 Years since, the Consideration £6, the same was laid out to him adjoyning to the last mentioned Tract, no Return appears.

Quaere, if any such sum appears in any of the Gov'rs Books to have been paid by the said Wm. Snead for 200 Acres as afores'd, the said Snead has Sold and Rel. by a Certain Instrument in Writing, As therein Mentioned, to the said Shad'k Walley, who desires this may be included in the Warrant of Survey aforesaid. Granted a Resurvey but not on these 200 Allow'd.

The Comm'rs, by Patent, granted 100 Acres Near Germantown to Thomas Fairman as p'r Patent dated 7th 9 mo., 1690, appears, the same being in right of William Stanley's purchase of 5,000 Acres.

Wm. Garret's Patent dated 2nd 8br., 1702, for 224 Acres was laid out by the late Comm'rs Warr't dated 9, 4 mo., 1683, Soon after the date of the first Warrant, Vide the New Commissioner's Min's, page 134.

At a Session of the Commiss'rs at Philadelphia 19 and 20, 8ber, 1702.

Present, Edw'd S., Gr. O., Tho. S., J. L., Secretary.

John Kinsey's Tract proving to be 539 Acres to 300 of which he had a right, 200 of it on purchase and 100 on Rent, which he buys off at £22 10s p'r C't for the 300, there is allowed 30 Acres and 9 Acres for the other 200, ye whole to be paid is £67, to be paid 1st 9br., 1703.

Wm. Powel agrees for 10 Dead Trees on the Gov'rs Land at 3s 6d apiece, to be paid in a month.

Captain Finney's Land, 250 A's, to be resurvey'd forthwith and a Patent granted if it Can be made appear Clear.

David Lloyd produces a Request to the Comm'rs dated 17 Inst., under the hand of Jos. Growdon, his Father-in-Law, that they would grant the said David a Warr't to himself and Wife for 1,000 Acres, and Warr'ts to take up the Remainder due to him. Granted 3 mo.

Edm'd McVeagh requests a Resurvey on 250 Acres bought of Peter Bainton, 70 of Silas Crispin and 31 more of said Silas, joyning in one Tract in Dublin Township, extending his lines to the westside line of Sasqueh. Road.

James Clayp. and Robert Tur., by Patent, dated 30, 3 mo., 1686, granted to Sam'll Bennet, first purchaser, 246 Acres on Skuylkill joyning on James Clayp. Sam'll Bennet, by Indorsem't on the said Patent, Dated 1, 4 mo., '86, granted all his Estate, Right and Title into the said Land unto Rob't Longs., his Heirs and Assigns for ever, he, the said Rob't Longshore, by another Indorsem't on the s'd Patent, dated 1 Apr., '87, for the Consideration therein Mentioned, Granted and Sold unto Richard Townsend, his Heirs and Assigns forever, All his Estate, Right, Title, Property and Interest of, in and to the said Land. He desires a Warr't of Resurvey and Patent. Granted, he paying for the Overplus (if any) as we can agree.

Jonathan Cockshaw producing 2 Returns of Survey, one for 500 Acres another for 480 Acres (in right of Richard Baker, granted, to Hannah Musgrove, now Price, Adm'x cum Testamento Annexo of Tho. Musgrove's Estate, Vid. Min's Sec's Office, Requests Patents granted to the said Hannah for the Uses of the last Will and Testament of the said Tho. Musgrove.

Mary, Widow of James Hayworth, produces a paper in P. Pemberton's hand, Signed by the Gov'r, granting to the said James a Tract of Land in New Town, Bucks, between Benj. Roberts and Jonath. Eldridge, at £20 p'r C't, to be paid or secured at taking out the Warrant, the s'd James is since Dead and his Widow Sues. Ord'd a War't, her Father being Security with her.

John Ogle producing a Return for 512 A's, granted pa. Ordered that it be confirmed by Patent, and that for the 12 Acres Measured in he gives 30 Shill'g above the £62 10s, Viz: £64.

Peter Anderson producing a Return for the 50 Acres granted pa. Desires a Patent. Granted.

The Prop'ry, by Deeds dated 21 and 22 8br., 1681, Granted to Wm. Neale, of the Parish of St. Olave, in Surry, Wool Stapler, 250 Acres, who by Indenture dated 20, 10br., 1683, Granted to Geo. Walker, of the parish of St. Savior, in Southwark, Fellmonger. all the said Land. Geo. Walker, by Indorsem't on s'd Ind. dated 20th Xbr., 1701, Granted all the s'd 250 A's, 4 A's Lib. L. excepted (which were taken up), to Wm. Garret, of Darby, Coun. Ch., Yeoman, who requests a Warrant for a City Lott; it falls in Mulberry Street, No. 185, between 7th and 8th Streets, North 99 foot, but if granted More Commodious he will take half. Granted.

Phil. James, by Deed Poll, dat. 26 Mar., 1701, granted to Geo. Guest, of Philad'a, Cooper, 20 foot of the Water Lott, part of the 40 foot granted to said Phil. James by Patent Mentioned, Desires to purchase the Reversion.

The Commissioners, by Patent, dated 3 Apr., 1689, Granted to Griff. Jones 71 foot of Bank before his Bank on Walnut Street, Bounded Southw'd with s'd Street, Nw'd with then Vacant Lotts. Gr. Jones, by Deed Ind., 10, Xbr., '89, granted to Nath. Sykes 25 foot thereof next the said Street, who by Assignm't Indorsed, dated 1, 8br., 1690, granted the same to Sam'll Atkins, who by a Deed dated 21 Jan'y, 1692, Convey'd the bank, and raising an Annuity of £4 p'r Ann. out of the water Lott, Sold the said Annuity to John Saunders of Philadelphia,

Bricklayer, who by Deed, dated 18, 6 mo., 1693, Convey'd the same to Robert Yeldale, of Philad'a, Cooper. Griff. Jones, out of the said Patent, Granted to Wm. Salway 20 foot, bounded now N'wd with Robert Jones, Sw'd with the above Wm. Salway, by Ind. 2, 2 mo., '93, Sold to Tho. Chaunders, whose Widow and Adm'x, Frances Chaunders, Sold to Samuel Carpenter, who by Deed Ind. 30 July, 1702, in exchange for the Annuity of £4 abovesaid, sold to Rob't Yeldal the Bank only, so that he holds 45 foot, bounded Nw'd with Robert Jones, Sw'd with Walnut Street, Ew'd with the 30 ft. Cartway, now King Street, the Reversion of this only, without recitals, to be Granted to R. Y. The Title from Fran. Chaunders to Sam'll Carpenter being Wholly lame as p'r last Deed Appears.

The Prop'ry, by L. and Rel., dated 22d and 23d Mar., '81, Granted to Tho. Holme 5,000 Acres, who deceasing, left two Daughters, Elenor, Marryed to Jos. Moss, and since to Jos. Smallwood, and Enter marryed to Silas Crispin, whom the said Tho. left Ex'or of his last Will, and the said Elenor, his Daughter, and Jos. Smallwood released to the said Silas all Claims Whatsoever to any part of the said Estate.

The Prop'ry, by L. and Rel., dated 22, 23 Mar., 1681, granted to Samuel Claridge, of Dublin, Merch't, 5,000 A's, and by a Deed dated 15 Aug., '82, Sold off the Rent of the said Land from 1s p'r C't to Ditto p'r M., and on the Back of the said last Deed Assigns the same to Tho. Holme, Assm't 18 May, '86.

Silas Crispin, Heir as Aboves'd, affirms that Tho's Holme purchased of the s'd Sam'll Claridge the whole said 5,000 A's, that 3,000 of it a least is taken up by him and that the Release being not to be found 'tis presumed the Assm't is Indorsed thereon as on the other deed.

The Prop'ry by Lease and Rel. dated 11 and 12 8br., '81, granted to R. Corslett, of Bristol, Goldsmith, 1,000 A's, who, by a blind Assm't, Indorsed, dated 1, 8br., '88, made over the same to Tho. Holme,—Of the aforegoing 11,000 there being about 8,000 taken up. Silas Crispin who is under an Obligation to his Brother and Sister Smallwood of £1,000 to procure them 1,000 Acres, Requests a Warr't for the same and Offers Security to pay for it in case their Right to S. Claridge's Land be not made appear. Granted.

At a Session of the Comm'rs at Philadelphia 2d 9br., 1702.

Present, Edward Shippen, Griffith Owen, James Logan, Secretary.

John Fisher purchased by Deed dated 25th 9br., 1701, of Thomas Hall a Tract of Land Cont. 421 acres in Sussex on great

Creek, Granted to the s'd Thos. for the said Quantity by the Prop'rs Patent, dated 26, 1 mo., '84, being assigned to the said Thomas by Rich'd Peaty, to whom it was granted and laid out by Order of Capt. Edm'd Cantwell, in which Patent there being a Small point left out before his house he prayes a Resurvey that may take the same in and a New Patent. Granted a Resurvey according to the old lines and to Survey the s'd Point, to be granted for its Value.

Sussex Court granted 15, 1 mo., '81, to Wm. Planner 1,000 a.'s on Slaughter Neck as by Warrant under L. Watson's hand and County Seal, 6, 8 mo., '83, which was located by him on the said Neck, but being Survey'd there was laid out but 600 a's, which he sold to Tho. Price, as by Record of Sussex Court, 8, 7 mo., '85; but the said Return of Survey Mentioning Mispain Creek instead of Slaughter by Mist'e, Planner, to make a Title, procured of the Comm'rs a Warrant of Resurvey dated 7, 2 mo., '86, to rectify the said mistake and make returns, accordingly directed to Wm. Clark, whose deputy, Jos. Barkstead, executed the same 26th 2d Month, 1687, upon which he requests a Patent. Granted.

The Comm'rs, by Patent dated 29, 9 mo., '85, Confirmed to Robert Longshore 500 acres, first granted to him (as 'tis said in the patent) as purchas'r, which Land he sold off again to Several and is in the hands of Tho. Rutter 200, who affirms he paid the Prop'ry £10 in Smith's Service for it, he requests a Resurvey of his 200, but the whole 500 is to be resurvey'd and Wm. Harman's 50 a's also.

Upon the Return of Wm. Jenkins' Warr't, granted on 437 a's, there being 20 acres Overplus above allowance, 'tis Ordered to be cutt off and a Patent granted on the Rem'dr.

Mem'dum to have two men Chosen for Allen Foster's Land.

———

At a Session of the Commissioners at Philadelphia the 9th 9 mo., 1702.

Present, Edward Shippen, Griffith Owen, Thomas Story, James Logan.

Jonathan Eldridge haveing his Land resurveyed, laid out for 250 a's, in Newtown, Bucks, by the Propr's Warrant, but found to Contain 289 a's, of which 20 being allowed by law, for the 19 he agrees to pay 8 Shillings p'r acre. Ordered a Patent.

Mem'dum to Survey the Gov'rs Mannor house. Wm. Stockdale's to make it 1,000 acres and sett off to John Grubb his 200 a's, taking in Wm. White's Land.

Wm. Jenkins' Tract, designed to be laid out for 250 a's in

Haverf'd, being part of John Poyer's Purchase of 750 acres, falling short 60 acres, and he having a Tract of 250 of his own purchase in Duffein Mawr, 'tis agreed and Ordered that he shall have a Resurvey on the said Last 250 acres and to make up the same to the said 60 acres.

Agreed with Jonathan Mifflin for fifty Cord of Wood, to be cutt of the Dead and Blasted Trees on the Gov'rs Manor of Springettsberry, within a Mile and a half of the said Jonathan's dwelling house, the bodies of White Oak being fitt for timber excepted, at 18 pence per Cord.

Hippolytus Le Fevre, of Newcastle, purchased of Marg't Sherry a Front Lott in Newcastle, 1695, purchased of James Williams, 92 purchased of Hans Codeny 5 mo., 1682, who sold the said Lott to the said Williams; bounded Eastward with Henrick Will'ms, South the Strand and Westw'd with Gisbert Dickson, and N. with Land Street, which being resurvey'd by the Propr's General Warrant and James Logan's Particular Order, is found to contain 51½ foot, for which he desires a Patent. Granted. Rent, bushell p'r 100 p'r ann.

Richard Hough procured a Warrant from this Board dated 24, 9br., 1701, for taking up 375 acres of Land, a late purchase in England, also having a right to 100 acres by his Wife Margery, Daughter of John Clows, purchaser of 1,000 acres, by one pair of Deeds, dated   , and of 500 by one other pair, dated   , who took up in part thereof 500 a's in one Tract in Makefield, Bucks, and 700 in another Tract on the Branches of Nesham., of which 300 being left untaken up, by his Will dated the   , the said John revised 100 a's to his said Daughter Margery, and the other 200 acres to his Daughter Sarah, Wife of John Bainbridge, and Rebc., Married to John Lambert, but deceased, and he, the said Rich'd, requesting that the said 100 acres might be survey'd to him together with the said 375 acres, the same was granted, and thereupon he produced a Return of 475 acres, laid out by J. C., in Bucks, for which he requests a Patent, and that there may be all the Priviledges expressed therein Granted in the first Deed of Sale from the Prop'ry in England. Granted a Patent.

Richard Hough having bought of the Propr'y a Tract of Vacant Land in Makefield, then reputed 300 acres, but sold for more or less for £40, already paid, for which Land the Prop'ry also granted him a War't dated 30, 9 mo., 1700, and the said Rich'd having also a right to 90 acres adjoyning, purchased of Wm. Beaks, he produces a Return of Survey for the said Vacant Land, and the said 90 acres cont'g in the whole 475 acres, for Which he requests a Patent. Granted.

The late Commis'rs, by Letters Patents under their hands

and Lesser Seal of the s'd Province, granted to Philip Rich'ds of Philad'a, a Certain Lott on or before the Bank of Dellaware River, in Philad'ia, aforesaid, in breadth 27 foot and in length 250 foot, bounded Westw'd with Dellaware front Street, Northward with Nathaniel Allen's, Southw'd with Alex'dr Parker's Lott and Eastw'd with the said River at the extent of 250 foot, to hold to the said Philip Richards, his Heirs and assigns for ever, Yielding during the space of 51 Years from the 26, 11 mo., 1688, Yearly 2 English Shill's and 9d, and at the expiration of the said space the Yearly Rent of the said Lott, with the buildings and Improvem'ts to be Valued and one-third part of the said Value to be paid to the said Wm. P., his Heirs, &c., forever hereafter, as by the Patent, dat. 24 Dec'br, 1692, appears, and the said Philip Richards, by Ind're dated 1st 6 mo., 1693, bargained and Sold the said Lott, with the app's to Daniel Cook, of Philad'a, Carpenter, To Hold, &c., by Vertue whereof and of the Laws of this province the said Daniel Cook became Seized of the said Lott and Made his last Will and Testament, dated 8, 7br., 1699, and appointed John Farmer, Watch Maker, and Jos. Kirl, Marriner, both of Philad'a, Ex'ors thereof, by the s'd Will authorising them, the said Ex'ors, to sell his House, Lands and Lotts, and all things else that he had, to pay his Just Debts.

The said John Farmer and Jos. Kirl, by Ind're dated 1, 12 mo., 1699, granted the said Lott., &c. to Thomas Masters, his Heirs and assigns, &c.

Thomas Masters Requests to purchase off the Reversion of that part of the said Lott Situate on the East Side of King's Street.

Hippolytus Le Fevre requests the Bank before his two front Lotts in Newcastle, which is granted.

A Warr't to John Hughes for 50 acres in the Neck of Springfield.

Philip Roman Requests a Patent on the 900 a's Mentioned pa.

Thomas Buffington purchases 100 a's in the Vacancy in the forks of Brandy Wine, to take it from Line to Line on both sides of the Creek, price £16 and a Bushell of Wheat, to pay Xmas or Interest; gives Security.

John Morris producing 3 Returns from the Office, each for 500 a's, Requests a Patent for the whole if it may be, if not that, it may be Confirmed however.

Robert Vernon having a Warr't from the Propr'y for 285 acres, he desires to Purchase 315 More to make it 600 acres for a Settlem't to two of his Sons and Chooses the N. East side of Brandywine, beyond the Barrens, for which he at last offers

£10 p'r 100, complaining much of his loss in not being Suffred to take up his Land before. Granted for Several Considerations as Requested, provided the Land be realy as represented and not culled; John Hope, of Chester County, purchases 200 a's ot that Land which was Ja's Stanfield's heading Peter Dix's, at £15 p'r 100 and a Bushell of wheat; to have it at one end.

At a Session of the Commissioners at Philadelphia 23d and 25th 9th Month, 1702.

Present, Edward Shippen, Griffith Owen, Thomas Story, James Logan.

Francis Lovelace Granted to Jan. Jansen 100 acres of Land between Marcus Kill and Haerwijek's Kill, on Dellaware, now the County of Chester, 10th 2 mo., 1673, and by another Instrument of the said date to John Hendrickson 100 acres, the said Instrum't in a Receipt under Phil. Lehnman's hand together with the former, but that was returned to them by Jenner, the other not, and in said Receipt, Verbatim, Philadelphia, 5, 3 mo., '83: Rec'd then 2 Patents from Jno. Jansen, one for 100 acres for himself, the other for 100 acres for John Hendrickson, the half of Which Jno. Jno'son hath bought of him, both dated the 10th of the 2 mo., 1673, witness my hand.

PHILIP TH. LEHMAN.

Daniel Linsye, by Ind're dated 11 Mar, '94, Owned to have sold to John Johnson one Moiety of 150 acres between Marcus and Haerwijek's Kills, which the said Daniel Purchased of Michael Isard by   , to whom it was granted; the said Daniel granted it to William Falle, Successor of the said Johnson, in right of his former Sale.

John Johnson deceasing, by his last Will dated 16 Mar., 1684-5 devised his Estate to his Wife Elenor and Children, who have Sold it to Philip Roman and Robert Langham, all the said 225 acres, who have or are to have distinct Deeds for their parts, and being resurvey'd by Isa. Taylor by the Gen'rl Warrant, each desire a Patent. Granted when the Deeds and Isard's Rights are produced.

Isaac Few requests to purchase 600 acres of Land on the west side of Brandywine, adjoyning on Wm. Brown, formerly s'd to be taken up by Francis Smith, 200 a's, John Brown 200 a's and Widow Pierce 200 a's, but is thrown up, as the said Isaac affirms, upon the same Terms with John Hope, viz: £15 p'r C't and a Bushel of wheat Rent, to be paid 25th 10br. next.

T. Bye's Patent to be stopt till James Streater's business is Settled.

Caleb Pusey, for his son-in-law, Hen. Worley, requests the grant of that Tract which was Rawlinson's, beyond Brandywine joyning on the Tracts granted to Hope and Few.

Griff. Jones' Tract to be resurvey'd and the Indians Settled.

Jos. Kirl having a Lott of 25 foot in the right of Collins, Wm. Bowlin 2 Lots of 15 foot, in right of John Blunston, 31 foot, George Wood 20 and from Gov'r Markham 100, and Philip England's Land, all to be resurvey'd they say to the River.

The Comm'rs grant to John Bowater 250 a's in right of Fincher's Land that he quitts in the Welch Tract, out of the Tract formerly laid out to Griff. Jones and 150 on purchase at £30 p'r 100, to be paid 25th 1 mo. Next, with Interest for 3 Months.

Margaret Cook producing a Return of a Lott in the High Street, 32 foot in breadth, joyning on the fifth Street, in right of Francis Burroughs, Purchaser of 1,000 acres, Requests a Patent. Granted.

Richard Few, purchaser of 500 acres, Sold to James Jacobs 10 acres of Liberty Land, which s'd James Jacobs Sold to Adam Roades, but no Deed. Deed to be made dated   A Warrant thereupon to Adam Roades and to be Confirmed with Pennock's Land, Clothworker, of Sawley, in Darby.

Tho. Whitby's Deeds, dated 10th and 11th Aprill, '82, for 500 acres, which s'd 500 acres and app's he convey'd by Lease and Rel., dated 22, 23 July, 1687, to John Roades, of Windgrave, in the County of Darby, Engl., Corbwainer. Jno. Roades deceasing, made his Sons, Adam and Jos., Ex'ors, but Adam Refused, Jos. took out Letters, vid. 28th 10 mo.

Judge Guest purchased of Francis Cook, of Ja's Claypoole's Land 150 a's, the Old Plantation, 200 acres laid out in 1684 and 180 in 1685, in all 530 acres, which he procured to be resurvey'd and taking in 22 acres of New Land, contains in all 538 acres, 150 thereof on old Rent, 200 thereof being taken up soon after the Propr's arrival is likewise allowed on Old Rent, but 180 thereof being by a Warrant, 1685, is judged to be a penny Sterling p'r acre, for all which he requests a Patent and agrees to pay £10 for reducing the s'd Tract to the same Rent with the rest, w'ch is granted.

Dirk Sipman, of Crevelt, County of Meurs, Merch't, by Lease and Rel., dated 9th and 10th Mar., 1682, purchased 5,000 acres of Land in Pennsylvania and by a Deed Ind. dated 1, 2 mo., 1683, purchased off the Rent and reduced it to one Shilling p'r 1,000. Govert Ramkes, of Crevelt, in the County of Meurs, in the Borders of Germany, Stay Maker, by Lease and Release, dated the 10th and 11th June, 1683, purchased of the Propr'y 1,000 acres, and by a Deed dated 11 June, '83, reduced the Rent to 1s Quitrent, and by a   , Vid. 8 Xbr., Dirk Sipman Sold the s'd 6,000 acres to Mathias Van Bebber, as he affirms, Vid. next day's Min's, 1, 10br., he appointed Jue. Vanbebber and Henry Sellen his attorneys, who, because the other had passed no regular Deed, only sent a Letter in credence of that Letter by Deed dated 1, 10br., 1702. Granted to Matt. Vanbebber.

Katherine Haverlaw, according to Min's taken by the Propr'y, by. J. Grey, A. D. 1701, held 300 acres on great Creek, between John Collinson and Simon Pawlin's purchased by her late husband, Antho. Haverlaw, of Antho. Creyger, by an Instrum't dated 7, 5 mo., 1679, who had the same from New York, and by will devised the same to his Wife for her life and after to his Children. Requests that the said 300 acres be resurvey'd together with 200 of Vacant lying between said Land and Nehem. Field, which Jno. Hill says they always paid Rent for, and now desire to have. They have lost their Deeds Since said Minutes were taken, by their House being burnt. Granted a Resurvey and Patent on the Return of the 300 acres, the other to be Considered.

At a Session of the Commissioners at Philad'a 30th 9br., 1702. Present, Edward Shippen, Griff. Owen, James Logan.

Mary Fletcher having Obtained a Warr't of Resurvey on her Land in Oxf'd Township, where she held 215½ acres, It is found to Contain 266 acres; she agrees to pay £30 for the Overplus in a little time. See for the Title Phil. Min's, Oxford Township, first pur. from Robert Adams 104, and from the same 111½ of Hen. Wad.

Wm. Harmer Caveats ag'st a Patent being Granted or any further progress being made in the Office of Property towards granting a Patent to Tho. Rutter and others, purchasers in the Tract of 500 acres first granted to Robert Longshore, above the Germantown, till the said Wm. with his Evidences can be heard, together with the said Rutter and others.

The Survey and Settlem't of the Welch Tract being Considered, 'tis Ordered that Rowland Ellis be Confirmed in 577 acres, Edw'd Jones, Senr., in 402 acres, Edw'd Jones, Junr., in 125 a's, Griffith Owen in   and Hugh Roberts in 338, John Roberts 262, Robert David 346, Hugh Roberts 441, and Richard Jones 157. In case Fincher and Hastings can be accommodated which is to be Endeavoured w'th all expedition, Evan Jones 361, Ellis David 409, Thomas Jones 587, Cadwallader Ellis 310, which likewise interfere in part with the former, also all in Duffein Mawr.

Ordered that a Warrant be Issued to David Powel to Resurvey all the Lands lying within or Ever Reputed to belong to Whitpain's Township, with all the Lands above Gwynedd and between it and Bucks' Line, also a Second Warrant for all the lands lying between the German Township and Skuylkill, and try the German Town out lines, and to Resurvey the Manor of Springfield in another Warrant, with Lands adjoyning, also a Third War't for the Neck between Delaware and Skuylkill below Philadelphia.

A Warrant also to Resurvey Pennsbury Manor to David Powel or to make Return of the Survey he made by the Prop'rs Ord'r upon the same.

At a Session of the Commr's at Philadel'a, 1, Xbr., 1702.

Present, Griffith Owen, Tho. Story, James Logan.

Thomas Jones Procured of the 'Prop'ry a Warr't dated 17, 5 mo., '83, for 250 a's of Land said to be purchased in Chester County, being, as is affirmed in Consideration of work done for the Gov'r, also a Return for the s'd Land, dated 13th 4 mo., '90 Survey'd 24, 5 mo., '83; taken out of the Records.

The said T. Jones also procured a Warr't from the Prop'ry dated 17, 8 mo., '83, for a Lott on Skuylkill, for which he produces a Return under Robert Longshore's hand, Sold to Wm. Davies, Mason, lies on Sassafras Street 49½ foot.

He also purchased of James James, by Deed Poll dated 8, 4 mo., 1695, fifty acres adjoyning to the former, being part of 300 acres Sold said James by Magdalen and Jno. Kinsey, on penny Rent. Requests a Resurvey on the whole 300 acres and a Patent. Granted a Resurvey.

Thomas Masters Making application to buy off the Reversion of his Bank Lot of 40 foot 9 inches, first granted to Albertus Brandt and since by Several Mean Conveyances, came into the Possession of Thos. Masters, Ordered that for £20 7s 6d a Patent be accordingly Granted.

Ordered that John Gardiner, in Consideration of his Trouble as Woodranger, have 20 Cord of Wood of the Dead Trees on the Mann'r.

Walter Faucet having Long had a difference with Edward Pritchett and by a Tryal at Chester Court having Obtained a decision Concerning his Moiety of a Tract of 100 acres on Delaware and Crum creek, upon a Resurvey of the whole there is found to be 38 acres Overplus, of which the said Walter Claims, also a Moiety, but for which not agreeing With the Comm'rs for the same, he Offering Only £20 and they Demanding £25, It is Order'd that

At a Session of the Commissioners at Philadelphia the 7th and 8th 10th Month, 1702.

Present, Edward Shippen, Thomas Story, James Logan.

Wm. Mark, T. Ellis and John Goodson, by a Patent dated 18th 2 mo., 1688, granted and Confirmed to Mary Bradnell, Renter, 200 a's granted by a Warrant dated 4, 12 mo., 1685, and Survey'd to her 17, 3 mo., '86, Situate, bounded by John Goodson's and R'd Whitpain's Land, in the County of Philadelphia, at 1d Sterling p'r acre. Requests a Resurvey. Granted.

The Proprietary, by Deeds 18, 19 August, '81, granted to Jno. Day, 1,250 a's, in part of which W. M. granted a Warrant dat. 5, 8 mo., '82, for 500 a's, in part of which the Surveyor General laid out one Tract of 210 a's, Resurv'd and Confirmed pa.   , for the other 290 acres James Atkinson produces a Draught under Tho. Fairman's hand; bounded by Coll. Rich'ds and Jno. West, Bartre's and Fuller's, and Rob't Turner's. Requests a Resurvey. Granted.

M. van Bebber having, as in pa.   , gained a Title to all D. Sipman's Land, alledges that there was 5,000 acres Laid out in one Tract, Joyning on An. Robinson's Land, as is Mentioned in its Return, now Edward Lane's, and one Jacob Telner's, as by the Return of that Land, but no Return Can be found; he requests a Resurvey on that Tract. Granted if to be found Vacant there and has Ever been Survey'd.

And to Resurvey in the Liberties what has been laid out in right of the said Purchase, Vid. pa.   , following.

Walter Faucet agrees to give £25 for the 38 acres Overplus in his Tract, Mentioned 1st Inst., and 40s to Reduce the Rent of his 50 acres to 1s p'r C't.

There having been a Tract of Land of 1,260 acres, or thereabouts, Laid out to Richard Snead in Chester County, within the Bounds of the Welch Tract, on which the Welch have made some Settlem'ts, and therefore and because it was an Incroachm't he is Oblieged to Resign One Part of it to the s'd Settlers and take the Remainder below, for which Richard Parker, his attorney, Requests a Warrant and to take up the rest in anot'r Convenient place. Granted.

———

At a Session of the Commissioners at Philad'ia, 14th Xbr.

Present, Omnes.

Matth. Van Bebber producing the following Paper, vid. Paper:

In pursuance of which 'tis said there was laid out in the Liberties of Philad'ia 50 acres, which yet lie Vacant, and 10 acres to Jacob Isaac's father to the said Matthias, on which

MINUTE BOOK "G." 341

he requests a Warrant, also for the acre In the City granted to D. Sipman and the ⅓ acre granted to said Jac. Isaacs, all which he hath a Right to and the ⅓ acre for Gov't Ramkes. Jac. Isaacs, by Deed dat. 12 Xbr. Inst't, granted the Lotts and Liberty Land to his Son Mathias.

The Proprietary having Sold to Jno. Grey (al's Tatham) 5,000 a's of Land, w'ch with the rest of the said Tatham's Estate, Tho. Revel, of Burlington, is become invested with a power to dispose off, as in pa. is at full recited, of which said 5,000 a's the s'd T. R., by a Deed dated 20th Ap., 1702, Sold and Convey'd one Moiety, viz: 2,500 a's to Wm. and Tho. Stevenson, being formerly Located and Survey'd on the Branches of Neshem., Coun. Bucks. Tho. Stevenson, for himself and Brother, Requests a Resurvey and Patent. Granted, he paying, &c.

The Ockanickon or Crum Creek Indians having removed from their old habitation before the Prop'rs Departure, by his Order Seated, by Caleb Pusey, Nicholas Pyle, Nat'll Newlin and Jos. Baker on the Tract in Chester County, formerly laid out to Griff. Jones, but now Vacant. But the said Indians expressing great uneasiness at the uncertainity of their Settlem'ts, pressed and Several times Urged the Neighbouring Friends that they might be Confirmed in Some particular place unter certain Metes and Bonds, that they Might live no more like Dogs, as they expressed themselves.

Richard Davies, of Welch Pool, Coun. Montgom'ry, Gent., having by Ind'd, L. and Rel., dated the 14, 15 7br., '81, purchased 5,000 acres by Ind. of L. and Rel., dated 19, 20 June, '82, Convey'd of the same 100 acres to David James, then in the Parish of Glaseram, in the County of Radnor, Weaver, which said 100 acres was taken up by the said David in Radnor, in this province, and he being possessed thereof, died and left behind him Mary James, his Sole Child and Heiress, who by an assignm't indorsed on said Ind're, dated 22d 10br., 1702, assigned and made over the said 100 a's of Land, with the Ind're and all, her Right, Title and Interest in and to the same to Stephen Evans, of Radnor, Yeoman.

David Meredith also purchased of the said Davies 100 a's, and of the Comm'rs 250, all which was laid out to him in Radnor, and out of the same he sold to Stephen Evans 150 a's, by Deeds dated 20th 5 mo., '91, Vid. Welch Min's.

There was also laid out of said David James at the same time with the aboves'd 100 acres of purchase, the like quantity of Head Land at a penny p'r acre, by War't dated 19, 1 mo., '83, as p'r Warrant in the Records appears, which said 100 acres the said Mary James, his Heiress, hath sold to s'd Stephen Evans also.

MINUTE BOOK "G."

Jno. Steven, for his Father, St. Evans, requests a Resurvey on the whole to his Father, and to purchase off the penny Rent, which is granted, but no arrears being paid, he pleads that for some Services done to the Prop'ry he, the Prop'ry, promised him a Kindness and thereupon he petitioned him before his departure for a remission of the said arrears, but offers to pay the Consideration Money of the purchase, viz: £11, and for the arrears will give Bond to pay what the Prop'ry will not remitt. Granted and a Patent on the Return, he paying. &c.

Tho. Cartwright affirming he purchased of John Priestner 2 Tracts of Land in the forks of Chester Creek, about 5 Miles from the River Delaware, laid out to the said Priestner upon New Rent, by Vertue (as 'tis s'd) of a War't from the Prop'ry recorded in the Office, dated 1, 8br., '83, for 200 a's, Requests a Resurvey. Ordered that when the said Tho. produces any proof that he realy purchased the said Land of Priestner before his decease (w'ch otherwise is escheated, Pr. having no Heirs) a Warrant shall be granted.

Joshua Morgan requests 100 adjoyning or near to the 100 a's lately granted to Wm. Brakyn, on Mill Creek, near Whiteclay, on the same terms, viz: for £12 10s, and to be paid 25th Xbr, 1703, with Interest for 1 Year and a bushell Rent, Informs that he is Seated on 200 acres leased to him by Jno. Champion for 9 Years at £3 p'r ann., which has been entred on about 11 Years without any grant or Survey.

James Atkinson Enters his Caveat against the granting of a Patent to Tho. Fairman, or any under his Right, for a Certain Tract adjoyning on Barns and Fuller, in or near   , first returned to John Day but afterwards taken up in Stanly's right and now Claimed by Tho. Fairman.

———

At a Session of the Commissioners at Philadelphia the 28th and 29th Xbr, 1702.

Present, Edward Shippen, Thomas Story, James Logan, Secretary.

Peter Thomas produces a Deed dated 8, 4 mo., '97, from Geo. Willard to himself for 500 acres, part of 1,500 laid out to Tho. Brassey in Willis Town, which s'd 500 acres in s'd Deed is s'd to be laid out to said P. Thomas out of said Tract of 1,500 acres, Requests a Resurvey. Granted, but the Title in the Chester Min's Inq. Williston a Patent, viz: how it came from Brassey to Willard.

Edward Burk having made good his Title to 200 a's near Springfield Manor 19th 3 mo. last, Now produces a Deed from

Zech. Whitpaine, dated 9, 5 mo., '88, to Nich. Skull for 100 acres of land adjoyning to the other 200 acres, reciting therein that it is a Moiety of 200 acres granted to Wm. Harmer, late purchaser, by Patent from the Commiss'rs, dated 26, 2 mo., '86, and by a Deed dated 9, 11 mo., '87-8, Convey'd by the said William Harmer to s'd Whitpaine, his Heirs, and [the whole 200 Requests a Resurvey upon the whole 300, Viz: this 100 and the other 200. Granted]. Nic. Scull, by a Deed dated 21, 9br., '98, Convey'd the first 200 acres together with the said 100 to said Edward Burk.

Richard Whitfield, by Ind'r dated 20, 6 mo., '90, granted to Patrick Robinson two Several parcels of Land in Tacony, the one of 70 acres, the other of 4 acres, which Indentures recites that the said 2 parcels were in possession of he said R'd Whitfield by Vertue of a Deed of Conveyance for 200 a's from Peter Yokum, dated 19, 10 mo., '83, acknowledged and Recorded and Indorsed thus: I will Confirm the within Deed by Patent to Rich'd Whitfield, his Heirs and assigns. Wm. Penn. P. Robinson, by an Indenture dated 1, 4 mo., '91, Convey'd the said two parcels to John Tyzack.

Erick Mullikar, by Ind. dated 21, 1 mo., '89, Convey'd to John Tyzack all that his Lott of Land upon Quessionaman Creek, Containing with the Marsh thereunto belonging, &c., about 74 acres, more or less.

Jno. Tyzack, by Ind'res of L. and Rel., dated 4 and 5 days of Xbr, 1697, Mortgaged to Ann Moore, of Stepney, in the County of Middlesex, Widow, all that Brick Messuage or Tenem't, and also that Tract of Land Situate at the mouth of Tacconinek Creek, in the County of Philadelphia, being the 2 aforesaid Tracts, for £615 18s 9d, which not being paid, Wm. Reed, with his Wife, Ann, Elizab., Rachael, Naomi Moore, all Daughters and Coheiresses of the said Ann Moore, joyntly with John Tyzack, by L. and Rel., dated 6 and 7th February, 1700, Gave, Granted, Released and Confirmed all the said Messuage and Tenem't to Sam'l Finney, of Cheatam Hill, in the County of Lancaster, Merch't, now of this Province, who requests a Patent for the same according to the Present Bounds and Contests, having been tried by David Powell and found to be rather Difficient than abound.

Wm. Reynolds, of the Lime Kills, agrees to pay 20s for a hog unmarked, Killed by Mistake. Accepted.

Jos. Roads, with his elder brother Adam, proving a Right in their deceased Father to Thos. Whitby's Lott, the said Jos. produces the probate of his said Father's Will, dated 20, 8br, 1701, in which he made the said Adam and Jos. E'ors of his said Will. But Adam refusing, the whole was Committed to Jos.

by Letters of administration from the Court, who thereupon desires a Warrant for the Lott. Granted, but not Confirmed till he produce the Release from his elder Brother, who is Heir.

Ordered that a Warrant be forthwith Issued to lay out tenu Thousand acres in 2 or 3 Several Tracts.

Peter Anderson having taken out a Warrant of Resurvey on Peter Hansen's Land, Granted by vertue of a Patent dated 4, 10 mo, '86, from the Commiss'rs, J. Clayp. and R. Turner, to his Father, Hans Hansen, for 425 Acres, Who, by his Will dated 11 August, '96, in these words, vid. infra. devised to the said Peter his Plantation on Aplin Island, with all the said Island and Land belonging thereunto, the Marsh excepted, which Marsh he divided among his 3 eldest Sons, Hans, s'd Peter and Joseph, Ex'ors of the said Will, being resurvey'd, is found to Contain upon the Surveyor's Review 596 Acres, wherein is Contained 130 Acres Overplus after Allowance of 40 A's by Law for which he agrees to pay after the Rate of £15 p'r C't to be paid 25th 10br. 1703, with Interest, viz: £20, Vid. Newc. Min's, Desires a Patent which is granted therein to have and to hold all the fast land to the s'd Peter Hansen and the Marsh to the Uses in the S'd Will Mentioned:

First I give unto my Son Peter Anderson the whole mentioned Island whereon I now live with all the lands and Improvements thereto belonging or appertaining to that Tract of Land, excepting the Marsh there to belonging, And for the said Marsh I give and Bequeath to my said Son Peter and my Son Hans Hansen and my Son Jos. Hansen to be equally divided among my 3 Sons. Proved before John Donaldson and James Claypoole 17, 9br., '96.

Upon application made by Judge Guest for the purchase of 1,500 A's in the great Swamp, 'Tis Ordered that a Warr't be granted to the said Judge with the first for Land in the said Place and that no land be Survey'd there to any Purchaser (Griff. Jones excepted) before him, Consideration to be not above £12 p'r C't and under the said sum if it be granted for less before 3 mo. next to any other.

The Prop'ry having granted to David Powel 400 Acres of Land before his Departure, to be paid for as he should agree with the Comm'rs to whose favour he recommended him in this Particular, with Orders under his hand that it should be under the Value, and upon a Survey being found to Contain 506 Acres, 'tis Ordered that the said David pay for the same £80, 25, 1 mo., 1704, and that he pay by portions as he can Raise it both before and after that time.

Isaac Woods, of the County of Philadelphia, produceth the Counter part of an Indenture of Partition between Francis

Searl and John Carver, dated 5 June, 1700, which said Indenture recites that, whereas the said Searl and Carver had Joyntly purchased of Jos. Fisher, Ex'or of the last will and Testament of Tho. Terwood, by Indr. of Bargain and Sale dat. 1, 9br., '97; 200 Acres of Land Situate in the County of Philadelphia, joyning on the Land of Jos. Knight and the Tract hereafter Mentioned, also that the said Searl and Carver purchased Joyntly of Silas Crispin in the Capacity of Ex'rs of the last will and Testament of Tho. Holme, by Indr. dated 10, 10br., '97, 500 Acres joyning on the above and running Northwest by Mares Manor, therefore they, the said Searl and Carver, by Indr., did make a Partition of both the said Tracts between them, And the said J. Carver did thereby Grant unto the said Fr. Carver all the said first 200 Acres together with 182 Acres part of the aforesaid 500 Acres adjoyning to the former, to hold to him, his Heirs,&c.,in Severalty as his full part or Share of which the said Francis being so possessed did Bargain and Sell the same to the said Is. Woods, who, suspecting there may be overplus, requests a Resurvey and a Patent. Granted, he paying for the Overplus and making Terwood's Title good, &c. The Deed from Searl to Woods is to be now made; Deed from Fisher to Searl, &c., Recorded Philad'ia, Book E, 3 Vol. 5, pa. 101, from S. Crispin, B. E., 3 Vol. 5, page 317.

Signed a Commission to John McDonald to be Ranger from the South Branch of Brandywine to George's Run, for all Wild Horses, Cattle and Swine from Christina and a Line by the Bridge Westw'd for Strays, Newc. excepted, with a proviso to Secure Alph. Kirk's Commission also.

Mem'dum, 1st January. Sealed a Deed to George Reed for 215 A's of Land.

At a Session of the Commissioners at Philadelphia 4th 11th Month, 1702.

Present Omnes.

The Comm'rs, W. M., R. T., J. G., S. C., by Patent dated 13, 12 mo., 1690, Granted to Humphrey Murray a Bank Lott over against his Front, Con. 42 foot 9 Inches in breadth, bounded Northward with Chestnut Street and Southward with a Vacancy of which he hath sold to Tho. Oldman, all the up'er half, and requests to purchase off the Reversion of the Lower. Granted.

To Mathias Van Bebber, Granted 36 foot in the high Street, between the 3d and 4th, enclosed now or formerly by Wm. Snead in lieu of all his Claim and Demand whatsoever, in right of the Prop'ry's Grant of 1 Acre and $\frac{2}{3}$ upon Sipman's,

Ramke's and his Father's purchase of 7,000 Acres, provided it be Clear.

Ordered at the Request of Clem't Pumstead that there be Warrants granted for the use of himself, Brother and Sisters, being Seven in all.

The Prop'ry, by Patent dated 4, 4 mo., 1684, Confirmed to Caleb Pusey a Lott in breadth 49½ foot, and in length 220 foot, in the North side of Walnut street, bounded Westward with the fifth Street, Eastward Vacant, in right of s'd Caleb's Purchase. Caleb Pusey, by Indorsem't on s'd Patent, 19, 9br., 1690, Assigned the said Lott to Daniel Jones, of Philadelphia, Cordwainer, who, by Deed p. dated 23 June, '96, Convey'd the same to David Lloyd.

The Prop'ry, by Warrant, dated 22, 9br., '83, granted to Roger Hughs, David Meredith, Rich'd Cook and John Lloyd, and to each a Lott proportionable to their purchase under R'd Davies, which being Survey'd between 4th and 5th in Chesn., the present Comm'rs, by Warr't dated 28th 2d mo. last, granted a Resurvey upon the said Lotts together with one other to David Price, Purchaser also Under R'd Davies by his Brother James. Roger Hughes, as recited in following Deed, Granted his Lott to David Meredith; R'd Cook and John Lloyd, their's to Da. Meredith and Stephen Evans, who, by a Deed dated 20, 9 mo., 1702, Granted all the aforesaid 4 Lotts to David Lloyd. Rent of Each 12d, Sterl.

David Lloyd being, by Vertue of the aforesaid seized of the aforementioned 5 Lotts, by Deed dated 23, 10br., 1702, in Consideration of £83 6s 8d, Granted all the afores'd 5 Lotts to Enoch Story, of Philad'ia, Merch't, to hold, &c., q'tt in the whole 247½. David Price Sold the aboves'd Lott to Wm. Thomas, who, for a Certain Consideration, sold it to Thomas Lloyd, but no Deed being made and D. Lloyd and Is. Norris, Ex'ors of Thos. Lloyd's Will, with power to Sell, &c., the said Price joyntly w'th El. Thomas, Relict of s'd Wm., by Deed dated 16 May, 1702, granted the said Lott to Isaac Norris and Da'd Lloyd, who, by Deed Poll, dated 20, 9br., 1702, granted the same in Consideration of £16 13d 8s to s'd Enoch Story, who requests a Patent for the whole Six in one, Containing 297 foot, at 6s, Sterling from 84.

The Comm'rs, by Warrant dated 4th 7 mo., 1685, Granted to Wm. Brown 300 Acres on Rent which warrant was executed by Tho. Pierson 19th 12 mo., '85-6, as by return under his hand in the Office Appears, and was entred and built on as is said forthwith and was Confirmed by Patent to the said Brown, dated 4, 7 mo., '88. William Brown resigned all his right to Joel Baily by Assignm't on said Patent dated 16, 10 mo., '92, who Assigned to Tho. Hope who enters upon it and is to Clear the Arrears of Rent which is 17 years to the first month next at 37s 6d p'r ann. is £31 17s 6d.

Ordered that the Office of Ranger for the County of Philad'ia be given to Robert Reading upon Jonas Potts laying it down, he giving Security for its just discharge.

Jos. Hansen having Obtained a War't for a Tract of Land reputed 300 Acres, pa.   , and having resigned it to Isaac Scheffer by Indr. dated 7th July, 1702, Granted all his Right and Title to the said Land to said Isaac Scheffer, who desires a Patent upon it with A Marsh formerly Granted.

George Dakeyne, Surveyor of Newc., requesting a Small Tract of Cripple reputed about 40 or 50 Acres, adjoyning to the Tract of 600 Acres already granted, Ordered that a Warrant be granted him for the said Land, he paying for the same after the rate of 12s p. C't, and the Rent of his other Tract, viz: 10 Shill's, Country Money p. C't.

Christian Arenson having obtained a grant from us for 100 Acres more to be added to a hundred, the right of which he purchased of Peter Oldson on the same Terms with that granted to said Peter, viz: at £16 p'r C't with a bushell of wheat Rent. Ordered that a Warrant be granted.

Rec'd a Bond from Abr. Brewster for £30, from Jos. Moor for £30, from Walter Faucet £26, 15s payable 10 Mar. and a penal Bill.

Joel Baily, now of Chester County, near Robert **Pyle**, requests a Grant of 200 Acres Vacant land on the South of Brandywine adjoyning to Peter Dix and William Brown's, or any other vacant Land thereabouts. Ordered that Land be very Sparingly Sold for the future in the County of Newc. and all other such places where there is but little left, but that the said Joel Baily have the preferrence of what land thereabouts is to be disposed of. Commission to Tho. Pierson and John Andrews both dated 2d Ins't.

At a Session of the Commissioners at Philadelphia 11th and 12th 11 Month, 1702.

Present Omnes.

The Prop'ry, by L. and Rel., dated 17 and 18 8 br., '81, granted to Sam'll Jobson, of the Parish Mary Magdalen's, Bermoadsey, C. of Surrey, Felmonger, 1,000 A's, and by Deeds of the same date to Humphrey South, of London, Merchant, 1,000 A's, who, by Deeds of L. and Rel., dated 1 and 2d January, 1684, Granted to said Sam'll Jobson 250 Acres.

Wm. Markham and John Goodson, by Patent, dat. 9, 5mo., 1687, Granted to Sam'll Jobson 920 Acres of Land Situate on the Northwestmost bounding line of the Welch Tract, all the other bounds are lines of Trees, said to be granted by a Warr't, dated 26, 5 mo., '86, Survey'd 7, 4 mo.,'87. The said Comm'rs by Patent, dated the same day, Confirmed to Sam'll Jobson 1,000 Acres, C. County, begining at a Corner of Tho. Barker's Land, W. S. W. 500 p's, by a line of Trees N. N. W. 320 p's, E. N. E. 500 p's, &ca, and no other Certain bounds.

Sam'll Jobson, by a Deed of Gift, dated 3d Feb'y, '99, Granted the said 1,000 Acres, his own purchase, and 250 A's of South's purchase, to his Son Michael Jobson, who requests a Resurvey and Patent.

Ordered a Patent to Jonathan Eldridge.

Ordered that a Patent be renewed to Joshua Hastings, formerly Confirmed to James Atkinson by Patent 28, 6 mo., '88, in right of Edw'd Samway, and by Said Jas. Assigned 24, 7ber, '97, to said Hastings, to be bounded between Isr. Hobbs and Jos. Wilcox.

W. Howel having had a Resurvey on his Tract, purchased from Tho. Fairman for 800 Acres, and there being 2 lines, the one making it 900 the other 7, and there being also 800 Acres adjoyning being formerly Telnor's, 400 thereof, 762 now Thos. Rutter's and Company in which there is overplus 22 Acres At least. Ordered the Possessors of said Land agree for their Overplus and that Wm. Howel have what they pay as they can agree.

Mom'dum, that the Prop'ry, in one order directed to the former Comm'rs, dated 12, 9 mo., '86, produced to us, did Order 300 Acres to be laid out to Sam'll Martin, acknowledging that he had Sold him that Quantity, and in another Certificate under his hand date 25, 8 mo., 1696, declares that he had given 200 A's formerly to Sam'll Martin, who Assigned the Deed to Thos. Bye, but it appeared afterw'ds to the Prop'ry that he had given the whole 300 Aforementioned.

Mem'dum, that Tho. Ellis is affirmed by David Powel to have taken out a Patent just at his going to England for 100 A's which Seems not accounted for to the Proprietary.

Mem'dum, that 'tis agreed between Robert Wharton, present husband of Rachel, Daughter of Tho. Ellis, who purchased of her brother, Humphrey Ellis, 250 A's left him by his Father, the said Thomas, on one hand, and Sam'll Carpenter and Owen Thomas, agents for Bartho. Rawles, in behalf of s'd Rawles on the other hand, by the Consent of the Comm'rs that the Warr't of Resurvey Obtained by the said O. T., bearing date 16, 12 mo. last, 250 Acres for s'd Bartho. Rawles, in Right of s'd Thomas Ellis be Executed by running an Equal partition line thro' the Middle of a Certain Tract laid out for 500 A's to s'd

Tho's Ellis, in Duffein Mawr, dividing the same into two Equal Moieties, and that Bartho. Rawles shall enjoy the Moiety on which the Improvem't made by said Owen Shall happen to be, And that the Difference of the Value of the s'd two Moieties be referred to four indifferent Men, now mutually chosen between the s'd parties viz: Da'd Morris, Rich'd Hayes, Edw'd Rees and Rob't Jones, to whome, or any 3 of them agreeing, the s'd parties fully and absolutely refer the whole Controversy and Differences between them about the said Land, and that the said persons, so chose, shall have full power to award and Determine the Said Difference in every respect, and by their Award ye s'd parties afores'd shall for ever be absolutely concluded.

Rich'd Worthington requests 66 foot on the fourth Street joyning to Edw'd Ship's Park, of 66 foot in br. on s'd Street on the back of Gicock and Bowcher's Lotts. Rent a 5s, Sterling.

Ordered a Warrant to Tho. Bye for 12 Acres of Liberty Land belonging to Pask's, Crew's and Limkin's Purchase of 250 Acres each, all invsted in the said Tho. and his Son Nath'l.

Mem'dum, that the Comm'rs be cautious in granting to John Prew 100 Acres which he is Shortly to apply for, he being about to sell it and will not be able to pay.

Richard Nicolls, Gov'r of N. Y., by Patent dated January 1st, 1667, granted to Rob't Ashman and his Associates, viz: Rob't Ashman, John Ashman, Tho. Caleb, Carman Duncan, Will'm Francis Walker, Thos. Llewellin, Frederick Anderson, Joshua Jacob and Thos. Jacob all that parcel of Land Commonly known by the name of Passayuncke on Delaware by the side of Skuylkill, containing, by Estimation, 1,000 Acres, be it more or less, bounded on the South with the Main River, on the West with the Skuylkill, on the North with Peter Rambo's Plantation, on the East with a parcell of Land called Molbee's Land, under the Rent of 10 bushells p. Ann. with a Mem'dum added that John Ashman,   first planters, should have the greatest proportion of Land according to their stocks and Ability.

John Ashman, by a Writing under his hand, dated 30 July, 1607, granted to Andrew Bankson all his Land taken up or untaken up in Passayunk, of this, being 100 A's, he sold to the Minister 80 A's and to Mathias Holston 3 Acres, So he holds 17.

Francis Jacob and Tho. Jacob, by the name of Jacocks, Sons of Old Tho. Jacobs, by Deed poll, dated 16, 7br.,' 82, Granted to Andrew Bankson, his Heirs and Assigns, a Tract between Moyamensen and Passayunk, part of Tho. Jacob's Lott, by agreem't, cont., by Estimation, 10 Acres more or less, but is 17.

Laur. Cock and John Snowdon having purchased Fred. Anderson's right, sold to said Andr. by Indenture, dated 26 Apr., '81, three Lotts of Ground in Malbour's poynt, each, as A. B. informs, cont. 17 Acres, being part of Passa. Grant.

Jan Claster Paarde, Cooper, by Deed, dated 26 April, 1681, granted to A. Bankson one Lott or Share of Land, Marsh and Meadow of s'd Passa., being the 5 Lot from Sickhansincks, running up the Cripple toward Maymensinck 80 p's, being Carman's Share.

Lasse or Laur. Cock, by deed, dated 10, 8ber, '87, Granted to said Andr. 35 Acres upon Seckhansincks Creek, Swamp, &c., being p't of Dun. Williams and others, of his own part, 'tis thought, of his overplus. Said Laur. Cock, by Deed, dated 30 Aug't, 1694, Granted to said Andr. 100 Acres of Marsh joyning on A. B's fat Land, Moyamensen and Holland'rs Creek, being part of 875 A's of Marsh, Swamp, &c., granted s'd Cock by Pat t. from the Commiss'rs.

Peter Cocks, by Deed, dated 10, 8br., 1687, granted to s'd Andr. 17 Acres on the Eastw'd of Andr. Bankson's Land.

Matthias Holston, by Deed, dated 15 July, '85, Granted to said Andr. 17 A's of Land in Malbour's point, bounded Northw'd on Lawr. Cock, Ew'd with And. Bankson's Lott, the whole being 170 A's, fast Land, viz: 10 Lots of 17 Acres each, 100 A's Marsh, with their Meadow being about 24 A's, shall further appear clear. Desires a Resurvey and Patent. Granted a Resurvey and Patent as it

———

At a Session of the Commissioners at Philadelphia the 18th 11th Month, 1702.

Present, Griffith Owen, Thomas Story, James Logan, Secretary.

The Prop'ry, by Patent, dated 31, 5 mo., 1684, Granted to Wm. Wood, Purchaser, 100 acres joynnig on the Land of Wm. Sharlow and Company, and the river Skuylkill, and by another Patent of the same date, granted to William Sharlow and Wm. Wood, Purchasers, one hundred Acres, beginning at a Corner Tree of John Bowles' Land, and joyns on the river Skuylkill and the other recited Tract, both which Several parcels the said Wood and Sharlow having Conveyed to Hugh Roberts, his 3 Sons Rob't, Owen and Edw'd, by Edw'd, request a Resurvey and new Patent. Ordered a Resurvey forthwith and a Patent when the Deed to Hugh Roberts is produced, and 'tis fully agreed among the said Brethren in whose name the said Patent shall be granted both in Blockley Township.

The Prop'ry, by L. and Rel., dated 2 and 3 May, '82, granted to Allen Foster and Mary, his wife, 1,100 Acres of Land, and they, by Deed, dated 14, 3 mo., '84, Granted to Tho. Fairman, as is recited, 600 Acres, parcel of the said Land, who, by Deed, dated 7, 11 mo., '98, Sold to James Plumley, Coun. Philad'ia, Yeoman, a Tract located in South'ton Township, Bucks, joyning on the s'd Townsh. Line and John Rush's Land, cont. 582 Acres, and the s'd J. Plumley, by Deed Poll, dat 26, 11 mo., '98-9, Granted the s'd Tract to John Morris, who requests a Resurvey.

Martha Durant producing a return out of the office for 402 Acres above the Welch Line, in part and pursuance of a Warr't granted for 600 Acres, and requests a Patent. Ordered a Patent Accordingly, if it appears by the Surveyor that the land be realy Vacant.

Ordered a Patent to Matthias Van Bebber on 2 Lots, one in the 2d another in the High Street, in full of the Warr't dated 14 day 10 mo. last, from ourselves.

Ordered a Patent to Jos. Sharpless for his Land, the 90 Acres of Overplus being cutt off, both Tracts in one Patent except they be Large.

John Henry Sprogel agrees to give for the 100 Acres granted to him by the Prop'ry in the Manor of Springfield £40 and Interest from the date of Survey till the same be paid, either here or in England, 50 p. C't Exch. Ord'd a Patent.

John Fincher, who has quitted 455 Acres of his Land in the Welch Tract to the true Welch Owners, has the same quantity laid out by David Powel on which he is to have a Patent. Ordered that a Patent be granted to John Fincher for the said 455 Acres, and 300 A's that are left of his former Tract, ye Title as Follows:

The Prop'ry by L. and Rel., dated 15 and 16, 10 br., '81, Granted to Francis Fincher, of Worcester, Glover, 1,000 Acres, entered in the list 1,250.

The Prop'ry, by L. and Rel., dated 25 and 26 7br, '81, granted to Alex'dr. Beardsly, of Worcester, Glover, 500 A's, who, by Indorsem't on the Release, dated 27, 8mo., '83, sold the same to the said Fra. Fincher.

In right of s'd Fincher's Purchase there was laid out on Skuylkill 500 A's and in the Liberties 25 A's, and by a Warrant, dated 7, 2 mo., '85, the remaining 475 Acres together with 490 A's in right of Beardsly by a Warr't 2, 4 mo., '85, were laid out together; 11, 7 mo., '92, was granted to Mary Fincher, who deceasing, left her Estate among her Children, Armil, John, Joshua, Rebecca. now wife of Wm. Corker, and Sarah, Wife of Dan'll Flower, who, making a Partition of the

Estate, the aforesaid Tract of 965 Acres (250 sold to John Bowater first deducted), the Remaind'r 715 fell to Josh. Fincher and his Brother John. Joshua, Wm. Carter and Rebecca, Daniel Flower and Wife Sarah, by a Deed, dated 19, 10 mo., released to the said John their whole Right and Interest in and to the Premisses to John Fincher.

The said Tract, falling within the Welch bounds, 'tis Ordered that there be confirmed of the same 300 Acres to John and 415 A's now laid out by David Powell in full, the said John to pay Rent, &c., for the said 300, but for the Remainder none, and therefore w't he has been out must be reimbursed. Ordered a Warr't to lay out 415 Acres with Allowance de novo and a Patent for the whole.

Ordered a Patent to James Wallace for 500 Acres in full of his 1,000 with 15 A's over for which Tho. Withers pays 30 Shilling, viz: £10 p. C't.

There being two tracts of Land in the forks of Chester Creek laid out to John Priestner at a penny p. acre the said John, by an Imperfect writing, dated 28, 9br., '86, is said to have granted the same to Cha. Brooks and Tho. Cartwright. Cha. Brooks Sold to John Haywood and he to Robert Eyre, who, with his Wife Ann, 10, 7 br., '91, Sold to Tho. Cartwright the said Brooks' Share. He now requests a Resurvey and is desirous to purchase off the Rent. Granted.

George Palmer having been above 16 Years a Prisoner in Maqueness and now returned, having lost all advantages that might have accrued to him by his father's purchase (of 5,000 acres) to 800 of which, by his will, the said George hath a Right, requests the Comm'rs would Commiserate his Condition and favour him in the Location of the said Land.

Ordered that all the favour within the Commiss'rs power shall be shewn to the said George in the said Location and that when he hath pitched on the County the Surveyor Shall have directions accordingly.

George Palmer and John Palmer, Sons of George Palmer purchaser of 5,000 acres, Caveat against granting a Patent to Jos. Growdon for his Land on Neshamineh untill they can have a Fair hearing for 500 a's laid out in the Bounds of the Lands he claims to their Mother, the Widow Palmer, about which there is a Controversy depending.

There having been Survey'd to Sam'll Allen 500 acres in South'ton, Bucks, granted by said Sam'll in his Will, dated 14, 10 mo., '99, granted of the same 200 acres to his Son, Sam'l Allen, and 300 a's to his Grandsons, John, Sam'll and Rich'd Parkers, who have all Sold to Tho. Sisom and he to Dan'll Pritchet, but no Deed past. Sam'll Allen having a right to take up 160 acres more by the same Will, he granted it to said Sisom, who Requests a Resurvey and Patent. Ordered a Resurvey forthwith, and when all parties have made a Deed to said Pritchet a Patent shall be granted.

The Comm'rs granted to John Prew a Warr't dat. 18 Feb'ry, '92-3, for 100 a's in Rockland joyning on the land where he lives, on New Rent, directed to James Claypoole, who never Survey'd it, but said John has entred and Cleared, he had 100 acres More.

The same Comm'rs, by Warrant of the same date, granted to Oliver Cope likewise 70 acres adjoyning on the Land where he lived, being 130 acres. They request a Confirmation of the s'd Land. Granted to John Prew 60 a's, not to Come Eastward of his old line, and to Wm. Cope, son and Heir of said Oliver, 45 acres not to exceed his Western line nor to come over the King's Road, but to take in all the Land between the said Prew's Eastern Line and Cope's Western Line, their head Lines and the King's Road, provided it take in no more than the said quantity, and if it should, then to leave the Vacancy above the Road. Rent 1d p. acre.

John Grubb affirms he purchased of Conradt Constantine his right to a Warr't from the Gov'r for 70 acres in the C. of Newc., dat. 5, 10 mo., '83, which warrant the said John caused to be Executed on the Land below Naaman's Creek, desired by Jasper Yeats, and of which he produces a draught Under J. Peirson's hand, and there is another also in the Office but Seems not allowed of. The said Grubb offers to resign the said Land to the Prop'ry in Exch. for a Small parcel on the North East Side of the Land he now holds and between the line of it and Isaac and David's Run.

Ordered that in Consideration that the Land on Naaman's Creek is Valuable and much desired by some that Sue for it, who would bring in another Title upon it, the said parcel be granted as requested, provided it exceed not 50 a's and that the said John Grubb procure a full release from C. Constantine for the Land afores'd.

———

At a Session of the Commissioners at Philadelphia 25th and 26th 11 mo., 1702.

Present, Griffith Owen, Thomas Story, James Logan.

The Prop'ry, by Patent dated 21, 5 mo., '84, confirmed to Lasse Andrews, Wm. Stille, Andrew Bankson and John Matson, their Heirs, &c., a certain parcel of Fast Land in Moyamensynck beginning at a Corner Hickery of Passayunck, running by Passa. Line North 272 p'ches to a Corner Spanish Oak of

Passa. Lands, then N. E. 116 p'ches to a Swamp Oak in Shackhanoing, the Corner of Wicac, Lands, then S. E. by S. by Wic. Lands 300 p'ches to a white oak by the Swamp, thence by the Swamp to a Corner Mulberry on Ranakens' hook, thence by said hook to an Oak Saplin, thence by the Swamp to the first hickery by Several Courses, First granted to Martin Clensmith, Wm. Stile and Lawr. Andrews from Alexander Haynoyassa, Gov'r of South River in America, by Patent 3 June, '64, and Resurvey'd by Propr's Warrant dated 13, 4 mo., '83, to the said first persons in 4 equal Shares, q'ty 525 acres in the whole, and by the same patent also two parcels of Meadow, the one beginning at a Corner Marked Spanish Oak in Holland'rs Creek, thence S. W. 93 p'ches to a Black Oak by Hay Creek, thence N. W. 40 p'ches to an Oak on a Swamp, thence by the Swamp to an Ash on said Holland'rs Creek, thence to the first Oak, the place of beginning, being 32 a's. The other beginning at a Poplar on Hay Creek, thence E. by S. 83 p'ches to an Ash by the Swamp, thence by the same 176 p'ches to a black oak on Rosamond Creek, thence N. by W. 160 p'ches to the place of beginning cont. 31 a's, the whole 63 acres granted to said first persons from Upland Court for 100 a's, but took by them for the whole, being 588 acres, was granted to be held in equal Shares among the said L. A., W. S., A. B. and J. M.

Andrew Bankson holds his ¼, John, Son of Wm. Stille, holds his, Andrew Wheeler holds Lasse Andrews', and the Widow Nailor, Relict of John King, holds Matson's.

Andrew Bankson desires a Resurvey on his ¼ in the same Warr't with Passayunck, John Stille his Share also to be resurvey'd.

Lawr. Andrews, by his last will, dated 17, 5 mo., 1689, devised all that his House and Plantation in Moyamensinck to Michael Nelson, Sen'r, and Andreas Wheeler, with all Orchards, Meadows, Pastures and App's whatsoever, equally between them.

M. Neilson by Deed dated   , Granted to s'd Wheeler all his right and Title in and to the said Plantation, who requests a resurvey and Patent and that each may have the 50 acres of Swamp formerly granted by the Prop'ry, Survey'd and Confirmed. Granted 3 Warrant.

The Comm'rs, by Patent dated 12, 4 mo., '89, Granted to Dan'll Smith 32 a's of L. Land granted by Warrant dated 24, 9 mo., '86, beginning at a Corner post of Tho. Callowhill.

Also by Patent of the same date they granted to s'd Smith 8 a's in right of Tho. Hatt, beginning at a Corner post of the above. Rand. Spakeman requests a Resurvey on the whole. Granted.

Benjamin Furlow having been agent for the Prop'ry in disposing of all his Lands sold to Foreigners and having always been in expectation of Lib. Land but has obtained None as Yet, and having wrote several times closely about it, and now again to his attornies, Dan'l and Justus Falkner, as by his Letters produced appears. Ord'd that a positive Warr't be granted for 50 a's W. Side of Skuylkll, not to prejudice any further Grant from the Prop'ry if Obtained, and to lay out such Lotts as fall to him.

The Prop'rs, by L., and Rel. dated 22 and 23 March, 1681, granted to Rob't Turner 5,000 acres of Land at the yearly Rent of 1s p. 100, and Ind'r. dated 15 August, '82, Released to the said R. T. 45s of the said Rent to the end that 5 shillings only should be paid for the whole 5,000 a's, and by like Indentures dated 3 and 4 July, '82, granted to John Gee, of King's C., in Ireland, Tanner, 2,500 a's at 1s p. 100, his Heirs and assigns, and Jno. Gee by like Ind'res, dat. 8 and 9 Sept'r, 1685, granted the said 2,500 a's to the s'd Rob't Turner, and by like Ind'res, dated 3 and 4 July, '82, the Prop'ry granted to Jos. Fuller, of King's C'ty, in Ireland, his Heirs, &c., 1,250 a's at 1s p. 100, and the said Jos. Fuller by like Ind'res, dated 29 and 30 7br., '85, granted the s'd 1,250 a's to Robert Turner, and by like Ind'res dated 3 and 4 July, '81, the Prop'ry granted to Jacob Fuller, of the said County, his Heirs, &c., 1,250 a's, who by like Ind'res, dated 8 and 9 Mar., 1685, Granted to Rob't Turner, his Heirs, &c., who became Interested by the said Several Deeds in 10,000 a's, part whereof was granted to the s'd Robert Turner by 4 Several Warr'ts from the Prop'ry, 1st dated 17, 5 mo., '83, for 1,000 a's, the 2d 14, 12 mo., '83, for 5,600 a's, the 3d 16, 3 mo., '84, for 720 a's, the 4th 16, 3 mo., '84, for 500 a's, in all 7,820 a's, all which was Laid out in one Tract in Philadelphia County.

Robert Turner being so Seized of the said 7,820 acres of Land afores'd, by Deed Poll dated 10, 1 mo., '98-9, granted the same to Wm. John and Thomas Evan, both of the County of Philadelphia, Yeomen, to hold to them, their Heirs and assigns for Ever under the yearly Quittrent accruing.

Wm. John and Tho. Evan, by Several deeds dated 5, 4 mo., 1699, Granted to:

Ellis or Da'd Pugh 220 Acres now found to Cont. 231 Overplus.

	Acres.	Overplus.			
Evan Hugh,	100	110			
John Hugh,	500	648	98	£19	12
John Humphrey,	450	561	66	13	4
Rob't ap Evan,	5,005	1,034	484	96	16
Edward Faulk,	400	712	272	54	08

	Acres.	Overplus.		
Robert Jones, ...	500	720	170	34
Robert Evan, ...	200	250	30	6
Evan ap Hugh,*	400 ⎫			
Da'd Pugh,*	200 ⎬	1,068	298	59 12
Edw'd Pugh,*	100 ⎭			
Cadwall'dr ap Evan, . .	500	609	59	11 16
Owen ap Evan, ...	400	538	98	19 12
Rob't ap Hugh, ...	200	232	12	2 8
Wm. John, ...	1,900	2,866	776–767	153 8
Tho. Evan, ...	700	1,049	†279	55 16
Will'm John, ...	‡150	322	157	31 8
Evan Rob't, ...	100	110	. . . .	. . . .
Hugh Griffith, ...	300	376	46	9 4
	7,820	11,436	2,846	569

* Brother; ye 2 Latt'r dead; Evan holds all and is found.
† All'd 9 A's for Ellis Da'd.
‡ In anoth'r pla'e.

Bound.	Oblig.	Cond.
Wm. John, Rob't John, Edw'd Faulk,	£370 5 5	£185 2 8½
Rob't John, Wm. John, Edw'd Faulk,	69 9 7½	34 14 9¾
Edw'd Faulk, Rob't John, Wm. John,	94 15 8½	47 7 10¼
Tho. Evan, Cadw. ap Evan, Rob't ap Hugh, ...	102 1 5½	51 0 8¾
Cadw. ap Evan, Tho. Evan, Rob't ap Hugh, ...	31 1 7½	15 10 9¾
Rob't ap Hugh, C. E., T. E., ...	7 15 10	3 17 11
Owen ap Evan, Robert Evan, ...	35 3 8	17 11 10
Robert Evan, Owen ap Evan, ...	181 1 7	90 10 9¾
Rob't Evan, Evan ap Hugh, ...	14 19 10	7 9 11
Evan ap Hugh, Rob't Evan, ...	119 13 5½	59 16 8¾
Jno. Humphry, Jno. Hugh, ...	38 6 8	19 3 4
Jno. Hugh, Jno. Humphry, ...	36 13 7½	18 6 9¾
Hugh Griffith & Son, ...	22 17 9½	11 8 10¾
Rob't John, ...		£3
Owen ap Ev., ...		5
Wm. John,*		15
Tho. Ev.*, ...		10
Rob't Evan, ...		10
Jno. Hugh, ...		5
Edw'd Faulk, ...		10
Evan Pugh, ...		5
		£63

* P'd by to Ja. Log.

MINUTE BOOK "G." 357

The Prop'ry granted to Geo. Palmer 5,000 Acres by L. and Rel., dat. 21st and 22 Apr., '82, who, by his last Will, gave to his Wife 1,000 And to his 5 Children, Geo., Jno., Thos., Wm. and Elizabeth, now wife of Ralph Jackson, each 800 A's. Elizabeth Sold 500 A's of her's and has the remaining 300 in Whitpains Township, the Widow has 500 at the head of Moreland and 500 in dispute on Nesham. Wm. has his share in Whitpains T'p, and in the same place John has 300; there is also laid out 80 Acres of Lib. Land to be allowed out of said John's, the whole laid out is 2,980 besides that in dispute. There remains untaken up to Geo. 800, to Tho. 800, and to John 420, for which they desire War'ts. Ordered that Geo. his share be laid out according to the Order of 18 Inst't in the most Commodious place in the Great Swamp or elsewhere, and two Warrants to John and Thomas for theirs.

Ordered a Patent to H. Sproegel, he giving a Bill for £26 13s 4d Sterl., to be paid in England with Security.

At a Session of the Commissioners at Philadelphia 1 and 2, 12th Month, 1702.

Tho. Brock having a Right to 22 Acres of Land in Bristol Township as at large appears in the Secretaries Minutes, under S. Carp'r, 28, 5 mo., 1701, upon a Resurvey there is found 30 A's, 48 p'ches, out of which 2 A's being allowed there remains 6 A's, 48 p'ches to be p'd for. Agreed to pay. Ordered a Patent to said Tho. upon a due Return for s'd

Henry Pierce produces a return of 200 A's Survey'd 18, 12 mo., 1685-6, by Tho. Pierson in pursuance of a Warr't for Tho. Holme dated 14, 2 mo., '85, (as is recited therein) to James Widdows Situate on the West Side of Brandywine about 5 Miles.

Peter Taylor producing a Return of Resurvey of 421 A's upon his Tract of 350 by a Warrant dated 6, 1 mo., 1700-1, also a Return of 229 Acres of New Land on a War't for 265 A's, dated 10th 10br. last. Ordered a Patent.

Ordered a Patent to Benj. Furly on 1,000 Acres in Bucks, and Patents on 2,900 Acres More in Philadelphia County.

Jos. Richards, of Witny, in Oxf'd Coun., purchased of the Prop'ry 500 A's by L. and Rel., dated 11 and 12, '81, in right of which there was Survey'd to him by Cha. Ascomb a Tract joyning on Wm. Woodmansey and Meadow laid out for the said quantity of 500 Acres.

There being 150 Acres of Overplus found in Matthias Fosses' Tract and about 50 A's Vacant adjoyning in Christ'a Hundred near Geo. Harland's, Jacob's Vander Cullen applying for it, 'tis offered at £18 p. C't.

Appointed that John Beal, Jos. Rich'ds, Sen'r and Jun'r, and Ewd'd Carter meet the 22 and 23 dayes Instant before the Commissioners.

Ordered that a Patent be granted to Jeremiah Cloud for 500 A's and the Overplus, leaving out those two Small Sleps that fall in Chester C'ty, and that John Prew be not Suffred to invade his Lines.

Ordered a Patent to Tho. Hollworth for 400 Acres.

The Prop'ry, by Deeds of L. and Rel., dated 23 and 24, 1 mo., '81, granted to Elizabeth Lovett 250 Acres and Sold to Edm'd Lovet, in Province, 50 A's more, all which was Confirmed to him by Patent 27, 5 mo., '84. Samuel Smith Intermarryed with the said Elizabeth and by Deed Poll dat'd 10, 8 mo., 1700, the said Sam'll and Elizab. granted to the said Edw'd 150 A's part of her said purchase and part of the Afores'd Patent by which he became Seized of 200 A's and procured a Resurvey thereon together with 2 Small Tracts of Vacant Land by Warr't dated 11, 11 mo., 1700, upon the execution of which there was found 333 Acres. He further produces an Order under the Prop'ry's own hand to J. L. in these Words:

20th, 8 mo., 1701.

James Logan: These are to require thee to draw up a Warrant for two hundred Acres of Land for George Brown, of the County of Bucks, as a Purchaser and prepare a Patent for me to Execute if possible before I goe, else to be done by the Comm'rs when gone. Also lett Edm'd Lovett his Pat't including his Overplus having Satisfied me for the same.

Requests a Patent and the Warr't for Brown. Both granted.

Daniel Williamson and Evan Lewis, Ex'ors of Tho. Norbury's Estate, have, by Deed to be drawn, dated this Instant, Convey'd to Ellis Hughes the said Tho.'s whole Tract found on Resurvey to Contain 200 Acres of which there is 190 Acres due to the said Tho., the other 10 cutt off on the Creek.

Whereas the Land agreed to be given to J. Grubb between his Land and Is. and Da'ds Run is found to be part of the Land purchased of Wm. Stocdale, w'ch we have not power to grant.

Ordered that the s'd agreem't be Void.

Ordered that the grant of Prud. West, page 93, be declared Void, she not having Complyed with the agreement and is since deceased.

Agreed with John Lea for £10 for his Overplus, viz: 30 Acres above the 100 granted to him in Concord.

Joel Baily applying for 200 A's at the Back of Peter Dix, South of Brandywine. Ordered that it be not Sold til Is. Few resign the 600 he bought which we are informed he is about to doe, and then that the Price be sett £20 p. C't. Rent as it can be had.

Ordered that a Patent be forthwith passed to Capt. Finney for his Land bought of John Tyzack for 150 Acres, found upon a Resurvey to Contain 187 Acres, it being found that the 100 A's he purchased from the Prop'ry encroach'd upon T. Lloyd's Lands which he has Since bought and upon a Resurvey was found Deficient in quantity by that Means.

At a Session of the Commissioners at Philadephia fifteenth 12th Month, 1702.

Present, Edward Shippen, Thomas Story, James Logan.

The Prop'ry, by Patent, dated 6, 5 mo, '84, Granted to Rich'd Lundy 200 Acres of Land Situate in the County of Bucks at a penny p. Acre, laid out 10, 6 mo.. '82-3. R'd Lundy by Ind'r, dated 8, 7 mo., '85, Granted the said Land to Jacob Telnor, his Heirs, &c.,* Who, by Deed, dated 1, 6 mo., '98, Granted the same to Albertus Brandt and his Wife Susannah, who, by their Deed, dat. 4, 2 mo., 1700, granted the same to Arth. Cook. Marg't Cook and John Cook, Heirs of the s'd Arthur, by Deed, dated 19, 5 mo., 1700, Convey'd the s'd Tract to Edw'd Wanton of Situate in Plymouth, in New England.* While the above Land was in Jacob Telnor's possession, the Prop'ry, by a Writing under his hand dat. 9, 8 mo., '93, Released all the Quittrents from the begining and granted them at 2s p. C't Sterl., from that time.

Tob. Dymocke having procured a Warr't of Resurvey dat. 27, 12 mo., 1700, on 250 Acres, and another Warr't of the same date to take up the like quantity in full of 500 A's, the purchase of Nath'l Hardin; the first being executed is found to Contain 300 A's, viz: 30 A's above Measure, he requests the same may be deducted according to Law, out of the other that is to be taken up, which is granted and a Patent upon the 300. For the Title See Secretaries Office 24, 12 mo., 1700. Ordered a Warrant for 220 Acres recalling the former.

Tob. Dymocke, for Edw'd Wanton, requests a New Patent for the s'd Land being resurvey'd by J. Cutler and found to Contain 203 A's without Warrant. Granted.

Ordered that a Patent be granted to Wm. Howel for the Land he holds that is out of dispute and that Da. Powel make returns of the said Land accordingly, and Also of the other 800 A's with an Accot. what Overplus is contained in Each Man's present possession.

Matts. V. Bebber producing a Return of Resurvey on his

Warrant for 5,000 Acres, the same is found to Contain 6,166, of which 5,500 being his due by purchase and a Cl of Law, and 251 remaining untaken up of his other 1,000 (there having been laid out in Germantown to Dirk Sipman 588 A's, and to Gov't Ramkes 161), all which making 5,751 A's and deducted out of 6,166 there remains 415 A's overplus for which he agrees to pay £60, the whole to be at one Sh. p. M.

He further produces a Return of 70 A's Lib. Land resurvey'd in pursuance of our Warrant dated 14, 10ber last, in right of D. Sipman, 10 in right of Gov't Ramkes and 10 in right of Jacob Isaacs, his Father, all which he requests may be Confirmed to him. Ordered that Patents be granted accordingly.

Whereas there was Survey'd to Joshua Hastings on Skuylkill a Lott in right of his purchase which he, the said Joshua, Sold by Deed dated 19, 6 mo., 1700, to Wm. Edw'ds, who, by a Deed, dated the next day, viz: 20th, Granted the same to Tho. Story.

Tho. Story requests the said Lott may be confirmed to him with the whole Bank to the water side, which is Granted.

Ordered that the Prop'ry's Pleasure be inquired concerning the 1,000 Acres granted to the said T. Story by Patent, dated 8, 2 mo., 1700, Situate above the Manor of Highlands which land is now all Survey'd away, the Prop'ry also gave a receipt for £33 6d 8s Consideration Money thereof.

Application being made by Geo. Dakeyne in behalf of 6 persons that would Settle, each with their Families, at Conestogoe.

At the request of Edw'd Shippen, That, whereas he hath purchased of Wm. Gieach a Small Lott in the 3d Street at the foot of his pasture and another of John Martin, and there being a third Vacant there all Situate between the end of Walnut Lotts and his pasture, requests the whole to be granted in Fee, extending to the fourth Street for which agrees to pay £17 10s, including all arrears, the Rent to be 2 Shill's for the whole. Ordered a Warrant for the same and Patent on the Return.

The Prop'ry, by Lease and Rel., dated 19 and 20 Mar., '82, granted to Wm. Bennet, in Longford in the Parish of Harmondsworth, Coun. Mid'sex, yeoman, 1,000 Acres of Land, he, by his last will, dated 9 August, '83, devised to his Daughter Ann and her Heirs for ever 200 Acres, and to his Daughter Rebecca and her Heirs 200 Acres. Ann Bennet and Rebecca B., by their Deed Poll, dated 5 July, 1700, granted to Wm. Stevenson, of West Jersey, Yeom., all their Right, Title, &c., in the said Land with, a Covenant for further Assurance, in pursuance of which Covenant they procured a Warr't from the Prop'ry dat. 15, 6 mo., 1700, to take up the said Land which was executed and Returned by the Surveyor Gen'll, Situate on the South Side of Brandywine, Chester, of which Ann, deceased, and her Sister Sarah, wife of Rob't Edw'ds, of Burl'ton, Cooper, and the said Rebecca, since intermarryed with John Scholah, of the Coun. Burl., Jer., becoming her Heirs, by a Deed Poll dat. 13 Apr., 1702, joyntly with their husbands further Convey'd the said Land as locateed to said William Stevenson, who, by Deed poll, dated 14 Apr., 1702, granted the same to Sarah Pennington, who requests a Confirm. Granted.

At a Session of the Commissioners at Philadelphia 22 and 23, 12th Month, 1702.

Present, Omnes.

Peter Dix having procured a Warrant for 300 acres on the South side of Brandywine for £50, which he hath paid, and having, by agreem't, taken up the whole vacancy there, which proves 554 a's, viz: 254 above the grant. Agreed that he shall have the s'd 254 a's for £45 and a Patent be granted for the whole.

Joseph Cloud, Sen'r, requesting a Vacant piece of Land left by Chest'r County Line out ot the Manor of Rocklands, joyning on Nathan'll Newlin's 200 acres and Henry Gunston, the same is granted for £45, to be paid in 30 days.

Ordered a Patent on 225 acres Survey'd to Wm. Lovet and Jam's Wood in pursuance of our Warrant for said Quantity dated

Robert French having purchased of Maj'r Donaldson his 2 front Lotts in the Strand in Newc. of 60 foot each, requests the Bank before the same. Granted.

The above Jos. Cloud having proved himself to have come into the Country a Servant to John Bezer, with the first Setlers. Ordered a War't for his 50 acres of head Land.

The Comm'rs having Sold to Hugh Roberts 200 a's and granted a War't for 100 thereof, dat. 1, 4 mo., '88, to Kath. Thomas, to whom he sold the s'd quantity, to be laid out in the Welch Tract. Thomas, in behalf of himself and his Brother Cadw., Ex'ors of the said Kath, Their Mother, requests a Warrant for the said Land. Granted w'th a proviso that it be not taken up.

Robert French producing a Return on 487 acres for 500 purchased of Maurice Liston by Deed dated   , also proved a right to 178 acres between himself and Maj'r Donaldson, as by Newc. Min's appears, which proves 312 a's, and having purchased Maj'r Donaldson's right to his share p. writing, dat. , (both to be produced), of w'ch there is allowed 17 acres for Measure and 13 a's to Make up the other Defficiency, there remains 104 acres, for which he agrees to pay £10 and requests a Patent for both in one, which is granted.

Ordered a Warrant of Resurvey on 85 a's purchased by the said Rob't of Wm. Hawkins, laid out in right of a grant to Alex'dr Chance, assigned to Geo. Martin, whose widow, adm'x, Sold it to said Hawkins, Situate between said Robert's Land and Geo. Martin's on S. W. Branch of Duck Creek.

The Prop'ry granted to Wm Cecil, of Longcomb, Coun. Oxford, Carp'r, 250 a's of Land by Ind'r. dat. 11 and 12, 8br., '81, in pursuance of which Th. Holme Issued a Warrant (which is produced) dat. 11, 6, 1682, directed to Cha. Ashcomb, to Survey to the said Wm. Cecil 247 acres Contigious to Edward Carter's Land on the South Side of Upland Cr., and by the return of said Carter's Land uuder Tho. Holme's hand, now in the Secretaries' Office; the said Carter's L'd is bounded by the said Wm. Cecil's Land, running E. N. E. 400 p's on the same. It further appears by an acc't under Ch. Ashcomb's own hand, of what returns he had made into Tho. Holme's Office, that he had Survey'd to the said Wm. Cecil 125 acres and to Anthony Weaver the same Quantity, who purchased it of Wm. and Came Over with Orders to take up the Remainder as Well as his Own Share; it also appears by an acc't under Rob't Longshore's hand of what returns had been made by Ch. Ashcomb into ye said Tho's Office. Upon a Suit of the said Tho. ags't the said Ch. for his fees, that such returns were made by all which it appears that such a Survey was duly made.

But Jos. Richards, purchaser of 500 a's, having First taken up and also Obtained a Confirmation of the whole said Quantity, further produces a Patent under the Prop'rs hand dated 25, 5 mo., '84, for that very Tract that is presumed to have been laid out to Cecil as aforesaid.

Ann Cecil, Widow, and Tho. Cecil, son of the said Wm., by Ind'r. of Lease dated 25 February, '85, demised one Moiety of the said 250 a's to Jos. Richards, of New Esale, in the parish of Witney, Coun. Oxon, Mason, for the Space of 999 Years from the date of the said Lease, and the said Jos., by Indorsm't on the said Lease, dated 9, 4 mo., '91, assigned the said Moiety, located in Aston T'p, to Edward Carter, of the said Township, in Ch. Coun., Yeoman, for the term then not Expired, who Claims thereby, and Jos. Richards, Sen'r, by his s'd Pat't.

The Prop'ry Issued a Warr't of Resurvey, dat. 26, 7 mo., 1701, for Resurveying the whole Tract of 1,000 a's, of which Jos. Richards, Sen'r, was purchaser of 500 acres, E. Carter 250, and Wm. Cecil 250. Jos. Richards gave of his 500 acres, by Deed dat. 10, 1 mo., '91, to his son, Nath'll Rich'ds, who sold it to R'd Barnard.

Wm. Cecil, by Ind'r. of Lease and Release, dat. 20 Feb'y, '81, granted to Anth. Weaver, of Charlbury Par., Coun. Oxon, Blacksmith, 125 acres, the Moiety of his 250 a's, who deceasing, left his Brother, Wm. Weaver, his Heir, who by his deed dated the last February, 1702, Granted the same to Humphry Scarlet, of the County of Chester, who by Deed dated 2d 1 mo., '92, Sold 75 acres thereof to Nath'll Richards, who Sold this 75 acres together with the above mentioned 100 acres by Indenture, Dated 14, 1 mo., '93-4, to the said Rich'd Barnard, whose Widdow Frances now holds the same for her son and Heir, Rich'd Barnard, and is found on resurvey to Contain exactly 175 acres, the Just Complem't.

Humphry Scarlet holds the remaining 50 and is found to Cont. 52. Jos. Rich'ds, Sen'r, holds his remaining 400. Robert Carter, Son of Edw'd Carter, holds his 250 and Claims the aforesaid 125, and upon Resurvey is found to Contain 380 acres.

Humphry Scarlet also purchased of John Kinsman, of Chich'r Coun. Che'r, Original Purchaser, 50 acres, bounded by his Deed dated 3, 4 mo., 1690, for Which together with his other 52 he requests a patent. Ordered that the same be granted, the first part of 52 acres, according to Is. Taylor's Return, the other 50 according to the Bounds of the Deed.

Ordered also a Patent to R'd Barnard, Heir to R'd aforesaid, for 175 acres, according to the said Bounds.

Rob't French haveing Obtained an Execution for £75 In Kent County against the Estate of George Martin, had Part of the Same levied On 180 acres of Land in the said County, Called Golden Grove, Joining On Francis Iron's, Near the S. West Branch of Duck Creek. Requests a Resurvey upon the whole.

Jos. Pennock, Son of Christopher Pennock, deceased, and Heir of all the Lands untaken up or Indisposed of, of Wm. and George Rogers, their Purchase of 5,000 acres, haveing Come into this Province to Look after his Father's Estate and the said Land, and being about to Return to Ireland, Requests Warr'ts to take up the Remainder, which is Computed to be about   But because 'tis uncertain Whether the said Christopher may not have taken up more than Warrants or Returns may appear for in the office, Ordered that Warrants be Granted to the said Joseph for   acres.

Jno. Gibbons, of Ches. County, Turn'r, having Long disputed a Priviledge with Jeremy Collet to the takeing up 200 acres of Land in Rocklands, in which the said Jeremy had Entered and Cleared a part of and having at Length Come to an agreement with the said Jerem., By an arbitration, who thereupon has quitted all Claim to the said Lands as by an award of the arbitrators duely Executed and dated 23 Inst. appears.

Ord'd that a Warrant be Granted to the said John Gibbons for 200 acres, he Paying for the Same £60 at or before ye 10, 2 mo. next.

Bartho. Coppock, Jun'r, haveing Purchased of Jno. Nixon 300 acres, P't of his Own Purchase, and of Thomas Hope 109 acres being Part of Ebenezer Langford's Purchase, both Contigious and Situate in Mapple T'p. in C. County, Requests a resurvey On both In one, and will Produce his title with the Return in order to a Patent.

A Warrant to Mau. Llewellin to Resurvey 500 acres of Holland's Purchase, Vid. Wel. Min's.

The Prop'ry, by L. and Rel., dat. 17 and 18, 8ber, Granted to John Tovey, of London, Grocer, 1,250 acres of Land in the Province.

John Tovey and Abiah Taylor, of Harwell, in Coun. Berks, Mercer, By L. and Rel., dat. ye 5 March, 1701, Between the said John Tovey and Abiah Taylor and Caleb Tovey, of Henley on Thames, Malster, did each of them Grant and Transferr to the said Caleb Tovey all that the said 1,250 acres of Land in this Province, then belonging to the said John, and the Reversion of a Certain Messuage, being the Right Of the said Abiah To have and to hold the said Caleb, his Heirs and assigns, to the Uses following, viz: the said 1,250 a's to the Only use and behoof of the said Abiah Taylor, his Heirs, &c., and the said Messuage to the Only use and behoof of the said John Tovey, his Heirs, &c.

The Prop'ry, by an order under his hand and Seal, dated at London, 27, 4 mo., 1702, directed to his Comm'rs E. S., G. O. and J. L., Required us to Grant Warrants to Henry Child, Purchaser of 1,000 acres in his Own Right and to said Abiah Taylor, Purchaser of 1,250 acres, in Right of the said Tovey, for taking up the Same and to Pass Patents When Returned, according to Custom and Regulation.

Upon which the said Abiah requests Warrants for the said 1,250 a's.

Ordered two Warrants to the said Abiah for 500 acres each (he having sold the Other 250 to R'd Lewin.)

———

At a Session of the Comm's at Philad'a 5 and 6, 2 mo., 1703. Pr't, Ed'd Shippen, Griff. Owen. Jas. Lo.

The Prop'ry, by L. and Rel., dat. 1 and 2 August, 1681, Granted to Antho. Elton, of Yatesbury, in the County of Wilts,

Yeoman, 500 acres of land. Antho. Elton deceasing, his Son and Heir, Antho. Elton, of Burlington, in W. N. Jersey, Yeoman, by Deed Poll dated 12, 9ber, 1702, sold to Edward Smout 400 a's, Called the Remainder of the said Purchase.

John Wheeler, of the said Purchase, has by Warrant, dated 1, 10 mo., '86, taken up 100 acres Situate in Bucks and Joyning on Wm. Say. There is also 8 acres Taken up in the Liberties, the remaining 392 acres the said Edw'd Smout requests to take up.

Ordered that a Warrant be granted for the s'd quantity.

Benjamin White, Youngest Son of Geo White, whose Purchase is Mentioned Pag. 45, by Deed Poll dated 24, 12 mo., 1702, sold to Jere. Langhorn, of Bucks, his share there, mentioned to be 250 a's, for which the said Jere. Requests a Warrant. Granted if to be laid out forthwith and not allowed already.

Dan'l and Justus Falkner Producing D. Powell's return of a Warrant for 50 a's Lib. Land Surveyed to Benj. Furly. Ordered a Pat't thereupon when Examined in the Office together with an High Street Lott of 132 foot as it fell in the Draught.

Present, T. Story.

Jno. Arthur requesting a Grant of some Land in the Man'r of Gilberts, agreed with him for 500 a's to be laid out in the upper end or side regularly with the whole lines of the said Man'r at £20 p'r 100. In Part of which he is to Pay what he Can Procure in Hand; to Pay Interest for the whole from the date of the Warrant and give Sufficient Security for the rest, the Whole to be Paid 25th 1 mo., 1704.

Sam'l Carp'r, attorney for Alexand'r Parker, Produceing a Warrant from the Comm'rs dat. 11, 6 mo., '85, for laying out the said Alexander 1,250 acres, which both he and Tho. Fairman, the Survey'r, affirm was Surveyed adjoining to the said Samuel's land, together w'th Samuel's, but upon Inquiry the said Alexand'r is found to be Purchaser Only of 1,000 acres. Samuel Carpenter, in behalf of his Constituent, Craves a Resurvey on ye said 1,000 acres, deducting the Liberty Land. Granted.

Isaac Few, haveing by Deed dat'd 28 day of 5 mo. last, Corveyed to Robert Pennell and Benjam'n Mendenhall, both in the County of Chester, Yeoman, all his Right, title and Interest in and to 600 acres of Land on Brandywine Granted to the said Isaac by us at £15 p'r C't., of which they have duely Paid, and there being also a Small Parcell of Vacant Land between the same and the Land of Geo. Harland, Judged to Contain about 50 a's. The said Robert and Benjamin request a Warrant for the said Vacant Land upon the Same Terms with the Other. Granted to be Paid upon Survey.

Abiah Taylor haveing Come over on Purpose to Settle in this Place and not finding any Convenient, requests that he may take up the Rem'r of that Vacant tract Where Tho. Buffington is seated in Right of the Purchase of Jn. Tovey, mentioned Pa. ; but this not being to be granted 'tis Offered in Consideration of his Sufferings in Comeing into this Place that he shall have the said Land, Paying for the Same £7 10s p'r C't in Each, at or before 24, 4 mo. next; 20 ac's Lib. Land to be deducted.

Rich'd Halliwell Produceing a return for 400 a's of Land surveyed in the County of Newc., in Pursuance of the Prop'rs Warrant for the said Quantity, requests a Patent for the Same. Granted, it appearing Clear and Claimed by no Other Person.

John Chandler haveing Purchased 132 foot On the High Str., being S. Carp'rs Lott and 3 lotts on Mulberry Street, each 49½ foot, Viz: E. Crew's, Pask's and Simkins, between 4 and 5 streets, of Th. Buy, There is left a Vacancy of about 44 foot, the whole Length of the said 3 lotts, Between the Ends of each which he requests to Purchase, and agrees to give £5 for the Same and 1 Shilling sterl. quitt Rent from 1 mo. last, Provided he finish the Whole before 3d Month next.

At a Session of the Comm'rs at Philad'a 12 and 13, 2 mo., 1703. Present, Griff. Owen, James Logan.

Rich'd Few, Original Purchaser of 500 acres, sold to Jas. Jacob ten acres of Land to be laid out in the liberties but never Conveyed it, and thereupon the said Jacob sold the Same to Adam Roades, of Darby, in Coun. Chester, but being unable to make any title Isaac Few, Son and Heir to the said Rich'd Few, and the said James Jacob, by one deed, dated 24, 9ber, 1702, did Joyntly Convey to the said Adam Roades the said 10 ac's of Lib. Land, who requests a Warrant Or take up the same adjoyning On the Land he Purchased of Christopher Pennock.

Jno. Simcock, Purchaser of 5,000 a's, haveing a Right to One Lott in the Front of 102 foot, and another in the High Street of 132 foot, both which were laid out, he bequeathed them to his son and Heir, Jacob Simcock, who requests a Confirmation of the Same. Granted a Warrant to be issued.

In Right of Jno. Simcock's aforesaid Purchase there was laid out to him two tracts in Ridley Township, one for 1,100 acres and the Other 1,000, beside 200 bought of John Test and 10 acres more added, adjoyning Overplus from the Prop'ry, being in the whole 2,310. Of which he has sold to Cha. Whiteacre 100, Jno. Stedman 110, Jno. Halliwell 100, Vincent Cordwell 100, Sam'l Hall 100, Henry Swift 80 a's, and Wm. Smith 60 a's, and has remaining 1,660 acres, On which Jacob Simcock requests a Resurvey, haveing the whole Right to the same as follows:

Jno. Simcock's, by Deed of Gift Dated   , gave to his said Son 940 acres, being the remainder of the Tract of 1,100 acres (100 being first Sold to John Halliwell and 60 to Jo'n Stedman), of which 940 he has sold to s'd Stedman, 50 more to Cordwell 100, To Hall 100 and to W. Smith 60, and has of the s'd Tract 360 Remaining. Jno. Simcock, out of the Tract of 1,210 acres sold to Cha. Whitacre 100 acres and to H. Swift 80 acres and the remaining 1,030 he, by his last will, Dated   , Bequeathed to his said Son Jacob, and Order'd a Resurvey as Requested.

The Settlers in the Welch Tract Produceing the following returns in Pursuance Of the severall Warrants issued last year Requests Patents for the Same as follows: Rowland Ellis Purchased of Rich'd Davies 1,100 a's, of w'ch he had 500 remaining in Meirion and 483 in Goshen (ye Other 117 sold), Which Proved in Meirion 881 a's, in Goshen 341, the whole 1,222 and is 39 a's Over pl., for which he agrees to Pay £12, 10s, and a patent is Ordered thereupon. He is to Pay for the Over pl. 12 Shillings p'r acre.

Jno. Rob'ts, of his Purchase of J. Thomas and Ed'd Jones, had 306½ a's, Part in Goshen and Part in Meirion, which being Resurveyed proves in Meirion 108 and in Goshen 262, the whole, 370, which is 33½ Over, of which 25 In Meirion and 8½ in Goshen also 150 in right of Rich'd Davies, which Proves but 130, And therefore 20 must be discounted Out of the Above and there remains 13½ Acres of the above to be Cutt Off, Also 60 a's of Andreas Wheeler, which Proves 113 and is 47 Over; lies in the Libertys, to be Cutt Off.

Hugh Roberts, of John Thomas and E. T. 67¾ and of Jno. ap John and T. W. 482, in the whole 549¾, also in Right of s'd Jno. ap John 200 and in Right of Peter Young 500, both Granted by One Warr't from the Prop'ry, 3, 7 mo., 1701, And in Right of the Society 100 a's, the Whole 1,349¾, in right of which there is laid out in Goshen 338 to themselves and in the said Place in the same right Possesst by Cadwallader Ellis 295 acres, the whole 633, for the Other 549¾, and is 80 acres Over. Patent to be On 338 Acres in the said Right, the Other 295 acres to Cadwallader Ellis, to be granted to said Cadwallader himself; the Deed not being yet made is to be Produced when Done.

See 28, 4 mo., pa.

Rob't David, of Jno. Thomas and E. Jones 509½ a's, in Goshen 234½, in Meirion 274½, the first of which Proves 846, the Other, by Deed dat. 11th June, 1702 (Proves 280 a Patent for those Two), Upon a former Bargain Purchased of Richard Thomas 88½ a's, being Part of his Father's Original Purchase of 5,000 a's, Viz: R'd ap Thomas, which quantity added to the said 234½, with the allowance by Law of 23 acres, makes up the Complem't of 346 Acres.

Griffith John of Jno. Thomas and E. Jones 194¼ Acres in Meirion, Proves 192 , Rich'd Jones of Jno. Thomas and Edw'd Jones 137½ a's, in Meirion 156¼, and is 6¼ a's Over. And in Goshen Between himself and his Brother Evan 153¼, which being Resurveyed is found to Contain 346 a's and is 178 a's Over.

A Return of a Warr't 11, 6 mo., 1702, to Wm. Crosdale, being Produced for 250 acres, new Survey in Salberry Township. Ordered a Patent if the Grant was Clear.

Geo. Willard haveing Produced a right to 346 a's near Southampton, in Bucks, which being Resurveyed, and the Overplus cutt Off, there is Returned 374 A's, viz: 20 a's allowed by Law, on 250, and 8 a's is found in the tract of 100, On which they request a Patent to the said George Willard. Granted the title to be Inspected in the Min's.

Jno. Gardner, by Order and in behalf of Abiah Taylor, requests a Warr't to take up the Proportion of Liberty Land belonging to John Tovey's Purchase of 1,250 a's, Mentioned Pa. Ord'd that a Warr't be Granted for 20 a's in right and in full of the said Purchase and that because the Liberty Land is like to fall short On the West side of Skuylkill, as well as the East, Therefore that for the future there Be but Sixteen Acres allowed for Every Thousand On the West Side of Skuylkill.

Shadrach Wally Produceing a return of a's resurveyed in Pursuance of our Warr't for 923 a's, in which 90 being allowed for Measure, there Remains 833 a's to be Paid for, for which he agrees to give £30 p'r C't, One-half Payable 25th 10ber next, and the rem'r 24, 4 mo. next Ensueing, with Interest from the 1st of the 3d Mo. next, Vid. Min's 6, 8ber, 1702, And thereupon requests a Patent.

The Prop'ry, haveing Ord'd that there should be laid out to Jonathan Hayes 1,100 a's in Lieu of that laid out to Benja. Chambers in the Manor of Williamstadt, 490 thereof being in right of John Chambers, Purchaser of 500 a's By deed dat. 19 and 20 Jan'y, '81, and 610 in right of Benja. Chambers, Purchaser of 1,000 a's by Deeds 24 and 25th Jan'ry, '81, and Tho. Fairman having undertaken to find him Other Land he at Length fixed on a tract laid out formerly to Rob't Jeffe On Penny Rent for 1,500 Acres and By his Widow resigned And Another tract above adjoyn'g, Bearing Fra. Smith's name in the Mapp, the Survey of which Land, if Ever made, is Void, the said Smith haveing no right to Land in this Province. Ordered therefore upon a full Agreem't with the said Jonathan that in Lieu of the said 1,100 a's there be laid out to him in the said Place ye said quantity with the allowance of Ten p'r C't, Viz: 1, 210 acres, close Measure, in One Entire Piece, extending the whole breadth and beginning at which end he shall think fitt, And that a Warr't be granted forthwith, with a Patent On the return, the Widow Jeffe releasing her right to the said tract In Williamstadt, Also that the Widow Jeffe be reimbursed the Charges of Survey of the said Land, Pursuant to the Governor's former Orders thereon.

Granted to Wm. Snead 4 Lotts On the South of Mulb. Street of 49½ foot each, Extending to the High Street Lotts, for 7 years from the first Month last, at the yearly Rent of 12 Shillings, Prov. money, p'r Annum, and Ordered a Warrant upon the Same to be a title to him.

William Clark requesting the Grant of a small Parcell of Marsh On the South side of Pothooks Creek, in the County of Sussex, divided from a Plantation of the said William's By a small Creek, the Whole not Exceeding Forty Acres, which is granted at Bushell Wheat Per Annum.

The Prop'ry, by L. and Rel., Produced to us, dat. 29 and 30, 2 mo., '83, sold to William Puryer 1,000 acres, who Conveyed the Same to Rob't Fairman by deed dat. 2 8ber, '89, who duely Constituting his Brother Thomas his Attorney, the said Thomas took up 500 a's in the Township of Dublin, as by a return appears, and by deed dat. 8, 10ber, 1687, sold of the same 100 a's to R'd Willington, who sold to Rich'd Wastell, Who sold to Rich'd Busby, who sold it to Jos. Paul, By deed, dat. 15, 9 mo., who requests a Resurvey upon the same.

The said Thomas Fairman, also of the said tract, sold 86 acres To Abrah. Pratt By deed dated 20th 7 mo., 1690, Who also requests a Resurvey On the said Lands.

The Prop'ry, by Pat't, dat. 26, 1 mo., '84, Granted to Jno. Ogle a tract of Land of 430 acres situate on the North side of white clay Creek Called the Hopyard at One Bushell of wheat p'r Annum p'r 100 a's, And One year's Value at Every Alienation. John Ogle making his last will and Testament in writeing dat.   , made Eliz'th, his wife, Ex'r thereof, who, after the said Testator's decease, by deed Poll, dat. 9, 11 mo., '86, Granted and sold the whole said tract to Peter Yocom, Of the County of Philadelphia. Peter Yocom haveing Mortgaged the said tract of Land for Certain Sum of Money to Charles Saunders of, which Sum, before his decease, he had Paid the greater Part, John Guest, Esqr., of Philad'a, Paid the rem'r of the said Sum to Sarah. Widow and Ex'rx of the said Charles, who thereupon released and Conveyed the said tract of Land to Judith Yokom, widow of the said Peter, the said Judith, widow and Ex'rx, Peter Yokom, Son and Heir, and John Hans Stellman, Joint Ex'rx with the said Widow, to said Peter Yokom deceased, by deed, dat. 12, 7ber, 1702, sold and Conveyed the said tract to the said John Guest, which tract being resurveyed By Thomas Pierson in Pursuance of Our General Warrant the Same is found to Contain 769 Acres in which 40 a's being allowed for Measure there remains 299 a's to be Paid for at £10 p'r C't p'r Agreement, for all which he requests a Patent. Granted.

Tho. Ogle, by deed, dat. 10 Feb., 1702-3, Son and Heir of John Ogle aforesaid, released the said Land to the said John Guest, his Heirs, &c.

The Comm'rs haveing, by their Warrant, dat. 31, 10ber, 1701, Granted to Joseph Moore, of Newcastle, Wheelright, 400 a's of Land at £12 10s p'r C't, Which, being in Pursuance of ye said Warrant Surveyed to the said Joseph's two tracts, One whereof Containeth 145 a's adjoyning On the Above mentioned Hopyard, the s'd Joseph in Consideration of £5 12s Paid to himself and £18 10s secured to be Paid to the Prop'ry's Use by his deed Poll dated 30 Jan'y, 1702-3, Granted and sold to the Said John Guest the said tract of 145 acres for which he requires a Patent. Granted.

Ordered a Patent to Peter Cock for 404 a's Part of Lasso Cock's 1,000 Acres taken up out of Laetitia's Man'r, He paying according to the Govern'r's Order £30 p'r C't with Interest from the date of resurvey, viz: £40 6s and Interest.

At a Session of the Comm'rs at Philad'a 19 and 20, 2 mo., 1703.

Present, Griff. Owen, Tho. Story, Ja's Logan, Secr'ry.

Thomas Ellis took up a tract laid out for 735 acres, but upon an Old Survey found to Contain 819 acres, in upper Meirion, which was sold to John Williams, by Deed, dat.   , By Daniel Humphreys, Adm'r to said Thomas. John Williams, by deed, dated 20, 11 mo., 1701, Conveyed to Robert Lloyd, of Meirion, 409½ Acres, One Moiety thereof On which he desires a Resurvey. Granted.

Charles Whiteacre haveing requested to Purchase 300 a's in the tract In West Town, Chest'r, Granted him the 2 Corners next Brassey's tract, by the two side Lines of the Indians' Land, reputed About 300 Acres, and what Else may Accommodate him Without Injuring the rest of the tract, be it More

Or less, for £35 p'r C't, £5 to be abated On the first 800 A's to be Paid in 3 m'ths with Interest after 1, 3 mo. next. Rectifye this by 1st, 9ber Next.

Welch Returns.

Thomas Jones, Robert Jones and Cadwall'r Jones, Sons of John Thomas, Orig'l Purchaser of 5,000 Acres with Ed'd Jones, of w'ch he resurveyed 1,250 a's to himself and had 1,225 thereof taken up in the Libertys and One Moiety of the Rem'dr, viz: 612½ in Meirion and as much in Goshen, haveing Procured a Warrant of Resurvey On ye said tracts, that in Meirion is found to Contain 679 a's, viz: 6½ a's above measure and the Other 635 in Goshen, no Overplus, both to be confirmed to the said 3 Sons, their father haveing, by will, Dated , Granted the Same to them, no Sum.

Cadwallader Morgan haveing a Warrant of resurvey On 202½ a's Part of Edw'd Jones and Jno. Thomas' Purchase, the Same is returned to Contain 222½, On which a Patent is Ordered, the return being Examined.

Edw'd Jones, Jun., haveing Procured a resurvey on 306½ Acres in two tracts, viz: 153¼ in Goshen, it is found to Contain Only 125 a's And is 28 a's deficient, the Other 153¼ in Meirion is found to Contain 188, viz: 20 a's Over to make up the Other On w'ch a Patent is Ordered to Ed'd Jones, Senr., to whom he has sold the whole By deed dat. , the returns being first duely made from the Office. Ordered a Patent forthwith, the Deed at D. Ll's.

Edw'd Jones, Senr., haveing a warrant on 157¼ a's in Meirion, which Proves but 150 and is 1¼ deficient, and On 153 in Goshen together with 200 more, In Right of R. Thomas, for which there is returned 402 a's and is 34 Over, Out of which 1 being deducted there remains 33 to be Paid for, for w'ch he agrees to Pay £6 8s to be Paid 1 mo. next. Ord'd all in one Patent, Vid. Wel. Min's.

Ord'd, upon severa Long debates with George Gottshick, who married Evan Oliver's Daughter, that there be Paid to the Heirs or Ex'rs of the said Evan £14 5s in full of £20 of (which the said Evan formerly Rec'd £5 15s), Being in full Satisfaction for 4 year's Service as Woodranger at £5 p'r Ann., as is Proved to us by the former Comm'rs, to be Paid in Some kind of Goods. Also that the 4 Acres On which the House Stands be Confirmed to Joseph Oliver, Son and Heir Of the said Evan (if anything Can be Produced for it).

The Prop'ry, by Lease and release, dat. 13 and 14 July, 1681, Granted to Thomas Rowland 2,500 Acres, whose Brother and Only Heir, Jno. Rowland, By deed, dat. 9, 7 mo., 1690,

Granted 500 acres to Gilbert Wheeler, of Bucks, of which 400 a's was laid Out above Highlands and Conveyed to John Pidcock by deed, dat. 21, 3 mo., 1701, this was laid Out to Pidcock in '84 but never Conveyed to him before, there is an Overplus which he desires to be Cutt off, and a Patent Granted.

William Jenkins haveing a resurvey On 250 a's in Duffryn Maw'r, which being resurveyed, Proves 378 to 275 acres, of which he haveing a right and there being a Deficiency in his tract in Haverford of 60 A's to be added which is 335 a's, there remains 43 a's to be Cutt Off in the said Duffryn Maw'r, w'ch is to be forthwith Done; Also his Overplus in Abington to be Cutt Off with all Expedition.

Ord'd that the Hund'd Acres formerly laid out to Henry Sproegal be Confirmed to him by Patent, he giveing the said Land in security for the Payment of £26 13s 4d sterling, in England, or Value thereof here before 1, 3 mo., with Interest from 25, 10ber last.

John Blunston haveing Procured a resurvey On 240 Acres in Willis Town, Coun. Chester, in Pursuance of Our Warr't dated 29, 7ber last, for John Browne, requests a Patent On the Same to the said Browne. Granted.

Aaron James requesting also a survey on the Other tract of 240 a's in West Town, Ches, Coun., mentioned in the Same min's with the foregoing, viz: 29, 7ber Ultimo, and a Patent On the return, w'ch is granted and Ord'd thereupon that Ja's Taylor makes returns of the Warrants of Resurvey upon the Survey he some few years agoe Made thereon.

The Prop'ry, by deeds of Lease and release, dat. 10 and 11 April, '82, Granted Tho. Whitbey, of Sawle, in the County of Darby, Cloath worker, 500 a's who, by Indenture, Dated 23 July, '87, sold the said 500 a's to John Roades, who, by Deed, dat. 12, 1 mo., 1700, Granted the said 240 a's to the said Aaron James.

Joseph Richards haveing   last Entered a Caveat against Confirming a Certain tract of Land laid out for 100 a's To William Woodmansey to Jno. Beales, the Present Possessor thereof, upon the late Resurvey made by Isaac Taylor on the Same in Pursuance of the Prop'ry's Warrant, and this being the day apppointed for the hearing the said Jos. Richards' objections, both he And the said John Appeared, and all his said objections, together with the Arguments On the Other side being fully heard and Considered, 'tis resolved that the said resurvey is Just, Legal and regular and Ought to be Confirmed to the said John Beale according to the Lines now returned by the said Surveyor, and thereupon it is Ordered by a Quorum of the Comm'rs that the said Lines be Confirmed to the s'd John

Beale, he Paying for the 22 Acres of Overplus found therein, £15. [Note, that by a Min'e of the 11 of December, 1704, the Overplus is sold at £5, and the Rent of the whole, 5 Pecks of Wheat.]

At a Session of the Comm'rs at Philad'a 3d 3 mo., 1703.
Present, Griff. Owen, Tho. Story, Jam's Logan.

Richard Hill Produceing a Patent under ye Com'rs hands, dat. 24 Feb'ry, 1692-3, for 100 A's of Land granted to Tho. Lloyd (as 'tis affirmed) In Consideration of his surrender of a tract Joyning On the south Line of the Town, sold by the said Comm'rs for an Encouragement to Edm'd Shippen, surveyed 15, 1st Mo'th and year, by a warrant of the Same Date, and Conveyed by a deed, dated 25, 1 mo., '93, from the said Tho. Lloyd to John Delaval, who, by his will, Dat.   , left the Same to his wife, Hannah, Present wife to the said Richard, who thereupon requests a Resurvey, which is granted.

Edward Smout Produces a return of Survey under Walter Wharton's hand for 280 a's laid Out on the Northside of Apoquinim, On the Lower side of Drawyers Creek, said to be recorded in the records of Land in Newc., fo. 83, as by a Certificate Dat. 26 July, 1678, To Rolaff Anderson, also a deed dat. 7 March, '87, from John Walker And Wybrech Walker, his wife, for 200 a's of Land Between Apoquin. And Drawyers Creek by the Marsh called the High Hooks, said and Intended by the said Deed to be the Same recited as aforesaid, which Deed also recites that the said Land was sold and made Over by the said Rolaff Andries to Jno. Walker and Wybreck and Conveys the Same to Richard Noble, of Delaw'e, with a Certain Parcell of Meadow or Marsh Containing 100 a's recited to have been grant'd to Jan. Sierick's Pr'decessor to the said John Walker by Pat't, from Gov'r Fra. Lovelace, dat. 4 Aug't, 1671, to hold the said 200 a's of Fast land and 100 a's of Meadow to the said Rich'd Noble, his Heirs, &c. Also a Deed dat. 28 June, '90, from the said Rich'd Noble for 500 a's of Land Called the High Hook and the Holt.

Present, Ed. Shippen.

Thomas Lloyd, by deed, dated 5, 6 mo., '91, Granted to Robert Owen, of Meirion, 548 acres in Meirion, being Part of Charles Lloyd's and M. Davies' Purchase, And the said Robert deceasing devised it by his last will to the Son Evan Owen, In whose behalf Jno. Roberts, Trustee for the said Ev., requests a Resurvey. Granted.

The Prop'ry, by L. and Rel., dat. 22 and 23 8ber, '81, Granted to Rich'd Collet, of Walthamstow, in Essex, husbandman, 500 a's, which by a Warr't from the Prop'ry dat. 1, 7ber, '83, for the said quantity In Byberry, On which he requests a Resurvey. Granted.

The Prop'ry, by deed dat.   , Granted to Edw'd Jefferson, of Ashwell, In the County of Hertford, Malster, and Mercy, his wife, 1,500 a's of Land, and the said Edw'd deceasing, the said Mercy, his Widow, Intermarrying with Tho. Phitty, the s'd Tho. and Mercy, by deed, dat. 7, 10ber, '85, Granted to John Day of the said Place and County, 200 a's, Part Of the aforesaid of which said 100 a's the said Jno. Day, then of the County of Burlington, yeom., by deed, dat. 9, 11 mo., '90, Granted to Hen. Paxon, of Neshamineh, 100 Acres to be laid out, for which He requests a Warrant. Ordered And a Patent thereon.

Rich'd Walter haveing a right to 100 a's and a Warr't thereon, 75 thereof Purchased of Rob't David in One tract and 25 in another is found to Contain 117 a's, viz: 7 acres Over, for which he agrees to Pay 15s p'r Acre.

At a Sesion of the Comm'rs at Philad'a 17 and 13, 3 mo., 1703.
Prst., Edw'd Shippen, Griff. Jones, Jam's Logan.

John Paul bringing a return of his 100 a's which Proves 116, of which 6 are to be Paid for, he agrees to give 24s, and requests a Patent.

Abrah. Pratt also Produceing a return of 96 A's for 85 of the Overplus, for which 5 is allowed for Roads and 4 to be Paid for after the Same rate, he agrees to give 53s 4d for the Same, and thereupon requests a Patent. Granted to both.

George and John Palmer, Sons of George Palmer, deceased, Orig'l Purchaser of 5,000 a's of Land in this Province, haveing, on the 18th 11 mo., last, Entered a Caveat at this Board against Confirming to Jos. Growden, by Patent, that tract of Land on Neshaminey Creek called his Man'r, untill they Can be heard and Make appear their Claim to One Parcell of 500 a's Surveyed there to their Mother, the Widow Palmer, as they averr, in right of the said Original Purchase within the bounds of the said tract, as now Claimed by the said Jos. Growden. And The said Joseph Growden haveing not hitherto Prosecuted his claim and request for a Confirmation, the said Caveators Complain they are kept Of from a hearing for w't they Judge their Right, They therefore now Produce A Warr't with Sundry Cert's Concerning the said 500 a's upon w'ch, according to Method, they Crave a resurvey in their Own right and for their use. But This Board Considering the Claim which Jos. Growden is said always to have made and Still makes to the said Land, Tis Ordered that the Secretary give notice to the said Jos. Growden, of the said Geo. and John's claim, and that he be required to make appear before this Board on the 24th or 31st Instant, his right to the said Parcell of Land now claimed by the said Palmers, he, the said Jos. haveing never hitherto Produced to this Board any Certain title to the said Land by Survey, Or upon failure thereof that a Warrant of Resurvey be granted to the said Geo. and John Palmer upon the title that they have now Produced.

John Parsons Produceing a return under Israel Taylor's hand for 450 acres, Surveyed in Warminster in the County of Bucks, in Pursuance of the Com'rs' Warr't recorded in the Office, dat. 18, 9br., '86, for 500 Acres Granted to William Lawrence, Purchaser of the said quantity, The s'd Wm. Purchased the said Land for £25 of the Prop'ry in this Place, which Paul Saunders Declares was P'd in Cloathes, and Offers further Evidence, and thereupon requests Confirmat'n. Ord'd that a Warrant be granted to resurvey ye Same and a Patent On the return if not Exceeding 500 acres. Wm. Lawrence is Dead, And Jasper Laur. apprent. w'th P. Y., his Heir.

Upon Philip England's Complaint, Ord'd that Jos. Kirl, Wm. Bowlin and he be heard On 3d day Morning the 25th Instant.

Francis White, Son of George White, haveing a right to 250 acres, as was made appear Pa. , in Sa. Baker's request, desires a Warrant for ye Same, which is granted.

David Powell haveing sold a tract granted to him by the Prop'ry for 500 a's to Sundry Persons as follows, viz; To Ja's Pugh 150 a's, which upon resurvey Proves 159 a's; to David Pugh 150, which Proves 162; to Hugh Samuel 100 a's, w'ch Proves $100\frac{1}{4}$ a's, and to John Evans 100 a's, which Proves 122 and Contains 12 a's Overplus to be Cutt off, there is also left Out in the Same tract a Parcell of Barrens said to be about 16 acres, but is Judged to be more.

The Prop'ry, by L. and Rel., dat. 12 and 13 July, 1681, Granted to Jno. Barber, of Shipley, in the County of Sussex, yeom'n, 2,500 acres of Land. Jno. Barber, by his last will and Testament, dat. 20, 7 mo., '82, Produced and Proved, devised his whole Estate, both real and Personal, in England and Pensilvania (some few Legacies Excepted), to Eliz'th, his wife, Eldest Daughter of Jno. Langhurst, to be disposed of by her, since Marryed to Robert Webb, deceased, who by deed, dat. 4 May, 1703, Granted to Jno. Guest, Esq'r., $666\frac{2}{3}$ acres thereof, and by deed of the same date the like quantity to David Lloyd, the said Jno. Guest and David Lloyd request each a warrant for taking up the Same. Ordered that Warr'ts be granted accordingly.

The Prop'ry, by L. and Rel., dat. 3 and 4 May, '82, Granted to Rich'd Thatcher, deceased, One thousand acres, and the said Rich'd. in his life time, by his last will, dated 13, 8 mo., '90, duely Proved, devised to his Sons, Bartholomew Thatcher and Jno. Thatcher, a Certain share of the said 1,000 a's, as well surveyed as unsurveyed, upon w'ch there being formerly 650 a's taken up and 350 remaining unsurveyed, w'ch fell to their Part, they, the said Bartholomew and Jos., by their deed Poll, dat. 6, 1 mo., 1700-1, directed to Edw'd Pennington, Conveyed the s'd 350 a's to Sam'l Beakes, of the County of Bucks, yeom'n, haveing first Procured a warrant for the Same from the Prop'ry, dat. 1, 12 mo., 1700-1, directed to Edward Pennington, w'ch warr't being executed by John Cutler and duely returned into the Office, the said Sam'l Beakes requests a Confirmation of the Same. Granted.

Wheeler and Says' Land laid out in the beginning of '87. The Comm'rs, viz: Wm. Markh. and Jno. Goodson, by their warr't, dat. 29, 1 mo., '89, Granted to Jno. Champion, Jno. Latham, Christ'r White and John Reynolds 1,000 acres of Land in Newc. County, On Rent; in Pursuance whereof there was Surveyed 800 a's, Only 400 thereof On St. George's or thereabouts, assigned on the Back of the Warr't by C'r White and Jno. Champion to Amos Nichols, and 400 on Mill Creek, now in the Possession of Edw'd Green and Thomas Lewis. The s'd Champion haveing a right By the said Grant to 200 a's more, Entered upon a tract adjoyning w'th out Survey and has made Improvem'ts upon the Same and Is since deceased. Christopher White, adm'r to the s'd Champion and Guard'n of his Orphans, being their Grandfather, Requests a Conf. of the said 200 a's in behalf Of the said Orphans. Granted, they Paying new rent for the Same Since '89, and thereupon Ord'd a Warrant for the Same, Expressing the Conditions.

The Prop'ry, by L. and Rel., dat. 10 and 11, 8ber, '81, Granted to Hen. Sleighton, of London, Turner, 250 a's in right of w'ch there was laid out to the said Sleighton, at the Instance of Edward Blake, a tract in the Middletown, In the County of Chester. Henry Sleighton, by L. and Rel., dat. 4 and 5 Aug'st, 1702, Conveyed the whole said 250 acres to Jno. Sotcher, of the County of Bucks, who thereupon Craved a Resurvey, which is Granted.

The Prop'ry, by L. and Rel., dat. 1 and 2 Aug'st, 1681, Granted to Wm. Smith, of Bromehouse, in the Par. of Brumham, Coun. Wilts, yeom'n, 1,250 a's of Land.

Wm. Smith, by L. and Rel., dat. 19 and 20, 8ber., '81, Granted to Benjam'n Shill, of Rowd, in the County of Wilts, yeoman, 125 a's, whose Only Son and Heir, Jonathan Shill,

MINUTE BOOK "G." 377

by Ind'rs of Lease and Release, dat. 17 and 18 August, 1702, Granted to Wm. Walter, of the City of Chichester, in Sussex, all the said 125 a's, to hold to him, the said Wm. Walters, his Heirs, &c., for Ever to the following uses, viz: 5 acres thereof to the Only use of Stephen Stapler, late of Emsworth, in the County of South'ton, Butcher, his Heirs and assigns for Ever, and the remaining 120 a's to the Only use and behoof of Hannah, wife of Jno. Hammond, of the Parish of St. Pincrass, near Chichester, Needlemaker, her Heirs, &c. Wm. Walter, by his Letter, dat. 20 of Aug't, 1702, by and w'th the Consent of the s'd Hannah, Constituted and appointed the s'd Stephen Stapler and Jno. Sotcher, of Pensilvania, to be his att'rys to Enter upon, take up, lett, sett, &c , the whole said 120 a's of Land, who thereupon Crave to Purchase 125 a's more to be addded to the Same, for w'ch they agree to Pay forthwith £12 10s and a Warr't for the whole 250 acres. Which is Granted.

The Prop'ry by his Pat't dat. 1st 5 mo., '85, Confirmed to Jno. Woods. of the County Of Bucks, 478 a's in falls T. together with an Island Over ag't the Same, at a Bushell p'r C't, whose Son Jos. now Enjoys it.

The Prop'ry also by his Pat't, dat. 31, 5 mo., '84, Granted unto Dan'l Brinson 205 acres adjoyning to the former at the said rent. Dan'l Brinson, by Ind re dat. 22, 11 mo., '85, Conveyed to the said Jno. Wood One Equal half Part of the said tract adjoyning On his Other, now also in the said Son's Possession. being in all 583½ acres, which being both resurveyed there is found in The first 558½, besides the Island, w'ch Contains 81½ acres, of which 40 being allowed there remains 40 acres, for w'ch he agrees to Pay £14. The Other Proves 217 acres in the whole, of which 108½ (no Overplus) to be added to the foregoing and Confirmed in One Patent at 1 shill'g st'l. p'r C't, he paying 4s p'r C't for reduc'g the rent and £15 for the Overplus; that is in the whole £37 to be Paid. One-half 24, 4 mo., and the Other On the 25, 1 mo. next, with 9 months Interest. Patent Ordered thereon.

This day the Comm'rs Conferred with the Surveyors of the sev'l Counties Concerning the Price and Pay for resurveys On the Propr'ys acc't, upon which those Especially of Chester, viz: Isaac Taylor and Hen. Hollingsworth, remonstrated that they Cou'd not afford to Proceed in the work and do it Effectually by running round and exactly Plotting Every Small tract with all the subdivision of the whole County and reduce the Same into general Draughts and Pay the Chain Carriers and bear all the Other Charges themselves under £3 for Every Thous'd not already Resurveyed by Warrant, On agreement from the People.

But this appearing a high rate and likely to advance to a great Sum and charge to the Prop'ry, the Comm'rs hesitated upon the Same but after further Consideration Offered fifty shill's for Every Thousand as aforesaid.

But this not being agreed to, it was at Length Concluded, That the said Survey'rs should vigorously Proceed to finish the resurvey Of the whole Province, and that they should be paid as they found their work deserved when finished, and that in the meantime they should be Supplied by the rec'r with such sums of money as they Indispensably wanted to bear their Charges, and should as they Proceeded in their work have Some reasonable Security for what they might be Judged to have Earned by assigning to them bonds Or good debts of their Neighbours, Or Some Other good reasonable Pay as shou'd be at the respective times agreed On; And the said Survey'rs did thereupon agree to proceed accordingly under Obligations to Survey for the Prop'ry alone and to deliver no Person what soever a Draughts or Plotts of any Parcell of Land whatsoever but to return their work duely into the Survey'is Office at Philad'a and to keep secret their whole Proceed'gs, Otherwise than as they may be directed by the Comm rs.

At a Session of the Comm'rs at Philad'a, 24, 3 mo., 1703.
Prst., Edw'd Shippen, Griff. Owen, Jam's Logan.

Edw'd Smout and his first wife, Eliz. Prigg, having both Come in Servants to Major Jasp. Farmer, the said Edw'd Requests his and his s'd Wife's headland, viz: 100 acres, to be laid Out with his Other in Chester County, which is granted.

Peter Thomas haveing On the 28th 10br., ulto., Procured a Warrant of resurvey On 500 acres, Part of T. Brassey's Purchase, he now Produces a return thereof from the Office, by which 'tis found to Contain 528 acres, On which he requests a Patent. Granted.

John Hart haveing Procured a Warrant of Resurvey from the Prop'ry, dated 9, 3 mo., 1701, on 441 acres in right of his Purchase, Produces a return from the Office making it to Contain 484 acres, of which 40 being allowed in Measure there remains 3 a's to be Paid for, for which he agrees to Pay 40 shillings and a Patent is Ordered thereupon. Vid. Secr'rys Off., 29, 1 mo., 1701.

Jno. Austen Produceing a Warrant from the Office dat. 12, 7 mo., '84, signed Thom's Lloyd and Ja's Clayp. for 100 acres of Land to Eliz'th Pott, near the Welch, being her and her Daughter's head-right, requests a Resurvey in Order to a Confirmation. Granted, the rent being settled One-half at a

Penny p'r acre and the Other half at a half Penny for her Daughter, being a Servant.

Martha Kiete Produceing a return of a Warr't of resurvey from the Prop'ry, dat. 29, 1 mo., 1701, On 200 acres, Part of 400 acres, the Purchase of her former husband, Dan'l Middlecot, which now Proves 279 acres, of which 20 being allowed for Measure there remains 59 to be Paid for, for which Richard Prichard agrees to Pay Eight shillings p'r acre. Bond to be Given to pay in 3 Months.

The Prop'ry, by L. and Rel., dat. 28 and 29 March, '82, granted to Robert Greenaway, of London, Mariner, 1,500 acres, who by one Pair of Indentures of Lease and release, dat. 3 and 4 Aug't, '82, Granted to Charity Pott, of New Gravel Lane, in the Parish of Pants Shadwell, Coun. Middlesex, vid. 500 acres, Part thereof. And by like Indentures dat. 3d and 4th Aug't, '84, viz: the same date, the said Robert Greenaway Granted to Thomas Maleigh, of London, apoth., 500 acres more, Part of the aforesaid. The s'd Rob't, By like Ind'rs, dat. 6 and 7, 8br., '84, in Consideration of £193, 19 Shill's Sterling. further Granted to the said Thomas Maleigh 500 acres more, the Remainder of the said Land, On a Proviso that if the said Sum should Be duely Paid by the s'd R. Greenaway to the said Maleigh On the 7th 8ber, 1685, the said Grant should be void, which being impossible, the said Maleigh held ye s'd 500 a's together w'th his Other 500 first Purchased, in all One thousand acres, and by the said Thomas's and his son's directions to their attorney, N. Puckle, as by Lett'r of attorney dat. 2d March, 1701, Impowering him to lett, sett, sell or demise. It is said that Charity Pott, By her will, bequeathed her 500 a's To Thomas Maleigh, Jun'r, who therefore now claims the whole and desires a resurvey On the Front Lott, Produceing an old return of the Survey thereof Joyning On Samuel Carpenter's and on his High Street Lott, also On his Liberty Land and a Warr't of Resurvey On the whole 1,500 a's formerly laid out in Bucks by Isr. Taylor, directed to him to make returns thereof.

Granted 2 Warrants, One On the Land and another On the Liberty Land and Lotts. Quitt Rents due from first Location.

Daniel and Justus Falkner, attorneys for Benjamin Furlow, Produceing returns, one for 1,000 acres Resurveyed in Coun. Philad'a, fomerly Confirmed by Patent, another for 100 acres resurveyed in Bucks, another for 1,900 a's surveyed in the County Philad'a by T. Fairman, in Pursuance Of Our Warrant dat. 16, 12 mo., 1701, and One Other Warr't for 50 acres of Lib. Land, laid out by D. Powell in Pursuance of Our Warrant, dat. 26, 11 mo, 1702, for all which they Crave Patents. Ord'd accordingly, and that in the Patent for that in Philad'a the former Pat't be recited.

Ordered 2 Patents to Edw'd Jones, Vid. 19, 2 mo..

The Prop'ry by Inde're of sale, dat. 9 Jan'y, 1682, reciteing as therein is recited and for the Consideration therein mentioned, released unto the said Benjamin Furlow, his Heirs and assigns for ever, the yearly Rent of 45 Shillings, p't of the yearly Quitt Rent of One Shilling, for Every 100 of 5,000 acres Purchased of the said Prop'ry, to the End that the Yearly Q. Rent of 5 Shill's Only should from thence forth be Payable for the s'd 5,000 to the Prop'ry and his Heirs for Ever.

At a Session of the Comm'rs at Philad'a, 31st 3 mo., 1703.
Prst., Edw'd Shippen, Gr. Owen, Jas. Logan.

Thomas Ashton, of the County of Bucks, requesting to Purchase 100 a's of Land Vacant between Newtown Lotts and the backs of the River lotts, for which he agrees to Pay £36, and the Office to bear all Charges On the First of the sixth Month next, and gives bond with Abra. Hooper for the Payment of the Same. Vide Min's 27, 7ber, 1703.

At a Session of the Comm'rs at Philad'a, 7th and 8th 4 mo., 1703.
Prst., Edw'd Shippen, Griff. Owen, Jam's Logan.

John Pitts, of Maryland, haveing Procured his tract of Land of 500 a's in Newc. County, to be Resurveyed, is found to Contain 527 acres, and discovering a Certain tract of Vacant Land adjoyning, which upon a Survey is found to Contain 287 acres, he requests Geo. Dekeyne to Purchase the Same and agrees to give as Others. In Answer to which the Price is Sett £12 st'l. p'r acre, to be Paid in Bills, i. e., £34, 8s in the whole, of which the Sec'ry is Ordered to advise him.

Jos. Growdon making application for 1,000 acres more in Right of his Own and Father's Purchase of 10,000 acres, Ordered that the same be granted if upon Examination of his Overplus and what is already taken up Or granted, he have a right to so much.

Nath'l Puckle Produceing One return of 450 a's laid out to himself In Philad'a County, In Pursuance Of the Propr'ys Warrant dat. 8, 6 mo., 1701, In Right of William Wade, Requests a Pat't. Granted. The said Nath'l also Produceing One Other Return for 200 a's laid Out in the s'd County to Joseph Tanner, In Pursuance Of the Prop'ry's Warrant, dat. the Same day, On w'ch he also Requests a Patent, and is Granted.

Whereas there was formerly laid Out to R'd Ingels, of Philad'a, Gent., 600 acres of Land by Mistake, within the

Welch tract and Confirm'd to the said R'd by Pat. from the Comm'rs, dat. 14, 2 mo., 1686, to which s'd tract Nath. Puckle, by Virtue of One deed Ind'd Of the said Ingels, dat. 11, 3mo., '86, Conveying the same to James Brook, of Philad'a, Merchant, and One Other Deed from the said Brook, dat. 22 July, '98, Conveying the same to Said Nath'l, who claims the whole Right. And Whereas that spott with a Considerable Quantity adjoyning has been by Virtue of Regular Warr'ts Surveyed to R'd Thomas, who has Conveyed Part thereof to Other Purchasers, some of whom have actually made settlements thereon, and thereby the said two claims Interfere, each Pretending the Principal Right, for accommodation of which it is agreed that because the said tract laid out to Ingels lies Cross the Range of all the Other Lands there, which, if rectifyed, would Leave sufficient Room for the s'd R'd, there being a resurvey Granted on all the said tract, Ordering the said quantity of 600 a's to be Regularly laid out to Nath'l Puckle, rangeing with the Other Settlements as Conveniently as may be and that the Rem'r be laid out to the said R'd Thomas, upon which a Warrant is forthwith Ordered, and that in Granting the New Patent the Old One be resigned for the said 600 a's.

Adam Birch haveing 3 years ago Settled On the Skuylkill above Gilberts by toleration from the Prop'ry, but never yet could obtain a title, w'ch he has Often sollicited, now earnestly Presses that he may Be at some Certainty, and Craves, as he always expected, 700 a's at £10 p'r C't, which the Comm'rs not thinking fit to grant have at Length Proposed and agreed that he shall have 500 a's in the Place he is now settled, takeing In for his breadth his whole Improvements from the hither side of his Rye Field to the upper side of his wheat Field and extending backwards sufficient to take in the said Quantity. And that the said Adam shall Pay for the Same £70, of w'ch £20 to be Paid 1st mo., 1705, £20 more 1st mo., 1706, and £30 1st mo., 1707, with Interest from 1704, upon which a Warrant is Granted.

Jonathan Cockshaw Produceing a return of 500 a's surveyed in Caln Towns'p, County Chester, to Tho. Musgrave's Children, by Virtue of a Warr't granted to said Cockshaw 5, 3 mo., 1702, and another return of 400 arces laid out to the Same Children by Warr't dat. 7th 8ber., 1701, Joining On the Corner of the Other, requests a Patent On them both in One, w'ch is Granted.

Richard Worrall Obtained of the Prop'ry a Grant of 500 a's in Dublin Township in One Patent, dat. 17, 5 mo., '84, of which he sold to Tho. Fairman by Deed dated , 250 acres. Thomas Fairman by Deed dat. 10, 8br., '89, sold 100 a's to Henry Hayward, and by Deed dat. 24, 9 mo., '94, sold to

Hugh Gold 50 acres of this and 50 a's of Overplus, and by Deed dat. 20, 5 mo., '94, 100 a's To Thomas Kitchen, all which is now in the Possession of Several, as follows, viz: Thomas Kitchen 100, R'd Mason 100, George Burson 100, and Requests a Resurvey according to the Subdivisions, which is granted, Only his Title to the 500 acres to be further Inquired into. Vid. Philad'a Min's.

Silas Crispin Producing a Return of 1,000 a's Surveyed in Philad'a County in Pursuance of Our Warrant, dat. 26, 8br., Ultimo. Ord'd a Patent, He giveing Bond, as mentioned in the Min., Pa.

John Roberts, Miller, and Martha Keite haveing for some time Past had a Controversy about the Partition Lines between their Lands, because of which and for Other Reasons there has been a Resurvey On both tracts, and the Lines returned according to the Opinion of a Jury that sat upon an action of Trespass brought by said Rob'ts Concerning the said Line. It is Ord'd that the said Returns be rec'd and a Patent granted to Martha Keite.

Nath'l Puckle Producing a Return of a certain tract resurveyed to Thos. Maleigh by Israel Taylor in Pursuance of Our Warrant, dat. 31st ulto., On 1,476 acres, which Proves 1,622 of which the Overplus, 146, Is allowed for Measure, and makes up the Quantity aforesaid, upon w'ch He Craves a Patent to the s'd Thomas, Senior and Jun'r, affirm'g the title is wholly in him. Ordered accordingly that a Patent be Granted to saip Maleigh, Sen'r and Jun'r, in Greenaway's Right, with the Salvo that are Legally Possessed w'th any Part thereof, duely derived from s'd Greenaways.

Cadwallader Morgan Producing a return of 222½ acres in Meirion, Resurveyed in Pursuance of Our Warrant, dat. 22, 10 mo., 1701, for 202½ acres, Requests a Pat't On the Same, which is Granted.

Hugh John Produceing a Return of 92 acres resurveyed in Pursuance of Our Warrant, dat. 22, 10br., 1701, On 76½ acres, in w'ch there is 8½ acres Overplus. He agrees to give 12s 6d p'r acre and Requests a Patent, which is Granted.

At a Session of the Comm'rs at Philad'a, 14, 4 mo., 1703.
Prst., Edw'd Shippen, Griff. Owen, Jam's Logan.

The Board haveing granted to Isaac Few 600 acres On Brandywine, in Consid'rn of £90, which is Paid, the said Isaac, by a Deed Ind'd 23, 1 mo. last, Granted and transferred all his Right and title to the said Land to Robert Pennell and Benj. Mendenhall, of the County of Chester, yeomen, their Heirs and assigns, who Produceing a return of the Survey, request a Patent upon the Same to them. Granted.

The Prop'ry, by L. and Rel., dat. 1st and 2d Aug'st, '81, Granted to Ralph Withers, of Bishopstanning, in the County of Wilts, yeoman, 500 a's, who 'tis said left all to his Heir, Jason Withers, who by his last will and Testament dat. 4 March, 1700, devised all his Estate, in w'ch the s'd Lands are said to be included (some few Legacies Excepted), to his Uncle, Jno. Hall and his Cousin Jos. Hall, the former of which Claiming this, appointed by a Publick Notarial Instrument, dat. 5 Mar., 1701, Abrah. Scott his attorney, who Requests a Warrant to take up the said Land. Granted.

Welch of Newcastle.

Howel James Produces a return of 1,040 acres laid out in the County of Newcastle to himself, in Pursuance of the General Warrant for 30,000 acres there (40 to be allowed in Measure if the Prop'ry Please, Otherwise not), w'ch said Land R'd Davies and Da'd Evan have by their Deed, dat. 27th June, 1702, assigned to the said Howel James. Also Produces a return of 315 acres Surveyed in the said Place to Edm'd Kinsey, assigned by the s'd Richard Davies and David Evan, On both which Patents are requested. Granted, they giveing good Security for the Money.

The Prop'ry, by Lease and rel., dat. 24 and 25 Jan'y, 1681, Granted to Hen. Child, of Coleshill, in Amersham, County Hertford, Yeoman, 500 acres, also by Other Like Deeds dat. 2d and 3d Feb'ry, '87, Granted to the said Henry 500 a's, who upon the Prop'rys Order to us, entered 15, 1 mo. last, requests Warrants to take up the Same. Ordered.

Jno. and Geo. Palmer Continue their Caveat ag't a Confirmation of that 500 a's they Claim on Neshamineh till they Can determine the Controversys Otherways.

Allen Foster haveing appointed Hen. Mallows and Wm. Hibbs to determine On his Side the Value of his Overplus Land, Jno. Carne and ———— ———— are appointed On the Prop'rys behalf On the Other hand to settle the Price of the Overplus, With Orders to Cutt Off what is unimproved between Geo. Northrap and Benj'n Duffield.

At the Request of Judge Guest that we would Encourage him to Make a Settlement half way Between Whiteclay Creek and Nottingham, as a Conveniency for travellers and himself by adding a Suffic't Quantity to 666⅔ acres already granted him. Granted 333⅓ acres to be added In the said Place at 2 Bushells of wheat p'r Annum; to be seated in One year after the Grant, Otherwise to be void.

William Rodney, in Behalf of Wm. Wilson, Sheriff of Kent, Requesting the Grant of One Hund'd and Twenty acres, adjoyning On Wm. Rodney and Edward Starkey, above the King's Road. 'Tis Granted at £6 p'r C't, to be Paid In 3 months, On Old Rent.

Evan Jones (By his wife) Produceing a return of 300 a's Surv'd by Tho. Pemberton and Certifyed by Wm. Clark, laid out in Kent County in Pursuance of a Warrant from Kent Court, dat. 24, 7ber, '81, for 400 a's, To the said Evan, in right of which there Was laid Out Only the said 300. He requests a Pat't On the Same, which is Granted, but is Caveated ag't by Jno. Jones Vintner.

The Prop'ry, by Lease and Rel., dat. 12 and 13, 7br., '81, Granted to Wm. Salloway, of Taunton Deane, Coun. Sumerset, Sergemaker, 250 a's. Wm. Salloway, by deeds of Lease and Rel., dat. 27 and 28 June, '83, Conveyed the said 250 a's to Mathew Perrin, Of Taunton aforesaid, Merchant. The Prop'ry, by L. and Rel., dat. 13 and 13 of 7br., '81, Granted to Francis Herford, of Taunton aforesaid, Sergemaker, 250 a's, who by Deed, dat. 27 and 28 June, '83, Conveyed the said 250 a's to Mathew Perrin aforesaid, who thereupon became Possessed of the whole Right to 500 a's in this Province, which Quantity, Lib. Land deducted, viz: 490 acres, was by Virtue of a warrant dat. 24, 7 mo., '84, laid Out in the County Philad'a, near the Lime kill and duely returned into the Office. Mathew Perrin, by his last will and Testament, dat. 18th March, '95, devised the said land to his wife in the words: Also I Give and Devise all my Lands, Tenem't and Hereditaments in Pensilvania unto the said Edith, my wife, and her Heirs for Ever, as by attested Copies of the said Deeds and Will appears. The said Edith Perrin Intermarrying with Edw'd Watts, formerly of Bristol, now of Taunton, the said Edw'd and Edith, by an Instrument dat. 28 July, 1699, Constituted James Logan, then of the City of Bristol, Gent., but Intending for Pensilvania, their true and Lawfull attorney, with full Power to demand, Levy, &c., all their debts, Rights, &c., In America. To Enter on all their Lands and to Contract for, Bargain and dispose of the Fee and Inheritance of all and Singular their Houses, Lands and Hered'ts, whereof they Or the s'd Edith stood seized of the Gift of the said Mathew Perrin, Deceased, in Pensilvania aforesaid. James Logan Procured a Warrant of Resurvey, dat. 8, 11 mo., 1700, On the said Tract, which was executed and returned By the Sarvey'r Gen'l and is found to Contain 540 acres and 28 p's, On which the said James Requests a Patent. Granted.

James Cooper Produceing a return of 300 a's of Serv'ts Lands laid Out in Pursuance Of Our Warrant, Requests a Patent thereon.

At a Session of the Comm'rs at Philad'a, 22, 4 mo., 1703.
Prst., Edward Shippen, Griff. Owen, Jam's Logan.

Nath'l Puckle, attorney for Jos. Tanner, Original Purchaser of 500 a's by Deeds dat. 2 and 3 Feb'ry, '81, Requests a Warrant to take up the Lott appurtenant to his Purchase, being No. 155, and is the Corner On the East of the 5th Street from Delaw. and South of Chestnut Street. Granted.

Nath'l Puckle haveing in the 6 mo., 1701, Proved his Right to Wm. Wade's Purchase in the Secretary's Office, the Front Lott of which was sold to Benj'n Chambers, but the High street seems not taken up yet, is Entered Between Chris'r Pennock's or W. Rogers' and Geo. Willard's in J. Blackwell's, Rent Roll, On Which therefore he requests a Warrant, which is granted, with a Provisoe that the said Lott be not taken up all ready.

Howel James Producing a Pat't under the Gov'r's hand dat. 12, 4 mo., '84, for 500 acres of Land in Bristol Township, C. Philad'a, Joyning on Taconinck Creek to Jno. Barnes, Original Purchaser of the said quantity, laid Out 5, 1 mo., '83, By a Warrant dat. 26th 12 mo., '82, also An Ind're dat. 3, 6 mo., '87, from the said Jno. Conveying the said 500 acres to Edw'd Batsford, of Philad'a Coun., Yeoman, also an Ind're dat. 10, 9br., '91, under the hands and Seals of Patr. Robinson, Hen. Wandy and Wm. Salway, Constituted Attornies Joyntly and Severally by the s'd Edw'd Bratsford by Virtue of a Letter of Attorney, Dat. 29 July, Proved, Impowered to sell the said Plantation and to sign, seal and deliver Deeds for the Same as in the said Deed is recited, Conveying the said 500 a's (for £125) to Howel James, then of Radnor, who being, by Virtue of the aforesaid, in Possession thereof, Requires a Resurvey On the Same, Which is Granted.

Wm. Davies and David Evan, undertakers for the Welch Settlement in Newc. County, by an Ind're, dat. 27 June, 1702, transfer their Rights to James James, of the County of Philad'a, Yeom., all their Right and Int'st to 1,246 A's of the Welch Tract in the said County, of the Survey of which a Return is Produced, and thereupon Desires a Pat't to himself he Answering for the Same, According to ye Gen'l Agreem't of £12 10s p'r C't, w'ch is Granted.

At a Session of the Comm'rs at Philad'a, 28th 4 mo., 1703.
Idem ut Supra

Wm. Markham, R. Turner and J. Goodson, Comm'rs, by Pat't, dat. 19 March, '93-4, Granted to Barnabas Wilcox, his Heirs. &c., a Bank of 30 foot in br., and 250 foot Deep, bounded

25—Vol. XIX.

N. W'd with Tho. Fess, and S. w'd with Henry Woods' Lott, said Barnabas Wilcox deceasing left his Son George his Heir, who deceasing without issue, Jos. Wilcox became Heir to the said George and upon a division of the said Barnabas's Estate, in Pursuance of his Will, the said Lott was allotted to Abigail, who, Intermarrying w'th Sam'l Powell, of Philad'a, Carp'r, the said Jos. Wilcox, by Indorsem't on said Patent, dat. 17 Feb'ry, 1701, assigned the said Lott to the said Samuel and Abigail in Part of the said Abigail's Portion, the said Sam'l Powel Requesting to Purchase the Reversion of the said Lott, agrees to Pay £15 at takeing up the Patent and 15 in 9br. next. Samuel Powel Requesting to Purchase a lott Situate between Tho. Cross's now Jam's Swaffer's and Jno. Martin's, On the South side of Walnutt Street, being the 3d Lott W. w'd of the third Street and is now Vacant, Agrees to Pay £15 at 3 mo's and Requests a Warrant a Patent.

Ord'd That a Warrant be Granted to Robert Heath for the Front and High Street Lotts Appurt't to Thomas Woolrick's Purchase.

There being laid Out to Hugh Roberts 633 acres in all in Goshen in right of 1,349¾ a's in right of sev'l Purchases, viz: 67¾ in Right of Jno. Thomas and Edw'd Jones. 482 in Right of John ap John and Tho. Wynne, 500 a's in Right of Peter Young and 100 a's in Right of a Purchase by the Society. Ord'd that the Remaind'r of the whole said Quantity be laid Out in the Place Now Appropriated in Duffryn Mawr, viz: 716 Acres, and that first a Warr't Be granted for the 100 acres.

Ann Calley (in the list Crawly) being Orig'l Purchaser of 500 acres, Francis Smith, of Brandywine (being Recommended by the Prop'ry to the Sec'ry Particularly before his Departure), Desires in her behalf a Warrant to take up the Land, the Prop'ry haveing Granted the Same while here.

Ord'd that R'd Stockton Pay £15 on the whole for Interest of his first Bond of £450 and that the Other £6 12s 10d be Remitted On the Prop'ry's Order to Be kind to him, &c.

David Lloyd and I's Norris, Ex'rs of the last will and Testament of Thomas Lloyd, Complaining that the Crd'rs of that Estate, Especially those In England, are Very sharp upon them and that they Can by no means Answer them unless they Can be favoured in Takeing up what Lands belong to the said Estate that are yet untaken up, Especially that they may have the Priveledge of takeing up that thou'sd Acres Granted by the Prop'ry at his Departure in exchange For the like quantity On Indian River in Sussex, may be Taken up Part in the Welch tract, viz: 500 acres where it may be found and the Remainder be located On A vacancy near Gwynedd, Which in

Considerat'n of the Difficulties the said Ex'rs Labour under, and to Prevent this dishonour likely to Accrue upon the Disappointment of the said E'rs, is granted as Requested, deducting Only Out of the tract of Gwynedd What Overplus is found in their tracts in Bucks or Elsewhere.

They also Request that Tho. Lloyd's Purchase of his Brother Charles and Marg't Davies, May be adjusted, which upon Enquiry is as follows: The Prop'ry by L. and Rel., dat. 14 and 15, 7br., '81, Granted to Charles Lloyd and Marg't Davies 5,000 a's, Charles Lloyd, by an Instrument, dat. 6, 4 mo., '83, assigned to Thomas Lloyd his full Share of the said Purchase, viz: 2,500 acres. Charles Lloyd and Marg't Davies Joyntly, by a Deed, dat. 29 June, '83, Granted to Joseph Harries, of Wallbrook, in London, 1,250 acres, and the said Jos. Harries, by a Deed, dat. 23 May, '88, granted the said 1,250 acres to Francis Smith, Plaisterer, who sold the same to the said Thomas Lloyd, but deceased before he Could make a title, And therefore Wm. Smith, his Son and Heir by Deed Poll, dat. 21, 10br., '93, Conveyed and Confirmed the said 1,250 a's to the s'd Thom's Lloyd, to hold to him, his Heirs, &c., by which Conveyance he became seized of 3,750 a's to be laid out in the Welch tract. Of the said Land there was laid out in One tract in Meirion 1,100 a's sold to sundry Persons, viz: to Wm. Cuarton 200 a's, to Da'd Pugh 118 a's, to D. Price 118 a's, to Rob't Owen 540, to E. Rees 125 acres, there was also taken up 100 a's of Lib. Land, there is 145 acres of Lib. Land taken up, now B. Chambers, and 100 a's more above Meirion sold to Tho. Davies, being in all 1,301. There is also granted to the said Ex'rs, by the Present Comm'rs, in One Tract, 2,215 a's, out of which they have Confirmed at the Instance Of the Comm'rs to some Of the English Purchasers who claimed a right in the said Land, viz: To Thomas Bowater 69 acres, to Wm. Swaffer 150 acres, to Jno. Craxon 110 acres, in all 329 a's, which must be discounted out of the said Tract, so that there Remains 1,886 a's to which 1,300 Acres being added is 3,186 Acres, which deducted Out of 3,750 there remains 564 acres to be taken up In the said Tract, for which a Warrant is Ord'd together with the Other 1,000 acres, also 370 Acres for the allowance of 10 p'r C't which is granted not of Right but in favour to the said Thom's Lloyd. And a warrant is Ordered for a vacancy in Gwynedd instead of the Welch Tract, being about 5 or 600 Acres, and the rest to be made up in the s'd Tract and the Other 1,000 acres, his whole Due is 934 a's. See above, Liberty Land.

Judge Guest haveing On the 15th Ulto., Obtained a Grant of $333\frac{1}{3}$ acres to be laid Out adjoyning to $666\frac{2}{3}$ acres, Part of Jno. Barber's Purchase, further Presses that the said Land is not Sufficient for his Design in making Settlem'ts in the said Place halfway between Whiteclay Creek and Nottingham, and that for his Services he alledges to this Government he has been a great Sufferer without Any Manner of Compensation He therefore Prays that this Board will Grant to him One thous'd A's more at a Bushell p'r C't, and that the Rent of the Other 333⅓ be reduced to the Same Rent. All which being Considered, And being Argued On the One hand that he has really been a Sufferer And exposed himself for the Service of the Governm't, and On the Other hand that this Board are not Judges of the Prop'ry's munificence and Cannot Grant On Any other Terms than what is mentioned in Our Commiss'n, but that the said Judge Guest Exhibiting In his Request that he Designs to make a Considerable Settlement there w'ch will be much for the Improvement of the Place, 'Tis Ordered that the said Judge Guest Shall have 500 a's in the Place aforesaid to be added to the said 666⅔ Acres under the yearly Rent of One Bushell of Wheat p'r C't and that he be Obliged to build and make a good Settlem't upon the Same before the first of Decem'r, 1704.

Jacobus Vanderculin upon Skuylkill desireing to Purchase Part of the Overplus found in that Tract of Matthias De Tosse in Christina Hundred together with about 50 Acres out of a Vacant Tract Adjoyning, Offers £15 p'r C't, £10 thereof to be Paid in hand, £10 more next Spring and the Rem'r in fall, with interest from the 1st of 7br. next.

Granted accordingly, Provided that the Land taken out of the vacant Tract Render not the rest of less Value and more unsaleable and upon that Condition Ordered a Warrant Accordingly.

Edw'd Edwards, Son of Alexander Edwards, Caveats ag't Job Bates, that a Patent of Confirmation be not granted him for his Land till he Can be heard, for Reasons assigned in his Caveat this day Entered.

The Prop'ry haveing, by deeds of L. and Rel., dat. 5 and 6, 7br., 1687, Granted to Eliz'th Symes, Spinster, 500 acres of Land (which, by a Rasure in the Deed, were made a thousand but in the list is Only 500), who, Intermarrying with Jno. Martin, of Philad'a, Taylor, and deceasing, the said John Procured of the Prop'ry a Warr't to take up 492 acres in the Rights aforesaid. John Martin in his Life time made his Last will and testam't dat. 8, 9br., 1702, and therein gave and bequeathed all his Estates, Lands, Goods, Chattles and Credits To Tho's Chaulkley, of Philad'a, Sawyer; Ralph Jackson, of Philad'a, Smith, and Jno. Meachiner, of Philad'a County, Yeoman, to be Equally divided between them and to be for the use of them and their Heirs for Ever, and ordained the s'd Tho. Cha., R. J. and J. M., Ex'rs of his s'd will, and dyed, the s'd Ex'rs Produceing a return of Survey of the s'd 492 acres requests a Confirmation, which is granted.

At a Session of the Comm'rs At Philad'a, the 2d 6 mo., 1703. Pres., Griff. Owen, Thomas Story, Jam's Logan.

Jos. Wood haveing in the year 1701 Procured a Resurvey on a tract of Land in Newc. County, On George Creek, reputed to Cont. 400 a's, but upon a Resurvey Proved more and therefore there was Cutt Off from it about 180 acres of Overplus and the rest Confirmed by a Patent, the said Jos. Now Requests that the said Land may be granted to him and that he may be Considered for his Charges of Resurveying, discover'g and Cutting of the Said Overplus, Upon w'ch 'tis Granted at ^{b} £12 p'r C't On the Usual Rent. A Provisoe that it shall not be a Presedent for Lands there, being but $\frac{2}{3}$ of the Value and a Warrant is Ordered thereupon and a Patent On the Return.

The s'd Jos. also Requests a Grant of about 24 acres lying Between his New Plantation and some Land he Purchased of Artman Haim. Ord'd that the Survey'r be wrote to About it.

Thom's Fairman haveing laid Out Certain tracts of Land to himself in that Part of Whitpains Township Called the Overplus of it, sev'l Parcels by Virtue of Warr'ts in Right of Stanley's Purchase amounting in the whole to 1,000 a's including that 200 acres Contested Between him and Job Goodson, and 200 more Granted by Patent On Rent to Mary Bradwell, But the sa'd Tho. not haveing a right to So much as he took up upon Stanley's Purchase for Reasons given in the Sec'ry's Office 1, 8 mo., 1701, and Mary Bradwell haveing a Right as afores'd, He Purchased of the s'd Mary the said Rent Land by an assignment on tne said Pat't dat.   , and has agreed w'th Job Goodson for the 200 a's in Contest as in Pa.

, And now renews the Request he has often made to the Prop'ry that he may Locate 1,000 a's of Stanley's Purchase On the said Tract, which the Prop'ry Granted On Ship board at his Departure, Only 'tis Thought fit to Reserve that Of Bradw'ls, and Accordingly a Warrant is Granted as Requested.

At a Session of the Comm'rs at Philad'a, 9th 6 mo., 1703. Omnes.

John Wood, uncle to the Orphans of R'd Bonsal, Produces a return of Survey in Pursuance of the Prop'ry's Warr't of Resurvey, dat. 8, 12 mo., 1700. On 100 acres of Land in King-

sess. Purchased by R'd Bonsal by Ind're dat. 2d July, '96, of
Enock Enockson, Heir to his Father, Garr't Enockson, Who
Purchased the Same of Hans Mounson, as by a Cetrtificate
under Thomas Holme's hand dat. 29th 5 mo., '83, mentioning
the Deed to have been deliv'd to him but was mislaid, yet advises that the Survey'r give in the Bounds that the Possessor
may make good his Claim, and the said return being for 104
acres a Patent is Requested upon the Same.

Ord'd that because the Title seems equal with the rest Of
the Swedes, that the Prop'ry by granting a Resurvey, Approved it, a Patent being granted to Jacob, Benj'n and Enock
Bonsal, the Orphans of the s'd Rich'd. Rent a Bushell of
wheat from the first Survey.

Jacob Simcock Producing a return for his Father's Front
and High Street Lotts in Pursuance of Our Warrant Dat. 14,
2 mo., last, also Producing An Old return Out of the records
of the Ofiice of a Bank lott Over against the Front, surv'd 15,
12 mo., '89, by Virtue of Warr't of the Same date, of 102 foot
mentioned also in the new Returns. Requests a Patent for the
Same. Ordered a Pat't for the High Street and Front lotts
and another for the Bank.

Welch Returns.

Stephen ap Evan haveing a right to 250 acres, 100 thereof in
Right of R'd Davies and 150 bought of David Meredith, Purchased of the Com'rs. Also to 100 acres, as he says, of Rent
Land bought of Mary James, Daughter of David James. In
the General return of Radnor Township there is found 432 acres
and Contains 47 acres Over, if the Survey be true; the Rent
Land he buys of at £11 and is to Pay arrears from '84 Inclusive;
the Overplus he Pays a Noble an acre. A Pat. is Ordered, he
Proving a Right to rent Land, a Due return being Produced
from I. T.

David Meredith haveing a right to 200 acres, 100 thereof in
Right to R'd Davies and 100 in Part of his Purchase of the
Comm'rs, upon resurvey is found to Contain 257 and is 37 Over,
for which he Pays a Noble p'r acre, and a Patent is Ordered
upon a Due return.

Marg't Jermain haveing a right to 100 acres Purchased of
Jno. Evans, Purchased of R'd Davies, is found to Contain 152
acres and is 42 acres Over, for which her Son Jno. Jermain,
agrees to Pay a Noble Per acre and a Patent is Granted.

John Morgan haveing a right to 450 acres, 100 thereof In Right
of R'd Davies, Purchased of Jno. Evans, 100 more in the Same
Right, Purchased of Ellis Jones and 250 of Ed'd Jones in the
Same Right. Upon Resurvey 't's found to be 474, for which a

Patent is Ordered upon a due Return (no Overplus). He has sold of this 80 acres to Hen'y Lewis, now Jno. Worrall's, but is to be included all in One Return as before said and Confirmed to said Morgan.

Edward David haveing Purchased of Jno. Evans 50 acres of Rent Land by Deed dat'd 19th July, '97, being Part of the 100 acres that he took up for himself and his Son by a Warrant dat. 19, 1 mo., '83, also to 100 a's Purchased of Wm. Davies by Deed Dat. 19 July, '97, being Part of R'd Davies Purchase for William Davies' title. See Chest'r Min's, Radnor T.

Which Two Parcells upon Resurvey are found the first to Contain 55 a's, the Rent of which he Purchases at £5 10s. Arrears are Paid to 1702, all to 9d; the rent of the Other 100 he is also to Produce acquittances for to 1702. The Other is found to Contain 100 acres, for both which a Patent is ord'd. Rent to Commence from March last.

Abel Robert, Son of Robert Ellis, of Radnor, Purchaser of 100 a's from Dav'd Powel, by Deed Poll dat. 1, 6 mo., '93, being now Possessed thereof the Same Is found to Contain 108 a's. On which a Patent is granted, Provided Dav'd Powell Produce an old Patent, which he says he Obtained, Or Other good title to the Same, but from 84 Patent not yet Requested.

David Evan haveing a Right to 200 acres Purchased of Howel James and his Son Purchased of Thomas Wynne, being Part of Jno. ap Jno. and said T. W's Purchase, the same is found 225 acres and is 5 Over, for which he agrees to pay a Noble p'r acre, Prove it more or less. Also a Right to 150 Purchased of Wm. Davies by Deed dat.   , as he says. Title to Be searched in Chest'r Min's, Radnor. Also to 312½ in Right of R'd Davies, 5,000 acres above Newtown; the same is found to Contain 357 and is 15 a's Over, for which he agrees to Pay 5 Shill's p'r acre. A Patent upon These 3 several Tracts in One upon a Due Return.

John Longworthy Produces a Patent from the Prop'ry to himself, dat. 4, 6 mo., '84, for 200 acres in Radnor, Survey'd 25, 10 mo., '83, by Virtue of a Warrant dat. 18, 3 mo., '83, at 1s p'r C't, of which he sold 100 a's to Hugh Williams. Also a Deed Poll dat. 28, 12 mo., '83, for 100 acres from David Evan to Harry Rees, of Radnor, reciteing that David Powel by Deed dat. 10, 7 mo., '87, Recorded Book E., Vol. 5, Pa. 672, Conveyed the Same to Philip Evan, of the said Place, whose Brother and Heir ye said Da'd Evan was and Is.

Granted to the said Dav'd Powel by a Patent to be Produced. Also a Deed from the said Henry Rees dat. 27, 11 mo., '86, for the said Land, by w'ch he became possessed of 200 acres, which being Resurveyed is 238 a's and is 18 acres Over, for which he Pays 6s 8d p'r Acre as the Rest.

A Warrant to be granted forthwith to Robert Heath for 2 Lotts in right of Thomas Woolrick.

The Prop'ry, by L. and Rel., dat. 3 March, '81, Granted to Thomas Rowland, of Acton, in the County of Chester, England, Yeoman, 1,000 a's, and the said Thomas, by his last will, devised the said 1,000 acres to his 3 Sons, Thos., James and John, and deceased, and constituted Alice Rowland, his wife, Ex'r of the said will, who by her Letter of Procuration dat. 10 May, 1701, appointed Jno. Worrall, of Edgemont, att'ry, to take up the said Land for the Uses aforesaid. It appears that Jno. Dalton took up 500 a's in Part of the said Land and therefore the said Jno. Worral requests a Warr't only for the Other 500 a's, which is Granted.

There being Surveyed to Thomas Wickersham 480 acres of Land On the Southside of Brandywine, Chest'r County, in Right of Hum. Killenbeck, by Virtue of the Prop'rys Warrant, dat. 21, 1 mo., 1700-1, a Patent is Ord'd thereon, Pursuant to the Min's of that time; Vid. if a Patent be not Done.

Nicholas Waln haveing by Our warr't dat. 23, 12 mo., 1701, Procured a Resurvey on 44 acres of Lib. Land, Purchased by George Walker, made up of the Several Purchases recited Pa. 72 and 73; also On 172 acres Purchas'd of Joshua Carp'r, made up of the following Rights, viz: as is recited In Joshua's Deed, To said Nicholas 80 acres, Granted by Patent dat. 21, 9br., '91, to Josh'a Carp'r, being that Granted to Robert Longshore, for w'ch He gave bond, 8 acres Granted by the Prop'rys Warrant: 83 to Fran's Smith in Right of his Purchase, who by Deed dat. 17, 3 mo., '92, sold the Same to Joshua Carp'r; 20 acres sold by Andr. Robinson To Jos. Carp'r by Deed dat. 14 Aug't, '94, Conveyed By the Ex'rs of Wm. Taylor, late and by Pet. Taylor, now of Chest'r Coun., Orig'l Purchasers of 1,250 a's, to Wm. Waite by Deed dat. 10, 10br., '88, who by Deed dat. 17, 7br., '94, Wm. and M. sold to Andr. Robinson 8 acres Granted by Patent 11 Aug't, '92, to Charles Pickering in Right of Jno. Southworth and Charles Pickering by Deed Dated 16 Aug't, '92, Conveyed the Same to Joshua Carp'r, Rent 1s p'r C't; 40 acres Granted by a Warrant dat. 11, 3 mo., '86, Surv'd 20 Inst., to Cha. Pickering and Confirmed by Patent, dat. 1, 5 mo., '86, to said Charles in right of Wm. Rakestraw, Conveyed by said Pickering to Jno. Redman, of Philadelphia, Bricklayer; 12 acres Granted by Pat't dat. 8, 7br., '87, to Thomas Minshall in Right of his Own Purchase and by deed dat. 12, 10br., '87, Conveyed by Samuel Buckley, att'ry to said Thomas, to said John Redman, who by Deed dat. 3, 7 mo., '91, Convey'd both the said 40 a's and 12 acres to the said Joshua Carpenter, Together with 4 acres more Granted by Patent dat.

20 Mar., '90, to John Hucks, of London, Cheesemonger, whose attorney, Walter Faucet, by assignment indorsed On said Patent dat. 2, 4 mo., '91, Granted the Same to Caleb Pusey, who by Ind're dat. 20, 6 mo., '91, Conveyed it to John Redman, who Conveyed to Jos'a Carp'r as aforesaid, 172 acres, all Conveyed by said Jos'a Carp'r to said Nich's Waln by Deed dat. 8, 7br. '97. Recorded in Book E., 3, Vol. 5th, Pa. 59, at Philad'a, also 44 acres of G. Walker.

The said Nicholas also Purchased 40 acres Granted by the Prop'rys Warrant dat. 29, 3 mo., '84, Surv'd 2, 6 mo., '84, and Confirmed by Patent dat. 29, 1 mo., '88, To Silas Crispin, Purchaser, who by Assignment Indorsed, dat. 20 4 mo., '95, Conveyed the Same to Nich. Rideout, of Philad'a, Last maker, who by Deed dat. 31, 3 mo., '96, Convey'd the Same to Nicholas Waln. 80 acres Granted by the Prop'rys Warrant dat. 6, 4 mo., '84, Surv'd 24, Confirmed by Patent dat. 25, 4 mo., '84, To Thomas Rudyard in Right of his Own Purchase sold him by And. Robeson By Deed dat.   , And by the s'd Andrew Conveyed to Griff. Jones by Ind're dat. 12th 8 mo., '89, and by Griff. Conveyed to Nich. Waln By Deed Dat. 10, 1 mo., '98, together with 5 acres more out of said Griff's Other Land, Out of which said 80 acres N. Waln sold 60 acres to Thomas Mitchener, and has 20 thereof remaining. 80 acres Granted by Patent dat. 27 May, '91, to Chr. Taylor Purchaser, who sold the Same (as is Recited) to Thos. Lloyd in his Life time, Whose Ex'rs, Is. Morris and Da. Lloyd, by Deed Dat. 20, 3 mo., '97, Conveyed the Same to said Nich's Waln. Out of these last 80 acres and the 40 a's Granted to Silas Crispin and the foresaid Tract of 20 a's Granted to Wm. and P. Taylor's, N. Waln sold to Ellis Jones 103 acres, and has therefore of his Purchase of G. Walker, Jos'a Carp'r, Nich. Rideout, Griff. Jones and T. Lloyd, Ex'rs, 258 a's remaining.

He Purchased also of Griff. Jones by Deed dat. 24, 7 mo., '97, 50 acres more being Part of Several Purchases made by said Griff. of Jos. Growdon, Tho. Holme and Wm. Salway, w'ch with the aforegoing makes 308 a's. He has also Purchased of the Com'rs 80 acres Granted by Our Warr't dat. 25, 12 mo., 1701, in Right of R'd Penn, 8 acres in Right of Jno. Carver, Granted by Our said Warrant, dat.   Conveyed by Carver by Deed dat. 30, 2 mo., 1700. Also 8 acres Granted by Our said Warrant in Right of Thomas Crosdale, conveyed by Wm. Crosdale, Son and Heir and Thomas Crosdale, 2d Son of the said Thom's by Deed Dat. 28, 6 mo., '98, to said Nich. Waln.   acres Granted to Randal Spakeman, adm'r On Dr. Smith's Estate, by Our Warr't dat. 7th 11 mo., 1701, 8 acres thereof In Right of said Daniel's Purchase of 500 acres, 8 acres

in Right of Thom's Logan's and Sus. Bayly's Purchase of 500 acres and 8 acres in Right of Wm. Isaac and 4 acres in Right of Hen. Barnard and 4 acres in right of Jno. Rety, Conveyed by the said Thomas Fairman, Sheriff of Philad'a, to said N. Waln, by Deed dat. 18th Jan'y, 1702-3, Being taken in Execution for a debt due from D. Smith to the Prop'ry.   acres Granted by Our Warr't dat. 25, 12 mo., 1701, to Jno. Swift, 8 acres thereof In Right of himself and 8 acres in Right of Wm. Bingley, Conveyed by the said Jno. to the s'd Nich's by Deed dat.   .   acres Granted by Our Warrant dat. 4, 6 mo., 1702, to James Streator in Right of Geo. Jackman, Conveyed by Deed from the said James to the s'd N. W., dat   .
acres Granted by Prop'rys Warrant dat. 16, 2 mo., 1701, to Rob't Heath in Right of Tho. Woolrick, Conveyed by s'd R't by Deed Dat.   .   acres Granted by Warr't Dat.
, to Th. Bye, sold by the said Tho. to N. Waln by deed dat.

At a Session of the Comm'rs at Philad'a, 23, 6 mo., 1703.
Prst., Edw'd S., Tho. S., James Logan, Sec'ry.

The Prop'ry, by L. and Rel., dat'd 18th 19th 8br., 1681, Granted to Charles Bathurst, of London, Salter, and Grace, his wife, 1,250 a's. Cha. deceasing and Grace Surviving, by Ind're dat. 22 and 23 Mar, 1702, 2do. R. Reg'ae An'ae, Granted to Susannah Cadman of Rotherhith, Coun. Surry, Spinster, for £20, the whole said 1,250 acres of Land, with the app's, and the s'd S. Cadman, by her Letter dat. 26 March, 1703, Constituted Jos. Brown, of Cohanzy, In Salem Co'ty, Jersey, her attorney, to take up the said Land, who thereupon Requests Warr'ts, Produceing also a Letter from the Prop'ry to the Com'rs Ordering us to grant it forthwith. Ordered that 2 Warr'ts be granted for the Land.

Jno. Jones having Caveated against Evan Jones, Req'ts 4, 4 mo. last. It is Ordered that this afternoon be appointed to hear them.

James Cartt, Att'ry to James Petoe, of Bristol, Requests a Res'y on 490 Acres of Land Situate above Gwynedd, Confirmed to the said James by Pat. dat. 12, 9 mo., '88-9, Which is Granted.

John Hugh Produceing a return of 257 Acres Resurv'd by Our Warrant On a Tract of 250 a's dat. 13, 2 mo, 1702, Requests a Patent, which is Granted.

There haveing Long been Obstructions to the Settlement of the Swanson's Land On Skuylkill, being in the whole 600 a's, 200 thereof Now in the Possession of John Hoodt, 200 More in the Possession of Jno. Callow and the upper 200 is to be Confirmed to Ann Swanson, widow of Andrew Swanson, and Chris'r Swanson, Eldest Son of the said Andrew. John Callow Purchased of James Thomas, of Philad'a, Merchant, 100 Acres, who Purchased of Woolla Swanson, to whom 200 a's, Part of the said 600, fell, and the said James sold to said Callow. Lydia Swanson, relict and Adm'x and Jno. Swanson and Peter Swanson, Eldest and second Son of the said Woolla. Sw., By Deed Poll, dat. 3, 4 mo., '96, Conveyed the said 100 acres, together with 100 more, Viz: 200 in all, to Jno. Callow, of Skuylkill. Ord'd a Resurvey On the Several subdivisions and Patents to the Possessors, they Paying for the Overplus if Any above the allowance.

Ellis Ellis haveing a Warrant of Res. dat. 18, 12 mo., 1701, On two Parcells, Cont. in the whole 330 acres, it Proves 425 and is 65 a. Over, for which He Agrees to Pay 7s 6d P'r Acre, and a Patent is Ordered.

Dan'l Humphries, of Haverf'd, haveing a Res. On 200 or 200¾ in Haverford which Proves 241 and Cont. 21 Acres or 20¼ Overplus, for which he agrees to Pay 8s p'r Acre.

Mem'dum, a Warrant to J. Parsons Ord'd 17, 3 mo. last, and to H Staples. Ord'd 18, Ditto.

Upon the Application of Sam'l Carp'r and Tho. Fairman, Attorneys to the London Company, that in Pursuance of the Prop'ry's Order we would approve of the Survey of Certain Lands made by the said Thomas in Pursuance Of the Prop'ry's Warrant to him dated 17 Aug't, '99, 'Tis Ord'd that One Draught of 1,360 a's in Newcastle County, and One Draught of 7,500 acres above the Falls, and one Draught of 21,500 a's in said County of N. C., in Two Tracts, and One Draught of 3,700 a's in s'd County, be rec'ed and Entred in the Survey'r's Office, they Paying the Fees, and returned into the Sec'ry's Office, Certifyed by Jacob Taylor.

Whereas there is a difference Between Evan Jones, of Kent County, and the Assignees of Jos. Growdon about the Division Line of Two Tracts of Land lately Resurveyed, the One Tract by Geo. Dakyne and the Other By Jonas Greenwood, Survey'rs, which Difference being heard and debated By the Com'rs, they have Ord'd that both the said Survey'rs goe On the Line Aforesaid and Compare the same with the Orig'l Patent Granted To Whitwell for a thous'd acres, also with Evan Jones's First draught of his Survey as also w'th the former Resurveys of the said Growdon's Land, and that the Lines of the said Orig'l Patent, if it breaks in upon the s'd ——— Evans' Claim, shall be Peremptory Notwithstanding the s'd Claim, But if not and the said Evans' first Survey be Prior to the said Jos. Growdon's Resurvey that the Lines Of the said Survey shall stand and the s'd Survey'rs are Required to make their Return Accordingly, dat. at Phila'd 23, 6 mo., 1703.

By Order of the Rest of the Comm'rs.

JAMES LOGAN.

To George Dakyne, Survey'r of the County of Newcastle and To Jonas Greenwood, Survey'r of Kent County.

William Howel haveing formerly Procured a Warr't Of the Comm'rs for 50 acres of Headland to his Serv't, Micah Thomas, which was Executed as is affirmed by Thom's Fairman, in Whitpains Township, upon a Special Warrant, he now Craves a Resurvey and Confirmation, which upon Sundry Considerations in favour of the said Wm. is Granted, he being Obliged in a bond of £60, in the year 1693, to make a Title. A Resurvey is ord'd thereupon.

At a Session of the Comm'rs at Philad'a, 30th 6mo., 1703.

Prst., Edw'd Shippen, Thomas Story, James Logan.

Justus Falkner, attorney of Benajm'n Furly. Produceing a return of 1,000 acres in Chest'r County, said to be in Pursuance of our Warr't dat. 16, 12 mo., 1701, and the Same Land appearing to be an Encroachm't upon the Welch Tract within their Settlements and already granted to David Lloyd and Is. Norris, the Same is Rejected and disapproved of and thereupon 'Tis Ordered that the Same be Certifyed by Indorsement On the said Return under ye Comm'rs hands, which is accordingly Done.

John Budd Claiming a right to 2,500 acres, a Moiety of Jno. Tatham's Purchase, it was apprehended that said Tatham had taken up 2,500 a's in One Tract and 500 in another near the Same In Bucks, but the said Tract of 500 a's Proveing to be laid Out To Thom's Phillips in Right of Jefferson's Purchase of   a's, 'tis thought the s'd John Craves a Warrant for the said 500 a's, which is Granted.

Thomas Johns, One of the New Welch Settlers of the Tract of 30,000 a's, Produceing a return from Geo. Dakyne of 632 a's, 140 Perches, survey'd to the said Thomas John, Requests a Confirmation of the Same. Ord'd that when a return is regularly Produced Out of the Office and a Deed from the Undertakers, a Patent be Granted, he giveing good Security for the Payment of £78 2s 6d, One Moiety 15, 8br. next and the Other 12 months after.

Wm. Huntley desireing to Purchase 200 acres at the Head of Peter Dix's Land beyond Branaywine, Joyning on Thomas Withers, agrees to Pay £40 at a Shilling p'r C't Rent. Granted,

Provided Joel Baily may also be accommodated with the like quantity if he desires it, On the Same Terms. He is to Pay £20 in 3 months and the rest 1 mo., 1705, with 15 Months Interest, if he Can no Sooner.

The Prop'ry, by L. and Rel., dat. 24 and 25 Jan'y, '81, Granted 1,500 acres of Land to Samuel Fox, of Rochester, in Kent, Taylor, who, by Ind're of L. and Rel., dat. 8 and 9 Jan'y, '85, Granted to Rich'd Whitpain, Citizen and Butcher, of London. The Prop'ry, by L. and Rel., dat. 29th and 30th April, '83, Granted to James Claypoole, of London, Merchant, 1,000 acres, who, by Ind're dated 16th and 17th July, 1683, Conveyed the Same to Jno. Marsh, of London, Merch't, who, by Ind're dat. 25th and 26th Jan'ry, '85, again Conveyed the Said Land to said R'd Whitpain. The Prop'ry, by L. and Rel., dat. 10th and 11th Aug't, '82, Granted to Charles Marshall, of Tetherton, Coun. Wilts, Practitioner in Physick, 5,000 acres of Land, who by Ind're dat. 1st and 2d Aug't, '83, Granted to said R'd Whitpain 1,000 acres, Part of the aforesaid. The s'd Charles also Conveyed 1,000 acres more, P't of the aforesaid, to Mary Davy, of London, Spinster, who by Ind're of Lease and Release dat. 25 and 26 Aug't, '86, Conveyed the Same (being then Located by Thomas Holme in the County of Philad'a) to the s'd R'd Whitpain. Copies of the 4 last under the Prop'ry's hand and seal Certifyed. The Prop'ry, by L. and Rel., dat. 17th and 18th 8br., '81, Granted one thousand acres to Sabian Coles, of London, Merchant, who by Ind'r dat. 1st and 2d 7br., '84, Conveyed the Said Land to said R'd Whitpain.

The Prop'ry, by L. and Rel., dat. 17 and 18, 8br., '81, Granted to Jno. and Joseph Moore, of London, Merch'ts, 1,000 acres, who by L. and Rel., dat. 12 and 13th 9br., '84, Conveyed the Same to the said R'd Whitpain. The Prop'ry, by L. and Rel., dat. 17th and 18th 8br., '81, Granted 1,000 acres to Humphrey South, of London, Merchant, who by Ind're of L. and Rel., dat. 1st and 2d Jan'y, '84, Granted 500 acres of the Same to s'd R'd Whitpain, the rest he granted to Barker and Jobson, of all which authentick Copies are Produced, Certifyed under the Prop'rys hand and seal, by which s'd sev'l recited Deeds the said R'd Whitpain became Invested with a right to 7,000 acres of Land in this Province. In Pursuance Of the above Rights there was by Virtue of 5 sev'l Warr'ts from the Prop'ry, dat. 28, 4 mo., '83, 5 Several Lotts laid out in the Front Street, bounded Northw'ds On James Claypoole's and thence Proceeding Thom's Barker 20 foot, Jno. Moore 20 foot, Sabian Cole 20 foot, then Wm. Frampton Interposses, again Samuel Jobson 20 foot, Humphrey South 20 foot, And 5 several High

Street Lotts On the South Side, between the 3d and 4th Street, On the Corner of 4th Street, beginning Eastw'd w'th Tho. Barker 26 foot, Sabian Cole 26 foot, Jno. Moore 26 foot, Sam'l Jobson 26 foot and Hum. South 26 foot. Note, Tho. Barker and Samuel Jobson, by Ind're of Lease and Rel., dat. 14 and 15th Oct'r, '85, joyntly Conveyed to the said R'd Whitpain all their Front Lotts on Dellaware, which they Erroneously Call 60 foot, Situate Between Wm. Frampton's and James Claypoole's lett out (as is s'd, but wrongfully in the Deed) to said Barker and Jobson in Right of their Purchase of 2,500 acres of Land, 1,000 each from the Prop'ry himself and 250 acres more each from Humphrey South, as is there Recited, which tho' Wrong in the recital yet Vested with all their Right to their 2 Lotts. By the s'd Warrants there was also laid out 5 lotts in the Liberties of 16 acres, each Joyning on Griff. Jones' to the N. N. W., and On Thomas Bowman to the East N E., beginning On said Jones', Hum. South 16 acres, Tho. Barker 16 acres, Jno. Moore 16 acres, Sabian Cole 16 acres and Samuel Jobson 16 acres, heading Said Bowman at One End and Vacant at the Other. By warrant from the Comm'rs dat. 26, 5 mo., '86, at Gr. Jones' Inst'e, there was granted to Thomas Barker and Comp. 920 acres, but in the Location is to Humph. South and Company, in the County of Chester, Joyning On the Welch Tract, Surv'd 27, 4 mo., '87, and by a warrant from the Comm'rs dat. 10, 12, '84, at the said Griffith's Instance, there was Laid out in said Co'ty to Thomas Barker and Comp'y 1,000 acres, and to Samuel Jobson and Company 1,000 acres, in the County of Chester, surv'd 24th 12 mo., '84., By 5 Warr'ts More, all dat. 28, 4 mo., '83, from the Prop'ry there was granted to John Moore, Tho. Barker, Samuel Jobson, Sabian Cole and Hum. South each 400 acres, in all 2,000, which was laid Out in Chester County, Joyning On R'd Collet's, which several Parcels make up the whole Complem't of 5,000 acres, 3,000 of which being R'd Whitpain's Right, he takes the first ment'd 920 and the last 3,000. Charles Marshall haveing himself Purchased 5,000 acres, is Called in the Warrants C. M. and Company, Purchasers of 6,000 acres, and in the Surveys they are Made to be Thom's Cox, Jno. Beasley, Charles Marshall, Jonas Smith, Rich'd Whitpain and Mary Davy, who had each 914 acres laid out in the County of Philad'a, in a tract laid Out for 5,500 acres, 9th 12 mo., '84, In Pursuance of a Warrant from the Prop'ry dat. 29th 3 mo., '84, for the said Quantity, and being Resurveyed, the whole was laid Out to R'd Whitpain in Right of Fox, and 'tis Supposed, Claypoole 2,500 acres in the Lower Part of that Township. Charles Marshall's Lotts fell On Skuylkill, the Front is the South Corner of Walnut Street, 122 foot, Surv'd

15, 9 mo., '83, and the High Street was laid Out the Same day; the Other 500 a's was laid out 13, 12 mo., '84, On Skuylkill, to Cha. Marshall and Company. Rich'd Whitpain being Vested with the said 7,000 acres, In his Last will and Testament, dat. 27 Ap'l, '89, appointing his wife, Mary Whitpain, his Ex'rx, Willed and declared that his house in the Front Street, of 60 foot in breadth and 56 foot depth, and his Plantation of 4,000 acres, Called Whitpain's Creek, with 100 acres Liberty Land and 250 or thereabouts in the County of Chester, and 500 acres to be taken up, Should be sold by his Ex'x as far as Necessary for the Payment of his debts. The said Ex'x by Ind're dat. 30 July, '89, Granted and Conveyed to Jno. Elridge, of the Parish of St. Mary Hill, London, Distiller; Wm. Ingram, of London, Salter; Jno. Blackhall, of London, Drap'r; Jno. Wase, of London, Clothworker, to have and to Hold to them, their Heirs, Ex'rs and assigns for Ever, all the said Messuages, Lands and Tenements (the last 500 acres, which the said R'd Whitpain had a right to Take up, Excepted), and all her s'd husband's Estate whatsoever, for the satisfyeing of the Cred'rs and Answering the said R'ds debts. Ingram and Blackhall, the Surviving Trustees, by their Instrument of Procuration, dat.   , appointed Tho. Storey, Rees Thomas and Ja's Logan att'ys to Receive Into their hands all writeings and Deeds belonging to said Estate, to Enter upon the Same and dispose of it according to the Trusts aforesaid. The said attorneys Crave Resurvey On all the Lands and Confirmation in Order to Sale, Which is Granted.

Recital of T. F.'s Deed to his Brother Robert, Fa. Shackamaxon, dat. 23, 6 mo., 1703, 256 acres, Part of 327 Sold by Mich'l Leyson, al's Nelson, to Tho. Child and Rob't Everndon, by Deed dat. 31, 8br., '99, Recorded Philad'a, B. E., 3, Vol. 5, pa. 323, and by them Conveyed to said T. F. by Deed dat. 4 June, 1700, which 327 acres are Part of 462½ acres granted or Confirmed to said Mich'l by Pat. from the late Comm'rs, dat. 4 March, '91, under the Yearly Rent of One Bushell of wheat, which said 462½ acres were the said Mich'ls dividend of a Tract held formerly by him in Joint Tenancy with Peter Cock by virtue of a Patent dat. 3 May, 1671, Granted to them by Gov'r Lovelace for about 600 acres.

The Comm'rs haveing Granted a Warrant to Mary Heyworth, dat. 26, 8br. last, for a Parcell of Vacant Land in Pursuance of the Prop'ry's Orders, at £20 p'r C't, which Now Proves upon the return 278 a's. Ord'd that her first Bond of £150 be given up and that she give a Bond to John Satcher for £45 12s, and a Bill On Will'm Ward'r for £10, and that thereupon she have a Patent.

At a Session of the Comm'rs at Philad'a, 27th 7br 1703. Omnes.

The Comm'rs, W. M., R. T. and J. G., by Patent in Paper, dat. 7, 5 mo., '84 (Recorded in the Office B. A., No. 1, Pa. 73), Confirmed to Ebenezer Langford 500 acres of Land on Darby Creek, in Chest'r Coun., Granted by the Prop'rys Warrant, dat. 5, 8 mo., '83, Surv'd the Same day to the said Eb. La.; the s'd Ebenezer Langford, of Antigua, by his Letter of attorney, dat.   , and Recorded in the Sec'rys Office at Philad'a, Book, 1, No. 1, Pa. 73, Impowered Edward Hunlock, of W. N. Jersey, Mercht, to Sell One tract of Land in the said Province, bounding On Darby Creek, who thereupon by his Ind're dat. 1, 9br., '94, Conveyed the said Tract, being the above, to James Stanfield. The Said James, by Ind're dat. 8, 3 mo., '96, Conveyed to Thomas Hope, of the County of Chester, 100 acres, Part of the aforesaid. The said James Stanfield is also said to have sold of the said Tract 100 acres to Jno. Fincher, who Sold the Same to Hen. Hams, of Ch. County, but Stanfield Conveyed it to the said Hams, No Deeds haveing Past to Fincher, And Hams, by Exchange, Granted $8\frac{7}{8}$ acres of the said Tract to Thomas Massey, of Chester Co'ty, all which Deeds are said to be recorded in the Rolls of Chester County. And Thomas Massey, by Deed Poll dat. 13, 6 mo., 1703, Conveyed the said $8\frac{7}{8}$ acres to said Thomas Hope, Tho. Hope, by Ind're dat. 31, 6 mo., 1703, Conveyed to Bartho. Coppock, Jun'r, of Spring, Coun. Ch'r, the s'd 2 several Parcells of 100 acres and $8\frac{7}{8}$ acres together with One Other Parcell In the Welch Tract.

The Prop'ry, by his Warr't dat. 6, 8br., '83, Granted to John Nixon to Take up in Ch. County 374 acres, in Pursuance of which there was Survey'd to the said Jno. in One Tract On Ridley Creek, 74 acres, and in another On the West side of Darby Creek 300 acres, as appears by Copies from the Survey'rs Office, which last Tract of 300 acres bounds On the above $108\frac{7}{8}$ a's. Jno. Nixon, by Deed dat. 12, 2 mo., '87, conveyed the said 30 acres to the said Barth. Coppock, who being Possessed of the said 3 Parcells, Procured the Same to be Resurveyed by Virtue of Our Warrant dat. 23, 12 mo., 1702, and is found Now to Contain 448 a's, On which he req'ts a Patent and is accordingly Ordered. There is Paid for the Survey £2 4s 8d To 1s. Taylor.

The Prop'ry, by Ind're of L. and Rel., dat. 8 and 9, 9br., '81, Granted to Leonard Fell, of Beakley, in Furnis, in the Co'ty of Lancaster, Yeo'n, 500 acres of Land, and the s'd Leonard Fell by a Deed of Gift, dat. 6th April, '99, Granted the said 500 acres to Wm. Norcross, of Alston, in the County of Lancaster, husbandman, who On Board the Britannia, in his Voyage from Liverpool to Pensilvania, made his Last will, dat. 12, 6 mo., '99, and Granted Of the said Land to Each of his 4 Children, Jno., Wm., Sarah and Thomas Norcross, 60 Acres, and the rem'r to his widow dureing her Widowhood, but in Case of Marriage to Revert and be divided among his said Children, and made his Wife Eliz'th and his Son Jno. Ex'rs, but the Latter Not being of age the Widow took Letters of adm'rn dureing his Minority, and Craves a warrant to take up the said Land. Granted.

Thomas Ashton Produceing a return of 100 a's in Bucks, in Pursuance of Our Warrant dat. , And haveing Paid the Consideration Money, he desires a Patent, which is Granted.

———

At a Session of the Comm'rs at Philad'a, 4th 8 mo. 1703.
Omnes.

Granted to Jno. Chandler 50 foot on the S. of Mulberry Str., beween his Lotts and Wm. Snead, for 7 years at 5s St'l. p'r Ann.

Samuel Richardson Produceing a return of 1,160 acres, Resurv'd In Pursuance of the Prop'rys Warrant, dat. , On a tract laid Out for 1,000 a's In right of Thomas Bowman, of w'ch he claims 100 for allowance and the Other 60 in Right of what he has yet to take up. Ordered that In Case he Prove his Right to said 60 acres a Patent be Granted.

Sam'l Browne and Jno. Blunston Produceing a return of 240 a's, in Pursuance of Our Warrant dat. 29th 7br., 1702, resurveyed to Jno. Browne, now of this Province, son of Jno. Browne, dec'd, req'ts a Patent. Granted for the title, vid. Min's 29, 7br., dit. The Prop'ry, by L. and Rel., dat. 19 and 20 Mar., 1681, Granted to Jno. Alsop, of Inquestry, Coun. Stafford, Yeom'n, 1,000 acres, who by Deed Poll dat. 19 July, '84, granted said 1,000 acres, with all its app'ts, to Thom's Tunnicliff, of Haughton, in the County of Stafford, Yeoman.

The Prop'ry, by Patent dat. 12, 4 mo., '84, Granted to Anthony Weston a Certain Lott in Chestnutt Street, On the North side, situate btween the 3d and 4th Streets, bounded to the Eastw'd with Jno. Austin's, W'd Vacant, N'wd with High Street Lotts, no dimensions, Granted by Warr't dat. 28, 5 mo., '83, Surv'd the day following, Rent 5s Ster. yearly, and was built upon. Upon Judg'ts Obtained ag't the said Anth. Weston, for debts and a writt of Venditione Exponas thereupon, directed to Thomas Farmer, H. Sheriff of the County, the said Sher. On the 24th 9br., 1701, Sold the Same to Jno. Budd, Up-

26—VOL. XIX.

holsterer, in Pursuance of the Law of this Province, &c. John Budd sold the Same to Tho. Fairman, but not Conveyed, and therefore upon the said Thomas' sale of the Same to Nath'l Webb, of Philad'a, Cooper, The said Jno. and Thomas, by their Ind're dated 25 June, 1703, Joyntly Conveyed the Same to the said Nath'l Webb, who req'ts a New Patent On the Same. Ganted, See the Deed with David Lloyd.

Granted to Thomas Evan, of Meirion, 500 a's On the Upper side of Gilberts, at £20 p'r C't, running the whole breadth if he take it.

The Prop'ry, by L. and Rel., dat. 23 and 24, 7ber, '81, Granted to Philip Ranings, al's Rakeings, of Lyneham, in the County of Wilts, shoemaker, 250 acres of Land, and the said Philip, by Indorsement on the Rel., dat. 8, 10br., '96, assigned and made Over 125 a's, being One Moiety of the aforesaid, to Jno. Mendenhall, of Concord, Coun. Chest'r, Yeoman, the whole being then Located in the said Tows'p of Concord. Jno. Mendenhall, by Deed dat. 9, 8br., 1703, Conveyed to Jos. Edw'ds, of the Same Township, all the s'd Tract of 125 a's, with all his right and title therein, The said Tract being Resurveyed Contains 150 a's, 125 p's.

Jno. Harding, Original Purchaser of 500 acres, by a Deed of Sale dat. 27, 4 mo., '83, as is Recited in the following Patent, Conveyed 250 acres, P't of the aforesaid, to Jno. Mendenhall, the Same being laid out 13, 12 mo., '82, by Virtue of the Prop'rys Warrant, dat. 6th Of the Same Month, and in Pursuance of the said sale the Prop'ry Confirmed the Same by Patent, dat. 26, 4 mo., '84, to the said Jno. Mendenhall, who by Indorsement on s'd Patent, dat. 1, 4 mo., '86, Assigned the said 250 acres to his Brother, Benj. Mendenhall, by Deed dat. 14, 1 mo., '93-4, Conveyed 50 a's of the s'd 250 a's to The s'd Jos. Edw'ds, w'ch being resurvey'd, is found to Contain 58 acres, 20 P's. Jno. Kingsman, of Chichester, by Deed dat. 14 Mar., '93-4, Conveyed to the s'd Jos. Edw'ds 100 a's in Thornbury, Joyning On the Above 50 a's, being Part of Jno. Simcock's Tract of 1,500 a's, of which he granted Part to the said Kingsman, with his wife, the said Simcock's Daughter, and the said 100 a's being Resurveyed is found to Contain 110 a's, 145 Per's, all these lying Contiguous. The said Jos. Edwards req'ts a Patent On the Whole, being 319 acres, and is 19 Acres Over, which is offered at £7, and if he accept a Patent is Granted. See 1st 9ber. next.

Benj'n Mendenhall's remaining 200 acres being Resurveyed is found to Contain 244 a's and is 24 a's Over, for which he agrees to Pay £7 10s, and a Patent is Ordered, the return to be had from Jacob T.

MINUTE BOOK "G." 403

Robert Lloyd Produces A Return of 482 acres Resurveyed in Meirion, in Pursuance of Our Warr't, dat. 20, 2 mo. last, for Resurveying 409½ Acres, One Moeiety of 819 Acres, Part of Thomas Ellis's Land, On which said 432 a's the said Robert Craves a Patent. Granted, Vid. Welch Min's, 19th 2 mo. last. The said 819 acres is made up of 625 acres bought of L. Owen, R. Owen, Ellis Morris, and Ellis ap Hugh, of Robert Davies' Purchase, and 84 a's of Overplus and Part of the Original Purchase.

Memorandum, to settle John Fincher's Land.

David Lloyd, in behalf of Joseph Growdon, Produceing a return of 1,000 a's, Survey'd In Bucks, in Pursuance of Our Warrant, dat. 8, 4 mo. last, upon which he req'ts a Patent. Granted to Lawrence Growdon, by the Name of L. G., of Anstel, Coun. Cornw., Gent., who by Deeds of L. and Rel., dat. 24th and 25th of 8ber, 1681, Purchased of the Prop'ry 5,000 acres, and by Deeds of the Same Date, Jos. Growdon, His Son, by the Name of J. G., of Trevoze, Coun. Cornwall, Gent.

In Pursuance of Our Grants to T. Ll's Ex'rs, there is Surveyed to them, viz: D. Ll. and Is. Norris, in Gwynedd, 654 acres in the Welch Tract out of Ellis David's 203 a's, and in One Large Tract in Right of the Land Surrender'd On Indian River 1,000 acres; there is also Out of Evan Jones's in the Welch Tract, 178 acres, mak'g In the whole 2,035 a's and is 101 acres above their due, for which they are to Pay £20, And 2 Patents are Ord'd, One for the 1,000 a's in the Welch Tract in Chest'r Co'ty, the Other for 654 in Gwynedd, In Philad'a Coun.

Ordered to Judge Guest, upon his Earnest Application for a Lott in the City, That there be granted to him 150 foot between the 3d and 4th Street, situate Midway Between Sassafras and Vine street, viz: leaving 200 foot for Sassafras Street Lotts and 285 for Vine street Lotts, to be held at 10s st'rl. p'r Annum for Ever; also all the remaining 385 foot extending to Vine street, upon a Lease of 21 Years, On the Same Rent with the former.

This Day agreed by all the Comm'rs with Jacob Taylor that he shall have £70 Certain for his Yearly Sallary, he finding himself in all Necessaries and that James Logan take Care as Sec'ry that he be duely Paid the Same Out of the Survy'rs Office, and where the money is obtained in the Several Survey'rs hands for their work done On the Prop'ry's Account, and what is not Paid into the Office than then the s'd James Logan as Rec'r who Ought to Pay the Survey'rs for their said Work, shall Out of the Prop'ry's Effects make Good the said Sum to the said Jacob; Also that a Commission be granted to the said Jacob Taylor to make his works in his Office the more Authentick.

The Prop'ry, by L. and Rel., dat. 11 and 12, 8br., 1681, Granted to Wm. Bowman, of Wandsworth, Coun. Surrey, Glazeier, 5,000 acres, in Right of which there was Taken Up 500 acres in Bristol Township, near the Liberties, by a Warr't from the Prop'ry, dat. 26, 12 mo., '82, Surv'd 5, 5 mo., '83, Pat'd 12, 4 mo, '84, also 300 acres in Bucks, on Delaware, Joyning On Tho. Rudyard, by a warrant from the Prop'ry, dat. 26, 8br., '83, Surv'd 3d, 7 mo, '84, Conf'd By Patent 29, 11 mo., '84, also 80 acres of Liberty Land, now Griff. Jones', by the Prop'ry's Warrant, dat. 12, 8 mo., '83, Surv'd 19, 1st, mo., Pat'd 5, 2 mo., '86; also a Front Street Lott or the High Street, by War't dat. 19, 4 mo., '83, Surv'd 26th, Do., Pat'd 20, 11 mo., '84, both recorded; also 1,000 a's In Chester County. The said William Bowman, by his Instrum't of Procuration, dated 8th April, '82, Constituted his Son Thomas Bowman, his sole Att'y, to take up, sell and dispose of all the said Land, who by Ind're dat. 3d 5 mo., '86, in Consid'rn of £340 Sterling, Conveyed the whole said Premisses to Samuel Richardson, then of Jamaica, Bricklayer, who afterwards sold to Char. Pickering, of this Province, 3,000 a's which, with the Aforement'd Tracts taken up, make up in the whole 4,880 acres.

The Prop'ry, by his Warrant, dat. 11, 8br., 1701, Granted to David Powell, of Bristol Township, to take up 242 a's, by him bought of Edw'd Lane, being in Right of his Father, Wm. Lane's Purchase of 500 a's, of w'ch 250 were taken up in Bristol Township, and 50 more adjoyning, he bo't of Jno. Bowyer, Being Part of Walter King's Purchase, and by Deed dated 2, 4 mo., '99, Convey'd the said Messuage, Mentioned to be 300 a's, but they affirm 'twas Only 250, and that the 50 acres ment'd in the Min's dat. 10th, 1 mo., 1700-1, were sold out of the Located Land, and the whole 242 to be taken up were in Right Of Lane (the s'd 50 a's were sold to the Pietists). D. Powell, by the name of Da. Powell, of Bristol Towns'p, Coun. Philad'a, Yeoman, Granted the said 242 Acres, being Located in the Townsh'p of Caln, Coun. Chester, and returned duely to his Son-in-Law, Lewis Lewis, of the Township of Newtown, Yeoman, by Deed of Gift Dated 5, 8br., 1703, On which he requests a Patent. Granted, if it appears that the said 50 acres were sold of The located Land and not the Other. Ord'd forthwith, the said Lewis to give £5 Bond in Case there be not a right to it.

Of R'd Davies' Purchase Tho. Ellis bo't of Mesne Purchases, Viz: of Lewis Owen, Rowl'd Owen, Ellis Maurice and Ellis Pugh 625 a's, which, with 194 more, Dan'l Humphreys,

Adm'r of said Estate, sold to Jno. Williams, who by Deed dat. 10, 5 mo., 1700, sold 200 thereof to Jno. Evan Edwards, Of Radnor.

The Comm'rs Granted to David P. 500 a's by Patent dat. 4, 4 mo., '86, Out of which by Deed Dat'd 22d 5 mo., '87, he Conveyed to said Jno. Evan Edward 100 a's, We, by Our Warrant dat. 28, 2 mo., 1702, Granted a Resurvey On the said Two tracts, which being returned, the first Contains 200 Only, and the Other 123 a's, of which 13 A's being Overplus, he agrees to give the Com'on Rate, viz: 6s 8d. A Pat. is Ord'd On both In One.

David Powell, by Deed dat. 17, 3 mo., '90, Conveyed 100 acres to James Pugh, and By Deed dat.   , Conveyed to Wm. Davies 200 a's, who by Deed Dated 22, 6 mo., '90, sold 50 thereof to said James, upon which 150 we Granted Our Warrant, dat. 28, 2 mo., 1702, and being executed, it was found to Contain 162 a's, On which a Pat. is Ordered.

Wm. Davies sold the Other 150 To Griffith Miles, and He to Phil. Phillips, but No Conveyance, therefore the said William Davies, Griff. Miles and Phoebe Phillips, Relict of the said Phillip, Conveyed the Same to David Pugh, which being Resurveyed by Our Warrant, dat. 28, 2 mo., 1702, is found to Contain 174 Acres and is 9 a's Over, for which he agrees to Pay £3, and A Patent is Ord'd. The s'd Pat'ts with the rest of Radnor, Ord'd 6 mo. last, to be done forthwith being Promised in a Fortnight.

Friends, appointed by the Meeting, Applying to this Board for a Lott in Right of George Fox's Original Purchase of 1,250 a's, It is Agreed that there should be granted to them 25 foot Out of the Lott formerly sett Out to Thomas Brassey, but Griffith Jones haveing Purchased Jno Simcock's Lotts and being Now Possessed of 25 foot Joyn'g On Day's Lott in right of Antho. Tompkins', and being desirous to have his Lott lie Contiguous, It is Agreed Between him and the Com'rs that the s'd Griffith shal' have 25 foot Adjoyning On the South side of his Lott, Purchased of Jno. Simcock, for which He is to Make Over and Convey to the Prop'ry the said 25 foot of Tompkins', with the Bank, Upon his doing of which a Patent is Ordered.

Granted also to ye said Griff. Jones to Inclose the remaining Part of the Lott formerly laid Out to Tho. Brassey, being 77 foot, by extending his Own Fence by it To R'd Thomas's Lott, upon Condition that he shall Grub the Same and Convert it into Pasture untill It shall Otherwise be disposed of, and then the said Griff. Shall have Leave to take of his Fence in Any time within Ten days after Warning.

Mem'dum, to Write to Geo. Dakyne about 200 Acres vacant Land Joyning On J. Yeates for him, also to Cause David P'l to make a return of the Overplus of R'd Roberts' Land To John Fincher, and to make up his Complement Elsewhere in Pursuance of Our Warrant.

Ord'd a Patent To Thomas Roberts and Cadwallader Jones for their Land in Meirion forthwith, and that in Goshen to be differed.

Ord'd a Patent to Dav. Lloyd for 1,000 acres of his Father-In-Law's Purchase; the Deed from J. G. to him to be made, date (Blank), and on 666 A's, as Returned.

It haveing been made appear that Tho. Jno. Evan, Sen'r, of Radnor, really Paid for his 250 a's, On which, with 50 a's more, he held a Resurvey, Ord'd 24, 9 mo. last, and haveing cleared the Quitt Rents of his Other 50 a s to the 1 mo., 1702, Craves a Patent On the return of his Warrant, being 340 acres, On Com'on Rent, and agrees to Pay £5 10s for Reduceing the Rents of the said 50 a's, and £3 6s 8d for the 10 acres Overplus, which is Granted, The title of the 50 a's as follows: David Kinsey, by Warrant dated   , took up 300 a's in Radnor On Rent, who deceasing, his widow, Magdalen, and Heir, Jno. Kinsey, by Deed dat 14, 9ber, '90, sold the Same to James James, of Radnor, Yeoman, who by Deed dat. 8, 4 mo., '95, sold 50 thereof to said Thomas Jno. Evan.

At a Session of the Comm'rs at Philad'a, 9 br., 1st, 1703.
Prst, Edward Shippen, Thomas Storey, Jas. Logan.

James Widdows Obtained a Warrant from the Comm'rs dat. 14, 2 mo, '85, for 200 a's On New Rent, in New C. County, which was executed by T. Pierson 18, 12 mo., '85-6, as by a regular return Appears. The said Land J. Widdows, by an Instrument under his hand, dat. 6, 12 mo., 1702-3, Acknowledges to have sold to Henry Pierce, who hath lived On it about 12 years, and being willing to Clear all Arrears, requests a Patent, which is granted, When Is. Taylor has tried the Measure which he is forthwith to Do. There is due to the 1st mo. Next £22 10s, of which was Paid to Ellis Gibbs, in '98, 6 Bushells at 7s, is 42s, and 4 Bushells to Col. Emps., in 1700, at 5s is 20s, in the whole £3 2s, remains £19 18s, which he is forthwith to Pay.

James Claypoole, by L. and Rel., dat. 13th, 14th 7 mo., 1681, Purchased of the Prop'ry 5,000 a's of Land, for 1,000 of which there was a Warrant granted by the Prop'ry, dat. 12, 5 mo., '84, which was Executed (as in Our Account) 30, 7 mo., '84, (Vid. E. P's Acco't of Warrants and returns), in Chester

County, near Duffrien Mawr. Francis Cook, Adm'r de bonis Non, of James Clayp.'s Estate, together with George, Joseph and Francis Claypoole, by their dat. 5, 1 mo., 1700, Conveyed 1,000 acres of the said Tract to Adam Roades, who requests a Resurvey.

In Pursuance of Our Warrant dat. 18, 3 mo. last, to Cha. Whiteacre there is Surveyed and returned 400 a's, for which 'tis Now Agreed that Jos. Baker, of Edgemont, and Francis Yarnall, of Springfield, both of Chester County, are to Pay £133 On the 1st of the 1 mo. next, with Interest from the 1st of the 7 mo. last, the said Charles haveing released the whole said Land To the said Francis, and a Patent is Ordered to the said Francis for the whole forthwith. Deed from Charles to Francis dated this Day.

Whereas it Appears by Original Deeds Produced to us 2 mo., 1702, that John Harries, of Goatacre, was An Original Purchaser of 1,500 Acres, Notwithstanding he is not in the List, the said Dates bearing date in 7 br., '81. It is Agreed a Lott shall be Granted to the said John in Lieu of his Front and High Street Lotts, viz: 3 Lotts of 50 foot each On the So. side of Mulberry Street, near Wm. Oxley's, to extend 300 foot towards High Street Lotts, and a Warrant is Ordered, Vid. P. 13.

Wm. Clayton Produces an acc't of a return Out of the Office of a Lott of 251 foot in Length and 51 In breadth, bounding On Longhurst Street and Thom's Fitz Waters, surv'd 22, 2 mo., '84. Will'm Cloud, Original Purchaser of 500 a's, by a Warrant dat. 30th 9 mo., '83, who by Deed dat. 28, 8ber, '98, Conveyed the Same to William Clayton, of Chichester, who req'ts a Resurvey and Patent. Granted.

Ord'd a Patent to Jos. Edw'ds On all his Land, he Paying £6 8s 8d for the Overplus, Vide 11th Ulto., forthwith.

Nath'l Thornton Produces a Patent from the Prop'ry, dat. 16, 4 mo., '84, for a Lott On Skuylkill 100 foot in breadth and 176½ foot in Length bounded N. W'd with Mulberry Street, E. w'd with 4th Street, S. w'd with Eb. Smith's Lott, W. w'd Vacant, Granted by a Warrant 12, 8 mo., '83, Surv'd 28, 12 mo., '84, to Milicent Hodgkins, Rent 2s 6d Sterling. M. Hodgkins, by Indorsm't dat. 30, 9 mo., '91, assigned The Same to Evan Morris; also a Patent from the Prop'ry to Wm. Harwood, dat. 4, 6 mo., '84, for a Lott On Skuylkill, between the 3d and 4th Street, 49½ foot in breadth and 306 foot Long, bounded Northward with Back lotts, E. w'd with Ja's Clayton's Lott, S. w'd with Mulberry Street, W. w'd vac't, Rent 6d Sterling Per annum, assigned by said Wm. Davies by Indorsem't On said Patent, 26th 10br., '90. Evan Morris Sold the first Lott to said Wm. Davies without Convey'ce, and

Wm. Davies sold both Lotts to Mich'l Walton, who sold the Same to said N. Thornton. The said Morris Davies and Walton therefore by a Joint Deed, dat. 25, 12 mo., '98-9, Conveyed the said Lotts to said Natha'l Thornton. The said Wm. Davies also Procured a Warrant from the Comm'rs, dat. 11th March, '92-3, directed to Thomas Holme for surveying to him Two Half Squares near Owen Faulk's lott On Schuylkill, On the Same Terms as Wm. Carter an Others have Taken up (which the s'd Thornton affirms was at 2s p'r acre for 21 years Only, from the Grant, Inq'e in the Min's of that time Or of Wm. Carter). Wm. Davies, by a Small Paper Under his hand, dat. 28, 1 mo., '99, assigned all his Right, both to that and 5 a's More, being in the whole 10 acres, to the said Nath'l Thornton, who requests some further Confirmation of the Same, Upon which 'tis Ordered that the said Nath'l Thornton Paying

The Prop'ry, by L. and Rel., dat. 19 and 20 March, '81, Granted to Jno. Alsop, of Inquestry, in the County of Stafford, Yeoman, 1,000 acres of Land, who by deed dated 19 July, 1684, Granted the whole said 1,000 acres To Thomas Tunnicliffe, of Haughton, in the said County, Yeoman, appurtenant to the s'd Purchase, a Lott fell in Delaware Front Street, and a High Street Lott, Surv'd 29, 5 mo., '86, by Warrant 26th said Mo. and year. Thomas Tunnicliffe by Ind're dat. 13, 10 mo., '87, Conveyed to Robert Longshore, Coun. Philad'a, yeom., 16 acres of Lib. Land, Part of the said Purchase, and Joyning on Robert Grenaway's, together with the said Front Lott, 20 foot and 4 Inches, bounded North with James Kinneryl's, South with a Vacant Lott, and the said High Street Lott, being in breadth 26 foot, in Length 306 f't, bounded E. w'd vacant, W.sw'd with 5th Street, N. w'd with H. Street, Consid. £15 See this Deed, Rec'd Bo. E., 1, Vol. 5, pag. 62.

Rob't Longshore, by Deed Called Ind're, dat. 9th 8ber, '86, Conveyed the said Front Lott To Thomas Bull, of Philad'a, Merch't (Deed Rec'd E., Vol. 5, pa. 490), who by Indorsement On the said Deed, dat. 25th 7ber, 1703, Conveyed the Same to Richard Bull, of the County of Gloucester, and Prov. of New Jersey, Yeoman, who Req'ts a Patent, and is Granted.

Mem'dum, Jno. Fincher with D. P.

---

9 mo., 8 [1703.]

Present, Edw'd Shippen, Gr. Owen and James Logan.

Jos. Wood haveing Purchased the Lott adjoyning On his House in Newc., which was Direck Harmensen's, since Intermarried with James Sinnexon, of the said James and Direck and Anna Harmenson, her Sister (vid. Newc. Min's in Maj'r Donaldson's), Req'ts a Warrant for the Bank, But Joannes Jordin, of Newc., claiming 18 foot of it, his said Claim is first to be heard.

Rich'd Thomas Produces a return of a High St. Lott of 132 foot in Right of his Father's Purchase, and of 51 foot in the Front Street, the latter in Pursuance of Our Warrant, for which he requests a Patent. Granted.

Griff. Owen haveing had a Resurvey on 401½ a's in Goshen, the Same is found to Contain 775 acres, of which 40 being allowed for Measure, there Remains 333½ to be Paid for, which he agrees to allow, and Craves a Patent, which is Ordered.

Philip Howel haveing by Deed dat. 18, 2mo., 1702, Purchased the Rights to the Head Land of Humphrey Edwards, who Came into this Province Serv't To Jno. ap Edwards, Jeremy Osborn and his wife Eliz'th, formerly Day, both Servants to Griff. Jones, Jacob Willis Serv't to William Cloud, Evan Williams Servant to Thomas Ellis, and Marg't, his wife, formerly Richard, Serv't to John Bevan, Edm'd McVeagh Servant to Thomas Holme, and Alice, his wife, formerly Dickinson, Servant to Ja. Harrison, Abraham Pratt, Jane Pratt, Tho. Pratt and John Pratt, Servants to the Society, Requests Warrants To Take it up.

Reuben Ford makeing it appear that he Came In a Servant to Jno. Gibbons and Duely Served his Time, Requests a Warrant. Granted.

Edward Griffith haveing a Warrant On 300 acres in Two Tracts Produces a return, by which One Tract is found to Contain 217 acres and the Other 117 acres, which is 7 acres Overplus, for which he agrees to Pay £2 10s, and a Patent is Ord'd forthwith.

Mem'dum of E. Jefferson's sale of 200 acres of his Purchase to John Day, of which 100 is Granted to Hen. Paxton by Warr't 3d 3 mo., 1703.

The Prop'ry, by deeds dat. 26, 7br., '81, vid. Rolls Bo. A., vol. fo. 82, Granted to Edm'nd Bennett 1,000 acres, who by warrant dated 1st 12 mo., '82, Took up 300 a's In Bristol Township, in Bucks, and the said Edm'd by his last will, dat. 5, 7ber, '92, Granted his whole Estate to his wife Eliz'th Bennett, who by her deed dated the 22, 3 mo., 1702, Conveyed 100 a's, Part thereof, to Wm. Crosdale. The said Tract being resurveyed is found to Contain 151 a's, for the Overplus of which he Offers £10, being Barren. A Patent is granted, the Consideration to be for Services done and No Sum.

Mem. Consult the Comm'rs about 50 acres, P't of about 7 or 800 for a meeting Place, also about 200 in Marsh, Criple, &c. See if G. D. has wrote about it. Write about Jacobus Vanderculing 200 acres of Matth. Defosse; Inquire of him of his Mother-In-Law, Lydia Swanson. Jno. Gregg also desires The Same Overplus.

Sam'l Nichols a patent. Omitted, refers To pa. 297.

6th 10ber [1703.]

Present, Edw'd Shippen, Tho. Storey and James Logan.

Granted to George Harmar, Taylor, 12 Cord of fal'n wood at 20d p'r Cord.

Mem'dum, to write to Allen Foster and B. Duffield to End their business.

10ber, 27 [1703.]

Present, Edw'd S., Griff. O., Jam. Logan.

The Govern'r of York by Patent dat. 11 Jan., 1667, Granted a Certain Lott in Newc. Strand of 60 foot Between To Henrick Jansen Van Evertson, who by assignment dat. 28, 9br., '71. made Over the Same to Cornels Josisson, whose widdow Geertia and Garrit Otto, her husband, made Over the Same by another assignment dat. 5th 9br., '78, to Jan. Harmson, whose Daughter, Dirreck or Dorcas, Intermarrying with James Sinnexen, and his Other Daughter Ann, by Deed dat. 8 June, 1703, Conveyed the Same to Jos. Wood. But Cornel. Josisson leaving a Daughter, Anna Maria, the true Heiress of the said Lott, who Intermarried with Jos. Moore, of Newcastle County, Millwright, they, the said Jos. and Anna, his wife, by an Instrument dat. 20 Febr'y, 1702, released their Whole right to the said James Sinnexen and Dorcas, his wife, and Ann Harmsen, who Conveyed as abovesaid. Jos. Wood Requests a Warrant for the Bank Ground.

Rob't Asheton, Produceing the Prop'ry's Deed to his Father's Children, ment'd Pa. 103. On which Deed the Prop'ry, under his hand, by Indorsement thereon, Ordered that the said Robert shall take up 1,500 Acres thereof; requests Warr'ts To take up 1,000 a's more of the Same. Granted in 2 warrants. The Children are Rob't, Francis, Mary, Rachel and Jno., the last dead.

At a Session of the Comm'rs at Philad'a, 3d 11 mo., 1703.

Prst., Edward Shippen, Tho. Storey, Jam's Logan.

Jno. Parsons Produceing a Return of Survey of 558 a's, Resurveyed to Wm. Watson, in New Bristol Township, Upon a

MINUTE BOOK "G."   411

Warrant for 490 Acres and is 19 a's Over Measure, for which he Agrees to Pay £3 16s, and req'ts a Pat't, Granted.

Tho. Prior Produces a Deed from Tho. Fairman, dat. 27, 10 mo., 1701, Granting 200 Acres of Land to Silas Prior, Part of Tho. Harley's Purchase, for which He Requests a Warrant. Granted.

Jno. Evans, Sen'r, of Radnor, Produces a return of 300 acres Resurveyed by a General Warrant, should Contain 250, and Consists of 150 acres, the rem'r of 350 Acres bo't by him of R'd Davies, and the 50 a's bo't of R'd Davies by R'd Corn, and sold by his Son to said John, and 50 a's of Rent Land, being one Moiety of 100 Acres taken up, 'tis Supposed by himself, is 25 acres Overplus, for which he is to Pay £8 6s 8d, and for Reduceing the Rent £5 10s, and Requests a Patent On the whole, w'ch is Granted, vid. Welch Min's.

11 mo., 10th [1703.]

Present, Omnes.

Tho. Prior Producing an Instrument under the Lesser seal and William Markham's hand, dated 31, 8 mo., '89, designed for a Patent for 30 foot of Bank to Nath'l Allen, between the Lotts of Philip James and Philip Richards, Granted by Warrant, dat. 20, 11 mo., '88, Surv'd 27 s'd Mo. to s'd Nath'l. This said Lott Nath'l Allen, by his last will, dat. 21 Aug't, '92, devised to his Daug'r, Lydia, Present wife of Tho. Prior, the Upper half of this Lott was sold To Jos. Kirl by the Mother (it Seems wrongfully), the Other Moiety said Thom's Craves to have Confirmed and would buy off the Reversions; is to give £16 10s.

Edward Baily Purchaser of 250 acres, by Deeds dat. 23 and 24 May, '82, by his Instrument dated 18, 3 mo., '83, Constituted Philip Ruming his Att'y, To take up his said Land, which he did, and now Craves the Lott Appurtenant To it. It is No. 187, falls between Mulb. Street and Sassafr., and 6th and 7th Street from Delaware.

Phil. Ruming, being also himself Purchaser of 250 a's, by Deeds dated 23d and 24th 7ber, '81, but not Entered in Any of the List, haveing Some Right by his said Purchase to a lott, Craves One to be granted in the Same Place with the Other.

An Affid't is Produced under a Justice's hand, Nath'l Newlin, made by Nath'l Park and Jno. Sanger, that R'd Farr and Mary, his wife, both Came in Servants to Jno. Bezer in the year '81, by which they Claim their Headland. The said R'd and Mary, by their Deed Dat. 24, 10 mo. last, granted all their Right to the said Land To. Jos. Cloud, Who Requests a Warrant To take up the Same. Granted.

Griff. Jones Produces a Patent dat. 10, 6 mo., '87, from William Markham and Jno. Goodson for 500 acres of Land in the County of Bucks, Joyning On Robert Turner's Land, Granted by the Prop'ry's Warr't, dat. 21, 8 mo., '83, and Surv'd 6, 4 mo., '84, and Confirmed by said Patent to Anth'y Tomkins by Deed dat. 22, 6 mo., '87, Conveyed the same to said Griff. Jones, Rent 1s p'r C't. The said Land being Res'd by Virtue of Our General Warrant is found To Contain 550 acres, for which he requests a New Patent, Including the said allowance. Granted.

Mary Southworth Intermarrying with Hen. Molineux, of Liverpoole, In Cheshire, Yeoman, the said Henry, by Ind're of L. and Rel., dat. 15th and 16th Ap., 96, Granted to R'd Woodworth, of this Province, a Certain Lott in the third street from Delaware (Granted by Patent from the Prop'ry, dat. 31, 5 mo., '82, Recorded Book A, fo. 24), to said Mary Southworth, and 8 a's of Land in the Liberties Appurtenant to a Purchase s'd to be made by s'd Mary of the Prop'ry, by Virtue of Ind're dat. 15 Aug't, '82, of 500 a's, for which said 8 a's of Lib. Land the Comm'rs. Ja. Claypoole and Robert Turner, Granted a Warr't dated 3, 1 mo., '85, together with 8 a's more in Right of Jno. Southworth's Purchase of the like Quantity, and was Surv'd near Griff. Jones' at first, as appears by a Cert. of R. Longshore's Survey, but Jno. Southworth's was afterwards removed and laid Out to Char. Pickering and sold To Josh'a Carp'r. Now N. Waln's the whole 16 a's notwithstanding remain unsurveyed to Any Other Person, and therefore the said Woodworth Requests a warrant to take up the said 8 acres. Granted.

Wm. Lambal, of Reading, Coun. Berks, Mealman, Purchaser of 625 a's of Land, by deeds from the Prop'ry, dat. 29, 30 June, 1688, by Instrum't dat. 2 May, 1702, declares that he granted Away of the same 100 a's to Jno. Bundsen, 100 a's to R'd Thatcher and 100 a's To Jos. Gilpen, and kept the remaining 326 to himself, for takeing up of which, and his City Lott, he appointed by the s'd Instrument the s'd Jos. Gilpen his Att'y, Who Requests the Grant of a Lott. The Purchase being Out of Time No Lott belongs to it, yet the Prop'r, by his War't in the Office, dat. 19, 4 mo., '84, Granted a Lott to the said W. in Right Of the Purchase aforesaid, which tho' not then Surv'd, it is Ordered that the said Warr't be renewed To Geo. Emlyn if Requested. Lott sold to Geo. Emlyn by J. Gilpen in Wm. Lambal's name by deed, dat. 28 Instant, to be signed.

Wm. Clayton Produceing a return in Pursuance of Our Warrant, dat. 1st, 9ber last, for resurveying a Lott laid Out to William Cloud. A Patent is Ordered upon the Same.

The Prop'ry Granted a Warrant dat.   , Produced to us to Jam's Pugh for a Lott in Chestnutt Street.

Mem'dum, To Allen Foster and B. Duffield to End their business.

Mem'dum, that in right of Jno. Hendrickson's Patent for 400 a's, on which they Claim 700, there is held by Jno. Hendr. 160 a's 20 Perches by Jno. Bartleson 160, 20 ps., By And'w Hendricks 164 a. 18 Ps., and by Jno. Bartleson, distinct from his Other, 103 a. 110 P's. more, Resurveyed by Hen. Holts.

Morton Mortonson, Muthys Muttison and Another had a Pat't for Amos Land for 200 a's at 2 Bushells, but holds above 700 acres, 'tis recorded In Philad'a, William Markham haveing given a Copy.

Edw'd Jones Produceing a return of 165 a's surveyd beyond Schuylkill In Pursuance of the Prop'ry's Warr't, dat. 9, 8ber, 1701, 'tis Concluded That he shall Pay £150 for the same, of which £50 being Paid, the Other to be answered forthwith, with Int. from the 1st of ye 9 mo. last. A Patent is Ordered forthwith.

Ord'd that unless Benj'n Chambers Appear the 2d day next and Either Pay or give Security for the 350 a's Purchased about 2 years agoe, the Warrant be Entirely Vacated.

The Inhabitants of Newcastle Town haveing Presented a Petition that a Certain Parcell of Marsh On the South West End of said Town might be added to the 1,000 acres Granted to them By the Prop'ry for a Com'on, of which Com'on the said Marsh they Declare has Always been Reputed a Part, notwithstanding it has lately been divided from the Same by a Grant made To Wm. Houston : Which s'd Petition being Considered 'tis Ordered that the said Marsh be Preserved for the said Town and upon No Terms be granted to Any Other Person untill we hear further of the Pro'ry's Resolution By himself Or Son in Relation to Such Affairs, and that the said Petition be Indorsed Accordingly.

James Claypoole and Rob't Turner, by their Warr't dat. 6, 4 mo., '85, Granted a Warrant to John Kingsman to take up 142 a's in the County of Chester, in full of his Purchase of 500 a's, which was Imaginarily laid Out in Edgemont near Jno. Browne's, and upon a Res. is found to Contain Only 135 a's, for which requests a Patent. Granted. He was Original Purchaser, as Pr. Deeds dat. 8th and 9th, 7ber, '81.

Peter Jansogoe Produces a Copy of a return from Thomas Pierson, Said to be in Obedience to Wm. Welch's warrant, dat. 15, 2 mo., '84 (To whom it is directed), for 150 a's laid out 19, 2 mo., '84, to Anthony Wallis, Scituate On Scott's run, on Georges Creek, which being Resurveyed is 153 acres. Wallis is dead without issue, and said Peter haveing Married His Sister has lived On it for some years Past, Offers to Pay the rent, w'ch Is £18 15s, and Must also Pay for the Survey 23s 6d. at 4d p'r acre, from the date of Survey, and Requests a Patent, which is granted.

Isaac Taylor a Draught of a Small Tract of Land On the Eastermost Corner of Concord Township, Containing 100 a's, because of It's great Barrenness, Requests to Purchase it, and Agrees to give £18 for it, upon w'ch 'tis granted and a Patent Ordered thereupon. Ordered a Patent, Mentioning the General Resurvey by Virtue of a Warrant dat. . And that this Being found there Vacant, I. T. Requested it, &c. No Warrant Particular.

Richard Reynolds, of Newcastle, by Geo. Dakyne Presenting a Petition for a Certain vacant slip or Lott of Ground Joyning On the said Town, Containing, as 'tis said, not above An Acre, under the Yearly Rent of a Bushell Of Wheat. Ordered that it be further Considered.

Wm. Horne Requesting a Grant of a Small Spott of Land On the King's Road near Jos. England's and the Road Crossing it to Maryland for A meeting house and burying Ground for Friends thereabouts, granted 10 acres in the said Place to Jos. England and Wm. Horne for the said Use Under the Rent of One Penny yearly if demanded.

George Dakeyne haveing Obtained a Grant of 600 Acres first of the Prop'ry and then by Our Warrant On Red Lyon Creek at 10s, Country Money, p'r C't, Req'ts to buy of the Same to a Bushell of Wheat p'r C't. Granted at £5 p'r C't, he Paying for the two Past years. He also Produces an Ind're dat. 10, 10ber, 1701, from Geo. Moore, of Newc., for 150 acres of Land adjoyning On the former, s'd to be Granted By an Old Warrant to the said George and Surveyed by Robert Wharton about Twenty Eight years Agoe.

Jos. England, by said Dakeyne and several former Letters Makeing Application for 1,000 acres of Land On the hithermost Corner of the Govern's Mann'r, in Newc. and Kent County, Agrees to Pay down for the Same One Hundred Pounds Silver Money and a Bushell of Wheat p'r C't Rent upon which It is Granted to be Cutt Out in One Intire Piece in the said Corner.

---

11 mo., 17th [1703.]

Present, Omnes.

Richard Nichols, Esqr., Governor of New York, by Instrument, dat. 15 Feb'y, '67, Granted to Peter Alricks two Islands

MINUTE BOOK "G." 415

in Delaware River On the West Side thereof and About Southward from the Island Commonly Called Mattiniconck, the bigger of the two formerly Called Kipp's Island, and by the Indian Name of Koomenakinckkouck, Containing about a Mile in Length and a half a mile in breadth, And the Other lying some w't to the North of the former about half a mile in Length and a quarter of a mile in breadth, also A Small Creek near the Leser of the said Islands fit to build a Mill thereon, runing up A Mile within Land with Liberty to Vest A Mill thereon where it shall be most Convenient as also a Convenient Proportion of Land On Each Side of the said Creek for Egress and Regress yielding, &c., (two Bushells of Wheat) as a Quitt Rent, but these words in Crotchets are by a Rasure in Another hand, said Instrument recorded the day and year abovesaid by M. Nichols, Sec'ry. Peter Alricks, by Deed, dat. 17, 11 mo., '82, Conveyed all the said Premises and Pat. In Consideration of £175, Bills of Exchange, to Samuel Bordin, his Heirs, &c.; Samuel Bordin In Consideration of £275 10s Sterling, granted all the said Premisses to Jos. Bordin, of the Town of St. Michaels, in Barbad., by an Ind're dat. 6, 1 mo., '88-9, upon a Mortgage for the Payment of said Sum On the 25th March, '92, with a Covenant to Pay the Same. The said Covenant not being Performed Jno. Sutton, Sole Ex'r of the last will of s'd Jos. Burdin, at a Court held for the County of Bucks 19, 8 mo., '99, recovered of Sam'l Burdin, late of the said County of Bucks, and Heir of the said Samuel and Fra. Rawle, his Adm'r as well ye s'd Sum of £275 10s, as also £133 3s 4d of Like money (Strl.), for damages of Nonperformance of said Covenant, and by a writ of Execution dat. 26, 12 mo., 1701, Samuel Beaks, the Sheriff of the said County, Seized all the said Premises and returned the Same, upon which a writt of Venditione Exponas dat. 20, 1 mo., 1701-2, was granted. And being appraised, Wm. Biles, Sheriff of the said County, By Deed, dat. 17, 2 mo., 1702, Conveyed the Same in Consideration of £521, Money of Pensilvania, to William Fishbourn, his Heirs, &c. Wm. Fishbourn, by Deed, dat. 10, 4 mo., 1702, Conveyed the Same to Samuel Carpent'r. These Islands are made by the River Delaware On the East and Some small Gutts Running Between the said Land and the Lands of Ralph Boom 100 a's now 116, Thom's Bills 100 a's, William Hammers 100 a s, as they are Called, which Gutts make a Considerable Quantity of Criple thro' which they Run, and thereupon the Bounds are not very Certain, as far as the Gutts Can be traced these are allowed to be the true bounds; but Samuel being for all the Criple up to the Adjacent Fast land, But it is Ord'd that Inquiry Be made how far the Possessors of the Adjacent Lye Claim To, and if any Vacant Criple be Left that Samuel have the Preference and that for settling the Rent Application be made to the Records of New York and According thereunto that the Same be granted in a New Patent when the business of the Criple Can be Settled.

In Page 45-50 is Shewn the Title of Old Renters of Bristol Township where 200 acres are allowed to Jno. Otter, And in the Min's of the Office of Property, 8. 6 mo., 1701, the whole title is Entered, for said 200 acres invested In said Samuel, Vid. Pa. 70 at Large and being resurveyed and returned by Virtue of a Warrant from us dat. 21, 11 mo., 1701, is found to Contain 335 a's and is 115 Over Measure. In the said Pa. 70 and by said Warrant was also Resurveyed 33 acres found to Contain 38 acres And is found 2 a's Over.

In Pa. 50 also is Recited the Title to 190 acres for 14 of which D. L. and I. N. are to Pay. Then Invested in the said Ex'rs together with 572 acres for 500 and is (22 Over Measure) of Griff. Jones' Purc'e, both which the said Ex'rs, D. L. and I. Norris, by Deed Poll, dat. 20 Jan'y, 1701-2, Conveyed to said Sam'l Carpenter, Consid. £218 for the whole 762 Acres, the first Of These is On Old Rent and the Other On New, Settle the Overplus w'th the said Ex'rs. In Pa. 34 is Recited also Thomas Yardly's Title to 50 Acres w'ch being Resurveyed is found to Contain 59 Acres Over.

Silas Crispin, under the Denom. of Sole Ex'r of the last will and Testament of Thomas Holme, deceased, Conveyed to Hen. Johnson, Carp'r, of Philad'a, by Deed, dat. 9th June, 1699, a Tract of Land in Bristol Township for 660 acres Joyning On the heads of the Land last Granted, and Fra. Richardson's, said In s'd Ind're to be granted by Warrant from Wm. Mark., dat. 12, 7 mo., '82. Surve'd 26 said Mo., returned 18, 5 mo., '88, Into the Sec'ry's Office, for the said Quantity in Right of his, the said Thom. Holme's Purchase of 5,000 acres by Deed dated   . Hen. Johnson, by Deed, dat. 24, 12 mo., 1701-2, Conveyed the said Land To Jos. Liddon, Coun. Philad'a, husbandman, Consid'n £240, for the Payment of which said Jos. Mortgaged the Same again to the said Hen. by Ind're dat. 25, 12 mo., 1701-2, s'd Jos. Liddon sold the said Land to Sam'l Carp'r who released the Mortgage aforesaid, and thereupon said Hen. Johnson, Silas Crispin and Jos. Liddon, by One Joint Deed Ind'd, dat. 5, 10br., 1702, Conveyed the whole said 660 acres to said Samuel, and for a further Confirmation Ellenor Smallwood, Eldest Daughter of said Thomas Holme, the True Heir, and Jos. Smallwood, her husband, Confirmed the same to Samuel; but this Tract being Resurveyed by Virtue of the General Warrant is returned by Jno. Cutler in the

Draught Deficient, Cont. but 547 acres, Upon which Samuel Carpenter desires a Warrant of Resurvey More Narrowly to Enquire The bounds According to the Old returns made into the Sec'ry's Office, Which is Ordered. Also that Jno. Cutler be Required to Send An Ac't of the bounds of the Islands as aforesaid.

Wm. Markham, Robert Turner and Jno. Goodson, by Patent, dat. 5th Jan'y, 1692, Granted to Charles Pickering 2 tracts of Land, the One Situate between James Scott's, Israel Holmes and Brandywine, also a Small tract of Land On Rattlesnake Creek and Christina Stalcup's Land, Cont'g 85 acres, Granted by Warrant from the Comm'rs dat. 29, 8 mo., '84, and laid Out 30, 4 mo., '85, Rent at Newc. 1 Bushell of wheat p'r C't. Cha. Pickering, by Deed. Dat. 28 March, '94, Granted the said two tracts To Andrew Robeson, Jos. Willcox, Esqr's, and Jno. Moore, Gent., Consi'n £60. Andrew Robeson deceasing, the surv'rs request a New Patent, Ord'd that it be Enquired whether the Indians Lay claim to it and what's the Measure, and if free and no Overplus 'tis Granted.

Anth'y Morris, Mayor of Philad'a, In behalf of the Corporation mak'g Application to this Board that the Streets of this City May be Regulated by a Concurrent Authority, both of the Comm'rs and said Corporation. 'Tis Ordered that Dav'd Powell forthwith Survey exactly According to the first Projection and mark out the bounds of all those Streets that have run Irregularly in upon each Other w'th the Assistance of Some fitt Persons Appointed by the Corporation.

11 mo., 24 [1703.]

Present, Edward Shippen, Griff. Owen and James Logan.

Christ'r Taylor, by Deed Poll, dat. 10, 7 mo., '85, Conveyed To Thomas Potter, of Shrewsberry, in East Jersey, Husbandman, 500 acres of Land in Bucks, According to a Draught thereof Entered in the Survey'r's Office, being Part of the said Chris. Purchase. Tho. Potter, by Deed Poll, dat. 6, 7 mo., '93, Granted the said land To Tho. Lloyd. Adjoyning to the said tract there lay a Small Parcel Containing About 100 a's formerly claimed by Hen. Paxon in Right of Some Purchase, but Now Relinquished, which being Resurveyed together with the former the whole is found to Contain 638 Acres, which D. Ll. and I. N. requests to be Confirmed to them 538 acres In Right of Taylor, and the Other 100 in Right and Lieu of Other Lands In the Welch Tract. Granted.

Wm. Asby, of Hayes, Coun. Northamp., husbandman, by L. and Rel., dat. 2 and 3d, 10ber, '81, Purchased of the Prop'ry

500 acres of Land, who Conveyed the whole said Land To Thom. Mercer, of Chester County, who, by Deed Poll, dat. 11, 8ber, 1703, Granted the Lott Appurtenant thereunto to Geo. Emlyn, Requests a Pat. Granted. It falls in the Draught 2d beyond the Str. On Sassafras N. side.

Benjamin Duffield Produces a Deed Ind'd, dat. 18 Feb'y last, from Allen Foster for 111 acres bounded On George Northrap's Land being Part of 500 a's Granted to said Allen by Pat. dat. 29, 5 mo., '84, formerly granted To the said Benj. by Deed, Dat. 5 July, '85, Now again Confirmed in Pursuance (as 'tis said) of a Clause in the former Deed for further Assurance and thereupon Claims a Pat. This being the Vacancy so Long Contested between the said Ben'n and Allen On the One hand, and Ja. Harrison On the Other, And there being An Overplus in Allen's said Tract Benj'n Requests that this May be Confirmed to him, Allen Paying for his Overplus and for The Preference of haveing it in the said Place, he Offer 5 £'s. Allen Haveing Appointed Wm. Hibbs and Hen. Mallows we now appoint John Carver and Thomas Fairman to sett a value On the Overplus, Remembering the Prop'ry is to Pay £20 To James Harrison for Relinquishing his Pretences there. App'd 15th Next Month.

Ord'd that Publick Notice be given in Print to Summon all Persons who Claim any Lotts Or Parcells of Ground in the City Philad'a back of the second Street from Delaware and in the Bank at Either End of the Town, to bring in their resp'ive Claims to the Sec'ry's Office between and 3d Mo. Next, where attendance is to be given from 10 to 12 and from 3 to 6 every day.

12 mo., 15 [1703.]

Present, Idem ut Supra.

The Prop'ry, by Deeds of L. and Rel., dat. 3d and 4th July, 1699, Granted to Jno. Willmer, of London, Silkman, 3,000 acres between the River Susquehannah and Delaware under the yearly Rent Of 10s strl. for the whole, Royal Mines Excepted, to begin to be Paid 7 years after the takeing of it up. Jno. Willmer, by L. and Rel., dat. 1 and 2d Feb'y, 1702, Granted and Conveyed all the said Land To Randal Janney, his Heirs and Assigns, but Imperfectly, In Considrn. of £120 to be Paid in 2 years after, and if not Paid the Grant to be Void. Of this Land there are two Tracts taken up Cont. 500 acres each, by War'ts from the Prop'ry, and Randal req'ts Warrants for the rest. Ordered two Warrants for five Hundred Acres each To D. P. and I's T.

William Rodney Produceing a return of Survey of 598 acres Surv'd by Virtue of a Warrant for 500 a's and Our Order for a Small Piece of Vacant Land to the Survey'r to be added to it. Granted him a Patent for the whole at 6 Bushells p'r A., he Paying 3 £'s. Jos. Woods Caveats ag't David Evans. Return being Pat'td till heard.

Judge Guest finding his Last Warrant for 1,200 a's Cannot be Executed according to It's Tenor, and has Procured Only 666⅔ a's to be Surv'd by Hen. Hall in Same Vacancy, as 'tis said, near the tract of 30,000 acres in Newc. County, Req'ts that he may have the whole laid Out there, and Offers for the Rem'r above the said 666 acres what reasonable Price shall be sett above a Bus'l p'r C't. Ordered that it be Considered.

Wm. and Peter Taylor, Purchasers of 1,250 Acres of Land, had a right to 33 foot in the High Street On Delaware side; Peter Taylor with Jno. Powell, by the Consent of his wife and Mary Taylor, sole Daughter and issue of said Wm. Taylor, by Deed, dat. 10, 1 mo., '92-3, Granted the said High Street Lott to Robert Longshore, who dying Intestate, and his widow, Marg't, Intermarrying with Tho. Jennett, and the said Longshore's Personal Estate not being sufficient to Ans'r the debts, by Order of Court, the said Tho. and Marg't, by Deed, dat. 13, 10ber, '97, sold and Conveyed the said Lott to Wm. Lawrence, of Philad'a, Taylor, and the said Peter Taylor and Jos. Taylor, Son, and Eliz'th Powel, Daughter of Wm. Taylor, deceased, and Jno. Powell, her husband, and Samuel Robinet with Mary, his wife, the Other Daugh'r of s'd Wm. being all his Children and Heirs by Deed, dat. 14, 10ber., '97, Released the said Lott to Will'm Lawrence, and there being 7 foot of a Vacancy adjoyning, we, by Warrant, dat. 23, 1 mo., 1701-2, Granted the Same to said Wm. Lawrence for £7, which is Surv'd and returned, and he Claims a Patent for these together. Ord'd a Patent accordingly.

Henry Lewis, of Haverford, Yeoman, haveing Purchased of Humphrey Ellis 79 acres of Land, Part of Jno. Burges' Purchase of 750 a's, Mentioned in the Welch Min's, desires a Warrant to take up the Said 79 acres, Vid. Title in Welch Min's.

12 mo., 22d [1703.]

Present, Edw'd S., Griff. O. and Jas. Logan.

Ord'd that a Patent be granted to Obiah Taylor for his Two Tracts, he hav'g Paid £32 5s for the Priviledge of the 430 acres where he lives, the return to be made forthwith by Is. Taylor.

Ord'd a Patent to James Thomas according to agreement for his 100 a's In Sussex.

Woola Swanson, by Deed Poll, dat. 5 Jan'y, '91, Granted To James Thomas 2 acres of Land Joyning On Philip South's Line and Delaware, 13 p'rs In breadth On the River, and about 26 or 27 p'rs In Depths, to Contain 2 a's, with allowance for the Street, the said Land is Part of Wickakoe lands to be divided Between the 3 Swansons, James Thomas Requests a Resurvey and Patent On the said land, which is granted.

Ditto, 28 [1703.]

Idem ut Supra.

Judge Guest not being able to find Out any such Land as he requested, and had a Grant of 19th 5 mo., Ultimo, and therefore Quitting it, req'ts in Lieu thereof 500 acres of Vacant Barrens, N. west of his Plantation Called Westminster.

Griff. Jones, in behalf of Jno. Cook, Produces a warrant of the Prop'ry, dated 24, 8 mo., '83, To Arthur Cook for a Lott of 40 foot Front in Skuylkill Front Street, In Right of the said Arthur's Purchase, which Purchase

Ord'd a Patent to Jno. Bevan on his Two Tracts of 508 a's returned Instead of 618½ acres. Vid. Welch Min's for the Title.

Do. 29 [1703.]

The Comm'rs, by Warrant dat. 23, 12 mo., 1701, Granted to Henry Sellen and Leonard Arets to take up 4,675 a's of Land in the County of Philad'a.

John Streipers, Purchaser of 5,000 a's, at 11 p'r M., Henry Sellen, of Kresheim, in the German Township, Conveyed to Leonard Arets 275 acres, Part of the said Tract, by Deed dat. 23 March, 1702-3. The Prop'ry, by Deeds of L. and Rel., dat. 10 and 11th June, '83, Granted to Leonard Arets 1,000 acres at 12d p'r C't, and by Ind're dated 11th June, '83, Rel'd the said Rent to 12d p'r M, of which said Land he Claims 225 acres yet untaken up. Thomas Holme (as 'tis said), in Pursuance of a Warrant from the Comm'rs, dat. 10, 9ber, '85, directed to Thomas Holme, Ordered to be laid Out to said Leonard Arets 534 acres in the Township, laid Out to Jac. Filner and Company, for which there was Surveyed 500, and is now again Resurveyed, and thereupon he req'ts a Patent. Granted, but See Arets' Title before Of the One thous'd. He has 500 In Germ't. This 225 and Den. Kender's 275.

Ordered a Patent to Jno. Streipers On the Other 4,400 a's, if Clear.

In Adam Roades' Tract there being 191 acres Overplus, Ordered to be left to Men to Cutt Off.

MINUTE BOOK "G." 421

Samuel Seller haveing 17 acres Overplus in a tract of 180 acres In Derby, Joyning On Mill Creek, not far from the Road, 'tis Ord'd that it be Cut off forthwith and a Pat. hastened, Or Else left to Men; ye latter he app'ts R'd Nailor and Is. Taylor.

Offered to Al. Adams 66 acres of Overplus Marsh for £12.

By Virtue of a Warrant from the Governor, dat. 2, 5 mo., '83, there was Surv'd To Wm. Sharlow 500 a's, Coun. Philad'a, On West side Skuylkill, of which Sharlow's Attorney sold 150 acres to Robert Jones, Pa. One Hund'd and Twelve, at Large, which being Resurveyed he requests a Patent, which Is Granted.

Ordered that Tho. Fairman and Jno. Mifflin Sett a Price Or Cutt Off Jno. Roberts' Overplus 6th day Next.

The Prop'ry, by Ind're of Lease and Rel., dat. , Granted 10,000 acres of Land To Nicholas Moore, his Heirs, &c., Rent 1sh. p'r 1,000, Sterling, in Right Of which Purchase, Pursuant to the Prop'rys Warrant, dat. 25, 5 mo., '84, there was laid Out the Same day to the said Nicholas 7 lotts in Philad'a, viz: 4 lotts on Delaware side and 3 On Skuylkill Side, the 1st On Delaware side Contains 50 f't in Breadth and 60 f't in Length, On the Second Street, bound N. w'd with the Dock street, Southw'd and E. w'd with the New Cutt Or Dock and To the W. w'd with the Second Street. The 3 Other Lotts On Delaware Side Cont. In breadth 102 f't; the first Containeth In Length from the 2d Street to the 3d Street 495 f't, the 2d Lott Cont. in Length from the 3d Street to the 4th Street 396 f't, the 3d Lott Cont. In Length from the 4th Street to the 5th Street 396 f't, w'ch s'd 3 lotts are bounded E. w'd and W. w'd with the before Mentioned Streets, N. w'd with Dock Str. and Southw'd with the Free Society Of Traders' Lott, the 3 Lotts On Skuylkill Side Cont. In breadth 102 foot, and the 1st of them Cont. in Length from the Front Street to the 2d Street, the 2d Lott Cont. in Length from the 2d Street to the 3d Street, the 3d Lott Cont. in Length from the 3d Street to the 4th Street, all which said 3 lotts are bounded E. w'd with ye said Streets, N. w'd with Dock Street and Southw'd with the said Society's Lotts, which said Nicholas Moore dyed Seized of and the said 7 Lotts, whereby the Same Came to Samuel Moore. Son and Heir of the said Nicholas Moore, and Mary, his wife w'ch said Smauel afterward, dyed, but first being at the age of 21 years and Upwards, viz: On the 6th day of 9ber, '94, byhis last will and Testament In Writeing, duely Executed and Proved On the 14th Same Month and year, did make Thom's Holme, of Phil'a, Exec'r of his said will, Impowering him to make sale of as much of his real Estate as might the Legacies given by the said Will as thereby appears. The said

Thomas Holme, by Deed Poll dated the 25th February, 1694, reciteing as therein Recited, and for the Consid'n therein mentioned, granted the said 7 Lotts, with their app'ts, To Nehemiah Allen, of Philadelphia, Cooper.

Will'm Markham, Robert Turner and Jno. Goodson, by warrant dated 21, 11 mo., '93, Granted to George Palmer, Jno., Thomas and Wm. Palmer, sons of Geo. Palmer, dece'd, and Eliz'th, his wife, who in his Life Time, Purchased of the Prop'ry 5,000 a's, In Pursuance of which said Warrant there was laid Out the Same day to them, the said George, Jno., Thomas and Wm., in Right Of the said Purchase a Certain bank Lott, in breadth 102 f't and in Length 250 f't, bounded W. w'd with Delaware Front Street, N. w'd with John Longhurst Lott, E. w'd with Delaware at the said Extent of 250 f't, and Southward with Jno. Fuller's Lott, said George, the Father, besides the said 4 Sons, left a Daughter named Eliz., now Married to Ralph Jackson, all by his wife Eliz., now also liveing, the said Jno, Tho., Wm. and Ralph Jackson, and Eliz'th, his wife, by Deed Poll dat. the 24 day of April,   , In Consideration of £48, Granted the Norther most Part of the said Lott, Cont. in breadth 76½ f't and In Length 250 f't, to Benj'n Chambers, of Phila., Yeoman, &c., who desires a Patent. Granted. The Remaind'r of the said Bank Lott being 25½ f't in the Possession of the said George Palmer.

---

2 mo., 3d 1704.

Present, Edw'd Shippen, Griff. O. and Jam's Logan.

There being an Overplus of 191 acres in the Tract formerly laid Out To Claypoole in the Welch Tract, now Ad. Roads', He appoints Michael Blunston and Jno. Hoodt, and ye Comm'rs appoint R'd Thom's and Da'd Powel to sett a Price Or Cutt it Off the 11th Instant.

Upon a full agreement with R'd Thomas Concerning the allowance upon his Land Taken up, It is Concluded and Ord'd that he shall have the full allowance On all the Land he has taken up, viz: 3   , for which he is to Pay Rents for the Whole, viz: 3 from the first laying Out of the Welch Tract.

The Prop'ry, by Warrant dat. 17th 3 mo., Granted to Marg't Atkinson in Right of her late husband, Chris'r Atkinson, 500 acres, which were surv'd 23d 6 mo. following. Marg't Atkinson. Ex'x of her said husband, by Deed dat. 8, 4 mo., 1702, Granted the said Land to Jos. Gilbert, of Bensalem, In Bucks, who req'ts a Patent thereupon. Ord'd a Patent to said Gilbert with a Special Restriction to be in Right Only of Chris'r and Jno. Atkinson of 1,500 acres, for which see Pat't to Wm. Atkinson, dat 12, 8 mo, 1702.

Agreed that Robert Heaton, Sen'r and Jun'r, may have the Priviledge of buying 2 Vacant Slips adjoyning on 100 of Rob't Heaton, Sen'r, On both sides, And that John Cutler agree with them for it and take the Pay Towards his Resurvey.

Present, ut Supra.

The Prop'ry, by Ind'res of L. and Release, dat. , Granted to Jno. Rowland 2 acres, To Hold, &c., in Right of which Wm. Markham, Rob't Turner, John Goodson and Samuel Carpenter, Comm'rs, by Patent dat. 22d June, in the 5th year of Wm. and Mary, Granted the s'd 190 a's, and the said 10 Acres of Land, Part of the said   acres To John Smith, of Bucks County, in this Province, Blacksmith, to Hold, &c. The Prop'ry, by Ind're dat.   , Granted to James Harrison 5,000 acres to Hold, &c., said James, by Ind'res of L. and Release, dat. as therein Mentioned, Granted 100 acres, Part of the said Harrison's Purchase, to Randal Blackshaw, &c. Said Randal, by Deed dat. 20 June, '93, Conveyed the said 100 acres to the said Jno. Smith, &c., who was thereby Possessed of 300 acres. The said Jno. Smith, by Deed Poll dat. 15, 1 mo., 1696, Granted the said 300 a's To Hen. Baker, and the said Hen., by Deed Poll dat. 1st 7ber, '98, Granted the said Premisses To Wm. Biles. The Prop'ry, by Warrant dat. 4, 5 mo., 1685, Granted to Christ'r Bennet 100 acres in Pursuance whereof the said 100 a's were laid Out the 6, 10ber, '84, in Bucks County, to said Bennet, and s'd Chr. Bennet Sold the Same to Ch. Bringham, who sold to Jos. Cross, who sold to Jno. Smith, who gave his Obligation to Henry Baker, dat. 28 March, 1696, with Condition Underwritten that He, the said Smith, His Heirs, &c., should at all Times Thence forth acquitt Or Otherwise save harmless, as well the said Baker, his Heirs and assigns, as the s'd 100 a's sold to him Or Intended to be sold, to the Use of the Said Baker, his Heirs, &c., for Ever, from all Bargains, Sales, &c., made before delivery of said Bond, done or suffered by said Smith, Cross, Bringham Or Bennet, Or any Other Person Claiming by, from or under them, Or any of them.

It is said that Baker sold the last 200 acres to the said Wm. Biles.

Mem'dum, that Nath'l Douglas, of Philad'a, Gave Benjamin Chambers, Coll'r, a Bill dat. 27, 3d mo., '99, for £4 13s 9d, which by B. Cs' rec'pt, dat. 10, 9 mo., '99, Indorsed, was Paid, and is acknowledged to be for 15 Years Quitt Rent for Five Hundred acres sold by Isr. Hobbs To John Colley. Benjamin Chambers also gave a rec't dat. 5, 8 mo., 1700, for 10, 6, In full for a Bank Lott of 20 f't, and the above 500 acres to 1 mo. Last.

Israel Hobbs, by Deed dat. 27, 1 mo., '99, Granted to Jno Colley, Hatter, his 500 a's, Confirmed to him by Patent dat. 4, 6 mo., '84. Jno, Colley, by Deed dat. 6th August 1700, Conveyed One-half of the above Land to Will'm Johnson, Koenan and Hunradt, Johnson Koenan, of Philad'a, Yeom'n, and by Deed dat. 1, 1 mo., 1700-1, Sold the Other Moiety to Renier Tyson, of German Town.

Present, Idem.
The Prop'ry sold Nicholas Waln 1,000 acres of Land by Deeds dat. 21 and 22d April, '82, of which there was laid Out 250 On Nesham., Now John Stackhouse's, 250 acres more On the Other side of Nesham., viz: South Side, and 250 more To Hen. Walmsley, Son of Tho. Walmsley, in his Right Lib. Land, and the rest Jeded Allen bought, Not taken Up that we know of, that of Walmsley, Francis Searle, and desires a Resurvey. Nicholas Waln Conveyed 150 acres to Henry Walmsley, Son of Tho. Walmsley, by Deed dat. 10th 1 mo., '86, by Deed of the Same Date 100 a's To Thomas Walmsley, Brother to said Henry.

Samuel Carpenter, in the Name of Thomas Lloyd and Samuel Carpenter, Ex'rs of the Last will and Testament of Sarah Ekeley, Sole Ex'x of Jno. Ekley, deceased, by Deed Poll dat. 18, 4 mo., '94, Conveyed to Dav'd Lewis 100 a's of Land in Haverford, 166 p's in L. and 95 ¾ Ps' in br., under the bounds, but Stakes, who desires a Res., and to have his Exact Quantity Made up if to be had there. Granted.

The above Land of 250 acres, P't of Nich. Waln's Purchase, laid Out To Walmsly, being Res'd by Jno. Cutler, is found to Contain Only 228 a's, but Jno. Cutler Informing that Ev. Griffith's Tract adjoyning has Overplus, he requests a Warrant to Take up his full right. Ord'd a Warrant to Survey it and make up the Quantity out of the adjacent, if Griff. agree, if not, Ord'd that the Pay the Money for the said twenty Two acres.

Mem'dum, that Wm. Fisher, formerly Fish, is said by Nich, olas Waln to be no Purchaser, nor Cha. Lea, but he Suspects they have both Claim'd Under Wm. Crosdale's 1,000 acres, who Notwithstanding has taken up the whole, the whole Deeds being To him.

The Comm'rs, by Patent dat. 10, 5 mo., '91, Signed Only by Wm. Markham and Robert Turner, Granted to Jno. Longhurst 51 f't of Bank, bound'd N. w'd with Sassafras Street, Southward with Palmer's Lott, Surv'd 5, 5 mo., '90, by Warrant of the Same Date, Rent 5s for 51 years, then Prout, alia. Jno. Longhurst, by Ind're dat. 28, 5 mo., '91, for £15 granted the said Lott to Andrew Robeson, of Philad'a, Merch't. Andrew Robeson, by Indorsement On the said Deed, dat. 20, 11 mo., '91-2, for 5sh. Granted it To Nath'l Lampleigh, Boat builder, who sold half thereof to James Parrock, Ship Carp'r, by Deed Poll dat. 5, 4 mo., '99, for £35, and the Other half To Jno. Henrickson, of Philad'a, Boat Builder, by Deed Poll of the Same date, 5, 4 mo., '99, and s'd Henrickson, by Deed P. dat. 1, 1 mo., 1702-3, Conveyed his Moiety to the s'd Parrock, who now holds and requests a New Patent In his Own Name, the first being Signed Only by Two of Three Commissioners. Granted.

Wm. M., R. T. and J. G., by pr'p Patent, dat. 6 Apr., '94, Ganted to Jno Jennet, of Philad'a, a Lott On the Bank in Philad'a, as 'tis said in the Patent, but beyond James West's Lott, as is affirmed, of 50 foot in breadth and 250 foot in Length, bounded (it should be N. w'd in the Pat., but is) S. w'd w'th Tho. Longston's Lott, S. w'd with Jam's Portis' lott (Poultess), Paying from the 24, 1 mo., '90, for 51 years 5sh. st'rl. yearly, and then, as Other Bank lotts not Recorded, belongs to Sam'l Spencer's wife.

Ord'd a Pat. to Philip England up to the Front Street On this side Skuylkill for all the Land below it, according to the Tenour of the former Draught, D. Powel to Regulate this with all Speed.

Rich'd Thomas, of his 5,000 a's Purchased by his Father, has sold to Philip Howel 700 a's, to Rob't W'ms 500 a's, to Edward Jones 200 acres, to Hugh Rob'ts 100 acres Lib. Land, to Da. Howel 200 acres, to Rob't David 86¼ a's, in all 1,786¼ acres. has taken up and is Patented 1,665 acres, which Make 3,451¼, and there remains 1,548¾, To which 320 Being added, allowed to him (for which he is to Pay Rent for the whole 3,200 from the first Location of the Welch Tract as well P'r agreement), for the 1,665 acres already Patented as for the Rem'r, makes 1,868¾, to be Confirmed forthwith, he Paying the said arrears.

3 mo., 1 [1704.]

Present, Idem ut Supra.

David Evan, of Radnor, being Possessed of a Tract of 200 acres In Right of Tho. Wynnes, Purchase being Part of 250 acres Confirmed by the said Thomas by Patent from the Prop'ry, dat. 29, 5 mo. '84 (vide Chester Min's, Radnor, Pa. 25), the said Tract was Resurveyed and found to Contain 232 acres and is 12 acres Over. He Possesses also a Tract of 150 acres bo't of Wm. Davies, Title as follows: The Prop'ry, By Deeds dat. 16 and 17 June, '82, sold to Richard Davies, of Welch Pool, in Montgomeryshire, 1,250 acres, who sold 100 acres thereof To Thos. Jones, of Laulanread, in Elvel, Coun. Radnor, who deceasing, bequeathed the Same by Will to his Nephew, Jno. Jones, who by Deed dat. 30th 8ber, '85, Conveyed the Same to Wm. Davies. Rich'd Davies, of his great Purchase of 5,000 acres, made 7ber, '81, Conveyed 200 acres thereof To Evan Oliver, whose Lawfull Heir (as 'tis said), in the following Deed, Conveyed Part thereof to the said Wm. Davies, who by Deed Poll dat. 18 Jan'y, 1702, Conveyed 50 acres, Part of the said 200, to the said Dav'd Evan, together with the aforegoing 100 acres, in One Parcel, which being res'd is found to Contain 165 acres. He requests a Patent for this and the aforegoing 232 acres. He has a right to 154 acres above Radnor, for which he has a Patent, dat. 27, 11 mo., '87, but is Located On a Tract Granted before to Wm. Wood, Jos. Wood's Father, by Patent of a Prior date, if y'rfore he Lose the said Tract of 154 acres, the above 12 acres is to be allowed it P't, if not, he is to Pay £4, viz: 6s 8d P'r acre, and Now gives Bond for it, Either to be Paid Or given Up as aforesaid, and a Patent is Ordered forthwith.

The Prop'ry, by Deed dat. 21st and 22d 8ber, Granted to Tho. Zachary, of Lond., Practitioner of Physick, 500 acres of Land, and the said Thom., by Deeds dat. 18 and 19 May, '88, Conveyed the Same To Thomas Hackney, of Lond., Gent. Thomas Hackney, by his Last will, dat. 23d Aug't, '92, Proved at Burlington, not mentioning the said Land, Constituted his Daughter, Sarah Evans, of West Jersey, widow, Edward Cowper, of Northampton, in England, and John Ellington, of Willingborough, In Northamp., Ex'rs of his will, the said Daughter, Now wife of Darby Green, Blacksmith, requests a Warrant to take up the said Land. Granted.

Mem'dum, to Settle B. Duffield's business for Ja. Atk., as ord'd 24, 11 mo. last.

Judge Guest requesting an answer to his Motion of the 28th 12 mo. last, It is Resolved and Concluded that He shall Enjoy the Benefit of all Our former Grants where they May be had exactly, according to their Tenour, that This Board will not further Concern themselves more than to Confirm By Patent all Such Surveys as have been or shall be regularly made in Pursuance of Our Warrants.

Randal Blackshaw, Purchaser of 1,500 acres, took up in Falls T., Bucks, 500 acres, of which he sold to Ralph Cowgill by Deed dat. 11 mo., '94, 112 acres, And Ralph Cowgill, by Deed dat. 1, 1 mo., '96, Conveyed the Same To Jos. Kirkbride. Randal Blackshaw, by Deed dat. 1, 1, '96, Conveyed To the said Jos. Kirkbride 290 acres, Part also of the said Tract, being with the foregoing 402 acres, the remaining Part of the said Land,

reputed 100 acres. Will'm Biles Possesses the said 400 acres (as
reputed), by Warr't from the Prop'ry, dated   ,
was Res'd and found to Contain   a's, and his   Over,
besides allowances, for which he Offers but £10, Quitting all
Other Claims or desires. It May be Valued Or Cut Off.

3 mo., 15 [1704.]
Present, ut Supra.

There haveing been laid out to Peter Cock On the East side
of Skuylkill, and where the City now stands, by Robert Noble,
Surveyor, 100 acres, as by a Certificate and return under Noble's
hand appears, dat. 28 July, '80, Upon the first Laying Out of
the City the said Cock Surrendered the Said Land in Ex'ch.
for 200 acres On the West side of Skuylkill, for Laying Out of
which, by the Gov'rs Order, the Surveyor Gen'l, T. H., by
Warrant dat. 25, 5 mo., '84, Ordered the said Quantity to be
laid Out as aforesaid, which was accordingly Executed Soon
after but not duely return'd till 18, 12 mo., '98, by D. Powel.
This Land, by agreement, Pays half a Bus'l P'r 100 acres Only.
Lasse Cock, Eldest Son of, and Erick Cock, both Ex'rs of said
Peter Cock, by Deed Ind'd dat. 10 10br., '98, Conveyed the said
200 acres To Thomas Jenner, Husband of Marg't, Daughter
of said Peter Cock, In Part of her Portion. Said Thomas
Jenner and his wife Marg't, by Deed dated 7, 1 mo.,
'98-9, Conveyed the said 200 a's of Land to Benjamin
Chambers for £71, to Hold to him, &c., James Clayp. and
Robert Turner, Comm'rs, by Pat. dat. 14, 2 mo., '86, granted
To Wm. Hearne, of Philad'a, 100 acres of Land Joyning On
the above, Surv'd 6, 6 mo., '85, by Virtue of Capt. Markham's
warrant, dated 7, 6 mo., '82, at 1 Penny st'rl. p'r annum, and
Wm. Hearn, by Deed Poll dat. 28, 9 mo., '99, for £57 7s Conveyed the said Land to Benjamin Chambers. The Comm'rs,
Samuel C., Wm. M., Robert T. and J. G., by Pat. dat. 29, 7ber,
'92, Granted to Thom's Lloyd 100 acres of Land in the City
Liberties In Right and Part of Cha. Lloyd and Mag't Davies,
their Orig'l Purchase of 5,000 acres, laid Out 23, 2 mo., '92, by
a Warrant of that Day, also By another Patent of the same
date viz 29, 7br., '92, The said Comm'rs Granted to the said
Thomas Loyd 45 a's of Fast Land and Criple in the said Liberties, laid 23, 2 mo., '92, by a Warrant of the Same date, no
Consid'n ment. Is. Norris and Thomas Lloyd, Ex'rs of the
said Thomas Lloyd's last Will and Testament, by Deed dat. 8,
1 mo., 1699, 700, for £110, Conveyed the said Two Tracts To the
said Benj'n Chambers. The Comm'rs, W. M., R. T. and J. G.,
by Patent dat. 5, 8 mo., '94, Granted to Dan'l Humphrey 100

acres of Land within the Liberties, laid Out in 2 parcells of Fifty Each in Pursuance of several Warrants To the Welch, F. D's, viz: Henry Lewis, Charles Bevan, Thomas Ellis, Jno. Bevan, Wm. Howel, Lewis Davies, Evan Thomas, Wm. Jenkins and Jno. Griffith, Purchasers, and the said Dan'l Humphreys, Together with Jno. Bevan, for himself, Charles Bevan and Eliz'th Prichard, Wm. Howel for himself and Evan Thomas, Wm. Jenkins for himself and Tho. Griffith, and Lewis David being Interested therein, Conveyed One Parcel thereof, being 50 Acres, by Deed dat. 2d 5 mo., 1700, to Benjamin Chambers for £33 10s. Robert Turner, by Deed dat. 6 July, '97, for £20 Conveyed to Thom's Jenner, of the County of Philad'a, the Proportion of Lib. Land belonging to the Purchase of Jno. Gee and Company, of 5,000 a's, for the Takeing Up of the said Lib. Land there was a warrant issued, dat. 14, 4 mo., '83, Which was Executed About the year '90, as is alledged of ye said Proportion, being 100 acres. Thomas Jenner, by Deed dat. 6, 1 mo., '99, Conveyed 50 Acres, the Other 50 Acres Jno. Gardner Possesses, all the said Land being 545 acres. B. Cham., has cleared to the last 1st mo., Except the last 50, for which He is to Pay from the year 1690. Only he has Paid 2 years in his book, given in 13 Inst., and 3 more said day, and now Pays 2, and all the said Land being Res'd 'tis found to Contain the Exact quantity, as laid Out for, viz: 545 a's. He requests a Patent for the whole, and to reduce it to An Even Rent, which is granted, He Paying £11 for Reduceing 100 a's of Penny Rent Land, And 40 shill's for bringing the Bushell of Wheat for 200 acres To 1 shilling p'r C't, i. e., 2 Shillings Strl., And a Patent is Ordered On the whole.

The Prop'ry haveing granted to the Heirs of Jos. Milner a Warrant of Resurvey, dat. 31, 1 mo., 1701, On 296 acres and On 300 A's and Another dat. 31, 3 mo., 1701, On 250 Acres, which it Appears now should have been Only 200, all Entered in Bucks' min's, the whole Compleating 796 acres, being res'd by Jno. Cutler, by a General Warrant 'tis found to Contain 1,108 acres, and is 233 acres Over Measure, which is Ord'd To be Cutt of and a Pat. Granted for the Rem'r, $\frac{2}{3}$ to Jno. Milner and $\frac{1}{3}$ to Mary, Sarah and Rachel Milner, each a like share, to be grounded On the Order of the Orphans' Court to be Produced.

Thomas and Mercy Philips, by Deed dat. 26, 6 mo., '85, Conveyed to Rob't Ingle, of W. Jersey, 100 Acres of Land, Part of Mercy Jefferson's, because She Joins in the Deed for 40sh., and Robert Ingle, by Deed dat. 17, 3 mo., '87, Conveyed it to Wm. Waite, who Obtained a Warr't for the Same, dat. 22, 1 mo., '89-90, and had it renewed Again from the Prop'ry. It was Located at that Time, but not finished.

There haveing been Survey'd to Mary Heyworth 278 acres in Bucks County, in Pursuance Of Our Warrant, dat. 26, 6 mo., 1702, at £20 p'r C't, being in the whole £55 12s, She desires a Patent Granted.

There being 2 Parcells of Vacant Land Adjoyning On both Sides of a Hundred Acres of Robert Heaton, which with the Overplus of ye s'd 100 a's, Contain 310 acres; s'd Robert Heaton Purchased 158 thereof, and young Robert Heaton, his Son, 152 Acres, for which they are to Pay £56 to Jno. Cutler On the Prop'ry's Acc't for Resurveys, the Land being Exceeding Barren and Poor. That to Robert, senior, is to be Confirmed together with 100 acres More, now Measureing 110, which he took up 20 Years ago and Paid for it at the Prop'ry's last departure, Just as he was going Away, he alledges, and produces the rec't of £10 and £3 5s for work at Pensbury, and there remains £2 14s 6d, Including the Rent. Also 284 acres Granted by Patent from the Comm'rs dat. 18, 3 mo., '86, to Robert Holdgate, for 250 acres, Being his Orig'l Purchase in England and by him Conveyed to said Robert, Sen'r, by Deed Dat. 19, 3 mo., '86, for £20, In which Tract there Being 14 A's he Agrees to Pay £4 12s. Also 266 Acres laid Out for 246 a's to Alex'dr Giles, and afterwards, by Virtue of A Warrant dat. 18, 2 mo., 1702, In Right of Hen. Bailey's Purchase, vid. Min's, and Conveyed by Mary Lovet and Dorothy Giles, Daughters and Heirs of the said Alexander, by Deed dat. 5th June, 1703, to the said Robert, who desires a Patent for the whole, being 818 acres. And Is Granted.

The Other 152 Acres are to be Confirmed to Robert Heaton, Jun'r, Together with Another Tract as folows: The Prop'ry, by Deeds of L. and Rel., dat. 21 and 22d 2 mo., '82, Granted to Tho. Crosdale 1.000 acres of Land, of which 250 A's were for Acc't of Thomas Stackhouse, who sold the Same to Nich's Waln, who sold his Interest to Robert Heaton, Sen'r, and thereupon Wm. Crosdale and Jno. Crosdale, Sons of the said Thomas, with Tho. Stackhouse and Nich's Waln, Joyntly, Conveyed the said 250 acres to said Robert, Senior, by Deed dat. 8th 2 mo., 1702. The Prop'ry, by L. and Rel., dat. 13 and 1?, 2d Mo., '82, Granted to James Dillworth 1,000 acres, of which 500 were laid Out On Nesham'a Creek by Warrant from Wm. Markham, &c., On the 9th Month, '82, and thereof the said James Conveyed 440 acres To the said Robert Heaton for £270 by Deed dat. 12, 8 mo., '97, the Other 60 Acres Matthias Wildman holds. The said 2 Tracts being 690 Acres, together with the said 60 Acres, being Resurv'd, Are found to Contain 925 acres, of which 65 being allowed for Heaton's (for Wildman's has no Overp.), there remains 110 acres Overplus to be Paid for at £40 p'r C't, i. e., £44, which added to the Other 755, makes 865 acres One-half Of which (being Conveyed to Robert, Jun'r, by his Father, By Deed dat.   ), is to be Confirmed to said Robert, Junior, Together with the Other 152 Acres, to be returned by Jno. Cutler In One Tract, 584½ acres, and the remaining 432½ Acres to be Confirmed by Patent to Robert, Senior. Ord'd Accordingly.

A return Of Our Warrant dat. 24th Ulto., being Produced for 250 Acres, res'd to Hen. and Thomas Walmsly, a Patent is Ord'd to them forthwith, the return to be bought in from Ja. Taylor. Promised in a fortnight, See 24th 2 mo. Last.

The Prop'ry, by Deeds of Le. and Rel., dat. 3 and 4 July, '82, Granted To Jno. Scarborough, of London, Blacksmith, 250 Acres, which by Warr't from Thomas Holme in '82, was laid out With 250 Of Nicholas Waln, On Nesham. Creek, In two Long Strips, which Proveing Inconvenient, were Cutt Off across and divided into two Parcells Endwise. Jno. Scarborow, Son of the said John, by Virtue of a Power of Attorney, duely Proved, dat. 15th 8ber, '96, Conveyed to Adam Harker 110 acres, by Deed dat. 6th 1 mo., 1700-1, the remaind'r of the said 250 Acres, haveing before Sold to Henry Huddleston 80 acres and Thomas Barnes 60 Acres. In Divid'g this Land Between Nicholas W. and Scarborow the Line was run unequally, he took into said Neshamin. above his Share and left Scarborow's deficient 23½ Acres, which Deficiency fell in the said Harker's Parcell. Jno. Stackhouse being now Owner of Nich. Waln's Land and said Harker being at difference, they Chose Arbitrators, J. Growdon, Wm. Paxon, Thomas Harding, Jer. Langhorne, Thomas Beans, and Jno. Cowgill, On Bonds of £40 Each to End the difference, and the said Arbitrat'rs Awarded that the said Stackhouse should give to the said Harker 30 acres Out of his Tract to make up this Deficiency, 23½ thereof being duely Wanting And 5 More allowed for, the 2 On the 100, and said Harker requests that the Survey'r may execute the said Award and make returns thereof, that a Patent be Granted.

The Prop'ry, by Pat. dat. 24, 4 mo'th '84, Granted to Daniel Jones a Lott in Walluut Street, Northside, 68 f't br.; 255 f't Long. bounded Northw'd with back Lotts, Eastward vac't Lotts, S. w'd Walnutt Street, Ww'd vac't. Granted By Warrant 20th 1 mo, '83, Surv'd 27th said Month and year, Rent has been 5 English Shillings To Dan'l Jones, Renter, but is made by a Manifest Rasure to 1 Shilling Purchaser. Record'd Fol. 6, 30th 5 mo., '84.

The Prop'ry, by Pat. dat. 30, 5 mo., '84, Granted to Jno. Hodgekinson, Purchaser, a Lott of 49½ foot br., 220 f't Long, bounded N. w'd back lotts, E. w'd vacant, S. w'd Wallnutt Street, W. w'd with the Above, Granted by Warr't dat. 9, 2 mo., '83, surv'd 1, 1 mo., '84, Rent 1 Shilling by a Rasure, but has been more. Recorded Book A, Fol. 157.

James Clayp. and Robert Turner, by Pat. dat. 2, 4 mo., '85, Granted to Dan'l Jones, Renter, a Lott 37 f't br., 255 f't Long, bounded N. w'd back lotts, W. w'd Vac't, E. w'd Dan'l Jones' lott and Southw'd Wallnutt Street, by Warrant 13, 8 mo., '84, Surv'd 20th day, Same Month, Rent 5sh. strl. Rec'd Bk. A, fo. 108.

Henry Nellson, of Bucks (by Jno. Cutler), requesting to Purchase a's of Land, Situate between Jos. Milner and Jonathan Ellridge's Land, Agrees To give for the Same £45, to be Paid One-half In hand and the Other after a Year, Without Interest, the Draught to be made forthwith by J. C. Patent Is Ordered. P'd £10 1s 5th 4 mo., is to Pay the Remainder of the 1st Payment in Wheat 7ber Next.

Thom's Asheton requesting Above the 100 acres Purchased last year 133 Acres adjoyning, in the whole 233 acres, agrees to give £50 for it, to be Paid 1, 12 mo., 1705-6, without Interest, the Land to be Security.

John Jones, of Brandywine, requesting (by Jno. Child) to Purchase 100 acres beyond Brandywine Joyning One Fran. Smith's Land, 'tis offered for £18 Ready Money and 1 Shilling Rent.

Ord'd a Pat. to Robert Jones on 165 acres, for 150 In Right of Sharlow. See Min. B., P. 112.

A Warr't for Geo. Fox's Lib. Land, a warr't for Lewis and a warr't for W. P.

The Prop'ry, by Patent dat. 21, 4 mo., '84, Granted to James Chick, Renter, a Lott in the City in br. 49½ f't and 306 f't Long, bounded N. w'd Back lotts, E. vacant, S. Mulberry Street, W. 4th Street from Sk. Granted by war't 16, 6 mo., '83, Surv'd 23 Ditto, Rent 2s 6d by a Rasure.

And by Another Pat. dat. 24, 4 mo., to Jno. Goodin a Lott in Philad'a between 4th and 5th Str. from Sk., in br. 49½ foot and 306 f't L., bounded N. Back lotts, W. vacant (but Joyns on the Above), and sur'd with Mul. St., warr't dated 17, 2 mo , '83, Surv'd 7, 8 mo., '84, 2s 6d strl. By a Rasure, both in the Possession now of Wm. Carter, Sold him by Geo. Smedley.

---

4 mo., 26th [1704.]

Present, Edw'd Shippen, Griff. Owen and James Logan.

The Prop'ry, by Deeds of Le. and Rel., dat. 14 and 15th 7br., '81, Granted To Thomas Wynne and Jno. ap Jno. 5,000 acres,

Thomas Wynne, of his Share, sold To Richard Orme, of Radnor, 150 acres, but not Conveyed it. Jonathan Wynne, Son and Heir of the said Thomas, by Deed dat. 2d 4th Inst., Conveyed the said Land to s'd Richard Orme. Ordered A Warrant for Takeing up the Same. He is seated On a Tract near that Quantity, which he hoped to have, But it is now Confirmed to Laetitia Penn.

Ordered Warr'ts for the Remainder of Fra. Plumstead's Land, Entered 8ber, 1702. Granted 2 Warrants, remains 1,500, Supp.

The Comm'rs Grantd To Timothy Clement a lott On the Bank of Philad'a, 30 f't in br. and 250 f't Long, bounded N. w'd with R'd Wall's Lott, S. w'd vacant, Confirm'd by Patent dat. 27 August, '90, which Lott was Conveyed by said Clement to P. Robison. This 250 f't from the Front Str. fell short of the River, because of It's bending in that Place, and therefore P. R. makeing Application Again to the Comm'rs they caused A New Regulation to be made, said to be dat. 2 May, '91, which fixed the Cartway of 30 f't, Now King Street, 150 f't distant from the Front and Granted 250 more from thence into the river, and in Pursuance thereof Granted a Patent for the said 30 f't, 150 f't In Length between the Front Street and Cartway, Rent for Ever 1s 6d Strl.; also 250 f't from the Cartway Into the River, Rent yearly 3 sh. Sterling, for 51 years from these On third, To revert, &c., And Other Usual Cove'ts, &c., And'w Rudman, Possessor.

The Comm'rs, by Warrant dat. 19, 9 mo., '90, Granted to Rich'd Wall a Bank lott of 30 f't br. and 250 f't Long bounded N. w'd with R'd Townsend's Lott and S. w'd with the Above; this was never Patented, as they say. Jno. Wall, Son and Heir Of the said Rich'd, by an agreement under his hand and Seal, dat. 21 Jan'y 1703-4, Granted all his Right to the above Lott to sa'd Andrew Rudman, who requests a Patent On the Same Terms with that above To P. Robison. Granted a Patent as above.

The Comm'rs, by Patent dat. 29, 7 mo., '91, Granted To Peter Sherboro 29½ f't in br. and 150 foot deep, bounded N. w'd and S. w'd vacant, Rent 1s 6d strl., Without Any Reserve for Time. Surveyed 20, 4 mo., '91.

And by Pat. dat. Same day, viz: 29th 7ber, '91, they Granted to Jeremiah Elfreth a Lott of the Same dimensions, viz: 29½ foot and 150 f't, bounded N. w'd with P. Robeson's and S. Vacant, Rent 1s 6d Strl., No Reservat'n, Surv'd 20, 4 mo., '91. And to the Same Jer. Elfreth a Patent 1st 8ber, '91, for a Bank lott Opposite to the above 44½ f't br. and 250 f't Long, bounded N. w'd With Tim. Clements, E. W'd with the River, S, with Peter Sherboro's and N. w'd with the 30 f't Str., Rent for 51 years from the 25, 2 mo., '91, 4s 6d, and then ⅓ to revert, this is now Rudman's. Peter Sherboro had also a Patent for a Bank lott of the Same dimensions with the above, viz: 44½ f't, now Rich'd Tucker's.

Note that the 2 Patents between Front Street and the Cartway are but for 59 f't both, But the Bank is for 89 f't. Quer., Who has the Other Fifty Foot?

Ord'd forthwith Da'd Williams' Land to be Inquired into about the Overpp. and Settled.

Upon reading the Petition of Jonathan Wynne for the rem'r of his Father's Purchase, Ordered that it be Inquired into.

Da'd Williams haveing a Claim to 500 acres of land Purchased (as 'tis s'd) of Coll. Markham, being Part of Maj'r Jasper Farmer's Overplus, the said Land was in Pursuance of a warrant from this Board, dat. 22d 9ber, 1703, resurveyed by Thom's Fairman, and found to Contain 780 Acres, and is 230 Over Measure. Thomas Fairman haveing also a Claim and Right to 1,250 acres, One-fourth Part of the said 5,000, The said Land was by Virtue of a warrant dat. 28, 2 mo., 1702, resurveyed by said Fairman and found to Contain Only 1,096 acres, and is 154 acres short, Which Edward Farmer, in behalf of his Nephew, T. Farmer, and his Assignee, Dav'd Harry, requests may be made up Out of the said Overp. of David Williams.

Note, that the Prop'ry, by his Patent under the great seal, dat. 31, 11 mo., '83, Granted To Jasper Farmer and his two Sons, Rich'd and Jasper Farmer, 5,000 acres On Skuylkill, On Part of the Lands Called by the Indians Umbilicamenca, without Any Other Location, Only that ye Prop'ry himself marked the Place and Tree with his Own hands, which as surveyed at first Contained some Thou'ds of Overplus, and on part of that the said Wm.'s Land was laid Out divideing T. F's Land from the rest of ye Tract. Ord'd that Dav'd Williams be Summoned to appear next 2d day to treat about his Overplus.

Edw'd Reece haveing a right to 205¼ acres of Land in Meirion, the Same was Resurveyed by Virtue of a Warr't dat, 16, 10 mo., 1701, and found to Contain Only 190 acres, and is 15¼ acres short. The said Ed'd haveing also 150 a's in Goshen sold it to Ellis David, and 'tis found to Contain Overplus, Out of which Edward is willing to take his said Deficiency, and thereup. a Pat is Ord'd for the rest in Meirion. Vid. Welch Min's.

Evan Harry haveing a right to 164 acres ('tis said now 179), but by the Warrant does not appear so, q'd vide, dat. 18th 12 mo., 1701, Page 84, had 214 Acres in Meirion upon the Resurvey. For the difference about the 15 acres D. Powel to be Consulted. Inquire Into all his Titles.

Isaac Gellias haveing Purchased 5,000 acres, Original sold his Right To Thomas Hudson, Also Jno. Cole, sold his right to 1,000 acres to the said Hudson.* Gellias' Land being laid out in '84, near Percassin, in Bucks, was sold to Wm. Lawrence, Jno. Tallman, Jos. Thorn, Samuel Thorn and Benjamin Field, all of Long Island, about the year '96 or '97, and Cole's 1,000 acres being laid out near Henry Baker's, is Possessed by Jno. Jackson, On the River.

The Prop'ry, by his Warrant dat. 15, 1 mo., '84-5, Ordered the Lotts appurtenant to the said Purchase to be laid Out. Cole's is in Number 20 and Gellias' On the South End of the first Street, both On Skuylkill. Ord'd that a Warrant be renewed.

Jno. Parker Produceing a return of Survey of 492 acres, Surv'd according to the Min's In the Sec'ry's Office, 7ber, 1701, In Right of Mary Southworth. Ord'd a Patent thereupon; he has given Security.

Evan Jones Produceing A return of Survey On his Land, Entered 14, 4 mo., 1703, which makes it Contain 410 acres. Ord'd that the Old Warrant and return be Produced, and Jonas Greenwood and Geo. Dakyne be both forthwith wrote To about it.

At the request of James Proteus and Ellinor Sykes, formerly Tain, both Servants to Wm. Wade, for the Headland. Ord'd Two Warrants.

Jno. Reece, of Haverford, haveing an Overplus of about 50 acres, offers 8 shillings P'r Acre, 'Tis Offered at 10sh.

Jacob Regnier, Esqr., haveing a Title to Some Lotts where the Pott house is built, of 133 f't in the whole in br. between the 4th and 5th Streets In Chestnut. He requests the Preference in Purchasing An adjoyning Lott of 30 f't Or thereabouts, w't ever vacancy there may be disposed off. Rich'd Hill requests this also. Ordered that the first Suitor have the Preference, he giveing as much as the Other.

Wm. Markham and Jno. Goodson, by Pat. dat. 3, 3 mo., '89, Granted To Jno. Claypoole, of Philad'a, Gent., a Lott on the Bank 52 f't In Br. and 250 f't, being bounded N. w'd with Wallnut Str. and S. w'd with James Clayp's Lott, Rent 5s Ster. for 51 years from the Date and the $\frac{1}{3}$ To Rivert. Wm. M., S. Carp'r, R. Tur., and J. Goodson, Granted also Another Patent for the Same Lott to James Clayp., dat. 15, 7ber, 1690. Jno. Claypoole, by Ind're dat. 20, 7ber, '90, Conveyed the above Lott To Patrick Robinson, of Philad'a, Gent., who by

---

*Error vid. 15th 9ber following.

Deed dat. 3d 10 mo., '90, Conveyed To Jno. Duplonoys, of the Same Place, Baker. the Just and Equal Southermost half Part of the said Bank lott, which said half Part doth Contain in br. 26 f't and in Length 250 f't, bounded N. w'd with the Other half Part of the said Lott, E. w'd with Dela. River, at the said Extent of 250 f't, Southward with a Lott then of Jno. Tyzack, and W. w'd with the Front Street, &c. The said Jno. Duplonoys, by Ind're dat. 25, 5 mo., 1692, Conveyed the said Southermost half Part of the Bank Lott aforesaid to Thom's Mast'rs, of Philad'a, Carpent'r, said Mast'rs, by Deed Poll dat. 31, 5 mo., 1695, Conveyed the Same To Thomas Test, of Philad'a, Innholder. The s'd Patrick Rob., by Ind're dat. 25th Jan'y, 1691-2, Granted the Other Moiety of the said Bank lott To Jno. Whitepain, of Philad'a, Mer't, who by Ind're dat. 17, 3 mo., '92, Conveyed the Same to the said Jno. Test, Whereby he became Possessed of the whole said Bank Lott. The s'd Jno. Test, by Deed Poll dat. 26, 1 mo., '98, Granted To Sam'l Carpent'r the whole said Bank lott and buildings thereupon Erected, And the s'd Samuel, by Ind're dat. 25th 2 mo., 1704, Conveyed unto Hen. Badcock a Certain Piece of the said Lott, with a Messuage Standing thereupon, Containing in br. 52 f't and in Length from the East Side of Delaw're Front Street to the West side of King Street, bounded Eastw'd with the said Str., E. w'd w'th Jas. Clayp.'s Lott, W. w'd with Front Street and N. w'd with Wallnut Street, under the Rent of £3 5s, Part of the Ground rent, Payable To Andrew Robeson, &c.

5 mo., 3d. [1704.]

Pres't, Idem.

The Prop'ry, by Deeds of L. and Rel., dat. 22d and 23d Aug't, '82, Granted To Andrew Sowle, Citizen and Stationer, Of London, One thousand acres of Land, of which there is Five hundred Surveyed Near the Lime Kilns. William Bradford, of New York, requests a Warrant, in behalf of Tacee Sowle, to take up the remaining 500 acres, Chester. Granted.

W. M. and T. Ellis, by Warrant dat. 17, 1 mo., '87-8, Granted to Jos. Ambler To take up a lot In Chestnut Str., On Rent. In Pursuance of which There was Surveyed a lot of 40 f't In br. bounded W. w'd with Benjamin Roberts' Lot, On the 24, 1 mo., '88, west of this lies a Lott of 25 f't Grant'd To Hugh Marsh, Renter, as p'r a Return under Rob't Longshore's hand Appears, Surv'd 23d 1 mo., '88, to s'd Marsh in Pursuance Of a War't from the Comm'rs Of the Same date, the said Lot was sold and Past thro' Several hands, and is Now all In the Possession of Dan'l Flower, Carpenter, who requests a Patent for the Same. Ordered in Ambler's Right, Rent 5s strl. p'r Annum from survey.

Jno. Swift Produces a return of Resurvey On a Tract in the County of Bucks, laid Out for 492 acres, but Proves 580, and is 89 acres Over, About which the Comm'rs not agreeing, Ordered that Jno. Cutler and   view it and Sett a Price, Or Cut it Off, with Peter Chamberlain and Thomas Morris.

Hugh Marsh haveing a right to 500 acres of Land Confirmed To him By Patent, he sold, as is said, 200 acres to Wm. Waite, who sold it To Jos. Holding, but there being Overplus in it, Holding Procured a warrant from the Comm'rs dat. 19, 1 mo., '87-8, for the said Overplus, to be laid Contiguous to that Tract of Land said Holding then lived Upon, which he formerly bought of Wm. Waite, in Pursuance of which Warrant the said Land was Resurveyed and laid Out as aforesaid, Containing 250 Acres. And the s'd Land was Taken in Execution and Conveyed To Jno. Nailer by Jos. Growdon, by Deed dat. 13, 1 mo., '94, no waranty against himself and Claiming under him. This 200 and 250 being res'd is found to Contain 445 acres Only. He requests a Confirmation, but the Overplus Never being sold that appears, it Cannot be granted. 'Tis Ordered that the Possessor be Ejected Or Sued In Order to Lay A foundation for a Title.

John Budd Produceing A return of 500 acres of Land, Surv'd upon Our Warrant, Joyning On the Tract near Brandyw., of 30,000 acres, Together with that Surv'd for Jno. Guest, Requests a Patent.

Eliz'th Webb, formerly wid'w of Jno. Barber, Purchaser of 2,500 acres, haveing sold to Dav'd Loyd 666⅓ Acres and to Judge Guest 666⅓ acres, has now by Deed dat. 4th May, 1704, Conv'd the remainder, 666⅓ acres, To Thomas Fairmar, who requests a Warrant to take up the Same.

Ordered that Edward Farmer's and Dav'd Williams' business Be forthwith Dispatched.

By Virtue of a Warrant from the Comm'rs dat. 20th 8 mo., '84, now in the Office, there was Surv d, as is alledged, 500 acres To Nathaniel Stanbury (in right of Arthur Cook, late Purchaser of 5,000 a's) in the County of Bucks, and bears his Name in the Map. He Requests a Resurvey. Granted.

Ordered that a Warrant be renewed to Judge Guest for 500 acres of Land in Lieu of that of which he was disappointed, to be beyond all Settlements and Surveys, at the Instance of the Gov'r and sev'l Others.

———

5 mo., 10 [1704.]

Present, Griff. Owen and James Logan.

Will'm Woodland, Son of Jno. Cole's Sister, Produces a Rel. from the Prop'ry for 1,000 Acres of Land, dat. 10th 7ber, '81, Sold to said John Coles, of Catcoat, in the Parish of Moorlinch, Coun. Somerset, Sergemaker, together with A rec't for the Money of the Same Date. This Woodland Claims the Land, but 'tis that which Thomas Hudson Claims. Vid. 24th Ultimo.

Do. Geo. Foxe's business forthwith. The Deeds from Griff. Jones To the Govern'r for 25½ f't of Front and Bank bounded , in Exchange for 25½ f't Front and Bank To be Confirmed to said Griff. by Patent, bounded . Warr't for the Lib. Land at the request of Sa. Car., Antho. Morris and D. Llo.

Inquire what Overplus there is in Wid'w Haverd's, Thom's Howe's and Nathan Thos's Lands. D. P. Surveyed.

6 mo., 14th [1704.]

Haveing Agreed with Jos. Wilcox to give him £40 for his Deficiency, We Offered 2 lotts On the 3d Str., Joyning To his Own On 2d Str., at £5 p'r and 1 sh. Quitt Rent, and 27 foot adjoyning to his Lott beyond the Town from Front to 2d Str. at 12s 6d per f't In Part of Pay.

Of the 10,000 Acres Granted to the Swedes On Mahanatawny, Rich'd Roades has 800 acres, Justa Justason 1,000 acres, Matthias Holston 900 acres, Morton Morton 1,200, Peter Boon 1,000 acres.

Jno. Archer requesting a Grant for 10 acres of vacant Marsh upon Darby Creek, Joyning to his first Lands, 'tis Granted to him for £10, to be Paid the 9th of 7ber Next. Void.

Ord'd To John Harper 5 acres of Lib. Land left unsurveyed to him of his 500 acres Of Purchased Land.

Jno. Bentley, of Whiteclay creek, Purchases 100 Acres Of Land Joyning On his Own Land and said Creek at £16 and Bushell of Wheat Rent, to be Paid 24th 7ber, 1705.

Ordered a Patent to Eliz'th Sands for 500 acres granted by Warr't, 11 8ber, 1703.

7ber, 11th [1704.]

Ieidem.

Silas Crispin, of 11,000 Acres Purchased, To Thom's Holme 5,000, by Samuel Claridge 5,000, and By Rich'd Crosby 1,000, vid. Min's, brings in an acco't of 1,581 remaining Untaken up, and Craves a Warrant for 1,000 of it, which is Granted, He giveing Bond as Before. See 8ber, 26, 1702.

Do., 26th [1704.]

Iediem.

Draw a Warrant to Samuel Powel for a Lott Ord'd 28, 4 mo., 1703. And a Bank Patent as there Ordered.

Ordered a Pat. To Jno. Buckley, of Rockland, upon his return of 200 Acres, he Paying £20 in the whole, with the Arrears of Quitt Rent for 30 acres. See 14, 7ber, 1702.

Ordered a Pat. to Evan Jones on his res. of 410 acres in Kent Coun., formerly laid Out for Only 300 acres by a Warrant for 400 acres, and now by the addition of Some Swamps and woodland Points make up the said Quantity, for which He is to Pay Rent for the whole from the first Survey, that is 4 Bus'ls p'r ann. from ye 1st Execut'n of ye warr't. For ye title see for ye Orig'l Warr't to Jones.

The Prop'ry, by Ind'res of L. and Rel., dat. 24 and 25, 11 mo., 1681, In Consid'n of £20, Granted 1,000 acres to Benja'n Chambers, of Bearstead, Coun. Kent, Turner, Rent 1 sh. st'rl. p'r C't. The said Prop'ry, by like Deeds of the Same date and like Consid'n, 500 acres To Hen'y Green, of Maidston Coun. Kent, Rent 1 sh. St'rl. p'r C't p'r Annum. The s'd Prop'ry, by like deeds of the Same date and Consid'n Granted 1,000 acres To James Hunt, of Bearstead aforesaid, Weaver, Same Rent. By Warrant from the Comm'rs, dat. 1, 4 mo., '88, there was laid Out 13, 7ber following, to said Benj'n Chambers, in Right and as a Part of his Own Purchase aforesaid, 374 acres In the County of Chester, by Warrant of Like Date laid Out the Same Day to said Henry in Right of his said Purchase, 492 acres, in the s'd County, which said Henry by a writeing dat. 19, 6 mo., 1682, sold his said Purchase When laid Out to said Benj'n, if said Green Came not himself to Pensilv'a. By warr't of the Same date there was laid out the Same day To James Hunt, in Right of his said Purchase, 980 acres in the said County, which the said Hunt, by Deed dat. 1st 4 mo. last Past, in Consideration of £100, Pensilv'a Money, Granted to said Benjamin Chambers, Jam's Portes, and Nathan'l Sykes and Ellinor, his wife, by Deed dat. 11th 5 mo. Last, in Consideration of £6, Pensilvania money, Granted 100 acres of Headland To the said Benjamin, which by 2 warr'ts, both dat. the 10th day of the Mo'th and year last Mentioned, was laid Out to the said Jno. Portes and Ellinor Sykes the 12th Sep'r last, it being Headland due to them as Servants. The Comm'rs, by Warrant dat. 31, 10br, 1701, at Benjamin Chambers's request Granted him To Take up for himself and Henry Green 150 acres On the Northside Of the Kentish Tract, near Brandyw., at £12 p'r C't, but there was Surv'd In Pursuance of said Warrant the 12th of 7ber last Only 115 acres. The Com'rs, by Warrant of Like date and upon the Same Terms With the last Mentioned Warr't Granted Benjamin Chambers to take up in behalf of Peter Blond and James Hunt about 200 acres at the Eastern Corner of and adjoyning To the said Kentish Tract, but in Pursuance thereof 335 acres was laid Out the 12th of 7ber last, all which said Parcells of 374 a's, 492 acres, 980 a's, 100 acres, 115 acres and 335 acres, Containing Together 2,396, were Resurveyed as they now Lye Contiguous in One Tract, and found to Contain 2,470 acres in the whole.

8 mo., 9th [1704.]
Present, Edw'd Shippen, Griff. Owen and Jam's Logan.

Joseph Ashton, of Dublin Township, desireing to Purchase 1,000 acres of Land in the Mannor of Gilberts, begin above the dry Hollow Vale about   Perches above Perquecominck Creek, and running backwards Till it Interfere with the said Creek, leaving besides the said hollow all That Tract On which the Prop'ry resolved to build a Town, agrees to Pay for the Same £235 On the 25th of March Next; to have Leave also to Fix an Dam Over Pequeominck, Provided that he does not divert the Course of the Creek any further than to accommodate a Mill Race. A Warrant and Patent is Ordered.

By Vertue of Warrant dat.   , there was Surv'd to Eliz'th Steedman 50 a's of Land in Springfield, Chester, by Charles Ashcom, 16 8br, '82, as by his return appears, which being resurveyed is found to Contain 51 acres. El. Steedman, by her Deed acknowledged in Chester Court 5th 4 mo., '88, Conveyed the Same To Peter Thomas, who wants a Pat. Thereupon at 1d Ster. p'r an. Granted. He Paid to Coll'r Pusey 27. 1 mo., '94, 23s 6d, to Sam'l Jennett 7s 9½d, 19, 1 mo., '96-7, and 21, 2 mo., '99, to Do. £2 7s 10d in full for Do. Due from that Time.

Ord'd a Patent to Eliz. Sands for 500 acres in Bucks, Granted by a War't dat. 11th 8ber, 1703, In Right of the Same Quantity Granted by the Propr'ys Lease and Release. dat. 8th and 9th 9ber, To Samuel Fell.

In Pursuance of Our Warrant dat. 26th October, 1702, Ord'd 5th 8ber, Ditto, There was Resurveyed a Tract On Nesham. for 400 acres, Now made 440, there being Thirty acres Cutt off Joyning on Jno. Crosdale. Ordered a Patent To Hannah Price for the use of the Children, see 20th 8ber and oth'r Pat's.

Israel Taylor Out of a Patent Granted to his Father, Christ'r, dat. 15, 5 mo., '84, for 500 acres Consid'n to Christ'r Wetheril, 150 acres by Deed dated 10th 4 mo., '85, and the Comm'rs,   and Robert Turner, by their Warrant dat. 17, 9 mo , '84, Granted to the said Christ'r 50 acres of Land, paid for here To Ja. Harrison, as is Certifyed by Phil. Pemb., and was laid Out adjoyning to the above On Nesham. These 200 acres being resurveyed is found to Contain 236 acres, and is 26 acres Over, for Which he agrees to give £9, and Requests a Patent. Granted.

---

8 mo., 31st [1704.].

Present, Omnes.

Rich'd Cantwell and Wm. Dyre, with Severall Other Petitioners, near Apoquin Creek, requesting a Tract of Land for accommodating a chapel of the Church of England and a Glebe for the Support of their Minister. 'Tis Ordered that 10 acres be granted for the said use Upon the Same Terms as in the 11th mo. Last as was granted To Jos. England and Wm. Horne, viz: at 1d Per acre.

William Smith, of Bristol, in England, Merchant, by Ind'res of Lease and Release, dat. 18 and 19, 12 mo., 1703, Granted unto Thomas Paschal and Hen. Flower, both of the City of Philad'a, Gent., 250 acres of Land lying in Chester County. This was Part of 1,000 acres, his first Purchase finish it.

Samuel Allen, Purchaser of 2,000 acres from the Prop'ry, Conv'd 100 acres of Land lying in Bucks County, adjoyning to the Land of James Boyden, to Charles Plumley, and also 100 acres of Land untaken up. Wm. Plumley, Son and Heir of the said Charles, did grant the said 2 Parcells of 100 acres each To Henry Paxen, of the said County, Yeom'n, To Hold, &c., as by Deed dat. 10, 12 mo., 1688, app's. The last Mentioned 100 acres were laid Out to the said Henry in New Town, Coun. Bucks, In Right Of the said Sam'ls Purchase. S'd Samuel, by his last will and Testament, in Writeing, dat. 14, 10ber, 1699, devised severall Parcells of Land To Several Persons therein Named, Makeing no Mention Of the 100 acres aforesaid, and haveing Never made any actual Conveyance of the Same To the said Plumley Or Paxon, did Devise In these words, viz: Item, all the rest of my Estate, real and Personal, whatsoever they Be, I Give To my Son-In-Law, Thomas Sisom, with my Daughter, Priscilla Sisom, they Paying Out of the Same 40s to Martha Dawson, as by the said Testament may appear, and Whereas the s'd Thomas Sisom and Priscilla, his wife as well for the Consideration money formerly Rec'd by the said Samuel Allen, as for the Sum of 50 sh. to them Paid by the said Henry Paxon, Granted and released to the said Henry Paxon the said 100 acres so mentioned to be laid Out to him as aforesaid, by Deed dat. 16. 9ber, 1703, Doth fully appear, which was Resurveyed by a General Warrant and found to Contain 114 acres, being 4 acres Overplus. A Patent to be made, Paying 6 sh. p'r acre for the said Overplus.

9ber, 15th [1704.]

Will'm Biles Produces a rec't dat. 24, 2 mo., '83, for £100 for 5,000 acres rece'd of Thomas Hudson, and another Rec't dat. 2d March, '85, for £10 for 500 acres sold to said Hudson, and another dated 25th May, '85, for £10 for 500 acres sold to Jacob Hall, which they say Hudson bought of Hall, and another rec't dated 25th Ap'l, '83, for £18 for buying off the yearly Rent of 45 sh., and another of the same date for £9 for buying off £1 2s 6d, and the Consideration Mentioned in a Pair of Ind'res.

Will'm Markham and Jno. Goodson, Comm'rs, by their Warrant dat. 6th 3 mo., '89, Granted To John Tyzack 40 f't of Bank On the S. side of Will'm Salway's Lott, Now Anthony Morris's, which said Lott Thomas Farm'r, Sherr. of Philad'a, in Consideration of a debt recovered by Eliz'th Robinson (of £37 10s and £3 Charges), made Over to Jacob Regnier by a Deed Poll. dat. 1 July, 1703, vide Deed Predict. He requests a Confirmation. Granted.

Finish a Patent to Peter Hansen for his Tract and Overplus, for the Titles See before.

Agreed p'r J. L. at Newc. with Neal Cook that he shall have a Pat't for the 200 acres Granted To Jno. King, and for his Own Two Hund'd, now Res'd as found To Contain 300 a's, and is 80 acres Over. He agreed at Newc. To give £3 for 20 acres, w'ch He thought was all, and 20 sh. the Survey. See Whether He will give Proportionably for the rest. Geo. Dakeyne is to Send Up the Title p'r J. L. at Newc.

Agreed formerly with Tho. Paschal, Jun'r, for £7 10s for the Overp. of William Jenkins' Father-in-Law's Land, being 43 acres; his right Is 250, allow'ce 25 acres, 60 acres for his Deficiency in Haverf'd; the Title is Entered about 8, 10 or 12 mo's agoe.

Will'm Mark., R. Tur. and Jno. Goodson, by a Pap'r Pat. dat. 5th 11 mo., 1692, Granted To Charles Pickering 411 acres of Land in 2 Tracts, the One Containing 326, the Other 85 a's, both Situate On Brandywine Creek, Granted to the said Charles by the former Comm'rs by warrant dat. 29th 8 mo., '84, Surv'd 20th 4 mo., '85, Rent a Bushell of Wheat for Every 100 acres. Charles Pickering, by Deed Poll dat. 28 March, '94, for £60, Conveyed the said Land To Andrew Robeson, Jos. Willcox and Jno. Moore, all of Philad'a; Robeson dying, by Survivorship the Other Two Claim the Whole and request a Confirmation. If there be no Overplus Granted by the Lines of the Old Pat't, Unless they P. for a New res. Inquire Whether Clear of Indians.

---

10 mo., 11th [1704.]

Present, Omnes.

The Gover'r Recommended to the Board To Consider of Some Suitable Compensation to Judge Guest for his Trouble in holding Courts in This Governm't, being a p'son Necessary in the pr'sent Administra'n, and that deserves Encouragement, And Represents that notwithstanding he knows it To be the business of the Country, And It is unjust and unreasonable that it should Lie upon the Prop'ry, Yet rather than that nothing should be done, the Prop'ry having recommended his Affairs to his (the Gov'rs Care), He believes it would not displease the Prop'ry that in the Mean Time till further Provision should be made, This Board should Contribute. This being Taken into Consideration, ye Comm'rs find it belongs not to them nor that it will be Warrantable in them by Virtue of Any Power they Stand Invested w'th to make Any Grants On this Score, Yet Are Willing that all favour be Shewn to the said Judge in Any request he has to make as far as shall be Consistent with Our Commission.

Richard Hill haveing formerly Purchased a Right from Jno. Kinsey, of a Lott of 40 f't, or thereabouts, in Chestnut Str., the 2d Lott Northside beyond the 5th Street, formerly granted To James Pugh, and by him sold To Kinsey.

And Now haveing Purchased of Ephraim Allen, Husband of Eliz'th, Relict of Jeremiah Powel, his Right To a lott On the said 5th Street, Adjoyn'g On the former, 40 f't br. and 178 foot Deep, Granted To said Jeremy, Renter, by a warrant from the Comm'rs dat. 27, 4 mo., '89, and Surv'd 4, 5 mo., '89, requests a Confirmation of both, and to Purchase another Vacant Lott of 60 f't Adjoyning up to the Pott house.

Jos. England Informing that He is Like to be molested in the Possession of 1,000 acres of Land bought in the Prop'ry's Mannor, near Duck Creek, for which he has Paid great Part of the Consideration Money, And yet that the said Land is Entered On by One Sewell, of Maryland, by Virtue of An Old Grant from that Province, and being unwilling To Contest it, Craves the Bargain May be Void and that his money be returned, Yet being desirous to Purchase Land for his Children, he Offers To take the Old Plantation On Duck Creek, formerly Called Holding's, first laid Out to Chr. Ellot, in Lieu of its being reputed 500 acres.

Agreed therefore with the said Jos. that he shall have the

said Plantat'n, Containing not Above the said Quantity of 500 acres, with the Allowance made by Law, and that the Land is first to be Escheated at ye said Jos.'s Charge (this being to be Ordered with as little Charge as Possible), and a Patent to be granted thereupon.

Ordered a Commission of Escheat forthwith To Wm. Tonge.

Ord'd To Will'm Dyer 100 acres of Land Adjoyning On Humph. Best, at 1d ster. p'r Acre, Provided We Grant Wm. Horn 500 acres there, Otherwise Sell 1,000 acres To Dyer, Cantwell and Monroe. Inquire about this Land.

Edw'd Beeson, of the County of Newc., Produces an Authentick Copy of An Ind're dat. 11 Mar., 1703, from Dan'l Wharley and his wife, Mary, reciteing that the Prop'ry by his Ind'res, dat. 17 and 18, 3 mo., 1681, Granted to Mary Pennington, ye younger, Of the woodside, Par. Agmondsham, Coun. Bucks, Spinster, 1,250 acres of Land in this Province in the usual form, all which the said Dan'l, with whom the said Mary Intermarried, And his wife, by said Ind'res, Granted to s'd Edward, his Heirs, &c. Part of the above Land being Laid Out, Ordered Warrants of Resurvey thereon where to be found and for ye Lotts and Lib. Land Appurten't to it.

Agreed by James Logan, at Chester, with Wm. Swaffer, to Confirm to him 150 acres headland Granted by the Prop'ry's Warr't, dat. 4, 2 mo., '83, for 150 acres, 50 thereof To Rob. Cadwell and his Daug'r Mary, now wife to said Swaffer, and her serv't, Sarah Stedman, who relinquish'd her Right, rent 2d p'r a'c. The Mother dying, It Came All to The Daughter; a Pat. to be made to the Husb'd and Daugh'r at 1s p'r C't, he haveing Given Bond with Security for £7 10s for reduceing it, and for all Arrears of Quitt Rents to Mar. next, what is above 150, not Exceeding 15 allowed by Law.

A Pat. to Jno. Beale, of Coun. Chester, for 132 acres, 100 thereof taken Up On Old Rent, 10 allowed by Law; for the remaining 22, being very Stoney and Barren, He gives £5 Rent, of the whole 5 Pecks Of Wheat, for the Title See him and Jos. Richards, Apr. or May, 1703.

---

10 mo., 27 [1704.]

Present, Omnes.

Agreed with Wm. Horn, of the County of Newc., for 1,000 acres of Land Near Blackbirds Creek, On the N. side of the Queen's Road, Joyning On Wm. Dyre's Plantation, for £8 10s p'r C't, and is to give Bond for £56 13s 4d Sterling, To be Paid 3 mo. Next.

Rob. Heaton having Purchased 250 acres of R'd Thatcher's Purchase In Bucks, and being res'd is found to Contain 280

Acres, of which 10 Is Overp., for which He Agrees to Pay £3 8sh. in Consideration that He was obliged to Pay £4 12s for 14 acres before. This to be Paid at May Fair.

---

12 mo., 19th [1704.]

Present, Omnes.

Nathaniel Puckle Produceing a Warrant from the Prop'ry for 3 lotts on Dela'e and 3 lotts on Skul. to Philad'a Ford, ye said 3 lotts Standing each behind ye Other, dat. 25, 5 mo., '84, req'ts a Resurvey. Granted.

The Prop'ry, by Pat. dat. 4, 6 mo., '84, Granted To Samuel Carp'r 204 f't of Bank to hold for 51 years under the Rent of 20sh., Country Money, and afterw'ds to be valued, and $\frac{1}{3}$ to be Paid yearly. Sam'l Carpent'r haveing Sold Wm. Trent 60 f't of this between the Cartway and the Front Str., desires in Pursuance of ye Prop'ry's Grant that he May have the Priviledge of buying it Off at the usual Rates, which, in Consideration of Samuel's merit in the Bank.

Samuel Powel's Warrant, bounded with J. M. and Tho. Cross, Now Swaffer, E. and hasten his Bank.

A Warr't to Jno. Parsons for the Corner Lott for 21 years at 5s Sterling.

Gover r Andros, by his Patent dat. 25 March, '76, in these words grant'd Jurian Hartsfielder a Tract of Land Called Hartsfield, On the W. side of Delaware River, at the Lower Side of Cohoesinck Creek, the which by Virtue of a Warrant hath been laid Out to Urian Hartfield'r. The said Land begining at the mouth of a Small Creek Or River Called Coo-ah-que-nunque, and from thence running Up the Several Courses of the said Run to the North End of Cooahquenunque Bridge, From Thence North and by W. along by the W. side of a Piece of Meadow Ground 112 Perches To a Corner Markt black Oak, standing at the Upper End of the said Meadow Ground, from thence N. E. 184 Perches by a Line of Marked Trees To a Corner marked White Oak, standing at the S. W. side of a Branch of Cohoesincks Creek, from thence down along the several Courses of the s'd Branch and Creek to the main River Side, and finally along the River side to the Place of Begining, Containing and laid Out for 350 acres of Land. The s'd Governor Grant'd to the said Jurian Hartsfielder, his Heirs and Assigns, the afores'd Parcell of Land and Premisses, with all and Singular the Appur'ces, To Have and To hold the said Parcel of Lands and Prem'es unto the said Jurian Hartsfielder, his Heirs and Assigns, unto the Proper use and behoof of the said Jurian Hartsfielder his Heirs and assigns for Ever, he makeing Improvement On the said Land According to Law, and Continueing in Obedience by Conforming himself According to the Laws of this Government, yielding and Paying y'rfore yearly to his Royal Highness 3½ Bus'ls Good Winter Wheat Unto such Officers, &c., for his Royal Highness's use. Date, ut Sup'a, Indorsed a Deed Poll from Jurian Hartsfielder and Marg't his wife, By their Marks, dat. 15th March, 1679, Conveyed To Hannah Salter, widow, all the within mentioned Land, saveing 100 acres sold to Andries Johnson next to the Creek, Called Oxenhose, for a Valuable Sum. The Deed is Good. Hannah Salter Gave a Deed in these words Literatim the 23d of the 4 mo., 1681 : Know all Men by these Presents that I, Anna Salter, of Toakony, Widow, have Indorsed the within written Deed of mey Land by Coakanake Creek To the Possion of Daniel Peage and his Heirs for Ever, all my Right, Interest, by Contract Or Wrighting, as Ever I had granted To myself Or Any Persons for me for a Consid'n Or Contract made Betwine the s'd Parties, 100 Skipfulls of Wheat, Payabell and togeather as the said Dan'l Peag Obligation To Anna Salter, aforesaid, finely by these Presents Acquit'g myself, my Heirs, Exe'tors, Administrates or Assignes, of all Rig'ts or Properties whatsoever. Witness my hand and seal.

Test,

THOMAS FAIRMAN,
JUDITH NARBOLE,
GEORGIUS SIGNSELDER.

Patent from the Prop'ry To Dan'l Pegg, dat 26, 1 mo , '84, under the same bounds, Verbatim with the first Grant, but the Quan'y, by a Rasure, is made 450 acres. Dan'l Pegg, by Ind're dat. 11th of Jan'y, 1690, Granted To Thomas Smith, of the County of Philad'a, Yeoman, all that his Northerly Just and Equal Moiety and half Part of the said Dan'l Pegg his 334 Acres of Land, Be the Same more Or less, Lying at the North End of Philad'a, Deed p'r Pat. Rob.

Thomas Smith Deceasing, Tho's Sisom Married the Widow, and the whole Tract being resurveyed is found to Contain   acres, of which   acres are Over Measure. Thomas Sisom, In behalf of Smith's Children, Craves To Purchase One Moiety of it, Also the Priviledge of Pegg's Part in Case none Of them will buy Their's. 'Tis Offered at 50sh. p'r Acre, Recerveing 20 acres to be laid Out Adjoyning the Prop'ry's Mill.

Isaac Wiltbank, of Lewis, Petitioning (by James Thomas) for a small Parcell of Land left Out between his Land and a Branch of Pagan Creek, Containing about 30 Acres for the Conveniency of a Bridge Over the Creek to his Land. Granted, He Paving After the rate of £20 p'r C't.

Thomas Tilton, of Slaughter Neck, in Sussex, Petitioning (by Jno. Thomas), for 100 Acres of Marsh in ye s'd Neck to Accom'odate his Land, which is 400 acres. Granted 50 acres at 1d p'r acre.

Wm. Dyre haveing formerly Applyed for a Parcell of Land in Newc. County, Near Blackbirds Creek, of which an Expectation was given him, but being Since disposed of To Wm. Horn, He req'ts to take up 200 Acres On New Rent, as had been Proposed To him, Adjoyning on Best and Wheeldon, which is Granted and a Warrant Ordered.

At a Session of the Comm'rs Held 26th 12 mo., 1704.
Prst., Omnes.

Ordered One Patent to Jos. Pike On 500 Acres in Philadelphia County, Surv'd by David Powel, and One Other Patent On 1,000 a's In the said County Now returned.

Upon Will'm Biles' request for Thomas Hudson's Lotts Of Maxfield, Coun. Chester, Granted To the said Thomas by the Prop'ry's Warrant, under his hand and seal, dat. Granting him the lots belonging to ye Purchases of Isaac Gellias and ——— Cole, as mentioned In the Min's.

Robert Marsh haveing a Grant of 500 acres by Patent from The Prop'ry, dat. 16, 5 mo., '84, Granted To Wm. Waite (now of Phil'a) 200 acres of it, who sold to Jos. Holding, who leaveing the Country, in debt, several Executions were taken against his Estate and levied upon his said Land.

Holding, when In Possession of the said 200 acres, understanding there was Overplus in the said Marsh's Tract, haveing first Obtained his free Leave and Right, Applyed to the Comm'rs for a resurvey On the s'd Tract, requesting that the Overplus may be laid Out in One Piece Contiguous to his Land, which they Granted by their Warrant, dat 19, 1 mo, '87-8, Executed 26th 8ber, '88, and found to be 250 acres, as p'r Return in the Office Appears. This Overplus, tho' Never Paid for being afterwards Accounted Holding's Land, was Taken In Execution with the Other 200, being in the whole 450 acres, and so sold By the Sherriff of Bucks to Jos. Growdon, who by his Ind're dat. 13, 1 mo., '94, Conveyed the whole to Jno. Nailor, of Southampton. Said Nailor Agrees to Pay the Price of the said Overplus as then rated at the time of the Grant, with Interest to this time, and req'ts a Patent On the whole 450 acres According to Jno. Cutler's return, which is granted. He Pays £35 for the whole. [Dispatch this and gett the return from J. T. the Patent to be finished In 5 days].

The Prop'ry Granted To Rebecca Cadwell for herself And

To her Daughter Mary, and her Serv't, Sarah Stedman, each 50 Acres serv'ts Land by a warrant dat. . The Servant Quitted all her Pretences, So that Rebecca Enjoyed it all, and dying, left it to her Daughter Mary, now wife of Wm. Swaffer. This Land being resrv'd is found to Contain 180 acres, he gives £7 10s to reduce the Quitt Rent to Common Rent and £5 for the Overplus, and req'ts that the whole be returned. Granted to himself and wife. Gett the Return of Jacob Taylor.

At a Session of the Comm'rs held the 19th 1st mo., 1705. Present, Edward Shippen, Griffith Owen and James Logan.

A Warrant to Edward Jennings, Servant To Jno. Harding, In 1682, by Cert. from Phil. Roman.

The Comm'rs, by Warrant dat. 23. 1 mo., '88, Granted To Hugh Marsh, Renter, a Lot In Chestnut Street of 35 foot, which was Surveyed To him the Same day, as by Warrant and return in the office. Marsh sold his Right to Richard Hilliard, who Sold to Wm. Trotter, Who built upon It, But No Deeds Ever Past. William Trotter deceasing, left 3 children, and his Widow, Rebecca (together with Mary Port, Relict of Richard Hilliard, Concurring with her), requests a Patent To herself In her husband's Right. Marsh is in Maryland and has often declared his readiness to Pass Any Necessary writing, as they Alledge, but he Never haveing Improved it nor Paid Any rent, which is the Only Consideration of the Grant, and Trotter haveing built On, a Patent is Ordered to said Rebecca in Right of Her Husband. Rent 5 sh's Ster. p'r Annum.

Andrew Paterson haveing A right by Survey to 600 Acres in the New Swedish Tract of 10,000 acres sends a Certificate under his hand (Witnessed by Jno. Gardner and David Powel that he has assigned all his Right To Jacob Culin or Josvan Koolen and Req'ts this Board to Confirm the said land to Jacob. Granted.

The Prop'ry, by Patent, dat. 17, 5 mo., '84, Confirmed To Richard Worral, Purchaser, 500 acres, in Right of his Original Purchase laid Out 20, 2 mo., '83, By Virtue of Wm. M's Warrant dat. 20, 7 mo., '82, to said Richard, In Dublin Township. The said Richard as himself Owns before us, sold Thomas Fairman 200 acres, Part of the said Tract, and Granted a Deed for It, but it Cannot be found. Thomas Fairman sold 100 of This To Henry Howard, 100 more To Thomas Kitchen, and 50 To Wm. Waite, but there being Some More Land in that Place vacant the said Thomas haveing laid out their 600 Acres for himself In right of Allen Foster, and to Accommodate Worrall quitted the Place To him, by which Means there was y't Vacancy. T. F. further Purchased of Walter King 100 acres in Right of which he was to take up ye said Vacancy but never had Any Survey, Yet Ventured to Sell 50 acres of it to Hugh Gooda, whose Only Daughter and Child George Burson Married, and bought the Other 50 of Waite so that he Possesses 100 acres, and Tho. F. Requests that in Pursuance.

Offered to Jno. Vaughan the Adjacent vacant Land upon his Tract in Sussex at £12 p'r C't, viz: so much as will Make it Even and Regular but No more, a Warrant issued.

Ordered upon a Cert. of the Prop'ry's Letter To Thomas Wright, Sent by the s'd Thomas To T. Storey, that a Patent be Granted to Jos. Pike for the 10,000 Acres in the Same Words with these of the Deed from the Prop'ry.

The Prop'ry, by Lease and Release, dat. 9th and 10th May, '82, Granted To Edw'd Blendman, of Shiptonmallet, Coun. Somersett, Clothier, 1,000 acres now all Taken up, also the Front lot by Jos. Paul to whom he Conveyed his whole Right by Assignm't. Indorsed dat. 23 Jan'y, '88. The Comm'rs Granted to J. Paul a warrant dat. 22, 12 mo., '89-90, for Takeing Up the Lotts which was Executed in Front Street and returned, and In High Street also 'tis s'd but not returned, J. Paul Craves a new warrant On the High Street Lott.

Governor Francis Lovelace, by Patent, dat. 10 Apr., 1673, Granted To John Johnson 100 acres of Land in Marcus Kill, and he, by Deed, dat. 28 Feb'y, '81, Granted the Same To Jno. Test, of Upland, who by Deed Dat. 14 March, '81, Granted it to Nathaniel Evans. The said Governor by Patent, dat. same day, Granted James Justason, under the Name of Jems Juste, 100 acres, who, by Deed, dat. 12, 1 mo., '78-9., Sold a Part of it to Alb't Hendrickson, who by Deed 26th 9 mo., Sold the same to Wolla Derickson, who, by Deed, 5, 6 mo., '84, Sold to Jno. Child, who also Marrying Eliz'th, Sole Daughter and Heiress of said Nath'l Evans, Enjoys all the said Land.

Jno. Harding, of Chichester, Yeoman, by an Instrument under his hand and Seal, dat. 26, 3 mo., '83, In Consideration of £28 15s Granted his Right And Title to his Land (old Sneed's Land) lying Between Middle Neck and Harwick Run, being 2 Parcells Lyeing Between Nath'l Evans and Morton Cornutes' Land, ye Other Between the said Morton's and John Johnson's Land with the Marsh and all the App'res thereto belonging To Jno. Bezor, of Chichester, afores'd, Yeoman, his Heirs and Assigns for Ever. Albert Hendrickson by Instrum't, dat. 30, 6 mo., '83, Grant'd a Certain Piece of Marsh in Harwick, to the s'd Jno. Bezor, his Heirs, &c., Jno. Hendrickson, of Philad'a, Shipwright, and Frances, his wife, Daughter of the said Jno. Bezor, deceased, in Consid'n of £30, Granted the said Parcells of Land, Meadow, Marsh and swamp, reputed to

Contain about 100 acres, to Jno. Child, of the County of Chester, Yeoman, his Heirs, &c., as by Deed Poll, dat. tne last of Sep'r, '94, appears, all which Parcells of Land (Except the Parcell Lyeing Between Jno. Johnson's and Morton's Land) were resurveyed As they are Contiguous, and found To Contain 240 acres, being the Same quantity the said Parcells were heretofore found To Contain in the first Resurvey of them made by Charles Ashcom, requests a Patent. Granted.

Richard Hill and Anthony Morris makeing Application to this Board in behalf of the Monthly meeting of Friends of Philad'a, and by their appointment that whereas Coll. Wm. Markham, dec'ed, haveing Procured (as 'tis said), a Patent to himself, signed by himself and One Other Commiss'r Only, for a lott in the High Str., Joyning on the 2d Street, Out of which Pat. the said Coll. Markham granted To Friends a Certain Part of the Same to build a meeting house, and is the Same where the great meeting House Now Stands, but Suspecting the Validity of the Title they therefore request a Confirmation from this Board, Alledgeing and Pleading that the Prop'ry had formerly Granted Ground for a Meeting house at the Center, upon which they built very much to their Charge, Inconveniency and Damage, and have Since left it Entirely, throwing it up again To the Prop'ry, and further that the Prop'ry allways Expressed a Willingness to furnish them with Ground for a meeting house, and was Accordingly ready to Confirm this to them himself at his Departure, but was neglected, all which being duely Considered, especially that the Prop'ry haveing no where Else Granted Friends any Place for a meeting house that is now of any Service To them, and that he Accounted himself Obliged in favour to them to Grant a Convenient Place, Therefore It is Ordered that a Patent be Granted for so much as they now hold in the Place aforesaid Without any regard had to the said grant Of Markham to himself being Illegal and Irregular, Or Any Title derived therefrom.

Jno. Welch, of Coun. Philad'a, Blacksmith, Produceing A return of Survey for 530 Acres in the Welch Tract, Ordered a Patent forthwith, Considerat'n Money for 530 a's (10 allowed) at £12 10s p'r C't, £65.

3 mo., 7th [1705.]

Ieidem.

Ord'd a Patent to Geo. Palmer for his 800 acres in the Great Swamp, and that the Other Land adjoyning, marked by T. F. for Jno. and Thomas Palmer, Be not disposed of to Any Other Purchaser till the said Jno. have Notice.

Geo. Palmer, Son of Geo. Palmer, dec'ed, haveing a Right to 25½ f't of Bank, remaining of Palmer's whole lott Granted by Warrant dat. 21, 11 mo., '92-3, (the rest being Confirmed upon Transfers To Benjamin Chambers by Pat't dat. 8, 3 mo., 1704), Requests a Patent. Granted this forthwith.

Nath'l Edgecomb, One Of the Attorneys, with Samuel Carpenter, to Jos. Wassey, of London, Mariner, Produces a return of 250 acres Surv'd 19, 1 mo., '83, to said Jos. by Warrant dat. 12, 7, '83, In Dublin Township, resurveyed by J. Andr. and Contains 251 acres. Req'ts a Patent to Wassey. Ordered upon the res., they Paying for it, A New Return to be given Out by Jacob Taylor forthwith.

Richard Davies Conveyed to Marg't James, Par. Newchurch, Coun. Radnor, Spinster, 200 acres by Lease and Release, dat. 19 and 20 June, '82, laid Out In Radnor, from T. H., 18, 5 mo., '83.

Ph. Tho. Lehnman rec'd 29th 5 mo, '84, of Samuel Miles £5 for the Purchase of 100 acres, formerly (as 'tis recited) laid Out to him On Rent by the Same Warrant.

Ellis Jones Takeing Fifty Acres On Rent by the Same Warrant assign'd his right to it to said Samuel Miles 16, 9 mo., '93.

Samuel Miles Marrying the S'd Marg't James, now holds the whole said Land, Except 92 acres sold to his Brother, Rich'd Miles, and therefore has 258 acres remaining, which being Surv'd Contains 352 acres, and is 69 acres Over, at 6s 8d p'r Acre and Interest for 18 mos.

Ellis Jones's 50 acres to be cleared for £5 10s, Rent to 1 mo. Last, £6 11s 3d. Jones Pays on 9th 9ber, 9 mos., viz. £3, 1s to be added to the Other is £18 11s, deduct £3 10s assumed by S. Miles, remains £5 1s. Miles Pays £23 and £3 10s for Jones, w'th £3 10s 3d Rent, in all £30 0s 3d, and 18 mo.'s Interest for £23 is 55s 6d. Sum £32 15s 6d. Pat. Ordered On 352 Acres.

Richard Davies also sold to Richard Miles (vid. Welch Min's) 100 a's (Deeds same Date with M. James's), and bought of Samuel Miles 92 a's, resurveyed Contains 233 acres, being 22 acres Over at the Same rate, Is £7 6s 8d, Interest 17s 7d, in all £8 4s 3d. Patents Ordered.

Ordered 50 acres To Isabel Clift, servant To Jos. Fisher in '82.

15th, Do. [1705.]

Ieidem.

There being 50 acres of Land laid Out On Rent 22, 8 mo., '83, Warrant 20, 8 mo., to Daniel Williamson, Confirmed to John Howel, in 400 a's, by Patent from the said Prop'ry, dat.

25, 5 mo., '84, being 300 acres, late Purchase of Jno. Howel, 50 acres of Rob't Taylor's Purchase given s'd Dan'l by said Rob't, his Master. He Complains that these 50 acres were designed to him as his headland and Produces Some Certificates of it, and that the rent was made 1d p'r Acre Only till he was Out of his time, as was said at the issueing the Patent; that Only being 50 a's, the Exact allowance of a Servant, and Taken up dureing the time of Servitude in his Own Name, upon all which he requests that it may be allowed at ½d p'r acre. Due for Rent 21 years in all £6 11s 3d. Paid £18 in '91; at 15d p'r sh. is now £1 1s 7d, remains £5 2s 8d at 1d, Granted to him to release at £5 p'r C't. is 50 for reduceing it and the whole is £7 19s 8d, to be Paid by Daniel Williamson to Clear It. Daniel Williamson sold his right to the whole 100 acres to Josiah, deceased, who sold it to Richard Thomson, who now holds it. Jno. Howel is dead and left his Land (as 'tis said) by will to his Dau'r Mary, who is married to Jos. Powel. A Deed must be made from Howel's Heirs or Devisees, Signed also by Thomas Massey, Jos. Taylor's Ex'r and Dan'l Williamson to Thomson.

Title of the Last:

The Prop'ry, by Pat. dat. 25, 5 mo., '84, Granted a Tract of 400 acres, Coun. Chester, to Jno. Howel, Late Purchaser, laid to said Jno. 300 a's of his Own Purchase, 50 acres in Part of Robert Taylor's Purchase and 50 a's to Daniel Williamson on Rent; these last Parcells were both for Dan'l Williamson, Brother in Law to Howel and Servant to Taylor, who gave his said Servant 50 acres Free Land and took up the Other 50 for his Headland. No Deed from Howel to Williamson, Jno. Howel is now dec'ed. Made a will to be Produced, by which they say he devised all his Land in the Patent to his Daughter Mary, now wife of Jos. Powell. D. Will. sold to Josiah Taylor, who is dece'd, and left Tho. Massey, of Chester County, Ex'r, and In trust for his Children, but before his decease sold to Richard Thomson 100 acres in Lieu of this 100, but is made up of P't of this and P't of 200 Others. J. Howel, in a Codicil of his will added these words; furthermore, It is my mind and Will that my Ex'rs shall Confirm and make a Lawfull title of 100 acres of Land To my Brother-in-Law, Dan'l Williamson, his Ex'rs Or assigns, Only The said Dan'l Paying the Quitt Rent that is Or shall be due upon the s'd 100 acres of Land, the said 100 acres being One of the 400 acres mentioned in My Patent, 50 acres in Part of Robert Taylor's Purchase Land and 50 acres more for Dan'l Williamson upon Rent, Proved 19th June, 1703, before Jno. Moore, dat. 31, 11 mo., 1702-3, Ex'rs Jacob Simcock and Charles Whiteaker.

Do., 18th [1705.]

Richard Price Produced a Certificate under Thomas Fairman's, Joseph Ashton's and Dan'l Street's hands that himself and E. Dun, his wife, Came serv'ts into this Province in 1682 to Will'm Stanley and thereupon desired a warrant to take up for himself and Wife 100 acres, which was Ordered.

The Prop'ry, by Ind're of L. and Rel., dat. 19 and 20, 1 mo., '82, Granted To William Bennett 1,000 acres of Land in this Province. Will'm Bennett made his last will and Test. dat. 9th Aug't, '83, and devised among Other Things 200 a's, Part of the said Purchase, to his Daughter Eliz'th in Fee, and 200 a's More of the said Land to his Daughter Rebecca in Fee, and 200 a's more to his Daughter Ann in Fee, and 200 a's more to his Daug'r Sarah in Fee, and of the Same Testament did make his wife Rebecca Sole E'x, and dyed, after whose decease his said Daughters Eliz., Rebecca, Ann and Sarah became Interested in an undivided Right of and in the said Land to them devised as aforesaid, being in all 800 acres, P't of the said 1,000 acres, and the Other 200 Residue ther_of is now Vested in ye said Rebecca and Sarah by Survivorship and Remains undivided from the 400 acres so belonging to the said Rebecca and Sarah as aforesaid.

Thomas Williams, of Burlington, in West Jersey, Intermarries with the said Rebecca, Relict of the said William Bennett, and Robert Edwards, of Burlington aforesaid, Cooper, Intermarries with the Said Sarah, One of the Surviveing Daughters and Heir of the s'd Will'm Bennett, and Thomas Scholah, of Annanick, in Coun. Burlington, Yeoman, Intermarries with Rebecca, the Other Surviv'g Daughter and Heir, who all of them by a Deed Poll Dated 27, 1 mo., 1703, in Consideration of £80, Pensilv'a Money, Granted 440 acres, Part of the said 1,000, Situate In New Town, in Bucks, To Ezra Crosdale, of Middle Town, Coun.   , yeoman. He, the said Tho's Williams, and Rebecca, his wife, the said Robert Edwards and Sarah, his wife, and the said Jno. Scholah and Rebecca, his wife, by Deed Poll dated 11th May, 1702, in Consid'n of £10, Pensilvania Money, Granted the last mentioned 200 acres being the Residue of the said 1,000 acres, To the said Ezra Crosdall, to hold to him, his Heirs, &c., which said 200 acres of Land by Vertue of a warrant dat. 19, 8 mo., 1702, was Located in Soulberry Township, Coun. Bucks, and by a Certain Warrant of the Like Date with the last mentioned for laying Out to the said Ezra a Certain Quantity of Vacant Land Situate in New Town at the Upper End of his Tract of 400 acres, there was Surv'd the 8, 3 mo., 1703, in the Same Place, a Certain Parcel of Land Cont. 90 acres. The said 440 a's were first of all Located

Sometime about the year 1684 for 400 a's, but being res'd by a Warrant dat. 15, 10ber, 1701, is found to Contain 440 acres.

1 mo., 27 [1705.]

Iediem.

Whereas Judge Guest has Taken frequent Occasions of Complaining to the Gover'r against the Board and Pleads that he has been greatly Injured by our not Suffering him to take up the Land Granted To him 19th 5 mo., 1703, viz: the additional 500 acres as he desired, and that the war't for Other 500 acres in Lieu of the former granted in June last will not Suit him for a final Conclusion, therefore of the difference 'tis agreed before the Governor that this Board shall choose 2 persons and the s'd Judge 2 other persons to whom it shall be fully left to agree upon an Equivalent in quantity of that Land Lying at the head of Isaac Scheffers' Tract in Newc. County, Considering the real Value of the s'd 500 acres then granted, with all the Circumstances and Conditions attending it, and the real Value of the Said Land the Judge now Pitches upon, w'ch agreement of theirs Shall fully Conclude both this Board and the Judge for Ever. And this Board chuses Jno. Budd and Isaac Taylor and Judge Guest Chooses Capt. Samuel Finney and Jos. Pidgeon to Judge of the whole matter, by whose Judg't all Parties Engage to Stand.

The Prop'ry, by L. and Rel., Granted 250 acres of Land To Thomas Wolfe, which was by a warrant from the Prop'ry dat. 1, 7ber, '83, laid out the 22d of the Same Month and year, In Bristol Township, in Coun. Bucks, and Confirmed by Patent from James C'aypoole and Robert Turner, late Comm'rs, dat. 22, 11 mo, '84, to the said Thomas Wolfe, to hold, &c. The said Thomas Wolfe, by Ind're dat. 8, 1 mo , '85, Granted 130 acres, Part of the said 250, to Antho. Burton to Hold, &c., the said 130 acres was also res'd by Virtue of a Warrant from the Present Comm'rs dat. the 10, 5 mo., 1702, and found to be 142 a's and $\frac{3}{4}$, which the said Anthony Req'ts may be Confirmed to him by Pat. Q't Rent Cleared to 22d 1 mo., 1704-5.

2 mo., 2d [1705.]

Present, Omnes.

A Petition from the Inhabitants of Lewis requesting a Resurvey On the Town by a Warrant of this Board was Granted.

A Petition from Henry Pennington setting forth that he had no Land tho' a Family of Children, and therefore requesting a Warrant for 400 acres; read and Granted for the said Quantity of fast land in One Tract where not Taken up at 1d English p'r acre.

The Prop'ry, by Deeds of L. and Release, dat. 16 and 17 June, 1682, Granted To Rich'd Pender, of Northshields, in the Coun. of Northumberland, Miner, and Jos. Williamson, of Hexam, in the said Co'ty, Groce:, their Heirs, &c., 500 acres of Land in this Province, as p'r Deeds recorded Rolls Office, Philad'a, Book B, Vol. 2., Pa. 177, 178. S'd Pinder and Williamson, by Deeds dat. 2 and 3 June, 1684, Granted the said 500 acres to Dan'l Toaes, of Stockton, Coun. Durham, M'r and Mariner, his Heirs, &c., for Ever, as p'r deeds record'd Ibid, Pa. 175, 176 appears. Daniel Toaes, by Ind'd L. and Rel., dat. 7th and 8th 8ber, '84, Granted the said 500 acres, reserveing the City Lotts and Lib. Land to himself, to Jno. Chapman, of his Heirs, &c., in Right of which 500 acres was laid Out to Said Chapman in Wright's Town, in Bucks, the   day of   by a Warrant from the Comm'rs, dat.   , of which s'd Chapman sold 100 acres, and the remaining 400 being res'd is found to Contain in the whole with the Town lott In Newtown 536 acres, which being 96 acres Over measure, his Son and Heir, Jno. Chapman, agrees to Pay £24 in 3 months, and a Patent is Ordered.

2 mo., 9th [1705.]

Omnes.

Toby Leech haveing appeared before this Board 4th 12 mo., 1701-2 (as p'r Min's), desireing a Confirmation, it was Ordered then that his Land and Jno. Ashmead's should be res'd, which haveing been Done, he now applies for a Pat. to himself and Jno. Ashmead, But the Board not being yet fully Satisfyed and demanding further Satisfation he Produced Everard Bolton and sev'l Other Evidences, which made it appear that the whole 1,000 a's were really Purchased Land, and shews a Probable reason for the Surveyor's Incurring the Mistake in the return, viz: that Rich'd Wall, who is first named in the Warrant, took up Over and above the 1,000 a's 100 acres more upon rent (w'ch they say Notwithstanding was Purchased off afterwards), and none of them being Purchasers in Engl'd, but Pay'g their money here, thro' mistake might be thus Occasioned, and 'tis now Ord'd upon ye whole to the said Qua'ty of 1,000 a's Purchased be allowed and further Confirmed as Requested, Pat's haveing been formerly granted for all but Ashmead's, but Some of them are burnt.

4 mo., 18th [1705.]

Pres't at a Session of the Comm'rs, Edw'd Sh., Griff. Owen and Ja's Logan.

Jonathan Wynne, Son and Heir of Thom's Wynne, alledging that his Father's Joint Purchase with Jno. ap Jno. of 5,000 acres was not fully taken up, Craves a Warrant for 400 acres in the Welch Tract, if to be had, or elsewhere if not. Granted with a Provisoe in the War't that it be released In Case they have had or sold there whole Complem't.

Shadrach Wolley requests to have a Patent for his Land, he giveing a Bond and Robert Heaton for Security for Payment for the Overp. at £20 str. p'r C't, according to former agreement, p'r min's of 13, 2 mo., 1703, q. v. Title is in Min's 6th 8ber, 1702.

The Prop'ry haveing granted to Robert Robinson, Renter, 150 acres In Providence T'p, Coun. Chester, by Pat. dat. 30th 5 mo., '84, Surv'd 10, 1 mo., '83, by Warrant dat. 19, 12, '82, at 1d p'r acre. Said Robert sold the said Land to David Jones, of the said Place who deceasing, left all to his wife Mary and his Children. 'Tis now all Possest by his Eldest Son, Thomas Jones, who desires to Purchase off the Rent, which upon favour Promised him by the Prop'ry is Granted at £10 p'r C't.

The Prop'ry, by L. and Rel., dat. 2d and 3d Feb'ry, '81, to Will'm Tanner, of Uxbridge, in Middlesex, Tanner, 500 acres of Land (also 500 acres To Jno. Tanner, of Lovelane, in London, Distiller, by like deeds of the Same date as is recited in the following Deed): Wm. Tanner and Jos. Tanner, by L. and Rel., dat. 20 and 21 June, '83, Conveyed the said 1,000 acres to Benj'n Clark, Citizen and Stationer, of London. The said Benj'n Clark made his last will, dat. 15, 8ber, '89, and granted all his Estate (save One Legacy) to his Son, Benjamin Clark (then and now) of Jersey, s'd Clark, by Letter dat. 17 May last, appointed Sam'l Nichols, of Philad'a, to be his attorney, to take up the Lott and Lib. Land belong'g to Wm. Tanner's Purchase. Ordered a Warrant for this Lott to be renewed, 'tis No. 153 In the Draught, and is that laid out to Jno. Loyd, lately claimed by D. Loyd. There was a Pat. On it before. Ordered a Warrant Elsewhere, and for the Lib. Land Inquire.

The Prop'ry, by L. and Rel., dat. 14 and 15 June, '82, Granted To Jos. Jones, of Southampton, Coun. South'ton, Blacksmith, 500 acres of Land. Jos. Jones, by Ind're dated 4th July, '87, Granted the said 500 acres together with half an acre in the City Phila'a to Peter Chamberlain, of Busleton, Coun. South'ton, husbandman. The said Peter Req'ts the Lott appurtenant to the said Purchase, as also the Lib. Land. Jos. Jones is not in this List, but Jno. Swift Offers his Oath ('Tis said) that it was bo't at the Same Time with his and the Other Purchasers of South'ton. 'Tis therefore Ordered that a lott be Granted to him, But Lib. Land he Can't have.

The Prop'ry Granted to Jno. Martin, Par. Millbrook, Coun. South'ton, Malster, 500 acres of Land by Deeds dat. , who sold to Robert Priestmal, Ship Carpenter, one-half thereof for 999 years, and to Will'm Jennings, of the Town and Co'ty of South'ton, Schoolmast'r, the Other Moiety thereof, for the said Term of 999 years, which last Moiety was Surveyed to the s'd Martin in South'ton Township, in Bucks. Will'm Jennings, by his will, dat. 8 of May, '94, devised all his Estate to his wife, Margery Jennings, who by her Letter of attorney, dat. 19 of Ap., 1701, appointed Peter Chamberlain, of Peniel, in Pensilv'a, husband'n, to sell and dispose of all her Land in Pensilvan'a. The above Land being resurv'd is found to Contain 225 a's in the Township and 25 a's in the Townstead, Exact measure 250 acres. Said Chamberlain req'ts a Pat. to Margery Jennings on a Res'y Ordered upon a New return as Requested.

Present, Ieidem.

Samuel Jennings Produces a Letter from the Prop'ry dat. 26, 1 mo., 1704, in favour of Thomas Edwards, to the Comm'rs Ordering his Land, being 1,000 a's of an Original Purchase with the appurtenant Lotts, to be Taken up as favourably as May be and Ordered that Warrants be Issued as they shall Req't, according to regulation; the Lotts fell on Skuylkill.

Geo. Gottschick, Son-In-Law to Evan Oliver, Produces a warrant under the Prop'ys hand and Seal, dat. 16, 5 mo., '84, for said Oliver's 4 acres of Lib. Land and 6 in right of 200 to be added to it On Rent, he req'ts a Confirmation of It. The rent is agreed at a Shill., Country Money, ffor the 6 acres, rent of the whole, £6 p'r annum. The Pat. to be made to Eliz., wife of Geo. Gottshick, and Evan Oliver, Daug'r and Coheiresses of Evan Oliver. Ordered a resurvey On the 10 acres and a Patent when returned.

The Prop'ry by an Instrument Intended for a release, dat. 18, 11 mo., 1701, sold to Geo. Beale, of Guilford, in Surrey, yeoman, 3,000 acres of Land between Delaware and Sassq'a at 1d p'r C't acres, Sterl., to be Paid 7 years after Location. Geo. Beale, by his instrument of Procuration, dat. 1 June, 1704, appointed his Nephew, Will'm Beale, his attorney, to take up it, who being come Over, requests Warrants for it. Granted 2 Warrants for 1,000 acres each.

Nicholas Smith, of Newc. County, wanting Land to Settle On, requested (at Newc.) of Ja's Logan a Grant for 200 a's at 1d Sterling p'r acre. Granted.

Jno. Cocks, of Newc. County, desireing to take up 250 acres of vacant Land adjoyning to his Own, for which he agrees to

Pay £18 p'r C't, and to give his Plantation for Security for that and the arrears of his Rent. Granted.

Geo. Dakeyne requesting that his land may be made Contiguous to Elk River Road, for which he agrees to Pay £18 p'r C't. Granted, Provided It Exceed not 60 acres.

Peter Anderson haveing a right to   acres In Newc. County, w'ch being resurv'd Proves Only   acres, req'ts a Warrant for his Deficiency. Grant'd.

Jno. Monroe being desirous to settle on some Land adjoyning on that req'ted by Nich's Smith, req'ts a Warrant for 300 acres at 1d p'r acre. Granted.

5 mo., 2d [1705.]

Ieidem.

James Claypoole haveing given the Prop'ry an Obligation for £100 ster. in the year 1682 or 3 for a 2d 5,000 of Land, as is believed, of which 300 acres are disposed of and 2,000 acres with the Deeds for it in the adm'r, Francis Cook's hands, he Proposed to Pay 1,000 acres of Land Taken up in Bucks for the 3,000 disposed, but Can offer no further.

Andrew Bankson requesting a Grant for a small Tract of Swamp Joyn'g upon his Fast Land in Passyunk, near Manienson, Cont. about 14 acres, he requests this in Part of the 50 acres of Criple granted him by the Prop'ry, But the Board finding it not Reasonable Propose it to him at 20s p'r acre, which he at Length accepts of and agrees To and is to give Bond Payable next Spring.

A Warrant being requested to Lay out the Bounds of the Dock and 30 f't Street of each side, as it was at first laid out in Philad'a, from its first Extreme to the upper End of It. Is granted.

Proposed a Rope walk to Jno. Walker, behind Wells' Lott, at 40s Sterling, p'r an. for 21 years, not Exceeding 4 acres, Or in Case it be more at 10sh. Sterling Per acre. Ordered a Warrant for the breadth of Wells' Lott about 1,500 f't, Lott makeing Even acres.

5 mo., 16th [1705.

Ieidem.

James Claypoole, Purchaser of 500 acres, took up by several Warrants 4,580 acres, and again by a Warrant dat. the 7, 9ber, '85, 500 acres more, which by his will dat. 5, 12 mo., '86, he bequeathed to his Son Nath'l, and he, by his Deed dated 9th 1 mo., '88, sold it To Jno. Crapp, who by Deed dat. 4, 7ber, 1705, sold it again for £60, viz: £12 p'r C't, to Will'm Streipers. James Claypoole had not a right to this 80 acres by his first Purchase, but being a Purchaser of a 2d 5,000 acres, of which 2,000 remains untaken up in the admin'rs hands, but the adm'r, Francis Cook, refuses to meddle with it. 'Tis Ordered that a Patent be granted for the said 500 acres to Streipers, Paying the Quitt Rent, And Jno. Crapp giveing an absolute Bond for the 80 acres Over at the rate of £12 p'r C't (viz: £9 12s 0d), which Bond is to be Paid in 6 m'ths in case the Said 200 acres are not to be Taken up. Vide James Claypoole's Will, and Inquire for the dates of the above Deeds Either to Crapp Or Streipers.

James Atkinson haveing recovered of his Daughters-in-Law, Jno. Days' Children, at Chester Court, a Tract of Land among the Welch reputed to Contain 300 acres, upon a Resurvey was found to Contain   acres, which he Desires to be Confirmed to him and is granted, he Paying the Overplus, 3 sh. p'r acre. the Price at which the Jury had appraised the Rem'r.

5 mo., 23 [1705.]

Ieidem.

The Friends appointed by the Monthly Meeting of Philad'a to Procure a Confirmation of ye Ground on which the Meeting house and School house Stand.

The Prop'ry, by his warrant dat. 29, 1 mo., '84, Granted To Thomas Brassey and the Comm'rs. W. M., R. T., S. C. and J. G, by their Patent dat. 10, 10ber, 1690, Confirmed to him 3 Parcells of Land in the T'ship and C'ty of Chester, Cont'g 200 acres in the whole (which was in Lieu of the said Brassey's Lott, Lib. Land in Philad'a, appurtenant to his Purchase of 5,000 acres. Thos. Brassey dyed seized of the above Land, and left 2 Daughters behind him, to whom he left all his Estate, viz: Rebecca, wife of Thomas Thomson, of Salem, In West Jersey, and Mary Married To Francis Worley, of Chester Co'ty, Pens'a; Rebecca dyed Possessed of her Moiety undivided, and T. Thompson, by Deed dat. 22, 7ber, '97, Granted her Part to Caleb Pusey Fra.. and Mary Worley, by Ind're dat. 29 July, 1700, Conveyed their Other Part To Sam'l Carpenter, and by Deed dat. 13th 9ber, 1702, (haveing a Legal Claim upon their Sister's Other Moiety by survivors'p), released their Right In it To Caleb Pusey. Samuel Carpenter, by Deed dat. 20th 10ber, 1704, Conv'd his Moiety to Caleb Pusey, who is Possessed Of the Whole and desires a Pat., which is granted. These Tracts being resurveyed are found deficient But must Pass for the Whole 200 acres.

Jno. Gibbons' Purchase of 500 acres Gave his Son, Jno. Gibbons, his City Lott, who Joyntly with his Father, by Ind're dated 26, 12 mo., 1703, Granted the said Lott to Jos. Shippen. Edw'd Brown, Purchaser of 500 acres, Conveyed his City Lott to Nath'l Lamplugh and Thomas Ducket.

Thomas Ducket dying, Nath'l Lam., by Right of Survivors'p, Conv'd the said Lott to s'd J. Shippen by Ind're made 26 March, 1705. The Prop'ry, by his Warrant dat. 6, 8 mo., 1701, Granted to Katherine, Relict of Swan Swanson; Anne, Relict of Andr. Swanson, and Lydia, Relict of Woola Swanson, each of them a lot In Philad'a in Considerat'n That their s'd Husbands were antient Inhabitants, &c. The said Katherine, Ann and Lydia, by 3 sev'l Ind'res, all dat. 28, 12 mo., 1703, Conveyed all the said 3 Lotts (viz: each of them her Own respectively) To said J. Shippen. This Board haveing granted to said J. Shippen the greater Part of a Square of Land for a Pasture for 21 years by Warr't dat.   . He req'ts 5 Lotts may be laid within the s'd Pasture. He also Purchased of Jos. Willcox and Jno. Moore the 3 Corner Lotts On the 4th Street, left by Charles Pickering to be disposed of by them, His Ex'rs to Pay his debts, who sold them P'r Ind're dat. 10 August, 1704, to said Shippen.

Jno. Burge, Purchaser of 750 acres, by Ind'res dat. 24th and 25th 8ber, '81, took up In Haverford 260 acres (designed for 300) and 250 In Another Tract and 240 more to take up. Jno. Burge dyeing, left his whole Estate to his wife Sarah, who After Intermarried with Jno. Eckley. The Prop'ry, by Deeds dat. 14 and 15, 2 mo., '82, Granted to Edward Pritchard, of Almely, Coun. Pembroke, Glover, 2,500 acres, who, by Deeds, dat. 1, 9ber, '82, Sold 1,250 thereof to Jno. Eckley, of the Lee, in Kimbolton, Coun. eod'm, 1,200 whereof was Surv'd 24, 2 mo., '84, by a Warrant dat. 13, 1 mo., '84, and Confirmed by Patent dat. 18, 3 mo., '85, under the great seal, together with the other 1,250 Acres, To Edward Pritchard and Company. Jno. Eckley deceasing devised his whole Estate to the said Sarah, his wife, Relict of Jno. Burge, who, by her last will, left all the said Land, in Thirds, to her Son, Will'm Burge, and Daughter, Mary Burge, since Intermarr'd with Wm. Trent, and Daughter Sarah Eckley. Wm. Burge and Wm. Trent Obtained of this Board a warr't dat. 24th 9ber, 1702, for Resurveying the first 2 Tracts and Laying Out the Overplus, but the first 1,200 acres of which they have with their Sister, One Moiety Containing 1,610 Acres upon a Resurvey, they request that the deficiency, 240 acres, be laid Out on The said Overplus According To Law, w'ch is Granted.

The Prop'ry, by Ind're, dat. 24 and 25 days of the 11 mo.,

1681, Granted To Amy Child, of Hertford, in Coun. Hertford, Spinster, 500 Acres of Land in this Province, to Hold, &c., to which Purchase belonged several Lotts in Philad'a by Virtue of Certain Commissions which the Prop'ry Granted to the first Purchasers, Pursuant whereunto by Virtue of Our Warrant pat. 29, 10ber, 1701, there was Surv'd the 9th 12 mo. next after, unto Charles Read, of the City of Philad'a, Merchant, in right of her, the said Amy, to whom the said Charles Read was at that time Married, a Certain Lott of Land in the said City, bounded On the East with a lott of Hen. Willis, on the N. w'th back lotts, On the W. with a Vacant Lott, and on the South with Mulberry Str., Cont'g In br. 100 f't and in Length 306 f't, the rent 2s yearly, w'ch said lott was granted and sold by the said Chas. Read and Amy, his wife, to Jno. Willis, Brumingham, in Coun. Chester, Yeoman, To Hold As by Deed Poll dat. 26, 1 mo., 1702, Acknowledged in Court at Philad'a The 12 day of 8ber, 1702, appears, a Pat. is Ordered On this Lott and another bought by the s'd Jno. Willis of his Father, Henry Willis, for which ask Jacob Taylor a return to have both lotts in One, Q't R't Last Lott 1sh , Vide Comm'rs large Min. Book, Pa. 93, also Inquire of Jacob for Jno. Willis's ret'n for 275 acres of Land, for the title see same Min. Book Pa. 109.

The Prop'ry, by L. and release, sometime about the month of 7ber, 1681, Granted 5,000 acres to Jno. Simcock, his Heirs, &c., 1,350 acres thereof was laid Out in 1684 in the W't End of Thornburry, in Coun. Chester, Jno. Simcock, by Deed, dat. 10, 4 mo., 1701, Granted 500 acres thereof to Jno. Yearsley, his Heirs, &c., The s'd Yearsley, by Deed, dat. 24th 3 mo., 1702, Granted to s'd Jno. Willis 280 acres, P't of the said 500 a's, to Hold, &c., The said Jno. Willis sold 25 a's, Part of the said 280, to Hen. Neale and 30 To John Stringer and 57 To Jno. Davis, there remains by the res., in the Possession of said John Willis, Only 225 a's of the s'd 280 acres, Which being res'd, together with the said 350 a's, by a General Warrant, dat. 25, 1 mo., 1702, and was found to Contain 445 a's, also by the said Warrant the said 25 acres was res'd Scituate in Brumingham and Cont. 25 a's, Just So that the s'd Jno. Willis is Possessed in all of 470 Acres.

Val. Hollingsworth haveing Taken up 1,000 acres for himself and Children, of which 200 for his son Tho. in 1683, he req'ts a Patent On it and 20 acres of Marsh laid Out for him at 2 Bus's Wheat p'r C't it was laid out at 1d p'r Acre; But Thomas believing that the rent had been reduced to 2 Bus's, Sold his Land, w'th a Covenant to make it good at that rate. To the Purchaser; That he may be able therefore to Comply w'th his Bargain he Offers to give Bond to the Prop'ry for £8, Or £5

6s 8d sterling in Case He will not be Pleased to Let it go at the said rate. Granted a Pat. On said Conditions; Bond to be Payable 25th 10ber, 1706, Rent for the 200 acres 4 Bus'ls, mention No Time And for the 20 acres.

The Prop'ry Granted to Robert Lucas 200 acres in Bucks by Warr't dat. 27, 12 mo., '82, for which there was laid Out by Dav'd Powel 244 a's, Paid for to James Harrison as p'r Note under his hand.

Robert Lucas, by his will, dat. 6, 10 mo., '87, Proved at Philad'a 21, 10 mo., 1703, Bequeathed his said Land to his wife Eliz'th, who, by Deed, dat. 6, 10 mo., '97, Sold the Same to Robert Lucas, his Heirs, &c., and Giles Lucas and Edw'd Lucas, By the Same Deed, released to the s'd Robert, who, by Deed, dat. 1st April, 1704, Conveyed the Same to Edward Lucas, his Brother. In this Tract, upon a resurvey by the Gen'l Warrant, there is found 322 acres, Cont'g 58 acres Overplus, which is To be Confirmd to him, Consideration £18.

The Prop'ry also Confirmed to the said Rob't Lucas 177 acres in ye falls T'p, On Delaware, by Pat. dat. 31, 5 mo., '84, upon Old Rent, being taken up by An Order from Sir Edmond Andros, but Surv'd by a Warrant from the Prop'ry, dat. 9, 3 mo., '84, R. Lucas, by his above mentioned will, left the said Land and Plantat'n To his Sons, Edward and Robert; Robert, by his Deed, dat. 4th 10br, '97, Conveyed all his Moiety and share thereof to his Brother Edw'd, who, by his Deed, dat. 20, 2 mo., 1705, Granted the Same to Robert Harvey, then of ye County of Burlington, in Jersey, Yeoman, Who, by the said Edward, requests a Patent To himself. This haveing been resurv'd Contains 204 Acres and is 12 Acres Over, or y'rabouts, which is Offered at 6s p'r acre; But Gilbert Wheeler's Plantation adjoyning, wanting 2½ Acres, he may have it off if he will Pay the Survey.

Ieidem. 6 mo., 27th [1705.]

Samuel Finney and Isaac Taylor, Two of the Arbitrators appointed Between this Board and Judge Guest, being Authorized by Mutual Agreement and Consent, instead of ye Other 4, haveing brought in their Award, Signed under their hands, Adjudging to the said Guest 250 acres of that Land in Newc. Co'ty in Lieu of his 500 a's in Chester Co'ty, in Pursuance of a Min. of this Board the of s'd mo. last. 'Tis Ordered that a Warrant be granted Accordingly and a Patent upon the return.

Will'm and Jos. Philips being Purchasers, by the List, of 1,250 acres, 'tis said, dying, left the Land to Thomas Barker, in behalf of whom, Griff. Jones, upon Barker's Letter, appears and requests Warrants for takeing it up. Granted that Warrants be issued in said Philips's Right without Any Mention Made of Other Purchasers.

Rich'd Halliwell and Rich'd Clark, both of Newc., appearing by themselves Or their Attorneys for the Bank before their Lotts in Newc., each haveing a Part of the Front of Jno. Cann's Lott, it Appears as follows: At ye time of the Prop'ry's Grant of the Petition to Newc. Inhabitants, Owners of ye Front Lotts, Jno. Cann, Jun'r, not then of Age, was Possessed of the whole Front Lott of 60 f't Part of this, viz: f't be sold to J. Van. Gezel in   , who sold to C. Empson, who, by Deed, dat.   , 1702, sold to Ric'd Clark. The Deed from Empson To Clarke, as 'tis s'd, mentioning the Bank Lott also, but was razed before Passing the Court by Consent, but there is no mention of the Bank to Van Gezel, Or Any Deed App's to him, but what is dat. in   November, 1703; Richard Halliwell Produces a Deed dat. in July, 1703, for the Other Part of the said Lott, as also the whole Bank lott of 60 f't In breadth and 630 f't Deep, mentioned in the Deed upon which each Claiming their Proportionable Part of the Bank. Upon Mature Consid'n Adjudged to the   Upon an Affid't made by Benjamin Chambers before a Justice that Sam'l Miles, who now appear'd before ye Board, Came a Serv't into this Province to ye Society in the year 1682, 'tis Ord'd upon his h'ble Req't and Suit that a Warrant be granted him for his headland.

Mem'dum, To make a Patent to Neal Cook for that Land which was formerly Jno. King's, who dyed before he took out his Patent from the Sec'ry's Office, y'rfore where the Same now Lyes, Signed. Neal is to Produce Jno. King's Will and a Deed from the Devisee To him.

7 mo., 3d [1705.]

Pres't, G. Owen, Thom. Storey and James Logan.

Toby Leech took up 350 acres allowed to be On Purchase, he sold 100 acres and bo't 200 of Geo. Shoemaker, laid Out to Richard Hall by a Pat. burnt with his Others and y'rfore holds 450 acres which Measures 575, he Offers 6s 8d p'r Acre Or desires a View According to Law, vid. 9, 2 mo. last, and 4th 12 mo., 1701, to be Considered.

Ordered to Jno. Ashmead, Son and Heir of Jno. Ashmead, deceased, Purch'r of 250 acres, a Pat. On his Land On Cheltenham Adjoyning To Toby Leech, now Measureing 269 acres, upon his New Return.

A Patent to Rich'd Wall, Jun'r, for 100 acres in Chester

Coun., Being Produced, in which the rent is changed from 1d p'r Acre to 1sh. 'p'r C't by a Rasure, it was fully Examined and sev'l witnesses (Especially Edward Bolton and Toby Leech), Appearing to Prove the Payment of the Purchase money, 'tis Conclud'd that the Rasure was made upon a mistake, At first in the Patent and by the same hand that drew, And therefore it is allowed to be Authentick.

The Prop'ry, by L. and Rel., dat. 11th and 12th 8ber, 1681, Granted To Rich'd Haunds, of Swanford, in the County of Oxon, husbandman, 1,000 acres of Land in this Province, to Hold, &c. The said Rich'd Haunds, by Ind'res of L. and Release, bearing Date the 13 and 14 days of 10ber, 1700, Granted the said 1,000 acres of Land to Henry Hays, of Fullvell, in said County, Carp'r, to Hold, &c., req'ts Warrants to Take up 500 acres and a Lott and Lib. Land Appurtenant to the Purchaser aforesaid. The Lotts Lye On Skuylkill Side.

The Prop'ry, by L. and Release, dat. 2d 6 mo., '81, Granted 500 acres of land to Rich'd Few, of Market Lavington, in the County of Wilts, Shoemaker, to hold, &c., And the said Few, by Ind're, dat. 14 and 15, 7ber, '81, Granted unto Joan Teif, of Market Lavington, aforesaid, Widow, 250 acres, P't of the said 500, to Hold, &c. The said Joan afterwards Intermarried with Robert Silvester, of Horseley, In the County of Gloucester, Mercer, who, by their Ind're of L. and Release, dat. 31st of Aug't and 1 Mar., 1683, sold the said 250 acres to Hen. English, of Horseley, aforesaid, Weaver, The said Hen'y, by an Indorsement On the last ment'd release, Yielded up And surrendered the Said 250 a's to Gyles Knight, of Byberry, in the County of Philadelphia, in Pensilvania, husbandman, for the use of his Sons, Jos. and Thom's Knight, heirs and Assigns for Ever, to be Equally divided between them when they are in Age, No Date nor Seal to this Idle Piece of writeing, desires a Patent, this 250 Acres is returned in a General Draught of Warminster Township as the Same was resurv'd by Jno. Cutler, But the Bounds not being Mentioned make it So Imperfect no Patent Can be made by it.

In renewing the Warrant for Robert Quarton, Insert for Assistants, George Perce, Jos. Baker, Reece Tho. and Reece Henry.

A Pat. To Jno. Scarborow for 500 acres or thereabouts of Amy Childs, Min's 18th and 19th 3 mo., 1702, makeing Mention Of the Alteration of the Lines because C. Read sold it under Other Bounds. Also for a lott to himself now Surv'd, Min's Ibid. to Call for them at the Fair.

A Patent To Robert Heaton for $\frac{1}{2}$ of 690 Acres and 65 allowance and 110 Overplus makes 865 in $432\frac{1}{2}$, the 690 is made up of

440 of Dilworth's and 250 of T. Stackhouse's, vid. min's 16, 3 mo., 1704, his Son Robert has a Patent for the Other Moiety. Bond for £32 17s 6d Payable 16th May, 1705, with 15 mo's Interest, this to be ready In Ten Days.

---

8 mo., 22d [1705.]

Ieidem.

Nath'l Puckle, Attorney to Philip Ford, of London, haveing formerly Produced to this Board a letter of Attorney from said Philip together with a Draught of 5,000 acres of Land said to be laid Out to his Father In Right of his Original Purchase within the Man'r of Gilberts, request'g thereupon a Confirmation of the said Land, to which req't it was Objected that the Man'r was Land Appropriated to the Prop'ry in Pursuance of the Original Concessions Agreed to by the Purchasers for Laying Out of Lands in this Province, and the Prop'ry for this Reason had as Indisputable a right to the said Land as his Proper demesne As Any Purchaser had to his Located and Patented Lands, and further that the said 5,000 acres were never Surveyed to Philip Ford as the Method of Locating Lands Indispensably Requires; But that the Draught was only Prickt off from One of the Printed Maps, w'ch Map is now in this town to be seen with Penholes Exactly Answering those in the Draught then Produced to us, The said Natha'l Nevertheless Produceing Another Later Letter from the said Philip desireing him to Insist on his Claim to the said Land, He now further Desires the Answer of this Board to his req't for a Confirmation of the said Land by Pat. as formerly returned and req'ts Our Positive Answer to be sent to his Constituent, which being fully Considered 'tis the resolution of this Board that without direction from the Prop'ry whose right is Invaded by the aforesaid Imaginary Survey we Cannot Proceed to a Confirmation of the s'd Land, but because 'tis Insisted On that Philip Ford duely Paid the Charges of the Survey'r's Office as fully as if the Land had been Actually Surveyed and had an Expectation that he was fully Secured of it in that Place without further trouble, Or Otherwise Might by the Same Care and Expence have Taken it up as advantageously at that time Elsewhere in the Province, 'Tis therefore referred Entirely To the Prop'ry himself at London to direct in it, with whom the said Philip may have A full and ready Opportunity to treat about it, and He is desired to treat with the Prop'ry accordingly and to Present him a Copy of this Minute, which is Ordered to be forthwith delivered to the said Att'ny who Came Over hither with recommendations To This

Board from the Prop'ry to be assistant to him in behalf of many Others of his Countrymen in finding Out Some Convenient tract or tracts of Land in this Province for seating a Considerable Number of Families, acquainted the Board that he had Spent much time in Viewing all the Considerable Surv'd Tracts in the Government belonging to the Prop'ry, as well as Lands that were still vacant and unsurveyed, and now further acquainting us that he designs speedily to return to England to acquaint his Employers what Progress he had made, Desires To know what Quantities they may Expect to take up in the Man'r of Gilberts and Wm. Penn, Jun'rs, and Laetitia's Mann'r, near Brandywine, To which 'tis answered that if Philip Ford have no Claim there, in ye first There May be 10,-000 a's, and in the Other 25,000 acres Certain if they agree for it in time.

Dan'l Falkner, by Order of Benjamin Furly, Informs that by the said Benjamin's Letter he finds the Prop'ry had Promised him 2 lotts in the City Philad'a, for his 2 sons, Jno. and Arent Furly, and gave him an Expectation that he had wrote to the Sec'ry about it, y'rfore, by his Petition, Requests the said lotts, but the Sec'ry nor any Other Person haveing Rec'd any Orders about them 'tis referred till Such Orders arrive.

The Prop'ry by a Certain Grant or Patent, dat. 22, 12 mo., '82, Granted 200 a's of Land on Red Lyon Creek, in ye Co'ty of Newc., To Hans Coderus, his H'rs, &c., Paying yearly for Ever 2 Bus'ls of wheat, the s'd Hanse Conveys ye Same To Hendrick Vandeburge to Hold, &c., as p'r Deed, dat. 10, 11 mo., '83, appears; the said Hendrick Conveys the said 200 acres unto Maj'r Will'm Dyre, of the said Province, to Hold to him, his Heirs, &c., as by Deed Dat. 22d June, 1686, May appear. The said Wm. Dyre became Possessed, of the s'd Land and made his last will and Testament in Writeing and in the same devised the said 200 acres of Land To his Younger Son, James Dyer, and after dyed. Rich'd Halliwell, by a Letter of attorney, dat. 15 January, 1702-3, Sold the Said Land to Geo. Dakeyne to Hold, &c., Consid'n £70, as p'r Deed, Dat. 1, 11 mo., 1703, appears and acknowledged in Court the 15th May, 1705. The Court of Newc., by an Order dat. 6th and 7th Days June, 1682, Granted Geo. Moore Leave To Take up 300 acres of Clear Land in the said County, and he Seating and Improveing the Same according to Law and the Gov'rs Directions. The said Geo. Moore, by Deed dat. 10, 10ber, 1701, sold the said 300 acres to the said Geo. Dakeyne, and Whereas by Virtue of a General Warrant for resurveying of Land in the said County the said 200 acres was resurv'd by Thomas Pierson and found to Contain the Same quantity.

And Whereas by Virtue of a Warrant from the Present Comm'rs, dat. 28, 11 mo., 1703, There was granted to the said Geo. Dakeyne 600 acres of Land On Red Lyon at 10 sh. p'r C't for Ever, as also Ordered to be resurv'd to the s'd Geo. Dakeyne the s'd Land by him Purchased of Geo. Moore, which was accordingly Performed and found to Contain together   acres, all w'ch s'd Parcell of Land of 200 acres, of 600 a's and of 300, being Contiguous in One Tract, are Scituate upon Red Lyon Run, in the said County of Newc. S'd Dakeyne req'ts a Patent, he haveing formerly agreed To Pay for Purchasing Off the Rent of the said 600 acres to the Rent of a Bushell of Wheat.

Samuel Carpenter haveing with Others Petitioned the Prop'ry that they might have the Priviledge of Purchasing Off the Reversion of their Bank lotts. He was Pleased to Grant their request as in Pa.   appears, Provided they Purchase in 12 Months after the Date of the said Petition, but the said Samuel deferring to take Out a Patent as was Proposed, He now requests that upon his Selling 69½ f't of half Bank To Sam'l Herriott, of this Place, being that Part of his Great Lott where the Globe Tavern Stands, he desires he may still have the Same Priviledge of Purchasing and Clearing the said Quan'ty according to his Contract with the said Herriott, which Otherwise will be Void. Granted upon Paying Interest from the Times of Paym't appt'd by the Prop'ry, and Ordered that the Patent be antedated.

Jno. Key being the first born in Philad'a, Petitions the Board y't according to the Prop'ry's Promise, as is said, he may have a lott in the City and 500 acres of Land Granted him, being Now of age. A Warr't from the Prop'ry, dat. 26, 3 mo., 1683, appears for a lott to his Father, which they Say was laid Out in Mulberry Street. Ordered therefore that a Warrant be issued for resurveying the said Lott, but Nothing appearing for the aforesaid Pretended Promise of Land, 'Tis referred to the Prop'ry.

Sam'l Thawley, by Geo. Dakeyne, req'ts a grant of 200 a's of Land in the Forest near Duck Creek at 1d p'r acre, to be seated forthw'th. Granted.

A Small Quantity of Land, about 200 acres, lying adjcaent to the Plantation Sold To Jos. England, in Newc. Co'ty, On the N. W't Branch of Duck Creek, Thos. Graham, of that Place, desires to Purchase it at £15 p'r C't, Payable the 10th March next, which is Granted.

A Small Tract of 30 acres lyeing between his Land and the Welch Tract is Granted to Wm. Wallace of £5 and so Proportionably.

Ordered a Patent to Edward Cole for a lott of 80 acres in Swanwick, formerly Ambrose Baker's, whose Daughter he Married, and had that for his Portion; for the Title See Newc. Min's, To w'ch add 25 a's of vacant Land sold him for £7 10s.

Geo. Pownel, by L. and Rel., dat. 21 and 22d of Mar., 1681, Purchased of the Prop'ry 1,000 acres of Land, for which the Lib. Land has not been yet Taken up. Rowland Pownell, his Eldest Son, desires a Warrant for the said Lib. Land for his Brother Geo., To whom it was alloted upon a Division of the Estate among themselves, their Father dyeing Intestate. Ordered a Warrant for 16 acres Over Skuylkill, if It be found Vacant.

There being a Small Parcell of Marsh, about 2 acres, Situate On the S. W't End of Newc. Town, Joyning On Alricks' Lott, Which was formerly ('tis said) Granted to Peter Alricks On Condition that he would drain it, but he nor any for him haveing Perfcrmed this Condition, tho' above 20 years ago, and ye Place being a great annoyance to the Inhabitants, 'tis now Granted to George Dakeyne upon his Petition upon Condition that he shall drain and Improve it with a Good Dyke and Trenches in 12 Months. and shall Pay the Prop'ry One Bushell of Wheat for Every 2 acres, and so Proportionably above One Bushell, but not under, for a Quitt Rent.

Brian McDonald haveing by Virtue of a Warrant dat. 18, 9 mo., '85, for 400 acres Taken up, 200 in Part thereof in the year '89-90, Surv'd to him by James Bradshaw's Order, dat. the Same day, by Henry Hollingsworth, as by the return 8, 1 mo., '89-90. He also Procured a Grant of this Board by Warrant, dat. 21, 10ber, 1703, to take up the adjoyning Vacant Land, reputed to be about 200 acres More, at £12 10s p'r C't, which Proves to be 354, and the Other 200 holds 239, Of which the Overplus, 19 acres, added to the former makes 373 acres, at the s'd Price amounts to £46 12s 6d. He also requests to reduce the Other 200 acres from the former Rent to a Bushell of Wheat, which is Granted for £16, viz: £8 p'r Ct'; this added to the former makes £62 12s 6d in the whole. besides arrears of Rent On the 200 On New Rent. Ordered a Pat. for the whole 593 acres at a Bushell of wheat hereafter p'r C't, add the Interest to this time, £5 10s.

Mem'dum, That Jos. Asheton's Bargain with the Comm'rs for 1,000 acres of Land in Parkeming is to be transferred to Abraham Bickley, of Philad'a, Merchant, and Ed'wd Lane, of Parkeameing, Yeoman.

---

9 mo., 19th [1705.]

Ieidem.

The Prop'ry, by L. and Release, dat. 26 and 27 July, 1681,

Granted to Jas. Hill, of Beckington, Coun. Somerset, Shoemaker, 500 acres of Land of w'ch there appears 442 a's, by the Sur'rs Office to be taken. His Only Son and Heir, Rich'd Hill, req'ts an Order for his Lib. Land and Lott, w'ch is No. 130, on Delaware. Ordered a Warr't for them.

This Board haveing Ordered Warr'ts for Wm. and Jos. Philips for their 1,250 acres Upon the application of Griff. Jones, He and George Heathcoat, in Behalf of Tho. Barker (to whom they say it was left by said Jos. Philips, Son and Heir of Wm., In his will appointing the said Thomas his Ex'r), requests a Warrant for their Lotts and Lib. Land. The lotts fall on Skuylkill. Ordered a Warrant for 2 lotts and 20 acres of Lib. Land.

John Hen. Kursten, Citizen and Woolen Draper, of Langere Salza, in Thuringen, Produces a Deed Translated by Dan'l Pastorius and Certifyed, dat. 5th August, 1704, from Frederic de Redegoldt, Colonel and Essay Master Generall of the Province of Pensilv'a and Terr's annexed, in Ameri'a (so runs ye Deed), for 750 a's of Land, Part of 10,000 acres purchased of the Prop'ry, as is said, in England, by the said Redegoldt, to be taken up between the Rivers Susq'a and Delaw'e, Rent Free for 7 years. Lawrence Chris'r Nohren has a like Deed from s'd Redegoldt for 250 acres, Certifyed also by Dan'l Pastorius, which 2 quantities they desire Warrants to Take up. Ord'd Warrants and that before any Confirmat'n Redegoldt's Deeds or Copies of them be Produced. Warrants to Dan'l Powel and Is. Taylor both.

Jno. Lewis, of Maryland, requesting by Jos. England, a Grant of 200 acres of Land near the New meeting house near Duck Creek, upon Rent, Intending to Settle there. 'Tis Granted at 1d Sterling p'r acre, To be Settled In 12 mos.

10 mo., 15th [1705.]

J. Logan, Solus.

Thom's Rees, of Haverford, Caveats ag't Granting a Pat. To Dav'd Lewis, of the Same Place, for a Tract of Land, Part of a Tract Granted To Jno. Bevan and sold by Ralph Lewis to Said David, untill the Lines be adjusted, w'ch Is now in hand.

10 mo., 24th [1705.]

Present, Griff. Jones, Edw'd Shippen and Jam's Logan.

The Prop'ry sold to Will'm Stanley 5,000 acres of Land, of which himself, Wid w and Children sold To Thomas Fairman a Certain Quantity, about 3,750 acres, vid. Sec'ry's Min's, 1701, T. F. Procured of the Comm'rs, W. M. and J. G., a Warrant dat. 10, 5 mo., '89, for Laying out to him 500 acres Purchased of said Stanley, as recited in the Warrant; this was laid Out in Philad'a County, Near Whitpains Township, next to the 800 acres laid out To Tyzack, Now Captain Finney's; being resurveyed, it Contains 511 acres. Ord'd a Pat. To T. F. upon the return, he Paying for the Resurvey.

Andr. Bankson's Warrant, , to Gertrude Bankson, widow, and Dan'l, her Son, Vid. 2, 5 mo.,

28th 11 mo [1705.]
Ieidem.

Captain Sam'l Finney haveing frequently Sollicited for a vac't Lott where it may be found, to build a Stable On for Accommodateing his Horses when he Comes to Town, and haveing made Inquiry where Any Lotts May be found Vacant, Pitches upon a lott next above the Lott now in the Possession of Gabriel Wilkinson, In the 3d Str., between Sassafras and Vine Str., on the E't side of the 3d Str., w'ch Lott is 55 f't in br. and 196 f't In Depth, Offered in Consideration of his many Services at half a Crown Sterling p'r Annum, and a Warr't and Pat. for it, Warr't dat. this day.

Griff. Jones Produceing the Pat. Granted by the Prop'ry at his Departure To Edward Shippen and 15 Others for the Tract of Land lying above the Welch Tract, Called Pickering's Mines. Complains that there is an Error in the Survey of it, for that upon the Resurvey to make a Partition of the Tract among the sev'l Claimers, it was found that the Lines in the Woods Do not agree w'th those In the Pat., and therefore he reqt's it in Behalf and by the appointment of the rest Concerned A New Patent, According to the Bounds as now found in the Field, which is Granted, Provided it Exceed not the Quantity Granted in ye Prop'ry's. The said Griff. Jones likewise Acquaints the Board that the Corporation has appointed 2 Persons, of whom He is One, that the Church of England has also appointed 2 Others, and Friends meeting 2 more, to req't of the Comm'rs a grant of Some Convenient Vacant Lott Of Land within the City for a Publick and Com'on burying Place, of w'ch the Place is at Present wholly unprovided, and desires to know when the Comm'rs will meet to receive their Application, w'ch he reqt's may be before the Sec'ry Goes down into ye Lower Co'ties, but the Comm'rs not designing to meet again before that time, nor thinking it Proper to Concern themselves in it, It is Concluded they shall

Take One of the Squares laid out for the Publick Service, viz: that On Wallnutt Street, next Delaware, and a Warrant is Ordered forthwith accordingly.

Dav'd Powel representing that he has spent much time, Labour and money in Resurveys and Other Services for the Prop'ry, for which he has never yet rec'ed Any Compensation, Except that 500 a's in the Welch Tract, for which his Bond still Lies out, desires that for his better Security, seeing He Craves No Other Pay than Land, that there may be a tract of about 1,000 acres laid aside in the Welch Tract, which may lie Secure from Other Surveys till Such time as his Acc'ts are made up, which he will Endeavour Speedily to Compleat. Ordered in Pursuance of the Prop'ry's Grant at his Departure that such a tract be Accordingly laid Out to lye by as afores'd; Provided always, that there be no Land included therein which will be wanted by any Other Purchasers to Compleat their Rights and Purchases in the said Tract.

Henry Hayes desireing a Convenient Lott to build On has Pitcht on a vac'y of 33 foot between 3d and 4th Streets on the South side, for which he resigns his 2 Lotts On Skuylkill side, belonging to Rich'd Hound's 1,000 a's, and Pays £15 to the Prop'ry with all Other Charges, let his Pat. be dispatched w'thout delay, he's given full Security.

Isaac Taylor Produces Certif.'s that Mary Hickman, now wife of Jos. Edwards, Came into this Province Servant To Jno. Hardin in the year 1682; also that Jas. Widows Came in a Servant To Jno. Bezor; That Marg't Smith, wife of Ric'd Venn, Came in a Servant To Rich'd Few, and that Christian Steward, now wife of Jno. Pullen, Came a Serv't To Nathaniel Allen, and that Wm. Thomas Came In a Serv't To Thomas Barker, Consigned by him to Rob't Wade, and fur. that all the said Persons duely Served out their Times in this Province, and also Exhibits Deeds from the several Persons aforesaid for their Rights To their resp'ive Shares of Headland, viz: 50 acres each from Mary Edwards and her husband, dat. 30, 1 mo., 1704; from James Widdows the same date; from Christian Pullen and her husb'd 28, 1 mo., 1705; from Richard and Marg't Venn 3 April, 1705; from William Thomas 29, 7ber, 1705, and Desires a Warrant To take up the said Rights.

---

1 mo., 11th [1705.]

At a Session of Comm'rs held 11th 1 mo., 1705-6. Prst., Edw. Ship., Griff. Owen and James Logan.

The Prop'ry, by L. and Rel., dat. 26 and 27, 7ber, '81. Granted to Edward Martindale, of Bristol, Merchant, 1,000 acres of

Land, which the s'd Edward, by Deeds, dat. 5 and 6 June, '83, Granted to Joshua Cart, of Tewksbury, in the Coun. of Glouces'r, Sadler, now of Bristol, the said 1,000 acres which he has left by will to his Eldest Son Samuel, Of this there was Surveyed by Thomas Holme 21, 9 mo., '83, by Virtue of a Warrant from the Prop'ry, dat. 12, 8 mo., '83, to said Joshua 300 acres in Abington, which being resurveyed Contains 341 acres, of which 11 acres being Overplus are allowed in Part of his Purchase, 20 Acres more being deducted for Lib. Land. Ord'd a Pat. for the whole of the said Tract and a Warr't for the Remainder, many of the Counties being 669 acres.

Thomas Masters haveing formerly Purchased Griff. Owen's Plantation and finding Occasion to Extend a Fence off for Marshy Ground thro' which his bounds Run upon Higher Ground and by that means to Come in upon the Land held by Thomas Sisom in which Land there is Some Overplus as is Entered, before the s'd Sisom Consenting under his hand that Thomas Masters may have 10 or 12 acres to Accommodate him, It is agreed that he shall have that Parcell Surv'd by Thomas Fairman, Containing 13 acres at ye rate of 40s p'r Acre, and a Pat. is Ordered to Thos. Masters for the Same.

— —

1 mo., 18th [1705.]

Ieidem.

Henry Johnson Produceing a Certificate of Survey from Rob't Longshore for 40 f't of Bank before the Prop'ry's Land, Surv'd 24, 1 mo., '89-90, by Vertue of a Warr't dat. 22d of the Same month, On which he has been several years seated, requests a Patent, which is Granted; Rent from the Survey 4sh. Sterling with ¼ of the Value To revert after 51 years from said Survey as Other Bank Patents,

Mich'l Jobson, by Consent of this Board, Procured that Part of his Father's Front lot Which Joyns upon the 2d Str. and runs back to the Dock to be resurv'd According to the Regulation made by the former Comm'rs with Thomas Budd, he Produces the return Containing on the S. side 40 f't And On the N. side 29 f't and 20 In Front, and Produces also An Acquittance from the Wid'w Budd for her late Husband's Charge in Wharfing, upon w'ch He requests a Grant of the said Land by Pat. to his Father, Which is Granted, Rent 6d Sterling yearly.

Agreed with Joshua Tittery for the Vacancy next the 3d Street at the Back of his Two Lotts in the Second Street at the rate of 4s p'r foot, whatever the Quantity be, less or more, under the usual rent of 1sh. Sterling p'r 50 f't, to give Bond upon Takeing Out the Patent, which is to be done with all speed.

The Comm'rs, by Patent, dat. 26, 7 mo., '87, Granted To Thomas Howard a lott On ye N. side of Mulberry Street Cont. 49½ f't which the said Thomas left to his Son Benjamin, who left it to his Wid'w, with whom Geo. Harmar Intermarried, And upon this, sold to Wm. Oxely, but the Title being weak, Geo. Harmar requests a Confirmation by a New Patent both himself and Wm. Oxely haveing Made Considerable Improvements upon it, the Rent being 5sh. ster. p'r Ann. 'Tis allowed, the arrears being now near the Value of the Lott the Improvem'ts Excepted, which Are Truly Harmar's and Oxly's, and therefore 'tis Granted.

Granted To Jno. Furness half a square upon Vine street between the 5th and 6th Streets from Delaware at 20sh. p'r A. for 14 years, a Warrant Ordered.

Hugh Laft, by his Friend, Jno. Gilbert, requesting a Patent for 200 Acres In Mispellan hundred, in Kent County, Surveyed by Order of Wm. Clark, of which he produces a return upon A Warrant for Old rent, Granted.

Charles Brooks, of the County of Chester, Yeoman, by Deed, dat. 12, 10ber., '93, for the Consideration therein Mentioned; Granted 150 Acres to Robert Chamberlain, laid Out by Warr't dat.   , in Ashton T'p, to Thom's Brassey In right of his Original Purchase of 5,000 acres, which said Brassey Granted the said 150 acres to Andrew Job, his Heirs, &c., and the s'd And'w Job Granted the Same to s'd Brooks, his Heirs, &c., who granted the Same to Rob't Chamberlain. The Prop'ry, by Pat., dat. 22d, 5 mo., '84, Granted 200 acres of Land (laid out in Concord, in Coun. Chester, by Warrant dat.   ), To Thomas King, Paying 1d p'r Acre ster. for Ever, the s'd King, by Deed, dat 4, 4 mo., '87, Granted 100 a's, Part of the said 200, to Rob't Chamberlain aforesaid, for the Warrants of the above Land, Vide ye warrants in ye Surv'r's Office, as also the Returns, the Q't R't to be reduced to 1sh. ster. p'r C't, Cons n £12 Pens'a Money. Thomas Cartwright Exchanges With Rob't Chamberlain 10 a's of Land Adjoyning the N. E. side of the said 150 Acres for the Like Quantity, the aforesaid Tracts were resur'd by a Warrant from the Present Comm'rs, dat. 20, 3 mo., 1703, and found to Contain 251 acres, requests a Patent, Granted. Ask J. Taylor for the Resurvey.

Sold Robert Perce 50 acres of Land Partly vac't, Partly the Overplus of Samuel Barker's Land upon Brandywine for £10 and ½ Bus'l of Wheat Rent, the money to be Paid the 1st of March, 1706-7.

Sold Thomas Cutler 101¾ Acres of Overp. in Southampton,

Bucks, for £36, being the Overp. of 200 acres Rent land laid Out On Rent To Jno. Gilbert in '83, sold by Jno. Gilbert To Hugh Marsh, by Deed, dat.   , who assigned it To Edw'd Cutler, p'r Indorsement, dat.   , Tho., his son, now holds it, his Father being dead, the Pat. To be for this 321¾ In 2 Tracts, one for 220 at a penny Per acre, the Other 101¾ at 1sh. p'r C't, T o be dispatched forthwith.

Ordered a Patent To Will'm Biles for 472 acres in 2 Tracts, 1 of 343 acres for 300, made up of Rowland's and Bennett's, and the Other of Harrison's, the Other 129, for 100, Bennet's is at ½ Sterling p'r Acre, Consideration for the Overplus being Barren £5, and for reduceing the Rent £5 5s, Min's at Large 2d Mo., 1704.

Sam'l Carpenter, Pa. 70, Shewed his right To A Small Lott in Bristol of 63 f't, Part of a tract of about 9¼ Acres of Land, One Moiety of 18½ a's Granted To Jno. Smith by Jno. White, p'r Deed dat. 6, 1 mo., '96-7, To whom the said Land was Granted (as P. Pemb. Informed) by Pat. J. Smith, p'r Deed, dat. 8, 1 mo., '96-7, Conv'd the said 9¼ acres To John Town, of Buckingham (Now Bristol), weaver, Deborah Town, Adm'x to her husband, Conveyed, by Deed, dat. 13, 4 mo., 1705, To Chas. Levally, of Bristol aforesaid, Cooper, by due Course of Law and by Order of the Orphans' Court, 15 2 mo. Inst., all the remainder of the said 9¼ Acres beside what Samuel Carpenter had Purchased before, Pa. 70. Charles Levally sold to Rob't Shaw, of the Same Place, by   dat.   , Who Conveyed to Sam'l Carp'r, p'r Deed dat.   , so that Samuel Now holds all the s'd 9¼ Acres. John Smith, by Deed, dat. 8, 1 mo., '96-7, Conveyed To Thomas Musgrove 3 Small Parcells of Land in the Place aforesaid, Cont g In the whole about 4½ A's, being a half Part of the Other moiety of the said 18½ Acres. Hannah Price, Relict and Ex'x of the last will and Testam't of Thomas Musgrove, with her husband, Dav'd Price, by Virtue of her former husband's will, by Deed, dat. 15, 10ber, 1702, Conv'd the said Parcell To Willliam Fishbourn, who, by Deed, dat. 16, 10ber, 1702, Conv'd the Same To Samuel Carpenter, who thereby holds 14 acres, P't of the 18½ A's aforesaid. In Pa. 70, also is recited Samuel Carpenter's title to 8 acres, P't of 30 left by S. Clift, p'r Will, To Jos. English, the Other 22 acres T. Brook Conv'd To Samuel Carpenter, p'r Deed, dat.   . This 30 Acres now Contains 38 acres and is 5 a's Overplus, Sam'l Carpenter holds the Old Rent Land.

160 a's Sold of Samuel Clift's, bo't of D. Ll. and I. N., res'd, to be Paid by D. L. and I. N.,	190,	over	14
200 a's of Jno. Otter's,	335,	over	115
30 of Jos. English's, Part of Clift's being T. Brook's and 8 bo't before,	38,	"	5
25 of Russel's, Compr'hended in the 38 a's in ye Draught which is made up of This and ye 8 a's bo't of English and Brook,	30,	"	3
50 a's of Yardley's,	53		
And Marsh to be Purchased in it,	6,	"	6
14 A's being ¾ of Jno. White's,	14		
479 at Old Rent, the whole Is,	700,	"	34
3½ A's of Peter White, Pa. 71,	3½	"	163
482½ Purchase,			56
			219
547 of Thomas Holmes,	547		
572 of Thom's Lloyd's,	606		
	1,788½		
Islands,	300		

Samuel Carpenter Pays for the Overp. of Otter's 115 and Lloyd's 14, and 56 and the Other 8 and 34 more than 666 (for now 'tis found 700) in all 227, £70 8s 0d, and for the 6 acres of Marsh £6.

The Prop'ry, by Ind're of L. and Release, dat. 11 and 12th 8ber, 1681, Granted 1,250 acres of Land To William Pardoe under the yearly Q't R't of 1sh Sterling p'r C't, the said William Pardoe, by an Indorsement On the s'd release, dat. 5, 3 mo., 1683, Assigned and sett Over the said 1,250 Acres to Jno. Waite, late of Worcester City, but In the said Indorsement these is not Ment'd, Either Heirs or assigns. Sarah Waite, of Philad'a, Spinster, Daughter of the said John, requests a Warrant To Take up the remainder of the said Land untaken up, being 325 acres, the rest being Taken up, it's said, In Chester County in two tracts, One of 500 acres the Other of 400, and 25 acres in the Liberties, the said John left 2 sons, Jno. and Jam's, both dec'd, Jno, left a Son named Benjamin, now Liveing. James Dyed Intestate Without issue.

By Virtue of a Warrant , there was laid Out To Thom's Clifton 200 acres of Land in Concord at 1d p'r Acre, Clifton Sold To Francis Chads and Chads To Rich'd Farr, he sold Jam's Hayward 50 a's of this and 26 Acres To Ralph Pyle, By Deeds. dat. 8. 7 mo., 1705, and Holds 124 which Measure 132

Acres On New Rent. Ralph Pyle Purchased also 11 a's of Edward Jennings by Deeds, dat. , who Purchased of Thomas Woodward, who Purchased of Jerem. Collet, who Purchased of Jno. Haslegrove, whose Father, Jno. Haslegrove was first Purchaser of 1,000 acres, to whom there was laid Out there 500 acres, Warr't 6, 12 mo., '82; A Pat. is Ordered to Ralph Pyle for his 26 years and these 11 acres in One tract, Rent for both Together 2s 4d Sterling, And a Patent To Rich'd Farr for the Other 132 at 1d p'r Acre, Rent from '84.

The Prop'ry, by Deed, dat. 16, 5 mo., '91, Granted To Jno. Kinnerly, of Shevington, Coun. Chester, Cheese Factor, 375 Acres of Land in this Province Towards the river Susquehanna (for £12 10s) under the yearly Rent of 1s p'r C't, to be Paid upon Takeing up and seating the s'd Land. John Kinnerly, by Deed, dat. 12, 12 mo., '96, Granted the said Land to Constantine Overton, of Ogleton, Coun. Chester, Yeom., his Heirs, &c., (for £5), C. Overton haveing Agreed to Sell the said Land to Vincent Cadwell ot this Province, the said Vincent desires a Warr't to Take up the same.

3 mo., 13th [1705.]

Ieidem.

Ord'd Warrants for the Rem'r of the 3,000 acres of Land Granted to Wm. Ashton's Children and Robert Ashton's request, there is allready Taken up One thous'd Three hundred and fourteen acres.

Henry Lewis haveing A right to 180 acres in the Welch tract, by his Father Henry Lewis's Purchase of Lewis David and 79 by Humphrey Ellis's Purchase under John Burge, these being Together, 259 were laid out together In the great valley but found, upon a Resurvey, to Contain 352 Acres with allowance of 25, it makes 248 and leaves 68 acres Overp., he has also 50 acres of Overp. in his Tract in Haverford laid Out for 400 acres but Cont. 490, for this Agrees to give £24 5s and for the Other 68, being mostly Barren, £5 in the whole, £29 5s Rent due for the first 259, 54sh. 4½d Sterling or £4 10s 7½d, Pensilv'a, for the title See the Min's about 2 years agoe, Or Welch Min's.

David Morris Purchased of the Comm'rs, 1687, 50 acres of Land for which 15, 2 mo., 1696, he Paid Samuel Jennings £5 and then Paid him 7 years' Q't R't for the said Land, 4s 4d, Warrant To Thomas Holme dat. 24, 11 mo., 1687, Surv'd by Dav'd Powell but Contained then 71 Acres Instead of 50, and now. upon Resurvey, Contains 90, Of which 40 must be Cutt Off and the Remainder Confirmed.

The Prop'ry haveing granted Jno. Grubb 4 Acres for a ta in yard and the Comm'rs, W. M., Rob't T. and J G., by Warrant, dat. 1 Apr., '93, Granted the Same, but 'twas Never laid out. Ordered that it be Surv'd and laid out as at first Granted between ye Lands of Thomas Gilpen and Isaac Savoy.

Jno. Grubb, with Wm. Drewit, appeared Together at the Board requesting that the 108 acres of Land Entered in Rockland's Min's To Jno. Grubb may be Confirmed to him by Pat., Jno. Grubb haveing Sued said Will'm, Adm'r upon the Estate, for a title, and now by Consent desire a Pat. as aforesaid.

In Pursuance of a Grant from the Prop'ry, under his hand, dat. 1, 9ber, 1701, In the Sec'ry's Custody, Granted To Dav'd Powell 300 a's of Land in the Welch tract at £12 p'r C't, bounded by D. Mered.'s late Grant, Griff. Jones and James Atkinson, a Warrant forthwith.

Ordered a Warrant for the Prop'ry for the 15,000 acres laid Out in Rockland.

Upon the request of Tho's Storey Granted him the Back lotts Between Matthias Vanbebber and Vine str. on the 3d Str. at 12d sterling for Every 10 f't p'r Ann., also all that Lott between Wills' lott Vine Str., Jno. Willcox's and the 3d Street, Contained at the Same rate Proportionably with the Other.

---

3 mo., 21 [1705.]

Nath'l Puckle, in behalf of Philip Ford, produces an Authentick Copy of a Warr't from the Prop'ry, dat. 30, 3 mo., 1684, Ordering a resurvey in ye s'd Philip's behalf On the S'd Lands between Jos. Growdon and Nath'l Allen, and to Survey to him 300 a's there. Also a return under T. Fair.'s hand of the Said Warr't upon which the said Nath'l Craves a Pat. to Philip Ford. Ordered that an Inquiry be made whether this Land as returned be free from Other Claims and Particularly that Jos. Growdon have notice of it before the said request be Granted.

Samuel Carpenter Produces a Pat. from W. M., R. T. and J. G., dat. 29, 3 mo., '91, for 104 a's of Land On Old Rent, being made up of 100 acres in Right of Gunner Rambo and 4 a's Purchased of the Comm'rs for 4 or £5 unpaid, vid. Comm'rs Min's, about 24, 11 mo., '90, the date of the Warrant; also a Deed dat. 2, 7ber, 1700, from Jno. Bowyer, Shipwright, for 25 a's Adjoyning on the above, being Part of Shakamaxon Land, Granted by an Old Pat. to Peter Cock, who gave this (as p'r Recital in S'd Deed) w'th Other Land unto Gunner Rambo, intermarrying with the said P. Cock's Daug'r, and the said Gunner Conv'd 100 a's, P't thereof To the said Jno. Bowyer, by a Deed dated 17 July, '99; 80 a's Granted by Pat. dat. 29, 3mo., 1691, to the said Samuel, being his Proportion of Lib.

Land Granted by Warrant dat. 2d 9 mo., '83, from the Prop'ry, and Surv'd the Same Day, rent 1sh. Sterling p'r C't. 30 a's Granted By Patent from the Comm'rs dat. 23, 11 mo., '87–8. To Rob't Turner In right of Jam's Harrison, Purchaser of 5,000 a's, the said R. T., by Deed Ind'd, dat. 14, 3 mo, '95, Conveyed the said Land to Israel and Jos. Taylor, Sons, and Mary (wife of Jno Busby), Daughter of Christ r Taylor, Israel T. and Jos. Taylor, by Deed, dat. 10, 4 mo., '98, Conveyed their Right in the said Land to the said Jno. Busby, and Mary, his Wife, who, by their Deed duely Acknowledged, dat. 10, 4 mo., '98, Conv'd the whole said 80 acres To Samuel Carpenter; Rent 1sh. p'r C't.

Francis Lovelace, Esqr., formerly Gover'r of N. Y., by Put. dat. 3d May, 1671, Granted a Tract of Land Called 300 acres at Shackamaxen to Peter Cock at a Bus'l of Wheat p'r C't, and who deceasing, the same descended to Lawrence Cock, Son of S'd Peter, who, by Deed, dat. 30th March, 1676, Granted the Same to Eliz'th Kinsey, Now wife of Thomas Fairman, who both Granted 2 par'ls of 100 and 6 acres To Samuel Carpenter as by Deed dat. 27, 3 mo., 170, appears.

Granted to Griffith Nichols 200 acres of Land lying about the Welch tract In Newc. County, at 3 Bush'ls of Wheat p'r C't p'r an num.

Granted To Thos. Russel 100 a's in Newc. Co'ty, beyond the Welch Tract, for £20, One Moiety Payable To the first 9ber next, the Other In 12 mo. after, With Interest.

Sam'l Robinet and Jno. Powel, who Intermarried with the 2 Daughters of Wm. Taylor, dece'd, Produce the Prop'ry's Deeds of L. and Rel., dat. 2d and 3d March, '81, To Wm. and Peter Taylor, both of Sutton, in the County Palat., of Chet'r, husbandmen, for 1,250 a's Of Land. Peter has all his Moiety, Wm. has 350 acres and 10 acres Lib. Land, and by a writing Intended for a will, dat. 6, 1 mo., 1683, Grants the Rem'r untaken up to his Daughters (viz: Eliz. Powel and Mary Robinet) they request a Warrant.

———

4 mo., 8th [1706.]

James Logan, Solus.

Sold Evan Powel about 180 or 200 a's, formerly Taken up by one, Lyborn, but deserted, adjoyning On the Land of Jos. England, near Duck Creek, at £15 p'r C't, he Paying all Charges.

The Prop'ry, by L. and Rel., dat 23 and 24 Apr., 1683, Granted to Thomas Hudson, of ye Co'ty of Chester, in England, yeo., 5,000 a's of Land at 1s Sterling p'r C't, vid. Infra, which, By a Warrant from ye Prop'ry, dat. 26, 12 mo., 1684, was laid out in the County of Bucks, Vide Infra. William Biles, by vertue of a Power of attorney from said Hudson, dat. 19 Aug't, 1697, and recorded in the County of Bucks, Conveyed the said 5,000 acres to Wm. Lawrence, Jno. Tallman, Jos. Thorn, Samuel Thorn and Benjamin Field, all of Long Island, Yeomen, who request a Patent for the Same. The Prop'ry, by Ind're, dat. 25 Apr., '83, for £18, released the Q't R't of 45sh., so that 5s Only remained to be Paid. The said 5,000 acres were first laid out by Isr. Taylor in Bucks County, but afterwards regulated by Phin. Pemberton, according to whose Survey the said Pesons have divided the Tract among them and Desire a Pat., but The Land Cont'g 5,680 acres. it Can't yet be Confirmed.

Jonathan Baily, of Lewis, haveing Purchased of Wm. Clark about 100 acres of Land, P't of 112 acres Granted by Ne. York to Corn. Verhoff (vid. Title in Sussex Min's), desires to Purchase the Marsh lyeing Between the s'd Land and Canary Kill, for which he is to Pay 5sh. p'r acre p'r agreement with J. Logan. Ordered a Warrant.

Agreed (p'r Do. J. L.) with Toby Leech for his 80 acres of Overplus at £32, Unless it be referred to Persons. The Patent to be finished.

The Commr's, by Warrant dat. 27, 4 mo., '89, Granted To Jeremy Powel, Renter, a Lott in Chestnutt Str., of 40 f't in breadth, which the said Jeremy's relict and Ex'x Bargained and sold To Richard Hill, Surv'd 4th 5 mo., '89, Rent 5sh. The said Comm'rs also Granted To James Pugh by a Warrant, dat. 27, 4 mo., '89, a lott of 50 f't, adjoyning On the above, who sold his right To the Same To Jno. Kinsey, who sold to s'd Rich'd Hill, rent 5s. There is also a vacancy of 60 f't next adjoyning to the above, which is sold by James Logan for £18 to the s'd Rich'd, or 6s p'r foot, Rent 1s. Desires a Grant of the whole by Patent.

Benjamin Chambers haveing Purchased of the Prop'ry 1,000 acres of Land, the Lotts appurtenant to Which Purchase fell On Delaware Side, and the said Benj'n haveing also by Deed dat. 1, 4 mo., '88, Purchased of James Kinnerly all the lotts and Liberty appurtenant to the Original Pucrhase of 1,500 acres, made by the said James Kinnerly and Hen. Maddock. The said Benjamin haveing never taken up the High Str. Lotts appurtenant to the said Purchases, req'ts a warr't for Takeing up the Same. Kinnerly's and Maddock's right falls next To Jefferson's, On the North side, between the 7th and 8th Str., the place where the said Benjamin Desires To Take up the Lotts aforesaid.

For the agreements made with the Indians of Brandywine See the Entry made 23d 7ber, 1707.

7 mo., 9th [1706.]

Omnes.

John Eastborne Complaining to this Board that haveing Obtained a Warr't for resurveying his 300 acres of Land where he lives, in the County of Bucks, directed To Jno. Cutler, Survey'r, The s'd Jno. had never duely executed the Warrant, and therefore req'ts that he may be Ordered to Execute the said Warr't, Or that it may be directed to some Other Surveyor. Ordered that Jno. Cutler, who Upon a Summons from the Board appeared, shall again fully Execute the Warrant formerly directed to him for Resurveying Jno. Eastborne's Land.

8 mo., 30th [1706.]

P., James Logan.

Agreed with Jno. McDonald for a tract of Land Cont'g 200 acres in Christina Hundred, laid out formerly to Philemon Murfy at 1d p'r acre, but quitted, and now sold to s'd Jno. for £20 p'r C't and 1s Ster. Q't R't.

8 mo., 29th [1706.]

At a Session of the Comm'rs 29th.
Prst., E. Shippen, Griff. O. and Jas. Logan.

Agreed with Wm. Hudson for a Strip of Lotts lyeing Between the Ends of the High Str. and Mulberry Str. Lotts, between the 5th and 6th Str. from Del., Containing about 48 f't and in Length from 5th to 6th Str. for £12 10s, with Interest, to be Paid from the date of the Warrant, and 2s Sterling Q't R't p'r annum.

Jno. Eastborne laid before the Board at Cert. of Jos. Ashton's, whom the Gov'r, By a Dedimus and his hand and seal, had Impowered to attest the Evidences required by the Comm'rs Warrant, to be Called upon resur'g the s'd Jno's Land, in which Cert. the said Jos. declares, that being Present upon the Spott, at the res. he attested some Certain Evidences, who disposed that a Line they Shewed was the true Old Line which divided the Land Sold Wm. Waite, who first Purchased Jno. Nailor's 200 a. of Hugh Marsh from the Other 300 now held by J. Eastborne, but that the Surveyor would run no Other Line than the Same he had run before. A Paper under the Surv'r's hand was also Produced, in which he Owned that the Line shewed by the Evidences was the former Old Line of Wm.

Waite's Land, but that the whole tract being res'd, the Lines were altered by Consent between Hugh Marsh and Jos. Holden, the then Possessors and that the several tracts were Sold To Nailor and Eastborne by that New Line, and therefore that was the True One. The whole Matter being Largely debated, and it being made appear that the Line In Controversy was the Division Line Only Between J. Eastborne's 300 acres and J. Nailor's, formerly Holden's 200 acres, w'ch division Line was not returned nor touched within the resurvey made By Rob't Longshore by Virtue of the Comm'rs Warrant, and by him returned into the Sec'ry's Office, and the said Eastborne Grievously Complaining that the resurvey made by Jno. Cutler On Jno. Nailor's Land had Proved very Injurious To him in running that Division Line, which touched not the Overplus and in which the Prop'ry was no way Concerned. He therefore requests that his Land may be yet resurv'd according to the Tenour of Our former Warrants by Some Skillfull Surv'r of another County, who has never been Concerned in that tract, which request being Considered Together with the reasons urged, 'tis Ordered that a Warrant be directed To Isaac Taylor, Surv'r of the County of Chester, to res. ye said John Eastborne's Land.

9b'r, 16th [1706.]

Granted To Edward Beeson liberty to Settle On a tract near Nottingham, On which Tho. Taylor was settled, and the refusal of it is Promised him, given him for this under Ed. S., T. S. and J. L's hands.

---

11 mo., 26 [1706-7.]

Present, Omnes.

The Board Takeing into Consid'n the disposal of the Surv'rs Gen'ls Office, upon a full Consid'n of the Circumstances of the said Office, and the ability of Jacob Taylor, formerly revisor of the Same, think fit to appoint the said Jacob Surv'r Gener'l of the s'd Province and County of Newcastle, Kent and Sussex, and 'tis Ordered that a Commission be accordingly Granted to him for the Same, the Master of the Rolls takeing Security to the Prop'ry of himself, the Sec'ry, James Logan, and his Brother, Israel Taylor, who offer themselves to that Purpose for the said Jacob's Just discharge of the Trust reposed in him in the Sum of £500.

Rob't Wharton haveing long Sollicited the Board for a Confirmation of his Land in the great Valley, and now Complaining that Our Irregular Grant On a resurvey of 250 a's of Land to Barth. Rowles, in Right of Thomas Ellis (whereas there was none ever Surv'd to him there, nor did the said Rowles Ever Purchase any of the Prop'ry), has Occasioned great Disturbance and Loss to the said Robert in Particular, and Owen Thomas, who has Taken Possession of the said Land in Behalf of B. Rowles, likewise appearing (upon an appointment made for them both this day), it was demanded of him Whether he would acquiesce in a Division of the 500 acres according to a former agreement made at this Board by him in behalf of B. Rowles, By which it was Ordered that 250 acres of Land should be sett apart out of T. Ellis's Purchase, notwithstanding no Conveyance or assignm't appears, if so, the Commr's would Confirm to Rob't Wharton Only 250 acres and let 250 acres more be sett apart for the said Rowles, but the s'd Owen refusing to Come to an accommodation and the said Robert Complaining that whereas his Father-in-Law, Thomas Ellis, had duely Purchased many years agoe and Paid for 500 acres of Land, w'ch were yet unconfirmed To him, he had been to this day kept out of it greatly To his Loss and Damage and with Great Injustice to his Particular Concerns, and to the Estate of the said Thomas Ellis, and this, Principally by means of the Comm'rs Takeing upon them to set apart Land,for said Rowles Out of Thomas Ellis's Purchase, with which this Board is no way Concerned, nor has there Ever been any Privity between the Prop'ry and the said Rowles in Relation To the said 250 acres, and therefore he Craves Justice of the Board and a Confirmation of the whole Land aforesaid in Right of Thos. Ellis, which right he solely Claims to make good, which he produces a Deed from Humphrey Ellis, Son of the said Thomas Ellis, dat. 1, 1 mo., 1702, for 200 a's left by the said Thomas to the said Humphrey by will dat. 1, 11 mo., 1688, and Duely Proved. Also a Deed from Ellis Ellis, Eldest Son and Heir of the said Thomas, dat. the 29th 11 mo., 1703, assigning to the s'd Robert the whole said 500 acres, which Includes the last ment'd 250 acres and the Other 250, also claimed in behalf of Rowles, upon Condition that the s'd Robert shall Pay and make Good to the said Rowles all debts and dem'ds due from the Estate of the said Ellis to the s'd Rowles. Whereupon 'tis Ord'd that the whole said 500 a's be Confirmed To Rob't Wharton upon the Foundation of the said Deed from Ellis Ellis, but that at the Same time a Bond be taken of the said Robert to grant 250 acres of the s'd Land, Including the House built by Owen Thomas, as soon as any p'rson Shall appear that is duely Qualifyed to receive the Same in the s'd Rowles' behalf, Provided that the Other 250 a's to be resurveyed by the said Robert shall be as valuable and Commodious in all respects as the 250 a's to be by him Granted to Rowles.

The said Owen Thomas Produced to the Board a Pat. signed by Wm. Markham and Thomas Ellis, dat. 30, 6 mo., 1688, Granting 100 acres of Land To Humphrey Thomas, late Purchaser, laid out 12, 5 mo., 1688, by a Warrant from the said Com'rs dated 22d 4 mo., '88, beginning at a Corner Post of Humphrey Ellis's Land, running N. N. W. 400 pr's to a Corner, then W. S. W. 40 p's To a post, then S. S. E. 400 p's, then E. N. E. 40 p's, which Land the said Owen Claims a right to and desires it may be laid Out On Part of the aboves'd 500 acres, but D. Powel, the Surveyor appearing, declared that the said Land, notwithstanding it was thus Granted, was never Surv'd nor marked Out, nor has Hum. Ellis any Land thereab'ts at that Time, So that the whole Boundaries were uncertain and unfixt, and that T. Ellis Procured this Patent in a hurry, as he well remembers, Just as he was leaving this Province and Embarqueing for England, but there was Land Enough very near adjoyning to Lay that Pat. upon. Ordered that Robert Wharton, as heir To Thomas Ellis, further Pay for 100 a's of Land at the Old rate of £5 p'r C't, w'th Interest from September, One thous'd Seven hund'd and One.

Sam'l Preston, In behalf of Rees Wolfe, of Sussex, requesting that we would Grant To the said Rees a Warr't for 200 a's of Land in the Forest, In the s'd County, lyeing upon Bracey's Beach, On the North side and above the Bridge, upon New Rent, viz: a 1d Sterling p'r acre. Ordered that the said Land be Granted accordingly.

Sold Sam'l Baker 54 acres of Overplus In Wright's Town, in Bucks, being the Surplusage of 40 acres, bought with 100 acres more, by his Father, of James Harrison, and is Part of ye s'd James's Original Purchase for £12.

A Cert. is Produced under the hand of N'l Newlin, of Chester Co'ty, Justice, that Jno. Sangers and Rich'd Farr, upon their attestation, did Declare that Nath'l Parke and his wife Elenor, and Jno. Martin, his Son-in Law, all Came In Servants to Nath'l Evans in the y'r 1681, whereupon the s'd Nath'l, for himself and his said wife, and the said Jno. Martin, request their Proportions of Headland, which is Granted In Two Warrants.

A Survey of a Bank Lott To Ja's Coults in Newcastle.

A Resurvey of 600 acres of Land in Dover Hundred, Kent County, formerly In 2 Parcells, to Stephen Paraddee, lately Purchased of Rich'd Levick, Vid. Title In James Logan's Min's of Kent.

The Prop'ry, by Deeds of L. and rel., dat. 9th and 10th March, 1682-3, Granted To Jno. Streipers, of Kaldkirchin, Coun. Juliers, Borders of Germany, Merch't, 5,000 acres, and by Deed

1st April, 1683, released 45s of the yearly Rent and left 5s remaining. By the Comm'rs Warrant, dat. 15, 12 mo., '83, and the Propr'y's Order from Crevelt, there was Surv'd to him in the Liberties 50 a's of Land, which Contains no Overplus and Harry Sellen and Leonard Arets, his attorneys, desire a Pat. for the Same. Granted. Henry Sellen, attorney to the said Jno. Streipers, by L'res, dat. at Crevelt the 13th May, 1698, Proved and recorded at Germantown by Deed Poll dat. 23d 1 mo., 1702-3, Granted to Leonard Arets 275 a's, Part of the said 5000, a's. The Prop'ry, by L. and release dat. 10th and 11th June, 1683, Granted to the s'd Leonart Arets, then of Crevelt, Coun. Meurs, 1,000 acres, and by Deed dat. s'd 11th June, releas'd 9s of the Rent. Deeds Produced. Of the said 1,000 acres there remain'd 225 a's to take up, which added to the 275 acres before ment'd make it 500 acres, which by Virtue of an Old warrant, dat. 10th 9ber, 1685, was laid Out first and since resurveyed, On which he desires a Pat.

The Prop'ry, by L. and release, dat. 1st and 2d March, 1681, Granted To Matthew Grange, of Lastock, Gratam, in the County Palat'e, of Chester, husbandman, 100 acres of Land which haveing never been taken up, and he now a Resident in New Jersey, desires a Warrant.

The Comm'rs haveing Granted to Judge Guest a Certain Part of a Square bounded with Vine Str., the 3d and 4th Str from Delaware, at 10s strl. p'r ann. for 21 years, which together with another Parcell then Granted him in Fee, he Conv'd To Thomas Storey, the said Thomas requesting to Purchase the Inheritance. The Comm'rs being all together did agree with him for the Inheritance and Reversion of the s'd Land for £20, to be paid in 12 mo's, with Interest, the Same rent to Continue.

Also for that Tract beyond Vine Str., lyeing Between the Same and Jos. Willcox Rope Walk, in depth the whole Distance, already Granted him behind Will's Lotts, to the uttermost Parts of the aforementioned Lotts Granted To Judge Guest, which, in the whole, is 446 f't, under the yearly Rent of 6d Sterling for Every 10 f't. viz : 22s and 3d Ster. for the whole. a Pat. To be made to him all together.

———

2 mo., 10th [1707.]

Sold Robert Oldham 100 acres of Land Joyning On Will'm Huntley for £20, to be Paid in 12 mo's, with Interest Rent as Huntley's.

The Prop'ry Sold Arthur Cook 5,000 acres of Land, as appears of a Rec't under his hand for £125 Consid'n Money, dat. 16, 6 mo., 1684, at Lewis. Arthur Cook Purchased also of

Fran's Burrows, of Boston, In New England, 1,000 a's for £20, by Deed poll dat. 26th 9ber, '84, which said 1,000 acres the said Fran's Purchased of the prop'ry by Deeds dat. 29th and 30th March, 1682, by the Name of Francis Burroughs, of Lond., Milliner. The said Arthur's Wid'w, Marg't Cook, purchased off Jos. Growdon 400 a. by Deed dat. 16th 9 mo., 1700, by which they have a right To 6,400 a's of This.

Granted by pat. from J. Cl. and R. T., dat'd 1, 4 mo., '86, warr'ts 4, 6 mo., '84; 28, 2 mo., '86, Survd' 1, 3 mo., '86,
In Bucks, ... 2,000
In New Town, Bucks, now T. Hillborne's, vid. his Pat., 500
Sold Nathan Stanbury, laid out in Bucks, ... 500
Near the Cold Spring, Sold Jno. Surkett, ... 400
In Chester, sold Edward Wanton 800, and Nath'l King 700, both in one Tract, ... 1,500
                                                       ─────
                                                       4,900

Besides the above 4,900 acres there was laid Out in Chest'r Co'ty near Brandywine, by a warr't, 1st 8ber, 1687, from Wm. M. and J. Goodson the remaining 1,500 a's, which the said Wid'w affirms was taken from her and the like quantity of Barrens put upon her, w'ch She refuses, and desires new Warrants to take it Elsewhere. Which request being Considered, and it being made fully ap'ear that the Land Confirmed to Arthur Cook was not the tract Surv'd to him (as D. Powel, who first laid the Same Out, affirms and declares), but was rem'd by Rob't Longshore, into the most Barren part of the whole Country, where it is not Judged to be worth even the arrears of Rent incumbent On it. 'Tis Therefore Granted that she shall have new Warr't for takeing up the s'd Land, w'ch She requests may be in 3 sev'l parcels of 500 a's each, 2 to Ezekiel Harland and the Other to Rich'd Buffington.

The Prop'ry, by L. and Rel., dat. ye 11th and 12th days 8ber, 1681, Granted To Wm. Pardoe, of the City of Worcester, Merch't, 1,250 acres of Land, which Land by Indorese't On the release, not sealed, but signed before Witnesses, he assigned to Jno. Weight, late of Worcester, but nothing of Heirs, &c., Ment'd. Of this there has been Taken up 900 a's, of w'ch there was laid in the Welch Tract a large part, near 700 acres 'tis said. Ordered a Warrant in Right of Wm. Pardoe at the request of Sarah Weight, Daughter of the said Jno. The whole right (if Duely Conveyed from Pardoe) belongs to said Sarah and her Brother, Jno. Weight's Children.

Thom's Langhorne, of Littendale, in ye County of Westmoreland, by Deeds of L. and Rel., dat 7th and 8th 9ber, '81, purchased of ye Prop'ry 500 acres of Land, which about the year 1685 were said to be located near Brandywine, But proved very Barren and unfit for Cultivation, his Son and Heir, Jeremiah Longhorne, disowns it, and claims a Warrant to Take up the said quantity where it may be had. Granted a Warrant.

The Prop'ry also by Deeds dat. 7th and 8th June, 1682, Granted To Thomas Cam, of Camsgill, Coun. Westmoreland, Gent., 500 acres, for which the said Thomas req'ts a Warr't. Granted.

Francis Nichols, Gover'r of Ne. York, by Pat. dat. 25th 10ber, 1667, Recorded In Philad'a Pat. Book A., p. 222, Granted to the Inhabitants of Taoconinck. Caspar Fish granted his share, or proportion of the s'd Land, being 150 acres, to Lawrence Cock, who by Deed dat. 25, 9 mo., 1679, Conveyed the Same To Anna Salter, upon which Deed are Indorsed these words in the Prop'ry's Own hand (I shall Confirm by pat., and till then Doe Confirm the Within assignm't to the Party To whom it is Conveyed, as it is Conveyed, given at Philad'a, 16, 3 mo., '84, Will'm Penn). Anna Salter Impowered Richard Whitfield, Thomas Fairman, Rob't Storey, Jno. Hart, Charles Pickering and Patrick Robinson, whom she appointed the Ex'rs of her last will, dat. 7th 9 mo., 1688, duely proved to sell and Convey all her Lands, &c. Thomas Fairman and John Hart, ye Surviveing Ex'rs, by Deed dat. 10th Jan'ry, 1704, Granted 130 a's of the said Land to Henry Mallows, for which they request a Pat. Granted.

Agreed p'r James Logan, with Jonas Potts, for 200 acres of Land in Gilbert's, to be held for 5 years Certain, at £8 p'r Annum, and to have the refusal of it when to be sold, and if he takes it not, but 'tis sold to another, then that Purchaser to allow him for his Improvement.

———

4 mo., 12th [1707.]

Jno. Lobe, by L. and Rel., Purchased of the Prop'ry 1,000 acres, and by like Deeds, dat. 9th and 10th Aug't, 1684, Granted the Same to Sam'l Levis and Wm. Garret, with the appur'ces, haveing Taken up the Front Lott, they Crave that in the High Str. Granted a Warrant.

Sir Edm'd Andros, by Pat. dat. 20th August, 1679, Granted to Rob't Higenot and Jno. Crue 900 acres of Land in Sussex Co'ty, which is now in the possession of Jno. Crue, Mary Dyne and Jacob Colluck, but the Bounds being uncertain and Confused they Crave a resurvey, which is granted.

14 mo., 6th [1707.]

Agreed, p'r Jas. Logan, with Jos. Kirkbride, for his Overplus, being 130 acres, for £15. 'Tis Exceeding Barren and *he prop'ry Promised it to him for Nothing, vid. Min's, 2 mo., 1701.

4 mo., 28th [1707.]

The Prop'ry, by Deeds of L. and Rel. (as p'r Recital), dat. 21st and 26th Aug't, 1681, Granted to Jam's Parke, of Southwarke, Coun. Surrey, Cheesemonger, 500 Acres of Land.

The said James, by Ind're dat. 7th and 8th 7ber, 1683, Granted to Rob't Hodkins, of Southwarke aforesaid, Waterman, 250 Acres, Part of the s'd Purchase. Tho's Chalkly, in behalf of the said Ex'rs of the said Rob't, requests a Warr't for Takeing up the said Land. Granted.

5 mo., 3d [1707.]

At a Session of the Com'rs Held 5 mo., 3d, 1707.
Prst., T. S., G. O., Jam's L.

George Dakeyne haveing by Virtue of sev'l Warrants from this Board res'd The greatest Part of the County of Newcastle On the prop'ry's Account, makeing in the whole about 85,000 a's and demanding his pay According to ye Agreements made with the Survey'rs 17th 3 mo., 1703, Entered these Min's. He is allowed £200 for the s'd resurvey, he being at all manner of Charges, and Completing Cantwell's Lands and the Prop'ry's rec't is to allow him the s'd Sum.

5mo., 19th [1707.]

Jno. Buckley being An Original Purchaser of 250 a's of land, and Oliver Cope, of the Same Quantity, in this province, the said Jno. and Wm. Cope, Son of the s'd Oliver, req'ts Warr'ts for takeing up the Lotts Appurtenant to the said purchases. They both fall On Delaware, Buckley's is No. 135, Cope's 179, in The City Draught.

Thomas Storey haveing Purchased divers lotts in the 2d Str. and 3d Str. of Philad'a, upon Delaware side, between Sassafras Str. and Vine Str., and there being Some Vac't Lotts adjoyning, hath requested the priviledge of fenceing in Such of those Vac't Lotts adjoyning as he may have Occasion for, w'ch

MINUTE BOOK "G. 487

Accordingly was granted to him by the Comm'rs, to hold the
Same till such Time as there may be Occasion to dispose of
the said Vacancies to Purchasers Or Others.

---

5 mo., 21 [1707.]

James Logan.
Fran's Lovelace, Esqr., Governor of New York, by Pat. dat.
10th Mar., 1670, Granted to Hans Manson a Certain Tract of
Land On the West of Skuylkill, then Called but 1000 acres, but
being res'd According to the Method of those times after the
Grant by Order of Capt'n Edm'd Cantwell, was found to Contain 1,100 a's, which s'd 1,100 a's the s'd Hans Manson, by
Deed dat. 29 Apr., 1681, Granted to Peter Peterson Yocomb,
his Heirs, &c. The s'd Yocomb, by Deed Poll dat. 30 Apr.,
1681, Granted 270 Acres of the said Land To Jonas Nellson, his
Heirs, &c., and 580 a's more thereof being res'd 16, 10 mo., '84,
to him by the Prop'ry's Warrant, dat. 25, 5 mo., '84, were
Confirm'd to the said Yocomb with 30 a's of meadow by Pat.
from Ja's Claypoole and Rob't Turner 22, 11 mo., 1684, and the
remaining 250 a's Granted to Jonas Nelson by his last will,
duely proved, bearing date the 14th of Jan'ry, 1691, devised
100 a's of the said Land to his Son, Mouns Jones, to his Son
Niels 70 a's, and to his Son Andreas 100 a's, being the whole
said 270 Acres, to them, their Heirs and assigns for Ever. The
said 270 a's being res'd in the 2d Mo. last, is found to Contain
272 Acres Only, of which 8 a's is Marsh and the s'd Mouns,
Niels and Andreas, request the Same to be Confirmed by Pat.

---

5 mo., 21st [1707.]

The Prop'ry, by his Warr't dat. 23d 9ber, 1683, Granted To
Wm. Nicholas a lott in the City, to be laid Out where the
Prop'ry shall Order, which On the 29th of the said Month and
year was Surv'd to him in Chestnut Str. Between Wm. Stanly's and James Cooper's, as p'r Cert. In the Office, in br. 50 f't
and 178 f't In Length. Wm. Nicholas, by Ind're 28th 7 mo.,
1685, Granted all the aforesaid Lott to Wm. Hudson, of the
County of Chester, Mason. Wm. Hudson Granted of the said
lott. 14 f't In br., to One, Christ'n Harrison, and rem'r, being
36 f't, by Deed Poll, dated 7th March, '94, he granted to Jos.
White, of Salem, in Jersey, yeoman, who by Indorsement On
the said Deed, Granted the Same To Wm. Hall, of the Same
place, Merchant. Wm. Hall Granted the s'd Lott to Jno.
Whitpaine, who deceasing before payment, for want thereof
the same, was again returned and released by the Ex'rs to the

s'd Will'm Hall, who thereupon sold, but did not Convey ye Same to Edward James, who therefore haveing an Equitable Title in the s'd Lott, Joyned with the said Wm. Hall and Conveyed the said Lott by their Joint Deed, dat. 17, 1 mo., 1701, To Robert Burrows, who desires a Patent for the Same. The Comm'rs, by warr't dat. 22d 1 mo., 1689-90, Granted To Wm. Rakestraw 100 f't of Bank Joyning on James Wast's, at the North End of the Town, On the Same Terms on which they were granted to Others, in Consideration of his dissappointment of the Front lott of 51 f't, belonging to the Orig'l purchase of 2,500 acres, made by Robert King, who throwing up the Same again, the said Wm. Purchased the whole right of Philip Ford, but before he had so done or before Notice was given thereof, the Prop'ry, upon King's relinquishing his right, Sold or gave 30 f't, part of the said 51 f't, To Wheeler, of Boston, who built upon it the House at the Lower End of the Front Street, now belonging To Edward Shippen. The s'd Wm. req'ts a Pat. On the said Lott.

5 mo., 28 [1707.]

Present, Thomas Storey, G. O. and Jas. L.
Rob't Wharton, Jno. Reece and Dav. Morris appeared about their Lands and they were Ord'd Immediately to be Surv'd.

6 mo., 15 [1707.]

Abiah Taylor haveing Purchased of Jno. Tovey, Orig'l Purchaser of 1,250 Acres of Land in this province, Conveyed by Ind'res of L. and rel., dat. 6th and 7th Apr., 1702, 250 a's, Part of the said 1,250, To Rich'd Lewin, of Drayton, Coun. Berks, yeoman. Rich'd Lewin, of Anne Arundel Co'ty, in Maryland, Son and Heir of the s'd Rich'd Lewin, by Deeds Ind'd, Dat. 26 March, 1707, Granted and Conveyed the said 250 acres to Walter Pomphrey, who by Indorsement dat. 5th May last, assigned it To Henry Hollingsworth, who assigned to Geo. Robinson, of Newark, Coun. Newc., who requests a Warrant for the said Land.

6 mo., 15th [1707.]

Jacob Tellner, Ori'l Purchaser of 5,000 acres of Land, by Deeds from the Prop'ry dat. 9th and 10th March, 1682, Recorded in Philad'a Rolls, B. A., Vol. pa. 194, Granted To Herman OpdeGraef, Derick Opd.G. and Abraham OpdeGraef, 3 Brothers, 2,000 a's by Deeds dat. 15 and 16, 2 mo., '88, recorded

Ibid., Bk. C, 2d, Vol. 3d, pa. 95-6-7, and the Same Jacob Telner, by Deed of Rel., dat. 4th Apr., 1689, record'd, Ibid., folio 124-5 of the Same book C. 2d, further Confirmed the said 2,000 a's, and Particularly 800 thereof, under bounds in Germantown. Abraham OpdeGraef, by Deed, dat. 4, 1 mo., 1689, Grant'd to Jacob Shoemaker, of Germantown, 125 acres, p't of the above 2,000 a's in Sev'l p'rc'ls, viz: Parcels in Germantown the One Cont'g 21¼ Acres and the Other 28¾ acres, being both together 50 a's, and 50 a's In Krisheim, the Other 25 In Crevelt. Jacob Shoemaker, by Ind're of Bargain and seal, dat. 4th 9ber, 1693, Conveyed the first ment'd 2 parcels, makeing 50 acres, mongst Other Lands to Heifert Paper, of Germantown husband n, Who, by Deed, dat. 29,, 9ber, 1705, Conveyed the s'd 50 a's to Sam'l Richardson, R'd Townsend, Tho's Potts and Sam'l Cart, all of ye County of Philad'a, Yeo'n, to Hold, &c., a Pat. is desired to the s'd 4 Persons.

Herman OpdeGraef being possessed of his part or portion of the said Land by Deed dat. 4, 8ber, 1701, Conveyed 390¾ Acres To Cornelius Siverts, of Germantown, Glasier, being then located In Telner's Township, laid Out by warr't from ye Comm'rs 6, 9 mo., '85. Dirk OpdeGraef, by his last will duely proved relicted to his Ex'r, Nilken OpdeGraef, his whole Estate, who, by Virtue thereof, has since Sold One Moiety of his Share in the said Township (which Share was likewise 390¾ acres) To Abraham OpdeGraef, her Brother, And the Other moiety being 195⅜ to the Other Brother, Herman, by Deed, dat. 29, 7ber, 1701, Corn's Siverts, his Heirs and Assigns for Ever. The s'd Siverts requests a Patent for the whole said 586 acres in One Tract as they Lye Contiguous; Rent 1sh. p'r 1,000.

The Prop'ry, by his Warrant, dat. 4, 6 mo., 1684, Granted To Peter Yocom 500 acres Of Land at ½d p'r Acre, whom Thom's Holme, Surv'd Gen'l, Ordered to be laid out On the W't side Skuylkill above all the Welch Townships, not Interfereing With the 12 miles square belonging to Ralph Fretwell, and Accordingly was Surv'd by Dav'd Powell, but fell within Part of that Tract appropriated To Laetitia Penn in right of her Original Purchase of 5,000 a's, which tract including divers Other Lesser Quantities before Surv'd to Other Persons. The Prop'ry Ordered that the s'd Lesser Quantities should be Confirmed to these persons, and accordingly Samuel Carpenter and Jam's Logan, Attorneys for the Trustees of Wm. Aubry, Are to Confirm the said Land, 250 a's thereof to Jno. Hughs, To whom Peter Yocom, in his lifetime, Sold the Same, and the Other 250 a's to the said Peter's Children to whom, by will, he left the Same.

Henry Stretcher and Jno. Millington, by Deed, dat. 3d May, '88, Granted the said Fisher's Island, in the Broadkill Marshes, To Thomas Wynne and Eliz'th, his wife. Tho. deceasing, Eliz'th, the Survivor, Granted the s'd Island, by Deed of Gift, 1, 12 mo., 1693, to Thomas [Fisher] and Margery, his wife, Daughter of the s'd Eliz'th, and to their Survivor and their Heirs begotten by the s'd Thomas On the s'd Margery. The Prop'r, by Warrant, dat. 12, 5 mo., 1701, Granted a resurvey On the Same w'ch was Executed the Winter following, and the s'd Island is found to Contain 175 acres to be Confirmed for £10. This was Certainly Granted Away by the Govern't of New York.

Dennis Rochford in right of Thomas Herriot, Original Purchaser of 5,000 a's, by Warrant from the Prop'ry, dat. 1st 7ber, 1683, Took up a high Street Lott On the North Side Between 4th and 5th Str. from Dela. Execution was levied by Jno. Claypoole, Sheriff of Philad'a, upon the said Lott upon An Action of Jno. Murray and Wm. Bevan, Adm'rs on the Estate of Rob't Shepherd, Ag't Wm. Carter, Adm'r On Mary Rochford's Estate, for £26 with Costs, recovered 7, 4 mo., 1692, ag't Den's Rocheford himself, but not levied till by Another Order of Court 4th June, 1696, and the s'd Sherriff sold the said lott to Dav'd Giffing for £100 by Deed Dated 7, 7 mo, 1697, who requests a Confirmation with An Addition of the Vac't Slip Between it and Mulberry Str. lotts, for w'ch he Pays £5.

The Prop'ry, by his Pat., dat. 26, 1 mo., 1684, Confirmed to Thomas Hall a Certain tract of Land in the County of Sussex Called Maidenhead Thicket, Scituate On the South side of the great Creek Cont. 421 acres, Granted and Surv'd by Order of Capt. Cantwell To Rich'd Peaty, who Assigned the same Over To the s'd Thom's Hall to whom it was thereupon Confirmed. And the said Thomas, by Deed Poll, dat. the 25, 9ber, 1701, Conv'd the s'd Land to Jno. Fisher, of ye Said Co'ty, Planter, his Heirs, &c., to whom the s'd Land was resurveyed by Warrant from ye Comm'rs dat. 1, 10ber, 1702, and Cont. 446 Acres, he requests a Pat. Ordered.

7 mo., 23d [1707.]

Omnes, Present.

Sam'l Cart haveing, 4, 2 mo., 1706, Procured a Warrant for the remainder of the 1,000 acres his Father Purchased of Edw'd Martindale, viz: for 669 Acres to be Yet Taken up there is discovered a Certain tract of 400 a's in the County of Bucks Appropriated to that right, On w'ch Samuel req'ts a resurvey, w'ch is Granted.

MINUTE BOOK "G." 491

Be it Remembered that On the 10th Day of 7ber, Ano., 1706, All the Comm'rs being Present, at the repeated Complaints of the Inhabitants On Brandywine Whose Lands have never been purchased of the Indians the Comm'rs Agreed with Sheekonickan, the Chief of the Indians there, to buy off their Claim for £100 of Pensilv'a money, of which a Considerable Part is paid as p r Waste book in Several Places.

Jno. Spencer, Orig'l Purchaser of 250 acres of Land as appears by the List, by Virtue of a Warrant from the Surv'r Gen'l, dat. 11, 7 mo., 1682, took up 125 acres of Land in the County of Bucks upon Neshaminie On the N. side, and Soon after dyed, Possessed thereof, Surv'd 10, 6 mo., 1683, and no more Appearing to Be Taken up in right of the said Purchase his Eldest Son, James Spencer, req'ts a warrant for takeing up the remaining 125 acres. The Prop'ry, also, by his Warrant in the Surv'r's Office, dat. 2, 5 mo., 1683, Granted to the said Jno. Spencer to take up a lott in the 3d Str. from Dela. in right of the Purchase aforesaid which Warrant haveing never been executed (both the Said Jno. and his wife haveing lost their lives by an Inundation of the said River Nesham. in the year 1684, Or thereabouts), the said James req'ts the Same to be renewed, both Granted.

Geo. Dakeyne having procured a warr't of this Board, dat. 15th 9ber, 1705, for a Certain piece of Marsh in the Town of Newc., on Certain Terms, Conv'd all his right to ye Same to Sam'l Lowman, by Deed, dat. 24th 9ber last, haveing first Obtained a release from ye Alricks's who had a prior Claim there to, s'd Lowman req'ts a Confirmat'n of the s'd Marsh.

Jon'n Wynne haveing A Right to the Remainder untaken up of his Father's purchase of 200 acres, it appears upon the best Inquiry that Can be made at Present that there is no more than 1,550 a s of it laid Out, he therefore req'ts a Warrant for the remaining 600 a's and 40 a's of Lib. Land to Compleat his purchase, his Brother-in-Law, Edw'd Jones, Sen'r, haveing taken up 10 acres; see the Welch Min's. Granted a Warr't for 600 acres to be laid Out in the Welch Tract Or Elsewhere, he likewise req'ts a warrant for 40 a's of Lib. Land, And his High Str. lott not being yet Taken up.

Michael Izzard, son of Mich'l Izzard, deceased, Claiming the Old House and Lott at the Center where Geo. Geddis lives, which has been Long supposed to be Escheated, An Inquisition of Escheat is to Pass upon it, for 'tis supposed to have been Sold to One Clark, who dyed without Heirs, &c., Intestate.

The Prop'ry, by L. and Rel., dat. 26th and 27th 7ber, '81, Granted to Wm. Lane, of the City of Bristol, Grocer, 500 acres of Land in Right of which there was Surveyed On the 29th 11 mo., 1685, in the 3d Str. from Dela. a lott of 55 f't in br'd. Edward Lane, Son and Attorney of the said Will'm, by Deed, dat. 25th Apr., '89, Granted the said Land To J. Jennett, of Philad'a, Taylor; Wm. Lane, by Ind're of L. and rel., dat. 23 and 24, 8ber, 1689, Granted the said 500 acres to said Edward; Jno Jennett, by his last will, dat. 10, 7ber, '99, Granted Among Other Things the said Lott to his Wid'w and Ex'r, Bridget, with power To sell, &c; And Ed'd Lane by Deed dat.

The Prop'ry, by Deeds of Lease and release, dat. 3d and 4th May, 1682, Granted To Thomas Phelps, of Limerick, in Ireland, Merchant, 1,000 Acres Of Land, and by Deeds of the Same Date to Rich'd Pearce, of the Same Place, Apothecary, the Same Quantity, and by Deeds of the same date to Sam'l Tavernor, of the Same Place, Merch't; the like Quantity, and by Like Deeds of the same date to Thom's Pearce, of the Same place, Mer't, ye like quantity; and 'tis supposed by Deeds of the Same date, to Ja's Craven, of the same place, Merch't, the Same Quantity. Jno. Phelps, of Bristol, Son and Heir of Jno. Phelps, Samuel Tavernor, Thom's Pearce for himself, and Rich'd Pearce, his Father, by Lease and release, bearing date the 23d and 24th days of Aug't, Granted all their said 4,000 a's To James Shattick and Edward Lane, of the province of Pennsilv'a, Whereupon they request Warrants to take up the Same; of this Land there was 2,000 Acres Taken up by Christ'r Pennock, what remains is to be granted. The Prop'ry by L. and Rel., dat. 11th and 12th 8ber, '81, Granted To Thomas Padget, of ye City of Bristol, Mealman, 500 a's of Land, and ye s'd Padget, by Deeds, dat. 21 and 22 Jan'y, 1703, Granted ye s'd lands to ye s'd James Shattick, of ye same prov'ce of Pensilv'a, yeom'n; he desires warrants for Takeing up ye Same.

The Prop'ry, by L. and Rel., dat. Twenty-Sixth and Twenty-seventh days of September, One thous'd Six hund'd and Eighty-One, Granted to Joane Dixon, of the City of Bristol, wid'w, 500 a's, who, by Deeds, dat. the 29th February and first March, One thous'd seven hund'd and three, Granted the s'd Land to Jam's Shattick, yeoman He desires Warrants.

The Prop'ry, by his warrant, dat. 2d 11 mo., 1683, Granted To Thomas Constable, of the Parish of Diskeard, in the County of Cornwall, Gent., 500 acres of Land, for which Nich. Waln, about five years after Paid £24 in p't. The Said Land was Laid Out On Nesham. together with 200 more To Walter Bridgeman for which, by the s'd Nicholas, there was Paid £9 10s; by Order of the Comm'rs the said Land was Subdivided, there being Overplus in it and 550 Acres sett off To Thomas Constable. The said Thomas, by Ind're, dat. 18 10ber, 1703, for £70 Strl. Sold and Conv'd the said 500 acres to Jas. Shattick, of the County of Philad'a, yeoman, who desires a Confirmation. All the principal of the Consideration Money, Except 20sh., was paid 5 years after it was due, upon which, deducting Interest, that Sum of £24 is reduced to £17 10s. Principal Paid and there remained £7 17s 2d, of which the Interest to this time is.

Alex'r Molleston, Jun'r, p'r Jacob Colluck, requests the Grant of a Small Slip of Marsh lying Between his Land and the Whorekill Creek for which he is willing to Pay 10s p'r Acre and Common Rent.

The Prop'ry, by Deeds, dat. 9th and 10th May, 1682, Granted to Edw'd Blenman, Sen'r, of Shipton Mallet, Coun. Somerset, Clothier, 1,000 acres of Land. Edw'd Blenman, by Ind're, dat. 10th 7 mo., 1685, for £6, Granted to Jos. Paul, of Ilminster, in the said County, Sergeweaver, 250 acres, Or One 4th p't of the whole Said 1,000 acres, to Hold, &c.; And Again, by an Indorsement On the Release, dat. 23d Jan'ry, 1688, Granted the whole said 1,000 Acres to the said Jos. in Consid'n Of £12. By Virtue of a Warrant, Dated 4 mo., 1704, there was Surv'd to the said Jos., in right of the s'd Purchase, 492 Acres in the County of Bucks, for which he desires a Pat.

Will'm Willson, Sherriff of Kent C., by Deed Poll, dat. 8th Aug't, 1704, made over unto Thomas England, of Phila'da, Merch't, One Tract of Land Called great Geneva, Cont. 600 a's, and One Tract Called Howell's Lott, Cont'g 1,000 a's, On Dover Creek, and One Moiety of a tract Called the Improvement, Cont'g 600 acres, On Duck Creek, all Lyeing In Kent County, and Contains 2,200 acres, in lieu in part of a debt of £200 Sterling recovered at Kent Court to 9ber, 1702, of Griff. Jones, of the s'd County, adm'r of the Estate of Jno. Howell, late of Stockton, in Bishop Durham, Mariner, due from the said Howel to Jacob Decow, late of the Parish of Hemingbrough, in the County of York, dece'd, whose Daug'r Hannah, sole Surviving Ex'r of his last will and Testament, the s'd Thomas England, Marr'd, and requests a Warrant of resurvey On the said 1,000 acres In Order for a pat.

The Prop'ry, by Deeds of Lease and release, dat. the 22d and 23d Mar., 1685-6, Granted To Jno. Dwight, of Fulham, Coun. Middlesex, Gent., his Heirs, &c., 500 acres of Land in this Province, Consid'n £22, after Jno. Dwight's decease his Ex'x and Relict, Lydia Dwight and Sam'l Dwight, and Philip Dwight, his only Sons, by their Joynt Deed, dat. ye 22 and 23d May, 1707, Conveyed all the said Land To Jno. Talbot, of Burlington, in New Jersey, for a Competent Sum of money (no Sum ment'd), who Desires a Warrant.

At a Session of the Comm'rs 14th 5 mo., 1708.
Pres't, Omnes.

The Prop'ry Granted To Evan Davies 500 acres of Land in Kent Called Betty's Fortune, On One of Duck Creek Branches, first Granted by Ord'r of Court in 1679, Surv'd 16, 11 mo. following, and Confirmed by the Prop'ry, dat. 26th 1 mo., 1684, Rent at Dover 10, 1 mo., 1 Bushell of wheat p'r C't. Evan Davies, by Deed dat. 20, 6 mo., 1684, Granted the said 500 acres, together with 175 acres more, being a plantation Called Shrewsbury, Situate in the s'd County On Lethe Creek (said to be granted by an Order of Kent Court), To James Wells, of the s'd County, to have, &c., James Wells deceasing, his 2 Sons, Jno. and Thomas, and his Daughter, Katherine Wells, being his Heirs, by their Joynt Deed, dat. 21, 8ber, 1701, Granted the s'd 2 tracts To Griff. Jones, of Philadelphia, His heirs and assigns for Ever, who, by Deed, dated   , Conveyed the said Land To Wm. Morton, of the said County of Kent, and his Heirs, &c. The Prop'ry, by Pat. dat. 9th 8ber, 1701, Confirmed unto Wm. Morton and Wm. Rodney, Joyntly, a Certain tract of Land Called London, On the N't Side of Little Creek, in the said County, Cont. 1,300 a's, first Confirmed by said Edm'd Andros to John Stevens, and Will'm Morton and Will'm Rodney, by their Deeds of Partition dividing their s'd Land, Wm. Rodney Confirmed to the said Wm. Morton a part of the said tract, Called London, Containing 600 a's, More Or Less, To hold to him and his Heirs. Wm. Morton, by his last will, dat. the 12 Jan'y, 1700, Granted To Jno. Richardson, his wife's Son, 50 a's of his Land, and to Wm. and Marg't Hirons, Children of Simon Hirons, a Certain Tract of Land, described, but the Quantity not Named, and to his Servant, Tho. O' Horell, 50 acres, and all the rest of his Land he gives To Samuel Berry, Jno. French and Rob't Parter, to be Equally divided Between them, and appointed Simon Hirons and ye s'd three persons to be his Ex'rs, but all the rest renouncing under their hands and Seals, adm'n was granted to Jno. French alone by Gov'r Evans, 11 Ap., 1705. The words Heirs not being In any of the Grants, in the will, and therefore the Severall Estates being Only for Life, and the Estate Proveing more Indebt than the Goods and Chattles would Pay, Jno. French, the adm'r, Req'ts the reversion Of the whole, for which he agrees to give Sixty Pounds.

---

5 mo., 24th [1708.]

Will'm Garrett haveing made Out his title To 250 acres of Land, Purchased by Wm. Neal 11th 3 mo., 1702, of which 200 a's are taken upon with 4 a's (besides allowance) and 4 a's of Lib. Land, he desires a Warrant for the remaining 42 a s. Granted This Day.

Do., 26th [1708.]

Abiah Taylor, in behalf of Jno. Cox, desires to Purchase 150 a's of Land adjoyning to his Own in the Forks of Brandywine for w'ch he is to Pay £24 next Fair, and he has leave to Settle it immediately; ye land bounds On Abiah's 2 tracts of Land On both sides and Isaac Taylor's new Surv'd Land.

6 mo., 2d [1708.]

A Warrant To Thomas Tresse for the Bank of Jno. Hendricks Lott, now belonging To his Daughter and Heiress, Joanna, wife of Sam'l Weaber, Of whom he is buying it.

A Warrant To James Miller for the Bank before his Front Lott in Newc., req'ted by Jos. Pidgeon and Jam's Rolfe.

6 mo., 31st [1708.]

Present, Comm'rs.

Fran's Lovelace, Governor of Ne. York, by Pat. Entered in the records with Blank Date, Granted To Francis Whitwell, a tract of Land then reputed to Contain 400 acres, which being afterwards resurveyed about the year 1684, by ——— Mitchell, was returned for 1,000 acres. Fran's Whitwell dyeing, Wm. Southbe and Wm. Barry, adm'rs of his Estate, did, pursuant to the Laws then In force, Convey the Said Land, then Called 1,000 acres, to Jos. Growdon by Deed dat. 19, 11 mo. 1684. Jos. Growdon, By a warr't from the Comm'rs, dat. about the year 1686, procured the Same to be resurv'd and was found to Contain near 1,500 a's, but this Survey never was returned. Afterward the s'd Jos. Selling the s'd Land to James Steel and Thomas Sharp, they Procured it to be resurv'd more Exactly by warrant from this Board, dat. 20th Inst., upon the return of which it was found to Contain 1,340 acres, which being divided into 3 p'cels, the said Jos., by Deeds (dat. 1st and 2d 7ber, 1708), Conveys 714 acres to James Steel, and 626 acres To Tho's Sharp, of Kent County. This said Land haveing been Mortgaged by Jos. Growdon to the Owner of the Ship Isabelle, w'ch m'tgage He is Obliged To Clear; the respective Shares are to be released Only To Sharp and Steel, they Paying the rents.

The Prop'ry, by L. and rel., dat. 24th and 25th 8ber, Granted to Francis Plumstead, of the Minories, in Lond., Iron monger, 2,500 acres of Land. Fran's Plumstead, by Deeds dat. 2d and

3d of Feb'ry, 1707, Granted all the said Land To [Richard] Hill, his Heirs, &c., for £111 Sterling, with all Town Lotts, City Lotts, Lib. Land, &c. The land is laid out in Bucks County and Confirmed to Fran's Plumstead, the Lib. Land and 2 lotts on Delaware side are also laid out but not Confirmed. Rich'd Hill requests a warrant of Resurvey On the said Lib. Land, and Patents for that and the lotts.

The Comm'rs, by Warrant dat. 2d 10ber, 1684, Granted to Will'm Gregory 50 acres of head land in Right of his Servitude, and 50 a's On Rent. By will dat. 20th 6 mo., 1703, he left this to his wife for the maintenance of her Children, On Provisoe that she should not Marry, and when she did, to his son, Jno. Gregory, who is now possessed of it, being resur'd 'tis found to Contain 123 acres, for which he requests a Pat't, and 'tis granted, he paying all arrears for the whole 123 acres, and to Continue So hereafter.

8 mo., 11 [1708.]

Present, Griff. O., Tho. Storey and Jam's Logan.

Granted unto Peter Bizallon, Indian Trader (upon his humble request), free Liberty to build to himself a house and plant necessary fields for his Own Use on any of the Lands above Conestoga, not Possesst Or made use by the Indians, To be held by him dureing the Prop'ry's and Governor's pleasure Or his Lieuten't Or Comm'rs, and nolonger, he paying One Deer Skin yearly for the privilege.

Patent to Jos. Kirkbride for Five hundred and seventy-five a's. Min's Taken 2 mo., 1701.

8 mo., 15th [1708.]

The Prop'ry, by Deeds of L. and rel., dat. 28 and 29 of June, 1683, Granted To Nath'l Branson, of the parish of Soning, in the County of Berks, Shoemaker, 1,250 a. of Land, his Heirs, &c.

The s'd Nath'l Branson, by Deed dat. 28th Aug't, 1707, Granted all the s'd Land to his Son William Branson, his Heirs and assigns for Ever.

By Virtue of a Warrant from the Court at Upland, laid Out for Will. Jecox, a tract of Land Called Mount Seipput, Situated and being On the W't side of Delaware River, and on the East side of Skuylkill, beginning at a Corner Marked Gum Tree of Peter Rambo's Land, Standing by s'd Creek, from thence E't by N'h by said Rambo's Line of Marked Trees 160 Per's to a Corner marked Black Oak, from thence due W't by a Line of Markt Trees 170 p's to a Corner markt Black Oak, Standing by the side of Skool Creek, at the Mouth of a small run, from thence down the s'd Creek On sev'l Courses 200 P's to the first ment'd Gum, Containing 200 acres of Fast Land, Surv'd the 20th of May, 168 , p'r Rich'd Noble, Surveyor of Upland Court.

This Land has never yet been seated, Jecoxs' haveing almost Ever Since lived near Morris's River, in Jersey, at Island, nor are any Q't R'ts paid. Nath'l Baldwin Sollicits a Confirmation In behalf of s'd Jecock's, yet liveing. Said N. B. works with Jno. Bowers, Cooper, Jno. Gilbert's Son-in-Law. The Land by the Draught lies Between Peter Rambo and Rich'd Tucker, and I suppose is in Springetsbury.

———

11 mo., 7th [1708.]

About the year 1685 or 6 Wm. Guest Obtained One Grant for 50 a. On New Rent, In Newcastle County, near the Great Run, w'ch flows into Redclay Creek, and another Grant for 200 acres, all w'ch he sold to One Phileman Murfy, who sold 50 acres of it To Brian McDonald, and resigned the rest, as 'tis said, to One of Brian's Children, but without makeing any Improvements or paying Rent he left the Country. Jno. McDonald, Some time last year, viz: 1707, Agreed with James Logan for all this Land at £20 p'r C't, and 1s ster. Q't R't from that Time, according to which Bargain he requests a regular Grant and Confirmation.

Mem'dum, that On the 10th day of Jan'y, 1708-9, Wm. Snowdon. in the presence of Sam'l Carpenter and Caleb Pusey, did declare that Wm. Jecox had £60 Offered to him for his right to the s'd 200 acres of Land which he Claims near Philad'a by Virtue of a Survey by Rich'd Noble.

———

Do., 20th [1708.]

There haveing been a tract of 1,000 a's Surv'd To Benj'n Furly in the Welch tract, which has been granted since to D. Lloyd, and Is. Norris, in behalf of Thomas Lloyd's Estate, Jno. Henry Sproegle, to whom Dan'l Falkener, as attorney To said Benjamin, by Virtue of a power, dat. 23d Apr., 1700, recorded in Philad'a, Book D., 2, Vol. 5, pa. 17, &c., Granted his right to all the said Land, as also grant'd 1,000 acres more in Bucks, and 50 a's more untaken up, of the whole 5,000 a's, by Deed dat. 30, 6 mo., 1708, req'ts a warrant to take up the s'd 1,000 acres. Granted.

Cornelius Empson representing that there is a small Piece of vac't Land at the Upper End of Cheese and Bread Island, in a Neck between Whiteclay Creek and Redclay Creek, and Between the Lands of the said Island and that formerly belonging to Abraham Man, being the Same Spot, he sayes On which his mill Stands, placed there by Mistake, and desires the refusal of it. Ord'd a warrant to be directed to Is. Taylor, Henry Hollingsworth and Geo. Dakeyne first to Survey it.

Dan'l Williamson is Ord'd to have a pat., ment'd the 14th 3 mo., 1705, for which he pays £3 13s 4d, Consid'n Money, and £7 6s 0d in the whole for Q't R't.

Upon the resurvey of Cornelius Empson's Land, a dispute ariseing Concern'g the Bounds of that Island Called Bread and Cheese Island, w'ch was granted by Rich'd Nichols, by Pat. dat. 3d Aug't, 1668, To Thomas Jackson, Wooley Poulson and Thomas Snelling, by the Name of an Island, altho. it does not now appear to be Surrounded With Water, the persons Concerned it, Particularly Edward Robinson and Matth. Peterson desire a resurvey of it according to its true Bound.

---

12 mo., 14th [1708.]

At a Session. Present, Edward Sh., Griff. O., Jam's Logan.

Will'm Jecoxs, who is mentioned On the Other side, appearing himself, Claims either the 200 a's of Land w'ch were Surv'd to him in the year 1681, by Order of Upland Court, and are adjoyning to the N't Boundaries of ye Town, Or that he may have due Satisfact'n made to him for it, Upon which an Inquiry into the Survey'r's Office being made, it appears that the Prop'ry By his Warrant dated 16th 9mo., 1683, Granted to the s'd Jecox to take up 200 acres anywhere in the County of Philad'a Or Chester, but was never laid Out to him, and now Insists upon Satisfaction, Which being Considered, and Par'larly that the Prop'ry has been Obliged to make large Grants to Such Others as were disappointed of their Lands in Or near the place where the City Now Stands, Particularly Rich'd Tucker, the Swansons, Rambos, &c. It is Ordered he Shall have a Grant of 400 acres, to be Taken up as Other new Lands are, and upon the Same Terms, which he accepts in full Satisfaction and Gives his Bond to repay in Case it appear that he has hitherto directly Or Indirectly Rece'd any Manner of Satisfact'n for his said disappointment.

---

1 mo., 10th [1708-9.]

Sold by James Logan to Evan Will'm 500 a's of Land at Parkeominck, The same that was Adam Birche's, but is thrown up By him, for £125, With 3 mos.' Credit, without Interest, and from thence for 9 mo's upon Interest.

Sold to Jacob Vandegrift, Dan'l Cormuck, Albert Van Zant,

MINUTE BOOK "G." 499

500 acres of Land, with One hund'd acres of Marsh (if to be had) adjoyning On the meeting and St. Geo's Creek, in Newc. County, for £22 10s p'r C't, at 3 Equal payments in 3 years, each at the End of One year.

Do., 21 [1708–9.]

The Prop'ry, by Deeds of L. and Rel. dat. 11 and 12 July, 1681, Granted To Jno. Pennington, of Woodside, in the Parish of Agmondisham, Coun. Bucks, Gent., 1,250 a's Of Land in this Province, who by Ind'res of Lease and release, bearing date 1 and 2d May, 1704, Granted unto Jno. Clark, of Rotherhith, in the Co'ty of Surry, Blockmaker, all the s'd Land by him, his Heirs, &c. In right of This Jno. Estough desires Warr'ts for their Lands, as well those surv'd, as the Other Untaken up.

2 mo., 7th [1709.]

The Prop'ry, by Deed Poll dat. 15th 7ber, 1695, for £25, Granted to Jno. Pierson, of Hoveningham, in the County of Suffolk, Yeom'n, and his Heirs, &c., for 1,000 years, 750 acres of Land in this province, between Delaware and Susq., with all Lands, Isles, mines, minerals, Woods, Fishings, Hawkings, Huntings, Fowlings, and all Other Royalties, Profits, &c., Royal mines Excepted, and by Deed Poll, dat. 16, 7ber, 1695, release the same, but no Longer than the said 1,000 years under the yearly Rent of 1sh. p'r C't, to be Paid in Seven years Survey. But by an Indorsement under hand and Seal On ye Release, dat. 12 Apr., 1696, for a Competent Sum of Money released the whole Q't R't aforesaid of 1s p'r C't To the said Jno. Pierson, &c., for Ever. Jno. Pierson, by Deeds dat. 28 and 29 May, 1706, for £30, Granted the said Land to Thomas Hayward, al's Howard, and his wife Mary, &c., but the Deeds are to be renew'd from Pierson, haveing Come to an accident, he desires a Warrant, which is Granted.

Jonas Greenwood, in Behalf Of Others, makes the following req'ts: 100 acres to Will'm Copes upon the head of Touchberry's Neck, in Sussex; 100 a's To the Widdow Thorrald betwixt Dundee and Isaac's Branch, in Kent, both these to be Granted at 1d sterling p'r acre, granted 4th 5 mo, 1709; 50 acres To Jno. Swallow On the Tract Called Coventry, in Kent, to be granted On Such Terms as Jo'as Greenwood shall agree.

Charles Buckworth, Jno. Comb and Marcus, desireing to seat themselves On Land near Mahanatawny, Liberty is Granted them, they Purchasing the Same w'thin 12 mo's, as p'r a License Entered in the Book of Warrants. Anth'y Lee, late of Darby, makeing the Same req't has Liberty to Settle about 8 or 9 miles above Mahanatawny On the Same Terms.

Jno. Roades, of Sussex, by articles dat. 7th March last, Sold To Thomas England a tract of Land Called the New Forrest, near Rehoboth, laid Out for 580 acres, Granted By Order of Sussex Court 11, 11 mo., 1681, and Surv'd 25, 8 mo., 1682, and Confi'd by the Prop'ry's Patent 30th 1 mo., 1684, To Jno. Roades. But this Land being tried by Jonas Greenwood 'tis found Deficient. Roades has much Overplus In his Other Tracts adjoyning, wherefore Thomas England desires a resurvey and an Order to make up the Deficiency.

The Prop'ry, by Deeds of Lease and release, dat. 26th and 27th Sep'r, 1681, Granted To Edw'd Erberry of Bristol, Sopemaker, 500 a's of Land, which was once taken up, but by the Surv'r Otherwise disposed of, he Comeing over to this Country with his Son, was lost in Virginia, his Daughters, Eliz'th Jones, Widow, Mary Leach, Widow, and Ann Erberry, Single Woman, appoint Rob't Packer, of Philad'a, to be their attorney, who req'ts a Warrant to take up the said Land.

7 mo., 9th [1709.]

Present, Edw'd Shippen, Griff. O. and Jam's Logan.

Henry Hollingsworth, of Chester County, Survey'r, haveing pr'sented to the Rec'r Gen'l his acc't of Surveys, Resurveys and Other Services done for the Prop'ry and his Children, for which he demands according to the s'd acc't £243, and the said demand appearing much too Large, the Comm'rs met to Consider it, and after hearing all his many allegations of his great Fatigue and the disbursements which he had been obliged to make, after a full Examination of Every article, they thought fitt to reduce the whole To One Hundred and Seventy Six pounds 5s. of the Old Currency, according to the acc't by them Stated, which they agreed (if he would acquiesce), should be made good to him, includeing what he had Already rec'd, But the s'd Henry Insisting upon it, that tho' he was willing to abate as much as he could w'th any Justice to himself and Family, Yet he Cou'd not afford to accept of this Proposal, and therefore desired that he might have a grant of Some Land to make it up. It was at Length agreed Between the Comm'rs and him that he shou'd accept the said Sum of £176 5s In full pay from the Prst. Rec'r, and that he might apply to the Prop'ry for any further additional Grant of Land, upon his arrival, that if he should think fit of himself, Graciously and not Otherwise, To make to Him.

Geo. Harland desires a Patent On 200 acres In Brumingham, sold him December, 1701, to his Son-in-Law Henry Hollingsworth, also Four hundred and seventy acres On New Rent in Kennet, which he has Cleared.

7 mo., 14th [1709.]

At a Session of the Comm'rs held the 14 September, 1709.
Prst., Edw'd Shippen, Griff. Owen and James Logan.
With Caleb Pusey, Rich'd Hill and Samuel Preston.

The Swedes, who Presented that abusive Petition to the assembly Concern'g their Lands, haveing desired a Meeting with the Comm'rs, divers of them met at the Sec'ry's Office, and being demanded what it is they Complain off, they said that the Prop'ry at his first Comeing Into this Province Promised them that he would be as a Father To Them, and that he Came not to Lessen Or Take away their Rights, but to Confirm them to them, but that Soon after he demanded a Sight of all their Pat's, which were delivered To him, that these had been detained from Them, and that many of Them had a Considerable P't of the Lands they hold by these Pat's taken from them, and that they were obliged To pay for the Lands they held Greater Q't R'ts than they had formerly Paid, which they Conceived to be greatly to their wrong. They were asked Concerning their allegation that they knew not they were Obliged to pay any Quit Rents to the Prop'ry, being Servants to the Crown. To this they answered that they knew not to whom they Ought to pay their Q't R'ts, that they were willing to Pay them to the Prop'ry if it appeared that he had a Right to them, which they said had not been hitherto made appear To Them. They were taxed hereupon with presumption in pleading Ignorance now in this Matter after they had lived 27 years under the Prop'ry's Government and Could not be but Sensible that the whole Country had been granted to the Prop'ry by a patent from King Charles the 2d, and that by all Men it had been acknowledged to be solely his, that he had the sole disposal of Lands in it and all the Queen's Subjects here had from that time acknowledged him their Land Lord and prop'ry, as well as Governor. They were told that when the Prop'ry took their patents he Intended a Kindness to them in it designing Nothing but to give Them Certain and Unquestionable Titles for what was very uncertain and doubtfull before. That all those who applyed To him had Such patents for all the Lands they Possessed before, and if Every One of them had not Procured the like it was Entirely their Own Faults That the Sec'ry, as he declared, neither now has nor never had One of their patents nor did he Ever demand any further Or greater Rents of them than a Bushel of Wheat for Every 100 a's of Land they held, that This was the Original Contract with the Government of York for their lands at first, and therefore no Pretence whatsoever, Should Excuse Or Exempt them from the Obligation. That if any of their Lands had been Taken from any of them, as it was a private Injury to that Person, so it must be Considered.

Matthias Netzilius and Jno. Hendrickson Complained in particular that Rich'd Tucker and Wm. Smith had unjustly Obtained One-half of the said Land which was now the said Matthias's right, and that Charles Ashcomb had as unfairly taken Off 300 acres from His tract, for which they In Particular desired Reparation. And the Comm'rs promising them to hear and Consider their Particular Complaints at a Conven't Time next week, they all Withdrew without haveing any further to say.

Jno. Estough Desires a Warrant of Resurvey On the Lands of Wm. Shardlow, purchased Joyntly with Wm. Wood, but Since divided by a writt of Partition, w'ch Lands are half the Lib. Land, half of 500 acres On Skuylkill, half of 2,000 acres in East Town, in the Welch Tract, allow'd by the Welch, and half the Remainder of 138 acres adjoyning that, have not been disposed of, besides which they Sold. 600 acres in Darby. Granted.

Edward Green, by Virtue of several Orders of Newcastle Court, Took up 2,500 acres of Land near the Road and not far from George's Creek, in the said County, and by Deeds, dat.   , Sold ye Same To Jno. Scott, whose Son and Heir, Walter Scott, of Bohemia, in Maryland, by Deed dat. Granted the Same to Matthias Vanbebber, who requests resurvey and Patent. Rec'ts are Produced for Payments of Quitt Rents in full To 1691 at Old Rent. Granted.

These are to certify that the foregoing Sheets Contained in this Book, No. 16, in the whole, amounting to four hundred and eight-five Pages, are true Copies of the originals found in the office of the Secretary, and that the same were carefully compared with the said originals by me dureing my appointment as recorder of Warrants and Surveys under the act of assembly passed in the 33d Year of his late Majesties' Reign, entiutled "an act for recording Warrants and Surveys and for rendering the real estates and Properties within this Province more secure."

p. JO'N HUGHES.

Signed in the Presence of

THO'S LEITH,
JOHN MORTON,
SAMUEL RHOADS,
JAMES WRIGHT,
HENRY WYNKOOP.

MINUTE BOOK "H."

MINUTES OF PROPERTY BEGINNING 9TH DAY OF THE SECOND MONTH, 1712. THIS IS BOOK "H." IN THE SECRETARIES OFFICE.

At a Meeting of the Commissioners of Property at Philadelphia the 9th day of the Second Month, 1712.

James Logan, being lately returned from England, presented to the Commissioners hereinafter named, and convened for that purpose, a Commission from the Proprietary under the great Seal of the Province, bearing date the 9th of November last past, also an Instrument under the hands and Seals of all the Trustees named for raising a certain Sum of Money out of this Province, which has been duly proved here, and with the s'd Commission entered upon record, both of which were read in the following words, viz't.

[The Proprietor's Commission under the Great Seal.]

William Penn, Esquire, True and absolute Proprietary and Governor in Chief of the Province of Pensilvania, and Counties of Newcastle, Kent and Sussex, upon Delaware: To all to whom these presents Shall come Sends Greeting, To the End that during my necessary absence from my Said Province and Counties, All persons who have a right and Just Claim to any Lotts, Lands or Hereditaments therein by Purchase from me in England, or otherwise, which have not hitherto been Surveyed and confirmed to them, may obtain the same, And that all others who would Make further Purchase or take up any vacant Lands may be accommodated, and all other Matters necessary for the Improvement or Settlement of the said Province and Countys may be as fully and amply transacted as if I were personally present there; Know Ye that I have thought fitt to appoint, and do by these presents nominate, Constitute and appoint my Trusty and well beloved ffriends, Edward Shippen, Samuell Carpenter, Richard Hill, Isaac Norris and James Logan, all of the said Province, in whose Integrity and prudence I do very much confide, to be my proprietary Deputies or Commissioners of Property, to have the care and management of all my lands and Estate in the Said Province and Counties, Giving hereby and Granting to my Said Deputies, Edward Shippen, Samuell Carpenter, Richard Hill, Isaac Norris and James Logan, full Power and Authority by Warrants under their hands, or the hands of any three of them, and my provincial Seal, to Grant and Cause to be laid out to all persons duly applying for the Same, all Such vacant Lands and Lotts of Land in the Said Province or Counties as have been heretofore legally Purchased of me or of persons duly Impowered by me, or hereafter shall be so Purchased or Rented by any Contract made, or to be made with me or my said Deputies. I do also by these presents Grant to my Said Deputies full power and authority for me and in my name by Instruments under their hands, or the hands of any three of them, and my Greater Provincial Seal, to Grant and Confirm to all and every Such person and persons, all Such Lands and Lotts of Land as aforesaid after they Shall be duly laid out and Surveyed according to the regulation for the laying out and Surveying of Lands and Lotts in the said Province and Counties; To hold to Such person or persons and their heirs or Executors and assigns for Such Estate and Estates, and under Such Rents and Services to be reserved to me and my heirs as have been or hereafter with my Said Deputies Shall respectively be agreed for, all which Instruments for granting and confirming of Lands and Lotts, Tenements and Hereditaments that have been or Shall be purchased or Rented as aforesaid, be'g past under my Great'r Seal and entered upon record in the Rolls Office of the Said Province. I do by these presents, for me and my heirs, fully and absolutely ratifie, Confirm and make valid to all Intents and Purposes according to the respective Tenours of the Same to be firm, unquestionable and indefeazable Titles to the respective Grantees and their heirs and assigns, and Shall be Good, Effectual and available in the Law against me and my heirs and assigns according to the true meaning and Intent of every Such Grant respe'ly, Provided always, that nothing Contained in any Such grant or Instrument Shall be contrary or Repugnant to any written Instructions which I Shall at any time Give to my Said Deputies, which Instructions Shall be Publick and upon record in the Rolls Office of the said Province, and for the further Encouragement of Purchasers of Larger Tracts of Lands in the said Province and Counties I do by these presents Grant to my Said Deputies my full power and Authority for me and in my name by Such Instruments as aforesaid to erect, or Cause to be erected, any Larger Tracts or parcells of Land in the Said Province or Counties into Mann'rs for holding of Court Barons and View of ffrankpledge, according to the powers Granted unto me for that purpose by the Royall Letters Pattent of King Charles, the Second, of happy memory. I do also hereby Authorise and Impower my Said Deputies, Edw'd Shippen, Samuell Carpenter, Richard Hill, Isaac Norris and James Logan, or any three of them, by comm'n under their hands and my Provincial Seal, to constitute and appoint all Officers as Surveyors, Rangers and Such others who are immediately Concerned in the affairs of my Lands or Estate, or in whom any trust may be reposed for executing any matter or thing between me as Proprietor of the said Province or Counties and any of the people thereof, and to do and execute, or Cause to be done or Executed, all and every Such Act and Acts, thing and things whatsoever necessary for the regulating, well ordering and Securing or managing of any of my Proprietary affairs in the said Province or Counties, or any affairs depend'g between me and any of the ffreeholders, Tennants or Inhabitants thereof as fully and amply to all Intents and purposes as if I were personally present. And I do hereby Specially Authorize and Impower the Said Edward Shippen, Samuell Carpenter, Richard Hill and Isaac Norris, or any three of them, to make up, State and Settle all accounts now depending between me and the said James Logan as my receiver Generall, or that hereafter may depend between me and him or my other Receivors, and upon adjusting and Setling the Ballance for me, and in my behalf to give him a Discharge or Discharges, which Shall be Valid and Effectual, and I do hereby, for me and my heirs and Executors, fully and absolutley ratifie and Confirm whatsoever my Said Deputies, or any three of them, Shall do in pursuance and in the due Execution of these presents. In Witness whereof I have hereunto Sett my hand and Caused my Great Seal of the Said Province to be affixed this 9th 9ber, 1711.

This Indenture made the tenth day of November, anno Domini 1711, and in the Tenth year of the Reigne of our Sovereign Lady Ann, Queen of Great Britain, &c., Between William Penn, Proprietary and Governor of the Province of Pensilvania, in America; Henry Gouldney, of London, Linnen-Draper; Joshua Gee, of London, Silkman; Silvanus Grove, of London, Merchant; John Woods, of London, Merchant; Thomas Callowhill, of the City of Bristoll, Merchant; Thomas Oade, of the Said City of Bristoll, Gentleman; Jeffery Pennell, of the Said City of Bristoll, Merchant, and John Field, of London, Haberdassher, of the one part, and Edward Shippen, Samuell Carpenter, Richard Hill, Isaac Norris and James Logan, of Philadelphia, in the Province of Pensilvania, Merchants, of the other part.

Whereas by Indentures of Lease and release, bearing date respectively the Sixth and Seventh days of October, in the year of our Lord one thousand seven hundred and Eight, made, or mentioned to be made Between William Penn, by the name of William Penn, the Elder, of London, Esquire, and William Penn, of London, Gentleman, Son and heir apparent of the Said William Penn, the Elder, of the one part, and the said Henry Gouldney, Joshua Gee, Silvanus Grove, John Woods, Thomas Callowhill, Thomas Oade, Jeffery Pennell and John Field and Thomas Cuppage, of Lambstone, in the Parrish of Whitchurch, in the County of Wexford, in the Kingdom of Ireland, Gentlemen, Since deceased, of the other part, on Consideration of Six thousand and Six hundred pounds in the Said recited Indenture of Release, mentioned to be paid unto the Said William Penn, the Elder, and of Tenn Shillings to the said William Penn, the younger, as in the Said Indentures of Release is mentioned. They, the Said William Penn, the Elder, and William Penn, the younger, did Grant, Release and Convey unto Henry Gouldney, Joshua Gee, Silvanus Grove, John Woods, Thomas Callowhill, Thomas Oade, Jeffery Pinnell, John Field and Thomas Cuppage, and their heirs and assigns forever, All That Tract of Land or province called Pensilvania, in America, and all and every the ffields, woods, Rivers, Duties, Mannors, Territories and Hereditaments therein or thereunto belonging, and all the rents, arrears of Rent, Services, Issues and proffits thereof, and all that the Town of Newcastle, otherwise called Delaware, and all that Tract of Land lieing within the Compass or Circle of Twelve Miles about the Same upon the River Delaware, in America, and the Said River and the Soil thereof, together with all rents, arrears of rent, Services, Royalties, Liberties and Priviledges thereunto belonging, and all that Tract of Land upon Delaware River and Bay, beginning Twelve Miles South of the Towne of Newcastle, otherwise called Delaware, and Extending South to the Whore Kills, otherwise called Capen Lopen, and all Rent and arrears of rent thereof (Saving all rents and liberties reserved to his late Royall highness, James, Duke of York, and his heirs), and all other the Lands, Tenements and Hereditaments of them, the said William Penn, the Elder, and William Penn, the younger, or either of them, within the said Province, Townes, Tracts of Land and Territories aforesaid, or any of them (Except the said William Penn, the Elder, and William Penn, the Younger, the Mannor of——and four thousand acres of Land thereunto belonging, and Except five thousand acres of land which were Conveyed by the Said William Penn, the Elder, to the s'd William Penn, the Younger, by lease and release, dated the one and Twentieth and two and Twentieth days of October, in the year one thousand Six hundred Eighty-one), and Excepting all messages, Lands, Tenements, City Lotts, and Town Lotts and hereditaments conveyed by the Said William Penn, the Elder, to Tobias Collet, Michael Russell, Daniell Quare and Henry Gouldney by Lease and release, dated respectively the Eleventh and Twelfth days of August, one thousand Six hundred ninety-nine, and except five thousand acres of Land Granted and Conveyed by the Said William Penn, the Younger, to Isaac Norris and William Trevil and their heirs, and all other Lands Granted by the said William Penn, the Elder, for which quitt rents and other Rents are reserved, And all the Estate, Right, Title, Interest, Trust, possession, Property, Claim and demand whatsoever of them, the Said William Penn, the Elder, and William Penn, the Younger (except as before mentioned to be excepted of into or out of the Same Premisses), with a Proviso in the Said recited Indenture of release Contained for making void the Same upon the payment of the Sum of Six thousand and Six hundred pounds, and Interest thereof at the rate of Six pounds p. Cent. p'r annum, on the Eighth day of October last past, before the date of these presents, and by the Said recited Indenture of Release the said William Penn, the Elder, did agree that in Case the Said Sum of Six thousand and Six hundred pounds, with the Interest, Should not be paid on or before the 8th day of October last; then the Said Henry Gouldney Joshua Gee, Silvanus Grove, Jno. Woods, Thomas Callowhill, Thomas Oade, Jeffery Pennell, John Field and Thomas Cuppage, or the Survi'rs of them, Should and might Sell and dispose of any Part of any or all the said Premisses for the Best price they or their Agents or Att'ry could get for the Same, and by the Said recited Indentures of Release the said William Penn the Elder, did assigne unto the Said Henry Gouldney, Joshua Gee, Silvanus Grove, John Woods, Thomas Callowhill, Thomas Oade, Jeffery Pennell, John Field and Thomas Cuppage, their Executors, administrators and assigns, all and every the quitt rents, rents, arrears of rent, Sum and Sums of money due or grow due to the Said William Penn, the Elder, within the Said Province, Tract of Land and Prem'es, and all Bonds, Bills and Securities for money due to him in the Said Province, and all other Debts therein due to him from his Deputies, Secretarys, Receivers, Stewards, Surveyors, Officers, Servants, Tennants, or any other person or persons whatsoever, and by the Said Recited Indenture of Release the Said William Penn, the Elder, did make and appoint the Said Henry Gouldney, Joshua Gee, Silvanus Grove, John Woods, Thomas Callowhill, Thomas Oade, Jeffery Pennell, John Field and Thomas Cuppage, and the Survivor or Survivors of them, and the Major Part of them, or of the Survivors of them, his True and Lawfull attorney and attorneys to ask, demand, Sue for, recover and receive for all persons whatsoever all and every, of rents, Debts, Securitys and Premisses therein mentioned to be assigned, and for that purpose to make and Constitute under them one or more Attorney or Attorneys, Agent or Sollicitor, to ask, receive and Sue for the Said Debts and premisses, and to do any other act or acts Concerning the Same, and by the Said recited Indenture of Release the Said William Penn, the Elder, did agree that it sh'od be lawfull for the Said Henry Gouldney, Joshua Gee, Silvanus Grove, John Woods, Thomas Callowhill, Thomas Oade, Jeffery Pennell, John FField and Thomas Cuppage, or the Survivor of them, or the major Part of the Survivors of them, their Attorneys or Agents and assigns, to remitt and Send all such Sum and Sums of money and Effects as Should be raised either by Sale of the Said Lands and Hereditaments, or by the Said Rents and Debts to London by Bills of Exchange, or in Merchandizes directly, or by way of Barbadoes and the Leeward Islands, or by any other ways howsoever, and to make Insurance upon the Same as they should think fitt at the hazard and Charge of the Said William Penn, the Elder, as by the Said recited Indentures of Lease and release, relation unto them respectively being had may more fully appear, And Whereas, the Said Sum of Six thousand and Six hundred pounds Principal Money, with a Considerable Sum for Interest, Still remains due; Now for the raising and paying off the Same pursuant to the Said recited Indentures of Lease and release and Mortgage, This Indenture witnesseth that the Said Henry Gouldney, Joshua Gee, Silvanus Grove, John Woods, Thomas Callowhill, Thomas Oade, Jeffery Pennell and John FField, Have and each of them hath (by and with the Consent of the said William Penn, the Elder, Testified by his being a Party to and Sealing and executing these presents), made, ordained, Constituted, authorized and appointed, and by these presents do, and each of them doth make, ordain, constitute, authorize and appoint the Said Edward Shippen, Samuell Carpenter, Richard Hill, Isaac Norris and James Logan, or any three of them, their and every of their true and lawfull attorneys and agents to Sell and Dispose of all or any Part of the Said Province, Lands, Tenements, Rents and Hereditaments by the Said recited Indentures of Lease and Release, Granted and conveyed, or mentioned to be conveyed, to the Said Henry Gouldney, Joshua Gee, Silvanus Grove, John Woods, Thomas Callowhill, Thomas Oade, Jeffery Pennell, John Field and the Said Thomas Cuppage, deceased for the best price that can be gotten for the

Same, and to ask, demand, Sue for, recover and receive of and from all Person and Persons whatsoever, all Bonds, Securities, Rent, Sum and Sums of money, Dues and Demands, or any of them, and to accept part in Satisfaction for the whole, and to give Good and Sufficient discharges and acquittances for the Same Debts, Rents, Sum and Sums of money, dues and demands, and in Case of non-payment to Sue, prosecute and defend for and concerning the Same Debts and premisses in any Court or Courts of Law or Equity, and the Said Henry Gouldney, Joshua Gee, Silvanus Grove, John Woods, Tho's Callowhill, Thomas Oade, Jeffery Pennell and Jno. Field, with the consent of the Said William Penn, the Elder, Testified as aforesaid, Do hereby Authorize, Impower and direct the Said James Logan and Isaac Norris Jointly or Severally, or the Surviv'r of them, his Executors and administrators, to receive, remitt and Send all Such Sum and Sums of money and effects as Shall be raised by the Sale of the Said Lands and premisses, or by the said Debts or otherwise in pursuance of these presents to London to the Said Henry Gouldney, Joshua Gee, Silvanus Grove, John Woods, Thom's Callowhill, Thomas Oade, Jeffery Pennell and John FField, or any Three of them, by Bills of Exchange or in Silver, or in Merchandizes directly, or by way of Barbadoes and Leeward Islands, or by any other Ways whatsoever, and to make Insurance of or upon the Same, And the Said Henry Gouldney, Joshua Gee, Sylvanus Grove, John Woods, Thomas Callowhill, Thomas Oade, Jeffery Pennell and John Field, do hereby Give and Grant unto the Said Edward Shippen, Samuell Carpenter, Richard Hill, I. Norris and James Logan, or any three of them, their full and whole Power and Authority as their agents or attorneys, which they or the major part of them can or may Grant to their Agents or Attorneys for the purposes aforesaid, by virtue of the Said recited Indentures of Lease and release, except as to the receiving and remitting Such Sum and Sums of money and Effects as Shall be raised, and do hereby declare and agree with Edward Shippen, Samuell Carpenter, Richard Hill, Isaac Norris and James Logan to make and Execute Such further Assurance and Conveyance of Such Lands, Tenem'ts, rents, Hereditaments, as they shall contract for or Sell to Such Persons as Shall Contract for or purchase the same with or from the said Edward Shippen, Samuell Carpenter, Richard Hill, Isaac Norris, James Logan, or the major Part of them, as Shall be reasonably devised, advised or required, and to ratifie and Confirm all and whatsoever Shall lawfully be done in pursuance of these presents, And the Said William Penn, the Elder, doth hereby ratifie and Confirm these presents, and the Power and Authority hereby Given to the Said Edward Shippen, Samuell Carpenter, Richard Hill, Isaac Norris and James Logan, or any three of them, and unto the said James Logan and Isaac Norris, or either of them, and doth hereby for himself, his heirs, Executors and administrators, Covenant and agree with the Said Edward Shippen, Samuell Carpenter, Richard Hill, Isaac Norris and James Logan, their heirs, Ex'ors and administrators that he, the Said William Penn, his heirs, Executors and adm'ors, shall and will Give and execute such further assurance and Conveyance of all or any Part of the said Premises which shall be sold pursuant to these presents to any Purchaser and Purchasers as shall be reasonably devised or required, and to ratifie and Confirm all and whatsoever Shall be lawfully done in pursuance of these presents. In Witness whereof the said Parties to these presents Have to these present Indentures Interchangeably Sett their Hands and Seals the day and year first above written.

    Wm. Penn,   Hen. Gouldney,
    Silvanus Grove,   Joshua Gee,
    Tho. Oade,   Jno. Woods,
    Jno. Field,   Tho's Callowhill.
    Jeffery Pennell,

 Sealed and Delivered by the within named Jno. Woods in the presence of us, Robert Pim, at Toms' Coffee house, Harbert Springett, in Birchin lane.

 Sealed and delivered, being first duly Stamped by the within named William Penn, Hen. Gouldney, Silvanus Grove, Jno. Field and Joshua Gee, in the presence of us,

    Thomas Norton,   Thomas Grey,
    John Annis,   Jos. Davis.

 Sealed and delivered by the said Thomas Callowhill, Thomas Oade and Jeffery Pinnell, in the presence of us,

    Brice Webb,   Sinan Baxord.
    Margaret Williams,

 Be it Remembered that the fourth day of the Second Month, in the year of our Lord one thousand Seven hundred and Twelve, before me, Nathan Stanbury, one of the Justices of the Peace of the City and County of Philadelphia, Came the above named Jno. Annis in his Proper Person and upon his Solemn Affirmation did declare and Say that he was personally present and Saw the within named Wm. Penn, Henry Gouldney, Silv. Grove, Jno. FField and Joshua Gee Sign, Seal, and as his Act and Deed, Deliver this writing or Instrument, and that his name Subscribed to the Same was of his own Proper handwriting. In Witness whereof I have hereunto Sett my hand and Seal the day and year first above written.

NATHAN STANBURY.

Be it Remembered that Charles Brockdon, Deputy Recorder of Deeds for the City and County of Philadelphia, was personally present when the above named John Annis did before the said Justice prove the Signing, Sealing and Delivery of the Said writing by the Said William Penn, Henry Gouldney, Silvanus Grove, John FField and Joshua Gee in manner and form aforesaid. Whereupon the said Justice having Certified the said Proofs, made the Day and Year in Manner and Form aforesaid, as the late Act of Assembly in that Behalf directs, did deliver the Said Writing to me to be entered of record, and the Same is recorded in the Inrollment Office at Philadelphia, in Book E., 7 Vol. and pa. 125, &ca., the ffourth day of the Second month, in the year of our Lord one thousand Seven hundred and Twelve. In Witness whereof I have hereunto sett my hand and Seal of my Office.

At a meeting of the Commissioners the Seventh of the 3d Month, 1712.

Present, Edward Shippen, Richard Hill, Isaac Norris, James Logan.

Joseph Growdon presented a petition to the Board Complaining that the Lotts due to his purchase of 5,000 Acres had not been regularly or duly laid out and thereupon Craved redress vide Petition.

He shews also that he brought into this Province 45 Servants, for each of whom he conceives he has a Right to take up 50 acres of Land. He requests also the Purchase of a small Piece of Vacant Land on Schuylkill River, next above the Cause'y, leading to B. Chambers' fferry, which Petition being read, the first and last were referred to farther Consideration, and upon the Second he is desired to produce his Right of Claim.

Thomas Story produces Deeds of L. and R. dated the 17th and 18th of 8ber, 1711, from Mary Coney, Daughter, devisee and Ex'rx of the last Will of Ann Coney, deceased, Sole daughter and heir to Henry Waddy, purchaser of 750 acres of Land in this Pro., by Deeds dated 25th and 26th of 7ber, 1681, Granting to the Said Thomas 188 acres of Land in Warminster, Coun. Bucks, also 12 Acres of Liberty Land in the city liberties, appurtenant to the s'd Purchase, together with one Second Street Lott of 51 foot in Breadth, bounding on Vine

Street, and one other lott further Back, 49 feet in Breadth and 198 feet in Length, both laid out in right of the Said Purchase of 750 acres, of all which he requests a Confirmation, but upon the Resurvey of the Land in Bucks 'tis found to Contain only 170 acres, and the Liberty Land being also resurveyed 'tis found to be deficient near two acres more; he therefore Craves a Warrant to take up those 20 Acres, which is Granted and this day Signed.

Ordered also a pattent for the Lib. Land and Lotts, including the Liberty Land of Richard Snead's purchase, lieing Contiguous to the other, and now Surveyed in a Tract. He also Craves a warrant of Survey on the Lotts belonging to Said Snead's purchase of 1,500 acres. Deeds from the Prop'r., dat. 26th and 27th 7ber, 1681.

Deeds from R. Snead to Th. Story, dat.   , for his whole purchase. Granted.

T. Story also produces a writing in paper with the Proprietor's name and the lesser Seal of the Province affixed to it, dated the 8th 2d month, 1700, Granting to the said Thomas one thousand acres of Land upon Delaware, above the manner of Highlands, also a Receipt for £33 6s 8d, dated 24, 4 Month, 1700, wrote in Thomas's own hand, as is also the aforement'd Grant, which Land being in the Poss'ion of Purchasers and other settlers on the same, he craves an Equivalent for it elsewhere.

But the word Highlands Twice in the Grant and once in the Receipt, being in every place on a manifest Rasure, he was asked the Cause, and upon Some further Discourse he declared the Matter thus: that the Proprietor at his last arrivall finding him here after Some time pressed him to stay in this Government, to be assistant therein, and particularly at the Councill Board; that upon this Motion Thomas objected that it might be looked on as irregular and unreasonable by the people that a person who was a stranger amongst them and very lately Come into the Place, and had no Interest in the Country, nor was so much as a ffreeholder, Shou'd be concerned in its Gov't To obviate which the prop'rr proposed that he wou'd make him a Grant which wou'd Shew him to be a ffreeholder, and accordingly desired him to draw an Instrument for it, which was done and dated as above Said; that in the 4th Month following, being to Enter into the Councill, he represented to the Proprietor that it wou'd be loss of So much time to him, which having nothing but his own Industry to depend on, he Cou'd not spare, that he must be considered for it; That thereupon the Prop. Gave him the above mentioned receipt, tho' he confesses he never paid anything upon it; That the Prop. in giving him directions at first for drawing the Grant, named two mannors to him, Gilberts and Highlands; that that on the river was pitched on, but that he mistook the name, Calling it Gilberts instead of Highlands, that this Mistake appearing it was rectified by a Rasure, as now appears.

[But here 'tis to be remembered that these rasures were made after, or at least not before the 24th of the 4th Month, the day the date of the Receipt, tho' the patent was Executed (as appears elsewhere) at least Ten Weeks before. 'Tis to be observed also that at the time T. S. was first introduced into the Councill his Commission was delivered to him and read at the Board, appointing him Keeper of the Great Seal, which was then put into his hands, and M'r of the Rolls, &c., as appears by the Minutes of the Councill of the 26th, 4th Month, 1700, p. P. Robinson.]

John Gumly, desiring to purchase a Piece of Vacant Land, formerly in the possession of one Francis Letts, in Bomboyhook, being between the lands of John Pound and Samuel Bayard, reputed to contain about 70 acres, which for want of Special Heirs are now fallen to the Proprietor, 'tis agreed that in Case it Shall be duly escheated at his Charge (not exceeding 5ct in the whole, to him, and the rest to be born by the Prop', he shall have it at Ten Shillings p. acre, and on these Terms a Warrant is Granted, dated this day.

John Cartlidge, a small Piece of Vacant Land in the upper Side of the Main Branch of Duck Creek, opposite to Some Land he has lately purchased of the Widow Green. But being found to be Improved and a Mill built on it by William Burrows, 'tis denied him unless he first purchase those improvements.

Griffith Nicholas requests leave to take up about 500 Acres near Elk River, where the Bounds of the Provinces are uncertain, for which he wou'd pay Rent; he offers three Bushells of Wheat p. c. p. annum.

———

At a meeting of the Commissioners 10th 3 Mo., 1712.

Present, Edward Shippen, Isaac Norris, Richard Hill, J. Logan.

The late Commisisoners having Granted to Brian and John McDonald a Tract of Land in Christina Hund. and Newc. Count. cont.   acres, Part of w'ch one Morton Justassen, Claiming by Purchase from William Jessox, who is said to have taken it up. The Said Morton, upon a Letter to him from the Secretary, appeared before the Board to make his

Claims and produce a Survey and Draught of 200 Acres of Land laid out to Wm. Jessox, Situate between William Guess and Francis Gilletts' land, Said to be Surveyed the 25th of the 6th Month, 1684, but is wrote (apparently) in Hen. Hollingsworth's Hand, 'tis directed to Wm. Welch, and Said to be in Obedience to his Warr., but their appears none either from him or the Commissioners, 'tis confessed to be on New rent, viz't a penny Sterl'g p. acre, but none appears to be paid.

The Commissioners, notwithstanding the Claim appears So very uncertain and Groundless, yet agree upon their paying the past Arrears of Quit rent to give the Claimer a New Grant for 200 Acres of the Vacant Land lieing in or near the Same Place. See the Copy of their Return taken literally p. K.

Mathias Pieterson, being possessed of 300 acres on the North Side of Christina Creek, which on resurvey Contains above 600 Acres, he desires that Andrew Justassen, who appears with him, may have the Overplus; they offer only Arrears of Quitt rent.

The Proprietor, by Deeds dated 5th and 6th 7ber, 1681, Granted to William Withers, of Bisshops Canning, in the County of Wilts, yeom., 500 Acres, which the said William, by Deed of Gift, dated 22d January, 1682, demised to his Son, Thomas Withers, for two thousand years, and to his heirs and assigns, &c. Thomas Withers, in the year 1683, coming over into this Province, took up the Said Land in the township of Chichester, but by giving way to Neighbors fell short of his Quantity by 68 acres. At the Proprietor's last Coming into this Province Tho's applied to him for the Said Deficiency, and obtained a Warrant dated 28, 10 month, 1700, for 100 acres, w'ch on the 27th 1st month following were laid out in the Township of Kennett and the County of Chester, and the Said Thomas desires a Pattent for the Same. By the Warrant p't of this 100 acres is said to be in right of his Father's purchase, and the other part (viz) 32 acres, to be yet purchased, but he acco'ts the prop'r Gave him the whole, he having no Allowance for Roads in his Tract of 432 Acres, and is disappointed of the Quantity Granted him in a much more valuable place; ordered a Pattent.

At a meeting of the Commissioners the 28th of the 3d Month, 1712.

Present, Edward Shippen, Samuel Carpenter, James Logan.

Randall Vernon having purchased of Thomas Powell 200 acres in Edgem't and claiming 100 more adjoining, in right of one, Sarah Dole, half a Servant's Land and half on rent, also another 100 in right of one, Rawlinson. on Rent, to w'ch not withstanding he is not at present able to prove a Suff'ct Title, and there being a vacancy adjoining between him and his next neighbor, so that the whole, including the 200 he has a right to and the other 200 that he claims, contains 531 acres. He desires a Grant of the whole Said quantity and agrees to pay in one Month, or interest on forbearance, Thirty pounds p. hundred acres, for all he cannot prove a right to the Satisfaction of this Board within the time aforesaid, vide his right entered.

Moses Key having some weeks agoe agreed for the Proprietor's 500 Acres in Marlborow, at £17 10s 0d p. C, viz't. £87 10s for the whole; he desires the Board to Confirm his Bargain and Grant him a Pattent thereon, w'ch is Granted. Moses Key having purchased of Thomas Moor, of Concord, 100 acres in that Township, taken upon rent, and by the Prop'rs Warrant, dated the 19th 7ber, 1701, resurveyed to the Said Thomas; he now produces a Return of that Resurvey, by which the Said Land is found to contain 120 Acres, and requesting a Pattent; he agrees to pay the arrears of Rent for the s'd 20 acres to this time, which for 28 years is £2 6s 8d sterling or £3 2s 3d of the p'sent Currency, and to Continue the Same Rent for the whole hereafter, and this Proposall being Equivalent to £40 p. C. for the Ten Acres which he might be obliged to purchase or cutt off; 'tis accepted and a pattent ordered. Deed from Thomas Moor to Moses Key, dated 23, 3 Month, 1702, passed in Court the 26th of the Same Month. Consideration for the whole £60.

———

At a meeting of the Commissioners, 31st 3 month, 1712.

Present, Edward Shippen, Samuel Carpenter, Richard Hill, Isaac Norris, James Logan.

The Board being Mett to Consider of Some Bills prepared by the Assembly to be passed into Laws, which Concerned the Proprietor's Estate, viz't one for Confirming Pattents and Grants, one for regulating the Lower Ferry, on Schuylkill, called B. Chambers's Ferry, and another for regulating the Ferries over Delaware and Neshamineh, they agreed on the necessary Amendm'ts to the first to be proposed to the Govern'r, which the Secretary was ordered to draw up to be laid before the Govern'r and Councill, and to be by him proposed in the Proprietor's behalf to the Assembly.

To the 2d B. Chambers appeared, and having Some time before made a proposal to the Board in writing that in Case the Comm'rs wou'd in the Proprietor's behalf agree to the

Bill then in agitation in his Favor, he wou'd advance to the propriet'r a sum of Money in Consideration of the Same, and this Matter having been discoursed at the last Sitting of the Board, he now further made it appear that having farmed or leased out the Said Ferry to a Tenant he rece'd no more than £32 p. annum for his House, Boats, wharfs and all his Conveniencies, out of which Benjamin himself made Good the repairs, that allowing out of this £8 p. ann. for the rent of the house, £6 for repairs and £3 for the Interest of about £40, which he will be obliged forthwith to lay out on the hither Caseway, there remains to him only £15 p. annum Clear profitt for all his Improvements in wharfs, roads, &c., of which he is willing to allow one-fifth part, But at length agreed to pay £50 down for the Prop'rs assent and his negotiation of the Act when passed here, with the Ministry at home.

The 3d Act being only for 7 years and the Proprietor's right appearing to be Sufficiently asserted in, it was agreed to.

Richard Darkin, of N. Jersey w'ch Sa. Carp'r, exhibited to the Board Deeds of L. and Release, dated the 6th and Seventh days of November, 1685, by which the Proprietor Grants unto Isaac Decow, of Draxabby, in the County of Yorke, Yeoman, in Consideration of one hundred pounds, Two thousand five hundred acres of Land, (to be laid out as in the other original Deeds) under the yearly rent of one Shilling for every one hundred acres.

Isaac Decow, by his Last Will and Testament, made the 23d 11 month, 1686 7, then in the County of New Castle, on Delaware, Gave and bequeathed unto his Dau'r, Elizabeth Decow, 250 acres of the Said Land; To his Son, John Decow, one thousand acres; unto his Son, Isaac Decow, one thousand acres, and to his Daughter Susannah the remaining 250 acres, and to them and their heirs and assigns forever by severall destinct Clauses in the Said Will.

Richard Darkin requests a Warr't for taking up that thousand left to John Decow, which is granted.

At a Meeting of the Comm'rs, 11, 4 month, 1712.

Present, Richard Hill, I. Norris, J. Logan.

John Cowgill, having by Deed dated 20, 12th month, 1698-9, Purchased of Wm. Crosdall and John Crosdall 200 acres of Land in Middletown, in Neshamineh, w'ch on the resurvey Contains 232 acres, of w'h 20 as being allowed by Law for the other 12 acres he agrees to pay ten Shillings p. acre and desires a Patent, which is Granted. This is p't of 670 acres Confirmed by Patent dat. 28 June, 1692, by W. M., R. P., and J. G. to Thomas Crosdall in p't (is Supposed) of one thousand acres Sold by Deeds of L. and Rel., dated 20 and 21st of Aprill, 1682, to T. Crosdall, of New Key, Coun. York.

John Le Dee and Some others having in the fall 1709 obtained leave to look out for Lands above Perquicominck, Chose a place Called Oley, about 50 Miles Distant from Philadelphia, and Settled thereon, but without any agreement or survey.

The said John, which Isaac de Turck and John FFrederickfields (all Germans), by further leave Granted them, procured the Surveyor (p. J. L. ord'r) to lay out to John Le Dee 300 acres, to Isaac de Turck 300 acres, to John FFrederickfields 500 acres, for which they agree to pay ten pounds p. hund'd.

Signed a warrant to Rich'd Darkin for 1,000 acres, to Jno. Decow, also a warr't to John Le Dee, I. de Turck and J. FFred. for 1,100 acres.

At a meeting of the Commisioners 20, 4 mo., 1712.

Present, Samuel Carpenter, Rich. Hill, Isaac Norris, James Logan.

Edward Guttridge having by three Severall Evidences proved that he Came into the Country a Servant and duly served his time to John Bezer, as by his Petition and the Deposition of his Evidences appears, a Warr't is Granted him for 50 acres of head Land at a half penny Sterling p. acre, and now Signed, dated the 8th 4th Instant.

John Littlejohn, of Naaman's Creek mill, desiring to purchase 200 acres of Land in Rocksland, near John Pierce's, 'tis agreed he Shall have the Same at £30 p. hundr'd, one-halfe to be paid next Philadelphia ffair, viz't 16th of the 9th m., and the other moiety the following fair, viz't 16, 3 mo., 1713, with Interest for the Last payment.

Hugh Davis being entered in the Comm'rs minutes 2d 12 mo., 1701, for 50 acres of head land and 50 more to be added on Purchase, now obtains a warrant for the Same.

Richard Webb produces the following Deeds, viz't:

The Proprietor, by Deeds of L. and Release, dat. 23d and 24th 7ber, 1681, Granted to Thomas Hayward, of Charlecott, in the County of Wilts, Serge maker, 250 acres of Land in this Province.

Thomas Hayward, by an Indorsement on the Release, dat. 11th of Jan'ry, 1710, assigned the Said 250 acres and all his Interest in the Said Deeds to Richard Webb and Elizabeth Webb, his wife, in Consideration of £9 sterl'g, paid in England. The Proprietor further by Deeds of L. and Rel., dated 2d and 3d of

April, 1686, Granted to Sam'll Hardy, of Badsly, in Hampshire, Clerk, 500 acres of Land; the Consideration money was first £20, and by an Interlineation is made £22; the rent also upon a manifest Rasure is one Shilling for the whole, but the Proprietor, upon Herb. Springet's Testimoney that the Deeds and Alterations therein were Genuine and of his hand writing, as by his Lett'r to the Proprietor here produced appears.

The Proprietor, by an Indorsement on the Release, done when J. L. was in London last, Certified that he allowed the Same. R. Webb requests warrants for these 750 a., and a Lott. Granted.

James Logan produced his right to Sundry Lands untaken up as follows:

The Proprietor, by Deeds of L. and Rel., dat. 4 and 5 of April, 1682, Granted to Henry Geary, of Chesham, in the County of Bucks, Yeoman, 500 acres of Land in this Province; Henry Geary, the Elder, of Urgenton, in the County Herford, Yeoman, Kinsman and heir to John Geary, deceased, who was Brother and heir to the first mentioned Henry Geary, by L. and Rel., dat. 24th and 25th of April, 1711, Granted all the Said 500 ac's, with all their app., to Ja. Logan, his heirs and assigns.

The Proprietor, by Deeds of Lease and Rel., dated 4th and 5th April, 1682, Granted to John Geary, the younger, in Dunsloe, in the Parish of Prig, in the County of Hertford, yeoman, 500 acres of Land in this Province, to hold to him and his heirs, &c.

John Geary, by his last will and Testament, dat. 28th March, 1696, Expressly Granted 500 acres of Land in Pensilvania to his Cousin, William Davy, who by Deeds of Lease and Release, dat. 24 and 25th of April, 1711, Granted all the Said 500 acres and app. to Ja. Logan, his heirs and assigns for ever.

The Proprietor, by Deeds of Lease and Rel., dat. 14 and 15 of 7ber, 1681, Granted to Hugh Lamb, of St. Martin's, in the ffields, Conn. Midd., Hosier, 250 acres of Land. The Propriet'r, also by like Deeds, dat. the 13th and 14th of 8ber, 1681, Granted to Edward Bettris, of the City of Oxford, Chirurgeon, 2,000 acres of Land in this Province, who by his Last Will, dated 29th Aprill, 1684, devised the Same to his Wife, Ann Bettris, and the Said Ann, by Deeds of Lease and Rel., dat. ye 14 and 15 of Aprill, 1685, Conveyed all the Said 2,000 acres and app. to the Said Hugh Lamb, his heirs and assigns. Richard Heynes, Merchant, of Lond., also by Deeds dat. 21st and 22d of March, 1682, Granted to the Said Hugh Lamb and his heirs, &c., 2,500 acres of Land in this Province, which Said 2,500 acres are recited in the Said Deeds to be part of 5000 acres Granted by the

Prop'rs W. P. by Deeds of L. and Rel., dat. 22 and 23d of August, 1682, to Mathew Marks, of FFolkstone, in the County of Kent, Carpenter, who by like deeds, dated the 12th and 13th of March, aforesaid, Conveyed the Same to s'd R. Heynes, his heirs, &c. Hugh Lamb being thus poss'ed of a right to 7,000 acres in the whole by his own Purchase of 2,500 acres, E. Bettris of 2,000 acres, and 2,500 from R. Heynes, made his last Will, dat. 20, 8ber, 1686, and by the Same Granted all the Said Lands to his Brother, Daniel Lamb, his heirs, &c., and Soon after died, and the Said Daniel died Intestate and without Issue, so that all the Said Lands Came to his Brother and heir, Joseph Lamb, who by Deeds Dated the 30th and 31st of 8ber, 1711, for £150, Granted all the Said 7,000 acres to James Logan, his heirs, &c.

The Said James having thus proved his Right to 8,000 acres, requests warrants for taking up the Same, which is Granted.

Signed warrants to Hugh Davies, Jno. Littlejohn, and Rich d Webb, dated this day.

At a Session of the Commissioners 25th 4th, 1712.

Present, Samuell Carpenter, Isaac Norris, James Logan.

Randall Vernon appearing to make Good his claim to the Lands mentioned 28th 3d mo. last, produces a Warr't from the Comm'rs, dated 25, 9th m., 1684, Granting to Sarah Dole 50 acres of head land, also another Warr't from the Same Comm'rs, dated 9th 10th mo., '84, Granting the Said Sarah 50 acres more, to be added to the former, and a Return under Cha's Ascome's hand for 100 acres Surveyed to Sarah Dole on Ridley Creek, at a Corner of Cha. Whiteacre's Land; he further produces a Deed from John Kaighin and Sarah, his wife, who was the said Sarah Dole, dat. 28, 3 mo., 1702, Granting all the Said 100 acres to the Said Randall Vernon, his heirs, &c.

He further produced some papers relating to another hundred acres he claimed in right of one, Rawlinson, but was able neither to prove Rawlinson's right to Land there, nor any right to himself from Rawlinson so that he must Purchase the Same according to the minute of 28, 3 month. Randall therefore having by his purchase from Thomas Powell p. Deed dat. , a Right to 200 acres of Purchased Land, and to 100 in right of Sarah Dole, upon rent, there remains, besides the 30 acres allowed for Roads, &c., to these 300 acres there remains 200 acres to be purchased by him at £30 p. Cent., which is £60, and 27 years rent for these 100 acres is £11 5s 0d sterling, also £7 6s 8d sterl'g for reducing the rent Land to 1sh. p.

C. is £18 11s 8d sterl'g, or £24 18s 7d in the whole to Clear the Said 100 acres and makes the Sum due from him £84 18s 3d, upon paying or Securing of which a Patent is ordered to him for the whole 531 acres.

William Shankland, of the County of Sussex, having Severall years agoe purchased the Plantation, which was Thomas Loyd's in the Said County, of Sam'll Preston, was to have the priviledge of some Marsh lieing on Pagan Creek, as being due in right of their Tenure of the Said Plantation, but Samu'll Grey having taken up the Greater part of it, the said Wm. now desires a Warr't for the remainder lieing between the Said Grey's land and Pagan Creek, and agrees to pay for the Same 716 of the p's't Currency, equall to Ten shillings of the old, p. acre. Granted.

Samuell Rowland, Sheriff of the County of Sussex, having a Plantation near Pagan Creek, at Lewis, in Sussex, and wanting the Accommodation of some Marsh lieing between the Ditch there and Mill Creek, desires the Priveledge of purchasing the same, But the Town of Lewis expecting a priviledge, the consideration of it is deferred, but he is promised the Refusal of it when to be disposed of; in the meantime he is allowed to use it.

The Proprietor, by deeds of L. and Rel., dat. 24th and 25th May, 1683, Granted to Wm. Cornethwaite, of Silverdale, in the County of Lancaster, Yeoman, and heirs, 500 acres in this Province, Rent 1 shill'g p. C.; Also by like Deeds and of the Same date the Prop'r Granted to Edward Atkinson, of Side, in the County of York, Yeoman, and his heirs, 500 acres at the Same rent. William Cornethwaite, by like Deeds, dated the first and Second April, 1686, Granted all his Said 500 acres and app. to John Cornwell, of the County of York, and Wm. Hudson, now of this place, and to their heirs, &c. Edward Atkinson also by like Deeds, dated   , granted his 500 acres to the Said J. Cornwell and Wm. Hudson in the Same manner. The said J. Cornwell and Wm. Hudson being thus Intituled to 1,000 acres, by a warr't from the Commis'rs took up the quantity on Brandywine in the 4th Month, 1687, as Jno. Cornwell acknowledges. William Hudson, in the year 1701, procured of the Prop'r a Resurvey on the said Land, as also an order for dividing the Same, w'ch was executed, and the land contain'g in the whole 1,132 acres, 566 acres thereof were by patent from the Proprietor, dated   , Confirmed to John Cornwell and 566 acres to Jno. Cornwell, but upon Some Misunderstanding the patents were never delivered, nor ye overplus p'd for. William Hudson now agrees to pay 40 shillings for his 16 acres of over measure, being the sum he agreed to give the Proprietor for it w'n here, but now makes it new money. Jno. Cornwell also agrees to the Same for his 16 acres, if in the Tract. They both represent to the Comm'rs that notwithstanding their Deeds are from Wm. Cornethwaite and E. Atkinson, yet John Blakelin was the p'son of whom they purchased, he having (by agreement only) bought the land, but no Deeds being made to him from said Cornethwaite and Atkinson they were made as above, and that in their purchase Jno. Blakelin Gave them a positive promise of Town Lotts as belonging to that Purchase, for which they Suppose the s'd Jno. had a promise from the Prop'r, being his Intimate acquaintance, and now request that the Board wou'd accordingly Grant them. Deferred.

William Hudson requests a pattent for 26 foot in the High street. Granted by warr't dat.   , and Surveyed to Rowland Ellis. Ord'd a Pattent to Rowland Ellis.

Samuel Carpenter produces Amor Strettell's Right to 5,000 acres of Land as follows: The Prop., by Deeds of L. and Rel., dat. 14th and 15th 2d month, 1682, Granted to George Shore, of Athlone, in the Kingdom of Ireland, Merch't, 5,000 ac's of Land in this Province, Rent 1 shill'g p. C., as appears by a Copy Signed by the Proprietor himself 22, 7 mo., 1703, in Perchment, and by other Good Testimonies. George Shore, by Deeds of L. and Rel., dat. ye 14th and 15th of Aprill, 1703, for £105, Granted all the Said Land to Amor Strettell, his heirs, &c., as appears by an attested Copy of the Said Deeds, but these Deeds are from Geo. Shore, of Athlone, felt maker, and under his Mark only.

Samuell Carpenter, that warr'ts may be Issued for this Land, There appears in the Office warrt's for 200 acres of Lib. land executed for 500 acres in the County of Philadelphia, also returned both these, dated in 1683, a warrant dated 27th Xber, 1683, for 20 acres to Phillipp England, who then was Shore's attorney, and for 1,000 acres, dat. 30th 7ber, 1684, but no return appears for it ordered. Ordered Warrants for 3,380 acres or thereabouts.

Signed warrants to Ja. Logan for 2,500 acres in right of H. Lamb, and for 500 acres in right of Henry Geary, and a warrant to Wm. Shankland for Marsh in Sussex.

At a Session of the Commissioners 16th 5th mo., 1712.

Present, Sam'll Carpenter, Rich'd Hill, Isaac Norris, James Logan.

The late Commissioners having Granted their warr't, dated the 24th day of the 4 mo., 1708, for laying out to John Talbott

500 acres of Land in right of John Dwight, Purchaser, in the year 1685, of the Said quantity, as is entered in the Minutes of that time; the said John Talbott, by Ind. dat. the 18th of July, 1709, for £40 Consideration, Granted and Conveyed all the Said 500 ac's, with his right to the Said Warrant, To Thomas FFairman, of Shakamaxon, &c., and his heirs and assigns forever. Thomas Fairman procuring of the Survey'r Generall an order to Execute the Said Warrant, laid it out on a Tract of Land in the County of Bucks, and by Deeds of Lease and Release, dated the 22d and 23d of December, 1710, for £175, money of this Province. Granted the Said 500 acres, located as aforesaid, to Bartho. Longstreth, of the County of Philadelphia, and his heirs, &c.

The Said Bartholomew having divers times applied to the Secretary for a Pattent on the Said Land, which has hitherto been deferred, Thomas Fairman not having as yet received the whole Consideration money, applies to the Board for the same. But the return being examined, and a due enquiry made into the location of the Said Land, it was found to be laid out on a Tract of Land near Southampton Township, which has hitherto been reputed to belong to one, John Rush, and is so entered in the printed Map of this Province. This Survey therefore proving irregular and indirect, the Board Cannott agree to Grant any Confirmation of the Same.

William Hudson renewing his application for Town Lotts, for which with J. Cornwell he applied last Session. The Board taking the Matter further into Consideration have thought fitt to agree that they shall have all the favour herein that can be Justly shewn, and that upon acco't of the Said Purchase Wm. Hudson shall be admitted to take up two Lotts in Mulberry Street, adjoining to those he has already purchased, or is about purchas'g there, on the easiest terms that may be Granted, he paying to John Cornwell one moiety of the value of the Said Grant.

James Cooper, of Philadelphia, Junior, having married the Widow of Henry Carter, late of the Same place, deceased, who purchased of R'd Hill part of the Great Lott in the 2d and High street, which was taken up by Coll. Markham, applies to the Board for a Confirmation of the Same, and proposes a Consideration to the Prop'r for the Grant to be paid by the Severall persons Concerned in that Said part of the Lott. The Board thereupon thought fitt to agree that in case the Said persons would advance to the Prop'r Twenty pistoles, a Release and Confirmation of the Said part should be forthwith made to them, that is for that whole part which Coll. Markham Granted to Thomas Loyd.

Joseph Kirl having procured of the Commissioners in his lifetime two warrants, dated ye 6th 2d month, 1702, one for Surveying to Rich'd Wood and Will'm Lovell in right of Rich'd Collins, first purchaser of 1,250 acres, the proportion of Liberty Land due to them, viz't 25 acres, and the other for laying out 225 ac's, the remainder of the whole purchase. Is. Norris now produces Deeds of Lease and Rel., dated the 26th and 27th of March, 1711, from Betty Lovel, sole Daughter and heir of William Lovel, late of the City of Bristoll, mariner, for all that Moiety of the said purchase belonging to Said Lovel, entered in the minutes 5th 11 m., 1701, pa. 49 (Consid'n £25 for the 635 acres), And thereupon requests that a warr't may be Granted him for his part, both for Liberty Land and the remainder unsurveyed, viz't, which is accordingly ordered.

At the survey of Notingham, H. Hollingsworth, the Surv'r, having obtained a grant of 500 acres to be laid out adjoining on the same terms with the rest, but never having taken out a warrant for it, he now applies for one and 'tis Granted on Condition that he pay all the arrears of Rent from the date to this time.

Signed a Warrant to the attorneys of Am. Strettell for 3,380 acres. A warr't to H. Hollingsworth for the return of 500 acres in Notingham.

At a Session of the Commissioners 30th 5th month, 1712.

Present, Richard Hill, Isaac Norris, James Logan.

The proprietor, by Deeds of L. and Rel., dat. 11th and 12th April, 1682, Granted to John Hecock, of the County of Stafford, husbandman, and Thomas Barret, Ditto, of Do., 875 acres of Land, of which 250 by agreement belonged to John Hecock and 625 being Barret's part, 'tis alledged was one-third thereof, viz't 208⅓ acres for his own acco't and the other two-thirds, viz't 416⅔, was purchased with the money of William Venables, for proof of which they produce an Instrument under the Said Barret's hand and Seal, disclaiming all right to the Said two-thirds, as is entered more at large in the Office of Property 7th 12 month, 1700, vid. min's.

Joyce Venables and FFrances Venables, Daughters and heirs of Wm., by Deed dated 21st Feb'ry, 1697, Granted all the Said Land belonging to their ffather by them Called 425 acres and ⅔, but is only 416⅔, to Andrew Heath, who by Deed Dated   , Conveys the Same to Thomas Stevenson and Chas. Brogden, who request a warrant for the Same. Granted.

The Prop'r, by Deeds of Lease and Release, dat. 26 and 27th July, 1681, Granted to William Lawrence, of Axbridge, County

Somus, Woolen Draper, 500 acres of land W. Law. (for £5), by Deed dat. 14th March, 1685, Granted one Moiety of the Said land to James Plumly, of Priddy, in Said County, Miner.

By virtue of a warr't from the Commissioners, dated 8, 9ber, 1686, for 500 acres there was laid out a Tract in Bucks, but returned for only 450 acres, there not being land enough in the vacancy on which the Said Warrant was executed.

James Plumly and Jasp. Lawrence, Son and heir of the Said Wm, by a Joint Deed, dated 7th 8ber, 1704 (for £30 ster'i'g), Granted all the Said 500 acres to Anthony Wheatly, of Bristoll, Grocer, who By an Instrument dated the 12th 8ber, 1704, Constituted James Shattick and Edward Lane, of this place, his attorneys. The Said Tract being resurveyed it holds 460 acres and there is found a vacancy between it and Geo. Willard's Land, which in reality was an overplus found in Willard's and thrown out by him, Containing 73 acres. James Shattick, in behalf of Anthony Wheatly, requests that the whole purchase may be made up by means of that 73 acres, which at first ought to have been within their Survey and then they wou'd have had it as their due, but now he offers £5 Consideration for it, having by mistake actually sold 500 acres, as supposing the whole to have been in the Tract at the rate of £20 old Curr. p. C't and must now make it Good.

Granted as requested and ordered a Pattent to Anthony Wheatly for the whole 533 acres, being a Narrow slip of 1,256 perches long and but 68 perches wide in full of Wm. Lawrence's Purchase of 500 acres.

Signed a pattent to Thomas Story for 170 acres in Bucks, dated 16th 5th month, Rent 1 shill'g p. C; A pattent to Thomas Story for 34 and ½ acres Lib. Land and 2 lotts, dat. 16, 5th mo., in right of Waddy and Snead; a pattent to H. De Turk for 300 acres at Oley, dat. 28, 5 mo.; A pattent to Martin Kindig for two thousand acres Tow'ds Susquehannah, laid out by virtue of the late Comm'rs warr't, dat.   , 8ber, 1710, Consid'n £5 sterl'g p. C., dat. 25th 5th month; A pattent to Moses Key for 120 acres in Concord on Rent, dat. 25th 5th Month; A pattent to Rowland Ellis for a lott of 26 foot in the High street, dated 27th 5th Month; A War.ant to Is. Norris for 125 acres in right of Collins, Lib. Land included, hodie.

A warrant to J. Logan for 4,500 acres in right of Edward Bettris and Matth. Marks, hod.

A warr't to J. Logan for Lib. Land and Lotts belonging to his purchases, hodie.

A warr't to Cha. Brogden for 416 acres and ⅔ in right of Barrett, &c., dated hodie.

A warr't to J. Logan for 500 acres in right of Jno. Geary.

At a Session of the Commissioners the 13th of the 6th month, 1712.

Present, Richard Hill, Isaac Norris, James Logan.

The former Commsisioners, by their warr'ts dated 25th 1st month, 1702, Granted to Jno. Willis 100 acres in Rocklands, in Chester County, for £25, w'ch he paid Thomas Hope by Deed dated 27th 1st mo., 1705, Sold to Said J. Willis 50 acres of Land in Bradford Township, surveyed to the Said Thomas about the year 1686, and was reputed to be his head right as a Serv't, but no Grant or warrant appearing nor any proof being made that he came in a Serv't in time it Cannott be allowed otherwise than at the full rent of a penny p. acre; and at those terms, J. Willis desires he may purchase off the Rent. There being a small vacant strip adjoining to this, Contain'g 36 acres, the Said John desires to purchase the Same, which is allowed him at 5s p. acre, and thereupon he desires a pattent of Confirmation on all the Said three pattents, viz't 100 acres already paid for, 50 acres (which being resurveyed makes 55 acres, the odd 5 of which are allowed by Law) for the reducing of which to Common rent he agrees to pay £4 17s 9d and the 36 acres for which he pays £9 for, these two Sums together with £7 4s 5d for arrears of quitt rents he gives Bond, Payable 25th 10th mo. next.

The Prop., by his warr't dat. 17, 3 mo., 1700, Granted to Wm. Cowper to take up 500 acres in the County of Bucks, which being executed by Ph. Pemberton, now upon a Division of the Same the land appears to be deficient in quantity, for rectifying of which a warr't of Resurvey is requested by his heirs. Granted.

The Proprietor having by Deeds dat. 20th and 21st Ap'l, 1682, Granted unto James Harrison 5,000 acres of Land in this Province, part whereof was laid out in Wrights Town, in the County of Bucks. Ph. Pemberton, by his Deed dat. 10, 12 mo., 1689 (as Husband to Phebe, Sole Daughter and heir to the Said James), 200 acres of the said Land Scituate between the other lands of James Harrison and that of Roger Longworth, in Consid'n of £12 unto James Radcliff, of the Said County, his heirs, &c. The Said James Radcliff's relict and Children, viz't Mary Baker, of Bristoll, Widow, the Said Relict, Rich'd Radcliff and Edward Radcliff, sons, and (Wm. Havhurst and) Rachell, his Wife, with Rebecca Radcliff, two dau rs of the Said James, by deed dated 15th 12th Month, 1704, for £46 Granted all the Said 200 acres to Jonathan Cowper, of the Said County, his heirs &c., and for a further Confirmation and to make Good the Deficiency of the Title, Israel Pemberton, as heir to the said Phebe Pemberton, true heir to the Said James Harrison, by his deed dated 7th 9ber, 1710, released all the Said Land to the Said Jonathan Cowper. But the Said 200 acres being resurveyed they are found to Contain 355 acres, of which 20 acres being allowed by Law, Jonathan Cowper desiring to purchase the overplus he agrees to give after the rate of £20 p. C't, provided the Board will agree to deduct out of it so much as Shall be found deficient in his ffather, Wm. Cowper's Tract, mentioned in the last minute aforegoing, which is Granted and a pattent ordered thereupon.

The Proprietor, by Deeds dat. 1 and 2 of August, 1681, Granted to Edward Bezer 500 acres of Land, the Lott appurten. to which Edw'd Bezer, Son and heir to the first mentioned Edward, by Deed dat. 1 May, 1708, Granted to John Willis, who requests a warrant for the Same, ordered as requested.

Edward Shippen, Gr. Owen and T. Story, a Quorum of the late Commissioners, by their order, dated the 20th of the first mo., 1710-1, Granted to Gabriel FFriend a Licence to feed upon an Island in Delaware at the Mouth of Schuylkill so many hogs as he Shou'd think fitt for one year, then next ensuing he paying to the Proprietor one fatt hogg of the value of 30 shill'gs or the Said Sum, and taking Care of the wood thereon. The Heirs of Andrew Boon,doe hereupon Complain to the Board alledging that the Said Andrew had always held the Said island, having first as they pretend purchased it of the Indians and afterw'ds obtained a Grant from Coll. Markham when L't Gov'r, to use it till the Prop'rs pleasure or that of his Comm'rs Shou'd be further known therein, and therefore Claim a Priority of Right or preference before all others. Both Parties appearing and debating the matter 'tis left to be further Considered.

Signed a Patent to Anthony Wheatly for 533 acres ordered the 30th ult. dated.

A Patent to John Willis for Three Tracts now ordered, dated this day.

A warrant to John Willis for a lott in right of E. Bezer, ord'd and dated to-day.

A warr't to the heirs of Wm. Cowper for a resurvey on 500 acres, ord'd and dat. to-day.

Andrew Sandall, minister to the Swedes of Philad'a County, presented a Petition Setting forth that there was a patent Granted by S'r Edmond Andros to Peter Mattson Dalbo for a Tract of Land on Schuylkill adjoining to Benjamin Chambers' fferry, bounded as is therein expressed, by which the Said Andrew and others always Conceived that the Said Land was bounded on that Side next Schuylkill by that River, including the adjoining Cripple and Flatts, but because there may be Some Dispute over the Said Cripple be included in the Same; he therefore requests a new Grant of the whole, including the Same.

Ordered that the Said Land be resurveyed and that the Said And'w (who is now in possession of the Said Tract by his Intermarriage with a Daughter of the Said Peter Matson Dalbo) may have the preference in purchasing the Said Land, he Giving a reasonable price for the Same.

At a meeting of the Commissioners 20th 6th mo., 1712.

Present, Samuel Carpenter, Rich'd Hill, Isaac Norris, James Logan.

The Proprietor having before his last departure granted to Patience Loyd, widow of Thomas Loyd, late of this Province, a Pension or allowance of Ten pounds p. annum, for which he gave her an order in these words, viz't:

To JAMES LOGAN, *my Secretary:*

These are to authorise and require thee to pay unto Patience Loyd, of Philadelphia, Widow, or her order or assigns, the Sum of Tenn pounds p. annum, by quarterly payments, viz't fifty Shill's a quarter, yearly, during her naturall life, and this Shall be thy Sufficient warrt. Give under my hand at Philadelphia the 27th day of October, 1701.

WM. PENN.

And the payment of the Said Money having been forbore for Some little time in the Said J. Logan's late absence from this Province, and not yet Complied with since his return, upon a Doubt arising whether the Proprietor's Transferring this Province, &c., and all Debts due to him therein to the Trustees does not Interfere with or make void the s'd order.

The Said Widow thereupon, by her friend, makes application to this Board praying that Since the Prop. has the Same Estate in the Province as formerly the Said order may be fully Complied with, &c.

And the Same being taken into Consideration 'tis the opinion of the Commissioners that the Said Order is as Valid and binding on the Secre'y as ever and therefore he is advised and directed to Comply with the Same.

Michael Rossel, formerly Miller at Bristol, in Bucks, by his last Will (of which he made Samuel Carpenter Executor) devised 400 ac's of Land then Surveyed in the upper part of the Said County and near the River to the Children of John Hough, and in pursuance of the Said Will the Said Ex'or, Samuell Carpenter, Granted the Said Children a Deed for the Same, But upon Inquiring into the Title of the Said 400 acres, tho' there are living witnesses that it was duly laid out to the

Said Rossell by the Surveyor and always accounted his, yet no Grant, warr't or order of any kind Can be produced for it, nor any proofs that it has been paid for or purchased, tho' the latter be no way doubted of, that is, that it was agreed for at least before Survey.

The Said Children wanting a Title, now apply to this Board sor the Same, and Since no proof Can be made of any payment the Said Land is allowed to them at the usual rate Lands were Sold at the time of the Said Survey, viz't £5 p. hund'd acres, with Interest for 25 years, w'ch triples the Said Sum and raise it to £15 p. ann.; this ought to be according to the present Currency and for divers Considerations 'tis allowed to them in the late Currency, and therefore upon their paying or Securing £60 of the Said Old Money, or £45 of the present, a Patent and Confirmation is ordered to them as they Shall desire.

David Brintnall producing Deeds dated the 31 of Aprill, 1682, for 250 acres Sold by the Proprietor to Alexand'r Mell, to which purchase the Said David is now by mesne Purchases invested with the Sole right and having obtained of the late Commissioners a warrant for the Said Land, dated ye 11th 8th month, 1710, he now requests a Lott in right of the Same. But the Said Alex'r not being named in the division of the City Lotts nor among the first purchasers, the Said request is referred to be further Considered.

At a Meeting of the Commissioners 10, 7ber, 1712.

Present, Samuell Carpenter, Rich'd Hill, Isaac Norris, James Logan.

John Maxwell (by his friend) desiring to purchase 200 acres of Vacant Land in the back parts of the County of Chester, adjoining or near to the Lands of D. Loyd and Thomas Davis, the Same is Granted to him at Tenn pounds p. hund'd, to be paid in three months, provided the Said Land be as is represented, viz't, but indifferent, of which the Surveyor is to Judge.

The Proprietor, by Deeds of L. and Rel., dat. 2 and 3d of March, 1681, Granted to John Clowes, of FFurnue Pool, in the Palatinate of Chester, Yeoman, a thousand acres of Land, and by like Deeds, dat. the 24 and 25th of April, 1683. Granted to the Said Jno. 500 acres more, who by last will dated 29th of the 11th Month, 1686, devised the Said 500 acres to his 3 Daughters, Margery, Sarah Bainbridge and Rebecca Clowes, and their heirs and ass., to be equally divided among them. The first mentioned thousand acres are all taken up, as also one hundred of the other 5 was taken up by Richard Hough, husband to the Said Margery, by a late warr't, and the Said Devises now request a warrant (by John Chapman, of Bucks), which is Granted, no further Surveys appearing.

In the year 1683 or about that time John Hill, late of Sussex, obtained a Warrant or Grant for 500 acres of Land to be laid out in the Said County on old rent, part of which was executed on Some Marsh in Broad kill Neck. But this Interfering with the Survey the Proprietor designed for himself in that place. He by a warr't dated 1st 8ber, 1701, ord'd the Said Survey to be regulated, and there was laid in that place only 255 acres. The Surveyor of the County presuming that the rest was to be laid out elsewhere, as it might be found Vacant, accordingly Surveyed two Small parcells in the Same right, the one Containing 93 acres and the other 111 acres, in the whole 204 acres. John Hill, by his last Will devised his whole real Estate to his wife (now his widow) Elizabeth, who requests a Confirmation of the Same and a Warr't for the remainder. To this the Board finding Cause to make Some objections, yet Since the Proprietor had Seen and allowed the Said Warr't for 500 acres it was thought fit to Grant her request and accordingly a Pattent is order'd for the Said 2 Parcells, she paying rent for the Same from the year 1683, and a warr't to be issued for the remaining 41 acres.

The late Commissioners having Granted ten thousand acres of Land to the Palatines, by their warr't dated   , 8ber, 1710; in pursuance thereof there was laid out to Martin Kindig (besides the 2,000 acres already confirmed to him and paid for) the like quantity of 2,000 acres towards Susquehannah, of which the Surveyor Generall has made a return.

The Said Martin now appearing, desires that the Said Land may be Granted and Confirmed by Pattent to Maria Warenbur, Widow, for whom the Same was taken up or intended and who is to pay the Consideration for it.

But upon further Consideration of the matter it is agreed among themselves that the said Land Shall be Confirmed to Daniel FFierre and Isaac Leffevre, two of the Said Widow's Sons, and the Consideration money, viz't £140, at £7 p. Hund'd, by agreement having been for Some time due, but is now to be paid down in one Sum; 'tis agreed that they shall pay only ten pounds for Interest, that is £150 in the whole.

Signed a Patent to Daniel FFierre and Isaac Leffevre for 2,000 acres, ordered to-day.

Signed a warrant to the heirs of John Hough, ordered to-day for 400 ac's.

Signed a warr't to John Maxwell for 200 acres, ordered to-day.

MINUTE BOOK "H."

At a meeting of the Commissioners 20th 8ber, 1713.

Present, Samuell Carpenter, Richard Hill, Isaac Norris, James Logan.

The Board having on the 16th of 5 mo. last agreed with James Cooper, Jun'r, and Richard Hill, Comm'rs, in behalf of themselves and others concerned in that part of the Great High Street Lott on the 2d Street (on which the meeting house Stands), which part Wm. Markham Granted to Some of the children of Tho. Loyd, deceased, that if they would advance Twenty Pistoles, to be paid down to the Proprietor's use, the Board would in Consideration of the merits of the said Thomas Loyd and his Services to this Governm't Grant and confirm the Same to Richard Hill, that the Purchas'rs under him might obtain a firm Title to the Severall Smaller parts which they Claim; the Said R. Hill represents that the Severall persons Concern'd in the Said Lott or Some of them have fallen so farr Short of the Contributions that were Expected from them that the Said Sum of 20 Pistoles Cannot be raised and therefore prays that an abatement may be made in the Said Consideration and that fifteen pistoles may be accepted in lieu thereof, as they among themselves at first proposed, tho' afterwards the Board raised to the number of twenty.

Which being taken into Consideration and fully debated it was at length resolved that upon the Said Richard's pay down Twenty pounds, Such regard should be had to the Said Thomas Loyd's Services that the Said part so Granted as aforesaid should be Confirmed, as desired, And accordingly the Said Rich'd Hill paying down the Said Sum of £20 a patent is forthwith ordered to him for the Said part, being one hundred foot on the 2d Street, bounded to the Southward with Strawberry Lane and in Depth 132 foot, bounded Eastward with the 2d street and Westw'd with Strawberry Alley.

The Proprieta'y, by L. and Release, dated 26th and 27th of July, 1681, Granted to James Hill, of Beckington, in the County of Somersett, Shoemaker, five hundred acres of Land in this Province, In right whereof there was Surveyed and laid out in Falls Township, in the county of Bucks, by virtue of a order from the Prop'r, dated 13th 9 mo , 1682, a Tract reputed to Contain 250 acres, which afterwards being by an order of the Commissioners, dat. 10, 10, 1694, Resurveyed was found to Contain 442 acres, and accordin'ly was returned into the Surveyor Generall's Office.

Richard Hill, Son of the Said James Hill, and his wife, by the name of (R'd Hill, of Bristoll, in the County of Bucks, in the Province of Pensilvania, Cordwainer, and Agnes his wife, he being the only Son and heir of James Hill, late of Burlington, in the Province of West new Jersey, deceased), by Ind. dated the 7th 3d month, 1712, in Considera'on of £150 Granted to Rich'd Hill, of Philadelphia, Merchant, all the Said 500 acres of Land so Granted to his ffather, James Hill, as aforesaid, and the said Tract of 442 acres as part thereof to hold to him, his heirs and ass. forever. The Said Richard Hill, of Philadelphia, Requests a warr't ordering the Said Tract to be exactly Resurveyed and that so much as it falls Short of his right, vizt., 492 acres (tne Liberty land being deducted), may be laid out to him elsewhere; he also requests a warr't for the 8 acres of Liberty Land and the City Lott appurtenant to the Said Purchase, which were Granted.

Richard Halliwell, of Newcastle, by his friend J. Moore, of Philad'a, Esqr., applying to the Board, represents that the Proprietor having at his last departure from this Province Granted to the Said Richard a warr. for taking up in the County of Newcastle four hundred acres of Land, the Same was executed on a Tract the Greatest part of which (as 'tis said) is the Right of Richard Cantwell and Henry Garretson, and therefore he requests that upon his Surrendering the Patent of Confirma'on Granted him for the Said Land, another Tract in the Said County, which he has procured the Surveyor to lay out, may be Granted and confirmed to him in lieu of the first mentioned, and the Board having fully Considered the Said request they came to this resolution upon the Same:

That Seeing it has not yet appeared to the Board by any Surveys of R. Cantwell's and H. Garretson's Lands that the Said 400 acres as at first Located are included either in the whole or in part within their true Bounds; the Said Cantwell and Garretson, tho' near relations to the Petitioner, having above all others in that County obstructed the Survey'r in the Discharge of his Duty in the late Generall resurvey made by vertue of a Law for that purpose, and Seeing the Said Land has upon the petitioner's own application and request been confirmed to him by Patent, therefore the present Commissioners cannot think it fitt to concern themselves further in it. But whereas 'tis apprehended that the late Survey or Second Location of the Said Land now presented to the Board is part of that Tract which has been Sett apart for the Proprietor's p'per use, being about the Distance of 8 or ten miles from New Castle Town and between the line of the Welch Tract and the River Delaware, upon which or any other Land the Surveyor had no power to enter without fresh orders for the Same, he having made a return of the first warr't Directed to him into the Office as he was required. 'Tis ordered therefore that the Surveyor of the Said County be Severely proceeded against for his Great Presumption and manifest breach of his Duty, and 'tis ordered that the Said Survey be not admitted.

Joseph Growdon's Petition, entered in the first of these minutes, being upon a late Complaint of his to the Lieut. Gov'r, taken again into Consideration, The Board came to a full Conclusion upon two of three requests made in the Same, viz't:

To the first that the p'sent Commissioners have no right or Authority to make any Variation from the Plan of the city Philad'a as 'tis laid down in the printed Draughts and References to the Same, that having been the Generall foundation of the Surveys and Titles to all or most of the Valuable Lotts in the Said City from the first Location thereof to this time, That the Purchasers having no Right to any Lotts in the City from any Grants or Concessions made by the Proprietor by his Deeds of Sale or otherwise in England (those concessions relating only to what are now called Liberty Lands), but only from his Grant after his arrivall here, what he then concluded on ought to be the Established Rule without any variation from it, inconsistent with the Primary Design. That tho' the lotts laid out on Society Hill (so called) prove now to be of less value than others nearer the middle of the Town (as now built), yet at the first allotment of them 'tis conceived they were understood to be much otherwise, The Society having Chosen that place for themselves and for the Bulk of their business, who were then Considered as the most capable and likely to improve and render any part of the Town Valuable, That this was the place where the Proprietor laid his own Sons and Relations Lotts with others that he had the Greatest regard for, and that if a Disappointment has Since happened it must now be born with by those Concerned, as one-half of the first Purchasers are obliged to bear with theirs whose Lotts have faln on Schuylkill Side, and are thereby become of little or no value, tho' the contrary was at first expected.

As to the third request, which is for a small piece of vacant Marsh land on the Schuylkill, near B. Chambers' Ferry, 'tis the Resolution of the Board that the Said Vacancy cannot, according to the Rules always observed by the Commissioners in Such cases, be granted away from those that hold the Tract between which and the River Schuylkill the Same lies and of which this vacancy has formerly been reputed a part, especially since Andrew Sandall, the Swedish Minister, who has a large Interest in the Said Tract, has also Petitioned the Board for the Same. As to the 2d Request, viz., for Lands in right of 45 Serv'ts imported by the Petitioner, the matter is referred to be further discoursed w'th him.

A complaint being made to the Board against Wm. Garrett, of the Township of Darby, for that having procured a Warr't from the Commissioners in the year 1709 for taking up 42 acres, the remainder of his purchase, and carrying the Said warrant to the Surveyor Generall, to whom it was directed, he artfully got it from him again and prevailed with Israel Taylor without any Authority to him derived to Execute the Said Warrant upon certain Surveyed Lands belonging to the Proprietor in Chester County, taking up only one acre of meadow in one place and about a mile's distance from it the other 41 acres; and the Said Garrett's Proceedings herein being Considered by the Board 'Tis ordered that both he and the Surveyor be forthwith proceeded against accord'g to Law, but that because said Garrett is under the Same profession w'th us, therefore that Some persons of Darby meeting be wrote to in order in the first place to Deal with himself and then if he make not Satisfaction to lay it before the meeting, And the Secretary is ordered to prepare a Letter to be Signed by all the Board.

The Proprietor, by pat't dat. 28, 3 mo., 1684, Granted to Thomas Cross, of Philad'a, a Lott in Walnutt Street, Contain'g 49½ foot in breadth, being the next but one beyond the 3d Street and 220 foot in length, Rent 1 shill'g p. ann. T. Cross, by deed dated 20th 8ber, 1697, Sold the Same to John Martin, who by Deed Poll dat. 14, 7ber, 1702, Sold the Same for £15 to John Budd, Sen'r, who by Deed dated 4, 1 m., 1702-3, Granted the Same for £17 to James Swaffer, who having built thereon, granted the Same with the Improvements for £115, by deed dated 5, 7ber, 1704, to John Knowles.

John Knowles finding in the Said Lotts 15 Inches of overplus, on which part of his house is built, desires to purchase the Said overplus and agrees to give one Shilling for each Inch, viz't 15 sh., and desires a patent for the whole, together with another Lott of 50 foot adjoin'g to it and lieing between that and the 3d street, first Granted by the Proprietor to John Test, by a warrt' dat. 29, 1 m., 1683, in consideration of Seven foot of Ground resigned by him to the Proprietor out of his front Lott, and the Said John, by deed dated 23 Ap'l, 1683, Sold the Same for £7 10s to William East, Master of the Governship Gulielma, whose Relict Esther, and Sole Daughter and heiress Elizabeth, with their present Husbands, Richard Cary, Citizen and Merchant Taylor of London, who married widow, and Thomas Jackson, of Dartford, Coun. Kent, Carpenter, Conveyed the Same by Deeds of L. and Release, dat. the 19th and 20th of 7ber, 1711, to James Logan for £10 sterl'g, who by Deed dated the 22d of September last granted the Same to the Said John Knowles. Granted and a Patent being prepared for the whole, dated the 30 of 7ber last; it was Signed by all the Commissioners.

The Proprietor, by L. and Release, dat. 1 and 2 of March, 1681, Granted to Wm. Smith, of Bromham House, in the County of Wilts, Yeoman, Twelve hundred and fifty acres of Land in this Province. Wm. Smith, by Deeds of Lease and Release, dat. 27 and 28 of April, 1683, for £10 Granted to Richard Hellyard, of Kingwood, in Hampshire, Yeoman, 500 acres, part of the Said 1,250, and to his heirs and assigns forever. In right of this 500 acres Richard Hellyard by warrt' dat. 29th 3m., 1683, took up in   , 300 acres, which was Surveyed the 30, 12 m., 1687, and the remaining 200 his relict, ——— ———, now the wife of Thomas Peart, being by her husband's Will.

James Logan having represented to the Board that the Proprietor having Impowered them, the rest of his Commissioners, to Settle all acco'ts with him, his receiver, he had for their Direction in a Paper wrote in his own hand and witnessed by divers p'sons in London (which paper was laid before the Board). The Proprietor had Expressed the allowances to be made to the Said J. L. for his Services, and particularly for the time Past before the date of the Said Paper in November last he had allowed one thousand pounds of the present Curreny of this Province, together with ten pounds p. ann. for eight years towards house rent for the meeting of the Council Commissioners and Transacting the Proprietor's business. That J. L. at making up his acco'ts upon his late Departure for England (being resolved to keep within very moderate bounds, that no refflection might be cast on him on that acco't in case he had miscarried in his voyage) had Charged the Prop'r only with one thousand pounds of the late Currency, which being Equal to Seven hundred and fifty pounds only of the present, there remains due to him of the Same (viz't of the new Currency £330, of which he has not yet rece'd or taken to himself much above the odd £30, as by the Books will fully appear Hereupon. He further represents that there being so great occasion to remit to England all the Effects that can be gott in on the Proprietor's acco't, he is very unwill'g to take to himself what is due to him out of those Effects, but on the other hand thinks it unreasonable that he should be kept much longer out of it, and therefore proposes to have part of it at least Secured to him in land. But that no Exceptions may be taken, and to prevent all Suspicions of his makeing himself advantages by this method, he proposes that having Sold out of the Rights to land, or originall Purchase which he lately bought in England, two thousand acres to two Severall persons here Since his arrivall, at a Price which he accounted the full value of it, viz't, at five pounds sterl'g or Six pounds thirteen Shillings and four pence of this Currency, for which Land he is to make a Title to the Purchasers out of his Said Rights. If, therefore, the Board in behalf of the Proprietor will be pleased to make the Said mesne Purchasers under him a Title to the Said Lands Directly from the Proprietor, discharging him from his obligation to make the Same Good to them out of those rights of his own he will take the Consideration money of the Said 2,000 acres, viz't, £133 6s 8d, as so much paid to him by the Proprietor.

Which proposal being taken into Consideration by the Board, and Particularly that this method wou'd be no hindrance to the Sale of the Proprietor's Lands, being only a Confirmation of Lands on the Proprietor's behalfe, which the mesne Purchasers without Such confirmation would otherwise as certainly hold, and that it is not in the Said J. L's Power to make any advantage to himself by this Method, 'Tis therefore fully agreed to, upon his further Proposall of giving his Bond for the Said Sum to pay the Same to the Proprietor in case so much Shall not upon a full Settlement of his acco'ts appear due to him, or Such part thereof as Shall not so appear due, which Bond upon Granting the Confirmations herein requested he is ordered to give accordingly.

The Proprietor, by his warrant dated 20th 1st mo., 1700-1, Granted to John Evans a hundred acres of Land on Mill Creek and the line of Rocklands upon Rent, which was Surveyed by H. Hollingsworth by order of the Surveyor Generall.

John Evans, by Deed Dated the 20th of August, 1708, Granted the Said Land to Evan Rees and his heirs for £20, who desiring a Confirma'on of the Same, the Secre'y has agreed with him that he Shall have a Grant thereof for £20 of the Present Currency, to be paid down in lieu of all pas rents, and that the Quitt rent for the future shall be only one Bushell of Wheat yearly.

Signed a Patent to John Knowles, dat. 30th 7ber, but ordered this day.

Signed a Warrant to Elizabeth Hill 24th 7ber, ordered the 10th, 7ber.

Signed a Patent to John Beckingham for 100 acres in Birmingham, Chest'r Coun., Granted by warrant from the former Board, dat. 18, 12 mo., 1701, for £25, old Currency, and 25 shill'gs for arrears of rent, viz't, £26 5s, old Currency.

At a meeting of the Commissioners 27th 8ber, 1712.

Present, Samuell Carpenter, Richard Hill, Isaac Norris, James Logan.

Maurice Lewellin produced a Deed, dat.   , from Ja's Thomas, of Meirion, Granting to him one hundred acres of Land in the Said Township whereon the Said James' ffather and himself had been Seated, on which Tract there being found by a late Resurvey 137 acres, he desires to Purchase the 27 acres of overplus remaining after Tenn acres are allowed for the hundred by Law. And 'tis agreed with the Said Maurice that the Same Shall be Granted to him together with a Confirmation of the whole Tract and Such as he holds adjacent (proving a Good Title to the Same), provided there be no overplus, he paying for the Said 27 acres fifteen pounds at the next Spring fair of Phialdelphia, and so proportionably Should there be more or less of the Said overplus when duly returned, w'ch is not yet done.

James Steel, of Kent County, Complains that in a pattent Granted in the year 1705 unto Evan Jones, of the s'd County, for 410 acres, upon a Resurvey there is Contained within the bounds of it a considerable quantity of the Tract he now lives on, called Whitwell's Chance, that the Said resurvey is altogether Irregular, the Surveyor having pretended to make up the addition to the 300 acres which Evan first held out of Certain broken points of Vacant Land and Marsh, when in reality it was made of Some of the best parts of the Said Tract, which he proves by producing the Originall Draught and return of the next adjacent Tract to the West, Called Benefield, and the old and first Courses of Whitwell's Chance, which are made to meet at the Creek and both Join at an old white Oake. He complains also that the Commissioners having issued an order, dated 23d of the 6th Month, 1703, directed to Geo. Dekeyne and Jonas Greenw'd for Examining the lines then Controverted between Whitwell's Chance and Evan Jones' Land; the Said order was kept from Geo. Dekeyne, who never was admitted to the knowledge of it, but that if the Said order had been executed it wou'd have fully discovered the mistakes that have been made, and therefore he prays that the Same order may Still be renewed; Which being taken into Consideration and the irregularity of Evan Jones' and the Surveyor's proceedings in his favour appearing fully to the Board, 'Tis ordered that the Said order of the 23d, 6 mo., 1703, may be renewed and revived and discited, with a warrant for that purpose to the Surveyors of the Counties of Chester, New Castle and Kent Jointly.

The Said J. Steel further represents in behalf of the heirs of Patrick Word, late of the Said County, that he, the Said Patrick, having about 30 years ago obtained a Grant (for which a warr't is now found in the Office) to take up land in Kent; he then Seated himself on a Tract called 600 ac's, That tho' they have no Evidence of the Survey of it, yet 'tis believed 'twas actually Surveyed by that warrant.

P. Word, by his last Will, left this Land to two Grand dau'rs, one of which is Dead without Issue, but the husband of the other (who also has not as yet any Issue) proposes to pay off the Quitt rents, which are almost all in arrear, if he may obtain a Patent of Confirma'on thereupon.

But an objection arising in favour of the next heirs by Blood in Case the p'sent Should die without Issue, 'tis proposed that the Petitioners obtain from under the hands of all Such p'sumptive heirs and those who may be Such their full Consent that a Patent Shou'd be so Granted, and upon producing Such a Certificate and paying the rents for the whole the land Contains from the first Grant of the warr't, a Pattent is ordered. See page 58.

J. Steel having been appointed by this Board Collect'r of the Prop'rs Quitt r'ts in the County of Kent, where he appears as an Agent for the Prop'r, by the Direction of the Sec'ry, &c. He represents that Timothy Hansen, Joshua Clayton and divers others have applied to him that they might take up upon Rent or Purchase Certain Parcells of vacant Marshes and fast Lands in Divers parts of the Counties, for which he desires the direction of the Board and to be Informed in Generall what encouragem't he may give to Such as Shall hereafter apply to him to take up Land. But the Board thought fitt only to give him one Generall Direction, viz't, to make the best Terms he cou'd with Such as wanted Such Lands or Marshes as are free to be disposed of.

Signed a Patent to Richard Hill for 100 feet in 2d Street, ordered 20th Inst.

Signed a Patt't to Rob't Pyle for 212 acres out of Rocklands, Granted by a Warr't dat. 1, 4 mo., 1709, for 200 acres at £30, old Currency, p. C., and now confirmed.

Signed a Warr't to Rich'd Hill for Resurveying 442 acres in Bucks, ord'd the 20th.

Signed a Warr't to Rich'd Hill for James Hill's Lotts and Lib. Land, order'd 20th.

Signed a Warrt' to Thomas FFairman for 200 acres, ordered 20th.

Signed a Warrant Renewing the order of the 23d 6 m., 1703, for J. Steel, order'd this day.

At a meeting of the Commissioners the 12th 9ber, 1712.
Present, Richard Hill, Isaac Norris, James Logan.

William Garrett, of Darby, appearing at the Board (by the Direction of the friends of that meeting to whom the Commissioners lately wrote Concerning him) in order to make Satisfaction for the offence for which he was complained against, Does before the Board acknowledge his Error and Condemn his Proceedings in taking up those 42 acres of Land mentioned in the Said Complaint in the manner he did it, To which Said Land, as located within the Said Surveyed Tract of the Proprietor's or within any part thereof, he renounces all manner of Claim for the future, directly or indirectly, Resolving to take up the Said Land elsewhere according to the Tenor of the warr't, and thereupon he desires the Commissioners to pass by his offence herein. In witness whereof he Signs this Minute with his own hand.

WM. GARRETT.

Hans Peterson, near Brandywine, producing the Copy of a Warrant from the former Commiss'rs, dat. 1st 6 mo., 1689, directed to Ja. Bradsh'w, Survey'r of Newcastle, for laying out to the Said Hans upon old rent 300 acres of Land where vacant near his own, in Consideration of the Indian Purch's, which he had made of a Tract on Brandywine before the Prop'rs time, of which 300 acres he says H. Hollingsworth, the Deputy Surveyor of that County, laid out to him only 150 acres of the Proprietor's Land, the rest being made up to him by 150 acres of the Mill Land, w'ch was his own many years before; he therefore desires this Board to grant him other 150 acres of the Prop'rs Land in lieu thereof, together with a Resurvey on all he holds.

But his Titles not appearing, Geo. Dakeyne is ordered by the Secret'y's Lett'r to Inquire fully into all his Claims, and Resurvey his Land as requested.

Signed a Pattent to Evan Rees, ordered 20th of Oct'r, for 100 ac's, Dat. ye 1st Inst.

At a meeting of the Commissioners the 19th of Nov'r, 1712.
Present, Richard Hill, Isaac Norris, James Logan.

Herman Groethousen, who a few years agoe came into this Prov., having had Deeds from the Prop'r for 500 acres of Land, applied to the late Commissioners (as Some of them inform) for the s'd, upon which a warr't was prepared for him, but instead of Calling for it he Seated himself on the Mannor of Springfield, in the County of Philad'a, which being rep'sented to the Board the Said Herman was Summoned to appear this day and produce his Authority for so Settling.

And for this he produces a Lease under the Proprietor's hand and Seall, bearing date the 30th of the 10th, 1709, for a thousand years, and a Release dated the next day, Granting to the Said Herman for ever five hundred acres of Land Clear of all Indian Incumbrances in the Province of Pensilvania, between the Rivers of Susquehannah and Delaware, there together, w'th all and every the Proffitts, Commodities and Hereditaments whatsoever unto the Same belonging, every acre to be admeasured and computed according to tne Statute, 33d Edw'd 1st, Royall mines and all others excepted [This is the whole Grant], paying yearly, and the s'd Herman doth for himself and his heirs Covenant and Grant to pay yearly as a Chief or quitt rent for every acre that Shall be taken up one penny Sterl'g, to Commence within 3 years after Seating. But in another Paper Signed by the Prop'r, dated the 30th of December, the Payment of the Said Rent is released till Seven years after Seating, and by an Indorsement on the Release of the Said 30th of 10, the Proprietor further Grants one-Twentieth part of all Royall Mines and two-fifth parts of all other Mines, they paying a Proportionable part of the Charge. The Proprietor also Reserves to himself, &c., free Liberty to Search for Mines in the Said Lands, and further by the Said Indorsement grants Liberty to Hawk, Hunt, Fish and fowl, &c.

This being the Sum of the whole Grant, in which no Particular Priveledge is mentioned, He is required to remove off from the Said Land, otherwise he must be proceeded against and ejected without Delay.

Because the Said Herman appears a stranger to our Constitution and he has laid out most of what he had on a Settlement made upon it, The Board has Considered and are willing to grant that he may enjoy his Improvements for Some years on a Reasonable Rent, He taking up his own 500 acres elsewhere.

———

At a meeting of the Commissioners the 10, 10 m., 1712.

Present, Samuell Carpenter, Richard Hill, Isaac Norris, James Logan.

Divers of the Inhabitants of the City of Phialdelphia and those of Northern Liberties, having this last Fall, by a Petition Represented to the Govern'r and Councill, that an order having been lately passed at that Board for laying out a new Road from the Northern end of the Town to Germantown, The S'd Road might much more commodiously be laid out from the End of the Front street to pass over the Mill Creek at the Gov'rs Mill Landing. w'ch wou'd Serve for the Road as well to Frankford as Germantown, and that divers Persons, viz't, The Petitioners and others, were so very Sensible of the Advantage of Such a Road that they had Subscribed Considerably towards the building of a Stone Bridge over the said Mill Creek at their Proper Charge, which Bridge is now very farr advanced.

But the undertakers Still wanting further Subscriptions it is Represented to this Board that Such a Bridge will be very much for the Int. and conveniency of the Govern'rs Mill, and therefore it is pray'd:

That the Commissioners would in the Proprietor's behalf Contribute Something towards the finishing of the Said Bridge, as the Gener'ty of those who have any Interest in that Road have already done, Which be'g taken into Consideration and the Proposall thereupon approved of and concurred with, 'Tis ordered that the Receiv'r pay Three pounds fifteen shill'gs of the Present Currency (divers others hav'g Subscribed the Same Sum), to the Said undertakers to promote so Good a work.

William Rakestraw, Jun'r, applying to ye Board for the Grant of a Small piece of Ground at the North End of the Town and about Eight or Nine streets back from Delaware for Erecting a Brick kill and Digging of Clay, 'tis agreed that he Shall be accommodated upon a Reasonable Consideratin, as well of Improvements to be made, as of yearly Rent, and is referred to the Secretary to fix the place, and after a full agreement 'tis allowed that he Shall have a Grant.

John Roads, near the mannor of Springfield, in the County of Philad'a, requests that the Board wou'd be pleased to grant him two acres of Ground in the Said Mannor for a short Term of years for building a School house for the accommodation of the Neighbourhood, wh'h is Granted.

Phinehas Pemberton having on his Death Bed the 1st of 1 mo., 1701-2, moved to the Secretary, who was then present with him, that he would procure a Grant to him from the Proprietor (which he had been given to Except) of that Small quantity of overplus which he Judged wou'd be found in his Tract of 800 acres in Wrights Town, in the County of Bucks, in Consideration of his attendance on the Proprietary's Gov'r in Council at Newcastle, in the 9th and 10th m'ths, 1700, at which time his absence from his Family and affairs proved Injurious to him, As also that the Quitt rents of his Lands Should be remitted to him during the time that Samuell Jennings was Rece'r Gen'll, in Consideration of his Perpetual assistance Given to the Said Samuel in Executing that Trust.

And Israel Pemberton, Son and heir to the Said Phinehas, having applied for a confirma'on of the Said Tract of 800 acres in Wrights Town, which Tract is now found by a Strict Resurvey to Contain only 896 acres, viz't, but 16 acres above his Right, and the allowance of Ten p. C. made by Law, he desires the Same may be Granted to him, and accordingly the Said 16 acres are granted as also the other part of the Said Phinehas's request, viz't, that the Quittrents of his Lands be remitted for the time herein before mentioned.

And a pattent being p'pared for ye s'd 896 a's, the Same is now Sig'd, dat. 8, 4m., 1713.

Geo. Smedley, of the County of Chester, desiring to Purchase 200 acres of that Vacant Land where Wm. Garrett took up those 41 acres, mentioned and Released by Wm. the 12th ult. ; his request is referred to furth'r consid'n.

At a meeting of the Commissioners the 31st 10ber, 1712.

Present, Samuell Carpenter, Rich'd Hill, Isaac Norris, James Logan.

John Carter, Brickmaker, being Possessed of those 5 Squares at the North End of the Town and about the 7th and 8th streets from Dela., which were formerly granted to B. Chambers for the Term of 21 years at 50 shill'gs p. ann., which Term expires the next first month, John Mifflin requests a Grant of them, the Said John Carter being at Present disabled to follow that Business. But the Said John having Still hopes of Conti'ng it (as he has informed Some of this Board), the matter is referred to further consideration, with a Promise notwithstanding to Said Mifflin that in Case Carter has them not he Shall have the Preference of all others upon Such reasonable Terms as he may hereafter be agreed on.

Jonas Potts having obtained of the late Commissioners a Grant of 300 acres in Gilberts mannor for Seven years under a Certain Rent, applies to the Board for the Priviledge of Purchasing it. But he is first ordered to pay the arrears due on his Lease, and after an Exact return of Survey of the whole mannor has been made, he may further apply for it and is to have the Preference of it before all others, he paying as good a price for it.

The Prop'r having many years ago Sent over into this Province one Martha Durant, a Relation of his own, with her husband, John Durant, and Children, She now, by her Petition to the Board Represents that being left a Widow and wholly destitute of all manner of Support She must of necessity perish for want or come upon the Publick, unless the Proprietor, upon whose Encouragement She and her family Transported themselves, shall think fitt to relieve and assist her, and being discoursed She Expresses a Great Inclan'on to do any manner of Business that She is Capable of for a Subsistance, if She cou'd be put into a way for it, adding that her Cousin, R. Assheton, was willing to advance Something for her if the Proprietor woud² do the Same.

And the Present miserable Circumstances of the woman being taken into Consideration, 'tis the opinion of the Board that She ought immediately to be relieved and Supported above want, that being a Relation of the Proprietor's, Sent over by him, She may not become a charge to the Publick; 'tis ordered therefore that R. Assheton be Treated with, and as She is desirous to keep a small Shop for Drams and Hucksters ware, that five pounds be immediately advanced to her by the Receiver, and that he use his best Care that She may not want.

Ordered that Robert Edwards, who is Seated on the mannor of Gilberts, be forthwith called on to know on what Right he pretends to hold that Land, having never hitherto paid any Consideration for it.

Ordered that the Business of overplus Lands be forthwith inquired into, in pursuance of the Late Law for Confirming Grants and Pattents, That a Copy of that Law be provided for the use of the Board and accounts of the overplus Lands found by the Late Resurvey be put into order, to be proceeded upon as the Said Law Directs.

At a meeting of the Commissioners the 7th of the 11th mo., 1712-3.

Present, Samuell Carpenter, I'ac Norris, James Logan.

Andrew Morton, Jno. Morton and Geo. Vanculin, of Ridly Township, in the County of Chester, being of the old Swedish settlers there, produce a Deed of Gift, dat.   , 170 , from their Uncle, Jno. Bartleson, Granting them 300 acres of Land near Stone Creek and Crum Creek, which by Mutual Bonds between Jno. Hendrickson and ye S'd Jno. Bartleson are agreed to be cut off and divided as in the s'd Bonds is Expressed, together with a Parcell of Marsh lieing between the fast land, one of the Creeks and the River, which Marsh they also Claim a Right to to make up the Deficiency which is in their other Lands, as they pretend.

The Said Persons request Pattents of confirma'on on the Said Land and their Share of the Marsh; Geo. Vanculin also desires a Pattent on 60 acres left him by his Father in the Said

Township, which was formerly held for 50 acres, but as he alledges from Some affidavits made of a Grant from Upland Court, Shou'd have been one hundred acres. But the Board taking into Consideration the uncertainty of the pres't Division of the Lands that were Bartlesons' from those of Hendrickson, and the Danger there may be of Disputes hereafter Concerning the Said Division, unless better settled, think fitt to defer Granting any Such Pattents untill a full Division be made and agreed to under their hands and Seals respectively for a foundation for the Pattents, and they are Directed forthwith to make Such a Division, after which their Claims of the Marsh, &c., are to be Considered.

William Fisher, of the County of Sussex, arriving from thence this morning, brings an acco't, as well Verbally as by Letters from Thomas Fisher, Collector of the Proprietor's quitt rents in the said County; that the Said Collector having last week distrained on a Parcell of Wheat belonging to Berkly Codd, who married the Widow of Luke Watson, Junior, deceased, for the Quittrents due from that Plantation, the Said Codd had Replevined it and Sent it up to Philadelphia for Sale, Boasting that now he would try the Proprietor's Title, &c.

J. Logan also informed that he had Early in the morning been with the Lawyers to take advice whether the Said Wheat cou'd be Seized here [advice having been brought to him of it before day] and had retained J. Moore in the Cause by Giving him a Guinea for a ffee, to prevent Codd's doing it by his fr'd here, to whom the Wheat is Sent, but that he found the Said Wheat Could not regularly be touched again in the Proprietor's behalf, Security having been Given at Lewis to answer for it at the Court, as by the Replevin (a copy of which is Sent up) appears.

The Board approved of the Said J. L's Early Care of giving the s'd Fee and thinking it adviseable and necessary that this affair be Carefully managed and the best Defence that Possible Can be made and in order thereunto 'tis concluded that an Express be immediately Sent to Andrew Hamilton, a Lawyer in Cecil County, in Maryland, who Generally attends our Courts below, to Engage him in the Cause.

William Fisher, of Sussex, by his Petition, requests a Grant of one hundred acres of Land on Hog Hammock, in the Bottom of Slaughter Neck, in the Said County, lieing Convenient to his other Land, as also of Fifty acres of Land in the Marsh of Parsymmon Hammock, adjoin'g to one hund'd acres, of which he is possessed. But the Board being unacquainted with the nature and Value of what is requested, think fit to defer it till further Information Can be had. In the meantime, as the Petit'r, by his Fidelity to the Proprietor, is Instituted to his Favour, 'tis Resolved that he Shall have the Refusall of these Lands (if free and Vacant) upon as reasonable Terms as they may be conven'ly Granted.

Ordered a Warr't to David Brintnall for a City Lott in right of Alexander Mell's Purchase, entered 20 of 6 mo. last; the Title is as follows:

The Proprietor, by Deeds of Lease and Release, dat. 31st March and 1st of Aprill, 1682, Granted to Alexander Mell, Son of Alexander Mell, late of Martin le Grand, in the County of Middlesex, Perfumer, 250 acres of Land in this Province. Alexander Mell, by a short Deed, dated the 22d of August, 1693, Granted the Said 250 acres of Land (for 20 shill'gs) unto Tho's Gibson, of the City of Lond'n, Pattenmaker, and his heirs, &c., who by Deed dated the 15th July, 1709 (for £3), Conveys the Same to David Brintnall, of Philadelphia, Shop keeper, his heirs and assigns for ever.

———

At a meeting of the Commissioners the 21st 11 mo., 1712-3.

Present, Samuell Carpenter, Richard Hill, Isaac Norris, James Logan.

Morris Lewellin Solliciting that a Pattent for the Land mentioned and the overplus agreed for the 27th of 8ber may be Issued, and having been Informed that D. Powell, of Philad'a, had desired to be heard by the Board before the Same was Granted, for which hearing this day was appointed by the Secretary; the Said Morris accordingly Came together with James Thomas, who Conveyed the Said Land, but D. Powell being prevented by Sickness from attend'g, James Thomas declares as follows, viz't: that upon his first Sale of that Land to Morris Lewellin, the Bargain was Drawn up in writeing, dated the last day of the 7th Month, 1705, that D. Powell, after this applying to him, told him he cou'd put him in a way to gett £8 or £10 by it and then proposed to purchase of him his Right to the overplus, that James Shewed David the Written Agreem't, upon w'ch David told him he had by that made over all his right and he would meddle no further in it, that afterwards David Sent him word he had thought of a way how he might Still Grant that overplus Safely, which was then or afterwards proposed to be by antidating a Deed for it to the other agreement with M. Lewellin, that accordingly a Deed was drawn which he Signed to D. Powell, and has his Bond for £8 Consideration, but avers the agreement was first made with M. Lewellin for the whole.

MINUTE BOOK "H." 545

The Board notwithstanding think fitt to order that D. Powell may be heard before the Pattent is Granted.

M. Lewellin produces a Return of Survey of the Said Hundred acres made by his Brother, David Lewellin, Surveyor, by the Secretary's Direction, by which the Said overplus is found to contain 30 acres, besides the allowance for Roads, &c., and therefore if the Same be granted to Morris he is to pay for the whole, accord'g to his first Agreement £16 13s 4d.

He produces the following Titles to his Lands, viz't: The Proprietary, by Deeds of L. and Release, dat. ye 16 and 17th days of June, 1682, granted to Rich'd Davies, of Welchpool, in the Co'ty of Montgom'ry, Gent., his Heirs, &c., 1,250 a's of Land in this Province. R'd Davies, by Ind. Tripartite, dated 19, 6 mo., 1686, granted for £32 16s to Stel, late of the Parish of Llancilis, Coun. Caemarthen, Yeoman, and Ellis Ellis, of Haverford, in Pensilvania, 410 acres, Part of a Tract laid (in Meirion) near the Township of Haverford, to hold to them and their heirs, &c., Ten Acres thereof to the use of Thomas Ellis; 100 acres to the use of Frances Howel and his Heirs, &c.; 100 acres to the use of Morgan David, his Heirs, &c.; 100 acres to the use of Francis Loyd, his Heirs, &c., and the other 100 acres to the use of James Thomas, &c.

James Thomas at his Decease left the Said 100 acres, then divided and cutt off from the rest, to his Son and Heir, James Thomas, who by the Name of J. Thomas, of ye Township of Whitland, in the Co'ty of Chest'r, Yeoman, by Ind. dat. 9th FFebbr'y, 1708, in Consid'n of £110 granted the same (including ye overplus) to Mor's Lewellin, of Haverf'd, his Heirs, &c.

Francis Howell, by his last Will, dat. 15th 1 mo., 1695, granted those Hundred acres alloted to him to his Son, Tho. Howell, &c., who by Deed Ind., dat. 17th June, 1708, in Considera'on of 5 sh. and Natural Affection, &c., granted the Said 100 acres, Messuage, &c., to the Said Morris, w'ch being Resurveyed is found to be Bare Measure.

The Prop'ry, by Deeds of L. and Rel., dat. 14 and 15th 6 mo., 1682, granted to Joshua Holland, of Chatham, in the County of Kent, Mariner, in England, Five thousand Acres of Land in this Province, and to his Heirs, &c. Joshua Holland, by his Power of Att'ry, dated 19th May, 1683, granted irrevocably to his Son John Holland, of Chatham, aforesaid, Shipwright, full Power to take up and dispose of to his own use and behoofe one Thousand Acres of the Said Land, who accordingly took up the Same near upper Meirion, and by Deed dat. 13, 3 mo., 1685, Conveyed 500 Acres, part thereof, to Geo. Collet, of Philad'a, Glover, his Heirs, &c., who by his Nuncupative Will in 10ber, 1685, gave the same to his Nephew, Nathaniel Pennock his Heirs, &c. Nath'll dying without Issue, his ffather, Chr. Pennock, administered on his Estate, and by Consent of Court Sold the Said Lands for Payment of his Son's Debts, and by Deed dat. 1, 1 mo., 1697-8, for £100 conveyed all the Said 500 Acres of Land to Morris Lewellin, of the Township of Haverford, Yeom'n, who by his Deed dat. 5 June, 1708, granted 400 thereof to his Son Morris Lewellin aforesaid.

The Said M. Lewellin, Jun'r, being possessed of 100 Acres from Ja. Thomas, with the Overplus included, sold by the Board 100 Acres from T. Howell, and these 400 Acres from his ffather, desires a Pattent of Confirmation on the whole, which is granted, when it appears that the 400 Acres have no Overplus.

A Warrt' of Resurvey, dat. 27, 12 mo., 1702, was granted on the whole 500 Acres from Holland, and 'tis found to contain Acres, but M. Lewellin's grant, his Son is said to Contain barely 400 Acres.

The Comm'rs, by their Warr't dated ye 28th of Jan'ry, 1701-2, granted to Paul Garretson, of the County of New C., one Moiety of a Vacant Tract of Land inclosed by the New Welch Line and the Lands of Judge Guest and Jno. Ogle, near White Clay Creek, provided the whole did not contain above 500 acres, in Pursuance whereof there was Surveyed to him a Tract of 230 acres, the other Moiety being at the Same time granted to James Harland, and about 60 Acres of the Same Vacancy to Sam'l Lowman at £12 10s p. C. and a Bushell of Wheat Yearly.

Paul Garretson, by Deed dat. the 28 of October last (having paid none of the consideration money) granted his Right to the Said Land and the Improvements made thereon to James Armitage and his Heirs, who offers to pay the Said Consideration money and ye Int. due thereon, and Requests a Patt't. Granted.

John Carter, Brickmaker, having had in his Poss'ion five Squares of Ground in Philad'a City, at the Northern Side thereof, w'ch were first granted to B. Chambers, in his Possession, on Part of which Brick kilns were erected, and the Lease having been for Some time expired, Jno. Mifflin, who last had the Last Kilns in his Possession under John Carter, desires to take ye Same on Rent, And by an Agreement with the Said John Mifflin the Said Kilns and Yard are now Granted him (with Ground Sufficient for digging of Clay) and all the Buildings erected thereon, to hold to him, his Executors, administrators and Assigns, for the space of Five Years from the First day of March next ensuing, for which he is to pay to the Prop'ry and Trustees use Five and Twenty Pounds on the

First Day of the third Month or May next and Five Pounds Yearly on the First day of the First Month in Every Year during the said Term, and the s'd John is to have Liberty to carry off anything that Shall be Standing thereon at the Expiration of the s'd Term, but proposes further to agree for a Piece of Ground near the Same Place for a Pasture, to be cleared and turned into Grass, to be held upon Rent for a Longer Term, the Priviledge of which is Promised him on such Terms as may be Agreed on.

The late Commissioners, by their Warr't dat. 23 of FFebr'y, 1702, granted to Thomas Jones and Cadwallader Jones, Executors of the last Will of Catharine Thomas, late of the Township of Meirion, their Mother, to take up in the Welch Tract one hundred Acres of Land, Part of 200 acres Sold by the former Comm'rs to Hugh Roberts, whereof one moiety was for the Said Catharine's use, In Pursuance of which Warr't there was Surveyed and laid out to the Said Executors in the said Welch Tract, Joining on the Lands of Mordecai Moore, John David, James Atkinson and Owen Roberts, the Said quantity of one hundred acres.

Thomas Jones and Cadwallader Jones, by their Deed Poll, dated the 14th of this Instant, in consideration of £20 granted the Said 100 acres to Thomas Rees, of Meirion, his Heirs and Assigns, who requests a Pattent thereon.

Ja. Logan having formerly produced to the Board an Order from the Proprietary, bearing date the 5th Day of December, A. D., 1711, directing y't those hundred acres of Land recovered Some Years agoe at the County Court of Philad'a, from the Estate of Robert Longshore, Should be deemed as City Liberty Land, &c., which order is in these Words, viz't:

To my Commiss'rs of Property for the Province of Pensilvania, &c.:

Whereas, Robert Longshore, late of the Said Province, obtained of Some of my former Comm'rs a Grant of Eighty acres of Land within the Liberties of the city of Philad'a, between Delaware and Schuylkill, and passed his Obligation to me for a Certain Sum that he wou'd restore the "like quantity within the Said Liberties, to be for the use of the Original Purchasers for whom those Liberties were alloted or intended.

"And Whereas, the said Rob't dying before he made good his said Contract, the Penalty of the Said Obligation (as it has been made known to me) was levied by Execution upon a certain Tract of Land then belonging to the Estate of the said Robert, adjoining or near to the said Liberties beyond Schuylkill, and Whereas the Liberty Lands of the Said city by Means of Such Practices have faln short and proved so deficient that divers Original Purchasers, as I am inform'd, cannot obtain their Right therein. I do therefore hereby order and direct you to all the said Land recovered of the Estate of Robert Longshore to be accounted as Liberty Land, in lieu of which it was taken and that my Secretary, James Logan, may be admitted if he desire it to take any Such Liberty Lands, as by Purchase he has a Right to, out of the Same. Given under my hand at London the 5th Day of Dece'r, 1711.

WM. PENN.

And the Board having by their Warrant, bearing date the 30th 5 month last, in Pursuance of the Said Ord'r directed the Surveyor Generall to lay out the Said Land to the said J. Logan in Right of the Purchases Mentioned in the said Warr't if there shou'd be Occasion for the same. He accordingly returned it as Liberty Land Surveyed to J. Logan in right of Hugh Lamb's Purchase of 2,500 Acres, Edw'd Bettris's Purchase of 2,000 acres, and Samuell Noyes' Purchase of 500 Acres, Compleating in the whole 5,000 Acres, to all which the said J. L. formerly proved his Right. At the Request therefore of the s'd J. Logan that the said Land might be confirmed to him by Pattent, the Commissioners have ordered that the Sheriff of Philad'a (from whom the Title to the Said Land must upon the aforesaid Execution be derived) do forthwith grant the said Hundred acres of Land to the s'd Ja. Logan, or to any other p'son or Persons for his use, and to his Heirs and assigns, without requiring in the Proprietor's behalfe, in whose Name the Action was commenced, any consideration for the Same, further than that he Shall be obliged to pay the arrears of Quitt rents heretofore due thereon, and a Warr't is Ordered to be drawn directed to the sheriff of Philad'a for this Purpose.

A Warr't in Pursuance of the Said Order was drawn and signed by Three of the Commissioners, dated the 24th Instant.

At a meeting of the Commissioners at Philad'a 11th 1st month, 1712-3.

Present, Richard Hill, Isaac Norris, James Logan.

The Proprietary, by Lease and Release, dated (as p. attested Copies produced by John Estaugh) the 21st and 22d of December, 1681, granted to Gilbert Mace, Citizen and Weaver, of London, and to his Heirs and ass's forever 500 acres of Land in this Province. Gilbert Mace, by Ind. of L. and Release, dated the 12th and 13th Days of May, 1684, for £5 5s granted 250 acres, Part of the said 500 acres, to John Marlow, of St.

Katherine's, in the County of Middlesex, Mariner, and to his Heirs, &c., forever, and by like Inds., dated the 23d and 24th of April, 1711, the said Gilbert (for £5 3s) granted the other 250 acres, with all Liberty Lands, Town Lotts, &c., thereunto belonging to the said John Marlow, his Heirs and ass's forever. Jno. Marlow, by like Ind's, bearing Date the 23d and 24th Days of May, 1709 (for £5), granted all those 250 acres first Purchased by him to Eliza Pace, of St. Katherine's aforesaid, Spinster, her Heirs and assigns forever. John Estaugh, in behalf of the Said El. Pace, requests a Warrant for taking up the said 250 acres of Land.

And in behalf of the said John Marlow he also requests a Warrant for taking up the other 250 acres, as also the Town Lott belonging to the whole 500 acres Purchased by Mace, which Lott falls on Delaware side, Numb'r . Ordered that warr's be granted accordingly.

Chr. Pennock, deceased, having proved a Right in his Son, Jos. Pennock, of 500 acres of Land in this Province, as by ye Minute of the Secretary's Office of Property, dat. 17th 12th mo., 1700-1, appears, one moiety of the said Land being the Orig'all Purchase of Francis Rogers, and the others the Purchase of Wm. Rogers, who granted their whole Right to Geo. Col'et, Uncle to the said Joseph, and there being found upon a search in the Surveyor's Office that there is taken up

	Acres.
in the Said Right in the City Liberties,	100
Beyond Brandiwine, in 5 Tracts, p. H. Holl.,	2,300
Ibid, in 2 Tracts, by H. Taylor,	1,250
On Schuylkill, an old Survey,	1,000
In the whole,	4,650

So that there Seems yet to remain untaken up 350 acres. The said Joseph Pennock Requests a Warr't for taking up the said quantity of Land, and Whereas the Proprietor, by his Warr't in the Year 1709, granted to Chr. Pennock to take up 200 Acres in the said Right out of the Overplus found to be in the last mentioned Tract of one thousand acres beyond Schuylkill, which Warr't notwithstanding was never Executed; the Said Joseph requests that he may be allowed to decline the said 200 acres and leaving the same to the Proprietor's Use, he now having no Interest in the said Originall Tract, and that the Board wou'd grant him to take up the whole Remainder of his Purchase, to be laid out in Chester County, according to the Common Method, which wou'd suit his occasions better than the Said overplus, tho' that in itself be more valuable than any that he can so take. Which request being Considered by the Board, 'tis granted that he Shall have a Warr't for what shall appear to be realy due to him, he resigning all Manner of Claim to the said grant of 200 acres in the aforesaid Overplus.

The Proprietor's Mill in the Northern Liberties, near Philad'a, having for Severall years past proved only a charge to him, without any Manner of Profitt, and none of the Severall Millars who have undertaken it having been able even to Subsist upon it, but have generally either failed or run away from it in Debt. It was Some time agoe thought advisable by the Comm'rs to dispose of it if a chapman sho'd Offer, and Tho. Masters, the nearest Neighb'r to it, having been treated with, the Commissioners at a casual meeting with the said Thomas lately, came to a full agreement with him for the Same, viz't, that the said Mill in the condition it now is, with the Thirteen acres of Land belonging to it and that Slip of Land which he has taken into his Plantation out of Springetsbury, now found to contain Eight acres, shou'd be granted to him in Consideration of Two Hundred and Fifty Pounds of the present Currency, one Hundred Pounds thereof to be paid in Hand and the other one Hundred and Fifty Pounds at next Philadelphia Fair, in Flour (that being at Present more Valuable than Money), at the Markett Price, and a Patent is accordingly to be granted to him for the Same.

Joseph Growdon renewing his application to the Board, requests (by his Letter now read) That in Consideration of the Proprietor's Encouragm't given him at First to transport himself and of his Severall Services in the Government Since his arrivall to this Time, the Board wou'd grant him Fifty Acres of Land for Each Servant imported by him (which were about 45 in Number), under the Common Yearly Quitt rent of one shill'g sterling p. Hund'd, But there being Nothing to be found in any of the Proprietor's grants that may Justify this, the said Request is Dismiss'd.

A Pattent to James Logan for 100 acres Liberty Land recovered from R. Longshore's Estate in Kinsess., was signed, Dated the 29th 11 mo. last, Rent 1 shill'g Sterling.

A Pattent to Joseph Cloud for 150 acres out of Rocklands, sold him by the former Comm'rs in 1703, was signed, dated 30, 11 m. last.

Signed a Warr't to Eliza Pace for 250 acres in Right of Gilbert Mace, dat. 12th Inst.

A warrant to Jno. Marlow for 250 acres in the same Right, dat. id.

A Warrant to John Marlow for a city Lott in the same Right, dat. id.

Richard James having by Geo. Dakeyne Requested a Grant of 150 or 200 acres of Land in the Forest, at the Lower End of Newcastle County, at a Penny p. acre, he having Seated on the same, 'tis granted him, he paying the Rent from the Time he Entered upon it, which is about Two Years agoe, and a warrant is Signed, dated 12th 1 month.

Joshua Clayton, of Kent County, desiring to purchase one Hundred a's of Salt Marsh, he agrees to pay Fifteen Pounds for the same within Three Months, and his Request being granted, a Warrant is signed for the same, date Id.

———

At a meeting of the Commissioners 6, 2d month, 1713.
Present, Richard Hill, Isaac Norris, James Logan.

James Steel and Thomas Sharp having discovered that the Bounds of the Tract of Land they bought of Jos. Growdon, called Whitwell's Chance, in Kent County, have been broke in upon as well by a Survey made by Evan Jones, already complained of, as by another made ih Favour of Geo. Martin; they by Means of the Warrant or Order from this Board, dated the 28th 8ber last, recovered the True Bounds of the Said Tract, and they now hold one Hundred acres of that Tract granted to the said Evan Jones and 130 acres granted to Geo. Martin (for 100 acres only) on the Northern side, whereupon the children of the said George being dispossessed of the said Land crave a warr't for taking up the like quantity in the Forest, which is granted to William Annand in Right of his Wife, Daughter to the said George, and her Brothers, they paying Rent from the First Survey of the aforesaid Land granted to the said George Martin, viz't for 30 years.

John Gumly having refused to hold that Land on Bombay Hook, for which he agreed and obtained a Warrant last 3d Month, John Pain, of Kent County (by James Steel), applies for the same and agrees to take in as much broken Marsh and Cripples adjoining as will make up the whole one Hundred acres, for which he is to pay Twenty Pounds in Three Months, and to be at all the charge of Escheating it if there be Occasion [that B. Gumly refused this Land as being rated, as they alledge, at double its value.]

Timothy Hansen, of Kent County, requesiting (by J. Steel) a quantity of Salt Marsh on the North Side of Litle Creek, fitt to accommodate his Plantation, 'tis granted that he may have any quantity there, not exceeding 250 acres, at Fifteen Pounds Purchase and a Bushell of Wheat Yearly p. Hundred.

John Dawson, of Kent County, requesting one Hundred acres of Land on Bradshaw's Branch, in the said County, where he has ventured to seat himself, 'tis granted him at a Penny Sterling p. acre p. ann., to be paid from the Time he Entered upon it.

By a Warrant from the Commissioners in 1687 there was surveyed in the Latter End of the Year 1689, to John Allen, a Tract reputed to contain 90 acres, but was granted for a Hundred, Situate in Bristol Township, in Bucks, at a Penny p. acre.

John Allen's Heirs granted all their Rights in this Land, being now found on the late Resurvey to contain 116 acres, to John Hall, of Bristoll, Cooper, and his Heirs. The Secretary last Summer agreed with J. Hall that they Should hold the whole said 116 acres, they paying Rent for the same from the Beginning, and so to continue without any Abatement for the allowance of 10 p. C., and accordingly J. Hall then paid all the arrears due on 87 acres thereof, and Ralp. Boon, by Discount for Work done at Pennsbury in 1700-1, paid the arrears also of the other 29 acres to the Year 1709 Exclusive.

'Tis hereupon ordered that Jno. Hall have a Pattent on the Said 116 acres.

Signed a Pattent to Caleb Prew for 160 acres in Rocklands on New Rent, formerly granted his Father, John Prew, dated this Day.

Signed a Pattent to John Hall for 116 acres, Ordered this day, dated the 9th.

Signed a Warrant to William Annand for 100 acres in Kent, ordered and dated this day. A Warrant to Timothy Hansen for 250 acres of Marsh in Kent, ordered and dated this day. A Warr't to John Pain for 100 acres in Bombay Hook, ordered and dated this day. A Warrant to John Dawson for 100 acres of Land on Kent, ordered and dated this day.

Jacob Stauber, late of Zurick, in Switzerland, applying to the Secretary to purchase 500 acres between the River Schuylkill and the French Creek, on the West Side of the said River, they agreed for the Same at £12 p. C., viz., £60, of which Tenn Pounds is to be paid in Hand upon the Warrant, £25 on the Tenth Day of October next and the remaining £25, with 6 months Interest, on the 10th of April, 1714.

Signed a Warrant to Jacob Stauber for the s'd 500 acres, dated 8th Instant.

At a Meeting of the Commissioners the 15th 2d Month, 1713. Present, Samuell Carpenter, Is. Norris, James Logan.

Edward Farmer having long pleaded in Bar of the Payment of his Quitr'ts, a Debt due to him for a Serv't of his Fathr's that went to Pennsbury, now applies to the Board and represents the Case as follows, viz't:

That the Proprietor in the year 1683, or thereabouts, desired of Edw'd's Uncle, Maj'r Jasper FFarmer, to assist him with a skilfull Carpenter for the building of Pennsbury, that accordingly he sent him one of his Serv'ts, named Geo. Booth, with a Large chest of Carpenter's Tools, belonging to his Said Master, that not long after this Serv't run away, and all the Tools being left at Pennsbury or disposed of by the Serv't, were also lost to their owner, his said Uncle, or more properly to him, the said Edward to whom upon his Father's Decease they belonged, being his Estate. Edward hereupon desires that some Allowance may be made him in his Rent, which being considered, 'Tis agreed and ordered that the Receiver Gener'll Discount w'th him Five Pounds out of the Rents due from his Lands, to be further consid'd [but it being since Discovered that Jasper FFarmer died in the Prop'rs debt, as appears by his Bond for £50, this Grant is Vacated. J. L.]

Edward Farmer obtained of the Former Commissioners a Grant of and Warrant for one Hund'd acres in the Mann'r of Springfield, adjoining on his other Lands, for which he was to pay Ten Pounds, but the Prop'rs Lett'rs forbid'g all Sales of his Mannor Lands arriving immediately after, he never had any Pattent or Confirmation of the same, But now desires it, together with one Hundred acres adjoining to be added to the other, for which he agrees to pay one Hundred Pounds of the Present Currency, one-half thereof the 25th of Nov'r next and the other half at the May ffair of Philad'a, A. D. 1714, And a Warrant is ordered thereupon.

The Assembly having last Summer passed an act Granting the fferry over Schuylkill to Benja. Chambers, his Executors and Assigns, for the Term of 21 years, for the Proprietor's consent to which by his Commissioners, he then paid £50; he now requests a Confirmation of the said Grant by Pattent from the Commissioners, an further prays that he may have an Addition of one acre on each Side of the Road out of the Vacancy betw'n the Swedes Land and the River.

Ordered that a Pattent be granted as requested for so much as is granted by the said act of assembly, but the Vacancy lieing between the Swedes Tract and the River being, as it appears, casually left out of the said Tract at the First Survey, is not (as yet) to be alienated from them.

Matthias Nitzilius, of Darby Township, having often complained to the Board, now renews the same as follows, viz., Sir

Edmond Andros, by Patent dated 25th March, 1676, granted to Henry Coleman and Peter Putcon a Tract on the Mill Creek, called one Hundred acres in the Patent, by the Courses and Distances as Expressed in the Said Patent contained at least Two Hundred acres out of the Bounds of this Tract. By some Mistake of the Surveyors the Proprietor granted to Richard Tucker one Hundred acres in Lieu of some Land that he had a Right to in the Tract laid out for the Mannor of Springetsbury, which is since come into the Hands of Sarah Smith, Widow of Thomas Smith, of Darby. M. Nitzilius having now, by Divers mesne Conveyances, the Sole Right to the whole originall Grant from S'r Edmond Andros, requests that this Board would in the Proprietor's behalf do him Justice, and either restore the Land his Predecessors have been deprived of Contrary to all Right, or grant him a Reasonable Satisfaction for it.

But the first of these being impracticable, the Board think fitt to propose to him that in Case he can Shew a Clear and full Right to all the Origin'll Grant, as is alledged, that then he Shall be favoured in any other Tract that he shall choose, the same being Vacant and Free to be disposed off.

Matthias Nitzilius' Title is as follows ·

Sir Edm'd Andros, by Pat't dated 25th March, 1676, granted to Henry Colem'n and Peter Putcon a Parcell of Land on the West side of Delaware River, on the Northwest side of a Creek called the Mill Creek, over against Carraconks Hook, beginning at a Corner White Oak on the Creek between this and Calcoon Hook, N. N. W. by Calcoon hook Land 290 Perches to a Marked Red Oak, thence N. E. by a Line of Marked Trees 128 p. to a corner Marked Black Oak on a Branch running into Mohorhoottink Creek, now Darby Creek, thence by the Branch and Creek to the Place of Beginning, containing and laid out for 100 acres of Land, as by the Return of the Survey, &c. The Rent one Bushell of Good Winter Wheat to his Highness's use to Such Person or Persons as Shall have Authority, &c. Recorded at Upland.

Peter Putcon, by an Indorsement on the Pat., dat. 12th 9ber, 1678, granted all his Right, &c., in the said land to Herman Johnson, &c., who by Deed dated 6th 8ber 1691, granted the same to Joseph Wood in the same Terms, viz't, all his Right, &c., in a Parcell of Land laid out for 50 acres, &c., formerly the Land of Peter Putcon, and sold by him to the abovesaid Herman Johnson, beginning at a White Oak on Darby Creek, thence N. N. W. 312 Perches to Calcoon Hook to a black Oak, thence E. N. E. 28 Perches by the Land of Jos. Wood to a stake, thence S. S. E. 300 Perches by Hen.

Coleman's Land to a stake, thence along ye the Swamp to the Place of Beginning, containing, as aforesaid, 50 acres.

J. Wood, by Deed dat. the next day, viz., 7, 8ber, 1691, granted the said 50 acres under the same Bounds to Otto Earnest Cock.

Henry Coleman, by Deed dated 21st 10 Month, 1696 (for £20,) granted to the said Otto Earnest Cock a Parcell of Land Containing 50 acres in the Township of Darby, part of 100 acres, &c., as before, the said Land beginning at a Corner Marked White Oak nigh the Creek side, between this and Calcoon Hook, thence N. N. W. by a Line of Marked Trees by Calcoon Hook Land 290 Perches to a corner Marked Red Oak, &c., as in the Pattent. This Deed Granting half of the whole (but by the name of 50 acres only), with all the Right, &c., of the said H. Coleman in and to the said 50 acres.

Otto Earnest Cock, by Deed dat. 18, 12, 1702-3, grants the whole said 100 acres by the Bounds of the Pattent to Matthias Nitzilius on his Marriage with his Daughter.

John Johnson, Son and Heir of Herman Johnson (as 'tis sayd), by Deed Dated 15th May, 1713, releases all his Right, &c., in and to the said 50 acres and overplus, &c.

By this it appears that M. Nitzilius had Right to no more than 50 acres, as he now holds it from Putcon, but has the whole of Coleman's and Herman Johnson's Heirs release to him may help him in the other.

Signed a Warr't to David Brintnall for a Lott, dated this day, ordered the 7th of the 11th month last, in right of Alexander Mell.

At a meeting of the Commissioners at Philad'a, 13, 3 mo., 1713.

Present, Samuell Carpenter, Richard Hill, Isaac Norris, James Logan.

John Frost, of the County of Bucks, having purchased that Tract in Newtown that was granted to Jonathan Eldridge, desires the Priviledge of Buying a small Vacancy lieing between his Land and the Creek, for which he agreed with the Secre'y at Pensbury to give Eight shillings p. acre, and now being found upon Survey to contain Six acres, 'tis granted at the said Price.

Joshua Story, of Newcastle, having been long treating with the Secretary for a Tract of Vacant Land near Major Donaldson's Plantation in the said County, containing between 3 and 400 acres, on part of which John Calvert, A. D.   , 1701-2, obtained a Grant for 200 acres at £20 p. C., old Currency, but threw up his Bargain, and the said Joshua having earnestly sollicited that he may have Time allowed for Payment, 'tis agreed that he shall have the Said Land for Thirty Pounds, p'sent Currency, p. Hund'd, to be paid without Interest the first of May, A. D. 1715, and a Warrant is ordered.

Jonas Arskin, of Newcastle, having requested the Priviledge of taking up Three hundred acres on North side of Otteraroe, about 3 or 4 miles from the Mouth of it, where a Small Improvement has been made, and having passed thro' sev'll Hands without any Right, is now purchased by the said Jonas, who desires to have a Survey thereon on a Grant from this Province, that he may assert the Proprietor's Right there. 'Tis granted as requested, at the yearly Rent of Two Bushells of Wheat for Each Hundred.

John Budd laid before the Board a Lett'r he had now rece'd from Hen. Hollingsworth, dated 3d Inst., informing that one John Bristow, with some others, who had seated themselves on that Tract called the Lond. Companie's, had obtained from Cha. Carroll, the Lord Baltimore's agent, an order to the s'd Henry (being lately made Surveyor of Cecil County, in Maryland), to Survey to them Two thousand acres of the said Land where they are now Seated, that he, the said Henry, was loth to be concerned in the Survey of any Lands formerly taken up by Rights of this Province, &c., that this Land being to the Northward of Otteraroe falls, not within Maryland, according to the Agent, C. Carroll's Claim, &c., and the said Henry desires that S. Carpenter and T. FFairman, Agents for the London Company, may be applied to, that Measures may be taken to prevent an further proceedings of the same kind.

'Tis ordered hereupon that the Secretary immediately Write to the said Surv'r, H. Holl., desiring him for the Reasons he has advanced in his own Letter to desist till he hear further from the agent, to whom the Matter is now to be represented, and the Secretary is further ordered to draw up a Lett'r to the said agent to be signed by all the Commissioners, a Copy of which is to be inserted in the Minutes of this day.

Jonathan Couper, of Bucks County, having purchased two hundred acres, Part of those thousand acres in Wrights Town, laid out to James Harrison, who first sold the s'd 200 acres to Will'm Couper, Father to the said Jonathan, and Phin's Pemberton, Son, and Israel Pemb., Grandson, to the said James, afterwards granted and confirmed the same. There was found by John Cutter's Resurvey of the said 200 Acres, made by order of Phinehas Pemberton, and in his Life time, 135 acres of Overplus, besides the Allowance for Roads, &c., which overplus the said Jonathan desires to purchase, and 'tis allowed to him at £20 p. C., and thereupon a Pattent ordered for the whole to him, in whom the Title from Wm. Couper shall appear to be duly invested. A Tract of Vacant Land adjoining, cont. 145 acres, is also allowed him at 15 p. C.

Thomas Thompson, Son of Christian Thompson, one of the first Settlers of Taconey Lands, being the first division of the s'd Lands, possessed of 160 Acres, as his share, for which he duly paid Rents to the Year 1689, and having now sold the said Land to Henry Mallows, a Pattent of Confirmation to T. Thompson is requested for the same, which is granted on their paying off the Arrears of Quitt rents to the Rec'vr Generall.

William Burrows, of Duck Creek, having about 12 Years agoe built a Mill on the said Creek, or a Branch thereof, 'tis now found to stand on a Piece of Vacant Ground belonging to the Proprietary, whereupon the said William's Heir and Namesake desires he may Purchase the same. Ordered that it be left to James Steel to sett a Price. Granted afterwards to the Children, p. agreement with J. L. for £10.

Mercy Green, Widow of William Green, of Duck Creek, deceased, produces a Return of one Thousand Acres, but cast up for 1,050 acres, on or near the s'd Creek, Surveyed by Richard Mitchell, by Vertue of two Warrants from St. Jones's Court, the one for 600 Acres, dated 17th 9ber, 1680, the other for 400 Acres, dated the 21st 7ber, 1681, which has never yet (she says) been confirmed by Pattent, and therefore she now desires one.

Ordered that Ja. Steel Examine Some of the Principall Lines of the said Land and if there be no overplus above the Allowance by Law, that then a Pattent be granted to the Person in whom the Right is.

John Jones complaining from Kent County that Jonas Greenwood has refused or delayed to lay out the Land for which by Agreement with the Secretary when in that Cou'ty he obtained a Warr't Mar., 1705-6, being one hundred acres at £8. 'Tis ordered that the Secretary write to said J. G. concerning it.

The Proprietary, by Deeds of L. and Release, dated 12th and 13th 7ber, 1681, granted to James Claypoole 5,000 acres of Land, which is wholly taken up and 80 acres over. To the End that the said J. Claypoole might be qualified for the office of Treasurer of the Society of Trade, he further agreed for 5,000 acres more, for which he gave Bond in the Year 1683, or thereabouts, in the Penalty of Two Hundred Pounds for the Payment of one Hundred sterl'g in Pensylvania, but not desiring to make use of the said last Purchase, he took five Severall Deeds for the same, Each for one thousand acres, in order to dispose of it to others, for 2 Thousand of which finding

Chapmen immediately, he took the Original Deeds in their names and the other 3 he took in his own, viz:

Deeds of L. and Release, dat. 29th and 30th of Aprill, 1683, to John Turner, Junior, of London, Merchant, for one thousand acres. Deeds of L. and Rel., of the same date, for the like quantity to Will'm Puryor, of Lond., Glazier. Like Deeds to the said Ja. Clayp. for the like quantity to himself, dat. 9 and 10th of March., 1682-3, And by like Deeds to the said James for the like quantity, dat. 29th and 30 Aprill, 1683, all which said Deeds are Recorded in the Rolls Office at Philad'a, in Book A., Vol 1, folio 171, &c., folio 122, &., folio 33, &., and fol. 140, &. They also produce the Originall Deeds, which bear date the 9th and 10th of March, 1682-3, but for the 5th Thousand acres they can produce neither originall nor Record.

Turner and Puryor, or their assigns, have already had their Lands. The late Commissioners, by their Warr'ts, dated , granted to FFra. Cook, Executor or adm'r of the said Estate, to take up one Thousand in Ja. Claypool's own Right, which Grant the said Francis sold to Dav'd Loyd.

To 2 thousand acres more, abating the 80 acres granted above, their Right upon their first 5,000 the said adm'rs, w'th J. Claypoole's Heirs, account they have a Right, but being unable to produce anything for it, 'tis believed that Ja. Claypoole sold one thousand acres and parted thereupon with the Originall Deeds for it, otherwise either they or their Record might be found with the Rest, and therefor untill the Said Deeds be produced no Grant can be made. But 'Tis Ordered that a Warr't be granted for what appears due, viz., 920 acres. Francis Cook, his Wife Mary Cook, Natha'll Claypoole and Joseph Claypooole, the Surviving Children of the Said James, by Deeds of L. and Rel., dated the 6th and 7th Inst't Grant and Release all the said 920 acres to George Claypoole, their Brother, in Consid'n of £36 9s 6d Sterl'g, which FFra. Cook orders the said George to pay to J. Logan, the Prop'rs Rece'r, and the Warr't is to be granted.

Robert Vernon having procured of the Proprietor in the Year 1700, his Warr't for taking up 285 acres, the Remaind'r of his Purchase, by an Agreement with the Commissioners, obtained their Warrant, dated 23d 9ber, 1702, for taking up 315 acres adjoining to the other to make up the whole 600 acres, but afterw'ds threw it up, and the whole Grant was by Consent made Void.

John Moor, of Concord, desiring to purchase the said Land, agreed for it with the Sec'ry for £50, one-half thereof to be paid in Hand, the other next, and a Warr't is ordered Signed and dated the 13th 3 Month, 1718.

Joseph Robinson, Brother of Geo. and James Robinson, near Brandywine, having agreed with the Secretary for 150 acres of vacant Land in Rocklands, for which he is to pay £40, part thereof in Hand and the remainder in Three Months, with 1 shill'g p. C. Quittrent. A Warr't is ordered.

Signed a Pattent to Thomas Thompson for 160 acres, ordered, dat. 6th Inst.

Signed a Warr't to Edward Farmer for 200 acres, ordered and dat. this day.

A Warr't to Joshua Story, ordered and dated this day, for ye Land in New C. Cou'ty.

A Warr't to Geo. Claypoole for 500 a's, ordered and dated this day.

A Warr't to s'd Geo. Claypoole for 420 acres, ye remaind'r of 920 a., now ordered.

A warr't to Jos. Robinson for 150 acres, dat. 14 Inst't, ordered the 13th.

A Warr't to the children of William Burrows for a Vacancy, ord'd this day, dat. 1, 4 m.

At a meeting of the Commissioners the 10th of the 4 mo., 1713.

Present, Samuell Carpenter, Isaac Norris, James Logan.

John Tatham, Son of John Tatham, Es'qr, late of Burlington, deceased, having against the Ensuing Court for the County of Bucks, renewed the Suit against Jos. Growdon for a Tract of Land on Neshamineh, of about 400 acres, which his ffather had about the Year 1686 purchased of the Proprietor in England, but he and his Successors have to this Time been kept out of Possession by the said J. Growdon. 'Tis ordered that J. Moore, of Philad'a, be employed in the Proprietor's behalf to defend that Cause, least upon loosing it the Damage fall upon the Proprietor, and the Secre'y is hereby directed to retain and pay the said J. M.

Griffith Nicholas having on the 7th 3 mo., 1712, requested a Grant of some Vacant Land between the Welch Tract and Elk River, in Newc. County, which he now finds exceeds not 2 or 300 acres, a Warr't is now Granted him at 3 Bush'ls p. C. acres Quittr t. A Warrant signed dated this day.

Isaac Leffevre, one of the Palatines, desiring to purchase Three Hundred acres of Land adjoining to the other Settlements made by his Countrymen near Conestoga, he agrees with the Secretary for the said Land at Ten Pounds p. Hund'd and common Rent, and a Warr't is granted, dat. 15th Inst.

Henry Hayes, of Chester County, desiring to purchase a Vacant Tract of Land lieing between the Tract laid out to the old Society of Traders and Hilltown, on the North of Abiah Taylor's Land, of which Isaac Taylor, by his Letter gives but a mean acco't, as being barren, &c. He agrees with the Secretary to give Twelve pounds Ten shillings p. Hundred, to be paid in Three months, and a Warrant is signed, dated the 22d Instant.

Sarah Green, widow of Thomas Green, late of Bromingham, in Chest'r County, desiring to purchase 225 acres of Land on the North East Branch of Otteraroe, agrees with Secretary for the same at £12 p. C., to be paid in three months, and a Warrant is granted for the same, dated 24th Instant.

Signed a Pattent to John FFredrickffulls for 300 a's, sold him at Oley, dat. 8th Inst.

A Pattent to Benja. Chambers for the fferry and an acre and half of Vacant Marsh, for 21 years from the 24th of June, 1712, at 1 shill'g pan., dat. 1, 10ber, 1712. Signed.

A Pattent to John FFrost for 6 acres in Newtown, granted 13th ult., 22d 3 mo. last.

A Pattent to Isr. Pemberton for 896 acres in Wrights Town, dat. 3, 4 mo. last, 1713.

At a Meeting of the Commissioners 22d 5 mo. 1713.

Present, Samuell Carpenter, Isaac Norris, Jam's Logan.

Daniel Pastorius being, by Deeds dat. 18 and 19 Jan'ry, 1682, from the Prop'r to Johan Wilhelm Uberfelt for one thousand acres of Land, and by Deeds from the said Uberfelt to himself, dated 11th July, 1683, Intituled to the said Quantity of Land in this Province, he had in the German Township, 107 acres thereof, and at the Propr'rs last arrivall there remained 893 ac. in part to be taken up. At the Sollicitation of Johannes Jawert and Daniel FFalkner, att'rys to those called the Frankfort Company, who purchased 25,000 acres in the whole, of w'ch the said Uberfelt's purchase was Part, there was surveyed to the said Company near Mahanatawny two and twenty thousand acres of Land in one Tract, in which the said Daniel's Part untaken up in right of Uberfelt, viz't, 893 acres, was laid with the rest, but without any Direction or Authority from the said Daniel, and was Confirmed by the Proprietor to the Survivors and Heirs of the FFranckford Company, all excepting Daniel, who notwithstanding he never alienated his Right to the said thousand acres which make a Part of the said 25,000 acres, is made no party to the said Grant or Pattent.

The said Daniel therefore desires of this Board a Warr't to take his remaining 893 acres, his Right to that quantity in the said Pattent not being granted to him but to others.

But his said Right being actually laid out in the said great Tract of 22,200 acres and granted from the Proprietor, 'tis objected that there he ought to take it and procure a Division upon it.

To this, by his Petition or Letter, dat. 28, 3 mo. last, now laid before the Board, he answers by Divers allegations that the Land was laid out there without his Application or Knowledge, and that it was never Granted to him but to others, and further insists that 'tis unreasonable to oblige him to take to Land that he cannot obtain but by a Course of Law, w'ch he is not capable to manage, and therefore desires a Warr't to take up what is due to him where he can find it.

But seeing those 893 acres laid out in his Right in the said great Tract must not be lost to the Proprietor, nor ought the Petitioner to be Disappointed of his Due, 'Tis ordered that a Warr't shall be granted him for the S'd quantity at the Rate of Seven pounds p. Hund'd acres, the Price at which the Palatines purchased theirs, and Some of the Board, viz't, I. N. and J. L., undertake to procure a Division as also to answer the Prop'r for the s'd Purchase Money, being £62 10s.

The Minister and Vestry, &c., of the Town of Newcastle, by their Petition, presented by Coll. FFrench, sett forth that they having been at Great Charge in Erecting a Church in the said Town find themselves at a Loss for want of a Convenient place for a Burying Ground or Churchyard, and therefore request this Board to Grant them one Hundred and Seventy ffoot Square of Ground Circumjacent to the said Church, to the Necessity of which the said Coll. FFrench Spoke, being authorized thereunto by ye s'd Petition, But the Matter being considered, 'tis referred.

George Smedley requesting to purchase two Hundred acres of Land adjoining to his Own, out of that Vacancy in Willistown (left by Gr. Jones throwing up 1,500 acres formerly surveyed to him there), in which he wou'd include the Survey of Forty-one acres, made by Will'm Garrett, which he resigned under his Hand in these Minutes the 12 of 9ber last, upon a Hearing of him and Wm. Garrett, who also desires the Priviledge of Purchasing there. His Request is granted, he paying this ffall £45 for the same, and a Warrant is ordered to the said George thereupon.

Moses Musgrove desiring to purchase Three hundred beyond the Surveys in the County of Chester, 'tis granted him at Ten pounds p. Hund'd. Part to be paid immediately after Survey and the Rest in 9 Months with 6 Months Intr'st.

William Fisher renewing by his Petition the same Request he made the 7, 11 mo. last, 'Tis ordered that he shall have the

Preference in what he desires before all others, but the Grant is for some Time suspended.

Jacob Kolluck, of Lewis, requests a warr't to resurvey a Parcell of Land in the Bottom of Angola Neck, containing about 80 acres, sold by Wm. Clark, deceased, to Jno. West, and by him to s'd Kolluck, with Liberty to take up what Vacant Land is bounding upon it, for which he is willing to pay a Reasonable Rate, also to take up on the same Terms one Hundred acres at the Head of Stuckberry Neck, of Both which the Preference is granted him, but no Warr't as yet ordered nor Agreement made.

William Garrett is allowed to take up the 42 acres due to him on his Original Purchase, out of that Vacant Land mentioned in the Grant this day to Geo. Smedley, provided he purchase as much as will make it up one Hundred, on the same Terms with the other Purchasers there, to be laid out adjoining to his Son Samuell Garrett's Land.

Signed a Pattent to B. Chambers for his fferry, dat. 20th 10ber last, pursuant to the Act of Assembly, together with an acre and halfe of Marsh on this side Schuylkill for accommodating his fferry in Landing Cattle, to hold for the Term for w'ch the fferry itself is granted, viz't, 21 Years, from 4 mo., 1712, and a Warr't is ordered for the Survey of the said Marsh.

Signed a Pattent to Jeremiah Cloud for 500 acres, besides the Allowance in Naaman's Creek, ordered 12th month, 1703, dat. 20, 5 mo. Instant.

Signed a Patt't to Jno. Key for a Lott in Sassafras str., ord'd 10ber, 1705, dat. 20 Inst.

Signed a Pat't to Jonathan Cowper for 638 a., ordered 13, 3 mo. last, dat. 20 Inst., Consid'n £74.

Signed a Pat't to Morris Lewellin for 100 a's, 130 a's and 400 a's in Meirion, ordered the   , dated 10th 4 mo. last, Consid'n for the Overplus, £16 13s 4d.

At a meeting of the Commissioners at Philadelphia, 29th 5 mo., 1713.

Present, Samuell Carpenter, Richard Hill, Isaac Norris, James Logan.

A Letter from Cha. Carrol, agent to the Lord Baltimore, directed to the Commissioners, bearing date the 9th of June last, in answer to that from them, dated 18th 3d mo., was read. The Comm'rs Lett'r was as follows:

PHILAD'A, 18, 3 mo., 1713.

CHA. CARROL, *Esteemed fr'd:*

The Proprietor of this Province having thought fitt to Constitute us his Proprietary Deputies to transact in his behalf the Affairs relating to his Estate here, we find ourselves oblidged to represent to thee, as principally concern'd for the Proprietor of Maryland, That notwithstanding there has been great Caution used on our Side not to break in on any Part of the Lands to the Southw'd to what you of that Province have always, as we understand, accounted yo'r Northern Bounds, yet lately (we are informed) Warrants have been issued to Survey not only Vacant to the Northw'd of those Bounds, but such as have for many Years been surveyed upon Old Purchases of Land in this Province, and entered upon by the Purchasers as an indisputable and unquestioned Right.

Since the first misunderstanding were over, upon the Grant of this Prov. to our Proprietor, as well those in Power as the Inhabitants in Generall, both in that and this, have lived amicably with each other, tho' the Boundaries were not certainly fixed, and now, seeing your Prop'r is, as we are informed, about surrendering his Gover't, as well as ours, we cann't but be of Opinion that it will be most adviseable to defer all such further Proceedings in these Cases till the Division can upon this Surrender be made by a Joynt Consent, and by the Intervention of the Authority of the Crown, which will then be Equally concerned in both.

This we believe cannot but be allowed as the Prudentest and most likely method to have it effectually settled, and for this Reason it must be not only the friendliest but the safest Part on both sides to forbear all further Surveys where there is Danger of Incroachm't, which we are apt to believe may at this Time be owing more to the private Views of Particular Persons than any Design in the or in such as are immediately concerned for ye L'd Baltimore.

We request thy Answer upon this Head, that nothing but what is amicable may be transacted on either side, which is heartily desired by

thy Real Loving ffriends,

SA. CARP'R,
R. HILL,
I. NORRIS,
J. L.

In Answer to the said Letter C. Carrol returned that he had rece'd the Commissioners Civil and amicable Lett'r, That from the Caution they Expressed he must believe it could not be they who had Granted large Tracts to the Southw'd of Octararoe, upon Lands granted from Maryland as Antient as that of this Province from the Crown, or that they were privy to or advising in seizing the Sheriff of Cecil County when in his Duty in the Execution of his Office on Lands many miles to the Southw'd of their Northern Bounds, but promises himself that no such Violence will be offered for the future, till affixed Settlement of their Northern and our Southern Bounds be made, which in his Opinion may with ease be done by the Rules of Art and Proper Instrum'ts to find the 40th Degree of Latitude without giving the Crown any Trouble, which he is informed has been heretofore done by able Artists and indisputably found to be a Great deal farther Northw'd than any of their Surveys, That the Information given as to their Issuing Warr'ts cannot be true, for that they Still follow their Antient, Constant Practice in granting Warrants without mention'g so much as the County, and leave it to, of him who purchases the Warrant, to direct the Survey, w'ch it may be rationally supposed he will do most for his own Safety by not runing out of the Bounds of the Province.

That he hopes it is not expected he should shutt up his Master's Office, but that while concerned it shall be his Chief Care to study all means that may lead him to act as well the just Part to his L'ps Interest as the friendliest and safest in Refere'ce to us and our People, their good Neighbours, with whom he has always been of Opinion it was necessary for our mutual Interest to cultivate a Sincere and Good understanding, that he is oblidged to us for our Belief, that what has been lately done may be owing more to the Private Views of Particular Persons than any Design in him, &c., but that he can see no further into this than that the People are willing to take their Titles from them who can make the most unquestionable, which he takes to be the Case of those Persons, that we may depend that as much Caution as we use to prevent misunderstandings shall Constantly be observed by him, &c.

Which answer containing nothing particular that is necessary to be replied to by the Board, 'Tis left to the Secretary.

Ordered that a Lett'r be wrote in answ'r to the Petition of the Minister and Vestry of New Castle informing them of the Objections made against their Request and the Inconveniences of it, for which this Board cannot grant it.

John Budd having before informed the Board of the Encroachm't made by Surveys from Maryland on a Tract of one thousand acres survey d to him near the Boundaries, requests that another Warr't may be granted him to take up the same quantity elsewhere, that he may not be quite disappointed of his Right in case he cannott hold it where first surveyed, but this is referred to be further considered.

The Grant of Geo. Smedley, as mentioned in the Minutes of the last Meet'g, is this day fully concluded for 200 a's at £22 10s

p. C., and that Wm. Garrett be accommodated as before expressed.

Signed a Warr't to B. Chambers for surveying an Acre and a halfe of Marsh, dated this day, in pursuance of the Grant in his Patt't and order of the 22d Inst't.

A Warrant to Roger Kirk, dated 3, 6 mo., for one Hundred Acres of Vacant Land in the County of Newcastle, between the Circular Line, the Mann'r of Stening and Jno. Houghton's Plantation, sold by the Secr. for £15, and a Bush'll of Wheat p. annum.

A Warr't to Daniel Pastorius, dat. 6, 6 mo., for 893 Acres, ordered last Sitting.

Warr't to John Orion for one Hundred acres in the Fork of Brandywine, sold him by the Sec'ry for £20, and 1 shill'g yearly Quittrent, dat. 25th 6 mo.

Warr't to Geo. Smedley for 200 Acres, ordered 29th 5th mo., dated 1, 6th.

Warr't to John Wyeth for about 50 Acres of Vacant Land in Bromingham, Coun. Chester, being between the Tract he is now possessed of and that of Joseph Gilpin, sold him by the Secretary at the rate of 5 shillings p. acre, in Three Months, dated 26, 6 Month.

Warrant to Wm. Garrett for 100 acres, mentioned the last sitting, dat. 6, 7ber. The Price of 58 acres sold him expressed in the warr't to be £12, but must be £13 1s.

Warr't to Cornelius Toby for two Hundred Acres in the said County of Kent, between the Lands of Wm. Denny and Wm. Reynolds, at a Penny sterl'g p. acre, formerly agreed to at James Steel's request, dat. 24th 7ber.

Warr't to FFrancis Hirons for one Hundred Acres in the said County of Kent, left Vacant between a Tract called Willis and that belonging lately to Jno. Powel, at a Penny p. acre, granted as the former, dated 24th 7ber.

Signed a Pattent to David Morris for 55 acres in Radnor, for 50 a's purchased by him for £5 of the Commissioners in 1689, and then laid out; the 5 acres is allowed for Roads, the Overplus being cutt off, dated 10th 7ber.

[Signed a Pattent to Jonathan Cowper for 638 acres, dat.] Entered before.

At a meeting of the Commissioners at Philadelphia, 30, 7ber, 1713.

Present, Samuell Carpenter, Richard Hill, Isaac Norris, James Logan.

Ordered that Warrants be granted to William Hudson and John Cornwell for a Lott to Each as usual, upon their former Requests. Entered in these Minutes, pa. 10.

John Furness, having in the Year 1701 been employed by the Prop'r to collect the two thousand Pounds Tax in the County and Town of Philad'a ' after Thomas FFarmer had tailed to discharge his Duty therein, demands Pay for 146 days riding at 6 shillings p. Day, and 55 days in the Town at 3 shill's, amounting in the whole to £57 9s of old Currency, and desires that Jno. Jones's Bond to the Proprietor for about £30, to whose Estate he is Indebted, may be delivered to him, and his own Bond, on which some Interest is due, upon which he promises to Collect the Remaind'r of the s'd Tax.

To this the Board agrees upon his Performance of that Condition, and making Good all he rece'd, but otherwise the Matter is to be further Consid'd.

John Longworthy produces a Paper wrote by the Proprietor's own Hand in these Words, viz., 25th 8ber, 1701:

Lett the Commissioners grant to John Longworthy, for his Three children, each one Hundred acres, to pay quittrent till able to purchase it off at a Settled rate.

WM. PENN.

And the said John further requesting that since he has so long deferred it, and 300 acres will Scarce be sufficient for his Sons, now grown up, he may therefore be allowed to take up 500 acres, three hundred thereof to be held at a Penny p. acre till he can purchase it at Ten pounds p. Hund'd, afterw'ds to be at the common Rent, and two Hund'd to be paid for in Years at the same rate of Ten pounds p. C't, and common Rent, with Int. for 1 year.

Clem't Plumsted, having with Geo. Fitzwater and Israel Pemberton, Purchased of Dan'l Pegg, Son of D. Pegg, deceased, a Parcel of Meadow and other Land for a Pasture at the Westernmost end of the said Pegg's Land, near the Town, he formerly requested that for the Conveniency of runing their ffence to better advantage on fast Land they might be allowed to take up a small strip out of the Proprietor's Mannor of Springetsbury adjoining, in length of their Western Line. Whereupon it was order'd Some one or more of the Board should View it least the Grant might any way incommode the rest of the Mannor Land adjoyning, and accordingly R. Hill having Viewed it, reports that in his Judgm't there can be no inconveniency in it, for that it takes in no Water belonging to the Proprietor's Land (Pegg's Bounds extending to the Western side of the Run) nor any Meadow of Value.

The said Request is therefore granted, they paying fifty shillings p. acre for the same.

Isaac Norris having purchased of Sam'l Carpenter his Plantation and Land near the Town, containing about 470 acres, whereof about 300 a's are upon Old Rent, viz., a Bushell of Wheat p. Hundred; he desires the Privilege of purchasing off the said Rent and reducing it to the common Quittr't of one shilling sterling p. C., as the Rest is held, w'h is granted at forty shillings p. Hund'd.

The s'd I. N. having also purchased of Arnold Cassell 160 acres of Liberty Land, being the Proportions of J. Claypoole's and William Stanley's Purchase of 5,000 acres each, also of Jno. Mitchener, his Plantation consist'g of divers small Parcells of Lib'ty Land, in the whole about 190 acres, all which 3 severall Purchases lie Contiguous, he desires a Pattent for the whole together, including those 7 acres he lately took up by a Warrt' from the Board in Part of ——— Collins' Right, by him also purchased, which is granted and a Pattent ordered accordingly.

The Land lately granted by Warr't, dat. 24th Inst., to Cornelius Toby, in Kent, being about one-third of a Piece of ordinary vacant Land there, James Steel requests that other 200 of it may be granted to David Strahan, who is now seated on a Corner of it, and the other 200 to Jno. Ellet, an Orphan, now under James's Care, on the same Terms with Toby's, viz., a Penny sterling p. acre, w'ch is also granted.

James Steel also requests a Pattent on 135 acres further discovered by Vertue of our Warr't, dat.   last, to have been within the Survey of Whitwell's Chance, where he now lives, on the same Terms w'th the Rest, viz't, paying the arrears of Rent from the first Survey. Granted.

Jonas Greenwood requesting a Grant for 2 or 3 Hund'd acres on the South side of the South west Branch of Duck Creek, between the said Branch and the Tract called the Exchange, upon Rent. 'Tis granted.

Warr'ts to John Longworthy and Clem't Plumstead, both ordered and dated this day.

———

At a Meeting of the Commissioners at Philad'a, 7th 8ber, 1713.

Present, Sam'll Carpenter, Rich'd Hill, Isaac Norris, James Logan.

Jacob Taylor having upon the Decease of Edward Penington been appoint'd by the late Commissioners Supervisor of the Surveyor Generall's Office, with a salary by Agreement, entered in the Commissioners Minutes ye   , of Seventy Pounds, old Currency, p. an., out of which all mann'r of Fees were to be discounted, represents that for the five years which he Officiated upon the said Terms there is considerable due to him, one Hund'd Pounds at least, according to his computation, Towards paym't of which he requests a Grant of five Hundred Acres of Land.

And Inquiry being made it appears that by any acco'ts that can now be made up there will be due to him at least the value of so much Land, but his acco'ts not having been Duly kept by him, he is ordered to make up acco'ts with those Surveyors who have not yet settled their acco'ts of ffees, with all possible exactness, and that reasonable allowances be made for the Deficiencys of Credit, the Price of the Land not to be und'r Ten pounds p. C.

James Jackson and Margarett his Wife, Grand Daughter of Patrick Word, deceased, having procured and sent up the certificate from the other children or Presumptive Heirs to the said Margar't, required in pa. 27 of these Minutes, 'tis agreed that upon their paying the arrears of Rent due, a Pattent be granted to the s'd James and Margaret, their Sister Honour being dead without Issue.

The Proprietor, by Deeds of Lease and Release, dat. 24th and 25th days of May, 1683, granted to Rob't Robinson, of Newby Stones, in the County of Westmoreland, Yeoman, 250 acres of Land in this Province, to hold to him, his Heirs, &c.— John Robinson, Son and Heir to the said Rob't, by Indorsement on the Release, dated ye 19th of the 1st Mo'th, 1712, assigned the said Land to Sarah Hallowfield, of Great Stockland, in the Parish of Morland and County aforesaid, her Heirs and assigns forever.

Sarah Hallowfield, by Caleb Pusey, requests a Warr't for taking up the Said Land.   Granted.

Signed a Warr't to Wm. Hudson for a City Lott, ord'd the 30th ult., dated this day.

A Warr't to Jno. Cornwell for a City Lott, ordered the 30th ult., dated this day.

A Warr't to Sarah Hallowfield for 250 Acres, ord'd and dated this day.

A Warr't to Jacob Taylor for 500 Acres, ordered and dated this day.

A Warr't to David Strahan for about 200 acres in Kent, ord'd ye 30th ult., dated this day.

A Warr't to J. Steel for Jno. Ellet for about 200 a's in Kent, ord'd the 30th ult., dated this day.

Isaac Decow having by his last Will (as is entered in these Minutes, pa. 6) devised 250 acres of his Purchase to his Daughter Susannah, who intermarried with Ambrose FFields, of the Pro. of New Jersey. They, the s'd Ambrose and Susannah, by Ind. dat. 17th 8ber, 1709, granted the same to her Brother Isaac Decow, who having by his Father's said Will a Right to one thousand acres before, in Right of w'ch there was laid out near Wrightstown, in Bucks, a Tract contain'g eleven Hund'd acres, of w'ch he held one thous'd in Right of the s'd Devise and the other Hund'd in Right of his said Purchase from his Sister, and sold the whole 1,100 a's to Tho. Stevenson. The remaining 150 acres the s'd Isaac, by Deed Poll bearing date 17th 9ber, 1709, granted to Jerem. Langhorn, of the s'd County, who requests a Warr't for the same. Granted.

Jeremiah Langhorn having taken up in Hilltown, in the County of Bucks, 500 acres in Right of his Father, Tho. Langhorn's Original Purchase of the said quantity, and one thous'd acres sold him by J. Logan in Right of Edw'd Bettris's original Purchase of 2,000 acres, has Sold 1,180 acres, viz't, his Father's 500 and 680 of the other Purchase, to Andreas Van Buskirk, in whose behalf he requests a Pattent for the same. Ordered.

Christopher Schleagel, late of Saxony, being desirous to Settle near the Palatines, towards Conestogoe, and to build a Mill upon a Run flowing into Conestogoe Creek, would take up one thous'd acres of Land in the said Place, and proposes to erect a Mill for the accommodation of ye Neighbour'g Inhabitants, provided he be allowed some Land for an Encouragement, Upon which it is agreed that he shall pay one Hundred pounds for the said thous'd acres (with the usual Quittrent) on the 25th day of the next first Month; But that if he build a Sufficient Grist Mill for the Service of the Inhabitants there by the latter end of the 3d Month following, Twenty Pounds of the said sum shall be abated to him.

John Musgrove desiring to purchase and take up Six Hundred acres of Land in Chester County, towards the Head of Octararoe, 'Tis granted to him for sixty Pounds, to be paid in 3 mo'ths from the Grant, viz., 28, 8ber, 1713.

Thomas Groom, Wm. Marshal and Tho. Kemball, all of the County of Philad'a, desiring to purchase 2,500 acres in the Tract called the great Swamp, in the County of Bucks, where they also propose to build a Mill. 'Tis granted them at Twelve Pounds p. Hund'd acres (and the usual Quittr't) for 2,250 acres of said Land, and the other 250 to be given in Case they build a good Grist Mill upon it next Summer, half the Consideration money to be paid next Summer fair, viz., 16th 3 mo., and ye Rem'dr in Six Months after.

Wm. Hudson having purchased or taken up upon Purchased Rights all the Lotts Lieing between the 6th and 7th Streets from Delaware, on the South side of Mulberry Street, excepting one of about 49½ foot, desires to purchase that one and agrees to pay seven Pounds Ten shillings for the same and one shill. sterl. yearly hereafter, which is granted on the said Terms.

Signed a Warrt' to Jer. Langhorn for 150 acres, dat. 17, 8ber last, ord'd pa. 59.

A Warr't to Chr. Schleagel for 1,000 acres, dat. 28th 8ber, ordered pa. 59.

A Warr't to Jno. Musgrove for 600 acres, dated 28th 8ber, ordered Ibid.

A Warr't to Tho. Groom, W. Marshal and Tho. Kemball for 2,500 a's ord'd Ibid, dat. 28th 8ber.

A Warr't to Wm. Hudson for a Lott dated 28th 8ber, ordered above.

Signed a Pattent to Is. Norris for 804 in the Libertes, &c., at 1 shilling p. C., dated 10th 8ber last, ordered pa. 57.

Signed a Pattent to Andreas Van Buskirk for 1,180 acres in Bucks, 500 of it in Right of Tho. Langhorn's Purchase of the same quantity and 680 acres, Part of a Thous'd sold Jeremiah Langhorn by J. Logan, in Right of Edw'd Bettris's Purch. of 2,000 acres, entered pa. 8, dated 15th 9ber, the whole sold to Buskirk by J. Langhorn.

John Brock, of Byberry, desiring to take up 500 acres of Land adjoyning on that granted to Tho. Groom, &c., in the Great Swamp, agrees to pay for it £60 or £12 p. C, in three months.

Signed a Warrant for the same this day, viz., the 2d 9ber.

James Chevers, of or near Concord, desiring to purchase 50 acres, Part of Rocklands left without the Circular Line and added to Concord, for w'ch he agrees to pay fifteen Pounds in Three Months. A Warrant is granted and Signed this day.

Richard Radcliffe, of the County of Bucks, desiring to take on Lease about a Hund'd acres of Land in Pensbury Mannor, between Bridge Creek and Geo. Heathcott's, Sa. Carp'r and J. L. agree with him that he shall have wh't he requests for Eleven Years, paying one third of all the Wheat, Rye, Oats, Barley that he raises and one-fourth of the Indian Corn, and shall leave ye Fences an Improvements in Repair and make no Waste of Timber, &c.

There having been Surveyed to Jno. Simcock in the Township of Caln, in Chest. Coun., 2,875 acre by Vertue of the Proprietor's L're to the Surv'r in 1701, but there having never been any Warr't for the same at the request of some of his child'n a Warr't is desired for a Return of the Survey, w'ch is Granted. Signed and dat'd this 4th 9ber.

Abiah Taylor desiring to take up two hund'd acres of Land adjoyning upon what he already holds, agrees to pay £12 p. C. in 3 Months.

Granted and a Warr't Signed, dat. 4th 9ber.

John Gregory, of Edgemont, having been disappointed in a Tract of Land for w'ch he had a Warr't in the Year 1709, agreed last Summer with J. L. for 200 Acres o very Course Vacant Land in the said Township at £18 p. C., and a Warrt' is granted to him for the same, the money to be paid in 12 Months after date. Signed ye Warr't for the s'd 200 a's and dated 8th 8ber last.

Granted to Nathan Dicks 300, or if he think fitt, 500 acres at the Head of Octararoe Creek, at Ten pounds p. C., to be paid forthwith after Survey.

Warrant Signed for the same 11th 9ber.

Granted to Elinor Cook, a poor Widow, lately arrived from England, one Hund'd acres of Land in Chester County, to be laid out beyond the other Surveys, for which she is to pay Ten pounds in one Year, without Int. Warrant dated this 18th 9ber.

Granted to Wm. Marsh, of the County of Chester, 300 acres of Land at the Head of Octararoe, near the place where he is seated, for which he is to pay £30 immediately after Survey at 3 years, Quittr'ts at 1 shilling p. C., because he has been so long setled thereon. Warr't signed and dated this 18th November.

Francis Yarnall desiring to purchase 150 acres of that Tract in Willistown, in the County of Chester, first taken up by Griff. Jones. but by him deserted for its Barrenness, agrees to pay £30 for the s'd 150 acres, being all that is left besides the Rocks themselves. Warr't dated this 18th 9ber.

Grace Chads, widow of FFrancis Chads, deceased, being apprehensive that a Neighbour of hers has a Design to break her Mill Dam upon Brandywine Creek, on pretence that the Land 'tis built on being the Soil of the River, belongs not to her and therefore desires a Grant of about 40 Perches of the soil of the said River for a Certain Term of Years and Moderate quittr't.

The Commissioners being all particularly Consulted hereupon Judge her request reasonable and 'tis allowed that she shall have 41 Perches of the said River for Nine Years at 4 shillings ster. p. an., one Perch thereof above the said Dam and the other 40 below, and a Pattent is now granted this 18th 9ber.

Signed a Pattent to George Smedley for 200 acres in Willis Town, ordered or entered pa. 57 and 55, dated 10th 9ber.

Signed a Pattent to Wm. Garrett for 100 acres in the same Tract with the foregoing. Granted pa. 52 and 55, dated the 11th 9ber.

Signed to Wm. Branson for a Lott in High street, near Strawberry alley, formerly granted by Pat. to Silas Crispin at £2 6s sterl. p. an., and from him derived.

William Markham having sold to Wm. Harwood a Part of that great High street Lott which he took to himself, as mentioned 20th 8ber, 1712, pa. 19 and 20, w'ch Part is 30 foot in Breadth on the 3d street, The same fell to his two Daughters, one of w'ch having by her att'ry sold her Moiety to Ebenezer Large, they find their Title deficient, and thereupon applying for a Confirmation for what they agree to pay £30, the charge of the Patt't included, but no otherwise, 'tis granted that they shall have the Lott of 30 foot on the 2d Street absolutely Confirmed to them for the s'd sum, of which J. L. takes only 6 shill. tow'ds ye Patt't and the other £29 14s is to be for the Proprietor's use. Patt't dated 4th 9th Instant.

Signed a Patt't to Morris Llewellin for 630 a's in Upper Meirion, and ye lower, granted pa. 26, dated 10th 4 mo. last.

Signed a Patt't to Joseph Robinson for 150 acres in Rocklands, grant. 13, 3 mo. last, pa. 49, dat'd 25, 9b., 1713.

Thomas Story having upon the Right of the Proprietor's Pattent to him for one thous'd a's of Land in the Mannor of Highlands, ment'd at large, fol. 1 of these Minutes, taken up the same quantity near the Settlem't of the Palatines, near Conestogoe, for w'ch the Comm'rs, he being one, granted a Patt't, dated 12 mo., 1711, to Israel Pemberton, to whom the s'd Thomas made over the same in Trust, that he might receive a Patt't it was made appear that the first grant of ye s'd thous'd a's was made only in Trust for the Proprietor's use, whereupon T. Story, by his Deed, dated   last, declared the s'd Trust and reconveyed those thous'd a's w'ch he last took up in lieu of the first in Highlands to the Proprietor, but having been at the Charge and Trouble of taking up the said Land he proposed to purchase the same and agrees to give the same Price that the Palatines did at the time this Tract, with theirs, was taken up, viz't, Seven pounds p. Hund'd and Int. and quittr'ts from Six Months after the Time the first Grant was made to the Palatines, and a Patt't is Signed to the s'd T. Story for ye s'd thous'd a's, dated the 9th of the 10 mo., '13, and for the Principall £70 and Int. he gives Bond to the Trustees as ususal, payable ye 10th of 8ber next.

20th 11 mo., 1713.

The Proprietor, by Deeds of L. and Rel, dated the 3d and 4th days of May, 1682, granted to Jno. Stevens, of Usington, in the County of Berks, Grocer, 250 a's of Land. Jno. Stevens, Son and Heir to the first mentioned Jno. Stevens, by like Deeds, dated the 7th and 8th June, 1708, granted the s'd 50 a's to Jno. Davies, late of Bermingham, Coun. Warwick, Taylor, and Mary his Wife, their Heirs, &c. Whereupon the s'd Jno. Davies requests a Warr't, w'ch is granted and dated this 20th 11 mo., 1713-4.

James Hamer, of the County of Philad'a, desiring to purchase 300 Acres of Land in the Mannor of Gilberts, next above that Part of it where Jonas Potts is setled, upon a Lease granted him about the Year 1708, agrees to pay Seventy-five Pounds for the same (or £25 p. C.) one Moiety thereof in Three Months and the other Moiety in Six Months after, with Int. for s'd Six Months, and a Warr't is signed, dated this 20th 11 mo., 1713-4.

Jonas Potts, at the same time with the forementioned James Hamer, desires that he may Purchase on the same Terms those 300 a's in Gilberts, which he held 5 years on Lease at £3, Old Currency, p. an., but before the above mentioned 300 Acres be laid out to J. Hamer he desires that 50 a's more may be added to the first 200 a's at the same rate, all which is granted, and the s'd J. Hamer agrees to begin so much Higher up provided that the Spott of low Land which otherwise might have faln within his Lines be left to him, which is mutually agreed between them. A Warr't to be granted.

Signed a Pattent to Geo. Harland for 110 acres in Christina Hundred, in the County of Newcastle, and for 283 acres in Two Tracts in Kennet, in the County of Chester, granted by one Warrant for 500 a's, dat. 28, 4 mo., 1690, at a Bushell of Wheat p. C. Ordered a Resurvey and setled by the Comm'rs 4th 12 mo., 1701.

Doct'r Mordecai Moore, of Maryland, having an Inclination to settle himself and Family in Philad'a, and to apply himself and his Servt's or Slaves to the raising of bright Tobacco in some of our lower Counties, if he can be accommodated with a Convenient Tract for the Purpose, preposes to take up in the Proprietor's Mannor on Duck Creek 3,000 acres if it may be granted. The Comm'rs are on the one Hand desirous to encourage such an undertaking, as tending to the advancem't of the Trade of this River and Governm't, but on the other they wou'd willingly decline the granting of any Lands there as far as may be, till a further Setlement of those Counties, but the said Doct'rs proposal being of great Importance the Commissioner agree,

That there be granted to the s'd M. Moore by Warr't in the usual Form Three thous'd acres at the North End of the said Tract, in an oblong Square by a Line Parralell to the head Line of the said Mannor.

That the said M. Moore, his Heirs and assigns, shall pay to the Propr'r and his Heirs one Penny sterling p. acre till such time as a Line shall be run by due Authority dividing the said Counties from Maryland, That immediately after runing the said Line the said M. Moore shall pay to the Proprietor or his Heirs Three Hund'd Pounds sterl'g, at London, for the said Three Thous'd acres, or proportionably after the rate of Ten pounds sterl'g p. Hund'd for so much thereof as shall to the Proprietor, after w'ch Payment the said Lands shall be held after the Rate of one Engl:sh shill'g p. C. yearly, That for so much of the s'd 3,000 acres as shall be Cutt off to Maryland, the like quantity Shall be added out of what shall be left Vacant in the Said Mannor, if any such be left, and shall be granted on the same Terms w'th the other, and lastly that in Case the s'd M. Moore proceed not without delay to improve the said Lands, this agreem't shall be Void, and upon these Terms a Warr't is to be granted, referring to these Articles, granted and dated ye 17th 12 mo., 1713-4.

Samuel Guildin, late of the Canton of Bern, in Switzerland, Minister to the Switzers, desiring to take up Eight Hund'd acres of Land in Strasburg, with the rest of his Countrymen, The Sec'ry agrees with him for the same at Ten pounds p. Hund'd, or Sixty pounds sterl'g, to be p'd in London in 6 Months after Survey, and a Warrant is granted, dated 1st 1 mo., 1713-4.

Ezekiel Harland agrees with the Sec'ry for the following sev'll quantities of Land to be granted to the following Persons at Ten pounds p. Hund'd and the usual Quittrent, viz't:

To Peter Collins 200 Acres for £20, to be paid the 29 of September next.

To William Buffington 250 acres for £25, to be paid at the same Time.

To John Buffington 250 acres for £25, to be also paid at the same Time.

The Proprietor, by Deeds of Lease and Release, dated 11th and 12th 8ber, 1681, granted to Thomas Dell, now of the Kensington, Coun. Mid'x, Yeoman, 500 acres of Land in this Province, and the s'd Thomas, by Deeds dated the 13th and 14th of 7ber, 1711, granted the same to his Son Thomas Dell, of this Province, to whom a Warr't is granted for taking up the said Land, dated 8th 1 m., 1713-4.

William Streipers, of White Marsh, desiring to purchase one Hund'd acres in the Mannor of Springfield, adjoining to Edw'd FFarmers last Grant, the Sec'ry agrees with him for the same at the rate of Eighty Pounds, one Moiety thereof, viz't, fforty pounds, to be paid down at the Time of Survey and the other Moiety next Winter, with Int. from s'd time, at Common Rent.

William Harmer desires the Priviledge of Purchasing 150 Acres in the same Mannor, w'ch is granted, but the Terms not fully settled.

The Proprietor, by Deed Poll under the Province Seal, bearing Date the 16th 5 mo, 1691, in Consid'n of £12 10s granted to Wm. Hyde, of Acton, in the County of Chester, in England, 375 Acres of Land in this Province, between Dela. and Susquehannah, Quittr't 1 shill'g p.C., to commence 5 Years after date, but afterwards 'tis covenanted in the Deed that the Rent Shall not be paid till after taking up and seating.

Richard Hyde, of London, Haberdasher, Son and Heir to s'd Will'm Hyde by Deed dated ye 22d of October, 1713, in Consid'n of £7 grants the said Land to John Salkeld, of this Province, who requests a Warr't for the same. Granted and dated ye 8th of the 1st mo., 1713-4.

The Proprietor, by short printed Deeds of Lease and Release, dated ye 3d and 4th of Ap., 1695, for £30 granted to Joseph Buckley, of London, Callender, Nine hund'd acres of Land in this Province for a Thousand years, under the Quittr't of 1 shill'g Sterl'g p. hundred, to commence 7 Years after tak'g up and seating. But on the Back of the Release the s'd Quittr'ts are released under Hand and Seal fore ever, Indorsement dated 12, 2 mo., 1695.

Joseph Buckley, Son to the s'd Joseph, requests a Warrant for the said Land, which is granted and dated 8th 1 mo.

The Prop'r, by Deeds of L. and Release, dated 14th and 15th 4 mo., 1682, granted to Rob't Barrow, of Kendall, in the County of Westmoreland, Mason, 300 acres of Land in this Province. Rebecca Shaw, Daughter and Heiress to the said Robert, requests (by her Friend Thomas Barmes) a Warrant to take up the same. Granted and dated 8th 1 mo., 1713-4.

The Prop'r, by Deeds of Lease and Release, dat. ye 1681, granted to Henry Comly 500 acres, in Right of w'ch (besides 200 acres taken up elsewhere) there was by vertue of a warrant for 300 acres, taken up a Tract above Southampton w'ch was returned for about 250 Acres, but it is since discovered that the said Survey was an abuse, for that there then was and still remains Sufficient of Vacant Land adjoyning to make up the s'd quantity and therefore his Son and Heir, Hen. Comly, requests a Warrant of Resurvey, with Orders to make up the s'd quantity, the full Compliment to which they have a Right, viz., 300 Acres, which is accordingly granted and dated the 15th 1 mo., 1713-4.

John Rumford, late of the Kingdom of Ireland, desiring to purchase 300 acres of Land on Schuylkill, above Thomas Millar's Mill, 'tis granted to him at £12 p. Hund' d, £20 thereof to be paid next 3d mo., and the remainder in 9ber next, and a Warrant dated the 19th 1 mo., 1713-4.

Isaac Taylor desires Warr'ts for the severall quaintities of Land hereinafter mentioned to the Persons following at Ten Pounds p. Hundred and common Quittr't, viz't, 1 shill'g p. one Hund'd acres, the Consid'n Money to be paid in Three Months after Survey, viz't:

To Michael Harland 250 acres, To Isaac Taylor 1,000, viz., a Thousand acres, To Richard Web 250 acres, To John Arnold 200 acres, To Jonathan Hayes 250 a's, To James Tregan 250 acres. All to be laid out in the County of Chester, and Warr'ts are dated for the said 6 Severall Parcells distinctly the 23d 1 mo., 1713-4.

Signed the following Pattents at severall Times, viz., To FFrancis Yarnal for 150 acres in Willistown for £30, dat. 1, 11 mo. last, ord'd pa. 61.

To Henry Pierce for 190 Acres at 1d p. acre in Kennet, on an old Grant to James Widows for 200 acres in 1686, dat. 15, 11 mo.

To Thomas Watson for 440 acres in Buckingham, granted to Michael Rossel, ord'd 20th 6 mo., 1712, and dated 15th 11 mo. last.

To William Hudson for 396 foot in Mulberry Street, on the South side, between 5th and 6th streets, and 354 ffoot in Depth, including a strip sold him in 1705; 150 ffoot granted to Ph. Roman in Right of John Harris, 49½ f't to Wm. Garret in Right of W. Neal, 49½ f't to R'd Webb in Right of Thom. Hayward, 49½ f't to D. Brintnall in Right of Alex'r Mell, 49½ f't in right of Cornthwait and Atkinson to himself, and 48 foot sold him for £7 10s.; the Warrants granted at severall times and the Patt't dated 1st 1mo., 1713-4.

To Clem't Plumstead for 500 acres, Part of a Thous'd given his Father, who was one of his Jury in 1668. Warr't dat. 23, 6, 1707; Pat. 1, 1 mo, 1713-4.

To Joseph Gilbert for 1,000 acres in Richland in Right of

Hugh Lamb, entered pa. 8 in J. Logan's Rights who sold the same, dat. 17, 3 mo., 1714.

To Ditto, J. Gilbert for another 1,000 acres adjoyning on the fformer and in the same Right, dated 18th 3 mo., 1714. Rent 1 sh'g.

To Joseph Hedges for 100 acres on Redclay Creek, Newc. Co'ty, Dat. 10, 2 mo., 1714, Rent 1 shill'g sterl. Granted for £20 by Warrant dat. 1702.

To Rowland Ellis and Anthony Morris for 50 a's in Blockley, &c., p't of And. Wheeler's, dat. 12, 1 m.

To James Pugh for 700 a's on the French Creek in Right of M. Marks, dat. 4th 9ber, 1713.

To Barthom Longstretch for 526 a's near Southampton, in Right of John Dwight, Rent £1 3s, the Warr't dat. 24, 4, 1708. Patt. 17, 8ber, 1713.

The sev'll Warr'ts following were signed at sundry Times, as the Persons to whom they were Granted applied and agreed for the Land in them mentioned:

To Robert Way 1,000 acres at £10 p. C., dat. 27th 1st mo., 1714; q't r't 1 p. C.

To John FFred 500 a's, same Price and date.

To William Branton 500 a's, Ditto.

To Charles Jones 250 a's, Ditto.

To Edward Bennett 500 a's, Ditto.

To Wm. Lewis 100 acres on rent, 1d sterl'g p. acre, all to be laid out in the County of Chester.

Thomas Andrews, late of Brockenborrow, in the County of Wilts, in Great Brit'n, now of West Jersey, having Purchased 250 a's of Land, Part of Enoc FFlowers' Purchase of 200 acres, mentioned in the Former Minutes, pa. 48, E. FF., by Deeds dated 21 and 22d days of 8ber, 1681, grants the said 250 acres to Wm. Player, of FFosket, in the said County, who by like Deeds, dated the 12 and 14th of Jan'ry, 1711, grants the same to the said Tho. Andrews, at whose Request a Warrant is granted and signed, dated the 7th 2 mo., 1714.

A Warrant to Peter Hatton for 800 acres at £10 p. C., dated ye 9th 2 mo. and signed.

A Warrant to Jacob Vernon for 1,000 acres, the same.

A Resurvey granted to Henry Comly on 8 acres Lib. Land, and Warr't dated the 24th 2d Month and Signed.

George Burston desires to purchase 2, 3 or 400 acres of Land in the Propr'rs Mannor of Gilberts, which is granted at £25 p. C., to be paid within Three Months after Location, with usual q't rent, 1s p. C. Warr't dated the 19th day of the 3 mo. and signed.

At a Meeting of the Commiss'rs the 26th 3 mo., 1714.
Present, Richard Hill, Isaac Norris, James Logan.

Tho's Masters being desirous to purchase the Piece of Land between the Mill Creek and the Land belonging to the Heirs of Tho. Smith and Daniel Pegg, deceased, if the same Might be Sold, which said Piece of Land was cut off from the above Land by a Resurvey and thrown up to the Propr'r, but least the said Heirs of Smith and Pegg should think themselves injured thereby or pretend to have any Right to the said Piece of Land, this Board orders that Notice be given them that they may appear the next 4th day of the Week, about the 10th Hour in the forenoon, before the Commissioners, that they may be heard.

Thomas FFairman desires that he might purchase one Thous'd acres of Land back in the Woods, which is granted him for one hundred Pounds, to be paid within one Year after this Date, and the usual q't rent of 1s p. C.

Thomas Fairman, in behalfe of his Son-in-Law, Jerem'a Hopton, produces an Instrum't under the Prop'rs Hand and Seal for 250 acres, which here follows Verbatim:

William Penn, Proprietor and Governor of Pennsylvania and Territories, To his loving Friends, Edward Shippen, Thomas Story, Griffith Owen and James Logan, Commissioners of Property for the same, Greeting:

Whereas, Edward Hopton, of London, Brewer, did buy of me Two Hundred and fifty acres of Land in Pensylvania, lieing Northward upon Pequession Creek, Eastward upon Delaware River, Southward upon Latitia Penn's Land and Westward towards the King's Road, for which he paid to my Order in England one Hundred and Thirty Pounds Sterling money thereof. These are to direct and require you to pass a Pattent under the Great Seal for the Same to the said Edward Hopton and his Heirs and assigns, according to the Power to you granted and by you Executed in the like Cases, for which this Shall be your Sufficient Warr't. Given und'r my Hand and lesser Seal at Kensington the Eighth day of the Eleventh Month, 1701-2.

WM. PENN.

Upon which a Resurvey is ordered to ascertain the Bounds and Quantity and a Pattent accordingly. The s'd E. Hopton hath granted the s'd Land to his Son, the said Jeremia Hopton.

Jonathan Baily, of Lewis, in Sussex, desires a Resurvey on a Tract of Land between Lewis and Rohoboth, which formerly belonged to a Person called Edward the Poor Workman, who granted the same to John Kipshaven and one Depra. The said Depra, in his life time, sold his part to the said Kipshaven, who afterward dyed and left only a Daughter, of whom Jonathan Baily purchased the same; he also desires to add Some Land Joining to the same at £10 p. C., and usual Quit rent of 1 Bussh. of Wh't p. C. Granted and a Warr't ordered.

Jacob Kollock, of Lewis, aforesaid, desires a Resurvey on two Tracts of Land in the County of Sussex, and to add to them some Vacant Land Joyning to them, for which he agrees to pay £10 p. C., or in Proportion, and usual Quitrent of 1 Bush. Wheat p. C. Granted and Warr'ts ordered, mentioned in Pag. 52 of these Minutes.

Signed a Warr't to Thomas Hawkins, of Duck Creek, for 100 a's of Land, on which he hath presumed to settle, to be held at 1d Sterl'g p. acre quit rent, dated this day.

Signed a Warr't to Wm. FFleming for 200 acres of Land on the West branch of Brandywine, Joyning to the Land where he dwells, for which he is to pay £30 and usual Quitrent of 1s p. C., dated this day.

Signed a Warr't of Resurvey to Sam'l Gilbert for the Compleating of his Tract of Land in Warminster, ordering the same to be made 246 acres, which of Right it should Contain, dated this day.

Signed two Warrants to Thomas Stevenson one for 250 acres in Right of Isaac Decow, being the Remainder of his Purchase of 2,500 acres, ment'd in Pag. ye 8th of these Minutes; the other for 250 acres in Right of George Smith, late of Bucks County, in this Province, deceased, which also compleats his Purchase of 2,500 a's, mentioned in the 45th Pag. of the former Minutes, dated this day.

Signed a Warr't of Resurvey to John Cowgill, of the County of N. Castle, on a Tract of Land in a Fork of Appoquiniming Creek, formerly granted and laid out to Francis Cook, of Philadelphia, and by him sold to the said John Cowgill, dated this day.

Signed a Patent to Hanna Emlen for 4 Lotts, laid out together on the South side of Sassafras Street, dated this day.

One of them in Right of James Hill, Purchaser of 500 acres.

A Second in Right of Wm. Ashby, Purchaser of 500 a's.

A Third in Right of Wm. Hichcock, Purchaser of 500 a's.

The Fourth in Right of Wm. Lamball, Purchaser of 625 a's.

Signed a Patent to John Brock for 300 acres in Byberry, purchased of Thomas FFairman, in Right of Wm. Stanly, dated this day.

Signed a Patent to Mary Crap for 1,100 a's of Land near Neshamena, in the County of Bucks, in Right of her Grandfather, James Claypoole, who gave the same to his Daughter Priscilla, Mother to the said Mary Crap, dated this day.

Signed a Patent to John Marlow for 250 acres on Paquea Creek, in Chester County, in Right of Gilbert Mace, mentioned in the 39th page of these Minutes, dated this day.

Signed a Patent to Eliz'th Pace for 250 acres on the abovesaid Creek and in the same Right, being the Remainder of Gilbert Mace's Purchase, dat. this day.

Signed a Patent to Andrew Haney for 356 a's of Marsh, Cripple and Swamp lieing in Passayunck, formerly granted to Lacey Cock, dated this day.

Signed a Patent to Wm. Burrows, of Duck Creek, for the Land whereon the Mill Stands, mentioned in the 47 pag. of these Minutes, dated 19th 3 mo.

Signed a Patent to Valentine Cock for 600 a's at Manatawney, being his and Mathias Nitzilius's Dividents of the Tract there laid out to the Swedes, dated ye 8th 3 mo.

Signed a Patent to Henry Comly for 318 acres in Warminster 300 in Right of his Father's Purchase and the 18 acres he pays for, Dated 26th 3 mo., ment'd p. 64.

At a Meeting of the Commissioners the 2d of the 4th Month, 1714.

Present, Richard Hill, Isaac Norris, James Logan.

Anthony Morris, on behalf of his Son James Morris, desires that a fformer Resurvey made on the Land where he, the s'd James, Dwells on Duck Creek, in Kent County, may be rectified, the same being altogether vicious and Contrary to the former Bounds of the whole Tract, which contains 12,000 a's, of which James Morris purchased one Moiety, but for want of the Conveyance of the said Moiety, which is recorded in the Said County, the Business is referred till the said Conveyance or Record of it can be had; he also craves a Grant for a Piece of Marsh that lies at the upper side of the said Tract on a Branch that runs into Duck Creek, which is also referred with the fformer.

Mary Stanbury produces a Judgment obtained at Kent Court aginst the Estate of Rich'd Michell, formerly Survey'r of that County, dece'd, for 500 acres of Land on the South side of the Main Branch of Duck Creek, purchased of ye s'd Michell by her former Husband Rob't Ewer, and paid for, but not conveyed. She desires a Warr't of Resurvey on the said Land, which is granted upon paying the Quittrents due on the same.

It is represented to this Board that one Nath'l Hall, lately come from New England to setle at Lewis, in Sussex, hath presumed without any Licence from hence to cutt and destroy Sundry Trees on the Cape; it's ordered that he be arrested in an action of £500 at the Propr'rs Suit for his so doing and that Care be taken that he may be prosecuted thereupon.

Signed a Warr't to John Reator for 156 acres of Land on Schoolkill and a small Island in the said River, dated this day.

The children of Tho. Smith being arrived at full age, as also the Eldest Son of Daniel Pegg, they appeared at this Board according to appointm't of the 26th 3 mo. last, and produced the Patent by which they hold their Land, wherein appears a Manifest Rasure on the quantity of acres, the Genuine Words being Three Hundred and fifty acres, but on the Rasure the Word "three" is taken out and the Word "ffour" put instead thereof, upon w'ch the Records were Examined and found that the Patent had not been Entered above a Year and that the Deputy Recorded had also entered a Memorandum near to that of the Pattent in these Words, that the Sevl'l Blanks in the last Proceeding Record were so left to denote that some Part of the Perchment whereupon the Originall thereof had been Writ seemed to be gone off and some Words thereby defaced by Mice or the like accident and at the quantity of acres appeared somewhat dubious from the Word [ffour], it being on a Rasure and Scarce legible as Such, and the Words [one Bushell of Winter] also upon a Rasure. It is ordered that Jacob Taylor do forthwith run the Line at the Extent of their Land, as it has formerly been done, and return the overplus into this Office.

At a Meeting of the Commissioners the 16th 4th month.
Present, Richard Hill, Isaac Norris, James Logan.

John Tank representing that Captain Palmer has caused an Ejectment to be brought against him for the Plantation on which he lives under colour of a Right derived from one Wilkins, and his Wife, who Claim under Jacob Young, by pretending that the woman was Young's Daughter, which Plantation notwithstanding has been understood to be Escheated to the Prop'r for want of Heirs to the Said Young. 'Tis therefore ordered that the Escheator be dire'ted to hold an Office on the said Land that a Due Enquiry may be made.

John Davis, whose Right from John Stevens for 250 acres of Land was entered before in these Minutes, pag. 62, he now desires a Warr't to take up a City Lott in ye same Right, w'ch is granted and a Warr't ordered, entered also for his Liberty Land, w'h is likewise granted and a Warr't ordered. Pa. 62 of these Minutes.

The 13th 6 mo., 1714.
Present, Rich. Hill, Isaac Norris, James Logan.

William Harmer desires a Warr't of Resurvey on 50 acres of Land formerly belonging to Thomas FFairman, Joyning to a Tract of Land laid out to Robert Longshore, in order to ascertain the Lines between the said Land and to add to the s'd Wm. Harmer's Land out of the Mannor of Springfield, about 150 a's, for which he agrees to pay after the rate of £75 p. C. A Warr't is ordered.

James Logan, the Proprietor's Receiver Gener'll for this Province and Counties, being disposed to resign the Collective Part of his Commission for the same, was pleased with the advice and Consent of the other Comm'rs to appoint James Steel to be Deputy Receiv'r Gen'll of the said Province and Counties, in order thereunto a Commission was brought to this Board and signed, dated the 30, 1 mo. last.

Signed a Commision to Wm. Crosdall and William Biles for Rangers of the County of Bucks, dated 10th 6th Month.

Signed a Patent to Samuel Guildin for 800 acres of Land at Strasburg, dated the 12th Inst't, Since by him relinquished.

Signed a Patent to Griffith Philip for 55 acres in the Welch Tract, in the County of Chester, dated the 26th 5th Month last; his Warr't is dated ye 10th 4 mo.

Signed a Patent to Edward FFarmer for 200 acres in the Mannor of Springfield, dated the 26th 3 mo last.

Signed a Patent to Job. Goodson for 235 acres in Philadelphia County, 200 in Right of his ffather's Purchase, the rest he pays for, dated 23d 5 mo.

Signed a Patent to John Longworthy for 500 acres at Manatawny, 300 at the Rent of 1d sterling p. acre, the other 200 he has purchased, dated 10th 6 mo.

Signed a Patent to Owen Roberts for 200 acres in the Welch Tract, in the County of Chester, in Right of John Thomas and Edward Jones, dat. 28, 5 mo.

Signed a Patent to Coll. John Evans for 607 acres in the great Valley, 500 acres in Right of Wm. Mordant, the Rest he pays for, dated 16th 3 mo.

Signed a Patent to John Rumford for 300 acres on Schoolkill, ment'd in the 64th pag. of these Minutes, dated the 3d 4 mo., 1714.

Signed a Pattent to James Steel for the Narrow Slip on the North side of the Tract of Land called Whitwell's Chance, mentioned in these minutes, 41 p., dated 8th 3 m. last, and in page 57.

Signed two Warr'ts to John Davis for a Lot and Liberty

Land in Right of John Stevens's Purchase, ordered the 18th 4th mo. last.

Signed a Warr't to John Garretson for 100 acres of Land, or thereabouts, in Newcastle County, at the rate of £25 p. C., dated 25th 4 mo. last.

Signed a Warr't to And'w Robeson, ord'd and dated this day for 500 acres.

To Silas Pryor, for 500 acres,
To Magnus Tate, for 300 acres, } At £10 p. C. Now granted and Warr'ts signed.
To Joseph English, for 500 acres,

Signed a Warr't to Wm. Cuerton for about 80 a's Joyning to his Plantation, near George's Creek, in New Castle County, at the Rate of £25 p. C, dated 25, 4 mo.

Signed a Warr't to David Powel for 200 Acres, Part of the Thousand acres granted to him by the Prop'r at his last departure from this Province, dat. 26, 5 mo.

Signed a War'rt to Jeremia Langhorne for 500 a's in Right of John Rowland and Priscilla his Wife (formerly Shepherd), and of Tho. Rowland, being the Remainder of all their Three Purchases, besides an addition purchased of the Comm'rs by the s'd Jno. Rowland to make up the said 500 a's, he having sold so much more than the said Purchase; dated this day.

Signed another to Jeremia Langhorne for 440 in Right of John Brock, late of the County of Bucks, deceased, being the Remainder of his Purchase, dated this day.

Signed a Warr't to Nathan Stanbury to resurvey 500 acres of Land on Duck Creek, ordered ye 2d 4 mo. last, dated ye 25th of the same.

The Prop'r, bv Indent'rs of Lease and Release, bearing date the 5th and 6th days of June, 1682, grants unto Tho. FFuller, of Peasnan, in the County of Sussex, 500 a's of Land, he dying, leaving only one Daughter, who married with Thomas Brewster, of Brandonferry, in the said County, who together by their Indent'rs, bearing date the 12th and 13 days of January, 1712, did grant and convey the said 500 a's of Land to Edward Whartnaby and Elizabeth his Wife, and they by their Deed, bearing date the 6th day of FFeb. then next following, grants the said 500 a's to Jeremia Simmons, of the City of London, Tufner, whose Son and Christopher Blackborne, his Attorneys, desire the same may be laid out, in ord'r to which a Warr't is ordered. Signed and dated this day.

Signed a Warr't to Wm. Streipers for his Son Leonard for 100 acres of Land in the Mannor of Springfield at £80, dated 25th 4 mo. last.

Signed a Pattent to Jacob Stauber for 510 a's at Oley Creek, dated the 9th 4 mo., 1714, a late grant to him, made for £60.

Signed a Patent to Capt'n Rich'd Anthony for 61 foot of Bank Lot first Granted to Zachary and John Whitpain, and since purchased by R. Anthony, who also purchased the Reversion of the same of the Commissioners at the Usual Rates, Patent dated 24th 4 mo., 1714.

Signed a Patent to Samuel Peres for 20 ff't of Water lott on the East side of King street, first granted with other Ground to Semercy Adams, and now confirmed to Samuel Peres, who has purchased the Reversion at the Common Rate. Patent dated the 24th 4 mo., 1714.

Signed a Pattent to Thomas Hayward for 1,000 acres in Chester County, 750 acres thereof in Right of John Pierson, mentioned before in these Minutes, and 250 acres granted to him by the Commissioners for £15, Pat. Dat. 16, 4th, 1714.

Signed a Patent to John Redmell for 94 acres of Land in the Prop'rs Mannor of Rocklands, lately granted to him for £37 10s, Pat. dat. 11, 6th mo., 1714.

Signed a Patent to John Gregory for 215 acres in Edgmont, a late Grant, for £38 16s, dated the 18, 9 mo., 1713, mentioned in page ye 61st.

Signed a Patent to Leonard Streipers for 100 acres in the Proprietor's Mannor of Springfield, a late Grant, for £80, dated ye 16th 6 mo., 1714.

Signed a Patent to Eliz'th Hill for 134 acres in the County of Sussex, being a fformer Grant to her Husband, dated 24th 6 mo., 1714.

Signed a Patent to Samuel Pound for 154 acres of Land and marsh on Bombay Hook Island, being the same that John Paine obtained a Warr't for but afterward relinquished it. The s'd Pound gives £32 16s, dated 13th 6 mo., 1714.

At a Meeting of the Commissioners the 15th 7 mo., 1714.
Present, Richard Hill, Isaac Norris, James Logan.

Joseph Heyton, Eldest Son and Heir of John Heyton, late of Nevis, deceased, desires that the Lot in the Second street, formerly laid out to his ffather, may be confirmed to him by Patent. It is ordered that the same be resurveyed and the quit rent of 5 shillings sterl'g p. Year be first paid, and a Patent provided to be then signed.

Benjamin Shurmer, lately arrived here from Bristol with a Design of setling in some of those American Collonies, with a Considerable Numb'r of Serv'ts, in order to raise Hemp, and having taken a Journey into the Lower Counties of this Governm't inclines to settle on the Proprietor's Man'r of FFrith, on the Head of Duck Creek, if the same may be granted,

MINUTE BOOK "H." 585

which is left to be further considered, and in the mean time the said Benjamin Shurmer is to look over the said Mannor and conclude what Part and quant'ty thereof will be Suff't for his undert'g and then ye Price for the same may be agreed.

At a Meeting of the Commissioners the 1st 8 month, 1714.
Present, Richard Hill, Isaac Norris, James Logan.

John Brewster, on behalf of the Inhabitants of the Town of New Castle, delivered a Petition from them to this Board humbly craving that the Marsh at the South End of the said Towne may be granted to them in proportionable Lotts in order that the same may be drained, which they suppose will conduce to the Health of the People. To which the Comm'rs returned the following Answer:

For the Generall Benefitt of the Town and rendering it more Healthy they Concurr with the Inhabitants desires to have that Marsh drained, but not being able to find upon Enquiry that it was ever granted away by the Propr'r, but on the contrary that it was reserved when the Grant of the common was made, they conceive they cannot answer the Trust reposed in them if they should alienate a Piece of Ground so Situate, and that by no very Chargeable Improvem't may be made Extream valuable, without some reasonable consideration, w'ch therefore they desire the Inhabitants to agree upon since it will be very well worth the Purchase, upon Which they propose that from George Dakeyne's Surveys an Estimate of the quantity as near as possible may be made, and that all the Inhabitants who are willing to undertake the Draining and reap the Benefitt of the Grant Subscribe to the quantity that each wou'd hold, after which a Warr't shall be Issued to the Survey'r Generall requiring him, by himself or Deputy, to lay out to every Particular Person their said respective quantity, with a Condition that they shall Effectually drain it within Some Such convenient Time as may be thought reasonable for that Purpose, and further that the said Persons, their Heirs, &c., shall be oblidged to keep the Ditches always in Repair, or otherwise the Person failing Shall forfeit their respective share. That a small quitrent shall be laid on each Lot in the Grant, and that a Further Generall Confirmation shall be granted, with a Draught of the whole annexed to be recorded and kept in the Rolls of the County.

Signed a Pattent to Joseph Heyton for his Lot in the Second street of Philad'a, ord'd ye 15th of the last Month and dated the 30th of the same (viz.), 7 mo., 1714.

At a Meeting of the Commiss'rs the 12th 3mo., 1714.
Present, Richard Hill, Isaac Norris, James Logan.

Caleb Pusey desires a grant for some Servants' Land which he hath purchased (viz.), of Edw'd Mayos, who came in Serv't to Wm. Bradford; of Wm. Smith, who came in Servant to the Propr'r, and of John Cowgill, who came Servant to Culbert Hayhurst, and also to consider some Services by him done for the Prop'r, especially in the Commission of Enquiry about Titles of Land in Chester County, which being considered by the Commissioners they agree to add to the 150 acres of Land, by the said Caleb Pusey Purch'd, 50 acres, and that he shall hold the whole at common Rent (viz.), 1s sterl'g p. C. Warr't is ordered.

Richard Hill and Isaac Norris desires that the Land due to them from ye Purchases of James Hill and Rich'd Collins, being 212 acres, w'ch remains untaken up, may be laid out to James Dickinson, and that there may be added to the same 388 acres at the Rate of £10 p. C., w'ch. is Granted and a Warrant ordered.

Thomas Wilson having purchased of Charles Hartford 1,000 acres of Land, being his Original Purchase, and there being 236 acres of the same, Formerly laid out to the said C. Hartford on the River Schoolkill, it is desired by the Said Tho. Wilson that the Remainder may be also laid out to him, being 764 acres, including his Liberty Land, and also that the City Lots belong'g to the said Purchase may be laid out to him likewise, which is Granted and Warrants ordered.

Signed the above mentioned Warr'ts to Thomas Wilson, dated 15, 8 mo., 1714.

Signed a Warr't to James Dickinson for 600 acres, ord'd 14th 8 m., dated ye 15 of ye same.

Signed a Patent to Thomas Wilson for a 20 foot Front Lott, Dated 26th 8 mo., 1714; 26 foot High street, do.; 236 acres for 216 a's on Schoolkill; 810 in Philad'a County and 20 a's in the City Liberty;

Signed a Pattent to James Dickinson for 600 acres in Phila'da County, granted to him 12th 8 mo., Dated ye 21 of the 8 mo., 1714.

Signed a Pattent to Joshua Clayton for 106 acres of Marsh in Kent County, granted to him the 11th of ye 1st month, 1712-3, dated 14, 8 mo., 1714.

Signed a Pattent to David Price for 300 acres in Blockley and Merion, purchased of Sundry Persons, and upon a Resurvey confirmed, dated 19th 8 mo., 1714.

Signed a Pattent to Thomas Miller for 155 acres in the County of Bucks, 90 acres thereof in Right of Jeffrey Hawkins's Purchase, and 65 a's now purchased for £13, dated the 5th 9b'r, 1714.

Signed a Pattent to Jacob Taylor for 400 acres of Land in Chester County, granted him for a Debt due from the Proprietor for his Service in the Office of Surveyor Generall, Ordered to him by a Warr't of the 8th 8th month, 1714.

Signed a Pattent to George Leonard for 300 acres at Octararo Creek, in Chester County, now granted for £30, dated ye 15th 9 month, 1714.

Signed a Pattent to Isaac Leffevre for 350 acres at Strasburg, in Chester County, a late Grant to him, at £10 p. C., dated the 25th 9th month, 1714.

Signed a Pattent to Robert Chalfont for 200 acres in Rocklands, granted for £50, dated the 1st 10th month, 1714.

Signed a Pattent to Caleb Offley for 300 acres of Old Rent Land, first granted to his ffather, Michael Offley, dated the 29th 9th Month, 1714.

Signed a Pattent to Jeremiah Langhorn for 1,390 acres in Hill Town, in Bucks County. 300 acres in Right of Edward Bettris, 150 in Right of Isaac Decow, 500 in Right of Jno. Rowl'd and Priscilla his Wife, and Tho. Rowl'd, 440 in Right of Jno. Brock, the remaind'r of all their Purchases. Dated 7th 10th mo., 1716.

Signed a Pattent to Mary Thorald for 150 acres of Rent Land in Kent, dated the 15th 10th month, 1714.

Signed a Pattent to David Powell for 200 acres at Manatawney, Part of the Proprietor's Grant to him at his last Departure from this Province, dated 10th 7 month, 1714.

At a Meeting of the Commissioners the 22d 10th month, 1714. Present, Richard Hill, Isaac Norris, James Logan.

The Proprietor, by Indentures of Lease and Release, bearing date the 29th and 30th days of 9ber, 1681, grants to Wm. Bryant and John Wisdom, both of Bucklebury, in the County of Berks, in Great Britain, 500 a's of Land Ye s'd Wm. Bryant, by like Inden'rs, dated the 26th and 27th days of Ap'l, 1713, grants 250 acres, P't of ye s'd 500 a's, to George Carter, late of Bucklebury afores'd, but now of this Province, who requests a Warr't for lay'g out ye s'd 250 a's, w'ch is grant'd and Sign'd this day, dat'd 15, 7 mo. last.

Isaac Self, of Market Lavington, in the County of Wilts, in Great Britain, by his Att'ry, George Chandler, of the County of Chester, in this Province, requests that he may take up 500 acres of Land in this Province, for which he produces the Prop'rs Receipt for the purchase Money, sayd to be rece'd by the s'd Isaac Self and Edward Guy, but the name of the latter (viz't, Edward Guy) is Scrawled out in three Places. The Date of the Deeds for the said Land are ment'd in the said Receipt to be the same of the Rece't (viz't), the 1st and 2d days of Aug'st, 1681, but it is to be noted that in the list of the first Purchasers Isaac Self and Edward Guy are made distinct Purchasers of 250 acres Each of them. Therefore a Warr't is Granted to locate the said Land, but it is not to be confirmed till the Originall Deeds or attested copies of them appears. The warr't dated 15th 7 month last and signed this day.

The following Warr'ts for Land lately granted are now Signed:
    At £10 p. C., To be paid within 3 mon s after Locat'n:
To Peter Dix 400 acres.
To James Clemson 500 acres.
To Thomas George 300 acres.
To Thomas Green 500 acres.
To George Pierce 225 acres.
To George Leonard 300 acres.
To Hugh Cristy 100 acres.
To James Todd 500 acres.
To Richard Mason 500 acres.
To William Pusey 500 acres.
To F'Fra. Evets and Jno. Butler 400 acres.
To Tho. Keald 100 acres.
To Archib'd McDonald 500 acres.
To Wm. Routledge 300 acres.
To Alexander Ross 500 acres.
To Richard Harrold 400 acres.
To Rich'd Craston 500 acres.
To Morris Rees 400 acres
To Wm. Beals 300 acres.
To Arthur Barrett 300 acres.
To John Grafton 250 acres.
To Robert Sinclair 400 acres.
To Ezekiel Harland   acres at £15 p. C.
*To David Powel 800 acres.
To Jos. Cox about 200 acres.
To John Batten 150 acres.
To Benj'n Burk and Jno. Potts 300 acres.
To John Grigg 300 acres.

---

   *That the above 800 acres granted to David Powel was by an order under the prop'rs Hand for 1,000 acres at the same Rate (viz.) £7 10s p. C., the present Currency, w'ch is £10 of the former, the other 200 being laid out before the said Order from the Proprietor was given at his last Departure from this Province.

To John Joder 450 acres.
To William Burny 250 acres.
To Eliz'th Clayton, came Serv't to Jno. Bezer in ye year 1682, 50 acres head land.
To Joseph English in Right of Jos. Mather and Wm. Smith, who came in Serv'ts w'th Phine's Pemberton, 100 acres head land.

The Propr'r, by Indentures of L. and Rel., dated the 11th and 12th days of 8ber, 1681, granted to John Marsh, of Nether Hayford, in the County of Oxford, in Great Britain, one thous'd a's of Land to be taken up in this Prov., Three Hund'd and fifty a's whereof being already out, the s'd J. Marsh, by his Att'ry, Joseph Kirkbride, by Deed dated ye 3d 1st month, 1711-2, grants and conveys the remain'g 650 a's to Joseph Jarvis, of the County of Chester, in this Province, who thereupon desires a Warrt' to lay out the same, w'ch is granted and now Signed.

Signed a Warrant to Caleb Pusey for 200 acres of Land, ordered the 12th 8 mo. last.

The Proprietor, by Indentures of Lease and Release, bearing date the 3d and 4th days of FFebruary, 1681, grants to Robert Jones, of Chotsbury, in the County of Bucks, in Great Britain, deceased, 500 acres of Land to be laid out in this Prov., who by his last Will and Testament, bearing date the 12th day of March, 1697, did give and bequeath all the said 500 acres of Land, &c., to Joseph Welch, Jun'r, late of Chesham, in ye s'd County of Bucks, since deceased, and to his Heirs, and there having been formerly laid out in the County of Chester, in Right of the s'd Purchase 280 a's, so y't there remains to be taken up to Compleat ye s'd Right or first Purchase 220 a's. Ann Welch, Relict and adm'x of the s'd Joseph Welch, and Guardian of John Welch, her Son by the s'd Jos. Welch, desires by her Att'ry that the said 220 acres of Land might be laid out for the use of her s'd Son together with a City Lot proportionable to the said Purchase, which is granted and the Warrants Signed this day.

At a Meeting of the Commissioners the 28th 10th month, 1714.

Present, Richard Hill, Isaac Norris, James Logan.

William Harmer and Thomas Rutter appeared and produced their Patentts and other writings belonging to the Land formerly Robert Longshore's and the 50 acres Joyning to the same, now in the Possession of the s'd W. Harmer, on which he desired a Resurvey from the Comm'rs 13th 6 mo. last. William

Harmer Earnestly desires that the Line between the s'd Lands might run by a Streight course, as his Pattent expresses, But Thomas Rutter opposes and says that the Said Line ought to go according to a small Run of Water that is mentioned in the Pattent to Robert Longshore, But because both the said Tracts of Land are already pattented and that the Difference between a Streight Line and the Courses of the small Branch or Run is so inconsiderable, the Comm'rs decline Meddling with it at present.

Andrew Hamilton prefers a Petition to this Board Setting forth that there is a certain Parcell of Land Containing about 200 acres on Little Creek, in the County of Kent, formerly belonging to one John Richardson, who was convicted of wilfull Murder and was accordingly executed, by w'ch means he presumes the said Land is forfeited to the Prop'r, and thereupon desires that it might be granted to him for such a Consid'n as Shall be or may be agreed on. 'Tis left to be further considered off.

Anthony Burton, Carpenter, who came in Serv't to ye Prop'r and served his Time at Pensbury, desires he may be granted to take up one Hund'd acres of Land allow'd him by ye Prop'r on acco't of his Service and not yet laid out to him. Granted and a Warr't ordered.

Jonathan Baily, of Lewis, in Sussex, petitions for 500 a's of Land and Marsh lleing between his Plantation and the Broad Creek, for which he offers £16 p. C. and the Common quitrent (viz.), one Bushell Wheat p. C. But till some other Information of the s'd Land and Marsh can be had it is referred.

Thomas Bedwell, late of the County of Kent, but now of Lewis, in Sussex, desires (by his Letter to J. Steel) that he might have a Grant of Two or three Bank Lotts on the Creek in Lewis, which he proposes to Improve, but there being no Such Grants in that Town for the Bank on the creek as yet, it is left to further Consideration.

The following Warrants were signed at severall Times:

To Samuel Davis, of Lewis, in Sussex, for about 40 a's of Marsh at 4s p C't.

	Acres.	
To Vincent Emerson, .	100	
Andrew Caldwell,, . .	200	
To John Clayton,. . ,	200	All on New Rent in Kent County.
To Matthias Greenwood,	200	
To William Stanton,. .	100	
To John Pleasington, .	100	

	Acres.
To William Darter,	200
To Tho. Geer,. .	300
To Tho. Davock, .	200
To Eiz'th Hill,. .	200
To John Walker, .	200
To Thomas Wilson,	200

All on New Rent in Sussex.

Signed a Warr't to James Hendricks for 1,000 acres near Strasburg at £10 p. C't.

To John Holland 100 a's in the Welch Tract, in Chester County, at £15.

To Peter Bellar 200 a's at Strasburg, at £10 p. C't.

To Robert Wilkins 200 a's above Manatawney, at £15 p. C.

To James McVeigh 100 a's in the great Swamp, at £15.

To Peter Wishart 300 a's in the Same Place, £40, the whole.

To Thomas Smith 500 a's at Susquehannah, at £10 p. C't.

To Thomas Richman 1,100 acres at Strasburg, at £10 p. C't.

Signed a Warr't to John FFalconer and Andrew Hamilton for 60 acres of liberty Land, being the Remainder of Charles Marshal's Originall Purchase of 6,000 a's, which the said John and Andrew are now possessed off, dated the 25th 1st Month, 1715.

At a Meeting of the Commissioners of Property ye 16, 12 mo., 1714-5.

Present, Richard Hill, Isaac Norris, James Logan.

Benjamin Shurmer having in page 72 of these Minutes requested a Grant of some Part of the Mannor of FFrieth, on the Branches of Duck Creek, for to plant and raise Hemp, being employed in that Business by William Donn and other Merchants of Bristol, in Great Britain.

This Board taking into Consideration the Importance of Such a Design and the Advantage that may accrue thereby to the Government, have granted to the said Benjamin for the Use of his Employers the quantity of 3,125 acres of Land, Part of the Said Mannor, to begin at the North E'st Corner thereof and runing from thence South 500 Perches, thence West 1,000 Perches, then North 500 Perches, and then East 1,000 Perches to the Beginning, for which said quantity of Land the said Benjamin, in Behalf of his said Imployers, now pays down to the Prop'rs Use £78 12s 6d, money of Great Britain, and is to pay for the same the yearly quitrent of one Penny sterl'g for every acre thereof till such time as Ten Pounds of like money shall be paid by the s'd Benjamin or his s'd Imployers to the Propr'rs Use for every 100 acres of the s'd 3,125 acres, and that then and for ever after such Payment. The s'd 3,125 a's shall be holden of the Prop'r under the yearly quitrent of one shilling sterling for every Hundred a's thereof and no more, whereupon certain articles of the afores'd agreement are now executed and a Pattent also granted to the said Benj. Shurmer in behalf of his said Imployers for the 3,125 acres of Land granted as afores'd The s'd Benjamin further desires a Grant of 1,000 acres more in the fforest of Kent County, on Rent, to be laid out in three Parcells, viz't, 500 in one Tract and the Remainder in two other Parcells, and also that he may have a Grant for 3 other Smaller Pieces of Land, two of w'ch Joynes on the East side of the s'd Mann'r and the other on the North side of Duck Creek, for w'ch he also agrees to pay the yearly quitrent of one Penny sterl'g for every acre thereof, the whole being granted as requested and Warrants for the same now granted.

George Clark, late of the City of London, but now of this Province, applyed to the Sec'ry for the Old Plantation formerly William Stockdall's, some Term on Rent, which is agreed on for five Years at £3 p. ann., upon which Leases are provided and signed, dated 29th 2 mo., 1715.

William Blakey, of the County of Bucks, having formerly agreed with Sam'l Carpenter, by order of the other Comm'rs, for the Plantation on the Mann'r of Pensbury, where Richard Wilson in his life time Dwelt, to hold the same on Lease for the Term of 12 years from the 1st mo'th last, at the yearly Rent of £12 p. ann., and that the said William Shou'd be allowed the two first years Rent to build on the said Plantation a good Logg House 24 foot long and 16 foot wide, which being built and the Leases according to the said agreement prepared they were signed, Dated the 1st day of the 1st month last.

Signed a Patt't to Peter Collins for 450 acres in Bradford Township, granted at £10 p. C't, dated 1st 12th month, 1714-5.

Signed a Pattent to Will'm Buffington for 350 acres in Bradford Township, granted at £10 p. C't, dated 1, 12 mo., 1714-5.

Signed a Pattent to Wm. Garrett for a City Lott in Right o John Love's Purchase, dated 16th 1st monh, 1714-5.

Signed a Pattent to James Jackson and Margarett his wife, for 750 acres of Land on the Southwest Branch of Duck Creek, ordered in the 58th page of these Minutes. Dated the 4th of the 3 mo., 1715.

Signed a Pattent to John Chandler for a city Lott now granted to him for £10, dated the 25, 5 mo., 1715.

Signed two Pattents to William Harmer for 382 acres in the

Mann'r of Springfield, one of them for 127 acres, dated ye 8th 11 mo., 1714-5.

The other for 255 a's, dated 10th 3 mo., 1715. The whole granted for £253 6s 8d.

Signed a Patent to George Pierce for 600 acres in Sadbury, in Chester County, dated 24, 3, 1715; 375 in Right of Jno. Hennerly's Purchase; 225 now granted for £22 10s.

Signed a Pattent to Clement Plumstead for 7¾ a's of Land in the Mannor of Springetsbury, granted him for an Addition to his Pasture for £18 12s 6d, dated 1st 11 mo., 1713-4.

Signed a Pattent to John Coe for 100 a's of Marsh on Lewis Creek, in Sussex, first granted to John Roades, of the same County, quitrent 1 Bush. of good Winter Wheat, dated 1715.

Signed a Pattent to Jonathan Bailey, of Lewis, for 668 acres of Land between Lewis and Rohoboth Bay, quitrent 1 Bushell of Good Winter Wheat p. C't, dated 25th 3 mo., 1715, upon a Resurvey.

Signed a Pattent to John Burges for 283 acres of Land in the Falls T'p, Part of James Hill's Purchase, mentioned in Page   of these Minutes, dated the 7th 4 mo., 1715.

Signed a Pattent to Roger Moon for 125 a's in the FFalls Township, Part of the next above mentioned Purchase, dated the Same Time.

———

At a Meeting of the Commissioners of Property the 8th 4 mo., 1715.

Present. Richard Hill, Isaac Norris, James Logan.

John Colly, on behalf of his Grand childen, the children of Henry Carter late of Philada', dece'd, requests a confirmation of 32 ffoot, Part of the great High street lott claimed by Coll. Markham, on the South end thereof, the said Henry having purchased the same in his life time, left it by his Will to his children (vid. p. 12). It is agreed that for £30, now paid or secured to the Prop'rs use, a Pattent being ready, is signed, dated 7 Ins't.

The Prop'r, by Ind'rs of Lease and Release, dated the   granted to John ap Evan   acres of Land. The John ap Evan, by Deed dated the   , grants 125 acres thereof to David Jones, whose Son and Heir, Daniel Jones, by like Deed, dated   , grants the same to Evan Powell, whose Son and Heir, John Powell, by his Deed, dated ye   , grants the s'd Land to John Remington, of Chester, in this Province, who by like Deed, dated   , grants the same to Joseph Redknap, who now desires a Confirmation, But

Joseph Growdon, in behalf of his Son and Daughter-in-Law, children of Samuel Bulkley, obje'ts against the Division of the said Land, there being the like quantity laid out with this to Math'w Jones, Grandfather to the s'd children, and therefore desires a Regular Division may be made, upon w'ch a Pattent is to be Granted to the s'd Jos. Redknap.

Gilbert Falconer represents that the Inhabitants of the Town of New Castle have wholly declined the accepting of those Terms preposed to them from this Board for draining the Marsh at the South West end of the said Town, and therefor desires that himself and Jasper Yeats may have a Grant for the said Marsh. The Commissioners being willing to promote so good an Undertaking that may Conduce to the Health of the said Town, Do agree that the said Marsh be forthwith granted to the s'd Jasper Yeats and Gilbert FFalconer on condition that Publick Notice Shall be given to the Inhabitants of the said Town to the End that so many of them as are willing to accept the Terms of this Grant and within two Months after the date thereof pay down to the said Jasper and Gilbert so much money as Shall be in Proportion to their Respective Shares or Lotts for the Purchase and Draining thereof, and the said Jasper and Gilbert do for themselves and such of their Neighbours as shall accept the same Terms with them, agree to pay down to the Prop'rs Use Twolve shillings for every acre thereof and the Yearly quitrent of a Half penny sterling for every acre, upon w'ch a Warrant is now Granted and Signed.

Joshua Hastings, first Purchaser of 1,000 acres of Land within this Province, desires a Resurvey on   , formerly laid out to him in Chester County it being the Remainder of his said Purchase. Granted and a Warr't Signed, dated   .

Harman Richman, late of Hamburg, but now of East Jersey, requests a Grant for 1,000 acres of Land in Strasburg, first laid out to John Rudolp Bundeli, who has since relinquished the same. The said Harman desires that 100 acres more might be added to make the Tract 1,100 acres, w'ch is granted him at £10 p. C., and a Warr't Signed, dat. 22, 8ber, 1715.

Samuel Baker, of Bucks County, desires that the 100 acres of Swamp Land obtained by his ffather, Henry Baker, of the former Comm'rs, which lies at the lower end of the Proprietor's Mannor of High Lands, might be Confirmed to him by Pattent. It is considered by the Secretary that the said Samuel having made large Improvements on the same Shall, upon his paying down to the Proprietor's Use £10, have a confirma'on.

The following Warrants were Signed at Severall Times to Robert Holgson and James Hendricks, two Warr'ts for 3,500 acres at Conestogo at £10 p. C't.

To Edward Gibbs 200 acres near Christina, at £20 p. C't.

To Arabella Crew, a Resurvey
To John Russel; the same } in Sussex.
To John Futcher, Ditto

To John Berry, Ditto
To Coll. John French, Ditto
To Edward FFretwell, Ditto
To Tim. Hanson, a Resurvey } in Kent.
   on the Land late of John
   Chant, D'tto on his plantation

                        Acres.
Henry Tuchberry,   200
Gilbert Marriner,   200
Tho. Davock, . .   200
Walter Read, . .   200 } All in Sussex, at 1d st'rl. p. acre.
Samuel Steward,   200
Tho. Painter, . .   200
Wm. Townsend, . 200
John Kinman, .   200

Signed a Warr't to Henry Warley for 600 acres Land granted to him in Chester County on some Convenient Creek for erecting a Mill, £10 p. C't.

Signed a Warrant to William FFisher for 50 acres of Marsh in Slaughter Neck, in the County of Sussex, granted to him for £7 10s.

Signed one other Warr't to Wm. FFisher for a small Island and as much Marsh as will make 150 acres, near to the above Grant, £22 10s.

———

At a Meeting of the Commissioners the 21st 10 mo., 1715.
Present, Richard Hill, Isaac Norris, James Logan.

Herman Groethausen, late of Germany, but now of this Province, having in the Year 1709 purchased of one, Coll. Rhedegelt, 9,000 a's of Land, to be laid out in this Province, upon which he repaired to London in order to transport himself and Family hither, and meeting with the Prop'r there, acquainted him with his Design. The Prop'r and he came to an agreement that upon Herman's Resigning of his Right which he purchased of Rhedegelt, he shou'd have in Lieu thereof 500 acres laid out amongst the Inhabitants at the yearly Rent of one Penny Sterling p. acre, for which the said

Herman took short Deeds of Lease and Release, dated the 30th and 31st days of December in the said Year, and soon after arrived in this Province and laid his Deeds before the Commissioners in order to have his Land laid out, but by his Deeds mentioning no Particular Place (only between the River of Susquehannah and Delaware, for laying out the same, there cou'd be no other Warr't granted but in the Common fform, which he not complying with, seated himself on the Mannor of Springfield, which soon after being made known to the Commissioners, they ordered him to remove from thence, but instead thereof he insisted on the Proprietor's Promises to him upon their agreements, and so went to England for Redress, and being now returned with some Depositions of his Resigning his Deeds for the said 9,000 acres for only 500 acres, and that at 1 Penny Sterl'g p. acre, and also with a Letter from Mrs. Hannah Penn to the Commissioners, directing them to make the said Herman Easie in his Setlement, they have thereupon ordered that 500 acres of Land be forthwith laid out to him within the said Mannor, including within the same his Improvement, and accordingly a Warrant is granted and Signed.

Coll. John FFrench desires a Confirmation for a small Piece of Land at his Mill, added for the Conveniency of the Race, and also for the 8 acres of Marsh laid out to him at the Lower end of the Town, which is granted in Consideration of   .

Thomas Masters having heretofore (p. 66) requested that he might Purchase the overplus Land thrown off from Pegg's and Smith's Land, lieing between that and the Mill Creek, it is now agreed that he shall have it at 45s p. acre, and that according to a former Order of this Board Jacob Taylor, the Survey'r Gen'll, do forthwith Survey the Same and return the exact quantity into the Secretary's Office.

12, 1 mo., 1715-6.

Present, T. Logan.

The Proprietor, by Indentures of Lease and Release, dated the   , Grants to John Clarke, of the Devizes, in the County of Wilts, in Great Britain, 500 acres of Land in this Province. His Son and Heir, John Clarke, of the same Place, by like Deeds, dated the 4th and 5th days of May, 1713, for £6 sterling, grants the said 500 acres to Rees Thomas, of Haverford, in this Province, who now desires Warrants to lay out the same with Lott and Lib. Land belonging to the said Purchase, which is granted and signed.

Randal Jenny, in his life time (viz.), in the year 1703, obtained of the then Commissioners two Warrants, dated the 3d and 4th days of the 1st month, 1703-4, for laying out to him one thousand acres of Land in Right of John Willmer's purchase of 3,000 acres. The said Randal, by his Indented Deed, dated ye 18th 9ber, 1708, grants the whole 3,000 a's to John Budd and his Sister, Sarah Murry. The above Warrants being executed by Henry Hollingsworth altogether Dissatisfactory to the said John Budd and Sarah Murry, they earnestly desire that they may be Suffered to resign the Land laid out by the said Henry, and that other Warr'ts for the like quantity to be laid out to them elsewhere might be granted to them. Ordered and signed, dated the 6th and 7th days of the 11th month, anno Dom. 1715-6.

The Proprietor, by Deeds of Lease and Release, dated the 7th and 8th days of 9ber, 1681, granted unto George Whitehead 500 acres of Land in this Province, who by his Deed Poll, dated 27th 7ber, 1686, granted the same to George Pratt, whose Heirs, Thomas Pratt and Ann Berry, with her Husband, John Berry, by their attorney, George Bows, all of Talbott County, in Maryland, by Deeds of Lease and Release duly executed. bearing date the 16th and 17th days of the 11th mo. last (by the said George Bows) conveyed all the said 500 acres of Land unto Evan Owen, of Philadelphia, who now requests Warrants for the same, with the Lott and Liberty Land belonging to the said Purchase, which are granted and Signed, dated the 25, 11 mo., 1715-6.

Signed the sev'll following Warr'ts at Sundry Times:

	Acres.	
Richard Friveller,	100	
Hans Graeff,	200	
Tho. Eldridge,	250	
John Whitesides,	200	
James Wright,	200	All in Chester County, grant. at £10 p. C't and 1s sterling quit-rent.
Benedictus Venerick,	200	
William Taylor,	250	
Joseph Hains,	100	
Thomas Clarke	300	
William Sherrard,	200	
Tho. Nicholls,	500	
William Cloud,	300	

Wm. Hakett, 150, N. Castle,
Mathew Corbet, 200, Ditto.
Patrick Broomfield, 200, Ditto.
James Griffin, 200, Kent.
Tho. Painter, 200, Sussex.   All these are att 1d sterling
William Morris, 200, Kent.   p. acre Rent.
Lewis Davis, 200, Ditto.
John Reynolds, 200, Ditto.
Mich'l Lober, 200, Ditto.
William Pearson, 200, Ditto.

Signed a Warrant to Edward Burrows, of N. Castle County, for 200 a's at £20 p. C.

To Gilbert FFalconar for 40 acres near A. Peterson's, at 4s p. acre.

To Abel Dodd for 150 acres near the K's Road, granted him for £17 10s p. C.

To Enoch Jenkin 150 acres near the Welch Tract, N. Castle County, £20 p. C.

To John FFrogg 100 acres near Christina, at £20.

To William Burney 250 acres near the same Place, at £50, the whole.

To Alex'r FFraiser 100 acres, Ditto, at £22 10s.

David Jones 200 acres near the Welch Tract, N. C., at £50, the whole.

The Proprietor, by Deeds of Lease and Release, dated the 7th and 8th days of the 2d Month, 1683, grants to Herman Hendricks, of Rotterdam, in Holland, 1,000 a's of Land to be laid out in this Province, at 1sh. sterling p. C't q't rent, and at the same Time by another Indenture for £3 sterling released Nine shillings of the q't rent on the 1,000 acres, so that only 1 shilling remains on the whole.

Herm. Hendricks, by an Indorsem't on the Back of the Release, dated the 16th day of the 2d Month, in the same Year, for £23 sterling sold and Transferred the said 1,000 acres to Arey Geritson, of Amsterd'm, Marriner, who by an Instrum't before a Notary Publick in Holland, dated 17th July, 1685, Sold the same Land to Reynier Jants, Veltermaker, who by a like Instrument, dated ye 5th of May, 1688, sold the same Land to Corn's Losvoll, of Colchester, in Great Britain, who by Indenture of Lease and Rel., dated the 19th, 20 of September, 1690, granted and conveyed the said Land to Jno. FFurley, Jonathan FFurley and Benjamin FFurley, all of Colchester aforesaid, and by like Indentures, dated the 1 and 2d of Jan'ry, 1713, the said Benj. FFurley, Anna FFurley, Widow of John FFurley, dece'd, Anna FFurley, Eliz. FFurley and Gertruda FFurley, Daughters of the said Jonathan FFurley, also deceased, granted the said Land to Tho. Spilman, of London, who also by Indentures of Lease and Release, dated the 1 and 2d days of FFebruary, in the said Year, 1713, granted the same 1,000 acres to John Evans, Esq'r., at whose request (by his ffather-in-Law, Jno. Moore) a Warrant is granted for laying out thereof, dated ye 16th 10 month, 1715.

Signed a Warr't to Sam'l Held for 180 acres near Brandywine, in Chester County, at £16 p. C't.

The Proprietor, by Deeds of Lease and Release, dated the 28th and 29th days of 8ber, 1681, granted to Ralph Kinsey, of London, 125 acres of land in this Province, whose eldest Son and Heir, John Kinsey, of London, aforesaid, be like Deeds dated the 11 and 12 days of FFeb., 1714, granted the same to Wm. Bradford, Jun'r, of New York, who desires Warrants to take up the said Land and the Lott belonging thereunto. Granted and signed.

The Proprietor, by Deeds of Lease and Release, dated the 10th and 11th days of 8ber, 1681, granted to John Beckley, of London, Perfumer, 250 acres of Land in this Province, who by his Deed, dated 10th day of 7ber, 1688, Conveyed the same to Tho. Place, of Edington, in the County of Somerset, in Great Britain, who by his Deed of Gift, dated 30th 6 mo., 1704, granted the said Land to his Son, Joseph Place, of Long Island, whose Son and Heir, Thomas Place, of the said Island, by his Deed, dated ye 2d day of 9ber last, conveyed the same to Mordecai Lester, Henry Seaman and Adam Mott, all of the said Island, who desire a Warr't for laying out the said Land w'ch is granted and Signed, dated ye 23, 9ber, 1715.

The Proprietor, by Deeds of Lease and Release, dated the 21st and 22d of Apr'l, 1682, granted to John Shiers, late of Grindleton, in Yorksh'r, in Great Britain, but now of this Province, 1,000 acres of Land, 500 acres whereof being formerly laid out in the County of Bucks; he now desires the Remainder, with the Liberty Land, may be surveyed to him, w'ch is granted and Warrants signed, dated ye 3d 3mo., and 23, 3 mo., 1715.

Signed a Warrant to Edward Roberts, of the County of Bucks, for 250 acres of Land in the Tract called the great Swamp, for £37 10s, the whole.

To John Edwards at the same time for 200 in the same Tract for £30, the whole.

Signed a Warrant to Jeffrey Burges, of the County of Bucks, for 200 acres in the Proprietor's Mannor of Highlands, for which he agrees to pay £60, the whole. Warr't 18th 9ber, 1715.

Signed a Warra't to David Potts for 100 acres in the Mannor of Springfield, for which he is to pay £80.

Richard Cloud for 650 acres on the Branches of Pequa Creek, in Chester County, for which he is to pay £78, the whole.

Rob't Edw'd in his life Time having seated himself on a Tract of Land near Parkcominck Creek, in Philadelphia County, upon his Decease, Rich'd Lewis, who intermarried with one of his Daughters, desires to purchase the same, there being in the said Tract 300 acres, for which he agree to pay £96 4s. A Warrant is granted and signed, dated the 19th 3 mo., 1715.

Agreed with Jonas Yocom for 300 acres of Land on School kill, near Manatawney, for w'ch he is to pay to the Proprietor's use £60, ye whole. The warr't granted and signed, dated the 22d 12 mo., 1714-5

Jeremia Carter having made it appear that he and his Wife came Servants into this Province in the Year 1682, and that Henry Swift and his Wife and Richard Whigsted came Servants about the same time and have sold their severall Rights to the said Jeremia, who now desires a Warr't for laying out the same, being 250 acres, which is granted and signed.

Signed a Pattent to the Children of Henry Carter for 32 foot of 2d street Lott, Part of Coll. Markham's Large Lott, being a Confirmation for the said 32 foot now granted by the Commissioners for £32, dated ye 10th 4 mo., 1715.

Signed a Pattent to William Burney for 250 granted him near Christina, in New Castle County, for £50, dated ye 10th 4 mo., 1715.

Signed a Pattent to Richard Lewis for 300 acres mentioned on the other side of this Leaf, dated the 9th 4 month, 1715.

Signed a Pattent to James Shattick for 492 acres in Right of Jon. Dickinson, mentioned in the former Minutes, dated 16th 4 month, 1715. Signed one other Pattent to James Shattick for 492 acres in Right of Thomas Paget, mentioned also in the said Minutes, dated the same day with the above.

Signed a Pattent to Joseph Buckly for 900 acres in Chester County, granted to his ffather from the Proprietor, ordered p. 64 of these Minutes, and dat. 22, 5 mo., 1715.

Signed a Pattent to Hugh Davis for 50 acres Headland, dated 27, 6 mo., 1715.

Signed a Pattent to John Funk for 250 acres, Part of the Tract laid out to the Palatines at Strasburg, Dated 30, 3 month, 1715.

Signed a Pattent to David Powel for a Lott in Walnutt street, granted to him by the Commissioners. Dated

Signed a Pattent to Margaret Miles for 60 acres of Land in

Radnor, reduced from 1d sterling p. acre to 8d, the whole, dated the 2d 10 mo., 1715.

Signed the severall following Warrants at Sundry Times:

To David and Tho. Gray, Resur.
To George Chambers, Resur.
To Edward Parker, Resur. } Resurveys to be made in Sussex.
To Edward Craig, Resur.
To James Drake, Resur.
To Robert Burton, Resur.

	Acres.
To Anderson Parker,	150
To David Smith, . .	200
To John Bennet, . .	200
Rich'd Hinman, . .	200
John Prettyman,. .	200
William Simmons, .	200
Samuel Hands, . .	200
Tho. Blizard, . . .	200
John Loftlands, . .	200
James Seaton, . . .	200

All in Sussex, granted at 1d sterl'g p. acre.

Alexander Molleson, of Lewis, in Sussex, desires to purchase two small Islands of Marsh in Lewis Creek, for which he agrees to pay five shillings for every acre Contained in them and the yearly quitrent of one Bushell of Good Winter Wheat in Proportion to one Hundred acres (The said Islands lieing before his own Land. Warrant ordered and Signed.

Signed a Pattent to Caleb Pusey for 500 acres in Chester County, 10, 1, 1715-6.

Signed a Pattent to William Pusey for 500 a's in Chester County, dated the 1, 10 mo., 1715.

I'd, 1 mo., 5th, 1715-6.

Thomas Roberts, Michael Atkinson, Rob't Gerald and John Moor desires that 200 acres of Land in the Tract called the great Swamp might be granted to each of them, for w'ch they agree to pay for every 100 acres upon the Survey £13 6s 8d, or Interest till they do pay. Granted and Warrants Signed.

Thomas FFairman in his life Time sold to John Rool, of Vanderwerf, 300 acres of Land near Shepack Creek, in Philadelphia County, but upon Examination it appears that Thomas FFairman had no Right to Sell it, the Same Land being fraudulently Concealed for severall years past by him for that Purpose, whereupon the said John Rool, of V'd'werf, desires a Confirma'on of the said Land, for which he agrees to pay Sixty-two Pounds fifteen shillings; £30 at the Survey and the Remainder Six Months after. Granted and Warrant signed, dated 3d 1 month, 1715-6.

Richard Jones, of Parkominck, desires to purchase 180 acres of Land on the East side of the Land late Edw'd Lane's and Joyning to his own Settlement, for which he agrees to pay forty Pounds, £20 on the 16th day of the 3d Month and the Remainder on the 16th of the 9 mo. next following, and if upon the Survey there Shou'd be more land than is above Expressed, he is to pay five shillings for every acre. Granted and Warrant Signed, dated 3d 1 mo., 1715-6.

Signed a Warrant to Daniel Harman for 200 a's in Chester County at £20, the whole, dated the 15th 1 month, 1715-6.

Signed a Warrant to John Evans, of Haverford, for 100 acres lieing between the Settlements of Abia Taylor, James Thomas and Lewellin Parry, in Chester County, granted for £12 10s, to be paid within 3 months after Survey.

Signed a Warrant to John FFincher for a Parcell of Vacant Land lieing between the Land of the London Company, Jno. Simcock and Peter Britain, for which he agrees to pay after of £13 p. C't and Usuall quitrent, dat. 23, 2, 1716.

Signed a Warrant to John Wright for the Lott and Liberty Land belonging to William Gibson's Purchase of 500 acres, dated 26, 2 mo., 1716.

Signed a Warrant to FFrancis Worley for 1,000 acres in Chester County at £10 p. C't. Signed a Warrant to Joshua Hastings for a Resurvey on 180 acres in Chester County, being the Remainder of his Purchase, dat. 23, 2 mo., 1716.

Signed a Pattent to John Salkeld for 400 acres in the County of Chester, 375 whereof was the originall Purchase of Richard Hyde, who Conveyed the same to John Salkeld, the other 25 acres he pays £2 10s for, dated 3 month, 1716.

Signed a Pattent to James Clemson for 600 acres in Chester County, 500 whereof is a late Grant to him at £10 p. C't, the other 100 was granted to William Lewis on Rent, who sold it to James Clemson, who reduced it to 1 shilling p. ann., dated 18th 3d Month, 1716.

Signed a Pattent to John Davis and Mary his Wife, for 250 acres, Coun. Chester, mentioned in p. 62, dated 21, 9ber, 1715.

Signed a Pattent to Coll. John FFrench for 583 acres of Land in Kent, first Granted to William Morton, of the said County, deceased, from whom it came to the said John FFrench by the last Will and Testament of the said William Morton, wherein he made him his Ex'or. It was first laid out for 500 acres and by a Resurvey made thereon by a Warrant dated the 29th 6th Month, 1715, was found 588 acres, which is now confirmed to him, paying quitrent from the first Survey 1 Bushell Good Winter wheat p. C't, the Pattent dated the 20th 7th month, 1715.

Joshua Hastings having often applyed for a Resurvey on 180 acres of Land in or near the Welch Tract in Chester County, it being the Remainder of his Originall Purchase, It is granted and a Warrant Signed, dat. 23, 2 mo, 1716.

Cornelius Wiltbank, of the County of Sussex, by himself and Samuel Preston has often requested a Grant for 100 acres of Marsh, situate on the North side of the broad Kill, which is now Granted to him at £15. Warrant signed the 10th 10ber, 1715.

James Steel having purchased a Certain Parcell of Land on the Head of the Middle or West Branch of Duck Creek, Part of a Larger Tract first granted to Henry Pearmain, desires a Resurvey on the same. Granted and a Warrant signed, dated 10th 2d Month, 1716.

Signed a Warr't to Daniel Cormick, of the County of New Castle, for about 40 acres Joyning to his Plantation, for which he agrees to pay 5s p. acre, dated 10th 2 mo., 1716.

Agreed with Joseph Wood, of Swanwick, for 2 Parcells of Land Joyning on his Plantation, supposed to Contain 208 acres, for which he agrees to pay £60 on the 25th 1st Month next, and if it exceed that quantity he is to pay in like Proportion for the Rest, quitrent one Bushell good Winter Wheat p. C't. Warrant Granted and Signed, dated 29th 3 month, 1716.

Joseph Growdon having often made application as well to the Proprietary as the Commissioners, Setting forth his great Disappointm'ts in not being allowed to take up Land on acco't of his Importing above Forty Servants into this Province at his own Charge, and also on acco't of his City Lotts being all laid out on Schuylkill side of the City, or as disadvantageous Place, as well as his Publick Services in the Government, all which the Proprietary ordered the Commissioners to enquire into, which having accordingly done, they do agree and order that a Warrant be forthwith drawn for laying out to the said Joseph two Thousand acres of Land, or one thousand acres (if he desires it) to be laid out in the Tract called the great Swamp, at Richlands, in Bucks County, the other thousand acres to be laid out to him in any Part of the Province where not already taken up nor appropriated, to be held under the yearly quitrent of one shilling sterling for every Hundred acres, which said two thousand acres of Land is to be in full Satisfaction of his Claim on the Importation of his Servants and for the Disappointment in the Location of his City Lotts and for his Publick services in the Government and of all other Dues and Demands whatsoever of or from the Proprietor. The Warrant is according drawn and signed the 20th 1 mo., 1715-6.

The Proprietor, by Indenture dated the 2d and 3d days of Xber, 1681, grants to John King, of Hadbury, in the County of Bucks, in Great Britain, 1,000 acres of Land in this Province. Joshua Hart, of Toncaster, in Northamptonshire, and Alice his wife (the said Alice being only Daughter and Heiress of the said John King, who is deceased), by their att'ry, Rich'd Robinson, of Philad'a, request that the s'd 1,000 acres might be laid out to them, as also the Lotts and L. L., which is granted, and the Warrant for the 1,000 acres signed, dated the 28th 2d month, 1716, and for the Lotts and L. Land, signed, dat. 10th 4 mo., 1717.

Israel Taylor and Joseph Taylor, Sons of Christopher Taylor, Original Purchaser of 5,000 acres in this Province, having obtained two Warrants for taking up the Remainder of the said Purchase, one of them dated the 6th 5 mo., 1692, the other 26, 8ber, 1709. Both of the said Warrants together contains 758 acres, which Compleats the said Purchase, which said Warrants having never yet been executed, they now request that they may Surrender them and that they may in Lieu thereof have the like quantity laid out to them with the addition of 242, which makes in the whole 1,000 acres; they agree to pay for the addition at the Rate of £10 p. C't. Warr't granted and signed, dated 7, 4 month, 1716.

Signed a Warr't to William Blackfan for 400 acres in Chester County at £10 p. C't, dated the 9th 4th month, 1716.

Capt. John Brinklo, of the County of Kent, having formerly obtained a Warr't from the then Comm'rs of Prop'ry (viz't), for laying out to him and Arthur Meston 200 acres of Marsh on Dover River, next below a Tract called Town Point, which was according executed, since which the said Arthur Meston deceasing, and the Marsh not divided nor Confirmed, nor no quitrents paid for ye same, the s'd John Brinklo desires that the said Marsh may be resurveyed to him, upon which he is ready to pay all arrears of quitrents. A Warr't signed accordingly, dated 12th 9 mo., 1716.

Signed the severall warrants following (viz't):

To Stephen Haregrove for 200 a's.
To John Jackson for 200 a's.
To John Newton for 200 a's.
To Edward Cock for 200 a's.
To William Jackson for 200 a's.
To Jno. Thompson for 200 a's, dat. 1, 6 mo.
To Rob't Blackshaw for 200 a's, 28, 5 mo.
To Edw'd Parnel for 200 a s, 1, 6 mo.
To John Coe for 200 a's, 18, 2 mo.
To John Hall for 200 a's, 18, 2 mo.
To Paul Williams for 200 a's, 8, 7 mo.

All in the county of Kent, at 1d sterling p. acre.

Shadrah Wally, William Buckham and John FFrost, on behalf of themselves and the other Inhabitants of Newtown in the County of Bucks, desires to purchase the Vacant Strip of Land lieing on a Branch of Neshamenah Creek, which extends itselfe into the Townsted, Supposed to Contain 30 acres. They agree to pay £10 for the 30 acres and in Proportion if it be more. Granted and a Warr't sign'd, dated 6th 6 Month.

Signed a Pattent to Coll. John FFrench for a Lott of Ground and Nine acres of Marsh in New Castle Town, and also ffour acres of Land at Christina for ye Conveniency of his Mill Race, requested by him in Page 82, dated 20, 4 mo., 1716.

Signed a Pattent to John Relof, of Vanderwerf, for 300 acres of Land granted to him, page 86, dated 4th Month, 1716.

Signed a Patent to Joseph Mather for a Lott of Ground in Sassafras Street in Right of John Russel, whose only Daughter and Heiress Joseph married, dated 26th 6th montn, 1716.

Signed a Patent to James Steel for 350 acres of Land, mentioned on the other side, dated the 10th 6th month, 1716.

Signed a Pattent to Jeffrey Burges for 200 acres of Land in the Prop'rs Mannor of Highlands, in Bucks County, granted to him the 18th 9ber, 1715, for £60. Patent dated the 7th 6th month, 1716.

Richard Tranter desires to purchase 200 acres of Land near Latitia's mannor in New Castle County, which is granted him at £16 p. C't, and a Bush. wheat quitrent for each Hundred, warranted, dated 14th 6th mon., 1716.

John Peel, of the County of New Castle, requests a Grant of a Parcell of vacant Land lieing between the Land of Erick Anderson, Andrew Cock and John Hendrickson, in Christina Hundred, supposed to contain about 150 acres. 'Tis agreed that he shall have it for £25, to be paid in 3 months after the date of the Warrant, and if the said Vacancy contains more he is to pay in Proportion, with the quitr't of one Bush. Wheat p. C't, &c. Warr't dated 16, 6 mo., 1716.

Signed a Warr't to Thomas Nixon for 200 a's in Chester County, dat. 22, 6 mo., 1716.

Signed a Warr't to Rich'd Carter for 200 a's, Ditto, dat. 22, 6 mo., 1716.

Signed a Warr't to Alex'r Bews for 400 a's, Ditto, dat. 22, 6 mo., 1716.

Signed a Warrt' to John FFarer for 400 a's, Ditto, dat. 22, 6 mo., 1716.

Signed a Warrant to Phil. FFierre for 300 a's, Ditto, dat. 24, 6 mo., 1716.

All these granted at £10 p. C't and 1sh ster. p. C't quit rent.

Coll. John FFrench, of the Town and County of New Castle, having purchased a Lott of Ground in the said Town, formerly belonging to Mathias de Ring, desires a Survey on the Same in order that it may be confirmed to him with his Marsh. Granted on his paying the quitrents due on the same. Warr't dated 15th 3 mo., 1716, included in his Patent on the other side of this Leaf.

Richard Townsend having obtained a Lott of Ground of James Logan in Right of Edward Bettris, Original Purchaser, desires a Warr't for laying of it out. Granted, dated the 30th 5th mo., 1716.

Signed a Warr't to William White for 150 acres on rent, in Sussex, dat. 14, 1 mo., 1716.

Signed a Warr't to FFrancis Vossell for 200 acres, Ditto, in Kent, dat. 8, 7, 1716.

Signed a Warr't to George Mills for 200 acres, Ditto, in Kent, dat. 8, 7 mo., 1716.

Signed a Warr't to Moses Brooks for 200 acres, Ditto, in Kent, dat. 5, 7 mo., 1716.

Signed a Warr't to John FFarker for 300 acres, Ditto, in Kent, dat. 8, 7 mo., 1716.

David Robert requesting to purchase 200 acres of Land between the Branches of Brandywine Creek, agrees to pay within three months £29 for the whole, and usual quitr't of 1sh ster. p. C't. Granted, Warr't signed, dated 27th, 7 mo., 1716.

William Cload, of the County of Chester, desires a Warr't for taking up the Lotts and Lib. Land belonging to the Original Purchase of 250 acres made by William Bezer, and also an addition to the Lott of his own Purchase, that the same may be in Proportion to Lotts now laid out to the like quantity of Lott purchased, which is granted and warr't signed, dated the 9th 6 mo. and 15th 7 month, A. D. 1716.

The Proprietor, by Indentures of Lease and Release, dated the 7th and 8th days of 9ber, 1681, granted to William Gibson, of London, Haberdasher, 500 acres of Land in this Province.

William Gibson, of London, Mercer, son and heir of the aforesaid William Gibson, by like Indentures dated the 25 and 26 days of FFebruary, 1713, for £40 sterl'g Conveys the said 500 acres, with the appurten'ces, to John Wright, then of Manchester, in Great Britain, but now of Chester, in this Province. The said 500 acres was laid out in Buckingham Township, in Bucks County, and a Patent granted for the same to Wm. Gibson in the Year 1701, but the city Lott and Liberty Land being not then granted, John Wright obtained a Warr't in the 2d month last for laying out the same and then granted the said Lott and Liberty Land to Is. Pemberton, vid. p. 86.

Signed a Warr't to Thomas Parker for 200 acres at 1d st. p. acre, dated 20, 7 mo., 1716.

Signed a Warr't to Jos. Dodd for 200 a's. Ditto. dated 20. 7 mo., 1716.

Signed a Warr't to Rob't Jenkins for 200 a's, Ditto, dated 20, 7 mo., 1716. All in the County of Sussex.

Signed a warrant to Anthony Lee, of Darby, for 300 acres of Land, to be laid out to him at Oley, at £12 p. C't and 1s sterling quitr't, dated 20th 8 mo., 1716.

Signed a Warr't to Anthony Pretter, of East Jersey, for 300 acres of Land near Conestogo, at £10 p. C't and usual quitrent, dated the 16th 9ber, 1716.

William Beckingham, John Beckingham, James Hayward and Sam'l Bishop Came Servants into this Province in or about the year 1682 and served their Time accordingly, as appears by attested Certificates, and have now respectively sold the Right belonging to them to their head Land unto Isaac Taylor, of the County of Chester, Survey'r, who thereupon request a Warrant to take up, being 200 acres Granted, dated 20th 7 mo., 1716.

The Prop'r, by Indentures of Lease and Release, date the , granted to Thomas Rowland, of

Signed a Warrant to Isaac Leffevre for 300 acres of Land at Strasburg, at £10 p. C't and 1 shill'g Ster. quitrent, dated 10th 8th month, 1716.

Signed a Warrant to John Carcy, of the County of Sussex, for 200 a's on Rent, at 1d ster. p. acre, dated 20th 9ber, 1716.

Signed a Warrant to John PettyJohn, of the County of Sussex, for 200 acres in the fforest of that county, on Rent 1d sterl. p. acre, dated 20th 9ber, 1716.

James Steel having purchased of George Carter the City Lott belong'g to the Original Purchase of William Bryant, mentioned in Page 75, desires a Warrant for laying out the same, which is granted and signed, dated 19th 9ber, 1716.

Daniel FFierre, of Strasburg, desires to purchase 600 acres

of Land near Pecque, in Chester County, for which he is to pay within three months after the date of the Warrant £10 for every Hundred and the usual quitrent of 1sh ster. p. C't. Granted and the Warrant signed, dated the 4th 8ber, 1716.

Signed a Warrant to Richard Dobson, of Sussex County, for 200 acres in the fforest of Sussex, on 1d Sterling p. acre, dated 14th 8th month, 1715.

Signed a Warrant to John Carey for 200 acres in the fforest of Sussex, at 1d Sterl'g p. acre, dated the 14th 8 month, 1715.

The Proprietor, by Indenture of Lease and Release, dated the 21st and 22d days of 9ber, 1682, granted to Samuel Barker, of Darbyshire, in Great Britain, 1,000 acres of Land in Province, who by his attorney, Thomas Wetherall, now desires the same may be laid out, which is granted and a Warr't signed, dated 24th 6 mo., 1716.

Signed a Patent to Captain John Brinkloe for 200 acres of Marsh, granted in Page 88, dated

Signed a Patent to George Vankulen for 2 Parcells of Land, one of them 60 a's, the other 125, being a Resurvey on old Swedes Grants in Ridley, in the County of Chester, dated ye 5th 9ber, 1715.

Signed a Patent to Samuel Scott for 107 acres of Rent Land in Bromingham, in Chester County, first laid out to Edmond Butcher, dat. 3 month, 1715.

Signed a Patent to William Hacket for 150 acres of Rent Land in the fforest of N. Castle County and on a Branch of Duck Creek, dated the

Signed a Warrant to John Gardiner, Jun'r, for 500 acres of Land near Conestogoe Creek, at £10 p. C't and 1sh sterling quitr't, dated 9th 12 month, 1716.

Signed a Patent to Thomas Dawson for 300 acres near Conestogoe at £10 p. C't and 1sh sterl., dated 10th 12 month, 1716.

The Proprietor, by Indentures of Lease and Release, dated the 11th and 12 days of August, 1699, granted unto Tobias Collet, Michael Russell, Daniel Quare and Hen. Goldney, 60,000 acres of Land in this Province, together with Nine Town or City Lotts, and thereupon also granted three Warrants, dated the 17th day of the same month, directed to Thomas FFairman, Surveyor, for laying out of the same, who in his life time surveyed and returned into the Survey'r Gen'lls Office the quant'ty of 47,129 a's, so that there yet remains unsurveyed to compleat the said Purchase the quant'y of 12,871 acres, whereupon Jno. Estaugh, agent to the Survivors of the said Persons, desires that the said Remainder be laid out to them in order that the said Purchase might be compleated, which is Granted by a Warrant signed and dated the 18th 8 month,

1716, and directed to Surveyor Generall to Cause it to be forthwith executed and returned (Thomas FFairman, who surveyed the above quantity of 47,129 acres, being since deceased). The first mentioned three Warrants from the Prop'r, as also the last from the Commissioners, are entered in the new Warr't Book, pa. 32, 35.

Signed a Pattent to Isaac Leffevre for 300 acres in Strasburg, mentioned on the other side of this Leaf, dated the 21st 9ber, 1716.

Signed a Patent to Edward Roberts for 250 acres in the Tract called the great Swamp, in Bucks County mentioned page 84, dated 21st 9ber, 1716.

Signed a Patent to Lionel Britain for a High street Lott, 66 f'tt on the Front and 306 f'tt Deep, in Right of Silas Crispin's Purchase, who sold the Same to Patrick Robinson, who exchanged 39½ f'tt in Breadth w'th Rob't Greenway for so much of his Lott as Joyned on his other Lotts, with which 26½ f'tt added to the 39½ makes up the 66 f'tt, which is now Confirmed to the said Lionel Britain instead of the first Grant to S. Crispin. Eliz'th Robinson, Widow of the said Patrick, Sold the said Land to L. Britain. Patent dated 20th 9ber, 1716.

Signed a Patent to Richard Townsend for a Lott of Ground in Sassafras street, mentioned in page 89, dated the 12th 7 Month, 1716.

The Proprietor, by Indentures of Lease and Release, dated the   Day of 1681, granted to Thomas Bond, of Woodacre, in the County of Lancaster, in Great Britain, 1,000 acres of Land in this Province, in Right whereof there has been laid out in the County of Bucks and in the Liberties of Philadelphia besides the usual allowance 724 acres, so that there remains to be yet taken up in the same Right 276 a's to compleat the said Purchase. The Right to which said Remainder being now Vested in Thomas Edward, of the County of Philadelphia, who purchased the same of the heirs of the said Thomas Bond, he requests a Warrant to take it up. Granted, signed and Dated the 13th 8th month, 1716.

Signed a Warrant to Joseph Booth, of the County of Kent, for 200 acres of Land in the fforest of the said County at 1d sterling p. acre Rent, dated 26th 12 mo., 1716-7.

Signed a Warrant to Moses Whitacre, of the County of Kent, for 200 acres of Land in the fforest of the said County at 1d sterling p. acre rent, dated 26, 12 month, 1716-7.

Signed a Warr't to Thomas Simmonds for 1 or 200 acres near Conestogoe at £10 p. C't and 1 shill'g sterl. quitr't, dat. 26, 12 month, 1716.

Signed a Patent to Thomas Eldridge for 50 acres in Caln Township, in Chester County, 250 acres in Right of Enoch FFlower, mentioned P. 66; the other 250 acres a new Grant to T. Eldridge for £25, dated 10th 1st month, 1715-6.

Isaac Taylor, of the County of Chester, Surveyor, produces Certificates under the Hands of Caleb Pusey and Henry Worley setting forth that Wm. Beckingham and John Beckingham came Servants into this Province in or about the year 1682 and served their Time with Joseph Richards, and that Samuel Bishop came in about the same and served James Sandilands, also a Certificate under the Hand of Nich. Pyle, certifying that James Hayward came also about the aforesaid Time and served Edward Bezer. The said Is. Taylor having purchased the severall Rights of the said Servants to their headland desires a Warrant to lay out the same, which is granted, signed and dated 20, 7ber, 1716.

John Cowgill desires the Grant of about 100 acres of Vacant Land near his other Tract in New Castle County, where he has planted a Tan Yard, vid. p'g. 123.

Signed a Warrant to John Robeson for one hundred acres of Land in Christina Hundred for £22 10s and a Bush'l of wheat qu'tre't, dated ye 4, 1 mo., 1716-7.

Agreed with George Grist for 150 acres in the Mannor of Rocklands for £50 and 1s 6d Sterling quitrent. Warrant signed and dated the 11th 6 mo, 1716.

Signed a Warrant to Charles Read and uxor for 2 Lotts of Ground beyond the 6th street from Delaware in lieu of the ffront Lott belonging to Thomas Bond's Purchase of 1,000 acres, which was by some Mistake Surv'd to some other Person; it fell by the allotm't above Chestnutt street, dated 29th 8ber, 1716.

Signed a warrant to John Griffith for a Parcell of Vacant Land near the Welch Tract in New Castle County, supposed to contain between 1 and 200 acres granted him for £22 10s p. C't and 1 Bush'l of Wheat quitr't, dated the 4th 1 mo., 1716-7.

Granted to Robert Courtney 150 acres of Land on the North side of Christina Creek at £22 10s p. C't and a Bushel of Wheat quitrent, Warrant signed and dated the 4th 1 mo., 1716-7.

Signed a Warrant to Benj. Shurmer for 600 acres on the Branches of Duck Creek and Blackbird's Creek, in the fforest of New Castle County, dated ye 1st 10 mo., 1716.

Agreed with John Bull, of Parkeomink, for 2, 3 or 400 acres of Land in that Part of the Mannor of Gilberts which makes a Corner by the Lines of the London Company and the Land late Edward Lane's, for £30 and the quitrent of 1sh sterl'g for each Hundred acres, to be paid within three months after the date of the Warrant, which is the 6th 1 month, 1716-7.

Signed a Warr't to Robert Prittyman for a Resurvey on his Plantation on the head of the Indian River, in the County of Sussex, dated 27, 3 mo., 1717.

Signed a Warrant to Robert Betts for 200 acres in Sussex, on Rent, 26, 3 mo., 1717.

Signed a Warr't to Tho. Prettyman for 200 acres, Ditto, Ditto.

Signed a Warr't to John Parsons for 200 acres, Ditto, Ditto.

Signed a Warrant to John Prittyman for a small Island of Marsh at the head of Rohoboth Bay at the yearly quitrent of a Bushell of Wheat, the whole, dated 27th 3 month, 1717.

Signed a Warrant to William Shankland for a small Island in Lewis Creek, of about Ten acres, at a Bushell of Wheat quitrent, dated the 27th 3 month, 1716-7.

Signed a Warrant to John Williamson for 150 acres in the fforest of New Castle, at the Yearly quitrent of 1d sterling p. acre, Dated the 6th 1st mo., 1716-7.

Colum Macnair, late of West Jersey, being desirous to purchase 200 acres of Land at Conestogo, it is granted to him for £20, the whole, and quitrent of 1sh Sterling for each hundred acres. Warr't granted and dated the 12th 4 mo., 1717.

Signed a Patent to Samuel Baker for 101 acres and 68 p's in the Mannor of Highlands formerly laid out to his ffather but was delayed a Patent because it was within the Mannor, But now for £10 consideration it is confirmed to said Samuel, dated the 6th 10 month, 1715.

Signed a Patent to Richard Thomas for 243 acres in the Welch Tract, in Chester County, in Part of 600 allowed him instead of the like quantity confirmed to him in New Town, which is claimed by the Heirs of Wood and Shardlow, the said Richard having released his Right of the said 600 acres to the Propr'r. The said Pattent is dated the 8th 1 month, 1716-7.

Signed a Patent to Edward Robinson and ux. for a Lott in Walnutt street, first laid out to John Tibby in Right of his Purchase of 250 acres, and since Sold to the said Edward Robinson and ux., quitr't 1sh Ster., dat. 24, 9ber, 1716.

Signed a Patent to Coll. John Evans for 1,000 acres, mentioned in Pag 83, dated 16, 10 month, 1716.

Signed a Patent to James Steel for 440 acres on the North side of the Murder Creek, in Kent County, first laid out to one Thomas Williams, and since by severall Grants is Vested in the said James in Trust for J. Logan, who paid the Consideration money for it but took the Deeds in his Name that he might the better take out a Patent. J. Logan being a Com'mr and with the Rest makes up but a bera Coram, dat. the 25, 1 month, 1717.

Signed a Patent to Vincent Emerson for 100 acres, mentioned in Pag. 77; it lies in the fforest of Kent County and held at the Yearly quitrent of 1d ster. for every acre, dated the 25th 1 month, 1717.

At a Meeting of the Commissioners of Property the 8th 2 month, 1717.

Present, Richard Hill, Isaac Norris, James Logan.

William Lawrence, of Philadelphia, preferred a Petition to the Board Setting forth that about the Year 1690 he purchased severall Lotts on Schulkill side of Philad'a, where he seated himself about the same Time, and that there lies a Parcell of Ground between the said Lotts and the River, which he desires might be now granted to him, because (as he says) other Persons holding Lotts thereabouts had the Priveledge to the said River.

But those Lotts held by the said William are located and patented, and that he hath no other Grant for any other Land there, nor hath it been a General Rule or Priviledge to others as he alledges, therefore his Petition is Dismissed.

William Carter, Wm. Lawrence and Michael Walton requests Confirma'ons on three Parcells of Land formerly (as they say) laid out by warrants from the fformer Commissioners on that side of Springetsbury Mannor, which Joyns to the City Philad'a.

That Claimed by W. Carter is said to be first laid out to one Lewis Thomas, for 9 years, the other Two Parcells to W. Lawrence and M. Walton; is said to be 6 acres in each of them.

But their pretended Grants being so very Short and Weak, and that the Prop'r always forbid the granting away any Part of the said Mannor, their Request is refferred to further Consideration.

Signed a Patent to John Goodson for a Bank Lott fifty foot Front, formerly laid out to himself at the North end of the Town, dated the 25th of the 1st Month, 1717.

Signed a Patent to James Morris for 600 acres of Land and Marsh on the South Side of the Main Branch of Duck Creek, mentioned in page 69 of these Minutes, dated the 12th of the 10 Month, 1716.

The Proprietor, by Patent dated 28th 5 month, 1684, confirmed to Tho. Howle 200 acres of Land at 1d sterling p. acre Rent (supposed to be in Southampton Township, tho' not mentioned in the Patent, nor so much as bounded on any other Land). Tho. Howle, by an Indorsement on the said Patent, gives the s'd Land to his Son Job Howle, by Deed dated ye 16 of 9ber, 1697, grants 100 a's, Part thereof, to ofte Hugh Ellis, and 50 acres more to FFrancis Eileston by Deed dated . The said H. Ellis and Francis Eileston, by Deed dated the 4th of March 1701, grants the said 150 acres to Philip Parker, and afterwards the said Job Howle, by an article dated ye 17th 8 mo., 1701, Bargains and sells the 50 acres to the said P. Parker, who by Deed dated the 15th FFeb., 1705-6, grants the whole to Daniel Robinson, who by Deed dat. 13th Xber, 1708, grants the whole to Patrick Ogleby, who running away, Griffith Jones and Hugh Lowden brought their actions of Debt against the said Land, and after Judgment was obtained the Sheriff of Bucks County (to wit), Wm. Biles, to answer the Debts due to Griffith Jones and Hugh Lowden, Sells the said Land by Deed the 9, Xber, 1712, to one William Jones, who by Deed dated the 13th FFeb., 1713-4, Conveys the said Land to Joseph Jones, now of Philad'a. Whereas there is a Vacancy of about 70 acres Joyning to the s'd 200 acres, the said Joseph desires a Grant of it, and that the whole might be confirmed to him by Patent. It is agreed that upon his paying off the arrearage of quitrent due on the 200 acres and paying 10sh p. acre for the 70 a's he shall have a Patent for the whole. Signed, dat. 10, 6 mo., 1717.

Tho. FFairman in his life time applied to this Board [See page 67] on behalf of his Son-in-Law, Jeremiah Hopton, for a Patent on 250 acres of Land on Potquessin Creek, Sold by the Proprietor to Edward Hopton, ffather of the said Jeremiah.

The Commissioners then ordered that the said Land Shou'd be Resurveyed and the Bounds of 250 acres fixed and then a Patent Should be provided, But a Certain Writing being brought to this Office, which was found in the Hands of Eliz'th, late Wife of Patrick Robinson (which here follows Verbatim), the Business is referred to a full hearing of the Commissioners:

I, Wollo Woolson, of the County of Philad'a, in the Province of Pensilvania, w'th Consent of Catharine my Wife, the thirteenth day of the fourth month, 1683, for me, my Heirs and assigns, grants my Just and Equal half Part of Six hund'd and forty acres of Land, with all its appurtences (which whole Six Hundred and forty acres of Land was by Order Surveyed to me and Lassey Lasson, equally betwixt us, and is in the Protracted Figure of the said Land called Pleasant Hill, as in the Copy of the said Survey under the Hand of Richard Noble at more Length appears), lieing in the County aforesaid, upon the River Delaware, having the

Lands of Peter Rambo, Jun'r, upon the Southwest, the creek called Poyquessing on the North East, and so backward in the Woods to Benj'n Acrod, Mar't, and his Heirs and assigns forever, for the Consideration of Two thousand two hundred Guilders or Fifty-five Pounds money of Pensylv'a, secured to be paid to me, my Heirs and assigns by two severall Bills, bearing date with these Presents. In Witness whereof I hereto set my Hand and Seal and hereby promise to acknowledge the same in open Court the next Time it shall be held at Philad'a for the said County.

Signed, sealed and delivered in the Presence of Lassey [his mark] Lasson, Pat. Robinson.

This Deed was Delivered and acknowledged in open court the 3d day of the 8th Month, 1683.

    The mark of Wollo Woolson. [SEALED.]

Test, John Southworth, Cl'k of the County.

It is Written on the Back of the foregoing Writing as followeth (viz.): Memorand'm, that upon the 13th day of the 4th month, 1683, the within Wollo Woolson gave to the within Benjamin Acrod actual Possession of the Lands within sold By Delivery of Turf and Twigg of the said Land to the s'd Benj. Acrod in Person, in Presence of Pat. Robinson and Lassey Lasson betwixt 3d and 4th Hours in the afternoon.

        PAT. ROBINSON,
        LASSEY × LASSON.

Recorded in the Office of Rolls and Publick Registry at Philadelphia, Vol. 3, Book E., folio 37. Signed by Pat. Robinson.

Jeremiah Hopton requests a Warrant for laying out to him the Lott and Lib. Land belonging to 250 acres purchased of the Propr'r by Rich'd Jordan, who sold the same to Edw'd Hopton, ffather of the said Jeremiah, the other Land being already laid out near Whitpain's Township, is now held by Abraham Daws. Alex'r Draper, of the County of Sussex, desires a Resurvey on the Pla'tation and Tract of Land where he dwells, w'th ye addition of some vac't Marsh and Points Joyning to the same. For ye Vac'cy he agrees to pay after ye rate of £15 p. C't and a Bush. Wh't quitr't, to be bound'd between ye Bay of ye s'd Land and Cedar Creek.

He also requests the same Priviledge for his Brother Henry Draper, whose Land lies on the South side of that of his Brother, the said Alexander's. The Marsh Joyns on the East to William FFisher's Marsh and on the West with A. Draper's Land. Both Granted and Warr'ts ordered, signed and dated the 10, 4 month, 1717.

Jno. Turner, of the County of Kent, desires to purchase 50 acres of Marsh upon Mispelan Creek, above a small branch of the said Creek, called the ffishing Gutt. Granted for £7 10s. Warrant signed, dated 21st 4 month, 1717.

The Proprietor, by Indentures of Lease and Release, dated the 7th and 8th days of 7ber, 1681, granted to Sarah Harsent, then of Worminghurst, in Great Britain, 500 acres of Land, to be laid out to her in this Province, which afterwards by a Warrant dated the 10th 10 mo., 1684, was surveyed near the Branches of Parqueaming, and her City Lott was laid out in the third street, where Sassafras street Crosses it, but the Liberty Land remains yet to be laid out. Sarah Harsent, by like Ind'rs, dated the 6th and 7th days of FFeb., 1716, for £40 Sterling, grants and conveys the whole purchase to Anthony Morris, who now desires a Warrant for the Liberty Land and that the Lott may be Resurvey'd, and so much Vacancy added as will make it the same Dimensions of other Lotts laid out in Right of Purchases of the like qua'ty, which is Granted. Warrant Signed and dated 20th 4 mo., 1717.

The Proprietor, by Short Deeds, intend'd for Lease and Release, dated the 7th and 8th days of the 11 mo., 1701, in Consideration of one Hundred Pounds, money of England (paid to Philip FFord), granted to George Beal, near Guilford, in the County of Surrey, 3,000 acres of Land between the Rivers Delaware and Susquehannah, at the yearly quitrent of one Penny Sterling for every Hundred acres, to commence Seven Years after Survey. William Beal, Nephew to the said George, in the year 1705, came over to this Province with a Power from his Uncle to take up the said Land, and then obtained an ord'r for Warr'ts to lay out 2,000 acres, of which there is only one to be found, and that not executed (the said William going hence was never heard of).

Jeremiah Langhorn, of the County of Bucks, in this Province, produces the said Deeds and a Letter from George Beal, dated the   , 1716, wherein he acknowledges an agreem't with the s'd Jeremiah for the whole 3,000 acres, and promises to confirm the same to him upon Payment of £120 Sterling, whereupon the said Jeremiah desires Warrants for laying out the whole 3,000 acres, w'ch is granted, to be in 3 Warr'ts (viz't), the former Warr't not Yet Executed is to be one and two more now made out for 1,000 acres in each Warrant, with the Restriction of only two Parcells of Land to be laid out by each Warr't which are Signed and dated the 24th and 25th of the 5th, 1717.

The Proprietor, by large Deeds of L. and Release, dated the 7th and 8th of 7ber, 1681, granted to Ann Cawley, of Rowde, in the County of Wilts, in Great Britain, 500 acres of Land in this Province. The said Ann, by her last Will and Testam't, devised the same to Richard Webb, of the same Place, who by like Deeds of Lease and Release, dated the 29th and 30th days of 8ber, 1707, granted the said 500 acres to Charles Mutell and John Child, who by their Indentures Tripartite, dated the 4th of 9ber, 1707, conveyed the said 500 acres to Samuel Perry and Abraham Allyes in Trust for the Children of FFrancis Gandouit, now of Philadelphia, Doctor of Physick, who desires a warr't for laying out 492 acres, the Lib. land and Lott being granted to Richard Hill, of Philad'a, Gent., which is granted and Signed, dated 10th 4th month, 1717.

The Proprietor, by Deeds of Lease and Release, dated the 21st and 22d days of 8ber, 1681, granted to George FFox 1,250 acres of Land in this Province. The said George, by his last Will and Testament devised the Lotts and Lib. Land for the use of ffriends here, which was confirmed to Samuel Carpenter, Rich'd Hill and Anthony Morris for that Purpose, by Patent dated the 26, 6 mo., 1705. The Remainder, which is 1,230 acres, he, by his said Testament, devised to Tho. Lower, John Rouse and Daniel Abraham.

The said Daniel Abraham and Nathanael Rouse, Son and Heir of Jno. Rouse, by their Deed (a Copie), dated the 21st of the 4 mo. (June), 1715, for £8 grants and Releases their Shares of the said Land to the said Thomas Lower, who now by his ffriend, D. Lloyd, desires a Warrant to lay it out, w'ch is granted and signed, dated the 22, 9ber, 1717.

Signed a Patent to Joshua Hastings for a lott of Ground in the 2d street from Delaware, laid out to Edw'd Samway, in Right of his Original Purchase of 500 acres, whose att'ry, FFranis Dove, sold the said Lott to James Atkinson, who conveyed it to the said Joshua, and being released to him by J. Logan, who purchased the whole Right of E. Samway, the same is now confirmed, dated 1st 3 mo., 1717.

Sign'd a Pat't to Dav'd Loyd for a lott in ye 2d str't, first laid out in the rig't of Wm. Smith's Purchase and since convey'd to the said David, dated the 1st 10 mo., 1716.

Signed a Patent to Israel Pemberton for 616 acres on Neshamenah Creek, the Remainder of the Purchase of Edward Samway, FFrancis Dove and Wm. Wigan, dated the 10th of 9ber., 1716.

Signed a Patent to Cha. Read and ux. for two Lotts of Ground in Walnut street, mentioned in pag. 92, dated 15, 1 mo., 1716-7.

Signed a Patent to Israel Pemberton for 2,000 acres of Land in Hill Town, in Bucks County; 1,500 acres in Right of Mathew Marks and 500 in Right of Edward Bettris (see page the 8th among J. Logan's Rights), dated the 1st 8ber, 1716.

Signed a Pat't to Is'l Pemberton for 256 a's, Part in Bristol Township and P't in the North'n Libertys of Philad'a (Viz't), 176 a's, Part of 500 a's first laid out to John Moon, in Bristol; 24 in R't of Dove, Wiggan and Samway; 20 laid out to M. V. Bebber in r't of some German; 16 laid out to Tho. Bond, Purchas'rs; Edw'd Edw'ds; 16 Henry Geary and John Geary; dated ye 10th 9ber, 1716. All in ye Liberties.

Signed a Patent to Israel Pemberton for 1,894 acres in Chester County; 1,000 acres on FFrench Creek and 894 acres in 2 Tracts on Pequea Creek (viz.):

460 acres in Right of Edw'd Bettris.
450 in Right of Hugh Lamb.
90 of John Geary's.
894 of John Geary and Henry Geary.

1,894

Dated the 1st 8ber, 1716. Se page 8 of these Minutes in J. L. Rights.

Signed a Patent to Israel Pemberton for 6 Lotts in Philad'a, between 6th and 7th streets from Delaware, and between Chesnut street and Walnut street, in Right of Henry Geary, Jno. Geary, Samuel Noyse, Wm. Gibson, Jno. Clarke and Edward Atkinson. Dated the 1st 8ber, 1716.

Signed a Warrant to Rob't Webb for 200 acres in Kent, dated the 24, 4 mo.

Signed a Warrant to Mark Manlove for 200 a's, Ditto, dated the 25, 1 mo., 1717.

Signed a Warr't to Jos. Booth, Jun r, for 200 acres, Ditto, dated the 19, 4, 1717.

Signed a Warrant to Richard Westley for 100 a's in Sussex, dated the 25, 1. All these are 1d sterling p. acre quitrent.

Signed a Warrant to Abraham Dubois for 1,000 acres of Land at New Strasburg, being Part of the 10,000 acres laid out to the Palatines in the Year 1710, dat. 17, 3, 1717.

Signed a Patent to FFrancis Rawle for 40 f'tt of Bank Lott at the North end of Philadelphia, first laid out to himself in the year 1690, dated 25, 3, 1717.

Signed a Patent to Anthony Lee for 400 acres at Oley, requested Page 89, dated the 26, 4 month, 1716.

Signed a Patent to Daniel FFierre for 700 acres at New Strasburg for £70, dated 25, 1 mo., 1717.

Signed a Patent to FFrancis Daniel Pastorious for 893 acres, laid out to him near Parkeomink Creek, granted in Page 51 forgoing.

Nicholas White, of the County of Chester, desires a Grant of a certain Parcell of Vacant Land lieing between the Lands of Dr. Jones, William Hudson and the Barrens of Goshen, supposed to contain 200 acres, which is granted him at £15 p. C't and usual quitrent (viz't), 1s, sterling. Warrant Signed and dat. 16, 3, 1717. The Consideration money to be paid in Three Months after the date of ye warr't.

Christopher Schlegle, of the County of N. Castle, desires to purchase 200 acres of Land back of Edw'd Green's Plantation in the said County, which is granted him for £50, to be p'd down at Survey or well Secured, and one Bush. of Wheat quitrent for each hundred. Warrant signed, dated the 1st 2d month, 1717.

Signed a Warr't to Jos. Cloud for 500 acres back in Chest'r Cou'ty, at £10 p. C't, dat. 1, 2 mo., 1717.

Signed a Warr't to Jno. Batten for 300 a's in the same Part, Same Price. 16, 3, 1717.

Signed a Warr't to Wm. Grimson for 100 a's on a Branch of Octararo at £12. 16, 3, 1717.

Signed a Warr't to Daniel Northington for 100 a's near ye Barrens of Goshen at £15. 16, 3, 1717.

Signed a Warrant to James Shattick for the Lotts and Liberty Land of the original Purchases of Thomas Pagget and Joan Dixon, being 500 acres, each of them dated the 11th day of the 4th month, 1717.

Signed a warrant to John FFrederickfulls, late of Oley, for 300 acres of Land Back in Chester County, at £10 p. C't and 1sh Sterling quitr't, dated 20, 3 mo., 1717.

John Hall, of the County of Kent, desires to purchase a Parcell of Vac't Marsh on the ffront of his Land on the South side of the South west Branch of Duck Creek, which is granted to him at the rate of £15 p. C't and the quitr't of a Bushell of Wheat, the Consideration Money to be paid within 3 months after the date of the Warrant for the same, now granted and signed, dated 1, 4, 1717.

Signed a Warr't to John Hilyard and Charles Hilyard for to resurvey to them the Tract of Land called the Exchange, Situate on the South side of the South west Branch of Duck Creek, first laid out to their ffather, dat. 25, 7ber, 1717.

Geo. Green, of the County of Kent, being desirous to purchase a p'rcel of Vacant Marsh that lies between the ffront of his Land and the South west Branch of Duck Creek, the same is granted him at the Rate of £15 p. C't and a Bushell of Wheat quitrent, the Consideration money to be paid within 3 months after the Date of the Warrant, which is now signed, dated the 25th 7ber, 1717.

Signed a Warrant of Resurvey to FFrancis Richardson on the Moiety of a Tract of Land in the County of Kent, first laid out to John Hill, late of the County of Sussex, for 300 acres, who sold one Moiety thereof to FFrancis Richardson, ffather to the said Francis, dated the 25th of 7ber, 1717.

Signed a Warrant to Peter Vossel for 200 acres in Kent County, dated ye 20, 6 mo.

Signed a Warrant to Wm. Wilson for 200, Ditto, 12, 8.

Signed a Warrant to John Macknot for 200 acres, Ditto, 30, 8.

Signed a Warr't to Rob't New for 200 acres, Ditto 30, 8.

Signed a Warr't to Waitman Siple for 200 acres, Ditto 30 8, 1717.

Signed a Warrant to James Thislewood for 200 acres, Ditto, 30, 8, 1717.

Signed a Warrant to Christop'r Siple for 200 acres Ditto, 30, 8.

Signed a Warrant to Patrick Kendal for 200 acres, Ditto, 30, 8.

Signed a Warrant to Tho. Walker for 200 acres in Sussex, 20, 6.

Signed a Warrant to Owen Hill for 200 acres in Sussex, 20, 6.

All these Grants are at the yearly Rent of 1d Sterlng for every acre.

Sam'l Holt, of Philad'a, att'ry of Henry Lloyd, of Queen's Village, in the Governm't of New York, desires a Warr't to resurvey a Certain Tract of Land in ye County of Suss'x, called the Maiden Planta'on, first survey'd to Wm. Durval for 1,000 a's and by him sold to John Nelson, of Boston, in New England, by Deed Poll dated ye 2d day of FFeb., 1687, who by Deed of Gift, dated ye 16 of 9ber, 1713, granted the same to his Son-in-Law, ye s'd Henry Lloyd. Granted, sign'd and dat'd ye 2, 9ber, 1717.

Signed a Warrant to John Williams for 200 acres in Sussex, 25th 9, 1717.

Signed a Warrant to Robert Heaton for 200 acres in Sussex, 20th, 6, 1717.

Signed a Warrant to Hugh Stevenson for 200 acres in Sussex, 25, 9, 1717.

All these are at 1d sterling quitrent p. acre.

Richard Painter, of th County of Sussex, having in the Year 1706-7, obtained a Warrant for laying out to him a Parcel of Vac't Land Joyning on other Land of his in Peach Blossom Neck, in the said County, which Warr't being never yet executed, and the said Richard having since purchased all the Surveyed Lands in the said Neck, w'ch lies under Direct Lines and therefore leaves out some Points of fast Land and Marsh between the said lines and the Branches on each side of the said Neck, he now desires a Resurvey on the whole, which is granted on such Terms as shall be agreed on, when it is to be confirmed to him. The Warrant is signed, dated ye 19th 2 mo., 1717.

Signed a Warrant to Griffith Thomas for 100 acres of Land between the Land late Richard Thomas' and the Barrens of Chester County, for £15 and 1 Shill. sterl'g quitrent, the £15 to be paid in one Month after the Date of the Warrant, w'ch is 10, 4 mo., 1717.

Owen Roberts having purchased of William Palmer and Tho. Palmer, the surviving Sons of George Palmer, deceased, Purchaser of 5,000 acres of Land in this Province, the Remainder untaken up of the said Purchase, being 500 acres, and thereupon desires a Warrant to take up the same, w'ch is granted and the Warr't signed, dated ye 12th of 7ber, 1715.

Richard Thomas, Son and Heir of Rich'd ap Thomas, having formerly obtained the Grant of a Lott of Ground on the River Schuylkil!, to be laid out to him in Right of his ffather's Purchase, besides those Lotts laid out to him on Delaware side of Philad'a, which Lott on Schuylkill not being survey'd to him, he now desires that he might resign his Right to the said Lott and that he wou'd instead thereof grant him one whole Lott in the Back streets on Delaware side. The Comm'rs considers his Disappointm'ts in not having his Lotts and Lands laid out to him before he came to age, grants his Request and a Warrant is signed and dated ye 25 of 7ber, 1717.

Signed a Warr't to Isaac Malin for 200 acres of Land near the Barrens of Goshen, in Chester County, granted to him for £15 and 1 shill. sterl'g for each hundred acres, to be paid within 3 Months after the date of the Warrant, which is the 22, 6 mo., 1717.

Signed a Warrant to Samuel Nutt for 400 acres back in Chester County for £40, the whole, and usual quitrent, to be paid in 3 months after the date of the Warr't, dated the 18th of 7ber, 1717.

Signed a warrant to John Stringer for 500 acres of Land back in Chester County at £10 p. C't, to be paid in three Months, dated 18th 7ber, 1717.

Signed a Warrant to Jos. Jones for resurveying the Land mentioned in Page 94, dated the 1st of the 5th month, 1717.

Signed a Warrant of Resurvey to Jacob Vandervere and his Kinsman, Jacob, ye Son of Corn. Vandervere, to resurvey to them 400 acres of Rent Land on the North side of Brandywine Creek, first laid out to the first mentioned Jacob and Cornelius by Vertue of a Warr't under the Hands of William Markham and John Goodson, dated the 27th of the 6th month, 1689, dated 29th 5 mo. 1717.

Signed a Warrant to Wm. Williams, of the Welch Tract, in N. Castle Co'ty, for 200 acres of Land near Obad'a Holt's, at £50, the whole, and a Bush'l of Wheat quitrent for each hundred, and also 200 acres more Joining on his Plantation at £40, the whole, and like quitrent, to be paid within three Months, dated 20th 9ber, 1717; also another Warrant to Simon James for 200 acres near the above mentioned, at £50, the whole, and like quitrent, to be paid within three months, dated 20th 9ber, 1717.

Signed a Warrant to Richard Beason for 500 acres in Chester County at £10 p. C't.

Signed a Warr't to Tho. Eldridge for 500 acres, both dated the 12th 10 month, 1716.

Signed a Warrant to David Jones for 150 acres of upland in Chester County at £20, the whole, and also one other Warrant to David Cadwalader in the same Place and at the same Price, both dated the 12th 10 mo., 1716.

Signed a Warrant to Isaac Taylor for 100 acres of head Land in Right of John Bromal and John Clews, who came Serv'ts into this Province, dat. 18th 7ber 1717.

Signed a Warrant to David Morris, of Marple, for 500 or 1,000 acres of Land near Conestogo at £10 p. C't, to be paid in 3 months, dated ye 12, 8ber, 1717.

Signed a Warrant to Richard Thomas for the remaining 357 acres of Land mentioned in Pag. 93, dated the 12th of 8ber. 1717.

Signed a Warrant to Samuel Lewis, of Darby, for 500 acres of Land to be laid out to him back in Chester County at £10 p. C't, in 3 Months, dated ye 16, 9ber, 1717.

David Lloyd, Ex'or of Tho. Lloyd, dece'd, desires that 329 acres of Land might be laid out to the Descendants of the s'd dece'd instead ot the like quantity resigned by him, and the other Ex'or to Bowater, Swaffer and Croxson out of a Tract in the great Valley in Chester County, which is granted and a Warr't signed, dated ye 22 of November, 1717.

The Proprietor, by Deeds of Lease and Release, dated ye 26 and 27 days of FFeb., 1681, granted to Rich'd Adams, of upper Heyford, in Northampton Shire, 500 acres of Land in this Province, quitr't one Shilling Sterling p. C't, as appears by Copies of the Deeds and Rece't for the Consideration money (viz.), £10, attested by John Vaston.

John Adams, Son and Heir to the said Richard Adams, by a Power of Att'ry proved here, authorises and appoints Hugh Sharp, of the County of Burlington, in West Jersey, to take up the s'd Land, whereupon he requests a Warr't for laying of it out, w'ch is granted and signed, dated ye 26th of 9ber, 1717.

Thomas Pierce, of Limrick, in Ireland, having formerly purchased of the Proprietor 1,000 acres of Land in this Province, had in the Year 1700, five hundred acres ye of laid out in the Tract called Limrick Township, and afterwards sold the whole to James Shattick, who now represents that ye said 500 acres laid out in Limrick is so very Stony and Barren that it will not yield him anything like the money he gave for it and therefore desires he may resigne and give up the same, and that the Comm'rs would grant him the like quantity in some other Place that is Vacant, for which a Warrant is ordered and signed, dated the 21st Xber, 1717.

Signed a Warrant to Christian Penerman and John George Trelinger for 60 A's of Land between the River Schuylkill and the FFrench Creek for £90 and usual quitr't, one-half of the Consideration money to be paid down at Survey and the other in 6 Months, dated 21st Xber, 1717.

Signed a Warrant to Samuel Saub for 200 acres at Oley for £12 p. C't, to be p'd in 3 months. 16, 9ber, 1717.

Signed a Warrant to Hans Snyder for 200 acres at Oley for £12 p. C't, to be p'd in 3 months. 26, 9ber, 1717.

Agreed with Martin Kundigg and Hans Heer of 5,000 acres of Land, to be taken up in severall Parcells about Conestogo and Pequea Creeks, at £10 p. Ct', to be paid at the Returns of the Surveys and usual quitrents, it being for settlements for severall of their Countrymen that are lately arrived here. The Warr't signed, dat. 22d 9ber, 1717.

Signed a Warr't to Hans Moyer for	350 a's.
Signed a Warr't to Hans Kaiggey for	100 a's.
Signed a Warr't to Chr'r Hearsey and Hans Pupather for	1,000 a's.
Signed a Warr't to Mich. Shank and Henry Pare for	400 a's.
Signed a Warrant to Hans Pupather for	700 a's.
Signed a Warrant to Peter Leman for	300 a's.
Signed a Warrant to Molker Penerman for	500 a's.
Signed a Warrant to Henry and John FFunk for .	550 a's.
Signed a Warrant to Christ'r FFransiscus for . . .	150 a's.
Signed a Warrant to Michael Shank for	200 a's.
Signed a Warr't to Jacub Lundus and Ulri'k Harvey for	150 a's.
Signed a Warrant to Emanuel Heer for	500 a's.
Signed a Warrant to Abr. Heer for	600 a's.
Signed a Warrant to Hans Tuber, Isaac Coffman and Melkerman for	675 a's.
Signed a Warrant to Mich. Miller for	500 a's.

All dated the 27, 7 ber, 1717, and most of it Surveyed in the following month. All at £10 p. C't, to be paid in three Months and usual quitr't.

Francis Cornwell, of Sussex County, in a Petition or Cavet Sets forth that his late ffather, FFrancis Cornwell, many Year since obtained a Grant for 100 acres of Marsh in the said County (on Rent, viz't, 1d Sterling p. acre), but by some supposed mistake either in the Patent or Returne his Neighb'r, David Gray, by a late Warr't hath run Considerably into the said Marsh, wherefore the said FFrancis desires a Warrant to resurvey the same and that he may have liberty to purchase the overplus, if any be within the Lines of his Patent, and desires that David Gray may not have a Confirma'on for any Part of the said Marsh till his Return be made and himself further heard upon the Premisses.

A Warrant of Resurvey is accordingly signed, dated ye 13th 11 mo., 1717.

Signed a Warrant to Daniel Brown for 200 a's
Signed a Warrant to Thomas Carlile for 200 a's
Signed a Warrant to John Ponder for 200 a's
Signed a Warrant to Peter Lucas for 200 a's

{ in the fforest of Sussex, dat. 13th 11 mo., 1717-8. All at 1d sterl'g p. acre.

At a Meeting of the Commissioners of Property the 21st of 9ber, 1717.

Present, Richard Hill, Isaac Norris, James Logan.

Samuel Preston, in behalf of Corn's Wiltband, desires that the 100 acres of Marsh laid out to the said Cornelius below Walton Huling's, in the Broad Kill Marsh in Sussex County, might be confirmed to him, w'ch has been delayed upon the Complaint of Margery FFisher, who alledged that the granting of the said Marsh to Corn's would be very Injurious if not ruinous to herself and Children, upon which enquiry being made by James Steel, who was lately in that Neighbourhood, and upon the same Marsh, says that it is surveyed at some distance from any of her Lines and that her Clamour is Groundless, and therefore a Patent to Cornelius is now signed, dated the 10th 8ber last.

MINUTE BOOK "H."

22, 9ber, 1717.
Pr'sent, only I. N. and J. L.

Martin Kundigg, Hans Heer and Hans FFunk, with severall others of the Palatines, their Countrymen, having applied to purchase Land near Conestogo and Pequea Creeks to accommodate those of them that are lately arrived in this Province, who are their Relations, ffriends or acquaintances, and whom they assure the Board are Honest, Conscientious People.

Their Request being Considered and the Circumstance of those People in Relation to their Holding of Lands in the Dominions of Great Britain were asked if they understood the Disadvantage they were under by their being born aliens, that therefore their Children could not inherit nor they themselves convey to others the Lands they purchase, according to the Laws of England, which may in such Case be extended hither. They answered that they were informed thereof before, however inasmuch as they had removed themselves and ffamilies into this Province they were, notwiths'g the s'd Disadvantage, willing to purchase Lands for their own Dwelling. It was further said by the Commissioners that it was their Business to sell and dispose of the Proprietors' Land to Such as would purchase it, yet at the same time they were willing to let them know, as they are aliens, the Danger that might ensue if not in Time prevented, also that some Years ago a Law was Enacted here and afterwards passed by the late Queen Ann, for enabling Divers aliens, particularly named therein, to hold and enjoy Lands in this Province, and that the like advantage might probably be obtained for those amongst themselves that were of good Report if a Petition were preferred to this present Assembly when they sit to do Business. With this advice they seemed pleased and desired to be informed with such a sitting of the Assembly would be, that they might preferr a Petition to them for such a Law as is above mentioned.

Signed a Patent to Hans Moyor for 700 acres of Land at Strasburg, granted him for £10 p. C't, dated the 30th 6 mo., 1717.

Signed a Patent to Julian Kirl for 83½ acres in Makefield, in Bucks County, 50 acres at ½d sterling p. acre, 30½ acres at 1d sterling p. acre, dated 1717.

At a Meeting of the Commissioners of Property the 2d 11 mo., 1717-8.

Present, Richard Hill, Isaac Norris, James Logan.

Andrew Hamilton having often applied for a Piece of

MINUTE BOOK "H."

Broken Low Ground at some Distance Northward of the Town Line for the Conveniency of a Pasture, which being taken into Consideration the Commissioners agree that he shall have about Twenty acres laid out to him for the Term of 21 Years, under the Rent of one Shilling Sterling, to be paid yearly, for every acre and at the Expiration of the said Term of 21 years the said Land is to be delivered up by the said Andrew Hamilton, his Ex'ors, adm'ors or ass's, well improved and under a good ffence to the Proprietor, his Heirs or Successors.

The Commissioners being informed that Matthias Vanbebber, from Maryland, taking with him Henry Hollinsworth, hath lately surveyed a Considerable Tract of Land near the head of Pequea Creek in this Province, including within the same the Old Sawannah Town, by vertue of Warr'ts from Maryland, and offering the People Settled under this Government to sell Lands to them in Right of Maryland and make them good Titles for the same. To prevent any further proceedings of the like Kind for the future, it is proposed that Speedy Measures be forthwith taken to dispossess all Persons Claiming Lands there under the said Right, also that a Reward of Ten pounds be publickly offered to any Person who shall apprehend any Surveyor Coming into those Parts to lay out Lands in a Maryland Right, and deliver him to the Sheriff or other Officer impowered for the Purposes in those Parts, y't they may be brought to Justice.

James Steel is ordered to be ready to go to Conestogoe with such Instructions as Shall be necessary to prevent the like Disorders for the Time to come.

Ordered a Warrant to lay out to Peter Chartier 300 acres of Land where his ffather is settled on Susquehannah River, it being at his ffather's request, at £10 p. C't and usual quitrent. Signed, dated this day.

A Warrant to Moses Comb, requested by his Brother-in-Law Peter Bizalion, for 200 acres among the other Surveys about Conestogo, at £10 p. C't. Signed, dated ye 30th Xber last.

Ordered that 500 acres be granted to Coll. John FFrench in or near the Sawannah old ffields, on Pequea Creek, as a Consideration of his Services to the Prop'r and his Interest, done and to be done in preventing the Incroachm'ts of Maryland on the Lands of this Province, and that five Guineas be paid to the said Coll. FFrench for his Expences in his last Journey to Nottingham and attending the Maryland Jury at North East, who were directed by the Comm'rs from England for forfeited Lands to make a Return of Coll. Talbot's

Mann'r between Northeast River and Otararoe Creek. The Warr't for ye 500 acres is signed and dated this day.

Jonathan Dickinson having long applied to this Board to purchase the Northern Part of Springetsbury Mannor, and Terms having been proposed to him last Winter in order to the same, it is now agreed and concluded that all that Part of the s'd Mannor wihch lies to the Northward of a Line to be drawn from the Cove below the Vineyard Tract to the Northwest Corner of Abraham Bickley's ffield, Shall be forth with granted him at one Pound Six shillings and Eight Pence Sterling p. acre, to be paid on his Bills in London, together with Interest for the same from the 24th day of the 4th month last past, in Consideration of which Interest money arising from former Proposalls made to him, all those $137\frac{1}{2}$ acres of the Vineyard Tract which he Claims, together with che Rest, Shall be confirmed to him, But that out of the Measure of the whole So much shall be allowed to him as the great Road passing through ye s'd Land shall be found to take up, to be computed at Sixty foot in Breadth, and the said Jonathan is to allow out of his Purchase a smaller Road leading out of the said great Road to the Remainder of the Mannor, to be laid near the said Corner of Abraham Bickley's ffield.

The late Settlements on and near Conestogo Creek hath made it necessary that the Indian ffields about the Town Should be enclosed by a good ffence to secure the Indians, Corn from the Horses, Cattle and Hoggs of those new Settlers that wou'd otherwise destroy it and thereby cause an uneasiness in those Indians. Wherefore 'tis ordered that the said ffence be forthwith made and that J. Logan pay for the same not exceeding Twenty Pounds.

Signed a Warrant to Rich'd Pearsal and Jeremiah Pearsal for 300 acres back in Chester County at £10 p. C't, to be paid in three Months. Signed a Warr't to Jno. Pearsal for 200 a's at the same Price, dat. 13, 10, 1717.

Signed a Warr't to Jno. Bromal for 400 a's, at   , dat. 25 9, 1717.

Signed a Warr't to Wm. Willis for 200 acres at £10 in 3 months, dat. 10, 8, 1717.

Agreed with Hans George Shutz and Mathias Ringer (two Germans) for 500 acres of Land on the West side of Schuylkill River, including the Old Plantation where Peter Bizalion formerly Dwelt, for which they are to pay one Hundred Pounds, fforty Pounds, Part thereof, on the Return of the Survey, now immediately to be made, and the Remaining Sixty Pounds at the Philad'a Fair in November next. Warr't Signed, dated ye 20th 11 mo, 1717-8.

Signed a Warrant to Mich'l Poughman for 400 acres at £10 p C't, dat. 20, 11, 1717.

Signed a Warrant to James Hammer for 200 acres at £10 p. C't, dat. 10, 8, 1717.

James Steel having Purchased of Joshua Tompkins and Evan Jones two Tracts of Land, Situate Contiguous on the South side of the South west Branch of Duck Creek, one of them was returned for 550 acres, the other for 470 acres, and there being a Narrow strip of Vacant Land on the lower Side of the said Tracts, next to the Land called Donby, he desires a Resurvey on the two Tracts and the addition of the Narrow strip, and that the whole may be returned together, which is granted upon his paying the like quitrent for the Addition as would have been due had the same been Surveyed with the Rest. The Warr't Signed, dated ye 24th day of Dec'r, 1717.

Signed a Patent to Morgan Jones for 250 Acres of Land in Concord. It was first laid out to Andrew Meclar at 1d sterling p. acre, and so continues, dated ye 10. 8ber, 1717.

Signed a Patent to Tobias Collet and others, the London Company, for 1,600 acres of Land in Two Parcells, on the River Schuylkill, Part of their Purchase mentioned in Page 91, dated the 9th 9ber, 1717.

Signed a Patent to Jeremiah Langhorn and John Chapman for 700 acres of Land in three Parcels, all in Bucks County, in Right of Isaac Decow, mentioned in page   , dated the 8, 7ber, 1717.

Signed a Patent to Martin Kundigg for 800 acres of Land at Strasburg, which was first laid out to Samuel Gulden on Certain Terms, which he never Complyed with, and therefore it was granted to the said Martin for £80, dated the 30, 10ber, 1714.

Signed a Patent to Thomas Sharp for 111 acres of Marsh lieing between his Land and Plantation and the Southwest Branch of Duck Creek. It being but ordinary broken Marsh, it is granted to him for paying the quitrent of a Bush. of Wheat p. C't, from the Time of the Prop'rs arrival here in the year 1682, and the same to Continue forever, dated the 20, 4 mo., 1717.

Signed a Patent to Claus Johnson for 150 acres of Land near Bebber's Township, being Part of the Thousand acres granted by the Prop'r at his Last Departure to David Powel, mentioned in Page   , dat. 9, 9ber, 1717.

Signed a Patent to John Grigg for 150 acres of Land on Brandywine Creek, Part of the Overplus in Mathias Defoss's Tract, released by Johannus Defoss to Jno. Grigg, who pays to the Prop'rs Use £22 10s, dated ye 18, 9ber, 1717.

Signed a Patent to Isaac Llefevre for 300 acres of Land at Strasburg, granted for £30, dated ye 16th 9ber, 1717.

Signed a Patent to Joan FForest for a Lott in Mulberry street, in Breadth 39 f'tt and in Length 306 f'tt, which being inclosed among the Lotts she purchased of the Willisses, is granted to her for £15, dated ye 10th 8ber, 1717.

Signed a Patent to Nathan Stanbury for 500 acres of Land on the South side of the Main Branch of Duck Creek, formerly belonging to Richard Mitchell, who dying in Robert Ewer's Debt, the Ex'ors or adm'ors of Mitchell assigned the said Land, in Kent Court, for Payment thereof, and N. Stanbury being Surviving Ex'or of Rob't Ewer, obtained a Resurvey on the said Land about 3 y'rs agoe and 'tis now Confirmed to N. Stanbury upon paying ye arrears of quitrent, dat. 30, 9, 1717.

Signed a Patent to Hans Pupather for 700 acres at £10 p. C't, near Conestogo, dat. 28, 9ber, 1717.

Signed a Patent to Hans Pupather and Ch'r Hearsay for 1,000 acres at £10 p. C't, near Conestogo, dat. 30, 9, 1717.

Signed a Patent to Daniel Herman for 450 acres at £10 p. C't, near Conestogo, dat. 30, 10ber, 1717.

Signed a Patent to Michael Shank and Hen. Pare for 400 a's at £10 p. C't, near Conestogo, dat. 31, 10ber, 1717.

Signed a Patent to Samuel Powel for 3 Lotts of Ground in the Third Street from Delaware, one of them in Right of Anthony Elton's Purchase of 500 acres, another in Right of John Wall and John Wallis's Purchase of 250 acres, the third being inclosed with the Rest is granted to him for £15, the whole upon the third Street, is in Front 133½ f'tt and 196 foot Deep, dated the 16th 9ber, 1717.

At a Meeting of the Commissioners of Property the 14th 11 mo., 1717-8.

Present, Richard Hill, Isaac Norris, James Logan.

Thomas Stevenson, of the County of Bucks, att'ry to Wm. Lawrence, Joseph Thorn, Benj. FField, John Talmon and Samuel Thorn, all of Long Island, Sets forth that the said Wm. Lawrence and others, about the year 169 , purchased of Wm. Biles, late of the said County, 5,000 acres of Land in the same County, belonging to one Thomas Hutson, whose att'ry he then was, and that the said William Lawrence, &c., never yet had the said Land Confirmed to them, and therefore desires a Patent may be now Granted for the same. But Tho. Shute, Andrew Hamilton, Geo. FFitzwater and James Steel being vested with the Right of the like quantity of Land, the Original Purchase of one Thomas Herriott, made of the

Prop'r, by Deeds Indented of Lease and Rel., dat. ye 10, 11 Xber and ye 13 and 14 8ber, 1681, objects, that in ye s'd Right of Tho. Herriott there was laid out in the year 1685 to Dennis Rockford, by the Survey'r Gen'lls Order on two Warrants, one for 1,200, the other for 3,000 acres, a Tract of Land Contain'g 4,200 a's, w'ch upon ye runing of ye Line y't divides the Counties of Philad'a and Bucks, was found Part in ye County of Philad'a and Part in the County of Bucks; y't Part w'ch fell in Bucks County prov'd to be ab't 3,000 a's, but ye whole was returned in one Tract. The s'd 3,000 a's some Time afterw'ds is supposed to be taken in by a Survey, presumed to be made by Israel Taylor of ye whole s'd 5,000 a's of Thomas Hutson.

Whereupon the said Tho. Stevenson produced a Power of Att'ry from the said William Lawrence and Company, and also Certain Instructions ordering him to lay the whole Matter in Difference before the Commissioners, desiring them to grant a full Hearing and then to determine to whom the s'd 3,000 acres Should be confirmed, and further that in Case the Comm'rs Shou'd not think fitt to take that Charge on them, Then the said Thomas Stevenson might leave the Matter in Difference to other Honest Men, to be chosen on Both Parts, and that the s'd Wm. Lawrence and others wou'd be Concluded by the Judgm't of those Men.

The Commissioners not thinking it Proper for themselves to undertake the Decision of the Matter in Controversy advises the Parties to chose other Persons as Arbitrators and leave the Difference to their Determina'on.

Signed a Warrant to Evan Owen for the Lott and Lib. Land belonging to Ann Cawly's Purchase of 500 acres, entered p. 95, dat. 3, 4, 1717.

At a Meeting of the Commissioners the 29th 11 mo., 1717-8.
Present, Richard Hill, Isaac Norris, James Logan.

Pursuant to what Tho. Stevenson, in behalf of Wm. Lawrence, Joseph Thorn, Benj. FFields, John Talmon and Samuel Thorn, laid before ye Commissioners the 14th Ins't, he, the said Thomas, on behalf of the s'd Persons, did nominate and Chose Jonathan Dickinson and Jeremiah Langhorn, and Tho. Shute and Partners did in like manner Chose Clem't Plumsted and Israel Pemberton on their Part and behalf to hear and determine the Difference on the said 3,000 acres in Controversy, both Parties hav'g oblidged themselves under the Hands and Seals to stand to the award of those men, who having after fully heard the allegations on both sides and

Viewed the sev'll Writings, Precepts, Surveys and Returns laid before them, unanimously agreed that the s'd 3,000 acres in Controversy, lieing in Bucks County, doth of right belong to the s'd Tho. Shute and Partners, Claimants under Dennis Rockford, to whom it was first laid out, and that the same ought to be patented to them. The award, und'r the Hands and Seals of the s'd J. Dickinson, Jerem. Langhorn, Clem't Plumst'd and Is'l Pemberton, is lodged in this Office, as also a full State of the Case affixed thereunto by the s'd Persons. Wherefore the s'd Tho. Shute, Geo. FFitzwater, Andrew Hamilton and James Steel having divided the whole 4,200 acres into sev'll Lotts or Shares, desires a confirmation to each of them for so much as they respectively hold (200 acres that were taken out of the same by Execution at the Suit of Andrew Robeson against the Estate of D. Rockford, then deceased, are to be Excepted). To which the Comm'rs agree that upon paying down the quitrents due on the whole, and for the Overplus found over and above the Ten p. C't, that Patents be accord'ly Granted, but first the Mem. Deeds from the Heirs of D. Rockford are to be laid before J. Logan that the Right of those Claimants may appear to be good.

A Petition from George Dakeyne to the Commissioners was read setting forth that he had often requested some Part of the Marsh and Cripple below Newcastle Town, about 16 acres, and that he had together with his House and Lots in that Town Mortgaged 6 acres of the said Marsh to Gilbert FFalconar, w'ch unless he can have the Grant and Liberty to sell the same to pay off the said Mortgage, he Expects to be intirely ruined by G. FFalconar. J. L. intends to answer this Petition by a Letter to George Dakeyne.

Joseph Wood, of N. Castle, has sent up an Information of Severall Tracts of Land in New Castle County, which are Valuable and might be disposed off to advantage, which he will either do for the Proprietor or take them to himself at a Price that might be worth his While to undertake it at. Referred to further Consideration.

Abraham Bickley Sets forth by his Request in Writing that there was 500 acres of Land, formerly laid to Wm. FFrampton in Right of Wm. Bowman's Purchase, near the Tract Called Pickering's Mines, and since upon a Resurvey and Division of that Tract the said 500 acres is taken in and confirmed to John Moor and Joseph Wilcox, and ye s'd A. Bickley being Vested with a Right to the said 500 acres, desires that it may be laid out to him in the nearest Vacancy to the Place where it was before Surveyed. Ordered that he produce his Deeds, which if Good, a Warrant is granted.

MINUTE BOOK "H." 631

Joseph Jones requests that 2 Bank Lotts formerly laid out to his ffather below Anth. Morris's Brew house, one Containing 20 foot ffront, the other 16 foot ffront, might be confirmed to him by Patent. Granted.

The Prop'r, by Ind'rs of Lease and Release, dated the 8th and 9th days of 7ber, 1681, granted to Ann Olliff, of Oxon, in Great Britain, wid'w, 500 acres of Land in this Province, quitrent 1 shilling sterl. p. C't. Ann Olliff, by her last Will and Testament, dated the 19th of March, 1682, did give and bequeath all her Estate (some Legacies Excepted) unto her only Daughter Jane Olliff, who afterward Intermarried with Robert Clarke, of London, Mault ffactor, since deceased.

Bartholomew Deeke, of the Parrish of St. Giles's, County of Midd'x, Baker, and Anna his Wife, who is the only Daughter of the said Rob't Clarke and Jane, his wife, by Deeds of L. and Rel., dated the 14th and 15th days of December, 1716, granted the said 500 acres of Land, with the appurtences, to James Robins, of Queen Hith, London, Meal ffactor, for £10, to hold, &c.

The s'd Ja's Robins, by a Power of Att'ry under his Hand and Seal, dated ye   , certified by a Notary Publick, and Witnesesd by Tho. Nixon and Rich'd Murry, appointed Capt'n Jno. Annis and Sam'l Robins, his Brother, dwelling in this Province, or either of them, to take up the same. Sam'l Robins requests Warr'ts for laying out ye s'd Land and Lott. S. Robins has sold the Lib. Land to Tho. Shute, vid. p. 124.

The Proprietor, by Lease and Release, dated the 26 and 27th days of 7ber, 1681, granted to Thomas Bailey, of Bristol, in Great Britain, 250 Acres of Land in this Province, quitrent 1sh sterl'g p. C't. The said T. Bailey, by like Deeds, dat. ye 8th and 9th days of May, 1713, for £5 granted the said 250 acres to Edward Roberts, of Philad'a, who now requests Warr'ts to take up the same with the Lott and Lib. Land.

Abr'm Bickley, pursuant to the foregoing Ord'r [p. 106], produces a Transcript from the Records of a Grant by Ind'r dated 5, 5 mo., 1686, for 1,500 acres of Land made by Samuel Richardson to Wm. FFrampton, being Part of Wm. Bowman's Purchase of 5,000 acres, whose Son, Tho. Bowman, sold the whole to Samuel Richardson.

One thousand acres whereof (is supposed) John Budd took in Execution for a Debt due from Wm. FFrampton. The other 500 acres was laid out near the Tract called Pickering's Mines, as aforesaid.

Tho. FFrampton, Son and Heir of the said Wm. FFrampton, by Ind'rs of Lease and Release, dated the first and Second days of Jan'ry, 1712, for the Consideration of £300, Money of West

Jersey, granted and Conveyed unto the s'd Abr. Bickley, his Heirs and assigns, all his Lands, Lotts, &c., in Pensilv'a, Jersey or elsewhere in America.

Signed a Patent to Hans Hawry for 300 acres of Land at Strasburg, 50 Acres of Head Land in Right of Jos. Mather and 50 acres Ditto in Right of William Smith; the other 200 acres are purchased.

The whole was laid out to Joseph English, who sold it to H. Hawry, who reduced the quitrent of the head Land to one sh. Sterling, the 100 acres the same with the Rest, dat. 18, 12, 1717-8.

Signed a Patent to Howell William for 106 a's of Land in Ughland. Granted to him for £10, dated 7th 1 mo., 1717-8.

Signed a Patent to Israel Pemberton for 316 acres in Bristol T'p, in Phild'a County,   acres Part of John Moon's Tract, the Rest of Liberty Land, dated the 16 November, 1717.

Signed a Patent to Wendall Bowman for 250 acres at Strasburg, being Part of the Tract granted to the Palatines in the y'r 1710, at 7 p. C't, dated 12th 1 mo., 1715-6.

Signed a Patent to Hans Moyor for 350 acres at Strasburg.

Signed a Patent to Melker Prenerman for 500 acres at the same Place, both granted for Ten pounds p. C't and dated the 30th day of November, 1717.

Signed a Warrant to Evan Owen for the Lott and Lib. Land belonging to the Purchase of Ann Cawley, entered in page 95, dated the 3d 4 month, 1717.

Signed a Warr't to Hubert Cassell for 250 acres on the West side of Schoolkill, at £10 p. C't, dated the 15th 12 mo., 1717-8.

Signed a Warr't to Jacob Steager for 150 acres on the West side of Schoolkill, at £10 p. C't, dated the 15th 12 mo., 1717-8.

Signed a Warr't to Jacob Knave for 200 acres on the West side of Schoolkill, at £10 p. C't, dated the 15th 12 mo., 1717-8.

Signed a Warrant to Jacob Hochstater for 250 acres at Strasburg, at £10 p. C't, dated ye 18, 12, 1717-8

Signed a Warrant to Jacob Kreytor for 250 acres at Strasburg, at £10 p. C't, dated ye 18, 12, 1717-8.

The Proprietor, in and about the first Month, 1682-3, granted to John Streipers, of the County of Juliers, in Germany, 5,000 acres of Land, in Right Whereof he was given to Expect Certain Lots of Ground in the City of Philad'a, the Right of which being now vested in Evan Owen, of the said City, he requests that the same may be laid out, which is granted and a Warrant signed for two hundred ninety-seven foot in Breadth or Front and the same Depth with other Lotts, to be located in Mulberry or Sassafras Streets, on Delaware Side, in full

Satisfaction of Lotts to the said Purchase, dat. 18th 12 mo., 1717-8.

Signed a Warrant to Martin Urner for 300 acres on the West side of Schoolkill, at £15 p. C't, dated the 28th 12 mo., 1717-8.

Signed a Warr't to Christ'r FFranciscus for 200 acres at Strasburg, at £10 p. C't, dated 5th 1 mo., 1717-8.

Signed a Warr't to Jeremiah Jermain for 250 acres in Ughland, in Chester County, at £12 p. C't, dated the 1st 1 mo., 1717-8.

Signed a Warr't to Morgan Jones for 400 acres on the Branches of Octararo Creek, in Chester County, at £10 p. C't, dated the same day with the forg'g Warr't.

Signed a Warr't to Griffith Jones for 200 acres in Kent at 1d sterling p. acre, dated the 6th 1 mo., 1717-8.

Agreed with Harman Casdorp, of Philad'a, Ship wright, and his Son for 500 acres of Land on the West side of Schoolkill, called Turkey Point, for one Hund'd Pounds, to be paid at or upon the Survey; the Warr't is made to the said Harman, dated the 6th 1st mo., 1717-8.

Richard Sherly, of the County of Kent, requests the Grant of a Point of Marsh Situate between the Murther Creek and Bawcom Brigg, suppos'd to contain about 60 or 70 acres. He agrees to pay after the Rate of fifteen Pounds, Pensylvania Money, and a Bushell of Good Winter Wheat. A Warrant is granted for the same and signed, dated ye 11, 1 mo., 1717-8.

Signed a Warrant to Richard Anderson for 100 acres in or near the Great Valley in Chester County, at £15, dated the 21, 4 mo., 1717.

Signed a Warrant of Resurvey to Timothy Hanson, of the County of Kent, to rectifie the lines of a Tract of Land Situate on the South Side of a Small Creek, Called Bawcom Brigg, in the said County, called Steyning, first laid out to Peter Bawcom and Richard Binks for Six Hundred acres, dated the 17th 1 mo., 1717-8.

Signed a Warrant to Thomas Pierson, Surveyor, for 54 acres of Land to Compleat the quantity of a Tract formerly held by him near Christina, which fell so much Short of what he had for divers Years p'd quitrents for, dated 25th 1 mo., 1718.

———

At a Meeting of the Commissioners the 18th 1 mo., 1717-8.

Present, Richard Hill, Isaac Norris, James Logan.

Application being made by Israel Pemberton, for himself and some others, that Edm'd Lovet, of Bucks County, for more than Thirty Years Since hath concealed a Patent that was granted him (as is p'sumed) by the Prop'r before his first

Departure from this Province, for a Certain Tract of Land near Pennsbury Mannor, which the Proprietor afterward gave him other Land in Exchange for and Confirmed the same to him by another Patent without taking up the fformer.

Edmund Lovet being in Town it was thought fit to send for him and know the Reason why he detained and kept in his Hands a Patent for which he had so long ago rece'd an Equivalent, who appearing at the Board it was further told him that the Land ment'd in the first being now in the Possession of sundry honest People they might in Time to come be disturbed in their Just Rights.

He confessed that he had such a Patent in his Keeping, but wou'd not give it up till Satisfaction Shou'd be made him for Exchang'g. The Commissioners told him that he had never made any Demands as was known to them, and in case anything was his due he shou'd make his Demand and it would be considered, but if he persisted to keep the Patent without Setting forth his Reasons for so doing, The Monthly Meeting whereunto he belongs Shou'd be applyed to, and if he refuse to submitt his Demand and deliver up the Patent to them if required, a due Course of law wou'd be taken to recover the same out of his Hands.

To which he only replied that he wou'd Consider of it.

Ruben Pownal, of Bucks County, desires the Grant of a small Island or two in Delaware River, lieing over against his Tract of Land in Makefield Township, for Range to his Cattle. Those Islands lie before Charles Read's Land, who ought to have them.

John Henry Kieursen having formerly purchased 100 acres of Land, Part of the 10,000 acres granted by the Prop'r to Coll. Rhedegelt, obtained a Warrant for laying of it out and afterward a Patent; but the Grant to Rhedegelt being then disputed a Bond was taken of Kieursen to pay   if the Grant to Rhedegelt did not appear Good, and now the s'd Kieursen supposing the same to appear Satisfactory, desires his said Bond may be deliv'd up to him.

Signed a Patent to Ewan Owen for 12 whole Lotts and 1 Single Lott of Ground' in Sassafras and the third streets on Delaware side of the city of Philad'a, in Rig't of Sundry Originall Purchases before entered in these Minutes, viz't, in Right of Sarah Hersent, Purchaser of 500.

The following Patents and Warrants were signed at Sundry Times as they were made out to the Grantees:

John Stevens and William Bezer 250 each.

Richard Ap Thomas in full of his Demand.

William Cloud 500.

Ann Cawly, 500.
Joan Dixon, 500.
Thomas Paget, 500.
George Whitehead, 500.
Thomas Rowland, 1,000, in full.
John Streipers, 5,000, Ditto. Patent dated the 12, 2 mo., 1718.

Signed a Patent to Thomas Symmons for 222 acres in the Great Valley, or Welch Tract, in Chester County, being the Remainder of his Grandfather of the same Name, his Purchase of 500 acres, the Rest being laid out in Haverford Township. Upon the whole there is found by the Generall Resurvey 43 acres of Overplus, for which he now pays £6 12s, it being very mean Land, as D. Powell informs. The Patent is dated the 10th 4 Month, 1718.

Agreed with Edw'd George for a Parcell of vacant Land in Radnor Township, Joining on the Land of Daniel Harry, supposed to contain about 2 or 300 acres, at £15, Pensylvania Money, p. C't and 1 shill. Ster. quitrent, the Consideration money to be paid within 3 months after the Date of the Warrant, which is the 25th 1 mo., 1718. Signed R. H., I. N., J. L.

Signed a Warrant to Joshua Calvert for 100 acres of Land in Rocklands, agreed for £30 and 1 Shill. Sterling quitrent, the Consideration to be paid in three Months after the date of the Warrant, w'ch is the 25th 1 mo., 1718.

Sold Robert Jones, of Parkeoming, 50 acres of Land on the Branches of that Creek, for £14. Warrant dated the 25th 1 mo., 1718.

Agreed with James Gibbons, of the County of Chester, for 1,000 acres of Land back in the Said County for one hundred Pounds, to be paid in three Months after the date of the Warrant and one Shilling Sterling quitr't each Hundred a's. Warr't dated the 25th 1 mo., 1718.

Signed a Warrant to John McDonald for 100 acres back of Chester County, for £10, to be paid in 3 Months, and 1 Shilling Sterling quitrent.

Signed a Warrant to Owen Powell for 250 acres in the FFrench Creek, for £30, to be paid in 3 Months, and 1 shill. ster. quitr't p. C't. Both Warrants dated the 25th 1 mo., 1718.

Signed a Warrant to John Moor, of Chester County, for 200 acres back in the said County, for £20, the whole to be paid in three Months time, and one shilling Sterl. each Hund'd quitrent. Dated ye 25, 1 mo., 1718.

Agreed with Joshua Cheesman for 100 acres lieing between Jos. Milner's and Edward Pennington's Land in Makefield Township, for £35, to be paid down or Interest from the date of the Warr't, and 1 Shill. Sterling quitr't. The warrant is signed and dated ye 29, 1 mo., 1718. [Thrown up by Joshua Cheesman who could not pay for it, & since sold to Jno. Knowls.]

Signed a Warrant to Isaac Watson for 200 acres in Sussex, dat. 31st 1 month, 1718, to be held at 1d Sterling p. acre Rent.

Signed a Warrant of Resurvey to James Steel to resurvey the N. west End of a Tract of Land first laid out to Tho. Peterson for 500 acres on a Branch of Duck Creek, in the County of Kent; 200 acres whereof ye said Tho. Peterson by Deed dated ye   , 168 , granted to Anthony Tomkins, whose son and heir Joshua Tomkins, by a like Deed dated the   , granted the same 200 a's to the said J. Steel, who also desiring the Grant of some overplus Land lieing between the said 200 acres and the South west end of the s'd Tract, which is already cutt off and now possessed by one John Reynolds. The same is granted to him upon paying the same quitrent with the 200 acres from the first Survey of the whole Tract, dated the 7th 2 mo., 1718.

James Steel having purchased the Proportions of Lib. Land belonging to the Originall Purchases of 500 acres made by Jno. Martin, of Middletown, in Chester County, and of 250 acres of Edmund Lovet and of 1,000 acres of Henry Child (four acres of which last Purchase remains yet untaken up) he desires the same may be laid out to him in the said Liberties, being in the whole 16 acres, and having produced his Deeds for the same his Request is granted and a Warr't Signed, dated ye 10th 6 mo., 1718.

William Clayton having of late applyed for the Land allow'd him on acco't of his ffather's Claim to the Lands granted to the Swansons, on the River Schuylkill, agrees now to take five hundred acres back in Chester County in full of all Demands on the same, upon w'ch a Warr't is now granted and signed, dated the 14th 2 mo., 1714.

Signed a Warrant to James Steel for Resurveying to him one Moiety of a Tract of Land Situate on the South side of the South west Branch of Duck Creek, first laid out to one John Cuff, for 400 acres and also to add to the same Moiety about 76 acres, the Remainder of Tho. Sharp's Tract, both Parcells now being Vested in the said James. The Warrant dated the 14th 2 mo., 1718.

Agreed with William Brinklo, of the County of Kent, for a Parcell of Marsh on the North side of Mispelon Creek, called the ffishing Gutt Island, at £15 p. Hund'd a's and a Bush. of Wheat quitrent, the s'd Marsh being supposed to contain about the quantity, for w'ch a Warrant is signed, dated

Signed a Warrant to John Clarke for 200 acres in Kent, dat. 10, 2 mo., 1718.

Signed a Warr't to Charles Bright for 200 acres, Ditto, dat. 14, 4 mo., 1718.

Signed a Warr't to Josiah Bradley for 200 acres, Ditto, dat. 14, 4 mo., 1718.

Signed a Warrt't to Sam. Wilson for 200 acres, Ditto, dat. 14, 4 mo., 1718.

Signed a Warr't to Henry Lewis for 200 acres, Ditto dat. 14, 4 mo., 1718.

Signed a Warr t to Mathew Parker for 200 acres in Sussex, dat. 26, 6 mo., 1717.

These 6 Parcells are at 1d Sterling p. acre quitrent.

Agreed with John Cadwallader for 200 acres of Land in Ughland, in the County of Chester, at £12 10s p. C't and 1 Shilling Ster. quitr't, for which a Warrant was signed, dated the 22d 9ber, 1715, but was neglected to be entered till now.

There was an agreement made in the Year 1713 with Moses Musgrove for 300 acres of Vacant Land in Chester County, at £10 p. C't and one Shilling Sterling quitrent, and a Warrant signed thereupon, dated ye 23, 5th month, in ye same Year. There was also an agreement made with John Musgrove in the said Year 1713, for 600 acres on Octararo River, at £10 p. C't, and 1 Shilling Ster. quitrent, and a Warrant signed, dated the 28th of October, in the same Year.

William Smith, of Wrights Town, in the County of Bucks, purchased of John Rowland 100 acres of Land about 20 Years agoe, and hath ever since claimed that quantity, Joining on his other Land in the same T'p, and now craves a Resurvey thereof in Order for a Confirmation, which is granted on his paying £5 to the Proprietor's Use, to which he agrees. The Warr't for the same is signed, dated the 10th 3 month, 1718.

Pursuant to the agreement made by the Commissioners with Jonathan Dickinson for the Northern Part of Springetsbury Mann'r, entered in Pag. 102 of these Minutes, A Warr't is signed for the same, dated ye 20th 4 mo., 1718.

William Hudson desires to purchase a Piece of vacant Ground w'ch is inclosed with his Lots on the North side of the High street, beyond the ffith Street from Delaware, which is granted him for £15 and quitrent from the year 1684. It is about 27 foot ffront on the High street and the Length or Depth of the adjoining Lotts, the Warrant dated the 10th 2 mo., 1718.

Signed a Warr't to Theodorus Eby for 300 acres of Land at Conestogo for £10 p. C't and 1 Shiling Sterling quitrent, dated ye 10th 3 mo., 1718.

Signed a Warr't to John Ponder, of Sussex County, for a Parcell of vacant Land Joining to his Plantation near the Broad Creek, at 1d Sterling p. acre quitrent, dated ye 20th 4 month, 1718.

Signed a Warr't to Richard Williams for 200 in Sussex, dated the 15th 4 mo., 1718.

Signed a Warr't to William Steward for 200 in Sussex, dated the 15th 4 mo., 1718.

John Nutter, of the County of Sussex, sets forth by his ffriend R. Shankland that a Tract of Land now in his Possession, situate in Slaughter Neck, first laid out for 1,000 acres, is found to be Short of that quantity, and having p'd quitr'ts for the same, desires a Resurvey thereof, and to make up the same quant'ty of a's out of ye Vac't Land or Marsh adjoining, w'ch is granted and a Warr't signed, dated ye 10th 3 mo., 1718.

James Steel having purchased a Lott of Ground on the South side of Mulberry street, between the 4th and 5th streets from Delaware, desires that a Vacant Lott and a Strip or Piece of Ground adjoyning thereunto might be granted to him, which is done for £15, and two shillings Sterling quitrent, to be paid from the year 1684 and a Warrant signed, dat. 18th 3 mo., 1718.

Signed a Patent to Tob't Collett, Dan'l Quare and Henry Gouldney, the Lond'n Company, for 5,553 acres at Conestogo and 718 acres in Marlborow T'p, in Chester County, dated ye 25th 4 mo., 1718.

Signed a Patent to Joseph Jones for 2 Bank Lotts at the lower end of Philad'a, first laid out to his ffather, Griff. Jones; one of them is 20 foot, ye other 16 foot ffront, dated 25th 1 mo., 1718, requested page 106.

Signed a Patent to Richard Anderson for 100 acres in Chester County, granted the 21st 4 month, 1717, Dated 31, 3 mo., 1718.

Signed a Patent to Nicho's White for 250 acres in Chester County, granted as it is Entered in Page 97 of these Minutes, dated the 10th 4 mo., 1718.

Signed a Patent to Henry Hayes, of the County of Chester, for 1,484 acres of Land in the Township of Caln and Marlborow in the said County, 1,000 acres whereof is Richard Hand's Originall Purchase, the other 484 a's he now pays £66 13s 4d, dated the 5th 9ber, 1717.

Signed a Patent to James Sutton for 145 acres in Makefield Township, 100 acres is head Land in Right of himself and one Hannah FFalkner, and the 45 acres he holds at 1d Sterling p. acre, dat. 20, 4 mo., 1718.

Signed a Warrant to Samuel Manlove, of Kent County, for 150 acres in the fforrest of that County, at 1d Sterl. p. acre quitr't, dat. 10, 7ber, 1718.

Signed a Patent to Hans Graef for 300 acres at Strasburg, in Chester County, a late Grant, for £10 p. C't and 1 Shill. Ster., dat. 16, 4, 1718.

Signed a Patent to William Hudson for the Piece of Vacant Ground ment'd Page 112, dated 10th 4 month, 1718.

Signed a Patent to John Cadwallader for 200 acres in Ughland, mentioned Page 111, dated 20th 6, 1718.

Signed a Patent to Gilb't FFalconar for 17 acres of Marsh in 4 Parcels at the lower End of Newcastle Town, mentioned page , dated 25, 5 mo., 1718.

Signed a Patent to Tho. Janvier for 6 acres, in 2 p'cells, of the same Marsh, dated the 1st 6 mo., 1718.

Signed a Patent to John Land for 4 acres of the same Marsh, dated the 1st 6 month, 1718.

Signed a Patent to Jasper Yeats for 19 acres, in 5 parcells, of same Marsh and Cripple, dated ye 25th 5 month, 1718.

Signed a Patent to Christopher FFranciscus for 150 acres of Land in Strasburg, dated 30th 9ber, 1717.

Signed a Patent to Hans Snider for 200 acres in the same Towns'p, dated ye 20th 5th Month, 1718.

Signed a Patent to Martin Urner for 356 acres on the West side of Schuylkill, granted as is entered in page 108, dated ye 10th 5 mo., 1718.

Signed a Patent to Jonathan Dickinson for 1,084 acres of Land, the Northern Part of Springetsbury Mannor, Entered page 102, dated 10th 5 mo , 1718.

Signed a Patent to David Jones, of New Castle County, for 260 acres on the South side of Christina Creek, mentioned page , dated the 15th 5th month, 1718.

Signed a Patent to Abiah Taylor for 200 acres, mentioned p. 60, dated the 20th of the 5th month, 1718.

Signed a Patent to Ezekiel Harlan for 346 acres in Kennet, granted him for £51 18s ; 224 acres at Doe Run, and 200 acres on Pecquea, at £10 p. C't, all in Chester County, dated ye 20, 4 mo., 1718.

Signed a Patent to John Bull for 300 acres in Gilb. Mannor, mentioned in Page 92, dated 25th 1 mo., 1718.

Signed a Patent to Joseph Lyn for 25 foot of Bank and Water Lott at the North End of Philadelphia, beyond the Penny pott house, first laid out to Tho. Langston, who by Deed dat. ye 4th Xber, 1690, granted the same to Tho. Sisom, who by Deed dated ye 15, 9ber, 1707, granted to Daniel Howell, by Deed dated the 6th June, 1717, granted ye said Lott to

Joseph Lyn, who now paying the arrears of quitrent hath it confirmed to him. The Patent dated ye 20, 4 mo., 1718.

Signed a Patent to Abraham Heer for 600 acres of Land at Strasburg, a late Grant, for £10 p. C't and 1 Shilling Sterling quitr't, dated ye 30, 9ber, 1717.

Signed a Patent to Tho. Baldwin for 200 acres, Part of the Tract laid out to James Hendricks, his ffather-in-Law, at Conestogo, dated ye 20, 5 mo., 1718.

Signed Warrants to Tho. Shute for the Liberty Land appurtenant to the Original Purchases of Samuel FFox 1,300, Ann Olliff 500 acres, and R'd Jourdan 250, being in all 36 acres in the Northern Liberties, dated ye 10 and 15, 3d month, 1718.

Signed a Patent to Thomas Shute for 120 acres in the Northern Liberties of Philad'a appurtenant to Sundry Original Purchases, viz't:

Dated 10th 5 mo., 1718. In Right of

William Bezer,	4
Tho. Rowland,	16
Tho. Paget,	8
Joan Dixon,	8
Ann Cawley,	8
Sarah Hersent,	8
Jno. Martin,	8
Edm'd Lovet,	4
Hen. Child,	4
Rob. Stevens,	4
Tho. Dell,	8
Wm. Bryant,	4
Sam. FFox,	24
Ann Olliff,	8
Rich'd Jordain,	4
Total,	120

Signed a Warrant to Charity Cammell for 100 acres near Manatawney, at £15, and 1 Shilling Ster. quitrent, dated ye 10th 2d month, 1718.

Signed a Warrant to Henry Pare for 300 acres at Conestogo, at £10 p. C't and 1 Shilling sterling quitrent, dated ye 10, 3 mo., 1718.

Signed a Warrant of Resurvey to Anthony Morris on the Land he purchased of Sarah Hersent, mentioned page 95, dat. 1, 3 mo., 1718.

Signed a Warrant to Hans Shank for 200 acres at Conestogo, at £10 and 1 Shilling sterling p. C't, dated 20th 3 mo., 1718.

Signed a Warr't to William Middleton for 100 acres near Pecque, at £10 and one Shilling Sterling.

Signed a Warrant to Owen O'neal for   a's, both dated 30, 4, 1718.

Signed a Warr't for 100 acres to John Blake in ye same Place, 25, 5, 1718.

Signed a Warrant to David Jones for 100 a's, Ditto, or near, 25, 5, 1718.

All these at £10 p. C't and 1 shilling Sterling p. C't.

Signed a Warr't to James PettyJohn for 200 acres in Sussex, at one penny Sterling p. acre Rent, dated ye 10th 5 mo., 1718.

Signed a Warrant to William Morgan for 100 acres above Manatawney Settlements, at £ , and one shilling Ster. quitrent, dated ye 12, 5 mo., 1718.

Signed a Patent to Anthony Morris for the Land he purchased of Sarah Hersent, mentioned page 95, upon the Resurvey whereof there was found 58 acres over and above the 500, and Ten p. C't for Roads and Highways (the liberty Land being first deducted), for which 58 acres The said Anthony agrees to pay £11 12s dated ye 20, 5 month, 1718.

Signed a Warrant to William Darter for 200 in Sussex at 1d Sterling p. acre quitrent, dated the 10th of the 5th month, 1718.

James Steel requesting the Grant of 1,000 acres of Land back among the late Surveys, it is granted him for £10 p. C't and 1 Shill. Sterling quitr't, to be laid out in one or more Parcells, and a Warrant is signed, dated ye 1st 7ber, 1718.

Signed a Warrant to John Turner for 200 acres in Kent.

Signed a Warrant to Nich's Macklander for 200 acres, Sussex.

Signed a Warrant to Jenkin Price for 200 acres, Ditto.

Signed a Warrant to William Simpson for 200 acres, Kent.

Dated 1, 7, 1718. All these at 1d Sterl'g p. acre quitrent.

Signed a Warrant to Rob't Wilkens for 150 acres above Conestogo.

Signed a Warrant to Tho. Rutter, Jun'r, for 500 acres back of Manatawney, both dated 1st 7ber, 1718. Both these are granted at £10 p. C't and 1 Shill. Ster. quitrent.

Signed a Warrant of Resurvey to Abraham Bickley, ordered in Page 106, he having produced his right by Deeds from the Heirs of FFrampton and to himself, dated the 10th 7ber, 1718.

Signed a Warrant to Anderson Parker for 150 acres of Land in Sussex, at 1 Penny Sterl. quitrent, dated ye 15, 7ber, 1718.

Cornelius Toby having purchased the Plantation late Henry Lands', on the Great Road leading to the Lower Countys below New Castle, requests the Grant of some vac't Land between the s'd Planta'on and Peter Anderson's, w'ch is granted to him at the Rate of £25 p. C't and a Bush. of Wheat quitr t. The Vacancy is supposed to contain about 50 acres. Signed, the Warr't dated ye 29, 7ber, 1718.

Signed a Warrant to Christopher Topham for 200 acres, Sussex, 29, 7, 1718.

Signed a Warr't to FFrancis Pope for 200 acres, Ditto, 30, 7, 1718.

Signed a Warrant to Geo. Bishop for 200 acres, Ditto, 30, 7, 1718.

Signed a Warrant to Rob't Prettyman for 200 a's, Ditto, 30 7, 1718.

These 4 Warrants are granted at 1d Sterling quitr't p. acre.

Signed a Patent to John Moor for 315 acres of Land in Chester County, granted him by Warrant of the 18th 3 mo., 1713, vid., pag. 49, dated ye 30th 7ber, 1718.

Hans Graef desiring to purchase about 1,100 acres of Land near Strasburg Towns'p, it is granted him at £10 p. C't and 1 Shilling Ster. quitr't, the Warr't dated the 4th day of 8ber, 1718.

Hans Line, of the same Township, requests the Grant of Nine hundred acres at the same Price and quitrent. Ordered a Warrant for the same, which is signed, dated the same with the above.

Samuel Nut, of Chester County, requests the Grant of 800 acres of Land back in the said County, for which he is to pay £10 p. C't and one Shilling Sterling quitrent. A Warrant is thereupon signed, dated 2, 8, 1718.

Agreed with John Henry Kiursen for 300 acres of Land at Oley, at £14 p. C't and 1 shill. Ster. quitr't, for w'ch a Warr't is signed and dated the 4th of 8ber., 1718.

The Proprietor's Kinsman, William Blackfan, hath often applied for a p'cell of Land to Setle himself upon, and upon some encouragement given him by the Comm'rs to Search for some Conven't Spott that might be Suitable for him, he pitches upon a Piece in the Mannor of Highlands, w'ch the Comm'rs are willing he Shall have at £20 each hundred and the quitrent of one Shilling Sterling, allowing two years for Paym't, and in the mean Time to get it released without if the Prop'r or his Successors sees meet. A Warr't for the same is granted and signed, dated the 30, 7ber, 1718.

Agreed with George Boon, Jun'r, of Abington, for 400 acres of Land at Oley, at £14 p. C't and one Shilling Sterl'g quitrent, for which a Warrant is granted, Signed and dated the 4th 8ber, 1718.

Signed a Warrant to Thomas Morgan for 400 acres on a Branch of Conestogo Creek, at £10 p. C't and 1 Shill. Sterl. quitrent, dat. 1st 9ber, 1718.

Signed a Warrant to Gab. Davis for 450 a's on the same Terms and date.

Signed a Warrant to Hugh Hughs for 500 acres, Ditto, Ditto.

These three p'cells were agreed for to be laid out on a Branch of Conestogo Creek, as aforesaid.

Richard Lundy, of the County of Bucks, having made it app'r by the Evidence of Joseph Mather that his present Wife (then Jane Lyon) came Servant into this Province with Phineas Pemberton and James Harrison and Served her Time accordingly, but never yet had her head Land laid out, therefore now desires it might be granted, w'ch is complyed with and a Warr't Signed, dated ye 10, 9ber, 1718.

Agreed with George Henton for 200 acres, the Back Part of the Proprietor's Lotts at Manatawney, at £15 p. C't and one shilling Sterling quitrent, for w'ch a Warrant is granted and signed, dated ye 1st 9ber, 1718.

Agreed with John William, of Merion, for 400 acres, with Marg't John for 400 a's, Lewis David 100 acres, all on a Branch of the FFrench Creek, and with Thomas Black for 100 acres at Conestogo for £10 p. C't and one shilling Sterling quitrent, and Warrants are according signed and dated the 18th day of 9ber, 1718.

Agreed with John Bown for 150 acres in Goshen, near Is. Malin's, at £24, the whole, and one Shilling and Six pence Sterling quitrent, for which a Warr't is signed, dated ye 18th 9ber, 1718.

Agreed with Christopher Wilson for 200 acres of Land on the South Side of Brandywine Creek, between the Lands of Vall. Hollinsworth and reputed Henry FFurniss', at £22 10s, and a Bush. of Wheat quitrent for each Hundred acres, for which a Warrant is signed, dated ye 8, Xber, 1718.

Rowland Fitzgerald requests the Grant of a Parcell of Vac't Land Joyning to his Plantation at White clay Creek, in Newcastle County, w'ch is granted him at the Rate of £20 p. C't and a Bush. of Wheat quitrent, ye Vacancy supposed to be about 50 acres. A Warrant for the same is signed, dated the 10th of Xber, 1718.

Agreed with Joseph Tucker for 200 acres of Land at Oley, for £14 p. C't and one shilling Sterling quitr't. Warr't signed, dated 12, Xber, 1718.

Signed a Warrant to Thomas Griffiths for 1,000 acres to be laid out back among the new Surveys, in one or more Parcells, at £10 and one shilling Sterl. quitrent p. C't, dated 20th Xber, 1718.

Agreed with George Boon, of Gwyned, Sen'r, for his Son George, for 400 a's of Land at Oley, for £14 p. C't and one shill. Ster. quitr't, ye Warr't dated ye 20th Xber, 1718.

Signed a Warrant to Henry FFunk for 100 acres on the Branches of Parkeoming, at £20, and one Shilling Ster. quitr't, dated 20th, Xber, 1718.

John Cartlidg having Seated himself between Conestogo Creek and Susquehanna River, desires the Grant of 300 acres, and also that he may fence in 200 acres more for Conveniency of Pasturage. The 300 acres are granted him at £10 p. C't and one Shilling Sterling quitrent and the 200 acres he is permitted to fence in and hold for Pasturage the Term of 14 Years, in Consideration of the Good Services he has done among the New Settlers of those Parts, as well as to the Indians, whose Town is very near to his Dwelling. A Warrant for the said Grant is signed, dated ye 11, Xber, 1716.

Edmund Cartlidg having purchased a Pretended Right of Christ'r Schlegle to a Tract of Land and an Ordinary Grist Mill on a Branch of Conestogo, which the said Christopher by not Complying with the Terms on which it was granted to him the Grant became Intirely Void. But the said Edmund having since built and erected a Good Mill on the Same Land desires the Grant of 400 acres to be laid out to him including his Buildings and Improvements, which is agreed at £10 p C't and one shilling Ster. quitr't, the Warr't Signed and dated 1, 8ber, 1717.

William Hanby, of Nottingham Township, is permitted to settle on the Propr'rs Lot in that Township and is to have the Preference of purchasing 200 acres thereof in a Regular Piece when the same is to be sold.

By Order of the Commissioners. J. L.

The Right of Richard Whitpain, dece'd, to 7,000 acres of Land in this Province, as well as to Certain Lots in the City Philad'a, being entered at Large in the Minutes of the 30th 6 mo., 1703, resurveys on the said Lands were then requested and granted but not executed, and the whole Right being since sold by the Surviving Trustee, mentioned in the said Minutes, to Wm. Aubrey, of London, who afterwards Conveyed the same to Rees Thomas and Anthony Morris, Jun'r, the whole affair has been Obstructed by the Claim of John Whitpain as Heir at Law to the said Richard, but the said John some Time before his Decease came to an agreement with the said Rees Thomas and A. Morris for a Certain Dividends of the Lands and Lotts or of the money which shall be raised by Sale thereof, Whereupon certain Deeds were executed to each other and soon after the said J. Whitpain made his last Will and Testament in Writing, of which he appointed his Wife Ann Whitpain sole Executrix, thereby giving to her full Power to act and do all things requisite in that affair, and dyed, and therefore the said A. Whitpain, R. Thomas and A. Morris desires that a Certain tract of Land in West Town, in Chester County, Part of the above Purchase, may be resurveyed in Order for a Patent.

The Deeds of Lease and Release from the Survi'ng Trustee (John Blackhall) to Will. Aubrey are dated the 27th and 28th days of 9ber, 1712, Consideration of the whole Purchase £300 Sterling. The Deeds from Wm. Aubrey to R. Thomas and A. Morris are dated the 24th and 25th days of April, 1713, granting the whole to them (500 acres all along excepted) for £500 Sterling. John Whitpain, upon Certain articles made between himself and R. Thomas and A. Morris, dated the 29th of May, 1718, agrees to pay them as soon as Money can be raised by Sale of the Premisses, £222 4s 5d, money of Pensylv'a, and to release ye whole Grant to them (except so much as his ffather Zach'a Whitpain disposed of in his life Time) upon their securing to him, his Ex'ors, &c., one full third Part of the Money arrising upon the Sales thereof. The Release is executed by him and his Wife, dated ye 26 of May, 1718.

There being a small Parcell of Vacant Land lieing between the North Line of Whitwell's Chance, a Tract of Land in Duck Creek Neck, in Kent County, and Dawson's Branch, supposed to contain about 40 acres, Joyn'g on Land belonging to James Steel, who requests a Grant of the same, w'ch is made him on some Terms to be hereafter agreed on. Warrant signed, dated 14th 2 mo., 1714. This ought to be in Page 115.

The Proprietor, by Deeds of L. and Release, dated the 29th and 30th of April, 1683, granted to James Claypoole 1,000 acres of Land, being the same mentioned in Page 48; the Deeds whereof did not then appear. J. Claypoole, by like Deeds dated the 26th and 27th days of June, the same year, granted the said 1,000 acres to Wm. Smith, of Middlesex, Shipwright. Wm. Smith, by like Deeds dated the 15th and 16th of 9ber, 1714, granted the s'd 1,000 acres to William Chadwicks, of Virginia, who by Other like Deeds dated the 29th and 30th of Xber, 1718, granted the same 1,000 to Wm. Allen and Tho. Shute, who desires a Warrant for taking up thereof.

The Proprietor, by his Patent, dated the 12th of 9ber, 1683, Granted and Confirmed to Henry Reynolds 200 acres on Naaman's Creek, quitrent half a Crown Silver Money, for the whole, and a Year's Rent on every alienation.

The Proprietor, by L. and Release, dated the 5th and 6th of 7ber, 1681, granted to George Andrews, of Rowde, in the

County of Wilts, Serge Maker, 250 acres of Land, quitrent 1 shill. Sterling p. C't.

George Andrews, by like Deeds dated the 16th and 17th days of the same Month, granted to John Hickman, of Bromham, in the said County, Woolcomber, 125 acres, Part of the said 250 acres, who by like Deeds dated the 30th and 31st of January, 1682, granted the said 125 acres to H. Reynolds, joyning on his other Land at Naaman's Creek.

The Proprietor, by L. and Release, dated the 12th and 13th July, 1682, Granted to George Strode 500 acres, quitrent 1 Shill. Ster. p. C't, who by like Deeds dated ye 21st and 22d of March, 1686-7, granted 200 acres (untaken up), Part thereof, unto H. Reynolds. Thomas Pierson, by a Return under his Hand, dated ye 10th 12 mo., 1685-6, Certifies that he has resurveyed a Tract of Land for Henry Reynolds on Naaman's Creek, containing 519 acres. H. Reynolds affirms the said 519 acres are made up of the above Parcells, but the Deeds of George Strode are dated a year after the Resurvey made by Tho. Pierson and mentions Land untaken up.

Henry Reynolds petitioned the Commissioners for a Resurvey on 250 a's of Land laid out to George Andrews and John Hickman in Chester County, in Order that he may lay a Warrant of 200 acres on the Overplus supposed to be in that Tract, which was granted by James Claypoole and Robert Turner and ordered to be done by Tho. Holme, dated the 6th 9 mo., 1685.

In Pursuance of the agreement made between Rees Thomas and Anthony Morris, Jun'r, and John Whitpain, entered on the Other side of this Leaf, they, the said Rees and Anthony, requests a Resurvey on a Tract of Land first laid out in Chester County to John Moor, Sabian Cole and Company for 2,000 acres, but Part thereof being irregularly run within the Lines of the Welch Tract, which is Since Confirmed to the Persons to whom it was surveyed, A Warant is granted to the said Rees and Anthony for the Remainder, dated the 30th of the 3d month, 1718.

The following Patents were Signed at Sundry Times as they were drawn and laid before the Commissioners and were entered in the List of Patents as they were delivered to the Recorder to be Sealed and Recorded:

Signed a Patent to Charles Brockden for 500 acres in Hill Town, in Bucks County, in Right of John and Thomas Rowland and Priscilla Shepard, antidated at C. Brockden's Request in Regard of a Sale made of the Land by him to another Person before the Patent was made, dated ye 9th of ye 2 mo., 1712.

MINUTE BOOK "H."	647

Signed a Patent to Andrew Sandel, the Swede Minister, for 12 acres of ffast Land and 7 acres of Cripple, lieing between his Share of the Land late Peter Dalbo's, whose Daught'r he married, and the River Schuylkill, for which he pays £11 16s 6d, dated ye , 1718.

Signed a Patent to David Powel for 200 acres near Manatawney, Part of the Proprietor's Grant to him at his Departure, dated ye 20th 5th mo., 1718.

Signed a Patent to James Hamer for 300 acres in the Mannor of Gilberts, above Parkeocoming, granted to his ffather, for £25 p. C't (see Page 63), dated 20th 5th month, 1717.

Signed a Patent to Geo. Claypoole for 45 acres in the Mannor of Springetsbury, 37½ in Right of Andrew Doz, ye Proprietor's Vigneron, and 7½ acres granted to himself, for £18 15s, dated ye 10th 5 mo., 1718.

Signed a Patent to John Sholl for 150 acres, a further Part of the thousand acres granted by the Proprietor at his last Departure to David Powell, dated the 20th 5th Month, 1718.

Signed a Patent to Rees Thomas and Anthony Morris, Junior, for 1,763 acres in Chester County, first laid out to John Moor, Sabian Cole and Company, Resurveyed by a Warrant dated the 30th 3d mo. The Patent bears date the 10th of the 5th month, 1718.

Signed a Pat't to Cha's Read and Ann his Wife, for 776 acres of Land in Makefield, Bucks County, the Original Purchase of Tho's Bond, Grandfather of ye s'd Ann, dat. 20, 5 mo., 1718.

Signed a Patent to Henry Pare for 300 acres laid out to him at New Strasburgh by a Warrant dated the 10th 3 mo., 1718, entered 114th Page of these Minutes, sold to him at £10 p. C't, Pat. dated ye 20th 4th month, 1718.

Signed a Patent to James Steel for a Lott in the 3d Street from ye River Delaware, at a Corner of Mulberry Street, in Right of William Bryant's Purchase of 250 acres, entered Page 90, the Patent dated ye 30th 10 mo., 1717.

Signed a Patent to Andrew Hamilton for 1,396 acres of Land in three Parcells, Situate on both Sides of the Line which divides the Counties of Philad'a and Bucks, being his Share of the Tract laid out to Dennis Rockford, entered in Page 105 and 106, dated the 25th 1 mo., 1718

Signed a Patent to George FFitzwater for 1,857 acres, being his Share of the above Tract laid out to Dennis Rockford, entered with the above, dated the same (viz't, 25, 1 mo., 1718).

Signed a Patent to Thomas Shute for 1,130 acres, his share of the said Tract laid out to Dennis Rockford, and entered together with the above, dated 25th 1 mo., 1718.

Signed a Patent to James Steel for   acres in two Parcels, being his Share of the above mentioned Tract laid out to Dennis Rockford, entered with the same and bears the same date with the above Patents (viz.), 25th 1 mo., 1718.

Upon a Resurvey and Division of the Whole Tract laid out to Dennis Rockford there is found to be within the same 258 acres of Overplus besides the quantity it was laid out at first, for which with Ten acres p. C't allowed is divided and apportioned to each Person's Share, who pays after the Rate of £20 p. C't for the said Overplus, as may be seen in each Person's account in the Proprietor's Books.

Gabriel Wilkinson having purchased the City Lotts belonging to John Buckley and Oliver Cope, which are laid out on the North side of Mulberry street, between the 5th and 6th Streets from Delaware, requested a Patent for the same some time ago, which was granted and signed, dated the 10th of the 1st month, 1715-6, but not delivered untill now, Vide Minutes of the

Signed a Patent to Jeremiah Hopton for the 250 acres of Land on Potquessin Creek, mentioned Page 94.

Signed a Patent to Richard Sherly for 54 acres of Marsh near the Murther Creek, in Kent County, mentioned Page 108, dated ye 10th 4 mo., 1718.

Signed a Patent to Hans Shank for 200 acres at Conestogo, mentioned Page 114, dated the 15th 5th month, 1718.

Signed a Patent to Antho. Morris for 600 acres of Land on this Side of Skepeck, 500 acres in Right of Sarah Hersent, 10 p. C't allowed upon the Resurvey 8 a's of Lib. Land deducted, there remains 58 acres Overplus, for w'ch A. Morris pays £11 12s. The Pat. dated ye 20th 5 mo., 1718.

The following Warrants were signed at Sundry Times as they were laid before the Commissioners:

To William Hews for 400 acres near Conestogo, at £10 p. C't, dated ye   day of

To John Morris for 200 acres,
To William Arey for 200 acres,
To Robert Davis for 200 acres,
} dated ye 13th of the 1st Month, 1717-8.

To William Dyre for 200 acres,
To Timothy Donovan for 200 acres,
To John Smith for 200 acres,
To Abr'm Parsly for 200 acres,
} All in Sussex County, at one Penny Sterling p. acre, dated ye 11th of the 1st Month, 1717-8.

Warrants signed to:
Abr'm Brooks for 120 acres.
Nich's Nickson for 200 acres.
John Townsend for 200 acres.
John Townsend, Jun'r, for 200 acres.

MINUTE BOOK "H."

FFrancis Alexander for 200 acres.
Benj. Shurmer for 200 acres.
All in Kent County, at one Penny Sterl'g p. acre, dated ye 6th of the 12th Month, 1717-8.

Signed two Warrants to Edward Roberts for the Land and Lott mentioned in Page 107, dated 4th 1st month, 1717-8.

Signed two Warrants to James Robins for the Land and Lott entered in Page 107, dated the 4th 1st month, 1717-8.

Richard Carter, of Conestogo, having requested the Grant of 200 acres of Land on or near to that Creek, the same is sold to him for £20, the whole, and one Shilling Sterling quitrent for each hundred acres. The Warrant signed and dated the first day of the first Month, 1717-8.

Signed a Warrant to James Steel for the Lib. Land belonging to the Original Purchase of Tho. Dell (being 500 acres), to the Purchase of Rob't Stevens (being 250 acres) and to the Purchase of Wm. Bryant (also 250 a's) which if laid out on this side of Schuylkill is 16 acres in the whole, if on the other side of that River then 20 acres, dated the 10th 2d mo., 1718.

William Tregan, of the County of Chester, requesting the Grant of 200 acres of Land back in that County, it is agreed that he shall have the same for £20, money of this Province, and one Shilling Sterling quitr't on each hundred acres. The Warrant Signed and dated the 25th 1 mo., 1718.

Peter Wisehart having formerly agreed for 300 acres of Land at the Great Swamp, in Bucks County, for £40, Money of this Province, for the whole, and 1 Shill. Sterl. for each hundred acres. A Warr't was made out and signed dated ye 6th of the 2d month, 1718.

At the Instance and Request of William Heddings, of the County of Chester, 200 acres of Land are granted to him back in the said County for £20, money of this Province, the whole and the yearly quitrent of one Shillng Sterling for each hundred acres. The Warrant being signed, is dated the 25th 1 mo., 1718.

John Cowgil having erected a Tan yard on a Branch of Black Bird's Creek, in Newcastle County, desires the Grant of 100 acres of Land on Rent, for Convenience and Security of the same for his Trade, which is Consented to at one Penny Sterling p. acre for ever, and a Warrant Signed, dated 1st 3d month, 1718.

Upon an agreement made with William Cloud, Jun'r, of Concord, for 300 acres back in Chester County, for £30, Money of this Province, for the whole, and one Shilling Sterling quitr't for each Hund'd acres. A Warrant is signed, dated the 16th 1st month, 1718.

Agreed with Mich'l Danagar, late of Germany, but now of this Province, for 300 acres of Land on or near Pecque Creek, in Chester County, for £30, Money of this Province, the whole, and the yearly quitrent of one shilling Sterling for each 100 acres. A Warr't for ye same is signed, dated ye 4th of 8ber, 171 .

The Prop'r, by Deeds of Lease and Release, dated the 2d and 3d days of March, 1681, granted to John Brown, of Kingsley, in the County of Chester, in Great Britain, Tanner, 250 acres of Land in this Province. John Brown, Son and Heir of the aforesaid John Brown, by like Deeds Dated the 1st and 2d days of the 12th month, 1710, granted the said 250 acres, with their app'rs, unto Joseph Helsby, now of this Province, who requested of the former Comm'rs a Warrant for taking up the same, which was granted, dated the 18th 8ber, 1712, Vide Page 140.

Signed a Warrant to Tho. Lucas for 200 acres in Kent.
    Ditto   to George Green for 200 acres in Kent.
    Ditto   to Art. Jansen and Kirk for 200 in Sussex.
All at one Penny Ster. p. acre. Dated the 10th of the 3d Month, 1718.

Signed a Warrant of Resurvey to Rees Thomas and Antho. Morris, Jun'r, on a Tract of Land in Chester County, requested Page 118, dated ye 30th 3 mo., 1718.

Signed a Warr't to Thomas Shute for the Lib. Land belonging to 500 a's, the Original Purchase of Ann Olliff and to 250 a's, the Purchase of Rich'd Jordan. In ye first he bought of Samuel Robins, att'ry of James Robins, entered in Pag. 122, the latter of Jeremiah Hopton, dat. 10, 3d mo., 1718.

Granted to Joseph Steman 100 acres of Land near Conestogo, for £10, Money of Pensylv'a, and one Shill. Ster. quitr't, dated ye 10th of the 3d Month, 1718.

Job Bunting, Son-in-Law to John Cowgill, having requested the Grant of 150 acres of Land on Rent near the Branches of Duck Creek, in New Castle County, a Warrant is made out to him for the same at one Penny Sterling p. acre, dat. 1, 3 mo., 1718.

Granted a Warrant to Christian Stone for 100 acres of Land at or near Conestogo, for £10, Money of Pensylvania, and one Shilling Sterling quitrent, dated the 10th of the 3d month, 1718.

Captain John Brinklo, of the County of Kent, having purchased of Coll. FFrench the Plantation and Tract of Land in the fforest of the said County, called the Cave, requests the Grant of 200 acres adjoyning thereunto at the same quitrent of the said Tract (viz.), one Bushell of Good Winter Wheat

MINUTE BOOK "H." 651

for each 100 acres from the Time of the Proprietary's first arrival in this Province, which is granted and a Warrant Signed dated the 30th 7ber, 1718.

Agreed with Thomas Edwards, of Chester County, for 500 a's back in the said County, for £50, money of the Province, for the whole, and one Shilling Ster. for each 100 acres quit rent. The Warrant signed, dated ye 18th 9ber, 1718.

Signed a Warrant to Simon Hirons, of the County of Kent, for 200 acres of Land in the fforest of the said County, at the Yearly quitrent of one Penny Sterl. for every acre, dated the 8th of Xber, 1718.

Agreed with Daniel Macfarsen, of Kennet Township, in Chester County, for 125 acres of Vac't Land Joyning on his Plantation, for which he is to pay £20, Money of this Province, and fifteen Pence Sterling quitr't. The Warrant is signed, dated the 10th of Xber, 1718.

Agreed with Tho. Rutter, of the County of Philad'a, for 500 acres of Land back of his Tract at Manatawney, being Ordinary Land and only fitt to Supply his fforage with Wood for Cole. He is to pay £50, Money of this Province, for the whole, and 1 Shill. Ster. quitr't. The Warr't Signed, dat. 31, Xber, 1718.

Signed a Warrant to William Allen and Thomas Shute for one thousand acres of Land, mentioned in Pag. 118, dated ye 31st of December, 1718.

Agreed with Edward Thomas for 250 acres of Land back in the County of Chester, for £25, money of this Province, for the whole, and one Shilling Ster. quitr't for each Hund'd a's, for w'ch a Warr't is signed, dated ye 10th of Xber, 1718.

James Letort having Seated himself on this Side of the River Susquehannah, between Conestogo and Paxtang, for Convenience of his Trade with the Indians, desires the Grant of 500 acres of Land to be laid out in a Regular Tract fronting on the said River, for which he agrees to pay £50 for the whole, Money of this Province, and one Shill. Ster. quitrent for each Hundred acres, dated 25th 1 month, 1719.

Signed a Warrant to Thomas Miller, (Millwright) for 200 acres of Land on a Branch of Manatawney Creek, for which he is to pay £27, Money of this Province, for the whole, and one Shilling Sterling quitrent for each Hundred acres. Dated 20th 3d month, 1719.

Signed a Warrant to Israel Pemberton for 4 acres of Lib. Land, the Proportion belonging to the Original Purchase of John Brown, being 250 acres, entered Pag. 123, dated 25th 1st Month, 1719.

Agreed with Hans George John, late of Germany, but now of this Province, for 100 acres of Land near the Branches of

Skepeck, for £16, Money of the said Province, and one shill. Ster. quitr't, dated ye 1st of the 3d month, 1719.

Agreed with Edward Ream for 200 acres of Land at or near New Strasburg, for £20, money of this Province, the Whole, and the quitrent of one shill. Ster. for each Hundred acres. The Warr't Signed, dated ye 1, 3, 1719.

Peter Bizalion having purchased a small Improvem't made by Nath'l Christopher on Susquehannah River, above Conestogo, desires to purchase 700 acres of Land, to include the said Improvem't, the whole being for Martha his Wife, Daughter of John Coomb, late of Philadelphia. It is agreed that 700 acres be laid out to the said Martha, the Wife of the said Peter Bizalion, in the Place afores'd, in a regular Tract fronting on the said River and to Include the said Improvem't and to extend so far back into the Woods as the Place will bear, for which the said Peter agrees to pay £70 for the whole and one Shill. Ster. quitr't for each 100 acres. The Warrant signed, dated ye 25th 1st Month, 1719.

Thomas Coats, Brickmaker, having long applied for a Piece of Ground for a Brick Yard, adjoining on the Old Brick Yard formerly held by John Mifflin, it is agreed that he Shall have three acres laid out in a regular Piece on the North West side of the s'd Old Brick yard, which he is to hold from the Term of fourteen Years from the first day of the 1st Month, 1718-9 under the yearly Rent of five Pounds, money of this Province, and at the Expiration of the said Term to Yield up the said three acres of Land with all the Earth or Clay Pits filled up and levelled, to all which he agrees and thereupon a Warr't is signed, dated the said first day of the 1 mo., 1718-9.

Agreed with David Davis, of Goshen, for 300 acres of Land near the Barrens of that Place and adjoyning to the Land of Ellis David, for which he is to pay five and forty Pounds, money of this Province, for the whole, and one Shilling Sterling for each Hundred acres. The Warrant Signed, dat. 12, 3d month, 1719.

Marcus Overholts having been seated by Tho. Fairman in his life time, on the West Side of Schuylkill, on 300 acres of Land w'ch he pretended to sell to him, but he dying before he cou'd make him a Title, he, the said Marcus, desires a Grant for the same Land, for which he agrees to pay Eight and forty Pounds, Money of this Province, for the whole, and one Shilling Sterling for each Hundred acres, whereupon a Warrant is signed, dated the 20th 3d month, 1719.

Agreed with John Humsted, of Skepeck, for 300 acres of Land on or near the Branches of Parkeacoming, for which he is to pay thirteen Pounds ten Shillings, money of this Province, and one Shilling Ster. quitr't for each Hundred acres. The Warr't is signed, dated ye 2d 3 mo., 1719.

Agreed with Henry Pannebaker, of Skepeck, for 500 acres of Land to be taken up on or near the Branches of Parkeacoming Creek, for w'ch he is to pay thirteen Pounds ten Shillings, money of this Province, and one Shilling sterl. quitrent for each Hundred acres, and a Warr't is signed, dated the 1st of the 3d month, 1719.

Agreed with Richard Gregory, of Oley, for 200 acres of Land in that Place, for which he is to pay Eight and Twenty Pounds for the whole, and one Shilling Ster. for each Hundred acres. The Warr't for the same is signed, dated the 1st of the 3d month, 1719.

Agreed with Derrick Jansen, of Germantown, for 800 acres of Land back of the Settlements and Surveys lately made, for which he is to pay after the Rate of thirteen Pounds Ten Shillings, money of this Province, and one Shilling Sterling quitrent for every Hundred acres. The Warr't for the Same is Signed, dated the 5th 3d mo., 1719.

Ralph Sutton, late of the County of Bucks, hath requested the Grant of 200 acres of Land at or near Oley, for which he is to pay eight and Twenty Pounds, money of Pensylvania, for the whole, and one Shilling Ster. for each Hundred acres. The Warrant is signed, dated the 26th of the 3d mo., 1719.

The Proprietary, by Deeds of Lease and Release, dated the 11th and 12th days of October, 1681 (as p. attested Copies under Tho. Grey's Hand, before Chief Justice Prat), granted to William Bacon, of the Middle Temple, Gent., 5,000 acres of Land within this Province, To hold to him, his Heirs and ass., under the yearly quitrent of one English Shilling for every Hundred acres. The said William Bacon, by like Deeds, dated the 19th and 20th days of FFeb., 1718, for £110 Sterling, granted and conveyed the said 5,000 of Land, City Lot, &c., to Humphrey Murry and John Budd, both of Philad'a, To hold to them, their Heirs and assigns forever, who request Warrants for laying out of the whole.

John Milner, Son and Heir of Joseph Milner, late of Makefield, in Bucks County, requests a Confirmation of his ffather's and Uncle Daniel Milner's Land in that Township, but there being a Sister of his yet living, and a Son of another Sister (that is deceased), Who Claims some Share of the said Land, the Divisions must be made amongst themselves before anything of that Kind can be done.

The Purchases are as follows:

Joseph and Daniel Milner's Purchase in England is . . .	250
Purchased in this Province, ...	300
Purchased of Edw'd Luff's Right, ...	296
Allowance on the Resurvey, ...	85
Overplus found in the Tract, ...	177
	1,108

The Commissioners, W. Markham and John Goodson, by Patent dated the 21st 11 mo., 1688, confirmed to Lancellot Lloyd two acres of Land near the Town of Philad'a, begining at a Post Standing on the side of the Run, thence East by a Line of Trees 528 foot, then S. 18, W. by the 2d street 180 foot, thence West by a Line of Trees 478 foot, then N. 18 deg'rs, East by the ffront Street 171 foot to the begining, granted by a Warrant, &c., laid out by the Survey'r Gen'll Order to L. Loyd, Renter, for erecting a Tan yard and following that trade thereon, Yielding and paying, &c., at Philad'a Eight English Silver Shillings yearly.

The Commrs., W. M., R. T. and J. G., by patent dated ye 6th Ap'l, 1693, granted to Griffith Owen 7 acres of Land begining at Post of Lance Lloyd's Land, thence E. by the same 43 p's, thence N. 18 Degrees, West 35½ p's, then N. 75, W. by Vine Street 37 p's, then N. 8 deg., E. 23 p's to ye begining, quit-rent [one Shilling, Silver money of Pensylvania, for each Hundred acres] for so are the Words in the Patent, which must be a Mistake. 'Tis much more likely one Shilling for each acre, w'ch it wou'd be were the word Hundred left out. Lancelot Loyd, by Indenture dated 29th 2 mo., 1692, for £5 granted all the said 2 acres to Hector Dicks, of West New Jersey, Tanner, who by a like Deed, dated ye 6th Jan'y 1695-6, for £8 13s granted the said 2 acres to Pat. Robinson, who by another like Deed, dated the 4th of June, 1696, for £9 Granted the same 2 acres to Robert Hawkes.

The Same Comm'rs, W. M., R. T. and J. G., by Patent dated the 25th 4th month, 1694, Granted to Gr. Owen, in Right of John Eckly, a Certain Lott of Ground containing in Breadth 50 ffoot and 320 foot in length, bounded Northward with Vac't Lotts, Eastw'd w'th ye 2d street from Schuylkill, Southw'd with Tho. Lloyd's Lott and Westw'd with the ffront street; the quitr't not legiable.

Tho. Lloyd and Samuel Carpenter, Ex'ors of the last Will and Testam't of Sarah Eckly, by Deed Poll dated 1st 4 mo., 1694, for £100 granted the said Lot with the Buildings thereon to Gr. Owen.

Griffith Owen, by Sundry Deeds dated in the 4 mo., 1694,

granted the 7 acres of Land, the Lott of John Eckly and a Lott of Phillip James's, unto the s'd Rob't Hawkes, who granted the same to Ruth Haddock together with the 2 acres first mentioned, who afterwards granted the whole to George Roach, who again granted to William Trent.

The Prop'r, by L. and Release, dated the 21st and 22 days of Mar., 1681, granted 1,000 acres of Land in this Province to Jno. Alsop, who by Deed dated ye 19th July, 1684, granted and conveyed the same to Tho. Tunnecliff, whose Kinsman and Heir at Law, James Tunnecliff, now possesses   acres in Makefield Township and desires a Confirmation on the same.

Peter Chamberlain having often applyed for a City Lott in Right of Joseph Jones, of Southampton, his Original Purchase of 500 a's of Land in this Province, w'ch has hitherto been refused him because J. Jones's Deeds from the Prop'r are dated about two Months after the Time the first Purchases expired, but John Swift affirming that J. Jones's Purchase was made and the Money paid at the Same Time with his, who was accounted one of the first Purchasers, The Comm'rs agree that P. Chamberlain Shall have Liberty to take up a Lott in the Back streets of Nine and forty ffoot and a half in Front and the Depth and Length the same with the adjoyning Lotts, which is to be in full Satisfaction of any further Demand on the said Purchase.

At a Meeting of the Commissioners the 4th of the 6 mo., 1719.

Present, Richard Hill, Isaac Norris, James Logan.

Andrew Hamilton having purchased of Richard Woodworth the back Part of his Lott in Chestnutt street, adjoyning to ye s'd Andrew's Garden, petitions the Comm'rs for the Grant of a Small Piece of Vac't Ground at the lower end of the said back Part, being about   foot broad and 30 foot Deep, or from the South end of the said Lott to the North ends of Walnutt Street Lotts, which is granted to the s'd Andrew in Consideration of Twenty Shillings, money of this Province, to be by him paid down and Sixpence Sterling quitrent to be paid for ever hereafter for the same.

The said Andrew further requests that the Parcell of low Ground granted to him, page 102, may be enlarged to 30 acres, and that he may therew'th enclose the Old ffield which lies between the same and the ffence of Abrah. Bickley's ffield or Orchard, and that the Commissioners wou'd grant him to hold the same for the Term of one and thirty Years under the

Same Rent in Proportion to the quantity which is mentioned in the said Minutes or otherwise, as they shall think expedient.

The Commissioners, taking into Consideration the Great Charge and Expence w'ch the s'd Andrew has been at and yet must be, in Grubing, clearing and ffencing the whole, agrees that the said Andrew Hamilton Shall hold the s'd low ground and Old ffield requested by him, which together makes Six and forty acres or thereabout for the said Term of one and thirty years from the Date of the said Minute, at and under the yearly Rent of one Shilling, present Currency, for every acre, and also to pay down Ten Pounds like Money to the Use of the Trustees. To all w'ch the said Andrew agrees, and thereupon a Warr't is ordered to be made out for surveying the same.

Signed Deeds of Lease and Release to Jon'n Dickinson for 1,084 acres of Land, being the Northern Part of the Mannor of Springetsbury, for which he had a Patent executed to him, dated ye 10th of the 5th month, 1718. Entered in Page 113.

John Hendrickson, of the County of N. Castle, produces an agreem't made with Secretary Logan in the year 1701, for one hundred acres of Land near Redclay Creek, in the said County, Part of a Tract formerly sayd to be laid out to one Robert Robertson, on Rent, and by him and his Heirs afterwards thrown up to the Propr'r, so that the s'd 100 acres were granted to ye s'd J. Hendrickson, 100 acres more of the same to his Brother-in-Law, Anderson Cock, and other 100 acres to James Williams, since dece'd, all on New Rent.

John Hendricks upon Making of his agreem't with Sec'y Logan gave his Obligation for the arrearage of quitr't, which he afterwards paid to G. Dakeyne, with Interest, in Cash, who only Charges himself with 30 Bushells of Wheat instead of the Cash, but never p'd that neither. Jno. Hendricks hath since purchased the Right to the 100 acres granted to James Williams, of his Widow (that was), now the wife of William Grimson, and has paid the arrearage of Rent and taken up J. Williams' Obligation, which was given for the same, but he complains that one James Waters, has made some sort of Purchase from the Heirs of Robertson and thereby threaten him with Trouble, wherefore he desires a Confirmation on the two Parcells he holds.

The Prop'r, by L. and Rel., dated the 22d and 23d days of Mar., 1685, for £22, granted to Tho. Parkhurst, Citizen and Stationer, of London, 500 a's of Land in this Province, quitr't one Shilling for the said 500 acres, but there is a Manifest Rasure which takes out ye Words [every Hundred acres of] and the alteration is made with Ink of a Different Colour from that the Deeds were Writ with.

The said Tho. Parkhurst, by like Deeds of L. and Rel., dated ye 1st and 2d days of August, 1709, for £5 granted the said 500 acres to Sam'l Bury, of St. Edmundsbury, in Suffolk, Clerk, To hold to him, &c., who by like Deeds, dated the 9th and 10th days of 8ber, 1716, for £10 granted the said 500 acres to John Head, of Philad'a, Joyner, and Rebeka his Wife, who again by other Deeds of L. and Release, dated ye 21 and 22d of July, 1719, granted and conveyed the same 500 acres to Derrick Jansen, of German Town, who now desires a Warr't to take up the same.

John Grigg, of Newcastle County, desires to purchase two Parcells of Land very uneven and Rockey joyning on the Tract where he dwells, contain'g 100 acres each Parcell. It was formerly laid out to Richard Grigg, who afterw'ds threw it up, having never seated nor improved it.

Agreed that John Grigg Shall have the two Parcells of Land for thirty Pounds and one Bushell of Wheat quitr't on each 100 acres.

Isaac Self, whose Right to 500 acres of Land is entered Page 75, hath now Sent over a Power of att'ry to Anthony Morris, dated ye 29th of August, 1717, together with John Gye, whose ffather, Edward Gye, was Joint Purchaser with the Grandfather of Is. Self, in the s'd 500 acres, to take up 250 acres, the other Part being already laid out in Chester County. A. Morrest requests a Warrant for the same, also for the Lott and Liberty Land belonging to the said Purchase.

The Prop'r, by L. and Release, dated the 9th and 10th days of 7ber, 1681, granted to John Coales, of Calcut, in Somersettshire, 1,000 acres of Land in this Province, quitr't one Shill'g Ster. p. Hund'd acres. John Coales soon after came into this Country and Settled at George's Creek, in New Castle Cou., but he dying before the Land was taken up, the same was claimed by one William Woodland, who was his Sister's Son and nearest of Kin to him, who administered on his Estate in N. Castle County and had the Original Deeds in his keeping during his life, but never took up the Land since William Woodland's decease. His Son and Heir, William Wooodland, who dwells near FFarlo Creek, in Maryland, by Deeds of Lease and Release, dated the 22d and 23d days of 8ber, 1719, granted the said 1,000 acres, with the appurtenances, to Samuel Powel, of Philad'a, Carpenter, who desires Warrants to take up the same, as also the Lotts and Lib. Land.

Charles Springer desires the Grant of 200 acres of Vac't Land near Samuel Barker's and Redclay Creek, on such Terms as the Comm'rs Shall think fitt, it being for Settling of his them Children, he having severall Sons and but little Land for

Matthias Peterson and Andrew Justice formerly applied to the Commissioners about the Overplus in Matthias's Tract (See pag. 3) and now the said Andrew again applies for a grant of the same, he having a Licence from Matthias in his life Time for his Settling thereon, as appears by his coming before the Commiss'rs with him for that Purpose. Andrew Justice proposes and is Willing to pay the arrearage of quitr't at a Bushell of Wheat p. C't from the Time of the first Survey till now.

Agreed with James Coal and Rich'd Bennett for 200 acres of Land to each of them adjoyning to or near Wm. Penn's Mannor, at £10 p. C't, one-half of the Money to be paid down and the other within Six Months after.

Richard Parker, Jun'r, of Darby, produces a Deed Poll, dat. 22d of Jan'ry, 1714, under the Hand and Seal of John Harrison, of Rocky Hill, in East Jersey, reciting one other Deed from Sam'l Thorn, of Long Island, dated the 7th day of May, 1712, who therein (is sayd to have) granted and Conveyed unto the said John Harrison at Moossehickamickon, being Part of the Tract Sold by William Biles, att'ry to Tho. Hudson, unto the said Sam'l Thorn and others on Long Island, contain'g 250 acres each (but they add the Overplus and make thereby each Lott 275 acres).

The said John Harrison, for £100, Jersey money, granted one of the above Lotts, No. 3, to Tho. Hunlock, of Burlington, who by another Deed dated the 17th 3 mo., 1714, for £77, Money of Pensylvania, conveyed the last mentioned Lott to Richard Parker and John Parker, and the said John Parker since dying without Issue, the said Lott, as well by Survivorship as by him, the s'd Richard being his Ex'or, is wholly vested in the said Richard, but the Same being within the Tract laid out to Dennis Rockford, or else taken by Tho. Stevenson in the same Right of Tho. Hudson, whereby the said Richard is deprived of holding the said Lott and therefore requests a 'Warrant to take up the like quantity elsewhere. Granted.

Peter Bizalion having purchased 500 acres of Land first granted by the Prop'r to Ralph Withers, entered in the fformer Minutes of the 4 mo., 1703-4. John Withers, only Surviving Brother of Ralph (who dyed without Heirs), by Deeds of L. and Release, dated the 21st and 22d days of May, 171 , for £20 Ster. granted the whole to John Bezer, of Chester County, who by other Deeds dated ye 2d and 3d days of Novemb'r, conveyed the whole to John Warder, but it is in Trust for Peter Bizalion. The Land is laid out near Brandywine Creek, in Caln Township; the City Lott is taken on the N. Side of Mulb. street, between 6 and 7 Streets from Delaware.

The Proprietor, by L. and Release, dated the 13th and 14th days of the 2d mo., 1682 (as p. Recital), granted to James Delworth 1,000 acres of Land in this Province, of which there was laid out to himself in Bucks County 500 acres. James Delworth, by Indenture dated the 5th of the 4 mo., 1686, for £25, conveyed to John Horner, of West Jersey, 480 acres, which with the Liberty Land compleats the whole Purchase. John Horner, by Deed Poll, Dated the 20th 12 mo., 1693, in Consideration of 300 acres of Land in West Jersey, exchanged and Conveyed the s'd 480 acres to Phinehas Pemberton, since dece'd. Israel Pemberton, Son and Heir of the s'd Phinehas, desires a Warr't for taking up the same.

Signed a Warrant to Andrew Hamilton for the Piece of Vacant Ground at the lower end of Richard Woodworth's Lott, entered Page 130, dated 5, 6 mo., 1719.

Signed one other Warr't to Andrew Hamilton for the Parcell of Land or low Ground with the Old ffield, entered with the above Piece of Ground in Page 130, dated the 5th of the 6th month, 1719.

Signed also a Warr't of Resurvey on 200 acres of Land at Little Creek, in Kent County, requested by Andrew Hamilton in Page 76, who since purchased the same of the Ex'or of John Richardson, deceased.

Signed a Warrant to Derrick Jansen for 50 acres, the Original Purchase of Thomas Parkhurst, entered Page 131, dated the 28th 6 mo., 1719.

Signed three Warrants to Humphrey Murry and John Budd.
The first for   2,000 acres, dated the 5th 3 month.
The Second for 0,080 acres of Lib. Land and Lotts; the same date.
The Third for   2,920 acres, the Remainder of William Bacon's Purchase.

5,000

Signed a Warrant to Peter Chamberlain for a City Lott, the Grant whereof is entered in Page 129, dated 26th 6 mo., 1719.

Signed two Warrants to Samuel Powel, the one for 984 acres of Land, the Purchase of John Coales, the other for 16 acres, the Proportion of Lib. Land and for the City Lotts. The Right of this Purchase is entered in Page 132, the Warrant dated the 5th of 9ber., 1719.

There being a Piece of Vacant Ground left on the West side of the third street from Delaware, at the North end of Griff.

Jones's High Street Lott, adjoyning on Some Lotts of Richard Hill, who now requests a Grant of the Same. It is agreed that he shall have the said Piece of Vacant Ground, being about 31 foot ffront on the third Street, and from the same extending to the burying Ground, paying down to Trustees Use Ten Pounds, money of this Province, and one Shill. Ster. quitr't forever.

Also a Piece of Vacant Ground lieing between Geo. Harman's Lott and a Lott of the S'd R. Hill, in the High street, of about Six foot in ffront and Depth of the adjoyning Lotts, is granted to him in Considera'on of five po'ds, to be p'd to ye Use of ye above sayd. A Warr't for both is signed, dat. 16th 7ber, 1719.

At a Meeting of the Commissioners the 32d of Xber, 1719. Present, Richard Hill, Isaac Norris, James Logan.

The Commissioners having been informed that the assembly of the Provinces of New York and the Jerseys had passed Severall acts for runing Division Lines between those Provinces and for finding out and fixing of the most Northerly Branch of Delaware River, the doing of which Concerns this Province very much, because that Branch is the Eastern bounds thereof; Whereupon the Comm'rs thought it expedient to order James Steel and Jacob Taylor to repair to Mackhackamack (a Dutch Town on the East Side of Delaware River), where certain Commissioners and Surv'rs from the above mentioned Provinces were appointed to meet, for which Purpose a Commission was provided, dated the 19th of the fourth month (last under the Seal of the Province and signed by the Comm'rs) and delivered to ye s'd James and Jacob, who thereupon Sett out on their Journey (in order to be present at the fixing of the most Northern Branch of Delaware) on the 20th day of the same Month, and returned again the 2d of the 6th Month following, an account of whose Journey and of the affair they went about is as followeth:

To the Commissioners of Property:

Whereas, by your Commission to us, directed under the Seal of the Province, bearing date the 19th of the 4th M'th, 1719, we were appointed to sett out on a Journey to Mackhackamack in Order to meet with Certain Persons who were appointed by the Goverm'ts of New York and New Jerseys, to repair to the said Place to find out and fix the Lat. of 41 degr. 40 m. on the Most Northerly Branch of Delaware River, and from thence to run a Division Line between those Goverm'ts over to Hudson's River.

In Pursuance whereof we sett out from Philad'a on the 20th day of the same Month and on the 24th day thereof we reached Mackhackamack, being Joined in our way by Jos. Kirkbride, John Reading, Tho. Wetherel and John Chapman. On the 27th day the Gentlemen from N. York (Viz't), Dr. Johnston, Coll. Isaac Hicks, Coll. John Hamilton, Captain R. Walter, Alane Jarret and James Alexander arrived there also (George Wilcox and John Harrison having been there some Days before). We mett with them at their Lodging, where the Business depending was debated. Their Commissions were Read, as was ours afterward, and enquiry having been made of Sev'll Indians, but more Particularly of Solomon Davis and Jacob Keykendal (two Indian Traders), about the Branches of the River Delaware that were between the s'd River, there called the ffishkill and Susquehannah. They all agreed in their Information that there were only some Small Brooks and Branches between the said Rivers, which they easily passed over as they Travelled, But no Branch any ways to Compare with the ffishkill, as they Call it. The said Solomon Davis and Jacob having, as well as those Indians, often Travelled between those two Rivers from one to the other, and therefore perfectly knew what Branches were to be found proceeding out of Delaware. Yet notwithstanding these Informations, which all the Commissioners and Surveyors seemed to believe to put the Matter beyond Dispute, they appointed Major John Harrison to travel over from the ffishkill to Susquehannah, who took with him Jacob Keykendal and an Indian for Guides, and soon after went on his Journey, which he undertook on foot.

In the mean while two or three Observations were taken by the Quadrant at Mackhackamack, by w'ch it was found we were about 17 Miles to the Southward of the Latitude, wherefore the Surveyors were ordered to proceed further Northward, which they did at some Distance from the River Delaware and Chained along as they went, and on the 7th day of the 5th Month we arrived at an Indian Town, Cashetang, which is Situate on both sides of the River about 37 miles to the Northwest of Mackhackamack. Here the quadrant was erected and daily plyed, but the Weather proving so very Wett and ffoggy that two Weeks were Spent before the Latitude was fixed, which was done about the 22d day, after which the Survey'rs returned to Mackhackamack ; the Rest of the Company returned a few days before for want of Provisions. Here we found Jno. Harrison returned from Susquehannah, who soon applyed himself to make a Draught of his Journey, and when the whole Company were returned from Cashetang and met together at Mackhackamack they were all of them so fully satisfied with the Report and Draught which he made of his Journey (on his Oath as we remember) and particularly of the Branches of Delaware, that not one Objection from any of them was further made against the ffishkill being the most Northerly Branch of Delaware River. Whereupon the same was so taken and deemed, and Indentures Tripartite were drawn, Certifying the same thing with a Draught of that Part of Delaware River where the Lat. of 41 deg. and 40 m. fell and was Settled, affixed to each Indenture, which were executed by all the Commissioners and Surveyors, (viz't), Coll. Isaac Hicks, Capt'n Rob't Walter and Alane Jarret for New York; Dr. Johnston, George Wilcox and James Alexander for East Jersey; Joseph Kirkbride and John Read'ng for West Jersey, on the 27th day of the said 5th Month and Witnessed by us, and then delivered to the Custody of each Party to be put on Record in the respective Provinces. These Instruments were executed as afores'd at the House of Thomas Swartwood, at the upper end of Mackhackamack, after which John Chapman, with some Chainmen, were imployed to run a random Line from Mackhackamack to Hudson's River, while the York and Jersey Gentlemen returned Home, and we on the same day (viz't), the 28th of ye 5th mo., left y't Place and arrived at Philad'a the 2d of the 6 month.

While we were upon this Journey we crossed the River Delaware at severall Places and Should have searched further into Pensylvania had not the Extremity of the Weather prevented us, so that we cannot give so Satisfactory account thereof as Cou'd be desired, yet as often as we had any View or Prospect from the Mountains over which we passed into Pensylvania we noted in what Manner it appeared to our Sight, which was continually Mountaineous, Rocky, and Variety of Hills, and but little low and Level Ground was seen by us on either side of the River after we passed Pahaquelan Mountains.

Truly Copied from the account delivered to the Commissioners of Property at their Meeting p.

         JAMES STEEL,
         JACOB TAYLOR.

Ordered that a Warrant be made out for Surveying to James Steel and Jacob Taylor four Hundred acres of Vacant Land, which is to be the Gratuity for their Journey to Mackhackamack and Cashetang

Isaac Norris having purchased the Rights of Cha. Marshall and Jonas Smith, which were laid out for 1,000 acres each in Philad'a County, and upon a Resurvey of the same finds a Defficiency in that Part laid out to Charles Marshall, which he desires may be made good to him out of the nearest Vacancy.

David Powel, Surveyor, having agreed for 3,000 acres of Va't Land to be take up back of the late Surveys on which he has Settled divers ffamilies of Palatines, to whom he has sold the whole 3,000 acres. The agreement was made with D. Powel in Sept., 1717, for three hundred Pounds, the Whole to be paid in three sev'll Paym'ts within one year, one hundred Pounds whereof he was to pay down, upon Which the Warrant was to be signed, but he not minding his Part of the agreem't proceeded to dispose of the Land and having learned the Date of the Warr't (tho' not Signed) made and executed Deeds to those Palatines and rece'd of them their ready money and Obliga'ons for what they Cou'd not pay down. The ready money (being at least one-half of what he sold the Land for) he converted to his own Use, and having nothing left to pay for the Land but those Palatines' Obligations, he earnestly requests that the Comm'rs wou'd be pleased to take those Obligations for Pay of those 3,000 acres of Land, who taking into their Consideration the Circumstances of those People to whom he has sold the said Land who are Settled thereon, and that they are an Honest, Industrious People, Do order J. Steel to take those Obligations into his Custody and give Notice to those Palatines that they do forthwith come in and alter the Property of those Obligations from D. Powel to the Trustees, upon their doing of w'ch the Warr't Granted to D. Powel is ordered to be Sealed and delivered to the Survey'r Gen'll, who is thereupon to deliver to each Person to whom the said D. Powel has Sold off the s'd Land, Returns or Certificates to the quantity of 3,000 acres and no more, in Order whereunto the said David Powel is to deliver to James Steel Exact and Distinct Draughts of each Man's quantity of Land, together with his Name, that he may be the Better able to settle this Crooked affair.

Thomas Shute Sets forth that he, together w'th Wm. Allen, having some Time agoe purchased 100 acres of Land, the remaining Part of James Claypool's last Purchase of 5,000 acres, entered Page 48, and having now found a parcell of Land on this Side Parkeawming, left unsurveyed by T. FFairman when he laid out the sev'll Purchases made by J. Shattick and E. Lane, desires that the said 1,000 acres may be Surveyed on the same Consideration, whereof he agrees to pay to the use of the Trustees fflfty Pounds.

Signed a Warr't to James Steel and Jacob Taylor for 400 acres of Land, ordered to them Page 137. James Steel having reported to the Commissioners that pursuant to their Order he has taken into his Hands the sev'll Palatines' Bonds from

David Powel, which amount to near the sum of money he stands indebted for the 3,000 acres of Land, and has sent Word to those People to come in and give other Obligations to the Trustees instead of those given to D. Powel, which are to be delivered cancelled to them upon their so doing, whereupon the Comm'rs have signed the Warr't to D. Powel for the 3,000 acres, and have ordered the same to be Sealed, which is according done. The Warrant bears date at the Time of the agreement, viz, 10, 7ber, 1717.

At a Meeting of the Comm'rs the 21st 11 mo., 1719-20.
Present, Richard Hill, Isaac Norris, James Logan.

There being an agreem't made some Years agoe with Jonathan Dickinson and some other Inhabitants of the City of Philad'a for the Improvement of some Parcells or quantitys of the Swamp or Cripple which lies below the said City, between the River Delaware, Wickaco and Moyamensing, in Pursuance whereof the whole Tract of Swamp, Marsh and Cripple has been carefully Surveyed and a Draught of the same laid before the Board, on which is described sev'll Parcells thereof formerly granted to the Prop'r unto Andrew Bankson, Benj. Bankson, John Stilly, Andrew Wheeler and Wm. Wells, as also two Parcells of meadow, one whereof is 32 acres, the other 31 acres, which together make 63 acres, being granted by the Prop'r in the Moyamensing Patent and are now claimed by John Stilly, And'w Wheeler, William Carter and the Heirs of And w Bankson, dece'd, which s'd 2 p'cells of Meadow being described in such ffigures by the Patent as do not agree with the Place where the Present Owners claim, it is proposed that if those Owners think fitt the quantity of 63 acres of Meadow shall be laid out to them in such regular Parcells as may accomodate them, provided they will release their Claim to the Location as it Stands in ye Patent.

The Comm'rs, Wm. Markham and John Goodson, confirmed to Joseph Walker a Piece of Ground in Phiad'a, begining at a Corner Post Standing on the North side of a swamp, which parts this Lott from Tho. Minshall's and John Tibby's Lotts, then North 18 deg. E. 40 foot, then South 72 d. [I suppose East] by Jane Blanchard's and Mary Southworth's Lotts 80 foot to a Corner Post Standing by the aforement'd Swamp, from thence up the Sever'll Courses to the Place of Begining, granted by a Warr't from ourselves, dated ye 13, 7ber, 1689, and laid out by the Surveyor Gen'lls Order the same day and y'r to Joseph Walker, Renter, quitrent five English Silver Shillings or Value in Com. Curr. Pat. dated the 3d 8ber, 1689.

The Prop'r, by Short Deeds of L and Release, dated the 10th and 11th days of the 1st month, 1694 (for £40 Ster.), granted to Joseph Peckover and Partners ['tis so expressed] 1,200 acres of Land in Pensil'a, clear of Indian Incumb's, between the Rivers Delaware and Susquehannah, quitr't one Shill. St'r. p. C't, to commence Seven Years after taking up. The said Jos. Peckover and Kathrin his wife, Jno. Hichcock and Mary his Wife (the s'd Mary and Kathrin being Sisters, who together with one Sarah Long, another Sister, advanced some Part of the Purchase Money and were to have some Shares of the said Land and therefore were in the Orig'll Deeds Called Partners), by Lease and Release, dated the 12th and 13th days of the first Month, 1715-6, for £30 Ster. granted and released the said 1,200 acres to Thomas Story, his Heirs and assigns forever, who by his att'ry, Wm. FFishborn, desires Warrants to take up the same.

The Prop'r, by Deeds of Le. and Release, dated the 22d and 23d days of the first Month, 1681, granted to John Brown, of Kingsly, in the County of Chester, 250 acres of Land in this Province. John Brown, Son and Heir of the s'd Jno. Brown, by like Deeds dated the 1st and 2d days of the Second Month, 1710, Conveyed the said 250 acres to Joseph Helsby, now of this Province, who had the same (or 246 acres) taken up at Ughland, and by his Deed Poll, dated the 3d of the 2d mo'th, 1717, granted the Lott and Lib. Land to Israel Pemberton, who desires a Warr't for taking up the Lib. Land, vid., pag. 123.

John Coats, Brickmaker, upon his earnest Request and ye Recommendation of sev'll Bricklayers, has obtained a grant for three a's of Ground for a Bricky'd, lieing by the Road w'ch leads to Wissahickon and joyning on James Logan's Pasture, for fourteen years, to commence from the first day of the first Month next, at Six Pounds p. ann., which he agrees to pay Yearly and to level all the Clay pitts which he shall digg for making of Bricks every Year, and to Surrender up the same with the Kills and Buildings at the Expiration of the said Term. A Warr't is ordered for laying out ye same.

At a Meeting of the Commissioners the 27th 11 mo., 1719-20. Present, Richard Hill, Isaac Norris, James Logan.

John Swanson, Christopher Swanson and Peter Swanson having procured a Cavet to be put into the Surv'r Gen'lls Office against any further Proceeding in runing out and Surveying the Swamp and Cripple near Hay or Hollanders Creek till their Right to the same Should be audited and contested [so are the words of the Cavet]. The Commiss'rs ordered that the s'd Swansons Shou'd have Notice of the s'd Meeting, w'ch accordingly was given to them in Writing some Days before the same.

The three Swansons, Wm. Tidmarsh, who is an under Purchaser, appeared and brought John Moor as Council to Speak for them, who asserted that the Swansons had an early Grant for the said Cripple and Meadow, included with 800 acres of Land granted to their ancestors in the year 1664, and was Survey'd anno 1675, but did not produce it. He further alledged that the Crown had excepted all former Grants and Possessions out of the Royal charter granted to the Prop'r, to which he affirmed with a great Deal of assurance, but Sec'y Logan producing that Charter und'r the Great Seal of England, Challenged John Moor to find out or produce any such Exception in that Grant, which when John Moor perceived was not in it, he then frankly confessed that he had never read it, tho' before he said that he had. The Swedes were told that there cou'd be no Grant of 1664, but what must be then taken under the Dutch Goverment, which afterw'ds became a Conquest and then a Surrender to England. Whereupon all the Inhabitants upon Delaware renewed their Grants from N. York, then Subject to the Crown of England, or upon our Prop'rs arrivall immediately addressed themselves to him for the same Purpose, who well knowing the little advantage the Country wou'd be to him with't Inhab'ts gave all necessary Encouragem't as well to those he found settled here as those that arrived during his Stay, and renewed their Grants as Application was made to him. They were further told that if they wou'd readily accept of the quantity of Mead'w and Cripple granted by the Prop r to the 3 Widows of the Swansons (some of their mother's) and cause the same to be regularly Surveyed and returned into the Surveyor Gen'lls Office and pay off the quitr'ts due on the same, they might yet have it, otherwise it wou'd be granted to some other Persons (two of those Widows being Dead to whom the Propr'rs Warrant was granted). To this they made no Direct answer but went Muttering out of the House.

About a Week before this Meeting John Swanson and Peter Swanson went with Jacob Taylor and James Steel into the Cripple below Wickaco and not only consented but ffreely assisted in runing and cutting a Line through the Same from the Bridge over Hollanders Creek to the River Delaw., upon a Course East 10 Degrees North.

Thomas Stevenson having in his life Time purchased of Jno. Talmon, of FFlushing, on Long Island, 1,500 acres of Land by Deed Poll, dated ye 11th of June, 1719, Part of 5,000 acres

MINUTE BOOK "H." 667

Sold by Will. Biles, attorney of Tho. Hudson, to Will'm Lawrence, Jno. Talmon, Sam'l Thorn, Joseph Thorn and Benj. FField, all of the same Island. The said Benj. FField, by Deed Poll dated ye 10th of the 4th mo., 1719, for £89, York Money, conveyed to the said T. Stevenson 1,000 acres, being his, the said Benjamin's, share of the said 5,000.

The said Joseph Thorne, by Deed Poll dated the 25th of July, 1718, for £30, Curr't money of America, Conveyed unto the said T. Stevenson 500 acres, a further Part of the said 5,000 acres.

The aboves'd Wm. Lawrence, by Deed Poll dated ye 11th June, 1719, for £57 10s, money of N. York, conveyed to the said T. Stevenson 500 acres, a further part of the said 5,000 acres.

The said Joseph Thorne, by another Deed Poll dated the 11th of June, 1719, for £60, money of N. York, conveyed unto the said T. Stevenson other 500 acres, which with what is above by him conveyed, makes his full Share of the said 5,000 acres granted to them by the s'd William Biles, as aforesaid.

By the above said Deeds it appears that T. Stevenson in his life Time was intituled to 4,000 acres of Land in the afore mentioned Right, and some Time after dyed, leaving his Wife and Joseph Kirkbride his Executors.

The whole 5,000 acres were formerly laid out in Bucks County, on the Line which divides that County and Philad'a County, but the Greater Part thereof being within the Lines of an Earlier Survey made to Dennis Rockford, entered at large in Pag. 105, the said Ex'ors desire Warr'ts to lay out so much as yet remains clear of the Claimants under D. Rockford and the Remainder of the said 4,000 acres where it can be found in the nearest Vacancy.

Samuel Allen, late of this Province, dece'd, Purchaser of 2,000 acres of Land in the said Province, had in his life Time Taken up in severall p'cells 1,840 acres, so that at the Time of his Death there remained untaken up 160 acres, which by his last Will and Testament in Writing, dated the 14th 10 mo., 1699, he bequeathed to his Grandson, Samuel Sisom, who about 10 y'rs since went to Sea in a small Sloop to Antequa, which was taken out of the Harbor in the Night and never was heard of Since.

John Sisom, only Brother to the said Sam'l, by Deeds Dated ye 21 and 22 days of the 1st mo., 1719-20, for £15 Conveyed ye s'd 160 acres to Tho. Shute, who now desires a Warrant to take up the same.

The Commissioners, S. Carpenter, Wm. Markham and John Goodson, by Pat. dated 25th 4 m., 1690, confirmed to Hugh

Marsh, Renter, a Lott of Ground on the N. side of Mulberry Street, in Length 306 foot and in Breadth 49 f't and a half, bounded N'd w'th Back Lotts, Eastw'd with Rob't Marsh, his Lott, S. w'd w'th Mulb. Street and West'd with James Potter's Lott, Rent five English Silver Shillings. The same Comm'rs, by another Patent bearing the same date with the foregoing, confirmed to Sarah and Hugh Marsh, in Right of Rob't Marsh's Purchase, one other Lott of Ground of the same dimensions of the foregoing, situate on the East side thereof and joyning thereto, quitr't one English Silver Shill. ye [one] Shill. being on a Rasure, yet seems to be right because Rob't Marsh was Purchaser of 500 acres.

Hugh Marsh, by assignments on the said Patent, dated the 1st of the 6 mo., 1692, did bargain, Sell and assign both the said Lotts unto James Poulters, who by Deed dated the last Day of the 12th mo'th, 1695-6, granted the above said two Lotts, together with one other Lott laid out to himself of the same Demensions with the fformer and Joyning on the West side of them, to Obadiah Holt, who by Deed Poll dated the 4th day of March, 1698-9, granted the said three Lots of Ground to Mary Shepard, who Still possesses them. The last mentioned Lott laid out to James Poulter is on Rent (viz't), five Shillings Ster. p. ann.

At a Meeting of the Commiss'rs the 5th 2d mo., 1720.
Present, Richard Hill, Isaac Norris, James Logan.

The Business of the Swamp and Cripple below the Town being laid out before the Board, Jonathan Dickinson being Present, desires that a Warr't may be granted to him for 200 acres of the s'd Swamp and Cripple already agreed to by the Commission'rs, as also for about 14 acres of Mead'w to the Southw'd of Wm. Carter's, which is laid out on the Southside of Hay Creek, to Extend from Wm. Carter's lower Corner on the Road laid out to the Point opposite to Glocester, about 50 Perches, and from thence to return at Right angles to John Bankson's Cripple, To which the Comm'rs agree and accordingly orders a Warr't to be made out for the whole Request, with Condition that the said Jonathan Shall pay down Ten shillings, money of this Province, for every acre and one Shilling Sterling quitr't for each hundred acres, and also that the said Jonathan, his Heirs or assigns Shall well and Sufficiently drain and bank the same so as to make it fit for Pasture or Mowing within Seven Years after the Date of the Warrant.

Our Present Gov'r, Wm. Keith, Esq'r, requests the Grant of about Ten acres of the s'd Swamp and Cripple lieing to the Southward of the Line w'ch divides the same from Wickaco Mead'w and Cripple and to ye Eastw'd of ye Road, laid out to the Road opposite to Glocester.

Andrew Hamilton desires the Grant of y't Part of ye Swamp and Cripple which lies to the Southward of the Piece requested by the Govern'r to the Northward of Little Hollanders Creek, and between the said Road laid out to the Point opposite to Glocester and the River Delaware, Supposed to contain about 55 acres.

Clement Plumsted, George FFitzwater and James Steel desires the Grant of a Parcell of the said Swamp and Cripple lieing between the abovementioned Road and the Bounds of a Parcel of Swamp, Mead'w and Cripple, by them purchased of Abel Noble, and to Joyn to the Northw'd on the Line of the Wickaco Meadow and Cripple, and to the Southward with the South Line of the said Abel Noble, Extended Easterly, containing about   acres.

There being a Warrant already ordered drawn to Evan Owen for about 47 acres of the said Swamp and Cripple lieing between Hay Creek and little Hollanders Creek, and between the s'd Road and the River Delaware, the same is signed.

There being also a Warrant ordered and drawn to Israel Pemberton for about forty acres of the said Swamp or Cripple lieing on the South side of Hay Creek and extending along the East Side of the above s'd Road 133 Perches to a small Gut or Branch which falls into Delaware, and from thence by the Side of the s'd River to Hay Creek, w'ch is likewise signed.

Thomas Chalkley produces Deeds of Lease and Release, dated the 2d and 3d days of 7ber, 1719, executed in London before 3 masters of Ships belonging to this City, being a Grant of 500 acres of Land in Warminster T'p, Surveyed to John Jones, of London, Glover, who was Original Purchaser thereof, who dying without Issue, his only Sister, Elizabeth Hilton, hath Conveyed the same to Tho. Chalkley by the aforesaid Deeds.

In the Year 1713 the said Eliz'th Hilton sent over a Power of attorney to Gilbert FFalconar to dispose of the said Land and also a Certificate of the Depositions of two Persons, taken before the L'd Mayor and Aldermen of London, under the City Seal, who deposed that the said Eliz. Hilton is the only reputed Sister and Heir of John Jones, late Citizen and Glover, of London, Dece'd. The said Power of attorney and Instrum't are now in the Office, as also a Return of the Survey of the Said Land under Tho. FFairman's hand, sent hither w'th the other Writings.

Thomas Chalkley desires Warrants to resurvey the Land entered on the other Side of this Leaf and to take up the Lott and Liberty Land appurtenant to the same.

At a Meeting of the Commissioners the 29th of the 2d Month, 1720.
Present, Richard Hill, Isaac Norris, James Logan.

The **Warrant** ordered the last meeting to Jonathan Dickinson for 200 acres of Swamp and Cripple and fourteen acres of Meadow is now signed, the Consideration for the same, as also for those quantities granted to Evan Owen and Israel Pemberton, is Ten Shillings, money of this Province, for every acre and one Shilling Sterling quitr't for 100 a's, or in Proportion thereunto for each quantity granted.

Jonathan Hayes in his life Time purchased 125 acres of Land of Rich'd Orm, who purchased the same of Humphrey Bettally, to whom the Same was conveyed by Tho. Wyn and John ap John. This 125 is Sayd to have been formerly laid out in one of the Welch Townships, but afterw'ds taken and held by some other Purchaser, so that it is not to be found that ever John Hayes or any Person under him has possessed it, Wherefore,

Richard Maris and Eliz'th his Wife, Evan Lewis and Mary his Wife (the s'd Elizabeth and Mary being Daughters and Heirs of John Hayes), by Deeds of L. and Release, dated the 8th and 9th days of the 2d mo'th last, granted and Conveyed the said 125 acres to Lewis Lewis, of Chester County, who desires a Warrant to lay out the Same back in the said County with the addition of 175 acres to be laid out with it, for which he proposes to pay £17 10s, money of this Province, and usual quitrent.

John Curtis having purchased the Plantation and Tract of Land formerly belonging to Peter Bizalion, Situate on the Murther Kill or Creek, desires to purchase the Marsh and Swamp which lies between the s'd Tract and the Creek, the upper Part whereof is very much broken and Mirey, it contains in the whole about one Hundred acres.

Coll. John FFrench having discovered a Parcel of Vac't Land containing about one Hundred acres, requests a Grant of the same at Such a Price as the Comm'rs Shall think fit to put upon it.

At a Meeting of the Commissioners the 9th of the 4th Mo'th, 1720.
Present, Richard Hill, Isaac Norris, James Logan.

MINUTE BOOK "H." 671

William Carter, John Stilly and Benjamin Bankson appeared according to Notice given them, and after some Time spent by their insisting on the 100 acres of Meadow mentioned in their Old Patent, to have been granted by order from Upland Court, concluded and agreed to release the two Parcels or quantities of Meadow as they are described in the said Patent and to accept and take in lieu thereof the like quantity, which is 63 acres in the whole, in such Parcells as each of them have a Right unto (Andrew Wheeler having in his life Time appointed where his Share Shou'd be), Whereupon the Draught of the whole Cripple, Swamp and Meadow being laid before the Board, the s'd William Carter, John Stilly and Benjamin Bankson did Chuse and appoint on the said Draught where each of their Shares Shou'd be laid, which is accordingly marked out on the Draught, and is ordered to be actually surveyed to them and fixed under certain Bounds in pursuance of a Warrant now ordered for that Purpose.

George Grigg having purchased a sort of Right to 50 acres of Land, Part of a Tract first laid out to George Hogg on New Rent, desires a new Grant of the Same and agrees to pay twelve Pounds, one-half down and half a Bushell of Wheat quitrent for the Future.

28th 5th Month 1720.

This Day John Estaugh, as agent to the London Company, in the Presence of Isaac Taylor and James Steel, came to the Office and ffreely resigned the Survey made on that Parcell of Land on the lower side of Naaman's Creek, between the King's Road and the River Delaware, for the like quantity to be laid out to the said Company in Rockland Mannor, upon w'ch an Order is now delivered to Isaac Taylor for surveying the same in the following Words:

FFriend Isaac Taylor: John Estaugh, as agent to the London Company, having resigned the Survey made on that Parcell of Land below Naaman's Creek, on Delaware River, for the like quantity to be laid out to the said Company Elsewhere. I therefore desire thee to survey to the s'd Company within the Mannor of Rocklands so much Land as is resigned, and make Returns of the same.

Thy real ffr'd,

JAMES STEEL.

James McVaugh produces a Deed under the Hand and Seal of Thomas Rogers, of Bensalem, in Bucks County, for 100 acres of Serv'ts Land, 50 acres in his own Claim and 50 acres his Wife (formerly Hannah Maugridge), also a Certificate under Benj. Chambers's Hand, who says that Tho. Rogers served his Time to the Society of Traders, but the s'd Hannah his Wife being dead long before the Date of the above Deed, he cannot pretend to have any Land on her acco't.

The Prop'r, by L. and Rel., dated ye 10th and 11th days of 8ber, 1681, granted to Tho. Cobb, of London, Shoemaker, 250 a's of Land in this Province, to hold to him, his Heirs and ass's forever, quitr't one shill. Ster. p. C't. Tho. Cobb, by like Deeds dated ye 13th and 14th days of FFeb., 1684, granted the s'd 250 a's to Chr'r Davison, Citizen and ffishmonger, of London (afterw'ds of this Province, Cagemaker), who obtained a Warr't for laying out ye same, dated ye 9th 4 mo., 1685, and some Years after by Deed dated ye 21st of March, 1709, for £50 conveyed the s'd 250 a's to Tho. Tress, und'r Certain Lines and Bounds said to be in Bucks County.

Thomas Tress, Nephew to the afores'd Tho. Tress, by Vertue of a Certain Instrument to him, made by the s'd Thomas, the Elder, by Indentures of L. and Release, dated the 18th and 19th days of August, 1719, for £20 conveyed the same Land to Jeremiah Langhorn under the same Lines and Bounds above mentioned, but the said Jeremiah upon Enquiry and Search reports that he cannot find any such Tract of Land as those Bounds describes, wherefore he desires a Warrant to lay it out elsewhere.

---

4 mo., 9th, 1720.

Emanuel Grubb and John Grubb, with Jacob Savoy, John Savoy and Peter Bilderbeck, came to the Office together and produced a Return of 600 acres of Land back from the River in Rockland Mannor, in Ephraim Harman's Hand, dated ye 19th 7ber, 1682, Said to be in Pursuance of a Warr't from N. Castle Court. The 600 acres are laid out to J. Grubb, Isaac Savoy and David Hendricks in Equal Shares. Is. Savoy and D. Hendricks dying, Jno. Grub, ffather to the s'd Emanuell and John, in his life Time claimed the whole by Survivorship, But the Proprietor when first here, having granted to Savoy and Hendricks two Tracts of Land on the other side of the River in Exchange for what they held in Rocklands, which was always understood to be in full Satisfaction for their whole Claim, and during their Lives they never made any further Claim. Wherefore Jacob Savoy, John Savoy and P. Bilderbeck were told that if they shou'd make Sale or Convey the 400 a's, P't of the 600, which they claim to any Person whatsoever the Lands which they enjoy in lieu thereof on the other Side the River wou'd be called in question, and that the

Prop'rs Will insist upon holding the Lands on this side. John Savoy says they have absolute Deeds for their Land on the Other side the River without any Conditions of Exchange, w'ch he promises to produce to the Office, till then the affair is respited.

9ber, 16, [1720.]

Jacob Savoy produced the Deeds mentioned on the other Page, one whereof is for 350 acres, granted for £30, Merchantable Pay at current Price, and other Good Causes and Considerations, the Proprietary thereunto Moving, quitr't 3 and ½ Bushels of winter Wheat Yearly on the 29th of 7br., unto the said W. P., his Heirs and assigns. Signed by James Nevil, agent. The Courses of the whole Tract are upon Rasures, as also is the quantity as often as mentioned and writ in a Different Hand from that of the Deed.

Also another Deed from James Nevil to John Hendrickson of one Tree Hook for 400 acres, consideration £32, quitrent 4 Bushells of Wheat. No Rasure on this.

Examined and Corrected p.

JO'N HUGHES.

These are to Certify that the foregoing Sheets contained in this Book, No. 17, in the whole amounting to Two hundred and thirty-two Pages, are true Copies of the Originals found in the Office of the Secretarys, and that the same were carefully compared with the Originals by me during my appointment as Recorder of Warrants and Surveys under the Act of Assembly passed in the 33d Year of his late Majesty's Reign, entituled "An Act for Recording Warrants and Surveys and for rendering the real Estates and properties within this Province more secure."

p. JO'N HUGHES.

Signed in the Presence of

THOS. LEETH,
JOHN MORTON,
SAMUEL RHOADS,
JAMES WRIGHT,
HENRY WYNKOOP.

MINUTE BOOK "I."

THIS IS BOOK "I" IN THE SECRETARIES OFFICE.

[Although thus designated, certain portions of this Minute Book duplicates the one prior.]

20th 7th mo., 1716.

Isaac Taylor, of the County of Chester, Surveyor, produces Certificates Under the hands of Caleb Pusey and Henry Worley Declaring that William Berkingham and John Berkingham came Servants into this province in or about the year 1682, and Served their Time to Jos. Richards, and that Samuel Bishop about the same Time came in and served James Sandilands. Also a Certificate under the hand of Nich. Pile Declaring that James Hayward came about the aforesaid Time Servant to Edward Bezer. The said Isaac having Purchased the Several Rights of the s'd Servants to their head Land, desires a Warrant to Lay out the same. Granted, Dated this day.

John Cowgill Desires the Grant of about 100 acres of Land Joyning on his other Tract, Near the branches of Duck Creek, in the County of New Castle, where he has planted a Tan yard, at 1d per acre rent.

At a meeting of the Commissioners of Property the 8th 2 mo., 1717.

Present, Rich'd Hill, Isaac Norris, James Logan.

Wm. Lawrence, of Philad'a, produced a Petition to the Board Setting forth that he, about ye Year 1690, purchased several Lotts on Schuylkill, where he seated himself about the same time, and that there lies a parcel of Ground between the said Lotts and the River Schuylkill which he desires may be now granted to him, because he says other Persons holding Lotts thereabout had the Priviledge to the River side, but those Lotts held by the s'd William are all located and Patented, and that he hath no other Grant for any other land there, nor hath it been a General Priviledge, as he alledges, therefore his Petition is dismissed.

Wm. Carter, William Lawrence and Michael Walton requests Confirmations on three Parcells of Land formerly (as they say) laid out by Warr'ts from the former Commissioners on that Side of Springetsbury Mannor which joins to the Town. That of Wm. Carter's is said to be first laid out to one Lewis

Thomas, for 9 acres, the other two p'cells to Wm. Lawrence and Michael Walton is said to be 6 ac. to each of them, but their pretended Grants being so extremely Short and Deficient and that the Proprietary always forbid the granting away any part of the Mannor, their request is referred to further Consideration.

Signed the following Patents:

A Patent to John Goodson for 50 foot Bank Lott formerly laid out to himself at the north End of the City. Dated the 25th 1 month last.

Signed a Patent to James Morris for 600 acres of Land and Marsh on the South side of the main Branch of Duck Creek, in Kent County, requested by his father Anthony Morris, in page 69 of these Minutes, the Survey being Rectified and the bounds thereof fixed according to the natural situation of the Tract. Dated the 12th of the 10th mo., 1716.

Mich'l Izard, Vid. Min. Prop'ty, 1790, about his Centre Lott.

The Prop'ry, by Patent dated 28th 5 mo., 1684, Confirmed to Tho. Howle, in Southampton Township (tho' not mentioned, the Survey being very near 200 a's of Land on rent (1d sterling p. acre). Tho. Howle, by Indorsm't on the said patt., Gives the Land to his Son, Job Howle, who by Deed Dated 16, 9br, 1697, grants 100 ac., part thereof, to Hugh Ellis, 50 acres more of the same granted by Job Howle to FFrancis Eccleston by Deed Dated   . The s'd Hugh Ellis and FFrancis Eccleston grants by Deed the 4 March, 1701, Grants the s'd 150 ac to Phillip Packer, and afterwards the said Job Howle by a certain article, dated 17, 8 mo., 1701, bargains and sells the remaining 50 acres to the s'd P. Packer, who afterwards by Deed dated ye 15 Feb., 1705-6, grants the whole to Dan'l Robinson, who by Deeds dated 13, Xber, 1708, Grants the whole to Pat. Ogleby, who Running away, Griffith Jones and Hugh Lowden brought their action of Debt against the s'd 200 acres of Land, and after Judgment obtained, the Sheriff, Wm. Biles, Grants the s'd Land to Wm Jones, who by Deed Dated 13 Feb., 1713, conveys the same to Step. Jones, Son of the s'd Griffith, the Sheriff's deed dated 9th Xber, 1712.

Thomas FFairman in his lite time applyed to this board on behalf of his Son-in-law, Jeremia Hopton, for a patent on 250 acres of Land on Potquessen Creek, Sold by the Proprietor to Edw'd Hopton, father to the s'd Jeremia. The Comm'rs then ordered that the s'd Land should be resurveyed and the bounds of 250 acres certainly fixed, and then a Patent to be provided, but a certain Writing being brought to the office, which was found in Eliz'th, late wife of Pat., Robinson's hands, which here follows (Verbatim). The business is referred to a full hearing of the Comm'rs.

I, Wollo Woolson, of the County of Philadelphia, in the province of Pennsylvania, with consent of Catharine my wife, the thirteenth day of the fourth month, 1683, for me, my heirs and assigns, grants my just and equal half part of Six hundred and forty acres of Land, with all its appertenances, which whole Six hundred and forty acres of Land was by order Surveyed to me and Lassey Lasson equally betwixt us, and is in the protracted ffigure of the said Land called Pleasant Hill, as in the Copy of the s'd Survey, under the hand of Rich'd Noble, at more length appears, lying in the County aforesaid, upon the River Delaware, having the Lands of Peter Rambo, junior, upon the South west, the Creek called Potquessing on the north east, and so backward in the woods.

To Benjamin Acrod, Mer't, and his heirs and Assigns forever, for the Consideration of two Thousand two Hundred Guilders, or fifty-five Pounds, money of Pennsylvania, Secured to be paid to me, my heirs and assigns by two several bills, bearing date with these Presents. In witness whereof I hereunto Sett my hand and Seal, and hereby promise to acknowledge the same in open Court the next time it shall be held at Philadelphia for the s'd County.

This Deed was dated and acknowledged. The mark of + in open Court the 3d of 8 mo., 1683.

WOLLO O WOOLSON.

Teste, John Southworth, Clerk of the County.

Signed, sealed and delivered in the Presence of [ye mark of]
LASSEY LASSON,
PAT. ROBINSON.

It is writ on the back of the foregoing Deed as followeth (viz.), Memorandum, That upon the 13th Day of Fourth month, 1683, the within Wollo Woolson gave to the within Benjamin Acrod actual Posession of the Lands within sold by Delivrie of Turf and Twigg of the s'd Land to the s'd Benjamin Acrod in P'son, in presence of Pat. Robinson, Lassey Lasson and betwixt the 3d and 4th hours in the afternoon, 5th 10 mo., 1684. Recorded in the office of Rolls and publick Reg'e at Philad'a, Vol. 5, book E., foll. 37.

PAT. ROBINSON,
The :: mark of LASSEY LASSON.

Signed by order.
PAT. ROBINSON.

The Prop'r, by Indr's of lease and release, bearing Date the 10th and 11th days of 8ber, 1681, Grants to Richard Jordain, of London, Shoemaker, 250 acres of Land. Rich'd Jordain, by like deeds, dated the 25th and 26th days of April, 1684, grants the s'd 250 ac. and premises to Edw'd Hopton, of London, Tripeman, in right whereof by Virtue of a Warr't from the Prop'r, dated 27th 1st mo., 1700, the 250 acres was Surveyed near Whitpain's Township. Jeremiah Hopton, Son and heir of Edward Hopton, desires a Warrant for the Lott and liberty Land appurtenant to the said Purchase.

Alexander Draper, of the County of Sussex, desires a resurvey on the Plantation and Tract of Land where he dwells, w'th the Addition of some Vaca't Marsh and Points adjoining to the same, for which said vacancy he agrees to pay to the Prop'r after the rate of £15 p. C't and the quitr't of one Bushell of good winter wheat, bounded between the Bay, the s'd Land and Cedar Creek.

He also requests the same for his Brother Henry Draper, whose land lies on the South side of the Land of Alexand'r, ye marsh joines on Wm. Fisher's Marsh to the East, and to the west on Alexand'r Draper's Land.

John Turner, of the County of Kent, desires 100 acres of Marsh for the Conveniency of mowing Hay, it lies upon Mispelen Creek, above a branch of the s'd Creek, called the great ffishing Gutt.

The Prop'r, by Ind'es of Lease and Release, dated ye 7th and 8th Days of 7b'r, 1681, granted to Sarah Hersent, then of Worminghurst, 500 acres of Land in this Province, which afterwards by a War'tr Dated 10th, 10br '84, was surveyed near the branches of Parqueaming, and her City Lott was laid out in the Third Street, where Sassafras street Crosses it, but the Liberty Land yet remains to be laid out.

Sarah Hersent, by like Ind'es, dated the 6th and 7th Days of FFeb., 1716, for £40 sterl., grants and Conveys the whole 500 acres of Land, City Lott and Premises to Anthony Morris, of Philad'a, who now desires a Warrant for the Liberty Land and that the Lott may be resurveyed, &c. Granted and a warr't signed, Dated——.

The Prop'r, by short Deeds intended for lease and release, dated the 7th and 8th days of the 11 mo., 1701, in Consideration of £100 money of Eng'd (p'd to P. FFord), granted unto George Beal, near Guilford, in the County of Surry, 3,000 acres of Land between the Rivers Dellaware and Susquenannah, at the yearly quitrent of 1d sterling for every Hundred acres, to commence 7 years after survey.

Wm. Beal, Nephew to the s'd George, in the year 1705, coming over with a power from his Uncle to take up the s'd Land, had then Warr'ts ordered him for 2,000 acres, of w'ch there is only one to be found, and that are not excepted (the s'd Will'm Going hence was never heard off).

Jeremiah Langhorn, of the County of Bucks, produces the said Deeds and a Letter from George Beal, dated   , 1716, wherein he acknowledges an agreement made with Jeremiah for the whole 3,000 acres, and promises to confirm the same to him upon payment of £120 Sterling, whereupon the s'd Jeremiah desires warr'ts for laying out of the whole, w'ch is granted in 3 Warr'ts (viz.), the former warr't not executed is to be one, and two more now made out for 1,000 acres each, with the restriction of but 2 parcels of Land to be laid out for each warr't. Signed, Dated 24th and 25th 5 mo., 1717.

The Prop'r, by (large) Deeds of Lease and Release, dated ye 8th 7ber, 1681, Granted to Ann Cawley, of Rowde, in the County of Wilts, 500 acres of Land. The said Ann, by her last Will and Testam't Gave and bequeathed the same to Rich'd Webb, of the same place, who by like Deeds of lease and Release, dated the 30th day of October, 1707, granted the said 500 to Charles Mutell and John Child, who by their Indenture tripartite, date ye 4th 9b'r, 1707, Conveys the s'd 500 acres to Samuel Perry and Abraham Allyss in Trust for the Children of Francis Gaudonet, now of Philad'a, Doct'r of Physick, who desires a warr't for laying out 492 acres, the 8 acres of lib'y Land and Lott being granted and laid out to Richard Hill, of Philadelphia.

The Prop'r, by Deeds of L. and Rel., dated 21, 22 days of 8b'r, 1681, Granted to George Ff'ox 1,250 ac. of Land in this Province, who by his last will and Testament bequeathed the Lotts and Lib'y Land to Friends here, and was confirmed to S. Carpent'r, Rich'd Hill and Anthony Morris, for their use, by Patent dated the 26th 6 mo., 1705, and the Remainder (viz.), 1,230 a's, he by the s'd Testament gave to Tho's Lower, John Rouse and Daniel Abraham.

The said Daniel Abraham and Nath'l Rouse, Son and Heir of the s'd Jno. Rouse, by their Deed (a copy) Ind'rs, dated ye 21 day of June, 1715, for £8 Grants and Releases there shares of the said Land to the said Tho. Lower, who now by his friend David Lloyd, requests a warrant for laying it out.

[This Minute should be entered before the following on the other leaf.] Cornelius Wiltbank, of the County of Sussex, having formerly applied for 100 acres of Marsh next below Walton Haling's line, in the broad Kill Marshes, obtained a Warr't and Survey on the same, whereupon Margery Green, then Widdow of Thomas Fisher, who dwells at some distance from the s'd marsh laid out to Cornelius, Came up to Philadelphia and made a grievous Complaint (or noise) that the marsh so laid out to him would be very injurious, if not ruinous to her and her Children, upon which it was ordered that enquiry should be made concerning its situation, which was done by James Steel, who was since the Survey upon the Spot, and says that the 100 acres of Marsh is laid out at some Considerable Distance from any part of her lines, so that her Clamour is groundless, and a Patent is ordered to Cornelius Wiltbank and now signed.

At a meeting of the Commissioners the 21, 9b'r, 1717.
Present, Rich'd Hill, Is. Norris, James Logan.

Martin Kundigg, Hans Heer and Hans FFunk, with several others of their Countrymen, the Palatines, having often applyed to purchase Land to accommodate those of them that are lately arrived in this Province and are their Relations, Friends or Acquaintance, who they assure the Board are honest, Conscientious People.

22d, 9b'r, 1717.
Present, only J. W. and J. L.

The Board taking into Consideration the Circumstances of those People in Relation to their holding of Lands in the Dominions of Great Britain, were asked if they understood the disadvantage they were under by Reason of their being born Aliens, that therefore their Children were uncapable of Inheriting what they purchased, according to the English laws, which in such Cases may be extended hither. They answered they were informed of it before, however inasmuch as they had removed themselves and families hither they were, notwithstanding the s'd Disadvantage, willing to purchase Lands.

It was further told them by the Commiss'rs that it was their Business to sell the Prop'rs Land to such as would purchase it, but were at the same time willing to let them know, as they (ye s'd persons) were aliens, the Danger that might ensue if not prevented, also that some years agoe a Law was here enacted and passed by the late Queen Ann for enabling Divers aliens, particularly named in the Law, to hold and enjoy Lands in this Province, and that the like advantage might be probably obtained for those amongst themselves that were of good report if a Petition were preferred to this present Assembly when they sit to goe upon Business. With this advice they seem'd pleased and desired to be informed when such a sitting of the Assembly was likely to be.

Signed the following warrants to the Palatines:

The Prop'r, by Indent'rs ot L. and Rel., dated 19, 20 Janu'ry, 1681, granted to Tho. Symyns, of the County of Pembrook, Gent., 500 acres of Land, 300 acres whereof was laid out in Haverford, which upon a Resurvey makes 372 acres, the other 200 acres was laid out in ye great Valley. Tho. Symyns, Grandson of the aforesaid Tho., desires a Resurvey on the last and that he may purchase the overplus. Granted.

The Prop'r, by Indent'rs of Lease and Release, dated ye 26th and 27th days of FFeb., 1681, granted to Richard Adams, of upper Hayford, in Worth'n Shier, 500 acres of Land, quitrent one shill. every Hundred acres, as appears by Copies of the s'd L. and Rel., and rec't for Consideration money (viz.), £10, attested by John Vaston. John Adams, Son and Heir of the s'd Rich'd Adams, by his Power of Attorney proved here, authorizes and appoints Hugh Sharp, of the County of Burlington, in West Jersey, to take up the s'd 500 a's. The s'd Hugh thereupon Requests a warr't to lay out the same.

At a meeting of the Commissioners the 2d 11 mo., 1717-8.
Present, Richard Hill, Isaac Norris, James Logan.

Andrew Hamilton having often applyed for a piece of broken low ground at Some distance Northward of the Town line for the Conveniency of a Pasture, which being now taken into Consideration, the Comm'rs agree he shall have about twenty acres laid out to him for the Term of 21 years, under the rent of one shilling sterling for each acre, and to be delivered up at the Expiration of the said Term under a good Fence, and the whole to be well improved at such delivery.

The Comm'rs being informed that M. V. Bebber, from Maryland, taking Henry Hollinsworth with him, he surveyed Land near the head of Pecquea Creek, in this Province, including within the same the old Shawana Town, by Virtue of warrants from Maryland, offering to the People settled under this Governm't to sell Land to them in Right of Maryland and make them good Titles for the same. To prevent any further proceedings of the like Kind for the future it is proposed that speedy measures be forthwith taken to disposses all persons claiming Lands there under the said right, also that a Reward of ten Pounds be publickly offered to any person who shall apprehend any Surveyor coming into those parts to lay out Land on a Maryland right, and deliver him to the Sheriffs or Officers impowered for the like purposes in those parts, that they may be brought to Justice, and therefore James Steel is ordered without delay to be ready to goe to Conestogo with such Instructions as will be necessary to prevent the like disorders for the time to come.

Ordered a War'rt to Peter Chartier for 300 a's of Land where his Father is now settled, being on his father's request, at £10 p. C.

A Warr't to Moses Comb for 200 a's among the other surveys.

Ordered that five hundred acres of Land be granted to Coll. John FFrench in or near the Sawanah old fields, on Pequea Creek, as a Consideration of his Services to the Proprietor and his interest, done and to be done in preventing the Incroachments of Maryland on the Lands of this Province, and that five guineas be paid to said Coll. French for his Expenses in his last Journey to Nottingham and attending the Maryland Jury of Northeast, who were directed by the Commissioners from England for forfeited Lands to make a Return of Coll. Talbot's Mannor between Northeast and Delaware.

Jonathan Dickinson having long applied to this Board to purchase ye Northern Part of Springetsbury Mannor, and Terms having been proposed to him last Winter in order to the same, it is now agreed and concluded that all that part of the said Mannor which lies to the Northw'd of a line to be drawn from the Cove below the Vineyard Tract to the northwest Corner of Abraham Bickley's field, shall be forthwith granted him at one pound Six Shillings and eight Pence Sterling p. acre, to be paid on his Bills in London, together with Interest for the same from the 24th day of the 4th Month last past, in Consideration of which Interest money arising from former Proposals made to him, all those $137\frac{1}{2}$ acres of the Vineyard Tract which he claims. together with the rest, shall be confirmed to him. But that out of the measure of the whole so much shall be allowed to him as the great Road passing through the said Land shall be found to take up, computed at sixty foot in breadth, and the s'd Jonathan is to allow out of his Purchase a smaller Road leading out of the s'd great Road to the Remainder of the Mannor, to be laid near the said Corner of Ab. Bickley's field.

The late Settlements on and near Conestogo Creek, hath made it necessary that the Indian fields about the Town should be inclosed by a good fence to secure the Indians' corn from the Creatures that would otherwise destroy it and thereby cause an uneasiness in those Indians.

Ordered that the said fence be forthwith made and that James Logan pay for the same, provided it exceed not Twenty pounds.

At a meeting of the Comm'rs of Property the 14th Day of the 11 month, 1717-8.

Present, Richard Hill, Isaac Norris, James Logan.

Thomas Stevenson, of the County of Bucks, Attorney to William Lawrence, Joseph Thorn, Benj. Field, Jno. Talmon and Sam'l Thorn, of Long Island, Setts forth that the s'd William Lawrence and others about the year 169 , purchased of William Biles, late of the s'd County, five thousand acres of Land in the said County, belonging to one Tho. Hudson, whose Attorney he then was, and that the said Wm. Lawrence, &c., had never yet had the s'd Land confirmed to them, and therefore desires a Pat. may be now granted for the same. But Thomas Shute, Andrew Hamilton, George Fitzwater and James Steel being invested with the right of the like Quantity of Land, the original Purchase of one Thomas Heriot, made of the Prop'r by Deeds indented of L. and R., dated ye   , 1681, objected that in the said right of Heriot there was laid out in the year 1685 unto Dennis Rochford by the Surv'r General's order on 2 Warr'ts, one for 1,200 and the other for 3,000 acres, a tract of Land Containing 4,200 acres, which upon the running of the line that divides the County of Philad'a and Bucks, was found part in the County of Philadelphia and part in the County of Bucks; that part which fell in Bucks County prov'd to be about 3,000 acres, but the whole was returned in one Tract, which said 3,000 acres Sometime afterwards is supposed to be taken in by a Survey, presumed to be made by J's Taylor, of whole said five Thousand acres of Thomas Hudson.

Whereupon the s'd Tho. Stephenson produced a power of Attorney from the s'd Wm. Lawrence and others, and also certain Instructions ordering him to lay the whole matter in Difference before the Commissioners, desiring them to grant a full hearing and then to determine to whom the s'd 3,000 acres should be confirmed, and also that in case the Comm'rs should not think fitt to take that Charge on them, that then the s'd Tho. Stevenson might leave the s'd Matter in Difference to other Honest men, to be chosen on both parts, and that they, the s'd Wm. Lawrence and others, would be concluded by the Judgment of those men.

The Comm'rs not thinking it proper for themselves to undertake the Decision of the matter, advises the parties to choose other Persons as arbitrators and leave the Difference to their Determination.

At a meeting of the Comm'rs of Property ye 29th 11 mo., 1717-8.

Present, Rich'd Hill, Isaac Norris, James Logan.

Pursuant to what Thomas Stevenson, in behalf of Wm. Lawrence, Jos. Thorn, Benj. Field, John Talmon and Sam Thorn, laid before the Commissioners the 14th Instant, He, the said Thomas Stevenson, on behalf of the s'd Persons, did then nominate and choose Jonathan Dickinson and Jeremiah Langhorn, and that Thomas Shute and partners did choose Clement Plumsted and Israel Pemberton on their part and behalf, to hear and Determine the difference of ye 3,000 acres of Land in Controversie, both parties obliging themselves under their hands to stand to the award of those men, who after having fully heard the allegations on both sides and viewed the several writings, precepts, Surveys and Returns laid before them, unanimously agreed that the s'd 3,000 acres in Controversie, lying in Bucks County, of right belongs to Thomas Shute and Partners, as Claimants under Dennis Rochford, to whom it was first laid out, and that the same ought to be Patented to them. The award, under the Hands and Seals of the s'd J. D., J. L., C. P. and J. P., being lodged in this Office, as also a full state of the case affixed thereunto by the said Persons, whereupon the s'd Thomas Shute, George Fitzwater, Andrew Hamilton and James Steel having divided the whole 4,200 acres into several Lotts or shares, desires a Confirmation to each of them for so much as they respectively hold (the 200 acres taken out of the same by an Execution at the suit of Andrew Robeson excepted). To which the Comm'rs agree that upon paying the quitrents due upon the whole and for the overplus Land found in each Lott over and above ye ten p. Cent., that Patents be according granted, but find the Mesne deeds from the Heirs of Rochford are to be laid before J. Logan, that the right to those Claimants may appear to be good.

A Petition from George Dakeyne to the Comm'rs was read, setting forth that he had often requested some part of the marsh and Cripple below N. Castle Town, about 116 acres, and that he had together with his house and Lotts in that Town mortgaged 6 acres of the s'd Marsh to G. Falconar, which unless he can have the Grant and liberty to sell the said marsh and Cripple to pay off the said Mortgage, he expects to be entirely ruined by G. F. J. L. intends to answer the Petition by a Letter.

Joseph Wood, of New Castle, sent up an Information of several Tracts of Land in that County which are valuable and might be disposed off to advantage, which he would either do for the Prop'r or take to them himself at a Price that might be worth his while, which is left to be further Considered.

Abr. Bickley setts forth by his request in writing that there was 500 acres of Land formerly laid out to Wm. Framton in Right of Tho. Bowmans near the Tract called Pickering's Mines, and since upon a resurvey and Division of that Tract the said 500 acres was taken in and Confirmed to John Moor and Jos. Wilcox, and the right to that 500 acres being now vested in the said Abraham, he desires it may be laid to him in the nearest Vacancy. It is ordered that he produce his Right, which if good, his request may be granted.

Jos. Jones requests that two bank Lotts formerly laid out to his Father below Anthony Morrisses Brew house, one of them containing 20 f'tt front, the other 16 foot, might be confirmed to him by Patent; he alledges that there was formerly a Patent for them both, but it is lost.

The Prop'r, by Deeds of L. and Release, dated the 8th and 9th days of 7b'r, 1681, granted to Ann Olliffe, of the City of Oxon, Widdow, 500 a's of Land in this Province, quitrent one Shill. Sterlin. Ann Olliffe, by her last Will and Testament, dated 19th of March, 1682, Did give and bequeath all her Estate (some Legacys excepted) unto her only Daughter Jane Olliffe, who afterwards intermarried with Robert Clarke of London, Malt factor, since deceased.

Bartholomew Duke, of ye Parish of St. Giles, Coun. Middl'x, Baker, and Anna his wife, who is the only Daughter of the said Robert Clarke, and Jane his wife, by Deeds of Lease and Release, dated 14th and 15th Decemb'r, 1716, Granted the said 500 a's of Land, with the appertenances, unto James Robins, of Queenhill, London, Meal factor (to hold, &c.).

The said James Robins, by a Power of attorney, under his hand and Seal certifyed by a notary Publick and witnessed by Tho. Nickson and Richd' Murrey, appoints Capt. John Annis and his Brother Samuel Robins, here in this Province, or either of them, to take up the same, &c. Samuel Robins requests Warrants to take up the said Land and Lotts, with the Lott and Liberty.

The Prop'r, by Deeds Indented of Lease and Release, dated the 26th and 27th days of 7b'r, 1681, granted to Thomas Bayly, of Bristol, in Great Britain, 250 acres of Land in this Province, quit. 1s Sterling p. C't.

The said Thomas Bayly, by like Deeds dated the 8th and 9th days of May, 1713, for £5 granted the said 250 acres to Edward Roberts, of Philad'a, who now desires warr'ts to take up the same, with the Lott and Liberty Land.

Abrah'm Bickley pursuant to the above order produced a transcript from the Records of a grant by Indenture, dated ye 5th 5 mo., 1686, for 1,500 acres of Land made by Sam'l Rich ardson to Wm. Frampton, being part of Wm. Bowman's purchase of 5,000 acres, whose son, Tho. Bowman, sold the whole to the said Samuel Richardson, 1,000 a's (I suppose) Jno. Budd took in execution for a Debt due from Frampton, the other 500 acres was laid near the tract called Pickering's Mines, as above said.

Thomas Frampton, Son and Heir of the said Wm. Frampton, by Indent'rs of L. and Rel., dated 1st and 2d days of Jan'ry, 1712, for the Consideration of £300, Money of West Jersey, granted and conveyed unto the s'd A. Bickley, his heirs and assigns, all his Lands, Lotts, &c., either in Jersey, Pensylv'a or elsewhere in America.

At a meeting of the Commissioners the 18th 1st month, 1717-8.

Present, Rich'd Hill, Isaac Norris, James Logan.

Application being made to the Comm'rs by Israel Pemberton himself, and that Edmund Lovet, of the County of Bucks, for above thirty years since hath concealed a Patent that was granted him (as is presum'd) by the Prop'r before his first Departure from this Province, for a certain Tract of Land near Pensbury Mannor, which the proprietor afterwards gave him other Land in Exchange and confirmed the same to him by another Patent without taking up the former.

Edmund Lovet being in Town, it was thought fit to send for him and know the Reason why he detained and kept in his hands a Patent for which he had so long agoe receiv'd an equivalent, and to let him know that the Land therein contain'd being in the Possession of Sundry honest People, they might in time to come be disturbed in their just Right. He confessed that he had such a Patent in his keeping, but that he would not give it up till he had satisfaction made him for exchanging those Lands. It was told him that he had never made any demand as was known to them, viz., the Commissioners, and that he ought in case he had any just claim to refer it to friends, if not, the meeting where he belonged to was to be next applied to, and in case he refused to submit his Demand to friends, that then a due course of Law should be taken to recover the said Patent out of his hand.

To which he only answered that he would consider of it.

Ruben Pownal desires the grant of a small Island or two in Delaware River, lying over against his land in Makefield, for conveniency of Range for his Cattle. This lies before C. Read's Land.

John Henry Kuirson having purchased 1,000 acres, part of ye 10,000 acres granted by the Prop'r to Coll. Rhedegelt, formerly obtained a warr't for laying out the same and afterwards a Patent, but the grant to Rhedegelt being disputed, a Bond was taken from Kuirson to Pay £ if this grant from Rhedegelt did not appear Good, and now the said Kuirson supposing the s'd grant to be sufficient, desires his bond may be delivered to him cancell'd, which is left to the Consideration off the Commissioners next meeting.

The right of Rich'd Whitpain's deed to 7,000 a's of Land in this Province, as well as certain Lotts in ye City Philad'a, being entered at large in the Minutes of 30th 6 mo., 1703. Re-surveys on ye Land were then requested and granted but not executed, but the said Lands being since sold by the surviving Trustee, mentioned in the said Minutes, to Wm. Aubrey, of London, who conveyed the same to Rees Thomas and Anthony Morris, Jun'r, the whole affair has laid dormant a considerable time by the claim of Jno. Whitpain as heir at Law to the s'd Rich'd. But the said John, sometime before his disease, came to an agreement with ye said R. T and A. M. for a certain divident of the Lands and Lotts, or of the Money that should be made by sale thereof, and thereupon certain Deeds were executed to each other, and soon after the said J. W. made his last Will and Testam't in writing, of which he appointed his wife Ann Whitpain sole Execut'x, giving to her full power to act and do all things requisite in that Affair, whereupon the said A. Whitpain, R. T. and A. M. desires that a certain Tract of Land in West Town, County Chester, might be resurveyed in Order to be Patented. The Deeds of L. and Release from Jno. Blackall, the abovesaid surviving Trustee, to Wm. Aubrey are dated ye 27th and 28th days of 9b'r, 1712, Consideration of the whole purchase, £300 Sterl.

Deeds of Lease and Release from Wm. Aubrey to Rees Thomas and A. Morris are dated ye 24 and 25 days of April, 1713, granting the whole to them (ye 500 a's all along excepted) for £500 Sterling.

Jno. Whitpain, upon certain Articles made between himself and Rees Thomas and Anthony Morris, dated ye 29th May, 1718, agrees with them to pay as soon as money can be raised by the sales of the premises £222 4s 5d, money of Pensylvania, and to Release ye whole grant to them, except so much as his father Zak'a Whitpain disposed of in his life time, upon their securing to him one full third part of the money arising from the sale thereof, the Release is executed by him and Ann his wife, dated the 26th May aforesaid.

PHILADELPHIA, 18*th*, 1 *mo.*, 1718-9.

William Hanby, of Notingham Township, is permitted to settle on the Proprietary's Lott in that Township, and is to have the preterrence of purchasing two hundred Acres thereof in a Regular Piece when the same is to be sold.

By Order of the Commissioners.

SAM. STEEL, *De. Sec'ry.*

The Propp'r, by his Patent dated 12th 9b'r, 1683, granted and confirmed to Henry Reynolds 200 acres on Naaman's Creek, quitr't half a crown, Silver Money, and a year's Rent on every Alienation.

The Propriet'r by Deeds of L. and Release, dated 5th, 6th 7b'r, 1681, granted to George Andrews, of Rowd, in the County Wilts, Sergemaker, 250 acres, q't r't 1s Sterl. p. C't. George Andrews, by like Deeds dated 16th and 17th days of the same Month, granted to John Hickman, of Bromham, in the said County, Woolcomber, 125 acres, part thereof, who by like Deeds dated 30th and 31st of January, 1682, granted the said 125 acres to the said Henry Reynolds, joyning on his other Land at N. Creek.

The Prop'r, by L. and Rel., dated 12th and 13th days of July, 1682, granted to George Strodd, of   , 500 acres of Land, q't r't 1s p. C't.

George Strodd, by Ind'r of L. and Rel., dated 21st and 22d of March, 1686-87, granted 200 acres, part thereof, untaken up unto the said Henry Reynolds. Thomas Pierson, by a return under his hand, Dated the 10th 12 mo., 1685-6, Certifies that he has Resurveyed a Tract of Land for Henry Reynolds on Naaman's Creek, containing 519 a's. Henry Reynolds says the above parcells make up that Tract, but the Deeds from Geo. Strodd are dated a year after the said resurvey and mentions Land untaken up.

Henry Reynolds Petitioned the Commissioners for a resurvey on 250 acres of Land laid out to George Andrews and John Hickman in Chester County, in Order that he might lay a Warr't of 200 acres on the overplus supposed to be in that Tract, which was granted by J. Claypoole and Robert Turner, and ordered to be done by Thomas Holme, dated 6, 9 mo. 1685.

The Prop'r, by Indentures of Lease and Release, dated ye 11 and 12 days of 8b'r, 1681 (as p. attested Copies under Tho. Grew's hand before chief Justice Pratt), granted to Wm. Bakon, of the Middle Temple, Gent., 5,000 acres of Land in Pensylvania, to hold to him, &c. The said Wm. Bakon, by like Deeds of L. and Release, dated the 19th and 20th days of FFeb., 1718, for £110 Sterl., granted and conveyed the said

5,000 acres of Land, with the Lotts and lib. Land, unto Humphry Murry and John Budd, both of Philadelphia, to hold to them, their heirs and assigns forever. The quitrent reserved is one Shilling for each Hundred acres. The said Humphrey and John desires Warr'ts to lay out the Whole.

John Milner, Son and heir of Joseph Milner, late of Makefield, in Bucks County, applys for a Patent on his Father's and Uncle D. Milner's Land in that Township, but there being a Sister of his yet living and a Son of another Sister (dece'd), and some sort of Division of the Tract made among themselves, it must be referred till the lines and quantities of the dividends are known before Patents can be made for it.

Vid. Min. Prop'r, 15, 3, 1704.

Jos. and Daniel purchased in England,	250 acres.
Purchased in this Province,	300
Purchased of Edw'd Luff's right,	296
Allowance,	85
	931 acres.

The Comm'rs, by Patent (Wm. Markham and Jno. Goodson), dated 21st 11 mo., 1688, Confirmed to Lancellot Lloyd 2 acres of Land near to the Town of Philad'a, beginning at a post standing on the N. side of a run, thence E. by a line of trees 508 foot, then S. 18 d. W. by the 2d Street 180 foot, thence W. by a line of trees 478 foot, thence N. 18 d. E. by the front Street 171 foot to the beginning, granted by a Warr't, &c., and laid out by the Surv'r General's Order to L. Lloyd, Renter, &c., fenceing it in and erecting a Tanyard and following that Trade thereon, yielding and paying, &c., at Philad'a, 8 English Silver Shillings yearly, &c. Lancellot Lloyd, by Inden'rs dated 29th 2 mo., 1692, for £5 Grants all the s'd 2 acres to Hector Dicks, of West New Jersey, Tanner, who by a like Deed dated ye 6th January, 1695-6, for £8 13s granted the said 2 acres to Pat. Robinson, who by another like Deed dated the 4th June, 1696, for £9 granted the said 2 acres to Rob. Hawks.

The Comm'rs, viz., William Markham, R. Turner and J. Goodson, by Patent dated 6th April, 1693, granted to Griff. Owen 7 acres of Land, beginning at a corner post of Lancellot Lloyd's Land thence E. by the same 43 p's, thence N. 3 d. E. 23 p's to the Beginning, quitrent one Shilling, Silver Money of Pensilv'a, for each Hundred acres (so it is in ye Patent), which must be a mistake, 'tis more likely one shilling for each acre, which it would be were ye word hundred lef' out. The same Comm'rs, W. M., R. T. and J. G., by Patent dated ye 25, 4 mo., 1694, granted to Griff. Owen, in right of Jno. Eckly, a certain Lott of Ground containing 50 f't in breadth and 320 in length, bounded N. ward w'th vac't Lot. E. w'd w'th ye 2d street from Schuylkill, to the S. w'd w'th T. Lloyd's Lott, &c., to the westw'd with the front street, quitrent not legible.

Tho. Lloyd and S. Carpenter, Ex'rs of the last will and Testament of Sarah Eckley, by Deed poll dated ye 1st day of ye 4th mo., 1694, for £100 granted the said Lott, with the Buildings, to Griff. Owen.

Griff'th Owen, by sundry Deeds, dated in the 4 mo., 1694, the 7 acres, the Lott of John Eckly and the Lott of Philip James, unto Rob. Hawks, who granted the same to Ruth Haddock, together with the 2 acres, who granted the same to George Roch, who again granted it to Wm. Trent, also.

The Prop'r, By L. and R. L., dated the 21 and 22 Days of March, 1681, granted to Jno. Alsop, 1,000 acres of Land in this Province. Jno. Alsop, by Deed dated ye 19th July, 1684, Granted the same to Tho. Tunnecliff. James Tunnecliff, as heir at Law to Tho. Tunnecliff and his Descendants, now possesses   acres in Makefield, who desires to have a Patent for it, which is to be hastened.

Edmund Grubb and his Brothers, together with the Heirs of Isaac Savoy and Daniel Herrick, came up to settle their Land, but J. Steel being just setting out on his Journey to Mackhackamock could not attend that Business, wherefore at his return the Office must be searched and those persons sent to when to attend again. They bring a Draught of their Land, called 600 a's, laid out by order of N. C. Court in 7b'r, 1682, by Eph. Harmen to J. Grub, Isaac Savoy and David Henrick in equal shares and proportions, as the Draught calls it.

At a meeting of the Comm'rs ye 4th 6 mo., 1719.

Present, Richard Hill, Isaac Norris, James Logan.

Andrew Hamilton having purchased of Richard Woodworth the back part of his Lot in Chestnut street, adjoyning to his Garden, petitions the Comm'rs for a grant to him of a small piece of vacant ground at the lower end of the same being about 26 foot and about 30 foot deep, or from the lower end of the said lot to the end of Walnut Street Lotts, which is granted in Consideration of twenty Shillings, Curr't Money, and Six pence Sterling quitr't and a Warr't ordered for the same.

The said Andrew further requests that the quantity of Low ground granted him in the former minutes, page   may be enlarged to thirty acres, and withal if the Comm'rs thought fit, to add to the same the old field that lies between the said Parcel of Low ground and the fence of Abraham Bickley's field or Orchard, and further that the whole may be granted him for 31 years from the date of the first Minute, under the same rent mentioned in the said Minute or otherwise, as they shall think fit. The Comm'rs taking into Consideration the great Charge the said Andrew has been at in grubbing, levelling, clearing and fencing of the whole, agrees that he shall hold the same, which will be in the whole about Six and forty acres, for the said Term of thirty-one years from the said date, under the yearly rent of one shilling, present Currency, for every acre and to pay down ten Pounds like money to the use of the Trustees, to which the said Andrew agrees and a Warr't is ordered for laying out the same.

A Deed to Jonathan Dickinson to release to him the Northern part of Springetsbury Mannor was now executed, a Patent being signed to him for the same sometime before and the Lease also.

25th 6 mo., 1719.

John Hendrickson, of the County of New Castle, produces an Agreement made with Secretary Logan in the year 1701, for one hundred acres of Land near Redclay Creek, part of a Tract formerly Laid out to one Robert Robertson, but by him or his Heirs thrown up, so that the said one hundred acres was afterward granted to said Hendrickson, one hundred Acres more to his Brother-in-Law, Andrew Cock, and one Hundred acres to James Williams, all on new Rent. J. Hendricks gave his Oblig. for ye arrears of Rent and had his agreement as above, afterwards he paid ye Oblig. to G. D., with interest, in Cash, tho' G. D. charges himself only w'th 30 bush. of Wheat received.

William Grimson, who dwells on the Road going to Conestogo, married James Wiliams' Widdow, who sold that 100 a's to John Hendricks, but has not actually conveyed it to him.

Needfull that J. Hendrickson get a Deed from Williams' heirs, and another from the Descendants of his Brother-in-Law so that the whole may be confirmed to him upon his paying the arrears of Rent and James Williams' Obligation.

7th 10, 1719.

Jno. Hendrickson has got a sort of Conveyance or agreement from under the hands and seals of Wm. Grimson and Mary his wife, dated ye 5th 7b'r, 1719.

Peter Chamberlain having often applyed for a Lott in right of Joseph Jones, of Southampton, his purchase of 500 acres which has hitherto been refused him because the Deeds are dated about 2 months after the time ye first Purchase expired, but John Swift affirming that purchase was made and the money paid at the same time with his, who had his Lot, the Comm'rs agree that Peter shall have one of 49 f't front in the back streets and usual length with other Lotts, which is to be in full satisfaction of that Purchase.

28th 6 mo., 1719.

The Prop'r, by Deeds of L. and R., dated 22d and 23d Days of March, 1685, for £22 granted to Tho. Parkhurst, Citizen and Stationer, of London, 500 acres of Land to be laid out in this Province, quitrent one shilling for the said 500 acres, but there is a manifest Rasure which takes out the words (every hundred acres of) in the Release and done with Ink of a Different Colour from that with which the deeds were writ. The said Thomas Parkhurst, by like deeds of L. and Release, dated the 1st and 2d days of August, 1709, for five pounds, Money of Great Britain, granted the said 500 acres to Samuel Bury, of St. Edmundsbury, in Suffolk, Clerk, To hold to him, &c. The said Samuel Bury, by like deeds dated ye 9th, 10th days of 8b'r, 1718, for £10 granted the said 500 acres to John Head, of Philadelphia, Joyner, and Rebecca his wife, their heirs and assigns forever, who by like Indentures dated the 21st and 22d days of July, 1719, granted the said 500 acres to Derrick Jansen, of Germantown, who now desires a warrant to take up the same.

John Grigg desires the Grant of 2 Parcels of ordinary stony Land, containing one hundred acres each, joyning on his Tract. It was formerly laid out to one Rich'd Grigg, who never seated but threw it up again, he offers £30 for the whole, and desires an answer. Since granted p. order of J. L.

Isaac Self, whose Right to 500 acres of Land is entered in page   of these Minutes, hath now sent over to Antho. Morris a Power of Attorney, dated the 29 day of August, 1717, severally with John Gye, whose Father, Edward Gye, was a joynt purchaser with the grandfather of ye s'd Jo. Self in the said 500 acres, to take up the remaining 250 acres, ye other parcell being already laid out in Chester County. Anthony Morris request a Warr't for the same, also for ye Lot and Lib. Land.

Maurice Litle requests the grant of 45 foot of Bank and water Lot next below the Dock, first laid out to Tunis Lynch, who assigned the same by Indorsm't on the Patt't to Jno. Hockin, but no quitrent ever paid for it; the said Hockin left this Province above 20 years ago and has not been since heard of.

5th 9 mo., 1719.

The Prop'r, by Deeds of Lease and Release, dated 9th and 10th Days of 7b'r, 1681, granted to Jno. Coals, of Calcut, in Summersetshire, 1,000 acres of Land in this Province, quitrent 1s sterling p. C't.

The said Jno. Coals soon after came into this County and settled at George's Creek, but dying before he had taken up his Land, the same was claimed by one William Woodland, who dwelt in Maryland, and was his Sister's Son and nearest Kinsman. W. Woodland administered on his Estate in Newcastle County and had in his keeping the original Deeds and rec't belonging to the said 1,000 acres, but never took it up. Since his Decease, his Son and Heir Wm. Woodland, who dwells near Farlo Creek, in Maryland, by like Deed dated ye 22 and 23 days of 8b'r last, granted all the said 1,000 acres of Land, with ye Appertenances, to Samuel Powel, of Philadelphia, Carpenter, who desires Warr'ts for the Lotts, Land and Lib'y Land, the original Deeds and rec t being also delivered unto the said S. Powel.

Charles Springer requests a grant of 200 acres of Land near Sam'l Barker's and Redclay Creek, being midlin Land, for the Settlem't of his Children. Math's Peterson and Andrew Justice formerly applyed to the Comm'rs about the overplus in Mathias's Tract (see page 3d of these Min'ts), and now Andrew Justice again request a Grant for the same, he having licence from Matt's in his lifetime for settling thereon, as appears by his coming before the Comm'rs with him and there giving of him leave so to do. Andrew is willing to pay the arrearage of Quitrent at a bush'l Wheat p. C't from the first Survey to this time.

Xber, 11, 1719.

By J. L's Ord'r Granted to James Coal 200 acres. To Rich'd Bennet 200 a's; both adjoyning or near to Wm. Penn, Jun'r, Marsh, at £10 p. C't.

Enq'r about Jos. Growdon's Survey of his 2,000 acres, last granted to him, which he has procured to be laid out in ye Swamp within the Propr's Tract. Martin Overholts, with some Palatines, desires to purchase about 50 a's there.

MINUTE BOOK "I."

Xber, 16th, 1719.

Rich'd Parker, of Darby, produces a Deed poll dated the 22d Jan'ry, 1714, under the Hand and Seal of John Harrison, of Rocky Hill, in East Jersey, reciting one other Deed under ye Hand and Seal of Sam'l Thorn, of Nasau (alias Long Island), dated the 7th day of May, 1712, who therein conveyed unto the said J. Harrison two Lotts of Land at Moosehickamickum, being part of the Tract sold by Wm. Biles, as Attorney to Thomas Hudson, containing 250 acres each, but they add the overplus and make each Lott 275 acres. The said Jno. Harrison, for £100, Jersey Money, grants one Lot, Numb'r 3, to Tho. Hunlock, of Burlington, who by one other Deed dated the 17th 3 mo., 1714, for £77, Money of Pensylvania, granted the same lot to Rich'd Parker and Jno. Parker, and the said Jno. Parker being since Dead, the said Lot, as well by Survivourship as by his, the said Richard, being his Exec'r, is wholy vested in the said Richard, but the same falling within the Tract laid out to Dennis Rochford, or else taken by Thomas Stevenson in ye same right as this was first granted, and the said Rich'd being thereby deprived of holding the same he desires a Warr't to take it up elsewhere.

Peter Bizalion having purchased 500 acres of Land first granted by the Prop'r to Ralph Withers, and mentioned in the former Minutes of ye 4 m., 1703-4, Jno. Withers, only Surviving Brother to Ralph, who dyed without Heirs, by Deeds of L. and Release, dated ye 21 and 22 days of May last, for £20 Sterling granted the whole to Jno. Bezer, of the County of Chester, who by like Deed dated 2d and 3d days of ye 9th last, granted the same to John Warder, but it is in Trust for P. Bizalion.

The land was laid out in the year 1703, at Caln Township. The Lot and Lib. Land is now desired to be laid out also.

Joseph Wood having had a Grant for a Tract of Land near N. Castle, first taken up by one Arnoldus Delagrange, but for about 30 years deserted, and not claimed by any other Person, desires a Commission of Escheat may be directed to some Person in Order that may have a Confirmation. Edw'd Farmer and Fisher's plant, Tho. Shute, &c., William Gray for a square, A. Bickly for FFrampton, a Piece for Pasture, Jno. Coats for a Brickyard, D. Powel, Wm Trent for the Strip before his house at Schuylkill.

Tho. Bird desires about 300 a's near the London Tract, enq're of J's Taylor.

The Prop'r by Deeds of Lease and Release, dated ye 13,14 days of the second Month. 1682 (as p. recital), granted to James Delworth 1,000 acres of Land, of which there was laid out in Bucks

County 500 a's to himself. The said James afterwards by Indent'rs dated ye 5th 4 mo., 1686, for £25 granted to John Horner, of West Jersey, 480 a's, of which with the Liberty Land is the remainder thereof. John Horner, by Deed Poll dated ye 20th of the 12 mo., 1693, for the Consideration of 300 acres of Land in West Jersey, exchanged and conveyed the said four hundred and eighty acres to Phinehas Pemberton, since deceased. Israel Pemberton, Son and heir of the said Phinehas, desires a Warr't for taking up the same.

At a meeting of the Comm'rs the 22d Xb'r, 1719.
Present, Rich'd Hill, Isaac Norris, James Logan.

The Comm'rs having been informed that the Governments of N. York and of the Jerseys had Passed several Acts for running a division line between those Provinces and fixing the most Northerly branch of the River Delaware, which concern'd this Province very much to see that branch rightly fixed.

Therefore they concluded it expedient to Order J. Steel and J. Taylor to repair to Mackhackamack, a Dutch Township on the E. side of Delaware River, where certain Comm'rs and Surveyors from the above mentioned Provinces were appointed to meet, for which Purpose a Commission was provided, dated ye 19th of ye 4 mo. last, and the said James and Jacob set out on their Journey the 20th of the same Month, and returned again the 2d of the 6 mo. following, an Account of whose Journey is as follows.

In Consideration of J. S. and J. T.'s Expence and Service in their Journey to Mackhackamack and Cacheetang, a Warr't is Ordered to lay out to them Six hundred acres of Land back in the Province, which is to be in full Satisfaction for the same.

David Powel having applied to ye Comm'rs that sundry bonds might be taken for his Debt of £300 to the Trustees for 3,000 acres of Land which he agreed with J. Steel for, and having since sold it to sundry Persons desires that they may have their Land confirmed to them, whereupon J. Steel is ordered to take the said bonds into his Custody and give notice thereof to the People concerned that they may come in and alter the property of those Bonds and take titles for their Land, and David Powel is ordered without Delay to give and deliver to James Steel exact and distinct Draughts and Accounts of every man's quantity of Land so far as will make up ye 3,000 acres. Isaac Norris sets forth that he has purchased the Rights of Charles Marshall and Jonas Smith, laid out for 1,000 acres each, but upon examining the lines and trying the quantities, he finds a deficiency of   a's in Marshall's, which he desires may be laid out to him in the nearest Vacancy.

John Budd and Humphry Murry having purchased a Right of 5,000 a's of Land, the original Purchase of William Bacon, of London, 2,000 a's being already surveyed or secured to be laid out, desires to have the Remainder laid out on the low Ground a little below Mackhackamack, which being considered was thought not convenient to be allowed and therefore they are ordered to take it up elsewhere in the Province where vacant.

Tho. Shute, &c., Sets forth that he, together with W. Allen, having sometime ago purchased of one Wm. Chadwick 1,000 acres, the remaining part of James Claypoole's last purchase of 5,000 acres, and having now found a parcel of Land that cannot well be called vacant, near Parkeoming Creek, craves that he may take the same in that Vacancy, and for that Liberty agrees to pay to the Prop'rs use Fifty pounds.

Abraham Bickly, whose right to 500 acres entered before, is also permitted to take up the same in the Vacancy near Parkeoming.

At a meeting of the Comm'rs of Property 21st 11 mo., 1719-20.
Present, Rich'd Hill, Isaac Norris, James Logan.

The Meadow, Marsh and Cripple below the Town being exactly resurvey'd and a draught thereof laid before the Comm'rs, and the several Grants made heretofore by the Prop'r to sundry Persons being laid down on the same, and there being yet a claim from the Swedes and Wm. Carter from the Movamensen Patent for 2 Parcels of Meadow of 32 and 31 acres, which together make 63 Acres, which being in their Grant described in such Figures as don't suit with the place, It is thought expedient if those Swedes think fit to lay out those two parcels of Meadow in a regular Manner, which may be much more to their advantage than it now is, their present Bounds being uncertain.

The Comm'rs (viz.), Wm. Markham and Jno. Goodson, confirmed to Joseph Walker a piece of Ground in Philad'a, beginning at Corn'r post standing on the North side of a Swamp which parteth this Lot from Thomas Minshal's and Jno. Tibby's Lot, Thence N. 18 d. E. 40 foot, Then South 72 d. by Jane Blanchard's and Mary Southworth's Lots 80 f't to a Corn'r post standing by the aforementioned Swamp, from thence up the several Courses thereof to the place of Beginning, granted by a Warr't from ourselves, dated the 13th of

7b'r, 1689, and laid out by the Surveyor General's Ord'r ye same day and year to Jos. Walker, Renter, and the said J. W. requesting, &c., Know ye, &c., To have, hold and Enjoy the said Lot, &c., of the Mann'r of Springetsbury. Yielding and Paying, &c., five English Silver Shillings, or value thereof in Coin Curr't, upon the first day of the first Month, dated the 3d day of 8b'r, 1689.

The late Prop'r, by short Deeds of Lease and Release, dated the 10th and 11th days of the first Month, 1694, for £40 Sterl., granted to Joseph Peckover and partners (so expressed) 1,200 acres of Land in Pensylv'a, clear of Indian Incumbrancy, between the Rivers Delaware and Susquehannah, Quitr 1 Shill. Sterl. p. C't, to commence 7 years after taking up.

The said Joseph Peckover and Katherine his wife, Jno. Hichcock and Mary his wife (the said Mary and Katherine being Sisters, who together with one Sarah Long, also another Sister, advanced some part of the purchase Money, and were to have some Shares of the said Land, and therefore were in the original Deeds called partners), by large Deeds of Lease and Release, dated the 12th and 13th days of the 1st Month, 1715-6 for £30 Sterling granted and released the said 1,200 acres to Thomas Story, his Heirs and assigns forever, who by his Attorney, Wm. Fishborn, desires warr'ts to take up the same.

The Prop'r, by Deeds of Lease and Release, dated the 22 and 23 days of the 1st Month, 1681, granted to Jno. Brown, of Kingsley, Coun. Chester, in Great Britain, 250 a's of Land in this Province.

Jno. Brown, Son and Heir of the said Jno. Brown, by like Deeds dated the 1st and 2d days of the 12 Month, 1710, granted the said 250 acres to Jos. Helsby, now of this Province, who by Deed Poll dated the 3d of ye 2 mo., 1717, granted the Lib. Land appertenant to the same to J. Pemberton, who desires a Warr't for taking up the same.

At a meeting of the Comm'rs of Property ye 27th 11 mo., 1719-20.

Present, Rich'd Hill, Isaac Norris, James Logan.

Jno. Swanson, Christ'r Swanson, Peter Swanson having procured a Cavet to be put into the Survey'r Gen'ls Office against any further proceedings in running out of the Meadow and Cripple at Weccoco till their Rights for the same should be audited and Contested.

The Comm'rs (for such are the words of the Cavet) ordered that the Swansons should have notice of the meeting, who with their Council, Jno. Moor, appeared. He asserted that the Swansons had an early Grant for the said Cripple and Meadow, included with 800 acres granted their ancestors in the year 1664, and was Survey'd anno 1675, but did not produce it. He further alledged that the Crown had excepted all former grants and Possessions out of the Royal Charter granted to the late Prop'r, to which Sec'ry Logan producing the Royall Charter under the great Seal of England, challenged Jno. Moor or any other to find out that exception, which he nor none else could do because there was no such exception therein.

The Swedes were further told that if they would readily accept of the quantity of Meadow and Cripple granted by the Prop'rs Warr't, they should have it, otherwise it would be granted to other Persons, to which they made no direct answer but went muttering out of the House.

Thomas Stevenson having in his life time purchased of John Talman, of Flushing, on Long Island, 1,500 acres of Land, by Deed Poll dated ye 11th of June, anno 1719, part of 5,000 acres sold by Wm. Biles as attorney of Tho. Hudson, to William Lawrence, John Talman, Samuel Thorn, Joseph Thorn and Benj. Field, all of the same Island.

The said Benjamin Field, by his Deed Poll dated the 10th day of the 4th Month, 1719, for £89, York Money, granted and conveyed one thousand acres to the said Tho. Stevenson, being his, the said Benjamin, Share of the said 5,000 acres.

Joseph Thorn, of Flushing aforesaid, by his Deed Poll dated the 25th day of July, 1718, for £30, Curr't Money of America, granted and conveyed unto the said Tho. Stevenson 500 a's, being also part of the above 5,000 acres.

William Lawrence, of Flushing aforesaid, by his Deed Poll dated the 11th of June, 1719, for £57 10s, Money of New York, granted and conveyed 500 acres, a further part of the said 5,000 acres, to the said Tho. Stevenson.

The abovesaid Joseph Thorn, by another Deed Poll dated the 11th day of June, 1719, for £60, Money of N. York, granted unto the said Tho. Stevenson 500 acres, which with what he granted to him before makes his full share of the 5,000 acres first granted to them by Wm. Biles.

By the aforementioned Deeds it appears that the said Tho. Stevenson in his life time was intitled to 4,000 acres of Land, and soon after dyed, leaving his wife and Joseph Kirkbride his Exec'rs, who now requests Warr'ts for laying out the whole. NOTE. The whole 5,000 acres was formerly survey'd and sold to the above Persons of Long Island by Wm. Biles, under certain Bounds, but the greater part being under an earlier Survey to Dennis Rochford, is taken by his assignees.

The Comm'rs, S. Carp., W. Mark. and J. G., by Pat. dated 25th 4 mo., 1690, confirmed to Hugh Marsh, Renter, a Lot of Ground on the North side of Mulb. Street, in length 306 f't, in breadth 49, bounded N. with back Lots, E. with R. Marsh, his Lot, Southward with Mulb. Street, and to the Westward with James Potter's lot, quitrent five English Silver Shillings.

The same Comm'rs by another patent dated the same day and year with the former, confirmed to Sarah and Hugh Marsh (in right of Robert Marsh's purchase) one other lot of Ground of the same dimentions with the foregoing, Situate on ye E. side thereof and joyning thereto, quitrent one English Silver Shilling, the (one) shilling being on a resurvey, yet seems to be right because Robert Marsh was a Purchaser of 500 acres. Hugh Marsh, by an assignment on each of the above Patents, dated the first day of the Sixth Month, 1692, Did Bargain, sell and assign the aforesaid Lotts to James Poulter, who by Deed the last day of the 12 Mo., 1695-6, granted the abovesaid 2 Lotts, with one other Lot laid out to himself, of the same Dimentions with the former and joyning on the West side of them, to Obediah Holt, who by Deed Poll dated the 4 day of March, 1698-9, Granted the said 3 Lotts to Mary Shepard, who now holds them.

The Lot laid out to James Poulter is a rent Lot, viz., 5 English Shillings.

Samuel Allen (late of this Province, dece'd), purchaser of 2,000 acres of Land, had in his life time taken up in several Parcells 1,840 acres, so that at the time of his Death there remained 160 acres untaken up, which by his last will and Testament in writing, dated the 14th of the 10th Month, 1699, he bequeathed to his Grandson, Samuel Sisom, who about 10 years since went to Sea in a small Sloop to Antequa, which was stolen and run away with in the night and never heard of since. Jno. Sisom, Brother to the said Samuel, as heir to him, by Deed dated ye   day of the first Month, 1719-20, for £15 Granted the said 160 acres to Thomas Shute, who now desires a warr't to take up the same.

Jno. Budd and H. Murry requests the grant of a parcel of the Cripple below the Town.

Charles Brockden desires the grant of a piece of Cripple adjoyning on the west side of his Ditch and the north side of the Creek at Moyamensing, supposed to contain about 4 or 5 acres, also of a Resurvey on his other Meadow, in Ord'r to a Confirmation.

John Coats, Brickmaker, upon his earnest request and the Recommendation of several Bricklayers, has obtained a Grant for 3 acres of Ground for a Brick Yard by the Road side which leads to Wissahiconk and joyning to J. Logan's Pasture, for 14 years from the 1st day of the 1st Month, at the yearly rent of £6, and to level the Ground where he diggs his Clay every year, and surrend'r the whole so levelled and the Killns.

At a meeting of the Comm'rs of Property 5th 2 mo., 1720.
Present Rich'd Hill, Isaac Norris, James Logan.

The business of the Swamp and Cripple below the Town being further debated, and Jonath. Dickinson present, He requests a Warr't for his 200 acres already concluded on by the Comm'rs, and the addition of about 14 acres to be laid out to the Southward of Wm. Carter's Lot on the south side of Hay Creek, and to extend from W. C. Corner fifty Perches southward along the said Road, and from thence by a line drawn at Right Angles to the East side of Jno. Bankson's Cripple. To which the Comm'rs agree and a Warr't is ordered according in the same manner as Rich'd Hill's, which is in Evan Owen's name, which is already made out.

Clem't Plumsted and G. Fitzwater request the Grant of the strip of Swamp that lies between their East line and the west side of the Road, as designed to be laid out, but the quantity of the strip not being known, the request is referred till it be measured.

Andrew Hamilton desires the Grant of that part of the Swamp which lies to the Southward of the Wiccaco line and between the said Road and Delaware River, above the Mouth of Little Holl'dr Creek.

George Claypoole desires the Grant of a few acres of the same Swamp.

Tho. Shute desires a parcel of the Swamp where the Comm'rs shall think fit to allot it to him.

J. S. craves the Favour of such a quantity of the Swamp as the Comm'rs shall think fit to appoint him.

Signed a Warr't to J. Steel and J. Taylor for 400 acres of Land in Consideration of their Journey and Expences to Mackhackamack and Cathetang, upon the Branches of Delaware River.

Tho. Chalkley produces Deeds of Lease and Release, dated the 3d and 4th days of 7b'r, 1719, Executed in London, before three Masters of Ships belonging to this place, purporting a Grant of 500 acres of Land lying in Warminster Township, surveyed to John Jones, of London, Glover, who was originally purchaser thereof, who dying without Issue, his only Sister Elizab. Hilton, hath Conveyed the same unto T. Chalkley by the Deeds aforesaid.

In the year 1713 the said E. Hilton sent a Power of Attorney to Gilbert Falconer to dispose of the said Land and also a Certificate of the Deposition of Two Persons taken before the s'd Mag'e and alderm., of London, under the City Seal, who deposed that the said Eliz. Hilton is the only reputed sister and Heir of John Jones, late Citizen and Glover, of London, Dece'd, &c. The said Power and Instrument is now in this Office, as also a Return under Thomas Fairman's hand, sent hither with the above Instrum'ts.

Upon the general resurvey of the Province there appears to be within the Reputed lines 958 acres, the overplus whereof the said Thomas desires to purchase, or that he may take his 500 acres with the usual allowance on which side he thinks fit, and a Warrant for the Lib. Land and Lot thereunto belonging.

Rich'd Nickson, of Little Creek, in Kent County, requests the grant of about 100 acres of Marsh below the said Creek, near or in the Fork of the Cattail Pond.

Wm. Miller, late of Ireland, desires the Grant of about 200 acres of Land near Susquehannah; acq't Is. Taylor of it.

Hans Weaver desires the Grant of about 500 acres on Conestogo Creek, about 4 miles above Hans Graef.

Arthur Park desires the addition of about 40 or 50 acres of Land joyning on the South End of his Tract in Chester County.

Lewis David, now of the Welch Tract, in N. C. County, desires to have the Grant of about 200 a's about the Branches of Conestogo; it's for himself and three or four Neighb'rs.

Christian Bloom desires about 150 acres joyning to Dan'l Fierre. Sam'l Swallont desires about 50 acres near the same place. John Henry Kuirson's business.

At a meeting of ye Comm'rs of Property 29th 2 mo., 1720.
Present, Rich'd Hill, Isaac Norris, James Logan.

Signed a Warr't to Jonathan Dickinson for 200 acres of the Swamp or Cripple below the Town, and also for about 14 acres of the hassack Meddow, next below Wm. Carter's lot on the South side of Hay Creek, ordered the last meeting.

Signed a Warr't to Israel Pemberton for forty acres of the said Swamp below Hay Creek, between the Road and ye River.

The Comm'rs agree and appoint to meet the second fifth day of the Week in every month.

David Lloyd having procured the Land granted to Geo. Fox to be laid out near Ughland, in Chester County, desires the grant of about 800 acres to be added thereunto.

Jonathan Hayes in his lifetime purchased 125 acres of Land

of Rich'd Orm, who purchased the same of Humphry Bettely, who purchased of Tho. Wyn and John ap John, which is said to have been laid out in some of the Welch Townships but afterwards taken and held by some other purchaser and not now to be found.

Rich'd Maris and Elizabeth his Wife, Evan Lewis and Mary his wife (the said Elizt'h and Mary being Daughters and Heirs of Jonathan Hayes), by Deeds dated 8 and 9 days of the 2 mo. last, granted and conveyed the said 125 acres to Lewis Lewis, of Newtown, in Chester County, who desires to have the same laid out to him and the Addition of 175 a's to be laid out with it, for which he is willing to pay £17 10s.

Jehu Curtis having purchased the Plantation and Tract of Land late Peter Bizalion's, on the Murther Creek, in Kent County, desires to purchase the Marsh which lies on the front of the Land on the said Creek, it being about 100 acres, but the upper part is very much broken and Mirey.

Tho. Morgan, of Haverford, and Jenkin Davis, of Radnor, desires about 1,000 acres of Land near or at the branches of Conestogo.

Coll. French desires the Grant of a small vacancy at Swanwick. supposed to be about 100 acres, also about 1,000 acres back of Notting'm, at the usual price.

At a meeting of the Comm'rs the 9tn 4 mo., 1720.

Present, Rich'd Hill, Isaac Norris, James Logan.

Wm. Carter, Jno. Stiles and Benjamin Bankson appeared before the Com'rs, and after some time spent by their insisting on the 100 acres of Meadow mentioned in the Patent to be granted by Order from the Court of Upland, concluded and agreed to release the two Quantities according to the old Location in the Patent, and to take their respective Shares in distinct Parcels, which are now set out and appointed in the Draught of the whole Cripple and Meadow, and is ordered to be laid out to them and fixed under certain bounds, and to be returned into the Survey'r General's office in pursuance of a Warr't to be drawn for that Purpose.

Jacob Kolluck desires the Grant of a small Island in Lewis Creek, a little above the Town nearest to the Cape side, containing about ten acres.

Also the Grant of a Vacancy joyning on his Land, formerly Capt. Avery's, in forked Neck, upon Rehobath Bay, likewise if Samuel Davis do not Hold the Island in Lewis Creek, for which he obtained a Warr't some time ago with Condition to pay for the same within a small Space of time, which he has not yet comply'd with, that he, the said Jacob, may have the same at a reasonable rate.

George Gregg having purchased a sort of Right to about 50 acres of Land, part of a Tract first laid out to George Hogg, on new rent, desires to make a purchase of it, and that it may be for the future at a bushel of Wheat in proportion to 100 acres. He agrees to pay £12 for the 50 acres, and after the same rate, be it more or less; upon his paying one-half of the Money an Order of Resurvey is to be made out.

Jno. Robinson having purchased a sort of a Right to 200 acres of Land which lies in Thomas Pierson's draught, in the name of Jno. Champion, but no warr't nor Return can be found for it in the office. He desires to have a grant of it upon moderate Terms; offers £30 for the 200 acres and a bush'l Wheat p. C't. Send him word by the way of Jno. Bickly, his Father-in-Law, or his Bro. James or George. Gourdon Howard desires the Grant of about 200 acres of Land near Nottingham.

Rich'd Sherly desires the Grant of about 50 or 60 acres of Land joyning on his line of his other Land, between Murther Creek and Bawcomb brigg. He is willing to give

PHILADELPHIA, 28th, 5 mo., 1720.

This Day John Estaugh, as Agent to the London Company, in the presence of Isaac Taylor, came to the office and freely resigned the Survey made on that parcel of Land on the Lower side of Naaman's Creek, and on the River Delaware, for the like quantity to be laid out to him in Rockland Mannor, upon which an order is delivered to I's. Taylor for Surveying the same.

PHILAD'A, 9th 6 mo., 1720.

To ffr'd I's. TAYLOR:

The Bearer hereof, Gourdon Howard, who has wrought for a considerable time for J. Logan, hath now obtained a grant for about one hundred acres of Land in some vac't place near Notingham. Please to Survey such a quantity to him and the warr't shall be ready.

J. S.

This is entered in the Letter Book and therefore crossed out here.

James McVaugh produces a Deed und'r the hand and Seal of Tho. Rogers, of Bensalem, in the County of Bucks, for 100 acres of Serv'ts Land, 50 acres thereof as belonging to himself and 50 acres belonging to Hannah his wife, formerly Hannah Maugaridge. A certificate under B. Chambers' hand says that said Rogers served his time to the Society of Traders, but the said Hannah being dead long before the above deed bares date, cannot have her head land.

The Prop'r, by Indentures of Lease and Release, dated the 10th and 11th days of Octob'r, 1681, granted to Tho. Cobb, of London, Shoemaker, 250 acres of Land in this Province, to hold to him, his heirs and ass. forever, quitrent 1 shill. p. C't. Tho. Cobb, by like Deeds dated ye 13th and 14th days of Feb'ry, 1684, granted the said 250 acres to Christopher Davison, Citizen and Fishmonger, of London (afterwards of this Province), who obtained a Warr't for laying out the same, dated the 9th 4 mo., 1685, and afterwards by Deeds dated the 21 day of March, 1709, for £50 granted the said 250 acres to Tho. Tress under certain lines and bounds in the County of Bucks.

Tho. Tress, Nephew to the above said Thomas, by vertue of a certain Instrum't to him, made in the life time of Tho. Tress, the Elder, by Indent'rs of Lease and Release, dated the 18th and 19th days of August, 1719, for £20 granted the said 250 acres to Jeremiah Langhorn, under the same lines and Bounds above mentioned, but upon enquiry there is no such Tract to be found in the place where it is described, wherefore the said Jeremiah requests a Warr't to lay it out elsewhere.

The Prop'r, by Deeds of Lease and Release (large), dated the 21 and 22 days of 8b'r, 1681, granted to Robert Lodge, of Macham, in the County of York, yeoman, 500 acres of Land in this Province, quitr't 1 Shill. Sterling for each Hundred acres.

Robert Lodge, by like Deeds dated the 11th and 12th days of August, 1686, for £25 Granted and conveyed the said 500 acres, with the app's, unto Rob't Whillon, of Snape, in the said County of York, now of this Province, who in the 10 and 11 mo., 1686-7, obtained Warr'ts for 250 a's and 500 a's, but no return appears to either, also for his Lot and lib. Land, which are laid out. He holds 300 acres in Dublin Township where he dwells, and the other 200 Rich'd Buffington holds in Chester County.

Jacob Collock desires the Grant of a small Island in Lewis Creek, at the upper end of the Town, near to a lot of his Son Jacob, for whom he intends it.

Nich's Hicks, of Springfield Mannor, desires the Grant of 100 acres of Land in the said Mannor for his Son, who would settle on the same, and that when a price is set for it he may have time for payment of the Money, and in the meantime to pay Interest for the same.

Tho. Tidball desires a piece of vac't Land in Rocklands, formerly seated by one John Pearse, who afterwards run away and left it. He proposes to give £32 p C't, or in proportion.

John Leatherbe having begun to build a Mill on a Branch of Tohickon, near the great Swamp, in Bucks County, by the persuasion of some of the Inhabitants there, now desires a Grant for the Land, it being vac't.

John Watson desires the Grant of about 300 acres, above Manatany 3 or 4 Miles, and till he can have such a Grant he desires that he may settle; leave given p. Sect'y L, 22, 7, 1720.

Wm. Brakin desires the Grant of 200 acres of Land in N. Castle County, Christiana Hundred, formerly Tho. Graves.

John Cottom desires the Grant of about 200 acres on Octorara, about 3 or 4 miles from Nottingham, who assigns it to Rich'd Tranter.

Rich'd Hughes desires about 200 acres near Nottingham. Speak to I's. Taylor, near young Wm. Brown's.

Widdow Prees desire her Lot may be confirmed to her near ye Centre.

4th 9b'r, 1720.

Edmund Grub and Jno. Grub, with Jacob Savoy, John Savoy and Peter Poilderbeck, came together and produced a Return of 600 acres of Land back from the River in Rochlands, in Ephram Harman's own hand, dated the 19th 7b'r, 1682, Said to be in pursuance of a Warr't from N. C. Court. The 600 acres are laid out to John Grub, Isaac Savoy and David Hendricks in equal shares. Is. Savoy and David Hendricks dying, Jno. Grub, Sen'r, in his life time claimed the whole by Survivorship when the Prop'r was last here, but the Prop'r having when first here granted to Savoy and Hendricks two Tracts in West Jersey, in the place called Penny Neck, in Exchange for their Lands on this side of Delaware, which was always understood to be in full Satisfaction for their whole claim, wherefore the said Jacob Savoy, Jno. Savoy and P. Poilderbeck were told that if they should make any Grant of the 400 acres, part of the 600 acres, their Lands which they enjoy in Penn's Neck will be called in Question, and that the Proprietary will insist upon holding the Lands on the side the River. Jacob Savoy says they have absolute Deeds without any Conditions of Exchange, which he says he will produce, till then the affair is referred.

16th 9b'r, 1720.

Jacob Savoy brought the above Deed for 350 acres of Land, the Consideration for which is £30, Merch'tble pay at current price, with other good causes and Consideration, the Prop'r thereunto moving, the quitrent 3 bush'ls of winter Wheat on every 29th of 7b'r unto the said W. P., his heirs and assignes. Signed by James Nevil, agent.

The Courses of the whole Tract is upon Rasures, as also the Quantity of acres in as many places as mentioned and the quitrent all writ in a Different Hand from that of the Deed.

Also another Deed from J. Nevil for 400 acres in West Jersey to John Hendrickson, of one Tree Hook. Consideration £32, quitrent 4 bush'ls of wheat, no Rasures on this.

Elisha Gatchal desires the Grant of about 50 or 100 acres of Land joyning on Nottingham for the Conveniency of some low ground to mow on.

John Curtis the grant of a parcel of vac't Marsh near George's Creek, for the conveniency of mowing Hay.

9b'r, 17, 1720.

Evan Powel, Hugh Morgan and some others from Nottingham inform that there is a strip of Land between the south line of Nottingham and the line which David Evans lately run from the mouth of Octorara, of about a mile broad. Those Persons who settled the said strip, some for many years, now desires a grant from hence to Survey the same to them, they having as they say applyed heretofore for Grants from this Office, which was delayed at that time because of the uncertainty of that time.

The Prop'r, by Patent dated 26, 1 mo., 1684, Confirmed to Joseph Cookson a Tract of Land on the North side of Whiteclay creek, in New Castle county, containing 219 acres, said to be first laid out to Jno. Can by the Prop'rs Warr't, who assigned to Jos. Cookson, the Rent 1 bush'l of Wheat for every 100 acres, to be paid at N. C. The words (one bush'l winter wheat) are on a Rasure, but seems to be writ in the same hand as the Patent. The present owner's name is Wm. Hughes.

Isaac Norris being at Burlington when E. Powel and the other Nottingham People requested the Grant of the above strip of Land, so that the Commr's could not meet about it, wherefore it was thought expedient by Secret'y Logan that J. S. should agree with those Persons and take that agreem't from under their Hands and then write to Isaac Taylor to Survey to each of their Settlements so much Land as will accommodate them, which is accordingly done.

Daniel Longanacre having the last Spring obtained a Grant for 200 acres of Land on the west side of Schuylkill, and then paid £16 of the money, presumed to set down within the lines of Joseph Pike's Land, and therefore cannot hold it, whereupon he request the Grant of about 200 acres adjoyning to G. Burson's, near Gilberts' Mannor. He is willing to give £25 p. C't, which if the Land prove ordinary he is to have it, if as Good as Burson's he is to pay more.

---

9 mo., 25th, 1720.

Antho. Morris, Jun'r, requests that he may purchase of the Reversion of his Bank and Water Lott where he dwells, being 77 foot in front, which according to the former computation continued to this time, amounts to about £138 12s.

---

9 mo., 29th, 1720.

John Buckly, Joseph Grub and Benjamin Moulder having purchased a Parcel of Land on the Lower side of Naaman's Creek, of John Estaugh, as Agent to the London Company, did before the said John's departure mutually agree with him that he should resign the said Land to the Proprietary Trustees, and y't they might take their Title from them, which the said John Estaugh did accordingly in this office ye   day of   , and thereupon had orders to Isaac Taylor to Survey to the said London Company the like Quantity of Land in any part of the Mannor of Rocklands that was not otherwise appropriated.

The said Jno. Buckly, Jos. Grub and B. Moulder therefore desire that they may hold the same Land at and under the priee they agreed with Jno. Estaugh, which is Granted, they paying two years Interest, which is from the time of their said agreement.

Agreed with Jno. Buckly for the old Plantation of Stockdel's at £3 p. ann. for 5 or 7 years.

Jno. Buckly says that Isaac Savoy and David Bilderbeck were seated on the Land where Stockdel's Plantation as 'tis called, when he first came into the Country in the year 1682, That they had but 50 acres each of them on the River's side, That soon after the Prop'r happening to come to Savoy's and Bilderbeck's House, they complained to him for want of Marsh, whereupon the Prop'r told them that he had Land and Marsh on the other side of the River which he would exchange with them for their Land on this side of Dellaware, which they were willing to do, and in order to which Rob't Wade and some other person were appointed to view their Land on this side and allow them so much on the other side ye River, and the Prop'r was to pay them for their improvements besides the Land as would Satisfy them, which was according done, whereupon the said Isaac and David removed over the River and had their Land confirmed to them there and never to his Knowledge made any claims to any Lands on this side Dellaware during their lives.

Hollyday, Minister, of Appoquinaming, requests the Grant of about 200 acres of Land joyning near A. Peterson, or another Parcel about the same quantity, Joyning on Hans Jacquet. He is dead and nothing done in it.

Robert Reddick and Jno. Camel desires the Grant of 100 acres of vacant Land joyning to Camel, being part of Judge Guest's Land in N. C. County.

Silas Prior requests 100 acres of Land in N. C. County for John Twiggs, joyning on Henry Suitgar's Tract.

David Lewis, of Haverford, having by a recommendation to Isaac Taylor about 2 years ago, procured 2 parcels of Land to be run about on a branch of Conestogo, Containing together 600 acres or thereabouts, for which he now desires a Warr't.

25, 1 mo., 1721.

James Smith and James Daniel, by the Intercession of Elisha Gatchel, are permitted p. Sect'y Logan to settle on some Lands near Nottingham, and that Isaac Taylor be ordered to lay out 200 acres to each of them.

Isaac Taylor, in behalf of his Son John, represents that there is about 500 acres of Land adjoyning to John in Thornsbury, kept under the Thumb of J. Baker, but is really none of his. He desires to purchase it and will make good pay.

John Buckly and B. Moulder were to give ten Shilings p. acre for the Land on Naaman's Creek Dam; agreed 26th 1 mo., 1719.

At a meeting of the Commissioners the 22, Xber, 1720.

John Songhurst produces original Deeds of Lease and Release, The Prop'r, to his Father, Jno. Songhurst, for 250 acres, dat'd 23 and 24 May, 1682. The Prop'r, to Jno. Burchal for 500 acres, dated ye 15 and 16 day of May, 82, whose Brother and Heir, Tho. Burchall, sold the same to Jno. Songhurst, the Father, by Deed of Lease and Rel., dated the 24 and 25th of July, '85. Jno. Songhurst alleges that there has been but part of the Land mentioned in the above Deeds yet laid out, therefore requests that a Warr't for the remainder may be granted to him.

But it seems strange that J. S. having lived so many years in the County should delay taking up any Land due to him till this time, wherefore the Comm'rs delays granting a warr't till further search be made.

Joseph Jones upon a late resurvey made on his Tract of Land in Richlands, als., the great Swamp, finds the length of the lines of that Tract to be different trom what they are said to be in ye Patent, but the Courses and Quantity of Land to be the same as are therein expressed, he therefore requests that the defect may be supply'd, which is done by an ample Endorsement on the Patent and Signed by A. H., I. N, and J. L.

Signed the several Warr'ts following (viz.):

To Andrew Hamilton for about 55 acres of the Swamp below the Town at 10s p acre.

To the Governor, Wm. Keith, Esq'r, 10 acres of the Swamp below the Town at 10s p. acre.

To Clem't Plumsted, Geo. Fitzwater and J. Steel ab. 18 acres at 20s p. acre.

All dated ye 20th of ye 12 mo., FFeb., 1719-20.

Christian Allebaugh being desireous to purchase 150 acres of Land in the Great Swamp where the Inhabitants are very desireous of his settling, he being a good weaver by Trade.

David Gibbon desires about 200 acres near Pickering's Tract, where he has made some Settlem'ts, he is willing to give £15 p. C't.

Jno. Mathews and James his Son, are permitted to Settle near the Musgrave's, at the Branches of Octoraro, and to have 200 acres each of them as soon as the Warr'ts can be signed, being recommended by the Musgrave's, and allowed to settle p. J. Logan.

Walter Walters, Evan Jones and Stephen Evans having with some others been back in the woods between Conestogo branches and Schuylkil! River to find out some convenient place of Settlement for themselves and families, for which they propose to take up in the whole about 2,000 acres, desires a Grant for the same. The above Evan Jones requests that Hugh Jones, of East Town, may have 1,000 acres of the above Tract.

Ew'd Green desires that one Christopher Hewston, may have the Grant of about 150 acres of Land, a vacancy between Wm. Ball's and Edw'd Green's Land, the said Hewston having seated on the same.

Elias Noerdine, of Appoquinoming, desires the Grant of about 200 acres of Land adjoyning to that lately granted to Johannes Jaquet, in the Neck between Appoq'g and Blackbird's Creek.

6 mo., 1721.

Peter Wents and Lawrence Switzer desires the Grant of about 1,200 acres of Land at a place called Sawcany, about 7 miles to the Northward of E. Oley.

7b'r, 21, 1721.

Wm. Kirkpatrick, of Christina Hundred, requests the Grant of about 200 acres of Land near the Widdow Houghton's, formerly seated by Jno. Day, and by him left, but never survey'd.

7b'r, 25, 1721.

John Read requests the grant of about 100 acres of Land near the Tract formerly laid out to Jno. Budd, to the Northward of the line run by the Lord Baltemore, where he has purchased some Improvem'ts made by another Person. Eli Gatchell has recommended him as an honest man and desire he may have his request.

8b'r, 27th, 1721.

Dav'd Nevan requests the Grant of a small vacancy lying between his Tract, formerly Geo. Read's, and the Land of Bryan McDonald, about   acres.

Tho. Price and Rees Price desires the Grant of about 1,000 acres between them, at the branches of little Conestogo.

28, Xb'r, 1721.

Nicho. Jones desires 100 acres near Octoraro. I have sent him the following noat (viz.), Nicho. Jones has apply'd to the office of p'pty for 100 acres of Land near Octoraro, where he has or intends to make a Settlem't, which application is entered in the said Office till he can have a Warr't for the Land.

Recommended p. Jno. Fincher.

J. S.

11 mo., 2, 1721.

In the year 1715 one Peter Hall, agreed for about 200 acres of Land near Jno. Houghton's, in Christina Hundred, on which he procured a Survey and made some improvement, but afterwards left it again and sold what he called his Improvem'ts to Silas Prior for about £15.

John Houghton in his lifetime applyed to this Office to purchase the same Land (it then being left void), and an expectation was given him, as also to his Widow since his decease, of their having it, but Silas Prior alleging the great Loss it will be to him if he cannot have the Benefit of P. Hall's agreem't, after having actually paid for his Improvem'ts as above, desires that he may be excepted and taken for the payment of the above agreem't, with Interest to this time, which is granted.

---

11 mo., 6, 1721.

The Prop'r, by Deeds of Lease and Rel., dated ye 17 and 18 days of 8b'r, anno 1681, granted to Wm. Kent, Citizen and Merch't Taylor, of London, 1,250 acres of Land in this Province, quitrent one shilling for every hund. acres.

The said Wm. Kent, by like deeds dated the 10 and 11 days of 7b'r, 1685, for £30 conveyed the said 1,250 acres to Walter Hill, of Bewdley, in the County of Worcester.

Walter Hill, by like Deeds dated the 28th and 29th of 7b'r, in the said year 1685, for £46 conveyed all the said 1,250 acres to Tho. Milner, of Kidderminister, in the same County of Worcester, Merch't, who by like Deeds dated 7th and 8th days of April last, Granted and conveyed the 1,200 acres to Jno. Davis of Philad'a, who desires warr'ts for taking up the same, with the Lotts and lib. Land.

John Seagar sets forth that he is seated on a Tract of Land to the Northward of Octoraro, upon a Right from Maryland, but since he is informed that it is under a Pensylvania Survey, and therefore desires from this office a grant for 360 acres, for which he is willing to pay the usual prices as Lands are granted at in those parts. This request is to be further considered of and inquiry made what Survey it is under. It is the same Land which John Budd took up and afterwards obtained other Warr'ts in the same Right. Vide these Minutes.

The Prop'r, by Deeds dated the 25, 8b'r, 1681, granted to Wm. Jenkins 1,000 acres of Land in this Province of Tenby, Coun. Pembroke, Emasculator.

Wm. Jenkins, by Indent'rs dated ye 3, 7, 1686, for £11, Money of Engl'd, granted to Francis Howel, of LLancilio, in the County of Carmarthen, 500 acres of the same, with the Proportion of lib. Land and the moiety of the City Lot.

Francis Howel, by his last Will and Test't dated the 15th of the 1st mo., 1685 (which could not be), gives and bequeaths unto Thomas Howel 300 acres of the said 500 acres. The said Tho. Howel, by Indentures dated ye 1, 7b'r, 1700, for £30 grants the said 300 acres unlocated to James Thomas.

David LLoyd and I's. Norris, by Deed Indented, dated the 10th 6 mo., 1706, granted to Ja's Thomas 156 acres, part of 1,000 confirmed to them by Patent in Right of Tho. LLoyd's deed, the Patent dated ye 25th 8b'r, 1703.

The Prop'r granted his Warr't for locating ye 300 a's ye 2 of 7b'r, 1700.

Of which J. Thomas has sold to Jno. Sharpless, ... 150
And to Joseph Coleman the Dwelling House and Plantation, ... 254
And has yet left 150
                                                            ———
                                                            554

The last 150 a's he has also sold to J. Coleman, and calls 100 a's of it the overplus of Tho. LLoyd's Land, being within his old lines, as his proposals of State, p. Vendue says.

12 mo., 26th, 1721-2.

Wm. Bowel desires the Grant of a square of Ground in the City between Mulberry and Sassafras Streets, and between the 9th and 10th Streets from Dellaware. He is willing to pay 40s Sterling p. ann., to commence from the first of the first Month next.

John Daniel desires the Grant of about 1 or 200 acres of Land on Rent between the Branches of Appoquinaming and Blackbird's Creek.

1 mo., 6, 1721-2.

Jno. Wyeth desires the grant of about 1 or 200 acres of Land adjoyning to David Brintnell's, near Marlborow, in Chester County; he says he can pay for it upon the Grant.

John Evan having some time ago requested the Grant of about 100 a's of Land joyning on the line of the Welch Tract, in Newcastle county, and now by an acc't brought up from several of the Neighbours they say it is very ordinary and without Water, therefore he is to have it at £12, if but 100 acres and in proportion if more or less, and a Bush. of Wheat quitrent.

Owen Thomas desires the Grant of about 600 acres of Land on the West side of Schuylkill above Joseph Pike's Tract.

The Prop'r, by Deeds of L. and Rel. (large printed), dated the 12th and 13th days of April, 1682, granted to Rich'd Wooler, of Golding lane, London, Tanner, 500 acres of Land in this Province, quitrent one shilling p. C't.

Dawson Wooler, Son and Heir of Tho. Wooler, who was Son and Heir of the said Rich'd Wooler, by Deeds of L. and Rel., dated 27th and 28th of May, 1714, for £12 Sterl. granted the said 500 acres, with the app'r., unto Sam'l Arnold, of London, upholder (To hold, &c.)

Sam'l Arnold, by his Power of Attorney, dated the 28th of May, 1714, directed to Gilbert Falconer and Clem't Plumsted, Authorises them to take up the said Land, wherefore they desire Warr'ts for the same (there was a Warr't granted by the Prop'r to Marg'rt Wooler for 490 acres and to Tho. Wooler for the lib. Land), vide old warr't book.

---

3 mo., 1, 1722.

John Butcher desires the Grant of about 50 or 60 acres of Land joyning on his Tract where he dwells, the Lands of Alex'r Adams and Philip Bavele, near Drawer's Creek, in Newcastle County. He is willing to give five Shillings p. acre, and to pay next fall. He has assigned his Pretence to Peter Laroux, Brother-in-Law to And'w Peterson.

Abraham Emmet, Jun'r, being possessed of 100 acres of Land in a fork of Elk River, which he purchased from a Maryland Survey, and now desires a Grant from this office to secure the same.

William Emmet desires a Grant of about 200 acres.

At a meeting of the Commissioners of Property the 16th day of ye 2d mo., anno 1722.

Present, Rich'd Hill, Isaac Norris, James Logan.

The Comm'rs having some days ago been informed that the Gov'r was gone towards Susquehannah River and had taken Jacob Taylor with him, which gave them some apprehensions of a design he might have on a parcel of Land on the other side of Susquehannah, where was supposed to be copper mine, whereupon they thought it expedient to send J. Steel with a Warr't under their Hands and Seals, dated ye 5th Instant, directed to himself and Jacob Taylor, authorizing them to Survey and lay out for the use of the Trustees (till the Mortgage Money and Interest due thereon should be paid and then to revert to the Heirs and Devises of the late Proprietary) the quantity of two Thousand acres of Land, inclosing within the lines of Survey the Land wherein is supposed to be the Copper Mine. J. Steel accordingly set out with the Warr't and met with J. Taylor at Conestogo, who readily accompanied him over Susquehannah, where after some opposition made by one John McNeal, by the Gov'rs Express order, as he said, they proceeded on the Survey on the 10th Instant and finished the same on the 11th, a Return whereof they now produce.

2 mo., 1722.

James Steel being appointed to attend Newcastle court, as he was setting out on his Journey thither from Philad'a, directed Sec'ry Logan to give George Dakeyne an order in writing to Survey to Coll. John French 300 acres of Land on Octoraro Creek, which he according did at Newcastle, a Copie whereof here follows.

George Waltham desires the Grant of about 200 acres of Land on the South side of Musmellon Creek, between Art. Verkirk and his Brother William Waltham.

Peter Higgat desires the Grant of about 200 acres between Thomas Read and Thunder Hill. If Elisha Gatchill and the old Inhabitants think well of his settling there, Isaac Taylor may run some lines for him when he goes that way, and Peter must come up and give security to the office.

Joseph Meredith desires the Grant of about 200 acres of Land on the west side of Tho. Griffith and on the North of James Morgan.

4 mo., 2, 1722.

Edw'd Green, Jun'r, desires the Grant of about 100 acres of Land between Wm. Brakin's and the Successors of Jno. Champion, in Christina Hundred. He is willing to give .
This is since granted to John Ball by order of Sec'ry Logan.

Joseph Kirkbride having purchased of Jeremiah Fowler and Wm. Thorn, both of Long Island, 500 acres of Land, part of Thomas Hudson's original purchase, already entered in these Minutes, desires a Warr't for laying it out. It is part of William Lawrence's share of that purchase, which was 1,000 acres, the other 500 were sold to Tho. Stevenson in his life time, whose Widdow and Exec'x has taken it up and sold it.

Wm. Davis desires the Grant of about 1 or 200 acres of Land near O. Roberts' Plantation at the French Creek, Recommended by O. R.

Gordon Howard desires the Grant of about 200 acres of Land about 2 Miles from Galbreith's Mill, to the Northward and near 4 miles back of Susquehannah River.

Sam'l Tomlinson requests 1 or 200 acres near Blackbird's Creek, in N. C. County.

Tho. Osborn, of Sussex county, desires the Grant of 200 acres of Land on the Branches of the Broad Creek.

The Comm'rs, S. C., W. M., R. T. and J. G., by Pat. dated ye 31st 7b'r, 1692, Confirm'd to Israel Harrison and John Ellice 435 acres of Land in two Parcells, joyning together on both sides of Christina Creek, about 2 Miles above the Bridge, about 60 acres whereof is now held by one David Thomas, the Remainder belongs to John Ellet, of Kingcessing, who now requests the addition of a parcel of vacant Land adjoyning to the N. W. side of the Tract to accommodate a Settlem't for his Son, who now dwells there.

John Asler, a Taylor, having some time ago made some Settlement near Arthur Parke, on the Branches of Octoraro, was afterward by some accident drowned at back Creek, he being a single man and leaving no child, his nearest kinsman, Wm. Foster, has taken upon him to pay his Debts, and therefore desires a Grant of about 300 acres where the Settlement is made, to prevent any other Person taking the same.

Edw'd Dougharty, who Married Mary Deadwood, from R. Hill's, by his wife, requested some time ago to settle near Stephen Atkinson's, above Conestogo Mannor, now desires that he may have 1 or 200 acres Granted to him.

Ex., 6 mo., 23, 1722.

John Ball having obtained a Survey about 9 years ago on a parcell of Land on Whiteclay Creek, in N. C. County, containing 103 acres, now desires that Survey may be allowed of, with the Addition of about 50 acres more out of the adjoyning Vacancy, which request is favoured by Secretary Logan, he paying £20 purchase and a bush'l of Wheat quitrent p. C't.

Tho. Powel, late of Providence, in Chester County, first purchaser of 500 acres of Land in this Province, in his life time by Deed of Gift did grant to his Son T. Powel, one-half of his Estate, Real and Personal, and the other half also after his and his wife's decease, which some time after happened, and the said Tho. Powel, ye Son, in Consideration of a sum of Money to be paid to his two Daughters, did by his last will give and bequeath all his Estate, Real and Personal, to his wife Sarah Powel, and soon after dyed, after whose decease John Powel and Joseph Powel, surviving sons and Heirs of T. Powel, the Elder, by Deed Poll bearing date ye   day of   , granted and Released the whole to the said Sarah Powel, who afterwards married with Peter Dicks, and then by their Deed dated ye 24th 6 mo., 1722, conveyed the Proportion of Lib. Land unto J. Steel, who requests a Warr't to take up the same.

Rees Jones, of the Welch Tract, in N. C. County, requests the Grant of a vacancy lying between his Land where he dwells and the Tract of John Holes.

Nich's Grainger, of Sussex county, desires the Grant of about 100 acres of Marsh lying within his Pasture in the south side of Musmellon Creek, between his first Land and the Creek, and that he may be favoured with a Warr't when the Comm'rs shall please to grant him the same.

In or about the year 1686 there was surveyed to one John Murray, about 300 acres of Land on the lower side of Christina Creek, 4 or 5 miles from N. Castle, on new Rent, which was afterward, as is said, sold to Wm. Hewston, who by his last Will and Testament bequeathed it to John Wilson, the then Presbiterean Minister at Newcastle, and after him to those that should succeed him in that Ministry, but Anthony Hewston having got the writings relating thereunto into his Hands offers to sell the same.

Abraham Emmit, Jun'r, has a desire to purchase it and would be advised how, for W. Hewston having absolutely devis'd it by Will, Anthony Hewston cannot claim it as William's Heir.

Sam'l Littler desires the Grant of about 300 acres of Land to the Northward of Nottingnam, for settling of his Sons (he having Six), 'tis among the Barrens. He is one of the first settlers and has continued in the interest of this Province against the Claims of Maryland; he is recommended by E. Gatchel.

Patrick Cammel requests the addition of 100 acres. Speak to J. Taylor on Susquehannah.

Sam'l Gilbert desires the Grant of about 200 acres next above the Land of John Jones in Warminster.

Tho. and Simeon Taylor request about 300 acres each to the Northward of Nottingham, Philip Taylor, of Thornsbury, is their Uncle and will see the Land p'd for. Let Philip hear.

———

17, 9 mo., 1722.

This was given to Rees Thomas upon his Brot'r illness:

I hereby certify that I did agree with Rees Thomas on behalf of his Brother, Wm. Thomas, for 200 acres of Land in Radnor, formerly held by Rees Prees on Rent, which agreem't is entered in the Land Office and I presume will be confirmed accordingly.

J. STEEL.

The price is forty Pounds for the whole in Consideration that Wm. Thomas also purchased ye right of Rees Prees.

———

At a meeting of the Commissioners the 20th 9th, 1722. Present, Rich'd Hill, Isaac Norris, James Logan.

The Officers of Maryland having in June last seized and taken into Custody Isaac Taylor, Survey'r of Chester County, and Elisha Gatchel, a Justice of the Peace for the same County, under pretence of their having invaded the Lands of or belonging to Maryland in Right of this Province; The said Persons applied to the Comm'rs not long after, representing that as they were most unjustly taken Prisoners for no other Cause than their acting in their Stations in the Service of the Prop'r of this Province, and are like to be at Charges which 'tis unreasonable they should defrey, seeing the Trouble they are and shall be put to in their defence, is more than they can well bear, and it was then the Opinion of the Commissioners that some Money should be advanced to them out of the Prop'rs Estate to support and encourage them in defending their cause, whereupon £3 7s 10d was then paid them, besides a Pistol given Thomas Reid towards paying for an Express to Philad'a on a like Occasion, four Pounds two Shillings paid Elisha Gatchell, expended by him for an Express to Annopolis and Philad'a, £4 paid John Barnes for going Express on the same Occasion to Annopolis, £2 8s expended by J. Logan and Rob't Ashton in their Journey to Cecil court on the same business, and fifteen shillings paid John Barnes this Month for an Express to Newcastle, in all amounting to £

It is considered that a further sum be advanced to the said Isaac and Elisha, not exceeding Ten Pounds for the present, towards supporting their Charges under their Confinem't in Cecil county, and to be further considered according to the Measures that shall be further taken by the Govern't of Maryland.

The Prop'r, by Deeds of Lease and Release, dated 26th and 27th of 8b'r, 1681, granted to Rich'd Webb, of Kingston, upon Thames, Linnen Draper, 1,000 acres of Land in this Province, quitrent 1 Shill. p. C't acres.

The said Rich'd Webb, by like Deeds dated the 1st and 2d day of Xb'r, 1684, Granted the said 1,000 acres to Abrah'm Bonyfield, his Heirs and ass. forever.

Abraham Bonyfield, Son and heir to the above said Abr. Bonyfield, By like Indentures dated the 22d and 23d days of June, 1722, Granted and Released the same 1,000 acres, with the app'es, unto Wm Passmore, his Heirs and Assigns forever. Wm. Passmore, by Deeds of L. and Rel., dated 8, 9, 5 mo., 1723, Conveyed 500 acres of the said Land to John Cartmell, of Rawcliff, in the Co. Lancaster. The Prop'r, by lease and Release, Entered in page 75, foregoing, granted to Wm. Bryant and Jno. Wisdom 500 acres of Land in this Province.

The said Bryant conveyed 250 acres to George Carter, who has had the same Surveyed in Chester county, and Jno. Wisdom dying without any division before made of the Land, Wm. Bryant, by right of Survivourship, has also granted the other 250 acres to Wm Passmore, who affirms that Wm. Bryant notwithstanding his right of Survivourship gave to the Children of John Wisdom their share of the purchase Money; he desires Warr'ts for it.

The Commissioners in the year 1713 Granted their Warrant to John Wyeth for 53 acres of Land near Brandywine, in Bromingham Township, with Condition that if he paid for the same in three Months after the Date thereof the Survey was to be Valid, otherwise to be void, but the said John has not, nor is ever like to do it, wherefore John Wilson, who has lately purchased Edw'd Bucher's Plantation, on which the 53 acres joyns, desires to have the same on reasonable terms and promises to make good pay.

Susannah McCane, Widdow, having made some Improvement on a piece of Land near Nottingham some time ago, seated by one Wm. Reynolds, She having three Sons able to work, requests the Addition of a small vacancy thereon adjoyning. Speak to J's. Taylor ab't it.

Hugh Durborow, Survey'r of Kent County, represents that several Persons have some years agoe seated themselves on the Back of the said County, near the Borders of Maryland, who have duly paid their respective Taxes and done their Duty in the said County, and that they are honest, quiet people, wherefore he requests that their Names may be entered in this office for their Settlem'ts till Warr'ts may be obtained for the same, whose names are as follows:

	Acres.		Acres.
Rob't Meredith,	200	John Wheeler,	200
Sam'l Willoughby,	100	Rich'd Tanner,	150
John Dill,	200	Mark Barden,	200
Hugh Parry,	100	Eph. Emerson,	200
James Anderson,	100	Lawrence Bedshold,	200
Dan'l Hudson,	100	Hugh Durborow,	200
Rich'd Parvis,	100		

These are seated near the Bear Swamp.

	Acres.		Acres.
David Shadley,	200	Wm. Anderson,	100
Tho. Folks,	100	Wm. Thompson,	100
John Shepard,	100	Henry Sap,	100
Charles Hudson,	100	Wm. Heron,	100

These are seated about the Black Swamp at ye Head of ye Murther Creek.

Fr'd HUGH DURBOROW:

According to thy request on behalf of the several Persons that are settled and desire to hold their Lands under the Prop'ry of Pensilv'a, I have made an entry in the Office in their Favour, that when Warr'ts may be had from hence those People may be secured in their Settlem'ts, provided they are within the Branches and running Water of Delaware.

Mich'l Hanlan having formerly agreed for some parcells of Land near Elk River, represents that he has but lately got the Surveys finished, tho' the returns bear date about the time of his agreement, and by Reason of the land lying near the Borders of Maryland he has met with some difficulty from them, wherefore he requests that he may be favoured in the Interest due on the Remainder of the Money, he having already paid a good part of it.

See for ye Return of Richl'd and Conestogo that they be returned.

The Land of J. Dickinson on the East side of the Road beyond R. Hill's is 330 acres.

At a meeting of the Commissioners the 16th 11 mo., 1722-3. Present, Rich'd Hill, Isaac Norris, James Logan.

Coll. John French having divers times represented to this Board that a parcell of Land joyning on Jos. England's, at Duck Creek, containing two Hundred acres, first laid out to one Sybrant Matthias Vulk, who by a power of Attorney appointed his Father-in-Law, Justa Andrees, to receive a certain Consideration of Adam Ishar, which seems to be paid to the said Attorney by one Robert Robinson, as appears by a Discharge under his Hand, and is therein said to be for 200 acres of Land, 130 acres whereof is therein mentioned to be then surveyed, the Discharge is dated 3d May, 1684. Edward Robinson, one of ye 7th Sons of the said Rob't Robinson, by a Deed under his Hand and Seal, dated the 7th January, 1718, granted and released the said 200 acres to Coll. French, who now earnestly requests the assistance of this Board to ratify the said Land in such Manner as they shall think fit.

Signed a Warr't of Resurvey to Coll. French for the above Land, the Warr't being drawn and dated the   day of   , 1719.

Philip Williams, with his Father-in-Law, Wm. Harmer, requests a Grant of 150 acres of Land, part of 500 acres reserved to the Prop'ry on the great Spring in Bucks County, for erecting a fulling mill, to which Sec'ry Logan has proposed that the Land must not be sold but leased for 7 years only, on Consideration that the said Philip pay down £10 at his entering on the Lands and the yearly rent of   , and that the said Philip may have the Liberty of purchasing the same within that Term upon such Conditions as may be then agreed on. The said Philip is to have liberty to cut necessary Timber and fire wood (Here is inserted diagram of the 150 acre tract).

John Kipshaven Johnson, of Sussex County, being vested with the Title of 560 acres of land on a branch of the Broad Creek, first laid out to Willam Clark by Vertue of ye Prop'rs Warr't and confirmed by the Comm'rs Patent to Honor Clark, Relict and Ex'x to the said Wm., under whom the said John holds, represents that the lines mentioned in the said Patent are different from the Situation of the Tract and contains short of the Quantity confirmed, as examined by Rob't Shankland, the Surv'r of Sussex, who has sent up a Plat shewing how it ought to lye; the said John requests that he may have a Re-survey and further Confirmation, the Draughts are left with J's. Taylor.

John Clough and Joseph Wells having purchased and seated themselves on part of George Burton's Tract of Land in Gilbert's Mannor, requests the Grant of about 200 acres belonging to the Prop'r on the upper side of the same. They are willing to give as much as any body and make good pay. This request is within Wm. Markham's Land.

John Robinson hath often applied for the old Plantation of Stockdell's, in Rocklands, for some terms on rent. which he requests may be as many years as can conveniently be granted, because the Buildings and Fences are much decayed. He proposes three Pounds p. ann. after the first year, which will be chiefly spent in putting the Plantation in Order. The rent to begin the first day of next first Month.

2, 2 mo., 1723.

Henry Reynolds, of Nottingham desires a small vacancy joyning on the west side of his Lot by the side of a Creek, supposed to contain about fifty acres, on which he, together with Messer Brown, designs to build a Grist Mill for the Conveniency of that End of the Township, as also the further Grant of a vacancy on the North side of the said Township of about one hundred acres.

Morgan Jones and some others dwelling near the further part of the Great Valley have recommended one William Anderson, for a small Vacancy of Land in that Neighbourhood for him to settle on, for teaching their Children to read and write. He also produced certificates from Virginia and Maryland of his behaviour there.

Sapience Harrison requests that he may have the Grant of about 200 acres of Land on ye Head of ye Deed Branch of Appoquinaming, in Newcastle County.

Rich'd Maclue desires the Grant of about 50 acres in Rocklands, recommended by Magnus Simmonds.

Philip Coolwine desires the Grant of 200 acres adjoyning to his other Land at Oley.

Joseph Hams having formerly appli'd for a parcell of Land near or adjoyning to the Land already Surveyed to him to the Northward of Nottingham, called Chestnut Hill, he now again requests that the same may be resurv'ed for him till a regular Grant may be had for it.

Casper, the Smith, desires the Grant of 100 acres where some Indians settled on Conestogo Creek, near   Mill.

Abraham Emmit recommends Alex'r Miller, Alex'r McConnel and John Scot as sober, industrious Persons, who requests about 3 or 400 acres for Settlements near Octoraro Creek, adjoyning on Tho. Reid.

Stephen Atkinson requests the Grant of a parcell of Land lying in the Barrens behind his Plantation, where is a conveniency for errecting a fulling Mill. Secret'ry Logan has writ to Isaac Taylor about it. Vide Book of Letters.

Tho. Dennis desires the Grant of about 200 acres in Chester County, near Doe Run and the Land of David Brintnall.

4th 7b'r, 1723.

John Twiggs requests a piece of Vac't Land Lying between the Land of James Rob, John Champion's and his own Land, supposed to contain about 50 acres.

Roger Kirk, son of Alphonsus Kirk, being seated on the South line of Nottingham, upon a Maryland Grant, desires notwithstanding that he may hold his Land being 200 acres under our Prop'r at the Common Tenure of those Settled in that Township.

Daniel Barker desires the Grant of about 100 acres of Land between the line of Henry Sintgar and Redclay Creek.

---

12 mo., 7, 1723.

Stephen Cornelius requests a small Vacancy between his Land, Joseph Hedges' and Jos. Barker's Land, at Redclay Creek. Stephen Cornelius has made over his right to this Land to Archebald McCallester, who is a Smith and dwells upon it, and is ready to pay the Prop'r for it. He desires a warr't to have it surveyed. It is a piece of broken land.

Xb'r, 29th, 1727.

Memorandum concerning Jonas Potts, taken from Sec'ry Logan's Entries. A Grant to Jonas Potts for 200 acres in Gilbert's, for 5 years for £3 p ann., the said Jonas to have the preferrence in purchasing (the improvem't excluded) at the rate or Value thereof at that time, dated 30th 3 mo., 1707.

Memorandum, that if Jonas Potts cannot purchase the Land, then the Person purchasing the same shall pay to J. P. for the Improvem'ts. Adjacent Land sold at that time at £25 p. C't, old currency.

William Williams desires the Grant of about 50 acres of Land jonying upon his Land in the Welch Tract, N. Castle County.

Wm. Smith, of Bristol, brass founder, by Deeds dated ye 26th and 27th days of ye 5 mo., 1681, purchased of the Prop'ry 500 acres of Land in this Province. His heirs and descendants by Indenture dated ye 15th 8 mo., 1692, granted the same unto Anthony Morgan, of Darby, in this Province, who by Deed Poll dated ye 4th 2 mo., 1724, granted the Lib. Land thereunto belonging unto Wm. Passmore.

---

3 mo., 7, 1724.

George Dandesson requests the Grant of a small parcell of Land about 3 or 4 miles from Sam'l Nut. He is recommended by him for an honest man.

Jacob Cook requests the Grant of about 100 acres at Oley, between Anthony Lee and Isaac De Turk.

Martin Mayley desires a Grant for about 100 acres in the Point in a fork of Conestogo Creek, near the Land called Wm. Willis'es, to make Tiles and Bricks.

Abraham England requests the Grant of about 200 acres near the Head of the Northwest branch of Duck Creek.

Tho. Nicholls requests, vid., his Papers in Box Letter N.

Nich. Schoonhover, from Sopus, requests the Grant of some low Ground on Delaware, between Pahaqualon and Machackamac.

Benj. Clark, of Stony Brook, requests in behalf of himself and Neigh'r to purchase the Tract of Land adjoyning to them.

James Lindley requests the Grant of about 500 acres of Land within the Tract called S'r Jno. Fagg's.

The late Prop'ry, by Deeds of Lease and Release, dated ye 17 and 18 days of 8b'r, 1681, granted to Tho. Ellwood, of Hunger Hill, in the County of Bucks, in Great Britain, 500 acres of Land in this Province, q't r't one shill. for each hundred acres, and by other like Deeds dated ye 24th and 25th days of Jan'ry, in the same Year, the s'd Prop'ry granted unto the s'd Tho. Ellwood and Mary his wife, other 500 acres in the said Province under the like quitrent.

Thomas Ellwood's wife dyed before himself, and by his last will and Testam't, dated the 21st day of the Month called August, 1712, duly proved (as p. a Copy produced here), did give and bequeath unto Isaac Pennington the said Lands in the following Words: Item., unto my young and hopefull Friend, Isaac Pennington, Son of my late Friend, Edw'd Pennington, deceased, and Grand son as well on the Father's side, unto my Dear and honoured Friend, Isaac Pennington, as on the Mother's side, unto my well beloved and much esteemed friend, Sam'l Jennings, late of West New Jersey, in America, dec'd, and to his Heirs and ass. forever, I Give and Devise all my Lands, Tenem'ts, and Hereditam'ts, with the app'es, lying and being within the Province of Pensylv'a, or elsewhere in America.

Isaac Pennington requests warr'ts for taking up ye s'd Land and Lotts.

Edw'd Robertson and Lucas Stedham produces the Transcript of a Patent from New York for 400 acres of Land, more or less, on the East side of Christina, bounded on the west with the Mill Creek, on ye East with the Bounds of Christina Town or Jno. Staliop's Land, laid out for four Soldiers (viz.), Rob't Scot, John Marshall, John Coumis and John Bowger, rent 4 bush'ls, Pat. dated 1st 8b'r, 1669.

Also a Deed Poll under the Hand and Seal of Justa Andries to Arnoldus Delagrange for the same, dated ye 16 of March, 1679-80, who has endorsed that he hath sold 200 acres to Lucas Stedham and 200 acres to Rob't Robertson by Deeds dated 16th 7b'r, 1684, and afterwards sold 158 acres to George Robertson, John Firkle and Rich'd Mankin by Deeds dated 18th of April, 1687, which he pretends to have done by Vertue of a resurvey. They, Edw'd Robertson and Lucas Stedham, desire the grant of some Marsh between their Lands and the Mill Creek and Resurveys on what they hold, that it may be confirmed to them. Let them know as soon as possible.

Sam'l Smith and Patrick Jack request a Parcell of Land at or near the Head of Octoraro, recommended by J. Grigg.

Xb'r, 1723.

Jno. Morton requests 200 acres of some Land fomerly called Paul Rose, lying near some Land survey'd to George Hogg at Brandywine. James Morton, his son, requests that he may hold the same, and now James Morton has sold his right in the same to William Dickson and John Springer.

Jno. Gregg requests that the Warr't granted to him some time since for 200 acres of Land (which could not be had) may be executed on a Vacant piece called the School house Land and ye remainder of D. Fosses'.

5 mo., 28, 1724.

Joseph Worth and Abr. Farington, both of Stony Brook, Jersey, request that they may have the Grant of the Prop'rs Tract of land adjoyning to their Settlements, and a meeting of Friends. They are willing to give as much for it as any other.

6 mo., 20, 1724.

Adam Fisher requests the Grant of about 30 acres of Marsh on the North side of the Murther Creek, joyning on the Marsh of Wm. Freeman, Nath. Hunn and Randal Donavan, that is an old request renewed.

Jos. Waterworth complains that divers Scots Irish are very Busy in settling about Octoraro Creek, which makes those Neighbours who settled there upon regular Grants very uneasy, who desire those people may be prevented from further settling.

7b'r, 14, 1724.

Alphonsus Kirk requests the Grant of about 10 acres, being between his own line, the line of Christ'r Wilson and Tho. Hollinsworth.

Roger Kirk, Son of Alphonsus, requests the Grant of about 100 a's near Fork of Octoraro.

Geo. Part requests about 150 acres near Christ. Francescus and Hans Loise, at Conestogo.

Geo. Mankin requests a proportionable part of the Marsh lying before the Land of himself, Edw'd Robinson and Lucas Stedham, it being all one Tract. Edw'd Robinson and L. Stedham have requested two pages foregoing.

Agreed with Frederick Antis for the Land called Darby Greens, in Limrick, about 300 and odd acres, at £22 p. C't; £30 to be p'd next 3 mo., and Interest for the rest till paid.

Abraham Parsly requests the Grant of the Vac't Marsh lying between his Land (late Nich. Grainger's) on Musmelon Creek and the said Creek. It will be necessary to resurvey the Land of Grainger and add thereunto the Marsh.

Alexander Adams having formerly purchased of Edw'd Smout 625 a's of Land near Drawer's Creek, called the Holt, and several years after Abraham Bickly, by 2 older Patents run into that Tract and took about 225 acres of the same, which the said Alex'r afterwards purchased of Abraham. Alexander requests that the Quantity may be made up to him out of some convenient Vacancy, which he has given to his Son-in-Law, Edw'd Gibbs, to whom he desires ye Warr't may be granted.

9b'r, 25, 1724.

Henry Harry requests a Confirmation on about 100 acres of Rent Land in Radnor, surveyed to his Father, Daniel Harry, in ye year 168 . He is willing to pay all the arrears of Rent. He is the only Son.

David and Jno. Lewis (Brothers) request the Grant of about 400 acres of Land between Octoraro and Pecque, near Geo. Leonard's.

John Sigfred requests the Grant of about 300 acres of Land above Oley when it is to be granted.

Christian Heer, of Conestogo, requests the Grant of about 50 acres of ordinary Land joyning to his other Land. Mich. Shank requests about 250 acres and Jacob Graeff about the same Quantity on or near Checasolungas.

Edw'd Robertson requests the Grant of 500 acres of Land on the Head of the further Branch of Elk River. Charles Hedge desires about the like Quantity about a mile to the Northward of the Indian Town, between the Head of Elk River and Octoraro.

Xb'r, 24, 1724.

John Smith, of Marlborough, requests the Grant of about 25 or 30 acres of Land joyning this Tract where he dwells. Isaac Taylor says it is but of little Value to any other Person. He is willing to give 4 Shill's p. ann. or less if it may be granted.

Henry Wark requests the Grant of a Settlem't near Conestogo or Shecassalungas. John Starret requests the same Liberty about the same places.

Elisha Gatchel requests in behalf of James Daniel that Parcel of land on a Branch of Elk River, containing about 150 acres near a place called Pine Tree Meadow, may be granted to him as soon as a Warr't can be had for it. The Land lies about 5 or 6 miles to the North of Lord Baltemore's line.

MINUTE BOOK "I." 725

Isaac Taylor requests in behalf of Rob't Green the Grant of about 50 acres of Land adjoyning on his Plantation on the Edge of Rockland Mannor, in Bromingham, it being a Parcell left when the Lands thereabout were granted to other Persons.

Eberherd Ream, of Conestogo, requests the Grant of about 200 acres of Land on a branch of that Creek, including a small Indian Settlem't, called Cocallico. He has the Indians' consent to settle and can pay the purchase Money down.

George Robinson requests the Grant of about 150 acres of Land in Rocklands for his Son Valentine, adjoyning on Tho. Babb's Plantation There is one Wm. Forehead, settled on it, without grant or licence.

Wm. Thomas requests the Grant of about 50 or 75 acres of Land in the Great Valley, joyning to his Land, late Griffith Phillip.

Andreas Bussert requests the Grant of above 150 acres between the Swedes' Tract and Tho. Rutter at Manatawny.

———

22d 11 mo., 1724.

Agreed with Peter Wents and Lawrence Switzer for one thousand or twelve hundred acres of Land at Sawcany, to be laid out in two Tracts joyning on each other, at Sixteen pounds p. hundred, which they are to pay one hundred pounds in Gold or Silver at the return of Survey, and the Remainder in one year after the Date hereof without Interest.

JAMES STEEL
PETER [his mark PW] WENTS,
LAWRENCE [his mark LS] SWITZER.

Friend NICHO. SCULL:

I have agreed with Peter Wents and Lawrence Switzer for one Thousand or twelve hundred acres of Land, Sawcany, to be laid out in two regular Tracts adjoyning to each other, which I desire thee to Survey and the Warr'ts shall be ready at thy return. For Jno. Sigfrad 300 acres.

Andrew Frazier requests the Grant of about 300 acres for himself and Arth. V. Kirk and his Son. It lyes between their fast Land and bald Eagle Gut, near the mouth of little Musmelon Creek.

Rob't Jones, of Merion, sets forth that he apprehends David Davis by a Warr't obtained 1719, has run some line or lines on or near his Tract in the Valley that very much incommodes his Intention of laying his Society Right next adjoyning to his own Tract, and therefore requests that if D. Davis' survey be as he apprehends it upon the return into the Office that he be prevailed on to accommod'e Rob't. Speak to Is. Taylor about it.

James Als Couradt, Rector, requests the Grant of a piece of land near Conestogo, joyning to Frederickfuls.

Henry Croswell and Alexander Evans requests the Grant of about 100 acres each to the Northward of Nottingham. Elicha Gatchel is requested to appoint their Settlem'ts.

Joseph Grub requests the Grant of the old place below the old Plantation of Jno. Grub, called Morgan's Plantation, no other person as yet having any Grant for it.

Philip Coolwin requests the Grant of 200 acres adjoyning to his tract at Oley, at £16 p. C't, to be paid in Gold, also Rodolph Storey requests 2 or 300 acres upon the same Terms.

Rich'd Story Trespasses on Doe run and interrupts Wm. Hamilton, who is building a Mill there; he appears and requests a Grant.

Darby Ryall requests a small parcel of Land in Marlborough, about 100 acres in Marlborough. Enquire of Is. Taylor, it joyns on him.

John Nich. Sents and Hans Yoder request the Grant of about 100 acres of Land at Sawcany.

---

1 mo., 6th, 1724-5.

Joseph Pennock requests the Grant of acres of the Tract called S'r John Fagg's, if to be disposed of.

John Hummit requests a Resurvey on a Tract of Land on the Murther Creek, first laid out and confirmed to Tho. Slidmore for 400 acres, to bound on the Creek and to take in the Marsh between the Fast Land and the Creek.

Wenlock and John Brinklo, sons of Wm. Brinklo, request the Grant of an Addition of Marsh and Points of Land between their Tract, the Stunt Kill and the Pond.

Ralph Needham requests the Grant of a Parcell of Marsh near Cuckold point, opposite Green's landing, on little Creek side, it being almost an Island made by Duck Creek; he would have about 100 a's.

Abraham Allen and Jethro Thompson each about 100 acres near Duck Creek.

Geo. Martin requests the Grant of 100 acres of Land in Duck Creek neck, adjoyning to the 200 acres laid out to Coll. Wm. Markham.

John Devor (recommended by J. McComb) requests the Grant of about 2 or 300 acres about 2 miles from Jno. Musgrave's, on Octoraro Creek. He had leave from J. L. to settle about two years since.

Jno. Boyle requests as above, he says Is. Taylor recommended him.

John Isaac Kline requests the Grant of about 20 acres, a Vacancy at the end of his 100 acres, bought of D. Powel at Skepack.

Rob't Bird requests the Grant of about 100 acres of Land joyning on the Tract called the Horse Hook, formerly belonging to Corn. Empson.

---

1 mo., 13, 1724–5

Duke Jackson (whip maker) requests the Grant of about 100 acres in the Great Swamp. The Spot he has pitched on is called Chestnut Hill; he may settle.

Tho. Pearl and Mary his wife, by Deed dated , 1709, granted to Fairman 200 acres, part of Wm. Smith, of Bromham House's purchase, who sold 500 acres thereof to Rich'd Hilliard, first husband to the said Mary.

Benj. Fairman and Susannah his wife, grants the same to Henry Trey. It is survey'd by a Warr't dated 1712, returned 1713.

John Taylor requests a Warr't for 263 acres, the remainder of Isaac Few's purchase, the Warr't to be in R. Few's name; he dwells at Kennet.

John Brinklo requests the Grant of about 100 acres of Marsh between his Land and Killingsworth.

Emanuel, Joseph, Sam'l and Nath'l Grub, sons of John Grub, produce the following Papers, viz., An Instrum't or Grant for 108 acres from Morgan Drewit to Thomas Gilpin, dated the 18th 6 mo., 1685 (being the Land where J. Grub's stone House stands by the River side.

Also a Deed executed by J. French, high Sheriff of N. Castle County, dated the 19th of July, 1707, to Jno. Grub for 175 acres, more or less, including the above, obtained by one Judgem't of Court, Tho. Bradshaw and Alice his wife, executʼx of Tho. Gilpin, against the Heirs of Morgan Drewit, and purchased by Jno. Grub. The Prop'r, by Warr't under his hand and lesser Seal, dated 19th 8b'r, 1683, Wills and requires Eph'm Herman to Survey to Jno. Grub 200 acres, part of 600 acres laid out before to him. Isaac Savoy and David Henrick also Return under H. Hollingsworth's hand, dated the 9th 3 mo., 1691, reciting a Warr't from the Prop'r 26th 4 mo., 1684, for four acres granted J. Grub for a Tan yard.

A Return under T. Pierson's hand for 70 acres of Land on the south side of Naaman's Creek, dated 12, 9 mo., 1684, to Conrad Constantine, who two days before gave his Bond to

Jno. Grub (in T. Pierson's hand writing), penalty forty Pounds, for conveying and making over all his Right, title and Interest of a certain piece of Land, containing 150 acres, according to the Tennor of a Warr't granted the said Conrad, dated ye 5th X mo., 1683, and a receipt of Edw'd Gibbs for 12 shillings for 4 years' quitrent due on the above 70 acres, but Tho. Pierson certifies under his hand ye 22, 12 mo., 1685-6, that John Grubb promised to resign that Land again upon the Prop'rs ordering him Land in another place. A Return under the Hand of Rich'd Tindell, dated March 12th, 1691, for fifty acres of Marsh on Jersey side, at the mouth of Ash Creek, also James Newell's receipt for £2 16s, in part for the said Marsh, dated 18 Feb., 1691-2.

Edw'd Hart requests the Grant of a Tract of Land back in ye Province. He Trades with the Indians and proposes to pay in Gold and Peltry.

Tho. Wilson, of Notingham, requests (p. Meser Brown) the Grant of about 40 acres of Land joyning on his Dwelling.

The Prop'r, by Deeds of Lease and Release, dated ye 26 and 27 days of 7b'r, 1681, granted to Charles Jones, Sen'r, and Charles Jones, Jun'r, of Bristol, 2,000 acres of Land in this Province, quitr't one Shilling for each 100 acres. Charles Jones, the Elder, by like Deeds dated the 3d and 4th days of 0b'r, 1711, granted the whole to Edw'd Shippen and Esther, his wife (Charles Jones, the younger, being for some time deceased). Esther Shippen, who survived her husband, Edw'd Shippen, by her last Will and Testam't dated the 4th of August, 1724, desires the untaken up Land in these words: I now for and concerning all the rest and residue of the said 2,000 acres of Land (over and besides the s'd 500 a's and 40 a's) whether the same is surveyed and Located or is yet to be located. I give and devise ye same unto Edw'd and Joseph, Sons of my Son-in-Law, Jos. Shippen, of Philad'a afores'd, Merchant, and to Margeret the daughter of my Son-in-Law, Edw'd Shippen, dece'd, and to their Heirs and assigns forever, to be equally divided amongst them share and share alike.

Tho. Lewis having formerly requested a Grant of some Land on Doe run, again applies for the same (about 300 acres) one Robert Henry, has presumed to make a Settlem't on or near the Spot he desired, who is ordered to remove.

George Martin requests the Grant of 100 acres of Land and Marsh joyning on the Land formerly Palmatary's, sold by Thomas Sharp to Rob't French, the Land requested is called the Brant Point.

Dan'l Boyden requests a confirmation of his Land in Bucks as soon as possible.

George Wilcox requests ye Grant of about 150 acres joyning on James Edward's, in Uckland.

---

3 mo., 17th, 1725.

John Parsons requests a Warr't for the remainder of Joseph Hall's purchase, who has purchased the same from Sam'l and Hannah Overton, to whom the former part was granted and laid out in Makefield. See from the rent roll the Quantity; he requests to have it adjoyning to him in Wrights Town.

At a meeting of ye Commissioners of Property the 12th 2 mo., 1725.

Present, Rich'd Hill, James Logan, Robert Asheton, Tho. Griffith.

Mary Davis, Widow and Execut'x of the last will and Testam't of John Davis, late of this City, dec'd, requests that the Warr'ts drawn in her husband's lifetime for 1,250 acres of Land, the original purchase of Wm. Kent, entered page , foregoing of ye Minutes, may now be signed in order that the Lands may be laid out. Signed for the whole purchase by R. H. and J. L.

---

2 mo., 14th, 1725.

Rob't Eyers requests (by David Herman) the Grant of a small parcell of Land near Pecque. He is a Cooper.

Jacob FFunck requests the Grant of about 50 acres adjoyning to his tract near Conestogo.

---

3 mo., 1, 1725.

Emanuel, Joseph and John Grub request that the Land claimed by their Father may be held amongst them.

Jno. Grub requests that when the old Plantation in Rocklands (Stockdell's) is to be sold, that he may have the preference in purchasing it. He says he made the same request some years agoe.

Benj. and Jno. Bankson request a confirmation on their Cripple and Swamp.

Daniel Fierre requests that the following names may be entered: Jonas La Rou 200 A's.

Geo. Robinson requests the Grant of about 20 acres which was first laid out for a meeting house, but never built on, it lyes on the side of his other land and therefore more convenient for him then another person.

Isaac Taylor requests a confirmation on the 250 acres he has purchased of Ezek'l Hanlan and paid for it in the office.

Hans Yost Hyde requests the grant of about 50 acres adjoyning to his Plantation on the south East side.

19, 3 m., 1725.

Memorandum, that Anthony Bretter produced a receipt under James Logan's hand for thirty Pounds, which the said Bretter acknowledged was paid equally between himself and John Frederickffulls for 300 acres of Land called the black Walnut Bottom, to be divided and held equally between them.

J. STEEL.

The Prop'r, by short Deeds of Lease and Release, dated the 3d and 4th days of April, 1695, Granted to Daniel Wharley, of Lond., Woolen Draper, three thousand acres of Land in this Province, clear of Indian Incumbrances, Between the rivers Delaware and Susquehannah, quitrent one shilling, English Money, to commence seven years after taking up and Seating. by an Indorsement on the said Release, dated the 12 day of April aforesaid, for a competent sum of Money, the said Prop'r Did Release the quitrent thereof from him, the said Prop'r, his Heirs and Ass., unto the s'd D. Wharley and his Heirs.

Daniel Wharley, eldest Son and Heir apparent of the afore said D. Wharley, by Indenture of Lease and Release, dated the 2d and 3d days of April, 1724, for £130 Sterling granted and released the said 3,000 acres of Land unto Rowland Ellis, Jun'r, his Heirs and Assigns forever, who requests Warr'ts for Surveying the same.

The Prop'r, by a short Deed Indented, for £12 10s granted to Geffry Alcock. of Ordsleyford, in the County of Chester, in G't Britain, 375 acres of Land to be laid out towards Susquehannah River, quitrent one shilling for every hundred acres. Geffry Alcock, by a like Deed dated ye 6th of Feb., 1723, for £16 granted and assigned the said Land to Peter Dicks, of Chester County, in this Province, who by Deeds of Lease and Release dated ye 21 and 22 days of 3 mo., 1725, for £60 conveyed the same land to John Leech and Isaac Leech, who now request a Warr't for the same.

The Prop'r, by Deeds of Lease and Release, dated ye 26 and 27 July, 1681, Granted to John Clare, of Froom Sellwood, in the County of Somerset, 500 acres of Land, quitr't one shilling for every hundred acres. Jno. Clare, only Son and Heir of the said Jno. Clare, for £20, by like Deeds dated ye 24 and

25 of January, 1723, granted and conveyed the said Land to Clare Rutty, of Melksham, in ye County of Wilts, who by other like Deeds dated ye 18th and 19th days of the 3d Month, 1724, for £50 granted and released the said 500 acres unto Morris Morris, of Abington, in this Province, who requests a Warr't for the same.

At a meeting of the Commissioners of Property the 20th 3 mo., 1725.

Present, Rich'd Hill, James Logan, Rob't Asheton, Tho. Griffith.

Charles Brockden requests a Confirmation of his Land, Cripple and Meadow lately resurveyed and laid out by Vertue of the Commissioners Warr't, granted upon the former Condiions.

Signed the following Warr'ts:

To Isaac Pennington for 1,000 acres, the original purhase of Thomas Ellwood, in two Warr'ts, dated this day.

To Edw'd, Joseph and Margaret Shippen, grand Children of Edw'd Shippen and Children of Joseph and Edw'd Shippen, for 1,360 acres in three Warr'ts, dated this day, the original Purchase of Charles Jones, Sen'r, and Charles Jones, Jun'r.

The Warr'ts drawn on Rowland Ellis are ordered to be altered, for that the Grant from Daniel Wharley, jun'r, to him appears not to be sufficient, there being other Children of D. Wharley, the Elder, which have not made themselves parties to the Grant made to Rowland Ellis.

The Prop'r, by Deeds (short) of Lease and Release, dated ye 3d and 4 days of April, 1695, for £20 Granted and released 600 Acres of Land between Delaware and Susquehannah, clear of Indian Incumbrances, unto Henry Thompson, of Westminster, Vintner, under the yearly quitrent of one shilling, English Money, for every hundred acres. The said Prop'r, by an Indorsem't on the said Release, dated ye 12th day of ye same month, for a Competent sum of Money, hath released the said quitrent to ye said Henry Thompson and his Heirs.

John Thompson, Son and Heir of the said Henry Thompson, for £20, by Lease and Release, dated the 22d and 23 days of Jan'ry, 1723, granted and released the said 600 acres of Land unto Humphrey Hill, of London, Merch't, his heirs and assigns forever, who by his Attorney, J. Logan, requests a Warr't for Surveying the same.

Charles Springer, in the Year 1719, requested for the Settlement of his Children the Grant of about 200 acres of Vacant Land near Sam'l Barker's and Redclay Creek, in New Castle

County, and now upon renewing of his request he is permitted by Sect. Logan to settle the same on Condition that when the Land Office is open he shall apply himself and agree for the same.

Edw'd Owen (D'r) requests the grant of a vacancy on the Head of his and his Brother's Land in Goshen, between that and the Barrens; there is one Jno. Williams settled on it, who is like to injure their Land very much and never able to pay for it.

Sam'l James (sometime in or about the first Month last) requested the Grant of 250 Acres of Land on White clay creek, formerly Surveyed to Wm. Burney, who deserted the same and has long since left the Province, and is still considerably in the Prop'rs Debt.

Moses Musgrave requests that the neighbourhood where he dwells may be Called Lisbon Township, also that Rob't Long, a shoemaker, may have about 100 acres.

John Hore, of Newcastle, requests the Grant of a parcel of Land on the Branches of Appoquinaming Creek, called the Church Branches, above the King's Road, on such terms as the Comm'rs shall think fit. J. Logan has ordered his requests to be entered in order for a Warr't.

John Willis requests the grant of 50 a's head Land, for which he produced the Certificate from 2 Justices. It is in right of Tho. Cooper, he would have it near his Mill.

The right of Rich'd Adams' purchase, entered in minute Book, p. 99, is entered to be in Jno. Adams, his son and Heir, but by the will now produced, Rich'd Adams gives and bequeaths the whole to his Son, Nicholas Adams, who by his Last Will and Testam't bequeaths the same unto his Kinsman, Rich'd Adams, son of his Bro'r, John Adams, to him, his heirs and Assigns forever.

Charles Hillyard requests the grant of 100 Acres of Vaca't Land joyning on the Tract of Cap't Ewens, on the South side of Duck Creek, he having formerly requested the like Grant of the Prop'r when last in Kent. Sect'ry Logan consents that he shall have orders to the Surv'r of Kent to examine the lines of the adjoyning Lands, and lay out 100 Acres if to be found Vaca't, or upon the Head of Rob'rt Draughton's Land.

At a meeting of the Commissioners of Property the 23d of the 5 mo., 1725.

Present, Rich'd Hill, James Logan, Rob't Asheton.

A Letter from Mrs. H. Penn, dated 22d 3d, 1724, in favour of Coll. French (directed to the Comm'rs), was laid before the Board, desiring them to grant to him their Warr't for so much vaca't Land as would with what he has already had make up to him fifty Pound p. Ann. for the time he has been Guardian of the Marches.

The Comm'rs taking the same into Consideration do think it necessary that Coll. French be present upon the occation, and therefore do order that Notice be given to him that the Comm'rs appoint to sit the 29th Instant in the afternoon.

———

At a meeting of the Commissioners of Property the 29th 5th, 1725.

Present, Rich'd Hill, Isaac Norris, James Logan, Rob't Asheton.

Coll. French being acquainted of this day's meeting, came up and gave in an Acc't of what Lands had been granted to him since the 5th Month, 1716, to which was added some Cash supplyed him by James Logan, and also an old Bond given by him in the year 1708, which being stated into an Account, as hereafter followeth, the allowance ordered by Mrs. Hannah Penn, the Ballance is given in Coll. French's favour, two Hundred Pounds, which is ordered to be discharged by some vacant Land in Newcastle County, to be forthwith granted for that Purpose and is to be in full Satisfaction for all services by him done to the date hereof.

———

At a meeting of the Commissioners of Property the 10 of the 6 mo., 1725.

Present, Rich'd Hill, James Logan, Rob't Asheton.

The Business of Coll. French relating to

———

8b'r, 29th, 1725.

Edw'd Robinson and Charles Hedge request the Grant of two parcells of Land on the Head of Elk River for 2 Settlem'ts for their Sons. Sect'ry Logan consents they may secure the same by making some small Improvements till Warr'ts can be had and then they are to pay as other People for the Land. They desire 500 Acres each.

George Carr requests the Grant of a piece of Land on the head or branches of Octoraro Creek. He is a Tanner by Trade and desireous of settling, he has disposed of his place to John Paten.

9b'r, 2d, 1725.

William Johnston and James his Son, request the Grant of a Settlement for each of them on a Branch of Pecquea, called Cattail run. Sect'ry Logan has consented they may settle till Warr'ts can be made out.

Philip David (recommended by Edw'd Roberts) requests the Grant of a piece of Land for a Settlement on the west Branch of Brandywine.

Matthias Stouffer (recommended by Christian Heer) requests the grant of a piece of Land near the Branches of Shecasalongo Creek.

Sam'l Verner (from Ireland) requests the Grant of a parcel of Land for a Settlement on Pecque, he has set down for some time. He produces good Credentials, both from our Friends in Ireland and others. Sam'l Verner being dead, his Son David requests the Grant, 200 A's.

Hugh Morrison and Tho. Paxton and Hugh Roberson and Lawrence Small request that they may Settle on the upper Part of Octoraro.

William Cleany produces a Draught and Certificate of 350 Acres of Land in Christina Hundred, surveyed to Oliver Mathews, from whose Son the said Wm. holds it. He requests a confirmation for it and is ready to pay the quitrent or purchase therein off.

James Harlan, Son of George Harlan, requests the Grant of about 500 A's of Land between Octoraro and Susquehannah and that he may settle till a Warr't can be had. The s'd James Harlan, by this Entry settled on the West Branch of Brandywine and has since made over his Interest to James Gibbons, who desires some lines to be run about it to keep off the Encroachers that are ready to invade the place.

8b'r 6, 1725.

James Paterson requests the Grant of about   a's of Land on the upper side of Octoraro Creek, near Tho. Reid's, he desires to make some Settlem't. Wm. Paterson, his Brother, requests the Grant of a Settlem't between the Creek and Henry Wark's, they are recommended by Elisha Gatchel and allowed to Settle by Sec'ry Logan.

The Prop'r, by Ind'rs of Lease and Rel., dated   , 1681, granted to Tho. Symens 500 Acres in this Province, which was laid out in Haverford and The Great Valley. John Symens, Son and Heir, as he calls himself, of Tho. Symens, by other Deed dated ye   of August, 1686, granted the whole to Tho. Marchant and Jane his wife.

Tho. Symens, Grandson to the said Thomas, the first Purchaser, came over about 7 years ago, and upon some evidence prevailed with the Comm'rs to Confirm 200 Acres laid out in the Valley, and now the deeds are produced and a Claim made for the Land by Jer'a Cowman, Jno. Warder and Owen Thomas, Attorneys of Tho. March't.

James Phillips requests a confirmation on about 100 Acres of Land laid out to G. Read and purhased of his Heirs by J. P. James Letort lived on it and makes some Claim to it, enquire of him.

Archebald Smith requests a Resurvey on a Tract of Land on the head of the Broad Creek, near the long Bridge, and to take in some Vacant Land adjoyning, the Land was first laid out to Wm. Clark.

9b'r 16, 1725.

Jno. Salkeld requests the grant of about 50 Acres of Swamp and Cripple adjoyning to the Southeast side of his Land, and if it be practible get it Surveyed as soon as possible, see for the Entry elsewhere. J. Salkeld requests the Addition to reach to the Barrens and that it may contain 100 Acres.

At a meeting of the Commissioners of Property the 28th 8b'r, 1725.

Present, Rich'd Hill, Isaac Norris, James Logan.

Signed a Deed to Charles Brockden for 42¼ A's of Land, Cripple and Swamp at Moyamensing (viz.), 24 A's and ¼ part of Moyamensing Patent, 18 A's overplus and an addition, for which he pays £11 5s 0d.

Rob't Jones (of Meirion) sets forth that he together with his Brothers are possessed of a Tract of Land in the Great Valley, confirmed to them by Patent by the former Commissioners, but there being no head line next the Barrens to be found, they understood that their Land joyned to a tract surv'd to D. LLoyd, but one David Davis, finding the lines of R. Jones' Patent did not reach (by the number of Perches) to D. LLoyd's land, obtained a Warr't above 6 years since for vacant Land adjoyning to the Tract of his Father, and thereupon obtained a Survey not only on the Head of his own Land but extended it between D. LLoyd's and R. Jones' Land. R. J's therefore requests that he may hold the Land which he always understood to be his own, and if the Quantity exceeds his right, he is willing to pay for it or secure it to himself by a Society Grant, which he has purchased. The Commissioners order that D. Davis be acquainted, they will hear what he can say in Objection to R. J's request.

9b'r 24, 1725.

Rich'd Ridgway, by an Instrum't or Deed dated ye 13 Instant, 1682, Bargained, sold and set over unto John Luff, his Heirs and Assigns forever, all his Right, Title and Interest of 100 Acres of Land, being the Moiety or half part of a Plantation which the said Rich'd Ridgw'y sold the other half to Daniel Gardner, lying between Sam'l Dark's and Lionel Britain's Plantation in Pensilv'a afores'd.

The same Land was resurveyed by John Cutler in 1702 and found to be 106 acres, and now of late the lines have been Try'd and are made to contain 120 Acres.

Gabriel Luff, nearest Kinsman of John Luff, who has been long Dece'd, by Deeds of Lease and Release, dated ye 7 and 8 days of 7b'r, 1724, for £25 15s, Money of Pensilv'a, Granted, Released and Confirmed the 100 (only) to Capt. James Gould, his Heirs and Assigns forever, who request a confirmation thereof by Patent and is ready to pay the Quitrent.

John William Lirunceller having purchased a Tract of Land of Alex'r Adams, requests the Grant of about 20 acres, a vacancy joyning on Readen Island Road and his said Land.

Adam Buckly requests the Grant of about 100 A's joyning on John Littlejohn's, and also a small Parcell joyning on his old Plantation.

Nich's White complains that upon Dr. Jones' running out his land he takes about 10 Acres of Nich's Land. He also requests the Grant of about 200 Acres on the east side of his Tract, and to have the Addition made for the Land taken from him by Dr. Jones, for which with the rest of his Tract he has honestly paid.

Alphonsus Kirk requests the Grant of 1,000 Acres of Land between the Lower Settlem'ts of the Dutch and Nottingham for Settlem'ts for his Sons.

He also requests the Grant of about 20 Acres for his Son Jonathan, adjoyning to his Land in Rocklands.

Mos. Musgrave requests the Grant of a piece of Land for John Cohalan, near the Branches of Octoraro.

Geo. Leonard having paid for his former Tract and is now settled between two Mountains on 140 Acres laid out to M. Musgrave, but is to be p'd for George, he requests the Grant of about 100 Acres more adjoyning to the other.

John Richardson requests the Grant of a parcel of Swamp or Cripple adjoyning on the upper part of his and Conrad

Constantine, on the North side of Christina Creek, on both sides of a small branch called England's Gut, and desires it may not be Granted to any other Person.

Benj. Ellis requests the Grant of a piece of Vac't Land in Goshen, joyning on Wm. Burg and Rees Thomas.

JOHN CADWALADER, of Horsham.

The Prop'r, by Deeds of Lease and Release, dated (p. recital) ye 1st and 2d days of August, 1681, granted to Rich'd Few, the Elder, of Market Levington, in the County of Wilts, Shoemaker, 500 Acres of Land to be laid out in this Province, quitr't 1 Shill. p. C't. The said Rich'd Few, by like Deeds dated ye 14th and 15th of 7b'r next after, granted 250 Acres, Parcell thereof, to Joan Self, of Market Levington, afores'd, her Heirs and Assigns forever. Robert Silvester and Joan his wife, of Horsly, in the County of Glocester (supposed to be Joan Self), by other like Deeds dated ye 1st 7b'r, 1683, granted and confirmed the said 250 Acres to Henry English, of the same place, broad Weaver. Henry English, by Indorsem't on the last memorand. Deed (very ill drawn) doth yield up and surrender all the within mentioned Tract of Land unto Giles Knight for the use of his two Sons, Joseph and Tho. Knight, to be equally divided between them.

JOHN CADWALADER, of Horsham.

The Prop'r, by Deeds of Lease and Release, dated 10, 11 days of 7b'r, 1681, granted to Rich'd Mills, of Bridgwater, in the County of Sumerset, Taylor, 250 Acres of Land, quitrent one Shilling p. C't.

The said Rich'd Mlils, by an ill drawn deed dated ye 8th 3 mo., 1701, for £3 doth Bargain and sell ye said 250 Acres to Aaron Pleas, of Eddington, in the said County, Malster, The same, quietly and peaceably to hold and enjoy according to all true Intent and meaning and without the interruption of the said Rich'd Mills, his Heirs or Ass. Aaron Pleas, by Indenture dated ye 11, 8, 1721, for £3 10s Granted and Confirmed ye said 250 Acres to C. Jacob, his heirs and Assigns forever.

Caleb Jacob, by Indentures of Lease and Rel., dated ye 30th and 31st of July, 1722 without reciting how or in what manner he came by his Right, for £40 granted and conveyed ye said 250 Acres to S'r Wm. Keith, his heirs and Assignes forever, who by like Deeds dated ye 12th and 13th of January, 1725, for £40 granted and released the said 250 Acres to Ebenezer Large, his Heirs and Ass.

Ebenezer Large requests warr'ts to lay out the same with Lot and Lib. Land.

Rob't Jones, of Skepack, brought the Money for his Bill,

but his Patent not being ready he is not to pay interest till he has it.

Sam'l Graves requests the Grant of about 200 Acres on Doe runn, near Isaac Taylor's Land, when

James Wood, recommended by Ebenezer Empson, requests the Grant of a piece of Land in Rocklands, towards Geo. Robinson.

Hugh Davis having obtained a grant for 50 Acres on rent and 50 on purchase, that on rent was laid out and confirmed to him in the year 1715, and the other not being then surveyed H. D. now requests that he may have it. Speak to I. Taylor to give Directions.

Timothy Hanson requests the grant of a piece of vac't Land lying on that North end of his Tract, where he dwells, and joyns on a Parcel bought by Joshua Clayton from some of the Hirons, there being about 100 Acres, as he supposes.

Paul, Peter and Anthony Jaquet, at Christian Ferry, request the Grant of a parcell of vac't Marsh joyning to the west side of their Land and on Christina Creek, containing about 40 Acres.

Joseph Skeen requests the grant of about 100 A's in ye Barrens, near Doe run.

Sam'l Hollingsworth requests the grant of 200 Acres of Land on a branch of Elkrin, near Thunder Hill, and about 200 Acres of S'r John Fagg's mannor on the Southwest Corner, and also that John Green may have the Grant of a Parcell of Vac't Land in Bromingham, parcell of Rocklands.

Edward Thompson requests the Grant of about 250 Acres of vac't Land on Pecquea road, about 4 miles beyond Tho. Moors' Mill.

Francis Hobson requests the Grant of about 5 or 600 Acres in S'r Jno. Fagg's Mannor when to be sold.

---

1 mo., 22, 1726.

John Parsons, having some Years ago purchased of the Comm'rs 150 Acres of Land on the North Part of Wrights Town, and there being about the like quantity on the west side of that 150 Acres lying under the name of Geo. Rigg and supposed to have been granted to him at a penny p. acre, but the said Rigg having been long since Dead and no grant to him for the said Land to be found, the said J. Parsons requests that he may have the priviledge of laying an old right, which he has purchased, upon the same.

Sect'ry Logan taking the request into Consideration has ordered that John Parsons be favoured in his request, and that upon paying some consideration in lieu of the Arrears of Rent that would have accru'd to the Prop'r had the same been held and occupied upon that foot, he may have the said Land confirmed to him with what he has before paid.

Dan'l Barker requests the grant of a piece of Land on Doe run, settled by Rich'd Story, who has sold his pretence to Daniel, who now agrees that Charles Springer shall have his Claim.

Johannes Vennoy, from Esopus, requests in behalf of himself and five others, his Neighbours, to purchase a Tract of Land on Dellaware, below Minisink.

Elisha Gatchel, by Consent of Sect'ry Logan, has procured three Tracts of Land to be surveyed on the running water of Connawowinga, an Acc't whereof he has lodged in this office, and John Hammond, who dwells on Octoraro, having a Tract on that Creek, has discovered a vacancy adjoyning thereto of about 100 Acres, which he desires may be granted to him, a Discription of it is also lodged with Elisha Gatchel's Papers.

Elisha Gatchel requests that when the common Lot at Nottingham is to be disposed of he may have the refusall.

———

2 mo., 11, 1726

John Henrickson (by his Brother-in-Law, C. Springer) requests the Grant of about 40 or 50 Acres of vac't Land adjoyning to him in Christina Hundred.

John Kay (first born) requests the Grant of a Parcell of Land adjoyning to Tho. Eldrige.

Martin Rucklefell (p. Letter from Is. Taylor) requests the Grant of a small Parcell of Land on the Barrens of Goshen.

David Smith (p. Rob't Shankland) requests the Grant of some vac't and overplus Land adjoyning to his Settlem't near Cedar Creek, or a Branch thereof, called Cypress Branch.

Owen Thomas requests that Morris Griffith may have the Grant of a parcel of Land in the Barrens of Willistown, where he has settled, when the same is to be disposed of. He (O. Thomas) also requests the Grant of a parcell of vac't Land Lying on the South East of his Land in the same Township. And also that Lewis William may be permitted to keep a small Settlem't he has made in the aforesaid Barrens till he can have a regular Grant and pay for the same.

David Moor requests the Grant of about 100 Acres of Vac't Land joyning on the south side of his Land, which he purchased of Caleb Pusey, on the Bridge above Wm. Marches.

Christopher Eaton requests the Grant of a Parcell of the Land claimed by Green and M. V. Bebberni N. C. County.

Emanuel Grub requests the Grant of about 100 Acres of Land on the N. E. side of his Tract on Cononawingo Creek and on the N. W. side of the said Creek, near Susquehanna.

James Miller (Son of Gawen) requests about 1,000 Acres of S'r John Fagg's Mannor when to be sold.

George Gotchick requests the Grant of a Parcel of Land supposed to be Va'ct, adjoyning to him in Abington.

Joseph Clapham requests the Liberty of Building a Grist Mill on a Branch of Pextang, which is also requested on his behalf by the few Neighbours thereabout Settled.

At a meeting of the Commissioners of Property ye 19th 3 mo., 1726.

Present, Rich'd Hill, Isaac Norris, James Logan.

Rees Thomas and Anthony Morris sets forth their right to 2,000 Acres of Land in Chester County and 4,500 in Philad'a County, formerly the Lands of Richard Whitpain, entered in the old minutes. The 2,000 Acres in Chester County has been resurveyed by Is. Taylor and found to be but 1,763 Acres, so that there is a deficiency of 237 Acres. They request a Warr't of Resurvey on the 4,500 in Philad'a County, and in case of a Deficiency that it may be with the above 237 A's laid out to them in some vacancy. Granted and a Warr't of Resurvey order'd.

4th mo., 8, 1726.

Allow'd p. J. L.

Joseph Jones, of Nottingham, requests the Grant of a Parcell of vac't Land joyning on a Settlem't of Charles Allen, near Conawingo Creek.

Joseph Jones has resigned his pretence in this Land to James King.

The late Prop'r, by L. and Rel., dated ye 11 and 12 days of 8b'r 1681, Granted to Jeremiah Waringe, of London, perfumer, 250 Acres of Land in this Province, quit'rt one Shilling p. C't. Jeremiah Waringe, of the Parish of Witney, in the County of Oxon, Mercer, by Lease and Release, as p. attested Copies by Edw'd Horne and Philip James, dated ye 2d and 3d days of 9b'r, 1721, for £11 granted and conveyed the said 250 Acres to Peter Rich, of Upton, in the Parish of Burford, in the said County, Paper Maker.

Peter Rich, by a Power of Attorney, dated the 1st day of March, Anno 1724, Witnessed by E. Horne and Ph. James, Impowered Wm. Tidmarsh, of Philad'a, to take up the said

Land, who requests warr'ts for the same with the Lot and Liberty Land.

William Moor supposing that there is some vacant Land between his lines and the Mannor of Bilton, procured the lines of both Tracts to be run, but upon examining the Office it is believed the same piece belongs to Bilton, and there being two Settlem'ts made y'r on by Persons who have no right thereunto, Sect'ry Logan thinks it proper to give orders to Wm. Moor to remove those Persons of the Premises, and that he may take care that no further Spoil be made there, and if at any time it is to be sold he may have the Preferrence of purchasing of it.

19th 6 mo., 1726.

Allowed p. J. L.

Tho. Caldwell, near Nottingham, requests the Grant of a piece of vac't Land adjoyning on the west side of the Tract late Rob't Ashton's, on the east side of Rob't Huchinson's Land, supposed to contain 100 Acres.

Elisha Gatchel and divers other Inhabitants in and about Nottingham have recommended Joseph Freizer to the Com'rs of Property as a man of a Sober Conversation and therefore desire that his request for a parcel of Land in that Neighbourhood to Settle on may be granted.

Geo. Garret requests the Grant of about 250 Acres in the Barrens of Goshen, recommended by Evan Lewis and John Taylor. J. Logan assents this Entry, but that G. Garret is to take no advantage hereof, but apply to the office for a further Settlem't when open.

The late Prop'r, by Deeds of Lease and Release (large printed), dated ye 11th and 12th days of August, 1682, granted to Thomas Roberts, ye Younger Son of Tho. Roberts, of London, Merch't, one Thousand Acres of Land in this Province, under the yearly quitrent of one Shilling p. C't.

Nathaniel Roberts, of Chatham, in the County of Kent, Turner, Brother and Heir at Law of Thomas Roberts, by like Deeds of Lease and Release, dated ye 18th and 19th days of 8b'r, 1723, for £30 sterling granted and conveyed the s'd 1,000 A's to Rich'd Murrey, of Philad'a.

The late Prop'r, by a short Deed Indented ye 16th 5 mo., 1691, for £12 10s Sterling granted unto Thomas Williamson, of Croton, in the County of Chester, 375 Acres of Land in Pensylvania, towards Susquehannah River, quitrent one Shill. p. C't, to commence at taking up and settling the same.

Jacob Littlemore, Son and Heir of Hannah Littlemore,

who was Sister and Heir of the said Thomas Williamson, by his Power of Attorney, dated the 22d Day of Feb, 1723-4, hath constituted and appointed Evan Lewis and Peter Dix, both of Chester County, to take up the same for his use.

The late Prop'r, by a short Deed Indented, dated ye 16 day of ye 5 mo., 1691, for £12 10s Granted 375 Acres of Land towards Susquehannah River to Henry Maydock, of Holm Hall, in the County of Chester, quitrent 1 Shill. p. C't, to commence at taking up and Sealing the same. Mordecai Maydock, Son of the said Henry, requests a Warr't to take up the same; 25 acres to be added by J. Logan's order, to be paid for.

Peter Rist requests the Grant of about 400 Acres lying near.

Joseph Branton requests that he may have the Grant of 650 Acres formerly laid out to Rob't Way, on Mill Creek, a Branch of Conestogo, but by him declined. He has given the descendants of R. Way satisfaction for the Charge of Survey, &c., and is ready to pay the Purchase Money to the Prop'r.

The late Prop'r, by Deeds of Lease and Release, dated the 11 and 12 days of 8b'r, 1681, Granted to John Boye, of Luckington, Coun. Wilts, Mercer, one Thousand Acres of Land, quitrent one shill. for every hundred Acres, as by Copies of the said Deeds ratified, recognized and confirmed by the said late Prop'r under his Hand and the lesser Seal of the Province, the 20th of ye Month called July, 1710, the said Deeds being affirmed to be consumed by Fire.

William Boye, of Titherington, in the County of Gloucester, Surgeon, Son and Heir of Francis Boye, late of the same place, Dece'd, who was eldest Brother and Heir of the said John Boye, by like Deeds of Lease and Rel., dated ye 24th and 25th of March, 1721, for £10 Granted and conveyed the said 1,000 Acres to Bovey Clark, of Thornbury, in the said County of Gloucester, Tallow chandler, his heirs and Assigns forever. The said Bovey Clark, by other like Deeds, dated the 22d and 23d days of March, 1725, for £30 Granted the said 1,000 Acres to John Packer, then of Moorton, in the said Parish of Thornbury, but now of this Province, who requests warr'ts to take up the same with the Lotts and Lib. Land.

Ulrick Burkhold, Hans Krow and Hans Leman request by Christian Heer some lands to settle on in their Neighbourhood, they being honest men and will pay.

The Friends, Inhabitants of Nottingham, having built a meeting house on the Publick Lot of that Township, request that they may have fifty Acres thereof laid out for the meeting's use.

Elisha Gatchel requests the Grant of about 300 Acres, the South part thereof, and Sam'l Littler   Acres near the North

End, and ——— Churchman a narrow strip at the North end of the Lot, the whole breadth.

James Daniel and Rob't Macke request a Parcell of Land for each of them to settle on, the former dwells at Whiteclay Creek, the other at Octoraro Creek, requested by y'r Minist'r Craighead.

Wm. Richardson requests the Grant of a Parcel of Land where he is already settled, about 200 Acres, near Pecque. Samuel Robinson requests the same Favour for about 200 Acres about a mile from the above Settlem't. Allow'd p. J. Logan.

The late Prop'r, by Deeds of Lease and Release, dated ye 1st and 2d days of March, 1681, Granted to Roger Beck, of Bryam Yard, in the County of Hereford, Ironmonger, five hundred Acres of Land in this Province, quitrent one Shilling for every hundred Acres. The said Roger Beck, by like Deeds dated ye 29th and 30th days of June, Anno 1721, for £24, Money of Great Britain, granted and released the said five hundred Acres, with the App'es, unto John Harris, of the Parish of Kings Swinford, in the County of Stafford, Butcher, who now requests warr'ts for the Land, Lib. Land and Lots.

Thomas John, of Nottingham, having some Years ago had about two hunderd Acres of Land surveyed to him in that Neighbourhood, has sold his right of the same to Thomas Hughs (Son-in-Law to Elisha Gatchel), and he to Wm. Reynolds, and upon the earnest Request of E. Gatchel this Entry is made.

Allowed p. J. L.

James King, Charles Allen and Josiah Pain, Kinsman of Jos. Kirkbride, having settled near Octoraro, desire that they may have some convenient quantities of Land surveyed to them and they will pay for the same, they being Persons in good Circumstances, as Joseph Kirkbride informs.

Henry Carpenter, of Conestogo, sets forth that one Henry Vinger, who some years ago settled on a parcell of Land near the Land of Herman Richman, by Isaac Taylor's appointm't, who was to have Survey'd the Land, as Henry says, but was prevented by his sudden return home, the said Vinger settled accordingly, and afterward dyed, leaving a Widdow and two Sons, who desire to have 200 Acres, but a Son of John Musgrove has since settled within that Land and Spoil'd the poor man's design. Write to Isaac Taylor about it.

Henry Carpenter requests the Grant of about 600 A's upon ye north branch of Conestogo.

John Kirkpatrick and Moses Ross request the grant of some Land near Octoraro Creek for Settlements for themselves.

Wm. Evans having seated at Octoraro on a piece of Land whereon John Devor sometime dwelt, requests the Grant of about 60 A's adjoyning on the same.

Alexand'r Ewens requests the Grant of a piece of Land on the Head of Cobourn's run for a Settlement.

Thos. Jackson (recommended in 7b'r last by Jos. Pennock and since by Elisha Gatchell) requests the Grant of a Parcel of Land near Octoraro Creek, which J. Logan consents he shall have about 200 Acres.

At a meeting of the Commissioners of Property ye 16 of the 11 mo., 1726.

Present, Rich'd Hill, Isaac Norris, James Logan, Rob't Asheton and Thomas Griffiths.

Isaac Norris produces Deeds from Ch. Marshall, Rich'd Whitpain, John Beasly, Tho. Cox and Mary Davy, who grants to Jonah Smith five hundred acres on Schuylkill, with all the City Lotts and Liberty Land apperten't to Six Thousand acres, said to be the original purchase of Ch. Marshall and Company. Jonas Smith being so seized dyed, and his only daughter Johannah, together with her Husband, Thomas Moor, by Deeds dated   , Granted the above mentioned Land, Lib. Land and Lotts, together with two other Tracts in Philad'a County, unto John Falconar and Andrew Hamilton, who by other Deeds dated ye   , Granted and conveyed all the above mentioned Land, Lib. Land and Lotts to Isaac Norris, who upon his purchasing the same had a Warr't for 60 Acres of Liberty Land, and it now appearing that there is Six and Thirty Acres of Lib. Land yet due to the said Is. Norris, he requests a Warr't to lay out the same.

The City Lotts belonging to the said purchase having been formerly laid out in the City on Schuylkill side but not returned so intelligibly as to find the certain Spots, He requests a Warr't to have the said Lotts fixed under certain bounds. The Commissioners consent that the Lots be lay'd out together in any place where Vac't and a Warr't Granted for the same.

Jonas Anderson, the Presbiterian Minister, who formerly lived at Newcastle, is desireous to settle among the People at Donnigall, and therefore requests the Grant of about 300 acres of Land for a Plantation. He having liv'd in repute amongst the People at N. Castle, may be of Service to the people where he is now going to settle, for w'ch reason Sect'ry Logan has ordered this Entry to be made in his favour.

Isaac Norris sets forth his right to 829 Acres of Land, the

Tract where he dwells being mostly made up of Liberty Rights, and by Jacob Taylor's resurvey of the same it appears that he has but 808 Acres in his Tract, so that he is deficient in the Quantity he ought to have, 21 Acres, for which he requests a Warr't. Granted.

The following Warr'ts were signed when the Comm'rs met ye 16th 11 mo., 1726. :
To John Packer for 984 Acres, in two Warr'ts.
To Ditto for Lott and Lib. Land.
To Rich'd Murry for 1,000 Acres, in 2 Warr'ts.
To Mordecai Maydock for 375.
Jacob Littlemore for 375.

2, 12 mo., 1726.

Allowed J. L.

James Buchanan and Alexander Allison, recommended from Elisha Gatchell, requests the Grant of two Parcells of Land formerly seated by Tho. Withers and James Langley, the latter on Octoraro Creek, opposite to Jonas Arskin, the other a little lower down the same Creek, they desire two Hundred Acres to each place.

Enoch Cummings requests the Grant of a piece of vacant Land joyning on his Tract in Kunboll's neck, in Sussex, where he dwells, supposed to contain about 50 A's.

Upon John Taylor's application to Secret'y Logan he is permitted to Survey for himself the Quantity of two Thousand Acres of Land back in Chester County, where the same may be found vac't, in 3 or 4 Parcells, in order that it may be confirm'd to him when the Office is open for that Purpose, at the Price that other Lands then unsurveyed will be sold for.

John Eby requests the Grant of a piece of vac't Land upon a Branch of Conestogo Creek to build a Grist Mill for the conveniency of the Neighbourhood.

Elisha Gatchel requests (on behalf of Rich'd Jones) a parcell of Land in the Barrens, near Nottingham, joyning to a Tract late Wm. Bail's, now Sam'l Whiting's, supposed to be about or near 200 Acres.

Daniel Ashcraft, of Wrights Town, requests the Grant of a Tract of Land in or near that Township, where Edw'd Milner is settled on presumption, if Milner does not purchase the same.

Alex'r Mongumry requests (by His Brother-in-Law, Wm. Halliday) the Grant of a piece of Land near Octoraro Creek for a Settlem't.

Thomas Johnson, who has purchased Thomas Falkoner's 250 Acres of Land at Pecque, desires the Addition of some vac't Land adjoyning to the same. Speak to Isaac Taylor about it.

James Armitage requests the Grant of a piece of vac't Land lying between Reynold Howel and George Gillespie, supposed to be about 9 or 10 Acres, Also a parcell of vac't Land lying between two Tracts called Fernsworth and Bishop's Choice, in Kent County, lying on both sides of the King's Road and on the North side of a branch of Murther Creek.

Hans Hess, of Conesotgo, requests a piece of Land for his Son Jacob between a Branch of Conestogo and Hans Ulrick, he also requests about 75 Acres joyning to his own Tract.

10th 1 mo., 1726-7.

Christop'r Topham requests the Grant of 200 Acres of Land lying about 2 miles to the west of William Darter, in the Forrest of Sussex County.

Thomas Haninger and Philip Sloong request the Grant of some Land for 2 Settlem'ts upon a Branch of Conestogo.

Mouns Jones (by his Son) requests the Grant of about 200 Acres about 8 miles above their Settlem't, on the other side of Schuylkill.

Hans Graeff requests the Grant of a piece of Land on Cocalico Creek (a branch of Conestogo) to build a Grist Mill for accommodating the Neighbourhood.

Hans Miller requests the Grant of 100 Acres on little Conestogo, recommended by Christop'r Franciscus.

Hugh Morrison requests the Grant of a piece of vac't Land ly ng to the West of Rob't Finney, near Octoraro about

---

8th 2d mo., 1727.

Elizabeth Dawson (Widow of James Dawson) requests the Grant of about 60 Acres of Land joyning on the west side of the land formerly laid out to her Husband, which she has been forced to sell to pay her husband's Debts.

Sebastin Byer and George Goodman request the Grant of a parcell of Land each of them near Conestogo.

11th 2 mo., 1727.

Allowed p. J. Logan.

Rob't Finney having purchased a Tract of 900 acres of Land of Michael Harlan, near Elk River, hath since procured two small parcells to be added to the same, containing together

200 Acres, which he now requests may be granted to him, as also about 150 Acres lying on the North East side of his tract.

Arthur Paterson requests the Grant of a Parcell of Land near Dunagall.

---

2 mo., 26th, 1727,

Peter Hastings and Sam'l Galbreath producing recommendations from El. Gatchel, Wm. Brown and others, of Nottingham, requests the Grant of two Parcells of Land in that Neighbourhood for Settlements.

Albert Henricks requests the Grant of about 200 Acres of Land between the old Settlem't of Francis Worley at Octoraro and Robert Baker.

John Grigg desires the continuation of his request entered some years since, enquire of Isaac Taylor how Christopher Wilson's lines interferes w'th Furnesses' Tract and to endeavour to accommodate John's request, also ye rem'r of Deffosses'.

George Grigg requests that he may have the grant of about 500 Acres in the Tract called S'r John Fagg's Mannor.

Tho. Dakeyne requests the Grant of a Parcell of vac't Land adjoyning or near his Land at Redlyon Branch, New Castle County.

John McNeile some time ago requested of Sec'ry Logan the Grant of a Parcell of Land at Donagal on Checasalungo Creek, and has now again by his Letter requested the same Favour in order that he may proceed to make some improvement.

John Cadwalader, of Horsham, requests the Grant of 250 Acres of Land in the great Swamp between John Lester and Jos. Gilbert.

Rich'd Edwards requests the Grant of a piece of Land for a Settlement near Nathan Evans's Mill, on a Branch of Brandywine, reccom'ded by D. LLewellen.

John Jordan requests the Grant of about 100 Acres of Land at Doe run, joyning his other Land, purchased of Tho. Nixon, and on the Land of Morgan Bryan.

Requested by Peter Bizalion the Grant of 200 Acres of Land adjoyning to the Tract where he dwells, 100 at each end of his Tract. Isaac Taylor present, allowed by J. Logan.

Joseph Rayle requests the Grant of about 200 Acres of vac't Land near or adjoyning to John Peel, on the Branches of Duck Creek.

Joseph Moor (recommended by Elisha Gatchel) requests the Grant of a piece of Land for a Settlem't about 2 or 3 miles from Tho. Reid's

Wm. Dickey requests the Grant of a small piece of vacant Land joyning to a Grist Mill he has lately built on the Land formerly granted to Nathan Dicks.

Rich'd Allison requests the Grant of 300 Acres at Dunnegall, this Entry allow'd p. Sect'ry Logan.

Evan James requests the Grant of about 80 Acres near Simon James', in Newcastle County, this was before requested by Tho. Dakeyne.

Cornelius Truax requests the Grant of a Parcel of vac't Land lying between Ward's neck and Moll's Tract, with some Marsh adjoyning.

Lewis William requests the Grant of a Piece of vac't Land joyning to his tract where he dwells in Whitland, in Chester County, being about 50 Acres, recommended by Wm. Paschall and allowed p. J. Logan.

Moses Musgrave obtained an order for surveying 300 Acres of Land, 140 Acres whereof being laid out on a Branch of Octoraro. He sold his Right to it to Roger Dyer, who sold the same to George Ledyard, who is now ready to pay for the same, and desires a Warr't for it in his own name, and to have the Addition of about 100 Acres adjoyning to the above.

Benjamin Roads, recommended by sundry Inhabitants of Conestogo, requests about 100 Acres of Land near a Branch of Conestogo.

The late Prop'r, by Deeds of Lease and Release, dated ye 9 and 10th of March, 1683, granted to John Streipers, of Kaldkircham, in the County of Juliers, on the Bord'rs of Germany, five Thousand Acres of Land in this Province, 4,448 Acres whereof were in the year 1703 Surveyed to him in the County of Bucks, and confirmed to him by Patent Anno 1705, and afterwards the said John Streipers dying an Alien, without Naturalization, his heirs were incapable of selling the said Land or taking a lawfull descent from him and the said Tract being so disadvantageously situated that the Agents of the said Heirs of Jno. Streipers could not make sale thereof to any purpose for their Constituants, whereupon James Logan being interested in a considerable Iron work in the said County of Bucks, which requires a large Tract of Land to supply the same with Timber, Wood, &c., made an Agreem't with Leonard Streipers, Reynier Tysen and Griffith Jones, the said Agents, for the Tract of 4,448 Acres, with the view of surrendering the same where it was located for the like quantity adjoyning to the Iron works, and in order for the Purpose a Petition was presen'd by the said Agents ot the Comm'rs of Property, and the case being also represented to the Widdow and John Penn, he, viz., John Penn, by his Letter of the 16 July, 1726, consents and agrees that in consideration that the purchase Money being p'd, the Heirs of Streipers ought to have the Land where it may be of advantage to them, and in regard of the advantage such an Iron work be to the Prop'rs Interest.

And the said J. Logan having actually paid to the Agents of the Heirs of John Streipers seventy-five Pounds, money of this Province, and to the Heirs themselves the further sum of £200 Sterling, and taken Deeds from all the Persons concearned, hath now released to the Commissioners of p'perty for the use of the Prop'r the said 4,448 Acres as the same is located and patented, and has accepted a warr't for the like quantity to be laid out to him in the Township of Durham, adjoyning to the Iron works there, which said Warr't is now actually signed, dated ye 15th of the 3d Mo'th, 1727.

R. Hill has J. L's Release of ye 4,448 Acres.

Present, I. N., J. L., 14th 4 mo., 1727, and approved by R. H. and T. G.

The Comm'rs, by 2 Warr'ts, Dated ye 20, Xb'r, and ye 11 of ye 12 Mo., 1719, Granted to Tho. Griffiths to take up fifteen Hundred Acres of Land which was laid out on Scheckasalungo Creek, in Chester County. The said Tho., by a Deed Poll dated the 20 of August, 1724, bargained and sold the said 1,500 Acres to Isaac Norris, to whom the same is now confirmed by Deed from the Comm'rs, dated ye 15th 4 mo., 1727, for £100 Sterling, bill of Exchange Drawn to J. Logan, Receiver Gen'l.

The Comm'rs, by a Warr't dated 2d 11 mo., 1717-8, Granted Peter Chartier to take up 300 Acres of Land on Susquahannah River, which was accordingly surveyed to him. He, the said Peter, by a Deed Poll dated ye 1, 9b r, 1719, granted and Assigned ye said 300 Acres to J. Logan, who by an Indorsm't on the said Deed granted and Assigned the same Land to Stephen Atkinson, his heirs and Ass., to whom the same is now confirmed, J. Logan having paid to the Trustees Thirty Pounds for the same deed from the Comm'rs to s'd Atkinson, dated the 15th 4 mo., 1727.

Enoch Cummings, of Sussex County, did in the 12 mo. last, request the Grant of a Tract of Land in Kimball's Neck, in ye said County, formerly laid out, as 'tis said, to one ———
———, long since deceased and without Heirs, wherefore he supposes ye same lyable to an Escheat, and now again desires a Grant of it when an Office may be had on the same, as he has also done by Letter dated in ye 2d Mo'th last.

John Harris requests (by John Warder) 500 Acres of Land above Pextang, on Susquahannah River.

Remember the Meeting House Lot at Nottingham, requested by Elisha Gatchel at the next meeting of the Comm'rs.

Abraham Emmit requests the Grant of a Tract of Land in a Fork of Octoraro Creek, intended for three Settlem'ts, and desires a Warr't as soon as possible.

Owen Thomas requests for and on behalf of his Brother, James Thomas, that he may have the Grant of a Parcel of vac't Land joyning on Wm. Crouche's and Wm. Lingard's, he, the said James having made some Improvem'ts thereon.

Jeremiah Shannon has sold to Tho. Harris a parcell of Land between Christina and Whiteclay Creek, to which Shannon has no right nor pretence, and it being vacant Harris desires to purchase it himself.

James Moor requests (by Wm. Halliday) the grant of a piece of vacant Land near Susquahannah and Octoraro.

Rob't Wright desires a Settlem't on Octoraro, requested by Wm. Halliday. He has several Sons, men Grown, who also desire Settlem'ts in that Neighbourhood.

James Allison requests the Grant of a Settlem't above Dunagall, on the place called Cornishe's Plains.

Henry Reynolds requests a piece of vac't Land near Nottingham, adjoyning on the Land late Thomas Chalkley's, now Geen Leiper's, containing about 150 Acres.

Abraham Emmit requests the Grant of 3 or 400 Acres of Land within the Tract called S'r John Fagg's Mannor, when the same may be had.

23d 7b'r, 1727.

Ent'red p. J. L. cons't.

Jonas Davenport having purchased an improvem't of one Leonard Milborn, an Inhabitant of Donagall, has the Consent of Secretary Logan that he, the said Jonas, may hold the said Improvem't with about 200 Acres of Land.

The said Jonas requests the Grant of 300 Acres on the upper side of the Mouth of Sawatara Creek, on Susquahannah River.

John Galbrith (by Jonas Davenport) requests the Grant of 200 Acres next above the 300 Acres requested by Jonas, entered before. This entry is only made as requested, but no grant thereon.

Wm. Wilkinson requests the Grant of about 200 Acres on ye N. E. side, adjoyning to his Settlem't back in Bucks County, on the Road to the Iron Works, called Durham.

John Barnet (recommended by Elisha Gatchel and Ab. Emmit, Jun'r), requests a piece of Land near Jos. Hickman's, on Pecquea, whereon is a small Improvem't, he desires 200 Acres

Simeon Taylor (recommended by Philip Taylor) requests the Grant of 100 Acres adjoyning to the like quantity surveyed some time ago to John White on the Barrens of Nottingham (but not paid for), under whom the said Simeon holds.

Hugh Thompson (recommended by Jno. Taylor) requests the Grant of a piece of vac't Land near Tho. Clark's, at Pecque.

Job Goodson produces a rece't under Tho. Holm's hand, witnessed by George Emlin, for twenty Pounds, in full paym't for ye Purchase of a vacancy of Land of ten foot in Breadth and 396 f't in length, adjoyning to the front Lot late of Alexander Parker, dated ye 17th 6 mo., 1694.

Henry Bare requests the Grant of about 100 Acres joyning on his Land at Little Conestogo.

Francis Wallis and Wm. Lindsey request the Grant for each of them a Settlem't on or near the Heads of Doe Run, Elk River and Whiteclay Creek, the Branches whereof meet very near.

Israel Peterson requests the Grant of about 40 Acres of vac't Land adjoyning to a Piece called Chestnut Hill, formerly Eb. Empson's.

James Turner, from Ireland (recommended by El. Gatchell and others), requests the Grant of a settlem't at Octoraro.

Joseph Hickenbotom and Joseph Sterman request a piece of vac't Land lying between their Plantations near Conestogo Creek mouth. They apprehend T. Perrin will apply for it.

Thomas Worth, Jun'r, requests the Grant of a Parell of va't Land lying in a Fork of Brandywine, bounded on the South with the Barrens, and on the West with the Indian Claims, and on the North va't, about 500 Acres.

Kelian Lan requests (by Anthony Breller) a parcell of Land at Mill Creek, Conestogo, for a Settlem't.

Anthony Breller requests the Grant for a piece of Land near his own Settlem't near the Dutch Mill.

John Creswell on behalf of himself and Rob't Stewart. requests the Grant of some Land for Settlem'ts at or near Octoraro Creek.

Jacob Ryfe, Ulrick Sawk, Rudolph Bane, Jacob Lighter, Jno. Snevelly and Jacob Snevelly and John Long and Casp'r Hoorn, Derrick Miller and Christian Crabill, recommended by several old Settlers.

Rich'd Carter (in behalf of his kinsman, Henry Knowland) requests the grant of 200 A's of land lying on the East side of

Lewis Lewis's, under the Barren Hills, at some distance from Conestogo.

John Bullagh requests the Grant of a Piece of Land in the Mannor of Rockland, if to be found vacant, recommended by E. Grub.

Robert Evans requests about 250 Acres of Land on the west Branch of Octoraro Creek for a Settlement, recommended by Wm. Branson.

The Prop'r, by L. and Rel., dat. ye 17 and 18, 8b'r, '81, Granted to Humphry South 1,000 Acres, who by like Deeds dated ye 1st and 2d of Jan'ry, Granted to Rich'd Whitpain and the rest, 500 Acres, to Barker and Jobson: Jobson, Grandson of ———— Jobson, by Deed dated ye   , Granted 125 Acres of his Grandfather's part to Rees Thomas and Antho. Morris, who also are vested with Rich'd Whitpain's right to the said first mentioned 500 A's, the whole right of Humphry South was laid out in Chester County, near the Welch Tract, but an earlier Survey made and Patented to Arthur Cook, takes in H. South's Land, wherefore the said Rees and Anthony request a Warr't to take up 625 Acres in right of Humphry South, and also 237 Acres in right of Jos. Moor, John Moor and Sabian Coal, which are wanting in a Tract of 2,000 Acres laid out in Chester County, and since Patented to the said Rees and Anthony for 1,763 Acres, for which 862 Acres they request a Warrant.

In the year 1702 there was granted to John Henry Sprogal 100 Acres in or near the Mannor of Springfield, which upon a late resurvey the same, or the greater Part, is found to be within a Tract formerly surveyed to Jonas Smith, but now belonging to Isaac Norris, and the right of the said 100 Acres being now vested in Arent Hassert, of Philad'a, Merch't, he requests that he may be permitted to take up the like quantity within the said Mannor next Schuylkill.

In or about the year 1703 there was surveyed and confirmed to Hannah Price, who was the Widdow of Thomas Musgrove, 500 Acres near the German Tract (as was then supposed), but upon running the lines of the said German Tract the said 500 Acres, or the greatest Part, is within the same, and the right being now vested in Nicholas Scull, of Philadelphia, he requests that he may be permitted to take up the like quantity of 500 Acres Eslewhere in the County of Philad'a that may be found vacant.

In the year 1715 Wm. Cloud obtained a Warr't for 300 Acres of Land to be laid out in Chester County, which by a writing under his hand he assigned his interest in the said Warr't to his Son, Joseph Cloud, who in the year 1718 had 200 Acres in vertue of the said Warr't surveyed to him on a Branch of Conestogo, and in the first Month, 1720, paid £10 in part, and since by Deed dated ye 1 of May, 1725, Conveyed all his right in the said Land to Nathan Evans, jun'r, of the said County, Millright, who has now paid of the remainder, with Interest and quitrent.

The said Nathan Evans requests the Grant of about 100 Acres joyning on the East side of the above mentioned 200 Acres to erect a Mill on, he also requests the Grant of a piece of Land for a Settlement for his Brother, Roger Evans, on the South side of his Tract.

Edward Thornbury (recommended by Charles Springer) requests the Grant of about 200 Acres on the upper part of Conestogo Creek, where he says he has discovered a vacancy.

Enoch Commings requests the Grant of a Tract of Land in Kimball's neck, in Sussex County, called New Harlem, about 3 or 400 Acres.

John Shankland requests the Grant of 200 Acres of Land joyning on his Father, Wm. Shankland, and George Chambers' lines, the Deep Valley and Mill Road.

Archebald Smith desires a Warr't of Resurvey and to rectify the lines of a Tract of Land lying near Longbridge Branch, in Sussex County, the Survey being so irregular that the lines neither meet nor make the Complement, and also that he may have the liberty of taking up some vacant Land joyning to the same, and also to take up 300 Acres in some vacant Place of the County. He also requests about an Acre or two joyning on his Land in Lewis.

Thomas Stokely requests the Grant of 100 Acres on Deep Creek, in Sussex, including Muskeal Savannah.

Joseph Cord requests the Grant of 200 Acres on Longbridge Branch, in Sussex County.

14th Xb'r, 1727.

Rich'd Beson and Daniel Smith, both of Nottingham, and Bona Griffiths, of the Mannor of Rocklands, request the Grant of each of them a Parcell of Land at or near Fishing Creek, which falls into Susquahannah (viz.) :

Richard Beson, for his Children, 1,000 Acres.

Dan'l Smith, for his Sons, 500 Acres.

Bona Griffith, 300 Acres.

In J. L's absence.

The late Prop'r, by L. and Rel., dated ye 23d and 24th 7b'r, 1681, granted to Enoch Flower, of Corsham, in the County of Wilts, 2,000 Acres of Land, of which E. Flower sold several

Pacrells of 250 Acres each. Wm. Mountjoy of Beddeston in the said County, eldest Son and Heir of Thomas Mountjoy, of the same place, Gent., Dece'd, by Deeds ot I. and Rel., dated ye 28th and 29th of July last (for 50), granted and Conveyed 250 Acres, part of E. Flower's purchase, to John Bond, of Abington, in this Province, reciting that E. Flower sold and conveyed the same to the said Tho. Mountjoy, but the Deed is not to be found.

The said Wm. Mountjoy has made affidavit before a master in Chancery that after his Father's Death the Deeds from E. Flower for the said 250 Acres came to his hands, but by some accident are lost, mislaid or destroyed, upon application made to Henry Flower, who dwelt several years with his uncle (the said Enoch), and was well acquainted with his affairs and came into this Province with him he, the said Henry, has certified under his hand that to the best of his remembrance his said uncle sold and conveyed 250 Acres of his said Purchase to the said Thomas Mountjoy, who was a Person of a Good Estate in the said County of Wilts, and having seen the Deeds from Wm. Mountjoy (which he remembers was the name of the Eldest Son of the said Thomas) to John Bond for the said 250 Acres, as also a Letter to himself concerning the same, It is his opinion the sale from Wm. Mountjoy to Jno. Bond is just.

William Brakin requests the Grant of a Pacrell of Land at Fishing Creek, near Susquahannah, and desires a warr't as soon as possible.

Rob't Love requests a parcel of vacant Land near Octoraro, he is recommended by Elisha Gatchel as an Honest, usefull man in that Neighbourhood.

Mathusalem Evans requests the Grant of about 100 Acres between his Plantation and Perkacy Hill.

Hugh Barkly and George Patterson (recommended by Abraham Emmit) request the Grant of a Parcell of vac't Land in a fork of Octoraro for a Settlem't each.

———

11 mo., 1727.

Richd' Empson requests the Grant of about 150 Acres of vac't Land on the North side of the main branch of Duck Creek, above the King's Road, joyning on the west side of the land formerly belonging to James Wyth.

Adam Buckly in his application to Sect'ry Logan has earnestly requested of him the Grant of the upper 200 Acres of Grub's Tract, so called, in Rockland Mannor, and offers £70 p. hundred Acres.

MINUTE BOOK "I."

Rowland Chambers presented a Petition to Sect'ry Logan, subscribed by 40 or 50 Persons, requesting the grant of about 10,000 Acres of Land at Sawhatara, near Pextang, for Settlem'ts for themselves and familys.

John Brookbaker requests the Grant of about 200 Acres joyning to Benj. Hearsy's Land on the little Conestogo Creek, he is ready to pay for it.

John Taylor (al's Hans Snyder) requests the Grant of about 100 Acres joyning on his Land near a Branch of Little Conestogo Creek.

John Littler, Son of Sam'l Littler, late of Nottingham, dec'd, desires to purchase a part of the Common Lot in that Township (formerly requested by his Father). Elisha Gatchel has recommended the young man to James Logan, who consents that his request shall be answered.

Nath'l Newlin obtained the Commissioners' Licence to purchase three hundred Acres of Land where Jos. Cloud (who is considerably indebted to the s'd Nath'l) is settled, near Pextang, on Susquahannah, desires the addition of 200 Acres adjoyning to the same in order to make the tract more Compleat.

Benedictus Venerick sells his 250 Acres to Christian Moyer, who is to pay all that is due on the same to the Prop'r, make a short Deed under the Warr't and Return.

John Sipple, of Kent, requests the Grant of 50 Acres joyning on the North side of his Settlem't, where he dwells.

George Robertson (called Mollasses) requests the Grant of a Parcell of Land in the Cattail Swamp, Kent County.

William Alexander (recommended by James Anderson), requests the Grant of a picee of Land for a Settlement at Dunagall.

Mich'l Jobson requests a Warr't for 125 Acres remaining of his Grandfather Jobson's Purchase made of Humphry South.

---

3 mo., 21, 1728.

Sam'l Hand, of Sussex County, requests the Grant of a piece of vac't Land opposite to his Mill on the Broad Creek.

Allowed p. J. L.

Alexander Ewens, by a very good certificate (as well as by E. Gatchel), is recommended for a Parcell of Land to settle on the Branches of Conewinga.

Timothy Hanson requests the Grant of about 150 Acres of Marsh on the East side of Taylor's Gut, which divides it from his other Marsh.

4 mo., 1728.

Roger Kirk having purchased the Plantation late Step. Stapler's, at Nottingham, requests the Grant of about 50 Acres of Barrens adjoyning on the North side.

Friends Pallsa Friends (a very odd name), who dwells with Dan'l Fierre, desires the Grant of a Piece of vac't Land on the N. side of Pecquea.

Wm. Parker requests the Grant of about 30 Acres of vac't Land lying between his Plantation in Duck Creek neck and Wm. Stanton's and John Dawson's.

Baptist Newcomb, of Sussex County (recommended by Rob't Shankland), requests the Grant of a piece of Marsh lying within his Pasture and adjoyning to the Land or marsh of John Fisher.

The Wife (or Widow) of Rich'd Dobson, of Sussex County, made application to Rob't Shankland (as he writes) for a piece of vac't Land which he undertook to enter for her, but he forgetting or delaying to do it, one John Chiltman, came to him and imposed so far on him as to procure an Entry for himself, and thereupon has taken the Land from the poor Woman who made the first application for it. R. Shankland says that Chiltham Knew that the Land was claimed by the Woman when he applyed to Rob't and affirmed there was no Claim on it.

6 mo., 23, 1728.

Anthony Woodward, on behalf of himself and Son Joseph, requests the Grant of about 400 Acres of Land in the County of Sussex, on Davock's Branch, which runs into the Broad Creek, (called Longbridge Branch).

Evan Jones, Ruth's Brother (of the great Valley), requests the addition of 200 Acres of Land between the upper end of his own Land and John Holland's side line. Speak to Jno. Taylor about it.

Adam Boyd, Minist'r of the Presbiterian Congregation near Octoraro, desires the Grant of about 150 Acres of Ordinary Land on the East side of the Tract where he dwells, being part of Wm. Pusey's Land that was formerly surveyed to him. Speak to I. Taylor for this and for Arthur Park.

The Prop'r, by Indenture dated the 16th day of the 5 mo., 1691, for £12 10s 0d granted to John Bradley, of Moberly, in the County of Chester, Yeom., 375 Acres of Land to be taken up towards the Susquahannah River, quitrent 1sh. p. C't (Royal Mines excepted). Jonathan Bradley, only Son and Heir of the said John (who is deceased), requests a warr't to take up the said Land. Jonathan Bradley, by Deeds dated ye 12 and 13th 9b'r, 1729, granted 75 Acres to Tho. Smedley.

David William (recommended by Joseph Pennock, with whom he served his time) requests the Grant of about 200 Acres of Land not far from Ann Roberts's Plantation.

Johannes Kitzmiller, late from Germany, having purchased the Consent of Nath. Evans to a piece of vac't Land on Little Conestogo Creek, where he had Licence to build a Mill, The said Johannes requests the grant of 3 or 400 Acres of Land adjoyning and is ready to pay for the same. Consented to p. J. Logan. Speak to I. Taylor to lay it out.

The late Prop'r, by Deeds of Lease and Release, dated ye 25th and 26th days of May, Anno 1682, Granted to John Snushold, of Chidington, in the County of Sussex, 500 Acres of Land, quitrent one Shill. p. C't. John Snushold dying Intestate, his nearest Kinswoman, Joan Beach, of Hove, in the same County, who was only Daughter of Rich'd Snushold, of Hackham, who was Brother and Heir of the said John Snushold, by her Attorneys, John Warder and John Sotcher, granted the said 500 Acres to James Steel, who desires a Warr't to take up the same.

This Minute should have been entered 25, 1 mo., 1726.

The late Prop'r, by Deeds of Lease and Release, dated ye 24th and 25th days of May, 1683, Granted to Lancellot Fallowfield, of Great Strickland, in the County of Westmoreland, Yeom., 250 Acres of Land, Quit. one Shill. p. C't.

John Fallowfield, Son and Heir of the said Lancellot, by Deed of L. and Rel., dated ye 29th and 30th days of Xb'r, 1726, Granted and Conveyed the said 250 Acres to his Son Lancellot Fallowfield, who by like deed dated 25th and 26th days of August, 1727, Granted and conveyed the said Land (under Coven'ts) to John Salkeld, of Chester, who desires a warr't for the same.

28th 12 mo., 1728.

Elisha Gatchel, on behalf of Rob't Reynolds, requests that he may hold a Settlement on Pecquea.

The right of George Shore's 5,000 Acres of Land being entered in the Minute Book of 1712, pag. 10, then vested in Amos Strettell, who by Indent'rs of L. and Rel., dated 3d and 4th days of 9b'r, 1721, granted ye whole to Abell Strettell, of Dublin, Merch't.

Wm. Till, of Sussex, requests the Grant of about 600 Acres of Land in the Broad Kill Neck for 3 of his wife's Relations (viz.), Thomas Groves, his Son Luke and daughter Mary, each 200

Acres. This Land appears to have been formerly surveyed, but to whom is not known and therefore must be delayed for further Enquiry.

George Dod having entered about 200 Acres of Land with R. Shankland, lying in the Forrest of Sussex, requests the same may be allowed him.

Casper Wister having often applyed to the Comm'rs for the Grant of 2,000 Acres of Land to be taken up back in the Province. They at length agreed that he should have 1,200 Acres for £133 6s 8d Sterling, for which he then passed his Bills of Exchange, payable to the Prop'ry Trustees in London, and for the 800 Acres he is to pay £128, Money of Pensilvania (in Gold), within Three months after the Date of the Warr't, which is of the 30th 11 mo., 1728-9

Tho. Chandler having lately had a Survey on 100 Acres of Land on the South side of Brandywine Creek, requests that he may have the Grant of about the like quantity of Vac't Land adjoyning added to the former.

George Grigg requests the Grant of about 150 Acres of the Overplus of Joannes Deffoss's Land in Christina Hundred.

The late Prop'r, by L. and Rel., dated ye 10th and 11th days of 8b'r, 1681, granted to Amos Nicholls, of the City of London, Distiller, as p. Recital, Acres of Land in this Province who by like Deeds dated ye 25th and 26th of April, 1682, granted 125 Acres thereof to David Hammond, of Radcliff, in the County of Middlesex, who again by like Deed dated 12 and 13 May, 1682, Granted the same 125 Acres to Eliz'th Meales, of London, Widdow, who by vertue of a Power of Attorney to her Son Sam'l Meales, of Philad'a, He granted the same Land to John Townsend, late of Philad'a, dec'd, who by his last will and Testament authorized and appointed Joshua Carpenter and Wm. Lee to sell the said Land after the decease of his, the said J. Townsend's wife, for the use of his Grand Children, and the said Joshua and William being since Dead, Elizabeth Carpenter, Widdow and Execut'x of the said Joshua, by Deed dated ye 4th of 8b'r last past, granted and conveyed the said 125 Acres to Andrew Hamilton, who desires a warr't for the same.

Dr. Sam'l Chew, of Maidson, in Maryland, and Peter Galloway, of the same Province, requests the Grant of about 3,000 Acres of the Mannor of Freith, on Duck Creek, for the same purposes as Dr. Moor formerly intended on his application in the minutes of Property.

John Bowman requests the Grant of about 200 Acres of Land on Beaver Creek, he is an honest man and will pay (says John Heer).

The Widow of Wolsey Burton, of Sussex, requests the Grant of the overplus Land within her Tract in Long Neck. The Widow Sanders, of the same County, requests the Grant of about 100 Acres of vac't Land between her and the Land late Rich'd Law's.

William Warrington requests the grant of 200 Acres of the Head of Pretty man's Branch, near the Road to Cow Bridge.

Christ'r Topham requests the Grant of 200 Acres adjoyning on the next above.

George Stewart requests the Grant of about 500 Acres of Land below the Fork of Sawatara Creek, 200 Acres for himself and 300 Acres for his Brother-in-Law, Lazerus Stewart.

John Cadwalader requests that he may have a Confirmation on about 250 Acres which he purchased of the Sons of Giles Knight, which was first Granted to Rich'd Few from the Prop'r very early it lies in Warminster. J. Logan is desirous it should be according to J. C's desire.

Nicholas Ridgley, who married a Daughter of Rob't French, late of New Castle, having in Right of his wife some Land in Duck Creek neck, in Kent County, requests the grant of a convenient quantity of marsh lying between the said Land and main Duck Creek.

Abr'm Emmit, jun'r, requests the Grant of about 300 Acres of Land near S'r John Fagg's Mannor, 'tis Claimed by the Heirs of Henry Hollingsworth, but upon search in this office no grant appears for it.

Allowed p. J. Logan.

Rob't Finney requests the Grant of about 600 Acres of vac't Land near Octoraro for Settlements for his two Sons, Rob't and Thomas, and for his son-in-Law, John McClanahan.

David Pugh, of Uchlan, having purchased a Settlem't of Elonar Cook, for which she formerly obtained a Warr't, requests the Grant of 50 Acres adjoyning to the same, he is ready to pay for it.

Joshua Hadley requests (by his Father, Simon Hadley) the grant of a quantity of Land on Fishing Creek, he desires 1,000 Acres.

George Stewart formerly obtained a Grant by warr't for 200 Acres on Susquahannah Rvier, for which he then paid £10, and afterwards obtained of Isaac Taylor a survey of some more Land adjoyning to the quantity of about 500 Acres, including the first 200 Acres, it lyes between the Land where John Gardner settled and the Land laid out to Rob't Wilkins. George desires a regular Survey and return on the whole and he will forthwith provide money to pay for the same.

Jacob Huber (by Jacob Moyer) requests the Grant of 150 Acres of Land (vacant) on the west side of Conestogo Creek.

Hans Hess requests the addition of about 50 Acres adjoyning to his Settlement near Conestogo.

14th 9b'r, 1730.

Joseph Jones, of Nottingham, having formerly obtained of Sect'ry Logan the Liberty of settling a piece of Land on Conywingo Creek but since finding it not very suitable for him, he, the said Joseph, relinquishes his Pretence in the same to James King, who being present, desires that about 500 Acres may be surveyed to him at the same place for Settlements for his Children.

John Carns requests the Grant of a picee of Land at Octoraro for a Settlement near John Rob.

Sam'l Preston requests the Grant of 100 Acres of Swamp Scituate on Hollander's Creek and Dam Creek.

The late Prop'r, by Deeds of Lease and Release, dated the 17th and 18th of Oct'r, 1681, Granted to Herbert Springet one Thousand Acres of Land in Pensilvania, quitr. one shilling for every hundred Acres, And by other like Deeds of the same date, whereof Copies are produced, the said Prop'r granted to the said Herbert Springet 500 Acres of Land in the said Province, under the quitrent of one shilling for each hundred Acres. Anthony Springet, Eldest Brother and Heir to H. S., by other like Deeds dated ye 5th and 6th days of June, 1729, granted the whole 1,500 Acres to John Page, of London, Gent. John Page, by like Indentures dated ye 28th and 29th of July, 1729, Granted the same 1,500 Acres to John Simpson, of London, Merch't.

The late Prop'r, by Deeds dated ye 24th and 25th days of April, 1682, Granted to Wm. Clark, of Westminster, Confectioner, 500 Acres of Land in Pensilvania, quitrent one shilling for every hundred Acres. Wm. Clark, by like deeds dated ye 21st and 22d days of 9b'r, 1720, granted the same 500 Acres to Rich'd Smith, of London, Pewterer, Who by other like Deeds dated the 12th and 13th days of Feb., 1728, granted the same 500 Acres to Wm. Allen, who requests a warr't for the same.

And'w Cox requests the Grant of about 200 Acres of Land in Caln, on the Back of Peter Bizalion's Tract. He is a Blacksmith by trade and is recommended by Sundry of the Inhabitants.

Joseph Pinnock requests that Rob't Burn may have the Liberty to settle on a Piece of vac't Land joyning to John Taylor's Land on Doe Run.

Thomas Hean requests to have the Grant of a Piece of Land near Cocalico, where he has settled and liv'd about 3 years, recommended p. Casper Wister as an honest man that will pay.

The late Prop'r, by Deeds of L. and Rel., dated ye 14th, 15th August, 1682, Granted to John Millington, of Shrewsbury, in the Coun. Salop, Baker, and Mary his wife, 500 Acres of Land in this Province, quitr't one shill. Sterl. p. C't.

John Millington, by his last Will and Testament, dated (as p. recital in the following Deeds) ye 20th April, 1689 (his wife being before deceased), devised the said 500 Acres to his Nephew, John Millington, and to the Heirs of his Body, and for default of such Issue, then to be divided between the Children of Mary Wilks and Rebecca Crudginton, and the said John Millington, the Nephew, also dying without Issue, Mary Hughs, Marth. Wilks and Damarose Wilks, the Children, of Mary Wilks, and Mary the wife of Sam'l Giles, and Ann Hughs, the Children of Rebecca Crudginton, together with the said Sam'l Giles, in and by Deeds of L. and Rel., dated ye 15th and 16th days of 7b'r, 1714, for £10 Sterl., grant and Release the said 500 acres, with the app's, unto Mordecai Moor, of Maryland.

Rich'd Moor, eldest Son of the said Mordecai, by Deeds dated ye 9th and 10th days of Xb'r, 1729, for £95 Granted the said 500 Acres to Ralph Assheton, of Philad'a, who by like deeds dated the 19 and 20th of 9b'r, and the 27th and 28th of Xb'r, 1730, Granted 250 Acres thereof to Squire Boon and the other 250 Acres to John Naglee, who desire warr'ts to take up the same.

---

11 mo., 1730.

Jonas Chamberlain desires about 50 Acres of Land near the Gap for to accommod'e his Trade, being a Tanner.

Enoch Cummings represents that there is an old Plantation lying on a Creek called Mill Creek, in the County of Sussex, it formerly belonged to J. Fisher, Grandfather to Enoch's wife, and there being now no heirs to whom it can Lawfully descend, he desires to have the Grant of it from the Prop'r.

Henry Snook, Christop'r Snyder, Conrad Himry, from Rariton, request the Grant of some Land about 7 miles above Durham for Settlements for themselves.

Mich'l Bare, recommended by X'n Heer, requests the Grant of about 200 Acres of Land near Cocalico.

John Warke (blacksmith) being settled on a Branch of Octoraro, desires to have 200 laid out to him.

William Loftin (by Elisha Gatchell) requests the Grant of a Parcel of Land for a settlement near Susquahannah, also on behalf of one James Crawford, who has settled on the Barrens of Nottingham, on a Branch of Elk River, and John Crawford likewise, adjoyning to the above.

Elisha Gatchell requests the Grant of two Parcells of Land in or near Nottingham, one containing about 150 Acres lying on the Crooked Brook, the other on the Road between Nottingham and Newgarden, of about the same Quantity.

Elisah Gatchell, on behalf of John Cristy, who was recommended to J. L. in the year 1726 for a Settlement, desires that he may hold the place whereon he is settled, near Octoraro, with a convenient Quantity of Land, as E. Gatchell thinks fit.

Rob't Barber, of Conestogo, requests the Grant of a Parcel of vac't Land next above the old settlem't of Peter Bizalion, at Pextang. J. L. consents to his request.

4 mo., 1731.

Jacob Kollock requests the Grant of about 200 Acres of Land in the Forrest of Sussex.

The Late Prop'r, by Lease and Rel., dated the 3 and 4th 3 mo., 1682, Granted to John Mason 1,000 Acres of Land in this Province, which has been already laid out, but Rob't Mason, surviving Son of the said John Mason, finding the Lib. Land belonging to the said Purchase not yet taken up, by Deed dated 15th 5 mo. last past, granted the same to John Ashmeade, who desires a warr't to take up the same.

8b'r, 2d, 1731.

James Buckley requests the Grant of about 200 A's of Land on the Branches of Octoraro, to build a Mill, as well for Merch'ts as the Countrey. This was afterwards confirmed to J. B. in Right of Sam'l Mickle's purchase made of the Children of Capt. Crispin.

Sam'l Hollingsworth (on behalf of his Kinsman, Wm. Andrees) requests the Grant of about 100 Acres of vac't Land in Kennet, between the Land late Ezkiel Hurlan's and James Wallis'. Speak to I. Taylor and write to Sam'l Hollingsworth about it.

Francis Reater, recommended by Philip Kuilwine and Peter Wents, requests the Grant of a piece of Land on Andeahalea Creek for a Settlem't.

Wm. Farrell requests the Grant of about 200 Acres near John Miller, Simon Graham and Tho. Clark.

MINUTE BOOK "I." 763

James Miller (Son of Gawen) having purchased a Tract of Land of John Taylor in the Great Valley, joyning to Caleb Pearce, requests the Grant of a small vacancy between his Land and Caleb's, supposing it to contain about 50 Acres.

12th, 9b'r, 1731.

Jacob Hyer (at the Instance of X'r FFranciscus) requests the Grant of a Parcell of Land on a Branch of Conestogo, called Carter's Branch.

1st mo., 17th, 1732.

Abraham England requests that he my have the refusal of the piece of Land formerly called Edw'd Owen's, on main Duck Creek.

James Miers and Abraham Wynkoop request the Grant of two small Islands, with a Quantity of Marsh to each, on Cedar Creek, in the County of Sussex, for Accommodating their Cattell.

3 mo., 1732.

Jabez Fisher, son of Thomas Fisher, late of Sussex County, requests that he may have the Grant of a Parcell of Vacant Marsh lying between his Plantation and Delaware Bay, and from the Broad Creek to Prime hook Bay, called Plum point Marsh.

Wm. Burton, of the Indian River, in Sussex (by Rob't Shankland's Letter), complains that Wm. Waple and Rich'd Poltney, on pretence of Entreys made w'th R. Shankland, have encroached on his Land. He desires no Grant may be made to those Persons till he may be heard.

Elisha Gatchel (on behalf of his daughter, Abigail Job) represents that her late Husband, Enoch Job, settled by Consent of the Commissioners on a piece of Land on the N. E. side of Nottingham, containing between 3 and 400 Acres, and the said Enoch being since Dead without Issue, and the Land not being regularly granted nor paid for, the said Elisha requests that his said Daughter may be allowed to hold the same upon satisfying the Proprietors.

Jacobus Bruin, Esq'r., Dr. John Hamilton, Joseph Wheeler, Tho. Quick and Hendrick Schoomaker presented a Petition (by Jos. Wheeler) to purchase some Parcells of vac't Land on this side Delaware of the Indians, who claim it, in Order to make Settlem'ts for themselves and to purchase the same from the Prop'r when it is to be sold. In answer to which Petition J. Logan writ the following Letter:

Friend JOSEPH WHEELER:

The Petition from Jacobus Bruin, Esq'r., thyself and others to our Commiss'rs, which thou delivered me some time since, requesting leave to purchase of the Indians and to settle some of the low Lands up the River Delaware cannot at present be granted, but it shall be noted on our minutes that when any of those Lands are to be disposed of, which I believe will be ere long, you may have the preferrence, in Case they should not be otherwise disposed of in England, of which I have no apprehension. In the mean time, as the Petition'rs cannot as yet settle these Lands themselves, they are desired not to suffer any other Person or Persons to seat them.

I am thy Loving Fr'd,

J. LOGAN.

PHILAD'A, 1, *Aug'st*, 1727.

These may Certify that James King obtained a Grant about 3 years ago for a convenient Tract of Land near Octoraro Creek, and therefore ought not to be disturbed by any incroachm'ts by other Persons. The said J. K. was also allowed to settle and Hold a Tract of Land at Conewingo Creek, where Joseph Jones had a Licence to settle before him.

J. STEEL.

PHILAD'A, 11*th* 9*b'r*, 1729.

---

6 mo., 1732.

Joseph Gregory requests for his Son the Grant of about 100 Acres of Marsh which lies within his Pasture near Salem, and that he may hold the Prop'rs Marsh and Land in Salem on Rent.

John Grigg requests the Grant of a piece of vac't Land between Brandywine and Squirrel Creek.

---

3 mo, 30th, 1739.

Joseph Comb having obtained a Survey on a Tract of 200 Acres of Land near that call'd Streipers, in Bucks County, and being now going for England to receive an Estate fallen to him, desires the Prop'rs forbearance till he may return with Effects to pay for the same; his wife and Children are to continue on the Land in his Absence.

Friend G. DAKEYNE:

The Bearer, J. Ball, has been favoured in his   by Sect'ry Logan, who is willing he shall have that 103 Acres of Land surveyed to him about 8 years ago, to which John now desires an Addition out of the vacancy that lies between that already surveyed and Wm. Brakin. If there be no other Claim I am willing he shall have his request if it exceed not 100 Acres.

J. S.

2d 6 mo., 1726.

Friend JONAS POTS:

I desire thee to deliver to the bearer hereof, John Head, all those black Walnut Loggs which thee some time ago secured for the Prop'rs use, and his rec't with this Order shall be thy suff't discharge for the same. From ffr'd

J. S.

Thereon Wm. Evan and Johannes Roseberry are settled near the County line on the Land called the Prop'rs 500 Acres, adjoyning to Rob't Ashton's.

The former Commiss'rs W. M., R. T. and J. G., by Pat. dated ye 25th 9b'r, 1691, confirmed to Peter Nelson 468 Acres of Land under the yearly quitr't of one Bushell of good Winter wheat for each hundred Acres, the Plantation and Land late Cap't Palmer's (now Wm. Ball's). Gunner Rambo, by Deed dated 26 June, 1697, sold to Major George Lillington, in 3 parcells, 183 Acres more, in Right of John Tank 8. Hans Lykill al's Nelson, by Deed dated 30th Aug't, 1697, sold to the said G. Lilington 175, and of Meadow 8. Tho's Fairman, by deed dated ye 19th Xb'r, 1698, granted to G. Lillington a small Island, 15. Andreas Lykell al's Nelson, by Deed dated 22d Jan'ry, '99, Sold to G. Lillington, of Meadow 10. Benj. Fairman, by Deeds dated 17, 18 Mar., 1728, Granted to Antho. Palmer, of Meadow 11. Anthony Palmer claimed under John Tank 27. Sold by Capt. Anthony Palmer to Wm. Ball, 620.

Oblig's delivered to And'w Hamilton 26, 2 mo., 1720. Daniel Cookson's since p'd and Deliver'd up. Capt. Rich'd Anthony part p'd and ye Oblig. returned. Jno. Holston p'd and Deliv'd up. Edw'd Smout part p'd and ye Oblig. returned 26th 3 mo., 1720 deliver'd to Andrew Hamilton, John Guest, Esq'r, his Obligation for £45.

Rich'd ap Richard, &c., Jno. Rees, Matt's Vanbeber's obligation since p'd and deliv'd up.

Delivered A. H., Henry Pennybaker's certificates and Return for the Land sold to H. G. Reiff.

John McDaniel informs that Matt's Peterson, Zachary Bartletson, Simon and John Eden, Tho. Nickson, P. Peterson, Lacey Horton, Charles Horton, James Butterfield, W. Homan, Cor's Corneliousson, Peter and Jacob Hendrickson destroys the Prop'rs Land and Timber in Penn's Neck, they threaten to shoot any that shall attempt to hinder them.

Patent Granted to Rob't Webb for 40 Acres Lib. Land, dated 28th 7b'r, 1691, appurten't to John Barber's Purchase, beginning at a Corn'r tree of John Daye's Land, thence W. S. W. 113 p's, then N. N. W. 56 p., then E. N. E. 113 p's, then S. S. E. 56.

Casper Lybeka, a Taylor, near John Shall, having about 20 Acres of Land, desires the Grant of Two Timber Trees on a piece of vac't Land near him, which he desires to Purchase.

The end of proprietary Book I, Compared and Corrected p.
JNO. HUGHES.

GENERAL INDEX.

[It has been deemed best to simply furnish an index of all surnames recorded in these minutes. In the case of the commissioners and other names of whom are mentioned on almost every page, the word, *general*, has been affixed.]

A.

Abraham, 616, 678.
Acrod, 614, 676.
Adams, 25, 28, 89, 260, 319, 338, 584, 621, 686, 712, 724, 732, 736.
Addis, 109.
Allen, 8, 9, 13, 17, 144, 172, 242, 250, 251, 268, 295, 305, 325, 335, 352, 411, 422, 424, 440, 442, 470, 476, 532, 645, 651, 663, 667, 695, 698, 726, 740, 743, 760.
Alloway, 144.
Alsop, 254, 255, 401, 408, 655, 689.
Alford, 309, 310.
Alricks, 414, 415, 466, 491.
Allyes, 616, 678.
Alexander, 649, 661, 662, 677, 755.
Allebaugh, 708.
Alcock, 730.
Allison, 745, 748, 750.
Ambler, 81, 274, 435, 436.
Andrews, 51, 57, 196, 239, 303, 309, 315, 347, 353, 354, 444, 450, 461, 485, 494, 526, 554, 577, 645, 646, 687, 718, 722, 762.
Anderson, 138, 233, 237, 246, 260, 331, 344, 349, 350, 373, 456, 605, 633, 638, 641, 717, 719, 744, 755.
Annis, 510, 511, 631, 684.
Annand, 552.
Anthony, 584, 765.
Antis, 723.
Appehon, 73, 593.
Apjohn, 670, 701.
Arskin, 251, 556, 745.
Arets, 270, 273, 274, 280, 420, 483.
Arinson, 347.
Arthur, 365.
Archer, 437.
Armitage, 546, 746.
Arnold, 576, 712.
Arey, 648.
Asby, 417, 579.
Ashcome, 7, 9, 14, 46, 47, 275, 286, 297, 357, 362, 439, 448, 502, 519.
Asheton, 19, 40, 282, 283, 303, 320, 380, 401, 410, 431, 439, 451, 467, 475, 479, 542, 716, 741, 744, 761, 765.
Ashmead, 86, 263, 454, 462, 762.
Ashman, 138, 349.
Askain, 208, 320.
Asler, 714.
Ashcraft, 745.
Atkinson, 25, 36, 39, 62, 68, 154, 155, 156, 157, 159, 205, 277, 306, 320, 340, 342, 348, 422, 426, 457, 475, 520, 521, 547, 576, 601, 616, 617, 714, 720, 749.
Atkins, 81, 161, 180, 331.
Aukes, 205.
Austen, 378, 401.
Aubry, 489, 644, 645, 686.
Avery, 701.

B.

Barker, 9, 26, 305, 348, 397, 398, 461, 463, 467, 470, 472, 608, 657, 692, 720, 731, 739, 752.
Baldwin, 23, 117, 249, 299, 300, 497, 640.
Baker, 45, 231, 232, 270, 271, 275, 298, 318, 331, 341, 375, 407, 423, 434, 466, 482, 525, 594, 611, 707, 747.
Barkstead, 51, 56, 333.
Badcock, 59, 97, 435.
Barclay, 71, 96, 754.
Barber, 74, 121, 241, 375, 387, 436, 762, 765.
Barnard, 86, 363, 394.
Bankson, 91, 349, 350, 353, 354, 457, 468, 664, 668, 671, 699, 701, 729.
Barnes, 99, 202, 214, 306, 342, 430, 575, 716.
Bainer, 178.
Basnett, 180, 181, 183, 184.
Baily, 196, 233, 234, 241, 292, 293, 327, 346, 347, 358, 394, 397, 411, 429, 477, 578, 579, 590, 593, 631, 684.
Ball, 204, 219, 224, 238, 251, 268, 327, 708, 713, 714, 764, 765.
Bainton, 249, 330.
Bates, 249, 296, 319, 388.
Barret, 261, 523, 524, 588.
Bannor, 261.
Baunse, 265.

INDEX.

Bales, 280.
Bail, 280, 745.
Bainbridge, 334.
Bartre, 340.
Batsford, 385.
Bathurst, 394.
Bartleson, 413, 542, 543, 765.
Barry, 495.
Baxord, 510.
Bayard, 513.
Barrow, 575.
Batten, 588, 618.
Bair, 622, 628, 640, 647.
Bawcom, 633.
Bacon, 653, 659, 687, 695.
Bavely, 712.
Barden, 717.
Babb, 725,
Barnet, 750.
Bane, 751.
Beardsley, 25, 160, 351.
Benett, 26, 33.
Bethell, 50.
Bevan, 67, 158, 322, 328, 409, 420, 428, 468, 490.
Berry, 68, 231, 494, 595, 597.
Bennet, 195, 215, 236, 255, 278, 284, 307, 330, 360, 409, 423, 451, 452, 472, 577, 601, 658, 692.
Beans, 207, 292, 385, 430.
Beaks, 213, 214, 267, 268, 334, 376, 415.
Bernard, 233, 234, 241, 243.
Best, 246, 443, 446.
Beckingham, 272, 273, 276, 535, 607, 610, 674.
Beeson, 280, 443, 480, 753.
Bezalion, 317.
Bettridge, 319.
Beale, 358, 372, 373, 443, 456, 588, 615, 677, 678.
Bezer, 361, 411, 448, 470, 517, 526, 606, 610, 634, 640, 658, 674, 693.
Beasley, 398, 744.
Bently, 437.
Bettris, 518, 519, 524, 548, 569, 570, 587, 606, 616, 617.
Bedwell, 590.
Bellar, 591.
Bebber, 617, 680.
Beckley, 599.
Bews, 606.
Betts, 611.
Benson, 621.
Benerman, 622.
Bettally, 670, 701.
Bedshold, 717.
Beck, 743.
Beach, 757.
Billopp, 33.
Bird, 70, 74, 693, 727.
Bittle, 231, 241, 275.
Biles, 234, 415, 682, 693, 697.

Bingly, 259, 278, 394.
Bickley, 467, 626, 630, 631, 632, 641, 655, 681, 684, 685, 690, 693, 695, 702, 724.
Bizalion, 496, 625, 626, 652, 658, 670, 693, 701, 747, 760, 762.
Bishop, 607, 610, 642, 674.
Binks, 633.
Bilderbeck, 672, 706, 707.
Blackfann, 16, 604, 642.
Blenman, 26, 317, 319, 448, 493.
Blackwell, 39, 43, 58, 385.
Blake, 40, 42, 48, 209, 254, 255, 376, 592, 641.
Blunston, 42, 251, 275, 288, 300, 326, 327, 337, 372, 401, 422.
Black, 107, 643.
Blardman, 120.
Blinstone, 153.
Blackburne, 203, 219, 313, 583.
Blan, 226.
Blackshaw, 277, 423, 426, 605.
Block, 329.
Blackhall, 399, 645, 686.
Blanchard, 664.
Blond, 438.
Blakelin, 521.
Blizzard, 601.
Blaned, 695.
Bloom, 700.
Boulton, 10, 202, 214, 263, 454, 462
Bowling, 35, 37, 227, 228, 337, 375.
Bowman, 42, 398, 401, 404, 627, 630, 631, 632, 684, 685, 758.
Bowls, 57, 350, 677, 711.
Bowyer, 58, 79, 276, 404, 476, 722.
Boulding, 60, 212, 237, 252, 253, 255.
Bowin, 113, 250, 326.
Boults, 167.
Bostock, 266, 271.
Bond, 275, 609, 610, 617, 647, 754.
Boswel, 286.
Bowater, 299, 337, 352, 387, 621.
Boome, 319, 415.
Bonney, 325.
Bowher, 349.
Bonsal, 389, 390.
Bordin, 415.
Boon, 437, 526, 552, 642, 644, 761.
Boyden, 440, 729.
Bowers, 497.
Booth, 553, 609, 617.
Bows, 597.
Bonyfield, 716.
Boyle, 727, 742.
Boyd, 756.
Brintnell, 9, 117, 118, 528, 544, 555, 576, 711, 720.
Bracy, 23, 35, 37, 41, 57, 63, 64, 71, 84, 482.
Bristow, 24, 57, 84, 556.
Bringley, 43.

INDEX.

Brown, 43, 56, 60, 112, 113, 237, 280, 281, 326, 336, 346, 347, 358, 372, 394, 401, 413, 458, 623, 643, 650, 651, 665, 696, 704, 719, 728, 747.
Brooks, 52, 305, 306, 352, 381, 472, 473, 606, 648.
Bradshaw, 65, 66, 68, 207, 326, 327, 467, 538, 727.
Brant, 78, 79, 80, 256, 273, 276, 339, 359.
Brincklo, 95, 604, 608, 636, 650, 726, 727.
Braine, 108, 114, 115, 135, 177, 178.
Bradford, 149, 295, 435, 586, 599.
Brock, 163, 253, 287, 357, 570, 579, 583, 587.
Brigham, 205, 238, 277, 423.
Bryant, 210, 317, 587, 607, 640, 647, 649, 716, 717, 747.
Brinsly, 228.
Brewster, 230, 246, 259, 264, 347, 583, 585.
Brotherton, 275.
Britton, 294, 602, 609, 736.
Bridgeman, 314, 492.
Brakin, 324, 342, 704, 713, 754, 765.
Bradnell, 340, 389.
Brassey, 342, 370, 378, 405, 458, 472.
Brinson, 377.
Branson, 496, 572, 577, 742, 752.
Brockdon, 511, 523, 524, 646, 698, 731, 735.
Broomfield, 598.
Bromal, 621, 626.
Brenerman, 632.
Bright, 637.
Bradley, 637, 756, 757.
Bretter, 730, 751.
Brookbaker, 755.
Bruin, 763, 764.
Bundeli, 594.
Burney, 589, 598, 600, 732.
Buffington, 24, 335, 366, 484, 574, 592, 703.
Butcher, 38, 324, 608, 712.
Burton, 51, 198, 201, 382, 447, 453, 590, 601, 719, 759, 763.
Budd, 56, 253, 288, 318, 396, 401, 402, 436, 453, 471, 533, 556, 564, 597, 631, 653, 659, 685, 688, 695, 698, 709, 710.
Buckly, 76, 90, 307, 324, 392, 438, 486, 575, 600, 648, 706, 707, 736, 754, 762.
Busby, 89, 174, 369, 476.
Buntes, 90.
Burbary, 95.
Butler, 140, 141, 588.
Bulkley, 142, 225, 594.
Burch, 165, 166, 381, 498.
Burges, 215, 226, 312, 318, 325, 419, 459, 475, 593, 599, 605.
Button, 293.

Burk, 311, 342, 343, 588, 737.
Burradale, 322.
Bull, 408, 610, 639.
Bundsen, 412.
Bullen, 470.
Burrows, 484, 488, 513, 557, 559, 580, 598.
Buckworth, 499.
Burston, 577, 706.
Buckham, 605.
Bunting, 650.
Bury, 657, 691.
Burchal, 707.
Bucher, 717.
Bussert, 725.
Burkhold, 742.
Buchanan, 745.
Bullagh, 752.
Burn, 761.
Butterfield, 765.
Byer, 746.
Byles, 26, 57, 83, 87, 196, 271, 277, 280, 291, 309, 415, 423, 427, 440, 446, 472, 477, 582, 613, 628, 658, 667, 675.
Byrn, 99.
Byfeld, 114, 115, 177, 178.
Bye, 229, 241, 267, 336, 348, 349, 366, 394.

C.

Carpenter Samuel (general).
Cart, 24, 78, 394, 470, 489, 490.
Cartmill, 25, 716.
Carter, 27, 33, 44, 47, 53, 57, 61, 78, 118, 161, 213, 269, 270, 300, 352, 358, 362, 363, 408, 431, 490, 522, 541, 546, 587, 593, 600, 606, 612, 649, 664, 668, 671, 674, 695, 699, 700, 701, 751.
Cartwell, 40, 333, 366, 367.
Callowhill, 66, 213, 214, 308, 354, 505, 506, 507, 508, 509, 510.
Calvert, 66, 233, 237, 555, 635.
Carpenter, 78, 255, 258, 280, 392, 393, 743, 758.
Cann, 85, 95, 461.
Cantrell, 88, 204, 214.
Carman, 138, 350.
Carre, 138, 733.
Carp, 202.
Carver, 205, 206, 207, 214, 345, 393, 418.
Caras, 207, 208, 281.
Cawdry, 221.
Catts, 247.
Cartlidge, 294, 301, 513, 644.
Caurton, 307.
Cartwright, 342, 352, 472.
Caleb, 349.
Carne, 383, 760.
Cawley, 386, 394, 615, 629, 632, 635, 640, 678.

49.—VOL. XIX.

INDEX.

Cadman, 394.
Cantwell, 440, 443, 486, 487, 490, 531.
Cadwell, 474.
Cam, 485.
Cary, 533, 607, 608.
Carroll, 556, 562, 563.
Cassell, 567, 632.
Caldwell, 590, 741.
Cadwalader, 621, 637, 639, 737, 747, 759.
Carlile, 623.
Casdorp, 633.
Cammel, 640, 707, 715.
Casper, 720.
Cery, 89.
Cecil, 362, 363.
Chambers, 11, 13, 17, 19, 26, 30, 32, 33, 34, 40, 45, 47, 57, 61, 62, 77, 126, 152, 208, 209, 225, 226, 232, 268, 269, 368, 385, 387, 413, 422, 423, 427, 438, 462, 478, 515, 541, 546, 553, 560, 562, 565, 601, 672, 702, 753, 755.
Chandler, 51, 62, 244, 280, 286, 366, 401, 587, 592, 758.
Chadd, 197, 213, 214, 243, 264, 270, 272, 474, 571.
Child, 216, 310, 364, 383, 399, 431, 448, 459, 463, 616, 636, 640, 678.
Chaffan, 221, 224, 253, 272.
Chevers, 221, 224, 253, 570.
Churchman, 280.
Chamberlin, 313, 436, 455, 472, 655, 659, 691, 761.
Chaunders, 332.
Champion, 342, 376, 702, 713, 720.
Chance, 362.
Chaulkley, 388, 389, 486, 669, 670, 699, 750.
Chick, 431.
Chapman, 454, 529, 627, 661, 662.
Chalfont, 587.
Chartier, 625, 681, 749.
Chadwicks, 645, 695.
Chiltham, 756.
Chew, 758.
Clemment, 31, 34, 68, 69, 73, 432.
Clark, 42, 50, 52, 74, 78, 85, 91, 92, 117, 193, 194, 195, 196, 197, 225, 300, 333, 369, 384, 455, 461, 471, 477, 491, 499, 562, 592, 596, 597, 617, 631, 637, 684, 719, 721, 735, 742, 751, 760, 762.
Claypoole, James, (general).
Clarridge, 45, 332, 437.
Cliff, 56, 61, 194, 236, 253, 254, 450, 473.
Clayton, 60, 277, 279, 407, 412, 537, 551, 586, 589, 590, 636, 738.
Cloud, 85, 265, 267, 268, 358, 361, 407, 409, 411, 412, 550, 562, 597, 600, 606, 618, 634, 649, 752, 755.
Clemison, 208, 588, 602.
Clanson, 247.
Clever, 278.

Clows, 334, 528, 621.
Clensmith, 354.
Clifton, 474.
Clough, 719.
Clare, 730.
Cleany, 734.
Clapham, 740.
Coburn, 10, 18, 38, 46, 257.
Collet, 28, 42, 43, 215, 293, 294, 300, 301, 325, 363, 364, 373, 398, 423, 424, 474, 507, 545, 549, 608, 627, 638.
Cooke, 33, 35, 38, 41, 56, 57, 68, 69, 72, 91, 98, 113, 119, 128, 129, 130, 131, 132, 133, 135, 136, 137, 143, 144, 145, 146, 147, 159, 160, 249, 274, 294, 318, 335, 337, 359, 407, 420, 436, 441, 457, 462, 483, 484, 558, 571, 579, 752, 759.
Countis, 35, 231.
Cock, 35, 36, 58, 62, 65, 73, 134, 135, 161, 296, 298, 324, 350, 370, 399, 427, 476, 485, 555, 580, 605, 656, 690.
Coxe, 37, 132, 167, 171, 350, 456, 495, 588, 744, 760.
Coats, 67, 329, 652, 665, 693, 698.
Cope, 76, 353, 486, 499, 648.
Collings, 83, 235, 287, 288, 337, 523, 524, 567, 574, 586, 592.
Copley, 107, 108, 109.
Coes, 182, 593, 605.
Comley, 210, 311, 575, 576, 577, 580.
Cooper, 220, 221, 224, 251, 272, 276, 280, 384, 487, 522, 530, 732.
Corsdale, 229.
Collier, 251.
Cobb, 255, 672, 703.
Coppock, 295, 316, 322, 364, 400.
Corsely, 301.
Cordry, 305, 307.
Cockshaw, 306, 328, 331, 381.
Constable, 314, 492.
Cowgill, 314, 318, 426, 430, 516, 579, 586, 610, 649, 650, 674.
Conway, 319.
Codeny, 334.
Collinson, 338.
Corker, 351.
Constantine, 353, 727, 728, 737.
Coles, 397, 398, 434, 437, 446, 466, 482, 646, 647, 657, 658, 659, 692, 752.
Cowper, 426, 525, 526, 556, 557, 562, 565.
Cordwell, 446.
Cornutes, 448.
Coderus, 465.
Colluck, 485, 493, 703.
Cormack, 498.
Coney, 511.
Cornethwaite, 520, 521, 576.
Cornwell, 520, 521, 522, 566, 568, 623.
Codd, 543.
Coleman, 554, 555, 711.

INDEX. 771

Colly, 593.
Comb, 625, 652, 681, 764.
Corbet, 598.
Cormick, 603.
Cord, 753.
Courtney, 610.
Coffman, 622.
Cottom, 704.
Cookson, 705, 765.
Coolwine, 720, 726, 762.
Cornelius, 720, 765.
Coumis, 722.
Conradt, 726.
Cowman, 735.
Cohalna, 736.
Croasdell (Crosdall), 20, 215, 217, 255, 260, 307, 308, 310, 312, 314, 321, 368, 393, 409, 424, 429, 439, 452, 516, 517, 582.
Crosby, 23, 298, 437.
Crews, 31, 149, 229, 349, 366, 485, 595.
Crispin, 35, 67, 139, 154, 156, 157, 159, 301, 307, 330, 332, 345, 382, 393, 416, 437, 572, 609, 762.
Crook, 38.
Cross, 38, 386, 423, 444, 533.
Crane, 108.
Croslie, 156.
Cromptoon, 251.
Crow, 329, 742.
Croslett, 332.
Creyger, 338.
Craxon, 387, 621.
Crapp, 457, 579, 580.
Craven, 492.
Cristy, 588, 762.
Craston, 588.
Craig, 601.
Croswell, 726, 751.
Craighead, 743.
Crouche, 750.
Crabill, 751.
Crudginton, 761.
Crawford, 762.
Curtis, 59, 69, 670, 701, 705.
Cumberland, 115.
Cuarton, 257, 387, 583.
Cutler, 281, 359, 376, 416, 417, 423, 424, 428, 430, 431, 436, 446, 463, 472, 478, 479, 480, 736.
Cuppage, 506, 507, 508.
Cutter, 556.
Cuff, 636.
Cummings, 745, 749, 753, 761.

D.

Day, 8, 23, 46, 122, 203, 205, 340, 342, 374, 409, 457, 709, 766.
Davison, 255, 672, 703.
Dalton, 392.
Dawson, 440, 552, 608, 746, 756.

Davis, 48, 87, 147, 153, 201, 202, 215, 227, 242, 251, 261, 268, 270, 276, 277, 302, 309, 316, 319, 328, 341, 346, 367, 373, 383, 385, 387, 390, 391, 397, 398, 403, 404, 405, 407, 408, 411, 425, 426, 427, 428, 450, 460, 494, 510, 517, 519, 528, 545, 573, 581, 582, 590, 598, 600, 602, 643, 648, 652, 661, 701, 710, 713, 725, 729, 735, 736, 738.
Dare, 106, 107.
David, 204, 205, 224, 242, 257, 268, 272, 276, 322, 327, 328, 338, 353, 367, 374, 391, 403, 425, 428, 433, 475, 518, 545, 547, 643, 652, 700, 734.
Dakeyne, 246, 247, 260, 327, 347, 360, 380, 395, 396, 406, 414, 434, 441, 456, 465, 466, 467, 486, 491, 498, 536, 538, 551, 585, 630, 656, 683, 713, 747, 748, 764.
Darkin, 516, 517.
Dalbo, 526, 527, 647.
Darter, 591, 746.
Davock, 591, 595.
Daws, 614.
Darter, 641.
Danagar, 650.
Daniel, 707, 711, 724, 743.
Dandesson, 721.
Davy, 744.
Davenport, 750.
Daylor, 755.
Denzy, 34, 35, 139, 202, 203.
Dewberry, 36.
Delavall, 60, 78, 79, 80, 81, 148.
Deane, 66, 67, 148.
Dennis, 74, 720.
Derickson, 130, 131, 132, 133, 134, 198, 448.
Dellbeech, 154.
Devor, 726, 744.
De Fosse, 388, 410, 627, 758.
Dewit, 475.
Decow, 493, 516, 517, 569, 579, 587.
De Turck, 517, 524.
Denny, 565.
Dell, 574, 575, 640, 649.
Depra, 578, 579.
Deeke, 631.
Delagrange, 693, 722.
Deadwood, 714.
Dixon, 84, 334, 492, 600, 618, 635, 640, 723.
Dire, 85, 197, 198, 201, 648.
Dillwin, 118, 119.
Dickinson, 257, 258, 259, 302, 317, 409, 586, 626, 629, 630, 637, 639, 656, 661, 668, 670, 681, 683, 690, 699, 700, 718.
Dicks, 264, 336, 347, 358, 361, 396, 571, 588, 654, 688, 714, 730, 742, 748.

772　INDEX.

Dillworth, 429, 463, 659, 693, 694.
Dill, 717.
Dickey, 748.
Doz, 32, 35, 44, 47, 52, 60, 61, 647.
Dowly, 47.
Donaldson, 233, 344, 361, 362, 409.
Dolby, 298.
Dove, 309, 616, 617.
Douglas, 423.
Dole, 514, 519.
Donn, 591.
Dodd, 598, 607, 758.
Dobson, 608, 756.
Donovan, 648, 723.
Dougherty, 714.
Drury, 84.
Drewitt, 236, 727.
Drake, 601, 736.
Draper, 614, 677.
Draughton, 732.
Dubois, 617.
Duckett, 23, 32, 33, 43, 47, 49, 52, 204, 238, 299, 458.
Dungan, 31, 91, 277.
Dunkley, 37, 41, 51, 92.
Dunn, 74, 207, 315, 316, 451.
Ducastle, 134.
Duplouvis, 134, 169, 170, 171.
Dungworth, 194, 195.
Duncan, 210, 349.
Dutton, 280.
Durant, 283, 351, 541.
Duffield, 383, 410, 413, 418, 426.
Duplonoys, 434, 435.
Durval, 619.
Duke, 684.
Durborow, 260, 717, 718.
Dwight, 493, 522, 577.
Dyer, 42, 322, 440, 443, 445, 465, 648, 748.
Dymocke, 359.
Dyne, 485.

E.

East, 38, 306, 533.
Eastburn, 289, 478, 479, 480.
Eaton, 306, 739.
Eby, 637, 745.
Eccleston, 675.
Edwards, 8, 31, 57, 61, 234, 249, 276, 279, 296, 297, 316, 319, 320, 322, 326, 361, 388, 402, 405, 407, 409, 452, 456, 470, 541, 599, 600, 609, 617, 651, 729, 747.
Edg, 46, 47.
Edgecomb, 449.
Eden, 765.
Eileston, 613.
Ekeley, 424, 459, 654, 655, 688, 689.
Ellis, Thomas, (general).
Ellis, 521, 524, 545, 577, 613, 713, 730, 731, 737.

Ellwood, 721, 722, 731.
Elfrith, 13, 66, 69, 70, 74, 81, 82, 321, 432.
Ellett, 75, 77, 442, 567, 568, 714.
Ely, 107.
Ellingsworthe, 149.
Elton, 319, 364, 365, 628.
Eldridge, 331, 333, 348, 399, 431, 555, 597, 610, 621, 739.
Ellington, 426.
Emlin, 38, 86, 291, 412, 418, 579, 751.
Empson, 45, 49, 240, 245, 280, 406, 461, 497, 498, 738, 751, 754.
Emerson, 590, 612, 717.
Emmet, 712, 715, 720, 750, 754, 759.
England, 25, 44, 46, 88, 211, 213, 285, 337, 375, 414, 425, 440, 442, 466, 468, 477, 493, 500, 718, 721, 763.
End, 98, 99, 100, 101, 102.
English, 253, 463, 473, 583, 589, 632, 737.
Enockson, 390.
Ernestchs, 41, 43.
Erickson, 247.
Erberry, 500.
Estaugh, 499, 502, 548, 549, 608, 671, 702, 706.
Eure, 63, 64, 95, 239, 303, 319, 352.
Evans, 276, 277, 309, 324, 341, 342, 346, 355, 356, 375, 383, 385, 390, 391, 402, 406, 411, 419, 425, 426, 448, 482, 494, 535, 582, 599, 602, 611, 705, 708, 711, 726, 744, 747, 752, 753, 754, 757, 765.
Everndom, 399.
Evets, 588.
Ewer, 580, 628.
Ewens, 732, 744, 755.
Eyers, 729.

F.

Fairman Thomas, (general).
Farmer, 25, 31, 33, 36, 37, 63, 89, 142, 283, 297, 304, 335, 378, 401, 433, 436, 441, 553, 559, 566, 575, 582, 693.
Fallows, 67.
Facter, 108.
Falkner, 218, 219, 243, 244, 249, 274, 365, 379, 396, 464, 497, 560, 638.
Faucit, 219, 239, 240, 241, 285, 286, 339, 340, 347, 393.
Falle, 336.
Faulk, 355, 356, 408.
Farr, 411, 474, 482.
Falconer, 591, 594, 598, 630, 639, 669, 683, 700, 712, 744, 746.
Farer, 606.
Farker, 606.
Faggs, 721, 726, 738, 740, 747, 750, 759.

INDEX. 773

Fallowfield, 757.
Farington, 723.
Farrell, 762.
Fenwick, 50.
Few, 336, 337, 338, 365, 366, 382, 463, 470, 727, 737, 759.
Fess, 386.
Fell, 400, 439.
Fecee, 727.
Flutcher, 194, 195.
Fitzwater, 9, 27, 32, 34, 35, 49, 122, 302, 407, 566, 628, 630, 647, 669, 682, 683, 699, 708.
Fincher, 43, 299, 337, 338, 351, 352, 400, 403, 406, 408, 602, 709.
Fisher, 71, 197, 199, 200, 214, 253, 268, 281, 300, 303, 321, 322, 332, 345, 351, 424, 450, 490, 543, 561, 595, 614, 622, 677, 678, 693, 723, 756, 761, 763.
Field, 198, 312, 313, 338, 434, 477, 505, 506, 507, 508, 509, 510, 511, 569, 628, 629, 667, 682, 683, 697.
Finney, 266, 268, 276, 305, 307, 330, 343, 359, 453, 461, 468, 746, 759.
Fishburn, 415, 473, 665, 696.
Filner, 420.
Fish, 485.
Fierre, 529, 606, 607, 617, 700, 729, 756.
Fitzgerald, 643.
Firkle, 722.
Fletcher, 93, 94, 140, 178, 338,
Flower, 140, 156, 169, 234, 287, 288, 351, 435, 440, 577, 610, 753, 754.
Fleckne, 169, 170, 171.
Fleming, 244, 579.
Fox, 35, 43, 68, 82, 268, 397, 398, 405, 431, 437, 616, 640, 678, 700.
Foreman, 68, 96, 111.
Foster, 81, 98, 99, 100, 101, 102, 178, 333, 351, 383, 410, 413, 418, 447, 714.
Forrest, 251, 320, 628.
Fosses, 357, 723.
Ford, 409, 444, 463, 464, 476, 488, 615, 677.
Fowler, 718.
Folks, 717.
Forehead, 725.
Fretwell, 13, 489, 595.
Fraes, 111.
French, 173, 178, 249, 282, 361, 362, 363, 494, 561, 595, 596, 602, 605, 606, 625, 650, 670, 681, 701, 713, 718, 727, 728, 733, 759.
Framton, 180, 181, 257, 397, 398, 630, 631, 641, 684, 685, 693.
Fredrickson, 250.
Fredrickfields, 517, 560, 618, 726, 730.
Friend, 526, 756.
Frost, 555, 560, 605.
Ffred, 577.

Frieth, 591.
Friveller, 597.
Frogg, 598.
Fraiser, 598, 725, 741.
Franciscus, 622, 633, 639, 723, 746, 763.
Freeman, 723.
Frey, 727.
Furnis, 13, 20, 28, 61, 200, 201, 267, 471, 566, 643, 747.
Fuller, 26, 44, 48, 70, 73, 306, 322, 340, 342, 355, 583.
Furly, 243, 244, 271, 274, 275, 357, 365, 396, 464, 465, 497, 598.
Furlow, 355.
Futcher, 595.
Funk, 600, 622, 624, 644, 679, 729.

G.

Gardner, 43, 44, 264, 274, 339, 368, 428, 447, 608, 736, 759.
Gale, 95.
Gallias, 96.
Garret, 202, 237, 244, 255, 306, 312, 330, 331, 485, 494, 533, 538, 541, 561, 562, 565, 572, 576, 592, 741.
Garretson, 260, 531, 546, 583.
Gandouit, 616, 678.
Gatchel, 705, 707, 709, 713, 715, 716, 724, 726, 734, 739, 741, 742, 743, 744, 745, 747, 750, 751, 754, 755, 757, 762, 763.
Galbreath, 747, 750.
Galloway, 758.
Gee, 36, 45, 88, 355, 428, 505, 506, 507, 508, 509, 510, 511.
Geetch, 59.
German, 71, 276.
Gellias, 434, 446.
Geddis, 491.
Geary, 518, 521, 524, 617.
George, 588, 635.
Geer, 591.
Geritson, 598.
Gerald, 601.
Genway, 609.
Gibbs, 29, 207, 406, 595, 724.
Gieach, 38, 324, 360.
Giles, 39, 251, 292, 429, 761.
Gibbons, 47, 94, 95, 96, 300, 301, 363, 364, 409, 458, 635, 708, 734.
Gilbert, 89, 251, 268, 269, 297, 381, 402, 422, 439, 463, 471, 472, 485, 497, 513, 573, 576, 577, 579, 706, 715, 719, 721, 747.
Gilpin, 273, 412, 475, 565, 727.
Gicock, 349.
Giffing, 490.
Gillett, 514.
Gibson, 544, 602, 606, 607, 617.
Gillespie, 746.
Goodson, John (general).

INDEX.

Goforth, 81.
Goss, 104, 105, 132.
Goodyear, 313, 314.
Gottshick, 371, 456, 740.
Gold, 382, 736.
Goodin, 431, 447.
Gouldney, 505, 506, 507, 508, 509, 510, 511, 608, 638.
Goodmen, 746.
Gray, 7, 26, 160, 317, 338, 341, 510, 520, 601, 623, 653, 693.
Grenaway, 24, 379, 382, 408.
Growdon, 27, 250, 254, 301, 302, 309, 330, 352, 374, 375, 380, 393, 395, 396, 403, 430, 436, 446, 476, 484, 495, 511, 532, 550, 551, 559, 594, 603, 692.
Grubb, 46, 62, 83, 333, 353, 358, 475, 672, 689, 704, 706, 726, 727, 728, 729, 740, 752, 754.
Griscom, 51, 53, 67, 294.
Green, 75, 226, 376, 426, 438, 502, 513, 557, 560, 588, 618, 650, 678, 708, 713, 725, 738, 739.
Grigg, 85, 410, 588, 627, 657, 671, 691, 702, 722, 723, 747, 758, 764.
Griffith, 96, 97, 272, 322, 328, 356, 398, 409, 424, 428, 582, 610, 643, 713, 739, 744, 749, 753.
Grunston, 224.
Grant, 232.
Grantham, 232, 233.
Groves, 322, 505, 506, 507, 508, 509, 510, 511, 757.
Greenwood, 395, 396, 434, 499, 500, 536, 557, 567, 590.
Graham, 466, 762.
Grange, 483.
Gregory, 496, 571, 584, 653, 764.
Groethousen, 538, 539, 595, 596.
Grumly, 551.
Grom, 569, 570.
Grafton, 588.
Graeff, 597, 639, 642, 700, 724, 746.
Griffin, 598.
Grist, 610.
Grimson, 618, 656, 690.
Grew, 687.
Graves, 704, 738.
Grainger, 715, 723.
Guest, 13, 17, 208, 217, 218, 245, 249, 250, 251, 260, 274, 280, 282, 283, 320, 325, 331, 337, 344, 369, 370, 375, 383, 387, 388, 403, 419, 420, 426, 436, 442, 452, 461, 483, 497, 514, 546, 707, 765.
Gunston, 221, 361.
Gumly, 513.
Guttridge, 517.
Guildin, 574, 582, 627.
Guy, 588.
Gye, 657, 691.

H.

Harrison, 7, 17, 83, 84, 88, 91, 95, 97, 155, 242, 308, 409, 418, 423, 439, 460, 472, 476, 482, 487, 525, 526, 556, 643, 658, 661, 693, 713, 720.
Hanson, 10, 233, 257, 311, 344, 347, 441, 537, 551, 552, 595, 633, 738, 755.
Hall, 22, 26, 111, 225, 332, 333, 366, 367, 383, 418, 441, 462, 487, 488, 490, 552, 580, 605, 618, 709, 710, 729.
Hastings, 24, 279, 299, 300, 338, 348, 360, 594, 602, 603, 616, 747.
Harland, 24, 39, 250, 260, 262, 263, 264, 271, 284, 357, 365, 484, 500, 546, 573, 574, 576, 588, 639, 734, 746.
Hardin, 34, 35, 86, 251, 402, 430, 447, 448, 470.
Harmer, 36, 38, 139, 143, 278, 338, 343, 410, 471, 575, 582, 589, 590, 592, 718.
Hardiman, 38, 159, 160.
Harde, 39, 72, 83, 518.
Hart, 43, 44, 71, 286, 378, 485, 604, 728.
Harris, 48, 122, 299, 387, 407, 576, 743, 749, 750.
Hartsfield, 57, 444.
Haslegrove, 81, 474.
Hamilton, 90, 543, 590, 591, 624, 625, 628, 630, 647, 655, 656, 659, 661, 669, 680, 682, 683, 689, 699, 708, 726, 744, 758, 763, 765.
Haines, 109, 114, 115, 177, 178, 518, 597.
Haughton, 113, 565.
Harlow, 142, 143.
Harley, 203, 411.
Haverd, 205, 279, 437.
Hayes, 208, 209, 272, 325, 349, 368, 369, 462, 469, 559, 576, 638, 670, 700, 701.
Haige, 210, 235, 321.
Hatt, 215, 234.
Halliwell, 222, 223, 366, 367, 461, 462, 465, 531.
Hayhurst, 229, 525, 586.
Hanse, 260, 344.
Harry, 277, 279, 297, 433, 635, 724.
Harker, 292, 430.
Harper, 311, 325, 437.
Hayworth, 331, 399, 429, 474, 517.
Harman, 333, 602, 672, 689, 704.
Haverlaw, 338.
Haywood, 352, 381, 407.
Haynoyassa, 354.
Hawkins, 362, 579, 586, 654, 655.
Hammond, 377, 739, 758.
Haim, 389.
Hams, 400, 720.

INDEX. 775

Harmenson, 408, 409, 410.
Hammers, 415, 627.
Hackney, 426.
Harvey, 461, 622.
Haunds, 462, 470, 601.
Hallowfield, 568.
Harwood, 572.
Hamer, 573, 647.
Hayward, 576, 584, 607, 610, 674.
Hatton, 577.
Haney, 580.
Hartford, 586.
Harrold, 588.
Hackett, 598, 608.
Haregrove, 605.
Hawry, 632.
Hayden, 638.
Hanby, 644, 687.
Haddock, 655, 689.
Haling, 678.
Hawks, 688, 689.
Hanlan, 718, 730.
Halliday, 745, 750.
Haninger, 746.
Hassert, 752.
Hand, 755.
Hadley, 759.
Hersent, 13, 615, 634, 640, 641, 648, 677.
Herriot, 27, 166, 466, 490, 628, 629, 682.
Helmns, 42.
Heathcoate, 74, 87, 88, 92, 131, 133 147, 148, 155, 177, 178, 305, 467, 570.
Herves, 106.
Herman, 138, 628, 727, 729.
Heath, 243, 261, 327, 386, 392, 394, 523.
Heaton, 256, 292, 308, 312, 321, 423, 429, 430, 443, 454, 463, 584, 585, 619, 643.
Heycock, 261, 523.
Herst, 265, 292.
Henricks, 266, 271, 307, 413, 495, 591, 595, 598, 640, 656, 672, 689, 690, 704, 727, 747.
Herick, 286, 689.
Hedges, 323, 577, 720, 724, 733.
Hendrickson, 336, 413, 425, 448, 502, 542, 543, 605, 656, 673, 690, 705, 739, 765.
Herford, 384.
Hearne, 427.
Heynes, 519.
Hellyard, 534.
Hennerly, 593.
Held, 599.
Herr, 622, 624, 640, 679, 724, 734, 742, 758, 761.
Hershey, 622, 628, 755.
Heddings, 649.
Helsby, 650, 665, 696.

Head, 657, 691, 765.
Hewston, 708, 715.
Heron, 717.
Henry, 728.
Hess, 746, 760.
Hean, 761.
Hill, 39, 68, 194, 323, 338, 373, 434, 442, 449, 467, 478, 496, 501, 503, 530, 535, 579, 586, 591, 593, 619, 710, 713, 731.
Hilliard, 43, 161, 162, 163, 172, 173, 176, 177, 447, 618, 727, 732.
Hibbs, 206, 383, 418.
Hicks, 207, 285, 301, 307, 309, 661, 662, 703.
Hilborne, 318, 484.
Hind, 320.
Hickman, 470, 646, 687, 750.
Higenot, 485.
Hirons, 494, 565, 651, 738.
Hichcock, 579, 665, 696.
Hinman, 601.
Hilton, 669, 699, 700.
Higgat, 713.
Hickenbothem, 751.
Himry, 761.
Holme, Thomas, Sur. Genr'l, 7, 8, 751.
Houghton, 21, 709, 710.
Hodgkins, 23, 255, 407, 430, 486.
Hobbs, 27, 33, 37, 49, 51, 141, 348, 423, 424.
Holmes, 34, 38, 45, 101, 102, 103, 154, 155, 156, 157, 158, 159, 180, 193, 195, 201, 208, 212, 213, 214, 216, 227, 266, 275, 295, 296, 298, 301, 306, 326, 332, 345, 357, 390, 393, 397, 408, 409, 416, 417, 420, 421, 422, 430, 437, 470, 473, 475.
Holston, 36, 349, 350, 437, 765.
Howell, 58, 59, 147, 229, 241, 260, 265, 271, 277, 293, 302, 315, 316, 320, 325, 328, 348, 359, 396, 409, 425, 428, 450, 451, 493, 545, 546, 612, 613, 632, 639, 675, 710, 746.
Hollingsworth, 65, 83, 207, 221, 244, 245, 263, 264, 265, 271, 275, 281, 298, 314, 377, 460, 467, 488, 498, 500, 514, 523, 533, 538, 549, 556, 597, 625, 643, 680, 723, 727, 738, 759, 762.
Hooper, 67, 380.
Hough, 83, 194, 195, 228, 271, 293, 334, 527, 528, 529.
Hoult, 107, 246, 260, 619.
Hollyman, 154.
Hogg, 222, 233, 246, 260, 315, 323, 671, 702, 722.
Hobson, 225, 738.
Howston, 265, 315, 323, 413.
Hoodt, 275, 394, 422.
Holding, 288, 436, 442, 446, 480.
Hoven, 319.

776 INDEX.

Hope, 336, 337, 346, 364, 400, 525.
Hollworth, 358.
Holland, 364, 545, 591, 756.
Holt, 413, 619, 621, 668, 698.
Horne, 414, 440, 443, 446, 659, 740, 751.
Holdgate, 429.
Howes, 437.
Howard, 447, 471, 499, 702, 713.
Horell, 494.
Hopton, 578, 613, 614, 648, 650, 675, 677.
Hodgson, 595.
Hochstater, 632.
Hockin, 692.
Horner, 694.
Hollyday, 707.
Holes, 714.
Hore, 732.
Horton, 765.
Homan, 765.
Hughes, 13, 92, 184, 268, 288, 293, 294, 302, 314, 322, 335, 346, 355, 356, 358, 375, 394, 403, 489, 643, 648, 673, 704, 705, 743, 761, 766.
Hudson, 19, 22, 57, 87, 271, 434, 437, 441, 446, 477, 479, 487, 520, 521, 522, 566, 568, 570, 576, 618, 628, 629, 637, 639, 658, 667, 682, 693, 697, 713, 717.
Hunt, 32, 34, 36, 75, 226, 247, 298, 312, 438.
Hughson, 39.
Hunlock, 47, 52, 53, 61, 63, 400, 658, 693.
Hulsted, 161.
Hussey, 210, 247.
Hutchinson, 243, 247, 327, 741.
Humphry, 276, 309, 328, 355, 356, 370, 395, 404, 427, 428.
Huddlestone, 292, 328, 430.
Hucks, 393.
Huntley, 395, 483.
Huber, 622, 760.
Huling, 623.
Humsted, 652.
Hunn, 723.
Hummit, 726.
Hurlan, 762.
Hybert, 251.
Hyde, 575, 602, 730.
Hyer, 763.

I.

Inians, 198.
Isaacs, 234, 241, 340, 341, 353, 360, 394.
Isard, 336, 491, 675.
Ingelo, 380, 381.
Ingram, 399.
Ingle, 428.
Ishar, 718.

J.

Jacquet, 707, 708, 738.
Jarret, 661, 662.
Jants, 598.
Jarvis, 589.
Jansogoe, 413.
James, 36, 40, 139, 165, 176, 275, 276, 325, 326, 331, 339, 341, 372, 383, 385, 390, 391, 406, 411, 450, 488, 551, 621, 636, 655, 688, 732, 740, 748.
Janney, 73, 280, 418.
Jamison, 94, 179.
Jacobs, 132, 138, 152, 249, 268, 305, 337, 349, 366, 737.
Janson, 205, 315, 336, 650, 653, 657, 659, 691.
Jawert, 219, 560.
Jacobson, 239, 240.
Jackson, 284, 290, 357, 388, 389, 422, 434, 498, 533, 568, 592, 605, 727, 744.
Janvier, 293, 315, 639.
Jackman, 321, 394.
Jack, 722.
Jecox, 496, 497, 498.
Jervais, 316.
Jefferson, 31, 374, 396, 409, 428, 478.
Jennings, 39, 44, 67, 72, 79, 82, 84, 90, 91, 282, 304, 447, 455, 456, 474, 475, 540, 722.
Jeff's, 44, 368.
Jenkins, 62, 209, 279, 300, 315, 317, 324, 328, 333, 372, 428, 441, 598, 607, 710.
Jennett, 81, 115, 116, 117, 419, 425, 439, 492.
Jenner, 127, 199, 213, 214, 227, 252, 253, 270, 310, 336, 427, 428.
Jessox, 513, 514.
Jermain, 390, 633.
Jeffries, 233, 234.
Jenny, 596, 597.
Jones, 8, 26, 39, 44, 51, 52, 53, 62, 70, 76, 77, 78, 81, 111, 117, 118, 134, 135, 136, 146, 147, 162, 171, 172, 173, 174, 175, 176, 213, 214, 220, 221, 223, 224, 236, 238, 251, 260, 265, 267, 272, 274, 276, 277, 279, 280, 284, 288, 305, 309, 313, 315, 316, 320, 331, 332, 337, 338, 339, 341, 344, 346, 349, 356, 367, 368, 371, 374, 380, 384, 386, 390, 393, 394, 395, 403, 404, 405, 406, 409, 412, 413, 416, 420, 421, 425, 426, 430, 431, 434, 437, 438, 450, 455, 461, 467, 468, 469, 475, 491, 493, 494, 500, 536, 547, 551, 557, 561, 566, 571, 577, 582, 589, 593, 594, 598, 602, 613, 620, 621, 627, 631, 633, 635, 638, 639, 641, 655, 660, 669, 675, 684, 691, 699, 700, 708,

INDEX. 777

709, 714, 715, 719, 725, 728, 731, 735, 736, 737, 740, 745, 746, 748, 756, 760, 764.
Jobson, 26, 182, 347, 348, 397, 471, 752, 755.
Joneson, 60.
Johnson, 222, 300, 336, 398, 416, 424, 445, 448, 471, 554, 555, 627, 661, 662, 719, 734, 746.
John, 224, 356, 368, 382, 396, 641, 643, 651, 670, 743.
Job, 280, 472, 763.
Jordan, 409, 614, 640, 650, 676, 747.
Josisson, 410.
Joder, 589.
Justason, 42, 437, 448, 513, 514.
Justice, 658, 692.

K.

Kaighm, 159, 519.
Kanning, 198.
Kaiggey, 622.
Kay, 739.
Kennerly, 26, 294, 298, 474, 478.
Keith, 36, 149, 668, 708, 737.
Kekwick, 110.
Kelpius, 219.
Keal, 233, 588.
Kelly, 237.
Kennedy, 237, 474.
Kender, 420.
Key, 466, 515, 524, 562.
Kemball, 569, 570.
Kendal, 619.
Kendig, 622, 624, 627, 679.
Keykendal, 661.
Kent, 710, 729.
King, 14, 19, 37, 48, 66, 113, 154, 155, 156, 157, 177, 178, 179, 180, 238, 251, 264, 274, 354, 404, 441, 462, 472, 484, 488, 604, 740, 743, 760, 764.
Kirk, 24, 251, 345, 565, 650, 720, 723, 725, 736, 756.
Kingsburrie, 29.
Kinsey, 38, 73, 242, 268, 325, 339, 383, 406, 442, 476, 478, 599.
Killingsworth, 98.
Killinbeck, 217, 392.
Kirl, 235, 267, 287, 288, 321, 335, 337, 375, 411, 523, 624.
Kiney, 330.
Kinsman, 363, 402, 413, 595.
Kiete, 379, 382.
Kitchen, 382, 447.
Kinneryls, 408.
Kirkbride, 426, 486, 496, 589, 661, 662, 667, 697, 713, 743.
Kindig, 524, 529.
Kipshaven, 578, 579.
Kieursen, 634, 642, 686, 700.
Kirkpatrick, 709, 743.
Kitzmiller, 757.

Kline, 727.
Knight, 308, 345, 463, 737, 759.
Knowles, 533, 534, 535.
Knave, 632.
Knowland, 751.
Konders, 270, 274, 312.
Koenan, 424.
Koolen, 447.
Kolluck, 562, 579, 701, 702, 762.
Kreytor, 632.
Krow, 742.
Kursten, 467.
Kuilwine, 762.

L.

Laykin, 24, 29, 40, 118.
Lawson, 44.
Lane, 50, 172, 173, 340, 404, 467, 491, 492, 524, 602, 610, 663.
Ladd, 65.
Lapthorne, 108.
Lamb, 114, 115, 177, 178, 518, 519, 521, 548, 577, 617.
Laschals, 135.
Landers, 200.
Langston, 201, 243, 639.
Land, 222, 224, 233, 278, 315, 316, 639.
Lawrence, 227, 228, 237, 270, 375, 419, 434, 477, 523, 524, 612, 628, 629, 667, 674, 675, 682, 683, 697, 713.
Langhorn, 229, 230, 265, 309, 365, 430, 484, 485, 569, 570, 583, 587, 615, 627, 629, 630, 672, 678, 683, 703.
Large, 319, 572, 737.
Lambert, 334.
Langham, 336.
Langford, 364, 400.
Latham, 376.
Lamball, 412, 579.
Lampleigh, 425, 458.
Laft, 471.
Lavally, 473.
Lawden, 613, 675.
Lasson, 613, 614, 676.
Landis, 641.
Laroux, 712, 729.
Langley, 745.
Law, 751, 759.
Lee, 24, 29, 196, 214, 218, 220, 358, 424, 499, 607, 617, 721, 758.
Leister, 40, 41, 42, 83, 599, 747.
Lewis, 66, 204, 272, 293, 322, 328, 358, 364, 376, 391, 404, 419, 424, 428, 431, 468, 475, 577, 600, 602, 621, 637, 670, 701, 707, 724, 728, 741, 742, 752.
Leasly, 76.
Loach, 86, 263, 454, 462, 477, 500, 730.
Leeth, 92, 502, 673.
Leamb, 106.
Leyman, 121, 622, 742.

INDEX.

Letort, 179, 180, 651, 735.
Lehnman, 210, 336, 450.
Levis, 241, 485.
Lewden, 247.
Le Fevre, 247, 334, 335, 529, 559, 587, 607, 609, 628.
Leyson, 399.
Lewin, 488.
Letts, 513.
Le Dee, 517.
Leiper, 750.
Levick, 482.
Leonard, 587, 588, 724, 736.
Leatherbe, 704.
Ledyard, 748.
Line, 59, 642.
Littell, 118, 691.
Lipet, 184.
Lichfield, 267.
Littler, 280, 715, 742, 755.
Linsye, 336, 751.
Limkin, 349.
Liston, 361.
Liddon, 416.
Littlejohn, 517, 519, 736.
Lindley, 721.
Lirunceller, 736.
Littlemore, 741, 745.
Lingard, 750.
Lighter, 751.
Lillington, 765.
Lloyd, 18, 38, 48, 63, 65, 81, 82, 88, 92, 118, 126, 141, 148, 159, 160, 200, 201, 235, 236, 258, 260, 267, 276, 294, 302, 307, 309, 320, 321, 324, 330, 346, 359, 370, 373, 375, 378, 386, 387, 393, 396, 402, 403, 406, 417, 424, 427, 436, 437, 455, 473, 474, 497, 520, 522, 527, 528, 530, 545, 557, 616, 619, 621, 654, 678, 688, 689, 700, 711, 735.
Llewellin, 138, 271, 272, 349, 364, 536, 544, 545, 546, 562, 572, 747.
Longshore, 41, 45, 53, 60, 73, 77, 78, 91, 118, 154, 155, 156, 157, 159, 164, 165, 202, 227, 228, 254, 255, 270, 278, 290, 304, 330, 333, 338, 339, 362, 392, 408, 412, 419, 435, 471, 480, 484, 547, 548, 550, 582, 589, 590.
Loftus, 56, 762.
Longhurst, 74, 121, 375, 422, 424.
Lovell, 83, 235, 288, 523.
Longworthy, 285, 391, 525, 566, 567, 582.
Logan, James, (general).
Love, 202, 529, 754.
Lockyer, 221, 222, 224, 247.
Lovelace, 239, 240, 266, 298, 336, 373, 399, 448, 476, 487, 495.
Lodge, 260, 703.
Lovet, 358, 429, 633, 634, 636, 640, 685.

Longston, 425.
Lobe, 485.
Lowman, 491.
Longstreth, 522, 577.
Lober, 598.
Losvoll, 598.
Loftlands, 601.
Lower, 616, 678.
Long, 665, 696, 732, 751.
Longanacre, 705.
Loise, 723.
Luke, 109.
Lukins, 273, 284.
Lucas, 303, 308, 312, 460, 461, 623, 650.
Lundy, 359, 643.
Luff, 654, 688, 736.
Lybeka, 766.
Lynes, 104.
Lymery, 108.
Lyborn, 477.
Lyn, 639, 640.
Lyon, 643.
Lynch, 691.
Lykill, 765.

M.

Markham, William (general).
Marsh, 13, 288, 397, 435, 436, 446, 447, 471, 472, 479, 480, 571, 589, 668, 698, 739.
Mason, 14, 205, 382, 588, 762.
Masters, 89, 147, 148, 258, 335, 339, 435, 470, 550, 596.
Maccoom, 41.
Marshall, 47, 52, 53, 62, 184, 251, 276, 397, 398, 399, 569, 570, 591, 662, 664, 694, 695, 722, 744.
Martin, 68, 70, 72, 75, 89, 274, 348, 360, 362, 363, 386, 388, 455, 482, 533, 551, 636, 640, 726, 728.
Martindall, 89, 470, 490.
Mannd, 152, 154.
Maydock, 199, 225, 294, 298, 313, 316, 478, 742, 745.
Marl, 210, 270, 311.
Matson, 219, 239, 240, 241, 353, 354.
Maline, 275, 620, 643.
Marjoram, 285, 312.
Marslender, 290, 329.
Maris, 293, 294, 322, 670, 701.
Massey, 298, 400, 451.
Manson, 487.
Maleigh, 379, 382, 721,
Mallows, 383, 418, 485, 557.
Mann, 325, 498.
Marks, 519, 524, 577, 616.
Maxwell, 528, 529.
Mace, 548, 549, 550, 580.
Marlow, 548, 549, 550, 551, 580.
Mayos, 586.
Mather, 589, 605, 632, 643.

INDEX. 779

Marriner, 595.
Macnair, 611.
Manlove, 617, 639.
Macknot, 619.
Mayor, 632.
Macklander, 641.
Macfarlan, 651.
Maugridge, 671, 702.
Mathews, 708, 734.
Maclue, 720.
Mankin, 722, 723.
Macke, 743.
McVeagh, 303, 330, 409, 591, 671, 702.
McDonald, 345, 467, 478, 479, 497, 513, 588, 635, 709.
McNeal, 712, 747.
McCane, 717.
McConnel, 720.
McCollester, 720.
McComb, 726.
McClanahan, 759.
McDaniel, 765.
Meedham, 51.
Mead, 108.
Metcalf, 207, 210.
Meredith, 277, 294, 302, 341, 346, 390, 475, 713, 717.
Merchant, 279, 734, 735.
Meres, 294.
Mendenhall, 365, 382, 402.
Meachiner, 388, 389, 393.
Mercer, 418.
Mell, 528, 544, 555, 576.
Meston, 604.
Melkerman, 622.
Meclar, 627.
Meales, 758.
Mitchell, 38, 495, 557, 580, 628.
Milner, 45, 428, 431, 635, 653, 654, 688, 710, 745.
Mincher, 47.
Millard, 83, 164, 165.
Milburne, 135, 750.
Miles, 141, 277, 405, 450, 462, 600.
Mickel, 157, 158, 159, 160, 762.
Minshal, 245, 264, 302, 392, 695.
Millington, 266, 267, 490, 761.
Mifflin, 334, 421, 541, 546, 547, 652.
Midlicot, 379.
Miller, 495, 576, 586, 622, 651, 700, 720, 740, 746, 751, 762, 763.
Mitchener, 567.
Mills, 606, 737.
Middleton, 640.
Miers, 763.
Morgan, 9, 13, 224, 227, 276, 342, 371, 382, 390, 391, 641, 642, 701, 705, 713, 721, 726.
Morton, 92, 437, 448, 401, 502, 542, 602, 673, 722, 723.
Moll, 315, 323, 748.
Moss, 332.

Moore, 25, 28, 34, 66, 88, 89, 92, 230, 231, 232, 239, 276, 305, 312, 324, 328, 343, 347, 370, 397, 398, 410, 414, 417, 421, 441, 451, 459, 465, 515, 543, 547, 558, 559, 573, 574, 599, 601, 630, 685, 642, 646, 647, 666, 684, 697, 738, 739, 741, 744, 747, 750, 752, 758, 761.
Mortamore, 38.
Morris, 59, 122, 146, 203, 210, 318, 323, 325, 335, 349, 351, 393, 403, 404, 407, 408, 417, 436, 437, 414, 449, 475, 488, 565, 577, 580, 598, 612, 615, 616, 621, 631, 640, 641, 644, 645, 646, 647, 648, 650, 657, 675, 677, 678, 684, 686, 691, 706, 731, 740, 752.
Molbee, 349.
Mounson, 390.
Molineux, 412.
Mortonson, 413.
Monroe, 443, 456.
Molleston, 493, 601.
Mordant, 582.
Moon, 593, 617, 632.
Mott, 599.
Moyer, 622, 624, 755, 706.
Moulder, 706, 707.
Morrison, 734, 746.
Montgomry, 745.
Mountjoy, 754.
Murray, 24, 43, 53, 81, 82, 236, 345, 490, 597, 631, 659, 684, 688, 695, 698, 715, 741, 745.
Musgrove, 305, 306, 327, 331, 381, 473, 561, 569, 570, 637, 708, 726, 732, 736, 743, 748, 752.
Mullikar, 343.
Muttison, 413.
Murfy, 478, 479, 497.
Mutell, 616. 678.

N.

Nailor, 219, 288, 289, 354, 421, 436, 446, 479, 480.
Naaman, 249.
Narbole, 445.
Naglee, 761.
Nellson, 36, 58, 70, 163, 164, 165, 287, 354, 399, 431, 487, 619, 765.
Nevell, 68, 673, 705.
Neughayon, 73.
Nepoughhas, 73.
Newcomb, 92, 193, 756.
Neech, 198.
Newlin, 216, 217, 218, 220, 221, 267, 314, 315, 316, 341, 361, 411, 482, 755.
Neal, 255, 306, 331, 460, 494, 576.
Netzilus, 502.
Newton, 605.
New, 619.
Nevan, 709.

INDEX.

Needham, 726.
Newell, 728.
Nicholas, 28, 38, 487, 513, 559.
Nichols, 137, 138, 292, 349, 376, 410, 414, 415, 455, 476, 485, 498, 597, 721, 758.
Nixon, 322, 364, 400, 606, 631, 648, 684, 700, 747, 765.
Nitzilius, 553, 554, 555, 580.
Noerdine, 708.
Noble, 38, 295, 373, 427, 497, 613, 669, 676.
Norris, 200, 235, 238, 253, 266, 289, 307, 320, 321, 346, 386, 396, 403, 416, 427, 497, 503, 662, 705, 711.
Norbury, 292, 293, 322, 358.
Northrop, 383, 303, 320, 418.
Norcross, 400, 401.
Nohren, 468.
Norton, 510.
Noyes, 548, 617.
Northington, 618.
Nutt, 379, 620, 638, 642, 721.
Owen, Griffith (general).
Otter, 13, 14, 17, 72, 236, 253, 318, 416, 473.
Ogle, 31, 230, 231, 232, 249, 250, 331, 369, 370, 546.
Olliffe, 43, 631, 640, 650, 684.
Oliver, 45, 60, 77, 81, 371, 426, 456.
Overton, 225, 474, 729.
Ogden, 245.
Oldson, 246, 259, 347.
Offly, 253, 587.
Orpwood, 305.
Osborn, 320, 409, 713.
Oldman, 345.
Oxleys, 407, 471.
Orme, 432, 670, 701.
Oldham, 483.
Opdegraef, 488, 489.
Oade, 505, 506, 507, 508, 509, 510.
Orion, 565.
Ogleby, 613, 675.
Oneal, 641.
Overholts, 652, 692.

P.

Paul, 26, 31, 115, 117, 120, 215, 317, 319, 369, 374, 448, 493.
Parsons, 27, 66, 67, 117, 199, 200, 202, 203, 204, 205, 265, 277, 375, 395, 410, 444, 611, 729, 738.
Patterson, 36, 447, 734, 747, 754.
Parker, 56, 109, 110, 145, 153, 165, 305, 335, 340, 352, 365, 398, 434, 494, 601, 607, 613, 637, 641, 658, 693, 751, 756.
Paxton, 84, 210, 261, 314, 374, 409, 417, 430, 440, 734.
Parkinson, 112, 113.
Parris, 135, 136, 137, 176, 177.
Pask, 229, 349, 366.
Palmer, 284, 290, 321, 352, 357, 374, 375, 383, 422, 424, 449, 581, 670, 765.
Pawlin, 293, 318, 338.
Paschal, 295, 440, 441, 748.
Paarde, 350.
Passa, 350, 353, 354.
Parke, 411, 482, 485, 700, 714, 723, 756.
Parrock, 425.
Pastorius, 467, 468, 560, 565, 617.
Pardoe, 474, 484.
Paraddee, 482.
Paper, 489.
Padget, 492, 600, 618, 635, 640.
Packer, 500, 675, 742, 745.
Passmore, 716, 717, 721.
Pannebaker, 653.
Paten, 733.
Pace, 549, 550, 580.
Paine, 551, 552, 584, 743.
Painter, 595, 598, 619.
Parry, 602, 717.
Pearmain, 603.
Parnel, 605.
Parsly, 648, 723.
Parkhurst, 656, 657, 659, 691.
Parvis, 717.
Pare, 751, 761.
Page, 760.
Peaty, 333, 394, 490.
Pennington, 13, 195, 196, 199, 228, 247, 262, 271, 284, 307, 361, 376, 434, 458, 499, 685, 722, 731.
Penn, William (general).
Penn, Maria, 13.
Penn, Lowther, Margarett, William, John and Anthony, 13. Hanna, 596.
Penn, Letitia 35, 84, 266, 293, 432, 489.
Pennock, 23, 28, 29, 262, 337, 363, 366, 385, 492, 545, 546, 549, 726, 744, 757, 761.
Pert, 24, 25, 534.
Peterson, 40, 41, 42, 49, 167, 168, 169, 222, 240, 241, 319, 498, 514, 538, 636, 658, 692, 707, 712, 751, 765.
Pegg, 59, 61, 182, 445, 566, 578, 581, 596.
Pemberton, 68, 84, 88, 92, 193, 197, 231, 235, 236, 242, 261, 292, 308, 312, 331, 384, 439, 477, 525, 540, 541, 556, 560, 566, 589, 607, 616, 617, 629, 630, 632, 633, 643, 651, 659, 665, 669, 670, 683, 685, 694, 696, 700.
Perril, 99.
Peters, 118.
Peller, 124, 125, 127.
Pennell, 365, 382, 505, 506, 507, 508, 509, 510.
Perrin, 384, 751.

INDEX. 781

Pender, 453.
Peres, 584.
Peel, 605, 747.
Petty, 607.
Perry, 616, 678.
Pearsal, 626.
Peckover, 665, 696.
Pennybaker, 765.
Pearl, 727.
Phipps, 30, 40, 225, 226, 268, 269, 313, 314, 317.
Philipps, 41, 103, 104, 265, 318, 396, 405, 428, 461, 467, 521, 725, 735.
Philley, 80.
Phitty, 374.
Phelps, 492.
Pickering, 7, 23, 78, 106, 107, 136, 137, 163, 173, 176, 177, 392, 404, 412, 417, 441, 459, 469, 485, 630, 631, 708.
Pillar, 35, 36, 38, 51, 67, 139.
Pierce, 40, 74, 217, 238, 239, 259, 336, 357, 406, 463, 472, 492, 517, 576, 588, 593, 622, 703, 763.
Pinyard, 95.
Pidgeon, 96, 114, 115,137,178,453,495.
Pierson, 10, 216, 259, 260, 307, 346, 347, 353, 357, 370, 406, 413, 465, 499, 584, 598, 633, 646, 687, 702, 727, 728.
Pike, 289, 446, 448, 705, 711.
Pidcock, 372.
Pitts, 380.
Pim, 510.
Plumstead, 324, 346, 432, 495, 496, 566, 567, 576, 593, 629, 630, 669, 683, 699, 708, 712.
Planner, 333.
Plumley, 351, 440, 524.
Player, 577.
Pleasington, 590.
Place, 599.
Pleas, 737.
Powell, 8, 25, 48, 50, 87, 149, 199, 201, 209, 216, 217, 238, 241, 242, 252, 253, 254, 255, 260, 266, 275, 279, 280, 291, 296, 299, 300, 314, 316, 330, 339, 343, 344, 348, 351, 352, 359, 365, 375, 379, 386, 391, 404, 405, 406, 417, 419, 422, 425, 427, 433, 437, 442, 444, 446, 447, 460, 468, 469, 475, 477, 478, 484, 489, 514, 519, 544, 565, 583, 587, 588, 593, 600, 627, 628, 635, 647, 657, 659, 663, 664, 692, 693, 694, 705, 714, 727.
Poulters, 52, 216, 425, 668, 698.
Portman, 231, 232.
Pomfry, 236, 488.
Polson, 247, 498.
Potts, 278, 286, 288, 347, 378, 379, 434, 485, 489, 541, 573, 600, 721, 765.
Potter, 321, 417, 668, 698.
Poyer, 328, 334.
Posey, 393.
Portes, 438, 447.
Pownell, 466, 634, 685.
Pound, 513, 584.
Ponder, 623, 638.
Pope, 642.
Poilderbeck, 704, 706.
Poltney, 763.
Prettyman, 601, 611, 642.
Priestmal, 455.
Prichard, 13, 203, 219, 239, 240, 241, 326, 339, 352, 353, 379, 428, 459.
Price, 97, 110, 276, 302, 307, 312, 328, 333, 346, 387, 439, 451, 473, 586, 641, 709, 752.
Preston, 199, 482, 501, 520, 603, 623, 760.
Priestner, 222, 342, 352.
Prosser, 284.
Prew, 349, 353, 358, 552.
Pratt, 369, 374, 409, 597, 687.
Prigg, 378.
Prior, 411, 583, 707, 709, 710.
Proteus, 434.
Pretter, 607.
Prees, 704, 715.
Pusey, 10, 17, 38, 46, 68, 267, 285, 286, 292, 293, 297, 312, 316, 337, 341, 346, 439, 458, 497, 501, 568, 586, 588, 589, 601, 610, 674, 739, 756.
Puckle, 180, 379, 380, 381, 382, 385, 444, 463, 476.
Puryour, 237, 238, 369, 558.
Pugh, 322, 355, 356, 375, 387, 404, 405, 413, 442, 478, 577, 759.
Putcon, 554, 555.
Pupather, 622, 628.
Pyles, 37, 341, 347, 474, 537, 610, 674.

Q.

Quary, 507, 608, 638.

R.

Rakestraw, 23, 27, 28, 37, 61, 136, 137, 392, 488, 540.
Rawles, 35, 50, 58, 59, 155, 212, 287, 348, 349, 415, 481, 617.
Ransted, 38.
Randal, 63.
Rambo, 70, 138, 296, 349, 475, 496, 497, 498, 614, 676, 765.
Radny, 85.
Rallis, 110.
Rawlinson, 337, 515, 519.
Ramkes, 337, 341, 346, 360.
Rakeings, 402.
Radcliffe, 525, 570.
Rayle, 747.
Redman, 136, 284, 320, 392, 393.

Reynolds, 172, 280, 343, 376, 414, 565, 598, 636, 645, 646, 687, 717, 719, 743, 750, 757.
Reese, 184, 224, 228, 322, 349, 387, 391, 433, 434, 463, 468, 488, 535, 538, 547, 588, 765.
Read, 216, 257, 259, 310, 343, 345, 459, 463, 595, 610, 616, 634, 647, 685, 709, 713, 716, 734, 735, 747.
Rety, 234, 241, 394.
Renier, 240, 434, 441.
Revel, 317, 318, 341.
Reading, 347, 661, 662.
Redegeldt, 467, 595, 634, 686.
Reator, 581, 762.
Redmell, 584.
Remington, 593.
Redknap, 593, 594.
Relof, 605.
Ream, 652, 725.
Reddick, 707.
Reiff, 765.
Rily, 10.
Richardson, 83, 194, 209, 210, 214, 235, 247, 259, 274, 280, 401, 404, 416, 489, 494, 590, 618, 619, 631, 659, 684, 685, 736, 743.
Right, 83.
Richards, 98, 99, 100, 101, 102, 107, 144, 145, 146, 165, 166, 167, 180, 181, 182, 183, 184, 257, 322, 328, 335, 340, 357, 358, 362, 363, 372, 411, 443, 610, 674, 765.
Rideout, 393.
Richman, 591, 594, 743.
Ringer, 626.
Ridgway, 736.
Rigg, 738.
Rich, 740.
Rist, 742.
Ridgley, 759.
Roberts, 8, 66, 67, 77, 108, 163, 176, 195, 214, 219, 221, 224, 256, 261, 265, 272, 295, 299, 306, 319, 322, 329, 331, 338, 350, 356, 361, 367, 373, 382, 386, 406, 421, 425, 435, 547, 582, 599, 601, 606, 609, 620, 631, 649, 684, 713, 734, 741, 757.
Rogers, 28, 262, 363, 385, 549, 671, 672, 702.
Robinson, 29, 33, 42, 46, 55, 69, 73, 93, 96, 97, 101, 102, 103, 105, 106, 111, 117, 118, 119, 121, 124, 125, 126, 127, 132, 134, 135, 137, 140, 141, 144, 146, 147, 148, 149, 151, 152, 154, 155, 156, 157, 159, 161, 163, 165, 167, 169, 171, 173, 176, 177, 178, 180, 213, 317, 321, 340, 343, 385, 432, 434, 435, 441, 455, 485, 488, 498, 559, 568, 572, 604, 609, 611, 613, 614, 654, 675, 676, 688, 702, 718, 719, 723, 725, 729, 733, 738, 743.

Rochford, 22, 24, 25, 26, 27, 57, 87, 166, 490, 629, 630, 647, 648, 658, 667, 682, 683, 693, 697.
Rowland, 29, 44, 52, 202, 204, 205, 238, 277, 305, 319, 371, 392, 423, 472, 520, 583, 587, 607, 635, 637, 640, 646.
Rossett, 31.
Roads, 65, 73, 92, 214, 232, 251, 326, 327, 337, 343, 366, 372, 407, 420, 422, 437, 500, 502, 540, 593, 673, 748.
Robeson, 74, 173, 392, 393, 417, 425, 432, 435, 441, 583, 610, 630, 683.
Rodney, 95, 96, 198, 201, 384, 419, 494.
Roystan, 104, 105.
Roach, 108, 655, 689.
Roynald, 172.
Rossel, 253, 473, 527, 528, 576.
Rowles, 272, 480, 481.
Robinet, 275, 419, 477.
Rolle, 289, 601.
Roman, 299, 335, 336, 447, 576.
Routledge, 306, 311, 588.
Rodman, 326.
Rolfe, 495.
Ross, 588, 743.
Rouse, 616, 678.
Robins, 631, 649, 650, 684.
Robertson, 656, 690, 722, 724, 734, 755.
Rob, 720, 760.
Rose, 722.
Rosberry, 765.
Rush, 35, 351, 522.
Russell, 39, 182, 321, 477, 507, 595, 605, 608.
Rudman, 269, 432, 433.
Rutter, 333, 338, 348, 589, 590, 641, 651, 725, 731.
Rudyard, 393, 404.
Ruming, 411.
Rumford, 576, 582.
Rucklefell, 739.
Ryner, 118, 119.
Ryall, 726.
Ryfe, 751.

S.

Salway, 26, 31, 46, 58, 81, 82, 83, 171, 172, 173, 174, 184, 332, 384, 385, 393, 441.
Sandelands, 35, 38, 68, 241, 610, 674.
Salford, 60.
Sawyer, 86.
Sager, 98, 233, 234, 241.
Savery, 98, 99, 100, 101, 102.
Sanders, 109, 114, 115, 272, 331, 369, 375, 759.
Salsbury, 122, 123, 124, 140.
Salter, 235, 238, 445, 485.

INDEX. 783

Say, 325, 365.
Samway, 348, 616, 617.
Satcher, 376, 399, 757.
Sanger, 411, 482.
Sands, 437, 439.
Savoy, 475, 672, 673, 689, 704, 706, 707, 727.
Sandall, 526, 527, 532, 647.
Salkeld, 575, 602, 735, 757.
Saub, 622.
Sap, 717.
Sawk, 751.
Scull, 53, 63, 225, 302, 311, 343, 725, 752.
Scott, 153, 255, 263, 323, 383, 413, 502, 608, 720, 722.
Scotehorn, 251.
Scarborow, 292, 310, 311, 312, 430, 463.
Scheffer, 311, 312, 347, 453.
Scholah, 361, 452.
Scarlet, 363.
Schleagel, 569, 570, 618, 644
Schoonhover, 721.
Sellars, 47, 52, 421.
Seconing, 73.
Sellwood, 97, 98.
Seaborne, 111.
Sellen, 273, 338, 420, 483.
Searle, 345, 424.
Sewell, 442.
Self, 587, 588, 657, 691, 737.
Seaman, 599.
Seaton, 601.
Seager, 710.
Shadley, 717.
Sharply, 25, 40, 91.
Sherlow, 42, 261, 288, 421, 431.
Shippen, Edward (general).
Shorter, 60.
Sherbono, 66, 69, 70, 74.
Shardlow, 169, 236, 237, 319, 350, 502, 611.
Sharp, 207, 300, 495, 551, 621, 627, 636, 680, 728.
Sharpless, 209, 217, 220, 227, 228, 231, 232, 270, 299, 313, 351, 711.
Sbaw, 253, 254, 473, 575.
Sherry, 334.
Shill, 376.
Sherboro, 432, 433.
Shoemaker, 462, 489, 763.
Shepherd, 490, 583, 646, 668, 698, 717.
Sheekonicken, 491.
Shattick, 492, 493, 524, 600, 618, 622, 663.
Shankland, 520, 521, 611, 638, 719, 739, 753, 756, 758, 763.
Shore, 521, 757.
Shurmer, 584, 585, 591, 592, 610, 640.
Sherrard, 597.
Shiers, 599.
Shank, 622, 628, 640, 648, 724.
Shute, 626, 628, 629, 630, 631, 640, 645, 647, 650, 651, 663, 667, 682, 683, 693, 695, 698, 699.
Sherly, 633, 648, 702.
Sholl, 647, 766.
Shannon, 750.
Simcock, 23, 43, 266, 293, 294, 297, 298, 315, 366, 367, 390, 402, 405, 451, 460, 570, 602.
Sibthorp, 23, 44, 48, 152, 153, 154, 254, 255, 323.
Sickhoys, 73.
Sibly, 89.
Simkins, 229, 241, 366.
Simson, 238, 259, 641, 760.
Simmonds, 279, 583, 601, 609, 635.
Siddon, 301.
Sipman, 337, 338, 340, 341, 360.
Sisom, 352, 440, 445, 470, 639, 667, 698.
Siericks, 373.
Sinnexson, 408, 410.
Signselder, 445.
Silvester, 463, 737.
Siverts, 489.
Sinclair, 588.
Siple, 619.
Sintgar, 720.
Sigfred, 724, 725.
Sipple, 755.
Skidmore, 41.
Skelton, 180, 182, 183, 184, 257.
Skeen, 738.
Slighton, 48, 376.
Slackhouse, 256.
Slidmore, 726.
Sloong, 746.
Smith, 44, 48, 57, 61, 67, 76, 85, 116, 120, 215, 229, 230, 233, 234, 235, 241, 243, 247, 251, 254, 271, 285, 293, 336, 354, 358, 366, 367, 368, 369, 376, 386, 387, 392, 393, 394, 398, 407, 423, 431, 440, 445, 456, 470, 472, 473, 502, 534, 554, 578, 579, 581, 586, 589, 591, 596, 601, 616, 632, 637, 645, 648, 662, 694, 707, 721, 722, 724, 727, 735, 739, 744, 752, 753, 760.
Smart, 148.
Smout, 160, 365, 373, 378, 724, 765
Smedley, 244, 245, 298, 312, 431, 541, 561, 562, 564, 565, 572, 757.
Smallwood, 301, 332, 416.
Small, 734.
Snook, 761.
Sneads, 71, 304, 329, 330, 340, 345, 369, 401, 448, 512, 524.
Snowden, 161, 243, 327, 350, 497.
Snelling, 498.
Snyder, 622, 639, 755, 761.
Snevelly, 751.
Southby, 23, 62, 68, 201, 255, 495.

INDEX.

Songhurst, 25, 707.
Southworth, 78, 142, 392, 412, 434, 614, 664, 695.
Sobers, 161, 162, 163, 176.
South, 347, 397, 398, 420, 752, 755
Soule, 435.
Spikeman, 33.
Spakeman, 56, 79, 216, 221, 234, 241, 243, 285, 290, 320, 354, 393.
Sparkman, 61.
Springett, 110, 518, 760.
Sproston, 266.
Springetts, 324.
Sprogel, 351, 357, 372, 497, 752.
Spencer, 425, 491.
Spilman, 599.
Springer, 657, 692, 723, 731, 739, 753.
Stockdale, 32, 86, 307, 333, 358, 592, 706, 719.
Storter, 35.
Stanly, 48, 52, 242, 247, 295, 319, 320, 330, 342, 451, 468, 487, 567, 579.
Stone, 105, 106, 650.
Standish, 159, 160.
Stanfield, 174, 175, 197, 213, 336, 400.
Stout, 184.
Story, Thomas (general).
Stevenson, 227, 228, 257, 318, 341, 360, 361, 523, 569, 579, 619, 628, 629, 658, 666, 667, 682, 683, 693, 697, 713.
Stanford, 236.
Stevens, 273, 284, 342, 494, 573, 581, 583, 634, 640, 649.
Streipers, 273, 280, 420, 457, 482, 575, 583, 584, 632, 635, 748, 749, 764.
Stacy, 282.
Stackhouse, 292, 309, 310, 312, 321, 424, 429, 430, 463.
Stanmore, 304.
Stapler, 306, 377, 395, 756.
Stanton, 310, 500, 756.
Stanbury, 319, 436, 484, 510, 511, 580, 583, 628.
Streater, 321, 394.
Stiles, 353, 354, 701.
Stedman, 366, 367, 439, 443, 446, 722, 723.
Stelleman, 370.
Starkey, 384.
Stockton, 386.
Stalcup, 417, 722.
Stringer, 460, 620.
Stretcher, 490.
Steel, 495, 536, 537, 551, 557, 565, 567, 568, 582, 590, 603, 605, 607, 611, 622, 625, 627, 628, 630, 636, 638, 641, 645, 647, 648, 649, 660, 662, 663, 666, 669, 676, 679, 680, 682, 683, 687, 689, 694, 708, 712, 713, 714, 725, 730, 757, 764, 765.

Strettell, 521, 523, 757.
Stauber, 552, 583.
Strahan, 567, 568.
Steward, 595, 638, 751, 759, 760.
Steager, 632.
Strode, 646, 687.
Steman, 650.
Stilly, 664, 671.
Starret, 724.
Storey, 726.
Stouffer, 734.
Sterman, 751.
Stokely, 753.
Sutton, 268, 269, 271, 638, 653.
Sumwayes, 309.
Surkett, 484.
Swift, 13, 52, 259, 260, 278, 280, 313, 316, 321, 366, 394, 436, 455, 600, 655, 691.
Sweetaples, 228, 237.
Swanson, 265, 394, 395, 410, 420, 458, 498, 636, 665, 666, 696, 697.
Swaffer, 386, 387, 443, 444, 446, 533, 621.
Swallow, 499, 700.
Swartwood, 662.
Switzer, 709, 725.
Symes, 388.
Sykes, 169, 331, 434, 438.
Sydon, 268.
Symyns, 680, 734, 735.

T.

Taylor, Isaac (general).
Tank, 68, 581, 765.
Tammany, 86.
Tanner, 225, 380, 385, 455, 717.
Tally, 238.
Tatham, 250, 317, 318, 341, 396, 559.
Tallman, 434, 477, 628, 629, 666, 667, 682, 683, 697.
Tavernor, 492.
Tulbot, 403, 521, 522, 625, 681.
Tate, 583.
Taylor, 587, 597, 602, 604, 639, 660, 662, 666, 712, 715, 741, 745, 751.
Telnor, 32, 33, 50, 171, 256, 340, 348, 359, 488, 489.
Test, 166, 167, 168, 169, 184, 250, 366, 435, 448, 533.
Terwood, 345.
Teif, 463.
Tholmain, 78, 86.
Thompson, 130, 131, 132, 133, 134, 451, 458, 557, 559, 605, 717, 726, 731, 738, 751.
Thornton, 143, 144, 407, 408.
Throckmorton, 180, 181, 257.
Thrattle, 267.
Thauten, 297.
Thorn, 434, 477, 628, 629, 658, 667, 682, 683, 693, 697, 713.

INDEX. 785

Thomas, 57, 195, 214, 221, 223, 224, 225, 261, 268, 269, 272, 275, 276, 277, 279, 286, 302, 322, 325, 328, 342, 346, 348, 361, 367, 368, 371, 378, 381, 386, 395, 396, 399, 402, 405, 409, 419, 420, 422, 425, 426, 437, 439, 445, 470, 481, 482, 583, 544, 545, 546, 547, 582, 596, 602, 611, 612, 620, 621, 634, 644, 645, 646, 647, 650, 651, 675, 686, 710, 711, 714, 715, 725, 735, 737, 739, 740, 750, 752.
Thatcher, 376, 412, 443.
Thawley, 466.
Thorrald, 499, 587.
Thislewood, 619.
Thornbury, 753.
Tibby, 33, 259, 611, 664, 695.
Tillery, 63, 70.
Tittery, 203, 214, 243, 471.
Tisen, 273, 274.
Tilton, 445.
Tidmarsh, 666, 740.
Tidball, 703.
Tindell, 728.
Till, 757.
Topham, 642, 746, 759.
Townsend, 27, 31, 35, 41, 60, 68, 286, 330, 432, 489, 595, 606, 609, 648, 758.
Toughis, 73.
Tom, 138.
Todd, 216, 217, 588.
Tomkins, 227, 405, 412, 627, 636.
Town, 254, 310, 472.
Toyer, 272.
Tovey, 364, 366, 368, 488.
Tonge, 442, 443.
Toaes, 453, 454.
Toby, 565, 567, 641.
Tomlinson, 713.
Trago, 46, 47.
Trotter, 140, 447.
Trent, 444, 459, 655, 689, 693.
Tresse, 495, 672, 703.
Trevil, 507.
Tregan, 576, 649.
Tranter, 605. 704.
Trelinger, 622.
Truax, 748.
Turner, 9, 31, 149, 225, 558, 614, 641, 677, 751.
Turner, Robert (general).
Tucker, 41, 43, 62, 66, 67, 316, 433, 497, 498, 502, 554, 643.
Tunnicliffe, 251, 254, 401, 408, 655, 689.
Turlow, 379, 380.
Tuchberry, 595.
Turk, 721.
Twiggs, 707, 720.
Tyzack, 32, 150, 151, 152, 321, 343, 359, 435, 441, 468.

50--Vol. XIX.

Tyson, 424.
Tyren, 748.

U.

Ungle, 115.
Uberfelt, 560.
Urner, 633, 639.
Ulrick, 746.

V.

Vaston, 621, 680.
Vandervere, 620.
Vanderburgh, 10, 30, 465.
Vangilder, 10.
Vandercoolin, 30, 357, 388, 410.
Van Bebber, 249, 320, 338, 340, 345, 351, 359, 475, 502, 625, 739, 765.
Vanderhyden, 311.
Van Everston, 410.
Vaughan, 447.
Van Gezel, 461.
Vandegrift, 498.
Van Zant, 498.
Vanculin, 542, 608.
Van Buskirk, 569, 570.
Verkirk, 713.
Vernon, 57, 285, 286, 299, 335, 514, 519, 558, 577.
Verhoofe, 196, 197, 477.
Venable, 243, 261, 285, 326, 327, 523.
Ven, 470.
Venerick, 597, 755.
Verner, 734.
Vennoy, 738.
Vines, 196.
Vincent, 289.
Vinger, 743.
Vossell, 606, 619.
Vulk, 718.

W.

Waddy, 26, 215, 338, 511, 524.
Waite, 26, 288, 392, 428, 436, 446, 447, 474, 479, 480.
Wall, 31, 34, 263, 432, 454, 462, 628.
Walker, 33, 103, 104, 117, 118, 119, 138, 197, 201, 242, 243, 255, 280, 306, 327, 331, 349, 373, 392, 393, 457, 591, 619, 664, 695, 696.
Wair, 34, 67, 106.
Watson, 68, 69, 76, 85, 197, 305, 316, 333, 410, 543, 576, 636, 704.
Warner, 72, 142, 143, 144, 231, 280, 303, 312.
Warriall, 86, 87.
Waln, 90, 206, 220, 255, 256, 277, 280, 292, 310, 314, 328, 392, 393, 394, 412, 424, 429, 430, 492.
Wager, 109, 110.
Wallis, 144, 146, 147, 294, 328, 352, 413, 466, 628, 751, 762.

INDEX.

Walter, 224, 374, 377, 661, 662, 708.
Watts, 265, 384.
Warder, 277, 658, 693, 735, 749, 757.
Ward, 310, 748.
Walley, 328, 329, 330, 368, 454, 605.
Wanton, 359, 484.
Wastell, 369.
Wade, 380, 385, 434, 470.
Wandy, 385.
Wase, 399.
Walton, 408, 612, 674, 675.
Walmsley, 424, 430.
Wassey, 449, 450.
Wast, 488.
Warenbur, 529.
Way, 577, 742.
Waters, 656.
Waler, 664.
Waltham, 713.
Waterworth, 723.
Wark, 724, 734, 762.
Waringe, 740.
Warrington, 759.
Waple, 763.
Webster, 10, 308.
Weston, 13, 226, 401.
West, 27, 28, 29, 273, 340, 358, 425, 562.
Wescard, 31.
Webb, 74, 120, 121, 122, 123, 124, 218, 275, 320, 375, 402, 436, 510, 517, 518, 519, 576, 615, 617, 678, 716, 765.
Weal, 136.
Weir, 152.
Welch, 208, 222, 320, 413, 449, 514, 589.
Weelbaucks, 322.
Weaver, 362, 363, 495, 700.
Wetheril, 439, 608, 661.
Wells, 457, 494, 664.
Weight, 484.
Westley, 617.
Wents, 709, 725, 762.
Wheeler, 23, 128, 131, 133, 261, 291, 305, 319, 321, 325, 354, 365, 367, 372, 461, 488, 577, 664, 671, 717, 763, 764.
Whitpaine, 32, 53, 63, 104, 114, 121, 126, 340, 343, 396, 397, 398, 399, 435, 487, 584, 644, 645, 646, 686, 740, 744, 752.
White, 56, 61, 104, 105, 117, 132, 143, 144, 152, 231, 254, 333, 365, 375, 376, 472, 473, 487, 606, 617, 638, 736, 751.
Whitehead, 97, 597, 635.
Whitacre, 220, 366, 367, 370, 407, 451, 519, 609.
Wheeldon, 246, 259, 446.
Whiteheart, 300.
Whitby, 326, 327, 337, 343, 372.
Whitfield, 343, 485.
Wharton, 348, 414, 480, 481, 482, 488.
Wharley, 443, 730, 731.
Whitwell, 495.

Whatly, 524.
Wheatly, 526.
Whartnaby, 583.
Whitesides, 597.
Whigsted, 600.
Whillon, 703.
Whiting, 745.
Williams, 42, 138, 224, 251, 276, 322, 334, 369, 370, 391, 405, 409, 425, 433, 436, 452, 498, 510, 605, 611, 619, 621, 638, 643, 656, 690, 718, 719, 721, 732, 739, 748, 757.
Willard, 49, 51, 76, 82, 118, 319, 342, 367, 385, 524.
Wilcox, 50, 60, 78, 104, 105, 127, 176, 210, 211, 226, 227, 232, 241, 348, 385, 386, 417, 437, 441, 459, 475, 483, 630, 661, 662, 684, 729.
Withins, 138.
Winder, 197.
Wilkinson, 212, 469, 648, 750.
Wickersham, 217, 220, 392.
Willis, 219, 265, 273, 279, 284, 285, 326, 409, 459, 460, 475, 483, 525, 526, 626, 628, 721, 732.
Wilburn, 253, 264.
Wilkins, 268, 278, 581, 591, 641, 760.
Withers, 294, 328, 352, 383, 396, 514, 658, 693, 745.
Wiggans, 309, 616, 617.
Williamson, 358, 450, 451, 453, 498, 611, 741, 742.
Willington, 369.
Wilson, 384, 493, 586, 591, 592, 619, 637, 643, 715, 717, 723, 728, 747.
Widdows, 406, 470, 576.
Willmer, 418, 597.
Wildman, 429.
Wiltbank, 445, 603, 623, 678, 679.
Wisdom, 587, 716, 717.
Wishart, 591, 649.
Willoughby, 717.
Wister, 758, 761.
Wilks, 761.
Wood, 77, 222, 223, 224, 235, 245, 261, 267, 287, 288, 290, 309, 312, 327, 329, 337, 344, 345, 350, 361, 377, 386, 389, 408, 410, 419, 426, 502, 505, 506, 507, 508, 509, 510, 523, 554, 555, 603, 611, 630, 683, 693, 738.
Worrell, 89, 219, 243, 285, 298, 299, 327, 381, 391, 392, 447.
Wollaston, 199, 253.
Wolfe, 205, 214, 322, 453, 482.
Woolman, 213.
Woodworth, 275, 412, 474, 655, 659, 689, 756.
Worthin, 328.
Worley, 337, 458, 595, 602, 610, 674, 747.
Worthington, 349.
Woodmansey, 357, 372.
Woolrick, 386, 392, 394.

INDEX.

Woodland, 437, 657, 692.
Word, 537, 568.
Woolson, 613, 614, 676.
Wooler, 711, 712.
Worth, 723, 751.
Wright, 30, 83, 92, 106, 107, 267, 291, 448, 502, 597, 602, 607, 673, 750.
Wynkoop, 92, 502, 673, 763.
Wynne, 279, 386, 391, 425, 431, 432, 433, 454, 490, 491, 670, 701.
Wyeth, 565, 711, 717, 754.

Y.

Yardly, 68, 195, 291, 416, 473.

Yokham, 60, 73, 266, 293, 343, 369, 370, 487, 489, 600.
Yeates, 105, 112, 135, 178, 233, 249, 329, 353, 406, 594, 639.
Yarnall, 266, 291, 294, 407, 571, 576.
Yeldale, 332.
Young, 367, 386, 581.
Yearsley, 460.
Yoder, 726.

Z.

Zeal, 196, 201.
Zachary, 426.

www.ingramcontent.com/pod-product-compliance
Lightning Source LLC
Chambersburg PA
CBHW052034290426
44111CB00011B/1508